The **Rough Guide** to

California

written and researched by

JD Dickey, Nick Edwards,
Mark Ellwood, and Paul Whitfield

with additional contributions from

Greg Ward

ROUGH
GUIDES

NEW YORK • LONDON • DELHI

www.roughguides.com

Contents

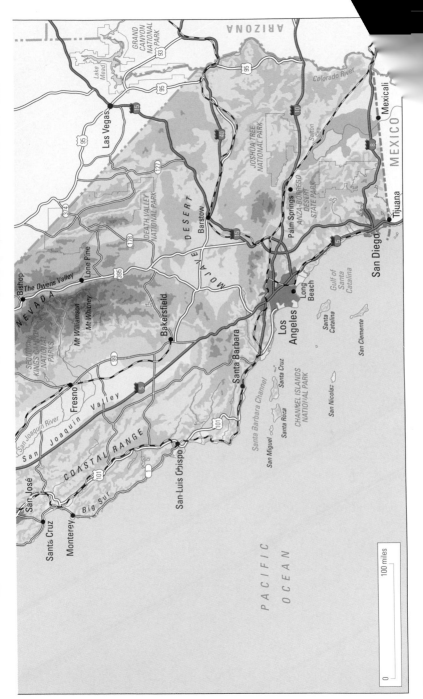

Introduction to
California

California is America squared. It's the place you go to find more America than you ever thought possible.

What's Wrong with America by Scott Bradfield

Perhaps no region of the world has been as idealized as California, and few, if any, actually manage to live up to the hype to the same degree. Justly celebrated for its sun, sand, surf, and sea, the state offers much more than that: towering mountain ranges, glitzy big cities, deep primeval forests, and charming historic hamlets.

As with the rest of America, California doesn't dwell too much on the past, and, in some ways, represents the ultimate "now" society: urban life is lived in the fast lane, conspicuous consumption is often paramount, and having the right hairstyle, wardrobe, tan, and income can count for a lot. But this is only one side of the coin, and once you get out of the cities, the landscape changes, giving way to dense groves of ancient trees, primitive rock carvings left by Native Americans, and the eerie ghost towns of the Gold Rush. A land of superlatives, California really is full of the oldest, the tallest, the largest, the most spectacular – all of which go far beyond local bravura.

It's important to bear in mind, too, that the supposed "superficiality" of California is largely a myth, created in equal measure by outsiders and Californians themselves – by San Franciscans contemptuous of LA's position as entertainment, theme park, and beach culture capital of America, and by Angelenos with a disregard for San Francisco as an outpost of snooty yuppies with pretensions to hipster, and hippie, culture. Still, while there may be plenty of such elements in both towns, the full range of peoples, cultures, and communities of California

cannot easily be reduced to any one stereotype – there's s[...]
much going on here.

Politically, California is probably the USA's most polarized state, [...]
to right-wing bastions like Orange County and San Diego and son[...]
the nation's most reactionary figures – Ronald Reagan and Richard Nix[...]
come to mind – yet also a principal source of America's most dynamic left
wing movements: environmentalism, women's lib, and gay and immigrant
rights. Some of the fiercest protests of the Sixties took root here, and in
many ways this is still the heart of liberal America, as California continues
to set the standard for the rest of the US (if not the world) regarding progressive action and social tolerance. The region is economically crucial as
well, with the cash-flush entertainment field dominated by California's film
and music industries, with financial services and real estate continuing to

California cuisine and wine

In much of rural California, the diner is king, with hamburgers, fries, and sodas the typical fare. However, the state also offers just about every gastronomic diversion imaginable, as well as a wide range of ethnic cuisines, which put to good use the fabulous array of fruit, vegetables, and cheeses grown and made here. This abundance, along with Mexican and Asian influences, led in the 1980s to the creation of **California cuisine**, a style with an almost obsessive devotion to the freshest local ingredients, tempered with a strong dose of French nouvelle cuisine – small portions, artful presentation. This may not sound so novel now, but at the
time it was revolutionary, and the spread of such ideas – featuring such signature dishes as blackened ahi tuna layered with sesame and mesclun salads with goat cheese and toasted walnuts – had national reach as well, encouraging regions from across the country to take another look at their indigenous cuisines and accomplish great new things with them.

The state's culinary rise has been matched by the improvement in its **wines**. Bulk wines for everyday quaffing are still the mainstay of California's industrial vintners (the state produces more than 17 million gallons of wine each year), but an ever increasing acreage is being planted by boutique wineries, particularly in the Napa (see pp.778–779) and Sonoma (see p.783) valleys north of San Francisco, but also around Santa Barbara County (see p.496). Growers are forever experimenting with different varieties and applying modern winemaking techniques to produce wines that challenge almost any in the world for both quality and price.

…fornia is known as the …lden State," a nickname …at derives from the Gold Rush days of the 1840s and 50s and is perpetuated by the golden poppy, or *Eschsholtzia californica*, which appears all over California each spring and is the state flower.

• California raised the flags of Spain, England, Mexico, and the short-lived Bear Republic before it was admitted to the Union on September 9, 1850, as the **thirty-first state**.

• Each year, California becomes home to more **immigrants** than any other state, most settlers hailing from Latin America and Asia, though with a smattering from Europe, Russia, and the Middle East, too. Almost a third of all immigrants to the US settle here.

• The **third largest state** in the US (after Texas and Alaska), California boasts an almost 700-mile-long coast along the Pacific and around 25,000 square miles of desert.

• Based on agriculture and the electronic, aerospace, film, and tourism industries, the state's **economy** is the strongest in the US. Indeed, if it were a country, California's economy would rank as **seventh largest** in the world.

• In US presidential races, California alone provides twenty percent of the **electoral votes** necessary for election – though these didn't help the last two state winners (Al Gore and John Kerry) from getting past George Bush to the Oval Office.

be fundamental economic bulwarks, and with all manner of politicians – whether from Texas or Massachusetts – dropping in to fatten their bankrolls with high-flying political fundraisers.

Where to go

California covers nearly 160,000 square miles: keep in mind that distances between the main destinations can be huge, and naturally you won't be able to see everything on one trip – even a comprehensive vacation may only just scratch the surface.

In an area so varied, it's hard to pick out specific highlights, and much will depend on the kind of

> **A land of superlatives, California really is full of the oldest, the tallest, the largest, the most spectacular**

vacation you're looking for. You may well start off in **Los Angeles**, far and away the biggest and most stimulating Californian city: a maddening collection of freeways and beaches, seedy suburbs and high-gloss neighborhoods, and extreme lifestyles. From Los Angeles you can head south to **San Diego**, the seventh largest city in America, complete with broad, welcoming beaches and a handy position close to the Mexican border, or inland to the Californian **deserts**, notably to **Death Valley** – as its name suggests, a barren, inhospitable landscape of volcanic craters and windswept sand dunes that in summer becomes the hottest place on earth. From here, it's a logical trip across into Nevada to the **Grand Canyon** via **Las Vegas**; though not actually in California, both spots are accessible from it and are, as well, among the star attractions in the US. An alternative is to make the steady journey up the **Central**

▲ Main Street King Kong, Universal Studio

Coast, a gorgeous run following the shoreline north through some of the state's most dramatic scenery, and taking in some of its liveliest small towns, notably Santa Barbara and Santa Cruz.

The Central Coast marks the transition from Southern to Northern California – a break that's more than just geographical. **San Francisco**, California's second city, is quite different from LA: the coast's oldest, most European-styled metropolis, it's set compactly over a series of steep hills, with wooden Victorian houses tumbling down to water on both sides. From here you have access to some of the state's most extraordinary scen-

▲ San Francisco's coastline and the Golden Gate Bridge

east in the national parks to the east, especially **Yosemite**, where
l waterfalls cascade into a sheer glacial valley that's been immortal-
by Ansel Adams – and countless others – in search of the definitive
scape photograph. Yosemite marks the highlight of the Sierras; south
m it are the worthwhile national parks of **Sequoia** and **Kings Canyon,** and north an interesting mix of quaint towns like Nevada City and
resorts such as Lake Tahoe.

North of San Francisco, the population thins and the physical look
changes yet again. The climate is wetter up here, the valleys that much
greener, flanked by a jagged coastline shadowed by mighty redwoods, the
tallest trees in the world. Though many visitors choose to venture no further
than the **Wine Country** and the Russian River Valley on weekend forays

California missions

Among the oldest European settlements in
California, its 21 **missions** were supposedly
established by the Spanish in the late eight-
eenth century in a burst of religious zeal
aimed at christianizing the local heathens.
In truth, each mission was accompanied by
a *pueblo*, or secular settlement, and, most
importantly, a *presidio*, or military fortress.
Masterminded by Franciscan Father Junípero
Serra, the entire network ran largely along
what was known as the *Camino Real*, or
Royal Road, from San Diego to Solano, just

north of San Francisco, ensuring that every mission was one day's ride
or hard walk from the next. This proximity enabled easy commerce and
communication along the chain.

The missions flourished for more than a hundred years, converting and
killing thousands of locals through a combination of forced evangelism
and smallpox. Eventually, when the missions were secularized under
Mexican rule in 1834, much of the land was given not to the indigenous
peoples, but to the Spanish-speaking *Californio* ranchers. The missions
continued to have a checkered reputation at least until the later Victorian
era, when sentimentalist writer Helen Hunt Jackson gave them an idyllic
gloss in her best-selling potboiler *Ramona* – a hugely influential book
responsible for the current image of missions as charming outposts of
quiet spirituality and quaintly austere architecture.

The largest and most populous settlement was San Luis Rey de
Francia (p.266) – its huge *lavandería*, or washing area, is now an
impressive sunken garden – while arguably the most famous is San
Juan Capistrano (p.178), which welcomes migrating swallows every
March. Visitors will find the most evocative, if not necessarily authentic,
sense of early settler life at the restorations at San Antonio de Padua
(p.517) and La Purísima (p.501).

from the city, it's well worth taking time out to explore the state's northernmost regions, which are split distinctly in two. The coastline is rugged and serene; the interior, meanwhile, is a volcano-scarred desolation that's as different from the stereotype of California as you could imagine.

When to go

California's climate can be as varied as its landscape: in **Southern California**, for one, you can count on endless days of sunshine from May to October, and warm dry nights – though LA's notorious **smog** is at its worst when

> California offers just about every gastronomic diversion imaginable

the temperatures are highest, in August and September.

Along the **coast**, mornings can be hazily overcast, especially in May and June, though you can still get a suntan – or sunburn – even under gray skies. In winter temperatures drop somewhat, but more importantly it can rain for weeks on end, causing massive mudslides that

Parks and preserves

California's fabulous array of **parks** and **preserves** are among the state's undisputed highlights, offering challenging but rewarding hikes, ideal camping, and an impressive range of trees, flowers, and wildlife. Superlatives abound: Death Valley (see p.369) has the lowest point in the Western Hemisphere and is the driest area in the US; the Bristlecone Pine Forest (see p.391) contains the world's most ancient trees; Mount Whitney (see p.386) is the highest peak in the 48 contiguous states and forms the eastern boundary of Sequoia National Park (see p.442), which in turn holds the largest trees in the world (the sequoias); and the north coast provides ideal conditions for growing the planet's tallest trees – the redwoods. Elsewhere, huge rock piles and strangely gnarled eponymous trees dot the desert of Joshua Tree National Park (see p.308), volcanic cones and lava tubes pepper Northern California, and the wondrous domes and spires of Yosemite (see p.457) are only rivaled for scenic wonder by Nevada's and Arizona's Grand Canyon (see p.353).

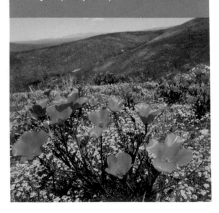

11

With an estimated 500,000 tremors detected annually in the state, California is a seismic timebomb, bisected by the most famous fault-line in the world, the **San Andreas**, which runs loosely from San Francisco to Los Angeles and marks the junction of the Pacific and North American tectonic plates. Given its fearsome reputation, though, it's not the most active fault at the moment – that honor goes to one of its connected faults, known as the **Hayward**.

While the 1906 **San Francisco earthquake** is the most infamous, it wasn't actually the quake itself that leveled the city but a careless homeowner cooking breakfast on a gas stove at the time; the ensuing fire raged for four days, razed 28,000 buildings, and left at least 3000 dead. Since then, there have been several significant shocks, most recently in 1989, when San Francisco again shook during the **Loma Prieta**, named after its epicenter close to Santa Cruz and respon-sible for the horrifying collapse of a double-decker freeway, and in 1994, when the **Northridge** quake tore through the north side of LA, rupturing freeways and leveling an apartment building.

Of course, everyone's waiting for the so-called **Big One**, a massive earthquake that, it's feared, could wipe out Los Angeles or San Francisco. Speculation has intensi-fied recently, since experts have pegged the interval between major ruptures in the southern reaches of the San Andreas at 140 years: the last such quake was Fort Tejon in 1857.

wipe out roads and hillside homes – most recently in 2005 in the hillside community of La Con-chita, north of LA. Inland, the **deserts** are warm in winter and unbearably hot (120°F is not unusual) in summer; desert nights can be freezing in win-ter, when it can even snow. For serious snow, head to the **mountains**, where hiking trails at the higher elevations are blocked from November to June: skiers can take advantage of well-groomed slopes along the Sierra Nevada mountains and around Lake Tahoe.

The coast of **Northern California** is wetter and cooler than the south, its summers tempered by sea breezes and fog, and its winters mild but wet. **San Francisco**, because of its exposed position at the tip of a peninsula, can be chilly all year, with summer fog often rolling in and chasing away what may have started off as a pleasant sunny day. Head a mile inland, though, and you're back in the sun.

	Jan	Apr	Jul	Oct
Death Valley				
(°F)	51	76	102	71
(°C)	11	24	39	22
Eureka				
(°F)	47	51	57	55
(°C)	8	11	14	13
Lake Tahoe				
(°F)	27	38	61	45
(°C)	-3	3	16	7
Las Vegas				
(°F)	45	63	86	66
(°C)	7	17	30	19
Los Angeles				
(°F)	56	63	73	67
(°C)	13	17	23	19
San Diego				
(°F)	56	62	70	66
(°C)	13	17	21	19
San Francisco				
(°F)	51	56	60	61
(°C)	11	13	16	16

34

things not to miss

It's not possible to see everything that California has to offer in one trip – and we don't suggest you try. What follows is a selective taste of the state's highlights: from its vibrant cities to its serene deserts. They're arranged in five color-coded categories, which you can browse through to find the very best to see and experience. All highlights have a page reference to take you straight into the guide, where you can find out more.

01 **Big Sur** Page **521** • Eyeball the secluded beauty of Big Sur's approximately ninety miles of rocky cliffs and crashing waves along the Pacific.

02 **Salvation Mountain** Page **316** • This only-in-California creation is a kaleidoscopic mound of concrete, bale, and vast quantities of paint, peppered liberally with Biblical quotes.

04 **Rafting on the Kern River** Page **423** • The Kern River offers some of the most thrilling whitewater rafting anywhere in the States.

03 **Bridalveil Fall** Page **472** • There's much stunning geology up and down the state, but nothing surpasses Yosemite Valley, where the awe-inspiring Bridalveil Fall cascade over six hundred feet of sheer rock.

05 **Balboa Park** Page **237** • San Diego's staggering collection of museums, lush greenery, and evocative Spanish Colonial buildings provides a wealth of opportunities for exploration.

06 Disney Hall Page **110** • Although Frank Gehry's architectural marvel was designed in 1987, it took sixteen years for it to finally get built, and today this inspired, sculptural creation seves as the monumental home of the LA Philharmonic.

08 Klamath Basin National Wildlife Refuge Page **854** • Each year, travelers from the avian world rest up in the gigantic sanctuary of the Klamath Basin before resuming their journeys along the Pacific Flyway.

07 Wind farms Page **325** • Californian wind farms like Tehachapi – home to over 5000 windmills and turbines – represent some of the world's most powerful sources of renewable energy and are spectacles which beget marveling.

09 Lava Beds National Monument Page **849** • Explore this striking chain of volcanic caves, lava flows, and craters in the Modoc National Forest, a natural monument to the 1872 war between the US and the Modoc Indians.

10 Tufa towers of Mono Lake Page **407** • See the fluffy, sandcastle-like tufa spires that have frothed up from below the surface of this fast-shrinking body of water.

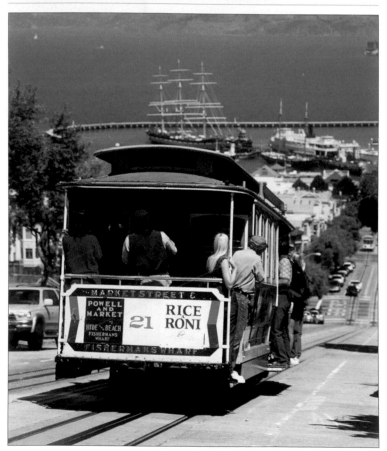

11 Riding a cable car Page **576** • No visit to San Francisco is complete without a ride on one of the city's cable cars, the best means of scaling the city's hills and enjoying the views.

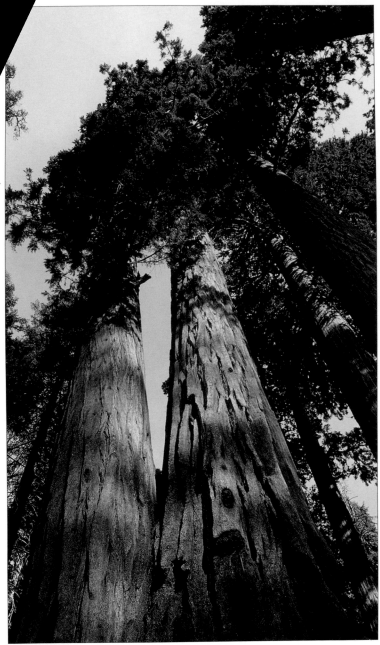

12 **Redwood National Park** Page **816** • The tallest trees in the world – some close to 400 feet high – preside over this dramatic national park, home to Roosevelt elk, black bears, and serene hiking trails.

13 The Chinese Theatre Page 130 •

A cherished relic of the Twenties, the Chinese Theatre recalls the glory years of Hollywood cinema, both with its Art Deco interior and the celebrity hand- and footprints pressed into the pavement outside.

14 Ride the Coast Starlight Page 489 •

While most visitors take to the highways, the best way to see the hundred-mile-long coast between Santa Barbara and San Luis Obispo is on the Coast Starlight train.

15 Bodie Ghost Town Page 409 •

Well past its 1880s gold-mining heyday, when it was the second largest town in the state, Bodie is now an intriguing time capsule of some 150 atmospheric wooden buildings.

16 La Jolla Page **249** • A glittering oceanside enclave where the San Diego elite reside in period revival mansions and where day-trippers come for the striking scenery, beachside coves, and quality museums.

17 The Third Street Promenade Page **149** • Sooner or later, all visitors to LA make their way to this Santa Monica pedestrian mall for its people watching, swinging nightlife, and fine dining options.

18 Gay Pride parade Page **635** • In late June, the Gay Pride parade takes over the streets of San Francisco's Castro district in exuberant fashion.

19 Mexican food Page **57** • Duck into a roadside *taqueria* or burrito joint to enjoy what's more or less the state's signature cuisine.

20 Surfing Pages **154** & **684** • From the gargantuan waves at Mavericks to the hot-dogging longboard mecca that is Malibu, California's consummate pastime can be enjoyed year-round on beaches all along its coast.

22 Whale watching Page **701** • Springtime is your best chance of seeing gray whales during their annual migration in the Pacific.

21 Hearst Castle Page **512** • O California's lavish dreams, none quite rivals William Randolph Hearst's monument to himself, which boasts a Mudejar cathedral facade and a private cinema.

23 Red Rock Canyon petroglyphs Page **396** • Once used as a backdrop in Spielberg's *Jurassic Park*, the canyon's rock formations present a panoply of aboriginal carvings.

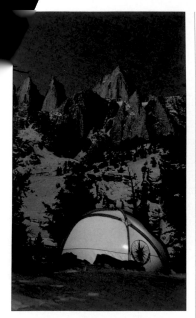

24 Hiking Mount Whitney
Page **386** • Hike the tallest mountain in the continental US, which sits right on the edge of Sequoia National Park.

25 Touring the Wine Country Page **770** • Sip
California's finest vintages on a trip to Wine Country, in Sonoma, Napa, Russian River, or Anderson valleys.

26 Cruising the Sunset Strip Page **142** • The Sunset Strip
has long been a choice LA place to hang out, jammed with groovy bars and clubs, swanky hotels, and towering billboards selling fashion, liquor, and starlets.

27 Centro Cultural Page **273** •
The eye-catching golf ball of a building in downtown Tijuana makes a good case for choosing culture over hedonism in the seedy town; while there, admire the impressive exhibits on Mexican culture and history.

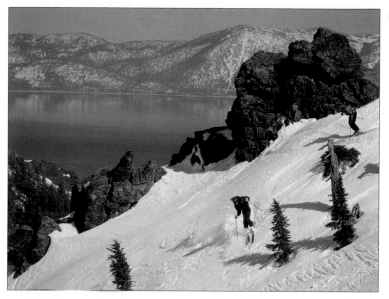

28 **Skiing and snowboarding at Lake Tahoe** Page **742** • Hit the renowned slopes around lovely Lake Tahoe, home to unbeatable downhill skiing and snowboarding.

30 **Berkeley's bookstores** Page **660** • The radical town holds a wide range of first- and second-hand bookstores, which make for an excellent day's browsing.

29 **Nevada City** Page **726** • One of the best preserved of the Gold Country towns, charming Nevada City is full of antique stores and quaint old buildings.

31 Cholla Cactus Garden Page
315 • One of the high points of any trip to Joshua Tree National Park is this cactus garden, a circular hike that takes in the unique jumping cholla.

32 La Purísima Mission
Page **501** • Just east of Lompoc, La Purísima reveals a faithful glimpse of late eighteenth-century mission life.

33 Viva Las Vegas Page **337** •
Just a patch of desert a century ago, Vegas has grown into the world's casino and resort capital, with replicas of whole cities in themed hotels like the *Venetian* along its famed strip.

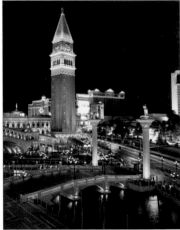

34 The Mojave National Preserve
Page **332** • The Mojave Desert can be shocking in its extremes and should not go unappreciated – some of the imposing sand dunes of the preserve, in the desert's eastern portion, rise as high as 4000 feet.

Basics

Basics

Getting there

The second largest state in the continental US, California presents an easy target for both domestic and international visitors. All the main airlines operate daily scheduled flights to San Francisco and LA from all over the world, and the state is easily accessible by road or rail throughout the year.

Generally, the most expensive time to fly is **high season**, roughly between June and August and around Christmas. April–May and September–October are considerably less pricey, and the rest of the year is considered low season and is cheaper still.

You can often cut costs by going through a **specialist flight agent** – either a consolidator, who buys up blocks of tickets from the airlines and sells them at a discount, or a **discount agent** who, in addition to dealing with discounted flights, may also offer special student and youth fares and a range of other travel-related services such as travel insurance, rail passes, car rentals, tours, and the like. Although there are no charter flights as such to the western United States, for some destinations, like Los Angeles, San Francisco, and Las Vegas, you may find it cheaper to pick up a bargain **package deal** from one of the tour operators listed below and then find your own accommodation when you get there.

Booking flights online

Many airlines and discount travel websites offer you the opportunity to book your tickets online, cutting out the costs of agents and middlemen. Good deals can often be found through discount or auction sites, as well as through the airlines' own websites, an increasingly simple and economic option.

Online booking agents and general travel sites

Note that many of the sites below have direct versions for the UK, Canada, Australia, or New Zealand by substituting .com with .co.uk, .com.ca, .com.au, or .com.nz respectively.

Ⓦ **www.cheapflights.com** Bookings for anywhere in the USA and a link for flights from the UK & Ireland.

Flight deals, travel agents, plus links to other travel sites.

Ⓦ **www.cheaptickets.com** Discount flight specialists; US only.

Ⓦ **www.etn.nl/discount.htm** A hub of consolidator and discount agent Web links, maintained by the nonprofit European Travel Network.

Ⓦ **www.expedia.com** Discount airfares, all-airline search engine and daily deals.

Ⓦ **www.gaytravel.com** Gay online travel agent, concentrating mostly on accommodation but some flights.

Ⓦ **www.hotwire.com** Bookings from the US only. Last-minute savings of up to forty percent on regular published fares. Travelers must be at least 18 and there are no refunds, transfers, or changes allowed. Log-in required.

Ⓦ **www.lastminute.com** Offers good last-minute holiday package and flight-only deals. Offers price-match guarantee.

Ⓦ **www.priceline.com** Name-your-own-price website that has deals at around forty percent off standard fares. You cannot specify flight times (although you do specify dates) and the tickets are non-refundable, non-transferable, and non-changeable.

Ⓦ **www.travelocity.com** Destination guides, hot Web fares, and best deals for car hire, accommodation and lodging, as well as fares. Provides access to the travel-agent system SABRE, the most comprehensive central reservations system in the US.

Ⓦ **www.travelshop.com.au** Australian website offering discounted flights, packages, insurance, and online bookings.

Ⓦ **www.travelzoo.com** Fast and efficient service for competitive flight deals originating in the USA or Canada.

From elsewhere in North America

Getting to California from anywhere else in North America is never a problem, for the region is well served by air, rail, and road networks. Flying remains the best but usually the most expensive way to travel;

taking a train comes a slow second and can even cost more. Traveling by bus is the least expensive method, but again is slow, and is much less comfortable than either by train or by plane.

By air

If you are flying to Los Angeles, most domestic flights land at the city's international **LAX** airport, though some touch down at the smaller airports at Burbank, Long Beach, Ontario, and John Wayne in Orange County. Visitors to San Francisco will probably use the main **San Francisco International Airport** (airport code SFO), as well as two others, both in the Bay Area: Oakland International (OAK), across the Bay, is easily accessible and **Norman J. Mineta San Jose International** (SJO), forty miles south, is a bit out of the way but has good connections with the western US, especially LA. Some carriers also fly to **San Diego's Lindbergh Airport** (SAN) nonstop.

As airlines tend to match each other's prices, there's generally little difference in the quoted fares. Published round-trip prices during the midweek in summer start at around $300 from New York and other eastern seaboard cities, slightly less from Midwest cities (and slightly more from Toronto and Montréal), although regular airline **promotions and savers** can nearly halve that price at slack times. What makes more difference than your choice of carrier are the conditions governing the ticket – whether it's fully refundable, the time and day, and, most importantly, the **time of year** you travel. Least expensive of all is a non-summer-season midweek flight, booked and paid for at least three weeks in advance, and they can be greatly discounted if booked many months in advance. Keep in mind too that one-way tickets are sometimes more expensive than round-trip tickets. Also, while it's good to check with the airlines directly to get a sense of their official fares, it's also worth contacting a reputable **travel agent**

Airlines in the US and Canada

Aer Lingus ☎1-800/474-7424, ⊛www.aerlingus.ie
Aeromexico ☎1-800/237-6639, ⊛www.aeromexico.com
Air Canada ☎1-888/247-2262, ⊛www.aircanada.com
Air France in the US ☎1-800/237-2747, ⊛www.airfrance.com; in Canada ☎1-800/667-2747, ⊛www.airfrance.ca
Alaska Airlines ☎1-800/252-7522, ⊛www.alaska-air.com
America West ☎1-800/235-9292, ⊛www.americawest.com
American Airlines ☎1-800/433-7300, ⊛www.aa.com
British Airways ☎1-800/247-9297, ⊛www.britishairways.com
Continental ☎1-800/523-3273, ⊛www.continental.com
Delta Airlines ☎1-800/221-1212 ⊛www.delta.com
Hawaiian Airlines ☎1-800/367-5320, ⊛www.hawaiianair.com
Iberia ☎1-800/772-4642, ⊛www.iberia.com
Icelandair ☎1-800/223-5500, ⊛www.icelandair.com
JetBlue ☎1-800/538-2583, ⊛www.jetblue.com
Lufthansa in the US ☎1-800/645-3880; in Canada ☎1-800/563-5954, ⊛www.lufthansa.com
Northwest/KLM ☎1-800/225-2525, ⊛www.nwa.com, ⊛www.klm.com
SAS ☎1-800/221-2350, ⊛www.scandinavian.net
Southwest ☎1-800/435-9792, ⊛www.southwest.com
United Airlines ☎1-800/241-6522, ⊛www.ual.com
US Airways ☎1-800/428-4322, ⊛www.usair.com
Virgin Atlantic Airways ☎1-800/862-8621, ⊛www.virginatlantic.com

to find out about any special deals or student/youth fares that may be available.

In addition to the big-name scheduled airlines, a few lesser-known carriers run no-frills flights, which can prove to be very good value, especially if you have a flexible schedule and can put up with a few delays. **JetBlue** often advertises flights from New York or Washington, DC, to several California airports for around $200 round-trip. **Southwest** flies from a host of Midwestern and Western cities at regular rock-bottom prices, especially using their Internet specials; six daily flights leave Chicago Midway for Oakland (they don't go directly to San Francisco) from $238 round-trip ($119 one-way) and four daily from Salt Lake City from $160 round-trip ($80 one-way). Their lowest fare out of Seattle to Oakland is $118 round-trip ($59 one-way), while LA to Oakland goes for as low as $78 round-trip ($39 one-way).

Travelers intending to fly from Canada are likely to find that, with less competition on these routes, fares are somewhat higher than they are for flights wholly within the US. You may well find that it's worth the effort to get to a US city first, and fly on to California from there.

By train

If you have a bit more money and hanker after a few more creature comforts (all the trains have private cabins and dining cars), or simply have the time and inclination to take in some of the rest of the US on your way to California, then an Amtrak **train** may be just the ticket for you. The most spectacular train journey of all has to be the **California Zephyr**, which runs all the way from Chicago to San Francisco (53 hours; departs 2.20pm daily) and comes into its own during the ride through the Rockies west of Denver. After climbing alongside raging rivers through gorgeous mountain scenery, the route drops down the west flank of the Rockies and races across the Utah and Nevada deserts by night, stopping at Salt Lake City and Reno. The next day the train climbs up and over the mighty Sierra Nevada, following the route of the first transcontinental railroad on its way into Oakland, where you change to a bus for the ride into San Francisco.

> For all information on **Amtrak fares and schedules**, and to make reservations, use the toll-free number ☏1-800/872-7245 or website ⓦwww.amtrak.com. Do not call individual stations.

Unfortunately the major southern cross-country route is no longer in operation, but two useful services are the **Texas Eagle**, which travels through chunks of the Mid-west and Southwest before eventually arriving in Los Angeles, and the **Coast Starlight**, which covers all of the West Coast between Seattle and Los Angeles.

Amtrak fares can be more expensive than flying, though off-peak discounts and special deals can make the train an economical as well as an aesthetic choice. A one-way cross-country ticket from New York to Oakland costs $208 on the day of travel, though it is only $133 if booked a month in advance. International travelers can take advantage of rail passes (see box, p.49 for a summary), while special deals and weekly rail sales for all comers are advertised on Amtrak's website (see box above). Although Amtrak's basic fares and passes are reasonable value, if you want to travel in a bit more comfort the cost rises quickly. Sleeping compartments, which include meals, small toilets, and showers, start at around $150 per night for one or two people.

By bus

Bus travel is the most tedious and time-consuming way to get to California, but, if you don't mind the discomfort, can save you a lot of money. **Greyhound** (☏1-800/231-2222, ⓦwww.greyhound.com) is the sole long-distance operator and has an extensive network of destinations in California. A one-way ticket from New York to San Francisco, bought seven days in advance, costs $109, while tickets purchased on the day of travel go for $169.

The best reason to go Greyhound is if you're planning to visit a number of other places en route; Greyhound's **Discovery Pass** (ⓦwww.discoverypass.com) is good for unlimited travel within a certain time, and costs $219 for seven days, $319 for fifteen

s, $419 for thirty days, and $589 for
xty days. Foreign visitors can buy better-
value **Ameripasses** before leaving home;
see box, p.49 for details.

An alternative, in every sense, is the San
Francisco–based **Green Tortoise** bus company; see box, p.50 for details.

By car

Driving your own car gives the greatest freedom and flexibility, but if you don't have one
(or don't trust the one you do have), one
option worth considering is a **driveaway**.
Companies operate in most major cities, and
are paid to find drivers to take a customer's
car from one place to another – most commonly between California and New York. The
company will normally pay for your insurance
and your first tank of gas; after that, you'll
be expected to drive along the most direct
route and to average 400 miles a day. Many
driveaway companies are keen to use foreign travelers, but if you can convince them
you are a safe bet they'll take something like
a $250 deposit, which you get back after
delivering the car in good condition. It makes
obvious sense to get in touch in advance,
to spare yourself a week's wait for a car to
turn up. Look under "Automobile transport-
ers and driveaway companies" in the *Yellow
Pages* and phone around for the latest offers;
or try one of the ninety branches of Auto
Driveaway, based in Chicago (☎312/341-
1900, ⓦwww.autodriveaway.com).

Renting a car is the usual story of phoning
your local branch of one of the majors (Avis,
Hertz, Budget, Thrifty, etc – listed on p.46),
of which Thrifty tends to be the cheapest.
Most have offices at destination airports, and
addresses and phone numbers are comprehensively documented in the *Yellow Pages*.

Also worth considering are **fly-drive** deals,
which give cut-rate (and sometimes free) car
rental when buying an air ticket. They usually work out cheaper than renting on the spot
and are especially good value if you intend
to do a lot of driving.

Package tours

Many operators run all-inclusive **packages** that combine plane tickets and hotel

accommodation with (for example) sightseeing, wining and dining, or excursions to
tourist sites. Even if the "package" aspect
doesn't thrill you to pieces, these deals can
still be more convenient and sometimes
even work out to be more economical than
arranging the same thing yourself, provided
you don't mind losing a little flexibility. With
such a vast range of packages available,
it's impossible to give an overview – major
travel agents will have brochures detailing
what's available.

Tour operators

Abercrombie & Kent ☎1-800/323-7308 or
630/954-2944, ⓦwww.abercrombiekent.com.
Well-tailored but rather upmarket tours.
Adventure Center ☎1-800/228-8747 or
510/654-1879, ⓦwww.adventure-center.com.
Hiking and "soft adventure" specialists.
Backroads ☎1-800/462-2848 or 510/527-1555,
ⓦwww.backroads.com. Cycling, hiking, and multi-
sport tours.
Holidaze Ski Tours ☎1-800/526-2827 or
732/280-1120, ⓦwww.holidaze.com. New
Jersey–based operation with Lake Tahoe deals.
Mountain Travel Sobek ☎1-888/687-6235 or
510/527-8100, ⓦwww.mtsobek.com. Conducts
hiking, kayaking, and rafting tours.
REI Adventures ☎1-800/622-2236, ⓦwww
.rei.com/travel. Climbing, cycling, hiking, cruising,
paddling, and multi-sport tours.

From Britain and Ireland

Though flying to California is pretty straightforward, choosing the best route can be
more complicated than you might think,
with prices fluctuating wildly according
to how and when you go. The majority of
budget options involve nonstop services
from Britain, although many others turn
out to be so-called "direct" flights, which
can land several times, waiting an hour or
so at each stop – a flight is called direct
as long as it keeps the same flight number
throughout its journey. The first place the
plane lands is your point of entry into the
US, which means you'll have to collect your
bags and go through customs and immigration formalities there, even if you're continuing on to California on the same plane.
This can be a real pain after a ten-hour
journey, so it's worth finding out before you
book a ticket.

Fares, routes, and agents

Although you can fly to the US from many regional airports, the only **nonstop flights** from Britain to California are from London, most of which land in LA, while fewer travel nonstop to San Francisco. The nonstop **flight time** is around eleven hours from London to San Francisco or LA; add an hour at least for each intervening stop on direct flights, twice that if you have to change planes.

Britain remains one of the best places in Europe to obtain flight **bargains**, though fares vary widely according to season, availability, and the current level of inter-airline competition. The comments that follow can only act as a general guide, so be sure to shop around carefully for the best offers by checking the travel ads in the weekend papers, on the holiday pages of ITV's *Teletext* and, in London, scouring *Time Out* and the *Evening Standard*. Giveaway magazines aimed at young travelers, like *TNT*, are also useful resources. The **Internet** is another valuable resource, and you'll often find good deals on any of the travel-based sites shown on p.27.

Stand-by deals (open-dated tickets you pay for and then decide later when you want to fly – if there's room on the plane) are few and far between and don't give great savings: in general you're better off with an **Apex** ticket. The conditions on these are pretty standard whomever you fly with – seats must be purchased seven days or more in advance, and you must stay for at least one Saturday night; tickets are normally valid for up to six months. Some airlines also do less-expensive **Super-Apex** tickets, which fall into two categories. The first are approximately £150 cheaper than an ordinary Apex

but must be bought 21 days in advance and require a minimum stay of seven days and a maximum stay of one month; the second are around £100 less than an Apex, must be purchased fourteen days in advance and entail a minimum stay of a week and a maximum stay of two months – such tickets are usually non-refundable or -changeable, at least the outward section. **"Open-jaw"** tickets can be a good idea, allowing you to fly into LA, for example, and back from San Francisco for little or no extra charge; fares are calculated by halving the return fares to each destination and adding the two figures together. This makes a convenient option for those who want a fly-drive holiday (see p.33).

For an overview of the various offers, and unofficially discounted tickets, go straight to an **agent** specializing in low-cost flights (we've listed some on p.32). Especially if you're under 26 or a student, they may be able to knock up to thirty percent off the regular Apex fares when there are no special airline deals. Agents will usually offer nonstop flights, or "direct" flights via another airport in the USA, although you may be offered other, stranger combinations (London–Los Angeles via Amsterdam, Manchester–Los Angeles via Paris for example) – all worth considering if the price is right.

Finally, if you've got a bit more time, or want to see a bit more of the USA, it's often possible to stop over in another city – **New York** especially – and fly on from there for little or no more than the cost of a direct flight to California. Also, with increased competition on the **London–Los Angeles** route, thanks to Virgin Atlantic among others and price wars between US carriers, the cost of a connecting flight from LA to San Francisco

Sample airfares from Britain

The prices given below (in £ sterling) are a general indication of the minimum transatlantic round-trip **airfares** currently obtainable from specialist companies; youth discount fares are cheaper. Remember to add £60–70 airport tax to these figures. Each airline decides the exact dates of its seasons. Prices are for departures from London to LA or San Francisco.

low	Nov–March (except Christmas)	200
shoulder	April, May, Sept, Oct	240
high	June–Aug, Christmas	540

One word of **warning**: it's not a good idea to buy a **one-way** ticket to the States. Not only are they rarely good value compared to a round-trip ticket, but US immigration officials usually take them as a sign that you aren't planning to go home and may refuse you entry. With increased airport checks, you are unlikely to be allowed even to board your flight to begin with.

has been brought down to less than £40. Many airlines also offer **air passes**, which allow foreign travelers to fly between a given number of US cities for one discounted price. For more details on long-distance travel within the US, see p.46.

Airlines

Air New Zealand ☎0800/028 4149, ⓦwww .airnz.co.uk
American Airlines ☎0845/778 9789, ⓦwww .aa.com
British Airways ☎0870/850 9850, ⓦwww .ba.com
Continental ☎0845/607 6760, ⓦwww .continental.com
Delta ☎0800/414 767, ⓦwww.delta.com
KLM/Northwest ☎870/507 4074, ⓦwww.klm.com

United ☎0845/844 4777, ⓦwww.ual.com
Virgin Atlantic ☎01293/450 150, ⓦwww .virgin-atlantic.com

Travel agents

Bridge the World UK ☎0870/443 2399, ⓦwww .bridgetheworld.com
eBookers UK ☎0870/010 7000, ⓦwww.ebookers .com, Republic of Ireland ☎1/241 5689, ⓦwww .ebookers.ie
Flight Centre UK ☎0870/890 8099, ⓦwww .flightcentre.co.uk
North South Travel UK ☎01245/608 291, ⓦwww.northsouthtravel.co.uk
STA Travel UK ☎0870/160 0599, ⓦwww .statravel.co.uk.
Trailfinders UK ☎020/7938 3939, ⓦwww .trailfinders.com, Republic of Ireland ☎1/677 7888, ⓦwww.trailfinders.ie
Travel Bag UK ☎0870/890 1456, ⓦwww .travelbag.co.uk
USIT Northern Ireland ☎028/9032 7111, ⓦwww .usitnow.com, Republic of Ireland ☎0818/200 020, ⓦwww.usit.ie
World Travel Centre Republic of Ireland ☎01/416 7007, ⓦwww.worldtravel.ie

Tour operators

Airtours UK ☎0870/238 7788, ⓦwww.airtours .co.uk. Multi-center holidays including

Flights from Britain

The following carriers operate **nonstop flights** from London to California (all from Heathrow):

Air New Zealand daily to Los Angeles.

American Airlines daily to Los Angeles.

Continental daily to Los Angeles and San Francisco.

British Airways daily to Los Angeles and San Francisco.

United Airlines daily to Los Angeles and San Francisco.

Virgin Atlantic daily to Los Angeles and San Francisco.

The following carriers operate **one-stop flights** from London to California (all from Gatwick unless otherwise stated):

American Airlines daily via Dallas to San Francisco, and daily from Heathrow via New York, Chicago, Los Angeles, or Miami to San Francisco.

Continental daily via Houston or Newark to Los Angeles, San Francisco, and San Diego.

Delta daily via Cincinnati or Atlanta to Los Angeles, San Francisco, and San Diego.

KLM/Northwest daily via Detroit or Minneapolis to Los Angeles and San Francisco.

combinations of Los Angeles, San Francisco, and Las Vegas.

American Holidays Northern Ireland ☎ 028/9023 8762, Republic of Ireland ☎ 1/673 3840, ⓦ www .american-holidays.com. All sorts of package tours to the US, including California, from Ireland.

Bon Voyage UK ☎ 0800/316 3012, ⓦ www.bon -voyage.co.uk. Flight-plus-accommodation deals in San Francisco, Los Angeles, Palm Springs, and Las Vegas.

British Airways Holidays UK ☎ 0870/240 0747, ⓦ www.baholidays.co.uk. City breaks in Los Angeles, San Diego, and San Francisco, and fly-drive deals (including motorhomes).

Contiki Travel UK ☎ 020/8290 6777, ⓦ www .contiki.co.uk. West Coast coach tours, aimed at 18–35-year-olds willing to party.

Explore Worldwide UK ☎ 01252/760 000, ⓦ www.explore.co.uk. Small-group walking tours, camping, or staying in hotels.

Holiday America UK ☎ 01424/224 400. Flight-plus-accommodation and fly-drive combinations.

Kuoni UK ☎ 1306/747 002, ⓦ www.kuoni.co.uk. Multi-center flight-plus-accommodation-plus-car deals featuring Los Angeles, San Francisco, and San Diego. Special deals for families.

Premier Holidays UK ☎ 0870/889 0850, ⓦ www .premierholidays.co.uk. Flight-plus-accommodation deals throughout California.

TrekAmerica UK ☎ 01295/256 777, ⓦ www .trekamerica.com. Touring adventure holidays, usually small groups in well-equipped four-wheel-drive vans.

United Vacations UK ☎ 0870/606 2222, ⓦ www .unitedvacations.co.uk. City breaks, tailor-mades, and fly-drives.

Virgin Holidays UK ☎ 0870/220 2788, ⓦ www .virginholidays.co.uk. Packages to a wide range of California destinations.

Packages

Packages – fly-drive, flight-accommodation deals, and guided tours (or a combination of all three) – can work out cheaper than arranging the same trip yourself, especially for a short-term stay. The obvious drawbacks are the loss of flexibility and the fact that most schemes use hotels in the mid-range bracket, but there is a wide variety of options available. Travel agents have plenty of brochures and information about the various combinations.

Fly-drive

Fly-drive deals, which give cut-rate (sometimes free) car rental when buy-

ing a transatlantic ticket, always work out cheaper than renting on the spot and give especially great value if you intend to do a lot of driving. On the other hand, you'll probably have to pay more for the flight than if you booked it through a discount agent. Competition between airlines and tour operators means that it's well worth phoning to check on current special promotions.

Northwest Flydrive offers excellent deals for not much more than an ordinary Apex fare; for example, a return flight to LA or San Francisco and a week's car rental (including basic insurance) might cost less than £300 per person in low season. Several of the other airlines listed opposite offer similar, and sometimes even cheaper, packages. It's also well worth checking what's on offer through the agents and tour operators listed opposite.

Watch out for hidden extras, such as local taxes, "drop-off" charges, which can be as much as a week's rental, and Collision Damage Waiver insurance (see p.46). Remember, too, that while you can drive in the States with a British license, there can be problems renting vehicles if you're under 25. For complete car-rental and driveaway details, see "Getting around" (p.45).

Flight and accommodation details

There's really no end of combined flight and accommodation deals to California. Drawbacks include the loss of flexibility and the fact that you'll probably have to stay in hotels in the mid-range to expensive bracket, even though less expensive accommodation is almost always available.

A handful of tour operators offer quite deluxe packages, of which Virgin Holidays are among the least expensive: for example, seven nights in San Francisco plus return flight costs around £550 in low season, £830 per person in high season. Discount agents can set up more basic packages for under £500 each. Pre-booked accommodation schemes, under which you buy vouchers for use in a specific group of hotels, are not normally good value.

Touring and adventure packages

A simple and exciting way to see a chunk of California's extensive wilderness, without being hassled by too many practical considerations, is to take a specialist touring and adventure package, which includes transportation, accommodation, food, and a guide. Some of the more adventurous carry small groups around on minibuses and use a combination of budget hotels and camping (equipment, except a sleeping bag, is provided). Most also have a food kitty of around £40 per week, with many meals cooked and eaten communally, although there's plenty of time to leave the group and do your own thing.

TrekAmerica (see p.33) is one UK-based company to offer such deals; a typical package would be the seven-day "Western Wonder" tour (San Francisco–Yosemite–Las Vegas–Grand Canyon–Colorado River–Los Angeles) from £379–454 excluding flights. Other operators are listed on the preceding page. If you're interested in backcountry hiking, the San Francisco–based Sierra Club (see box, p.69) offers a range of tours that take you into parts of the state that most people never see.

Flights from Ireland

Aer Lingus operates the only **nonstop flight** to Los Angeles from Dublin five times a week. The cheapest flights from Ireland – if you're under 26 or a student – are available from USIT. Student-only return **fares** to San Francisco or Los Angeles direct range from €380 to €600. Non-students can expect to pay €450 to €700. Flights via London may cost less, but you pay slightly more tax. Ordinary Apex fares are only marginally higher.

See p.32 for USIT contact details. Aer Lingus is at 40 O'Connell St, Dublin 1, and Dublin Airport (℡01/886 8888, ⊛www .aerlingus.ie), and Delta Airlines is at 24 Merrion Square, Dublin 2 (℡01/676 8080).

From Australia and New Zealand

If you are coming from Australia and New Zealand, there's very little price difference between airlines and no shortage of flights, either via the Pacific or Asia, to Los Angeles and San Francisco. Crossing the Pacific most flights are nonstop, with traveling time between Auckland/Sydney and LA twelve to fourteen hours, though some allow stopovers in Honolulu and a number of the South Pacific islands. If you go via Asia (a slightly more roundabout route that can work out a little cheaper), you'll usually have to spend a night, or the best part of a day, in the airline's home city.

Various **coupon deals** – available with your international ticket for discounted flights within the US – are good value if California is part of a wider US trip. A minimum purchase of three coupons usually applies and should cost under US$400. Tickets purchased directly from the airlines are usually at published rates, which are often more expensive than a round-the-world fare. Travel agents offer the best deals on fares and have the latest information on limited special offers, such as free stopovers, fly-drive-accommodation and Disneyland packages. Flight Centres and STA (which offer fare reductions for ISIC cardholders and under-26s) generally offer the lowest fares.

Airfares vary throughout the year, with seasonal differences generally working out between A/NZ$200–400. For most airlines, **low season** is from mid-January to the end of February and October to the end of November; **high season** mid-May to the end of August and December to mid-January; **shoulder seasons** cover the rest of the year, though all of this is complicated by periodic high prices during school holidays. Seat availability on most international flights out of Australia and New Zealand is limited, so it's best to book at least several weeks ahead.

Traveling from **Australia**, fares to LA and San Francisco from eastern cities cost the same, while from Perth they're about A$350 more. There are daily nonstop flights from Sydney, to LA and San Francisco on United Airlines and to LA on Qantas, for around A$1850 low season. In addition there are several airlines that fly via Asia, which involves either a transfer or stopover in their home cities. The best deals are usually on China Airlines (from A$1480) but there can be lengthy stopovers. If you don't want to waste the time, Cathay Pacific can get you there, via a transfer in Hong Kong, from around A$1610, and Air Tahiti Nui (via Tahiti) for around A$50 more. Look out for special deals from agents at slack times, which can see tickets to Los Angeles from Sydney go for as little as A$1250.

From **New Zealand**, most flights are out of Auckland (add about NZ$150–200 for Christchurch and Wellington departures). The best deals for the more direct Pacific routes are on Air Tahiti Nui via Tahiti (from NZ$1510), while on both Air New Zealand, to Los Angeles either nonstop or via Honolulu, Fiji, Tonga, or Papeete, and United Airlines, also nonstop to LA or San Francisco, cost from around NZ$1800. Air Pacific via Fiji, and Qantas via Sydney (though direct is cheaper) both start around NZ$1900–2000. Via Asia, Singapore Airlines offers the best connecting service to LA and San Francisco from N7$2000.

If you intend to take in California as part of a world trip, a round-the-world (**RTW**) ticket offers the greatest flexibility. In recent years, many of the major international airlines have aligned themselves with one of two globe-spanning networks: the "Star Alliance," which links Air New Zealand, Ansett Australia, United, Lufthansa, Thai, SAS, Varig, and Air Canada; and "One World," which combines routes run by American, British Airways, Canadian Airlines, Cathay Pacific, LAN Chile, and Qantas. Both offer RTW deals with three stopovers in each continental sector you visit, with the option of adding additional sectors relatively cheaply. Fares depend on the number of sectors required, but start at around A$2400 (low season) for a US–Europe–Asia–and–home itinerary. If this is more flexibility than you need, you can save $200–300 by going with an individual airline (in concert with code-share partners) and accepting fewer stops.

Airlines

Air New Zealand Australia ☎132 476, ⓦwww.airnz.com.au; New Zealand ☎800/737 000, ⓦwww.airnz.co.nz
Air Pacific Australia ☎1-800/230 150, New Zealand ☎800/800 178; ⓦwww.airpacific.com

Air Tahiti Nui Australia ☎02/9244 2899, New Zealand ☎09/308 3360; ⓦwww.airtahitinui-usa.com
Cathay Pacific Australia ☎131 747, New Zealand ☎09/379 0861; ⓦwww.cathaypacific.com
China Airlines Australia ☎02/9244 2121, New Zealand ☎09/308 3371; ⓦwww.china-airlines.com
Delta Air Lines Australia ☎02/9251 3211, New Zealand ☎09/379 3370; ⓦwww.delta.com
JAL Japan Airlines Australia ☎2/9272 1111, New Zealand ☎09/379 9906; ⓦwww.jal.com
Korean Air Australia ☎02/9262 6000, New Zealand ☎09/914 2000; ⓦwww.koreanair.com.au
Qantas Australia ☎131 313, New Zealand ☎9/357 8900; ⓦwww.qantas.com
Singapore Airlines Australia ☎0131 011, New Zealand ☎800/808 909; ⓦwww.singaporeair.com
United Airlines Australia ☎131 777, ⓦwww.unitedairlines.com.au; New Zealand ☎9/379 3800, ⓦwww.unitedairlines.co.nz

Travel agents

Budget Travel New Zealand ☎800/808 480, ⓦwww.budgettravel.co.nz. Major countrywide flight discounter.
Flight Centre Australia ☎133 133, ⓦwww.flightcentre.com.au; New Zealand ☎800/243 544, ⓦwww.flightcentre.co.nz. Near-ubiquitous high-street agency frequently offering some of the lowest fares around.
Holiday Shoppe New Zealand ☎800/808 480, ⓦwww.holidayshoppe.co.nz. Great deals on flights, hotels, and holidays.
STA Travel Australia ☎1300/733 035, ⓦwww.statravel.com.au; New Zealand ☎508/782 872, ⓦwww.statravel.co.nz. A major player in student, youth, and budget travel with branches in many universities.
Trailfinders Australia ☎02/9247 7666, ⓦwww.trailfinders.com.au. Knowledgeable staff skilled at turning up odd itineraries and good prices.
Travel.com.au Australia ☎02/9249 5444, ⓦwww.travel.com.au. Youth-oriented center with an efficient travel agency offering good fares, a travel bookshop, and Internet café.
Travel.com.au New Zealand ☎800/788 336, ⓦwww.travel.co.nz. Kiwi version of the youth-oriented agency above.

Specialist agents

Adventure World Australia ☎02/8913 0755, ⓦwww.adventureworld.com.au; New Zealand ☎9/524 5118, ⓦwww.adventureworld.com.nz.

Individual and small-group exploratory tours and treks.

Canada & America Travel Specialists Australia ☎02/9922 4600, ⓦwww.canada-americatravel .com.au. North American specialists – offering everything from flights and hotels to travel passes and adventure sports.

Journeys Worldwide Australia ☎07/3221 4788, ⓦwww.journeysworldwide.com.au. All US travel arrangements available.

Peregrine Adventures Australia ☎03/9663 8611, ⓦwww.peregrine.net.au. With offices in Brisbane, Sydney, Adelaide, and Perth, Peregrine

offers small-group active holidays from short walking and camping to longer overland trips through California.

Sydney International Travel Centre Australia ☎02/9250 9320, ⓦwww.sydneytravel.com.au. Individually tailored holidays, Disneyland passes, flights, and bus and rail tours.

Travelplan Australia Australia ☎02/9958 1888, ⓦwww.travelplan.com.au. Ski holiday packages in the Lake Tahoe region.

USA Travel Australia ☎02/9250 9320, ⓦwww .usatravel.au. Good deals on flights, accommodation, city stays, car rental and trip packages.

Red tape and visas

Under the Visa Waiver Program – designed to speed up lengthy immigration procedures – citizens of Andorra, Australia, Austria, Belgium, Brunei, Denmark, Finland, France, Germany, Iceland, Ireland, Italy, Japan, Liechtenstein, Luxembourg, Monaco, the Netherlands, New Zealand, Norway, Portugal, San Marino, Singapore, Slovenia, Spain, Sweden, Switzerland, and the United Kingdom visiting the United States for a period of less than ninety days only need a machine-readable passport and a visa waiver form. The latter will be provided either by your travel agency, or by the airline before check-in or on the plane, and must be presented to immigration on arrival. The same form covers entry across the land borders with Canada and Mexico as well as by air. However, those eligible for the scheme must apply for a visa if they intend to work, study, or stay in the country for more than ninety days.

Prospective visitors from parts of the world not mentioned above don't have it so easy. As well as a passport valid six months beyond your intended stay you'll need a **Non-immigrant Visa**. How you'll obtain a visa depends on what country you're in and your status when you apply, so contact the nearest US embassy or consulate (listed below). You'll be charged the equivalent of $100 simply to apply, and if successful may have to pay a further "reciprocity fee" depending on what your country charges US citizens for a visa. Visa applicants must now submit to a finger scan so you will almost certainly have to schedule an appointment at your nearest embassy or consulate. Non-immigrant visas will not normally be issued outside your home country, so apply before setting out. Expect

the whole process to take at least four weeks, longer if they have even the slightest reason to think you might be involved with terrorists. Application forms can be downloaded from the Department of State website (ⓦtravel .state.gov/visa/tempvisitors.html), which also has stacks of relevant information.

Whatever your nationality, visas are not issued to convicted felons and anybody who owns up to being a communist, fascist, or a drug dealer.

US embassies and consulates abroad

Australia

Canberra Moonah Place, Yarralumla, ACT 2600 ☎02/6214 5600, ⓔinfo@usembassy-australia .state.gov, ⓦusembassy-australia.state.gov

Melbourne 553 St Kilda Road, Vic 3004
①03/9526 5900, ⑥9510 4646
Perth 16 St George's Terrace, 13th floor, WA 6000
①08/9202 1224, ⑥PerthConsular@state.gov
Sydney MLC Centre, 59th floor, 19–29 Martin
Place, NSW 2000 ①02/9373 9200, ⑥9373 9125

Canada

for all visa applications and appointment
bookings call ①1-900/451-2788 ($2 a
minute) or visit ⑩www.amcits.com.
Calgary 615 Macleod Trail SE, Room 1000, AB T2G
4T8 ①403/266-8962, ⑥264-6630
Halifax Suite 904, Purdy's Wharf Tower II,1969
Upper Water St, NS B3J 3R7 ①902/429-2480,
⑥423-6861
Montréal 1155 St Alexandre St, PQ H3B 1Z1
①514/398-9695, ⑥398-0973
Ottawa 490 Sussex Drive, ON K1N 1G8
①613/238-5335, ⑩www.usembassycanada.gov
Québec City 2 Place Terrasse Dufferin, Québec
G1R 4T9 ①418/692-2095
Toronto 360 University Ave, ON M5G 1S4
①416/595-1700, ⑥595-0051
Vancouver 1095 W Pender St, BC V6E 2M6
①604/685-4311, ⑥685-5285

Ireland

Dublin 42 Elgin Rd, Ballsbridge ①1/668-8777,
⑥668-9946, ⑩dublin.usembassy.gov

New Zealand

Auckland 3rd floor, Citibank Building, 23 Customs
St ①9/303 2724, ⑥366 0870
Wellington 29 Fitzherbert Terrace, Thorndon
①4/462 6000, ⑥499 0490, ⑩usembassy.org.nz

South Africa

Cape Town 7th floor, Monte Carlo Building,
Heerengracht, Foreshore ①21/421 4280,
⑥425 3014
Durban Old Mutual Building, 31st floor, 303 West
St ①31/305 7600, ⑥305 7691
Johannesburg 1 River St, Killarney ①11/644
8000, ⑥646 6916
Pretoria 877 Pretorius St, Pretoria 0083 ①12/431
4000, ⑥342 2299, ⑩usembassy.state
.gov/pretoria

UK

Belfast Danesfort House, 223 Stranmillis Road,
BT9 5GR ①028/9038 6100, ⑥9068 1301
Edinburgh 3 Regent Terrace, EH7 5BW ①131/556
8315, ⑥edinburgh-info@state.gov. London handles
all visa applications for Scotland.

London 24 Grosvenor Square, W1A 1AE
①20/7499 9000; visa hotline (24hr; 60p a minute)
①9068/200 290, operator-assisted information
line (Mon–Fri 8am–8pm, Sat 10am–4pm; £1.30 a
minute) ①09055/444 546, ⑩www.usembassy
.org.uk

Embassies and consulates in California

Australia

Los Angeles 2049 Century Park E, 19th floor, CA
90067 ①310/229-4800, ⑩www.austemb
.org/Consulates/LosAngeles.htm

Canada

Los Angeles South Hope Street, 9th floor,
CA 90071-2627 ①213/346-2700, ⑥346-2767,
⑩www.dfait-maeci.gc.ca/can-am/los_angeles
San Francisco 555 Montgomery St, Suite 1288,
CA 94111 ①415/ 834-3180, ⑥5834-3189,
⑥sfran@dfait-maeci.gc.ca, ⑩www.dfait-maeci
.gc.ca/can-am/san_francisco

South Africa

Los Angeles 6300 Wilshire Blvd, Suite 600, CA
90048 ①323/651-0902, ⑩www.link2southafrica
.com

UK

Los Angeles 11766 Wilshire Blvd, Suite 1200, CA
90025 ①310/477-0031, ⑥481-2960, ⑩www
.britainusa.com/la/
San Francisco 1 Sansome St, Suite 850, CA
94101 ①415/617-1300, ⑥434-2018, ⑩www
.britainusa.com/sf/

Immigration controls

The standard immigration regulations apply
to all visitors, whether or not they are using
the Visa Waiver Program. During the flight,
you'll be handed an immigration form (and a
customs declaration), which must be given
up at immigration control once you land.
The form requires you cite your proposed
length of stay and to list an address, at least
for your first night. Previously "touring" was
satisfactory, but since September 11, controls have become more stringent and they
require a verifiable address
officials may insist yc
accommodation for
writing down a ⌐
from the appropr'

will probably get you through. The proposed implementation of the "Advanced Passenger Information System" will mean that you'll have to give this information at check-in, so be prepared.

You probably won't be asked unless you look disreputable in the eyes of the official on duty, but you should be able to prove that you have a return air ticket (if flying in), and enough money to support yourself while in the US; anyone revealing the slightest intention of working while in the country is likely to be refused admission. Around $300–400 a week is usually considered sufficient – waving a credit card or two may do the trick. You may also experience difficulties if you admit to being HIV positive or having AIDS or TB. Part of the immigration form will be attached to your passport, where it must stay until you leave, when an immigration or airline official will detach it.

Customs

Customs officers will relieve you of your customs declaration and check if you're

carrying any fresh foods. You'll also be asked if you've visited a farm in the last month – if you have, you may well have your shoes taken away for inspection. The duty-free allowance if you're over 17 is 200 cigarettes and 100 cigars, a liter of spirits (if you're over 21), and $800 worth of gifts. As well as foods and anything agricultural, it's prohibited to carry into the country any articles from Burma, Cuba, Iran, Iraq, Liberia, North Korea, Serbia and Montenegro, and Sudan, obscene publications and drug paraphernalia, or pre-Columbian artifacts. Anyone caught carrying drugs into the country will not only face prosecution, but be entered in the records as an undesirable and probably denied entry for all time. There are more details on the US Customs website Ⓦ www.customs.treas.gov.

Extensions and leaving

The date stamped on your passport is the latest you're legally allowed to stay. Leaving a few days later may not matter, especially if you're heading home, but more than a week or so can result in a protracted, rather unpleasant interrogation from officials, which may cause you to miss your flight and be denied entry to the US in the future.

To get an extension before your time is up, apply at the nearest US Citizenship and Immigration Service (Ⓦ uscis.gov) office; the address will be under the Federal Government Offices listings at the front of the phone book. The service will automatically assume that you're working illegally, and it's up to you to convince them otherwise. Do this by providing evidence of ample finances and, if you can, bring along an upstanding American citizen to vouch for you. You'll also have to explain why you didn't plan for the extra time initially.

Canadian citizens are in a particularly privileged position when it comes to crossing the border into the US. Though it is possible to enter the States without your passport, you should really have it with you on any trip that brings you as far as California. Only if you plan to stay for more than ninety days do you need a visa. Bear in mind that if you cross into the US by car, trunks and passenger compartments are subject to spot searches by Customs personnel. Remember too, that without the proper paperwork, Canadians are legally barred from seeking gainful employment in the US.

Information, websites, and maps

California's official tourism website (@www.visitcalifornia.com) is a reasonable starting point for advance information. Much of the same material is available in their free "tourism information packet," which can be ordered online, by calling ☎1-800/GOCALIF, or by contacting the California Office of Tourism, 801 K St, Suite 1600, Sacramento, CA 95814-3520 ☎916/322-2881 or 1-800/862-2543. Once you've arrived in the state, you'll find most towns have visitor centers of some description – often called the Convention and Visitors Bureau (CVB) or Chamber of Commerce: useful ones are listed in the Guide. These will give out detailed information on the local area and can often help with finding accommodation. Free newspapers in most areas carry news of events and entertainment.

Most bookstores will have a range of local trail guides, the best of which we've listed in Contexts, p.903.

Websites

Nowhere is more Net-savvy than California and almost anything you might wish to know (and a lot more besides) is available online. We've included the most useful websites throughout the Guide, and have listed a few sites below which should inspire further exploration.

Ain't It Cool News @www.aintitcoolnews.com. Self-confessed geek Harry Knowles offers up rambling film reviews and Hollywood insider secrets.
Backcountry Resource Center @pweb.jps.net/~prichins/backcountry_resource_center.htm. Superb noncommercial site laden with valuable information on backcountry skiing, climbing, and general outdoor interest with plenty of useful links.
The California Beerpage @www.beerpage.com. Accessible guide to California's microbreweries and beer festivals.
Caltrans: The California Department of Transportation @www.dot.ca.gov. Straightforward and informative, the Caltrans homepage contains current highway conditions, public transit schedules, information on traveling by bike, and more.
E! Online @www.eonline.com. Breathless, gossipy, and visually gorgeous site with pages full of star profiles and movie reviews.
LA Times @www.latimes.com. California's largest circulation newspaper and good source of current state news.
Rough Guides @www.roughguides.com. Post any of your pre-trip questions – or post-trip suggestions – in Travel Talk, our online forum for travelers.

Surfline @www.surfline.comt. US-wide surf site that's strong on California breaks, with daily surf reports, surfcams, and good local beta.
Variety @www.variety.com. The daily morning read of Hollywood insiders, full of news, reviews, previews, and the latest Tinseltown tales.

Maps

Tourist offices throughout the state supply good maps, either free or for a small charge, and, supplemented with our own, these should be enough for general sightseeing and touring. Rand McNally (see following page) produces a good low-cost fold-out map of the state ($4.95) and its Road Atlas ($8.99), covering the whole country plus Mexico and Canada, is a worthwhile investment if you're traveling further afield. For driving or cycling through rural areas, the Atlas & Gazetteer: Northern California and Atlas & Gazetteer: Southern California ($19.95 each; published by DeLorme, @www.delorme.com) are valuable companions, with detailed city plans, marked campsites, and reams of national park and forest information. Hikers should visit ranger stations in parks and wilderness areas, which all sell good-quality local topographic maps for around $4, and camping stores generally have a good selection too. The American Automobile Association (@www.aaa-calif.com), has offices in most large cities and provides excellent free maps and travel assistance to its members, and members of affiliated organizations elsewhere.

Map outlets

In the US and Canada

AdventurousTraveler.com ⓦ www.atb.away
.com

Book Passage 51 Tamal Vista Blvd, Corte Madera,
CA 94925 ☎ 1-800/999-7909, ⓦ www
.bookpassage.com

Distant Lands 56 S Raymond Ave, Pasadena, CA
91105 ☎ 1-800/310-3220, ⓦ www.distantlands
.com

Elliot Bay Book Company 101 S Main St,
Seattle, WA 98104 ☎ 1-800/962-5311, ⓦ www
.elliotbaybook.com

Get Lost 1825 Market St, San Francisco, CA
94103 ☎ 415/437-0529, ⓦ www.getlostbooks
.com

Globe Corner Bookstore 28 Church St,
Cambridge, MA 02138 ☎ 1-800/358-6013,
ⓦ www.globecorner.com

Map Link 30 S La Patera Lane, Unit 5, Santa
Barbara, CA 93117 ☎ 1-800/962-1394, ⓦ www
.maplink.com

Map Town 400 5 Ave SW, Calgary, AB T2P 0L6
☎ 403/266-2241 ⓦ www.maptown.com

Phileas Fogg's Books & Maps 87 Stanford
Shopping Center, Palo Alto, CA 94304
☎ 1-800/233-3644, ⓔ foggs@aol.com

Rand McNally ☎ 1-800/333-0136, ⓦ www
.randmcnally.com. Stores online and in
Massachusetts, Pennsylvania, Illinois, Texas, and
California (San Francisco, Irvine, and LA); call or
check the website for the nearest location.

Sierra Club Bookstore 6014 College Ave,
Oakland, CA 94618 ☎ 510/658-8083, ⓦ www
.sierraclub.org/store

Travel Bug Bookstore 3065 W Broadway,
Vancouver, BC V6K 2G9 ☎ 604/737-1122, ⓦ www
.travelbugbooks.ca

World of Maps 1235 Wellington St, Ottawa, ON
K1Y 3A3 ☎ 1-800/214-8524, ⓦ www
.worldofmaps.com

In the UK and Ireland

Blackwell's Map and Travel Shop 48–51 Broad
St, Oxford OX1 3BQ ☎ 01865/792 7922, ⓦ www
.blackwell.co.uk

Easons Bookshop 40 O'Connell St, Dublin 1
☎ 01/858 3800, ⓦ www.eason.ie

Heffers Map and Travel 20 Trinity St, Cambridge
CB2 1TJ ☎ 01223/568 568, ⓦ www.heffers.co.uk

Hodges Figgis Bookshop 56–58 Dawson St,
Dublin 2 ☎ 01/677 4754, ⓦ www.hodgesfiggis
.com

James Thin Booksellers 53–59 South Bridge,
Edinburgh EH1 1YS ☎ 0131/622 8222, ⓦ www
.jamesthin.co.uk

The Map Shop 30a Belvoir St, Leicester LE1 6QH
☎ 0116/247 1400, ⓦ www.mapshopleicester.co.uk

National Map Centre 22–24 Caxton St, London
SW1H 0QU ☎ 020/7222 2466, ⓦ www.mapsnmc
.co.uk, ⓔ info@mapsnmc.co.uk

Newcastle Map Centre 55 Grey St, Newcastle-
upon-Tyne NE1 6EF ☎ 0191/261 5622, ⓦ www
.newtraveller.com

Ordnance Survey Ireland Phoenix Park, Dublin 8
☎ 01/802 5300, ⓦ www.osi.ie, ⓔ custserve@osi.ie

Ordnance Survey of Northern Ireland Colby
House, Stranmillis Ct, Belfast BT9 5BJ ☎ 028/9025
5755, ⓦ www.osni.gov.uk

Stanfords 12–14 Long Acre, London WC2E 9LP
☎ 020/7836 1321, ⓦ www.stanfords.co.uk,
ⓔ sales@stanfords.co.uk. Maps available by mail,
phone order, or email. Other branches at 39 Spring
Gardens, Manchester M2 2BG ☎ 0161/831 0257
and 29 Corn St, Bristol BS1 1HT ☎ 0117/929 9966.

The Travel Bookshop 13–15 Blenheim Crescent,
London W11 2EE ☎ 020/7229 5260, ⓦ www
.thetravelbookshop.co.uk

In Australia and New Zealand

Auckland Map Centre National Bank Centre,
Shop 3, 209 Queen St, Auckland 1001 ☎ 09/307
7725, ⓦ www.aucklandmapcentre.co.nz.

The Map Shop 6–10 Peel St, Adelaide, SA 5000
☎ 08/8231 2033, ⓦ www.mapshop.net.au

Mapland 372 Little Bourke St, Melbourne, Victoria
3000 ☎ 03/9670 4383, ⓦ www.mapland.com.au

MapWorld 173 Gloucester St, Christchurch, New
Zealand ☎ 0800/627 967 or 03/374 5399, ⓦ www
.mapworld.co.nz

Perth Map Centre 884 Hay St, Perth, WA 6000
☎ 08/9322 5733

Insurance

Even though EU health care privileges apply in America, residents of the United Kingdom would do well to take out an insurance policy before traveling to cover against theft, loss, and illness or injury. Before paying for a new policy, however, it's worth checking whether you are already covered – some all-risks home insurance policies may cover your possessions when overseas, and many private medical schemes include cover when abroad. In Canada, provincial health plans usually provide partial cover for medical mishaps overseas, while holders of official student/teacher/youth cards in Canada and the US are entitled to meagre accident coverage and hospital in-patient benefits. Students will often find that their student health coverage extends during the vacations and for one term beyond the date of last enrolment.

After exhausting the possibilities above, you might want to contact a specialist travel insurance company, or consider the travel insurance deal Rough Guides offers (see box). A typical travel insurance policy usually provides cover for the loss of baggage, tickets, and – up to a certain limit – cash or checks, as well as cancellation or curtailment of your journey. Most of them exclude so-called dangerous sports unless an extra premium is paid: in America, this can mean scuba diving, whitewater rafting, windsurfing, and trekking, though probably not kayaking or jeep safaris. Many policies can be chopped and changed to exclude coverage you don't need – for example, sickness and accident benefits can often be excluded or included at will. If you do take medical coverage, ascertain whether benefits will be paid as treatment proceeds or only after return home, and if there is a 24-hour medical emergency number. When securing baggage cover, make sure that the per-article limit – typically under £500 – will cover your most valuable possession. If you need to make a claim, you should keep receipts for medicines and medical treatment, and in the event you have anything stolen, you must obtain an official theft report from the police.

Rough Guides travel insurance

Rough Guides has teamed up with Columbus Direct to offer you travel insurance that can be tailored to suit your needs.

Readers can choose from many different travel insurance products, including a low-cost backpacker option for long stays; a short break option for city getaways; a typical holiday package option; and many others. There are also annual multi-trip, policies for those who travel regularly, with variable levels of cover available. Different sports and activities (trekking, skiing, etc) can be covered if required on most policies.

Rough Guides travel insurance is available to the residents of 36 different countries with different language options to choose from via our website – Ⓦwww.roughguides.com/insurance – where you can also purchase the insurance.

Alternatively, UK residents should call ☎0800 083 9507; US citizens should call ☎1-800 749-4922; Australians should call ☎1 300 669 999. All other nationalities should call ☎+44 870 890 2843.

Health

Foreign travelers should be comforted that if you have a serious accident while you're in California, emergency services will get to you sooner and charge you later. For emergencies, dial toll-free ☏911 from any phone. If you have medical or dental problems that don't require an ambulance, most hospitals will have a walk-in emergency room: for your nearest hospital, check with your hotel or dial information at ☏411. The same is true for dental work.

Should you need to see a doctor, lists can be found in the *Yellow Pages* under "Clinics" or "Physicians and Surgeons." Be aware that even consultations are costly, usually around $75–100 each visit, which is payable in advance. Keep receipts for any part of your medical treatment, including prescriptions, so that you can claim against your insurance once you're home.

For minor ailments, stop by a local pharmacy, many of which are open 24 hours. Foreign visitors should note that many medicines available over the counter at home – codeine-based painkillers, for one – are **prescription-only** in the US. Bring additional supplies if you're particularly brand loyal.

By far the most common tourist illness in California is **sunburn**: south of Santa Barbara and in the state's interior, the summer sun can be fierce, so plenty of protective sunscreen (SPF 15 and above) is a must. Surfers and swimmers should also watch for strong currents and **undertows** at some beaches: we've noted in the text where the water can be especially treacherous. Note that despite the media's frenzied circling around the story of man-eating **sharks**, it's still a blip on beach safety compared with sunburn and swimming difficulties.

Travelers from Europe, Canada, and Australia do not require inoculations to enter the USA.

Costs, money, and banks

Despite the recent slowing of the US economy and the slight weakening of the dollar, the United States remains a fairly expensive place to travel and, with its large urban population, California is one of the pricier states. It is true that car rental, gas, clothes, and consumer goods are usually somewhat cheaper than in Western Europe and Australasia, but the benefit is often less than it seems once you've factored in the additional sales tax or added in the cost of rental-car insurance. At first, eating and drinking seem a bargain (and fast-food joints are), but in more upscale establishments, you'll be adding close to 25 percent to your expected total to cover taxes and tips. It soon mounts up.

For museums and similar attractions, the prices we quote are generally for adults; you can assume that **children** (typically aged 5–12 or 14) get in half-price.

Generally youth and **student cards** are of little benefit; take it if you have one, but don't make any special effort to get one.

Naturally, costs will increase slightly overall during the life of this edition, but the relative comparisons should remain valid.

Costs

Accommodation is likely to be your biggest single expense. A few hotel or motel rooms cost under $40, but it's more usual to pay between $50 and $80 for anything halfway decent in a city, though rates in rural areas can be appreciably cheaper. Hostels offering dorm beds – usually for $15–23 – are reasonably common in San Diego, Los Angeles, and San Francisco, but they are sparsely scattered around the state, besides which they save little money for two or more people traveling together. Camping, of course, is cheap and convenient around the national parks (ranging from free to about $18 a night per site), but is rarely practical in or around the big cities.

As for **food**, $15 a day is enough to get an adequate life-support diet if you are eating cheap and preparing some meals yourself, but $30 is more realistic if you are eating out at diners and budget Mexican places. For around $50 a day, you can dine pretty well. Beyond this, everything hinges on how much sightseeing, taxi taking, drinking, and socializing you do. Much of any of these – especially in the major cities – and you're likely to go through upwards of $75 a day.

The rates for **traveling around**, especially on buses and, to a lesser extent, on trains and even planes, may look inexpensive on paper, but the distances involved mean that costs soon stack up. For a group of two or more, **renting a car** can be a very good

investment, not least because it enables you to camp or stay in the ubiquitous budget motels along the interstate highways instead of relying on expensive downtown hotels.

Remember that a **sales tax** is added to virtually everything you buy except for groceries and prescription drugs; it is seldom included in the quoted price. The base rate is 7.25 percent, but some counties exact an additional tax of half to one percent. In addition, a bed tax is sometimes levied, so hotel rooms usually cost 10–12 percent more than the quoted price

Plastic money and cash machines

If you don't already have a **credit card**, you should think seriously about getting one before you set off. For many services, it's simply taken for granted that you'll be paying with plastic. When renting a car (or even a bike) or checking into a hotel, you may well be asked to show a credit card to establish your creditworthiness – even if you intend to settle the bill in cash. **Visa, MasterCard, Diners Club, American Express**, and **Discover** are the most widely used.

With MasterCard or Visa (including those issued by foreign banks), it is also possible to **withdraw cash** at any bank displaying relevant stickers, or from appropriate automated teller machines (ATMs). Remember that all cash advances are treated as loans, with interest accruing daily from the date of withdrawal; there is generally a transaction fee on top of this. However, you may be able to make withdrawals from ATMs in California

Exchange rates and US currency

Regular upheaval in the world money markets causes the relative value of the US dollar to vary considerably against the currencies of the rest of the world. At time of publication, the British pound buys $1.80; one Canadian dollar is worth 75¢; one Australian dollar is worth 70¢; one New Zealand dollar buys 65¢; and one euro is roughly equivalent to $1.20.

Bills and coins

US banknotes (typically $1, $5, $10, $20, $50, and $100) are all the same color and size so be sure to check what you are handing over; anyone frequently dealing with money usually states the denomination of the bill they have just received. The dollar is made up of 100 cents with coins of 1 cent (known as a penny, and regarded as worthless), 5 cents (a nickel), 10 cents (a dime), and 25 cents (a quarter). Quarters are very useful for buses, vending machines, parking meters, and telephones, so always carry plenty.

using your debit card, which is not liable to interest payments, and the flat transaction fee is usually quite small – your bank will be able to advise you on this. Make sure you have a personal identification number (PIN) that's designed to work overseas.

A compromise between travelers' checks and plastic is **Visa TravelMoney**, a disposable pre-paid debit card with a PIN which works in all ATMs that take Visa cards. You load up your account with funds before leaving home, and when they run out, you simply throw the card away (or reload with funds from your account either by phone or online). You can buy up to nine cards to access the same funds – useful for couples or families traveling together – and it's a good idea to buy at least one extra as a backup in case of loss or theft. There is also a 24-hour toll-free customer assistance number: ☎1-800/847-2399. The card is available in most countries from branches of Travelex (⊛www .travelex.com). For more information, check the Visa TravelMoney website at ⊛www.usa.visa .com/personal/cards/visa_travel_money.html.

Overseas visitors should also bear in mind that fluctuating **exchange rates** (see box, p.43) may result in spending more (or less) than expected when the item eventually shows up on a statement.

Banks and travelers' checks

It is worth carrying a second major credit card as a backup, but you may feel more comfortable with a wad of **US dollar travelers' checks**. These are the best way for both American and foreign visitors to carry money; they offer the great security of knowing that lost or stolen checks will be replaced. You should have no problem using the better-known checks, such as American Express and Visa, in the same way as cash in shops, restaurants, and gas stations. Be sure to have plenty of the $10 and $20 denominations for everyday transactions, and don't be put off by "no checks" signs, which only refer to personal checks.

With credit cards, cash cards, and travelers' checks, you may never need to visit **banks,** which are generally open from 9am until 5pm Monday to Thursday, 9am to 6pm on Friday, and some open on Saturday morning. Most major banks change **foreign**

travelers' checks and currency; though exchange bureaus, always found at airports, tend to charge less commission: Thomas Cook or American Express are the biggest names. Rarely, if ever, do hotels change foreign currency. **Emergency phone numbers** to call if your checks and/or credit cards are stolen are on p.72.

To find the nearest bank that sells a particular brand of travelers' check, or to buy checks by phone, call the following numbers: American Express ☎1-800/673-3782, Citicorp ☎1-800/645-6556, MasterCard ☎1-800/223-9920, Thomas Cook ☎1-800/223-7373, and Visa ☎1-800/227-6811.

Financial emergencies

Having money **wired** from home using one of the companies listed below isn't cheap, and should be considered a last resort. It is increasingly convenient though, both companies allowing someone to send you money simply by accessing their website and using a major credit card: the money should turn up at one of their agencies in around ten minutes. The more you send the lower the fees become (as a percentage of the sum sent): expect to pay around $65 to send $800.

You could also try having money wired directly from a bank in your home country to a bank in California, though this is becoming less viable as banks are insisting you first have an account with them.

Foreign travelers in difficulties have the final option of throwing themselves on the mercy of their nearest national **consulate**, which will – in worst cases only – repatriate you, but will never, under any circumstances, lend you money. See p.37 for the addresses of consulates in LA and San Francisco.

Money-wiring companies

Travelers Express Moneygram US ☎1-800/666-3947, Canada ☎1-800/933-3278, Australia ☎0800/666 3947, Republic of Ireland 0800/666 3947, New Zealand 0800/666 3947, UK 0800/8971 8971; ⊛www.moneygram.com. **Western Union** US and Canada ☎1-800/CALL-CASH, Australia ☎1-800/173 833, New Zealand ☎0800/005 253, UK ☎800/833 833, Republic of Ireland ☎66/947 5603; ⊛www.westernunion .com.

Getting around

Although distances can be great, getting around California is seldom much of a problem. Certainly, things are always easier if you have a car, but between the major cities there are good bus links and a reasonable train service. The only regions where things are more difficult using public transportation are the isolated rural areas, though even here, by adroit forward planning, you can often get to the main points of interest on local buses and charter services, details of which are in the relevant sections of the Guide.

By car

Driving is by far the best way to get around California. Los Angeles, for example, grew up and assumed its present shape after cars were invented, sprawling for so many miles in all directions that your hotel may be fifteen or twenty miles from the sights you came to see. Away from the cities, points of interest are much harder to reach without your own transportation; most national and state parks are only served by infrequent public transportation as far as the main visitor center, if that much. What's more, if you are planning on doing a fair amount of camping, renting a car can save you money by allowing access to less expensive, out-of-the-way campgrounds.

Drivers wishing to rent cars are supposed to have held their licenses for at least one year (though this is rarely checked); people under 25 years old may encounter problems, and will probably get lumbered with a higher than normal insurance premium. Car rental companies will also expect you to have a credit card; of the major companies renting new cars (see p.46), only Enterprise still accepts a hefty cash deposit ($500) as

an alternative. The likeliest tactic for getting a good deal is to phone the major firms' toll-free numbers and ask for their best rate – most will try to beat the offers of their competitors, so it's worth haggling.

In general, the lowest **rates** are available at the airport branches – $149 a week for a compact is a fairly standard budget rate, though they can go for little over $100. Always be sure to get free unlimited mileage and be aware that leaving the car in a different city to the one in which you rent it will incur a **drop-off charge** that can be $200 or more. However, many companies do not charge drop-off fees within California itself, so check before you book if you plan a one-way drive. If you are planning to venture outside California, inquire if there are any limitations; some companies don't allow travel beyond Reno or into Mexico, while others simply ramp up their insurance charges. Also, don't automatically go for the cheapest rate, as there's a big difference in the quality of cars from company to company; industry leaders like Hertz, Avis, and Budget tend to have newer, lower-mileage cars, often with air conditioning and stereo cassette decks or CD

Road conditions

The California Department of Transportation (CalTrans) operates a toll-free **24-hour information line** (T1-800/427-7623) giving up-to-the-minute details of road conditions throughout the state. On a touch-tone phone, simply input the number of the road ("5" for I-5, "299" for Hwy-299, etc) and a recorded voice will tell you about any relevant weather conditions, delays, detours, snow closures, and so on. From out of state, or without a touch-tone phone, road information is also available on T916/445-1534. Nevada Highways has a similar system on T775/793-1313. You can also check online at W www.dot.ca.gov/hq/roadinfo.

players as standard equipment – no small consideration on a 2000-mile desert drive.

Alternatively, various **local companies** rent out new – and not so new (as does the national Rent-A-Wreck company; see below for details) – vehicles. They are certainly cheaper than the big chains if you just want to spin around a city for a day, but you have to drop them back where you picked them up, and free mileage is seldom included, so they can work out more costly for long-distance travel. Addresses and phone numbers are listed in the *Yellow Pages*.

When you rent a car, read the small print carefully for details on the **Collision Damage Waiver (CDW)** – sometimes called a Liability Damage Waiver (LDW) or a Physical Damage Waiver (PDW) – a form of insurance which usually isn't included in the initial rental charge but is well worth considering. Americans who have their own car insurance policy may already be covered (check before you leave home), but foreign visitors should definitely consider taking this option. It specifically covers the car that you are driving, as you are in any case insured for damage to other vehicles. At $9–15 a day, it can add twenty to forty percent to the daily rental fee, but without it you're liable for every scratch to the car – even those that aren't your fault. Some credit-card companies offer automatic CDW coverage to anyone using their card; read the fine print beforehand in any case. Smaller companies may offer low-cost CDW that still leaves you liable for, say, the first $500 of any claim. Before stumping up for their optional Personal Accident Coverage (or similar), consult your travel insurance policy, which may cover you for a certain amount of rental vehicle excess, eliminating the need for this extra cost.

You should also check your **third-party liability**. The standard policy often only covers you for the first $15,000 of the third party's claim against you, a paltry sum in litigation-conscious America. Companies strongly advise taking out third-party insurance, which costs a further $10–12 a day but indemnifies the driver for up to $2,000,000.

If you **break down** in a rented car, there will be an emergency number pinned to the dashboard or tucked away in the glove compartment. You can summon the highway

patrol on one of the new emergency phones stationed along freeways (usually at half-mile intervals) and many other remote highways (mostly every two miles) – although since the highway patrol and state police cruise by regularly, you can just sit tight and wait. Raising your car hood is generally recognized as a call for assistance, although women traveling alone should be wary of doing this. Another tip is to rent a **mobile telephone** from the car rental agency (or from outlets at major airports) – you often only have to pay a nominal amount until you actually use it, and in larger cities they increasingly come built into the car. Having a phone can be reassuring at least, and a potential lifesaver should something go terribly wrong.

One variation on renting is a **driveaway**, whereby you drive a car from one place to another on behalf of the owner, paying only for the gas you use. The same rules as for renting apply, but look the car over before you take it, as you'll be lumbered with any repair costs, and a large fuel bill if the vehicle's a big drinker. The most common routes are between California and New York, although there's a fair chance you'll find something that needs shifting up the coast, from Los Angeles to San Francisco. See p.30 for further details.

Car rental companies

Alamo ☎1-800/462-5266, ⓦwww.alamo.com
Avis ☎1-800/230-4898; in Canada ☎1-800/272-5871, ⓦwww.avis.com
Budget ☎1-800/527-0700; in Canada ☎1-800/472 3325, ⓦwww.budgetrentacar.com
Dollar ☎1-800/800-3665, ⓦwww.dollar.com
Enterprise ☎1-800/726-8222, ⓦwww.enterprise.com
Hertz ☎1-800/654-3131; in Canada ☎1-800/263-0600, ⓦwww.hertz.com
National ☎1-800/962-7070, ⓦwww.nationalcar.com
Payless ☎1-800/729-5377, ⓦwww.paylesscar.com
Rent-A-Wreck ☎1-800/944-7501, ⓦwww.rent-a-wreck.com
Thrifty ☎1-800/847-4389, ⓦwww.thrifty.com

Renting an RV

Besides cars, Recreational Vehicles or **RVs** (camper vans) can be rented from around

Driving for foreign visitors

UK nationals can **drive** in the US on a full UK driving license (International Driving Permits are not always regarded as sufficient). The most important differences between driving in the US and in Britain is the need in the US to **drive on the right**. This can be remarkably easy to forget – some people draw a cross or tie a ribbon on their right hand to remind them. Once you have rented a vehicle, you'll find that **petrol** (US "gasoline") is fairly cheap, though California is one of the more expensive states for it; a self-served US gallon (3.8 liters) of **unleaded** costs between $1.90 and $2.40, depending on the location of the gas station. In California, most gas stations are self-service and you always have to pre-pay; full-service pumps often charge upwards of $0.30 extra per gallon.

There are several **types of road**. The best for covering long distances quickly are the wide, straight, and fast **interstate highways**, usually at least six-lane motorways and always prefixed by "I" (eg I-5). Even-numbered interstates usually run east–west and those with odd numbers north–south. Drivers **change lanes** somewhat frequently; in California, you are also permitted to stay in the fast lane while being overtaken on the inside, although common courtesy dictates that slower drivers stay to the right. A grade down, and broadly similar to British dual carriageways and main roads, are the **state highways** (eg Hwy-1) and the **US highways** (eg US-395). In rural areas, you'll also find much smaller **county roads**; their number is preceded by a letter denoting their county.

The maximum **speed limit** in California is 70mph, with lower signposted limits – usually around 35–55mph – in built-up areas, and 20mph near schools when children are present. If given a ticket for **speeding**, your case will come to court and the size of the fine will be at the discretion of the judge; $100 is a rough minimum. If the **police** do flag you down, don't get out of the car, and don't reach into the glove compartment, as the cops may think you have a gun. Simply sit still with your hands on the wheel; when questioned, be polite and don't attempt to make jokes.

As for other possible violations, US law requires that any **alcohol** be carried unopened in the boot (US "trunk") of the car, and it can't be stressed enough that **driving under the influence (DUI)** is a very serious offense. At **intersections**, one rule is crucially different from the UK: you can turn right on a red light (having first come to a halt) if there is no traffic approaching from the left, unless there is a "no turn on red" sign; otherwise red means stop. Stopping is also compulsory, in both directions, when you come upon a school bus disgorging passengers with its lights flashing, and not doing so is regarded as a serious infraction. Blinking red lights should be treated as a stop sign, and blinking yellow lights indicate that you should cross the intersection with caution, but do not need to come to a complete stop. And at any intersection with more than one **stop sign**, cars proceed in the order in which they arrived; if two vehicles arrive simultaneously, the one on the right has right of way. Two other rules to be aware of: it is illegal to park within ten feet of a **fire hydrant** anywhere in the US; in California, you have to **kerb your wheels** when parking on a hill.

$500 a week (usually with no or limited free mileage) in low season, often more than doubling in price in summer. Outlets are surprisingly rare, as people tend to own their RVs: **El Monte RVs** (☎1-888/337-2214, ⓦwww.elmonte.com) has a dozen or so California locations, mostly in the LA and Bay Area regions. Two of the larger national companies offering RV rentals are **Cruise America** (☎1-800/327-7799, ⓦwww.cruiseamerica.com) and **Moturis** (☎1-877/668-8747, ⓦwww.moturis.com). The Recreational Vehicle Rental Association (ⓦwww.rvra.org) has details of many member rental firms in the US and Canada on its website.

On top of the rental fees, take into account the **cost of gas** (some RVs do twelve miles to the gallon or less) and any drop-off charges, in case you plan to do a one-way trip across the country. Also, it is rarely legal simply to pull up in an RV and spend the night at the roadside – you are expected to stay in designated parks that cost around $25 or more per night.

By plane

A **plane** is obviously the quickest way of getting around California, and much less expensive than you may think. By keeping up to date with the ever-changing deals being offered by airlines – check with your local travel agent, read the ads in local newspapers, or search the Internet – you may be able to take advantage of heavily discounted fares.

Airlines with a strong route structure in the state include Alaska, American, Continental, Delta, Northwest, Reno Air, Southwest, and United. Phone the airlines for routes and schedules, then buy your ticket from a travel agent using the computerized Fare Assurance Program, which processes all the available ticket options and searches for the lowest fare, taking into account the special needs of individual travelers. One agent using the service is Travel Avenue (☏1-800/333-3335, ⊛www.travelavenue.com).

At **off-peak times**, flights between Los Angeles and San Francisco can cost as little as $40 one way (less than the equivalent train fare), though may require a booking to be made 21 days in advance.

By train

Unlike elsewhere in the US, traveling on the Amtrak **rail** network is a viable way of getting about California, thanks in great measure to the growing number of Amtrak Thruway buses, which bring passengers from the many rail-less parts of the state to the trains. Traveling by train is slightly more expensive than Greyhound, from $49 one way between Los Angeles and San Francisco, for example, but unlike on a bus, a smooth journey with few if any delays is a

near certainty. All the major cities are connected and the carriages clean, comfortable, and rarely crowded. Probably the prettiest route is the **Coast Starlight**, which winds along the coast between Santa Barbara and San Luis Obispo, a 100-mile coastline ride during which it's not unusual to see seals, dolphins, or even whales in the waters offshore. The other LA-to-SF Amtrak routes head inland, by bus to Bakersfield then by rail north through the dull San Joaquin Valley. Avoid these unless you are making for Yosemite National Park.

If California is part of wider travels, it may be economic to buy one of Amtrak's rail passes (see box opposite).

By bus

If you're traveling on your own, and making a lot of stops, **buses** are by far the cheapest way to get around. The main long-distance service is **Greyhound** (⊛www.greyhound .com), which links all major cities and many smaller towns. Out in the country, buses are fairly scarce, sometimes appearing only once a day; as a result, you'll need to plot your route with care. But along the main highways, buses run around the clock to a fairly full timetable, stopping only for meal breaks (almost always fast-food dives) and driver changeovers. Greyhound buses are actually less uncomfortable than you might expect, and it's feasible to save on a night's accommodation by traveling overnight and sleeping on the bus – though you may not feel up to much the next day.

It used to be that any sizeable community would have a Greyhound station; in some places, the post office or a gas station now doubles as the bus stop and ticket office, and in many others the bus service has been canceled altogether. Note that advance reservations, either in person at the station or on the toll-free number, are useful for getting cheaper tickets but do not guarantee a seat, so it's still wise to arrive in good time and join the **queue** at busy stations – if a bus is full you may be forced to wait until the next one,

For all information on Amtrak **fares and schedules** in the US, use the toll-free number ☏1-800/872-7245, or use the reservation facility on their website ⊛www .amtrak.com; do not phone individual stations.

Rail, bus, and air passes

Amtrak rail passes

Foreign travelers have a choice of two rail passes that cover California; the National Pass allows travel over the entire system, whereas the West Pass permits unlimited train travel in the western United States.

	15-day (June–Aug)	15-day (Sept–May)	30-day (June–Aug)	30-day (Sept–May)
National	$440	$295	$550	$385
West	$325	$210	$405	$270

On production of a passport issued outside the US or Canada, the passes can be bought at travel agents, or at Amtrak stations in the US. In the **UK**, you can buy them from Destination Marketing (℡020/7253 9009) or through Trailfinders (see p.32); in **Ireland**, contact USIT (see p.32); in **Australia**, Asia Pacific Travel Marketing (℡02/9319 6624) or Rail Plus (℡03/9642 8644); and in **New Zealand** passes can be purchased from almost any travel agent.

In addition, foreigners and US citizens alike can find great deals on the weekly **Rail Sale** promotions or invest in one of the new **California Rail Passes**: the Statewide pass allows 7 days of travel in a 21-day period for $159, while the Northern and Southern passes allow 5 days travel out of 7 in their respective areas for $99.

Greyhound Ameripasses

Foreign visitors and US and Canadian nationals can all buy a **Greyhound Ameripass** or **Discovery Pass**, offering unlimited travel within a set time limit: most travel agents can oblige or you can order online at ⓦwww.greyhound.com. They come in several durations and the fare for international visitors is slightly less. A seven-day pass costs $209 for foreign visitors ($219 for North Americans), ten days go for $259 ($269), fifteen days for $299 ($319), thirty days for $399 ($419), forty-five days for $479 ($439), and the longest, a sixty-day pass, is $539 ($589). All kids under 12 go half-price, and there are discounts of around seven percent for North American students and seniors (62+). No daily extensions are available. The first time you use your pass, the ticket clerk will date it (which becomes the commencement date of the ticket), and your destination is written on a page that the driver will tear out and keep as you board the bus. Repeat this procedure for every subsequent journey.

Air passes

All the main American airlines (and British Airways, in conjunction with its partners) offer **air passes** for visitors who plan to fly a lot within the US. These must be purchased in advance, and comprise between three and eight **coupons**, each valid for a flight of any duration in the US, though in many cases only one flight can be transcontinental. Rates start at around US$400 for three coupons, and $60 for each additional coupon; a little more if you are not traveling to the States with that airline.

There are also **Visit USA** fares only available to non-US residents. These can be substantially less than the standard fare for that flight, and it is certainly worth asking your travel agent, but in many cases there are discount fares available which undercut the Visit USA fare. If you just plan to buy one flight, good low-season fares from New York, Washington, and Boston to California are $300–350 round-trip; LA is marginally less expensive than San Francisco.

sometimes overnight or longer, although there is a policy that if more than ten people are unseated they will put on an extra bus.

Fares average 10¢ a mile, which can add up quickly; for example, $43 ($35 if purchased seven days in advance) from Los Angeles to San Francisco one way. For long-trip travel, riding the bus costs about the same as the train; considering the time (75 hours coast-to-coast, if you eat and sleep on the bus) it's not that much cheaper than flying. However, the bus is the best deal if you plan to visit a lot of places, and Greyhound's **Ameripasses** (see box on the previous page) can work out to be good value. There are also assorted three-, seven-fourteen-, and twenty-one-day advance purchase discounts, which can be useful for longer trips, though they seldom offer savings within California.

Greyhound produces a condensed **time-table** of major country-wide routes, but does not distribute it to travelers; to plan your route, pick up the free route-by-route timetables from larger stations, or consult Greyhound's website.

Smaller companies catering specifically to tourists come and go with alarming frequency. One currently operational is **AmeriBus** (℡954/923-1480, ⊛www.ameribus.com), which uses buses and minivans on a circuit from LA up the coast to San Francisco, inland to Yosemite, down to Las Vegas, and then back to LA. Services leave the major cities daily, so if you fork out $129 you've got unlimited travel around this loop for one month.

Bear in mind that fair distances can be covered for very little money – if also very slowly – using **local buses**, which connect neighboring districts. It's possible, for example, to travel from San Diego to Los Angeles for around $5, but it'll take all day and at least three changes of bus to do it. And of course, there's always the hippyish Green Tortoise, which runs between the major Californian cities (see below).

Cycling

In general, **cycling** is a cheap and healthy method of getting around all the big **cities**, some of which have cycle lanes and local

Greyhound's nationwide toll-free **information service** can give you routes and times, plus phone numbers and addresses of local terminals. You can also make reservations: ℡1-800/231-2222.

buses equipped to carry bikes, strapped to the outside, though San Francisco will test your legs. In **rural areas**, certainly, there's much scenic and largely level land, especially around Sacramento and the Wine Country.

Bikes can be **rented** for $20–30 a day, and $100–150 a week from most bike stores; the local visitor center will have details (we've listed rental options where applicable throughout the Guide). Apart from the coastal fog, which tends to clear by midday, you'll encounter few **weather** problems (except perhaps sunburn), but remember that the further north you go, the lower the temperatures and the more frequent the rains become.

For **long-distance cycling**, you'll need maps, spare tires, tools, panniers, a helmet (not a legal necessity, but a very good idea), and a good quality multispeed bike. Don't immediately splurge on a mountain bike, unless you are planning a lot of off-road use – good road conditions and trail restrictions in national parks make a touring bike an equally good or better choice. A route avoiding the interstates – on which cycling is illegal – is essential, and it's also wise to cycle **north to south**, as the wind blows this way in the summer and can make all the difference between a pleasant trip and a journey full of acute leg-ache. The main

---

Green Tortoise

One alternative to long-distance bus hell is the slightly countercultural **Green Tortoise**, whose buses, furnished with foam cushions, bunks, fridges, and rock music, ply the major Californian cities, running between Los Angeles, San Francisco, and on into the Pacific Northwest. (In summer, they also cross the country to New York and Boston, transcontinental trips which amount to mini-tours of the nation.) Other Green Tortoise trips include excursions to the major national parks (in 16 days for $659 plus $191 for food), the Northern California Loop (6 days for $299 plus $51 for food), as well as south to Mexico and Central America, and north to Alaska.
   Main office: 494 Broadway, San Francisco, CA 94133 ℡415/956-7500 or 1-800/867-8647, ⊛www.greentortoise.com.

Hitchhiking

The usual advice given to **hitchhikers** is that they should use their common sense; in fact, common sense should tell anyone that hitchhiking in the US is a **bad idea**. We do not recommend it, though it is practised commonly enough by hikers seeking access to Sierra trailheads and in certain parts of Northern California.

problem you'll encounter is traffic: wide, cumbersome recreational vehicles spew unpleasant exhaust in your face and, in Northern California, enormous logging trucks have slipstreams that will pull you towards the middle of the road. Be particularly careful if you're planning to cycle along Hwy-1 on the Central Coast since, besides heavy traffic, it has tight curves, dangerous precipices, and is prone to fog.

If you're camping as well as cycling, look out for **hiker/biker campgrounds** ($3–5 per person per night), which are free of cars and RVs, dotted across California's state parks and beaches. Many of them were set up in 1976 as part of the **Pacific Coast Bicentennial Bike Route**, running 1825 miles from the Mexican border to Vancouver, Canada. Sites are allotted on a first-come-first-served basis, and all offer water and toilet facilities but seldom showers. For more information, call ☎1-800/444-7275 or check with Hostelling International – USA (details on p.54); the Adventure Cycling Association (☎406/721-1776 or 1-800/755-2453, ⓦwww.adv-cycling.org) or the Sierra Club (see box, p.69).

Accommodation

Accommodation standards in California – as in the rest of the US – are high, and costs inevitably form a significant proportion of the expenses for any trip to the state. It is possible to haggle, however, especially in the chain motels, and if you're on your own, you can possibly pare costs down by sleeping in dormitory-style hostels, where a bed will generally go for $15–23. However, groups of two or more will find it only a little more expensive to stay in the far more plentiful motels and hotels, where basic rooms away from the major cities typically cost around $40 per night. Many hotels will only charge $5–10 each for a third or fourth adult on top of the regular price, reducing costs considerably. By contrast, the solo traveler will have a hard time of it: "singles" are usually double rooms at an only slightly reduced rate. Prices quoted by hotels and motels are almost always for the actual room rather than for each person using it.

However, with the exception of the budget interstate motels, there's rarely such a thing as a set rate for a room, most applying **seasonal** and often **weekend** rates. A basic motel in a seaside or mountain resort may double its prices according to the season, while a big-city hotel which charges $200 per room during the week will often slash its tariff at the weekend when all the business types have gone home.

Since cheap accommodation in the cities, on the popular sections of the coast, and close to the major national parks is snapped up fast, **book ahead** whenever possible, using the suggestions in this book. **Reservations** are only held until 5 or 6pm unless you've told them you'll be arriving late. Most of the larger chains have an advance-booking form in their brochures and will make reservations at another of their premises for you.

Wherever you stay, you'll be expected to **pay in advance**, at least for the first night and perhaps for further nights too, particularly if it's **high season** – generally summer, but most likely winter in desert and ski areas – and the hotel expects to be busy. Payment can be in cash or travelers' checks, though it's more common to give your credit card number and sign for everything when you leave.

Hotels and motels

Hotels and **motels** are essentially the same thing, although motels tend to congregate along the main approach roads to cities, around beaches, and by the main road junctions in country areas. High-rise hotels predominate along the popular sections of the coast and are sometimes the only accommodation in city centers.

In general, there's a uniform standard of comfort everywhere, with all rooms featuring one or more double or queen beds, plus bathroom, cable TV, phone, refrigerator, and a coffee maker. The budget places (costing around $40) will be pretty basic and possibly run down, but an extra $10–15 will get you more space, modern fittings, and better facilities, such as a swimming pool. Paying over $100 brings you into the realms of the in-room hot tub.

Microwaves and coffee makers are common, but only rarely will you find full cooking facilities in your room. Instead, an increasing number of hotels (and the better motels) provide a **complimentary breakfast**. Sometimes, this will be no more than a cup of coffee and a soggy Danish pastry,

but it may be a sit-down affair and likely to comprise fruit, cereals, muffins, and toast. In the pricier places, you may also be offered made-to-order omelets.

Enormous roadside signs make finding cheap hotels and motels pretty simple, and you'll soon become familiar with the numerous chains. Common budget-priced **chains**, including *Econolodge*, *Days Inn*, and *Motel 6*, offer rooms costing $35–50 (though in popular tourist areas $80 is more common). For mid-priced options ($50–100) try *Best Western*, *Howard Johnson*, *Travelodge*, and *Ramada*, though if you can afford to pay this much there's normally somewhere with more character to stay – when it's worth blowing a hunk of cash on somewhere really atmospheric we've said as much in the Guide. Bear in mind that the most upscale establishments have all manner of services which may appear to be free but for which you'll be expected to **tip** in a style commensurate with the hotel's status – ie big.

Discounts and reservations

During **off-peak periods**, many motels and hotels struggle to fill their rooms, and it's worth **haggling** to get a few dollars off the asking price. Staying in the same place for more than one night will bring further reductions, and motels in particular offer worthwhile discounts (usually ten percent) for seniors and members of various organizations, particularly the American Automobile Association (AAA). Members of sister motoring associations in other countries may also be entitled to such discounts. Additionally, pick up the many

Accommodation price codes

All the **accommodation** listed in this book has been categorized into one of nine **price codes**, as set out below. The prices quoted are for cheapest available room for two people in the high season. You can expect many places to jump into the next highest category on Friday and Saturday nights, and almost all lodging (except state and federally run campgrounds) is subject to additional local hotel taxes, which are generally around ten percent but may soar to twenty percent. For campgrounds, and hostels that offer individual beds or bunks, we have given the per-person price (excluding tax) along with a code for any private rooms.

❶ up to $40	❹ $70–90	❼ $150–200
❷ $40–55	❺ $90–120	❽ $200–250
❸ $55–70	❻ $120–150	❾ $250+

discount coupons which fill tourist information offices and look out for the free *Traveler Discount Guide*. Read the small print, though – what appears to be an amazingly cheap room rate sometimes turns out to be a per-person charge for two people sharing, and limited to midweek.

Bed and breakfasts

Staying at a **bed and breakfast** in California is a luxury. Typically, the bed-and-breakfast inns, as they're usually known, are restored buildings and grand houses in the smaller cities and more rural areas although the big cities also have a few, especially San Francisco. Even the larger establishments tend to have no more than ten rooms, often without TV and phone but with plentiful flowers, stuffed cushions, and a sometimes-contrived homely atmosphere. Others may just be a couple of furnished rooms in someone's home, or an entire apartment where you won't even see your host. Victorian and Romantic are dominant themes; while selecting the best in that vein, we've also gone out of our way to seek out those that don't conform.

While always including a huge and wholesome breakfast (five courses is not unheard of), prices vary greatly: anything from $70 to $250 depending on location and season. Most fall between $85 and $125 per night for a double, a little more for a whole apartment. Bear in mind, too, that they are frequently booked well in advance, and even if they're not full, the cheaper rooms that determine our price code may be already taken.

As well as the B&Bs listed in the Guide, there are hundreds more throughout the state, many of them listed on various **accommodation websites** such as California B&B Travel (@www.bbtravel.com), the California Association of B&B Inns (@www.cabbi.com), and B&B Inns of North America (@www.inntravels.com).

Hostels

At an average of $17 per night per person (though $23–27 in San Francisco and at Santa Monica in LA), **hostels** are clearly the cheapest accommodation option in California other than camping. There are two main kinds of hostel-type accommodation in the US: the internationally affiliated HI-USA hostels, and a growing number of independent hostels variously aligned with assorted umbrella organizations.

Altogether California has around twenty **HI-USA** hostels (the prefix is shortened to HI in "Listings"), mostly in major cities and close to popular hiking areas, including national and state parks. Most urban hostels have 24-hour access, while rural ones may have a curfew and limited daytime hours. HI also operates a couple of small "home hostels" in the state; though similar to other hostels you need to reserve in advance or there may be no one there to receive you.

Dormitory bed rates at HI hostels range from $15 to $27 for members. Nonmembers generally pay an additional $3 per night, so becoming a member will quickly pay off. Membership is international, but you are expected to join in your home country (see p.54 for contacts), something which will cost the equivalent of $20–30 annually.

Details of all hostels are listed in the *USA Hostel Directory*, available free to members (otherwise $3): pick one up at a hostel, order online, or request a copy from the HI National Office (℡301/495-1240, @www.hiusa.org). HI hostels don't allow sleeping bags though some will provide sheets as a matter of course. Otherwise, you'll need to rent a sheet sleeping bag (typically $2 a night) or bring your own. Few hostels provide meals, but most have **cooking** facilities. Alcohol and smoking are banned.

Particularly if you're traveling in high season, it's advisable to make **reservations**, either by contacting the hostel directly, or booking online (at least 48 hours in advance). There's also the IBN booking service (@www.hihostels.com), which helps you book certain big-city and gateway hostels through your home organization. San Diego, LA, and San Francisco hostels can be booked this way.

Independent hostels now number around fifty and are concentrated in the big cities. They're usually a little less expensive than their HI counterparts, and have fewer rules, but the quality is not as consistent; some can be quite poor, while others, which we've included in the book, are absolutely wonderful. In popular areas, especially LA, San Francisco, and San Diego, they compete fiercely for your business with airport and train station pick-ups, free breakfasts, and free bike hire. There is often no curfew and, at some, a party atmosphere is encouraged at barbecues and keg parties. Their independent status may be due to a failure to measure up to the HI's (fairly rigid) criteria, yet often it's simply because the owners prefer not to be tied down by HI regulations.

All the information in this book was accurate at the time of going to press; however, hostels are often shoestring organizations, prone to changing address or closing down altogether. Similarly, new ones appear each year; check the noticeboards of other hostels for news or consult hostel websites, particularly ⓦwww.hostels.com.

Youth hostel contacts

Australia YHA Australia ☎02/9261 1111, ⓦwww.yha.com.au
Canada Canadian Hostelling Association ☎1-800/663-5777, ⓦwww.hihostels.ca
England Youth Hostel Association ☎0870/770 8868, ⓦwww.yha.org.uk
New Zealand New Zealand Youth Hostels Association ☎800/278 299 or 03/379 9970, ⓦwww.stayyha.com
Northern Ireland Hostelling International Northern Ireland ☎028/9032 4733, ⓦwww.hini.org.uk
Republic of Ireland An Óige ☎01/830 4555, ⓦwww.anoige.ie
Scotland Scottish Youth Hostel Association, ☎0870/155 3255, ⓦwww.syha.org.uk
USA HI National Office ☎301/495-1240, ⓔmembers@hiusa.org, ⓦwww.hiusa.org

Camping

California **campgrounds** range from the primitive – a flat piece of ground that may or may not have a pit toilet and water tap – to others that are more like open-air hotels, with shops, restaurants, and washing facilities. In major cities, campgrounds tend to be inconveniently sited on the outskirts, if they exist at all.

When camping in national and state parks, as well as national forests, you can typically expect a large site with picnic table and fire pit, designed to accommodate up to two

vehicles and six people. It is usually a short walk to an outhouse and drinking water. Note that sites fill up quickly and it's worth reserving well in advance (see list below for contact numbers).

Naturally enough, prices vary accordingly, ranging from nothing for the most basic plots, up to $20 a night for something comparatively luxurious, and more like $22–30 if you want to hook your RV up to electricity, water, sewage, and cable TV. For comprehensive listings of these check out ⓦwww.californiacampgrounds.org and Kampgrounds of America (ⓦwww.koa.com).

There are plenty of campgrounds but often plenty of people intending to use them as well: take care over plotting your route if you're intending to camp in the big national parks, or anywhere at all during national holidays or the summer, when many grounds will be either full or very crowded. Vacancies often exist in the grounds outside the parks – where the facilities are usually marginally better – and by contrast, some of the more basic campgrounds in isolated areas will often be empty whatever time of year you're there. Often rural campgrounds have no one in attendance (though a ranger may stop by), and if there's any charge at all you'll need to pay by posting the money in the slot provided; save your small bills.

Look out too for **hiker/biker** or **walk-in** campgrounds, which, at $3 per person per night, are much cheaper than most sites but only available if you are traveling under your own steam.

Much of California is in the public domain, and, if you're backpacking, you can **camp rough** pretty much anywhere you want in the gaping wilderness areas and deserts. However, in the more heavily hiked areas (we've indicated the relevant areas in the text), you must first get a **wilderness permit** (almost always free), and usually a free **campfire permit** (even if you are using a cooking stove). Campfire permits are available from park rangers' offices and once obtained are usually valid for a year. You should also take the proper precautions – carry sufficient food and drink to cover emergencies, inform someone of your travel plans, and watch out for bears and rattlesnakes, as well as the effect *your* presence can have on *their* environment; see "Backcountry camping, hiking, and wildlife" on p.68.

see "Backcountry camping, hiking, and wildlife" on p.68.

Camping reservation contacts

National Forests National Recreation Reservation Service (NRRS) ☏ 1-877/444-6777 or 518/885-3639, ⊛ www.reserveusa.com.
National Parks (except Yosemite) National Park Reservation Service (NPRS) ☏ 1-800/365-2267, ⊛ reservations.nps.gov. Operational 7am–7pm Pacific Time.
State Parks California State Parks Reservations ☏ 1-800/444-7275 or 916/638-5883, ⊛ www.reserveamerica.com.
Yosemite National Park ☏ 1-800/436-7275 or 301/722-11257, ⊛ reservations.nps.gov. Operational 7am–7pm Pacific Time.

Long-term accommodation

Excluding San Francisco, **apartment-hunting** in California is not the nightmare it is in, say, New York: accommodation is plentiful and not always expensive, although the absence of housing associations means that there is very little really cheap accommodation anywhere except in very isolated country areas. Accommodation is almost always rented unfurnished, so you'll have to buy furniture; expect to pay at least $700 a month for a studio or one-bedroom apartment and upwards of $2000 per month for two to three bedrooms in Los Angeles or San Francisco. Most landlords will expect one month's rent as a deposit, plus one other month in advance.

By far the best way to find somewhere is to ask around – particularly near universities or college campuses, where apartment turnover is usually frequent. Otherwise rooms for rent are often advertised in the windows of houses, and local papers have "Apartments for Rent" sections. In **Los Angeles** the best source is the *LA Weekly* (⊛ www.laweekly.com), although you should also scan the *LA Times* classifieds. In **San Francisco** check out the *Chronicle* (⊛ www.sfchron.com) and the free *San Francisco Bay Guardian* (⊛ www.sfbg.com), *SF Weekly* (⊛ www.sfweekly.com), and the *East Bay Express* (⊛ www.eastbayexpress.com).

Eating and drinking

It's not too much of an exaggeration to say that in California – its cities, at least – you can eat whatever you want, whenever you want. On every main street, a mass of restaurants, fast-food places, and coffee shops try to outdo one another with bargains and special offers. Be warned, though, that in rural areas you might go for days finding little more than diners and cheap Mexican joints.

California's cornucopia stems largely from its being one of the most agriculturally rich parts of the country. Junk food is as common as anywhere else in the US, but the state also produces its own range of highly nutritious goodies: apples, avocados, dates, grapes, kiwi fruit, melons, oranges, and peaches are everywhere, plus abundant seafood, high-quality meat, and dairy goods. You'll rarely find anything that's not fresh, be it a bagel or a spinach-in-Mornay-sauce croissant (California's mix'n'match food concoctions can be as anarchic as its architecture), and even fast food won't necessarily be rubbish.

California is also one of the most **health-conscious** states in the country, and the supermarket shelves are chock-full of products which if not fat-free, are low-fat, low-sodium, low-carb, caffeine-free, and dairy-free. Much the same ethic runs through the menu of most restaurants, though you needn't worry about going hungry: portions are universally huge, and what you don't eat can always be "boxed up" for later consumption.

Breakfasts

For the price, on average $5–9, breakfast is the best-value and most filling meal of the day. Go to a diner, café, or coffee shop, all of which serve breakfast until at least 11am, with some diners serving them all day.

The breakfasts themselves are pretty much what you'd find all over the country. **Eggs** are the staple ingredient, served in a variety of styles and, in omelet form, with the occasional exotic filling (avocado, for instance). There is usually also some form of **meat** available: ham, bacon, or sausages. Some sort of toast or muffin invariably accompanies this.

If you wish, you can add **waffles**, **pancakes**, or **French toast** to the combination, consumed swamped in butter with lashings of sickly-sweet syrup, flavored to mimic the more delicate and expensive maple syrup. A concession to California's love of light food is the option of **fruit**: typically apple, banana, orange, pineapple, or strawberry, wonderfully styled and served on their own or with pancakes, though costing as much as a full-blown fry-up.

Lunch and snacks

Between 11am and 3pm you should look for the excellent-value **lunchtime set menus** on offer – Chinese, Indian, and Thai restaurants frequently have help-yourself buffets for $6–10, and many Japanese restaurants give you a chance to eat sushi much more cheaply ($8–12) than usual. Most Mexican restaurants are exceptionally well priced all the time: you can get a good-sized lunch for $5–8. In Northern California, watch out for seafood restaurants selling **fish'n'chips**: the fish is breaded and then fried, and the chips are chunky chipped potatoes rather than the matchstick french fries you normally find. A plateful is about $7. Look as well for **clam chowder**, a thick, creamy shellfish soup served almost everywhere for $4–5, sometimes using a hollowed-out sourdough cottage loaf as a bowl ($5–8).

As you'd expect, there's also **pizza**, available from chains like *Pizza Hut*, *Round Table*, and *Shakey's*, or local, more personalized restaurants. Most are dependable and have a similar range of offerings; count on paying around $12 for a basic two-person pizza. If it's a warm day and you can't face hot food, delis (see below) usually serve a broad range of salads for about $4.

For **quick snacks**, you'll find many **delis** do ready-cooked meals for $4–6 as well as a range of **sandwiches** which can be meals in themselves: huge French rolls filled with a custom-built combination of meat, cheese, and vegetables; **bagels** are also everywhere, filled with anything you fancy. **Street stands** sell hot dogs, burgers, tacos, or a slice of pizza for around $2.50, and most shopping malls have ethnic fast-food stalls, often pricier than their equivalent outside, but usually edible and filling. Be a little wary of the grottier **Mexican fast-food** stands if you're buying meat, although they're generally filling, cheap, and more authentic than the Tex-Mex outlets. There are chains, too, like *El Pollo Loco*, *Del Taco*, and *Taco Bell*, which sell swift tacos and burritos from $1 up. And of course the burger chains are as ubiquitous here as anywhere in the US: best to seek out the few *In-n-Out* burger chain franchises if possible, all made to order and as delicious as you'll find.

Restaurants

Even if it often seems swamped by the more fashionable regional and ethnic cuisines, traditional **American cooking** – juicy burgers, steaks, fries, salads (invariably served before the main dish), and baked potatoes – is found all over California. Cheapest of the food chains is the California-wide *Denny's*, although you'll rarely need to spend more than $12 for a solid blowout anywhere.

By contrast, though, it's **California cuisine**, geared towards health and aesthetics, that's raved about by foodies on the West Coast – and rightly so. Basically a development of French *nouvelle cuisine*, using the wide mix of fresh, locally available ingredients, California cuisine is based on physiological efficiency – eating only what you need to and what your body can process. Vegetables are harvested before maturity and steamed to preserve a high concentration of vitamins, with a strong flavor – and to look better on the plate. Seafood comes from oyster farms and the catches of small-time fishermen, and what little meat there is on the menu tends to come from animals reared on organic farms. The result is small but beautifully presented portions, and high, high prices: it's not unusual to spend $40 a head (or much more) for a full dinner with wine. To whet your appetite, starters (perhaps $8–10) include mussels in jalapeño and sesame vinaigrette, snails in puff pastry with mushroom purée, and, among main courses, roasted goat-cheese salad with walnuts, swordfish with herb butter, and *ahi* tuna with cactus ratatouille.

Restaurants serving California cuisine build their reputation by word of mouth; if you can, ask a local enthusiast for recommendations, or simply follow our suggestions in the Guide, especially in Berkeley, the recognized birthplace of California cuisine. Of other American regional cooking, **Cajun** remains in vogue. Also known as "Creole," it originated in Louisiana as a way of saving money by cooking up leftovers. It is centered on black beans, rice, and seafood, and is always highly spiced. There are a few relatively inexpensive places to find it (charging around $12 a dish, but its cachet has generally pushed prices up).

Although technically ethnic, **Mexican** food is so common that it often seems like (and, historically, often is) an indigenous cuisine, especially in Southern California. What's more, day or night, it's the cheapest type of food to eat: even a full dinner with a beer or margarita will rarely be over $15 anyw~~here~~ except in the most upmark~~et~~ ments. Californian M~~exican~~ ~~is usu~~our-dou~~gh~~ ally different,~~from~~ an accompani~~ments~~ makin~~g by han~~ wrapped around ~~(a taco); rolled, filled, and baked~~ ~~(an enchilada); or fried flat and topped with food (a **tostada**). One of the few

options for vegetarians in this meat-oriented cuisine is the **chile relleno**, a mild, green pepper stuffed with cheese, dipped in egg batter, and fried. Veggie burritos, filled with beans, rice, lettuce, avocado, cheese, and sour cream are another prevalent option for those averse to meat.

Other ethnic cuisines are plentiful too. **Chinese** food is everywhere, and during lunchtime can often be as cheap as Mexican. **Japanese** is more expensive and fashionable – sushi is worshipped by some Californians. **Italian** food is very popular, but can be expensive once you leave the simple pizzas and pastas to explore the specialist Italian regional cooking that has caught on in the last few years. **French** food, too, is widely available, though always pricey, and the cuisine of social climbers and power lunchers, rarely found outside the larger cities. **Thai**, **Korean**, **Vietnamese**, and **Indonesian** food is similarly city-based, though usually cheaper; **Indian** restaurants, on the other hand, are thin on the ground just about everywhere and often very expensive – although as **Indian** cuisine catches on the situation is gradually changing for the better, with a sprinkling of moderately priced Southern Indian food outlets.

Drinking

In freeway-dominated Los Angeles, the traditional neighborhood bar is as rare as the traditional neighborhood. There are exceptions, but LA bars ten~~d~~ to be either extremely preten~~ti~~ous, ~~of social drink-~~ neither ur~~g~~ent ~~boozing town, still~~ ~~that are fun to~~ ~~get an evening~~ if you don't ~~plan to get legless.~~ array of sp~~ot~~s in the ~~late~~ you'll find the normal To buy and consume alcohol in California, you need to be 21, and bars almost always have someone on the door checking ID: you'll probably need to be into your thirties before getting waved through automatically. Licensing laws and drinking hours are among the most liberal in the country (though laws on drinking and driving ar~~e~~ not). Alcohol can be bought and cons~~umed~~

any time between 6am and 2am, seven days a week in bars, nightclubs, and many restaurants. Some restaurants only have a beer and wine license, and many allow you to take your own bottled wine into a restaurant, where the corkage fee will be $5–10. You can buy beer, wine, or spirits more cheaply and easily in supermarkets, many delis, and, of course, liquor stores.

American beers fall into two distinct categories: wonderful and tasteless. The latter are found everywhere: light, fizzy brands such as Budweiser, Miller, Schlitz, and so on. The alternative is a fabulous range of microbrewed beers, the product of a wave of backyard and in-house operations that swelled in the late 1980s and has now matured to the point that many pump out over 150,000 barrels a year and are classed as "regional breweries." Head for one of the brewpubs (many are listed in the Guide along with breweries you can visit; see also the California Beerpage website listed on p.39) and you'll find handcrafted beers such as crisp pilsners, wheat beers, and stouts on tap, at prices only marginally above those of the national brews. Bottled microbrews, like Chico's hoppy Sierra Nevada Pale Ale and the full-bodied, San Francisco–brewed Anchor Steam Beer, are sold throughout the state, while Red Tail Ale is found throughout Northern California. Imported beers are of course available in most places as well. Expect to fork out $4–5 for a glass of draught beer, about the same for a bottle of imported.

If you're in

Californian w

may b be internationally known

are held in low reg llo and Paul Mas-

and are prod in barn that they

refineries. Most Coast,

of California's innume The

good, smaller wineries — which produce preu

oma valleys — which produce French-strain gra ast of quality of the roast, and offer a

dry wines made from French-strain gra

are widely, and rightly, regarded as the cradle of the Californian wine industry. Wines are categorized by grape-type rather than place of origin: the heavy and fruity Cabernet Sauvignon is probably the most popular red, along with the lighter Merlot and Pinot Noir. Among the whites, Chardonnay is very dry and flavorful, and generally preferred to Sauvignon Blanc or Fumé Blanc, though these have their devotees. The most unusual is the strongly flavored Zinfandel, which comes in white (mocked by wine snobs, but popular nonetheless), red, or rosé.

You can learn a lot about Californian wine by taking a winery tour, mostly including free tastings (although some charge $4–5 for a full glass or two), a number of which we've mentioned in the Guide. Alternatively, the visitor centers in popular wine-producing areas produce informative regional directories. The best lesson of all, of course, is simply to buy the stuff. It's fairly inexpensive: a decent glass of wine in a bar or restaurant costs $4–6, a bottle $10–20. Buying from a supermarket is better still – a tolerable bottle can be purchased for as little as $7.

Cocktails are extremely popular, especially during happy hours (usually any time between 5pm and 7pm) when drinks may be half-price and there's often a buffet thrown in. Varieties are innumerable, sometimes specific to a single bar or cocktail lounge, and they cost anything between $3 and $6.

An increasing alternative to drinking dens, coffee shops (look out for any joint with "Java" in the title) play a vibrant part in California's social scene, and are havens of high-quality coffee far removed from the stuff served in diners and convenience stores. In larger towns and cities, cafés will roast of quality of the roast, and offer a of espresso, cappuccinos, lattes, served straight, iced, organic, ps. Herbal teas and light the menu.

Communications

You'll have no trouble keeping in touch while in California. In rural areas the nearest public phone may be miles away, but phones are generally plentiful, mobile phone coverage is good, there is Internet access all over the place, and post offices are abundant.

Telephones

Californian **telephones** are run by a huge variety of companies, many of which were hived off from the previous Bell System monopoly – the successor to which is the nationwide AT&T network.

Public telephones generally work, and – in cities at any rate – can be found nearly everywhere. They take 5¢, 10¢, and 25¢ coins. The cost of a **local call** from a public phone (generally one within the same area code) is typically 35¢–50¢; when necessary, a voice comes on the line telling you to pay more.

Some numbers covered by the same area code are considered so far apart that calls between them count as non-local (zone calls) and cost much more. Pricier still are long-distance calls (ie to a different area code and always preceded by a 1), for which you'll need plenty of change. Non-local calls and long-distance calls are much less expensive if made between 6pm and 8am – the cheapest rates are after 11pm and at weekends – and calls from private phones are always much cheaper than those from public phones. Detailed rates are listed at the front of the telephone directory (the *White Pages*, a copious source of information on many matters).

Rates are much cheaper using **phone cards** – typically in denominations of $5, $10, and $20 – bought from general stores and some hostels. These provide you with a temporary account (just tap in the number printed on the card), and are a lot cheaper than feeding coins into a payphone, especially if calling abroad. There are many brands, some quoting long-distance rates as low as five cents a minute, but beware of the 50¢ connection fee only mentioned in the fine print. Making telephone calls from **hotel rooms** is usually more expensive than

from a payphone, though many hotels offer free local calls from rooms – ask when you check in.

Many government agencies, car rental firms, hotels, and so on have **toll-free numbers**, which always have the prefix ☏1-800, ☏1-888, ☏1-877, or ☏1-866. Within the US, you can dial any number starting with those digits free of charge, though some numbers only operate inside California: it isn't apparent from the number until you try. Numbers with the prefix ☏1-900 are pay-per-call lines, generally quite expensive and almost always involving either sports, phone psychics, or phone sex.

Phone numbers throughout this book are given with the area code followed by the local number: for local calls just dial the seven-digit local number; for anywhere more than a few miles away dial 1 followed by the area code and local number. For international calls to the US dial the country's international access number, then 1 and the area code and local numbers (see p.60).

Calling home

One of the most convenient ways of phoning home from abroad is via a **telephone charge card** from your phone company back home. Calls made from most hotel, public, and private phones will be charged to your account. Since most major charge cards are free to obtain, it's certainly worth getting one at least for emergencies; but bear in mind that rates aren't necessarily cheaper than calling from a public phone.

In the **US and Canada**, AT&T, MCI, Sprint, Canada Direct, and other North American long-distance companies all enable their customers to bill credit-card calls to their home number.

In the **UK and Ireland**, BT (☎0800/800 150, ⓦwww.bt.com) will issue free to all its customers the BT Chargecard, which can be used worldwide.

To call **Australia and New Zealand** from California, telephone charge cards such as Telstra Telecard or Optus Calling Card in Australia, and Telecom NZ's Calling Card can be used to make calls, which are charged back to a domestic account or credit card. Apply to Telstra (☎13 2200, ⓦwww.telstra.com.au), Optus (☎1300/300 937, ⓦwww.optus.com.au), or Telecom NZ (☎123, ⓦwww.telecom.co.nz).

Useful numbers

Emergencies ☎911; ask for the appropriate emergency service: fire, police, or ambulance.
Directory information ☎411
Directory inquiries for toll-free numbers ☎1-800/555-1212
Long-distance directory information ☎1- (area code)/555-1212
International operator ☎00

Calling home from California

Australia 00 + 61 + city code
Canada 1 + area code
New Zealand 00 + 64 + city code
UK and Northern Ireland 00 + 44 + city code
Republic of Ireland 00 + 353 + city code

Email and Internet access

One of the best ways to keep in touch while traveling is to sign up for a free Internet email address that can be accessed from anywhere, for example via YahooMail or Hotmail – accessible through ⓦwww.yahoo.com and ⓦwww.hotmail.com. Once you've set up an account, you can use these sites to pick up and send mail from any Internet café, or hotel with Internet access. Internet cafés are found in most towns of any size, but many travelers prefer the **free Internet access** provided by almost all public libraries. Generally, you just reserve a half-hour or hour-long slot and away you go. If neither of these options fit the bill, or you just need a fast machine with assorted peripherals, then find a commercial photocopying and printing shop (look under "Copying" in the *Yellow Pages*). They'll charge around 20¢ a minute for use of their computers, but you're guaranteed fast access. Most upscale hotels also offer email and Internet access – though again at a price.

If you are traveling with a laptop and want to get connected, browse ⓦwww.kropla.com, which gives details of how to plug your laptop in when abroad, phone country codes around the world, and information about electrical systems in different countries.

The spread of **wireless hot spots** all over the state (airports, cafés, and notably in *Starbucks* outlets) means anyone traveling with a Wi-Fi–enabled laptop or PDA should have no trouble getting connected in the populated areas. Out in the deserts and mountains you may go days without picking up a signal at all.

Mail services

Post offices are usually open Monday to Friday from 9am until 5pm, and Saturday from 9am to noon (sometimes 4pm), and there are blue **mailboxes** on many street corners. **Ordinary mail** within the US costs 37¢ for letters weighing up to an ounce; addresses must include an abbreviation denoting the state (in California "CA") and a five-digit number – the **zip code** – denoting the local post office. Letters that don't carry the zip code are liable to get lost or at least delayed; if you don't know it, phone books carry a list for their service area or check at ⓦwww.usps.com. The return address should be written in the upper left corner of the envelope.

Airmail from California to Europe generally takes about a week. Aerograms and letters weighing up to half an ounce (a single sheet) cost 70¢, and postcards cost 70¢ (50¢ to Canada and Mexico).

Letters can be sent c/o General Delivery (what's known elsewhere as poste restante) to the one relevant post office in each city, but must include the zip code and will only be held for thirty days before being returned to sender – so make sure there's a return address on the envelope. If you're receiving mail at someone else's address, it should include "c/o" and the regular occupant's name, or it is likely to be returned.

Rules on sending parcels are very rigid: packages must be sealed according to the instructions given at the start of the *Yellow Pages*. To send anything out of the country, you'll need a green customs declaration form, available from the post office. Postal rates for airmailing a parcel weighing up to 1lb to Europe, Australia, and New Zealand are $16–18.

The media

Every major urban center in California has its own newspaper, from the politically obsessed Sacramento Bee to the Hollywood hype of the *Los Angeles Times*. You'll also be able to pick up *USA Today*, the moderate if rather toothless national daily, while such East Coast stalwarts as the *New York Times*, the *Washington Post*, and the *Wall Street Journal* should be available in most towns, with a slight price premium. Until recently, the *San Francisco Chronicle* was arguably the most highly regarded of California's newspapers; however, since it became embroiled in a nasty ownership spat with its major competitor, the *San Francisco Examiner*, a couple of years ago, it's rather stumbled.

As in any North American town, the best place to turn for entertainment listings – not to mention an irreverent take on local government and politics – is one of the many freesheets available on most street corners. Since nightlife venues, clubs, and bars open and close so rapidly, they're the best source of up-to-date listings available. We've noted local titles in relevant towns throughout the text; note that many have online editions, too, so you can check them out before you travel.

Television

In California, you'll have access to all the usual stations: from major networks like ABC, CBS, and NBC to smaller netlets like the WB and UPN. Expect talk shows in the morning, soaps in the afternoon, and marquee name comedies and dramas during primetime. If that's all too maddeningly commercial-heavy, there's always PBS, the rather earnest, ad-free station, which fills its schedule with news, documentaries, and imported period dramas. The precise channel numbers vary from area to area.

There's a wider choice on cable, including CNN for news and music on MTV; well-regarded premium channels like HBO and Showtime are often available on hotel TV systems, showing original series and blockbuster movies.

Radio

Listening to the radio – and how its mix of stations changes during your travels (for example, a rapid increase in Christian pop stations) – is often one of the smartest ways to gauge the character of the local area. And as the land of the roadtrip, it's not surprising that California is well served by diverse radio stations. It's best to skip most specialty stations on the AM frequency – although AM chat shows, with their often angry, confrontational callers and hosts can be hilarious and illuminating, if not in the intended sense. On FM, you'll find the usual mix of rock, Latin, and R & B: stations are too numerous to list, although all-pop-rock stations KLLC (97.3 FM, known as 'Alice') in San Francisco and KROQ (106.7 FM) in Los Angeles are especially well known. Expect commercials interrupted by an occasional tune during drive time (6–9am and 4–7pm); also note that many stations have an astonishingly limited playlist – and songs in heavy rotation will often be played half a dozen times a day.

In Southern California, you'll also often come across Mexican stations (some local, others broadcasting from over the border), which can be enjoyable even for non-Spanish speakers.

A safe harbor if you're struggling to find satisfying local news is to tune to National Public Radio (NPR), the listener-funded talk station with a refreshingly sober take on news and chat (FM frequencies vary). To check for local frequencies for the World Service log on to the BBC (www.bbc.co.uk/world service/index.shtml), Radio Canada (www .rcinet.ca), or the Voice of America (www .voa.gov).

Public holidays and festivals

Someone, somewhere is always celebrating something in California, although apart from national holidays, few festivities are shared throughout the entire state. Instead, there is a disparate multitude of local events: art and craft shows, county fairs, ethnic celebrations, music festivals, rodeos, sandcastle-building competitions, and many others of every hue and shade.

Among California's major annual events are the **gay and lesbian freedom** parades held in June in LA and, particularly, San Francisco; the **Academy Awards** in LA in March; and the world-class **Monterey Jazz Festival** in September. These and other local highlights are covered in the text. In addition, California tourist offices can provide full lists, or you can just phone the visitor center in a particular region ahead of your arrival and ask what's coming up.

Public holidays

The biggest and most all-American of the national festivals and holidays is **Independence Day** on the Fourth of July, when the entire country grinds to a standstill as people get drunk, salute the flag, and take part in firework displays, marches, beauty pageants, and more, all in commemoration of the signing of the Declaration of Independence in 1776. **Halloween** (October 31) lacks any such patriotic overtones and is not a public holiday despite being one of the most popular yearly flings. Traditionally, kids run around the streets banging

on doors demanding "trick or treat," and are given pieces of candy. These days that sort of activity is mostly confined to rural and suburban areas, while in bigger cities Halloween has grown into a massive gay celebration: in West Hollywood in LA and San Francisco's Castro district, the night

Public holidays

January 1 **New Year's Day**
January 15 **Martin Luther King Jr's Birthday**
Third Monday in February **Presidents' Day**
Varies (usually early April) **Easter Monday**
Last Monday in May **Memorial Day**
July 4 **Independence Day**
First Monday in September **Labor Day**
Second Monday in October **Columbus Day**
November 11 **Veterans' Day**
Fourth Thursday in November **Thanksgiving Day**
December 25 **Christmas Day**

is marked by mass cross-dressing, huge block parties, and general licentiousness. More sedate is **Thanksgiving Day**, on the last Thursday in November. The third big event of the year is essentially a domestic affair, when relatives return to the familial nest to stuff themselves with roast turkey, and (supposedly) fondly recall the first harvest of the Pilgrims in Massachusetts – though in fact Thanksgiving was already a national holiday before anyone thought to make that connection. **Christmas Day** is another family occasion and is celebrated much as it is in other countries where there is a predominance of Christians, all preceded, of course, by commercial overkill.

On the other national **public holidays** listed above, banks and government offices are liable to be closed all day, and some shops may reduce their hours but otherwise things tick over pretty much as usual. The traditional **summer season** for tourism runs from **Memorial Day to Labor Day**, though California's benign weather extends that considerably, and the desert areas have their peak season through the winter.

Sports and outdoor pursuits

Nowhere in the country do the various forms of athletic activity and competition have a higher profile than in California. The big cities generally have at least one team in each of the major professional sports – football (though LA lost its last football team to Oakland in 1995), baseball, and basketball – as well as supporting teams in soccer, volleyball, ice hockey, wrestling, and even roller derby.

For foreign visitors, American sports can appear something of a mystery; one unusual feature is that in all the major sports the divisions are fixed, apart from the occasional expansion, so there is no fear of relegation to lower leagues. Another puzzle is the passion for **intercollegiate sports** – college and university teams, competing against one another in the Pacific-10 Conference, usually with an enthusiasm fueled by passionate local rivalries. In Los Angeles, USC and UCLA have an intense and high-powered sporting enmity, with fans on each side as vociferous as any European soccer crowd, and in the San Francisco Bay Area, the rivalry between UC Berkeley and Stanford is akin to that of Britain's Oxford and Cambridge.

And in California, where being physically fit and adventurous often appears to be a condition of state citizenship, the locals are passionate about their **outdoor pursuits**; the most popular include surfing, cycling, and skiing. When and where to enjoy any of California's most popular outdoor pursuits are detailed in the relevant chapters of the Guide, along with listings of guides and facilities.

Football

Professional football in America attracts the most obsessive and devoted fans of any sport, perhaps because there are fewer games played – only sixteen in the regular season, which lasts throughout the fall and is followed by the playoffs, culminating in the **Super Bowl** at the end of January. With many quick skirmishes and military-like movements up and down the field, it's ideal for television, and nowhere is this more apparent than during the **televised games** which are a feature of many bars on Monday nights – though most games are played on Sunday afternoons and evenings (and also shown on cable TV).

The game lasts for four fifteen-minute quarters, with a fifteen-minute break at half-time. But since time is only counted when play is in progress, matches can take at least three hours to complete, mainly due to interruptions for TV advertising. Commentators will discuss the game throughout to help your comprehension, though they use such a barrage of statistics to illustrate their remarks that you may feel hopelessly confused. Not that it matters – the **spectacle** of American football is fun to experience, even if you haven't a clue what's going on. Players tend to be huge, averaging about six foot five and weighing upwards of three hundred pounds; they look even bigger when they're suited up for battle in shoulder pads and helmets. The best players become nationally known celebrities, raking in millions of dollars in fees for product endorsements on top of astronomical salaries.

Teams and tickets

All major teams play in the National Football League (**NFL**), the sport's governing body, which divides the teams into two conferences of equal stature, the National Football Conference (**NFC**) and the American Football Conference (**AFC**). In turn, each conference is split into four divisions, North, East, South, and West. For the end-of-season playoffs, the best team in each of the eight divisions, plus two wildcards from each conference, fight it out for the title.

The Californian teams are the **Oakland Raiders**, who have promised much but delivered little of late; the **San Diego Chargers**, strong challengers for a play-off spot in 2004–5; and the **San Francisco 49ers**, who have recently been letting down the side's history which has seen them win five Super Bowls (a record shared with the Dallas Cowboys).

Tickets usually cost at least $60 for professional games and can be very hard to come by, while college games can be as low as $8 and are more readily available – check at the respective campuses covered in the text.

Booking tickets

NFL ☎ 212/450-2000, ⓦ www.nfl.com
Oakland Raiders ☎ 510/864-5000, ⓦ www .raiders.com

San Diego Chargers ☎ 619/220-8497, ⓦ www .chargers.com
San Francisco 49ers ☎ 415/421-8497, ⓦ www .sf49ers.com

Baseball

Baseball is often called "America's pastime," though the players' strike in 1994 left its image tarnished. The lustre has more or less come back, and after the threat of another image-shattering strike was averted at the last minute in 2002, home-run king Barry Bonds led the **San Francisco Giants** to their first World Series in thirteen years in an all-California match-up against the **Anaheim Angels**. The Angels, having never appeared in the showpiece before, came from behind to clinch the championship in the seventh game. Since then neither team, nor any of the other three California major leaguers (see below) has come near to the big prize.

Games are played – 162 each in the regular season – all over the US almost every day from April to September, with the division and league championships, followed by the **World Series** (the final best-of-seven play-off) lasting through October. Watching a game, even if you don't understand what's going on, can be at the very least a pleasant day out, drinking beer and eating hot dogs in the bleachers (unshaded benches) beyond the outfield; tickets in this area are cheap and the crowds usually friendly and sociable.

Teams and tickets

All major league baseball teams play in either the **National League** or the **American League**, each of equal stature and split into three divisions, East, Central, and West. For the end-of-season playoffs and the World Series, the best team in each of the six divisions plus a second-place wildcard from each league fight it out for the title. The 2002 Giants v Angels World Series was unique in being the first time both leagues' wildcards had reached the final stage.

California's other major league clubs are the **Oakland Athletic** (A's), **Los Angeles Dodgers**, and **San Diego Padres**. There are also numerous minor-league clubs, known as farm teams because they supply the top clubs with talent. Tickets for games cost $8–70 per seat, and are generally available on the day of the game.

Booking tickets

The Major Leagues ☎212/931-7800, ⓦwww.mlb.com

Anaheim Angels ☎1-888/796-4256, ⓦwww.angelsbaseball.com

Los Angeles Dodgers ☎323/224-1448, ⓦwww.dodgers.com

Oakland Athletics ☎510/762-2255, ⓦwww.oaklandathletics.com

San Diego Padres ☎619/881-6500, ⓦwww.padres.com

San Francisco Giants ☎415/972-2000, ⓦwww.sfgiants.com

Basketball

Basketball is one of the few professional sports that is also actually played by many ordinary Americans, since all you need is a ball and a hoop. The men's professional game is governed by the National Basketball Association (**NBA**), which oversees a season running from November until the playoffs in June. It is played by athletes of phenomenal agility; seven-foot-tall giants who float through the air over a wall of equally tall defenders, seeming to change direction in mid-flight before slam-dunking the ball (smashing it through the hoop with such force that the backboard sometimes shatters) to score two points. Games last for an exhausting 48 minutes of actual playing time, around two hours total.

The women's professional game is run by the **WNBA**; the season goes through the summer.

Teams and tickets

California's professional men's basketball teams consist of the **Los Angeles Lakers**, the **Golden State Warriors** (who play in Oakland), the **Sacramento Kings**, and the **Los Angeles Clippers**. The Lakers have ruled the NBA roost in recent seasons, collecting three consecutive titles up to 2002, though they lost in the 2003 semis and were beaten by Detroit in the 2004 finals. LA's **UCLA** once dominated the college game,

winning national championships throughout the 1960s; they emerged to win again in 1995. **USC, UC Berkeley**, and **Stanford** also field perpetually competitive intercollegiate teams, the last being the predominant force in the Pac-10 athletic conference in recent years.

Local **women's basketball teams** are in LA and Sacramento; tickets (beginning at about $8) are much more reasonable than the $50-plus for a decent seat at the men's game.

Tickets for NBA teams

The NBA ☎212/407-8000, ⓦwww.nba.com

Golden State Warriors ☎510/986-2200, ⓦwww.nba.com/warriors

Los Angeles Clippers ☎310/426-6001, ⓦwww.nba.com/clippers

Los Angeles Lakers ☎310/419-3100, ⓦwww.nba.com/lakers

Sacramento Kings ☎916/928-0000, ⓦwww.nba.com/kings

Tickets for WNBA teams

WNBA ☎212/688-9622, ⓦwww.wnba.com

Los Angeles Sparks ☎310/330-2434, ⓦwww.wnba.com/sparks

Sacramento Monarchs ☎916/928-3650, ⓦwww.wnba.com/monarchs

Ice hockey

Despite California's sun and sand reputation, **ice hockey** enjoys considerable popularity in the state, although most of the players are imported from more traditionally hockey-centric regions in Canada, Eastern Europe, and Scandinavia. A considerable rivalry has developed over the years between players from the United States and Canada, owing largely to Canada's fear of losing their long-time claim as the world's premier hockey nation – a fear that was somewhat allayed by Canada beating the USA in the 2002 Olympic Final. The domestic title is the **Stanley Cup**, contested by the playoff winners of the two **NHL** (National Hockey League) conferences (Eastern and Western), each comprised of three divisions of five teams. The season runs from October to June and, amazingly for such a fast and physical sport, each team plays several times a week. However, at the time of writing, nobody was playing at all due to a protracted dispute between owners and players causing a **lockout**, which was looking likely to completely wipe out the 2004–5 season and greatly damage the sport's image.

Teams and tickets

California boasts three NHL teams, and although none has ever won the big trophy, they still manage to draw considerable crowds; the **San Jose Sharks** sell out nearly every game and have become quite a force of late, reaching the quarterfinals of the Stanley Cup in 2002 and 2004; and the **Anaheim Mighty Ducks** came from nowhere to reach the Stanley Cup final in 2003. The **Los Angeles Kings** complete the trio. **Tickets** start at about $25.

Booking tickets

NHL ☎212/789-2000, ⓦwww.nhl.com
San Jose Sharks ☎408/287-7070, ⓦwww.sj-sharks.com
Los Angeles Kings ☎310/419-3160, ⓦwww.lakings.com
Anaheim Mighty Ducks ☎714/704-2700, ⓦwww.mightyducks.com

Soccer

In the main, the traditional American sports rule, but **soccer** is quickly gaining ground, especially as a participation sport for youngsters of both sexes. At the professional level, the successful US bid to host the 1994 World Cup led to the establishment of **Major League Soccer** (MLS; ⓦwww.mlsnet.com) in 1996, where twelve teams are divided into two conferences. The game continues to get injections of exposure with the national men's team qualifying for the finals of the World Cup both times since they hosted it and surprising everyone by making a spirited run to the quarterfinals in Japan/Korea 2002, where they narrowly lost to Germany. The **US women's team** have done even better, winning the Women's World Cup in 1999 and Olympic Gold in 2004. Unfortunately, WUSA (Women's United Soccer Association; ⓦwww.wusa.com), the sport's first professional league for women, lasted only three seasons before

lack of financial backing led to its suspension in 2003.

Teams and tickets

The **Los Angeles Galaxy** and **San Jose Clash** both play in the Western Conference of the MSL; having each reached the MSL Cup final, only to be beaten by DC United on both occasions, the Galaxy finally triumphed in 2002 with an overtime win versus the New England Revolution. The season runs through the summer and tickets cost $15–40.

Booking tickets

Los Angeles Galaxy ☎1-877/342-5299, ⓦwww.lagalaxy.com
San Jose Clash ☎408/985-4625, ⓦwww.clash.com

Outdoor pursuits

Surfing is probably the best-known Californian pastime, immortalized in the songs of the Beach Boys and Frankie Avalon. The California coast up to a little north of San Francisco, especially the southern half, is dotted with excellent surfing beaches. Some of the finest places to catch a wave, with or without a board, are at Tourmaline Beach near San Diego, Huntington Beach and Malibu in Los Angeles, along the coast north of Santa Barbara, and at Santa Cruz – where there's a small but worthy surfing museum. Individual beaches and outlets to hire equipment are covered in more detail in the text. **Windsurfing** is more commonly practised on lakes and protected inland lagoons, as the ocean is usually too rough, and again there are plenty of places to hire a board or get lessons.

Cycling is an extremely popular outdoor pursuit, with California home to some highly competitive, world-class road races, particularly around the Wine Country. The heavy-duty, all-terrain **mountain bike** was invented here, designed to tackle the slopes of Mount Tamalpais in Marin County. Weekend enthusiasts now put their knobby tires to use on the countless trails that weave throughout California's beautiful backcountry. Special mountain-bike parks, most of them operating in summer only, exploit the groomed, snow-free runs of the Sierra ski bowls of Lake Tahoe and Mammoth. In such places, and throughout California, you can rent bikes for $20–35 a day; see "Getting around," p.50, for more on general cycling and throughout the Guide for rental shops.

Skiing and **snowboarding** are also wildly popular, with downhill resorts all over eastern California – where, believe it or not, it snows heavily most winters. In fact, the Sierra Nevada Mountains offer some of the best skiing in the US, particularly around Lake Tahoe (see p.742), where the 1960 Winter Olympics were held. You can rent equipment for about $25–35 a day, plus another $40 to $65 a day for lift tickets. Details are given in the relevant sections. A cheaper option is **cross-country skiing**, or ski-touring. A number of backcountry ski lodges in the Sierra Nevada offer a range of rustic accommodation, equipment rental and lessons, from as little as $20 a day for skis, boots, and poles, up to about $200 for an all-inclusive weekend tour.

During the summer months, when the snows have melted and laid bare the crags of California's peaks, there is also a thriving **mountaineering** community, especially around Mount Shasta in the far north and in parts of the High Sierras. If you are not very experienced and do not have your own equipment, you can hire just about anything you might possibly need and get expert advice, lessons, or a guided expedition from numerous businesses that specialise in these areas.

California also has some of the world's best **rafting** rivers, the best of which cascade off the western side of the Sierra Nevada. Most rivers are highly seasonal, normally running best from mid-April to the end of June.

Rivers and rapids are classed according to a grading system, ranging from a Class I, which is painstakingly easy, to a Class VI, which is literally dicing with death. Trips can be as short as a couple of hours, taking in the best a river has to offer (or just the most accessible section), or can extend up to several days, allowing more time to hike up side canyons, swim, or just laze about on the bank. You might typically expect to pay around $100 for a four- to six-hour trip, going up to $150–200 a day for longer outings, including food and camping equipment rental. **Kayaking** is another popular water-based activity, both on the many rivers and, increasingly, in the ocean. Equipment rental starts at around $20 per hour or you might prefer an hour or two's guided kayaking from $60. Particularly good spots for both sports are outlined throughout the Guide.

Other outdoor activities include both fresh and salt water **fishing** – it's usually easier if you have your own gear but it can be rented in some places – and **horse riding**; many outfits offering equestrian fun are mentioned in the chapters. Prices vary more widely than for other activities, ranging from $40–100 for rides that might not differ all that much in length, so it's a good idea to skim through the places you will be visiting to see where the best deals are offered.

Finally, California offers virtually unlimited **hiking** opportunities, from coastal trails through dense forest paths to some stunning mountain ranges that are bound to test your stamina. All you need, of course, is some stout footwear and to be prepared for the possibility of some drastic changes in the weather. Serious backcountry hiking is dealt with separately in the following section.

Backcountry camping, hiking, and wildlife

California's landscape is one of the compelling reasons for visiting the state, with some of the most fabulous backcountry and wilderness areas in the US, coated by dense forests and capped by great mountains. While there are huge areas reachable only on foot, the excellent road system makes much of it easily accessible, aided by well-equipped and beautiful campgrounds right where you need them.

Unfortunately, it isn't all as wild as it once was, and the more popular areas can get pretty crowded. If you're thinking of joining the throngs, you can help preserve the special qualities of the environment by observing a few simple rules. For practical information on traveling through the deserts, see the box on pp.284–285.

The US's protected backcountry areas fall into a number of potentially confusing categories. Most numerous are California **state parks** (ⓦ www.parks.ca.gov), which include state beaches, state historic parks, and state recreational areas, often around sites of geological or historical importance and not necessarily in rural areas. Daily fees are usually $2–4, and can be as much as $14 but you are unlikely to save money by buying the **Annual Day-Use Pass** ($125) which is available online and at most parks.

National parks – such as Yosemite, Death Valley, and Joshua Tree – are large, federally controlled, and preserved areas of great natural beauty comprising several different features or ecosystems; entry fees are generally $10 per car (valid seven days), though Yosemite costs $20. These are supplemented by the smaller national monuments (free to $5), like Devil's Postpile, with just one major feature, and national seashores. If you plan on visiting a few of these, invest in a **National Parks Pass** ($50 from any national park entrance), which grants both driver and passengers (or if cycling or hiking, the holder's immediate family) twelve months' access to all the national parks across the country. The **Golden Eagle Pass** ($65) additionally provides nationwide access to national monuments, historic

sites, recreation areas, and wildlife refuges, though as few of these charge a significant entry fee it is usually better to buy the National Parks Pass and upgrade (for $15) if needed.

Excellent free **ranger programs** – such as guided walks, slide shows, and campfire talks – are held throughout the year. The federal government also operates **national recreation areas**, often huge hydro dams where you can jet ski or windsurf free of the necessarily restrictive laws of the national parks. Campgrounds and equipment-rental outlets are always abundant.

California's eighteen **national forests** cover twenty percent of the state's surface area. Most of them border the national parks, and are also federally administered (by the US Forest Service), but with much less protection. More roads run through national forests, and often there is some limited logging and other land-based industry operated on a supposedly sustainable basis.

All the above forms of protected land can contain **wilderness areas**, which aim to protect natural resources in their most native state. In practice, this means there's no commercial activity at all; buildings, motorized vehicles, and bicycles are not permitted, nor are firearms or pets. Overnight camping is allowed, but **wilderness permits** (usually free, though there's often a booking fee for advance reservations) must be obtained from the land management agency responsible. In California, Lava Beds, Lassen, Death Valley, Sequoia & Kings Canyon, Joshua Tree, Pinnacles, Point Reyes, and Yosemite all have large wilderness areas – 94 percent of Yosemite, for example – with only the regions and steamed to preserve a high concentration of vitamins, with a strong flavor – and to look better on the plate. Seafood comes from oyster farms and the catches of small-time fishermen, and what little meat there is on the menu tends to come from animals reared on organic farms. The result is small but beautifully presented portions, and high, high prices: it's not unusual to spend $40 a head (or much more) for a full dinner with wine. To whet your appetite, starters (perhaps $8–10) include mussels in jalapeño and sesame vinaigrette, snails in puff pastry with mushroom purée, and, among main courses, roasted goat-cheese salad with walnuts, swordfish with herb butter, and *ahi* tuna with cactus ratatouille.

Restaurants serving California cuisine build their reputation by word of mouth; if you can, ask a local enthusiast for recommendations, or simply follow our suggestions in the Guide, especially in Berkeley, the recognized birthplace of California cuisine. Of other American regional cooking, **Cajun** remains in vogue. Also known as "Creole," it originated in Louisiana as a way of saving money by cooking up leftovers. It is centered on black beans, rice, and seafood, and is always highly spiced. There are a few relatively inexpensive places to find it (charging around $12 a dish, but its cachet has generally pushed prices up).

Although technically ethnic, **Mexican** food is so common that it often seems like (and, historically, often is) an indigenous cuisine, especially in Southern California. What's more, day or night, it's the cheapest type of food to eat: even a full dinner with a beer or margarita will rarely be over $15 anywhere except in the most upmarket establishments. Californian Mexican food is generally different from what you'll find in Mexico, making more use of fresh vegetables and fruit, but the essentials are the same: lots of rice and pinto beans, often served refried (ie boiled, mashed, and fried), with variations on the **tortilla**, a thin maize or flour-dough pancake. You can eat it as an accompaniment to your main dish; wrapped around the food and eaten by hand (a **burrito**); filled and folded (a **taco**); rolled, filled, and baked (an **enchilada**); or fried flat and topped with a stack of food (a **tostada**). One of the few

options for vegetarians in this meat-oriented cuisine is the **chile relleno**, a mild, green pepper stuffed with cheese, dipped in egg batter, and fried. Veggie burritos, filled with beans, rice, lettuce, avocado, cheese, and sour cream are another prevalent option for those averse to meat.

Other ethnic cuisines are plentiful too. **Chinese** food is everywhere, and during lunchtime can often be as cheap as Mexican. **Japanese** is more expensive and fashionable – sushi is worshipped by some Californians. **Italian** food is very popular, but can be expensive once you leave the simple pizzas and pastas to explore the specialist Italian regional cooking that has caught on in the last few years. **French** food, too, is widely available, though always pricey, and the cuisine of social climbers and power lunchers, rarely found outside the larger cities. **Thai**, **Korean**, **Vietnamese**, and **Indonesian** food is similarly city-based, though usually cheaper; **Indian** restaurants, on the other hand, are thin on the ground just about everywhere and often very expensive – although as **Indian** cuisine catches on the situation is gradually changing for the better, with a sprinkling of moderately priced Southern Indian food outlets.

Drinking

In freeway-dominated Los Angeles, the traditional neighborhood bar is as rare as the traditional neighborhood. There are exceptions, but LA bars tend to be either extremely pretentious or extremely seedy, neither good for long bouts of social drinking. On the other hand, San Francisco is the consummate boozing town, still with a strong contingent of old-fashioned, get-drunk bars that are fun to spend an evening in, even if you don't plan to get legless. Elsewhere in the state you'll find the normal array of spots in which to imbibe.

To buy and consume alcohol in California, you need to be 21, and bars almost always have someone on the door checking ID: you'll probably need to be into your thirties before getting waved through automatically. Licensing laws and drinking hours are among the most liberal in the country (though laws on drinking and driving are not). Alcohol can be bought and consumed any time between 6am and 2am, seven days a week in bars, nightclubs, and many restaurants. Some restaurants only have a beer and wine license, and many allow you to take your own bottled wine into a restaurant, where the corkage fee will be $5–10. You can buy beer, wine, or spirits more cheaply and easily in supermarkets, many delis, and, of course, liquor stores.

American beers fall into two distinct categories: wonderful and tasteless. The latter are found everywhere: light, fizzy brands such as Budweiser, Miller, Schlitz, and so on. The alternative is a fabulous range of microbrewed beers, the product of a wave of backyard and in-house operations that swelled in the late 1980s and has now matured to the point that many pump out over 150,000 barrels a year and are classed as "regional breweries." Head for one of the brewpubs (many are listed in the Guide along with breweries you can visit; see also the California Beerpage website listed on p.39) and you'll find handcrafted beers such as crisp pilsners, wheat beers, and stouts on tap, at prices only marginally above those of the national brews. Bottled microbrews, like Chico's hoppy Sierra Nevada Pale Ale and the full-bodied, San Francisco–brewed Anchor Steam Beer, are sold throughout the state, while Red Tail Ale is found throughout Northern California. Imported beers are of course available in most places as well. Expect to fork out $4–5 for a glass of draught beer, about the same for a bottle of imported beer.

If you're partial to the internationally known Californian wines, like Gallo and Paul Masson, you may be surprised to learn that they are held in low regard on the West Coast, and are produced in plants resembling oil refineries. Most people prefer the produce of California's innumerable, and invariably good, smaller wineries. The Napa and Sonoma valleys – which produce predominantly dry wines made from French-strain grapes –

are widely, and rightly, regarded as the cradle of the Californian wine industry. Wines are categorized by grape-type rather than place of origin: the heavy and fruity Cabernet Sauvignon is probably the most popular red, along with the lighter Merlot and Pinot Noir. Among the whites, Chardonnay is very dry and flavorful, and generally preferred to Sauvignon Blanc or Fumé Blanc, though these have their devotees. The most unusual is the strongly flavored Zinfandel, which comes in white (mocked by wine snobs, but popular nonetheless), red, or rosé.

You can learn a lot about Californian wine by taking a winery tour, mostly including free tastings (although some charge $4–5 for a full glass or two), a number of which we've mentioned in the Guide. Alternatively, the visitor centers in popular wine-producing areas produce informative regional directories. The best lesson of all, of course, is simply to buy the stuff. It's fairly inexpensive: a decent glass of wine in a bar or restaurant costs $4–6, a bottle $10–20. Buying from a supermarket is better still – a tolerable bottle can be purchased for as little as $7.

Cocktails are extremely popular, especially during happy hours (usually any time between 5pm and 7pm) when drinks may be half-price and there's often a buffet thrown in. Varieties are innumerable, sometimes specific to a single bar or cocktail lounge, and they cost anything between $3 and $6.

An increasing alternative to drinking dens, coffee shops (look out for any joint with "Java" in the title) play a vibrant part in California's social scene, and are havens of high-quality coffee far removed from the stuff served in diners and convenience stores. In larger towns and cities, cafés will boast of the quality of the roast, and offer a full array of espressos, cappuccinos, lattes, and the like, served straight, iced, organic, or flavored with syrups. Herbal teas and light snacks are often also on the menu.

Gay and lesbian travelers

California's easy-going attitude is evident in its vibrant gay and lesbian scene. The heart of gay California (and, arguably, of gay America) is San Francisco, which has been almost synonymous with gay life since World War II, when suspected homosexuals, purged by the military at their point of embarkation, stayed put rather than going home to face stigma and shame. This, and the advent of gay liberation in the early 1970s, nurtured a gay community with powerful political and social connections.

San Francisco's gay, lesbian, bisexual, and transgender scene is easy to find; but there are also strong communities in Los Angeles, centered in West Hollywood, Palm Springs, and Santa Cruz, which has become something of a lesbian mecca in recent years. Be aware, though, that outside major urban centers and particularly in the deserts of interior California, attitudes may be more conservative and openness about your sexuality may provoke uneasiness from locals.

For a complete rundown on local resources, bars, and clubs, see the relevant headings in individual cities.

Contacts for gay and lesbian travelers

In the US and Canada

Damron Company PO Box 422458, San Francisco, CA 94142 ☎ 1-800/462-6654 or 415/255-0404, ⓦ www.damron.com. Publisher of the *Men's Travel Guide*, a pocket-sized yearbook full of listings of hotels, bars, clubs, and resources for gay men; the *Women's Traveler*, which provides similar listings for lesbians; and *Damron Accommodations*, which provides detailed listings of over 1000 accommodations for gays and lesbians worldwide.
Gayellow Pages PO Box 533, Village Station, New York, NY 10014 ☎ 212/674-0120, ⓦ www .gayellowpages.com. Useful directory of businesses in the US and Canada.
International Gay & Lesbian Travel Association 4331 N Federal Hwy, Suite 304, Fort Lauderdale, FL 33308 ☎ 954/776-2626 or 1-800/448-8550, ⓦ www.iglta.org. Trade group that can provide a list of gay- and lesbian-owned or -friendly travel agents, accommodation, and other travel businesses.

In the UK

Dream Waves Redcot High St, Child Okeford, Blandford DT22 8ET ☎ 0870/0422 475, ⓔ dreamwaves@aol.com. Specializes in exclusively gay holidays, including skiing trips and summer sun packages.
Madison Travel 118 Western Rd, Hove, East Sussex NN3 1DB ☎ 01273/202 532, ⓦ www .madisontravel.co.uk. Established travel agents specializing in packages to gay- and lesbian-friendly mainstream destinations, and also to gay/lesbian destinations.
ⓦ **www.gaytravel.co.uk** Online gay and lesbian travel agent, offering good deals on all types of holiday. Also lists gay- and lesbian-friendly hotels around the world.

In Australia and New Zealand

Gay and Lesbian Travel ⓦ www.galta.com .au. Directory and links for gay and lesbian travel in Australia and worldwide.
Gay Travel ⓦ www.gaytravel.com. The site for trip planning, bookings, and general information about international travel.
Parkside Travel 70 Glen Osmond Rd, Parkside, SA 5063 ☎ 08/8274 1222, ⓔ parkside@harveyworld .com.au. Gay travel agent associated with local branch of Harvey World Travel; all aspects of gay and lesbian travel worldwide.
Silke's Travel 263 Oxford St, Darlinghurst, NSW 2010 ☎ 02/8347 2000 or 1-800/807 860, ⓔ silba@magna.com.au. Long-established gay and lesbian specialist, with the emphasis on women's travel.
Tearaway Travel 1st floor, 155 Commercial Rd, South Yarra VIC 3141 ☎ 03/9827 4232, ⓦ www .tearaway.com. Gay-specific business dealing with international and domestic travel.

Women travelers

Practically speaking, though a woman traveling alone is certainly not the attention-grabbing spectacle in California that she might be elsewhere in the world (or even elsewhere in the US), you're likely to come across some sort of harassment. More serious than the odd offensive comment, rape statistics in the US are high, and it goes without saying that, even more than anyone else, women should never hitchhike alone – this is widely interpreted as an invitation for trouble, and there's no shortage of weirdos to give it. Similarly, if you have a car, be careful whom you pick up: just because you're in the driver's seat doesn't mean you're safe. If you can, avoid traveling at night by public transportation – deserted bus stations, while not necessarily threatening, will do little to make you feel secure, and where possible you should team up with another woman. On Greyhound buses, follow the example of other women traveling alone and sit as near to the front – and the driver – as possible.

Californian **cities**, especially San Francisco, can feel surprisingly safe, and **muggings** are an uncommon occurrence. But as with anywhere, particular care has to be taken at night, and a modicum of common sense can often avert disasters. Walking through unlit, empty streets is never a good idea, and you should take cabs wherever possible. The advice that women who look confident tend not to encounter trouble is, like all home truths, grounded in fact but not written in stone; those who stand around looking lost and a bit scared are prime targets, but nobody is immune. Provided you listen to advice, though, and stick to the better parts of a town, going into **bars** and **clubs** alone should pose no problems, especially in San Francisco and LA, where there's generally a pretty healthy attitude towards women who choose to do so and whose privacy will be respected. Only extremely unevolved specimens will assume you're available. If in doubt, gay and lesbian bars are usually a trouble-free alternative.

Small towns in rural areas are not blessed with the same liberal attitudes toward lone women travelers that you'll find in the cities.

If you have a vehicle breakdown in a country area, walk to the nearest house or town for help; don't wait by the vehicle in the middle of nowhere hoping for somebody to stop – they will, but it may not be the kind of help you're looking for. Should disaster strike, all major towns have some kind of rape counseling service available; if not, the local sheriff's office will make adequate arrangements for you to get help, counseling, and, if necessary, get you home.

The National Organization for Women (Ⓦ www.now.org) is a women's issues group whose lobbying has done much to affect positive social legislation. NOW branches, listed in local phone directories and on their website, can provide referrals for specific concerns, such as rape crisis centers and counseling services, feminist bookstores, and lesbian bars. Further back-up material can be found in *Women's Travel in Your Pocket* ($16; Ferrari Publications, PO Box 37887, Phoenix, AZ 85069 ☎602/863-2408), an annual guide for (lesbian) women travelers. Specific women's contacts are listed where applicable in the city sections of the Guide.

Directory

Addresses Generally speaking, roads in built-up areas are laid out to a grid system, creating "blocks" of buildings: addresses of buildings refer to the block, which will be numbered in sequence, from a central point usually downtown; for example, 620 S Cedar will be six blocks south of downtown. In small towns, and parts of larger cities, "streets" and "avenues" often run north–south and east–west respectively; streets are usually named (sometimes alphabetically), avenues generally numbered.

Cigarettes and smoking Smoking is a much frowned-upon activity in California, which has banned smoking in all indoor public places, including bars and restaurants. Cigarettes are sold in virtually any food shop, drugstore, or bar, and also from vending machines. A packet of twenty costs around $5, much cheaper than in Britain, though many smokers buy cigarettes by the carton for around $30.

Departure tax All airport, customs, and security taxes are included in the price of your ticket.

Drugs Possession of under an ounce of the widely consumed marijuana is a misdemeanor in California, and the worst you'll get is a $100 fine. Being caught with more than an ounce, however, means facing a criminal charge for dealing, and a possible prison sentence – stiffer if caught anywhere near a school. Other drugs are, of course, completely illegal and it's a much more serious offense if you're caught with any.

Electricity 110V AC. The insubstantial two-pronged plugs have now largely been replaced by a more sturdy three-pronged affair. Foreign devices will need both a plug adapter and a transformer, though laptops usually automatically detect and cope with the different voltage.

Floors In the US, what would be the ground floor in Britain is the first floor, the first floor the second floor, and so on.

ID Should be carried at all times. Two pieces should diffuse any suspicion, one of which should have a photo: driving license, passport, and credit card(s) are your best bets.

Measurements and sizes The US has yet to go metric, so measurements are in inches, feet, yards, and miles; weight in ounces, pounds, and tons. American pints and gallons are about four-fifths of Imperial ones, so a US gallon is only 3.8 liters rather than 4.5. Clothing sizes are always two figures less what they would be in Britain – a British women's size 12 is a US size 10 – while British shoe sizes are half a size below American ones for women, and one size below for men.

Time California runs on Pacific Standard Time (PST), which is eight hours behind GMT, and jumps forward an hour in summer (the last Sunday in April to the last Sunday in October), largely in step with the UK. In summer, when it is noon Monday in California it is 3pm in New York, 8pm in London, 5am Tuesday in Sydney, and 7am Tuesday in Auckland.

Tipping You really shouldn't leave a bar or restaurant without leaving a tip of at least fifteen percent and about the same should be added to taxi fares. A hotel porter should get roughly $1 for each bag carried to your room; a coatcheck clerk should receive the same per coat. When paying by credit card you're expected to add the tip to the total bill before filling in the amount and signing.

Videos and DVDs The standard format used for video cassettes in the US is different from that used in Britain and Australasia, though many modern VCRs will play both formats. DVDs also work to different formats around the world so when buying make sure that the disc will play on your machine back home.

Guide

Guide

Los Angeles

CHAPTER 1 # Highlights

* **Golden Triangle/Rodeo Drive**
For high-end consumers (and avid window-shoppers), this compact section of downtown Beverly Hills, featuring jewelry, fashion, and beauty merchants, is the main reason to visit Los Angeles. See p.143

* **Getty Center** A colossal, modernist arts center, the Getty is stuffed with treasures of the Old World and does much to help the city shake off its reputation as a culture-free zone. See p.147

* **Pacific Coast Highway** This sinewy stretch of Highway 1 winds around coastal cliffs and legendary beaches from Santa Monica to Malibu, where the views are stunning. See p.153

* **Rose Parade** If you are here on New Year's Day, check out this Pasadena procession of grand floral floats and marching bands, culminating in a momentous football game. See p.163

* **Disneyland** This monumental resort offers pricey hotels, monorails, and family-oriented rides of the original 1950s-era theme park and the newer California Adventure. See p.172

* **Musso and Frank Grill** This classically dark and moody watering hole has long been a favorite hangout for movie stars of the Golden Age and today's brattier celebrities. See p.186

△ The Getty Center

Los Angeles

Sprawling **LOS ANGELES** spreads across its great desert basin in an eye-popping, ear-blasting jangle of fast-food joints, shopping centers, palm trees, movie studios, and swimming pools, bordered by snow-capped mountains and the Pacific Ocean and stitched together by an intricate network of freeways crossing a thousand square miles of architectural, social, and cultural anarchy. It's an extremely visual city, colorful and brash in countless ways – a maddening patchwork like nowhere else on earth.

For all that, LA seems very familiar. The entertainment industry has been hyping the city ever since filmmakers arrived in the 1910s, attracted by a climate that allowed them to film outdoors year-round, plenty of open land on which to build elaborate sets, nearby landscapes varied enough to form an imaginary backdrop to just about anywhere in the world, and of course, the ever popular lures of cheap labor and low taxes. Since then, the money and glitz of Hollywood have lured countless thousands of would-be actors, writers, designers, and other budding artistes and celebrities to cast their lot in this hard-edged glamour-town, their triumphs and (more often) failures becoming intrinsic to the city's towering myths. So, too, has the threat of sudden disaster: floods, fires, and earthquakes are facts of life here, and the coexistence of both extremes – spectacle and tragedy – lends a perilous, almost unhinged personality to the city.

Some history

Originally settled by Chumash and Tongva peoples about a thousand years before the arrival of Spanish settlers in 1781, Los Angeles was named for the Spanish phrase for "**Our Lady Queen of the Angels**," not surprisingly later becoming a link in Junípero Serra's lengthy chain of 21 Franciscan missions (see p.10), as well as a staging ground for Spanish military expeditions. In 1821, Mexico gained control of California, and the entire terrain was subdivided into huge **ranchos** under the control of politically powerful land bosses, only to be swallowed up again during the Mexican–American War in 1847 by the US, which did everything it could to eradicate the society and government created by Spain and Mexico.

Up until the Civil War, LA was a multicultural burg of white American immigrants, poor Chinese laborers, and wealthy Mexican ranchers, with a population of less than fifty thousand. It wasn't until the completion of the **transcontinental railroad** in the 1870s that the city really began to grow, consistently doubling in population every ten years, with hundreds of thousands coming to live in what was billed as a Mediterranean-styled paradise. Ranches were subdivided into innumerable suburban lots, and scores of new

Ventura & Santa Barbara

Sacramento ▲

SAN FERNANDO

118

210

5

170

SIMI VALLEY · SAN FERNANDO VALLEY FREEWAY

118

23

SIMI VALLEY

NORTHRIDGE

SEPULVEDA BLVD

405

San Fernando Valley

VAN NUYS

NORTH HOLLYWOOD

HOLLYWOOD FREEWAY

CANOGA PARK

TOPANGA CANYON BLVD

VENTURA FREEWAY

NORTH HOLLYWOOD

101

101

ENCINO

SHERMAN OAKS

VINE

HOLLYWOOD

W. HOLLYWOOD

MULHOLLAND DRIVE

San Diego Freeway

TOPANGA CANYON BLVD

TOPANGA STATE PARK

BEL AIR

WESTWOOD

BEVERLY HILLS

LAS VIRGENES RD

SANTA MONICA MOUNTAINS

MALIBU CREEK STATE PARK

Getty Center

BRENTWOOD

UCLA

LACMA

KANAN DUNE RD

SANTA MONICA NATIONAL RECREATION AREA

PACIFIC PALISADES

SANTA MONICA

SANTA MONICA BLVD

SANTA MONICA FREEWAY

CRENSHAW

MALIBU

PACIFIC COAST HIGHWAY

1

405

CULVER CITY

1

Point Dume

Santa Monica Pier

VENICE

LINCOLN BLVD

INGLEWOOD

Venice Boardwalk

LAX

405

Santa Monica Bay

EL SEGUNDO

MARINE AVENUE

SEPULVEDA BLVD

BOULEVARD

Manhattan Beach

Hermosa Beach

HAWTHORNE

Redondo Beach

PALOS VERDES PENINSULA

N

- - - · - - - · Gold Line Light Rail
· · · · · · · · · · · Red Line Subway
- - - - - - - Blue Line Light Rail
- - · - - · - Green Line Light Rail
○ Station

0   10 miles

PACIFIC

Santa Catalina Island ▼

towns, like San Pedro and Santa Monica, sprang up. Meanwhile, land speculators marketed an enduring image of Los Angeles, epitomized by the family-size
suburban house (with a swimming pool and a two-car garage) set amid the
orange groves in a glorious land of sunshine.

More **boom years** followed World War II, when veterans, many of whom had
passed through on their way to the Pacific, came back to stay, buying government-subsidized houses and finding well-paid jobs in the mushrooming defense
and aeronautics industries, along with other work for oil, steel, and automotive
companies. Despite ongoing racial strife and increasingly dreadful pollution, in
many ways the period from the 1940s through the 1970s was LA's historic peak.
Along with heavy manufacturing, the entertainment and real estate sectors drew
ever-increasing numbers of people from around the country, and LA's population
exploded, turning the city into the nation's second-largest metropolis.

After the Cold War, though, Southern California was hit hard by cutbacks
in defense spending, particularly in the aeronautics industry. Unemployment
reached a peak of ten percent in the early 1990s, resulting in a spike in crime
and a pervasive paranoia in the suburbs. The **riots of 1992** (see p.118) exacer-
bated tensions, which were only increased by a pair of earthquakes and various
floods and fires in Southern California during the same period. With economic,
social, and racial troubles rampant, the city entered one of its darkest periods,
marked by the 1994 passage of **Proposition 187**, designed to deny Latino
immigrants access to social services (though later expunged by the courts).

In spite of the hostility, **Latino immigration** has continued to increase
dramatically, especially in Santa Ana and Garden Grove, and once-entrenched
white suburbanites now seek new refuges in distant "edge cities" like Rancho
Cucamonga and Palmdale, where their neighbors are state prisons stocked
with LA convicts from whom they once fled. Even in South Central, long the
center of African-American culture in the city, massive demographic upheaval
is taking place as traditional black neighborhoods become majority Latino,
with many of those newcomers arriving from some of the most impoverished
regions of Central America.

Unfortunately, LA's abiding racial animosities are nothing new, having been
with the city ever since its first settlement, and continuing in the barbarism
of some local police and the historic inability of the city's leaders even to
acknowledge or respond to the problem. Some residents, notably in the San
Fernando Valley and Harbor area, have pushed for **secession** as the answer to
the region's ills, though this simple-minded strategy has had little luck with
voters thus far. More liberal-minded residents have pushed for the strength-
ening of labor unions (with some limited success) and the election of a true
reforming mayor to solve the city's problems, specifically in the form of
Antonio Villaraigosa, who in 2001 stood poised to become LA's first Latino
mayor since the nineteenth century. Unfortunately, LA voters, stuck in their
conservative ways, gave the job to cheerless technocrat **James Hahn**, and the
city has been mired in scandal and malaise ever since.

Nonetheless, LA has regained its economic footing in the past ten years,
focusing on entertainment and real estate once more. About the only symbol

LA area codes

Because the Los Angeles region has eight telephone **area codes** – ☎213, ☎310,
☎323, ☎562, ☎626, ☎714, ☎818, and ☎949 – we have included the code before
each number.

of the hard-working old days is the port of LA and Long Beach, which handles more than sixty percent of the ocean-going cargo coming into the West Coast and remains an economic dynamo for Southern California. In LA proper, numerous glossy **museums**, many built during the past two decades, maintain the city as an international center of visual art, and the forest of Downtown skyscrapers attests to its key position as the high-finance gateway between America and the Far East.

Arrival

However you **arrive** in Los Angeles, and especially if you're not driving, you're faced with an unending sprawl that can be a source of bewilderment even for those who've lived in it for years. Provided you don't panic, this ungainly beast of a city can be managed and even navigated, if not necessarily tamed.

By plane

All European and most domestic **flights** use Los Angeles International Airport – always known as **LAX** – sixteen miles southwest of Downtown LA (☎310/646-5252, ⦾www.los-angeles-lax.com). **Shuttle buses** "B" and "C" serve their respective parking lots round the clock (disabled travelers should call ☎310/646-8021 for special lifts). If you're not planning to rent a car (if you are, see "Driving and car rental," p.91), local **buses** (the citywide MTA and individual lines to Santa Monica, Culver City, and Torrance) pick up by parking lot "C" – see pp.93–94 for more details.

The most convenient way into town is to ride a minibus such as **LAX Chequer Shuttle** (☎1-800/545-7745, ⦾www.laxchequer.com) or **SuperShuttle** (☎310/782-6600 or 1-800/258-3826, ⦾www.supershuttle.com), which run to Downtown, Hollywood, West LA, and Santa Monica (SuperShuttle also goes to Long Beach and Disneyland) and have signs on their windshields advertising their general destination. Fares vary depending on your destination, but are generally around \$25–30, plus tip. The shuttles run around the clock from outside the baggage reclaim areas, and you should never have to wait more than fifteen or twenty minutes; pay the fare when you board.

Taxis charge at least \$35 to West LA or Hollywood, \$90 to Disneyland, and a flat \$38 to Downtown; a \$2.50 surcharge applies for all trips starting from LAX. For more information check out ⦾www.taxicabsla.org. Unlicensed taxi operators may approach you and offer flat fares to your destination; such offers are best avoided. Using the **Metro** system to get to your destination from LAX is difficult. The nearest light-rail train, the **Green Line**, stops miles from the airport, and the overall journey involves three time-consuming transfers (very difficult with luggage) before you even arrive in Downtown Los Angeles. If you'd like to try anyway, shuttle service leaves from the lower level of the terminal to access the Metro stop at Aviation Station.

Most flights into LA use LAX, but if you're arriving from elsewhere in the US or Mexico, you can land at one of the **smaller airports** in the LA area – at Burbank, Long Beach, Ontario, or Orange County's John Wayne Airport in Costa Mesa. These are similarly well served by car rental firms; if you want to use public transportation, phone the MTA Regional Information Network on arrival (Mon–Fri 6am–7pm, Sat 8am–6pm; ☎1-800/COMMUTE, outside LA 213/626-4455 or 1-800/2LA-RIDE, ⦾www.mta.net), and tell them where you are and where you want to go.

By bus

The main **Greyhound** bus terminal, at 1716 E 7th St (☏213/629-8401, ⓦwww.greyhound.com), is in a seedy section of Downtown – though access is restricted to ticket holders and it's safe enough inside. There are other Greyhound terminals elsewhere in LA handling fewer services: in Hollywood, at 1715 N Cahuenga Blvd (☏323/466-6381); Pasadena, at 645 E Walnut St (☏626/792-5116); North Hollywood, at 11239 Magnolia Blvd (☏818/761-5119); Long Beach, at 1498 Long Beach Blvd (☏562/218-3011); and Anaheim, at 101 W Winston Rd (☏714/999-1256). Only the Downtown terminal is open around the clock; all have toilets and left-luggage lockers.

By train

Arriving in LA by **train**, you'll be greeted with the expansive Mission Revival architecture of Union Station, on the north side of Downtown at 800 N Alameda St (☏213/624-01710), from which you can reach Metrorail and Metrolink lines, and also access the nearby Gateway Transit Center, which offers connections to bus lines. Amtrak trains also stop at outlying stations in the LA area; for all listings, call Amtrak (☏1-800/USA-RAIL, ⓦwww.amtrak .com).

By car

The main routes by **car** into Los Angeles are the interstate highways, all of which pass through Downtown. From the east, I-10, the San Bernardino Free-way, and I-210, the Foothill Freeway, connect through the eastern suburbs and on to Phoenix; from the north and south, I-5 connects LA with Sacramento and San Diego. Of the non-interstate routes into the city, US-101, the scenic route from San Francisco, cuts across the San Fernando Valley and Hollywood into Downtown; Hwy-1, or the Pacific Coast Highway (PCH), follows the coast of California and takes surface streets through Santa Monica, the South Bay, and Orange County; and US-60, the Pomona Freeway, parallels I-10 through the eastern suburbs – though a bit slower it provides a less hair-raising interchange when it reaches Downtown.

Information

For free maps, accommodation suggestions, and general information, the Convention and Visitors Bureau (CVB) operates two **visitor centers**: Downtown, at 685 S Figueroa St (Mon–Fri 9am–5pm; ☏213/689-8822, ⓦwww.lacvb .com), and at the Hollywood & Highland mall, 6801 Hollywood Blvd (Mon–Sat 10am–10pm, Sun 10am–7pm; ☏323/467-6412). Other LA areas have their own bureaus: Beverly Hills, 239 S Beverly Drive (Mon–Fri 8.30am–5pm; ☏310/248-1000, ⓦwww.beverlyhillscvb.com); Long Beach, 1 World Trade Center, Suite 300 (Mon–Fri 9am–5pm; ☏562/436-3645, ⓦwww .visitlongbeach.com); Orange County, near Disneyland, at 640 W Katella Ave (daily 8am–8pm; ☏714/239-1340, ⓦwww.anaheim411.com or www .anaheimoc.org); Pasadena, 171 S Los Robles Ave (Mon–Fri 8am–5pm, Sat 10am–4pm; ☏626/795-9311, ⓦwww.pasadenacal.com); Santa Monica, at 1400 Ocean Ave (daily 10am–4pm; ☏310/393-7593, ⓦwww.santamonica .com), and in the Santa Monica Place mall, Colorado Blvd at Third St (daily

10am–6pm; ☎1-800/544-5319); and West Hollywood, in the Pacific Design Center, 8687 Melrose Ave #M38 (Mon–Fri 9am–5pm; ☎310/289-2525, Ⓦwww.visitwesthollywood.com).

All the centers offer free **maps** of their areas, but you'd do better to seek out our own laminated *Los Angeles Rough Guide Map* ($8.95). If you're in LA for a considerable period of time, you may want to invest in the thick, comprehensive *LA County Thomas Guide* ($19.95), the city's definitive road atlas, used by tourists and locals alike to navigate the bewildering maze of LA streets.

Newspapers and magazines

LA has just one **daily newspaper** of consequence: the *Los Angeles Times* (Ⓦwww.latimes.com), available from street-corner racks all over Southern California. The Sunday edition is huge, and its "Calendar" section contains the most complete listings of what's on and where, as well as reviews and arts and entertainment listings. Of the city's many **free papers**, the fullest and most useful are the *LA Weekly* (Ⓦwww.laweekly.com) and *Orange County Weekly* (Ⓦwww.ocweekly.com), featuring news, reviews, and listings with an alternative bent. Numerous small local papers covering individual neighborhoods, musical scenes, and political activism are available all over the city, especially at cafés and record- and bookstores. If all else fails, the touristy *Where LA* public-relations magazine can be found for free inside many hotel rooms.

To get a sense of how style-conscious LA sees itself, pick up a copy of the monthly *Los Angeles* magazine (Ⓦwww.lamag.com), packed with gossipy news and profiles of local movers and shakers, as well as reviews of the city's trendiest restaurants and clubs. There are also dozens of less glossy, more erratically published zines focusing on LA's diverse gay and lesbian culture and nightclubs.

City transportation

Wherever and however you're **getting around** LA, you should allow plenty of time to get there. Obviously, this is partly due to the sheer size of the city, but the confusing entanglements of freeways and the gridlock common during rush hours (or any hours) can make car trips lengthy slogs – and the fact that most local buses stop on every other corner hardly makes bus travel a speedy alternative.

Driving and car rental

Not surprisingly, the best way to get around LA – though by no means the only way – is to **drive**. Despite the traffic being bumper-to-bumper much of the day, the **freeways** are the only way to cover long distances quickly. The system, however, can be confusing, especially since each stretch can have two or three names (often derived from their eventual destination, however far away) as well as a number. Out of an eye-popping, four-level interchange known as "The Stack," four major freeways fan out from Downtown: the Hollywood Freeway (US-101) heads northwest through Hollywood into the San Fernando Valley; the Santa Monica Freeway (I-10) connects the northern edge of South Central LA with Santa Monica; the Harbor Freeway (I-110) runs south to San Pedro (heading northeast it's called the Pasadena Freeway); and the Santa Ana Freeway (I-5) passes Disneyland and continues to Orange County and San Diego. **Other area freeways** include the San Diego Freeway (I-405), following the coast through West LA and the South Bay (but not actually reaching San Diego); the Ventura Freeway (Hwy-134), linking Burbank, Glendale, and Pasadena to US-101 in the San Fernando Valley; the Long Beach Freeway (I-710), a truck-heavy route connecting East LA and Long Beach; the Foothill Freeway (I-210), skirting the suburbs at the base of the San Gabriel Mountains; and the San Gabriel River Freeway (I-605), linking those suburbs with Long Beach. For **shorter journeys**, especially between Hollywood and West LA, the wide avenues and boulevards are a better – sometimes the only – option, not least because you get to see more of the city.

All the major **car rental** companies have branches in the city (check the *Yellow Pages* for the nearest office or call one of the numbers listed on p.46), and most have their main office close to LAX, linked to each terminal by a free shuttle bus. A number of smaller rental companies specialize in everything from Gremlins to Bentleys. The best known, and one of the cheapest, is Rent-A-Wreck (☏310/826-7555 or 1-800/995-0994, Ⓦwww.rentawreck.com), at 12333 W Pico Blvd in West LA and seven suburban locations.

Parking is a particular problem Downtown, along Melrose Avenue's trendy Westside shopping zone, in downtown Beverly Hills, and in Westwood. Anywhere else is less troublesome, but watch out for restrictions – some lampposts boast as many as four placards listing dos and don'ts.

Public transportation

The bulk of LA's public transportation is operated by the LA County Metropolitan Transit Authority (**MTA** or **"Metro"**). Its massive **Gateway Transit Center**, east of Union Station on Chavez Avenue at Vignes Street, serves thousands of daily commuters traveling by Metrorail, Metrolink, Amtrak, and the regional bus systems. The Center comprises **Patsaouras Transit Plaza**, from which you can hop on a bus; the glass-domed **East Portal**, through which you can connect to a train; and the 26-story **Gateway Tower**, at which you can find an MTA customer service office (Mon–Fri 6am–6.30pm; Ⓦwww .mta.net) on the ground floor.

Metrorail and Metrolink

LA's **Metrorail** subway and light-rail system encompasses four major lines, though extensions are planned in coming years. A new **Orange Line** crossing the San Fernando Valley and linking Canoga Park with North Hollywood is scheduled for completion in August 2005. The latter area already provides the northern terminus for the underground **Red Line**, which heads south under the Hollywood Hills to connect Central Hollywood and Downtown (stopping at the Gateway Transit Center, as do all Downtown routes). Of more use to residents than tourists, the **Green Line** runs between industrial

---

MTA offices and information

For **MTA route and transfer information**, phone ☏213/626-4455 or 1-800/COM-MUTE (Mon–Fri 7.30am–3.30pm); be prepared to wait, and be ready to give precise details of where you are and where you want to go. Otherwise, you can visit MTA on the Web at Ⓦwww.mta.net or go in person to Downtown's Gateway Transit Center, Chavez Ave at Vignes St (Mon–Fri 6am–6.30pm), or to three other centrally located offices: at 515 S Flower St, on level C of Arco Plaza, Downtown (Mon–Fri 7.30am–3.30pm); 5301 Wilshire Blvd, Mid-Wilshire (Mon–Fri 9am–5pm); and 14435 Sherman Way, in the San Fernando Valley (Mon–Fri 10am–6pm).

El Segundo (from where you can pick up an LAX shuttle at Aviation Station; see p.89) and colorless Norwalk, along the middle of the Century Freeway. The **Blue Line** leaves Downtown and heads overland through South Central to Long Beach, while the more appealing **Gold Line**, another light-rail route, connects Downtown with northeast LA, Highland Park, and Old Pasadena, before ending at drab Sierra Madre. **Fares** are $1.25 one way, with one-hour-long transfers available for 25¢ and day passes available for $3. Trains run daily 5am–12.30am, at five- to six-minute intervals during peak hours and every ten to fifteen minutes at other times. No smoking, eating, or drinking is allowed while on board.

As one rail alternative, **Metrolink** commuter trains operate primarily inter-suburban to Downtown routes on weekdays, though can be useful if you find yourself in any such far-flung districts, among them places in Orange, Ventura, Riverside, and San Bernardino counties. Although casual visitors may find the service useful mainly for reaching the outlying corners of the San Fernando Valley, the system does reach as far as Oceanside in San Diego County, from which you can connect to that region's Coaster commuter rail (see p.226) and avoid the freeways altogether. One-way fares range from $3.50–11.25, depending on when you're traveling (most routes run during daily business hours, often to LA in the morning and back to the suburbs in the evening) and how far you're going. For information on specific routes and schedules, call ☎1-800/371-LINK or visit on the Net at ⓦwww.metrolinktrains.com.

Buses

Car-less Angelenos not lucky enough to live near a train route have to settle for **buses**. Although initially bewildering, the MTA network is really quite simple: the main routes run east–west (eg, between Downtown and the coast) and north–south (eg, between Downtown and the South Bay). Establishing the best transfer point if you need to change buses can be difficult, but with a bit of planning you should have few real problems – though always allow plenty of time.

Free brochures are available from MTA offices, as are diagrams and timetables for individual bus routes, as well as regional bus maps showing larger sections of the metropolis. Buses on the major arteries between Downtown and the coast run roughly every fifteen minutes between 5am and 2am; other routes, and the **all-night services** along the major thoroughfares, are less frequent, usually every thirty minutes or hourly. At night, be careful not to get stranded Downtown waiting for connecting buses.

The standard **one-way fare** is $1.25, except for night routes (9pm–5am), when the cost is only 75¢; **transfers**, which can be used in one direction within the time marked on the ticket (usually three hours), cost 25¢ more; and **express buses** (a limited commuter service), and any others using a freeway, are usually $1.75–2.25, but can be as much as $4 depending on length of trip and the number of zones you pass through, as shown on station maps. Put the correct money (coins or notes) into the slot when getting on. If you're staying a while, you can save some money with a **weekly** or **monthly pass**, which cost $14 and $52, respectively (with monthly student passes for $27), and also give reductions at selected shops and travel agents. If you're staying about two weeks, consider a semi-monthly pass, sold for $27. Finally, "EZ Transit" passes give you the option of traveling on MTA and DASH buses, as well as Metrorail trains, for a flat $58 per month.

In the coming years, the MTA is planning to continue rolling out more of the new **Metro Rapid** routes throughout the region, offering modified bus service

MTA bus routes

MTA's **buses** fall into the route categories shown below. Whatever bus you're on, if traveling alone, especially at night, sit up front near the driver. Try and sit near a ventilation hatch, too, as the air conditioning can emit a pungent odor.

#1–99 – local routes to and from Downtown
#100–299 – local routes between other areas
#300–399 – limited-stop routes (usually rush hours only)
#400–499 – express routes to and from Downtown
#500–599 – express routes between other areas
#600–699 – special service routes (for sports events and the like)
#700–799 – Metro Rapid service

Major LA bus services

From LAX bus center to:
Beverly Hills #220
Downtown #42, #439
Long Beach #232
San Pedro #225
Watts Towers #117
West Hollywood #220 (for Hollywood change to #4 along Santa Monica Blvd)

To and from Downtown along:
Hollywood Blvd #2, #4, #10, #20, #21 (connect at La Brea Ave onto #212, #312 north)
Sunset Blvd #2, #302
Santa Monica Blvd #4, #304
Melrose Ave #10, #11
Wilshire Blvd #20, #21, #320
Olympic Blvd #28
Venice Blvd #33
Broadway #45, #46

From Downtown to:
Hollywood #2, #302
Beverly Hills #20, #21, #320
Santa Monica #4, #20, #434
Venice #33, #333
Getty Center #2, #302 (transfer at UCLA to #761)
Forest Lawn Cemetery, Glendale #90, #91
Exposition Park #38, #81
Huntington Library #78, #79
Burbank Studios #96
San Pedro #445, #446, #447 (transfer to DASH #142 for Catalina)
Manhattan Beach/Hermosa Beach/ Redondo Beach #439
Palos Verdes #444
Long Beach #60, #360
Orange County, Knott's Berry Farm, Disneyland #460

(along special #700 lines) with special red-colored identification, waiting kiosks with enhanced displays, and technology to reduce waiting times at green lights. There is no extra charge for these nine routes, and in Central LA they currently serve Wilshire, Ventura, and La Cienega boulevards, Vermont Avenue, Broadway, and the 405 freeway – though LAX is not yet connected. There are also the mini **DASH** buses, which operate through the LA Department of Transportation, or LADOT (☏808-2273 for area codes 213, 310, 323, and 818, ⓦwww.ladottransit.com), with a flat fare of 25¢. Six routes run through Downtown every five to ten minutes between 6.30am and 6pm on weekdays, and every fifteen to twenty minutes between 10am and 5pm on Saturdays and Sundays. Other DASH routes travel widely throughout the metropolis, including the Mid-Wilshire area, Pacific Palisades, Venice, and South Central LA, usually every fifteen to thirty minutes on weekdays, less often on Saturdays, and not at all on Sundays. The LADOT also operates quick, limited-stop routes called **commuter express**, though these cost a bit more (90¢–$3.10) depending on distance.

Other **local bus services** include those for Orange County (OCTD; ☏714/636-7433, ⓦwww.octa.net), Long Beach (LBTD; ☏562/591-2301, www.lbtransit.org), Culver City (☏310/253-6500, Ⓦwww.culvercity.org /depts_bus.html), and Santa Monica (☏310/451-5444, Ⓦwww.bigbluebus .com) – the latter two systems provide the best options for reaching the Getty Center (see p.147).

Taxis

You can find **taxis** at most terminals and major hotels. Otherwise call – among the more reliable companies are Independent Cab Co (☏1-800/521-8294), Checker Cab (☏1-800/200-1085), and United Independent Taxi (☏1-800/411-0303). Fares are set by the city at $2, plus $1.60 for each mile (or 40¢ per minute of waiting time), with a $2.50 surcharge if you're picked up at LAX. The driver won't know every street in LA but will know the major ones; ask for the nearest junction and give directions from there. If you encounter problems, call ☏1-800/501-0999, or visit Ⓦwww.taxicabsla.org.

Cycling

Cycling in LA may sound perverse, but in some areas, notably away from the freeways, it can be one of the better ways of getting around. There is an excellent **beach bike path** between Santa Monica and Redondo Beach, and from Long Beach to Newport Beach, and many equally enjoyable inland routes, notably around Griffith Park and the grand mansions of Pasadena (the LA River route, however, is justifiably notorious, loaded with broken glass and bands of budding criminals). For maps and information, contact the AAA, 2601 S Figueroa St (Mon–Fri 9am–5pm; ☏213/741-3686, Ⓦwww.aaa-calif.com), or the LA office of the state Department of Transportation, known as CalTrans, 120 S Spring St (Mon–Fri 8am–5pm; ☏213/897-3656, Ⓦwww.dot.ca.gov). The best place to **rent a bike** for the beaches is on Washington Street around Venice Pier, where you'll find numerous outlets, including Spokes 'n' Stuff, 4175 Admiralty Way (☏310/306-3332) and 1700 Ocean Ave (☏310/395-4748); in summer, bike rental stands line the beach. Prices range from $8–10 a day for a clunker to $15–20 a day or more for a mountain bike. For similar cost, many beachside stores also rent **roller skates** and **rollerblades**.

Walking and hiking

Although some people are surprised to find sidewalks in LA, let alone pedestrians, **walking** is in fact the best way to see much of Downtown and districts like central Hollywood, Pasadena, Beverly Hills, Santa Monica, and Venice. You can structure your stroll by taking a **guided walking tour**, the best of which are organized by the Los Angeles Conservancy (☏213/623-CITY, Ⓦlaconservancy.org), whose treks around Downtown are full of Art Deco movie palaces, once-opulent financial monuments and architectural gems like the Bradbury Building (see p.111). The group runs Downtown tours every Saturday, leaving the *Biltmore Hotel* on Olive Street at 10am (reservations required; $10); alternately, you can take Conservancy tours of Angelino Heights, Highland Park, and San Pedro for the same fee. You can enjoy guided **hikes** through the wilds of the Santa Monica Mountains and Hollywood Hills free of charge every weekend with a variety of organizations and bureaus, including the Sierra Club (☏323/387-4287, Ⓦwww .sierraclub.org), the State Parks Department (☏818/880-0350, Ⓦwww .parks.ca.gov), and the Santa Monica Mountains National Recreation Area (☏818/597-1036, Ⓦwww.nps.gov/samo).

Guided tours of LA

One quick and easy way to see LA is from the window of a guided bus tour, which can vary greatly in cost and quality. The mainstream tours carry large busloads around the major tourist sights and generally don't cover anything that you couldn't see for yourself at less cost. Specialist tours, tailored to suit particular interests, usually carry smaller groups of people and are often a better, quirkier value. Studio tours of film and TV production areas are covered on day-trips by most of the mainstream operators, though again you'll save money by turning up on your own.

Mainstream tours

By far the most popular of the mainstream tours is the half-day "stars' homes" jaunt. Usually including the Farmers Market, Sunset Strip, Rodeo Drive, the Hollywood Bowl, and, of course, the "stars' homes," this is much less enjoyable than it sounds – frequently no more than a view of the gate at the end of the driveway of the house of some has-been celebrity. These tours are typically the most visible, and the area around the Chinese Theatre is thick with tourists lining up for tickets. Other programs include tours around the Westside at night, to the beach areas, the *Queen Mary*, day-long excursions to Disneyland, and shopping trips to Tijuana.

Costs are $30–95 minimum per person, with some simple hour-long trips around Hollywood for around $15; assorted leaflets are strewn over hotel lobbies and visitor centers. You can make reservations at – and be picked up from – most hotels. Otherwise contact one of the following booking offices:

Hollywood Fantasy Tours 6671 Hollywood Blvd ☎323/469-8184, ⓦwww .hollywoodfantasytours.com.

LA Tours 1617 Gower St ☎323/460-6490, ⓦwww.latours.net.

Red Line Tours 6773 Hollywood Blvd ☎323/402-1072, ⓦwww.redlinetours.com.

Starline Tours 6925 Hollywood Blvd ☎323/463-3333, ⓦwww.starlinetours.com.

VIP Tours 9830 Bellanca Ave ☎310/641-8114, ⓦwww.viptoursandcharters.com.

Specialist tours

The specialist tours listed are also generally $30 or more per person. For more suggestions, pick up the free *LA Visitors Guide* from hotels and visitor centers.

Architecture Tours LA ☎323/464-7868, ⓦwww.architecturetoursla.com. Driving tours of the master buildings of the LA region, with packages focusing on Hollywood, West LA, Pasadena, and Downtown. Cost varies depending on itinerary.

Accommodation

Since LA has 100,000-plus rooms, finding **accommodation** is easy, and, whether you seek basic budget motels or world-class resorts, the city has something for everyone. However, finding somewhere low-priced and centrally located can be difficult, though not impossible. If you're driving, of course, you needn't worry about staying in a less than ideal location – a freeway is never far away. Otherwise you'll need to be more choosy about the district you pick, as getting across town can be a time-consuming chore.

Motels and the bottom-end hotels start at about $40 for a double, but many are situated in seedy or out-of-the-way areas, and often you'll gain by paying more for a decent location in any of a number of other non-chain, mid-range hotels. **Bed and breakfasts** are still uncommon in Central LA, and tend to be quite expensive, often fully booked, and sited in out-of-the-way places. For those on a tight budget, a handful of **hostels** are dotted all over the city, many

Architours ☎323/294-5821 or 1-866/227-2448, ⓦwww.architours.com. Walking, driving, and custom tours of the art and architecture highlights of certain parts of the city. Multi-day trips also available. Prices vary widely according to itinerary.

Black LA Tours ☎323/750-9267, ⓦwww.soulofamerica.com/tours/tour_la.html. Black historical and entertainment tours of once renowned Central Avenue and important sites for African-American society and culture. Prices vary.

Heli-USA 16303 Waterman Drive, Van Nuys ☎818/944-1445, ⓦwww.toflyla.com. Tours by helicopter of some of the more prominent visual sights in the region, such as movie studios, skyscrapers, and the Hollywood sign, for $150–270, with dinner packages available.

Neon Cruises 501 W Olympic Blvd, Downtown ☎213/489-9918, ⓦwww.neonmona .org/cruise. Popular, three-hour evening tours of LA's best remaining neon art, once a month on Saturdays, organized through the Museum of Neon Art. You may need to book months in advance. $45.

Off 'n Running Tours 1129 Cardiff Ave ☎310/246-1418. Curious four- to six-mile jogging tours of the stars' homes and various jaunts around Beverly Hills and West LA. $50.

SPARC tours: the Murals of LA 685 Venice Blvd, Venice ☎310/822-9560, ⓦwww .sparcmurals.org. Thoroughly enlightening tour of the "mural capital of the world." Along with being an excellent resource center, SPARC conducts two-hour mural tours ($400), personalized to your interests and sometimes including discussions with the artists.

Studio tours

For some small insight into how a film or TV show is made, or just to admire the special effects, there are guided tours at Warner Bros Studios ($35; ⓦwww .burbank.com/warner_bros_tour.shtml), NBC ($7), Sony ($20; ☎323/520-TOUR), and Universal ($50; ⓦwww.universalstudioshollywood.com), all of which are near Burbank except for Sony, which is in Culver City. If you want to be part of the **audience** in a TV show, Hollywood Boulevard, just outside the Chinese Theatre, is the spot to be: TV company reps regularly appear handing out free tickets, and they'll bus you to the studio and back. All you have to do once there is be willing to laugh and clap on cue.

in good locations, though at some stays are limited to a few nights. Surprisingly, there are a few **campgrounds** on the edge of the metropolitan area – along the beach north of Malibu and in the San Gabriel Mountains, for example – but you'll need a car to get to them. **College rooms** are also sometimes available for rent during student vacation time: contact UCLA Interfraternity Council (☎310/825-7878) or USC's off-campus housing office (☎1-800/USC-4632, ⓦhousing.usc.edu) for more information.

LA is so big that if you want to see it all without constantly having to cross huge expanses, it makes sense to divide your stay between several **districts**. Downtown has both chic, swank hotels and basic dives; Hollywood has similar options, with roadside motels providing cheap and adequate rooms; more salubrious West LA, Santa Monica, Venice, and Malibu are predominantly mid-to-upper-range territory, with the odd hostel here and there. Among options further out, the South Bay and Harbor Area carry a good selectio~~n~~ mid-range hotels (and a hostel) strung mostly along the Pacific C~~~~

It's only worth staying in Orange County, thirty miles southeast of Downtown, if you're aiming for Disneyland or are traveling along the coast: hotels under $75 a night are uncommon and you must book at least a week in advance, especially if a convention is in town. In Anaheim, unfortunately, many of the plentiful rooms along Katella Avenue and Harbor Boulevard are decrepit and depressing, even though they charge up to $100 a night. A far better alternative is the handful of hostels and coastal campgrounds in easy reach.

Since visitor centers don't make accommodation **reservations** (though they will offer information and advice), you can only book a room through a travel agent or by phoning the hotel directly. Ask if there are special weekend or midweek rates.

The hotels are listed below by **neighborhood**, with specific options for gay and lesbian travelers listed on p.210. In case you're arriving on a late flight, or leaving on an early one, we've also listed a few places to stay near the airport: cheap hotels near LAX are blandly similar and generally around $40–75, but most have complimentary transportation to and from the terminals.

Airport hotels

Days Inn 901 W Manchester Blvd ☎310/649-0800 or 1-800/231-2508, ⊛www.the.daysinn.com. Modern hotel with clean rooms and an outdoor pool in a grubby neighborhood by the 405 freeway. Offers free parking and free LAX shuttle. ❹

Quality Inn 5249 W Century Blvd ☎310/645-2200 or 1-800/228-5151, ⊛www.qualityinn.com. Featuring ten floors of comfortable, well-equipped rooms and a restaurant and bar, this motel also offers free LAX shuttles every fifteen minutes and a location a half-mile west of the 405 freeway. ❺

Renaissance 9620 Airport Blvd ☎310/337-2800, ⊛www.renaissancehotels.com. The best of the higher-end accommodations close to LAX, along a hotel row. With wood-and-marble decor, ample rooms, and luxurious suites with Jacuzzis, plus on-site pool, spa, and health club. ❽

Travelodge LAX 5547 W Century Blvd ☎310/649-4000, ⊛www.travelodge.com. Reliable chain motel with continental breakfast, airport shuttle, and on-site *Denny's* – good value for the area. ❸

Downtown and around

See the map on p.105 for hotel locations.

Downtown LA Standard 550 S Flower St ☎213/892-8080, ⊛www.standardhotel.com. Located in a former oil-company building, the latest branch of LA's self-consciously trendy chain features sleek, modern furnishings and quirky decor, but is best for its rooftop bar. Although billed as a "business hotel," the party scene is pretty much constant. ❻

Figueroa 939 S Figueroa St at Olympic Blvd ☎213/627-8971 or 1-800/421-9092, ⊛www .....hotel.com. Colorful, distinctive hotel with

attractively furnished rooms in a retro Spanish style, 24hr coffee shop, pool, and spa. ❻

Los Angeles Athletic Club 431 W 7th St ☎213/625-2211, ⊛www.laac.com. This brick-and-terracotta charmer is one of Downtown's better Beaux Arts buildings. While still home to an exclusive club, the top three floors make up a hotel with 72 nicely furnished rooms and nine expensive suites; a real plus is free use of the club's track, pool, exercise equipment, and handball and basketball courts. ❼

Millennium Biltmore 506 S Grand Ave at 5th St ☎213/624-1011 or 1-800/222-8888, ⊛www .thebiltmore.com. Neoclassical 1923 architecture combined with modern luxury, with a health club modeled on a Roman bathhouse, cherub and angel decor, and a view overlooking Pershing Square. Significantly cheaper rates on weekends ($50–100 less). ❾

Miyako Inn 328 E 1st St ☎213/617-2000, ⊛www.miyakoinn.com. Despite the grim, concrete-box exterior, this business-oriented hotel offers rooms with fridges, a spa, and Internet access, plus there's a karaoke bar. ❻

New Otani 120 S Los Angeles St ☎213/629-1200 or 1-800/421-8795, ⊛www.newotani.com. Business hotel featuring spacious suites, a good restaurant with Asian cuisine, and the small Japanese Garden in the Sky, which uses the traditional technique of "borrowed scenery" to incorporate existing views into the design. ❻

Omni Los Angeles 251 S Olive St at 4th St ☎213/617-3300 or 1-800/327-0200, ⊛www .omnilosangeles.com. Fancy Bunker Hill hotel with plush rooms, swimming pool, and weight room. Adjacent to MOCA and the Music Center. ❽

Westin Bonaventure 404 S Figueroa St ☎213/624-1000 or 1-800/228-3000, ⊛www

.westin.com. Modernist luxury hotel with five glass towers that resemble cocktail shakers, a six-story atrium with a "lake," and elegantly remodeled, conic-shaped rooms. A breathtaking exterior elevator ride ascends to the rotating *Bona Vista* cocktail lounge. Suites upwards of $2000. ❽

Hollywood

See the map on p.124 for hotel locations.

Dunes Sunset 5625 Sunset Blvd ☎323/467-5171. On the dingy eastern side of Hollywood, but far enough away from the weirdness of Hollywood Blvd to feel safe; adequate motel rooms and good access to Downtown. ❸

Holiday Inn Hollywood 2005 N Highland Ave ☎323/876-8600, ⓦwww.holiday-inn.com. Chain hotel with prime location three blocks from the center of the action, with pool, spa, gym, and Internet access. ❹

Hollywood Metropolitan 5825 Sunset Blvd ☎323/962-5800 or 1-800/962-5800, ⓦwww.metropolitanhotel.com. Sleek high-rise in central Hollywood. Good value for the area, with decent rooms and disabled access. ❹

Hollywood Roosevelt 7000 Hollywood Blvd, between Highland and La Brea ☎323/466-7000, ⓦwww.hollywoodroosevelt.com. The first hotel built for the movie greats in 1927. The place reeks of atmosphere, with renovated rooms and a "History of Hollywood" exhibit on the second floor. Also offers a Jacuzzi, fitness room, and swimming pool. ❼

Orchid Suites 1753 Orchid Ave ☎323/874-9678 or 1-800/537-3052, ⓦwww.orchidsuites.com. Roomy, if spartan, suites with cable TV, kitchenettes, and heated pool. Very close to the most popular parts of Hollywood and adjacent to the massive Hollywood & Highland mall. ❹

Renaissance Hollywood 1755 N Highland Blvd ☎323/856-1200, ⓦwww.renaissancehollywood.com. The hotel centerpiece of the new Hollywood & Highland mall, with upscale rooms and suites, and prime location in the heart of Tinseltown. ❼

West LA and Beverly Hills

See the map on pp.136–137 for most hotel locations.

Avalon 9400 W Olympic Blvd ☎310/277-5221, ⓦwww.avalonbeverlyhills.com. Located in south Beverly Hills, three long blocks from Rodeo Drive, a hipster-oriented hotel with cozy rooms and hip, modern furnishings, along with in-room CD players, fax machines, VCRs, and fitness club. The poolside bar is where the young elite pose in their black togs. ❽

Bel Air 701 Stone Canyon Rd ☎310/472-1211 or 1-800/648-1097, ⓦwww.hotelbelair.com. The nicest hotel in LA bar none – and the only one in Bel Air – in a lushly overgrown canyon above Beverly Hills. Go for a beautiful brunch by Swan Lake if you can't afford the rooms, which can reach $500 a night. ❾

Beverly Hills Hotel 9641 Sunset Blvd ☎310/276-2251 or 1-800/283-8885, ⓦwww.beverlyhillshotel.com. The classic Hollywood resort, with a bold pink-and-green color scheme and Mission-style design, and surrounded by its own exotic gardens. Rooms feature marbled bathrooms, VCRs, Jacuzzis, and other such luxuries, and the famed *Polo Lounge* restaurant is also on the premises. ❾

Beverly Hilton 9876 Wilshire Blvd ☎310/274-7777 or 1-800/922-5432, ⓦwww.hilton.com. Despite its high-profile chain status and excellent location near downtown Beverly Hills, this upscale hotel offers few surprises, though it does have one of the few remaining *Trader Vic's* bars. ❽

Beverly Laurel 8018 Beverly Blvd ☎323/651-2441. The hotel coffee shop, *Swingers* (see p.181), attracts the most attention here, primarily as a hangout for locals and inquisitive tourists. No-frills accommodation, with very basic rooms, but a good location. ❹

Bevonshire Lodge 7575 Beverly Blvd ☎323/936-6154. Well situated for both West LA and Hollywood, not far from Fairfax district. All of the functionally decorated motel rooms come with a refrigerator, and for a few dollars more you can have a kitchenette. ❸

Chateau Marmont 8221 Sunset Blvd ☎323/656-1010, ⓦwww.chateaumarmont.com. Exclusive Norman Revival hotel, which resembles a dark castle or Hollywood fortress and has hosted all manner of celebrities. Largely suites and bungalows. ❾

Claremont 1044 Tiverton Ave ☎310/208-5957. An amazingly good deal for the area, this cheerful and inexpensive little hotel sits very close to UCLA and Westwood Village. Rooms are fairly basic, but the main difficulty is the lack of parking. ❸

Grafton 8462 Sunset Blvd ☎323/654-6470, ⓦwww.graftononsunset.com. Mid-level boutique hotel with attractive furnishings, in-room stereos and VCRs, plus a pool, fitness center, and complimentary shuttle to nearby malls and businesses. ❻

Le Montrose 900 Hammond St ☎310/855-1115, ⓦwww.lemontrose.com. West Hollywood hotel with Art Nouveau stylings, featuring rooftop tennis courts, pool, and Jacuzzi. Most rooms are suites with full amenities. ❽

Le Parc 733 N West Knoll ☎310/855-8888 or 1-800/578-4837, ⓦwww.leparcsuites.com. West Hollywood apartment hotel in cozy neighborhood setting (but not far from the action), with studios, suites, rooftop pool and Jacuzzi, and a view of the hills. **8**

Maison 140 140 S Lasky Drive ☏ 310/281-4000, ⓦ www.maison140.com. High-profile entry for swank hipsters, boasting rooms with CD and DVD players, Internet access, and nice appointments, plus salon, bar, fitness room, and complimentary breakfast. **6**

The Standard 8300 Sunset Blvd ☏ 323/654-2800, ⓦ www.standardhotel.com. Amazing style, though not much substance, at this famed hipster "party hotel" offering extra-spartan rooms furnished with beanbags, swinging outdoor pool and bar, and a goofball design with Astroturf floors and other bizarre decor. **7**

Santa Monica, Venice, and Malibu

See the map on p.150 for hotel locations.

Bayside 2001 Ocean Ave, Santa Monica ☏ 310/396-6000, ⓦ www.baysidehotel.com. Just a block from Santa Monica beach and Main Street. Bland exterior, but generally comfortable rooms – some with ocean views, fridges, Internet access, and kitchenettes. **4**

Cadillac 8 Dudley Ave, Venice ☏ 310/399-8876, ⓦ www.thecadillachotel.com. Stylish Art Deco hotel and hostel on the Venice Boardwalk. Although the suites are nice, some of the lower-end rooms are spartan and have few amenities. On-site sundeck, pool, gym, and sauna. Dorms **1**, hotel rooms **5**

Carmel 201 Broadway, Santa Monica ☏ 310/451-2469, ⓦ www.hotelcarmel.com. A good bet for decent rooms and suites near the beach, with the ocean two blocks away and the Third Street Promenade a block in the other direction. **6**

Channel Road Inn 219 W Channel Rd, Pacific Palisades ☏ 310/459-1920, ⓦ www.channelroadinn.com. B&B rooms in a romantic getaway nestled in lower Santa Monica Canyon (northwest of the city of Santa Monica), with ocean views, a hot tub, and free bike rental. Enjoy complimentary grapes and Champagne in the sumptuous rooms, each priced according to its view. **7**–**9**

Inn at Venice Beach 327 Washington Blvd ☏ 310/821-2557 or 1-800/828-0688, ⓦ www.innatvenicebeach.com. A good, basic choice for visiting Venice Beach and the canals, with simple, tasteful rooms featuring fridges and balconies. **6**

Loew's Santa Monica Beach 1700 Ocean Ave, Santa Monica ☏ 310/458-6700, ⓦ www.loewshotels.com. One of Santa Monica's chicest hotels, a deluxe, salmon-colored edifice overlooking the ocean and Santa Monica pier, and often

in demand as a film set. The finest rooms top $450, but lesser rooms are a bit cramped and overpriced. **9**

Malibu Hotel 22541 Pacific Coast Hwy, Malibu ☏ 310/456-6169, ⓦ www.the-malibu-motel.com. King-size beds and refrigerators make this roadside motel one of the less expensive choices in the area, with swimming pool and DSL connections. **6**

Malibu Riviera 28920 Pacific Coast Hwy, Malibu ☏ 310/457-9503. Quiet place outside town, less than a mile from the beach, with clean and basic rooms, a sundeck, and Jacuzzi. Fairly isolated from the rest of the city. **4**

Santa Monica Beach Travelodge 1525 Ocean Ave, Santa Monica ☏ 310/451-0761, ⓦ www.travelodge.com. Clean and basic chain lodging, excellent for its beach proximity. To save $10, try the less appealing units on the eastern edge of town, in a grim, colorless building, 3102 Pico Blvd (☏ 310/450-5766). **4**

Shangri-La 1301 Ocean Ave, Santa Monica ☏ 310/394-2791, ⓦ www.shangrila-hotel.com. Wonderfully restored Art Deco treasure overlooking Palisades Park and the Santa Monica beach, with clean and sleek, if basic, rooms. **7**

Viceroy 1819 Ocean Ave, Santa Monica ☏ 310/451-8711, ⓦ www.viceroysantamonica.com. Luxury item with great bay views and nicely appointed rooms with CD players, on-site pool, and lounge. The high-end rooms reach $500. **8**

The South Bay and Harbor Area

Hotel Hermosa 2515 Pacific Coast Hwy, Hermosa Beach ☏ 310/318-6000, ⓦ www.hotelhermosa.com. In a busy part of town, between Hermosa and Manhattan beaches, a sumptuous hotel with rooms starting at moderate prices (though rising up to $350 suites) and a short walk to the beach. **4**–**9**

Rodeway Inn 50 Atlantic Ave, Long Beach ☏ 562/435-8369, ⓦ www.rodewayinn.com. Inoffensive chain-motel accommodation not far from the marina and convention center, with Internet access, too. **4**

Sea Sprite Motel 1016 Strand, Hermosa Beach ☏ 310/376-6933, ⓦ www.seaspritemotel.com. Right next to the beach along a popular strip. Several different room options come with varying prices, including weekly rates for longer stays, plus units with kitchenettes and balconies. **5**

Seahorse Inn 233 N Sepulveda Blvd, Manhattan Beach ☏ 310/376-7951 or 1-800/233-8050. Faded exterior but clean and simple rooms. Further from the beach than others, but with a pool. **3**

Vagabond Inn 150 Alamitos, Long Beach ☏ 562/435-7621, ⓦ www.vagabondinn.com. One of the cheapest, most reliable of the chain lodging options in the area, with a pool, located just a few blocks west of the main downtown action. ❷

Westin Long Beach 333 E Ocean Blvd, Long Beach ℡562/436-3000, ⓦwww.westin.com. A solid bet for bayside luxury at affordable prices (cheaper when booked online), right by the convention center, with a spa, fitness center, and pool. ❻

Disneyland and around

Desert Palm Inn and Suites 631 W Katella Ave, Anaheim ℡1-800/635-5423, ⓦwww .anaheimdesertpalm.com. Large, comfortable rooms with refrigerators, microwaves, VCRs, and complimentary continental breakfast. ❺

Disneyland Hotel 1150 W Cerritos Ave, Anaheim ℡714/956-6400, ⓦdisneyland.disney.go.com /disneylandresort. Cookie-cutter rooms without much charm, but still an irresistible stop for many. The Disneyland monorail stops outside (theme park admission is separate). ❾

Disneyland Pacific Pier 1717 S Disneyland Drive, Anaheim ℡714/956-6425, ⓦdisneyland .disney.go.com/disneylandresort. Renovated concrete complex turned into overflow accommodation for park visitors; farther from the main theme park than its counterpart on Cerritos Ave, but shuttles are available and rooms are slightly cheaper, with the same amenities. ❼

Park Place Inn 1544 S Harbor Blvd, Anaheim ℡714/776-4800, ⓦwww.stovallshotels.com /park_place. *Best Western* chain hotel across from Disneyland, with the customary clean rooms and no-frills amenities. ❹

Pavilions 1176 W Katella Ave, Anaheim ℡714/776-0140, ⓦwww.pavilionshotel.com. Convenient chain hotel offering basic rooms with fridges, as well as a pool, spa, sauna, and shuttle to Disneyland. ❹

Stovall's Inn 1110 W Katella Ave, Anaheim ℡714/778-1880, ⓦwww.stovallsinn.com. Tasteful and clean chain accommodation near Disneyland, with on-site fitness center, pools, and spas, and in-room fridges and microwaves for extra. ❸

The Orange County Coast

Hotel Laguna 425 S Coast Hwy, Laguna Beach ℡949/494-1151, ⓦwww.hotellaguna.com. Atmospheric and comfortable, with luxurious appointments and location in the center of Laguna Beach. Price of room depends on quality of view. ❺–❽

Little Inn by the Bay 2627 Newport Blvd ℡949/673-8800, ⓦwww.littleinnbythebay.com. Eighteen comfortable rooms near Newport Beach in a renovated complex; the cheapest accommodation in the area, with in-room fridges,

microwaves, and complimentary breakfast. Close to Balboa Peninsula. ❹

Mission Inn 26891 Ortega Hwy, at I-5 ℡949/234-0249, ⓦwww.bbonline.com/ca /missioninnsjc. Twenty B&B rooms in San Juan Capistrano, offering continental breakfast, fridges, Jacuzzi, and a pool. ❻

Ocean View Motel 16196 Pacific Coast Hwy, Huntington Beach ℡562/592-2700. Family-run establishment with clean, comfortable rooms. Get a Jacuzzi in your room for an extra $15. Good deal for the area. ❸

Pacific View Inn 16220 Pacific Coast Hwy, Huntington Beach ℡562/592-4959, ⓦwww .pacificviewinn.com. Twenty beachside rooms with tasteful decor in a comfortable establishment; some rooms have ocean views and Jacuzzis. Continental breakfast. ❹

Seacliff Motor Hotel 1661 S Coast Hwy, Laguna Beach ℡949/494-9717 or 1-866/732-1400, ⓦwww.seaclifflaguna.com. Renovated motel with close ocean access, heated pool, and complimentary breakfast. Rates jump if you want a room with a sea view or a balcony. ❸–❼

Seal Beach Inn and Gardens 212 Fifth St, Seal Beach ℡562/493-2416, ⓦwww.sealbeachinn.com. Although located in an uneventful burg, a fine B&B offering nice cottages, villas, and suites – and one penthouse for $400 a night – with sumptuous appointments, two blocks from the sands. ❻

The San Gabriel and San Fernando valleys

Artists Inn 1038 Magnolia St, South Pasadena ℡1-800/799-5668, ⓦwww.artistsinns.com. Themed B&B with ten rooms and suites (some with spas) honoring famous painters and styles. Best of all is the Italian Suite, with an antique tub and sun porch. Located just two blocks from a Gold Line Metro stop. ❻

Ritz-Carlton Huntington 1401 S Knoll Ave, Pasadena ℡626/568-3900, ⓦwww.ritzcarlton .com. Landmark hotel, c.1900, luxuriously designed and discreetly tucked away in residential Pasadena. Suites start at $500, with more basic rooms for less than half the price. ❽

Safari Inn 1911 W Olive St, Burbank ℡818/845-8586. A classic mid-century motel, renovated but still loaded with pop-architecture touches (tiki and Googie styles). Features a pool, fitness room, Burbank airport shuttle, and in-room fridges, with some suites also available. ❺

Sheraton Universal 333 Universal Terrace, Burbank ℡818/980-1212 or 1-800/325-3535, ⓦwww.starwood.com. With the neighboring *Universal City Hilton*, 555 Universal Terrace

(☎818/506-2500, ⊛www.hilton.com), a large and luxurious hotel on the Universal Studios lot, with health club and elegant restaurant. Both ❼ **Sportsmen's Lodge** 12825 Ventura Blvd, Studio City ☎818/769-4700, ⊛www.slhotel.com. Old-time multistory motel remodeled for a new era and built around a pool, with Jacuzzi, quaint gardens, exercise room, on-site restaurant, thirteen suites

and hundreds of more basic rooms. The units also have fridges and Internet access. ❻ **Vagabond Inn** 1203 E Colorado Blvd at Michigan, Pasadena ☎626/449-3170, ⊛www.vagabondinn .com. Friendly budget chain motel, usefully placed for exploring Pasadena, with kitchenettes, pool, and continental breakfast. ❹

Hostels

Banana Bungalow 2775 Cahuenga Blvd W, in Cahuenga Pass ☎323/851-1129 or 1-800/446-7835, ⊛www.bananabungalow.com. Popular large hostel near Universal City and US-101, with free airport shuttles, city tours to Venice Beach and Magic Mountain, and a relaxed atmosphere. Outdoor pool, free parking, and as much beer as you can drink every second night for $3. Dorms $18–21, and more expensive private doubles $64. **HI-Anaheim/Fullerton** 1700 N Harbor Blvd at Brea, Fullerton ☎714/738-3721, ⊛www .hihostels.com. Convenient and comfortable, five miles north of Disneyland on the site of a former dairy farm. The hostel's excellent facilities include a grass volleyball court, golf driving range, and picnic area. There are only twenty dorm beds, so reservations are a must. Summer check-in 5–11pm; rest of year 4–11pm. Mornings open 7.10am–noon. OCTA bus #43 stops outside. Members $17, others $20. **HI-LA/Santa Monica** 1436 2nd St at Broadway, Santa Monica ☎310/393-9913, ⊛www.hihostels .com. A few blocks from the beach and pier, the building was LA's Town Hall from 1887 to 1889, and retains its historic charm, with a pleasant inner courtyard, ivy-covered walls, and a skylight – and 224 beds. Members $27, others $30; private rooms for $70 or more – the price includes laundry machines and huge kitchens. Smoking and drinking are prohibited. Reservations essential in summer; open 24hr. **HI-LA/South Bay** 3601 S Gaffey St #613, San Pedro ☎310/831-8109, ⊛www.hihostels.com. Sixty beds in old US Army barracks, with a panoramic view of the Pacific Ocean. Ideal for seeing San Pedro, Palos Verdes, and the whole Harbor Area. Open 7am–midnight. $17 members, $20 others; private rooms $38 per person. MTA bus #446 passes close by, but it's a two-hour journey from Downtown. You can also take the SuperShuttle from LAX. During Oct–April only open to groups of 15 or more. **Hollywood International Hostel** 6820 Hollywood Blvd ☎1-800/750-6561, ⊛www.hollywoodhostels .com. One of three good-value locations in the

area, with free tea and coffee, game room, gymnasium, patio garden, kitchen, and laundry. Offers tours of Hollywood, theme parks, Las Vegas, and Tijuana. Dorms $17, private rooms $40. **Hostel California** 2221 Lincoln Blvd, Venice ☎310/305-0250, ⊛www.hostelcalifornia.net. Twelve six-bed dorms with kitchens, pool table, big-screen TV, linen, and parking. Shuttle bus to and from LAX. $20; 30-bed mixed dorms for $12.75 per person. **Huntington Beach Colonial Inn Hostel** 421 8th St, Huntington Beach ☎714/536-3315, ⊛www .huntingtonbeachhostel.com. Four blocks from the beach and mostly double rooms. Sleeping bags allowed. Open 8am–11pm. Key rental after 1pm, $1 (plus $20 deposit). Dorms $21, private rooms $50; weekly rates $130. **Orange Drive Manor** 1764 N Orange Drive, Hollywood ☎323/850-0350, ⊛orangedrivehostel.com. Centrally located hostel (right behind the Chinese Theatre), offering tours to film studios, theme parks, and homes of the stars. Members $20, others $24, private rooms $40–56. **Orbit Hotel** 7950 Melrose Ave, West Hollywood ☎323/655-1510 or 1-877/ORBIT-US, ⊛www .orbithotel.com. Retro-1960s hotel and hostel with sleek Day-Glo furnishings and ultra-hip modern decor, offering complimentary breakfast, movie screening room, patio, café, private baths in all rooms, shuttle tours, and $20 per-day car rental. Dorms $18–21, private rooms $54–69. **USA Hostels – Hollywood** 1624 Schrader Ave ☎323/462-3777 or 1-800/LA-HOSTEL, ⊛www .usahostels.com. A block south of the center of Hollywood Boulevard, near major attractions and with a game room, private baths, main bar, Internet access, tours of the area ($5–7), and garden patio, as well as airport and train shuttles. Shared rooms $16–20 and private rooms from $40. **Venice Beach Cotel** 25 Windward Ave, Venice ☎310/399-7649, ⊛www.venicebeachcotel .com. Located in a historic beachside building, this colonnaded hostel (or "cotel") has dorm rooms for $16–18, and private rooms for $35–49.

LA area campgrounds

Reserve America (☎1-800/444-7275, ⓦwww.reserveamerica.com) processes reservations at many of the **campgrounds** listed below and can look for an alternative if your chosen site is full. It charges a $7 fee per reservation per night up to a maximum of eight people per site, including one vehicle.

Bolsa Chica Campground ☎714/846-3460. Facing the ocean in Huntington Beach, also near a thousand-acre wildlife sanctuary and birdwatchers' paradise, with fishing opportunities as well. $25–30 for campers with a self-contained vehicle. No tent camping. Add $9 to the rate for sites near the ocean.

Chilao Flat on Hwy-2 twenty miles northeast of Pasadena ☎818/899-1900, ⓦwww .fs.fed.us/r5/angeles. The only campground in the San Gabriel Mountains reachable by car, though there are others accessible on foot. For details contact the Angeles National Forest Ranger Station at 701 N Santa Anita Ave, Arcadia (☎626/574-1613). $12, with $5 vehicle pass; may be periodically closed due to bear activity.

Dockweiler Beach County Park 8255 Vista del Mar ☎310/322-4951 or 1-800/950-7275, ⓦbeaches.co.la.ca.us. On a noisy coastal strip, almost at the western end of the LAX runways. Mainly for RVs, tent sites by reservation only. A popular urban beach, which can get a little dicey on weekends. $25–32.

Doheny State Beach Campground 25300 Dana Point Harbor Drive ☎949/496-6171 or 1-800/444-7275. Often packed with families, especially on weekends. Located at southern end of Orange County, not far from Dana Point Harbor. $16–21, add $10 for beachfront sites.

Leo Carrillo State Park northern Malibu ☎818/706-1310 or 1-800/444-7275. Pronounced "Ca-REE-oh," near one of LA's best surfing beaches, 25 miles northwest of Santa Monica on Pacific Coast Hwy, and served twice an hour in summer by MTA bus #434. $15–20.

Malibu Creek State Park 1925 Las Virgenes Rd, in the Santa Monica Mountains ☎818/706-8809 or 1-800/444-7275. A rustic campground in a park which can become crowded at times. Sixty sites in the shade of huge oak trees, almost all with fire pits, solar-heated showers, and flush toilets. One-time filming location for TV show *M*A*S*H*, among other things. $15–20.

San Clemente State Beach Campground 3030 Avenida del Presidente, two miles south of San Clemente ☎714/492-7146 or 1-800/444-7275. A prime spot for hiking, diving, and surfing, around an area that was once home to Richard Nixon's "Western White House." $16–21, add $9 for beachfront sites.

Neighborhoods and orientation

As it spills over its vast, flat basin without clear divisions between neighborhoods or a centralized core, LA is far from a conventional city. Traveling from one end of town to the other takes you through virtually every social extreme imaginable, from mind-boggling coastal luxury to some of the worst inner-city poverty in the US – both partially the result of the city's explosive growth within an area of 465 square miles.

If LA has any kind of urban core, however, it is **Downtown**. Located in the rough center of the basin, its towering office blocks of Bunker Hill punctuate an otherwise unimpressive skyline. Still, with everything from avant-garde art to striking Art Deco buildings, Downtown offers a taste of almost everything you'll find elsewhere around the city, compressed into an area of small, easily walkable blocks. It's a good place to get your initial bearings and is the hub of the transportation network. The area **around Downtown** comprises an assortment of districts with little in common except for being adjacent to Downtown: the Victorian relics of the turn-of-the-century hilltop suburbs in Angelino Heights, the formerly quaint MacArthur Park neighborhood that now hosts the city's many Central American immigrants, the museum pocket of Exposition Park, and the impoverished sprawl of South Central LA.

Away from Downtown, you'll probably spend most of your time in the broad corridor that runs 25 miles west to the coast. Here are LA's best-known and most eye-catching districts, the first of which, **Hollywood**, has streets teeming with movie myths and legends – even if the genuine glamour is long gone. Neighboring **West LA**, the center of what is amorphously called the Westside, is home to the city's newest money – shown off in the incredibly expensive shops of Beverly Hills and the lively nightclubs of the Sunset Strip – and its western edge merges into **Santa Monica** and **Venice**, the quintessential Southern California of palm trees, white sands, and laid-back cool. The coastline itself is the major draw, stretching north from here twenty miles to the northern edge of LA and to **Malibu**, famous for its celebrity residences.

South along the coast from Venice, the three cities of the **South Bay** – Manhattan, Hermosa, and Redondo beaches – are quieter, mostly inhabited by middle-class commuters, and a long way in spirit from the more bustling and fad-conscious portions of the city. The beach bluffs and coves lead south to the **Harbor Area** – though despite recent facelifts and some mildly enjoyable resort areas, there's nothing to detain you in the South Bay for more than a few hours at a time, although **Long Beach** has such draws as the Aquarium of the Pacific and the *Queen Mary* ocean liner.

North of Downtown, the **San Gabriel and San Fernando valleys** stretch east and west until LA fades into desert, mountains, and ocean. The valleys (especially San Fernando) are distanced from mainstream LA life socially as well as geographically, their inhabitants the butt of Angeleno hick jokes. The chief reasons for venturing here include a number of worthwhile art collections in Pasadena, and a couple of working (and tourable) film studios, as well as the most famous of LA's cemeteries, Forest Lawn.

Orange County, southeast of the Harbor Area, is mainly depressing suburban sprawl, and almost the only reason most people come here is to visit **Disneyland**, the city's biggest single tourist attraction. If you're not keen on seeing the self-styled "happiest place on Earth" (or its neighboring theme park of Knott's Berry Farm), it's best to hug the Pacific and continue south, along the **Orange County Coast**, with its string of relaxed, libertarian communities, to San Diego.

Downtown LA

Nowhere else do the social, economic, and ethnic divisions of LA clash quite as loudly and visibly as in the square mile (bordered by the 10, 110, and 101 freeways) that makes up **DOWNTOWN LA**. In the space of a few short blocks, adobe buildings and Mexican market stalls give way to Japanese shopping plazas and avant-garde art galleries. Although it's long been the commercial focus of the city (and always the seat of local government), as businesses spread out across the basin in the postwar boom years, the area became more dilapidated, until its Victorian mansions decayed into flea-bitten boarding houses and the middle class finished their long march westward – almost completely disappearing from Downtown in the years after World War II. Various

DOWNTOWN LOS ANGELES

CESAR CHAVEZ AVENUE

HOLLYWOOD FREEWAY

El Pueblo de Los Angeles

Chinese American Museum

TEMPLE STREET

Our Lady of the Angels Catholic Church

Ahmanson Theatre

Mark Taper Forum

City Hall

Geffen Contemporary

Dorothy Chandler Pavilion

Japanese-American National Museum

Disney Hall

LA Times Building

MOCA

2ND STREET

Wells Fargo Museum

Angels Flight Funicular

LITTLE TOKYO

3RD STREET

Library Tower

BUNKER HILL

Bradbury Building

Japanese-American Cultural and Community Center

Central Library

Cole's Pacific

4TH STREET

SKID ROW

Los Angeles Theater

5TH STREET

Union Rescue Mission

PERSHING SQUARE

Red Line Metrorail

6TH STREET

7TH STREET

Orpheum Theater

GARMENT DISTRICT

Flower Market

8TH STREET

Cooper Building

Museum of Neon Art

9TH STREET

OLYMPIC BOULEVARD

Staples Center

● Metrorail Stations
--- Dash Mini-Bus Routes

0   500 yds

LA Convention Center

South Central LA

Hollywood

East LA

CAFÉS & RESTAURANTS	
Angelique Café	29
Café Pinot	16
Checkers	17
Ciao Trattoria	28
Cicada	25
Ciudad	15
Clifton's Cafeteria	27
Cole's Pacific Electric Buffet	23
Engine Co. No. 28	22
Grand Central Market	13
Grand Star	1
La Luz del Dia	8
L.A. Prime	14
Mandarin Deli	5
Mitsuru Café	10
Mon Kee's	7
Ocean Seafood	4
Original Pantry	30
Pacific Dining Car	20
Patina	9
Philippe the Original French Dip	3
Pho 79	6
Water Grill	19
Yang Chow	2
Yorkshire Grill	21
BARS AND CLUBS	
Casey's Bar	24
Mayan	31
Redwood	11
The Smell	12
Standard Hotel Bar	18
Stock Exchange	26
Top of Five	14

ACCOMMODATION	
Downtown LA Standard	E
Figueroa	H
Los Angeles Athletic Club	G
Millennium Biltmore	F
Miyako Inn	B
New Otani	A
Omni Los Angeles	C
Westin Bonaventure	D

revitalization initiatives from the 1960s to the 80s helped to create postmodern office towers and a rash of plush condos for young professionals, but these have ultimately only served to intensify the extremes. Still, there's more here than there once was, and the sparkling new museums and skyscrapers are testimony to just how much money and effort the power brokers have invested in the area's renovation and rebirth.

Each part of Downtown has its own history, cultural institutions, and architecture. Much of it can be seen on foot, starting with LA's rather bland historic and governmental heart at the **Civic Center**, crossing into the brasher, corporate-tower-dominated **Bunker Hill**, continuing past the street vendors, swap meets, and movie theaters of **Broadway**, and finally, if you have the nerve, skirting Skid Row and checking out the lively **Garment District**.

Downtown can easily be seen in a day, and if your feet get tired you can hop aboard the DASH buses that run every five to ten minutes on six loops through key areas (look for the silver-signed bus stops). Parking in lots is expensive on weekdays (around $8–10 per hour), but on weekends is more affordable (a flat

$5–8); street parking is a good alternative, except on Bunker Hill, where the meters cost at least $2 per hour. Downtown is the hub of the MTA networks and easily accessible by public transportation, especially around the grand colossus of Union Station.

❶ El Pueblo de Los Angeles and Chinatown

Just across US-101 from the current seat of local government at the Civic Center, you can get a glimpse of LA's early frontier days at **El Pueblo de Los Angeles**, 845 N Alameda St (daily 9am–5pm; free; ☎213/628-2381 or 628-3562, ⓦwww.ci.la.ca.us/ELP), the site of the original late-eighteenth-century Spanish settlement of Los Angeles, where the few early buildings that remain evoke a strong sense of LA's Hispanic origins – the rest is filled in with period replicas and a few modern buildings with kitschy Spanish Colonial facades. The plaza church, **La Placita**, 535 N Main St (daily 8am–8pm; ☎213/629-3101, ⓦwww.laplacita.org), is the city's oldest and has long served as a sanctuary for illegal Central American refugees (with immigration again becoming a potent political issue). If you'd like to take part in one of the church **masses** (occasionally with mariachi bands), they occur three or four times daily (Mon–Fri 6.30am, 8am, noon & 5.30pm, Sat 7.30am, 12.30pm & 5.30pm), with twelve Eucharist services on Sunday.

Along with its Mexican heritage, the pueblo also features the remnants of Chinese, Italian, and even French settlements. Of particular note, the **Chinese American Museum**, 425 N Los Angeles St (Tues–Sun 10am–3pm; $3; ⓦwww.camla.org), details the local history of Chinese settlement, society, and culture, visible with artifacts from the nineteenth and twentieth centuries such as revealing letters, photos, and documents, as well as a smattering of contemporary art and the re-creation of a Chinese herb shop c.1900. Also worth a look is the city's first **firehouse** (Tues–Sun 10am–3pm; free) – later a boardinghouse and saloon – which has a small but intriguing roomful of fire-fighting gear and dates back to 1884, though the handsome, colonnaded **Pico House**, LA's most luxurious hotel when it opened in 1870, is closed. **Olvera Street**, which runs north from the plaza (daily 10am–7pm; free; ⓦwww.olvera-street.com), is a curious attempt at restoration, contrived in part as a pseudo-Mexican village market and now comprising about thirty old-looking buildings. Taken over for numerous festivals throughout the year, like the Day of the Dead on November 2, when Mexicans traditionally honor the spirits of the departed (see p.203), the street is at its best on such communal occasions, and regularly features strolling mariachi bands, Aztec and Mexican-themed processions, and various dancers and artisans. Hourly tours (Wed–Sat 10am–noon; free) are also offered, starting from the information booth at 130 Paseo de la Plaza.

Like other historic districts around the country, Olvera Street is not simply a charming vestige that just happened to thwart ruin. Rather, its re-emergence was the work of one **Christine Sterling**, who, with other powerful citizens and help from the city government, tore down the slum she found here in 1926 and built much of what you see today, incorporating some of the salvageable historic structures. Working for the next twenty years to organize fiestas and popularize the city's Mexican heritage, she lived in the modest, early nineteenth-century **Avila Adobe** at 10 Olvera St – touted as the oldest structure in Los Angeles (from 1847), although almost entirely rebuilt out of reinforced concrete following the 1971 Sylmar earthquake. Inside the house are two museums (daily 9am–3pm; free): one featuring an idealized view of pueblo-era domestic life and offering information on Ms Sterling; the other, across the landscaped courtyard, telling the sanitized official story of the "History of the Water in Los Angeles" – ie, how local authorities connived to steal a water supply from upstate farmers (for the real story, see p.408). Across the street, the **Sepulveda House**, 125 Paseo de la Plaza (Mon–Sat 10am–3pm; free; ☎213/628-1274), is a quaint 1887 Eastlake structure that used to provide space for stores and a boardinghouse. Nowadays, it offers rooms highlighting different periods in Mexican-American cultural history (focusing on the Victorian era), shows an informative film (Mon–Sat 11am & 2pm) on the history of LA, and is the park's visitor center. Pick up self-guided tour brochures here and get more information on the 27 old buildings that have been fully or partially preserved, or at least reconstructed to match their earlier appearance.

Across from Olvera Street at 800 N Alameda St, **Union Station** echoes LA's roots in a rather different way. It's a striking mix of monumental Art Deco and Mission Revival architecture, finished in 1939, and occupies the site of the original Chinatown, whose residents were forced to relocate when construction on the station began. Although the building is no longer the evocative point of locomotive arrival and departure it once was, Amtrak and commuter rail still stop here, and the structure itself is in fine condition, with a spacious vaulted lobby, heavy wooden benches, and intact Art Deco signs. Once thronged with passengers, it now sees fewer trains per day, though you may spot the occasional movie crew – the station famously doubled as police headquarters in the film *Blade Runner*. The nearby **Gateway Transit Center** is less elegant, but more functional as the hub of the region's bus lines.

What is now **CHINATOWN** was established by 1938 along North Broadway and North Spring Street following its residents' abrupt transplant from the site of Union Station. It's not the bustling affair you'll find in a number of other US cities, however, and unless it's Chinese New Year, when there's a parade of dragons and firework celebrations, there's little point in turning up here except to eat. Apart from this, official Chinese culture consists of a handful of small shopping malls, where you can pick up an assortment of lanterns, teapots, and jade jewelry – aimed more at tourists than residents. (To get a truer sense of contemporary Chinese culture, visit Alhambra or Monterey Park, both lively ethnic suburbs located just beyond LA's eastern boundary.)

The Civic Center

South of the Santa Ana Freeway from Olvera Street, most of the **CIVIC CENTER** is a collection of plodding bureaucratic office buildings, one of which – the County Courthouse – became briefly famous during the O.J. Simpson trial. Standing out among the drab white boxes, LA's Art Deco **City Hall**, 200 N Spring St, is known to the world through LAPD badges seen in TV shows ever since *Dragnet*, and was until 1960 the city's tallest structure, though its silhouette is now dwarfed by the office blocks of Bunker Hill. The building's crown is as close as most visitors will ever get to seeing the Mausoleum at Halicarnassus, one of the seven ancient wonders of the world, which provided a curious, only-in-LA architectural inspiration. You can still get a good look at the inside of the building on its free tours, which include its 28th-story 360° observation deck (daily 10am–1pm; reserve on ☎213/485-4423, ⓦwww.lacityhall.org), but for a more in-depth, 1hr 45min view of the building and its architecture, the LA Conservancy offers monthly tours (first Sat of month 11am; $5; ⓦlaconservancy.org) as well.

On the south side of the Civic Center plaza, the **Los Angeles Times**, 202 W 1st St, provides free tours (by reservation only at ☎213/237-5757,

Little Tokyo and around

East of the Civic Center, the colorful shopping precinct of **LITTLE
TOKYO** provides the clearest evidence of the Pacific Rim money that
accounted for much new construction in LA during the 1980s. For a closer
look into the community, head for the **Japanese American Cultural
and Community Center**, 244 S San Pedro St (ⓦwww.jaccc.org), whose
Doizaki Gallery (Tues–Fri noon–5pm, Sat & Sun 11am–4pm; free) shows
traditional and contemporary Japanese drawing and calligraphy, along with
costumes, sculptures, and other associated art forms. The center also includes
the **Japan America Theater**, which regularly hosts Kabuki theater and
more contemporary groups. Located between the two and easy to miss, the
stunning **James Irvine Garden** (daily 9am–5pm; free), with a 170-foot
stream running along its sloping hillside, was named after its biggest financial
contributor. The garden really owes its existence to the efforts of two hundred Japanese-American volunteers who carved the space out of a flat lot,
turning it into the "garden of the clear stream" and making the area seem
a world away from the outside expanse of asphalt and concrete. From the
cultural center, a zigzagging pathway takes you through the Shoji screens,
sushi bars, shops, and rock gardens of the **Japanese Village Plaza** (daily
11am–9pm; ☏213/613-0588) – really just a glorified mall – and on to the
Japanese-American National Museum at First and Central (Tues–Sun
10am–5pm, Thurs closes at 8pm; $8; ⓦwww.janm.org), which houses exhib-
its on everything from origami to traditional furniture and folk craftwork to
the internment of Japanese Americans during World War II.

Across the street from Little Tokyo is the **Geffen Contemporary**, 152 N
Central Ave (same hours, prices as the Museum of Contemporary Art, to
which a ticket also entitles same-day entrance; see opposite) – an exhibition
space in a converted police garage, designed by local maverick Frank Gehry.
Initially developed as the temporary home of the Museum of Contemporary
Art, the museum's success was such that it was kept on as an alternative exhibition space to its more mainstream sibling.

Bunker Hill

Until a century ago the area south of the Civic Center, **BUNKER HILL**, was
LA's most elegant neighborhood, its elaborate Victorian mansions and houses
connected by funicular railroad to the growing business district down below
on Spring Street. As with all of Downtown, though, the middle class soon
moved to new, outlying suburbs to the west, and many of the old homes were
converted to boardinghouses, later providing the seedy backdrop for detective
films, notably the apocalyptic 1955 Mike Hammer film noir *Kiss Me Deadly*.
These structures were in turn wiped out by 1960s urban renewal and replaced
with a forest of grim, anonymous high-rises, which if viewed from the window
of a passing airplane, almost give Downtown the look of an urban center.

When it's in operation, the **Angels Flight** funicular is a bright and colorful memory of a long-departed era. These inclined train cars were removed
in 1969 during the urban-renewal period, but were restored in 1996. The
short section of railway leads up from the corner of Hill and Fourth streets to
the top of Bunker Hill. The funicular was closed in 2001 after the death of a
passenger in an accident, but is due to begin operation once more by 2006.

When and if it does, it's well worth a trip, as you view the Beaux Arts charm of older Downtown structures to the east, then are dwarfed by the office blocks of the **FINANCIAL DISTRICT**, which looms above you with austere modernity. Most of the fifty-story towers have shops and restaurants at their base – neon-lit shopping malls intended to provide a synthetic street-life for the brokers and traders, and about as dreary as you might expect. One of the few notable structures is the **Gas Company Tower**, 555 W Fifth St, a metallic blue building whose crown symbolizes a natural-gas flame on its side.

The Museum of Contemporary Art

Based at the California Plaza, a billion-dollar complex of offices and luxury condos, the **Museum of Contemporary Art** (MOCA), 250 S Grand Ave (Mon & Fri 11am–5pm, Thurs 11am–8pm, Sat & Sun 11am–6pm; $8, students $5, free Thurs; ☎213/621-2766, ⓦwww.moca.org), has become the leading institution for contemporary art in Southern California. It's not that its endowment is particularly huge – the Getty Trust could, if it were interested, easily outbid MOCA for any work it desired – but it does manage to represent an excellent selection of post-World War II American art in all its manifestations, from Abstract Expressionist to postmodern. Designed by showman architect Arata Isozaki as a "small village in the valley of the skyscrapers," it justifies a look for the building alone, its playful exterior a welcome splash of color among the dour skyscrapers, an array of geometric red shapes recognizable from the occasional TV commercials filmed here.

The complex is well worth a visit, even if its rooftop terrace, courtyard café, and gift shop sit in the shadow of the Plaza's looming office and condo blocks. One particular highlight is the weekly "Immersion" events (Thurs 5–8pm; free) that bring forth artists and lecturers to discuss their ideas, musicians to set the tone, and happy-hour cocktails to make it all go down more easily. To head straight for the art, go past the barrel-vaulted entrance pavilion on Grand Avenue, which opens out to an outdoor sculpture plaza, and follow the stairs down from the upper plaza to the smaller courtyard, between the café and the main entrance to the galleries.

Much of the gallery is used for temporary exhibitions and the bulk of the **permanent collection** is mid-twentieth-century American, particularly from the Abstract Expressionist period, including work by Franz Kline and Mark Rothko. You'll also find plenty of Pop Art, in Robert Rauschenberg's urban junk, Claes Oldenburg's papier-mâché representations of hamburgers and gaudy fast foods, and Andy Warhol's print-ad black telephone. Don't be surprised to find a few Minimalist creations, either, with drawings and photos of the massive earthworks of Robert Smithson as a definite point of interest when they're on view.

Many of the compelling ideas are expressed by the paintings and sculpture of the newer stars of the art world – Alexis Smith's quirky collages, Charles Ray's Amazon-sized mannequins, and Martin Puryear's anthropomorphic wooden sculptures. The museum is also strong on **photography**, and features the two-thousand-print collection of New York dealer Robert Freidhaus, exhibiting the work of Diane Arbus, Larry Clark, Robert Frank, Lee Friedlander, John Pfahl, and Gerry Winograd, as well as a few choice, and thoroughly disturbing, images by Cindy Sherman. Also not to be missed is the impressive selection of **Southern California artists**, which ranges from Lari Pittman's spooky, sexualized silhouettes to Chris Burden's disquieting performance-art imagery to Robert Williams' feverishly violent and satiric comic-book-styled paintings.

The theater on the lower floor of MOCA hosts some bizarre multimedia shows and performances, as well as the more standard lectures and seminars (☎213/621-2766 for details). The best time to visit the museum is during an evening concert in summer, when entry is free, and jazz and classical concerts are played outdoors under the red pyramids. At other times, a ticket to MOCA also entitles you to same-day entrance to the Geffen Contemporary, the museum's renovated-warehouse exhibition space on the east side of Downtown, and to the branch at the Pacific Design Center (see p.142) out in West Hollywood.

Disney Hall and Our Lady of the Angels

Just north of the museum, around the stodgy music and theater establishments of the Music Center, 135 Grand Ave (see "Performing arts and Film," p.204), **Disney Hall**, First Street at Grand Avenue, is LA's latest jewel of modern architecture, a headline-grabbing spectacle based on a 1987 design by pioneering architect Frank Gehry and strikingly prescient of his Guggenheim Museum in Bilbao, Spain. Delayed for many years, the Hall is a 2300-seat acoustic showpiece whose titanium exterior resembles something akin to colossal broken eggshells, or stylized habits worn by nuns, or various other images depending on your view. The LA Philharmonic (ⓦwdch.laphil.com) is based here, and with the Hall's rich, warm acoustics and features such as a colossal, intricate pipe organ, it may be the best place to hear music in the city, perhaps in all of California. Unfortunately, the self-guided **audio tours** (9am–10.30am, or 3pm if no matinees; $10; reserve at ☎323/850-2000) don't offer a look at the stunning auditorium itself, and only shunt you around the garden and anterooms of the building. For a look inside, you'll have to attend a concert.

One long block north of Disney Hall stands LA's other modernist colossus, the $200-million **Our Lady of the Angels** Catholic church, 555 W Temple St (Mon–Fri 6.30am–7pm, Sat 9am–7pm, Sun 7am–7pm; tours Mon–Fri 1pm; free; ⓦwww.olacathedral.org). The church, the centerpiece of the local archdiocese, is a truly massive structure in its own right – eleven stories tall and capable of holding three thousand people – and solidly built of concrete – which has led some critics to compare the church's fortress-like exterior to a prison. Still, the interior is the highlight, featuring tapestries of saints, giant bronze doors, ultra-thin alabaster screens for diffusing light, a grand marble altar, and $30 million worth of art and furnishings.

South of MOCA

To the south of MOCA, the **Wells Fargo History Museum**, 333 Grand Ave (Mon–Fri 9am–5pm; free; ☎213/253-7166, ⓦwww.wellsfargohistory.com), sits at the base of the Wells Fargo Center, and is one of nine such museums in the US. As with the others, it tells the history of Wells Fargo & Co, the bank of Gold Rush California and current international giant, and displays among other things a two-pound nugget of gold and a simulated stagecoach journey from St Louis to San Francisco.

A block away, the shining glass tubes of the **Westin Bonaventure Hotel**, 404 S Figueroa St (see "Accommodation," p.98), have become one of the city's most unusual landmarks since the late 1970s. The only LA building by modernist architect John Portman, the structure is built with a flurry of ramps, elevators, concrete columns, and catwalks in a soaring atrium that is one of the city's most eye-popping interiors. Make sure to ride in the glass elevators that run up through the atrium and climb the outside walls (showcased in Clint

Eastwood's *In the Line of Fire*), giving views over much of Downtown and beyond.

From the Westin's rotating skyline *Bona Vista* lounge, you'll get a bird's-eye view of one of the city's finest buildings, the **Richard J. Riordan Central Library**, 630 W Fifth St (Mon–Fri 10am–8pm, Sat 10am–6pm, Sun 1–5pm; tours Mon–Fri 12.30pm, Sat 11am & 2pm, Sun 2pm; ☎213/228-7000, ⓦwww.lapl.org/central), named for LA's billionaire mayor of the 1990s. Built in 1926, the library was the last work of architect Bertram Goodhue (who also designed much of the campus of Pasadena's CalTech University), and its striking, angular lines set the tone for many LA buildings, most obviously City Hall.

In exchange for planning permission and air rights, the developers of the **Library Tower** across Fifth Street – the tallest office building west of Chicago – agreed to pay some fifty million dollars toward the restoration of the library. Now owned by Wells Fargo, the cylindrical tower is occasionally open to tours run through operators such as Red Line Tours (see p.96), and features Lawrence Halprin's huge **Bunker Hill Steps** at its base, supposedly modeled after the Spanish Steps in Rome. From the *Source Figure*, one of Robert Graham's creepy nude sculptures, at the top, the steps curve down Bunker Hill between a series of terraces with uninspiring outdoor cafés and boutiques. If you don't feel like walking, the Steps also feature a less appealing escalator.

Broadway and Pershing Square

Though it's hard to picture now, **Broadway** once formed the core of Los Angeles's most fashionable shopping and entertainment district, brimming with movie palaces and department stores. Beyond the handful of jewelry merchants who've stuck around since the old days, today Broadway is largely taken over by the clothing and knickknack stores of a bustling Hispanic community, which operate out of the ground floors of otherwise empty hundred-year-old buildings, the salsa music and street culture making for one of the city's most electric environments. You get a taste of the area amid the pickled pigs' feet, sheep's brains and other delicacies inside the indoor **Grand Central Market** (daily 9am–6pm; ⓦwww.grandcentralsquare.com), on Broadway between Third and Fourth. It's a real scrum but without a doubt the best place (at least for carnivores) to enter into the spirit of things.

The **Bradbury Building** (Mon–Sat 9am–5pm; free), across the street, marks a break from the mayhem of the market, its magnificent sunlit atrium surrounded by wrought-iron balconies, and open-cage elevators operating on opposite sides of the narrow court, with elaborate staircases at either end. The whole place is an art director's dream – not surprisingly, most of the income for this 1893 office building is generated by film shoots: scenes from *Blade Runner* and *Citizen Kane* were both filmed here. Tourists are only permitted in the lobby, but it's worth a look for the great view up. (Los Angeles Conservancy tours often begin here; see p.95 for more information.)

Aside from the street life, the best things about Broadway are the great movie palaces of the **Theater District**, some of whose "enchanted realms" still function today. Although Hollywood has some of LA's most noteworthy grand moviehouses, many would argue that those located Downtown are beyond compare, and, while many are not restored, constitute one of the last remaining urban pockets of classic cinema architecture in the country. Several structures are especially noteworthy: next to the Grand Central Market, the opulent 1918

Million Dollar Theater, 307 S Broadway, its whimsical terracotta facade mixing buffalo heads with bald eagles in typical Hollywood Spanish Baroque style, was originally built by theater magnate Sid Grauman, who went on to build the Egyptian and Chinese theaters in Hollywood. It's now closed to the public, and its projector has been removed; still, there's always talk of refurbishing it someday.

The **Los Angeles Theater**, 615 S Broadway, is even more extravagant: built in ninety days for the world premiere of Charlie Chaplin's *City Lights* in 1931, it crowned what had become the largest concentration of film theaters in the world and is often considered the best movie palace in the city, and one of the finest in the country. The theater's plush lobby behind the triumphal arch facade is lined by marble columns supporting an intricate mosaic ceiling, while the 1800-seat auditorium is enveloped by trompe l'oeil murals and lighting effects. It's no longer open to the public for regular screenings, but a June program called Last Remaining Seats draws huge crowds to this and the nearby **Orpheum Theatre**, 842 S Broadway, to watch revivals of classic Hollywood films, many from the silent era. If you're in town at the time, don't miss it (tickets $20 per film, often with live entertainment; call ✆213/623-CITY for details). Finally, the monumental Renaissance Revival charm of the **State Theatre**, 630 S Broadway, is on display during occasional film screenings and public events; check entertainment listings for details.

With the advent of TV, the rise of the car, and LA's drift to the suburbs, the movie palaces lost their customers and fell into decline. An underground parking lot was built in **Pershing Square** in an attempt to bring the crowds back – it failed. The redesign of the square itself, unfortunately, has turned the public park into a bleakly synthetic space only a bureaucrat could love. Inspired by the work of Mexican architect Luis Barragan, the square's bright purple campanile is its only highlight.

Despite the bleakness, some of the buildings around the square have – albeit after years of neglect – emerged in fine form. The most prominent of these, the **Biltmore Hotel** (now in the *Millennium* chain; see "Accommodation," p.98), stands over the west side of the square, its three brick towers rising from a Renaissance Revival arcade along Olive Street. Inside, the grand old lobby that was the original main entrance has an intricately painted Spanish-beamed ceiling that you can admire over a pricey glass of wine. A block south, the Art Deco **Oviatt Building**, 617 S Olive St, is another sumptuous survivor. The ground floor housed LA's most elegant haberdashery, catering to dapper types such as Clark Gable and John Barrymore. The elevators, which open onto the street-level lobby, are still worth a look, featuring hand-carved oak paneling designed and executed by Parisian craftsman René Lalique. Also striking is the intricate 1928 design of the building's exterior, especially its grand sign and its looming clock above.

Four blocks to the south, the adulterated visage of Mona Lisa smiles at you through blue-and-yellow tubing at the **Museum of Neon Art**, 501 W Olympic Blvd (Wed–Sat 11am–5pm, Sun noon–5pm; $5; ✆213/489-9918, ⓦwww.neonmona.org). Offering a small exhibition space featuring classic neon signs, more modern interpretations of the noble gas and a range of bizarre kinetic art, the museum is best for its monthly bus tours of LA's neon highlights (see p.97). Finally, three blocks to the southwest, the LA **Convention Center** and the **Staples Center** are sleek modern structures that have led the way for the redevelopment of what is now called **South Park**; however, despite the area's name, there's nothing particularly irreverent or free-spirited about the place – visit only for conventions and Lakers games.

The Eastside

A block east of Broadway, LA's old financial district along **Spring Street**, between Fourth and Seventh streets, was once at the center of the city's commerce and banking in the early twentieth century, then was depopulated and abandoned by the 1980s. In the past few years, however, it has slowly re-emerged as a center for upmarket loft housing. Behind these Neoclassical facades you can find a handful of interesting nightclubs, galleries, and theaters, though one impediment to the neighborhood's revival is its closeness to **Skid Row**, just a few blocks east. This downtrodden area has a more than slightly threatening air, and as a longstanding seedy neighborhood, also has a few arty associations to match. The Doors posed here for the cover of their *Morrison Hotel* album, and Charles Bukowski was just one luminary of the booze'n'broads school of writers who've used the bars and poolrooms as a source of inspiration.

South of Skid Row, the lively **Garment District** – or, according to the city PR machine, the Fashion District (℡213/488-1153, ⑳fashiondistrict.org) – offers a respite from the bleak streets and attracts an energetic multi-ethnic crowd for its cut-rate shops and bargains on fabrics, for as little as $2 per yard. The **Cooper Building** (℡213/627-3754, ⑳www.cooperdesignspace .com), which takes up most of the Ninth Street block between Santee and Los Angeles streets, is famous for its occasional designer sample sales and houses at least fifty stores where you'll find big markdowns on outfits that might normally be out of your price range. Nearby, at the atmospheric **Flower Market**, 766 Wall St (Mon, Wed & Fri 8am–noon, Tues, Thurs & Sat 6am–noon; entry $2, Sat $1; ⑳www.laflowerdistrict.com), you can mingle with the wholesalers and buy flowers for a fraction of the high-street prices.

Around Downtown

When you leave Downtown you enter the LA sprawl, and the area **around Downtown** is united by little more than freeways and large distances separating the major points of interest. Cumulatively, there's quite a bit worth seeing, in areas either on the perimeter of Downtown or simply beginning here and continuing for many miles south or west. The districts immediately northwest of Downtown, **Angelino Heights** and **Echo Park**, are where the upper crust of LA society lived luxuriously at the turn of the last century in stylish Victorian houses (now either preserved or decrepit), vivid indicators of the prosperity of their time, just as the nondescript drabness surrounding them now evidences the blight that later befell the area. Much the same applies to the zone around **MacArthur Park**, which contains some of the impressive commercial architecture that set the visual tone for the city in the 1920s, as well as some of its current, and most notorious, drug-dealing havens.

The other areas that surround Downtown are each a ten- to forty-minute drive away from the next. Directly south of Downtown, the long succession of low-rent housing developments is interrupted only by the nearly walled-off **USC campus**, populated by conservative, well-coddled students, and the neighboring **Exposition Park**, with acres of gardens and several excellent museums. Beyond here lies one of LA's most depressed areas, the vast urban bleakness of **South Central LA**. A counterpoint to the commercial vibrancy of Downtown, this district surrounds the main route (I-110) between Downtown and the Harbor Area, and has a few isolated spots of interest; it's generally a place to visit with caution or with someone who knows the area, though is safe enough in daytime around the main drags.

More appealing is colorful **East LA**, the largest Mexican-immigrant enclave outside Mexico, a buzzing district of markets, shops, and street-corner music. It's less hectic northeast of Downtown, where, on the way to Pasadena, amid the preserved homes of **Highland Park**, the **Southwest Museum** holds a fine and extremely comprehensive collection of Native American artifacts.

Angelino Heights and Echo Park

Long before there was a Malibu or Beverly Hills, some of the most desirable addresses in Los Angeles were in **ANGELINO HEIGHTS**, LA's first suburb, just northwest of Downtown off US-101, laid out in the flush of a property boom at the end of the 1880s on a pleasant hilltop. Though the boom soon went bust, some of the elaborate houses that were built here, especially along **Carroll Avenue**, have survived and been restored as part of an officially recognized "Historic Preservation Overlay Zone" – about as close as LA gets to having an architectural-preservation district. There's more than a dozen compelling houses in all, and most merit a look for their catalog of late-Victorian details – wraparound verandas, turrets and pediments, set oddly against the Downtown skyline and occasionally used in ads for paint, among other things. The best of the lot is the **Sessions House**, no. 1330, a Queen Anne masterpiece with Moorish detail, decorative glass, and a circular "moon window." On the first Saturday of the month, you can take a two-and-a-half-hour tour of the neighborhood through the LA Conservancy (Sat 10am; $10; reserve at ☏213/623-CITY, ⓦwww.laconservancy.org), and visit the interiors of two of these classic homes as well.

At the foot of the hill, to the west of Angelino Heights, **ECHO PARK** is a small oasis of palm trees and lotus blossoms set around a lake. In the large white **Angelus Temple** on the northern side of the lake, the evangelist **Aimee Semple McPherson** used to preach sermons to five thousand people in the 1920s, with thousands more listening in on the radio. The first in a long line of media evangelists, "Sister Aimee" died in 1944, but the building is still used for services by her Four Square Gospel ministry, who dunk converts in the huge water tank during mass baptisms. In Roman Polanski's film *Chinatown* detective Jake Gittes follows the town water boss to a clandestine meeting here, spying on him in a rowboat – the kind which you can still rent (along with paddleboats; typically $10 per hour) from vendors along Echo Park Avenue, running along the eastern edge of the lake.

MacArthur Park and around

Wilshire Boulevard leaves Downtown between Sixth and Seventh streets as the main route across 25 miles of Los Angeles to Santa Monica's beachside Palisades Park. It was named after another of the city's colorful, larger-than-life characters, the oil baron, entrepreneur, and socialist Gaylord Wilshire, who, aside from his petroleum profits, made a fortune selling an electrical device that claimed to restore graying hair to its original color. Wilshire used his money to buy up a large plot of land west of Westlake Park, later renamed **MACARTHUR PARK**, through the center of which runs his eponymous thoroughfare, previously known as the "Old Road."

A century later, the park has fallen into disrepair and remains a venue for drug deals after dark. Despite the grim background, however, the park can be agreeable at times, and the adjacent Red Line Metrorail connection has turned its scattered patches of green and seemingly idyllic lake into the closest relief from Downtown.

Much more inviting, the one functional museum of some note in the area can be found nearby at 403 S Bonnie Brae St, where the **Grier-Musser Museum** (Wed–Sat noon–4pm; $6, kids $3; Ⓦ home.comcast.net/~gmuseum) provides a glimpse of the luxurious furnishings and stylish architecture of the nineteenth century, overflowing in six rooms with all manner of Victorian bric-a-brac and precious decor.

Half a mile west of MacArthur Park, the **Bullocks Wilshire** department store, 3050 Wilshire Blvd, is a stunning monument to 1920s Los Angeles and the most complete and unaltered example of Zigzag Art Deco architecture in the city. Built in 1929, in what was then a beanfield in the suburbs, Bullocks was the first department store in LA built outside Downtown and the first with its main entrance at the back of the structure, adjacent to the parking lot – catering to the automobile in a way that was to become the norm in this car-obsessed city. Transportation was the spirit of the time, and throughout the building, triumphant murals and mosaics of planes and ocean liners glow with activity in a studied celebration of the modern world. The building was badly vandalized during the 1992 riots and closed for five years. It has since reopened as the law library of adjacent **Southwestern University**; to reserve space on the library's periodic Tea & Tour events, visit Ⓦ www.swlaw.edu /bullockswilshire.

The **Ambassador Hotel**, just past Vermont Avenue at 3400 Wilshire Blvd, is another landmark of the boulevard's golden age. From the early 1920s to the late 1940s, when the hotel was the winter home of transient Hollywood celebrities, its *Cocoanut Grove* club was a favorite LA nightspot. The large ballroom hosted some of the early Academy Award ceremonies, and was featured in the first two versions of *A Star is Born* – though the hotel's most notorious event occurred on June 5, 1968, when **Bobby Kennedy** was fatally shot in the hotel kitchen while trying to avoid the press after winning the California presidential primary. Now closed to public view, the building's demolition was held up for years as a result of a legal feud between LA's school district (LAUSD) and Donald Trump, a fight won by the LAUSD. As of 2004, most of the structure is still due to be demolished, with perhaps a section or two saved for posterity. Across the street, another of LA's landmarks sits in a perversely altered state. The **Brown Derby** restaurant, once the city's prime example of programmatic architecture (or buildings shaped like objects – in this case, a hat), has now been relocated to the roof of an adjacent mini-mall, repainted, redecorated, and now all but unrecognizable.

Wilshire Boulevard continues west into the so-called "Miracle Mile" (see p.138), while two blocks south of Wilshire, between Vermont and Western, **Koreatown** is home to the largest concentration of Koreans outside Korea. In reality, and five times bigger than Chinatown and Little Tokyo, the comparison is unfair, for Koreatown is an active commercial district, not just a tourist sight, and home to restaurants, bars, theaters, community groups, banks, and shopping. The **Korean Cultural Center**, in the Miracle Mile at 5505 Wilshire Blvd (Mon–Fri 9am–5pm; free; Ⓣ323/936-7141, Ⓦ www.kccla...) is the place to begin. Along with a museum displaying art gallery with craftwork from Korea and local immigrants, the center puts on periodic theatrical and of fine art, folk work and rotating exhibits performing arts prod...

The USC campus

The **USC** (University of Southern California) **CAMPUS**, a few miles south of Downtown along Figueroa Street, is an enclave of wealth in one of the city's poorer neighborhoods, South Central LA. USC, or the "University of Spoiled Children," is one of the most expensive universities in the country, its under-graduates thought of as more likely to have rich parents than fertile brains. Indeed, the stereotype is often borne out, both by their easygoing, suntanned, beach-bumming nature, and by USC being more famous for sporting prowess than academic achievement. Alumni include O.J. Simpson, who collected college football's highest honor, the Heisman Trophy, and some of Richard Nixon's henchmen like H.R. Haldeman. There have been attempts to inte-grate the campus population more closely with the local community, but USC continues to be something of an elitist island, right down to its own fast-food outlet, as most of its students are cheerfully oblivious to the substantial blight around them.

Though sizeable, the campus is reasonably easy to get around. You might find it easiest to take the free 50min **walking tour** (leaving on the hour Mon–Fri 10am–3pm; by reservation at ☎213/740-6605, Ⓦwww.usc .edu). Without a guide, a good place to start is in the **Doheny Library** (Mon–Thurs 8am–midnight, Fri 8am–5pm, Sat 9am–5pm, Sun 1–10pm), an inviting Romanesque structure where you can pick up a campus map and investigate the large stock of overseas newspapers and magazines on the sec-ond floor – though UCLA (see p.146) has a better selection. Another good place for general information is the **Student Union** building, across the quadrangle from the library.

Of things to see, USC's art collection is housed in the **Fisher Gallery**, 823 Exposition Blvd (Tues–Sat noon–5pm; free; Ⓦwww.usc.edu/org/fishergallery), focusing on a wide range of art, from international and multicultural to avant-garde and contemporary. Elsewhere, you can see smaller shows of students' creative efforts, as well as retrospective shows featuring the models, blueprints, and sketches of internationally famous architects, in the **Helen Lindhurst Architecture Gallery**, in the USC School of Architecture, 850 W 37th St (Mon–Fri 10am–6pm; free), while the **Helen Lindhurst Fine Arts Gallery**, room 103 in the same complex (Mon–Fri 9am–4pm; free), focuses on con-temporary and experimental works from student and regional artists. Finally, the campus is also home to the **School of Cinema–Television**, a mainstream rival to the UCLA film school in Westwood. Although Steven Spielberg ~~ı~~ldn't get in to USC when he applied as an aspiring director, today his name later~~w~~ed here, and writ large on the wall of the sound-mixing center he thoug~~h~~d. You'll find little reason to linger for more than a few minutes, and con~~t~~ little more to see than big Hollywood names on the drab brick foreign fli~~c~~ ~~b~~ildings. You can, however, sometimes catch a good classic or School at 3~~5~~ U~~S~~ nearby **Eileen Norris Cinema**, just south of the Cinema Between 393~~½~~le Pkwy.

Coliseum, its glory ~~p~~osition Park, sports fans may want to stop at the has seen its football team long ~~s~~t. The site of the 1932 and 1984 Olympic Games to much excitement ~~(~~ ~~m~~), and recent decades, with the Raiders American .collegesports.com), and ~~e~~ ~~r~~ USC home games are still played here headless commemorative ~~s~~ ~~i~~mum; ☎213/740-GOSC, Ⓦusctrojans worth a look. ~~n~~d arch on the facade and muscular, ~~ı~~ugh interest to make the place

Exposition Park

Across Exposition Boulevard from the USC campus, **EXPOSITION PARK** is, given the grim nature of the surrounding area, one of the most appreciated parks in LA, incorporating lush landscaped gardens and a number of good, or at least adequate, museums. It's large by any standard, but the park retains a sense of community – a feeling bolstered by its function as a lunchtime picnic place for school kids. After eating, their favorite spot tends to be the **California Science Center** (daily 10am–5pm; free, parking $6; ⓦwww.casciencectr.org), set among a cluster of **museums** off Figueroa Street at 700 State Drive (unless otherwise stated, all daily 10am–5pm; free), a multimillion-dollar showcase for scientific education, not unlike such museums elsewhere in the US. With scores of working models and thousands of pressable buttons, some of the museum's highlights include a walk-in microscope and a giant talking robot that offers simple biology instruction – keep in mind, though, that three of the museum's attractions, including a "high-wire" bicycle, motion simulator, and rock-climbing wall, cost an extra $7 each. In the same complex, an **IMAX Theater** (tickets $7.50, kids $4.50; information at ⓣ213/744-2015) plays a range of documentaries on a gigantic curved screen. Nearby, the **Air and Space Gallery** (Mon–Fri 10am–1pm, Sat & Sun 11am–4pm; same admission with Center) is marked by a sleek jet stuck to its facade, offering a series of satellites and telescopes, a slew of airplanes and rockets, and the menacing presence of an LAPD helicopter "air ship" – to complement their constant drone in the skies above.

To the south, head for the stimulating **California African-American Museum**, 600 State Drive (Wed–Sat 10am–4pm; free; ⓦ www.caamuseum .org), which has diverse, temporary exhibitions on the history and culture of black people in the Americas, as well as a good range of painting and sculpture from local and national artists. Not far away, the **Natural History Museum of Los Angeles County**, 900 Exposition Blvd (daily 10am–5pm; $9; ⓣ213/763-3466, ⓦwww.nhm.org), has much appeal as the home of the park's biggest collection, as well as its most striking building and best museum overall – an explosion of Spanish Revival architecture with echoing domes, travertine columns, and a marble floor. Foremost among the exhibits is a tremendous stock of dinosaur bones and fossils, and some individually imposing skeletons (usually casts) including the crested duckbilled dinosaur, the skull of a Tyrannosaurus Rex, and the astonishing frame of a Diatryma – a huge prehistoric bird incapable of flight. Exhibits on rare sharks, the combustible native plant chaparral, and a spellbinding insect zoo – centered on a sizeable ant farm – add to the appeal. In the fascinating pre-Columbian Hall are Mayan pyramid murals and the complete contents of a reconstructed Mexican tomb, while the Californian history sections document the early (white) settlement of the region during the Gold Rush era and after, with some amazing photos of Los Angeles in the 1920s. Topping the whole place off is the gem collection, several breathtaking roomfuls of crystals, and an enticing display of three hundred pounds of gold, safely protected from your prying fingers. On a sunny day, spare some time for walking through Exposition Park's **Rose Garden** (daily 10am–5pm; free). The flowers are at their most fragrant in April and May, when the bulk of the 45,000 annual visitors come by to admire the 16,000 rose bushes and the overall prettiness of their setting.

South Central LA

Lacking the scenic splendor of the coast, the glamour of West LA and the history of Downtown, **SOUTH CENTRAL LA** is comprised of such

Cops, riots, and scandals

Los Angeles has had a longstanding reputation as having one of the most brutal and insensitive police forces in the nation – the **LAPD** – whose paramilitary tactics were developed under 1950s super-cop William Parker and allowed to flourish under later chiefs, most notoriously the 1980s champion of reaction, **Daryl Gates**. The methods of Gates during the economic boom years of the 1980s presented a frightening spectacle: the department's own tank bashing down the walls of alleged (often innocent) drug suspects, its helicopter gunships patrolling the skies over South Central LA, and its chief himself proudly arguing, in front of Congress, that casual drug users should be taken out and shot. Gates was allowed to get away with these quasi-fascist antics only for so long, though. The unexpected acquittal in 1992 of five white Los Angeles police officers, charged with using excessive force after they were videotaped kicking and beating black motorist **Rodney King** (after pulling him over for speeding through the suburb of Pacoima), could almost have been calculated to provoke a **violent backlash** in LA's poverty-stricken ghettos. What few predicted, however, was the sheer scale of the response to the verdict, which was partly – and ironically – fueled by the almost total lack of a police presence during the first evening's bloodshed. The violence and anger far surpassed the Watts Riots of 1965 (see p.120), beginning in South Central LA with motorists being pulled from their cars and attacked, and quickly escalating into a chaos of arson and shooting that spread across the city from Long Beach to Hollywood. Before long, the arsonists around town gave way to looters, who became the focus of the national media's attention, openly stealing stereos, appliances, and even diapers from large and small retail stores. Ultimately, it took the imposition of a four-day dusk-to-dawn curfew, and the presence on LA's streets of several thousand well-armed US National Guard troops, to restore calm – whereupon the full extent of the rioting became apparent. The riots, some of the worst urban violence seen in US history, left 58 dead, nearly 2000 injured, and caused an estimated $1 billion worth of damage. A second federal trial, on charges that the officers violated Mr King's civil rights, resulted in prison sentences for two of the officers.

Although ignited by a single incident, the riots were a very real indication of the **racial tensions** in a city whose controllers and affluent inhabitants have traditionally been all too ready to turn a blind eye to social problems – and it didn't help that the trial occurred in right-wing Simi Valley, best known for its large population of retired cops. Prompted by the Rodney King case, the Christopher Commission was set up to investigate racial prejudice within the LAPD. Sadly, its recommendations had all too blatantly not been implemented by the time of the **Rampart police scandal**. In 2000, the police department's gung-ho militaristic culture was once again on display, this time in the form of elite CRASH units sent to investigate drug-related crimes around the MacArthur Park and Temple-Beaudry barrios. Accused by ex-cop-turned-informant Rafael Perez of all manner of vigilante actions – from framing suspects for drug arrests to beating innocent civilians to shooting suspects in cold blood – most of the alleged perpetrators in blue walked away from the charges, the momentum for their conviction either dissipating by a lack of social outrage or a lack of interest on the part of the local district attorney. Since then, even though New York's trailblazing former police chief **William Bratton** has been brought in to turn things around, almost nothing has changed. Gang violence in 2004 is again on an upswing, this time with many more Latino suspects than before (given the ground-swell of immigration), and a longstanding truce between rival gangs was allowed to expire, letting blood flow freely in the streets once more. However, since much of South Central is well off the radar screen of upscale white Los Angeles, and bland technocrat mayor James Hahn evinces little interest in controlling violence in the hood, the problems continue to fester and worsen – waiting for the next spark to send LA up in flames once more.

neighborhoods as **Watts**, **Compton**, **Inglewood**, and **Crenshaw**, but hardly ranks on the tourist circuit – especially since it burst onto the world's TV screens as the focal point of the April 1992 **riots** (see box opposite). Still, it's an integral part of the city, especially in terms of size: a big, roughly circular chunk reaching from the southern edge of Downtown to the northern fringe of the Harbor Area. The population was once mostly black, but is increasingly Hispanic and Asian, and the dislocations resulting from immigration have made for surprising trends and more than a little racial hostility. As a whole, South Central doesn't look so terribly run down at first sight, mostly made up of detached bungalows enjoying their own patch of palm-shaded lawn. But this picture is deceptive and doesn't conceal for long the fact that many residents are poor, and have very limited chances of climbing the social ladder and escaping to the more affluent parts of the city.

Watts

The district of **WATTS**, on the eastern side of South Central, achieved notoriety as the scene of the six-day **Watts Riots** of August 1965 (see box, p.120). Despite the district's violent and troubled history, there is one valid reason to come here, to see the internationally famous, Gaudí-esque **Watts Towers**, sometimes called the Rodia Towers, at 1765 E 107th St – one of Southern California's most important visual landmarks, and also one of its most frustrating to access. Constructed from iron, stainless steel, old bedsteads, and cement, and decorated with fragments of bottles and around 70,000 crushed seashells, these striking pieces of street art were built by Simon Rodia, who had no artistic training, but labored over the towers' construction from 1921 to 1954, refusing offers of help and unable to explain either their meaning or why he was building them. Once finished, he left the area, refused to talk about the towers, and faded into obscurity. Although compelling, the site is open by appointment only; call or visit the adjacent Watts Tower Arts Center, 1727 E 107th St (Tues–Sat 10am–4pm, Sun noon–4pm; free; ℡323/860-9964, Ⓦwww.wattstowers.net), for more information. One good time to come is during the September Day of the Drums Festival, or the October Watts Towers Jazz Festival, both signature events in the city, which take place at the adjoining **Cultural Crescent Amphitheater**; call the Arts Center for details and program listings.

About five miles north, the **Dunbar Hotel**, 4225 S Central Ave, marks the first US hotel built specifically for blacks and patronized by almost every prominent African American from the 1930s through the 1950s. Lying on a strip that once hosted many classic diners and nightclubs, the hotel is only visible in its restored lobby and facade, as it is now a home for the elderly (information through the OASIS senior center; Mon–Fri 9am–5pm; ℡323/231-6220). It does, however, feature occasional art exhibits open to the public, and hosts the Central Avenue Jazz Festival in August (more details at ℡213/847-3169).

Compton and Inglewood

Between Watts and the Harbor Area, only a few districts are of passing interest. Despite its fame as the home of many of LA's rappers – NWA, for example, sang venomously of its ills on their album *Straight Outta Compton* – not to mention of tennis phenoms Serena and Venus Williams, **COMPTON** is not a place where strangers should attempt to sniff out the local music scene. History buffs secure in their cars, however, might enjoy a stop for the free conducted tours at the **Dominguez Ranch Adobe**, 18127 S Alameda St (Sun & Wed 1, 2 & 3pm; ℡310/631-5981), a restored mission that chronicles the social

The Watts Riots

The **Watts Riots** of 1965 began with the arrest of a 21-year-old unemployed black man, **Marquette Frye**, on suspicion of drunken driving, which gave rise to charges of police brutality and led to bricks, bottles, and slabs of concrete being hurled at police and passing motorists during the night. The situation had calmed by the next morning, but the following evening, both young and old were in the streets, giving vent to an anger generated by years of unfair treatment by Chief William Parker's militarized LAPD – and other white-dominated institutions. Weapons were looted from stores and many buildings set alight; street barricades were erected, and the events took a more serious turn. By the fifth day, the insurgents were approaching Downtown, which – along with the fear spreading through white LA – led to the call-out of the National Guard: 13,000 troops arrived, set up machine-gun placements and road blocks, and imposed an 8pm-to-dawn curfew, causing the chaos to subside. In the aftermath of the uprising, which left 36 dead, one German reporter said of Watts, "It looks like Germany during the last months of World War II." Much of it still does – Watts is by far the ugliest part of South Central LA, and the promises of investment made after 1965 never amounted to much.

ascent of its founder, Juan José Domínguez – one of the soldiers who left Mexico with Padre Junípero Serra's expedition to found the California missions – whose long military service was acknowledged in 1782 by the granting of these 75,000 acres of land. As the importance of the area grew, so did the influence of Domínguez's descendants, who became powerful in local politics. The six main rooms of the 1826 adobe are on display with their original furnishings, or at least replicas of them, and are well worth a look for anyone intrigued by the pre-American period in California.

Closer to LAX, on the other side of the Harbor Freeway, **INGLEWOOD**, unenticing in itself, is home to the **Hollywood Park Racetrack** (☎310/419-1500, ⓦwww.hollywoodpark.com), a landscaped track with lagoons and tropical vegetation, and, next door, **The Forum**, the 17,000-seat arena that was the former home of both the LA Lakers (basketball) and the LA Kings (hockey). These days it's been converted into one of the country's biggest megachurches, owned by Faithful Central Bible Church, though concerts are still occasionally held here during the week (see "Listings," p.216). Nearer to the 405 freeway, two gems of pop architecture are worth a look: **Randy's Donuts**, 805 Manchester Blvd (☎310/645-4707, ⓦwww.randysdonuts.com), an iconic fast-food drive-though operation that's famed for its giant rooftop donut, and **Pann's**, a mile north at La Tijera and Centinela boulevards (☎310/337-2860, ⓦwww.panns.com), one of the last true Googie coffee shops around, with a pitched roof, big neon sign, exotic plants, and wealth of primary colors. If you have a taste for more historic architecture, make sure to check out the **Centinela Adobe**, just south of *Pann's* at 7636 Midfield Ave (Wed & Sun 2–4pm; free; ☎310/649-6272), an 1834 structure whose earthen bricks were made at the site, and which is loaded with period antiques and Victorian furnishings.

Crenshaw

As a general rule, it's not a good idea to venture into South Central looking for entertainment, unless you're with a local. The **CRENSHAW** district and adjacent **Leimert Park**, on its western fringe around the intersection of W 43rd Place and Degnan Boulevard, may be an exception. Where the old center of African-American culture was once along Central Avenue, it is now here,

Horseback riding in the Santa Monica Mountains

specially with the recent tide of Hispanic immigration pushing more black residents to the western side of South Central. Crenshaw and Leimert Park feature a number of restaurants, fine book and record stores, and an uneventful shopping mall. Two notable sights include the striking **Leimert Theater**, 3300 43rd Place (☎323/291-7321), also known as the Vision Theatre, which features a towering oil-derrick sign with neon accents, and is in occasional use as a performing-arts center; and the **Museum in Black**, 4331 Degnan Blvd (Tues–Sat 11.30am–6pm; donation; ☎323/292-9528), exhibiting a wide range of African-American art and history, including slave-purchasing documents that date back nearly three hundred years. Beyond Crenshaw, the black upper-middle class resides in **Baldwin Hills**, a picturesque district marred by a slew of oil wells, which was one of the sites for the 1932 Olympics, though few relics remain.

East LA

Of the many Hispanic neighborhoods all over LA, one of the most longstanding is **EAST LA**, which begins two miles east of Downtown. There was a Mexican population here long before the white settlers came, and from the late nineteenth century onward millions more arrived, coming here chiefly to work on the land. As the white inhabitants moved west towards the coast, the Mexicans stayed, creating a vast Spanish-speaking community that's one of the most historic in the country.

Other than the lively markets, street life, and murals, however, there are few specific "sights" in East LA. The best plan is just to turn up on a Saturday afternoon – the liveliest part of the week – and stroll along **Cesar Chavez Avenue**, formerly Brooklyn Avenue, going eastward from Indiana Street, checking out the wild pet shops, with free-roaming parrots and cases of boa constrictors, and **botanicas shops**, which cater to practitioners of Santería – a religion that is equal parts voodoo and Catholicism. Browse amid the shark's teeth, dried devil fish, and plastic statuettes of Catholic saints, and buy magical herbs, ointments, or candles after consulting the shopkeeper and explaining (in Spanish) what ails you. Only slightly less exotic fare can be found in **El Mercado de Los Angeles**, 3425 E First St (daily 10am–8pm; ☎323/268-3451), an indoor market somewhat similar to Olvera Street (see p.106), but much more authentic.

Guadalupe, the Mexican image of the Virgin Mary, appears in mural art all over East LA, nowhere better than at the junction of Mednik and Cesar Chavez avenues. Lined with blue tile, it now forms an unofficial shrine where worshippers place fresh flowers and candles.

Non-Hispanic visitors are comparatively thin on the ground in East LA, but you're unlikely to meet any hostility on the streets during the day – though the wild steer clear of the rough and very male-dominated bars, and avoid the area after dark.

Highland Park

North of Downtown, towards the foothills, completed in 1941 the **Pasadena Freeway** curves along a dry riverbed charming greenery munity whose name it bears. The freeway, LA's first, was LA. Be aware that this two Seco Parkway, as it was designed to be lined with exit ramps so short and sharp ntings – an idea not very suitable for a place like to take the recently comp roadway has stop signs on the on-ramps, and Station, which loosely follows eed limit is 5mph. It's a much better move line light rail from Downtown's Union Old Pasadena and beyond.

Just off the road, two miles from Downtown, **HIGHLAND PARK** has a number of exuberantly detailed Victorian houses brought together from around the city to form **Heritage Square**. This fenced-off ten-acre park at 3800 Homer St (grounds Fri 10.30am–3.30pm, Sat & Sun noon–3pm, tours on the hour Sat & Sun noon–3pm; $6; ⓦwww.heritagesquare.org) has been derided by some critics as an architectural "petting zoo." The strip uncomfortably sites a railway station next to an octagonal house next to a Methodist church, and although the buildings are interesting enough, the park's freeway-adjacent home is a less than ideal spot to escape into a Victorian world of buggies and gingerbread.

Just beyond the next freeway exit, at 200 E Ave 43, the **Lummis House** (Fri–Sun 1–4pm; free; ⓦwww.socalhistory.org) is the well-preserved home of Charles F. Lummis, a publicist who was at the heart of LA's nineteenth-century boom. An early champion of civil rights for Native Americans, and one who worked to save and preserve many of the missions, Lummis built his home as a cultural center, where the literati of the day would meet to discuss poetry and the art and architecture of the Southwest. He built it in an ad hoc mixture of Mission and Medieval styles, naming it *El Alisal* after the many large sycamore trees that shade the gardens, and constructing the thick walls out of rounded granite boulders taken from the nearby riverbed, and the beams over the living room of old telephone poles. The solid wooden front doors are similarly built to last, reinforced with iron and weighing tons, while the plaster-and-tile interior features rustic, hand-cut timber ceilings and homemade furniture, all a fitting reflection of its rugged owner, one of the few individuals to reach LA by walking – from Cincinnati.

The Southwest Museum

Although many people in LA scarcely know about it, the **SOUTHWEST MUSEUM** (Tues–Sun 10am–5pm; $7.50; ⓦwww.southwestmuseum.org), which rises castle-like below Mount Washington, was Charles F. Lummis's most enduring achievement and is well worth an afternoon's visit. Half a mile north of the Lummis House (with its own Gold Line light-rail stop), the museum is the oldest in Los Angeles, founded in 1907. Its name is a bit deceptive – there are displays of Native-American artifacts from all over North America, with exhibits of pre-Columbian pottery, coastal Chumash rock art, and a full-sized Plains Indian Cheyenne teepee. Its traveling exhibitions, educational programs, and theatrical events have made it an international center for indigenous American cultures; the museum shop features Navajo rugs, kachina dolls, and turquoise jewelry, as well as an extensive selection of books and publications. Nearby, the **Casa de Adobe**, administered by the museum, is a 1917 attempt to recreate a Mexican hacienda, featuring a small museum of its own that details LA history up to the nineteenth century. The Casa is only open for special events (call ☎323/221-2163 for more information). Note that the Southwest Museum and Griffith Park's Museum of the American West (see p.133) offer a joint ticket for $12 – though you'll probably need a car to get to both easily.

Hollywood

If a single word epitomizes the American dream of glamour, money, and overnight success, it is **HOLLYWOOD**. Ever since movies and their stars became international symbols of the good life, Hollywood has been a magnet to

▲ Lake Hollywood

HOLLYWOOD

Griffith Park

0 ____ 200 yds

N

John Anson Ford Theater

Hollywood Bowl

Hollywood Bowl Museum

Hollywood Heritage Museum

Chinese Theatre

Hollywood Entertainment Museum

Hollywood and Highland Mall

Erotic Museum

Egyptian Theatre

Frederick's of Hollywood

Hollywood History Museum

Motion Picture Production Office

Knickerbocker Hotel Site

Capitol Records Tower

Pantages Theater

Hollywood & Vine

Hollywood Athletic Club

Hollywood Palladium

Crossroads of the World

Hollywood High School

Cinerama Dome

FRANKLIN AVENUE

HOLLYWOOD BLVD

SUNSET BLVD

West Hollywood

Hollywood Memorial Cemetery & Paramount Studios ▼

millions of tourists on celebrity-seeking pilgrimages and an equal number of hopefuls drawn by the prospect of riches and glory. Even if their real chances of success were infinitesimal, enough people were taken in by the dream to make Hollywood what it is today – a charged combination of optimism and despair.

In reality, Hollywood was more a center of corruption and scandal than the city of dreams the studio-made legend suggests. Successful Hollywood residents actually spent little time here – leaving as soon as they could afford to for the privacy of the hills or coast. Even by the 1930s Hollywood had developed into a gritty district rife with prostitution and petty thievery, and subsequent decades only accelerated the decline. Although the area continues to be a secondary center for the film business, with technical service companies like prop shops and equipment suppliers abundant, all the big film companies (other than Paramount) relocated long ago to places like Burbank, leaving Hollywood in isolation, with urban blight, drug dealing, and seedy adult bookstores becoming the harsh reality clouding the more glamorous fantasies. Things have brightened up slightly in the past few years, however, with public and private capital financing the construction of new tourist plazas and shopping malls – places which, in their focus on the golden age of moviemaking, try to take the tarnish off the Hollywood myth once more.

Approaching from Downtown via Sunset Boulevard, **East Hollywood** offers the first taste of the district, an assortment of cheap housing and low-rent businesses with a few interesting sights scattered here and there, among them **Los Feliz**, which has become a trendy place to live and socialize, with a number of eye-catching modernist homes glittering above in the hills. Further west, **Central Hollywood** is the signature part of the area, a compact zone loaded with movie history, and swamped by an eccentric street mix of social derelicts and star-struck tourists. You'd have to be totally uninterested in film lore to find the place dull, though. Protecting Hollywood from the outside world, the slopes of the Santa Monica Mountains contain **Griffith Park** – several thousand acres of nature offering rugged hiking trails and busy sports and picnic grounds, which form a scenic northern edge to the area. Beyond the park to the west, the **Hollywood Hills** hold exclusive homes perched on snaking driveways that are the most tangible reminders of the wealth generated in the city – and the brand-name celebrities that have sprung from it.

East Hollywood: Silver Lake and Los Feliz

Typically unseen by most visitors, **EAST HOLLYWOOD** finds its focus near the eastern intersection of Hollywood and Sunset boulevards, and is mostly inhabited by Hispanic immigrants who have yet to fulfill the American dream, with the dingier parts of Sunset contrasting dramatically with the chic western side of the strip. Still, even here, the perimeter neighborhoods bordering the hills are highly sought after, the streets around Beachwood Avenue have evolved into popular places to live and hang out, and upscale Mediterranean-style homes clutter the hillside.

Four blocks north of Sunset, **SILVER LAKE** was once home to some of Hollywood's first studios, since converted into restaurants and galleries, or at least warehouses and storage units. Walt Disney opened his first studio at 2719 Hyperion Ave in 1926 (now a parking lot), and the Keystone Kops were dreamed up in Mack Sennett's studio at 1712 Glendale Blvd (now a storage facility), when the zone was known as **Edendale**, and where just a single sound studio now remains. Another faded bit of movie history can be found in the vicinity of 930 Vendome St, where a lengthy stairway was a location for Laurel and Hardy's 1932 flick *The Music Box*, in which the lads tried to haul a piano up the many steps, to predictable effect. Otherwise, there are no official "sights" in Silver Lake, except for a collection of interesting modernist houses in the hills designed by the likes of Richard Neutra and R.M. Schindler, highlighted by John Lautner's **Silvertop**, 2138 Micheltorena St (best viewed from 2100 Redcliff Drive), an eye-grabbing marvel with projecting roofs and balconies, wraparound glass windows and sweeping concrete curves. The district is also known as the hip, edgy counterpart to West Hollywood: a gay-oriented spot that, with its cozy bars, quirky dance clubs, and alternative leftist bookstores, caters to a more working-class, Hispanic crowd than the whiter, more upscale, and better-known western end of Hollywood.

Nearby **LOS FELIZ** has fair-sized Hispanic and gay contingents, too, and on summer nights its bars are full of students from the local **American Film Institute** campus (Los Feliz Blvd at Western Ave) and would-be bohemians from the Hollywood Hills. Tim Burton's *Ed Wood* was partly shot, and premiered, at the architecturally impressive **Vista** movie theater, just off Hollywood Boulevard near Virgil – across from the 1916 site of D.W. Griffith's *Intolerance* film set, which featured giant pillars and elephant statues, and has since been "re-created" in the Hollywood & Highland shopping mall further west (see p.129). **Hollyhock House**, on a small hill close to the junction of Vermont Avenue at 4800 Hollywood Blvd (Wed–Sun tours on the half-hour

A history of Hollywood

Strangely enough, Hollywood started life as a **temperance colony**, created to be a sober, God-fearing alternative to raunchy Downtown LA, eight miles away by rough country road. Purchased and named by a pair of devout Methodists in 1887, and allegedly home to the country's largest Presbyterian church, the district remained autonomous until 1911, when residents were forced, in return for a regular water supply, to become an LA suburb. The film industry, then gathering momentum on the East Coast, needed a place with cheap labor, guaranteed sunshine, and a diverse assortment of natural backdrops to enable pictures to be made quickly, and most importantly, a distant spot to dodge Thomas Edison's patent trust, which tried to restrict filmmaking nationwide. Southern California, with its climate, scenery, and isolation, was the perfect spot. A few offices affiliated to Eastern film companies appeared Downtown from 1906 and the first true studios opened in nearby Silver Lake, but independent hopefuls soon discovered the cheaper rents on offer in Hollywood. Soon, the first **Hollywood studio** opened in 1911, and within three years the place was packed with filmmakers – many of them, like **Cecil B. DeMille**, who shared his barn-converted office space with a horse, destined to be the big names of the future.

The industry expanded fast, bringing riches and fame – with momentum provided by the overnight success of DeMille's *The Squaw Man*, filmed inside the former barn itself – and now reopened as the **Hollywood Heritage Museum**, 2100 N Highland Blvd (Sat & Sun 11am–4pm; $3; ☎323/874-4005, ⓦwww.hollywoodheritage.org), exhibiting interesting antiques and treasures from the silent era. Yet moviemaking was far from being a financially secure business, and it wasn't until the release of D.W. Griffith's **The Birth of a Nation** in 1914 that the power of film was demonstrated. The film's racist account of the Civil War and Reconstruction (the KKK are the "heroes" and independent-minded blacks the "villains") caused riots outside cinemas and months of critical debate in the newspapers (Woodrow Wilson approvingly described it as "writing history with lightning"), and for the first time drew the middle classes to moviehouses – despite the exorbitant $2 ticket price. It was also the movie which first perfected the narrative style and production techniques that gradually became standard in classic Hollywood cinema.

Modern Hollywood took shape from the 1920s on, when film production grew more specialized, the "**star system**" was perfected, and many small companies either went bust or were incorporated into one of the handful of bigger studios that came to dominate filmmaking. The **Golden Age** of the studio system was at its peak from the 1930s through the late 1940s, when a Supreme Court ruling put an end to studio monopolies owning their own exhibitors and theaters, and employing shady techniques such as "block booking," wherein theaters were forced to screen a slate of crummy, B-grade throwaway flicks in exchange for running the studios' major films. Despite lean years from the later 1950s until the 1970s, and the onslaught of competition from television, Hollywood slowly rebounded until, in the modern era, the studios have become simple adjuncts to global media empires. Whatever the structure of the business, the film industry's enduring success is in making slick, unchallenging movies that sell – from Rhett Butler romancing Scarlett O'Hara to Yoda dueling with a light saber. Ultimately, of course, no matter how much lip service Hollywood pays to the "**independent cinema**" (mainly by purchasing brash upstarts like Miramax), it's been big names, big bucks, and conservatism that have kept the town alive. The film industry today rarely thinks about taking artistic risks, even as it regularly takes unnecessary financial ones.

12.30–3.30pm, Wed–Fri by reservation only at ☎323/644-6269, ⓦwww .hollyhockhouse.net; donation), was the first of architect Frank Lloyd Wright's contributions to LA and was largely supervised by his student, Rudolf Schindler, later one of LA's pre-eminent architects. Covered with Mayan motifs and stylized, geometric renderings of the hollyhock flower, the house, completed in 1921, is an intriguingly obsessive dwelling, whose original furniture (now replaced by detailed reconstructions) continued the conceptual flow. The bizarre quality of the building was obviously too much for its oil heiress – and socialist – owner, Aline Barnsdall, who lived here only for a short time before donating both the house and the surrounding land to the city authorities for use as a cultural center, now the **Barnsdall Art Park**. Renovated in the past five years and featuring a number of galleries devoted to the work of regional adult (and child) artists, the complex makes for a pleasant stop while you're waiting for the Hollyhock tour to begin.

Another Wright building, the 1924 **Ennis-Brown House**, looms over Los Feliz at 2655 Glendower Ave. One of four of his local structures to feature "textile" concrete block, its ominous, pre-Columbian appearance has added atmosphere to more than thirty film and TV productions, from Vincent Price's *The House on Haunted Hill* to David Lynch's *Twin Peaks*. The house is open for 90min tours (Tues, Thurs & Sat 11am & 1.30pm; $20; reserve at ☎323/660-0607, ⓦ www.ennisbrownhouse.org), which lead you around its rather cramped interiors and hallways, as well as a striking Great Room with its high ceiling.

Further into the hills, Richard Neutra's **Lovell House**, 4616 Dundee Drive, is a set of sleek, white rectangles and broad window bands that looks quite contemporary for a 1929 building, making it one of LA's landmarks of early modernism. Curiously, the house was used as the 1950s home of pimp and pornographer Pierce Patchett in the film *L.A. Confidential*. More garish is the **Sowden House**, 5121 Franklin Ave, a pink box with concrete jaws designed by Frank Lloyd Wright's son Lloyd, which isn't open for tours, and it's probably just as well – this was the mid-century home of the man reputed to be one of LA's most fiendish murderers, according to his own son, who detailed the evidence in the 2003 book, *Black Dahlia Avenger*. Ironically, the house is now the headquarters of an organization devoted to world peace.

Central Hollywood

The few short blocks of **CENTRAL HOLLYWOOD** contain the densest concentration of faded glamour and film mythology in the world, a pervasive sense of nostalgia that makes the area deeply appealing in a way no measure of commercialism can diminish. The decline that blighted the area from the early 1960s is slowly receding in the face of prolonged efforts by local authorities – including repaving Hollywood Boulevard with a special glass-laden tarmac that sparkles in the streetlights and inviting all manner of new malls to take root here. Nevertheless the place still gets hairy after dark, away from the main tourist zones, when the effects of homelessness, drug addiction, and prostitution are more evident, and petty thieves go hunting for the odd purse or wallet. The contrasting qualities of dimmed glamour, modern hype, and deep-set seediness also make Hollywood one of LA's best spots for funky bar-hopping and night-clubbing, with a range of cheap, affordable options.

Along Hollywood Boulevard

HOLLYWOOD BOULEVARD is, of course, the axis of all the accumulated movie lore, and if you follow it west, the first notable sight is the junction of **Hollywood and Vine**, a juxtaposition of street names that still tingles the spines of dedicated movie buffs. During the early golden years (1910s–20s), the rumor spread that any budding star had only to parade around this junction to be spotted by big-name film producers or directors (the major studios were in those days all concentrated nearby), who nursed coffees behind the windows of neighboring restaurants. In typical Hollywood style, the whole tale was blown wildly out of proportion, and while many real stars did pass by, it was only briefly on their way to and from work, and the crossing did nothing but earn a fabulous reputation. For a commemoration of the era, you'll have to proceed underground to the local **Red Line** subway stop, which is decorated with all sorts of film-related geegaws and memorabilia.

Much of the pavement along this stretch of Hollywood Boulevard is marked by the brass nameplates of the **Walk of Fame** (officially beginning at Hollywood and Vine). The laying of the plates began in 1960, instigated by the local chamber of commerce, which thought that by enshrining the big names in radio, television, movies, music, and theater, it could somehow restore the boulevard's faded glamour and boost tourism. Although the newspapers do announce induction ceremonies for such worthies as Billy Bob Thornton, dubious choices are often made as well; the Rolling Stones, for example, took decades to gain a star, long after they were past their prime, while such questionable picks as TV's *Rugrats* cartoon characters are enshrined frequently. Selected stars have to part with several thousand dollars for the privilege of being included: among them are Marlon Brando (1717 Vine St), Marlene Dietrich (6400 Hollywood Blvd), Michael Jackson (6927 Hollywood Blvd), Elvis Presley (6777 Hollywood Blvd), and Ronald Reagan (6374 Hollywood Blvd).

Other Hollywood icons can be found just off the Walk; at 1750 N Vine St, for one, the **Capitol Records Tower** resembles a stack of 45rpm records and serves as the music company's headquarters, its 1950s design supposedly inspired by an offhand Johnny Mercer remark. Nearby, at 6233 Hollywood Blvd, the **Pantages Theater** has a bland facade but one of the city's greatest interiors, a melange of Baroque styling that mainly sees touring stage productions these days. Also in the vicinity, the bulky **Knickerbocker Hotel**, 1714 Ivar Ave, now an apartment complex, was where the widow of legendary escapologist Harry Houdini conducted a rooftop seance in an attempt to assist her late spouse in his greatest escape of all. During the 1930s and 1940s, the hotel had a reputation for rooming some of Hollywood's more unstable characters, and a number of lesser names jumped from its high windows; in the 1950s the likes of Elvis Presley and Jerry Lee Lewis stayed here. A block away, at 1817 Ivar Ave, stands the flea-bag boardinghouse where author and screenwriter Nathanael West lived during the 1930s, after coming west to revive his flagging financial situation – and ultimately failing. Gazing over the street's parade of extras, hustlers, and make-believe cowboys, West penned the dark satirical portrait of Hollywood, *The Day of the Locust*, the apocalyptic finale of which was inspired by Hollywood Hills wildfires in the summer of 1935 (and which includes a character with the oddly prescient name of Homer Simpson).

Back on Hollywood Boulevard, at no. 6608, **Frederick's of Hollywood** is a local landmark. Opened in 1947, it has been (under-)clothing Hollywood's sex goddesses ever since, and many more mortal bodies all over the world through its mail-order outlet. Inside, the **lingerie museum** (Mon–Fri 10am–9pm, Sat 10am–6pm, Sun noon–5pm; free) displays some of the company's corsets, bras, and panties, donated by a host of famous wearers, ranging from Liz Taylor and Lana Turner to Cher and Madonna. If you're sufficiently fired up by all of these displays, wander another block down to the recently opened **Erotic Museum**, 6741 Hollywood Blvd (Sun–Thurs noon–9pm, Fri & Sat noon–midnight; $13; ⓦ www.theeroticmuseum.com), Hollywood's latest attempt to contextualize (and make a profit off of) the sleaze that's available for free on the streets outside. The museum is something of an intellectual attempt to probe the mysteries of sex, libido, and the like, but what most tourists come here for is the chance to take a peek at a dirty movie (in the "Projections" room) without a crowd of raincoat-wearing perverts lurking nearby. Other sections – covering sex and technology, biology, art, and so forth – have the same effect, making what were formerly secret fantasies into wall displays and enticing taboos into scientific dogma.

If the sex museum is just one of several that have opened in various US cities in the past few years, the **Egyptian Theatre**, 6708 Hollywood Blvd, is a unique, essential Hollywood icon: the very first Hollywood premiere (*Robin Hood*, an epic swashbuckler starring Douglas Fairbanks Sr), took place here in 1922. Financed by impresario Sid Grauman, the Egyptian was a glorious fantasy in its heyday, modestly seeking to re-create the Temple of Thebes, with usherettes dressed as Cleopatra. This great old building was damaged in the 1994 earthquake, but has since been lovingly restored by the American Cinematheque film foundation, and now plays an assortment of Hollywood classics, documentaries, avant-garde flicks, and foreign films to small but appreciative crowds (typical ticket $9). Tourists, however, are encouraged to check out a short documentary, presented hourly, chronicling the rise of Hollywood as America's movie capital (Sat & Sun 2pm & 3.30pm; $7; ⓦegyptiantheatre .com). Alternatively, you can get the grand tour of the theater itself in hour-long in-depth visits to sights like the backstage dressing rooms and projection booth, usually presented twice monthly in the middle of the month (10.30am only; $9; call for details at ⓣ323/461-2020 ext 115). Much less appealing, the eastern corners of the Hollywood and Highland intersection feature a handful of dreary tourist traps – wax museum, oddities gallery, world-record exhibit – that are worthwhile only if you're very easily amused.

West of the Egyptian, the **Hollywood & Highland** complex (ⓦwww .hollywoodandhighland.com), on the northwest side of the eponymous intersection, must rank as one of LA's most frustrating attractions. After nearly a billion dollars of investment and the relocation of the Oscars to the specially designed **Kodak Theatre** on site, this towering beacon of commerce – which was supposed to revitalize Hollywood and give the district a cultural renaissance – is no better than your average suburban mall. Its chosen theme is the Babylonian set from the 1916 D.W. Griffith film *Intolerance*, from which the mall borrows heavily in its super-sized columns, elephant statues, and colossal archway. Unrivaled in film history for almost fifty years, the

Hollywood impressions at the Chinese Theatre

Opened in 1927 as a lavish setting for premieres of swanky new productions, the **Chinese Theatre** was for many decades *the* spot for movie first nights, and the public crowded behind the rope barriers in the thousands to watch the movie aristocrats arriving for the screenings. The main draw, of course, has always been the assortment of **cement handprints** and **footprints** embedded in the theater's forecourt. The idea came about when actress Norma Talmadge accidentally – though some say it was a deliberate publicity stunt – trod in wet cement while visiting the construction site with owner Sid Grauman, who had established a reputation for creating garish movie palaces with gloriously vulgar designs based on exotic themes. The first formally to leave their marks were Mary Pickford and Douglas Fairbanks Sr, who ceremoniously dipped their digits when arriving for the opening of *King of Kings*, and the practice continues today. It's certainly fun to work out the actual dimensions of your favorite film stars, and to discover if your hands are smaller than Julie Andrews' or your feet are bigger than Rock Hudson's (or both).

movie was Hollywood's first real financial disaster, helping to ruin the career of its director and making the movie studios permanently wary of taking any sort of creative risks.

One site that the mall has almost ruined is the **Chinese Theatre**, 6925 Hollywood Blvd, which has for no good reason been swallowed up by the complex and expanded into a multiplex (beyond the three theaters pre-dating the mall). This was another of Sid Grauman's showpieces from the early days of the movie biz, and whereas it was once derided as Hollywood hokum designed to draw in the rubes for fancy viewin', it has since become a movie-palace icon with few peers. As for the building, it's an odd version of a classical Asian temple, replete with dubious Chinese motifs and upturned dragon-tail flanks, and the lobby's Art Deco splendor and the grand chinoiserie of the auditorium make for interesting viewing. Afterward, on the street outside the theater, you can hop aboard a tour for a look at the "homes of the stars" (see p.96), along with hundreds of other sightseers.

To catch a movie in the making, cross the road to the **Motion Picture Production Office**, 7038 Hollywood Blvd, 5th floor (Mon–Fri 8am–6pm), which issues a "shoot sheet" every weekday ($1–2), detailing exactly what's being filmed around town that day, and what kind of access you can expect as a lookey-loo. A few doors down, the **Hollywood Roosevelt**, 7000 Hollywood Blvd, was movieland's first luxury hotel (see "Accommodation," p.99). Opened in the same year as the Chinese Theatre, it fast became the meeting place of top actors and screenwriters, its *Cinegrill* restaurant feeding and watering the likes of W.C. Fields, Ernest Hemingway, and F. Scott Fitzgerald, not to mention legions of hangers-on. In 1929 the first Oscars were presented here, beginning the long tradition of Hollywood rewarding itself in the absence of honors from elsewhere. Look inside for a view of the splashing fountains and elegantly weighty wrought-iron chandeliers of its marble-floored lobby, and for the pictorial **History of Hollywood** on the second floor. The place is thick with legend: on the staircase from the lobby to the mezzanine Bill "Bojangles" Robinson taught Shirley Temple to dance; and the ghost of Montgomery Clift apparently haunts the place, announcing his presence by blowing a bugle. Surviving lounge divas like Eartha Kitt still put on the occasional show at the hotel's cabaret.

Across the street, the **Hollywood Entertainment Museum**, 7021 Hollywood Blvd (summer daily 10am–6pm, winter Thurs–Sun 11am–6pm; $10; ☎323/465-7900, ⓦwww.hollywoodmuseum.com), unlike what its name might suggest, is far from compelling. It occupies a lower level of the crudely "futuristic" Hollywood Museum Center. Although showcasing the full set of the TV show *Cheers* and the bridge of the Enterprise from *Star Trek*, along with rotating exhibitions and various antiques and curios from Hollywood history, the museum is a rather amateurish collection of odds and ends from old TV programs and movies, presented without context or any real purpose. Somewhat better is the **Hollywood History Museum**, 1660 Highland Blvd (Thurs–Sun 10am–5pm; $15; ⓦthehollywoodmuseum .com), which exhibits on its four levels the fashion, sets, make-up, and special effects taken from a broad swath of movie history, with particular focus on the latest Hollywood spectaculars. There's also a number of items from the Golden Age, though the museum doesn't quite have the classic focus of the old Max Factor Museum, which closed in the 1990s in the same space. Indeed, even though located in America's film capital, both museums pale in comparison to the much better Museum of Television and Radio in Beverly Hills (see p.144).

Along Sunset Boulevard

Paralleling Hollywood Boulevard to the south is another famous stretch nearly as steeped in movie legend, **SUNSET BOULEVARD**, which sports both contemporary decay and countless sites for Tinseltown nostalgia. For example, although there's not much at the corner of Sunset and **Gower Street** today, during the industry's formative years unemployed movie extras would hang around here hoping for a few days' work with one of the small B-movie studios, helping the junction earn the nicknames "Gower Gulch" and "Poverty Row." Another remaining shard of the boulevard's old-time glory can be found at no. 6360, where the huge, white **Cinerama Dome** was built in 1963 to exhibit giant three-projector films on a curved screen, and is now part of a larger retail complex of theaters, shops, and eateries called ArcLight (⊛www .arclightcinemas.com). Luckily, you can still see (single-projector) blockbusters in the dome on a large, curved screen – as fun and engaging a cinematic experience as any in LA – and occasionally even view such three-projector flicks as *This is Cinerama!* Nearby, the delectable Spanish Revival-style building at 6525 Sunset Blvd was, from the 1920s until the 1950s, known as the **Hollywood Athletic Club**. Another of Hollywood's legendary watering holes, the likes of Charlie Chaplin, Clark Gable, and Tarzan himself (Johnny Weismuller) lounged beside its Olympic-sized pool, while Johns Barrymore and Wayne held olympic drinking parties in the apartment levels above, with the Duke himself prone to chucking billiard balls at passing automobiles below. After standing empty for 25 years, the building reopened in 1990 as a pool hall, bar, and restaurant, only to close again at the end of the decade – though it opens for special parties and events (⊛www.hollywoodathleticclub.com).

The grouping of business offices at **Crossroads of the World**, 6672 Sunset Blvd, isn't much to look at these days, but when finished in 1936, was one of LA's major tourist attractions and one of the very first local malls. The central plaza supposedly resembles a ship, surrounded by shops designed with Tudor, French, Italian, and Spanish motifs – the idea being that the shops are the ports into which the shopper would sail. Oddly enough, time has been kind to this place, and considering the more recent and far brasher architecture found in the city, this has a definite, if muted, charm. (The facility is open during regular business hours during the week.) However, it can be seen in its full glory in the 1997 film *LA Confidential*, which also uses the nearby *Formosa Café* (see p.193) and *Frolic Room* bar, 6245 Hollywood Blvd, as period emblems of 1950s LA swagger. Finally, nearby **Paramount Studios**, entrance at 5555 Melrose Ave, is best known for its gate – famously seen in the film *Sunset Boulevard* – though since 9/11, tours are no longer offered.

Hollywood Forever

Not surprisingly for a town obsessed with marketing and PR, even the cemeteries are renamed to draw the crowds. Thus the former Hollywood Memorial Park has been reincarnated as **HOLLYWOOD FOREVER**, a few blocks below Sunset at 6000 Santa Monica Blvd (daily dawn–dusk; free; ⊛www .hollywoodforever.com), though the graves have luckily been kept in the same places. Overlooked by the famous water tower of neighboring Paramount Studios, the cemetery displays myriad tombs of dead celebrities, most notably in its southeastern corner, where a cathedral mausoleum includes, at no. 1205, the resting place of **Rudolph Valentino**. In 1926, 10,000 people packed the cemetery when the celebrated screen lover died aged just 31, and to this day on each anniversary of his passing (23 August), at least one "Lady in Black" will likely be found mourning – a tradition that started as a publicity stunt in

1931 and has continued ever since. While here, spare a thought for screen star Peter Finch, who died in 1977 before being awarded a Best Actor Oscar for his film *Network*. His crypt is opposite Valentino's and tourists often lean their butts against it while photographing the marker of the "White Sheik."

Fittingly, outside the mausoleum, the most pompous grave belongs to **Douglas Fairbanks Sr**, who, with his wife Mary Pickford (herself buried at Forest Lawn Glendale), did much to introduce nouveau-riche snobbery to Hollywood. Even in death Fairbanks keeps a snooty distance from the pack, his ostentatious memorial (complete with pond) only reachable by a shrub-lined path from the mausoleum. One of the cemetery's more recent arrivals was **Mel Blanc**, "the man of a thousand voices" – among them Bugs Bunny, Porky Pig, Tweety Pie, and Sylvester – whose epitaph simply reads "That's All, Folks."

As you enter the cemetery, you will notice the many tightly packed rows of glossy black headstones with Orthodox crosses and Cyrillic lettering. These mark the resting places of Russian and Armenian immigrants, who increasingly populate the graveyard just as their living counterparts populate Central and West Hollywood.

Griffith Park

Built on land donated by Gilded Age mining millionaire Griffith J. Griffith, vast **GRIFFITH PARK**, between Hollywood and the San Fernando Valley (daily 5am–10.30pm, mountain roads close at dusk; free), offers gentle greenery and rugged mountain slopes, a welcome respite from the chaos of LA. The largest municipal park in the country, it's also one of the few places where the city's many racial and social groups at least go through the motions of mixing together. Above the landscaped flat sections, where the crowds assemble to picnic, play sports, or visit the fixed attractions, the hillsides are rough and wild, marked only by foot and bridle paths, leading into desolate but appealingly unspoiled terrain that gives great views over the LA basin and out towards the ocean.

There are four **main entrances** to Griffith Park. Western Canyon Road, north of Los Feliz Boulevard, enters the park through the **Ferndell** – as the name suggests, a lush glade of ferns, from which numerous trails run deeper into the park – and continues up to the **Griffith Observatory**, 2800 E Observatory Rd, familiar from its use as a backdrop in *Rebel Without a Cause* and numerous low-budget sci-fi flicks such as *The Amazing Colossal Man*. An icon of LA, and one of the city's most enjoyable spots, the observatory is unfortunately closed for renovation until 2006, including its Hall of Science, planetarium, laserium, and massive telescope. Until then, more modest exhibits are on view at a satellite facility in the northeast section of the park (Tues–Fri 1–10pm, Sat & Sun 10am–10pm; free; information at ☏323/664-1191, ⊛www.griffithobs.org).

Hiking in Griffith Park

The steeper parts of **Griffith Park**, which blend into the foothills of the Santa Monica Mountains, offer a variety of **hiking trails**. You can get maps from the **ranger station**, at 4400 Crystal Springs Rd (daily during daylight hours; ☏323/662-6573) – also a good spot for bike rental from Spokes 'n Stuff and the starting point for guided hikes and atmospheric evening walks, held whenever there's a full moon. The rangers also have maps for drivers that detail the best vantage points for views over the whole of Los Angeles, not least from the highest place in the park – the summit of Mount Hollywood. Note, however, that you are not allowed access to the Hollywood sign, which sits on the slope of Mount Lee to the west – tempting, but illegal to access.

Descending from the observatory on Vermont Canyon Road (effectively the continuation of Western Canyon Rd) brings you to the small **bird sanctuary**, set within a modest-sized wooded canyon. Across the road is the **Greek Theatre** (☎323/665-1927, ⓦwww.greektheatrela.com), an open-air amphitheater that seats nearly five thousand beneath its quasi-Greek columns – though if you're not going in for a show (the Greek is a venue for big-name rock, jazz, and country music concerts during the summer), you'll see just the bland exterior.

The **northern end** of the park, over the hills in the San Fernando Valley, is best reached directly by car from the Golden State Freeway, although you can take the park roads (or explore the labyrinth of hiking trails) that climb the park's hilly core, past some of its wildlife lurking in the brush. Caged animals, meanwhile, are plentiful in the **LA Zoo**, 5333 Zoo Drive (daily 10am–5pm, summer closes 6pm; $10, kids $5; ⓦwww.lazoo.org), one of the biggest zoos in the country and home to more than 1600 creatures, dividing its animals by continent, with pens representing various parts of the world. Despite the zoological inventory and layout, it's still not terribly impressive, especially in comparison to its San Diego counterpart (see p.241). Even less intriguing is the nostalgic **Travel Town Museum**, 5200 Zoo Drive (Mon–Fri 10am–4pm, Sat & Sun 10am–5pm; free; ⓦtraveltown.org), touted as a transportation museum but more a dumping ground for old trains and fire trucks, most of them presented without context or purpose. Bounding Griffith Park's northwest rim, **Forest Lawn Hollywood Hills**, 6300 Forest Lawn Drive (daily 8am–5pm; ⓦwww.forestlawn.com), is a cemetery of the stars that, while not quite as awe-inspiringly vulgar as its Glendale counterpart, is no less pretentious, with showy grave-markers and fancy memorials to such esteemed figures as Buster Keaton, Stan Laurel, Marvin Gaye, and Charles Laughton, as well as the likes of Andy Gibb, Liberace, and Jack Webb.

Museum of the American West

Sharing a parking lot with the zoo, the **Museum of the American West**, near the junction of the Ventura and Golden State freeways at 4700 Western Heritage Way (Tues–Sun 10am–5pm, Thurs closes 8pm; $7.50, students $5, combo ticket with Southwest Museum (p.123) for $12; ⓦwww.museumoftheamericanwest.org), was founded by Gene Autry, the "singing cowboy" who cut more than six hundred discs beginning in 1929, starred in blockbuster Hollywood Westerns during the 1930s and 1940s, became even more of a household name through his TV show in the 1950s, and died in 1999 after a very lengthy career. Autry fans hoping for a shrine to the man who penned the immortal *That Silver-Haired Daddy of Mine*, are in for a shock, however. The **collection** – from buckskin jackets and branding irons to Frederic Remington's sculptures of turn-of-the-century Western life and the truth about the shootout at the OK Corral – is a serious and credible attempt to explore the mindset and culture of those who colonized the West. The museum includes engaging sections on native peoples, European exploration, nineteenth-century pioneers, the Wild West, Asian immigrants, and, of course, Hollywood's versions of all of the above. Catholic missionaries, gunslinging criminals, tribal medicine men, Romantic painters, and Tinseltown directors are but a few of the colorful figures the museum honors, and sometimes criticizes.

The Hollywood Hills

Apart from offering the chance to see the endlessly flat expanse of the LA basin, the views from the **HOLLYWOOD HILLS** feature perhaps the oddest, most opulent, selection of properties to be found anywhere. Around these canyons and slopes, which run from Hollywood itself into Benedict Canyon above Beverly Hills, mansions are so commonplace that only the half-dozen fully blown castles really stand out.

Mulholland Drive, named after LA's most renowned hydro-engineer, runs along the crest, passing some of the most famous sites: Rudolph Valentino's extravagant **Falcon Lair** (1436 Bella Drive), Errol Flynn's **Mulholland House** (7740 Mulholland Drive), and the former home of actress Sharon Tate (10066 Cielo Drive) – and studio of Trent Reznor of Nine Inch Nails – where some of the Manson family killings took place. Guided tours (see p.96) can point out which is which, but for the most part you can't get close to the most elaborate dwellings, and none is open to the public. Plus, there's a number of run-of-the-mill million-dollar residences belonging to an assortment of luminaries, visionaries, former politicians, and movie moguls, most visibly in **Mount Olympus**, a high-kitsch real-estate tract loaded with faux palazzos, pseudo-Roman statuary, goofy marble urns, and snarling stone lions. Doubtless the most bizarre sight, though, is the **Chemosphere**, 776 Torreyson Drive, a giant UFO house hovering above the canyon on a long pedestal, designed by quirky architect John Lautner and now home to irreverent publisher Benedikt Taschen, who sometimes throws outrageous parties in its alien confines.

There's no real way to explore in depth without your own car and a knowledgeable friend to help pinpoint the sights, spread widely across every hillside. You could use one of the guided tours, but for the most part you're better off doing your own exploring, preferably with a copy of the latest *Thomas Guide* map and, if possible, a detailed and updated guide to LA architecture. You can always pick up one of the ubiquitous "homes of the stars" maps sold on street corners and in souvenir shops, and guide yourself through the hills with a real map as a supplement, though you'll probably be more likely to spot Tom Arnold lounging in a hot tub than Tom Cruise.

The Hollywood sign

The **Hollywood sign** began life on the slopes of Mount Lee in 1923 as little more than a billboard for the **Hollywoodland** development and originally contained its full name; however, in 1949 when a storm knocked down the "H" and damaged the rest of the sign, the "land" part was removed and the rest became the familiar symbol of the area and of the entertainment industry. Unfortunately, the current incarnation has literally lost its radiance: it once featured 4000 light bulbs that beamed the district's name as far away as LA Harbor, but a lack of maintenance and an abundance of thievery put an end to that practice.

The sign has also gained a reputation as a suicide spot, ever since would-be movie star Peg Entwistle terminated her career and life here in 1932, aged 24 – no mean feat, with the sign being as difficult to reach then as it is now. Less fatal mischief has been practiced by students of nearby Caltech, who on one occasion renamed the sign for their school. More unsavory acts of sign desecration have also occurred, most of them too asinine and numerous to mention. Because of this history, there's no public road to the sign (Beachwood Drive comes nearest, but ends at a closed gate) and you'll incur minor cuts and bruises while scrambling to get anywhere near. In any case, infrared cameras and radar-activated zoom lenses have been installed to catch graffiti writers, and innocent tourists who can't resist a close look are also liable for a steep fine. For a much simpler look, you can check out the sign from your computer by visiting ⍟www.hollywoodsign.org.

Lake Hollywood

Hemmed in among the hills between Griffith Park and the Hollywood Freeway, **LAKE HOLLYWOOD** is a small piece of open country in the heart of the city. The clear, calm waters, actually a reservoir intended for drought relief, are surrounded by clumps of pines in which squirrels, lizards, and a few scurrying skunks and coyotes easily outnumber humans. You can't get too near the water, as metal fences protect it from the public, but the footpaths that encircle it are pleasant for a stroll, especially for a glimpse of the stone bearheads that decorate the reservoir's curving front wall. The lake has figured in a few Hollywood films, notably the disaster epic *Earthquake*, which showed the dam bursting and flooding the basin to devastating effect, another in a long line of LA-apocalypse movies.

You can only reach the lake by car. Although opening and closing times vary widely throughout the year, the lake **access road** is generally open from 7am until noon and 2pm until 7pm on weekdays, and 7am until 7.30pm on weekends: to get to it, go north on Cahuenga Boulevard past Franklin Avenue and turn right onto Dix Street, left into Holly Drive and climb to Deep Dell Place; from there it's a sharp left on Weidlake Drive. Follow the winding little street to the main gate.

The Hollywood Bowl

Near the Hollywood Freeway at 2301 N Highland Ave, the **HOLLYWOOD BOWL** is an open-air auditorium that opened in 1921 and has since gained more fame than it probably deserves. The Beatles played here in the mid-1960s, but the Bowl's principal function is as the occasional summer home of the Los Angeles Philharmonic, which gives evening concerts from July to September (information at ℡323/850-2000, ⓦwww.hollywoodbowl.org), along with the pops-oriented Hollywood Bowl Orchestra. These events are less highbrow than you might imagine, many of them featuring spirited crowd-pleasers like *Victory at Sea* and the *1812 Overture*, as well as selections of smooth jazz, film music, and other inoffensive fare. Although not a choice spot for lovers of fine music, the venue can still be fun, with ticket prices starting at $1 (and up to $100 and beyond). If you're really broke, come to the Bowl during summer mornings (Tues, Thurs & Fri 9am–noon) and listen to rehearsals for free. More about the Bowl's history can be gleaned from the video inside the **Hollywood Bowl Museum** (July to mid-Sept Tues–Sat 10am–8pm, Sun 4–7.30pm; mid-Sept to June Tues–Sat 10am–4.30pm; free; ℡323/850-2000) near the entrance. It's not an essential stop by any means, but is worth a visit if you have any affection for the grand old concrete structure. With a collection of musical instruments from around the world, the museum also features recordings of notable symphonic moments in the Bowl's history and architectural drawings by Lloyd Wright, Frank's son (more famous for his Wayfarer's Chapel, p.157, and spooky Sowden House, p.127), who contributed a design for one of the Bowl's many shells. The fifth and newest of these dates from the summer of 2004.

West LA

What is loosely called the Westside of Los Angeles begins immediately beyond Hollywood in **WEST LA** – a broad, general area that is, confusingly, also a small city district near the 405 freeway – which contains some of the city's

N

Art and Design Museum

WEST HOLLYWOOD

Schindler House

Pacific Design Center

Cedars-Sinai Hospital

Beverly Center

Beverly Hills

ACCOMMODATION

Beverly Laurel	H
Bevonshire Lodge	G
Chateau Marmont	B
Grafton	A
Le Montrose	D
Le Parc	E
Orbit	F
The Standard	C

CAFÉS & RESTAURANTS

Astro Burger	11
Barefoot	53
Barney's Beanery	7
La Boheme	18
Ca' Brea	63
Cajun Bistro	3
Campanile	66
Canter's Deli	41
Carlitos Gardel	10
Chianti Cucina	32
Chin Chin	6
Cobras and Matadors	51
Duke's	16
El Carmen	58
El Compadre	2
El Coyote	52
Erewhon	50
Flora Kitchen	61
French Quarter	8
Genghis Cohen	31
Gumbo Pot	59
Inaka	57
India's Clay Oven	67
Jar	47
Jerry's Famous Deli	46
Kate Mantilini	62
Locanda Veneta	54
L'Orangerie	24
Lucques	36
Mark's	25
Matsuhisa	64
Mel's Diner	4
Mickey's	26
Mimosa	48
Mishima	55
Noura	35
Newsroom Café	43
Nyala	72
Pink's Hot Dogs	30
Real Food Daily	40
Surya	60
Swingers	49
Tail o' the Pup	44
Talesai	71
Tommy Tang's	34
Yukon Mining Company	20

BARS AND CLUBS

7969	9
Cat Club	15
Conga Room	69
Doug Weston's Troubadour	38
El Rey Theatre	68
Formosa Café	21
House of Blues	5
Jones	12
Key Club	13
Largo	42
Lava Lounge	1
Molly Malone's	65
Mother Lode	29
Nova Express	45
The Palms	23
Parlour Club	19
The Plaza	28
Rage	27
The Roxy	14
Snake Pit	37
St. Nick's	56
Tempest	33
Tom Bergin's	70
Ultra Suede	39
Viper Room	22
Whisky-a-Go-Go	17

most expensive, and exclusive, neighborhoods. Bordered by the Santa Monica Mountains to the north and the Santa Monica Freeway to the south, and Hollywood and the beach cities to the respective east and west, the swath of West LA, perhaps more than anywhere but the beaches, best embodies the stylish images that the city projects to the outside world. Actually, the reality is often less dazzling: away from the showcase streets are the usual long, residential blocks, only marginally less drab than normal with their better-tended lawns, more upscale supermarkets, and tastier fast food.

One of the best reasons to come to West LA is the impressive collection of the **LA County Museum of Art** (LACMA), on the eastern perimeter of the **Fairfax District**, and forming the centerpiece of the resurgent cultural zone touted as the **Museum Mile** (sitting at the west end of the classic 1930s auto strip known as the Miracle Mile). West of Fairfax Avenue and north of Beverly Boulevard, **West Hollywood** is known for its art and design, loaded with posey restaurants and boutiques, and is surprisingly small-scale, except for a giant design center at its core. **Beverly Hills**, a little farther west, is less friendly but more affluent: you may need an expense account to buy a sandwich but it's a matchless place to indulge in window-shopping on the way to the more roundly appealing **Westwood**. The main activity in this low-rise, Spanish Revival, pedestrianized area has always been movies – seeing them rather than making them. The original Art Deco palaces still retain most of their original glory, and are a hop from the **UCLA Campus**, home to a number of galleries and museums, and altogether more engaging for visitors than the fortress atmosphere of USC. The **Sepulveda Pass** forms the western edge of West LA and leads the visitor to the essential **Getty Center** and the **Skirball Cultural Center**, both positioned high above the basin's turmoil.

Fairfax Avenue and the Miracle Mile

Between Santa Monica and Wilshire boulevards, **FAIRFAX AVENUE** is still the backbone of the city's Jewish culture. Apart from temples, yeshivas, kosher butcher shops, and delis, there's little actually to see here, but by local standards it's a refreshingly vibrant neighborhood, and easily explored on foot.

From Wilshire, Fairfax continues north to the longstanding wooden structures of the **Farmers Market**, 6333 W Third St (Mon–Fri 9am–9pm, Sat 9am–8pm, Sun 10am–7pm; free; Ⓦ www.farmersmarketla.com), a rabbit warren of fast-food stalls and produce stands. Started in 1934 as a little agricultural co-op during the Depression, the market has since expanded to the point where it now sees 40,000 visitors *daily*, and has engendered a monstrous new mall next door: **The Grove** (Ⓦ www.thegrovela.com), a three-level, $100 million colossus that offers branches of all the major chain stores, making parking spots that much more scarce, and expensive. To the east on Third Street, pleasant **Pan Pacific Park** once featured the wondrous Pan Pacific Auditorium, a masterpiece of late Art Deco architecture and filming location for the Olivia Newton John kitsch classic *Xanadu*. Although the structure burned down in a 1989 fire, a hint of its breezy architectural style is still visible in the lettering and curving pylon of an adjacent sports facility. Also at the site is a moving **Holocaust Memorial**, featuring six black-granite columns (each representing a million Jews killed by the Nazis) inscribed with the events taking place in that dark period from 1933 to 1945.

Back at the corner of Fairfax and Wilshire, the premier property development of the time, the **MIRACLE MILE**, stretched along Wilshire eastward to La Brea Avenue and is still lined with faded Art Deco monuments. At this corner, the **May Company** department store was built in 1934 and has been compared to an oversized, golden perfume bottle ever since; its main contemporary function is as the site of **LACMA West**, an exhibition annex to the larger museum down the road (daily noon–5pm, Sat & Sun opens 11am, closed Wed; $9, good for LACMA admission; see below). When this annex isn't showing big-ticket blockbusters, it presents a good selection of experimental work, historic and contemporary pieces by Native American artists, and children's art in a special gallery – with pieces made to be jumped on, played with, and laughed at.

Most of the old department stores that once lined the Miracle Mile have long since closed, but look out for the old site of **Desmond's**, 5514 Wilshire Blvd, a former department store consisting of a Zigzag Moderne tower stepping up from a streamlined two-story pedestal and, just east of La Brea Avenue on Wilshire, the 1929 black-and-gold **Security Pacific Bank**. The bank gives you a small hint of what LA's greatest Art Deco structure, the **Richfield Building** Downtown, must have looked like before it was summarily destroyed in 1968. The most vibrant classic building may be the **El Rey Theater**, 5519 Wilshire Blvd, a thriving concert venue (see "Live music," p.99) with a yellow-and-red design, sleek king's head and flashy neon marquee, unmistakable amid its modern concrete-box neighbors.

LA County Museum of Art

The **LA County Museum of Art**, 5905 Wilshire Blvd (Mon, Tues & Thurs noon–8pm, Fri noon–9pm, Sat & Sun 11am–8pm; $9, students $5; ⓦwww .lacma.org), comprises a rather ugly cluster of oversized beige-and-green blocks, which were plopped down along the Miracle Mile in 1965 and have been mostly dismissed or scorned ever since. Because of this disregard, the museum plans to undergo a massive rebuilding project. Unless you come during a period of reconstruction (the schedule is still up in the air), make sure to check out as much of LACMA's wide-ranging stock of art as you can, some of which is among the best in the world. And if you arrive on a Tuesday before 1pm, check out the schedule of classic Warner Bros films playing in the **Leo S. Bing Theater**, where you can see anything from a film noir to a screwball comedy for only $2 (regular, evening, ticket prices are $9).

LACMA is enormous, and there's no way you could see it all in one trip; you're best off either focusing on the contemporary art and traveling exhibitions in the **Anderson Building** (the concrete block on Wilshire Boulevard) or diving into the fine selection of Old Masters and world art in the **Ahmanson Building** (the concrete block on Ogden Drive). The central attractions here are undoubtedly the **European art rooms**, which begin with a good overview of Greek and Roman art and continue into the medieval era with religious sculptures and ecclesiastical ornamentation, notably a series of stone carvings of the Passion cycle. The Renaissance and Mannerist eras are represented by compelling works such as Paolo Veronese's *Two Allegories of Navigation*, great Mannerist figures filling the frame from an imposing low angle, El Greco's *The Apostle Saint Andrew*, an uncommonly reserved portrait, and Titian's *Portrait of Giacomo Dolfin*, a carefully tinted study by the great colorist. Northern European painters are well represented by Hans Holbein's small, resplendent *Portrait of a Young Woman with White Coif*, a number of Frans Hals' pictures of cheerful burghers, and Rembrandt's probing *Portrait of Marten Looten*.

Alongside many excellent collections of Southeast Asian sculpture and Middle Eastern decorative arts in the Ahmanson Building, the **Fearing Collection** consists of funeral masks and sculpted guardian figures from the ancient civilizations of pre-Columbian Mexico. Where the museum really excels, however, is in its specializations, notably the prints and drawings in the **Rifkind Center for German Expressionist Studies**, which includes a library of magazines and tracts from Weimar Germany, and the **Pavilion for Japanese Art**. Currently the only attractive building on the site, the pavilion was created by iconoclastic architect Bruce Goff to resemble the effects of traditional shoji screens, filtering varying levels and qualities of light through to the interior. Displays include painted screens and scrolls, ceramics, and lacquerware, rivaling the collection of the late Emperor Hirohito as the most extensive in the world, and viewable on a gently sloping ramp that spirals down to a small, ground-floor waterfall that trickles pleasantly amid the near-silence of the gallery.

Other Museum Mile attractions

Beyond LACMA, the roof combs of the Japanese art pavilion make a playful reference to the tusks of a model mastodon sinking slowly into the adjacent **La Brea Tar Pits**, a large pool of smelly tar ("la brea" in Spanish). Tens of thousands of years ago, such creatures tried to drink from the thin layer of water covering the tar in the pits, only to become stuck fast and preserved for modern science. Millions of bones belonging to the animals (and one set of human bones) have been found here, with some of them reconstructed in the next-door **George C. Page Discovery Center** (daily 9.30am–5pm, Sat & Sun opens 10am; $7, students $4.50; Ⓦ www.tarpits.org). At the Center, you can spot the skeletons of your favorite extinct Ice Age–era creatures, from giant ground sloths to menacing saber-toothed tigers – in fact, it was a petroleum geologist, William Orcutt, who found the modern world's first such tiger skull here in 1916. Tar still seeps from the ground, but most of the sticky goo oozes behind chain-link fences.

On the opposite side of LACMA, across from LACMA West at 6060 Wilshire Blvd, the **Petersen Automotive Museum** (Tues–Sun 10am–6pm; $10, parking $6; Ⓣ 323/930-CARS, Ⓦ www.petersen.org) offers three floors loaded with all kinds of motorized vehicles, with periodic exhibits on topics like the golden age of custom cars (the original "tangerine-flake, kandy-kolored streamline baby" in Tom Wolfe's parlance) in the 1950s and 1960s, and "million-dollar" vehicles like the 1919 Bentley and 1961 Ferrari. The ground floor features an asphalt path that takes you on a journey through the city's vehicular past, from crude early-twentieth-century flivvers and seminal hot rods that raced on dangerous wooden tracks, to a classic 1930s gas station, post–World War II gas guzzlers, and so on.

The last significant museum on the Museum Mile is the **Craft and Folk Art Museum**, 5814 Wilshire Blvd (Wed–Sun 11am–5pm; $3.50; Ⓦ www.cafam .org), which has had some difficulty staying open, but if you're interested in this sort of thing – handmade objects from rugs to paintings to mugs to clothing, often with a multicultural twist – it's worth a look if you're in the area. The fairly limited gallery space also hosts a few rotating exhibitions, among them pottery bowls and vases designed by Picasso, international carnival costumes, and local examples of "low-rider" bicycles.

West Hollywood

Between Fairfax Avenue and Beverly Hills, **WEST HOLLYWOOD** has become synonymous with social tolerance and upmarket trendiness, even though it was for many years notorious for its after-hours vice clubs and debauchery. Things

A trip to Culver City

South of West LA and east of Venice you can find one of LA's most overlooked spots, **CULVER CITY** – one of the towns that helped give rise to the American movie industry in the 1910s. Much of this tradition is still visible at the gates of the old Triangle Pictures, 10202 Washington Blvd, the early studio of film pioneer and producer **Thomas Ince**, who was a major figure in the industry until he was mysteriously killed on William Randolph Hearst's yacht. Triangle became MGM by the 1920s, which in turn was swallowed up by Sony. Unfortunately, most of the glorious backlot was torn down, so if you go on a tour of the facility (for which call ☏323/520-TOUR; Mon–Fri 9am–3pm; $20), you'll have to be content with sauntering through massive, often empty soundstages and sets for such TV shows as *Jeopardy!* Fans of *Gone With the Wind*, however, may recognize Ince's other former complex, now the **Culver Studios**, up the road at 9336 Washington Blvd – predictably, this Colonial Revival "mansion" is no more than a facade.

While you're in the area, take a look at the **Hayden Tract**, LA's premier showplace for modern, deconstructivist architecture, lying near Hayden Avenue and National Boulevard and featuring the stunning work of avant-garde master builder **Eric Owen Moss**. A few of his more striking works include Pittard Sullivan, 3535 Hayden Ave, a giant gray box with massive wooden ribs; 8522 National, featuring a jangled-up facade with a white staircase leading to nowhere; The Box, just to the east, another gray box, this one with a riveted cubic window that looks ready to tumble down to the street below; and the huge Samitaur, 3457 S La Cienega Blvd, massive gray warehouse-like offices with gnarled, jagged points and a truly freakish sense of geometry.

If movie history and weird architecture aren't enough for you, top off your trip with a visit to the always bizarre **Museum of Jurassic Technology**, 9341 Venice Blvd (Thurs 2–8pm, Fri–Sun noon–6pm; $6; ⓦwww.mjt.org). As much an art museum as a science center, this institution has little to do with distant history or roving dinosaurs. Rather, it features a great range of oddities from the pseudo-scientific to the paranormal to the just plain creepy. Several regularly rotating exhibits include a trailer-park art display, showing various junk collections next to tiny models of RVs and mobile homes about to be swallowed up by the earth; depictions of folk superstitions, with a memorable image of dead mice on toast used as a cure for bedwetting; written and oral narratives of crank scientists and researchers, many of whom have reputedly disappeared under strange circumstances or gone mad; a strange re-creation of a Baroque-era museum run by a Jesuit scholar; and a series of unearthly insects, like an Amazonian bug that kills its prey through the use of a giant head-spike. However, if you assume the museum is merely the work of a local eccentric, consider that its creator David Wilson was a 2001 winner of a MacArthur "Genius" Award, due largely to his enterprising work for this quirky institution.

changed in 1983, however, when the autonomous city of West Hollywood was established, partly to clean up the place and partly to represent the interests of gays, pensioners, and renters. There are still sleazy areas around La Brea Avenue in the east, but much of the rest has smartened up considerably, from the new sculpture garden down the median of **Santa Monica Boulevard**, the district's main drag, to the flashy dance clubs and designer clothing stores in the rest of the neighborhood. By way of contrast, the eastern end of the boulevard has become home to a large and growing contingent of Russians, many of whom don't mesh too well with the libertine scene around them.

Melrose Avenue, LA's trendiest shopping street, runs parallel to Santa Monica Boulevard four blocks south, a streetscape where neon and Art Deco abound among a rash of secondhand clothiers, exotic antique shops, avant-garde galleries, record shops, and high-attitude restaurants. Since the 1990s, though, a crush of designer boutiques has been gaining ground at the expense of the older, quirkier tenants, the result being a less iconoclastic feel to the strip and more of a homogenized, touristy atmosphere. The west end of Melrose is a rather snooty precinct, with furniture shops and art galleries spread out around the hulking, bright-blue glassy mass of the **Pacific Design Center**, a design marketplace near San Vicente Boulevard, known as the "Blue Whale" for the way it dwarfs its low-rise neighbors, along with its counterpart, a geometric emerald monolith known as the "Green Giant." The center also features a Westside branch of the **Museum of Contemporary Art** (Tues–Fri 11am–5pm, Thurs closes 8pm, Sat & Sun 11am–6pm; free; Ⓦwww.moca.org /museum/moca_pdc.php), focusing on architecture and industrial and graphic design with a sleek, modern bent, and often participating in multi-site exhibitions with the two Downtown branches (see p.108 and p.109).

The stylistic extremes of Melrose Avenue are also reflected in the area's domestic architecture. Four blocks east of La Cienega Boulevard, the 1922 **Schindler House**, 835 N Kings Rd (Wed–Sun 11am–6pm, tours on the hour Sat & Sun 11.30am–2.30pm, and by appointment; $6), was for years the blueprint of California Modernist architecture, with sliding canvas panels designed to be removed in summer, exposed roof rafters, and open-plan rooms facing onto outdoor terraces. Coming from his native Austria via Frank Lloyd Wright's studio to work on the Hollyhock House (p.125), Schindler was so pleased with the California climate that he built this house without any bedrooms, romantically planning to sleep outdoors year-round in covered sleeping baskets on the roof; he misjudged the weather, however, and soon moved inside. Now functioning as the **MAK Center for Art and Architecture**, the house plays host to a range of avant-garde music, art, film, and design exhibitions (program information at Ⓣ323/651-1510, Ⓦwww.makcenter.com). Modern-architecture enthusiasts can also visit Schindler's historic **Mackey Apartments**, 1137 S Cochran Ave, south of the Miracle Mile (tours $5; reserve at Ⓣ323/651-1510), a 1939 geometric white assemblage that looks much more contemporary than it actually is.

Four blocks west of the Schindler House, **La Cienega Boulevard** divides West Hollywood roughly down the middle, separating the chic trendies on the Hollywood side from the establishment couturiers on the Beverly Hills border. La Cienega ("the swamp" in Spanish) holds a mixture of LA's best and priciest restaurants and art galleries, and passes the huge **Beverly Center** shopping mall at Beverly Boulevard – a nightmarish fortress of brown plaster that is nonetheless the city's main consumer icon. A smaller, but more appealing, structure, and one that managed to survive the wrecking ball by some adroit repositioning, is **Tail o' the Pup**, the world-famous hot-dog stand shaped like a (mostly bun) hot dog, which was moved a block away from La Cienega to 329 San Vicente Blvd to make way for a hotel.

Further south, on the Beverly Hills border at 333 S La Cienega, the Academy of Motion Picture Arts and Sciences' **Margaret Herrick Library** (Mon, Tues, Thurs, & Fri 10am–6pm; Ⓦwww.oscars.org/mhl) is a non-circulating research library that holds a huge hoard of film memorabilia and scripts inside a Moorish-style building that was once a water-treatment plant.

Sunset Strip

Above West Hollywood, the roughly two-mile-long conglomeration of restaurants, plush hotels, and nightclubs on Sunset Boulevard has long been known as the **SUNSET STRIP**. These establishments first began to appear during the early 1920s, along what was then a dusty dirt road serving as the main route between the Hollywood movie studios and the West LA "homes of the stars."

F. Scott Fitzgerald and friends spent many leisurely afternoons over drinks here, around the swimming pool of the long-demolished *Garden of Allah* hotel; and the nearby *Ciro's* nightclub was the place to be seen in the swinging 1940s, its husk surviving today as the original *Comedy Store* (see p.207). With the rise of TV, the Strip declined, only reviving in the 1960s when a scene developed around the landmark *Whisky-a-Go-Go* club, which featured seminal rock bands such as Love and Buffalo Springfield, as well as the manic theatrics of Jim Morrison and The Doors. Since then, the striptease clubs and "head shops" have been phased out, and this fashionable area now rivals Beverly Hills for entertainment-industry executives per square foot. Some tourists come to the strip just to see the enormous **billboards**: fantastic commercial murals animated with eye-catching gimmicks, movie ads with names like Jet Li in gargantuan letters, and self-promotions for only-in-LA characters like the busty blonde "Angelyne," who can often be seen looming over Tinseltown in all her Day-Glo splendor.

Greta Garbo was only one of many stars and starlets to appreciate the quirky character of the huge Norman castle that is the **Chateau Marmont** hotel, towering over the east end of Sunset Strip at no. 8221. Built in 1927 as luxury apartments, this stodgy block of white concrete has long been a Hollywood favorite for its elegant private suites and bungalows (see "Accommodation," p.99). Howard Hughes used to rent the entire penthouse so he could keep an eye on the bathing beauties around the pool below; and the hotel made the headlines in 1982 when comedian John Belushi died of a heroin overdose in the bungalow that he used as his LA home. Across the street, the **House of Blues**, no. 8430, is a corrugated tin shack, with imported dirt from the Deep South, that is one of the area's chief tourist attractions, although it pales in comparison with the more authentic scene found around the **Whisky-a-Go-Go**, no. 8901, and the **Roxy**, no. 9009, both of which still offer shows from some of the loudest and angriest rock and punk bands. Other spots, like the **Viper Room**, no. 8852, and the **Sunset Hyatt**, no. 8401, have also established their own sordid histories – Johnny Depp's trendy lair for rockers is the spot where River Phoenix OD'd, and the upscale hotel was the staging ground for the lurid antics of The Who and Led Zeppelin – who took to racing motorcycles down its hallways. Finally, for a dose of chic WeHo art on this convulsive strip, check out the **Art + Design Museum**, in a business complex at 8650 Sunset Blvd (Mon–Sat 10am–6pm, Sun noon–6pm; free; ⓦwww.aplusd.org), which puts on rotating exhibits of the latest trends in art, photography, and architecture, with most of the famous international names represented.

Beverly Hills

Probably the most famous small city in the world, **BEVERLY HILLS** has over the years sucked in more than its fair share of wealthy residents. Predictably, it's not a particularly welcoming place outside the major tourist zones, especially if your clothes don't match the elegant attire of the residents – the pets in Beverly Hills are better dressed and groomed than some of the people elsewhere in LA. Of course, visitors are expected to stroll the designer boutiques of Rodeo Drive, if only to press their noses against the glass. Just don't try to make off with any of the fancy merchandise: Beverly Hills has more police per capita than anywhere else in the US.

Beverly Hills divides into two distinct halves, separated by the disused train line down Santa Monica Boulevard. Below the former tracks is the flashy **Golden Triangle** business district, which fills the wedge between Santa Monica and Wilshire boulevards. **Rodeo Drive** cuts through the triangle in a two-block-long, concentrated showcase of the most expensive names in international fashion. It's a dauntingly stylish area, each boutique trying to outshine the rest: none as yet charges for admission, though some require an invitation. Avoid the tourist trap of **Two Rodeo** at Wilshire, a faux European shopping alley that is the height of pretentious kitsch, its phony cobblestoned street really hiding a parking lot below. For a complete overview of the shopping scene, including Rodeo Drive and beyond, take a trip on the **Beverly Hills Trolley** (July & Aug Tues–Sat noon–5pm; May–June & Sept–Nov Sat noon–4pm; $5), which offers tourists a 40-minute glimpse of the town's highlights, departing hourly from the corner of Rodeo and Dayton Way; also worthwhile is the special Art & Architecture trolley tour (May–Dec Sat 11am; $5; information at ☎310/285-2438), a 50-minute trip through the city's aesthetic high points. Even more appealing is the **Museum of Television and Radio**, 465 N Beverly Drive (Wed–Sun noon–5pm; $10 donation, kids $5; ⓦwww.mtr.org), which features a collection of more than 75,000 TV and radio programs and presents rotating exhibits on such subjects as political image-making in an age of high-tech propaganda, famous advertising characters from the twentieth century, and the best of radio and TV sitcoms, dramas, and thrillers. As LA's first real attempt at providing a media museum of scholarly value, the institution succeeds, even though the city still awaits a decent film museum.

Above Santa Monica Boulevard is the upmarket part of residential Beverly Hills, its gently curving drives converging on the florid pink-plaster **Beverly Hills Hotel**, on Sunset and Rodeo (see "Accommodation," p.99). Built in 1913 to attract wealthy settlers to what was then a town of just five hundred people, the hotel's social cachet makes its *Polo Lounge* a prime spot for movie execs to power-lunch. In the verdant canyons and foothills above Sunset, a number of palatial estates lie hidden away behind landscaped security gates. **Benedict Canyon Drive** climbs up from the hotel near many of them, including, at 1040 Angelo Drive, Harold Lloyd's **Green Acres**, where the actor lived for forty years. With its secret passageways and large private screening room, the home survives intact, though the grounds, which contained a waterfall and a nine-hole golf course, have since been broken up into smaller lots. One of the few estates in the area that is open to the public is the wooded **Virginia Robinson Gardens**, 1008 Elden Way (tours Tues–Thurs 10am & 1pm, Fri 10am; $10, students $5; by appointment only at ☎310/276-5367), which holds six acres of flora, with more than a thousand varieties, including some impressive Australian king palm trees.

The grounds of the biggest house in Beverly Hills, **Greystone Mansion**, are now maintained as a public park by the city, which uses it to disguise a massive underground reservoir. The fifty-thousand-square-foot manor was once the property of oil titan Edward Doheny, who was not only a huge figure in LA history, but was also a major player in the Teapot Dome scandal of the 1920s. Although the house itself is rarely open (except for political fundraisers and filming music videos), you can visit the sixteen-acre **Greystone Park** (daily 10am–5pm) at 905 Loma Vista Drive, which affords fine views of the LA sprawl and its attendant pollution.

Century City

The bland high-rise boxes of **CENTURY CITY**, just west of Beverly Hills, were erected during the 1960s on what was the backlot of the 20th Century-Fox film studio. The district's main focus, as is so often the case in LA, is a large shopping mall, the **Century City Shopping Center**, 10250 Santa Monica

Blvd, loaded with upscale boutiques and department stores, but still a rather grim display of 1960s corporate modernism. To the southwest, look through the front gates of the still-functional **20th Century-Fox** studios to catch a glimpse of the intact New York City street set used for the filming of *Hello Dolly!* – though don't bother trying to get inside the place unless your cousin's a production assistant.

Less frivolously, just east of Century City, below Beverly Hills, an inauspicious white building houses the **Simon Wiesenthal Center for Holocaust Studies** at 9786 W Pico Blvd. The US headquarters of the organization devoted to tracking down ex-Nazis, the center has an extensive library of Holocaust-related documents, photographs, and accounts – but the main draw for visitors is the affecting **Beit HaShoa Museum of Tolerance** (April–Oct Mon–Thurs 11.30am–6.30pm, Fri 11.30am–5pm, Sun 11am–7.30pm; Nov–March Fri 11.30–3pm; $10, students $7; ⓦ www.wiesenthal.com/mot), an extraordinary interactive resource center aimed at exposing the lies of revisionist historians. The most technologically advanced institution of its kind, it uses videotaped interviews to provide LA's frankest examination of the 1992 riots and leads the visitor through re-enactments outlining the rise of Nazism to a harrowing conclusion in a replica gas chamber.

Westwood and UCLA

Just west of Beverly Hills, on the north side of Wilshire Boulevard, **WEST-WOOD** is one of LA's more user-friendly neighborhoods, a grouping of low-slung Spanish Revival buildings that went up in the late 1920s under the name **Westwood Village**, along with the nearby campus of the nascent University of California at Los Angeles (UCLA), which had moved from East Hollywood. It's an area that's easily explored on foot and one very much shaped by the proximity of the university. Because of its ease for pedestrians, the neighborhood has limited parking; for minimum frustration, find a cheap parking lot and dump your vehicle there for a few hours while you explore. Otherwise you'll be constantly feeding a meter or risking a sizeable parking ticket.

Broxton Avenue, Westwood's main drag, is one of West LA's top spots for record stores, video-game arcades, and diners, with some of the pricier eateries crowding out their lower-rent counterparts in recent years. It's also a big movie-going district, with thirty or so cinema screens within a quarter-mile radius. Much of the original Spanish design has survived the intervening years of less imaginative construction, though the ordinary businesses of the old days have been replaced by fancy boutiques and designer novelty shops. The spire at the end of the street, at 961 Broxton Ave, belongs to the 1931 **Fox Village** theater, which, together with the neon-signed **Bruin** across the street, is sometimes used by movie studios for sneak previews of films to gauge audience reaction – you'll not fail to be impressed by the theaters' elegant Art Deco architecture. South of the village, Westwood at Wilshire Boulevard exploded in the 1970s and 1980s with oil-rich high-rise developments, leading to a change of scale that would seem bizarre anywhere outside of LA. Modest detached houses sit next to twenty-story condo towers in which penthouses with private heliports sell for upwards of $12 million.

Inside one of the towers on the corner with Westwood Boulevard, the **UCLA Hammer Museum**, 10899 Wilshire Blvd (Tues–Sat 11am–7pm, Thurs 11am–9pm, Sun 11am–5pm; $5, kids free, Thurs free to all; ⓦ www .hammer.ucla.edu), comprises a sizeable art stash amassed over seven decades by the flamboyant oil tycoon **Armand Hammer**. Art critic Robert Hughes called the paintings here "a mishmash of second- or third-rate works by famous names," but while the Rembrandts and Rubenses may be less than stunning, the nineteenth-century pieces like Van Gogh's intense and radiant *Hospital at Saint Remy* more than make amends. In any case, under the management of neighboring UCLA, the institution has recently become nationally acclaimed for its insightful, sometimes risk-taking contemporary, avant-garde, and multicultural exhibits.

Across Wilshire from the museum, at the end of the driveway behind the tiny Avco cinema, at 1218 Glendon Ave, you'll find Hammer's speckled marble tomb sharing the tiny cemetery of **Westwood Memorial Park** with the likes of movie stars Peter Lorre and Natalie Wood, wildman jazz drummer Buddy Rich, and, to the left of the entrance in the far northeast corner, the lipstick-covered plaque that marks the resting place of Marilyn Monroe. You can also see some of these stars on the radiant mural inside the **Crest Theater**, 1262 Westwood Blvd, notable as well for its brash neon marquee, advertising the best moviehouse outside the Village.

The UCLA campus

The **UCLA CAMPUS** is the dominant feature in Westwood, a group of lovely Romanesque Revival buildings spread across well-landscaped grounds. It's worth a wander if you've time to kill, particularly for a couple of good exhibition spaces. The Student Union building, at the north end of Westwood Boulevard, half a mile north of Westwood, has a bowling alley, a good bookstore, and a "rideboard" offering shared-expense car rides; and there's also a decent coffeehouse in Kerckhoff Hall, just behind.

Before embarking on your exploration, pick up a **map** from various information kiosks scattered around campus. Of things to see, the **Powell Library** (Mon–Thurs 7.30am–11pm, Fri 7.30am–6pm, Sat 9am–5pm, Sun 1–10pm; Ⓦwww.library.ucla.edu) has a spellbinding interior with lovely Romanesque arches, columns, and stairwell, and an array of medieval ornament to complement its ecclesiastical feel. At the northern end of campus, the large **Franklin D. Murphy Sculpture Garden** (always open; free) has seventy works made between 1930 and 1980 by such major names as Jean Arp, Henry Moore, Barbara Hepworth, Henri Matisse, Jacques Lipchitz and Isamu Noguchi, as well as other notable works including Auguste Rodin's *Walking Man*, a stark nude composed of only a torso and legs; Gaston Lachaise's Amazonian *Standing Woman*, a proud, if grotesque, 1932 sculpture; and George Tsutakawa's *OBOS-69*, an odd example of fountain art resembling abstracted TV sets. Free garden tours are available by reservation at Ⓣ310/443-7040.

Just to the east, UCLA's **film school** is less industry-dominated than its counterpart at USC, and has produced offbeat filmmakers like Francis Ford Coppola, Alison Anders, and Alex Cox; it also has one of the most extensive collections of old films and TV programs in the world, examples of which are shown to the public in the James Bridges Theater (tickets usually $7). Check the bulletin board in the lobby, phone Ⓣ310/206-FILM, or visit Ⓦwww.cinema.ucla.edu for the current schedule. Also worth a look is the nearby **Fowler Museum of Cultural History**, Bruin Walk at Westwood Plaza (Wed–Sun noon–5pm, Thurs closes 8pm; free; Ⓦwww.fmch.ucla.edu), which offers an immense range of multicultural art – including ceramics, religious icons, paintings, and musical instruments – with some political works thrown in for good measure. The museum's highlights include a worldwide selection of native masks, more than ten thousand textile pieces from different cultures, and an extensive collection of African and Polynesian art and various folk designs.

The Sepulveda Pass, Getty Center, and Skirball Museum

The gap through the Santa Monica Mountains known as the **SEPULVEDA PASS** is best known for the 405 freeway that cuts through it. Starting at Sunset Boulevard just northwest of UCLA, the pass divides several of LA's most exclusive residential zones. **Brentwood**, to the west, is an insular enclave best known for being the former home of O.J. Simpson and his murdered wife Nicole; to the east, **Bel Air** is a hillside community that is similarly well-heeled and boasts a particularly fine hotel, the *Bel Air* (see p.99).

A short distance away to the west, Getty Center Drive leads up to the monumental **GETTY CENTER** (Sun & Tues–Thurs 10am–6pm, Fri & Sat 10am–9pm; free, parking $7; Ⓦ www.getty.edu), a gleaming complex that towers over the city as oil baron J. Paul Getty once towered over his competitors. Although parking reservations are no longer required, for some arriving by cab provides a simpler alternative. For buses, you'll need to take MTA line #761 from UCLA, and can access that campus from Downtown via line #2 or #302. There are also other lines that serve the Getty from Culver City (Ⓣ310/253-6500, Ⓦ www.culvercity.org/depts_bus.html), and Santa Monica (Ⓣ310/451-5444, Ⓦ www.bigbluebus.com).

Designed by arch-modernist Richard Meier, the center was built for about $1 billion and was a decade in the making. Originally, Meier planned for the whole museum complex to be constructed from white metallic panels – his signature style – but protests from the Brentwood neighbors below forced him to redesign part of it in travertine, in the end a good aesthetic choice for its classical appeal. Although the Getty Foundation plunked down a ten-figure sum for the Center, it still has billions in reserve and must, by law, spend hundreds of millions each year from its endowment. Thus, it plays an elephantine role on the international art scene and can freely outbid its competitors for anything it wants.

Getty started building his massive collection in the 1930s, storing much of it in his house until the Getty Museum opened in 1974, on a bluff overlooking the Pacific Ocean. That site is now closed, but will reopen in Fall 2005 as the **Getty Villa**, a showcase for the foundation's antiquities (see p.153). As the main museum's collection is, not surprisingly, determined by the enthusiasms of Getty himself, there's a formidable array of ornate furniture and **decorative arts**, with clocks, chandeliers, tapestries, and gilt-edged commodes, designed for the French nobility from the reign of Louis XIV, filling several overwhelmingly opulent rooms. Getty was much less interested in **painting** – although he did scoop up a very fine stash from the Renaissance and Baroque periods, including works by Rembrandt, Rubens, and La Tour – but a large collection has been amassed since his death, featuring all the major names from the thirteenth century to the present: drawings by Raphael and Bernini, paintings of the Dutch Golden Age, and a handful of French Impressionists, to name just a few. The museum's biggest catch is probably Van Gogh's *Irises*, which was snatched up for a still undisclosed sum. Elsewhere in the museum, there's an extensive and highly absorbing collection of **photographs** by Man Ray, Laszlo Moholy-Nagy, and other notables, along with a respectable assortment of **sculpture** from the seventeenth to the nineteenth centuries. The museum also boasts a wide collection of **drawings**. Among the best are Albrecht Dürer's meticulous *Study of the Good Thief*, a portrait of the crucified criminal who was converted on the cross; his *Stag Beetle*, precise enough to look as if the bug were crawling on the page itself; Giovanni Piranesi's dramatic image of a ruined, but still monumental, *Ancient*

Port; and William Blake's bizarre watercolor of *Satan Exalting over Eve*, an expressionless devil hovering over his prone captive.

From the museum, continue up the Sepulveda Pass until you come to the **Skirball Cultural Center**, 2701 N Sepulveda Blvd (Tues–Sat noon–5pm, Sun 11am–5pm; $8, students $6; ⓦwww.skirball.org), which devotes its attention to the history, beliefs, and rituals of Judaism. Concentrating on the more mystical elements of the faith, the fairly absorbing center hosts a range of exhibitions and lectures designed to illuminate the American Jewish experience. It also features a wide collection of artifacts, everything from an early copy of the Declaration of Independence to a replica of a Holy Ark (a cabinet for Torah scrolls) from a German synagogue.

Santa Monica Bay

Set along a twenty-mile strand of white beaches and home to some of LA's finest stores, restaurants, and galleries, the small communities that line the **Santa Monica Bay** have none of the smog or searing heat that can make the rest of the metropolis unbearable. The entire area is well served by public transit and near enough to the airport, plus there's a wide array of accommodation, making the area a good base for seeing the rest of LA.

Santa Monica, lined by palm-tree-shaded bluffs above the Pacific Ocean, is the oldest, biggest, and best known of the towns. Once a wild beachfront playground and memorable location for many scenes from the underworld stories of Raymond Chandler, it's a self-consciously healthy and liberal community, which has enticed a large expatriate British community of writers and rock stars. Directly south, **Venice**'s beachfront boardwalk brings together a lively mixture of street performers, roller skaters, and casual voyeurs, while its remaining network of canals gives a hint of what the place used to look like, nearly a hundred years ago.

North from Santa Monica along the Pacific Coast Highway, **Pacific Palisades** is a gathering of hugely expensive houses clinging to the lower foothills of the nearby mountains, though there's really not much to see beyond some pioneering postwar architecture and **Will Rogers State Park**, holding the home and now museum of one of the legends of the American West. A few miles farther along the coastal road, **Topanga Canyon** offers more hiking, its reputation as haven of back-to-nature hippiedom gone, but still with a surprisingly wild set of trails leading into the deep, wooded canyons and sculptured rock outcrops of the Santa Monica Mountains. **Malibu**, at the top of the bay, twenty miles from Santa Monica and the northern and westernmost edge of the LA region, is a whole other world, studded with beach-colony houses owned by those who are famous enough to need privacy and rich enough to afford it, despite the constant threat of hillside wildfires. However, you don't have to be a millionaire to enjoy its fine surfing beaches, or the birds, seals, and whales that seasonally migrate offshore.

Santa Monica

For a lot of Westsiders not rolling in dough, **SANTA MONICA** represents the impossible dream – a low-slung, tolerant beachside burg with rent-controlled apartments and a relaxed air, with easy access to the rest of the city. Of course, the appeal is a paradox, because those same attributes tend to keep the place exclusive – a mix of expensive historic-revival bungalows and out-of-reach "apartments-for-life," coveted zealously by their lucky tenants under that same rent-control policy. However frustrating the place is to move into, Santa Monica is a great spot to visit, a compact, accessible, and friendly bastion of oceanside charm.

Lying across Centinela Avenue from West LA, Santa Monica splits into three distinct portions. The **town** itself, holding a fair chunk of Santa Monica's history and its day-to-day business, is mostly inland but is more interesting closer to the coastal bluffs. Just to the west there's the **pier** and **beach**, while **Main Street**, running south from close to the pier towards Venice, is a style-conscious quarter, with designer restaurants and fancy shops.

The Town

Santa Monica reaches nearly three miles inland, but most of its attractions lie within a few blocks of the beach. Make your first stop the **Visitor Information Office**, 1400 Ocean Ave (daily 10am–4pm; ☎310/393-7593, ⓦwww.santamonica.com), in a kiosk just south of Santa Monica Boulevard in **Palisades Park**, the famous, cypress-tree-lined strip that runs along the top of the bluffs and makes for striking views of the surf below. The visitor center's handy free map shows the layout of the town and the routes of the Santa Monica Big Blue Bus transit system, a useful Westside complement to the MTA network (☎310/451-5444, ⓦwww.bigbluebus.com). There's another visitor center in the nearby mall (see "Information," p.90), but this one's a bit more central.

Two blocks east of Ocean Boulevard, between Wilshire and Broadway, the **Third Street Promenade** is a pedestrian stretch long popular with buskers and itinerant evangelists, which underwent a successful refurbishment a decade ago and now attracts a lively crowd of characters. It's fun simply to hang out in the cafés, bars, and nightclubs, play a game of pool, or browse through the many secondhand and fine-art book shops – though chain retailers have virtually conquered the northern end of the strip between Wilshire Boulevard and Arizona Avenue. It's especially busy on weekends, when huge numbers of tourists and locals jostle for space with sidewalk poets, swinging jazz bands, and street lunatics, under the watchful eyes of water-spewing **dinosaur sculptures** draped in ivy. The mall is anchored at its southern end by the expensive **Santa Monica Place**, a white stucco pile that's among architect Frank Gehry's less inspired work. It has the usual assortment of chain stores and a mandatory food court.

Santa Monica has a number of fine **galleries** selling works by emerging local and international artists. **Bergamot Station**, the city's aesthetic hub, is a collection of former tramcar sheds at 2525 Michigan Ave, near the intersection of 26th and Cloverfield, which houses a multitude of small art galleries (most open Tues–Fri 10am–6pm; free). Many of LA's latest generation of artists have shown here, and the highlight is, of course, the **Santa Monica Museum of Art**, in Building G-1 (Tues–Sat 11am–6pm, $3; ⓦwww.smmoa.org). This is a good space to see some of the most engaging and curious work on the local scene, in temporary exhibits ranging from simple paintings to complex, space-demanding installation art. Among the regular galleries, don't miss the **Gallery of Functional Art**, Building E-3 (free; ⓦwww.galleryoffunctionalart.com), which offers an array of mechanical gizmos and eccentric furniture like cubist lamps and neon-lit chairs. Further inland, if you want to check out more adventurous art, the **Side Street Projects**, 1629 18th St (Wed–Sat noon–6pm; free; information at ☎310/829-0779), is another of the town's ambitious young art spaces – involving both education and exhibition – which forms a part of the **18th Street Arts Complex**, 1639 18th St (ⓦwww.18thstreet.org),

VENICE & SANTA MONICA

WILSHIRE BOULEVARD
ARIZONA AVENUE
SANTA MONICA
SANTA MONICA BLVD
BROADWAY
COLORADO AVENUE
OLYMPIC BOULEVARD
SANTA MONICA FREEWAY
MICHIGAN AVENUE
DELAWARE AVENUE
PICO BOULEVARD
BAY STREET
GRANT STREET
PACIFIC STREET
PEARL STREET
CEDAR STREET
PINE STREET
MAPLE STREET
OCEAN PARK BOULEVARD
OAK STREET
HILL STREET
ASHLAND AVENUE
SUNSET AVE
MARINE STREET
NAVY ST
OZONE ST
MACHADO ST
ROSE AVENUE
FLOWER AVENUE
SUNSET AVE
VERNON AVENUE
INDIANA AVENUE
BROOKS AVENUE
BROADWAY
WESTMINSTER AVENUE
SAN JUAN AVE
SANTA CLARA AVE
CALIFORNIA AVENUE
PALMS BLVD
VENICE BOULEVARD
WASHINGTON AVENUE
MILDRED AVENUE
OLIVE AVENUE
ZANJA ST

Third Street Promenade
Visitor Center
Bus Station
Santa Monica Place
18th Street Arts Complex
Memorial Park
Woodlawn Cemetery
Santa Monica College
City Hall
Civic Auditorium
Bay Park
Hotchkiss Park
Joslyn Park
Los Amigos Park
California Heritage Museum
Ocean Park
Ballerina Clown Sculpture
Chiat / Day / Mojo
Race Through the Clouds
Westminster Park
Muscle Beach
Windward Colonnade
Beyond Baroque Arts Center
Venice Canals

Santa Monica Pier
Pacific Park
Santa Monica Pier Aquarium

P A C I F I C   O C E A N

Santa Monica Beaches
Venice Beach

Bergamot Station
Museum of Flying

ACCOMMODATION

Bayside	H
Cadillac	I
Carmel	C
HI-LA Santa Monica	B
Hostel California	K
Inn at Venice Beach	L
Loew's Santa Monica Beach	E
Santa Monica Beach Travelodge	D
Santa Monica-Pico Blvd. Travelodge	G
Shangri-La	A
Venice Beach Cotel	J
Viceroy	F

Venice Pier

0   600 yds

N

CAFÉS & RESTAURANTS				BARS & CLUBS	
Bagel Nosh	8	Joe's	35	14 Below	22	Rusty's Surf Ranch	21
Border Grill	3	Lighthouse Buffet	10	Anastasia's Asylum	4	Sugar	17
Café 50s	34	Mani's Bakery	23	Circle Bar	30	Temple Bar	5
Chaya Venice	32	Mariasol	20	Finn McCool's	26	Ye Olde King's Head	14
Chinois on Main	25	Michael's	2	Gotham Hall	13	Zanzibar	1
Crocodile Café	12	Norm's	19	Harvelle's	16		
Drago	7	Reel Inn	15	Library Alehouse	28		
Figtree's Café	33	Shambala Café	18	Mor	31		
Flower of Siam	24	Wildflour Pizza	27	Novel Café	29		
Gaucho Grill	9	Wolfgang Puck Express	11	Red Room Café	36		

a hip and modern center for various types of art, much of it experimental. The performance space **Highways**, 1651 18th St (☎310/315-1459, ⓦwww .highwaysperformance.org), is one such example in the complex (see p.208), showcasing edgy political and gender-based work.

Elsewhere inland, it's less easy to stumble upon Santa Monica's worthwhile sights. On the northern border, **San Vicente Boulevard**'s grassy tree-lined strip is a joggers' freeway, while south of San Vicente, the flashy eateries and boutiques of **Montana Avenue** are better for spotting B-list stars than for finding any bargains.

Santa Monica Pier and around

Jutting out into the bay at the foot of Colorado Avenue, the **Santa Monica Pier** (ⓦwww.santamonicapier.org) is a great example of an old-fashioned, festive beach-town hub, with a giant helter-skelter and a restored 1922 wooden **carousel** (March–Sept Mon–Thurs 11am–5pm, Fri–Sun 11am–7pm; Oct–March Thurs–Mon only; 50¢ a ride), with more than forty colorful hand-carved horses, featured in the 1973 movie *The Sting*. Although the familiar thrill rides of **Pacific Park** (June–Aug daily 11am–11pm, Sat & Sun closes at 12.30am; $20–22, kids $11; ☎310/260-8744, ⓦwww.pacpark.com) may catch your eye, featuring a rollercoaster and various other amusements, it's still a rather overpriced attempt to lure back the suburban families – you're better off saving your money for a real theme park. Better yet, visit the **Santa Monica Pier Aquarium**, below the pier at 1600 Ocean Front Walk (Tues–Fri 2–5pm, Sat & Sun 12.30–5pm; $5; ☎310/393-6149, ⓦwww.healthebay.org/smpa), where you can find out about marine biology and get your fingers wet touching sea anemones and starfish.

Just south of the pier, Santa Monica has its own miniature version of Venice's Muscle Beach: a **workout area** loaded with rings, bars, and other athletic equipment designed for would-be bodybuilders and fitness fans. If you'd rather match wits than compare biceps, visit the adjacent **International Chess Park**, a fancy name for a serviceable collection of chessboards that attracts a range of players from rank amateurs to slumming pros. Finally, a **bike path** begins at the pier and heads twenty miles south, a stretch that ranks as one of the area's top choices for cycling. On foot, you can wander south along the beach to Pico Boulevard and head two blocks inland to Main Street.

Main Street

The completion of the Santa Monica Freeway in 1965 brought Santa Monica's beachfront homes within a fifteen-minute drive of Downtown and isolated the bulk of the town from **MAIN STREET**, five minutes' walk from the pier. Here, the collection of novelty shops, kite stores, and classy restaurants now forms one of the most popular shopping districts on the Westside. Beyond shopping, eating, and drinking, though, there's not much to do or see. One of the few actual sights, the **California Heritage Museum**, 2612 Main St (Wed–Sun 11am–4pm; $5; ⓦwww.californiaheritagemuseum.org), is the city's effort to preserve some of its architectural past. Two houses were moved here to escape demolition: one house – the museum itself – hosts temporary displays on Californian cultural topics like old-time amusement parks, and permanent exhibits on regional pottery, furniture, and decorative arts, while the other house is known as the *Victorian Restaurant* (☎310/392-4956, ⓦwww.thevictorian .com) and serves tea on its patio at weekends. For a more comprehensive day of consumerism, you can travel between Main Street, the Pier, and the Prom-enade on the **Tide Shuttle** (every 15min; Sun–Thurs noon–8pm, Fri & Sat noon–10pm; 25¢; ⓣ310/451-5444), ponying up a mere quarter to hit many of the town's shopping highlights.

Venice

Immediately south of Santa Monica, fluidly connected by Main Street, **VENICE** was laid out in the marshlands of Ballona Creek in 1905 by developer **Abbot Kinney** as a romantic replica of the northern Italian city. Intended to attract artists to sample its pseudo-European air, this twenty-mile network of canals, lined by sham palazzos and waterfront homes, never really caught on, although a later remodel into a low-grade version of Coney Island postponed its demise for a few decades. With the coming of the automobile, many of the canals were filled in, and the area fell into disrepair, with most of the home sites being taken over by oil wells. This grim era features in Orson Welles' 1958 film *Touch of Evil*, in which derelict Venice stars as a seedy Mexican border town.

Kinney was, however, strangely ahead of his time. A few evocative shards of the original plan survive, and the bohemian atmosphere has since worked to draw in the artistic community he was targeting. Main Street, for instance, is home to the offices of advertising firm **Chiat/Day/Mojo**, just south of Rose Street, marked by Claes Oldenburg's huge pair of binoculars at the entrance and Frank Gehry–designed offices. Just to the north, the frightening **Ballerina Clown**, a gargantuan sculpture by Jonathan Borofsky, looms over a nearby intersection, its stubbly clown head and lithe body making for an unforgettably disturbing combination. Elsewhere, a strong alternative arts scene centers around the **Beyond Baroque Literary Arts Center and Bookshop** in the old City Hall at 681 Venice Blvd (Feb–July & Oct–Dec Mon–Fri 11am–6pm; ⓣ310/822-3006, ⓦwww.beyondbaroque.org), which holds regular readings and workshops of poetry, prose, and drama, while next door, SPARC offers pricey tours of some of the more remarkable murals around town.

Windward Avenue is the town's main artery, running from the beach into what was the Grand Circle of the canal system – now paved over and ringed by a number of galleries and the Venice post office, inside of which a mural depicts the early layout. Leading to the beach, the original Romanesque **arcade**, around the intersection with Pacific Avenue, is alive with health-food shops, used-record stores and roller-skate rental stands. Here and there colorful and portentous giant **murals** – depicting everything from a ruined freeway overpass cut short in midair to Botticelli's Venus in roller skates – cover the whitewashed walls of the original hotels, and of the Venice Pavilion on the beach. The few remaining **canals** are just a few blocks south, where the original quaint little bridges survive. It's a great place to walk around, though if you're in a car and wish to avoid the tiny, maze-like streets between the canals, there's only one way to see the area. Head north on Dell Avenue between Washington and Venice boulevards, a route that often draws a procession of slow-moving motorized gawkers. Also a short distance inland, much of **Abbot Kinney Boulevard** is a fine stretch for hanging out, sipping a latte, deciphering modern art, and having a bite in a smart eatery.

Still, it's **Venice Beach** that draws most people to the town, and nowhere else does LA parade itself quite so openly, colorfully, and aggressively as it does along the **Venice Boardwalk**, a wide pathway also known as Ocean Front Walk. Year-round at weekends and every day in summer it's packed with jugglers, fire-eaters, Hare Krishnas, roller-skating guitar players and, of course, teeming masses of tourists. West of Windward is **Muscle Beach**, a legendary weightlifting center where serious hunks of muscle pump serious iron, and high-flying gymnasts swing on the adjacent rings and bars. If you'd like to check the place out yourself, contact the Venice Beach Recreation Center, 1800 Ocean Front Walk, for more information (☎310/399-2775), or if you're a real weightlifting enthusiast, visit in July when the Bench Press Championships are held here, one of many such competitions taking place during the year. There are **rental shacks** along the beach for picking up skates, surfboards, or bikes, and plenty of merchants selling Day-Glo tube tops and wraparound sunglasses – if you really want to fit in with the athletic locals.

Incidentally, be warned that Venice Beach **at night** can be a dangerous place, and walking on the beach after dark is illegal in many stretches.

Pacific Palisades and Will Rogers State Historic Park

The district of **PACIFIC PALISADES**, rising on the bluffs two miles north of Santa Monica pier, is slowly but very surely falling away into the bay, most noticeably on the point above Pacific Coast Highway – otherwise known as "PCH." With each winter's rains, a little bit more of the bluffs gets washed away in mud slides, blocking traffic on PCH, and gradually shrinking the backyards of the cliff-top homes. Although there are few places of interest among the suburban ranch houses, a handful of the most influential buildings of postwar LA were constructed here. The **Eames House**, for example, at 203 Chautauqua St, was fashioned out of prefabricated industrial parts in 1947 as part of the influential Case Study Program. Only the grounds and exterior are viewable, by appointment only (Mon–Fri 10am–4pm; free; ☎310/459-9663, ⓦwww.eamesoffice.com). Also appealing is the **Schwartz House**, 444 Sycamore Ave, designed in 1994 by Pierre Koenig, whose unique design includes a black-steel frame and foundation pivoted at a 30-degree angle from the rest of the boxy gray house, making for an unusual Rubik's Cube effect, which also has the function of keeping the interior out of the glare of the rising sun.

A mile east along Sunset Boulevard is **WILL ROGERS STATE HISTORIC PARK** (summer daily 8am–dusk; rest of year daily 8am–6pm; free; ☎310/454-8212), a steep climb from the MTA bus (#2, #302) stop. This was the home and ranch of the Depression-era cowboy philosopher and journalist **Will Rogers**, one of America's most popular figures of the time, and renowned for saying that he "never met a man he didn't like." After his death in a plane crash in 1935, there was a nationwide thirty-minute silence. The overgrown ranch-style house serves as an informal **museum**, though this will be closed for renovation until 2006; when it reopens, it will likely be filled once more with cowboy gear and Native American art. The 200-acre park – which is still open – has miles of foot and bridle paths, including polo grounds where matches take place during the spring and summer (April–Oct Sat 2–4pm, Sun 10am–noon; free). Just north of Sunset Boulevard's intersection with PCH, the **Getty Villa** sits on a picturesque bluff overlooking the ocean. Once the site of the Getty Museum (now in West LA; see p.147), the villa will be reopening in Fall 2005 as a center for the Getty's considerable cache of antiquities, and the grounds have been remodeled to effect the look of a stylish hillside villa from the world of ancient Rome. Luckily, as with other facilities administered by this multibillion-dollar trust, the entrance should be free, though parking could be a problem (call for an update at ☎310/440-7300, or visit ⓦwww.getty.edu).

Topanga Canyon

Surprisingly for LA, **TOPANGA CANYON** provides an excellent natural refuge. With hillsides covered in golden poppies and wildflowers, a hundred and fifty thousand acres of these mountains and the adjacent seashore have been protected as the Santa Monica Mountains National Recreation Area. Park rangers offer free guided hikes throughout the mountains most weekends (information and reservations ☎818/597-9192), and there are self-guided trails through the canyon's Topanga State Park, off Old Topanga Canyon Road at the crest of the mountains, with spectacular views over the Pacific. If you'd like to find out more, contact the visitor center in neighboring Thousand Oaks, 401 W Hillcrest Drive (daily 9am–5pm; ☎805/370-2301, ⓦwww.nps.gov/samo).

The nearby community of **TOPANGA** was in the 1960s a well-known proving ground for West Coast rock music, when Neil Young, the Byrds, and other artists moved here and held all-night jam sessions in the sycamore groves along Topanga Creek. Few real bohemians are left, however, and most of the upscale residents just affect an enlightened, pseudo-hippie New Age style. If you'd like to revisit a bit of the old arty spirit, the **Theatricum Botanicum**, 1419 Topanga Canyon Blvd, is a wooded outdoor amphitheater known for its classical and modern plays, including well-regarded summer performances of Shakespeare ($15–25, kids $8; information and tickets at ☎310/455-3723, ⓦwww.theatricum.com). Before leaving the area, don't miss **Red Rock Canyon**, off Old Topanga Canyon Road via Red Rock Road (ⓦsmmc.ca.gov or www.lamountains.com), a stunning red-banded sandstone gorge that was formerly a Boy Scout retreat. Now a California state park, the colorful rock formations, surrounding gardens, and riparian wildlife give you a good reason to leave your car behind and go exploring.

Malibu

Everyone has heard of **MALIBU**, and while its upscale Hollywoodized image is not so very far from the truth, you might not think so on arrival. As you enter the small town, the succession of ramshackle surf shops and fast-food stands scattered along both sides of PCH around the graceful Malibu Pier don't exactly reek of money, but the secluded estates just inland are as valuable as any in the entire country.

Facing south by the pier, **Surfrider Beach** was a major surfing nexus in the 1950s, first gaining traction as the sport was brought over from Hawaii and early Southern California pioneers mastered it. However, it was really popularized in the 1960s by movies such as *Gidget* and *Beach Blanket Bingo*, starring the likes of Sandra Dee, Annette Funicello, and Frankie Avalon. It's still a big surfing spot: the waves are best in late summer, when storms off Mexico cause them to reach upwards of eight feet – not huge for serious pros, but big enough for you. Just beyond is **Malibu Lagoon State Park** (daily 8am–dusk), a nature reserve and bird refuge; birdwatching walks around the lagoon are offered some weekends. A small **museum**, 23200 PCH (tours Wed–Sat 11am–3pm; donation), gives you the historical rundown, from the Chumash era up to the arrival of Hollywood movie stars. If you must get a glimpse of the elite, visit the **Malibu Country Mart**, 3835 Cross Creek Rd, where A- and B-listers can often be found buying veggies or sipping espressos.

Much of **Malibu Creek State Park**, at the crest of Malibu Canyon Road along Mulholland Drive, used to belong to 20th Century-Fox studios, which filmed many Tarzan pictures here and used the chaparral-covered hillsides to simulate South Korea for the TV show *M*A*S*H*. The 4000-acre park includes a large lake, some waterfalls, and nearly fifteen miles of hiking trails, making it crowded on summer weekends but fairly accessible and pleasant the rest of the time (for information on camping here, see "Accommodation," p.103). Nearby **Paramount Ranch**, near Mulholland Drive at 2813 Cornell Rd, is another old studio backlot, with a phony railroad crossing, cemetery, and Western movie set used for, among other things, the interminable TV drama *Dr. Quinn, Medicine Woman*. Finally, a few miles west of Cornell Road, the glory days of the **Peter Strauss Ranch** are long past, when it was known as "Lake Enchanto" in the 1930s and 1940s, and boasted colorful rides and chic resort amenities. These days, little is left of the resort, but the site has become an excellent natural refuge with hiking trails and occasional exhibitions of sculpture, and classical and blues concerts (information at ☎818/597-1036).

Given Malibu's walled-off security and privacy, the **Barbra Streisand Center**, located in Ramirez Canyon Park north of Point Dume and PCH at 5750 Ramirez Canyon Rd (individual tours Wed 1–4pm, groups Tues & Thurs 1–4pm; $35; by reservation only at ☎310/589-2850, ⓦwww.lamountains .com), comes as a bit of a shock, a 22-acre complex of houses and gardens that the entertainer donated to the Santa Monica Mountains Conservancy in 1993. Amid extensive flower, herb, and fruit gardens, you can get a glimpse into her former residences, highlighted by the "Deco House," with its red-and-black colors, geometric decor, and stainless-steel panels taken from Downtown's Richfield Building, before that Art Deco monument was destroyed in 1968.

The beaches

Five miles up the coast from Malibu Pier, **Zuma Beach** is the largest of the LA County beaches, easily connected to the San Fernando Valley by Kanan Dume Road. Adjacent **Point Dume State Beach**, below the bluffs, is more relaxed, especially up and over the rocks at its southern tip, where **Pirate's Cove** is used by nudists. The rocks here are also a good place to look out for seals and migrating gray whales in winter, as the point above – best accessed by car or a longish path – juts out into the Pacific at the northern lip of Santa Monica Bay. **El Matador State Beach**, about 25 miles up the coast from Santa Monica, is about as close as you can get to the private-beach seclusion enjoyed by the stars, thanks to its northern location and an easily missable turn off PCH. Another five miles along the highway, where Mulholland Drive reaches the ocean, **Leo Carrillo** ("ca-REF-oh") **State Park** marks the northwestern border of LA County and the end of the MTA bus route (#434). The mile-long sandy beach is divided by Sequit Point, a small bluff that has underwater caves and a tunnel you can pass through at low tide, and is also one of LA's best campgrounds (see "Accommodation," p.103). Five miles farther on, at **Point Mugu State Park**, there are some good walks through mountain canyons, and campsites right on the beach.

The South Bay and LA Harbor

South of Venice, the charmless high-rise condos of Marina del Rey and the faded resort town of Playa del Rey offer little to interest visitors; beyond that, the coast – seen along the oceanside strip of Vista del Mar – is dominated by the perimeter of LAX, a huge oil refinery, and LA's main sewage-treatment plant. South of this industrial zone, however, is an eight-mile strip of beach towns – **Manhattan Beach**, **Hermosa Beach**, and **Redondo Beach** – collectively known as the **SOUTH BAY**. These are more low-slung, quieter, more suburban, and smaller than the Westside beach communities, and they're also well connected to the rest of the city – within easy reach of LAX and linked by regular buses to Downtown.

Visible all along this stretch of the coast, the large green peninsula of **Palos Verdes** is an upmarket residential area, while the comparatively rough-hewn working town of **San Pedro** is sited on the LA Harbor, the third-busiest cargo port in the world (after a pair in China) and still growing. On the other side of the harbor, **Long Beach**, connected to Downtown by bus #60, is best known as the resting place of the *Queen Mary*, even though it's also the region's second-largest city, with nearly half a million people. Perhaps the most enticing place in the area is **Santa Catalina Island**, twenty miles offshore and easily reached by ferry. It's almost completely conserved wilderness, with many unique forms of plant and animal life and just one main town, **Avalon**.

Manhattan, Hermosa, and Redondo Beaches

Along the South Bay cities' shared beach boardwalk known as **The Strand** (which ends at Redondo Beach), the joggers and roller skaters are more likely to be locals than poseurs from other parts of LA. Each city has at least one municipal pier and a beckoning strip of white sand, with most oceanside locations equipped for surfing and beach volleyball – regular world-class events for both sports are held here, and a two-week international surf festival occurs each August. The most northerly city, **MANHATTAN BEACH**, is a likable place with a healthy, well-to-do air, home mainly to white-collar workers whose middle-class stucco homes tumble towards the beach, uncluttered by high-rise hotels. These days, Manhattan Beach's **pier** is used mainly for strolling by tourists, but is also the site of the accurately named **Roundhouse**, sitting at the end, which houses a fine **aquarium** (Mon–Fri 3pm–dusk, Sat & Sun 10am–dusk; $2), a mildly interesting spot where you can look at crabs, eels, lobsters, squid, and – in their own "touch tank" – tide-pool creatures like anemones and sea stars. By contrast, the **Manhattan Beach Art Center**, 1560 Manhattan Beach Blvd (Tues & Sat 1–5pm, Wed 2–8pm, Thurs 2–6pm; free), presents contemporary work from regional artisans, working in media from glass to sculpture and photography. The art center lies across from **Polliwog Park**, a pleasant enough green space, which in the summer is one of the sites that hosts "**Shakespeare by the Sea**" (periodically Thurs–Sun 6, 7 & 8pm; free; Ⓦ www.shakespearebythesea .org), a series of local performances of the Bard at South Bay parks, including this and Point Fermin in San Pedro, among many others.

To the south, **HERMOSA BEACH**, across Longfellow Avenue, is more downscale than Manhattan Beach, its houses smaller and less showy, with a lingering bohemian feel of the 1960s and 70s in certain spots. It does, however, have a lively beachside strip, which is most energetic near the foot of the **pier** on 12th Street. Packed with restaurants and clubs (among them one of the South Bay's best-known nightspots, *The Lighthouse*; see p.199), this has long been a major hangout for revelers of all stripes. A good time to come is during the **Fiesta Hermosa** (Ⓦ www.fiestahermosa.com), a three-day event held over Memorial Day that's good for fun music (including surf rock), tasty food, and displays of regional arts and crafts.

Despite some decent strips of sand and fine views of Palos Verdes' stunning greenery, **REDONDO BEACH**, south of Hermosa, is much less inviting than its relaxed neighbor. Condos and hotels line the beachfront, and the yacht-lined King's Harbor is off limits to curious visitors.

Palos Verdes

A great green hump marking LA's southwest corner, **PALOS VERDES** is a rich enclave holding a number of gated communities, but can be enjoyable for the bluffs and coves along its protected coastline. **Malaga Beach**, by Torrance County Beach just south of Redondo, is a popular scuba-diving spot; **Abalone Cove**, reached from the parking lot on Berkentine Road, off Palos Verdes Drive, boasts rock and tide pools and offshore kelp beds with rock scallops, sea urchins, and, of course, abalone.

While you're in the area, don't miss **Wayfarer's Chapel**, 5755 Palos Verdes Drive S (Ⓦ www.wayfarerschapel.org), designed by Frank Lloyd Wright's son, Lloyd, as a tribute to the eighteenth-century Swedish scientist and mystic Emanuel Swedenborg. Its practical, modern function, though, is as LA's ultimate spot for weddings, the redwood grove around the chapel symbolically growing and weaving itself into the glass-framed structure. A few miles farther on, just before the end of Palos Verdes Drive, **Point Fermin Park** is a small tip of land poking into the ocean that is LA's southernmost point. Here, the squat wooden **lighthouse** (tours Sat 1–3.30pm; donation) is an 1874 Eastlake structure with a cupola that once contained a 6600-candlepower light which beamed 22 miles out to sea, and a whale-watching station lets you read up on the winter migrations. Bottle-nosed dolphins can often be seen during their fall departure and spring return, and there's also the less seasonally dependent thrill of spotting hang-gliders swooping down off the cliffs.

From the park, it's an easy stroll along Bluff Place and down the 29th Street stairway to Cabrillo Beach and the excellent **Cabrillo Marine Aquarium**, 3720 Stephen White Drive (Tues–Fri noon–5pm, Sat & Sun 10am–5pm; $5, parking $7; Ⓦ www.cabrilloaq.org), displaying a diverse collection of marine life that has been imaginatively and instructively assembled: everything from predator snails and the curious "sarcastic fringehead" to larger displays on otters, seals, and whales.

Finally, about ten miles inland on the peninsula and not really close to anything else worth seeing, the curious **South Coast Botanic Garden**, 26300 Crenshaw Blvd (daily 9am–5pm; $7; Ⓦ www.palosverdes.com/botanicgardens), was once the site of a huge landfill stuffed with 3.5 tons of trash, but has since been covered over and turned into a charming array of themed gardens filled with cacti, ferns, bromeliads, and several different types of palm trees, and even a small French-style garden. The only hint of its former life is its undulating terrain: unsettling evidence of the refuse slowly shifting below the surface.

San Pedro and Wilmington

From the Cabrillo Aquarium, three miles farther on along Bluff Place, the scruffy harbor district of **SAN PEDRO** stands in stark contrast to the affluence of Palos Verdes. It was a small fishing community until the late nineteenth century, when the construction of the LA Harbor nearby brought a huge influx of labor, much of it from Portugal, Greece, and Yugoslavia. Many of these, and their descendants, never left the place, lending a striking ethnic mix to the town. A good chunk of the district's nautical history is revealed in the **Maritime Museum**, on the harbor's edge at the foot of Sixth Street (Tues–Sat 10am–5pm, Sun noon–5pm; $3; Ⓦ www.lamaritimemuseum.org), housed in a grand WPA-Moderne structure that was the Municipal Ferry Building from World War II up to the early 1960s. These days, the old ferry tower is a storehouse for art and artifacts from the glory days of San Pedro's fishing and whaling industries, focusing on everything from old-fashioned clipper-ship voyages to contemporary diving expeditions. Farther north, the **SS Lane Victory**, in Berth 94, off Swinford Street (daily 9am–4pm; $3; ⓦ www.lanevictory.org), is a huge, ten-thousand-ton cargo ship that was built in the shipyard in 1945 for World War II, operated in Korea and Vietnam; today it's maintained by the Merchant Marine. A tour will take you through its many cramped spaces, including the engine and radio rooms, crew quarters, galley, and bridge.

Four blocks west of the Maritime Museum, old downtown San Pedro has been refurbished in recent years, thanks in part to the restoration of the opulent **Warner Grand Theater**, 478 W Sixth St (ⓣ310/548-7672, ⓦ www.warnergrand.org), a terrific 1931 Zigzag Moderne moviehouse and performing-arts center with dark geometric details, grand columns, and sunburst motifs, a style that almost looks pre-Columbian. Also part of the clean-up effort is the **San Pedro Trolley** (Fri–Mon 10am–6pm; $1), a collection of three classic 1908 Pacific Electric Red Cars (two replicas, one restored) brought back to life as a tourist route linking most of the city's major attractions, paralleling Harbor Boulevard and connecting the *SS Lane Victory* with the Cabrillo Marina at 22nd Street. Although it's accessible from the trolley, don't bother with the banal **Ports o' Call Village** – a dismal batch of wooden and corrugated-iron huts supposedly capturing the flavor of seaports around the world.

Between San Pedro and Long Beach (connected by LADOT bus #142) soar two tall road bridges, giving aerial views of oil wells and docks, and the vast Naval Supplies Center. Just inland, the community of **WILMINGTON** is the site of the Greek Revival **Banning House**, 401 E Main St (guided tours hourly Tues–Thurs 12.30–2.30pm, Sat & Sun 12.30–3.30pm; $3; ⓦ www .banningmuseum.org), the opulent Victorian home of mid-nineteenth-century entrepreneur Phineas Banning, who made his fortune when the value of his land increased astronomically as the harbor was developed. Through his promotion of the rail link between the harbor and central LA he also became known as "the father of Los Angeles transportation" – back when the local transportation system was one of the best in the world. While you're in the area, make sure to visit the **Drum Barracks and Civil War Museum**, 1052 Banning Blvd (hourly tours Tues–Thurs 10am–1pm, Sat & Sun 11.30am–2.30pm; $3; ⓦ www.drumbarracks.org), the Civil War–era federal staging point for attacks in the Southwest against Confederates and, later, Indians. The sole remaining (rickety) building houses a collection of military antiques and memorabilia, such as a 34-star US flag, and assorted guns, muskets, and weaponry, including an early prototype of a machine gun.

Long Beach

Combined with San Pedro, **LONG BEACH** is home to the third-largest port in the world, and biggest outside China – making it the point of entry for the majority of goods shipped (and then trucked) to the Western US. Once the stomping ground of off-duty naval personnel, the city's porn shops and sleazy bars lasted until the 1980s, when a billion-dollar cash infusion into the town led – in downtown at least – to a spate of new office buildings, convention center, hotels, and shopping mall, and a preservation campaign that has restored some of the best c.1900 buildings on the coast. Inland from downtown, however, it's a different story – grim, uninviting housing developments on the perimeter of South Central LA.

Running from Magnolia Avenue to Alamitos Boulevard and Ocean Boulevard to Tenth Street, **downtown Long Beach** offers a wide array of boutiques, antique dealers, and bookstores, many of them around a three-block strip known as **The Promenade**, lined with touristy restaurants and stores that can get quite busy on weekend nights. Two blocks west of the Promenade, at the terminus of the Blue Line light railway to Downtown LA, **Pine Avenue** has some of the city's best-preserved architecture – historic-revival buildings that have since been reborn as hotels, artists' lofts, galleries, and nightclubs. For a closer look at Long Beach's historic and architectural gems, preservation society Long Beach Heritage runs a bimonthly **tour** that begins at 315 W Third St, just a few blocks to the west (first & third Sat of month 10am–12.30pm; $5; reserve at ☎562/493-7019, ⊛www.lbheritage.org).

To the south, **Shoreline Village** is a waterfront entertainment belt that used to feature carnival rides and a carousel up to the 1940s, but is now mostly a ragtag collection of shops and restaurants. You can, however, explore the intriguing, though pricey, **Aquarium of the Pacific** (daily 9am–6pm; $19, kids $11; ⊛www.aquariumofpacific.org), which exhibits the aquatic flora and fauna of three distinct climates and regions from around the world, including the local Southern Pacific, Northern Pacific, and tropical zones. Nearby, the other major draw is the **Tallship American Pride**, a sleek, 130ft cutter which is a simulation of an 1848 vessel, offering tourists the chance for three-hour whale-watching outings (Sat 10am–1pm & 1.30–4.30pm; $30) or brunch and dinner cruises around the harbor (Sat 6–9pm, $49; Sun 10am–1pm, $42); by reservation at ☎714/970-8800, ⊛www.americanpride.org.

Ocean Boulevard leads away from Shoreline Village down to the **Breakers Hotel**, 200 E Ocean Blvd, a 1925 structure with twelve pink Spanish Revival stories topped by a green copper roof. Although the hotel itself is now used for senior citizens' housing, the top-floor *Sky Room* bar and restaurant (⊛www.theskyroom.com) is a good spot for a drink in self-consciously retro-1930s surroundings. A mile further on, the **Long Beach Museum of Art**, 2300 Ocean Blvd (Tues–Sun 11am–5pm, Thurs closes 8pm; $5; ⊛www.lbma.org), is a 1912 Craftsman home that is now the site of some of LA's more experimental modern artworks. Fringed by an abstract sculpture garden and featuring a decent collection of early modernism, folk art, and contemporary Southern Californian art, the museum is most interesting for its horde of **video art** – one of the country's biggest collections – from Nam June Paik's modified televisions, broadcasting only thin white lines, to Bill Viola's enigmatic video projections. Several blocks north of the ocean, the **Museum of Latin American Art**, 628 Alamitos Ave (Tues–Fri 11.30am–7pm, Sat 11am–7pm, Sun 11am–6pm; $5; ⊛www.molaa.com), is LA's only major museum devoted solely to Hispanic art. Showcasing artists from Mexico to South America, the collection includes big names like Diego Rivera and José Orozco, as well as newcomers using styles that range from social criticism to magical realism.

Between November and March, more than fifteen thousand whales cruise the "**Whale Freeway**" past Long Beach on their annual migration to and from winter breeding and berthing grounds in Baja California. Spirit Cruises, 429 Shoreline Village Drive (☎562/548-8080, ⊛www.spiritmarine.com), and Harbor Breeze, Dock 2, Rainbow Harbor (☎562/432-4900, ⊛www.longbeachcruises.com), operate good two- to three-hour whale-watching trips for $15–20.

The Queen Mary and Scorpion submarine

Long Beach's most famous attraction is, of course, the mighty ocean liner **QUEEN MARY** (daily 10am–6pm; $28 guided tours, kids $17; ⊛www.queenmary.com), acquired by the local authorities with the specific aim of bolstering tourism – which it has succeeded in doing, well beyond expectations. The *Queen Mary* lies across the bay, opposite Shoreline Village, and is accessible either by a lengthy walk or the free Long Beach Transit **shuttle** from downtown (information at ☎562/591-2301, ⓦwww.lbtransit.org). Now a luxury hotel, the ship's exhibits suggest that all who sailed on the vessel – the flagship of the Cunard Line from the 1930s until the 1960s – enjoyed the extravagantly furnished lounges and luxurious cabins, all carefully restored and kept sparkling. But a glance at the spartan third-class cabins reveals something of the real story: the tough conditions experienced by the impoverished migrants who left Europe hoping to start a new life in the US.

The *Queen Mary* site in recent years has become something of an entertainment complex, but the only new wrinkle that constitutes an actual attraction (beyond the big boat itself) is the **Scorpion submarine** (same hours and admission as *Queen Mary*, otherwise $10), which was until 1994 used in the service of the Soviet, and then Russian, navy, carrying a payload of 22 nuclear weapons and powered by diesel engines.

Santa Catalina Island

SANTA CATALINA ISLAND is an inviting mix of uncluttered beaches and wild hills twenty miles off the coast. Claimed by the Portuguese in 1542 as San Salvador, and renamed by the Spanish in 1602, it has stayed firmly outside the historical mainstream. Since 1811, when the indigenous Tongva Indians were forced to resettle on the mainland, the island has been in private ownership, and has over the years grown to be something of a resort – a process hastened by businessman William Wrigley Jr (part of the chewing-gum dynasty), who financed the Art Deco Avalon Casino, the island's major landmark, in the 1920s, and once made the island the spring-training base for the Chicago Cubs. The island is a popular destination for boaters and nature lovers, and its small marina overflows with luxury yachts and cruise ships in summer. Even so, tourism has been held largely at bay: the hotels are unobtrusive among the whimsical architecture and cars are a rarity, as there's a ten-year waiting list to bring one over from the mainland. Consequently, most of the three thousand islanders walk, ride bikes, or drive electric golf carts.

Arrival and transportation

Depending on the season, a round-trip **ferry** from San Pedro or Long Beach to Catalina Island's one town of any size, **Avalon**, costs about $40. Catalina Explorer (☎1-877/432-6276, ⓦwww.catalinaferry.com) and Catalina Express (☎310/519-1212 or 1-800/315-3967, ⓦwww.catalinaexpress.com) run several services daily. From Newport Beach (see p.176) to Avalon, the Catalina Passenger Service (☎949/673-5245) runs a daily round-trip for $44. If you get seasick or feel extravagant, **helicopter** services to Avalon, costing $136 round-trip (plus tax), are offered by Island Express (☎310/510-2525, ⓦwww.islandexpress.com) from Long Beach and San Pedro.

If you're interested in taking a **tour** of the island, one of the more reliable operators is the Catalina Island Company (☎1-800/446-0266, ⓦwww.scico.com), which offers tours of the Avalon Casino or downtown area (each $13.50) and two- to four-hour jaunts through the outback of the island ($29–79) – the only way to see the interior of Catalina without hiking. Cheaper tours of the same terrain are provided by Catalina Adventure Tours ($13–35; ☎310/510-2888, ⓦwww.catalinaadventuretours.com), which also offers combination trips with harbor cruises and glass-bottom-boat rides. **Golf carts**, for which you need a driver's license, and **bikes** (both banned from the rough roads outside Avalon) can be rented from stands throughout the island. Bikes run $20–35 per day, depending on the model, while golf carts are much steeper, at $35–40 per hour only.

The waters around Catalina are rich in yellowtail, calico bass, barracuda, and sharks. Catalina Island Sportfishing, 114 Claressa St (℡310/510-2420), runs **charter fishing trips** for around $100–120 an hour (though you can fish for free from the pier). EZ Ocean Charters (℡310/306-3006, @www .e-zoceancharters.com) has a sliding scale ($70–120 per hour) depending on the number in your party, and also offers cheaper sightseeing trips ($30 per hour). **Snorkel** and **scuba** gear is available for rent at Catalina Divers Supply, on the pier and at the Casino (℡310/510-0330 or 1-800/353-0330, @www .catalinadiverssupply.com), for $27 per day for a complete snorkel set, and $50 for the full scuba package.

Accommodation and eating

The cost of **accommodation** in Avalon hovers upwards of $100, and most beds are booked up throughout the summer and on weekends. The most interesting **hotel** is the *Zane Grey Pueblo*, 199 Chimes Tower Rd (℡310/510-0966 or 1-800/446-0271, @www.zanegreyhotel.com; ⑤–⑥), which has sixteen rooms overlooking the bay or mountains, with an enticing winter-season (Nov–March) weekday rate of $59. The cheapest overall is usually the *Atwater*, 125 Sumner Ave (℡310/510-2500 or 1-800/626-1496; ④), though there are also units here that reach $369. If you really have a bundle to spend, the *Inn on Mt Ada*, 398 Wrigley Rd (℡310/510-2030, @www.catalina.com/mtada; ⑨), is the final word in hilltop hotel luxury. The only true budget option is **camping** ($12 per person, kids $6). *Hermit Gulch* (℡310/510-8368) is the closest site to Avalon and thus the busiest. Four other sites – *Blackjack*, *Little Harbor*, *Parsons Landing*, and *Two Harbors* – in Catalina's interior (all bookable at ℡310/510-8368, @www .scico.com/camping) are usually roomier.

For **eating**, *Catalina Cantina*, 313 Crescent Ave (℡310/510-0100), is among the best, offering tasty and affordable Mexican staples washed down with margaritas, with live music on weekends.

Avalon

AVALON can be fully explored on foot in an hour, with maps issued by the **Chamber of Commerce** at the foot of the ferry pier (℡310/510-1520, @www.visitcatalina.org). The best place to begin is at the **Avalon Casino**, a 1920s structure that still shows movies, featuring mermaid murals, gold-leaf ceiling motifs, a grand Art Deco ballroom, and a small **museum** (daily 10am–4pm, Jan–March closed Thurs; $2.50; @www.catalina.com/museum .html) displaying Native-American artifacts from Catalina's past.

On the slopes above the Casino, the **Zane Grey Pueblo Hotel**, 199 Chimes Tower Rd (see above), is the former home of the Western author, who visited Catalina with a film crew to shoot *The Vanishing American* and liked the place so much he never left, building for himself this pueblo-style house. Its hotel rooms are themed after his books, and the pool is shaped like an arrowhead. Also striking is the **Holly Hill House**, 718 Crescent Ave (tours periodically offered; call ℡310/510-2414 for details), an 1890 Queen Anne cottage on a high bluff overlooking the bay, with an elegant and colorful conic tower and stylish wraparound verandas.

If possible, venture into the Catalina **interior**. You can take a tour (see p.160) if time is short; if not, free hiking permits are available in Avalon from the **Catalina Island Conservancy**, 125 Claressa Ave (daily 9am–5pm; ☎310/510-2595), which owns and manages 88 percent of the island's land; mountain biking requires a $60 permit, or $85 per family, from the same place.

The **wilderness** of the interior holds a wide variety of native flora and fauna, including the Catalina Shrew, so rare it's only been sighted twice, and the Catalina Mouse, bigger and healthier than its mainland counterpart thanks to abundant food and lack of natural enemies. There are also buffalo, descended from a group of fourteen left behind by a Hollywood film crew and now a sizeable herd wandering about the island. One place definitely worth visiting, a mile and a half inland from town at 1400 Avalon Canyon Road, is the **Wrigley Memorial and Botanical Garden** (daily 8am–5pm; $5), administered by the Catalina Island Conservancy. Here, all manner of natural delights are displayed on nearly forty acres, with a special emphasis on native, endangered plants, such as the local varieties of manzanita, ironwood, mahogany, and the wild tomato – a poisonous member of the nightshade family. Also fascinating is chewing-gum magnate Wrigley's own **cenotaph** (he's buried elsewhere), a striking monument of Georgia marble, blue flagstone, and red roof-tiles.

Northwest of Avalon, the small, isolated resort town of **Two Harbors** sits on a small strip of land that connects Cherry Cove and Catalina Harbor. With a large marina and campground, the town is suitable enough for outdoor activities like kayaking, snorkeling, and scuba diving, but there's little to really see.

The San Gabriel and San Fernando valleys

Running north of central LA, beyond the crest of the hills, lie two long, expansive valleys that start close to one another a few miles north of Downtown and span outwards in opposite directions – east to the deserts around Palm Springs, west to Ventura on the Central Coast.

To the east, the **SAN GABRIEL VALLEY** was settled by farmers and cattle ranchers who set up small towns on the lands of the eighteenth-century Mission San Gabriel, foothill communities which grew into prime resort towns, luring many here around the turn of the last century. **Pasadena**, the largest of the modest cities, holds many elegant period houses, as well as the fine **Norton Simon Museum**, and has become most notable for its **Old Pasadena** outdoor shopping mall, featuring dining, movie-going, and various cultural activities in stylish old buildings. Above Pasadena, the southern slopes of the San Gabriel Mountains are peppered with detritus from the resort days, and make great spots for hiking and rough camping, though you'll nearly always need a car to get to the trailheads. South of Pasadena, WASP-ish **San Marino** is dominated by the **Huntington Library and Gardens**, a stash of art and literature ringed by botanical gardens, that itself is worth a trip to the valley.

North of Downtown LA, and spreading west, the **SAN FERNANDO VALLEY** is *the* Valley to most Angelenos: a sprawl of tract homes, mini-malls, fast-food drive-ins, and auto-parts stores that has more of a middle-American feel than anywhere else in LA and is visually similar to much of inland Orange County. There are a few rather far-flung sights worth a look, but for most

Earthquake Central: The San Fernando Valley

The devastating 6.7 magnitude **earthquake** that shook LA on the morning of January 17, 1994, was one of the most destructive disasters in US history. Fifty-five people were killed, two hundred more suffered critical injuries; the economic cost was estimated at $8 billion. One can only guess how much higher these totals would have been had the quake hit during the day, when the many collapsed stores would have been crowded with shoppers and the freeways full of commuters. The quake, with its epicenter in the San Fernando Valley community of **Northridge**, eclipsed LA's previous worst earthquake in modern times, the 6.6 magnitude temblor of February 1971, which had its epicenter in Sylmar – also in the Valley.

Small earthquakes happen all the time in LA, usually doing no more than rattling supermarket shelves and making dogs howl. In the unlikely event a sizeable earthquake strikes when you're in LA, protect yourself under something sturdy, such as a heavy table or a door frame, and well away from windows or anything made of glass. In theory, all the city's new buildings are "quake-safe," though as the 1994 quake recedes in memory, the retro-fitting of older buildings seems to diminish in perceived importance. So when the inevitable "Big One," a quake in the 8+ range, arrives, no one knows exactly what will be left standing.

people, the main reason to come out here is to drop in on the tourable movie studios in **Burbank** and **University City**. Elsewhere, **Forest Lawn Cemetery** is a prime example of graveyard kitsch that's hard to imagine anywhere except in LA, and ultra-conservative **Simi Valley** is the home of the **Ronald Reagan Presidential Library** (daily 10am–5pm; $7; ⓦwww.reaganlibrary.com/pma), containing all the papers pertaining to the eight-year reign of the Gipper, as well as his memorial site, following on his death in 2004.

Pasadena

In the 1880s, wealthy East Coast tourists who came to California looking for the good life found it in **PASADENA**, ten miles north of LA and connected via the I-10 (Pasadena) Freeway, where luxury hotels were built and a funicular railway cut into the nearby San Gabriel Mountains, leading up to a resort and observatory on the mile-high crest. Many of the early, well-heeled visitors stayed on, building the rustically sprawling houses that remain, but as LA grew so Pasadena suffered, mainly from the smog which the mountains collect. The downtown area underwent a major renovation in the 1980s, with modern shopping centers being slipped in behind 1920s facades, but the historic parts of town have not been forgotten – unusual for LA. Maps and booklets detailing self-guided tours of city architecture and history are available from the **Pasadena Visitors Bureau**, 171 S Los Robles Ave (Mon–Fri 8am–5pm, Sat 10am–4pm; ☏626/795-9311, ⓦwww.pasadenacal.com). The town's most notable attraction, the New Year's Day **Tournament of Roses**, began in 1890 to celebrate and publicize the mild Southern California winters, and now attracts more than a million visitors every year to watch its marching bands and elaborate flower-emblazoned floats (see box, p.200). Also fascinating is the **Tournament House**, 391 S Orange Grove Blvd (tours Feb–Aug 2–4pm; free; ☏626/449-4100, ⓦwww.tournamentofroses.com), a pink 1914 Renaissance Revival mansion, formerly owned by gum king William Wrigley, that now serves as the administrative headquarters of the parade. If you like old Renaissance Revival estates, the place is well worth a look for its grand manor and surrounding gardens – containing up to 1500 types of roses.

△ The Tournament of Roses

Between Fair Oaks and Euclid avenues along Colorado Boulevard, the historic shopping precinct of **Old Pasadena** draws visitors for its fine restaurants, galleries, and theaters, and is accessible by light-rail connection on the Metro Gold Line (see p.93). Downtown Pasadena's most prominent architectural work and its municipal centerpiece, **Pasadena City Hall**, 100 N Garfield Ave (under renovation until 2007), is one of several city buildings in Mediterranean Revival styles, in this case Spanish Baroque, with a large, tiled dome and imperious facade with grand arches and columns. The local preservation society, **Pasadena Heritage**, offers periodic tours of the city's landmarks – including an excellent overview of Old Pasadena on the second Saturday of the month (Nov–June, Aug & Sept only; $10; reserve at ☎626/441-6333, ⓦ www.pasadenaheritage.org).

Just to the east of City Hall, a replica Chinese Imperial palace houses the **Pacific Asia Museum**, 46 N Los Robles Ave (Wed–Sun 10am–5pm, Fri closes 8pm; $7; ⓦ www.pacificasiamuseum.org), which has a wide range of objects from Japan, China, and Thailand, from ceramic artifacts to hand-woven garments to finely detailed scrolls. One particular highlight is the Courtyard Garden, with koi fish, marble statues, and trees native to the Far East. Just around the corner, at 490 E Union St, the three-story **Pasadena Museum of California Art** (Wed–Sun noon–5pm; $6; ⓦ www.pmcaonline.org) offers an eye-opening focus on the many aspects of the state's art world since it became part of the Union in 1850, in all kinds of media from painting to digital art.

The Norton Simon Museum

Although not as famous, the collections of the **Norton Simon Museum**, 411 W Colorado Blvd (Wed–Mon noon–6pm, Fri closes 9pm; $6, students free; ⓦ www.nortonsimon.org), are at least as good as the LA County or Getty museums. You could easily spend a whole afternoon or day wandering through the spacious galleries, as well as a sculpture garden inspired by Claude Monet's own Giverny.

The core of the collection is **Western European painting**. It's a massive collection, much of it rotated, but most of the major pieces are on view constantly. Highlights include Dutch paintings of the seventeenth century – notably Rembrandt's vivacious *Titus, Portrait of a Boy* and Frans Hals' quietly aggressive *Portrait of a Man*, and Italian Renaissance work from the likes of Botticelli, Raphael, Giorgione, and Bellini. There's also a good sprinkling of French Impressionists and post-Impressionists: Monet's *Mouth of the Seine at Honfleur*, Manet's *Ragpicker*, and a Degas capturing the extended yawn of a washer woman in *The Ironers*, plus works by Cézanne, Gauguin, and Van Gogh.

Unlike the Getty, the Norton Simon also boasts a solid collection of modernist greats, from Georges Braque and Pablo Picasso to Roy Lichtenstein and Andy Warhol. As a counterpoint to the Western art, the museum has a fine collection of **Asian art**, including many highly polished Buddhist and Hindu figures, some inlaid with precious stones, and many drawings and prints – the highlight being Hiroshige's masterful series of colored woodblock prints, showing nature in quiet, dusky hues.

Arroyo Seco

The residential pocket northwest of the junction of the 134 and 210 freeways, known as **ARROYO SECO**, or "dry riverbed" in Spanish, features some of LA's best architecture and some of the Valley's most worthwhile attractions. Orange Grove Avenue leads you into the neighborhood from central Pasadena and takes you to the **Pasadena Historical Society**, 470 W Walnut

St at Orange Grove Avenue (Wed–Sun noon–5pm; $5, kids free; Ⓦwww
.pasadenahistory.org), which has fine displays on Pasadena's history and tasteful
surrounding gardens, but is most interesting for the on-site **Feynes Mansion**
(tours Wed–Sun 1.30 & 3pm; free with admission). Decorated with its original
1905 furnishings and paintings, this elegant Beaux Arts mansion was once the
home of the Finnish Consulate, and much of the folk art on display comes from
Pasadena's "twin town" of Jarvenpää in Finland.

But it's the **Gamble House**, nearby at 4 Westmoreland Place (60min tours
Thurs–Sun noon–3pm; $8, students $5; Ⓦwww.gamblehouse.org), which
brings people out here. Built in 1908, this masterpiece of Southern California Craftsman architecture freely combines elements from Swiss chalets and
Japanese temples in a romantic, sprawling shingled house. Broad eaves shelter
outdoor sleeping porches, which in turn shade terraces on the ground floor,
leading out to the spacious lawn. With the same attention to detail, all the carpets, cabinetry, and lighting fixtures were designed specifically for the house; in
2004, the house completed a major renovation, repairing nearly a century of
decay to its wooden beams and shakes, and giving it back the full splendor of
its original rough-hewn look. The area around the Gamble House is filled with
at least eight other houses by the two brothers (the firm of Greene & Greene)
who designed it, including Charles Greene's own house at 368 Arroyo Terrace
(closed to the public).

Almost incongruously, the 104,000-seat **Rose Bowl** is just to the north, out
of use for most of the year but home to a very popular **flea market** on the
second Sunday of each month and, in the autumn, the place where the UCLA
football team plays its home games (Ⓣ310/825-2101).

Into the foothills

On the other side of the Foothill Freeway, **Descanso Gardens**, 1418 Descanso
Drive (daily 9am–5pm; $5, kids $1; Ⓦwww.descansogardens.org), in the nearby
city of La Cañada Flintridge, concentrates all the plants you might see in the
mountains into 155 acres of landscaped park, especially brilliant in the spring
when all the camellias, tulips, lilies, and daffodils are in bloom. From La Cañada,
the winding **Angeles Crest Highway** (Hwy-2) heads up into the mountains
above Pasadena, an area once dotted with resort hotels and wilderness camps.
You can hike up any number of nearby canyons and come across the ruins of
old lodges that either burned down or were washed away towards the end of
the hiking era in the 1930s, when automobiles became popular. One of the
most interesting trails is a five-mile round-trip following the route of the Mount
Lowe Railway, once one of LA's biggest tourist attractions, up to the foundations of "**White City**" – formerly a mountaintop resort of two hotels, a zoo, and
an observatory. Today, you'll see little more than crumbling walls, but the trail's
expansive views of the basin can be quite striking when smog isn't too much of
a problem. To follow the old route of the railway, drive north on Lake Avenue
until it ends at the intersection of Loma Alta Drive. Back on the pavement, the
Crest Highway passes through the **Angeles National Forest**, capped by Mount
Wilson, high enough to be the major siting spot for TV broadcast antennae, and
with a small **museum** (daily 10am–4pm; donation; Ⓦwww.mtwilson.edu) near
the 100-inch telescope of the 1904 Mount Wilson Observatory.

The Huntington Library and Gardens

South of Pasadena, **San Marino** is a dull, upper-crust suburb with little of
interest beyond the **Huntington Library, Art Collections and Botanical**

Gardens, off Huntington Drive at 1151 Oxford Rd (Tues–Fri noon–4.30pm, Sat & Sun 10.30am–4.30pm; $15, students $10; ⓦ www.huntington.org), based on the collections of Henry Huntington, who owned and operated the Southern Pacific Railroad – which in the nineteenth century had a virtual monopoly on transportation in California. Later the head of the Pacific Electric Railway Company, Huntington's "Red Cars" soon became the largest network in the world, and Huntington the largest landowner in the state, buying up farmland and extending the streetcar system at a huge profit. He retired in 1910, moving to the manor he had built in San Marino, devoting himself full time to buying rare books and manuscripts, and marrying his uncle's widow, Arabella.

You can pick up a self-guided walking tour of each of the three main sections from the bookstore and information desk in the covered pavilion. The **Library**, right off the main entrance, has a two-story exhibition hall containing rare manuscripts and books, among them a Gutenberg Bible, a folio edition of Shakespeare's plays, and the **Ellesmere Chaucer**, a c.1410 illuminated manuscript of *The Canterbury Tales*. Displays around the walls trace the history of printing and of the English language from medieval manuscripts to a King James Bible, from Milton's *Paradise Lost* and Blake's *Songs of Innocence and Experience* to first editions of Swift, Dickens, Woolf, and Joyce.

To decorate the **main house**, a grand mansion done out in Louis XIV carpets and later French tapestries, the Huntingtons traveled to England and returned laden with the finest art money could buy. Unless you're a real fan of eighteenth-century English portraiture, head through to the back extension, which displays, as well as works by Van Dyck and Constable, the stars of the whole collection – Gainsborough's *Blue Boy* and Reynolds' *Mrs Siddons as the Tragic Muse*. More striking, perhaps, are Turner's *Grand Canal, Venice*, awash in hazy sunlight and gondolas, and Blake's *Satan Comes to the Gates of Hell*, which is quite the portrait of Old Nick, in this case battling Death with spears.

Nearby, the **Scott Gallery for American Art** displays paintings by Edward Hopper and Mary Cassatt, and a range of Wild West drawings and sculpture, though for all the art and literature, it's the grounds that make the Huntington really special. The acres of beautiful themed **gardens** surrounding the buildings include a Zen Rock Garden, complete with authentically constructed Buddhist Temple and Tea House, and a Desert Garden with the world's largest collection of desert plants, including twelve acres of cacti in an artful setting; in Fall 2005, the Huntington plans to open an expansive **botanical conservatory** as well, which will serve as a showcase for regional and exotic horticultural techniques. While strolling through these assorted wonders, you might also call in on the Huntingtons themselves, buried in a neo-Palladian **mausoleum** at the northwest corner of the estate.

Along Foothill Boulevard

Parallel to the Foothill Freeway (I-210), **FOOTHILL BOULEVARD** was once best known as part of Route 66, still a strip with much nostalgia attached to it. The freeway stole Route 66's traffic and glory, and following Foothill Boulevard out of Pasadena nowadays leads to the town of **Arcadia**, whose **LA County Arboretum**, 301 N Baldwin Ave (daily 9am–4.30pm; $5; ⓦ www.arboretum.org), contains many impressive gardens and waterfalls, flocks of peacocks, and, of course, a great assortment of trees – arranged according to their native continents. The site was once the 127-acre ranch of "Lucky" Baldwin, who made his millions in the Comstock silver mines in the 1870s, then settled here in 1875 and built a fanciful white Victorian palace along a palm-treed lagoon (later used in the TV show *Fantasy Island*) on the site of the 1839 Rancho Santa Anita. He also bred horses, and raced them on a neighboring track that has since grown into the **Santa Anita Racetrack** (racing Oct to early Nov & late Dec to late April, Wed–Sun, post time 12.30pm or 1pm; $5; Ⓦwww.santaanita.com), one of the more glamorous racetracks in California.

Directly north of Arcadia, the city of **Sierra Madre** lies directly beneath Mount Wilson and is worth a visit if you're a hiker, as the seven-mile round-trip trail up to the summit is one of the best hikes in the San Gabriel range. (The trailhead is 150 yards up the private Mount Wilson Road.) Southwest of Sierra Madre stands the valley's original settlement, the church and grounds of **Mission San Gabriel Arcangel**, 428 S Mission Drive (daily 9am–4pm; $5; Ⓦsangabrielmission.org). Still standing at the corner of Mission and Serra in the heart of the small town of **San Gabriel**, the mission was established here in 1771 by Junípero Serra and the current building finished in 1812. Despite decades of damage by earthquakes and the elements, the church and grounds have been repaired and reopened, their old winery, cistern, kitchens, gardens, and antique-filled rooms giving some sense of mission-era life. The city is peppered with compelling antique and historic-revival structures, and makes for an interesting, out-of-the-way walk if you have an hour; to check out a suggested self-guided **tour**, visit Ⓦwww.sangabrielcity.com.

Glendale

Jumping many miles west, to the opposite side of the San Gabriel Valley and the gateway to the San Fernando Valley, **GLENDALE** lies eight miles north of Downtown LA and was once a fashionable suburb. Now it's a nondescript bedroom community, though there are a few reasons to come here. For one, the marvelous **Alex Theatre**, 268 N Brand Blvd, is an undeniably appealing piece of green-and-yellow Art Deco with a towering pylon (and now serves as a performing arts venue and site for the Last Remaining Seats festival; see p.208 or Ⓦwww.alextheatre.org); the **Brand Library**, 1601 W Mountain St (Tues & Thurs 1–9pm, Wed 1–6pm, Fri & Sat 1–5pm; free), is a striking 1902 confection with white "Islamic" domes and minarets, now an arts library set in a pleasant park; and the **Casa Adobe de San Rafael**, 1330 Dorothy Drive (summer Sun 1–3pm, rest of year first Sun of month 1–3pm; free), is an old adobe set among birds of paradise, magnolias, and eucalyptus trees, designed in 1871 for LA County's first sheriff.

Forest Lawn Cemetery

Without a doubt, though, Glendale is best known for its branch of **Forest Lawn Cemetery**, 1712 S Glendale Ave (daily 8am–5pm; free; Ⓦwww .forestlawn.org), founded in 1917 by one Dr Hubert Eaton, and still the place to be seen dead, its pompous landscaping and pious artworks attracting celebrities by the dozen. It's best to climb the hill and see the cemetery in reverse from the **Forest Lawn Museum**, whose hodgepodge of historical bric-a-brac includes coins from ancient Rome, Viking relics, medieval armor, and a mysterious sculpted Easter Island figure, discovered being used as ballast in a fishing boat in the days when the statues could still be removed from the island – it's the only one on view in the US. Next door to the museum, the **Resurrection and Crucifixion Hall** houses the biggest piece of Western religious art in the world: *The Crucifixion* by Jan Styka – an oil painting nearly 200ft tall and 50ft wide – though you're only allowed to see it during the ceremonial unveiling every hour on the hour.

From the museum, the terrace gardens lead down past sculpted replicas of the greats of classical European art, and on to the **Freedom Mausoleum**, home to a handful of the cemetery's better-known graves. Just outside the mausoleum's doors, Errol Flynn lies in an unspectacular plot, rumored to have been buried with six bottles of whiskey at his side, while nearby is the grave of Walt Disney, who wasn't frozen, as urban legend would have it. Inside the mausoleum itself you'll find Clara Bow, Nat King Cole, Jeanette MacDonald, and Alan Ladd, all close to each other on the first floor. To the left, heading back down the hill, the **Great Mausoleum** is chiefly noted for the tombs of Clark Gable and Jean Harlow.

A number of other Forest Lawn cemeteries continue the style of the Glendale site, notably the Hollywood Hills branch in Burbank. The others, in Covina Hills, Cypress Beach, and Long Beach, are best avoided.

Burbank and the studios

Although Hollywood is synonymous with the movie industry, in reality most of the big studios moved away long ago. Much of the grimy business of actually making films goes on over the hills in otherwise boring **BURBANK**, just west of Glendale, which has a media district bustling with production activity – most of it off-limits to the general public, including Disney and its **Studio Office Building**, 500 S Buena Vista St, a clumsy effort from Michael Graves that features five of the Seven Dwarves propping up the building's roof. By contrast, **Warner Bros**, Warner Boulevard at Hollywood Way, offers worthwhile "insider" tours of its sizeable facilities and active backlot (Mon–Fri 9am–4pm; $35; reserve at ⊤818/972-TOUR, Ⓦwww.burbank.com/warner_bros_tour.shtml), and **NBC**, 3000 W Alameda St (Mon–Fri 9am–4pm; $7; ⊤818/840-3537), allows 90min tours of the largest production facility in the US, and gives you the chance to be in the audience for the taping of a TV program (phone ahead for free tickets), such as Jay Leno's *Tonight Show*.

The largest of the backlots belongs to **Universal Studios**, whose four-hour tours (summer daily 8am–10pm; rest of year daily 10am–6pm; $50, kids $40; ⊤818/508-9600, Ⓦwww.universalstudioshollywood.com) are more like a trip around an amusement park, with high-tech rides, stuntman shows, and "evening spectaculars" based on current movies. The theme rides are based on the studio's more popular films, including *Back to the Future* (a jerky trip on a motion simulator), *Jurassic Park* (close encounters with prehistoric plastic), *Terminator 2* (a 3-D movie with robot stuntmen) and *Spiderman Rocks!* (a

North Hollywood

The **North Hollywood Arts District** (Ⓦwww.nohoartsdistrict.com), located around Magnolia Blvd between Burbank and the Western San Fernando Valley, and accessible by a nearby Metro Red Line station, was named "NoHo" by county bureaucrats as a play on New York's SoHo. While the name is a transparent ploy to drum up the tourist trade, and the district has nothing on Manhattan, it's still a lively enough spot that's well worth a trip if you're in the area, with no less than thirty live theaters and plenty of coffee shops, galleries, bookstores, restaurants, and odd little boutiques to attract your interest. There are even, here and there, flashes of the creatively anarchic spirit that once flourished on Melrose Avenue and still does in places like Silver Lake and northeast LA. This despite the fact that the district has almost nothing to do with the more rambunctious Hollywood, except the name.

musical version of the blockbuster). You never actually get to see any filming, though. Also part of the complex is **Universal CityWalk**, an outdoor mall that's free to all who pay the parking fee, where pop bands churn out MOR covers, street performers warble syrupy ballads, and giant TV screens run ads for the latest Universal releases.

The Western San Fernando Valley

On the **western end** of the San Fernando Valley, the Ventura Freeway (US–101) passes below the expensive hillside homes of **Sherman Oaks** and **Encino**, close to which **Los Encinos State Historic Park**, 16756 Moorpark St (Wed–Sun 10am–5pm; free), is all that remains of the original Native American settlement and later Mexican hacienda that were here. The high-ceilinged rooms of the 1849 adobe house open out onto porches, shaded by oak trees (in Spanish, "encinos") and kept cool by the two-foot-thick walls. Nearer the 405, the **Tillman Japanese Garden**, 6100 Woodley Ave in Van Nuys (grounds Mon–Thurs noon–4pm, Sun 10am–3.30pm, tours by reservation only Mon–Thurs; $3; ☎818/751-8166, ⓦwww.thejapanesegarden.com), is an enjoyable little spot, adorned with stone lanterns, bonsai trees, low bridges, a teahouse, and artful streams and pools.

West of Encino, Topanga Canyon Boulevard crosses the Ventura Freeway, leading south towards Malibu or north to **Stony Point**, a bizarre sandstone outcrop that has been used for countless Western shootouts, and is now a popular venue for LA's lycra-clad rock climbers. The area, though crossed by both Amtrak and Metrolink trains, certainly has a desolate spookiness about it, and it comes as little surprise to learn that during the late 1960s the Charles Manson "family" lived for a time at the **Spahn Ranch**, just west at 12000 Santa Susana Pass.

North of the Valley and beyond

At the north end of the Valley, the San Diego, Golden State, and Foothill freeways join together at I-5. Just east of the junction, **Mission San Fernando Rey de España**, 15151 San Fernando Mission Blvd (daily 9am–5pm; $5), had to be completely rebuilt following the 1971 Sylmar earthquake. Nowadays, there's a good collection of historic pottery, furniture, and saddles, and a replica of an old-time blacksmith's shop. Up the road in nearby Sylmar, the wondrous **San Sylmar**, 15180 Bledsoe St (Tues–Sat 9am–4.30pm; tours by reservation 10am & 1.30pm; free; ☎818/367-2251, ⓦwww.nethercuttcollection.org), is one of LA's most interesting museums, a storehouse for Wurlitzer organs, antique player-pianos, cosmetic paraphernalia, Tiffany stained glass, and classic

The LA Aqueduct

Just beyond Mission San Fernando, I-5 runs past two of LA's main reservoirs, the water of which has been brought hundreds of miles through the **California Aqueduct** from the Sacramento Delta, and through the **LA Aqueduct** from the Owens Valley on the eastern slopes of the Sierra Nevada Mountains. However, the legality of the arrangements by which Los Angeles gained control of such a distant supply of water is still disputed. Agents of the city, masquerading as rich cattle-barons interested in establishing ranches in the Owens Valley, bought up most of the land along the Owens River before selling it, at great personal profit, to the City of Los Angeles. These cunning tactics provided the inspiration for Roman Polanski's 1974 movie *Chinatown*. For more on the Owens Valley, see p.383.

French furniture, but most notably the **Nethercutt Collection**, a stunning showroom loaded with the finest array of automobiles imaginable – with classic Packards, Mercedes, Bugattis, and especially Duesenbergs.

Just north of the freeway junction in the town of **Santa Clarita**, the **William S. Hart Ranch and Museum**, 24151 San Fernando Rd (Wed–Fri 10am–1pm, Sat & Sun 11am–4pm, summer Wed–Sun 11am–4pm; free; ⓦwww.hartmuseum.org), holds a fine assemblage of Western history, featuring native artworks, Remington sculptures, displays of spurs, guns, and lariats, Tinseltown costumes, and authentic cowhand clothing, housed in a Spanish Colonial mansion with a surrounding 265-acre ranch. Continuing north, Hwy-14 splits off east to the Mojave Desert, while I-5 continues north past Valencia to **Magic Mountain**, 26101 Magic Mountain Parkway (summer daily 10am–10pm; rest of year Sat & Sun only 10am–8pm; $47, kids $30, $8 parking; ⓦwww.sixflags.com/parks/magicmountain), which has some of the wildest rollercoasters and rides in the world – a hundred times more thrilling than anything at Disneyland. Among them are the appropriately named Goliath coaster, full of harrowing 85mph dips, and Déjà Vu, a high-speed gut-wrencher that twists and jerks you in several different directions at once. The adjacent waterpark, **Hurricane Harbor** (same hours; $24, kids $17, or $57 for both parks; ⓦwww.sixflags.com/parks/hurricaneharborla), is another fun choice, providing plenty of aquatic fun if you don't mind getting splashed by throngs of giddy pre-adolescents.

Inland Orange County

Throughout America, the enclave of **ORANGE COUNTY** is the very image of the American suburb – as well as an insular, paranoid bastion of white flight. Still, even though this stereotype was true for much of the twentieth century (or at least since World War II), by the 1990s Orange County had begun to change: many of the old-line conservatives that first fled LA decades ago continued their flight to other, more sympathetic climes such as Arizona and Colorado, while the county itself welcomed a flood of new migrants from around the world. These changes are most visible in the cities in the inland part of the region, with Hispanics and Asians increasingly populating cities like Anaheim, Garden Grove, Santa Ana, and Westminster (the latter being a key center for Vietnamese expatriates). This trend has demographically shifted these places to the point that it's no longer amazing to find sections of the county that have a tolerant, even progressive, bent – a far cry from the days when the area was the vote-rich stomping ground for Ronald Reagan and Richard Nixon.

For most visitors, though, Orange County means **Disneyland**; though it only exists on roughly one square mile of land, it continues to dominate the **Anaheim** area and contribute to its commercial growth, and the boom doesn't look like it's slowing. Elsewhere, the thrill rides at **Knott's Berry Farm** go some way to restoring antique notions of what amusement parks used to be like; the **Crystal Cathedral** is an imposing reminder of the potency of the evangelical movement; and the **Richard Nixon Library and Birthplace** is a good spot to find out about the illustrious life and career of Tricky Dick. If you're a sports fan, note that baseball's Anaheim Angels play at Anaheim Stadium and hockey's Mighty Ducks play at Arrowhead Pond; the latter team is owned by the town's mouse-in-chief.

Disneyland

In the early 1950s, illustrator and filmmaker **Walt Disney** conceived a theme park where his internationally famous cartoon characters – Mickey Mouse, Donald Duck, Goofy, and the rest – would come to life, animated quite literally, and his fabulously successful company would rake in even more money from them. **DISNEYLAND**, 1313 Harbor Blvd (summer daily 8am–1am; rest of year Mon–Fri 10am–6pm, Sat 9am–midnight, Sun 9am–10pm; $50, $40 kids, parking $8; ☏714/781-4565, ⊛disneyland.com), opened in 1955, in anticipation of the acres of orange groves thirty miles southeast of Downtown LA becoming the next center of population growth in Southern California.

These days Disneyland is still world-renowned as one of the defining hallmarks of American culture, a theme-park phenomenon with the emphasis strongly on family fun. Thus while it has been known for people to cruise around Disneyland on LSD, it is not a good idea; the authorities take a dim view of anything remotely antisocial, and anyone acting out of order will be thrown out. In any case, the place is surreal enough without the need for mind-expanding drugs.

Practicalities

Disneyland is about 45 minutes by **car** from Downtown LA on the Santa Ana Freeway (I-5). By **train** from Downtown (there are ten a day), it's a thirty-minute journey to Fullerton, from where OCTD buses will drop you at Disneyland or Knott's Berry Farm. By **bus**, MTA #460 from Downtown takes about ninety minutes, and Greyhound runs twelve-to-fourteen buses a day and takes 45 minutes to get to Anaheim, from where it's an easy walk to the park.

As for **accommodation**, most people try to visit Disneyland just for the day and spend the night somewhere else, or at home. If you must stay, we've listed some reasonable options on p.101; alternately, the *HI-Anaheim/Fullerton* hostel is the cheapest bet in the area (see p.102). Your culinary options in Disneyland are more limited: a massive central kitchen produces all the **food** that's eaten in the park (you're not permitted to bring your own), unloading popcorn, hot dogs, hamburgers, and other all-American junkfood from the many stands by the ton. For anything healthier, you'll need to leave the park and travel a fair way. The "Eating" listings on p.182 suggest some of the more palatable options.

The main park

Not including the new California Adventure annex (see opposite), the Disneyland admission price includes all the rides, although during peak periods you might have to wait in line for hours – lines are shortest when the park opens, so choose a few top rides and get to them very early. From the front gates, **Main Street** leads through a scaled-down, camped-up replica of a bucolic Midwestern town, filled with souvenir shops and diners, toward **Sleeping Beauty's Castle**, a pseudo-Rhineland palace at the heart of the park that isn't much more than a giant, walk-through prop. **New Orleans Square**, nearby, contains the two best rides in the park: the Pirates of the Caribbean, a boat trip through underground caverns, singing along with drunken pirates, and the Haunted Mansion, a riotous "doom buggy" tour in the company of the house spooks. In **Adventureland**, the antiquated Jungle Cruise offers "tour guides" making crude puns about the fake animatronic beasts creaking amid the scenery, and Tarzan's Treehouse is little more than a movie tie-in with ramps and catwalks circling around the trees. Much more appealing is the nearby **Indiana**

Jones Adventure, involving an interactive archeological dig and 1930s-style newsreel leading up to the main feature – a giddy journey along 2500ft of skull-encrusted corridors in which you face fireballs, burning rubble, venomous snakes, and, inevitably, a rolling-boulder finale.

Less fun are the contiguous areas of **Critter Country** and **Frontierland**, the smallest and most "all-American" section of the park, supposedly taking its cues from the Wild West and the tales of Mark Twain, with the less savory and more complex elements carefully deleted or sanitized. The main attraction, Big Thunder Mountain Railroad, is a drab, slow-moving coaster, while Splash Mountain at least has the added thrill of getting drenched by a log-flume ride, and Tom Sawyer Island offers an elaborate playground with treehouses, caves, and canoes. Continuing counterclockwise around the park, **Fantasyland**, across the drawbridge from Main Street, shows off the cleverest, but also the most sentimental, aspects of the Disney imagination: Peter Pan, a fairytale flight over London, and It's a Small World, a tour of the world's continents in which animated dolls warble the same cloying song over and over again. Tots who just can't get enough saccharine can wander into **Toontown**, a cartoonish zone thick with slow-moving bumper cars and other plodding amusements – aimed only for the under-10 set and generally unbearable for older, thrill-seeking visitors.

Fantasyland mercifully gives way to **Tomorrowland**, Disney's vision of the future, where the Space Mountain rollercoaster zips through the pitch-blackness of outer space, and R2D2 pilots a runaway space cruiser through George Lucas's Star Tours galaxy. This fun zone has been updated somewhat in recent years, with new rides like the Jules Verne–inspired Astro Orbiter and recent additions such as Innoventions, which comes larded with a lot of futurist babble but is really little more than a fun opportunity to look at, and play with, the latest special effects. In addition to these attractions, **firework displays** explode every summer night at 9pm, and all manner of parades and special events celebrate important occasions – such as Mickey Mouse's birthday.

The California Adventure

Opening in 2002, the **CALIFORNIA ADVENTURE** is technically a separate park but is connected to the main one in architecture and style – although it's much less popular and of middling interest to most visitors. Aside from its slightly more exciting rollercoasters and better food, the California Adventure is really just another "land" to visit, albeit a much more expensive one – you cannot get access to both parks with a single-day admission ticket. Instead, you'll have to shell out another $50 or plunk down $98 for a two-day pass that covers both (even kids are charged $78 for this).

The lack of visitors is telling: it's hard to justify spending the money when most of Disneyland's classic, and memorable, attractions are on the other side of the park. That said, there are a handful of highlights if you're looking to visit both areas. **Grizzly River Run** is a fun giant-inner-tube ride, splashing around through various plunges and "caverns"; **Soarin' Over California** is a fairly exciting trip on an experimental aircraft that buzzes you through hairpin turns and steep dives; and the **Pacific Pier** zone has a slew of old-fashioned carnival rides that faintly recall the wilder, harder-edged midways of California's past.

Knott's Berry Farm

It's hard to escape the clutches of Disneyland even when you leave: everything in the surrounding area seems to have been designed to service the needs of its visitors. However, some prefer the more traditional **KNOTT'S BERRY FARM**, four miles northwest off the Santa Ana Freeway at 8039 Beach Blvd (summer Mon & Sun–Thurs 9am–11pm, Fri & Sat 9am–midnight; rest of year Mon–Fri 10am–6pm, Sat 10am–10pm, Sun 10am–7pm; $45, kids $30; ⓦwww .knotts.com). This relaxed, though still pricey, park offers a sprawling sideshow of rollercoasters and carnival rides that, unlike Disneyland, can easily be seen in one day, as long as you concentrate on the coasters, which now make Knott's second only to Magic Mountain (see p.171) for number of thrill rides per acre. Although there are ostensibly six themed lands here, several of them, namely the **Ghost Town** and **Indian Trails**, consist only of mid-level carnival rides, fast-food stands, and dodgy history displays. **Camp Snoopy** is the Knott's equivalent of Disney's Toontown, and just as tedious, while the so-called **Wild Water Wilderness** isn't really a theme area at all, but simply a showplace for the moderately exciting Bigfoot Rapids giant-inner-tube ride.

Simply put, you should spend most or all of your time in just two areas: **Fiesta Village** – home to Montezooma's Revenge, the original one-loop coaster, and Jaguar, a high-flying coaster that spins you around the park concourse – and especially the **Boardwalk**, which is all about thrill rides: the Xcelerator, a 1950s-themed rollercoaster; WindJammer, two racing coasters looping and dipping around each other; Supreme Scream, a delightfully terrifying freefall drop; and the Perilous Plunge, a hellish drop at a 75-degree angle that's far more exciting than any old log-flume ride. The Boardwalk, Knott's version of a carnival midway, with its death-defying rides and vomit-inducing thrills, easily puts Disney's Pacific Pier (see p.172), with its softer-edged, toddler-friendly attractions, to complete shame.

The adjacent Knott's water park, **Soak City USA** (May–Sept only, hours vary but generally 10am–8pm; $25, kids $13, $15 for entry after 3pm; ⓦwww .knotts.com/soakcity), offers 21 rides of various heights and speeds, almost all of them involving the familiar water slides – either with or without an inner tube – that can really bring out the sweltering masses on a hot summer day.

Around Disneyland

To the south of Disneyland, the giant **Crystal Cathedral**, just off the Santa Ana Freeway on Chapman Avenue (tours Mon–Sat 9am–3.30pm; free; ⓦwww.crystalcathedral.org), is a Philip Johnson design of tubular space-frames and plate-glass walls that forms part of the vision of evangelist Robert Schuller, who, not content with owning the world's first drive-in church (next door to the cathedral), commissioned this dramatic prop to boost the ratings of his televised sermons – raising $1.5 million for the construction of the building during one Sunday service alone. A more worthwhile attraction, perhaps, lies in the nearby, unappealing burg of **Santa Ana**, where the splendid **Bowers Museum of Cultural Art**, 2002 N Main St (Tues–Sun 11am–4pm; $14, kids $8; ⓦwww.bowers.org), features a great range of anthropological treasures from early Asian, African, Native American, and pre-Columbian civilizations. Showcasing artifacts as diverse as ceramic Mayan icons, hand-crafted baskets from native Californians, and highly detailed Chinese funerary sculpture, the museum is an essential stop for anyone interested in civilizations outside the West. A same-day ticket also allows entry to the adjacent **Kidseum** (Sat & Sun 11am–4pm), a less invigorating look at the same subject, made easily digestible for bored youngsters.

North of Disneyland, bland **Fullerton** is the site of the esteemed **Muckenthaler Cultural Center**, 1201 W Malvern Ave (Wed–Sun noon–4pm;

$5, kids free; ⓦwww.muckenthaler.org), located in an attractive 1924 Renaissance Revival mansion and hosting a wide range of international multicultural art, with Native American art and textiles, African craftwork and jewelry, and contemporary Korean ceramics only a few of the highlights. There are also countless examples of decorative arts, drawings, and textiles from around the world – and, this being Southern California, an annual display of "automotive art" in the spring, with many colorful car-related illustrations and designs.

The Richard Nixon Library and Birthplace

Mickey Mouse may be its most famous resident, but Orange County's favorite son is the 37th US president, Richard Nixon, born in 1913 in what is now the freeway-caged **Yorba Linda**, about eight miles northeast of Disneyland. Here, the **Richard Nixon Library and Birthplace**, 18001 Yorba Linda Blvd (Mon–Sat 10am–5pm, Sun 11am–5pm; $8, kids $3; ⓦwww.nixonfoundation .org), is an unrelentingly hagiographic library and museum that features over-sized gifts from world leaders, amusing campaign memorabilia, and a collection of obsequious letters written by and to Nixon. In 2004, the new **Loker Center** opened on the premises, the high points of which are a miniature, 70ft replica of the White House – looking strangely like an imperial dollhouse – and the re-creation of the **East Room** of that executive mansion, replicated in architecture and decor. It's an ironic tribute, given that Nixon was always uncomfortable in Washington and did all he could to escape it. Even in death, he avoided lying in state (unlike Ronald Reagan) and made provision for his memorial service to take place here, where he's buried.

It's in the constantly running archive radio and TV recordings that the distinctive Nixon persona really shines through, from his notorious Checkers Speech to his disastrous debates with John F. Kennedy. Throughout the museum, Nixon's face leers down in Orwellian fashion from almost every wall, but only inside the **Presidential Auditorium** (at the end of the corridor packed with notes attesting to the former president's innocence in the Watergate scandal) do you get the chance to ask him a question. Many possibilities spring to mind, but the choice is limited to those already programmed into a computer. Ten or so minutes after making your selection, Nixon's gaunt features will fill the overlarge screen and provide the stock reply – though "I am not a crook" is never one of the correct answers.

The Orange County Coast

The **ORANGE COUNTY COAST**, a string of towns from the edge of the LA Harbor area to the borders of San Diego County 35 miles south, is suburbia with a shoreline: swanky condos line the sands, and the ambience is easygoing, affluent, and conservative or libertarian depending on the area. As the names of the main towns suggest – **Huntington Beach**, **Newport Beach**, and **Laguna Beach** – there's no real reason beyond sea and sand to go here. But unlike most of LA's beach districts, the communities here don't stand shoulder-to-shoulder but are a few miles apart. The one place that genuinely merits a stop is just inland at **San Juan Capistrano**, site of the best kept of all the Californian missions. Further on, there's little to see before you reach adjoining San Diego County, but the campground at **San Clemente** provides the only cheap accommodation along the southern part of the coast.

The fastest way to **travel** from LA to San Diego skips the coast by passing through Orange County on the inland San Diego Freeway, the 405. The coastal cities, though, are linked by the more appealing **Pacific Coast Highway** (PCH), part of Hwy-1, which you can pick up from Long Beach (or from the end of Beach Boulevard in Anaheim), though it's often busy in the summer. OCTD bus #1 rumbles along PCH roughly hourly during the day, though Greyhound connections aren't so good: San Clemente gets ten buses a day and San Juan Capistrano gets two in the early morning, but there are none to Huntington, Laguna, or Newport beaches. Amtrak connects Downtown LA (or Disneyland) to San Juan Capistrano, though you can travel all the way along the coast from LA to San Diego using local buses for about $5 – but you should allow a full day for the journey. A slightly pricier, but more worthwhile, transit option is the Metrolink commuter train line (see "Public transportation," p.92), which not only connects Downtown LA with Orange County down to San Clemente, but continues on to Oceanside in San Diego County, from where you can pick up that region's Coaster and connect to Downtown San Diego.

Huntington Beach

HUNTINGTON BEACH is the first place of note on the Orange County Coast, the wildest of the beach communities, and one that you don't need a fortune to enjoy. It's a compact town composed of engaging, ramshackle single-story cafés and beach stores grouped around the foot of a long pier, off PCH at Main Street – also the place where the **Surfers Walk of Fame** commemorates the sport's towering figures. Otherwise the beach is the sole focus: it was here that California surfing began, imported from Hawaii in 1907 to encourage day-trippers to visit on the Pacific Electric Railway. You can check out the **International Surfing Museum**, 411 Olive Ave (Oct–May Thurs–Mon noon–5pm; June–Sept open daily; $3; Ⓦwww.surfingmuseum .org), which features exhibits on such legendary figures as Corky Carroll and Duke Kahanamoku, historic posters from various world surfing contests, and an array of traditional, contemporary, and far-out boards, including one shaped like a Swiss Army Knife. If all this appeals to you, see the full glory of the sport at the **Pro Surfing Championship**, a world-class event held each June. In October, the largely blonde and suntanned locals celebrate a plausible **Oktoberfest** with German food and music, and the burg is also a surprisingly good place to stay, with Orange County's cheapest beds in a **youth hostel** three blocks from the pier (see "Accommodation," p.102).

Several miles north, nature lovers won't want to miss the **Bolsa Chica State Ecological Reserve**, PCH at Warner Avenue, a sizeable wetland preserve. Taking a one-and-one-half-mile loop tour will get you acquainted with some of the current avian residents of this salt marsh, including a fair number of herons, egrets, and grebes, and even a few peregrine falcons and endangered snowy plovers. Self-tours are free, and guided tours are available on the first Saturday of the month (9–10.30am; $2; groups by reservation at Ⓣ714/840-1575, Ⓦwww.amigosdebolsachica.org).

Newport Beach and Corona Del Mar

Ten miles south of Huntington, **NEWPORT BEACH** could hardly provide a greater contrast. With ten yacht clubs and ten thousand yachts, this is upmarket even by Orange County standards, an image-obsessed town that people visit to acquire a tan they can show off on the long stretches of sand or in the bars alongside. The beach is spread around a natural bay that cuts several miles inland, and although there are hardly any conventional "sights" in town, the place to hang out is on the thin **Balboa Peninsula**, along which runs the three-mile-long strand. The most youthful and boisterous section is about halfway along, around **Newport Pier** at the end of 20th Street. North of here, beachfront homes restrict access, but to the south, around the second of Newport's two piers, the **Balboa Pier**, is a tourist-friendly zone that holds a marina from which you can escape to Catalina Island (see p.160). Away from the peninsula, Newport Beach is home to the **Orange County Museum of Art**, 850 San Clemente Drive (Tues–Sun 11am–5pm, Thurs closes 8pm; $7, free Tues; ⓦ www.ocma.net), a surprisingly good institution that stages engaging exhibitions of contemporary work.

Just a few miles along PCH from Newport, **Corona Del Mar** is worth a short stop for its good beach and the **Sherman Library and Gardens**, 2647 East PCH (daily 10.30am–4pm; $3; ⓦ www.slgardens.org), devoted to the horticulture of the American Southwest and raising many vivid blooms in its botanical gardens, including cacti, orchids, roses, and an array of different herbs. Between here and Laguna Beach lies an unspoiled three-mile-long coastline, protected as **Crystal Cove State Park** – perfect to explore on foot, far from the crowds.

Laguna Beach

Six miles south of Crystal Cove, nestled among the crags around a small sandy strip, **LAGUNA BEACH** developed late in the nineteenth century as a community of artists, drawn by the beauty of the location. You may need a few million dollars to live here nowadays, but still there's a relaxed and tolerant feel among the inhabitants, who range from millionaires to middle-class gays and lesbians. The scenery is still the great attraction, and despite the upswell in population, Laguna remains relatively unspoiled with a still-flourishing arts scene in the many streetside galleries.

PCH passes right through the center of Laguna, a few steps from the small main **beach**. From the beach's north side, an elevated wooden walkway twists around the coastline above a conserved **ecological area**, enabling you to

Laguna Beach festivals

Laguna hosts a number of large summer **art festivals** over six weeks in July and August. The best known – and most bizarre – is the **Pageant of the Masters**, in which the participants pose in front of a painted backdrop to portray a famous work of art (or in some cases, a famous movie poster). It might sound ridiculous, but it's actually quite impressive and takes a great deal of preparation – something reflected in the prices: $20–75 for shows that sell out months in advance. You may, however, be able to pick up cancellations on the night (shows begin at 8.30pm; ⓣ949/494-1145 or 1-800/487-3378, or ⓦ www.foapom.com for more information). The idea for the pageant was hatched during the Depression as a way to raise money for local artists, and the action takes place at the Irving Bowl, close to where Broadway meets Laguna Canyon Road, a walkable distance from the bus station. The pageant is combined with the **Festival of the Arts** (daily 10am–11.30pm; $5; information as above) held at the same venue, featuring the work of 150 local artists.

The excitement of both festivals waned in the 1960s, when a group of hippies created the alternative **Sawdust Festival**, 935 Laguna Canyon Rd (July & Aug, 10am–10pm; $6.50, season pass $12; ⓣ949/494-3030, ⓦ www.sawdustartfestival .org), in which local artists set up makeshift studios to demonstrate their skills. It is now just as established, but easier to get into than the other two.

peer down on the ocean and, when the tide's out, scamper over the rocks to observe the tide pools. From the end of the walkway, make your way by the posh beachside homes and head down the hill back to the center. You'll pass the excellent **Laguna Art Museum**, 307 Cliff Drive (daily 11am–5pm; $9; Ⓦlagunaartmuseum.org), which offers fine exhibitions drawn from its stock of Southern Californian art from the 1900s to the present. A few miles further is less-touristy **South Laguna**, where the wonderfully secluded Victoria and Aliso beaches are among several below the bluffs.

Finally, about two and a half miles inland from downtown Laguna Beach is one sight not to be missed by lovers of sea life, the **Friends of the Sea Lion Marine Mammal Center**, 20612 Laguna Canyon Rd (daily 10am–4pm; free; Ⓣ949/494-3050), a rehabilitation center that lets you watch as underweight, injured, or otherwise threatened seals and sea lions are nursed back to health.

Dana Point

From South Laguna, it's possible to see **DANA POINT**, a town and promontory jutting into the ocean about four miles south. It was named after sailor and author Richard Henry Dana Jr, whose *Two Years Before the Mast* described how cattle hides were flung over these cliffs to trading ships waiting below, and did much to romanticize the California coast while still viewing it with a wary eye. He ended his voyaging career here in 1830, and there's a statue of him and a replica of his vessel, *The Pilgrim*, at the edge of the harbor, on the grounds of the **Ocean Institute**, 24200 Dana Point Harbor Drive (Sat & Sun 10am–4.30pm; $5.50; Ⓦwww.ocean-institute.org), which offers marine-biology cruises and public visits during which you can view oceanic wildlife, from lobsters to anemones, in glass-enclosed tanks.

San Juan Capistrano

Further south, and three miles inland along the I-5 freeway, most of the small town of **SAN JUAN CAPISTRANO** is built in a Spanish Colonial style derived from **Mission San Juan Capistrano**, Ortega Highway at Camino Capistrano in the center of town (daily 8.30am–5pm; $6; Ⓦwww.missionsjc.com), a short walk from the Amtrak stop. The seventh of California's missions, founded by Junípero Serra in 1776, the mission was within three years so well populated that it outgrew the original chapel. Soon after, the **Great Stone Church** was erected, the ruins of which are the first thing you see as you walk in – and make up one of the top endangered historical sites in the world. The huge structure had seven domes and a bell tower, but was destroyed by an earthquake soon after its 1812 completion, and the ruins themselves are now decaying rapidly, requiring up to $20 million in projected restoration. For an idea of how it might have looked, see the full-sized replica – now a church – just northwest of the mission.

The rest of the mission is in an above-average state of repair. The **chapel** is small and narrow, decorated with Indian drawings and Spanish artifacts, set off by a sixteenth-century altar from Barcelona. In a side room, the chapel of **St Pereguin** is a tiny room kept warm by the heat from the dozens of candles lit by miracle-seeking pilgrims who arrive here from all over the US and Mexico. Other restored buildings include the kitchen, smelter, and workshops used for dyeing, weaving, and candlemaking. There's also a rather predictable **museum** (open during mission hours; free), giving a history of the Spanish in California and displaying odds and ends from the mission's past.

The city is further noted for its **swallows**, popularly thought to return here from their winter migration on March 19. They sometimes do arrive on this day – along with large numbers of tourists – but are much more likely to show up as soon as the weather is warm enough, and when there are enough insects on the ground to provide a decent homecoming banquet.

San Clemente

Five miles south of San Juan Capistrano down I-5, **SAN CLEMENTE** is a pretty little town, its streets contoured around the hills, lending an almost Mediterranean air. Because of its proximity to one of the largest military bases in the state, **Camp Pendleton**, it's a popular weekend retreat for military personnel, and is also home to some of Orange County's better surfing beaches, especially toward the south end of town, and has a reasonable campground, too (see "Accommodation," p.103). It's here, around the city's southern tip, that San Clemente had a brief glimmer of fame when President Richard Nixon convened his **Western White House** here from 1969 to 1974, regularly meeting with cronies and political allies. The 25-acre estate is located off of Avenida del Presidente and is visible from the beach – though off limits if you want a closer look.

Eating

Whatever you want to eat and however much you want to spend, LA's **restaurants** leave you spoiled for choice. **Budget food** is, of course, plentiful here, ranging from historic diners to street-corner coffee shops and cafés to big-franchise burgers. Almost as common, and just as cheap, **Mexican food** is the closest thing you'll get to an indigenous LA cuisine. The options are almost endless for quick and cheap meals, and include free grub available for the price of a drink at **happy hours**. Many of the city's **higher-end restaurants** serve superb food in consciously cultivated surroundings, driving up their prices on the back of a good review, and typically specializing in French, Italian, Japanese, or **California cuisine** – the latter the signature style of top-notch LA eating since the 1980s, blending world cuisines into an eclectic, harmonious brew.

As any tourist knows, LA is littered with **celebrity-owned** outfits, but the food is usually so unremarkable we haven't listed them. For chowing down, celebrity watching, or just enjoying a nice view, you're better off practically anywhere else.

Budget food: coffee shops, delis, diners, and drive-ins

Budget food is everywhere in LA, at its best in the many small and stylish **coffee shops**, **delis**, and **diners** that serve soups, omelets, sandwiches, and burgers; it's easy to eat this way constantly and never have to spend much more than $6 for a full meal. There are, of course, the franchise fast-food joints on every street, though the local chains of **hamburger stands** (many open 24hr) are always much better.

Unfortunately, the best of the 1950s **drive-ins**, such as *Tiny Naylors* in Hollywood, have been torn down. However, some spots, such as *Pann's* near Inglewood, continue to cater to fans of old-fashioned formica **diners**, with their neon signs, boomerang roofs, and classic steak-and-eggs breakfasts.

LA restaurants

Downtown and around

Cassell's Hamburgers 3266 W 6th St ☎213/387-5502. No-frills takeout hamburger stand that some swear by, serving up nearly two-thirds of a pound of beef per bun. Closes at 4pm.

Clifton's Cafeteria 648 S Broadway ☎213/627-1673. Classic 1930s cafeteria, the last remaining of a chain of six, and with much bizarre decor: redwood trees, waterfall, and mini-chapel. The food is traditional meat-and-potatoes American, and cheap, too. Open until midnight.

Cole's Pacific Electric Buffet 118 E 6th St ☎213/622-4090. As the name suggests, this place has been here a very long time – since 1908, making this LA's oldest extant restaurant. The decor and food haven't changed much since then, either, with the dark-wood paneling, and ancient fixtures mirroring the rich, hearty French dip sandwiches loaded with steak, pastrami, or brisket – a dish invented at this very spot.

Grand Central Market 317 S Broadway ☎213/624-9496. Selling plenty of tacos, deli sandwiches, and Chinese food, plus a few more exotic items, like pig's ears and lamb sweetbreads. A recent renovation makes this a fun, cheap place to eat.

Langer's Deli 704 S Alvarado St ☎213/483-8050. "When in doubt, eat hot pastrami" says the sign, though you still have to choose from more than twenty ways of eating what is easily LA's best pastrami sandwich. Open daylight hours only in a dicey spot; curbside pick-up available.

Original Pantry 877 S Figueroa St ☎213/972-9279. There's always a queue for the hearty portions of very meaty American cooking – chops and steaks, mostly – in this 24hr diner owned by former mayor Dick Riordan. The quirky, old-fashioned brochures are also worth a look.

Philippe the Original French Dip 1001 N Alameda St ☎213/628-3781. 1908 sawdust café that invented the eponymous sandwich, which is served loaded with turkey, ham, lamb, or beef – an amazingly good and filling treat for less than $5.

Picholine 3360 W 1st St ☎213/252-8722. A European twist on old-fashioned comfort food, in this case a solid selection of sandwiches with upmarket ingredients – pesto, sun-dried tomato, etc – and sides of pasta to go with the mouth-watering fare. All for under eight bucks.

Yorkshire Grill 610 W 6th St ☎213/623-3362. New York–style deli and neighborhood fave since 1947, with big sandwiches and friendly service for under $10. Lunchtime is crowded with yuppies and locals; get there early, since it closes at 4pm (Sat 2pm).

Hollywood

Astro Burger 7475 Santa Monica Blvd ☎323/874-8041. Not just burgers, but sandwiches and even veggie meals are the appeal of this lower-Hollywood diner – along with the late hours, until 3am weekdays, 4am weekends.

Du-Par's 6333 W 3rd St ☎323/933-8446. A longstanding LA institution, located in the Farmers Market, which draws a whole host of grizzled old-timers for its greasy breakfasts and heavy-duty cheeseburgers. Make sure to sample a piece of pie – they come in a full range of bright colors and flavors.

Fred 62 1854 N Vermont Ave, Los Feliz ☎323/667-0062. Designed like something out of the 1950s – with a soda fountain, streamlined booths, and 24hr operation – the restaurant offers stylish, affordable California-cuisine twists on familiar staples like salads, burgers, and fries, and a tempting array of pancakes and omelets.

Mel's Drive-In 8585 Sunset Blvd ☎310/854-7200. Calorie-packing milkshakes, fries, and, of course, burgers make this 24hr diner an essential stop if you've got the late-night munchies.

Pink's Hot Dogs 709 N La Brea Ave ☎323/931-4223. The quintessence of chili dogs. Depending on your taste, these monster hot dogs are lifesavers or gut bombs. Open til 2am, or 3am weekends.

Roscoe's Chicken and Waffles 1514 N Gower St ☎323/466-7453. An unlikely spot for Hollywood's elite, this diner attracts all sorts for its fried chicken, greens, and thick waffles. Listen to the ringing pagers and cell phones as you wait in line for breakfast with movie-industry big shots. One of several area locations.

Tommy's 5873 Hollywood Blvd ☏323/467-3792. One of the prime LA spots for big, greasy, tasty burgers – and, many would say, the best. Located right off the 101 freeway through Hollywood. 24hr.

Topz 8693 Santa Monica Blvd ☏310/659-8843. A local chain of fast-food joints that focuses, somehow, on the healthier side of eating burgers, hot dogs, and french fries, with lo-cal cooking oils and lean meats on the culinary agenda.

Yukon Mining Company 7328 Santa Monica Blvd ☏323/851-8833. Excellent 24hr coffee shop with comfort food and a curious clientele – don't be surprised to see a crowd of newly arrived Russians, neighborhood pensioners, and glammed-up drag queens.

West LA

The Apple Pan 10801 W Pico Blvd ☏310/475-3585. Grab a spot at the counter and enjoy freshly baked apple pie and nicely greasy hamburgers across from the imposing Westside Pavilion mall. An old-time joint that opened just after World War II.

Barney's Beanery 8447 Santa Monica Blvd ☏323/654-2287. Two hundred bottled beers and hot dogs, hamburgers, and bowls of chili served in a hip, grungy environment, which used to be a haunt of Jim Morrison's. Open until 2am.

Canter's Deli 419 N Fairfax Ave ☏323/651-2030. Huge sandwiches for around $7 and excellent kosher soups served by famously aggressive waitresses in pink uniforms and running shoes. Open 24hr. Live music on Tuesday nights in *Canter's* adjoining "Kibitz Room."

Duke's 8909 Sunset Blvd ☏310/652-3100. A favorite haunt of visiting rock stars (the *Roxy* and *Whisky-a-Go-Go* clubs are up the street), this place attracts a motley crew of night owls and bleary-eyed locals.

Jerry's Famous Deli 8701 Beverly Blvd ☏310/289-1811. The most engaging of the many *Jerry's* locations in LA, featuring a sizeable deli menu and open 24hr. Occasionally, celebrities stop in to nosh.

John o' Groats 10516 W Pico Blvd ☏310/204-0692. Excellent cheap breakfasts and lunches (mostly staples like bacon and eggs, oatmeal, and waffles), but come at an off hour; the morning crowd can cause a headache.

Kate Mantilini 9109 Wilshire Blvd ☏310/278-3699. Tasty, upscale versions of classic American diner food, served up in a stylish interior designed by edgy architectural firm Morphosis. Open until 1am weekdays, 2am weekends.

Nate 'n' Al's 414 N Beverly Drive ☏310/274-0101. The best-known deli in Beverly Hills, popular with movie people and one of the few reasonable places in the vicinity. Get there early (opens 7am) to grab a booth.

Oki Dog 5056 W Pico Blvd ☏323/938-4369. An essential LA stop for all lovers of "red hots," in this case wieners wrapped in tortillas and stuffed with all manner of gooey, super-caloric ingredients – from pastrami to cheese to chili.

Swingers in the *Beverly Laurel Motor Hotel*, 8020 Beverly Blvd ☏323/653-5858. Affordable American comfort food – with a few eclectic vegan and pan-Asian offerings – served in a strangely trendy motel environment, luring a large crowd of hipsters and poseurs, as well as a few movie-star wannabes.

Tail o' the Pup 329 N San Vicente Blvd ☏310/652-4517. Worth a visit for the roadside pop architecture alone – a squat little wiener trapped in a massive concrete bun – though the dogs and burgers are good, too.

24-hour eats

These places satisfy hunger at all hours. For full restaurant reviews, see the appropriate sections.

Bob's Big Boy 4211 W Riverside Drive, Burbank ☏818/843-9334 – p.183

Canter's Deli 419 N Fairfax Ave, West LA ☏323/651-2030 – p.181

Fred 62 1854 N Vermont Ave, Los Feliz ☏323/667-0062 – p.180

Jerry's Famous Deli 8701 Beverly Blvd, West LA ☏310/289-1811 – p.181

Mel's Drive-In 8585 Sunset Blvd ☏310/854-7200 – p.180

Original Pantry 877 S Figueroa St, Downtown ☏213/972-9279 – p.180

Pacific Dining Car 1310 W 6th St, Downtown ☏213/483-6000 – p.185

Tommy's 5873 Hollywood Blvd, Hollywood ☏323/467-3792 – p.181

Yukon Mining Company 7328 Santa Monica Blvd, West Hollywood ☏323/851-8833 – p.181

Santa Monica, Venice, and Malibu

Bagel Nosh 1629 Wilshire Blvd, Santa Monica ℡ 310/451-8771. With an ambience straight out of the 1960s, a neighborhood favorite for its size-able breakfasts of omelets and bagel sandwiches, picked up from an old-fashioned short-order counter.

Café 50s 838 Lincoln Blvd, Venice ℡ 310/399-1955. No doubts about this place: Ritchie Valens on the jukebox, burgers on the tables.

Café Montana 1534 Montana Ave, Santa Monica ℡ 310/829-3990. Eclectic menu is highlighted by solid breakfasts, excellent salads, and hearty grilled fish, in an upmarket section of Santa Monica.

Crocodile Café 101 Santa Monica Blvd, Santa Monica ℡ 310/394-4783. Pizzas, sandwiches, and burgers are the dining allure at this inexpensive nouveau fast-food spot, part of a local chain.

Norm's 1601 Lincoln Blvd, Santa Monica ℡ 310/450-0074. One of the last remaining classic diners, this local chain has nine other LA branches and serves breakfasts and lunches for around $5. Great Googie architecture, too.

Rae's Diner 2901 Pico Blvd, Santa Monica ℡ 310/828-7937. Classic 1950s diner with heavy comfort food. Its turquoise-blue facade and interior has been seen in many films, notably Tony Scott's *True Romance*.

Reel Inn 18661 PCH, Malibu ℡ 310/456-8221. Seafood diner by the beach, with appealing prices and a good atmosphere. Also at 1220 W 3rd St, Santa Monica (℡ 310/395-5538).

The South Bay and Harbor Area

Blueberry Hill 5735 E PCH, Long Beach ℡ 562/986-4455. Hefty helpings of good, old-fashioned comfort food, a spot where the burgers are chunky and mouthwatering, the onion rings are stacked high, and the fries come coated in thick gravy.

East Coast Bagels 5753 E PCH, Long Beach ℡ 562/985-0933. Located in a dreary mini-mall, but with an excellent, wide selection of bagels, ranging from New York staples to California hybrids like the jalapeno-cheddar bagel stuffed with cream cheese.

Hof's Hut 6257 E 2nd St, Long Beach ℡ 562/598-4070. One bite of the *Hut*'s juicy Hofburger and you know you've found the real deal. Three other Long Beach locations, and seven in Orange County.

Johnny Reb's 4663 N Long Beach Blvd, Long Beach ℡ 562/423-7327. The waft of BBQ ribs,

catfish, and hush puppies alone may draw you to this prime Southern spot, where the portions are large and the price is cheap.

The Local Yolk 3414 Highland Ave, Manhattan Beach ℡ 310/546-4407. As the name suggests, everything done with eggs, plus muffins and pancakes. Breakfast and lunch only.

Pier Bakery 100 Fisherman's Wharf #M, Redondo Beach ℡ 310/376-9582. A small but satisfying menu with jalapeno-cheese bread and cinnamon rolls. Probably the best food in this touristy area.

Disneyland and around

Angelo's 511 S State College Blvd, Anaheim ℡ 714/533-1401. Straight out of *Happy Days*, a drive-in complete with roller-skating car-hops, neon signs, vintage cars, and, incidentally, good burgers.

Heroes 305 N Harbor Blvd, Fullerton ℡ 714/738-4356. The place to come if you're starving after hitting the theme parks, a spot to knock back one of the countless beers available or chow down on items like hamburgers, beef stroganoff, or meatloaf.

Knott's Chicken Dinner Restaurant located just outside Knott's Berry Farm at 8039 Beach Blvd, Buena Park ℡ 714/220-5080. Serving cheap and tasty meals for over 65 years. People flocked here for delicious fried-chicken dinners long before Disneyland was around, and they still do; there's also a mean boysenberry pie.

Mimi's Café 18342 Imperial Hwy, Yorba Linda ℡ 714/996-3650. Huge servings, low prices, and a relaxing atmosphere down the street from the Nixon Library. Part of a sizeable chain in Los Angeles and Orange counties, and popular in both.

Orange County Coast

The Cottage 308 N Coast Hwy, Laguna Beach ℡ 949/494-3023. Hungry beachgoers can choose from filling American breakfasts, or else affordable seafood, pasta, and chicken dishes at lunch and dinner.

Crab Cooker 2200 Newport Blvd, Newport Beach T949/673-0100. The hefty plates of crab legs and steaming bowls of chowder make the long lines here a bit more bearable.

Duke's 317 PCH, Huntington Beach ℡ 714/374-6446. Stick to staples like steak and salad at this frenetic beachside favorite, which is best for its prime location near the pier.

Harbor House Café 34157 PCH, Dana Point ℡ 949/496-9270. Worth seeking out for its prime breakfasts, particularly the over-stuffed, gut-busting omelets – a huge slew of them, with a veritable laundry list of options.

Jack Shrimp 2400 W Coast Hwy, Newport Beach ☎949/650-5577. One in a chain of Cajun dinner establishments in various spots along the Orange County Coast, with an appealing assortment of spicy seafood and fairly authentic Louisiana staples.

Ruby's 1 Balboa Pier, Newport Beach ☎949/675-RUBY. The first and finest of the retro-streamline 1940s diners that have popped up all over LA – in a great location at the end of Newport's popular pier. Mostly offers the standard burgers, fries, and soda fare.

Zinc Café 350 Ocean Ave, Laguna Beach ☎949/494-2791. A popular breakfast counter offering simple soup-and-salad meals and other light fare. Good for a day on the sands.

The San Gabriel and San Fernando valleys

Art's Deli 12224 Ventura Blvd, Studio City ☎818/762-1221. Longtime film-industry favorite (mainly for old-timers, not for the nubile), with a good range of hefty, scrumptious sandwiches and soups.

Bob's Big Boy 4211 W Riverside Drive, Burbank ☎818/843-9334. The classic chain diner, fronted by the plump burger lad, and a veritable pop-architecture classic, saved from demolition through the efforts of Googie preservationists. 24hr.

Dr Hogly-Wogly's Tyler Texas Bar-B-Q 8136 Sepulveda Blvd, Van Nuys ☎818/780-6701. Long lines for some of the best chicken, sausages, ribs, and beans in LA, despite the depressing surroundings in the middle of nowhere.

Fair Oaks Pharmacy and Soda Fountain 1526 Mission St, South Pasadena ☎626/799-1414. A fabulously restored old-fashioned soda fountain with many old-time drinks like lime rickeys and egg creams – a historic 1915 highlight along the former Route 66.

Goldstein's Bagel Bakery 86 W Colorado Blvd, Pasadena ☎626/792-2435. If money's tight, feast on day-old 15¢ bagels; otherwise enjoy what some call LA's best bagels, made in a New York style. In the Old Pasadena shopping district.

Law Dogs 14114 Sherman Way, Van Nuys ☎818/908-3234. Another of those only-in-LA establishments, this one serving up adequate hot dogs from a basic food stand, but with the added attraction of free legal advice (Wed 7pm) dished out by the attorney-proprietor.

Pie & Burger 913 E California Blvd, Pasadena ☎626/795-1123. Classic coffee shop, with primo cheeseburgers and excellent fruit pies, served fresh and hot to your gullet.

Porto's Bakery 315 N Brand Blvd, Glendale ☎818/956-5996. Popular and cheap café serving Cuban flaky pastries and sandwiches, rum-soaked cheesecakes, muffins, Danishes, croissants, torts, and tarts, and cappuccino.

Rose Tree Cottage 395 E California Blvd, Pasadena ☎626/793-3337. Scones, shortbread, and high tea in a country-home setting so thoroughly English that it's the West Coast HQ of the British Tourist Board. Reservations are essential.

Wolfe Burgers 46 N Lake Ave, Pasadena ☎626/792-7292. Knockout gyros, chili, tamales, and burgers – a longstanding Valley favorite.

Mexican and Latin American

LA's **Mexican** restaurants offer the city's best – and most plentiful – foodstuffs, serving tasty, healthy, and filling meals for as little as $5. Those in East LA are some of the finest, though you can find a good selection of both authentic and Americanized fare all over the city. **Caribbean** food is less visible but, when sought out, can be quite rewarding, especially in its Cuban incarnation. The cuisine of the rest of **Latin America** is also increasingly popular, whether it be a mix of flavors and spices from Central American countries like Honduras and Nicaragua, a tasty blend of local seafood and native Peruvian cuisine (aka "Peruvian seafood"), or the hot, garlicky platters of Argentine beef that have found aficionados throughout the Westside.

Downtown and around

Burrito King 2109 W Sunset Blvd, Echo Park ☎213/484-9859. Excellent burritos and tasty tostadas from this small stand; open until 2am.

Ciro's 705 N Evergreen Ave, East LA ☎323/267-8637. A split-level cave of a dining room, serving enormous platters of shrimp and *mole* specials.

The *flautas* are the main draw, and they also offer takeout.

El Cholo 1121 S Western Ave ☎323/734-2773. One of LA's first big Mexican restaurants and still one of the best – offering a solid array of staples like enchiladas and tamales – despite the frequent presence of drunken frat-rats from nearby USC.

King Taco 1104 S Hoover St ☎213/738-9197. One in a chain of many such restaurants around Downtown, with many varieties of tacos – most of them quite savory.

La Luz del Día 107 Paseo de la Plaza ☎213/628-7495. Amid the throngs of trinket vendors on Olvera Street, this authentic Mexican eatery is worth seeking out for its fiery burritos, enchiladas, and stews, served in sizeable enough portions to make you sweat with delight.

Luminarias 3500 W Ramona Blvd, Monterey Park ☎323/268-4177. Dance to salsa and merengue between bites of seafood-heavy Mexican food. The Spanish name refers to honorary candles in brown paper bags. See "Live music," p.204.

Hollywood

Casa Carnitas 4067 Beverly Blvd, south of Hollywood ☎323/667-9953. Tasty Mexican food from the Yucatán: the dishes are inspired by Cuban and Caribbean cooking – lots of fine seafood, too.

Havana on Sunset 5825 Sunset Blvd ☎323/464-1800. Like the name says, everything is Cuban at this festive eatery, from the lively music to the rich, authentic meals of soups, seafood, and garlic-heavy entrees.

Mario's Peruvian Seafood Restaurant 5786 Melrose Ave ☎323/466-4181. Delicious and authentic Peruvian fare: supremely tender squid, rich and flavorful mussels, with a hint of soy sauce in some dishes.

Mexico City 2121 N Hillhurst Ave ☎323/661-7227. Spinach enchiladas and other Californian versions of Mexican standards served in red booths, with a great view of the street from the wall-length window.

Yuca's Hut 2056 N Hillhurst Ave ☎323/662-1214. A hidden jewel with good al fresco burritos.

West LA

Baja Fresh 475 N Beverly Drive ☎310/858-6690. Cheap, enjoyable chain serving Mexican food to a hungry crowd of window shoppers and movie-industry wannabes with an emphasis on "healthy" eating.

Carlitos Gardel 7963 Melrose Ave ☎323/655-0891. Seriously rich and tasty Argentine cuisine – ie, heavy on the beef and spices, with sausages and garlic adding to the kick.

El Compadre 7408 W Sunset Blvd ☎323/874-7924. With potent margaritas, live mariachi bands, and cheap Mexican standards, this is a music-loving gourmand's delight. One of several locations, most in more distant parts of the metropolis.

El Coyote 7312 Beverly Blvd ☎323/939-2255. An eatery known to practically every Westsider, for better or worse. Labyrinthine restaurant serving

heavy Mexican food, more than you can stand. But cheap and lethal margaritas are the primary draw to the gloomy setting.

La Salsa 1154 Westwood Blvd ☎310/208-7083. The place to come for fresh, delicious, soft tacos and burritos.

Versailles 10319 Venice Blvd ☎310/558-3168. Busy and noisy authentic Cuban restaurant with excellent fried plantains, paella, and black beans and rice. Also nearby at 1415 S La Cienega Blvd (☎310/289-0392).

Zabumba 10717 Venice Blvd, Culver City ☎310/841-6525. In a colorful building amid drab surroundings, this venue is a Brazilian favorite for its bossa nova music, Latin American–inflected pizzas, tasty seafood, and convivial atmosphere.

Santa Monica, Venice, and Malibu

Border Grill 1445 4th St, Santa Monica ☎310/451-1655. Good place to sup on shrimp, pork, plantains, and other Latin American–flavored fixings, with excellent desserts, too.

Gaucho Grill 1251 Third Street Promenade, Santa Monica ☎310/394-4966. One in a fine local chain of Argentine beef-houses, where the steaks come rich and garlicky, and the spices can bowl you over.

Mariasol 401 Santa Monica Pier, Santa Monica ☎310/917-5050. *Cervezas* with a view, hidden away at the end of the pier, with good, straight-forward Mexican staples. On weekend afternoons, the small rooftop deck affords a sweeping panorama from Malibu to Venice.

Marix Tex-Mex Playa 118 Entrada Drive, Pacific Palisades ☎310/459-8596. Flavorful fajitas and big margaritas in this rowdy beachfront cantina. Also at 1108 N Flores St, Hollywood ☎323/656-8800.

The South Bay and Harbor Area

Alegria Cocina Latina 115 Pine Ave, Long Beach ☎562/436-3388. Tapas, gazpacho, and a variety of *platos principales* served with sangría on the patio, and to the beat of live flamenco on weekends. Good location near the harbor in Downtown Long Beach.

El Pollo Inka 1100 PCH, Hermosa Beach ☎310/372-1433. Good Peruvian-style chicken, catfish, and hot and spicy soups to make your mouth water. For a closer visit, try the one at 11701 Wilshire Blvd, Westwood (☎310/571-3334).

Pancho's 3615 Highland Ave, Manhattan Beach ☎310/545-6670. Big portions of old favorites like tacos and burritos, and fairly cheap for the area. One of the few decent Mexican establishments down this way.

Taco Beach 211 Pine Ave, Long Beach ☎562-983-1337. As you might guess, fish tacos are the main draw here, though the rest of the eatery's south-of-the-border fare is also quite good.

The San Gabriel and San Fernando valleys

Don Cuco's 3911 W Riverside Drive, Burbank ☎818/842-1123. Good food, mainly familiar Mexican staples, with a great Sunday brunch. One of several in a Valley chain.

El Tepeyac 800 S Palm Ave, Alhambra ☎626/281-3366. Huge, luscious burritos and hot salsa bring true lovers of Mexican food out to this rather removed section of the San Gabriel Valley.

Izalco 10729 Burbank Blvd, North Hollywood ☎818/760-0396. Salvadoran cuisine presented with grace and style, from plantains and pork ribs to corn cakes and *pupusas* – a bit of a pleasant surprise for the area.

Kingston Café 333 S Fair Oaks Ave, Pasadena ☎626/405-8080. All the Caribbean favorites make an appearance here, including oxtail, plantains, jerk chicken, beans and rice, and other traditional specialties of Jamaica and other islands.

Señor Fish 618 Mission St, South Pasadena ☎626/403-0145. Somewhat drab-looking joint with great fish tacos and charbroiled halibut for under $10.

Xiomara 69 N Raymond Ave, Pasadena ☎626/796-2520. An upscale Old Pasadena eatery serving tasty Cuban and Latin American meals, with the accent on beef, pork, and fish entrees and a nice range of stews and colorful sauces.

American, California cuisine, and Cajun

American cuisine – with its steaks, ribs, baked potatoes, and salads – has a low profile in faddish LA, although it's available almost everywhere and may not even cost more than $15 for a comparative blow-out. More prominent – and more expensive, at upwards of $20 per entree – is **California cuisine**, based on local ingredients (though originating in San Francisco), more likely grilled than fried, and stylishly presented with a nod to nouvelle **French** cuisine. Another rage is spicy, fish-based **Cajun cooking**, available in its authentic form and often inexpensive.

Downtown and around

Angelique Café 840 S Spring St ☎213/623-8698. A marvelous Continental eatery in the middle of the Garment District, where you can sit on the quaint patio and dine on well-crafted pastries for breakfast or savory sandwiches, rich casseroles, and fine salads for lunch.

Café Pinot 700 W 5th St ☎213/239-6500. Located next to the LA Public Library, this elegant restaurant offers a touch of French cooking for its nouvelle California cuisine – one of the best known in LA for that style.

Checkers 535 S Grand Ave in the *Hilton Checkers* ☎213/891-0519. One of the most elegant Downtown restaurants, serving top-rated California cuisine, with rack of lamb and sea bass among the better offerings. If you're lucky, you can escape with a bill under $100.

Engine Co. No. 28 644 S Figueroa St ☎213/624-6996. All-American grilled steaks and seafood, served in a renovated 1912 fire station. Great french fries and an excellent wine list round out this classic local eatery.

L.A. Prime in the *Westin Bonaventure*, 404 S Figueroa St ☎213/612-4743. Plump slabs of tender Midwestern beef are the draw at this New York–style steakhouse, if you can stomach the bill, while the side orders and Strawberries Romanoff dessert hold their own. Fine views from the hotel's 35th floor.

Pacific Dining Car 1310 W 6th St ☎213/483-6000. Would-be English supper club where the Downtown elite used to cut secret deals, located inside an old railroad carriage. Open until 2am for (very expensive) steaks. Breakfast is the best value.

Patina 141 S Grand Ave ☎213/972-3331. Fancy, ultra-swank Disney Hall branch of one of LA's signature eateries, where you can devour pheasant in apple-champagne sauce, pork loin medallions, and other rotating items on the menu, if you're prepared to drop a wad of cash.

Water Grill 544 S Grand Ave ☎213/891-0900. One of the top-notch spots for munching on California cuisine in LA, or anywhere, with the focus on seafood, prepared in all manner of colorful and ever-changing ways. Extremely pricey, though.

Hollywood

Alex 6703 Melrose Ave ☎323/933-5233. Located between Hollywood and Mid-Wilshire, a California-cuisine take on French cooking, emphasizing the

185

usual delicious culinary experiments under dark decor and moody lighting.

Cha Cha Cha 656 N Virgil Ave ☏323/664-7723. Offering paella, black-pepper shrimp, jerk chicken, and other Caribbean treats. Also at 762 Pacific Ave, Long Beach ☏562/436-3900.

Hollywood Canteen 1006 N Seward St ☏323/465-0961. A dark club scene with fish, steak, and clam chowder – just the right ambience to make you feel like a Tinseltown big shot. Not as pricey as similar joints in the area.

Musso and Frank Grill 6667 Hollywood Blvd ☏323/467-7788. A 1919 classic, loaded with authentic Hollywood atmosphere and history in a dark-paneled dining room. The drinks (see p.194) are better than the pricey, mostly upscale diner, food.

Off Vine 6263 Leland Way ☏323/962-1900. Dine on eclectic Cal cuisine – pecan chicken, duck sausage, and Grand Marnier soufflé – in a renovated but still funky Craftsman bungalow. Popular among the snoots.

Patina 5955 Melrose Ave ☏323/467-1108. This dark, clubby, and ultra-chic place delivers exquisite California cuisine, taking duck, chicken, and pheasant, adding exotic spices and herbs, and throwing in the occasional kidney or calf's foot – more appetizing than it sounds.

Pig 'n Whistle 6714 Hollywood Blvd ☏323/463-0000. Historic 1927 eatery refurbished as a swank Cal-cuisine restaurant, with the emphasis on all things porcine, from ribs to pork roast to bacon. Although much of the old spirit and decor are the same, the prices are not: no diner has food this pricey.

Pinot Hollywood 1448 Gower St ☏323/461-8800. Upmarket American food crossed with nouvelle French, in a spacious environment with 24 types of martinis and Polish potato vodka. You may even spot a celebrity or two, lurking in the shadows.

vermont 1714 N Vermont Ave ☏323/661-6163. One of the best Cal-cuisine eateries to open in recent years. The entrees are predictable enough – roasted chicken, crab cakes, ravioli, etc – but the culinary presentation is effective and, on occasion, inspired.

Vida 1930 Hillhurst Ave, Los Feliz ☏213/660-4446. Despite the cringe-inducing puns on the menu – Thai Cobb Salad and the like – this is ground zero for LA's culinary hipster set, with a dark, quasi-Polynesian bar and succulent Cal-cuisine, like calamari (oddly served in a paper bag) and organic, hormone-free meat and chicken dishes.

West LA

Barefoot 8722 W 3rd St ☏310/276-6223. Good pasta, pizza, and seafood between Beverly Hills and the Beverly Center. Considering the prime location, very affordable.

Cajun Bistro 8301 Sunset Blvd, West Hollywood ☏323/656-6388. Funky, unpretentious Cajun joint on a central part of the strip that offers tasty Louisiana cooking – especially the jambalaya – without busting your wallet.

Flora Kitchen 460 S La Brea Ave ☏323/931-9900. Perhaps the city's best restaurant connected to a flower shop – in this case, the nearby Rita Flora. Apart from flowers, the key attractions here are the California cuisine–style sandwiches, made with a host of tasty, fresh ingredients.

The Gumbo Pot 6333 W 3rd St in the Farmers Market ☏323/933-0358. Delicious, dirt-cheap Cajun food in a busy setting; try the gumbo yaya (chicken, shrimp, and sausage) or the fruit-and-potato salad.

Jar 8225 Beverly Blvd ☏323/655-6566. A steakhouse that features all the usual red-meat fare with an inspired Cal-cuisine flair, throwing in different spices and exotic flavors to create an unusual, yet strangely traditional, result.

L'Orangerie 903 N La Cienega Blvd, West Hollywood ☏310/652 9770. Nouvelle California–style French cuisine; if you haven't got the $150 it takes to sit down, enjoy the view from the bar.

La Boheme 8400 Santa Monica Blvd, West Hollywood ☏323/848-2360. The dark, somewhat spooky decor is matched by the indulgent melange of Cal-cuisine flavors mixed with pan-Asian cooking, for a truly memorable experience.

Lucques 8474 Melrose Ave ☏323/655-6277. Expensive but tasty eatery that doles out comfort food for the culinary elite – ribs, chicken, and pork dishes that have an all-American flavor but also feature exotic sauces and ingredients.

Maple Drive 345 N Maple Drive, Beverly Hills ☏310/274-9800. Fine food from a large culinary palette, including tasty foie gras, meatloaf, and pork chops. If you're lucky, you might spot local celebs sneaking in for an oyster or two.

Maurice's Snack 'n' Chat 5549 W Pico Blvd ☏323/931-3877. Everything here is cooked to order: spoon bread or baked chicken requires a call two hours ahead, though you could just drop in for fried chicken, pork chops, grits, or salmon croquettes.

McCormick and Schmick's 206 N Rodeo Drive, Beverly Hills ☏310/859-0434. Swank seafood joint for business types known for a great weekend dinner special; part of an esteemed national chain.

Spago 176 N Cañon Drive ☎310/385-0880. Now that the original Sunset Strip branch of LA's most famous restaurant has closed, you'll have to go to this stuffy Beverly Hills location to get a taste of Wolfgang Puck's latest Cal-cuisine concoctions, among them designer pizzas.

Santa Monica, Venice, and Malibu

17th Street Café 1610 Montana Ave, Santa Monica ☎310/453-2771. Seafood, pasta, sandwiches, and burgers at moderate prices in a chic part of town. Nicely casual, unpretentious atmosphere.

Gladstone's 4 Fish 17300 PCH ☎310/573-0212. An inevitable tourist stop at the junction of Sunset Blvd, known best for its prime beachfront location – not for its heavily fried and breaded seafood or steep prices.

Granita 23725 W Malibu Rd ☎310/456-0488. If you can't get enough of Wolfgang Puck (see *Spago*, above), check out his Malibu entry – a heady mix of Cal-cuisine and Italian flavors. Delicious and pricey, and good for spotting a few names here and there.

Hal's 1349 Abbot Kinney Blvd, Venice ☎310/396-3105. Popular restaurant along a hip shopping zone in Venice, with a range of well-done American standards, including marinated steaks and salmon dishes.

Joe's 1023 Abbot Kinney Blvd, Venice ☎310/399-5811. One of the less heralded of LA's better eateries, offering appealing California-cuisine dishes (mixed with a dash of French cookery) using staples like crispy chicken, pork, and salmon.

Killer Shrimp 523 Washington Blvd, Marina del Rey ☎310/578-2293. When all you want is shrimp, and lots of it, this popular, somewhat dreary-looking spot is the place to come. For a pretty cheap price, you can happily stuff your maw with crustaceans.

Michael's 1147 3rd St, Santa Monica ☎310/451-0843. Longstanding favorite for California cuisine, and supposedly one of the restaurants that invented it, served here amid modern art. This venerable establishment always attracts the crowds for its steaks, pasta, and fowl – reservations are essential.

Saddle Peak Lodge 419 Cold Canyon Rd, Calabasas ☎818/222-3888. On the San Fernando Valley side of the Santa Monica Mountains, this is elite LA's nod to rustic hunting lodges, where exquisite California cuisine is presented below mounted game heads, and you can elegantly devour anything from venison to boar to antelope.

Italian, Spanish, and Greek

LA has a good number of eateries specializing in regional **Italian** cooking, especially around the Westside. The phenomenon of **designer pizza** continues to grow, featuring toppings such as duck, shiitake mushrooms, and other exotic ingredients. The problem with all this? It doesn't come cheap. A pasta dish in the average Italian restaurant can cost upwards of $15, and the least-elaborate designer pizza will set you back $10. **Spanish** food and tapas bars have also become popular, and pricey. In contrast, if you want **Greek** food, you'll have to look hard – restaurants are good but uncommon.

Downtown and around

Ciao Trattoria 815 W 7th St ☎213/624-2244. Housed in a striking Romanesque building, full of lovely historic-revival decor, a good choice for upscale, Northern Italian dining. Somewhat pricey, but not as bad as you might think.

Cicada 617 S Olive St ☎213/488-9488. Lodged in the stunning Art Deco Oviatt Building (see p.112), this Northern Italian restaurant offers fine pasta for half the price of its fish and steak entrees.

Ciudad 445 S Figueroa St ☎213/486-5171. Roast chicken and quinoa fritters are some of the highlights of this colorful Mexican-influenced Spanish spot, where the live Latin music competes with the delicious food for your attention.

Papa Cristo's 2771 W Pico Blvd ☎323/737-2970. Consider venturing to this grim neighborhood near the 10 freeway to sample the authentic delights at this Greek joint, where you can munch on delicious gyros and spanakopita or have a hefty meal of lamb chops or roast chicken without even spending ten bucks.

Hollywood

Chianti Cucina 7383 Melrose Ave ☎323/653-8333. Old-fashioned 1930s restaurant amid Melrose chaos south of Hollywood. Try the delicious ravioli or go with the well-crafted chicken and lamb dishes.

Louise's Trattoria 4500 Los Feliz Blvd ☎323/667-0777. Everybody in LA knows this chain: some love it for its good, mid-priced pizzas, some hate it for its overcooked, uninspired pasta. You decide.

Miceli's 1646 N Las Palmas Ave ☎323/466-3438. Hefty, old-style pizzas that come laden with gooey cheese and plenty of tomato sauce. It's hardly nouvelle cuisine, but you'll be too busy scarfing it down to notice.

Palermo 1858 N Vermont Ave ☎323/663-1178. As old as Hollywood, and with as many devoted fans, who flock here for the rich Southern Italian pizzas, cheesy decor, and gallons of cheapish red wine. If you like huge platefuls of spaghetti in chunky red sauce, this is the place.

West LA

Ca' Brea 346 S La Brea Ave ☎323/938-2863. One of LA's best-known, and best, choices for Italian cuisine, and especially good for *osso buco* and risotto. Getting in is difficult, so reserve ahead and expect to pay a bundle.

Campanile 624 S La Brea Ave ☎323/938-1447. Incredible but very expensive Northern Italian food – the likes of rosemary-infused lamb and butternut-squash ravioli – if you can't afford a dinner, try the dessert or the best bread in Los Angeles at the adjacent *La Brea Bakery*.

Cobras and Matadors 7615 Beverly Blvd ☎323/932-6178. A fine tapas restaurant just down the street from Pan Pacific Park, where you can sample all your favorite Castilian delights in a hushed, dramatic setting.

Delphi 1383 Westwood Blvd ☎310/478-2900. The place to come in West LA for authentic Greek cooking, from flavorful *dolmas* and tabouli to the hearty pitas and *souvlaki* – an unpretentious joint that offers plenty of food for a reasonable price.

Locanda Veneta 8638 W 3rd St ☎310/274-1893. Scrumptious ravioli, risotto, veal, and carpaccio – you can't go wrong at one of LA's previously quiet culinary joys. But be prepared to wait.

Mimosa 8009 Beverly Blvd ☎323/655-8895. French bistro cooking with an accent on pasta, making for savory offerings like seafood risotto, beef bourguignon and tagliatelle, and macaroni with prosciutto au gratin.

Santa Monica, Venice, and Malibu

Abbot's Pizza Company 1407 Abbot Kinney Blvd, Venice ☎310/396-7334. Named after the old-time founder of the district, this home of the bagel-crust

pizza allows your choice of seeds, tangy citrus sauce, or shiitake and wild mushroom sauce. Also at 1811 Pico Blvd, Santa Monica (☎310/314-2777).

Drago 2628 Wilshire Blvd, Santa Monica ☎310/828-1585. One of the better of LA's super-chic Italian eateries, offering various meats and pastas with eclectic ingredients and sauces, in an appropriately pretentious setting.

Valentino 3115 Pico Blvd, Santa Monica ☎310/829-4313. Some call this the best Italian cuisine in the US, served up in classy surroundings with great flair. For a hefty sum, you can be the judge.

Wildflour Pizza 2807 Main St, Santa Monica ☎310/392-3300. Serving up a great thin-crust pizza, this cozy little spot often draws the crowds.

Wolfgang Puck Express 1315 3rd St, Santa Monica ☎310/576-4770. On the second floor of a food mall, watch Promenade tourists below while munching on great pizzas and salads. One of a national chain.

The South Bay and Harbor Area

Alegria Cocina Latina 115 Pine Ave, Long Beach ☎562/436-3388. Quality tapas and gazpacho served with plenty of sangría on the patio, and to the beat of live flamenco every night, in a prime location in Downtown Long Beach.

L'Opera 101 Pine Ave ☎562/491-0066. Very swank Italian dining – mixed with a fair bit of California-cuisine style – in a historic old building near the center of Long Beach's Downtown activity.

Mangiamo 128 Manhattan Beach Blvd, Manhattan Beach ☎310/318-3434. Like the name says, "Let's eat!" Fairly pricey but worth it for the specialist Northern Italian seafood – and right off the beach, too.

Mykonos 5374 E 2nd St, Long Beach ☎562/434-1856. Authentic dishes and spirited nightly dancing at this unpretentious Greek eatery, where the gyros, souvlaki, and other favorites are served with culinary flair.

The San Gabriel and San Fernando valleys

Café Santorini 64–70 W Union St, Pasadena ☎626/564-4200. A fine mix of Greek and Italian food – capellini, *souvlaki*, and risotto – with a little Armenian sausage thrown in as well. Located in a relaxed plaza and offering some patio dining.

La Luna Negra 44 W Green St, Pasadena ☎626/844-4331. An affordable spot for mouth-watering tapas, including classic croquetas, paellas, and spicy seafood dishes – prepared in mostly traditional fashion.

Market City Caffè 164 E Palm Ave, Burbank
☎818/840-7036. Southern Italian cuisine featuring a range of Mediterranean delights, along with a
supreme antipasto bar.
Panzanella 14928 Ventura Blvd, Sherman Oaks
☎818/784-4400. Some of the best Italian cuisine
in LA, taking foodways from central Italy and adding a dash of California creativity, while staying

true to the simple, delicious character of traditional
pasta, rice, and beef dishes.
Spark Woodfire 11801 Ventura Blvd, Studio City
☎714/960-0996. A chic Italian eatery with a
California twist, though still remaining authentic
enough to serve up tasty pasta, pizza, and
prosciutto to a crowd of TV producers, B-list
actors, and locals in the know.

Japanese, Chinese, Thai, and Korean

LA's most fashionable districts offer great **sushi** bars and **dim sum** restaurants,
favored by foreign visitors and fast-lane yuppies alike, where you can easily eat
your way through more than $30. Lower-priced and less pretentious outlets
tend to be Downtown, where you can get a fair-sized meal for around $12.
There are also a good number of excellent **Thai** and **Korean** eateries – for
which you can expect to pay around $15 per meal, or up to $50 for some
top-notch Korean spots.

Downtown and around

Dong Il Jang 3455 W 8th St ☎213/383-5757.
Cozy little Korean restaurant where the meat is
cooked at your table and the food is consistently
good, especially the grilled chicken and BBQ beef.
Tempura dishes and a sushi bar are an added
draw.
Grand Star 934 Sun Mun Way, Chinatown
☎213/626-2285. While the traditional soups and
meat dishes here are flavorful and authentic, the
real appeal is the video karaoke on Sun, Tues, and
Wed. Also offers takeout.
Mandarin Deli 727 N Broadway #109
☎213/623-6054. Very delectable and cheap
noodles, pork, and fish dumplings, and other
hearty staples in the middle of Broadway's riot
of activity. Also at 356 E 2nd St, Little Tokyo
(☎213/617-0231).
Mitsuru Café 117 Japanese Village Plaza,
Little Tokyo ☎213/613-1028. Exotic snow
cones made with *kintoki* (bean paste) or milk
kintoki (sweet custard). Try the *imagawayaki*
– adzuki beans baked in a bun. Located in a
popular mall.
Mon Kee's 679 N Spring St, Chinatown
☎213/628-6717. Long-standing favorite for fresh
fish and rich, hearty seafood soups.
Ocean Seafood 750 N Hill St ☎213/687-3088.
Cavernous but often busy Cantonese restaurant
serving inexpensive and excellent food – abalone,
crab, shrimp, and duck are among many standout
choices.
Pho 79 727 N Broadway #120 ☎213/625-7026.
Great spot for noodles and authentic soups, a
Vietnamese chain without too many frills, but with
excellent flavors.

Yang Chow 819 N Broadway, Chinatown
☎213/625-0811. Solid Chinese restaurant, where
you can't go wrong with the Szechuan beef or any
shrimp dish.

Hollywood

Chan Darae 1511 N Cahuenga Blvd ☎323/464-
8585. Terrific Thai food, and the locals know it,
with a full range of scrumptious staples such as
tom yum soup and pad thai.
Jitlada 5233 Sunset Blvd ☎323/667-9809. In a
dreary mini-mall, but the spicy chicken, squid, and
seafood curries more than make up for the setting.
Affordable prices, too.
Joss 9255 Sunset Blvd ☎310/276-1886. Sitting
at the west end of the Sunset Strip, the Westside's
version of Chinese cuisine: pricey meals with rich,
complex flavors and a minimum of excessive color
and style – which, of course, makes it all very hip.
Sanamluang Café 5176 Hollywood Blvd
☎323/660-8006. You can't beat the cheap and
plentiful noodles at this nearly-all-night Thai eatery.
Shibucho 3114 Beverly Blvd ☎213/387-8498.
Seriously tasty, locally popular sushi bar just south
of Silver Lake; go with someone who knows what
to order, as the sole waitress doesn't speak English. Otherwise, the squid and eel are quite fine,
along with the famed *toro*, an expensive but delicious tuna delicacy.
Tommy Tang's 7313 Melrose Ave ☎323/937-
5733. Terrific, very chic Thai restaurant in a hot
shopping zone, and the incongruous setting for
Tuesday drag nights, when the male waiters can
be seen "en femme."
Vim 5132 Hollywood Blvd ☎323/662-1017.
Authentic Thai and Chinese food at low prices.

Especially good are the seafood soup and that old favorite, pad thai.

West LA

Chaya Brasserie 8741 Alden Drive ☎310/859-8833. Pan-Asian bistro with moderate-to-expensive prices and a chic clientele that lurches in to munch on fancy presentations of noodle, curry, and fish dishes. Worth a splurge if you like your Asian fare with LA trendiness.

Chin Chin 8618 Sunset Blvd ☎310/652-1818. Flashy but good dim sum café, a longstanding favorite and one of several around town. Open till midnight.

Chung King 11538 W Pico Blvd ☎310/477-4917. The best neighborhood Chinese restaurant in LA, serving spicy Szechuan food: don't miss out on the *bum-bum* chicken and other house specialties.

Genghis Cohen 740 N Fairfax Ave ☎323/653-0640. Familiar Chinese dishes with a Yiddish touch: the menu abounds with culinary puns, much like the restaurant's name. The Szechuan beef and *kung pao* chicken are good, as are the chicken wings served at lunchtime.

Matsuhisa 129 N La Cienega Blvd ☎310/659-9639. The biggest name in town for sushi, charging the highest prices for sea urchin, eel, black cod, and the like. Essential if you're a raw-fish aficionado with a wad of cash; otherwise you can dine two or three times at other fine, and much cheaper, Japanese restaurants.

Mishima 8474 W 3rd St ☎323/782-0181. Great miso soup and *udon* and *soba* noodles, at very affordable prices at this chic, popular Westside eatery.

Mori Sushi 11500 W Pico Blvd ☎323/479-3939. A quietly stylish spot that resists trendiness, but still offers up some of the city's finest sushi, often presented in spare and elegant arrangements, and almost always delicious.

The Sushi House 12013 W Pico Blvd ☎310/479-1507. Reggae and sushi coalesce in a small bar with limited seating. Try the "Superman," a rainbow-colored roll of salmon, yellowtail, whitefish, and avocado.

Talesai 9198 Olympic Blvd, Beverly Hills ☎310/271-9345. Excellent curried seafood, corncakes, and Cal-cuisine-leaning noodle dishes served to knowing gourmets in a drab strip mall.

Santa Monica, Venice, and Malibu

Chaya Venice 110 Navy St, Venice ☎310/396-

1179. Elegant mix of Japanese and Mediterranean foods in an arty sushi bar, with a suitably snazzy clientele.

Chinois on Main 2709 Main St, Santa Monica ☎310/392-9025. Expensive Wolfgang Puck restaurant, mixing nouvelle French and Chinese cuisine for a ravenous crowd of yuppie diners and self-appointed food critics.

Flower of Siam 2553 Lincoln Blvd, Venice ☎310/827-0050. Some swear by this spicy but succulent, authentic Thai food, guaranteed to set your tastebuds on fire and your eyes watering.

Lighthouse Buffet 201 Arizona Ave, Santa Monica ☎310/451-2076. All-you-can-eat sushi; indulge to your heart's content for around $10 at lunchtime or $20 in the evening.

Sushi Roku 1401 Ocean Ave, Santa Monica ☎310/458-4771. While the ambience here can be a bit on the stuffy side, this upscale eatery is worth visiting for its fine Spanish mackerel sushi, monkfish, octopus sashimi, and crab rolls.

The San Gabriel and San Fernando valleys

Genmai-Sushi 4454 Van Nuys Blvd, Sherman Oaks ☎818/986-7060. "Genmai" is Japanese for brown rice, but you can get soft-shell crabs in *ponzu* sauce, along with sushi and macrobiotic dishes.

Kuala Lumpur 69 W Green St, Pasadena ☎626/577-5175. Curried soups and tangy salads are some of the highlights at this Malaysian eatery, along with coconut rice and spicy chicken and other delectable Southeast Asian cuisine offerings.

Saladang 363 S Fair Oaks Ave, Pasadena ☎626/793-8123. Don't miss out on the pad thai, curry, and salmon at this chic spot, or the spicy noodles that would pass muster anywhere. The restaurant's annex, *Saladang Song*, offers even spicier, more exotic Thai concoctions.

Shiro 1505 Mission St, South Pasadena ☎626/799-4774. One of LA's few top-notch restaurants in South Pasadena, perhaps the only one. Seafood – particularly the grilled catfish and smoked salmon – is best here, prepared in an assortment of rich, tangy flavors.

Sushi Nozawa 11288 Ventura Blvd, Studio City ☎818/508-7017. Traditional, pricey sushi dishes served to trendy, masochistic regulars, who don't mind being berated by the famously imperious chef: if you sit at the bar, he will decide what you'll eat. Period.

Indian, Sri Lankan, and Middle Eastern

Indian and **Sri Lankan** food is increasingly popular in LA – with menus embracing uniquely Californian dishes. **Middle Eastern** places in LA encompass a good range of Levantine cookery, but tend toward the traditional, with the occasional Cal-cuisine tinkering thrown in for good measure. Most of the Indian and Middle Eastern restaurants in Hollywood or West LA fall into a fairly mid-range price bracket – around $10–15 for a full meal, less for a vegetarian Indian dish.

Hollywood

Electric Lotus 4656 Franklin Ave ☎323/953-0040. While somewhat cramped and located in a mini-mall, a fine choice for traditional staples – *pakoras*, *vindaloo*, curries, etc – at affordable prices.

Marouch 4905 Santa Monica Blvd ☎323/662-9325. Although located in a nondescript part of town, this fine Lebanese restaurant provides rich sustenance with its flavorful kebabs and *shawarma*, at very manageable prices.

Moun of Tunis 7445 Sunset Blvd ☎323/874-3333. Mouthwatering Tunisian fare presented in huge, multi-course meals, heavy on the spices and rich on the exotic flavors – plus regular belly-dancing.

New East India Grill 345 N La Brea Ave ☎323/936-8844. Southern Indian cuisine given the California treatment: impressive specialties include spinach curry, ginger chicken, curried noodles, and adventurous "parmesan naan."

Zankou Chicken 5065 Sunset Blvd ☎323/665-7845. The top Middle Eastern value in town (and part of a citywide chain), with delicious garlicky chicken cooked on a rotisserie and made into a delicious sandwich, plus all the traditional salads – tabouli, hummus, and the like.

West LA

Clay Pit 145 S Barrington Ave ☎310/476-4700. Some of LA's best Indian food, featuring delights like lamb-stuffed *keema naan* and a fine tandoori chicken – all for around $15, though prices have gone up since the restaurant moved from the Wilshire area further east.

Koutoubia 2116 Westwood Blvd ☎310/475-0729. Good authentic Moroccan lamb, couscous, and seafood.

Noura Café 8479 Melrose Ave ☎323/651-4581. Moderately priced Middle Eastern specialties. For beginners, the "taster's delight" plate – hummus, *baba ganoush*, tabouli, falafel, fried eggplant, zucchini, and stuffed grape leaves – is a good, filling bet.

Nyala 1076 S Fairfax Ave ☎323/936-5918. One of several Ethiopian favorites along Fairfax, serving staples like *doro wat* (marinated chicken) and *kitfo* (chopped beef with butter and cheese) with the delightfully spongy *injera* bread.

Shamshiry Grill 1916 Westwood Blvd ☎310/474-1410. Top Iranian restaurant in the area, offering scrumptious kebabs, pilafs, savory rice cakes, and exotic sauces.

Surya 8048 W 3rd St ☎323/653-5151. Just west of the Farmers Market, a scrumptious array of Indian flavors matched with borrowings from Japanese and California cuisines, where the tandooris and *vindaloos* come with the familiar curry sauces and less predictable ingredients like duck and sashimi.

The San Gabriel and San Fernando valleys

Burger Continental 535 S Lake Ave, Pasadena ☎626/792-6634. Although it sounds like a fast-food joint, this is actually one of LA's better Middle Eastern restaurants, where you can get mounds of chicken and lamb kebabs for no more than a few bucks.

Carousel 304 N Brand Ave, Glendale ☎818/246-7775. A Lebanese charmer in downtown Glendale, chock-full of Levantine cultural artifacts and deliciously authentic food, from roasted chicken and quail to several different kinds of kebabs.

Vegetarian and wholefood

As you might expect, LA has a great many **wholefood** and **vegetarian** restaurants, most of them on the consciousness-raised Westside. Some veggie places can be a good value, but watch out for the ones that flaunt themselves as a New Age experience and include music – these can be three times as much. Otherwise, for a picnic try the *Trader Joe's* chain – which supplies imported cheeses, breads, and canned foods – or the area's **farmers markets**, loaded with organic produce and advertised in the press. (For health-food stores, see "Shopping," p.213.)

West LA

Erewhon 7660 Beverly Blvd ⓣ323/937-0777. A good old-fashioned juice bar and deli, where you can gulp down as many wheatgrass concoctions and bee-pollen smoothies as you can stand.

Fountain of Health 3606 W 6th St ⓣ213/387-6621. Vegetarian chili and burgers are the highlights at this affordable eatery just south of Hollywood. Closes at 3pm. Mon–Fri.

Inaka Natural Foods 131 S La Brea Ave ⓣ323/936-9353. Located in the trendy La Brea district and featuring vegetarian and macrobiotic food with a Japanese theme. Live music on weekends.

Newsroom Café 120 N Robertson Blvd ⓣ310/652-4444. A prime spot to see B-list celebrities with A-list attitudes eating veggie burgers and drinking wheatgrass "shooters." Especially popular for lunching; also offers magazine racks (thus the name) and Internet terminals.

Real Food Daily 414 N La Cienega Blvd ⓣ310/289-9910. Avocado rolls, beet bisque, and salads draw a good crowd at this vegan restaurant, which also operates branches at 514 Santa Monica Blvd, Santa Monica (ⓣ310/451-7544), and 242 S Beverly Drive, Beverly Hills, (ⓣ310/858-0880).

Santa Monica, Venice, and Malibu

Figtree's Café 429 Ocean Front Walk, Venice ⓣ310/392-4937. Tasty veggie food and grilled fresh fish on a sunny patio just off the Boardwalk. Health-conscious yuppies come in droves for breakfast.

Inn of the Seventh Ray 128 Old Topanga Rd, Topanga Canyon ⓣ310/455-1311. The ultimate New Age restaurant in a supremely New Age area, serving vegetarian and other wholefood meals in a relatively secluded environment. Excellent desserts, too.

Mäni's Bakery 2507 Main St, Santa Monica ⓣ310/396-7700. An array of veggie treats – from sugarless brownies to meatless sandwiches – for breakfast or lunch are the draw at this coffeehouse and bakery. Look hard enough and you might see a weight-obsessed celebrity darting in. Also a good bakery and coffeehouse at 519 S Fairfax Ave, Wilshire district (ⓣ323/938-8800).

Shambala Café 607 Colorado Ave, Santa Monica ⓣ310/395-2160. Apart from organic chicken, the menu is meat-free, with shrimp, pasta, tofu, eggplant, and some very interesting seaweed dishes.

The South Bay and Harbor Area

Good Stuff 1300 Highland Ave, Manhattan Beach ⓣ310/545-4775. Healthy eating, vegetarian or otherwise, is the focus at this popular spot, with a range of filling sandwiches and fruit plates. One of five South Bay locations.

Papa Jon's 5006 E 2nd St, Long Beach ⓣ562/439-4333. Meatless Mexican entrees and garden burgers are the highlights of this quiet eatery, which offers totally vegan meals as well as an on-site market.

The Spot 110 2nd St, Hermosa Beach ⓣ310/376-2355. A staggering array of veggie dishes, based on Mexican and other cuisines, and free of refined sugar or any animal products.

Bars and clubs

Nightlife in LA can be among the best and most frenetic in the country, with options for serious drinking, partying, and debauchery available throughout the metropolis. Weekend nights are the busiest at the various bars and clubs, but during the week things are often cheaper, though rarely any less enjoyable. Everywhere, between 11pm and midnight is the best time to turn up. Where they exist, most cover charges range widely, depending on the night and the establishment (often $5–20). Except at all-ages, alcohol-free clubs, the minimum age is 21, and it's normal for ID to be checked, so bring your passport or other photo ID. For listings, check out the *LA Times*' Calendar section or the *LA Weekly*, available on Friday and Thursday, respectively.

You can find **coffeehouses** throughout LA, too, from grim hole-in-the-wall dives to sanitized yuppie magnets. Well-trafficked areas like Melrose Avenue, West Hollywood, and Santa Monica's Third Street Promenade are loaded with spots to grab a caffeinated jolt, as well as tea, food, and even alcohol in some cases. A few of the better ones may also offer more sublime amusements like art, music, poetry, or truly eye-popping decor.

Bars

As you'd expect, LA's **bars** reflect their locality: a clash of artists and financial whiz kids Downtown; serious hedonists and leather-clad rock fans in Hollywood; movie-star wannabes and self-styled producers in West LA; a batch of jukebox- and dartboard-furnished bars in Santa Monica (evidence of British expats) and the more oddball selection in Venice; and the random assortment of interesting, out-of-the-way spots in the valleys. A few hard-bitten bars are open the legal maximum hours (from 6am until 2am daily), though the busiest hours are between 9pm and midnight. During **happy hour**, usually from 5 to7pm, drinks are cheap and sometimes half price.

Downtown and around

Akbar 4356 Sunset Blvd ℡323/665-6810. A curious blend of patrons – manual laborers and bohemians, gays and straights, old-timers and newbies – frequent this cozy, unpretentious watering hole. Also presents occasional comedy and fringe theater events.

Barragan's 1538 W Sunset Blvd ℡213/250-4256. Actually a Mexican restaurant with reasonably palatable food, but allegedly producing the most alcoholic margarita in LA. Be alert for the dicey neighborhood, though.

Casey's Bar 613 S Grand Ave ℡213/629-2353. White floors, dark wood-paneled walls, and piano music on Wed and Thurs nights; something of a local institution.

HMS Bounty 3357 Wilshire Blvd ℡213/385-7275. An authentic dive experience. Advertising "Food and Grog," a grungy bar that's a hot spot for hipsters and grizzled old-timers – they come for the dark ambience, cheap drinks, and kitschy nautical motifs.

Redwood 316 W 2nd St ℡213/617-2867. Not overly flashy or eventful, but a solid Downtown choice for serious drinking and cheap all-American grub since 1943, attracting a mix of office workers, newspaper hacks, and only a few outsiders.

Standard Hotel Bar 550 S Flower St ℡213/892-8080. The poseur pinnacle in Downtown LA, a rooftop, alcohol-fueled playpen where the black-leather-pant crowd goes to hang in red metallic "pods" with waterbeds and sprawl out on an Astroturf lawn, amid modern corporate towers looming overhead. $20+ cover charge if you're not staying at the hotel.

Top of Five at the *Westin Bonaventure*, 404 S Figueroa St ℡213/624-1000. Thirty-five floors up, this constantly rotating cocktail lounge spins faster after a few of the expensive drinks, and offers an unparalleled view of the sun setting over the city.

Hollywood

Boardner's 1652 N Cherokee Ave ℡323/462-9621. A likably unkempt neighborhood bar in the middle of Hollywood's prime tourist territory, with a colorful history that dates back to World War II. Occasional guitar-poets provide the soundtrack.

Burgundy Room 1621 Cahuenga Blvd ℡323/465-7530. A classic place to get down and dirty with the old Hollywood dive-bar vibe, with minimal decor, stiff drinks, a growling crowd of regulars, decent DJs, and a rocking jukebox.

Cat 'n' Fiddle Pub 6530 Sunset Blvd ℡323/468-3800. A boisterous but comfortable pub with darts, British food (served until midnight on weekends), expensive English beers on tap, and live jazz on Sundays (7–11pm). See also "Live music," p.202.

Dresden Room 1760 N Vermont Ave ℡323/665-4298. One of the neighborhood's classic bars, best known perhaps for its nightly entertainment (except Sun), in which the husband-and-wife lounge act of Marty and Elayne takes requests from the crowd of old-timers and goateed hipsters.

Formosa Café 7156 Santa Monica Blvd ℡323/850-9050. Started during Prohibition, a creaky old Hollywood institution alive with the ghosts of Bogie and Marilyn. Imbibe in the potent spirits, but stay away from the insipid food.

Frolic Room 6245 Hollywood Blvd ℡323/462-5890. Classic LA bar featured in the film *LA Confidential*, decorated with Hirschfeld cartoons of celebrities and offering affordable drinks and a dark, authentic old-time ambience. Right by the Pantages Theater.

Goldfingers 6423 Yucca St, north of Hollywood Blvd ☏ 323/962-2913. Fascinating 1960s-kitsch design with striking black-and-gold lamé highlights. Drinks aren't bad, either, and nightly music is a mix of dance and acoustic stylings.

Good Luck Bar 1514 Hillhurst Ave ☏ 323/666-3524. A hip Los Feliz retro-dive, this hangout is popular for its cheesy Chinese decor and drinks straight from the heyday of *Trader Vic's*. Located near the intersection of Sunset and Hollywood blvds.

Lava Lounge 1533 N La Brea Ave ☏ 323/876-6612. Wallow in the cheesy retro decor and slurp down a glowing cocktail to the sounds of pounding rockabilly and freewheeling surf music. Especially fun is "Kinky Karaoke" on Sunday nights.

Musso and Frank Grill 6667 Hollywood Blvd ☏ 323/467-7788. If you haven't had a drink in this 1940s landmark bar (located in the center of the district), you haven't been to Hollywood. It also serves pricey diner food. See also "Eating," p.186.

Pinot Hollywood 1448 Gower St ☏ 323/461-8800. Nearly thirty types of martini and Polish potato vodka, served in airy surroundings with an upscale crowd. See "Eating," p.186.

The Powerhouse 1714 N Highland Ave ☏ 323/463-9438. Enjoyable, longstanding rockers' watering hole just off Hollywood Blvd; few people get here much before midnight.

Smog Cutter 864 N Virgil Ave ☏ 323/667-9832. Dive bar that attracts a mix of boozers and smirking Gen-Xers. Don't miss the Tuesday-night karaoke, which, like the liquor, can be pleasantly mind-numbing.

Tiki Ti 4427 W Sunset Blvd ☏ 323/669-9381. Tiny grass-skirted cocktail bar straight out of *Hawaii-Five-O*, packed with kitschy pseudo-Polynesian decor, on the edge of Hollywood.

West LA

Barney's Beanery 8447 Santa Monica Blvd ☏ 310/654-2287. Well-worn poolroom/bar, stocking over 200 beers, with a solid, rock'n'roll-hedonist history. It also serves all-American, rib-stuffing food; see "Eating," p.181.

El Carmen 8138 W 3rd St ☏ 323/852-1552. Faux dive-bar with a south-of-the-border theme, pushed to the extreme, with black-velvet pictures of Mexican wrestlers, steer horns, stuffed snakes, and much tongue-in-cheek grunge, as well as signature margaritas.

Jones 7205 Santa Monica Blvd ☏ 323/850-1726. Groovy, youthful scene with a colorful atmosphere and decent American cuisine, though the main

draw is the head-spinning drinks named after rock stars.

Molly Malone's Irish Pub 575 S Fairfax Ave ☏ 323/935-1577. Self-consciously authentic Irish bar, from the music – mostly grinding rock and Celtic folk – to the shamrocks in the foaming Guinness.

Parlour Club 7702 Santa Monica Blvd ☏ 323/650-7968. Located in WeHo's grimmer eastern side, a strange and stylish bar with a widely eclectic musical selection (from metal and rap to disco and electro) playing nightly and the occasional dose of creepy performance art.

St. Nick's 8450 W 3rd St ☏ 323/655-6917. A few blocks from the colossal Beverly Center mall sits this relaxed and unassuming neighborhood bar, with a decent selection of brews and a formidable jukebox.

Snake Pit 7529 Melrose Ave ☏ 323/852-9390. One of the better bars along the Melrose shopping strip, and not too showy, with a mix of jaded locals and inquisitive tourists.

Tom Bergin's 840 S Fairfax Ave ☏ 323/936-7151. Old-time drinking joint from 1936, a great place for Irish coffee (supposedly invented here), and less rough-and-ready than *Molly Malone's* down the road. You can spot the regulars from the pictures on the walls.

Santa Monica, Venice, and Malibu

14 Below 1348 14th St, Santa Monica ☏ 310/451-5040. At this casual bar, pool tables and a fireplace compete for your attention with rock, folk, and blues performers, who play nightly.

Circle Bar 2926 Main St, Santa Monica ☏ 310/392-4898. Old-fashioned dive bar that in recent years has lurched toward drawing in fashionable out-of-towners – and a lot of tourists. If you get plastered on the pricey drinks, Venice is well within staggering distance.

Encounter 209 World Way, at LAX ☏ 310/215-5151. A strange bar that lurks in the upper reaches of the boomerang concrete "Theme Building" in the LAX parking lot. Believe it or not, it's worth a visit to sample the potent, if pricey, Day-Glo drinks and watch the jets land.

Finn McCool's 2700 Main St, Santa Monica ☏ 310/452-1734. Despite the dubious name, a worthwhile Irish pub with a savory selection of Emerald Isle brews and neo-Celtic artwork, plus hefty platters of traditional food that require a pint of Guinness to consume properly.

Gotham Hall 1431 3rd St, Santa Monica ☏ 310/394-8865. The strong drinks and purple pool tables here attract a generally youthful set of drinkers, with a solid Hollywood contingent. Sometimes attracts interloping tourists from the Promenade with no flair for eight-ball.

Library Alehouse 2911 Main St, Santa Monica ☏310/314-4855. Presenting the choicest brews from West Coast microbreweries and beyond, this is a good spot to select from a nice range of well-known and obscure labels while munching on salty bar food.

Ye Olde King's Head 116 Santa Monica Blvd, Santa Monica ☏310/451-1402. British-heavy joint with jukebox, dartboards, and signed photos of all your favorite rock dinosaurs; don't miss the steak-and-kidney pie, afternoon tea, or the fish'n'chips.

The San Gabriel and San Fernando valleys

Amazon 14649 Ventura Blvd, Sherman Oaks ☏818/986-7502. A small wonderland of kitsch, in which you can knock back *Trader Vic's*–type tropical concoctions amid pseudo–South American and Polynesian decor: waterfalls, ferns, and so on.

Clearman's North Woods 7247 N Rosemead Blvd, San Gabriel ☏626/286-3579. A kitsch-lover's delight with fake snow on the outside and

moose heads on the walls inside; a great place to space out while listening to moody live torch singers and throwing your peanut shells on the floor.

The Colorado 2640 E Colorado Blvd ☏626/449-3485. A bright spot along a bleak Pasadena stretch. Salty bartenders, cheap drinks, and a couple of pool tables amid a decor based around hunting.

Cozy's Bar & Grill 14048 Ventura Blvd, Sherman Oaks ☏818/986-6000. Listen to blues on the weekend, or come by any time to throw darts, shoot pool, or knock back a few. A friendly, laid-back San Fernando Valley spot with a devoted clientele.

Gitana 260 E Magnolia Blvd, Burbank ☏818/846-4400. Giant entertainment complex in the shadow of a mall, with mixed drinks, pool tables, cigar bar, and eclectic tunes on the dancefloor, including salsa. Mixed crowd of tourists and locals.

Ireland's 32 13721 Burbank Blvd, Van Nuys ☏818/785-5200. One of San Fernando Valley's better spots for quaffing Irish drafts, powering down traditional stews and chops, and soaking in a fair amount of Emerald Island decor, shamrocks and all.

Coffeehouses

Coffeehouses in LA don't quite carry the same cultural cachet as they do in the Pacific Northwest or San Francisco, but they are good spots for socializing, whiling away the hours, and in some cases accessing the Internet. And the people you see conspicuously writing on their laptops are less likely to be budding poets or novelists than would-be screenwriters plotting bloody action flicks over caramel lattes.

All-Star Theater Café 6675 Hollywood Blvd ☏323/962-8898. Antiques store/café with a 1920s feel and overstuffed armchairs, inhabiting the historic 1936 Vogue moviehouse – very sleek and hip. Open 7pm–3am weekends.

Anastasia's Asylum 1028 Wilshire Blvd, Santa Monica ☏310/394-7113. Comfortable place with quirky decor and customers, and strong coffee and tea; also with nightly entertainment, of varying quality.

Bourgeois Pig 5931 Franklin Ave, Hollywood ☏323/962-6366. Self-consciously hip environment and overpriced cappuccinos – you really pay for the atmosphere of mirrors, chandeliers, and loveseats, but the tasty java and colorful atmosphere might make it worthwhile.

Cobalt Café 22047 Sherman Way, Canoga Park ☏818/348-3789. Grungy but hip coffeehouse in the Valley, with coffee, food, and live music – along with poetry readings.

Coffee Table 2930 Rowena Ave, Los Feliz ☏323/644-8111. Casual, unpretentious space with affordable coffees and relaxed surroundings – a nice antidote to the *Bourgeois Pig*, further west.

CyberJava 7080 Hollywood Blvd ☏323/466-5600, ⊛www.cyberjava.com. Located near the corner of La Brea Avenue, this spot offers DSL Internet access while selling Web surfers the usual range of smoothies, java drinks, and assorted sweets.

Highland Grounds 742 N Highland Ave, Hollywood ☏323/466-1507. The posiest of LA's coffee bars and something of a scene, serving iced latte, pancakes, and even beer. At night it's a club, with poetry and up-and-coming bands, and even a bit of alcohol.

Hot Wired Café 11651 Riverside Drive, North Hollywood ☏818/753-9929. Ultra-caffeinated java in a Valley joint with a range of curious entertainment, from Monday-night blues jams to comics and acoustic strummers several nights of the week.

King's Road Espresso House 8361 Beverly Blvd, West Hollywood ☎ 323/655-9044. Sidewalk café in the center of a busy shopping strip. Popular with the hipster crowd as well as a few interloping tourists.

Nova Express 426 N Fairfax Ave ☎ 323/658-7533. One of the grooviest coffee joints around, designed with retro-futuristic sci-fi decor, with weird colors and lighting, and additional curiosities like lava lamps and alien lounge and dance music most nights. Open till 4am.

The Novel Café 212 Pier Ave, Santa Monica ☎ 310/396-8566. Used books and high-backed wooden chairs set the tone; good coffees, teas, and pastries, though with many self-consciously studious patrons. Located near the Venice border.

Red Room Café 1604 Pacific Ave, Venice ☎ 310/399-1785. A coffeehouse with acceptably good beverages and snacks, but best for its actual artworks displayed for your perusal, in forms ranging from painting to sculpture to multimedia installations.

Sacred Grounds 399 W 6th St, San Pedro ☎ 310/514-0800. Although located a ways from central LA, this combo coffeehouse and club offers a sizeable stage for regional performers, with open-mike night, music jams, and even some marginal comedy acts.

Un-Urban Coffee House 3301 Pico Blvd, Santa Monica ☎ 310/315-0056. Another combination coffeehouse and performance space, with mostly alternative music and comedy.

Clubs

The **clubs** of LA may be among the wildest in the country. Ranging from posey hangouts to industrial noise cellars, even the more image–conscious joints are like singles bars, with everybody claiming to be either a rock musician or in the movies. Nowadays, many of the more interesting and unusual clubs are transient, especially those catering to the house, ambient, and rave scene. As a result, the trendier side of the club scene is hard to pin down, and you should always check the *LA Weekly* before setting out.

Most of the top clubs are either in Hollywood or West Hollywood. Beverly Hills is a lifeless yuppie desert; Downtown is home to a handful of itinerant clubs operating above and below board; and the San Fernando Valley's more rough–and–ready scene is usually confined to the weekends. For gay and lesbian clubs and discos, see p.211.

Downtown and around

The Echo 1822 Sunset Blvd ☎ 213/413-8200. Like the name says, an Echo Park scene with scrappy dance DJs spinning a range of old- and new-school favorites most nights, with rap on weekends and rock and retro DJs on Sundays.

Jewel's Catch One 4067 W Pico Blvd ☎ 323/734-8849. Sweaty barn catering to a mixed crowd of gays and straights and covering two wild dancefloors. A longtime favorite for many club-hoppers of all sorts. Especially busy Fri–Mon, though located in the middle of nowhere.

Mayan 1038 S Hill St ☎ 213/746-4674. Formerly a groovy pre-Columbian–styled movie palace, now hosting Latin rhythms and nonstop disco and house tunes on three dancefloors. Fri and Sat only, no jeans or sneakers.

Stock Exchange 618 S Spring St ☎ 213/489-3877. An attempt to broaden the Downtown club scene on a previously deserted stretch of road, spinning enough house, hip-hop, salsa, and disco tunes to make the crowd gyrate with abandon. Cover can reach $15.

Hollywood

1650 1650 Schrader Blvd ☎ 323/871-1650. Signature Hollywood dance club, which draws plenty of club kids for its rap, house, reggae, and retro DJs, with several party scenes sometimes going on at once in the house, at full volume.

Arena 6655 Santa Monica Blvd ☎ 323/462-0714. Work up a sweat to funk, hip-hop, and house sounds on a massive dancefloor inside a former ice factory. Gay-friendly scene, playing host to different, ever-changing club nights.

Avalon 1735 N Vine St ☎ 323/462-3000. Formerly *The Palace*, now converted into a weekend dance club spinning old-school faves, along with a dash of rock and retro, with the occasional big-name DJ dropping in.

Bar Sinister 1652 N Cherokee ☎ 323/769-7070. A collection of sprightly dance beats most nights of the week, then memorably spooky Goth music and anemic-looking vampire types on Saturdays ($10 if in costume). Connected to *Boardner's* bar (see p.193).

Blue 1642 N Las Palmas ☎ 323/462-7442. Goth, industrial, fetish freak-outs, and some retro-80s draw the pallid and neo-zombie contingent to this combo restaurant and club, nightly except Tuesdays and Thursdays.

The Conga Room 5364 Wilshire Blvd ☎ 323/938-1696. A high-profile celebrity investment results in a surprisingly appealing feast of Cuban food and Latin music, with weekend DJs to stir the salsa soul – but cover that can run up to $20 or more.

The Derby 4500 Los Feliz Blvd ☎ 323/663-8979. Restored supper club in east side of Hollywood with gorgeous high wooden ceilings and round bar that was one of the originators of the retro-swing craze, thanks to the movie *Swingers*.

Dragonfly 6510 Santa Monica Blvd ☎ 323/466-6111. Unusual decor, two large dance rooms, and house and disco club nights that are continually buzzing on Thurs–Sun nights; live music at other times.

Florentine Gardens 5951 Hollywood Blvd ☎ 323/464-0706. Stuck between the Salvation Army and a porno theater, but popular with the LA dance crowd, especially the under-21 set, for weekend DJ nights.

The Ruby 7070 Hollywood Blvd ☎ 323/467-7070. A wide range of feverish dance clubs Thurs–Sun, everything from retro-kitsch to grinding industrial to perky house and garage.

West LA

7969 7969 Santa Monica Blvd ☎ 323/654-0280. Classic WeHo dance club – a landmark for its frenetic assortment of gay-themed (but straight-friendly) shows, from go-go girls to male strippers to drag queens. Always one of LA's most colorful spots for dancing and grinding.

Carbon 9300 Venice Blvd ☎ 310/558-9302. Though hardly near anywhere you'd want to be, a good spot for eclectic nightly DJs, whose turntables glow with Latin, retro, jungle, drum & bass, hip-hop, soul, and rock beats, depending on the night.

The Factory 652 N La Peer Drive ☎ 310/659-4551. Mixed straight and gay crowd grooving to DJs spinning house and retro most nights of the week at what is still one of West Hollywood's more popular clubs.

Tempest 7323 Santa Monica Blvd ☎ 323/850-5115. After 10pm on weekends, the eclectic grooves start to spin here, from retro-funk and disco to the latest hip-hop to 1960s *Austin Powers*–style sing-a-longs.

Ultra Suede 661 N Robertson Blvd, West Hollywood ☎ 310/659-4551. The spot for superior retro-dancing on Wednesday and weekend nights, heavy on 1970s disco and 80s technopop. Neighbor to *The Factory* and draws much of the same mixed crowd.

Santa Monica

Mor 2941 Main St ☎ 310/455-6720. Nightly selections of techno, trance, house, and soul, mixing it up for groovy club nights most evenings in this hip lounge setting, and including the occasional rock, new wave, and retro throwbacks as well.

The Space 2020 Wilshire Blvd ☎ 310/829-1933. Ground zero for weekend retro vibes, a bar and lounge with backward-looking DJs massaging everything from 1980s electro, pop, and New Wave to spacey 1970s disco and funk to more contemporary breakbeats.

Sugar 814 Broadway ☎ 310/899-1989. Hard-hitting electronica, from big beat to house to techno, served up in a shiny and gorgeous glass-and-steel interior. Cover ranges widely per night, from $5–20.

Temple Bar 1026 Wilshire Blvd ☎ 310/392-1077. Popular, if chaotic, mix of different groove styles, from rap to R&B, with heavy doses of world beat thrown in as well. Always a fun, engaging scene.

Zanzibar 1301 5th St ☎ 310/451-2221. Nightly DJs spinning sounds with a house, funk and soul bent, but also with a bit of experimentation – anything from ragga to sci-fi techno to Euro-jungle.

The San Gabriel and San Fernando valleys

Bigfoot Lodge 3172 Los Feliz Blvd ☎ 323/662-9227. On the far side of East Hollywood in dreary Atwater, but a prime draw for its nightly DJs, who set feet to stomping with retro-rock and punk tunes, with glam, goth, thrash, and rockabilly sounds thrown in as well.

CIA 11334 Burbank Blvd, North Hollywood ☎ 818/506-6353. Or the "California Institute for Abnormal Arts," a truly odd venue where art and music collide, with curious visual installations (often based on circus clowns and freak shows) and sounds from punk to avant-garde.

Gitana 260 E Magnolia Blvd, Burbank ☎ 818/846-4400. Giant dance-and-dining complex with pool tables, cigar bar, and eclectic tunes on the dancefloor. Mixed crowd of tourists and locals.

The Muse 54 E Colorado Blvd ☎ 626/793-0608. Dance, funk, and hip-hop tunes mingle in this Old Town Pasadena tri-level club with nightly DJs and no less than eleven pool tables.

Live music

LA has an overwhelming choice of **live music** venues. Since the nihilistic punk bands of nearly thirty years ago drew the city away from its spaced-out slacker image, LA's **rock music** scene has been second to none. The old **punk** scene has been revitalized with up-and-coming bands, and heavy metal can be found here and there. The influence and popularity of **hip-hop** is also prevalent, whether mixed in dance music by Westside DJs or in its more authentic form in the inner city (best avoided by out-of-towners). Surprisingly, **country music** is fairly common, at least away from trendy Hollywood, and the valleys are hotbeds of bluegrass and swing. There's also **jazz**, best in the few genuinely authentic downbeat dives, while Latin **salsa** music can be found in a few Westside clubs.

There are always plenty of British and European names on tour, from major artists to independents, and an enormous number of venues. Most venues open at 8pm or 9pm; headline bands are usually onstage between 11pm and 1am. Cover ranges widely from $5 to $50. You'll need to be 21 and will likely be asked for ID. As ever, *LA Weekly* is the best source of **listings**.

Major performance venues

Cerritos Center for the Performing Arts 12700 Center Court Drive ☎1-800/300-4345, Ⓦwww .cerritoscenter.com. North of Long Beach, a top draw for mainstream country, gospel, classical, pop, and jazz acts – usually nothing too quirky or adventurous.

Greek Theatre 2700 N Vermont Ave, Griffith Park ☎323/665-1927, Ⓦwww.greektheatrela.com. Outdoor, summer-only venue with a broad range of mainstream rock and pop acts and seating for five thousand. Parking can be a mess, so arrive early.

Grove of Anaheim 2200 E Katella Ave ☎714/712-2700, Ⓦwww.thegroveofanaheim .com. Orange County concert space aimed at showcasing old-time performers and mid-level entertainers in soul, country, pop, rock, and jazz.

Hollywood Palladium 6215 Sunset Blvd, Hollywood ☎323/962-7600, Ⓦwww .hollywoodpalladium.com. Once a big-band dance hall, with an authentic 1940s interior, now a home to all manner of hard rock, punk, and rap outfits.

Kodak Theatre 6801 Hollywood Blvd, Hollywood ☎323/308-6363, Ⓦwww.kodaktheatre.com.

Part of the colossal Hollywood & Highland mall, a media-ready theater partly designed to host the Oscars, which it will for many years, as well as top-name pop and rock acts.

Staples Center 865 S Figueroa St, Downtown ☎213/624-3100, Ⓦwww.staplescenter.com. Big, glassy sports arena (home to the LA Lakers) that's also a good showcase for Top 40 rock and pop acts.

Universal Amphitheater 100 Universal City Plaza ☎818/622-4440, Ⓦwww.hob.com/venues /concerts/universal. A big but acoustically excellent auditorium with regular rock, pop, and Latin shows. Located on the Universal Studios lot.

Wiltern Theater 3790 Wilshire Blvd, Mid-Wilshire ☎323/388-1400, Ⓦwww.thewiltern.com. A striking blue Zigzag Art Deco movie palace, recently renovated and converted into a top performing space for standard pop acts as well as edgy alternative groups.

Rock venues

The Cat Club 8911 Sunset Blvd, West Hollywood ☎310/657-0888. Hard, meaty jams every night of the week, with the focus on rock, punk, and

What's on and tickets

The best sources of **information** are the *LA Weekly* and the "Calendar" section of the *LA Times*. You can buy seats for concerts or sports events from **Ticketmaster**, which has branches in Tower Records stores, and charge-by-phone numbers (☎213/480-3232 or 714/740-2000). A quick way through the maze of LA's **theaters** is to phone the **LA Stage Alliance** (☎213/614-0556, Ⓦwww.lastagealliance.com) and ask for the availability of discount tickets for a given show, under its LA Stage Tix program.

rockabilly – no surprise there, since owner Slim Jim Phantom is a former Stray Cat.

Doug Weston's Troubadour 9081 Santa Monica Blvd, West Hollywood ☎310/276-6168. An old 1960s mainstay that's been through a lot of incarnations. Used to be known for folk and country rock, then metal, now for alternative and acoustic lineups.

El Rey Theater 5515 Wilshire Blvd, Mid-Wilshire ☎323/936-4790. Although not as famous as its Sunset Strip counterparts, this rock and alternative venue is possibly the best spot to see explosive new bands and still-engaging oldsters. Also offers a variety of dance-club nights.

Gabah 4658 Melrose Ave, Hollywood ☎323/664-8913. Eclectic spot serving up a mix of reggae, funk, dub, and rock – even flamenco – with a mix of club and live-music nights. The dicey neighborhood leaves much to be desired; always let the valet take charge of your car.

The Joint 8771 Pico Blvd, West LA ☎310/275-2619. A dark, mirrored neighborhood venue with an assortment of B-grade screamers and, occasionally, decent rock and alternative groups.

Key Club 9039 Sunset Blvd ☎310/274-5800. A hot spot in the most lively section of the strip, attracting a young, hip group for its regular concerts in the rock, punk, and metal vein, with occasional lighter fare as well.

King King 6555 Hollywood Blvd ☎323/960-5765. A solid Hollywood bet for nightly concerts by chord-crunching rockers and for live dance music on weekends, with house, funk, rap, and retro-pop all on the DJ docket.

Largo 432 N Fairfax Ave, West LA ☎323/852-1073. Cozy cabaret with some unusual live acts, though mostly jazz, rock, and pop, often of the acoustic variety, with some comedy as well.

The Lighthouse 30 Pier Ave, Hermosa Beach ☎310/376-9033. Adjacent to the beach, this old favorite has a broad booking policy, which spans rock, jazz, and reggae as well as Monday-night karaoke and occasional comedy.

Mr T's Bowl 5621 N Figueroa Ave, Highland Park ☎323/960-5693. Former bowling alley, since been remodeled into a quirky bar with a regular crowd of hipsters and local characters. On weekends, there's live music, with a strong punk-rock-surfer bent.

The Roxy 9009 Sunset Blvd, West LA ☎310/276-2222. The showcase of the music industry's new signings, intimate and with a great sound system, on the western – but still frenetic – end of the strip.

The Smell 247 S Main St, Downtown ☎213/625-4325. A funky space with groovy art grunge, including strange decor, frenetic rock and punk

music, and a notoriously grim location.

Spaceland 1717 Silver Lake Blvd, Silver Lake ☎213/833-2843. Excellent spot to catch up-and-coming local and national rockers and other acts, including punk and alternative musicians.

The Viper Room 8852 Sunset Blvd, West Hollywood ☎310/358-1880. Great live acts, a famous owner, and a headline-hitting past. Expect almost any musician to show up onstage.

Whisky-a-Go-Go 8901 Sunset Blvd, West Hollywood ☎310/652-4202. Legendary spot, thanks mostly to The Doors, and important for LA's rising music stars. Mainly hard rock, though you might catch an alternative act now and then.

Country and folk venues

Boulevard Music 4136 Sepulveda Blvd, Culver City ☎310/398-2583. This unglamorous music store manages to host some fairly interesting folk acts on weekends, from roots country to delta blues, with international groups adding even more to the eclectic mix.

Cowboy Palace Saloon 21635 Devonshire St, Chatsworth ☎818/341-0166. Worth a trip to this distant corner of the San Fernando Valley for plenty of down-home country concerts and free Sunday BBQ fixings.

CTMS Center 16953 Ventura Blvd, Encino ☎818/817-7756, �🌐www.ctmsfolkmusic.org. The home base for the California Traditional Music Society, which puts on periodic performances throughout the year of ancient and modern folk music, offering education and training, monthly jam sessions (open to the public), and occasional concerts by visiting musicians.

McCabe's 3103 W Pico Blvd, Santa Monica ☎310/828-4497. LA's premier acoustic-guitar shop; long the scene of some excellent and unusual folk and country shows, with the occasional alternative crooner thrown in as well.

Rusty's Surf Ranch 256 Santa Monica Pier ☎310/393-7437. Offers not only surf music – and displays of old-time long boards – but also rock, pop, folk, and even karaoke. Always a popular spot for tourists, near the end of the pier.

Viva Cantina 900 Riverside Drive, Burbank ☎818/845-2425. A Mexican restaurant on the far side of Griffith Park, where you can hear some of LA's most engaging country, bluegrass, and honky-tonk artists performing nightly.

Jazz and blues venues

The Baked Potato 3787 Cahuenga Blvd W, North Hollywood ☎818/980-1615. A small but near-

January

1 Japanese New Year. Art displays, ethnic culinary offerings, and cultural exhibits at this annual Little Tokyo festival, centered around the Japanese American Cultural and Community Center (☏213/628-2725, ⓦwww.jaccc.org).

1 Tournament of Roses in Pasadena. A parade of floral floats and marching bands along a five-mile stretch of Colorado Boulevard. Coincides with the annual Rose Bowl game (☏626/795-9311, ⓦwww.tournamentofroses.com).

mid Martin Luther King Parade and Celebration. The civil rights hero is honored with activities at King Park, Baldwin Hills, and Crenshaw, and many other city locations (☏310/314-2188 in LA and 562/570-6816 in Long Beach).

February

early to mid Chinese New Year. Three days of dragon-float street parades, tasty food, and various cultural programs, based in Chinatown, Monterey Park, and Alhambra (☏213/617-0396, ⓦwww.lachinesechamber.org).

mid Mardi Gras. Floats, parades, costumes, and lots of singing and dancing at this Brazilian fun fest, the most colorful antics of which take place in West Hollywood (☏323/634-7811 or 310/289-2525).

mid to late Bob Marley Reggae Festival. A two-day event that exalts the reggae god with food, music, and plenty of spirit. At the Long Beach Convention and Entertainment Center (☏562/436-3661, ⓦwww.bobmarleydayfestival.com).

mid to late Queen Mary Scottish Festival. All the haggis you can stand at this two-day Long Beach celebration, along with highland dancing and bagpipes (☏562/435-3511, ⓦwww.queenmary.com).

end The Academy Awards. Presented at the Kodak Theatre in the Hollywood & Highland mall (see p.129). Bleacher seats are available to watch the stars arrive (ⓦwww.oscars.org).

March

early LA City Marathon. All over the streets around town you can cheer on the runners – or sign up to participate yourself (☏310/444-5544, ⓦwww.lamarathon.com).

mid St Patrick's Day. Parade along Colorado Boulevard in Old Town Pasadena, and another in Hermosa Beach (☏310/374-4972, ⓦwww.stpatricksday.org). No parade but freely flowing green beer in the "Irish" bars along Fairfax Avenue.

late Spring Festival of Flowers. An explosion of floral color is displayed at Descanso Gardens with different types of tulips, lilies, and daffodils, among others (☏818/952-4401, ⓦwww.descansogardens.org).

end Cowboy Poetry and Music Festival. Plenty of folk music from the Old West and accompanying cowboy poems – some excellent, some cornpone – are the highlights of this three-day Santa Clarita celebration, just north of LA (☏661/286-4078 or 1-800/305-0755).

April

early California Poppy Festival. Although located in a bleak northern valley, Lancaster's huge poppy reserve of 1800 acres draws big crowds to see its eye-blinding, fiery orange colors that appear every spring. The town festival presents local foodstuffs, folk art, and crafts to go with the blooms (☏661/723-6077, ⓦwww.poppyfestival.com).

Saturday before Easter The Blessing of the Animals. A long-established ceremony, Mexican in origin. Locals arrive in Olvera Street to have their pets blessed, then watch the attendant parade (☏213/625-5045).

weekend nearest 13 Thai New Year. The Wat Thai Temple in North Hollywood is the focus for this cultural celebration, with spicy food and authentic music, and many Buddhist monks (☎818/997-9657).

mid Long Beach Grand Prix. Scores of locals come out to watch the Indy cars race around Shoreline Drive (☎562/752-9524, ⊛www.longbeachgp.com).

late Fiesta Broadway. Lively music from Hispanic pop singers and tasty Mexican food are the highlights of this street fair along Broadway Downtown (☎310/914-0015, ⊛www.fiestabroadway.la).

May

5 Cinco de Mayo. A day-long party to commemorate the Mexican victory at the Battle of Puebla. Spirited parade along Olvera Street, and several blocks Downtown are blocked off for Latino music performances. There are also celebrations in most LA parks (☎213/625-5045).

mid NoHo Theater and Arts Festival. The San Fernando Valley district of North Hollywood has undergone a successful cultural renovation, and this fest provides the evidence: a cavalcade of music, food, poetry, theater, and dance (☎818/508-5155).

mid to late Venice Art Walk. A great chance to peer into the private art studios in town, where you can see the work of both big-name local artists and lesser-known up-and-comers – though it will cost you $50 (☎310/392-9255).

late UCLA Jazz & Reggae Festival. Spirited music, food, and activities take place on the campus (☎310/825-9912, ⊛www.studentgroups.ucla.edu/jazzreggae).

June

second weekend Irish Fair and Music Festival. Sizeable music, food, and cultural celebration held at Woodley Park in Encino, in the San Fernando Valley (☎818/501-3781, ⊛www.irishfair.org).

mid Playboy Jazz Festival. Renowned event held at the Hollywood Bowl, with a lineup of traditional and non-traditional musicians and groups (tickets ☎213/480-3232, ⊛www.playboy.com/arts-entertainment/features/jazzfest2005).

late Bayou Festival. Heaps of Creole food, wild paradoo, and plenty of high-spirited Cajun and Zydeco music at this colorful Long Beach event (☎562/427-3713, ⊛www.longbeachfestival.com).

late Gay Pride Celebration. Parade on Santa Monica Blvd in West Hollywood. Carnival atmosphere, hundreds of vendors, and an all-male drag football cheerleading team (☎323/860-0701, ⊛www.lapride.org).

July

4 Independence Day. The *Queen Mary* in Long Beach hosts a particularly large fireworks display, as well as colorful entertainment. Fireworks displays in many places in LA (☎562/435-3511 in Long Beach, or ☎323/848-6530 for West Hollywood's Plummer Park).

first weekend after 4 Lotus Festival. An Echo Park celebration with dragon boats, ethnic food, pan-Pacific music, and, of course, the resplendent lotus blooms around the lake (☎213/485-1310).

early July to late August Pageant of the Masters. Laguna Beach's signature street festival, which not only features the standard displays of food, arts, and dancing, but also living presentations of classic paintings – a unique Southern California spectacle (see p.177; ☎949/494-1145, ⊛www.foapom.com).

mid Old Pasadena Jazz Festival. In the historic Old Pasadena zone, a nice mix of mainstream jazz and tasty foodstuffs (☎818/771-5544, ⊛www.omegaevents.com).

late Central Avenue Jazz Festival. Celebration of both jazz and blues by big names and lesser-known performers, held in front of the historic Dunbar Hotel in South Central (☏213/847-3169).

August

early Festival of the Chariots. Another strange and unique LA phenomenon: giant decorated floats parade down Venice Boardwalk to the sound of lively music and the smell of ethnic food (☏310/839-1572, ⓦwww.festivalofchariots.com).

early International Surf Festival. Tournament and celebration in the South Bay that provides for an exciting three-day spectacle, which also includes volleyball, fishing, and sand-castle design (☏310/305-9546, ⓦwww.surffestival.org).

mid Long Beach Jazz Festival. At the Rainbow Lagoon park in downtown Long Beach, relax and enjoy famous and local performers (☏562/436-7794, ⓦwww.longbeachjazzfestival.com).

mid Nisei Week in Little Tokyo. A celebration of Japanese America, with martial arts demonstrations, karaoke, Japanese brush painting, baby shows, and performance (☏213/687-7193, ⓦwww.niseiweek.org).

late African Marketplace and Cultural Faire. Hundreds of arts and crafts booths and many different entertainers make up this annual celebration at Exposition Park in South Central LA. Runs to early Sept (☏323/734-1164, ⓦwww.AfricanMarketplace.org).

late Sunset Junction Street Fair. A spirited neighborhood party – always one of LA's most enjoyable fetes – along Sunset Boulevard in Silver Lake, with live music, ethnic food, and a carnivalesque atmosphere (☏323/661-7771, ⓦwww.sunsetjunction.org).

September

5 LA's birthday. A civic ceremony and assorted street entertainment around El Pueblo de Los Angeles to mark the founding of the original pueblo in 1781 (☏213/625-5045).

mid Koreatown Multicultural Festival. Dancing, parading, and tae kwon do exhibitions are the main events at this colorful Mid-Wilshire celebration (☏213/730-1495); also a celebration in Pasadena at about the same time (☏626/449-2742).

last two weeks LA County Fair. In Pomona, in the San Gabriel Valley. The biggest county fair in the US, with livestock shows, pie-eating contests, rodeos, and fairground rides (☏909/623-3111, ⓦwww.fairplex.com).

late Watts Towers Day of the Drum/Jazz Festival. Two days of community spirit and free music – a wealth of African, Asian, Cuban, and Brazilian drumming – with the towers as the striking backdrop. Taking place at the same time, and in the same location, the Jazz Festival is the most longstanding such event in LA (☏213/847-4646).

late through October Oktoberfest. Venture into Alpine Village, in the South Bay suburb of Torrance, to revel in Teutonic culture: hearty German food, music, and dancing abound (☏310/327-4384, ⓦwww.alpinevillage.net). Also a spirited event in the Orange County town of Huntington Beach (☏714/895-8020, ⓦwww.oldworld.ws).

---

legendary contemporary jazz spot, where many reputations have been forged. Don't come looking for bland lounge jazz/muzak – instead, expect to be surprised.

Catalina Bar & Grill 6725 Hollywood Blvd, Hollywood ☏323/466-2210. A jazz institution with plenty of style and atmosphere, with filling meals and potent drinks.

Cat 'n' Fiddle Pub 6530 Sunset Blvd, Hollywood ☏323/468-3800. An English-style pub with jazz

on Sundays from 7pm until 11pm; no cover. See also "Drinking," p.193.

Cozy's Bar & Grill 14048 Ventura Blvd, Sherman Oaks ☏818/986-6000. Listen to blues on the weekend, or periodically during the week, at this restaurant and lounge that also features karaoke, funk, and soul performances.

Harvelle's 1432 4th St, Santa Monica ☏310/395-1676. Near the Third Street Promenade, a stellar blues joint for more than six decades offering

October

first three weekends Catalina Island Jazz Trax. A huge lineup of major and rising stars in jazz perform in the historic surroundings of this island's beautiful Art Deco Avalon ballroom (☎1-888/330-5252, ⓦwww.jazztrax.com).

early Scandinavian Festival. Folk dancing with assorted foods and art, along with vivid displays of ethnic costuming. Held at Grand Hope Park in Downtown LA (☎213/661-4273, ⓦasfla.org).

second weekend LA Street Fair and Carnival. Free rock music, theater, and comedy on the streets of Sherman Oaks in the San Fernando Valley. At the same time as West Hollywood Street Festival, a display of handmade arts and crafts (☎310/781-2020).

31 Halloween Parade. A wild parade in West Hollywood, where all manner of bizarre and splashy outfits and characters are on display (☎310/289-2525). Or you can opt for the Halloween Shipwreck on the *Queen Mary*, which spends one day as a haunted ocean liner full of favorite ghouls and demons (☎562/435-3511).

November

2 Dia de los Muertos. The "Day of the Dead," celebrated authentically throughout East LA and more blandly for tourists on Olvera Street. Mexican traditions, such as picnicking on the family burial spot and making skeleton puppets, are morbidly upheld (☎213/625-5045).

Sunday before Thanksgiving Doo-dah Parade. Quintessential LA event that began as a spoof of the Tournament of Roses parade, with a cast of absurdly costumed characters marching through Pasadena (☎626/440-7379, ⓦwww.pasadenadoodahparade.com).

late Griffith Park Light Festival. Tremendous electrical spectacle along Crystal Springs Road in the park, with tunnels of light, thematic displays, and representations of familiar LA sights like the Hollywood sign. A hugely popular draw (☎213/485-8743).

December

1 Hollywood Christmas Parade. The first and best of the many Yuletide events, with a cavalcade of mind boggling floats, marching bands, and famous and quasi-famous names from film and TV (☎323/469-2337).

early Belmont Shore Christmas Parade. East Long Beach is the setting for holiday floats and marching bands (☎562/434-3066).

mid Christmas Boat Parade. Marina del Rey is the site for this annual, ocean-going display of brightly lit watercraft, supposedly the largest boat parade in the West (☎310/821-7614). Another big display takes place along Shoreline Village in Long Beach (☎562/435-4093).

---

different performers nightly and a popular band showcase on Monday nights.

House of Blues 8430 Sunset Blvd, West Hollywood ☎323/848-5100. Over-commercialized mock sugar shack, with good but pricey live acts. Very popular with tourists (also a branch at Disneyland; ☎714/778-2583). Cover can reach $40 or more.

Jax 339 N Brand Blvd, Glendale ☎818/500-1604. A combination restaurant and performing stage where you can take in a good assortment of jazz sounds, from traditional to contemporary. No cover.

Jazz Bakery 3233 Helms Ave, Culver City ☎310/271-9039. More performance space than club, the brainchild of singer Ruth Price. The best local musicians play alongside big-name visitors. In an actual former bakery building.

Knitting Factory 7021 Hollywood Blvd ☎323/463-0204. West Coast branch of New York landmark club, featuring a wide range of highly eclectic interpretation, much of it experimental or avant-garde.

Lunaria 10351 Santa Monica Blvd, West LA ☎310/282-8870. This restaurant's intimate lounge hosts nightly jazz performers playing a good range of styles, from swing to bebop. No cover.

Spazio 14755 Ventura Blvd, 2nd Floor, Sherman Oaks ☎818/728-8400. Swank Italian eatery that's one of the bigger-name spots for mainstream jazz, hosting regular nightly performances.

Salsa venues

Club Samba 701 Long Beach Blvd, Long Beach ☎562/435-6238. The first Saturday night of the month in winter and spring is the time for eye-opening samba performances, also taking place on weekly Saturday nights in July. Also with Monday-night samba classes.

The Conga Room 5364 Wilshire Blvd ☎323/938-1696. Live Cuban, salsa, and South American music throughout the week at this hip, lively club on the Miracle Mile, where the cover can sometimes be steep. See also "Clubs," p.197.

El Floridita 1253 N Vine St, Hollywood ☎323/871-8612. Decent Mexican and Cuban food comple-ments a fine lineup of Cuban and salsa artists, who play on weekends and jam on other nights.

Luminarias 3500 Ramona Blvd, Monterey Park, East LA ☎323/268-4177. Hilltop restaurant (see p.184) with regular live salsa reckoned to be as good as its Mexican food.

Zabumba 10717 Venice Blvd, Culver City ☎310/841-6525. In a colorful building amid drab surroundings, this venue is more bossa nova Brazilian than straight salsa, but it's still great, and very lively.

Reggae venues

Domenico's 82 N Fair Oaks Ave, Pasadena ☎626/449-1948. Old Pasadena Italian restaurant hosting reggae several nights a week.

Fais Do-Do 5247 W Adams Blvd ☎323/954-8080. Though it often hosts DJ nights of the dance, funk, and rap variety, this spot, between Downtown and Culver City, also presents weekend concerts from regional reggae and R&B acts.

Golden Sails Club Room 6285 E PCH, Long Beach ☎562/596-1631. Some of the best reggae bands from LA and beyond show up at this hotel on Friday and Saturday nights.

Performing arts and film

Despite the countless stereotypes about Southern California being a culture-free zone, in truth the city offers a wealth of **performing arts** options scattered throughout the basin. While it's true that the city's range of highbrow cultural offerings was at one time quite limited, confined to art-house cinemas and a handful of mainstream theaters, since then LA has firmly established itself in the performing arts field thanks to a renewed push from old-money and corporate interests.

LA boasts a world-class conductor and orchestra for **classical music**, along with less-familiar entities like chamber-music groups, and the fields of **opera** and **dance** are represented by several fine companies. **Theater** is always a growth industry here, with more than a thousand shows annually, plenty of actors to draw from, and a burgeoning audience for both mainstream and fringe productions. **Comedy** is a big draw, too, and it comes as no surprise that this is one of the prime entertainment options that first-time visitors seek out. Not surprisingly, though, it's **film** that is still the chief cultural staple of the region, and there is no shortage of excellent theaters in which to catch a flick.

Classical music, opera, and dance

LA has an increasing number of outlets for **classical music** and **opera**. The Los Angeles Philharmonic and LA Opera are the major names in the city, and perform regularly during the year at the Music Center Downtown, while smaller groups appear sporadically at different venues. Watch the press, especially the *LA Times*, for details, and expect to pay from $10 to $120 for most concerts, more for really big names. **Dance** in Los Angeles has its annual big event with the **Dance Kaleidoscope**, held over two weeks in July at the John Anson Ford Theater and organized by the Los Angeles Area Dance Alliance (☎323/343-5120) – a co-operative of LA dance companies that provides a central source of information. Otherwise check for performances at the **universities**, where many important names in dance have residencies.

Major venues

Alfred Newman Recital Hall on the USC campus, South Central ☎213/740-2584. A fine university venue for sonatas, concertos, and other classical works (usually Sept–May), with most tickets costing less than $20 – and even cheaper for students, around $12.

Disney Hall 1st St at Grand Ave, Downtown ☎323/850-2000, ⓦwdch.laphil.org. LA's most renowned cultural attraction (along with the Getty Center), which hosts the LA Philharmonic in a striking Frank Gehry design (see p.110) and has begun drawing tourists back to Downtown LA.

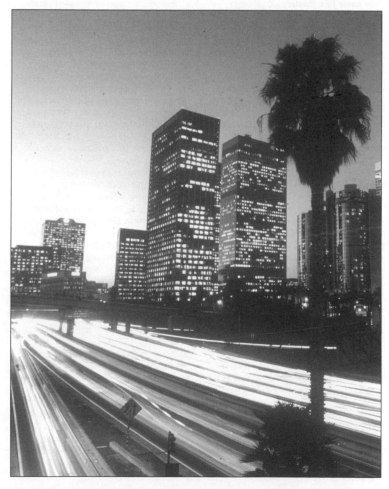

△ Los Angeles freeway at night

The **Dorothy Chandler Pavilion** in the Music
Center, 135 N Grand Ave, Downtown ☏ 213/972-
7211 or 972-7460, ⓦ www.musiccenter.org. Long-
standing warhorse of the arts community, used by
LA Opera and other top names.

The **Hollywood Bowl** 2301 N Highland Ave, Hollywood ☏ 323/850-2000, ⓦ www.hollywoodbowl
.org. Hosts the LA Philharmonic and Hollywood
Bowl Orchestra for open-air concerts, usually of
the pops variety, Tuesday through Saturday evenings from July to September.

Japan America Theater 244 S San Pedro St,
Little Tokyo ☏ 213/680-3700, ⓦ www.jaccc.org.
Dance and performance works drawn from Japan
and the Far East.

John Anson Ford Theater 2850 Cahuenga
Blvd, Hollywood ☏ 323/461-3673, ⓦ www
.fordamphitheater.org. Besides the summer Dance
Kaleidoscope, this open-air venue also has eclectic
productions by local groups and sporadic pop and
rock concerts.

Orange County Performing Arts Center 600
Town Center Drive, Costa Mesa ☏ 714/556-ARTS
or 949/740-2000, ⓦ www.ocpac.org. Orange
County home of the Pacific Symphony Orchestra
and Opera Pacific, as well as touring big names in
pop and jazz.

Pasadena Dance Theatre 1985 Locust St,
Pasadena ☏ 626/683-3459, ⓦ www
.pasadenadance.org. One of the San Gabriel
Valley's most prominent dance venues, hosting
diverse groups throughout the year.

Royce Hall on the UCLA campus, Westwood
☏ 310/825-9261 or 825-2101, ⓦ www
.performingarts.ucla.edu. Classical concerts,
often involving big names, occur at this splendid
historic-revival structure throughout the college
year (Sept–June, generally speaking).

The **Shrine Auditorium** 665 W Jefferson, South
Central LA ☏ 213/749-5123, box office at 655
S Hill St. Huge 1926 Moorish curiosity that hosts
touring pop acts, choral gospel groups, and countless award shows (but not the Oscars anymore).

UCLA Center for the Performing Arts office at
10920 Wilshire Blvd, Westwood ☏ 310/825-4401,
ⓦ www.performingarts.ucla.edu. Coordinates a
wide range of touring companies, and runs an "Art
of Dance" series with an experimental emphasis
(Sept–June).

Groups and institutions

Da Camera Society rotating venues throughout
LA ☏ 213/477-2929, ⓦ www.dacamera.org. This
organization's "Chamber Music in Historic Sites"
provides a great opportunity to hear chamber

works in stunning settings, from grand churches
to private homes, including Doheny Mansion, the
Biltmore and *Dunbar* hotels, and the beautiful
Canfield-Moreno estate. Ticket prices vary
depending on the venue.

LA Opera at the Music Center, 135 N Grand Ave,
Downtown ☏ 213/972-8001, ⓦ www.laopera.com.
Stages productions between September and June,
from heavy *opera seria* to lighter operettas. The
mainstream heavyweight in town.

Long Beach Opera at the Carpenter Center, 6200
Atherton St ☏ 562/439-2580, ⓦ www.lbopera
.com. Despite being eight years older than the
LA Opera, this alternative company presents the
freshest and edgiest work in town, from old pieces
by Monteverdi to craggy newer works by modernists like Bartok.

Los Angeles Chamber Orchestra rotating local
venues ☏ 213/622-7001 ext 215, ⓦ www.laco
.org. Appearing at UCLA's Royce Hall and
Glendale's Alex Theatre on one weekend per
month, the orchestra presents a range of chamber
works, not all canonical, from different eras.

Los Angeles Master Chorale at Disney Hall and
rotating venues, 135 N Grand Ave, Downtown
☏ 1-800/787-LAMC, tickets through Ticketmaster
☏ 213/365-3500, ⓦ www.lamc.org. Classic works,
along with lighter pops favorites, are showcased
by this choral institution.

Los Angeles Philharmonic at Disney Hall, 1st
St and Grand Ave, Downtown ☏ 323/850-2000,
ⓦ www.laphil.org. The one big name in the city
performs regularly during the year, and conductor
Esa-Pekka Salonen always provides a diverse,
challenging program, from powerful Romantic
works to thorny modern pieces.

Opera Pacific Orange County Performing Arts
Center, 600 Town Center Drive, Costa Mesa
☏ 949/474-4488 or 1-800/34-OPERA, ⓦ www
.operapacific.org. Performs mostly mainstream
grand opera and operettas.

Pacific Symphony Orchestra Orange County
Performing Arts Center, 600 Town Center Drive,
Costa Mesa ☏ 714/755-5788, ⓦ www
.pacificsymphony.org. Orchestra that draws big
crowds for its excellent, stylish performances.
Another attraction is the symphony's lower ticket
prices than its LA equivalent.

Pasadena Symphony at Pasadena Civic Auditorium, 300 E Green St ☏ 626/584-8833, ⓦ www
.pasadenasymphony.org. Veering between the
standard repertoire and more contemporary
pieces, this esteemed symphony provides plenty of
artistic sustenance for its audience.

Comedy

LA has a wide range of **comedy** clubs. While rising stars and beginners can be spotted on the "underground" open-mike scene, most of the famous comics, both stand-up and improv, appear at the more established clubs in Hollywood, West LA, or the valleys. These venues usually have a bar, charge a $10–15 cover, and put on two shows per evening, generally starting at 8pm and 10.30pm – the later one being more popular. The better-known places are open nightly, but are often solidly booked on weekends.

Comedy venues

Acme Comedy Theater 135 N La Brea Ave, Hollywood ☎323/525-0202. A fancy venue with sketch and improv comedy, as well as variety shows and theme-comedy performances.

Bang Theater 457 N Fairfax Ave, Hollywood ☎323/653-6886. One-person shows and long-form improvisation are the specialties at this small theater/comedy club, with the popular shows running on weekends. Cheap cover, often $5–10.

Comedy & Magic Club 1018 Hermosa Ave, Hermosa Beach ☎310/372-1193. Strange couplings of magic, dance, singing, and comedy. Jay Leno sometimes tests material here. Tickets can run up to $25, depending on the performer.

Comedy Sportz 733 Seward St, Hollywood ☎323/856-4796. Recently relocated to a new home, the purveyors of comedy competitions arranged like sports contests, with Saturday-afternoon shows for the kids and other theme events during the week.

The Comedy Store 8433 W Sunset Blvd, West LA ☎323/656-6225. LA's premier comedy showcase and popular enough to be spread over three rooms – which means there's usually space, even at weekends. Run by Pauly Shore's mom.

Empty Stage 2372 Veteran Ave, West LA ☎310/470-3560. Sometimes funny, sometimes irritating sketch comedy that draws upon long improvisational routines. Cast mainly with up-and-comers of varying hilarity.

Groundlings Theater 7307 Melrose Ave, West LA ☎323/934-9700. Another pioneering venue where only the gifted survive, with furious improv events and high-wire comedy acts that can inspire greatness, or groans.

Ha Ha Café 5010 Lankershim Blvd, North Holly-wood ☎818/508-4995. Amateur and even a few professional comedians face off for your amusement nightly, at this combination comedy club and café space around the NoHo Arts District.

The Ice House 24 N Mentor Ave, Pasadena ☎626/577-1894. The comedy mainstay of the Valley, very established and fairly safe; often amusing, with plenty of old warhorses and the occasional big name. Two-drink minimum.

The Improv 8162 Melrose Ave, West LA ☎323/651-2583. Longstanding brick-walled joint known for hosting some of the best acts working in the area in both stand-up and improv. One of LA's top comedy spots – so book ahead.

Improv Olympic West 6366 Hollywood Blvd ☎323/962-7560. In the heart of old Hollywood, a spot for those who like their improv drawn out and elaborate, with comedy routines more like short theater pieces than a set of wacky one-liners.

LA Connection 13442 Ventura Blvd, Sherman Oaks ☎818/784-1868. Cozy space for sketch comedy, improv, group antics, and individual jokesters. Seldom less than memorable.

The Laugh Factory 8001 Sunset Blvd, West Hollywood ☎323/656-1336. Stand-ups of varying standards and reputations, with the odd big name. Features a variable open-mike night.

Second City Studio Theater 8156 Melrose Ave, Hollywood ☎323/651-2583 ext 176. Nightly improv and sketch comedy, sometimes built around lengthy routines and theme performances. Mostly up-and-comers.

Theater

From huge Broadway shows to small avant-garde productions, LA has a very active **theater** scene. While the bigger venues host a predictable array of retread musicals and classics with an all-star cast of celebrities, more than a hundred "Equity waiver" theaters with fewer than a hundred seats can be found around the city, enabling non-Equity-cardholders to perform, and a vast network of fringe writers, actors, and directors to showcase their talent. **Tickets** are less expensive than you might expect: a big show will cost you at least $40 (matinees are cheaper), smaller shows around $10 to $30. Always book ahead (see box "What's on and tickets," p.198).

Fringe theaters

Evidence Room 2220 Beverly Blvd, Mid-Wilshire ☎213/381-7118. Edgy, startling works, alternated with more conventional modern dramas and comedies. Call to confirm listings and venue space.

Highways 1651 18th St, Santa Monica ☎310/315-1459. Located in the 18th Street Arts Complex, an adventurous performance space that offers a range of topical drama and politically charged productions, with a strong bent toward the angry, polemical and subversive.

Hudson Mainstage Theater 6539 Santa Monica Blvd, Hollywood ☎323/993-7199 or 323/960-4551. Socially conscious "message" plays alternate with more satiric, comedic works at this theater for upcoming actors.

Odyssey Theater Ensemble 2055 S Sepulveda Blvd, West LA ☎310/477-2055. Well-respected Westside theater company with a modernist bent, offering a range of quality productions on three stages for decent prices.

Powerhouse Theater 3116 Second St, Santa Monica ☎310/396-3680 or 866/633-6246. Cozy venue, worth visiting for the adventurous and risk-taking experimental shows.

Stages Theater Center 1540 N McCadden Place, Hollywood ☎323/465-1010. With three stages offering twenty to one hundred seats, an excellent place to catch a wide range of comedies and dramas, including re-stagings of canonical works and contemporary productions with either a mainstream or experimental bent.

Theatre West 3333 Cahuenga Blvd West, Hollywood ☎323/851-7977. A classic venue that's always a good spot to see inventive, sometimes odd, productions with a troupe of excellent young up-and-comers.

Theatricum Botanicum 1419 N Topanga Canyon Blvd, Topanga Canyon ☎310/455-3723. Terrific spot showing a range of classic (often Shakespearean) and modern plays amid an idyllic outdoor setting. Founded by Will Geer – TV's Grandpa Walton.

Major theaters

Ahmanson Theatre at the Music Center, 135 N Grand Ave, Downtown ☎213/628-2772. A two-thousand-seat theater hosting colossal traveling shows from Broadway. If you've seen a major production advertised on TV and on the sides of buses, it's probably playing here.

Alex Theatre 216 N Brand Blvd, Glendale ☎1-800/872-8997. Gloriously restored movie palace bedecked with green-and-yellow decor and neon spire, hosting a fine range of musical theater, dance, comedy, and film.

Coronet Theater 366 N La Cienega Blvd, West Hollywood ☎310/657-7377. Solid Westside choice that's home to the LA Public Theater and the Youth Academy of Dramatic Arts. Notable as the spot where mid-level Hollywood actors come to test new material.

Geffen Playhouse 10886 Le Conte Ave, Westwood ☎310/208-5454. A five-hundred seat, quaint Spanish Revival building that often hosts one-person shows. There's a decided Hollywood connection, evident in the crowd-pleasing nature of many of the productions.

Mark Taper Forum 135 N Grand Ave, Downtown ☎213/972-0700 or 213/628-2772. Theater in the three-quarter round, mostly known for its conservatism and adherence to the mainstream repertoire. Located in the Music Center complex.

Pantages Theater 6233 Hollywood Blvd, Hollywood ☎323/468-1770 or 213/365-3500. Quite the stunner: an exquisite, atmospheric Art Deco theater, in the heart of historic Hollywood, hosting major touring Broadway productions.

Pasadena Playhouse 39 S El Molino Ave, Pasadena ☎626/792-8672 or 626/356-7529. A grand old space that provides enjoyable mainstream entertainment. Actors are often a mix of youthful professionals and aging TV and movie stars.

South Coast Repertory 655 Town Center Drive, Costa Mesa ☎714/708-5555. Orange County's major entry for theater, where you can watch well-executed performances of the classics on the main stage, and edgier works by new writers on the smaller, 150-seat second stage.

Film

Major feature **films** are often released in LA months (or years) before they play anywhere else, and a huge number of cinemas show both the new releases and the classics – with fewer screens showing independent and foreign movies. Depending on where you go and what you see, a ticket will be from $6.50 to $10, with much higher costs for special events such as the Last Remaining Seats Festival (up to $20).

Classic moviehouses

Bruin 948 Broxton Ave, Westwood ☏310/208-8998. While smaller than it used to be thanks to aggressive remodeling, this 1930s moviehouse remains a city landmark for its wraparound marquee and sleek Moderne styling.

Chinese 6925 Hollywood Blvd, Hollywood ☏323/464-8111. With its large main screen, six-track stereo sound, and wild chinoiserie design, this Hollywood icon shows relentlessly mainstream films, but is still worthy of all the postcard images (see p.130).

Cinerama Dome 6360 Sunset Blvd, Hollywood ☏323/466-3401 or 464-4226. This white hemisphere has the biggest screen in California, a giant curved panel with slight distortion at the corners. Now part of a larger complex of theaters and shops called ArcLight (see p.131).

Egyptian 6712 Hollywood Blvd, Hollywood ☏323/466-FILM. Thanks to the American Cinematheque film group, this historic moviehouse has nightly showings of revival, experimental, and art films, and has been lovingly restored as a kitschy masterpiece of the Egyptian Revival – all grand columns, winged scarabs, and mythological gods (see p.129).

El Capitan 6834 Hollywood Blvd, Hollywood ☏323/467-7674. Whether or not you enjoy the typically kiddie-oriented fare offered here – thanks to its Disney ownership – the restored splendor of this classic Hollywood movie palace is bound to impress you.

Fine Arts 8556 Wilshire Blvd, Beverly Hills ☏310/652-1330. Proof that modern moviehouses don't necessarily have to be ugly concrete boxes. The simple exterior and lobby give way to a grandly opulent 1936 theater showing a mix of mainstream and art-house films.

Los Angeles 615 S Broadway, Downtown. Boasting an exquisite French Second Empire lobby, with triumphal arches lined by marble columns supporting an intricate mosaic ceiling, and an 1800-seat auditorium enveloped by *trompe l'oeil* murals. One of the all-time great moviehouses in the country, though only open to the public during the Last Remaining Seats film festival in June (tickets $20; see p.112).

Orpheum 842 S Broadway, Downtown ☏213/239-0939. Recently renovated, a spellbinding mix of French Renaissance and Baroque decor, with a pipe organ, brazen chandeliers, ornamental grotesques, nude nymphs, and grand arches in gold-leaf. Visible during the Last Remaining Seats festival, but also for periodic performing-arts events.

Rialto 1023 Fair Oaks Ave, South Pasadena ☏626/799-9567. A 1925 movie palace and historic landmark that also served as a theatrical stage and vaudeville locale, with Moorish organ screens, Egyptian columns, winged harpies, and a central Medusa head.

Village 961 Broxton Ave, Westwood ☏310/208-5576. One of the most enjoyable places to watch a movie in LA, with a giant screen, fine seats, and good balcony views, and a frequent spot for Hollywood premieres. The marvelous 1931 exterior features a white spire on top.

Warner Grand 478 W 6th St, San Pedro ☏310/548-7672. Restored 1931 Zigzag Moderne masterpiece with dark geometric details, great columns, and sunburst motifs – a style that almost looks pre-Columbian. Now a repertory cinema and performing-arts hall.

Art houses and revival cinemas

Bing at the LA County Art Museum, 5905 Wilshire Blvd, Mid-Wilshire ☏323/857-6010. Offers afternoon screenings of Warner Bros classics for just $3, as well as full-priced evening programs of classic, independent, foreign, art-house, and revival cinema.

Los Feliz 1822 N Vermont Ave, Hollywood ☏323/664-2169. Having successfully avoided a descent into the porn-movie market in the 1960s, the theater's three small screens show international and low-budget American independent fare.

New Beverly Cinema 7165 Beverly Blvd, Mid-Wilshire ☏323/938-4038. Not a particularly attractive theater, but a worthwhile one for its excellent art films and revival screenings, with some imaginative double bills.

Nuart 11272 Santa Monica Blvd, West LA ☏310/478-6379. Showing rarely seen classics, documentaries, and edgy foreign-language films, this is the main option for independent filmmakers testing their work, and sometimes offers brief December previews of Oscar contenders long before they're released nationwide. Be prepared to wait outside the theater in a lengthy line near the 405 freeway.

Old Town Music Hall 140 Richmond St, El Segundo ☎310/322-2592. An old-fashioned spot to see historic movies, with accompanying organ or piano music on some nights, this quaint theater is unfortunately sited in a grim industrial location south of LAX.

Silent Movie 611 N Fairfax Ave, Mid-Wilshire ☎323/655-2520. Offers an enjoyable mix of silent comedies and adventure flicks – Douglas Fairbanks swashbucklers and the like – along with darker fare like Fritz Lang's *Metropolis* and even the occasional talkie.

Sunset 5 8000 Sunset Blvd, West Hollywood ☎323/848-3500. This art-house complex sits on the second floor of the Sunset Plaza outdoor mall – former site of the legendary Schwab's drugstore – and shows a good assortment of edgy independent flicks.

Vista 4473 Sunset Drive, Hollywood ☎323/660-6639. A nicely renovated moviehouse with very eclectic offerings – from mindless action flicks to micro-budgeted indie productions – located near the intersection of Sunset and Hollywood boulevards.

Gay and lesbian LA

Although nowhere near as big as that of San Francisco, LA's **gay and lesbian scene** is well established. The best-known area is the city of **West Hollywood**, which is synonymous with the (affluent, white) gay lifestyle, not just in LA but all over California. The section of West Hollywood on Santa Monica Boulevard east of Doheny Drive has chic restaurants, shops, and bars, whereas **Silver Lake**, especially along Hyperion and Sunset boulevards, has much more of a vibrant ethnic and working-class mix. Surprisingly, perhaps, even Orange County has its pockets of gay and lesbian culture, centered mainly around the upscale confines of **Laguna Beach** and its trendy restaurants and bars.

Gay couples will find themselves readily accepted at just about any LA **hotel**, but there are a few that cater especially to gay travelers and can also be useful sources of information on the local scene. This is also true of a number of **restaurants** and various **bars** and **clubs**.

Resources

AIDS Project Los Angeles 611 S Kingsley Drive, Hollywood ☎213/201-1600, ⊛www.apla.org. Sponsors fundraisers throughout the year and a well-attended annual walkathon. Office open Tues, Wed & Fri 10am–5pm.

A Different Light 8853 Santa Monica Blvd, West Hollywood ☎310/854-6601, ⊛www.adlbooks .com. The city's best-known gay and lesbian bookshop, with art shows, readings, music events, and comfortable chairs for lounging.

Gay and Lesbian Community Services Center 1625 N Schrader Blvd, Hollywood ☎323/993-7400, ⊛www.laglc.org. Counseling, health-testing, and information. Publishes *The Center News*, a bimonthly magazine. Open Mon–Fri 9am–9pm, Sat 9am–1pm.

Gay Community Yellow Pages 1604 Vista Del Mar Ave, Hollywood ☎323/469-4454. Gay businesses, publications, services, and gathering places listed yearly; available all over LA.

One Institute and Archives 909 W Adams Blvd, South Central LA ☎213/741-0094, ⊛www .oneinstitute.org. The world's biggest library of rare

books and magazines, literature, artworks, and related information on gay and lesbian culture, social issues, and politics. Open Tues & Wed 3.30–9pm, Thurs & Fri 1.30–5.30pm, Sat 11am–3pm.

Hotels

Coral Sands 1730 N Western Ave, Hollywood ☎323/467-5141, ⊛www.coralsands-la.com. Cruisy spot exclusively geared towards gay men. All rooms face the inner courtyard pool. Also with on-site sauna, Jacuzzi, and gym. ❹

Holloway Motel 8465 Santa Monica Blvd, West Hollywood ☎323/654-2454, ⊛www .hollowaymotel.com. Typical clean roadside motel, if rather dreary looking. Comes with complimentary breakfast. Add $50 during holidays like Halloween and Gay Pride. ❺

Hollywood Metropolitan 5825 Sunset Blvd ☎323/962-5800, ⊛www.metropolitanhotel.com. Spanish-style hotel with a mix of small, comfortable rooms and larger suites, featuring the *Havana on Sunset* restaurant on site (see p.184). ❹

Ramada 8585 Santa Monica Blvd, West Hollywood ☎310/652-6400 or 1-800/845-8585, ⊛www

.thegayhotel.com. The self-styled "Gay Hotel," a modern place with clean and comfortable rooms, plus pool and gym, in the center of the community. **⑤**

San Vicente Inn 854 N San Vicente Blvd, West Hollywood ☎310/854-6915, ⓦwww.gayresort.com/sanvicenteinn. Small and comfortable bed and breakfast located just north of Santa Monica Boulevard, with pool, spa, and sauna. **⑤**

Restaurants

French Quarter 7985 Santa Monica Blvd, West Hollywood ☎310/654-0898. Inside the *French Market Place*, a New Orleans–theme restaurant with food that's more tasty than it is authentic.

Golden Bull 170 W Channel Rd, Pacific Palisades ☎310/230-0402. Enjoyable, if expensive, steak-and-seafood restaurant and bar that makes for a relaxed atmosphere near the ocean, not far from Santa Monica.

Marix Tex-Mex Playa 118 Entrada Drive, Pacific Palisades ☎310/459-8596. Flavorful fajitas and big margaritas in this rowdy beachfront cantina, which attracts mixed gay and straight crowds. An even livelier branch at 1108 N Flores St, West Hollywood ☎323/656-8800.

Mark's 861 N La Cienega Blvd, West Hollywood ☎310/652-5252. High-end establishment serving California cuisine, with especially good crab cakes, *osso buco*, and Australian lamb chops.

Woody's at the Beach 1305 S Coast Hwy, Laguna Beach ☎949/376-8809. Upscale bar and restaurant in Orange County serving quality California cuisine to a fairly well-heeled clientele.

Yukon Mining Company 7328 Santa Monica Blvd ☎323/851-8833. Colorful 24hr coffee shop where you're likely to see local drag queens, newly arrived Russians, and neighborhood pensioners.

Bars and clubs

7969 7969 Santa Monica Blvd, West Hollywood ☎323/654-0280. Legendary club back in business after closing due to fire for a few years, and offering high-energy dance tunes, frenetic DJs, and colorful theme-party nights.

Arena 6655 Santa Monica Blvd, Hollywood ☎323/462-0714. Many clubs under one roof, large dancefloors throbbing to funk, house, and hi-NRG grooves, and sometimes with live bands and mind-blowing drag shows. See also "Clubs," p.196.

Boom Boom Room 1401 S Coast Hwy, Laguna Beach ☎949/494-7588. The pulse-pounding name says it all: house and disco tunes spun by local DJs on weekends, male strip shows, and all kinds of other colorful performances and spectacles.

Jewel's Catch One 4067 W Pico Blvd, Mid-Wilshire ☎323/734-8849. Sweaty barn catering to a mixed crowd – gay and straight, male and female – all on two wild dancefloors.

Micky's 8857 Santa Monica Blvd ☎310/657-1176. Lively, pulsating scene with a full range of club nights, including the usual retro-70s and 80s dance-pop, thundering house and hip-hop beats, and even monthly swing and Dixieland bands.

Mother Lode 8944 Santa Monica Blvd ☎310/659-9700. Strong drinks, wild dancing to house and hi-NRG music, and periodic drag antics make this one of the more colorful and frenetic of WeHo's clubs.

Ozz Supper Club 6231 Manchester Blvd, Buena Park ☎714/522-1542. A lively dance club with booming house, disco, and salsa music on the weekends and assorted drag shows, cabaret music, and lounge performers as well. A gay standout in this Orange County burg.

The Palms 8572 Santa Monica Blvd, West Hollywood ☎310/652-6188. Mostly house and dance nights at West Hollywood's most established lesbian bar, which increasingly caters to a mixed crowd.

The Plaza 739 N La Brea Ave, Hollywood ☎323/939-0703. Nondescript little joint hosts funky drag shows to a multi-ethnic, mostly gay crowd.

Rage 8911 Santa Monica Blvd, West Hollywood ☎310/652-7055. Very flashy gay men's club and neighborhood favorite playing the latest hi-NRG and house to a long-established crowd. Drinks are fairly cheap.

Shopping

Shopping in LA is an art, and touring the more outrageous stores can be a great insight into LA life – revealing who's got the money and what they're capable of blowing it on. Besides the run-of-the-mill chain retailers you'll find anywhere, there are big **department stores** and mega-sized **malls** where most of the hardcore shopping goes on, and of course **Rodeo Drive**, two blocks of the world's most exclusive shopping. The trendiest boutiques line **Melrose Avenue**, between La Brea and Fairfax avenues; **Old Town Pasadena** boasts a few more upmarket chains; while the few blocks above Prospect on Vermont Avenue in **Los Feliz** are home to some of the underground's groovier shops.

LA also has a good assortment of **book** and **record stores**, and whether you're in search of a cozy secondhand shop or a megastore with all the new releases, plus a café to boot, you won't have a hard time finding it, especially in the trendiest shopping zones. There's an equally diverse array of **food stores**, from corner delis and supermarkets to exquisite cake stores and gourmet markets.

Department stores and malls

Each of LA's neighborhoods has a collection of ordinary **stores** and **mini-malls**. A step up from these in price and quality, though still good for general shopping, are **department stores**, which are often included within massive **malls** and resemble self-contained city suburbs, around which Angelenos do the bulk of their serious buying.

The malls

Beverly Center 8500 Beverly Blvd, West Hollywood ☎310/854-0070. Seven acres of boutiques, Macy's and Bloomingdale's, a multiplex cinema, and a *Hard Rock Café*, all in one complex that resembles a giant brown concrete bunker – trimmed in hideous green and purple.

Century City Marketplace 10250 Santa Monica Blvd, Century City ☎310/553-5300. An outdoor mall with one hundred upscale shops, and one of the better food courts around. The place to come to see stars do their shopping, and a spot to catch a first-run movie in excellent surroundings at the AMC Century 14 Theater.

Del Amo Fashion Square Hawthorne Blvd at Carson St, Torrance ☎310/542-8525. The South Bay's own super-mall, one of the country's largest, with five major anchor stores and a wealth of mid-level retailers and shoppers. Convenient location just south of the 405 freeway.

The Grove 6301 W 3rd St, Mid-Wilshire ☎323/900-8080. A giant, open-air megastructure in the vicinity of the Farmers Market; the latest variant of LA mall design, with all the usual chain retailers and restaurants, movie theaters, and a somewhat more stylish design than the typical "dumb-box" construction found elsewhere.

Hollywood & Highland at the same intersection in Hollywood ☎323/960-2331. Another colossal new mega-mall, with a design inspired by an ancient film set, but offering the same old corporate boutiques and trendy shops, and a cineplex connected to the Chinese Theatre.

Paseo Colorado E Colorado Blvd at S Los Robles Ave, Pasadena ☎626/795-8891. Two levels of (mostly chain) stores with street-front entrances, an open-air design that invites strolling, and several levels of housing built over the retailers to attract the truly hardcore spenders.

Santa Monica Place Broadway at 2nd St, Santa Monica ☎310/394-5451. Sunny, skylit mall with three tiers of shops and an outdated postmodern-pastel decor. The chain-link-walled parking garage is of minor note as an early Frank Gehry design experiment.

South Coast Plaza 3333 Bristol St, north of 405 freeway, Costa Mesa ☎714/435-2000. Orange County's main super-mall, with nearly three hundred shops, seven anchor stores, plus a good mix

Rodeo Drive

The black hole for expense accounts is **Rodeo Drive** in Beverly Hills, a solid line of exclusive stores lying on and just off the street itself. Some of the bigger names include Barney's, 9570 Wilshire Blvd (☎310/276-4400), Chanel, 400 N Rodeo Drive (☎310/278-5500), Giorgio Armani, 436 N Rodeo Drive (☎310/271-5555), Gucci, 347 N Rodeo Drive (☎310/278-3451), and Neiman-Marcus, 9700 Wilshire Blvd (☎310/550-5900). Nearby, **Two Rodeo**, the area's mock-European tourist trap, competes for buyers' attention in a more kitschy and less appealing fashion.

of retailers. You're sure to get a good workout from navigating the place.

Third Street Promenade between Broadway and Wilshire Blvd, Santa Monica. A rare successful attempt to lure back consumers to the heart of the city, packed on weekend evenings with mobs scurrying about to get to bookstores, fashion outlets, restaurants, and cinemas, amid throngs of itinerant musicians,

homeless folks, street lunatics, and ivy-covered dinosaur fountains.

Westside Pavilion Pico Blvd at Westwood Blvd, West LA ☎310/474-6255. Postmodern shopping complex with two different wings branching out from Westwood Blvd – an older, more typical mall to the east (under a hemispheric glass atrium) and a newer, more outdoorsy addition to the west. Overall, no real surprises though.

Food and drink

Since eating out in LA is so common, you may never have to shop for **food** at all. But if you're preparing a picnic, or want to indulge in a spot of home cooking, there are plenty of places to stock up. **Delis**, many open round the clock, are found in many areas; **supermarkets** are almost as common, some open 24 hours, or at least until 10pm. There are also **ethnic groceries** and more expensive **gourmet markets**, not to mention a bizarre collection of one-off outlets for all kinds of food oddities.

Bakeries and desserts

Cobbler Factory 33 N Catalina Ave, Pasadena ☎626/795-1005. Bakery selling a range of scrumptious, fruity cobblers from $5–35, depending on how huge you want them. Occupies a prime spot near Old Pasadena.

Diamond Bakery 335 N Fairfax Ave, West LA ☎323/655-0534. In the heart of the Fairfax District, this great old Jewish bakery provides a good number of traditional favorites, including cheesecakes, breads, and rugelach, and a legendary pumpernickel bread.

Hansen Cakes 193 S Beverly Drive, Beverly Hills ☎310/273-3759. Local institution with a collection of resplendently decorated, and very tasty, cakes.

La Brea Bakery 624 S La Brea Ave, West LA ☎323/939-6813. Perhaps LA's best bakery, selling everything from cheap sourdough rolls to thick, heavy breads made with olives, cherries, and cheese. Connected to the equally appealing *Campanile* restaurant (see p.188).

Mousse Fantasy 2130 Sawtelle Blvd #110, West LA ☎310/479-6665. A Japanese version of a French patisserie, featuring a range of tasty tarts and pastries, all found in a crowded strip mall. Particularly notable is the Green Tea Mousse cake – a curious-tasting concoction.

Röckenwagner 2435 Main St, Santa Monica ☎310/399-6504. A Westside culinary delight serving up a fine mix of California cuisine and nouveau German food, including chocolate desserts, rich pastries and scones, and hearty breads. Located in the Edgemar shopping complex.

Viktor Benes Continental Pastries 8718 W 3rd St, West LA ☎310/276-0488. The place to go for freshly baked bread, coffee cakes, Danish pastries, and various chocolate-oriented treats, and appreciative local fans know it. Five other area locations as well.

Delis and groceries

Bay Cities Italian Deli 1517 Lincoln Blvd, Santa Monica ☎310/395-8279. A gigantic store with piles of fresh pasta, spices, meats, sauces, and many French and Middle Eastern imports.

Bharat Bazaar 11510 Washington Blvd, Culver City ☎310/398-6766. One of several excellent Indian grocers around this stretch of Culver City, providing all the goods for making your own curries and *vindaloo*.

The Cheese Store 419 N Beverly Drive, Beverly Hills ☎310/278-2855. More than four hundred types of cheese from all over the world, including every kind produced in the US, with many of them suspended invitingly over your head. Typically high prices to match.

Claro's Italian Market 1095 E Main St, Tustin ☎714/832-3081. A compact but well-stocked haven of Italian wines, chocolate, crackers, and frozen meals, with a deli and bakery offering at least forty varieties of cookies. Worth the drive out to a distant section of Orange County.

Gastronom 7859 Santa Monica Blvd ☎323/654-9456. Despite the unpleasant name, a hearty Slavic market popular with just about everyone in the area, with smoked fish and caviar as the highlights. Visible evidence of the burgeoning Russian community.

Olson's Deli 5560 Pico Blvd, Mid-Wilshire
☎ 323/938-0742. Herring, meatballs, and assorted
sausages at this Swedish grocer, one of the few
Scandinavian food retailers in LA and definitely
worth a try.

Porto's Cuban Bakery 315 N Brand Blvd,
Glendale ☎ 818/956-5996. In a town that used
to be a major home of Cuban immigrants, this
throwback to the old days offers tasty baked
goods and desserts, along with flaky Cuban
pastries, cheesecakes soaked in rum, muffins,
Danishes, croissants, and tortes.

Say Cheese 2800 Hyperion Ave, Silver Lake
☎ 323/665-0545. A distinctive array of French and
other international cheeses, priced moderately to
steeply. The delicious sandwiches may be your
best bet.

Standard Sweets and Snacks 18600 Pioneer
Blvd, Artesia ☎ 562/860-6364. Good Indian
finger-food joint selling vegetarian *dosas* – a
South Indian crêpe-like delight – and appealing
sweets.

Books

LA is home to a great variety of **bookstores**, from chain dealers like Barnes
and Noble and Borders to some good **general-interest** booksellers, selling a
smaller but more well-considered selection of titles than the chains. The city
also has a wide range of **specialist** and **secondhand bookstores**, which will
help you find that obscure physics text or gardening tome you're looking for,
and may reward several hours' browsing along the miles of dusty shelves.

New books

Bodhi Tree 8585 Melrose Ave, West Hollywood
☎ 310/659-1733. Ultra-trendy Westside book
retailer in a chic part of Melrose, with a range of
New Age, occult, and psychobabble titles, including plenty of information on the healing power of
crystals, pyramids, and the like.

Book Soup 8818 W Sunset Blvd, West Hollywood
☎ 310/659-3110. Great selection, right on Sunset
Strip. Narrow, winding aisles stuffed pell-mell with
books, strong in entertainment, travel, and photography. Celebs are sometimes known to come in,
attempting to look studious.

A Different Light 8853 Santa Monica Blvd, West
Hollywood ☎ 310/854-6601. The city's best-
known gay and lesbian bookstore, with monthly
art shows, readings, and musical events. See also
"Gay and lesbian LA," p.210.

Dutton's 11975 San Vicente Blvd, Brentwood
☎ 310/476-6263. The best of the stores in this LA
chain, an ungainly complex built around a central
courtyard. Its aisles tend to be cluttered, but it's a
good store; just try to visit during the less-crowded
weekdays.

Hennessey and Ingalls 1254 3rd Street
Promenade, Santa Monica ☎ 310/458-9074. An
impressive range of art and architecture books
makes this bookstore the best in LA in its field,
though quite expensive.

Larry Edmunds Book Shop 6644 Hollywood Blvd
☎ 323/463-3273. Many stacks of books, a large
number of them out of print, are offered on every
aspect of film and theater, with movie stills and

posters. Located at the center of tourist-oriented
Hollywood.

Midnight Special 1318 3rd Street Promenade,
Santa Monica ☎ 310/393-2923. A large general
bookstore, with eccentrically filled shelves and a
broad focus on lefty politics and social sciences.
Always attracts a good crowd of regulars and
tourists.

Norton Simon Museum Bookstore 411 W
Colorado Blvd, Pasadena ☎ 626/449-6840. Prices
in this museum-attached store are lower than in
any other major art bookstore in LA, and the stock
is superb – often with sizeable volumes on artists
in the museum's collection.

Samuel French Theatre & Film Bookshop 7623
Sunset Blvd, West Hollywood ☎ 323/876-0570.
LA's broadest selection of theater books is found in
this local institution, along with a good collection of
movie and media-related titles. In the back room,
you can sometimes find discounted or used titles.

Taschen 354 N Beverly Drive, Beverly Hills
☎ 310/274-4300. Fun, edifying, and weird titles
that focus on everything from Renaissance art to
Americana kitsch to fetish photography. Cheap
volumes on both familiar and obscure subjects,
and even the coffee-table books are occasionally
affordable. Also features an art gallery, café, and
performance space.

Vroman's 695 E Colorado Blvd, Pasadena
☎ 626/449-5320. One of the Valley's major retailers, offering a good selection with a café. Although
there are no real bargains, other, smaller used-
bookstores can be found within a few blocks.

Secondhand books

Acres of Books 240 Long Beach Blvd, Long Beach ☎ 562/437-6980. Worth a trip down the Blue Line Metrorail just to wallow in LA's largest, and most disorganized, secondhand collection. You may not be able to find the exact title you're looking for, but chances are you'll stumble across something good.

Atlantis Book Shop 145 N San Fernando Blvd, Burbank ☎ 818/845-6467. History, fiction, and politics are some of the specialties, but especially the paranormal, extraterrestrial, and mythological.

Book Alley 611 E Colorado Blvd, Pasadena ☎ 626/683-8083. A handsomely designed bookstore with used volumes on a variety of subjects, with many of the books quite affordable. Store has expanded into a second building: Book Alley Too!, 696 E Colorado Blvd (☎ 626/795-0818).

Brand Book Shop 231 N Brand Blvd, Glendale ☎ 818/507-5943. Valley used-bookseller with a broad range of liberal-arts titles and particular strengths in entertainment, history, and politics. Located in the pulsing heart of downtown Glendale.

Cliff's Books 630 E Colorado Blvd, Pasadena ☎ 626/449-9541. With many narrow aisles of tomes on a wide assortment of subjects, this long-standing used-bookseller has a greater selection than some of its neighbors, though the prices are known to be a bit higher.

Cosmopolitan Book Shop 7017 Melrose Ave ☎ 323/938-7119. The cozier Westside equivalent to Acres of Books, a dealer loaded with thousands of titles stacked high on oversized bookcases, on a variety of subjects but especially strong on film and media.

Wilshire Books 3018 Wilshire Blvd, Santa Monica ☎ 310/828-3115. The best used-bookstore in LA for its size, which is quite small and cramped. Still, a solid collection of art, politics, religion, music, science, and other books, all well-organized.

Music

If anything, **record stores** are even more plentiful than bookstores in LA. While CDs are the dominant format, vinyl fans will be happy to find LPs in abundance, thanks in equal parts to diehard collectors and the constant need for "scratching" by club DJs. The selection below leans toward LA's more one-of-a-kind record stores, though chain lovers will inevitably be drawn to the huge Tower, 8801 Sunset Blvd (☎ 310/657-7300), and Virgin, 8000 Sunset Blvd (☎ 323/650-8666), megastores, both on the Sunset Strip.

Amoeba Music 6400 W Sunset Blvd, Hollywood ☎ 323/245-6400. A vast selection of titles – supposedly numbering around half a million – on CD, tape, and vinyl, which you can freely hear at listening carrels throughout the store. Also presents occasional in-store live music.

Aron's Records 1150 N Highland Ave, Hollywood ☎ 323/469-4700. Secondhand discs – all styles, all prices, and a sizeable stock, though nothing too out of the ordinary. Getting help can be a problem, as the place is often packed.

DMC Records 7619 Melrose Ave, Hollywood ☎ 323/651-3520. A prime spot to buy used CDs and, especially, vinyl. Local club-hoppers and DJs come here to stock up on the latest dance records and find more obscure tracks by little-known artists.

Heavy Rotation 12354 Ventura Blvd, Studio City ☎ 818/769-8882. Cheap prices for used CDs, cassettes, laserdiscs, and video games are one big draw for this San Fernando Valley dealer; the other is the interesting assortment of music-industry promotional records.

Penny Lane 12 W Colorado Blvd, Pasadena ☎ 626/564-0161. New and used records at reasonable prices. Always crowded, this local chain features listening stations from which you can sample up to a hundred eclectic discs. Also at 7563 Melrose Ave (☎ 323/651-3000) and 10914 Kinross Ave, Westwood (☎ 310/208-5611).

Poo-Bah Records 1101 E Walnut Ave, Pasadena ☎ 626/449-3359. Plenty of American and imported New Wave sounds, along with 1980s technopop and various other genres.

Record Surplus 11609 W Pico Blvd, West LA ☎ 310/478-4217. Massive LP collection of surf music, ancient rock'n'roll, 60s soundtracks, and unintentionally hilarious spoken-word recordings. Prices are excellent, with many CDs and cassettes offered for ridiculously low prices.

Rhino Records 1720 Westwood Blvd, West LA ☎ 310/474-8685. The biggest selection of international independent releases, stocked with rock, punk, funk, and everything else, not to mention the countless records put out by Rhino Records itself.

Vinyl Fetish 7305 Melrose Ave, West Hollywood ☎ 323/935-1300. Besides the punk and post-punk sounds, a good place to discover what's new on the LA music scene.

Listings

Airport information Bob Hope/Burbank ☎818/840-8847, ⓦwww.burbankairport.com; John Wayne/Orange County ☎949/252-5006, ⓦwww.ocair.com; LAX ☎310/646-5252, ⓦwww.los-angeles-lax.com; Long Beach ☎562/570-2600, ⓦwww.longbeach.gov/ airport; Ontario ☎909/937-2700, ⓦwww .lawa.org.

Amtrak Union Station, located Downtown at 800 N Alameda St, connects to Gateway Transit Center, an access point for local bus lines. Amtrak trains stop at the station and at outlying stations in the LA area; for all listings call Amtrak (☎1-800/USA-RAIL, ⓦwww.amtrak.com).

Automobile Club of Southern California 2601 S Figueroa St, South Central LA ☎213/741-3686, ⓦwww.aaa-calif.com. For maps, guides, and other motoring information.

Beach information Coastal weather conditions for Malibu ☎310/457-9701, Santa Monica ☎310/578-0478, South Bay ☎310/379-8471.

Bicycling information MTA ☎213/244-6539, ⓦwww.mta.net; the LA office of the state Department of Transportation, known as CalTrans, ☎213/897-3656, ⓦwww.dot.ca.gov; California Association of Bicycling Organizations ☎310/639-9348, ⓦwww.cabobike.org.

Coast Guard Search and Rescue Los Angeles/ Long Beach ☎562/980-4444, Orange County/ Newport Beach ☎949/834-3800.

Consulates Australia, 2049 Century Park East, Century City (☎310/229-4800, ⓦwww.austemb .org/losangeles.html); Canada, 550 S Hope St, 9th Floor, Downtown (☎213/346-2700, ⓦwww .dfait-maeci.gc.ca/los_angeles); New Zealand, 12400 Wilshire Blvd #1150, Westwood (☎310/207-1605, ⓦwww.nzembassy.com); UK, 11766 Wilshire Blvd #1200, West LA (☎310/481-0031, ⓦwww.britainusa.com/la).

Currency exchange Outside of banking hours, exchange offices are scattered inconveniently throughout town. Most reliable are those at LAX, hours vary by terminal (often daily until 11pm; ☎310/649-2801).

Dental treatment The cheapest place is USC School of Dentistry, 925 W 34th St (☎1-888/USC-DENT, ⓦwww.usc.edu/hsc/dental/patient_care), on the USC Campus, costing $50–200. Turn up and be prepared to wait all day. You can also get emergency treatment at the LA Dental Society, 3660 Wilshire Blvd #1152 (☎213/380-7669, ⓦwww.ladentalsociety.com).

Directory inquiries Local ☎411 (this is a free

call at pay phones); long distance ☎1, then area code, then 555-1212.

Emergencies ☎911. For less urgent needs: fire ☎323/890-4194; civil defense and disaster services ☎213/974-1120; police ☎213/625-3311; poison control center ☎1-800/777-6476; food poisoning reports ☎213/240-7821.

Hospitals The following have 24hr emergency departments: Cedars-Sinai Medical Center, 8700 Beverly Blvd, Beverly Hills (☎310/855-6517 or 423-8780, ⓦwww.csmc.edu); Good Samaritan Hospital, 1225 Wilshire Blvd, Downtown (☎213/977-2121, ⓦwww.goodsam.org); UCLA Medical Center, 10833 Le Conte Ave, Westwood (☎310/825-9111, ⓦwww.healthcare.ucla.edu).

Internet access Available from cyber-oriented coffee shops (see "Coffeehouses," p.195), the Newsroom Café (p.192), many city libraries, and sit-down terminals near flight gates at LAX. Outside of libraries, expect to pay around 10–25¢ per minute to browse the Web.

Mexican Tourist Office and Consulate 2401 W 6th St, 5th floor, Downtown (☎213/351-2069 or 1-800/44-MEXICO, ⓦwww.visitmexico.com). Call for general information or pick up a tourist card – necessary if you're crossing the border. Mon–Fri 9am–5pm.

Newspapers USC and UCLA have libraries holding overseas newspapers. Day-old English and European papers are on sale at Universal News Agency, 1639 N Las Palmas Ave (daily 7am–midnight), and World Book and News, 1652 N Cahuenga Blvd (24hr), both in Hollywood.

Pharmacies 24hr pharmacy at Kaiser's West LA hospital, 6041 Cadillac Ave (☎323/857-2151, ⓦwww.kaiserpermanente.org). Horton & Converse, 11600 Wilshire Blvd, West LA (☎310/478-0801), open daily until 2am.

Post office The main Downtown post office is at 760 N Main St (☎213/617-4405), north of Union Station. Zip Code is 90012; pick up letters Mon–Fri 8am–3pm; hours are Mon–Fri 8am–7pm, Sat 8am–4pm.

Smog LA's air quality can often be very poor and, especially in the valleys in late summer, sometimes quite dangerous. An air-quality index is published daily in the *LA Times*; if the air is really bad, warnings are issued on TV, radio, and in newspapers. For more information contact the South Coast Air Quality Management District (☎1-800/CUT-SMOG, ⓦwww.aqmd.gov).

Sports Baseball: the LA Dodgers (☎323/224-1-HIT, ⓦwww.dodgers.com) play at Dodger Stadium near Downtown; the Anaheim Angels (℡714/663-9000 or 1-888/796-4256, ⓦwww.angelsbaseball.com) at Anaheim Stadium in Orange County. Basketball: the Staples Center Downtown hosts the Lakers (℡213/480-3232, ⓦwww.lakers.com), and the woeful Clippers (℡213/742-7430, ⓦwww.clippers.com), as well as hockey's LA Kings (℡1-888/KINGS-LA, ⓦwww.lakings.com). LA's other hockey team, the Mighty Ducks, plays in Orange County at Anaheim's Arrowhead Pond (℡714/704-2500, ⓦwww.mightyducks.com). Football: Los Angeles has no professional football teams, but Pasadena's 102,000-capacity Rose Bowl (℡626/577-3100, ⓦwww.rosebowlstadium.com) is used for the annual New Year's Day Rose Bowl football game and is the home field for UCLA's football team (℡310/UCLA-WIN, ⓦuclabruins.collegesports.com). Rival USC also plays in historic digs, in the South Central location of the LA Coliseum (℡213/740-GOSC, ⓦusctrojans.collegesports.com).

Taxes LA sales tax is 8.25 percent; hotel tax variable, generally around 14 percent.

Traffic Check radio news channels for updates on which freeways are suffering from congestion; if a highway section is particularly immobile, a "SigAlert" will be issued, meaning "avoid at all costs." Radio stations emphasizing traffic reports include KNX 1070 AM; also try ⓦwww.sigalert.com on the Internet.

Travel details

Amtrak trains

Los Angeles to: Anaheim (10 daily; 40min); Fullerton (for Disneyland) (10 daily; 35min); Las Vegas (1 daily; 10hr, with bus connection); Oxnard (6 daily; 1hr 35min); Oceanside (10 daily; 1hr 50min); Palm Springs (2 daily; 2hr 35min); Sacramento (1 daily; 14hr); San Bernardino (1 daily; 2hr); San Diego (10 daily; 2hr 50min); San Francisco (3 daily; 9–12hr, with bus connection); San Juan Capistrano (10 daily; 1hr 17min); Santa Barbara (5 daily; 2hr 35min); Tucson (2 daily; 9hr 30min); Ventura (4 daily; 1hr 50min).

Greyhound buses

Los Angeles to: Las Vegas (18 daily; 5–8hr); Palm Springs (7 daily; 3hr 30min); Phoenix (10 daily; 7–9hr); Portland (5 daily; 20–23hr); Reno (9 daily; 12–15hr); Sacramento (12 daily; 7–10hr); Salt Lake City (4 daily; 15–16hr); San Diego (24 daily; 3hr); San Francisco (17 daily; 8–12hr); Seattle (5 daily; 25–28hr); Tijuana, Mexico (10 daily; 3hr 30min); Tucson (9 daily; 10–12hr).

2

San Diego and around

CHAPTER 2 # Highlights

✳ **Balboa Park** The museum centerpiece of San Diego, a 1400-acre green space loaded with history, science, and art, and crowned with the city's popular zoo. See p.237

✳ **Old Town State Historic Park** Stroll among these twenty-five preserved structures from mid-nineteenth century San Diego, and take in the adjacent re-creation of an eighteenth-century Mexican street market. See p.242

✳ **Mission Basilica San Diego de Alcalà** This complex features medieval stalls, a museum with Native American craftworks, and the state's oldest cemetery. See p.243

✳ **Villa Montezuma** A bizarre explosion of Victorian architecture in a classic 1887 home, the villa is loaded with stylized decor – and has a reputation for being haunted. See p.244

✳ **Mission Beach** The most free-spirited and hedonistic of the city's surfing beaches, with acres of bronzed flesh and bikini babes, chaotic bars, and even carnival rides. See p.248

✳ **Tijuana** This Mexican border town is a longtime favorite for its easy access from San Diego, the numerous bargains in its bazaars, and its shopping alleys. See p.271

△ The Gaslamp District, San Diego

2

San Diego and around

Lacking much of the urban chaos, social vitality, and national reputation of its neighboring megalopolis to the north, **San Diego** and its surrounding county represent the acceptable, conservative veneer of Southern California. Surpassed long ago by Los Angeles in the race to become the region's essential city, San Diego was for some time considered an insignificant blot between Los Angeles and Mexico, home only to right-wing pensioners and cloistered suburbanites. Although that stereotype still has a large measure of truth, San Diego also boasts considerable charm, with its gracefully curving bay, appealing oceanside vistas, clutch of fine museums, and big-name tourist attractions that rival anything in LA.

Outside San Diego County's eponymous urban center, you can find a host of compelling destinations. The **North County** includes the small, enticing coastal communities from the northern edge of San Diego itself to the Camp Pendleton marine base, as well as the vineyards and avocado groves that reach east into wilder mountain country. Beyond the tiny and insular beach towns, several deep forests and state parks are ideal for exploring via hiking trails and obscure backroads.

South of San Diego, there's little until you reach Mexico, where **Tijuana**, just 25 miles south, serves as a fine base for visiting **Baja California**. While it may be far from the most pleasant destination in Mexico, Tijuana nonetheless has an inescapable, if seedy, allure for thousands of day-tripping Californians every weekend. Moreover, with many of the border formalities waived for anyone traveling less than twenty miles or so into Mexico, quick visits to the party-heavy beach burgs of Rosarito and Ensenada are also a tempting draw.

Of course, there's also heavy traffic in the other direction, as countless Mexicans stream into Southern California, above and below official radar. Many are hotel and restaurant workers, but first- and especially second-generation immigrants are gradually becoming integrated into less menial levels of the workforce. However, unlike in LA, where Latino newcomers are beginning to flex their political muscle, those of San Diego County are largely ghettoized, still viewed by the blinkered white gentry as welfare-cheating detriments to society, rather than essential boosters of the local economy.

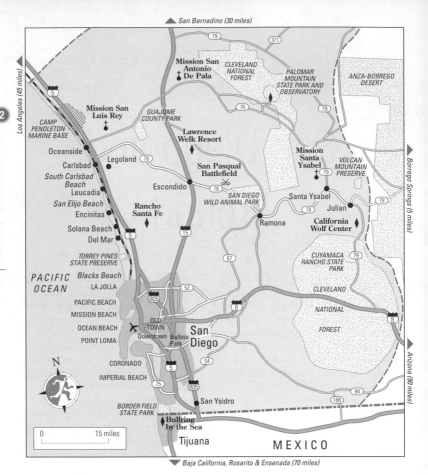

San Bernadino (30 miles)

Los Angeles (45 miles)

Borrego Springs (5 miles)

Arizona (90 miles)

Baja California, Rosarito & Ensenada (70 miles)

San Diego

Baking in the sun, its humidity tempered by ocean breezes, **SAN DIEGO** is an ideal holiday resort for hordes of tourists, most of whom arrive for its terrific beaches, major attractions like the San Diego Zoo and SeaWorld, and excellent museums in Balboa Park. More enterprising visitors may also wish to explore the city's historic Downtown, namely the Gaslamp District, whose style of preservation varies from architecturally considerate to commercially kitschy.

The traditional image of San Diegans as conformist, affluent, and Republican is true to a large extent – San Diego has as much in common with Salt Lake City or Phoenix as it does with Los Angeles or San Francisco. However, there's also been a few unexpected undercurrents in recent years, from the emergence and tolerance of a vibrant gay scene in Hillcrest to increasing numbers of liberal students and professionals. The presence of three college campuses – SDSU, UCSD, and USD – has also helped the city lose some of its rigid and reactionary character. Still, while the city's once-notorious smugness and orthodoxy has diminished, its insular civic character remains – critics such as Mike Davis have claimed that the town has one of the most corrupt political cultures in the nation, and recent scandals involving bribes, municipal kickbacks, and all manner of secret wheeling-and-dealing do little to help this image.

Obviously, the political culture is much less interesting to tourists than the sparkling weather. Paradoxically, though, for such a sunny place throughout the year, San Diego is susceptible to extended periods of overcast skies and light rain when you'd least expect it – the so-called "June Gloom" that's caused by a climatic anomaly and leaves visitors scratching their heads as they trudge through damp coastal sands.

Some history

The first European to land on Californian soil, Portuguese adventurer and Spanish agent Juan Rodríguez Cabrillo, put ashore at Point Loma, ten miles from today's Downtown San Diego, in 1542. White settlement didn't begin until two centuries later, however, with the building in 1769 of a Catholic mission – the first in California – and a military garrison on a site overlooking San Diego Bay. Later conflict between land-holding *Californios* and the fresh waves of settlers from the East led to America's capture of San Diego in 1847, an event contemporaneous with the Mexican–American War. However, the city missed out on the new mail route to the West and was plagued by a series of droughts through the 1860s, causing many bankruptcies and economic problems. Although the transcontinental Santa Fe Railroad link was short-lived – repeated flooding forced the terminus to be moved north to Los Angeles, depriving San Diego of direct rail service to the East – its establishment resulted in an economic boom through the 1880s. In 1915 came the first of two international expositions in Balboa Park, which were to establish San Diego's nationwide reputation.

In part because of its lack of direct railway access to the East Coast, the city has long been overshadowed by Los Angeles in trade and economic significance, though it has used its strategic seaside location to become a military stronghold. During World War II, the US Navy took advantage of the city's sheltered bays and made San Diego its Pacific Command Center – a function it retains.

However, it is San Diego's reputation as an ocean-oriented "resort city" that provides much of its modern relevance (at least to those not in uniform). Although it has a formidable population of more than a million people, making it the seventh-largest city in the US, for most visitors it's synonymous only with getting bronzed, yachting around the bay, surfing a killer break, and hanging out at the zoo.

Arrival and information

Motorists will find it simple to reach the city center from any of three interstate **highways**: I-5, the main artery from Los Angeles and the rest of California, follows the coast and the northern parts of the central city, hits

Downtown (with I-805 as a bypass that skirts it), and heads on to Mexico; from the east, I-8 runs by Old Town before terminating in Ocean Beach; and I-15, coming from inland San Diego County and Arizona, cuts through the city's northern and eastern suburbs. The road system in San Diego suffers from erratic planning, however, and often if you miss a freeway exit, you may be in for a long, frustrating detour; specific directions are essential. **Parking lots** are scattered around Downtown, and there's plenty of metered parking – free overnight, but not allowed on evenings reserved for street cleaning.

All forms of **public transportation** drop you in or near the heart of Downtown San Diego. **Trains** use the Santa Fe Railroad Depot, close to the western end of Broadway, while the Greyhound **bus** terminal is a bit more central at Broadway and First Avenue. Lindbergh Field **airport** (aka San Diego International) is only two miles from Downtown, and is connected to it by bus #992 ($2.25); the service starts around 5am and finishing around 12.30am. Given the short distance, **taxis** to Downtown aren't expensive ($8–10 one way), and quite a few hotels – even some of the budget ones – offer guests a free **airport limo** service. The main **car rental** firms all have desks at the airport (see "Listings," p.262).

A good first stop in the city is the **International Visitor Information Center**, near the bay at 1040 W Broadway (Mon–Sat 9am–5pm, Sun 10am–5pm; ☎619/236-1212, ⓦwww.sandiego.org, ⓔsdinfo@sandiego.org), which has maps, visitors guides, and other publications covering the arts and local golf courses. Another useful source for visitor information is the HI-AYH office inside the hostel foyer at 521 Market St (daily 7am–midnight; ☎619/525-1531, ⓦsandiegohostels.com/downtown.htm). For eating and entertainment information, the free, weekly *San Diego Reader* (ⓦwww.sdreader.com) can be found in many shops, bars, and clubs; the entertainment section of the *San Diego Union-Tribune* (50¢; ⓦentertainment.signonsandiego.com) is also useful.

City transportation

Despite its size, **getting around** San Diego without a car is slow but not terribly difficult, whether you use buses, the light-rail-like San Diego Trolley, or a rented bike. Traveling can be harder at night, with most transit routes closing down around 11pm or midnight. The transportation system won't break anyone's budget, especially with longer-term tickets and passes reducing costs over a few days or weeks. **Taxis** are also an affordable option: the average fare is anywhere from $5 for a jaunt around Downtown, to $10 for Coronado, to $15 or so to get up to the more northerly beaches (Ocean, Mission, Pacific).

Buses

The overarching **bus** system within San Diego County is called the Metropolitan Transit System (MTS), of which there are three major units; by far the most prominent is San Diego Transit Corporation, or SDTC (☎1-800/266-6883, ⓦwww.sdcommute.com), which offers typical one-way fares of $1.75 and $2.25, or up to $3.50 for the most distant routes; the exact fare is required when boarding (dollar bills are accepted). Transfers are often free, but those made between transit systems (bus-to-trolley, bus-to-Coaster, etc) will require the price of the higher fare. Service is reliable and frequent, particularly Downtown, which is known on route maps and timetables as "Center City." If you're headed to more outlying regions, other major operators include North County Transit District (fares $1.75; ☎1-800/COMMUTE, ⊛www.gonctd.com) and County Transit System (fares $2–4; ☎858/874-4001).

If you have any queries about San Diego's local buses, call the **Transit Store**, at First and Broadway (Mon–Fri 9am–5pm; ☎619/234-1060), for detailed timetables, the free *Regional Transit Guide*, and information on the Day Tripper Transit Pass and monthly passes. If you know your point of departure and destination, you can get automated bus information by phoning ☎619/685-4900.

The Trolley

Complementing county bus lines is the **San Diego Trolley**, often called the "Tijuana Trolley" because it travels sixteen miles from the Santa Fe Railroad Depot (departures from C Street) to the US–Mexico border in San Ysidro – a 45-minute trip. Fares are $1.25–3.00, depending on how long you stay on, and Day Tripper packages are also available (see above). One-way tickets should be bought from the machines at trolley stops, which also offer round-trip tickets; occasionally an inspector may request proof of payment. Of the two routes, the **Blue Line** is by far the most visitor-oriented, starting in the north with Qualcomm Stadium and Mission San Diego and continuing through to Old Downtown and Downtown San Diego, then turning south to Mexico. From the transfer station at Imperial and 12th, the trolley's **Orange Line** usefully loops around Downtown, but offers little else of interest other than to

Useful San Diego bus routes

The following buses regularly connect **Downtown San Diego** with the surrounding area:
Balboa Park #1, #3, #3A, #7 #7A, #7B, #25, #115
Coronado #901, #902, #903, #904
East San Diego #1, #7, #7B, #15, #15A, #115
Hillcrest #1, #3, #11, #16 #25
Imperial Beach #901, #933, #934
La Jolla #30, #34, #34A
Mission Beach #34, #34A
Ocean Beach #923
Old Town #3, #5, #5A,
Pacific Beach #30, #34, #34A
Point Loma peninsula #922 (transfer to #26 for Cabrillo NM)

commuters, darting out toward the eastern suburbs. Trolleys leave every fifteen minutes during the day (starting around 5am); the last service back from San Ysidro leaves at 11.30pm (or 1am Saturday night), so an evening of south-of-the-border revelry and a return to San Diego the same night is quite possible. Note that by 2006, a planned Mission Valley East extension will link both Blue and Orange lines into a giant loop, connecting near SDSU and Interstate 8.

The Coaster

North County San Diego is linked to Downtown via a simple commuter light-rail system called **The Coaster**, which includes eight stops from Oceanside through Carlsbad, Encinitas, Solana Beach, Sorrento Valley, and Old Town, ending up at the Santa Fe Railroad Depot. On weekday mornings, six trains run southbound, with the same number returning northbound for the late-afternoon and early-evening commute, while four trains make the trip on Saturdays. Fares range from $3.75 to $5.25 one way, $1.75 to $2.50 for seniors, and $105 to $144 for a monthly pass (information T1-800/COASTER, Wwww.gonctd.com). The Coaster also provides a good alternative way of reaching Los Angeles, with transfers at Oceanside onto the Metrolink commuter rail system (see "Public transportation" in Los Angeles, p.93), which links San Diego County all the way to Downtown LA and even up to Oxnard in Ventura County.

Cycling

San Diego is a fine city for **cycling**, with many miles of bike paths as well as some agreeable park and coastal rides. **Rental shops** are easy to find, especially around bike-friendly areas, and some outlets also rent out skateboards, rollerblades, and surfboards (prices for all start around $5–7 per hour, $12–20 per day; $25–35 per day for surfboards). Reliable outlets include Bicycle Barn, 746 Emerald St, Pacific Beach (T858/581-3665); Bike Cab, 641 17th St, Downtown (T619/232-4700); and Cheap Rentals, 3685 Mission Blvd, Mission Beach (T858/488-9070, Wwww.cheap-rentals.com), and 3221 Mission Blvd, Belmont Park (T858/488-5533). You can carry bikes on the San Diego Bay ferry for an extra 50¢, and on several city bus routes for no added charge. Board at any bus stop displaying a bike sign and tack your machine securely to the back of the bus. The Transit Store (T619/234-1060, Wwww.sdcommute.com) provides information on bicycle commuting, and distributes free passes that allow you to take your bike on the trolley. You can also order a regional bike map in advance of your trip from RideLink (☎1–800/COMMUTE ext 3, ⓦwww.ridelink.org/bicycle.html).

Accommodation

Accommodation is readily available in San Diego, with abundant hotels and motels, and a decent selection of hostels and B&Bs – only travelers with tents are likely to feel restricted, with just a few inconveniently located and comparatively expensive **campgrounds** from which to choose.

Downtown offers the best base if you're without a car and features two hostels and a batch of affordable hotels in renovated classic buildings – along with a few chic **boutique hotels** that have popped up in the last few years. Prices are more expensive at beach **motels** and hotels – and nearly stratospheric at the bigger-name golf-and-tennis resorts – though Ocean Beach and Pacific Beach have **hostels**, too. Another group of motels can be found around Old Town (useful if you're driving or just staying for a night while seeing the immediate area), and some of the cheapest motels line the approach roads to the city.

Bed and breakfasts are a popular option, especially in Hillcrest. Contact the Downtown visitor center (see p.224), or send $3.95 for the *Bed & Breakfast Directory for San Diego*, PO Box 3292, San Diego, CA 92163 (☎619/297-3130, ⓦwww.sandiegobandb.com).

If you're arriving in summer, when prices increase and availability is limited, it's wise to **book in advance**. The International Visitor Information Center Downtown (see p.224) has accommodation leaflets (many of which carry discount vouchers) and will phone hotels, motels, or hostels on your behalf at no charge.

Gay travelers are unlikely to encounter hostility in San Diego, and several hotels and bed and breakfasts are particularly noted for their friendliness (see "Gay and lesbian San Diego," p.261).

Downtown

See the map on p.234 for locations.

Bristol 1055 First Ave ☎619/232-6141, ⓦwww.thebristolsandiego.com. Centrally located boutique hotel with stylish modern decor and tasteful amenities – though the size of the rooms reflects the cheaper price. Still, with in-room CD players and Internet access, it's well worth a visit, especially considering the area. ❻

Comfort Inn Gaslamp 600 G St at Seventh Ave ☎619/238-4100, ⓦwww.comfortinn.com. Fairly unexciting but serviceable chain hotel, with cable TV, microwaves, wet bars, and fridges in each room. One of the more affordable bets in the popular Gaslamp District. ❻

Courtyard San Diego 530 Broadway ☎619/446-3000, ⓦwww.marriott.com. Perhaps the most stunning of the recent wave of historic renovations in town, this stylishly preserved 1920s Renaissance Revival bank is now home to upscale guestrooms and suites, and loaded with beautiful period detail in the lobby and even a conference room in an old-time bank vault. ❼

Horton Grand 311 Island Ave at Third Ave ☎619/544-1886 or 1-800/542-1886, ⓦwww.hortongrand.com. Classy, modernized amalgam of two century-old hotels, with fireplaces in most of the 132 recently renovated, antique-flavored rooms, staff dressed in Victorian-era costumes, on-site restaurant, and piano bar. ❼

J Street Inn 222 J St between Third and Fourth aves ☎619/696-6922, ⓦwww.thejstreetinn.com. Aimed at low-income travelers interested in longer-term stays in town (weeks or months). Centrally located near the Gaslamp District, Greyhound terminal, and the waterfront, this little gem has in-room microwaves, refrigerators, and cable TV. ❹

La Pensione 606 W Date St at India St ☎619/236-8000, ⓦwww.lapensionehotel.com. Great-value small hotel in a quiet area within walking distance of the core of the city center. The rooms, around a central court, are small but

CLAIREMONT MESA BLVD

163

AERO DRIVE

MURPHY CANYON ROAD

MISSION GORGE ROAD

NAVAJO ROAD

WARING ROAD

Qualcomm Stadium

✝ Mission Basilica
San Diego de Alcalá

8

San Diego River

MONTEZUMA ROAD

8

805

ADAMS AVENUE

15

163

EL CAJON BLVD

HILLCREST

UNIVERSITY AVENUE

30TH STREET

FAIRMOUNT AVENUE

EUCLID AVENUE

Marston House

see 'Balboa Park & San Diego Zoo' map

FLORIDA DRIVE

94

see 'Downtown San Diego' map

Villa Montezuma

MARKET STREET

47TH ST

Coronado Museum of History and Art

IMPERIAL AVE.

San Diego-Coronado Bay Bridge

NATIONAL AVENUE

5

HARBOR DRIVE

HIGHLAND AVENUE

8TH STREET

Coronado Naval Amphibious Base

75

SILVER STRAND

18TH STREET

ACCOMMODATION

Hillcrest & Old Town

Balboa Park Inn	23
Embassy Hotel	20
Friendship Hotel	18
Harbour House Resort	28
Heritage Park B&B	13
Hillcrest Inn	24
Old Town Inn	14
Park Manor Suites	27
Sommerset Suites	22
Studio 819	19
West Park Inn	29

Coronado

El Cordova	30
El Rancho	33
Hotel Del Coronado	34
Glorietta Bay Inn	31
Villa Capri by the Sea	32

Ocean Beach & Point Loma

Ebb Tide Motel	14
HI-San Diego (Pt. Loma) Hostel	25
Loma Lodge	19
Ocean Beach International Backpackers Hostel	21
Ocean Villa Motel	13

Mission Beach & Pacific Beach

Bahia Resort	12
Banana Bungalow	8
The Beach Cottages	9
Beach Haven Inn	2
Campland by the Sea	5
Catamaran Resort	10
Crystal Pier	6
Ocean Park Inn	7
Santa Clara Motel	9
Pacific Terrace	1
Surf & Sand Motel	3
Western Shores Motel	4

tastefully decorated and equipped with microwaves, fridges, cable TVs, and on-site laundry. ❸
Manchester Grand Hyatt One Market Place, at Harbor Dr ☎619/232-1234, ⓦwww
.manchestergrand.hyatt.com. The most prominent hotel along the waterfront (and among the biggest in the state), a pair of gleaming white slabs of luxury with all the top-notch amenities: pool, spas, health club, several restaurants and lounges, and rooms with expansive views of the bay. Also ground zero for conventioneers. ❽
Prava 911 Fifth Ave ☎619/233-3300, ⓦwww
.pravahotel.com. Affordable boutique hotel in the Gaslamp District with modern amenities in comfortable suites, plus kitchenettes and fridges, and on-site gym, spa, sauna, restaurant, and lounge. Housed in a nicely preserved classic structure. ❻
The U.S. Grant 326 Broadway between Third and Fourth aves ☎619/232-3121 or 1-800/237-5029, ⓦwww.usgrant.net. Across from Horton Plaza, Downtown's poshest address since 1910, and newly renovated with grand Neoclassical design, chandeliers, marble floors, and cozy but comfortable guestrooms and more capacious suites. The elegant ballrooms and swank conference rooms are also worth a peek. ❽
Wyndham Emerald Plaza 400 Broadway ☎619/239-4500, ⓦwww.wyndham.com. Upscale lodging for business travelers, with spacious rooms, pool, spa, and exercise facilities. Visually distinctive with its green-lit towers, looking like a high-rise relic from the go-go 1980s. ❽

Hillcrest, Balboa Park, and Old Town

See the map on pp.228–229 for locations. For Hillcrest, see also "Gay and lesbian San Diego," p.261.
Balboa Park Inn 3402 Park Blvd, Hillcrest ☎619/298-0823, or 1-800/938-8181, ⓦwww
.balboaparkinn.com. Elegant, gay-oriented B&B within walking distance of Balboa Park and the museums. The 26 themed suites (with oceanside, Impressionist, and Tarzan motifs, to name a few) have coffee makers and mini-fridges. Prices vary, depending on size and level of kitsch. ❺–❼
Embassy Hotel 3645 Park Blvd, Balboa Park ☎619/296-3141. Basic accommodation close to Balboa Park and with all the usual amenities – restaurant, some kitchenettes, and free in-room movies and local phone calls – for low rates. ❷
Heritage Park B&B 2470 Heritage Park Row, Old Town ☎619/299-6832 or 1-800/995-2470, ⓦwww.heritageparkinn.com. A restored Queen Anne mansion in Heritage Park, chock-full of Victorian trappings. Breakfast and afternoon tea

are included, and classic movies are shown nightly. Rooms and suites are in the usual lace-and-chintz style, with one small unit going for $125 per night. Otherwise ❼–❾
Old Town Inn 4444 Pacific Hwy, Old Town ☎1-800/643-3025, ⓦwww.oldtown-inn.com. Convenient location within a few strides of the Old Town's liveliest areas, offering complimentary breakfast and clean, simple rooms. ❹
Park Manor Suites 525 Spruce St, near Balboa Park ☎619/291-0999 or 1-800/874-2649, ⓦwww.parkmanorsuites.com. Renovated apartment complex that's nearly a hundred years old. The tasteful hotel suites feature kitchens and nice, large sitting areas, and continental breakfast is included. ❺
Sommerset Suites 606 Washington St, Hillcrest ☎619/692-5200 or 1-800/962-9665, ⓦwww
.sommersetsuites.com. Eighty well-equipped suites with kitchenettes and Internet access, offering pool, spa, central location, and complimentary breakfast. One of the better deals in the area. ❺
Studio 819 819 University Ave, Hillcrest ☎619/542-0819, ⓦwww.studio819.com. Standard but safe budget accommodation in the heart of Hillcrest near the freeway. Primarily a residential hotel for longer-term stays, it offers a microwave, kitchenette, and fridge in each room. Weekly rates for as little as $345. ❷
West Park Inn 1840 Fourth Ave ☎619/236-1600, Ⓕ619/231-4734, ⓦwww.westparkinn.com. Gay-friendly hotel with clean rooms, cable TV, refrigerators, and microwaves. Recently renovated, in a great location two blocks from the west entrance to Balboa Park. ❸

Coronado and Ocean Beach

See the map on pp.228–229 for locations.
Ebb Tide Motel 5082 W Point Loma Blvd, Ocean Beach ☎619/224-9339. Modest-sized, pet-friendly motel that's handy for the beach and features clean, adequate rooms with kitchenettes and cable TV. ❹
El Cordova 1351 Orange Ave, Coronado ☎619/435-4131 or 1-800/229-2032, ⓦwww
.elcordovahotel.com. The best deal in Coronado, but you'll need to reserve at least six months ahead for the lower-priced units. Spanish Colonial buildings from 1902, and arranged around lovely gardens. There's a pool, and some rooms have kitchenettes. Huge price spread, from cheap and basic units without a/c to grandly elegant suites for $750. ❺–❾
El Rancho 370 Orange Ave, Coronado ☎619/435-2251, ⓦwww.geocities.com/ranchomot. Small

but attractive motel with pleasant decor, and one of the cheapest deals on this side of the water. Rooms come equipped with microwaves and fridges, and some even have Jacuzzis. **④**

Glorietta Bay Inn 1630 Glorietta Blvd, Coronado ☏619/435-3101, ⓦwww.gloriettabayinn.com. Striking 1908 Edwardian mansion that's since been converted into swank modern rooms and suites, all with Internet access and complimentary breakfast, and some with kitchenettes and balconies. The place drips with period detail, from the antique chandeliers to the grand piano. **⑦**

Hotel del Coronado 1500 Orange Ave, Coronado ☏619/522-8000 or 1-800/468-3533, ⓦwww .hoteldel.com. The luxurious spot that put Coronado on the map and is still the area's major tourist sight (see p.245) – millions have been poured into the complex in recent years, and the striking rooms and suites, expansive bay views, and old-fashioned Victorian charm from 1888 still give the place much appeal. **⑧**

Loma Lodge 3202 Rosecrans St, Ocean Beach ☏619/222-0511 or 1-800/266-0511, ⓦwww .lomalodge.com. Among the best values in the district, a decent motel with an agreeable pool and complimentary breakfast; good for exploring the peninsula, but not close to the beach. **③**

Ocean Villa Motel 5142 W Point Loma Blvd, Ocean Beach ☏619/224-3481 or 1-800/759-0012. Handy for visiting the sands, and pet-friendly to boot; the ocean-view rooms feature kitchenettes, fridges, and microwaves; there's also a pool. **⑤**

Villa Capri by the Sea 1417 Orange Ave, Coronado ☏1-800/231-3954, ⓦwww .villacapribythesea.com. Old-style motel-like accommodation that has more going for it than you might expect at first glance from the road. Offers fourteen suites with pool, kitchenettes, Internet access, VCRs, and a homely feel in a classic 1950s structure with some modern style inside. Central location by the beach is another big plus. **⑥**

Mission Beach and Pacific Beach

See the map on pp.228–229 for locations.

Bahia Resort 998 W Mission Bay Drive, Mission Beach ☏858/488-0551 or 1-800/576-4229, ⓦwww.bahiahotel.com. Sprawling resort offering agreeable rooms and suites, plus a restaurant, pool, hot tub, tennis courts, and very close proximity to the beach. **⑥**

Beach Cottages 4255 Ocean Blvd, Mission Beach ☏858/483-7440, ⓦwww.beachcottages.com. Beside the beach, three blocks south of the pier,

this relaxing spot offers a wide range of accommodation. Most units have kitchenettes, all have fridges. Prices vary depending on season, but often motels **⑤**, studio units **⑥**, and cottages and apartments **⑧**.

Beach Haven Inn 4740 Mission Blvd, Pacific Beach ☏858/272-3812 or 1-800/831-6323, ⓦwww.beachhaveninn.com. Clean and tidy motel accommodation with comfortable, tastefully decorated rooms around a heated pool; continental breakfast included. One of the nicest places to unwind at the beach, and plenty cheap to boot. **④**

Catamaran Resort 3999 Mission Blvd, Pacific Beach ☏1-800/422-8386, ⓦwww .catamaranresort.com. A range of upscale units, from entry-level garden-view rooms to swank bayside suites; also with restaurant, bar, water sports, spa, Jacuzzi, and volleyball courts. **⑦–⑨**

Crystal Pier 4500 Ocean Blvd, Pacific Beach ☏858/483-6983 or 1-800/748-5894, ⓦwww .crystalpier.com. Quaint, deluxe cottages built in the 1920s and situated right on the pier. All units are suites with private decks and most have kitchenettes. Can get pricey, but you stay literally on the water. **⑦**

Ocean Park Inn 710 Grand Ave, Pacific Beach ☏858/438-5858, ⓦwww.oceanparkinn.com. Another solid beachfront choice, offering Internet access, microwaves, fridges, and complimentary breakfast, plus a pool and spa. Nothing too flashy for the price, but the central location is a good draw. **⑦**

Pacific Terrace 610 Diamond St, Pacific Beach ☏858/581-3500, ⓦwww.pacificterrace.com. Entrancingly chic accommodation on the beach, with rooms offering kitchenettes, fridges, Internet access, and sea-facing balconies, and suites with the full range of swanky amenities. **⑧**

Santa Clara Motel 839 Santa Clara Place, Mission Beach ☏858/488-1193. Adequate, no-frills rooms with kitchenettes. Won't win any style awards, but it is an easy walk from the sands and a half-mile north of Belmont Park. **③**

Surf & Sand Motel 4666 Mission Blvd, Pacific Beach ☏858/483-7420. Clean and cozy motel near the beach, with pool, cable TV, and mini-fridges or kitchenettes. **⑥**

Western Shores Motel 4345 Mission Bay Drive, Mission Beach ☏858/273-1121. Ultra-basic but clean and simple motel approximately two miles from the water. **③**

La Jolla

See the map on p.250 for locations.

Andrea Villa Inn 2402 Torrey Pines Rd ☏1-800/411-2141, ⓦwww.andreavilla.com.

Surprisingly affordable accommodation in this upscale town, offering kitchenettes and complimentary breakfast, plus pool and spa and easy access to area attractions. Rooms are on the basic side, but the location is the main draw. ❺

Grande Colonial 910 Prospect St ⊤858/454-2181 or 1-800/826-1278, Ⓦwww.thegrandcolonial.com. A Twenties landmark in the heart of La Jolla and a short walk from the cove. Vaguely Victorian decor in cozy but elegant rooms and a handful of larger suites, with excellent package deals – especially in winter. ❼

Hotel Parisi 1111 Prospect St ⊤1-877/4-PARISI, Ⓦwww.hotelparisi.com. Top-shelf boutique hotel with a New Age twist, offering "feng shui" design and rooms with balconies, CD and VCR players, and some ocean views. If all this luxury still doesn't relax you, call the hotel's resident shrink for advice. ❾

La Jolla Bed & Breakfast 7753 Draper Ave ⊤858/456-2066 or 1-800/582-2466, Ⓦwww.innlajolla.com. Designed in 1913 by early-modernist Irving Gill, a collection of fifteen themed rooms – topped by the $300-a-night Irving Gill Penthouse – with tranquil gardens, great service, and nice proximity to the beach and art museum. ❼

La Jolla Cove Suites 1155 Coast Blvd ⊤858/459-2621 or 1-888/LA-JOLLA, Ⓦwww.lajollacove.com. Kitchen-equipped rooms and suites right by the sea – some of the rooms have sprawling oceanfront balconies. Also with on-site Jacuzzi, pool, and complimentary breakfast. Basic studio units go for around $200, but for anything spacious you'll need to drop at least $100 more. ❽

La Jolla Inn 1110 Prospect St ⊤858/454-0133 or 1-888/855-STAY, Ⓦwww.lajollainn.com. Charming European-style lodge, well priced for the area, with ocean views (for a few dollars more), fridges, balconies, complimentary breakfast, and afternoon tea on the sundeck. The inn offers studios as well. ❻

La Valencia 1132 Prospect St ⊤858/454-0771 or 1-800/451-0772, Ⓦwww.lavalencia.com. Radiant pink favorite of Hollywood celebs in the 1920s. Today only a slightly less glamorous spot, but no less plush, with capacious rooms and suites that boast beautiful decor and nice sea views, plush an on-site pool, spa, and fitness center. ❽

Hostels

Banana Bungalow 707 Reed Ave, Pacific Beach ⊤858/273-3060 or 1-800/5-HOSTEL, Ⓦwww.bananabungalow.com. Although the rooms are small and drab, the beachside location, volleyball, cookouts, and lively atmosphere make it worthwhile. Free buffet breakfasts, Internet access, keg nights, and a communal kitchen are included. Six-person dorms run $18–20, private rooms for $49. Turn off Mission Boulevard at no. 4250, or take bus #34.

Grand Pacific Hostel 726 Fifth Ave between F and G sts, Downtown ⊤619/232-3100 or 1-800/438-8622, Ⓦwww.usahostels.com/sandiego/s-index.html. Well-placed hostel on the edge of the Gaslamp District. Six to eight beds per room with sheets and continental breakfast all for $20; doubles available for $48. Free bike use, organized tours to Tijuana, and a discount shuttle to LA make this one of the best city hostels.

HI-Point Loma Hostel 3790 Udall St, Ocean Beach ⊤619/223-4778 or 1-800/909-4776, Ⓦsandiegohostels.org/pointloma.htm. Well-run and friendly, though without the party atmosphere prevailing in other hostels. Located a few miles from the beach and six miles from Downtown (via bus #35), the hostel features a large kitchen, a patio, and a common room. Eight-bed (or smaller) dorms $17–20, private rooms for three or more, $42–48.

HI-San Diego Downtown Hostel 521 Market St at Fifth, Downtown ⊤619/525-1530 or 1-800/909-4776, Ⓦsandiegohostels.org/downtown.htm. Centrally located, especially good for the Gaslamp District and Horton Plaza. $17 for HI members, $23 for others, and private doubles from $44–55. Free coffee and bagels. No curfew.

Ocean Beach International Backpackers Hostel 4961 Newport Ave, Ocean Beach ⊤619/223-7873 or 1-800/339-7263, Ⓦmembers.aol.com/OBIhostel/hostel. Lively spot a block from the beach, offering barbecues, bike and surfboard rentals, and nightly movies. Space in a four-bed dorm $12–16, double rooms $20, all with sheets, showers, and continental breakfast. Tax included; must reserve online.

Campgrounds

Of the city's half-dozen **campgrounds**, only two accept tents. The best-placed of these is *Campland on the Bay*, 2211 Pacific Beach Drive (⊤858/581-4200 or 1-800/4-BAYFUN, Ⓦwww.campland.com), where a basic site starts at $35–51, though larger, more elaborate "Super Sites" – stuffed with more amenities – can run $115–242. *Campland* boasts a number of pools and hot tubs, as well as a marina, activity rentals, and a general store; it is linked to Downtown by bus #30. For a more serene alternative, San Elijo State Beach, Rte 21 south of Cardiff-by-the-Sea, offers fishing, hiking, and swimming, and campsites run from $11–25. Call ⊕760-753-5091 for information or ⊕1-800/444-7275 for reservations, or go to ⓦwww.reserveamerica.com.

The City

Like most other major cities of the West Coast, San Diego is set along a wide, curving bayfront, its climate among the most agreeable in the country and its atmosphere friendly and relaxed. Much more staid than Los Angeles (its hedonism on display mainly at the beaches), the city nonetheless has many of the same extremes of rich and poor – here analogous to oceanside and inland, respectively, with most of the prime-time tourist draws on or within a few miles of the water.

San Diego divides into several easily defined sections, the most prominent of which is **Downtown**, where anonymous high-rise bank buildings and hotel complexes stand beside older, often renovated structures from San Diego's earlier boom days, notably in the **Gaslamp District**, home to a number of worthwhile cafés and bars, and the epicenter of the Downtown party scene.

A few miles northeast, the well-maintained oasis of **Balboa Park** contains many of the city's major museums and the ever-popular San Diego Zoo, and is perfectly suited for strolls and picnics through acres of carefully tended gardens and natural greenery, set amid splendid Spanish Revival buildings from the 1920s. Just northwest of Downtown, **Old Town** is a somewhat isolated enclave where the first white settlement developed near the site of the original San Diego Mission, an area now featuring an array of modern shops and theme restaurants intended to evoke the style of Old Mexico; it's easily accessible via a convenient trolley stop. Other districts near Downtown don't have any official "sights," but can be interesting as well. **East San Diego** offers a large college campus that livens up what is an otherwise featureless sprawl, while northwest of Balboa Park, **Hillcrest**'s eclectic mix of yuppies, gays, bohemians, and artists makes it one of the city's best areas for dining and nightlife.

If you're mainly interested in pure relaxation, simple beach-bumming or a golf-and-tennis weekend, the **beach towns** and the pricey aquatic diversions of the **SeaWorld** theme park, both within easy reach of Downtown, are good for a half-day trip – or longer. There's nothing really essential here, unless of course you view San Diego as having little purpose beyond its beaches, surfboards, and bikinis.

Downtown San Diego

Loosely bordered by the curve of San Diego Bay and the I-5 freeway, **DOWNTOWN** is the inevitable nexus of San Diego and the best place to start a tour of the city. Kick-started in the late 1970s, various preservation and restoration projects have improved many of the area's older buildings (notably in the restaurant district of Little Italy; see "Eating," p.251), resulting in several pockets of stylishly renovated turn-of-the-century architecture, while the corporate towers left over from the boomtown 1980s and 90s showcase the city's bustling trade with the Pacific Rim and inflated real-estate market. Although Downtown is largely safe by day, at night it can be unwelcoming, with the financial zone becoming a high-rise dead zone. After-dark activities are therefore best confined to the popular and well-policed Gaslamp District.

Along Broadway

If you roll into town by train or trolley, you'll be dropped off at the **Santa Fe Railroad Depot**'s tall Spanish Colonial archways, which were built to welcome visitors to the 1915 Panama–California International Exposition in Balboa Park. With the bayfront just to the west, the depot's old historic-revival architecture provides a dramatic contrast to the postmodern contours of the neighboring **American Plaza**, an array of high-rise offices left over from the finance-fueled boom of the mid-1980s. The plaza encompasses a central terminal of the San Diego Trolley, as well as the Downtown branch of the **Museum of Contemporary Art**, or MCA San Diego, 1001 Kettner Blvd (11am–5pm; closed Wed; free; Ⓦwww.mcasandiego.org), which is a fine first-stop for anyone interested in contemporary art with a California twist. Although its permanent collection focuses on American minimalism, Pop Art, and the indigenous art of Mexico, its temporary shows are the real appeal here,

ACCOMMODATION

Bistol — L
Courtyard San Diego — A
Comfort Inn Gaslamp — D
Grand Pacific Hostel — E
HI-Metropolitan Hostel — K
Horton Grand — F

J Street Inn — C
La Pensione — B
The U.S. Grant — H
Wyndham Emerald Plaza — G
Manchester Grand Hyatt — I
Prava — J

CAFÉS & RESTAURANTS					
Alambres	16	Caffé Italia	1	Dobson's	7
Anthony's Fish Grotto	3	Candelas	25	Dublin Square	21
Bandar	10	The Cheese Shop	18	Filippi's Pizza Grotto	2
Bella Luna	17	Chive	20	Grand Central Café	5
Café Lulu	14	Croce's	12	Henry's Pub	19
Café Zzz	23	de' Medici	9	Karl Strauss Brewery	4

Martini Ranch	11		
Olé Madrid	15		
Onyx Room	8		
Rei Do Gado	6		
Sammy's Woodfired Pizza	13		
Taka	22		
Upstart Crow	24		

often involving irreverent imagery drawn from the intersection of pop-culture surrealism, ethnic subcultures, and regional socioeconomic problems, among many other topics. The museum also has a La Jolla branch (see p.249).

American Plaza marks the western end of **BROADWAY**, which slices through the center of Downtown and is most lively between Fourth and Fifth avenues, where the pedestrian traffic is a mix of shoppers, sailors, yuppies, the homeless, and tourists. Although this is hardly the free-spirited strip of LA's Broadway (much less New York's), there are still a few points of interest here and there. Many visitors linger around the fountains on the square outside **Horton Plaza**, between First and Fourth avenues south of Broadway (Mon–Fri 10am–9pm, Sat 10am–8pm, Sun 11am–7pm; Ⓦwww.westfield .com/us/centres/california/hortonplaza), a giant mall of some 140 stores and San Diego's de facto city center. Completed in 1985, Horton Plaza's quick success caused local real estate prices to soar and condo development to surge, and gave shopping-mall developer **Jon Jerde** the green light to put his stamp of neon-beckered, pop-art-flavored design on malls across the country – most prominently at LA's Universal CityWalk (see p.170). For better or worse, the complex's whimsical, colorful postmodern style, loaded with quasi–Art Deco and Southwestern motifs, is inevitably a colossal tourist draw, and its lack of a roof makes it ideal for the region's sunny climate. Although there's nothing on the retail front you won't find in every other American shopping complex, the 21-foot-tall **Jessop Clock**, on level one, is the one inescapable highlight, an intriguing antique from the California State Fair of 1907.

Further along, Broadway is rather uninviting until you reach a handful of the secondhand bookstores, such as **Wahrenbrock's Book House**, 726 Broadway (☏619/232-0132), supposedly the oldest and largest in the city, and the **Central Library**, 820 E St (Mon & Wed noon–8pm, Tues & Thurs–Sat 9.30am–5.30pm, Sun 1–5pm; Ⓦwww.sandiego.gov/public-library), which has regular book sales on the weekend and an extensive reference section, where you can pore over California magazines and newspapers. Tucked away on an upper floor, the **Wangenheim Room** (Mon, Wed & Fri 1.30–4.30pm or by appointment; ☏619/236-5807) holds the fascinating collection of turn-of-the-century patrician Julius Wangenheim. The collection includes Babylonian cuneiform tablets, palm-leaf books from India, silk scrolls from China, and many more global curios documenting the history of the written word.

If you have plenty of time to explore, another interesting diversion is the **Firehouse Museum**, six blocks north of Broadway at 1572 Columbia St (Thurs & Fri 10am–2pm, Sat & Sun 10am–4pm; donation; ☏619/232-FIRE), which is situated in San Diego's oldest firehouse and displays firefighting equipment, paraphernalia, and uniforms, with photographs vividly recalling some of San Diego's most horrific conflagrations, and the horses and firefighters who had to battle them.

The Gaslamp District

South of Broadway, the **GASLAMP DISTRICT** occupies a sixteen-block area running south to K Street, bordered by Fourth and Seventh avenues. The core of San Diego when it was still a frontier town, the district – known then as **Stingaree** after a stingray found in San Diego Bay – was rife with prostitution, opium dens, and street violence, a chaotic scene that played out beneath the wrought-iron balconies and Victorian gingerbread of the nineteenth-century piles lining the street. The area predictably decayed until its revitalization in the late 1970s under an intensive urban-renewal campaign, after which it started to mutate into the heavily tourist-oriented zone it is today.

What remaining flophouses and dive bars there are make a dramatic contrast with the nearby yuppie-centric cafés, antique stores, and art galleries – all under the glow of ersatz "gaslamps" powered by electricity. The focus of San Diego nightlife, especially on the weekend, the district's relatively high police profile is designed to keep the area clean and safe, and to keep the tourists coming. This flow of visitors has been lately ensured by the construction of **Petco Park**, Seventh Avenue at Harbor Drive (Ⓦsandiego.padres.mlb.com), which draws plenty of Padres baseball fans but has more limited options for parking. If you've come to play spectator, make an early trip on the Blue Line trolley (which passes alongside) – mass transit around game time resembles a rail-bound journey into deepest tourist hell.

Beyond the ballpark, the Gaslamp District is intriguing to explore, not least for the scores of late nineteenth-century buildings – rich with period detail and styles from Eastlake to Queen Anne, with some Spanish Colonial and Baroque Revival touches as well – in various stages of renovation. Few are better than the grandiose **Louis Bank of Commerce**, 835 Fifth Ave, an eye-popping Victorian confection from 1888 that's almost too busy for its own good, replete with carved wooden and terracotta bay windows, a sheet-metal frieze across the front, and a pair of squat, colorful little towers on top. This building is best examined – and the area's general history gleaned – during the two-hour **walking tour** (Sat 11am; $8, includes admission to the William Heath Davis House; Ⓣ619/233-4692, Ⓦwww.gaslampquarter.org/tours) that begins from the small cobbled square at Fourth and Island avenues.

The square is within the grounds of the **William Heath Davis House**, 410 Island Ave (Tues–Sun 11am–3pm; Ⓣ619/233-4692; $3), whose owner founded modern San Diego and built his saltbox-styled home here in 1850, believing that a waterfront location would stimulate growth (the fledgling city had previously been located a few miles inland and to the north – the site of Old Town San Diego; see p.241). Although Davis was initially wrong and had to leave the city in short order, eventually dying penniless, the more influential Alonzo Horton did manage to fulfill some of his goals for waterfront growth in later years. Copious with photographs, each room of the house commemorates a different period with its decor, and should be fascinating to anyone with an interest in Southern California history.

Even without the walking tour, there are a few other evocative sights in the area, including the **Horton Grand Hotel** (see "Accommodation," p.227), opposite the William Heath Davis House, created in the mid-1980s by cobbling together two older hotels, the **Grand Horton** and the **Brooklyn Kahle Saddlery** – where Wyatt Earp lived for seven years in the early twentieth century. Dating back to the 1880s, the hotels were carefully dismantled and moved about four blocks from their original sites. In the lobby of the *Horton Grand*, the small **Chinese Museum**, 404 Third Ave (Ⓣ619/544-1886; free), is a reminder of the once-thriving Chinatown area, where railroad laborers and their families lived.

The bayfront

The streets south of the Gaslamp District are now occupied by expensive condos and the San Diego Convention Center, a $165-million complex with a sail-like roof resembling the yachts in the nearby marina. Continuing north along San Diego's curving, enjoyable **bayfront**, the pathway of the **Embarcadero** runs a mile or so along the bay, curling around to the western end of Downtown. Although the route is favored by strollers, joggers, and kite-flyers, some tourists get no farther than **Seaport Village**, a predictable array of trinket shops and diners, in dire need of renovation to improve its exhausted 1970s feel. Beyond this, if you can't get enough of the US military on your TV set at home, clamber aboard for a tour of the **USS Midway**, 910 N Harbor Drive (10am–5pm, last admission 4pm; $13, kids $7; ☎619/544-9600, ⓦwww .midway.org), which permanently docked here in 2004 and now shows off its formidable collection of naval hardware and weapons to the public. Although touring the innards of an old-time aircraft carrier may not be for everyone – and can induce claustrophobia in spots – for those with a taste for naval combat from World War II to the first Gulf War (the life cycle of the ship), the experience is a memorable one, enhanced by the presence of flight simulators and seven old-time planes parked at the site. Other, more vintage, ships can be visited further north at the **Maritime Museum**, 1492 Harbor Drive (daily 9am–9pm, winter closes 8pm; $8; ☎619/234-9153, ⓦwww.sdmaritime .com), highlighted by the 1863 **Star of India**, the world's oldest iron sailing ship still afloat, and the **Californian**, a modern replica of an 1847 cutter, which served as a federal lawboat patrolling the Pacific during the heady Gold Rush days. However, the adjacent *Berkeley*, for sixty years a San Francisco Bay ferry, the *Medea*, a small steam-powered yacht, and the *Pilot*, an old commercial pilot boat, are of lesser appeal. Keep in mind that since most of these craft are sea-worthy, some may be cruising around elsewhere when you come to visit; call ahead to make sure the boat you seek will be on view.

Finally, architecture enthusiasts may enjoy the nearby **San Diego County Administration Center**, 1600 Pacific Hwy (Mon–Fri 8am–5pm; free; ☎858/694-3900), one of the more distinctive public buildings in California: a rich mix of Spanish Colonial and Beaux Arts styles, decorated with gold and azure tiles. From Harbor Drive you can walk right through the building's foyer to its main entrance, on the way viewing the eye-catching *Guardian of Water* statue and three interior murals.

Balboa Park and the San Diego Zoo

Although the 1400 sumptuous acres of **BALBOA PARK** feature one of the largest collections of museums in the US, the park's real charm is its verdant landscape of trees, gardens, promenades, and Spanish Colonial buildings – and of course, the ever-popular **SAN DIEGO ZOO**. A desolate stretch of cacti and scrubland until 1898, the park began to take shape when one Kate Sessions began cultivating nurseries and planting trees in lieu of rent. The first buildings were erected for the 1915 Panama–California International Exposition, held to celebrate the opening of the Canal, and memories of its success lingered well into the Depression, until in 1935 another building program occurred for the California–Pacific International Exposition. Five years later the park was in such sparkling condition that Orson Welles decided to film close-up shots here of Charles Foster Kane's monumental Xanadu enclave for the film *Citizen Kane* (especially prominent in the *News on the March* segment near the beginning of the movie).

Along El Prado

Most of the major museums flank **El Prado**, the park's pedestrian-oriented east–west axis, which encompasses the charming Plaza de Panama at the heart of the park, and is best explored from the west via Laurel Street and the Cabrillo Bridge. From this direction, the first institution you'll come to will be the handsome neo-Baroque folly of the **Museum of Man** (daily 10am–4.30pm; $6; ⓦwww.museumofman.org), which veers from the banal

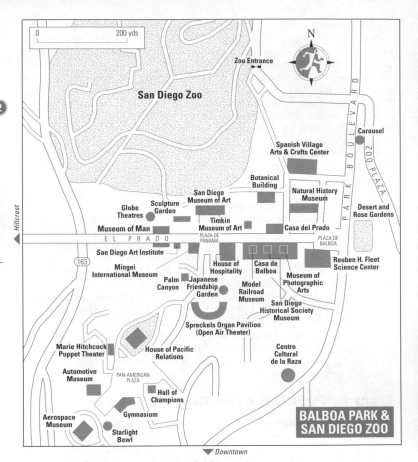

Hillcrest

Downtown

to the engaging to the bizarre, including demonstrations of tortilla-making and Mexican loom weaving, replicas of huge Mayan stones, interesting Native American artifacts, and various Egyptian relics. Just to the north, theater buffs will want to drop in on the **Globe Theatre** complex (see "Theater," p.259), while just across El Prado to the east, the **Mingei International Museum** (Tues–Sun 10am–4pm; $5; ⓦwww.mingei.org) has a rotating collection of folk art, featuring everything from weather vanes and carousels to furniture made from bottle caps. None of the exhibits is permanent, though previous exhibitions have focused on African, pre-Columbian, and Romanian art, as well as home-made toys and garments from around the world. Next door, the **San Diego Art Institute** (Tues–Sat 10am–4pm, Sun noon–4pm; $3; ⓦwww.sandiego-art.org) is a sporadically interesting venue for the works of its members, showcasing everything from pedestrian works by artists-in-training to unexpectedly fascinating mixed-media pieces and curious installation art.

To the east, the lovely **Plaza de Panama** is immediately adjacent, and on its north side lies the **San Diego Museum of Art** (Tues–Sun 10am–6pm, Thurs closes at 9pm; $9, kids $4; ⓦwww.sdmart.org), which is the main venue for any big shows that come through town – big-ticket collections from Egypt,

China, and the Vatican (to name a few) that usually charge a $5–10 premium beyond museum admission. In the permanent collection, there's a solid stock of European paintings from the Renaissance to the nineteenth century, highlighted by Hals and Rembrandt, matched by a fairly uninspiring American selection and a few bright rooms filled with modern works, especially by California artists. The biggest surprises are found amid the exquisitely crafted pieces in the Asian section, mainly from China and Japan but with smaller works from India and Korea. The **Sculpture Court and Garden** offers free exploration at any time, with a number of important works by artists like Henry Moore and Alexander Calder. There's also a pleasant, though pricey, restaurant nearby.

Just to the east, the **Timken Museum of Art** (Tues–Sat 10am–4.30pm, Sun 1.30–4.30pm; Sept closed; free; ⓦ www.timkenmuseum.org) stands out for its squat, drab modern design. While there are a sufficient number of interesting paintings to make the stifling, formal atmosphere worth enduring, most of the works – from the early Renaissance to the Impressionist era – are fairly minor, including those of Rembrandt and El Greco. More appealing is the museum's stirring collection of Russian religious icons.

Behind the Timken Museum to the north, the wood-ribbed **Botanical Building** (Fri–Wed 10am–4pm; free) dates back ninety years to the 1915 Exposition and features a fair selection of regional and tropical plants – making for a nice break from all the museums. On the south side of the Timken, the **House of Hospitality** hosts the visitor center (see box, p.240), while just to the House's east, **Casa de Balboa** is home to four museums, three of which are definitely worth a look. The **Museum of Photographic Arts** (daily 10am–5pm, Thurs closes 9pm; $6; ⓦ www.mopa.org) offers a fine permanent collection dating back to the daguerreotype and includes the work of Matthew Brady, Alfred Stieglitz, Paul Strand, and other big names; the **San Diego Historical Society Museum** (Tues–Sun 10am–5pm, Thurs closes 8pm; $6; ⓦ www.sandiegohistory.org), virtually next door, charts the booms that have elevated San Diego from scrubland into the seventh-largest city in the US within 150 years, focusing on topics such as the city's use as a Hollywood backlot; and the **Model Railroad Museum** (Tues–Fri 11am–4pm, Sat & Sun 11am–5pm; $5; ⓦ www.sdmodelrailroadm.com), the most curious of all, displays tiny, elaborately conceived replicas of cityscapes, deserts, and mountains, as well as the industrious little trains that chug their way through them – a must for all aficionados of miniature railways.

Continuing east, near the Park Boulevard end of El Prado, the **Reuben H. Fleet Science Center** (Mon–Thurs 9.30am–5pm, Fri 9.30am–9pm, Sat 9.30am–8pm, Sun 9.30am–6pm; Science Center $6.75, Science Center and theater or simulator $11.75, all three $15; ⓦ www.rhfleet.org) presents an assortment of child-oriented exhibits of varying interest, focusing on the glitzier aspects of contemporary science, as well as the expected IMAX theater. Predictably, the most impressive sensations are provided by the **Space Theater**'s dome-shaped tilting screen and 152 loudspeakers, which showcase stomach-churning trips into volcanoes, over waterfalls, and through outer space. More impressive and appealing, though, is the **Natural History Museum**, on the north side of El Prado at its eastern end (daily 10am–5pm; $9; ⓦ www .sdnhm.org), which features a great collection of fossils, a curious array of stuffed creatures, hands-on displays of minerals, and entertaining exhibits on dinosaurs and crocodiles. The more scholarly topics – on subjects such as the controversial links between birds and late-period, chicken-sized dinos – are interspersed with crowd-pleasing exhibits on chocolate, T Rexes, and other kid-friendly topics. A short walk behind the Natural History building, the

Balboa Park practicalities

Ideally, you should visit Balboa Park on Tuesdays, when free admission is offered for several rotating museums, usually two to four depending on the Tuesday (except if it's the fifth one in the month); don't come on Mondays, when the main collections are closed. The cheapest way to see the museums is to buy the $30 **Balboa Park Passport**, which allows admission to the park's thirteen museums and is valid for a week, although you can visit each museum once only. This passport, along with a $55 variant that includes the San Diego Zoo, is available at all the museums and at the **visitor center** (daily 9.30am–4.30pm; ☎619/239-0512, Ⓦwww.balboapark .org), located in the **House of Hospitality** on the Prado. This is the best place to find information about each individual museum, and to buy the useful Balboa Park map and guide for $1. If you're interested in a basic hour-long **tour** of the park, drop by the House on Fridays at 1pm, or for a more architecture-oriented journey, come by on the first Wednesday of the month at 9.30am; both walks are free.

The park, within easy reach of Downtown on **buses** #3, #7, #16, or #25, is large but fairly easy to navigate on foot – if you tire, the free **Balboa Park tram** runs frequently between the main museum groupings and the parking lots.

Spanish Village Arts and Crafts Center (daily 11am–4pm; free; Ⓦwww .spanishvillageart.com) dates from the California Pacific 1935 Expo and, of course, was designed in the style of a Spanish village. Some three hundred craftspeople now display their work in forty different studios and galleries, and you can watch them hard at work, practicing their skills at painting, sculpture, photography, pottery, and glass-working. From here, if you continue north you'll find yourself at the gates of the San Diego Zoo (see opposite).

Pan American Plaza and around

Needless to say, the attractions arrayed along El Prado are by far the highlights of the park, and only if you have a significant amount of time (or are a car, airplane, or sports enthusiast) should you venture very far south, in the direction of the **Pan American Plaza**. At the outset, the **Palm Canyon** and **Japanese Friendship Garden** reserves are pleasantly appealing, if not particularly essential, but the **Spreckels Organ Pavilion** (free Sunday concerts, 2–3pm; Ⓦwww.serve.com/sosorgan), is definitely worth a look, as the home of one of the world's largest pipe organs, with no less than 4500 pipes. And if you miss one of the concerts, you may be able to hear the house organist practicing through the closed metal grate. Continuing on to the north end of the plaza, the cottages of the **House of Pacific Relations** (Sun noon–5pm; free) comprise an international collection of kitsch that evokes a cut-rate version of Epcot Center – enjoy the proffered tea, coffee, and cakes, but don't expect any real multicultural education. More compelling are the **Marie Hitchcock Puppet Theater** (Wed–Fri shows at 10am & 11.30am, Sat & Sun at 11am, 1pm & 2.30pm; $3, kids $2; Ⓦwww.balboaparkpuppets.com), in the nearby Pacific Palisades building, with lively and festive productions, and the **Automotive Museum** (daily 10am–5pm; $7, kids $3; Ⓦwww.sdautomuseum .org), offering a host of classic cars and motorcycles, from old-time Model Ts and fancy Rolls Royces to more obscure models like the 1912 Flying Merkle cycle and the 1948 Tucker Torpedo – one of only fifty left.

At the southern end of Pan American Plaza, the cylindrical **Aerospace Museum** (daily 10am–4.30pm; $9; Ⓦwww.aerospacemuseum.org) not only showcases a worthwhile history of aviation – loaded with 69 planes like the Spitfire, Hellcat, and the mysterious spy plane *Blackbird* – but also presents

Star Station One, a hands-on demonstration imparting knowledge about the International Space Station. There's also a replica of the *Spirit of St Louis* in the entrance hall. Heading back north, on the west side of the Plaza is the **Starlight Bowl** (tickets Tues–Fri 10am–4pm, Sat noon–4pm; ⓦwww .starlighttheatre.org), a longstanding performance space for local operettas and musicals, while the **Hall of Champions** (daily 10am–4.30pm; $7; ⓦwww .sdhoc.com) is a sports museum stuffed with memorabilia from baseball to skateboarding, mainly of interest if you have a thing for old jerseys, helmets, and trading cards.

Visiting all the museums in Balboa Park could well leave you too jaded even to notice the unassuming round building on the edge of the area, beside Park Boulevard. This, the **Centro Cultural de la Raza** (Thurs–Sun noon–4pm; free; ⓦwww.centroraza.com), mounts thoughtful temporary exhibits on Native American and Hispanic life in an atmosphere altogether less stuffy than the showpiece museums of the park, focusing on murals, folk art, literature, dance, and theater.

The San Diego Zoo

The **San Diego Zoo** (daily: mid-June to early Sept 7am–10pm; early Sept to mid-June 9am–4pm; $21, kids $14; ⓦwww.sandiegozoo.org), immediately north of the main museums in Balboa Park, is one of the city's biggest and best-known attractions, possibly the premier zoo in the country. As zoos go, it undoubtedly deserves its reputation, with more than four thousand animals from eight hundred different species, among them very rare Chinese pheasants, Mhorr gazelles, and a freakish two-headed corn snake – as well as some pioneering techniques for keeping them in captivity: animals are restrained in "psychological cages," with moats or ridges rather than bars. It's an enormous place, and you can easily spend a full day here, soaking in the major sections devoted to the likes of chimps and gorillas, sun and polar bears, lizards and lions, and habitats such as the rainforest. Take a bus tour early on to get a general idea of the layout, or survey the scene on the vertiginous **Skyfari** overhead tramway. Bear in mind, though, that many of the creatures get sleepy in the midday heat and retire behind bushes to take a nap. Moreover, the much-hyped pair of visiting Chinese **pandas** (resident at the zoo until 2008) spend a lot of time sleeping or being prodded by biologists in the park's Giant Panda Research Station, where the creatures – including a newly arrived male – recently became parents to Mei Sheng, a very rare example of a panda born in the Western Hemisphere. Aside from this facility, there's also a children's zoo in the park, with walk-through birdcages and an animal nursery.

Regular **admission** only covers entry to the main zoo and the children's zoo; to add a 35-minute bus tour and a round-trip ticket on Skyfari, you'll need the $32 Deluxe Ticket Package. A $56 ticket (kids $38) also admits you to the San Diego Wild Animal Park (near Escondido; see p.267) within a five-day period. Finally, truly motivated tourists will enjoy all of the above, as well as admission to SeaWorld (see p.247), for the rather staggering sum of $92 (kids $67).

Old Town

In 1769, Spanish settlers chose what's now **Presidio Hill** as the site of the first of California's missions. After their military service, as the soldiers began to leave the mission and the presidio, or fortress, they settled at the foot of the hill. This settlement was the birthplace of San Diego, later to be administered by Mexican officials and afterwards by early migrants from the eastern US.

The area was preserved in 1968 as **Old Town State Historic Park** (locally referred to as "Old Town") and commemorates San Diego from the 1820s through the 1870s. Featuring 25 structures, some of them original **adobe dwellings**, the district's period atmosphere is somewhat diminished by the inevitable souvenir shops. Still, it's a good place to get a sense of the city's Hispanic roots away from its modern high-rises; thus, it's also somewhat out in the middle of nowhere, isolated from anything else worthwhile in town. Luckily, bus #5 or #34 or the Blue Line trolley from Downtown makes the place conveniently accessible; by car, take I-5 and exit on Old Town Avenue, following the signs. Alternatively, from I-8 turn off onto Taylor Street and left onto Juan Street; signs should prevent any confusion.

Most things in the park which aren't historical – the shops and restaurants – open around 10am and close at 10pm (though a number of the restaurants are open until midnight or later), but the best time to be around is during the afternoon, when you can enter the more interesting adobe structures with an excellent **free walking tour**, leaving at 2pm from outside the Seeley Stables, just off the central plaza. You can get details on this, and check out a scale model of Old Town circa 1872, at the **visitor center** (daily 10am–5pm; ☎619/220-5422, ⓦwww.sandiegohistory.org), located inside the **Robinson-Rose House**, where you can also pick up a fine walking-tour book.

Exploring Old Town

A number of the historic structures in the park are well preserved and display many of their original furnishings, giving a good indication of early San Diego life. Most of the houses are open daily from 10am to 4pm or 5pm and offer free admission. One of the more significant structures is the **Casa de Estudillo** on Mason Street, built by the commander of the **presidio**, José María de Estudillo, in 1827. The chapel in this most elaborate of the original adobes served as the setting for the wedding in Helen Hunt Jackson's overblown, though highly influential, romance about early California, *Ramona*. When the house was bought in 1910 by sugar baron J.D. Spreckels, he advertised it as "Ramona's Marriage Place." Next door, the **Casa de Bandini** was the home of the politician and writer Juan Bandini and acted as the social center of San Diego during the mid-nineteenth century. After California became part of the United States, the house became the **Cosmopolitan Hotel**, considered among the finest in the state, its many elegant period appointments still visible in the dining room; the site later became a grocery and a pickle cannery before its current incarnation as a Mexican restaurant. Of somewhat less appeal are the **San Diego Union Building**, where the city's newspaper began in 1868, and the **Seeley Stables**, stuffed with Old West memorabilia.

An idealized re-creation of an eighteenth-century Mexican street market, **Bazaar del Mundo**, abuts the state park. Though rife with tacky gift shops, it's enjoyable enough on a Sunday afternoon, when there's free music and folk dancing in its tree-shaded courtyard. It's also a fair place to **eat**: stands serve fresh tortillas, and the two sit-down Mexican restaurants are decent enough if you can grab an outside seat.

Just beyond the park gates on San Diego Avenue, the **Thomas Whaley Museum** (daily 10am–4.30pm; closed Tues in winter; $5; ⓦwww.whaleyhouse.org) was the first brick building in California and the home of Thomas Whaley, a New York entrepreneur drawn by the Gold Rush. It displays furniture and photos from his time, as well as a reconstruction of a courtroom from 1869, when the building housed the county courthouse. Oddly enough, the place has been officially stamped by the US Department of Commerce as haunted, possibly by one of the occupants of the neighboring **El Campo Santo Cemetery**. Once the site of public executions (Antonio Garra, leader of an 1851 uprising by the San Luis Rey Indians, was forced to dig his own grave here before he was killed), the inscriptions on the cemetery's tombs read like a *Who's Who* of late nineteenth-century San Diego, though the cemetery (Spanish for "holy field") is most renowned for being haunted by the ghost of "Yankee Jim" Robinson, hanged in 1852 by a kangaroo court for the "capital crime" of stealing a rowboat. More crime is on display around the corner at the **Sheriffs Museum** (Tues–Sat 10am–4pm; free), which starts its timeline in the early-American period and continues to the present day, showing the way in which county law enforcers have acted to control street crime with guns, batons, and helicopters, and the response in turn of criminals with guns, knives, and brass knuckles.

Just north on Juan Street, **Heritage Park** is where several Victorian buildings have been gathered from around the city and preserved, instead of summarily destroyed in a manic burst of urban renewal. They're now mostly shops and offices, and include the agreeable ecumenical grouping of an 1889 **Temple Beth Israel** and the contemporaneous **Christian House** – now a bed and breakfast (the *Heritage Park B&B*; see "Accommodation", p.230). The view of the harbor from the park is worth the climb, as is the walk along Conde Street, which lets you peer into the atmospheric, sculpture-filled interior of the **Old Adobe Chapel**, dating from the 1850s, used as a place of worship until 1917, and restored twenty years later.

Presidio Hill and Mission San Diego

The Spanish Colonial building that now sits atop **Presidio Hill** is only a 1929 approximation of the original 1769 mission – moved in 1774 – but contains the intriguing **Junípero Serra Museum**, 2727 Presidio Drive (Fri–Sun 10am–4.30pm; $5; ☎619/297-3258), which includes Spanish furniture dating back to the sixteenth century, along with various weapons, diaries, and historical documents pertaining to the leading Catholic missionary of California. The museum additionally lionizes the yeoman struggles of a few devoted historians to preserve San Diego's Spanish past in the face of dollar-hungry developers. The **Mormon Battalion Visitor Center**, nearby at 2510 Juan St (daily 9am–9pm; free), lets you relive, via artifacts, paintings, and multimedia, the 500-troop, 2000-mile saga of the Mormon Battalion March during the Mexican–American War – the longest US military infantry march in history.

Outside the Serra Museum, the striking **Serra Cross** serves as a modern marker on the site of the original mission. To find the actual mission, you'll need to travel six miles north to 10818 San Diego Mission Rd, where the **Mission Basilica San Diego de Alcalá** (daily 8am–4pm; $3 donation suggested; ⓦ www.missionsandiego.com) was relocated to be closer to a water source and fertile soil and further from conflict with Native Americans – which still didn't prevent Padre Luis Jayme, California's first Christian martyr, from being clubbed to death there in 1775. The present building (take bus #43 from Downtown), the fifth to be constructed on this site, is still a working parish church, offering confession, weddings, baptisms, and daily masses at 7am and 5pm (tours available Mon & Thurs noon & 2pm; by reservation at ☎858/565-9077). Walk through the dark and echoey church – the fourteenth-century stalls and altar were imported from Spain – to the **garden**, where two small crosses mark the graves of Native American neophytes, making this California's oldest cemetery. A small **museum** holds a collection of Native

American craft objects and historical articles from the mission, including the crucifix held by Junípero Serra at his death in 1834. Despite claims that his missionary campaign was one of kidnapping, forced baptisms, and virtual native slavery, Serra was summarily beatified in 1998 during a Vatican ceremony.

East San Diego and Hillcrest

Scruffy **EAST SAN DIEGO** is largely faceless suburban sprawl, only really of interest if you want to venture into its western fringes as far as 1925 K St, the site of **Villa Montezuma** (Fri–Sun 10am–4.30pm, also open Thurs in Dec; $5; ☎619/239-2211), doubtless one of the more unusual entries on the National Register of Historic Places. Ignored by most visitors to San Diego, possibly due to its location, the villa is a florid show of Victoriana, with a rich variety of onion domes and all manner of loopy eccentricities. Known to some as the "haunted house," it was built for **Jesse Shepard** – English-born but noted in the US as a composer, pianist, author, and all-round aesthete – and financed by a group of culturally aspiring San Diegans in 1887. The glorious stock of furniture remains, as do many ornaments and oddments and the dramatic stained-glass windows. It's a place that well reflects Shepard's introspective nature and interest in spiritualism, both of which must have been entirely out of step with brash San Diego through the boom years, or even today. To get to the villa without a car, either make the long walk (about 45min) from Downtown, take bus #3, #5, or #16, each stopping within about five blocks, or use the trolley, transferring to the Euclid Avenue line and getting off near 20th Street.

North of Downtown and on the northwest edge of Balboa Park, **HILLCREST** is a lively and artsy area, thanks to the wealthy liberals who've moved into the district in recent decades and the general sprucing-up of the place – predictably followed by skyrocketing rents that have driven lower-income bohemians out. Altogether, it feels rather more disconnected from the culture of San Diego in a way that, say, Haight-Ashbury in San Francisco or West Hollywood in LA do not. Perhaps its most familiar local characteristic is as the center of the city's **gay community**, with a handful of gay-oriented hotels (see "Gay and lesbian San Diego," p.261), and some colorful streetlife around University and Fifth. Easily reached from Downtown on bus #3 or #11, Hillcrest also has a cache of interesting cafés and restaurants (see "Eating," p.252), decent book and music shops, and an appealing collection of Victorian homes. Among these, and the only conventional "attraction" in the area, is the **Marston House**, 3525 Seventh Ave (Fri–Sun 10am–4.30pm; $5; ☎619/298-3142), a 1905 Craftsman charmer whose rustic Arts and Crafts design little resembles the later modernist work of its co-architect Irving Gill. Nonetheless, it has a warmly elegant late-Victorian feel, and is well worth a look for anyone with a flair for houses of the era.

The beaches

For many visitors, San Diego's renowned **beaches** are reason enough to visit – the idea of sand and surf being so fundamental to the California vibe that anything else seems superfluous. It's true that if you're after seclusion and any sense of privacy, you've come to the wrong place, but the beaches do live up to their reputation for top-notch sunbathing, surfing, and swimming, and if you have any other aim beyond heat, water, and sport, you'll probably be disappointed – unless, of course, you're here for SeaWorld.

Directly southwest of Downtown across San Diego Bay, **Coronado** is a plush, well-heeled settlement, best known as the site of a large naval base and a famous resort hotel. Just beyond, and much less upscale, **Imperial Beach**'s chief draw is simply the peace of its sands, and, if you have an equestrian bent, its nearby horse-riding trails.

Across the bay to the north, the rugged **Point Loma Peninsula** marks the entrance to San Diego Bay, with oceanside trees along its spine and a craggy shoreline often dotted by easily explored tide pools – though offering little opportunity for sunbathing. **Ocean Beach**, further north at the end of the I-8 freeway, was once known to be freewheeling, though is now tempered by tourists and well-heeled residents with little taste for chaos or debauchery. These days, some of Ocean Beach's former vitality has migrated to **Mission Beach**, eight miles northwest of Downtown, and the adjoining, and slightly more salubrious, **Pacific Beach** – "PB" – linked by an exuberant beachside walkway. Both beaches encompass a peninsula that provides the western edge of **Mission Bay**, known best as the site of the colossal tourist draw of **SeaWorld**, several miles inland. To see the area at its most chic and upscale, and to discover a few honest-to-God attractions that aren't beach-oriented, travel a few miles further north up the coast to stunning **La Jolla**, whose coastline of caves and coves is matched by short, litter-free streets lined with small coffee bars, art galleries, and a stylish modern-art museum.

Coronado

Across San Diego Bay from Downtown, the bulbous isthmus of **CORONADO** is a well-scrubbed resort community with **North Island Naval Air Station** at its western end, one of the reasons you're apt to see so many sailors and soldiers in town. Although the station was closed to the public after 9/11, if you'd like a closer look, you may be able to get past the gate on one of the Old Town Trolley tours (see box, p.226). Beyond this, although Coronado has an interesting New England air, with an assortment of cozy, "saltbox" houses, the town is of limited interest, save for a historic hotel and the long, thin beach – a natural breakwater for the bay – that runs south. Although you could trek way down to the base of the peninsula, a much simpler way to get here is on the **San Diego Bay ferry** (daily 9am–9pm; $2.25 each way, $2.75 with bikes), which leaves Broadway Pier on the hour, returning on the half-hour. Tickets are available on the pier at **San Diego Harbor Excursion**, 1050 N Harbor Drive (℡619/234-4111, ⓦwww.sdhe.com), which offers many other cruises for a range of budgets. From the ferry landing on First Street, shuttle bus #904 (half-hourly 9.30am–5.30pm; $1.25) runs the mile up Coronado's main street, Orange Avenue, to the *Hotel del Coronado*. Alternatively use bus #901 from Downtown. By road, you freely cross the **Coronado Bridge** (tolls were eliminated in 2002), its struts decorated with enormous murals depicting Hispanic life, best seen from the park under the bridge in the district of Barrio Logan.

The town of Coronado grew up around the **Hotel del Coronado**, 1500 Orange Ave (see "Accommodation," p.231), a Victorian whirl of turrets and towers erected as a health resort in 1888. Using Chinese laborers who worked round-the-clock shifts, the hotel was built to appeal to well-heeled enthusiasts of healthy living, as well as rich hypochondriacs. If you're in the neighborhood, the place is certainly worth a look, its expansive grounds still something of an elite playground. Through the lobby and courtyard, a small basement **museum** (free) details the history of the "Del," including its most notable moment, when Edward VIII (then Prince of Wales) met Coronado housewife Wallis Warfield Simpson here in 1920, which eventually led to their marriage and his abdication of the British throne. Also not to be missed is the tablecloth signed by Marilyn Monroe and the rest of the cast who filmed Billy Wilder's *Some Like It Hot* here in 1958, when it doubled as a ritzy Miami Beach resort. Outside are the sands upon which Monroe memorably flirted with Tony Curtis as he pretended to be a yachting playboy with a Cary Grant accent. A guided, hour-long **historical** tour (Mon–Sat 11am & 1pm, Sun 3pm; $15) takes in many of these highlights as it wends its way around the hotel, beginning in the lobby.

A less grandiose place to explore Coronado's past is the **Coronado Museum of History and Art**, 1100 Orange Ave (Mon–Fri 9am–4pm, Sat 10am–4pm, Sun 11am–4pm; $4; Ⓦwww.coronadohistory.org), which offers displays chronicling the town's early pioneers and first naval aviators, as well as its history of yachting, architecture, and ferries. For a look at the historical and architectural importance of the various buildings in town, the museum offers hour-long **tours** (Wed 2pm & Fri 10.30am; $8). Next to the museum, the **Coronado Visitor Center** (Mon–Fri 9am–5pm, Sat 10am–5pm, Sun 11am–5pm; Ⓣ619/437-8788 or 1-800/622-8300, Ⓦwww.coronadovisitorcenter .com) offers much useful information on the area.

Silver Strand State Beach to Mexico

Heading south of the *Hotel del Coronado* (bus #901), follow Silver Strand Boulevard and you'll find plenty of good spots to stretch out and relax – though few food and drink facilities – foremost among them **SILVER STRAND STATE BEACH** (daily 8am–dusk; $6 per vehicle), where you can rollerblade or bike in a pleasant atmosphere. There are camping facilities, but for RVs only. At the end of Silver Strand Boulevard, less-engaging **IMPERIAL BEACH** contrasts unfavorably with more upscale Coronado, and in any case is a full half-hour south of Downtown San Diego, nearly at the Mexican border. It does, however, have an enjoyable and fairly quiet beach, and the **US Open Sandcastle Competition** (Ⓦwww.usopensandcastle.com), one of the nation's largest such events in July, where you're apt to see anything from sea monsters and fairytale figures to sandy skyscrapers and the face of Elvis – at least until the next high tide. Nearby **Border Field State Park** (daily dawn–dusk; Ⓣ619/575-3613) was named for the place where surveyors from the US and Mexico agreed on an international boundary after their war in 1848; it's also compelling for its unexpected **Tijuana River estuary**, a brackish marsh that's home to pelicans, teal, and migrating waterfowl. You can access the beach from here, take in a ride along a horse trail, or enjoy a weekend tour of the natural beauty. The Mexican border is also located here, and immediately adjacent is the **Bullring-by-the-Sea**. If you have a taste for bloodsport, this is the place to indulge it, on Sunday afternoons during the summer – though you will pay dearly ($20–50; Ⓣ664/680-1808, Ⓦwww.bullfights.org/tijuana).

To return directly to San Diego from Imperial Beach, take bus #934 to the trolley and head north through dreary Chula Vista and National City.

Ocean Beach and Point Loma

Ruled by the Hell's Angels in the 1960s, **OCEAN BEACH**, six miles northwest of Downtown via bus #35 or #923, is a fun and relaxed beachtown that big-moneyed interests have been trying to develop for decades, with varying success. While the single-story adobe dwellings that were home to several generations of Portuguese fishing families as recently as the 1980s have virtually disappeared to make way for garish yuppie McMansions, the odor of over-development has otherwise been kept at bay in large measure (at least in the downtown area). Indeed, the quaint, old-time streets and shops near the coast have preserved some of their ramshackle appeal and funky character. The two big hangouts include **Newport Street**, where backpackers slack around at snack bars, surf and skate rental shops, and some of the best secondhand music stores around, and **Voltaire Street**, which true to its name has a good range of independent-minded local businesses. There is often good surf, and the beach itself can be quite fun – especially on weekends, when the local party scene gets cranking. Where Voltaire Street meets the waves, you can visit Ocean Beach's one major attraction, **Dog Beach**, the only sand-strip in the area where pooches are allowed to frolic without leashes – great for canines, if not necessarily for small children. South from the pier rise, the dramatic **Sunset Cliffs** are a prime spot for twilight vistas, though notoriously unstable – more than a few people have tumbled over the edge following an afternoon of excess on the beach.

Further south, the hilly green peninsula of **POINT LOMA** is mostly owned by the US Navy, which keeps it attractive, unspoiled, and largely inaccessible. To get here from Downtown, take the trolley to Old Town and pick up bus #26. After a long, tedious ride to the point's southern extremity, you reach **Cabrillo National Monument** (daily 9am–5pm; seven-day pass $5 per vehicle, $3 per pedestrian or cyclist; Ⓦwww.nps.gov/cabr), the spot where captain Juan Rodríguez Cabrillo and his crew became the first Europeans to land in California in 1542, though they quickly reboarded their vessel and sailed off. The monument's startling vistas, across to Downtown and along the coast to Mexico, easily repay the journey here. After enjoying the view, you can discover the marine life in the many tide pools around the shoreline, reached on a clearly marked **nature walk** beginning near the monument. Also nearby, a visitor center (daily 9am–5pm; free with admission) has information on the history and wildlife of the point, and lies near the **Old Point Loma Lighthouse** (daily 9am–5pm; free with admission), whose historical tours lead you past replica Victoriana and equipment from the 1880s. As it was, the structure's main purpose was ultimately unfulfilled: soon after it was built, it was discovered that its beacon would be obscured by fog, and another lighthouse was erected at a lower elevation.

Facing the Pacific on the southwest-facing cliffs of the lighthouse, a sheltered viewing station with telescopes makes it easy to see the November-to-March **whale migration**, when scores of gray whales pass by on their journey between the Arctic Ocean and their breeding waters off Baja California.

Mission Bay and SeaWorld

Heading northwest from Downtown toward the coast, you pass through a drab, cheerless zone – frequented by sailors for its strip clubs and by tourists for its cheap hotels – before reaching **MISSION BAY**, whose mud flats quickly become landscaped lagoons and grassy flatlands crowded with watersports fanatics. (From Ocean Beach, Mission Bay is accessible by crossing the San Diego River on Sunset Cliffs Boulevard.) The source of Mission Bay's popularity is, of course, the formidable amusement park **SEAWORLD** (daily: mid-June to Labor Day 9am–dusk; rest of year 10am–dusk; $49.75, children \$39.75, parking \$7; Ⓦ www.seaworld.com), the San Diego branch of an entertainment colossus that stretches from California to Texas to Florida, which you can reach by taking SeaWorld Drive off I-5, or bus #9 from Downtown. Although the entrance fee is very steep, SeaWorld is San Diego's most popular attraction for its undeniable kid-friendly appeal. But for adults, experiencing the local sea life by whale watching and snorkeling may be much more rewarding, and a lot cheaper. The park's entry price demands that you allow a full day to make it worthwhile; amazingly enough, the Skytower and Bayside Skyride attractions charge an extra \$3 per ride – so don't assume \$50 is all you're going to spend, especially after costs for the pricey junkfood are figured in.

Highly regimented, SeaWorld has numerous exhibits and events, including the killer-whale shows that make up Shamu Adventure (where you shouldn't sit in the first fourteen rows unless you're prepared to be soaked by belly flops from a high-flying orca); Forbidden Reef, stocked with moray eels and stingrays; the Wild Arctic, populated by walruses, beluga whales, and polar bears; and the Shark Encounter, where sharks circle menacingly around visitors walking through a submerged viewing tunnel. Some of the park's latest attractions, however, have devolved into the sort of standard-issue theme-park fare that includes the likes of giant-inner-tube rides, motion simulators, sky trams, and "haunted" lighthouses, though if you've come here for this sort of diversion, you're better off just sticking to Disneyland.

Mission Beach and Pacific Beach

Simply put, the biggest-name public beaches in San Diego are **MISSION BEACH**, the peninsula that separates Mission Bay from the ocean, and its northern extension, **PACIFIC BEACH**. If you aren't up for bronzing on the sands, you can always nurse a beer at one of the many beachfront bars while observing the toasty sands overrun with scantily clad babes and surfboard-clutching dudes. Or you could rollerblade or bike down **Ocean Front Walk**, the concrete boardwalk running the length of both beaches, and the fastest way to travel when summer traffic is bumper-to-bumper on Mission Boulevard.

After much effort, city authorities have mostly succeeded in curbing the hedonism and drunken debauchery long associated with this classic slice of Southern California beachlife, including approving the revitalization of the once-derelict **Belmont Park**, near the southern end of Ocean Front Walk at 3146 Mission Blvd (Mon–Thurs 11am–10pm, Fri–Sun 11am–11pm; rides \$2–4; Ⓦ www.belmontpark.com). Although there are ten official rides, the two main attractions, both from 1925, are the **Giant Dipper** rollercoaster, one of the few of its era still around, and the **Plunge**, once the largest saltwater plunge in the world, and the setting for famous celluloid swimmers Johnny Weismuller and Esther Williams. These days, the two main draws are also supplemented by an assortment of lesser carnival thrills, swimwear stores, a pricey fitness center, and countless seaside snack joints.

By following Mission Boulevard north, you cross from the spirited amusements of Mission Beach into the more sedate Pacific Beach, where expensive oceanside homes with tidy lawns suggest haute-bourgeois refinement, though there's still plenty to enjoy. A serviceable beach, for one, around Crystal Pier is a decent spot for a suntan, while **Garnet Avenue**, running inland from the pier, is lined by funky eating joints and nightspots. For many, though, Pacific Beach is synonymous with **surfing**, as one of the prime strips of coastline in the area specifically marked for it. Indeed, a mile north of the pier, **Tourmaline Surfing Park**, La Jolla Boulevard at Tourmaline Street (☎619/221-8100), regularly pounded by heavy waves, is reserved exclusively for the sport, as well as windsurfing – but no swimmers are allowed. If you don't have a board, a good alternative is a few miles north, **Windansea Beach**, a favorite surfing hot spot that's also fine for swimming and hiking alongside the oceanside rocks and reefs.

La Jolla and around

"A nice place – for old people and their parents," wrote Raymond Chandler of **LA JOLLA** (pronounced "La Hoya") in the 1950s, though that didn't stop him from moving here (his former house is at 6005 Camino de la Costa) and setting much of his final novel *Playback* in the town, renaming it "Esmeralda." Since Philip Marlowe concluded his last case, La Jolla has been infused with scads of new money, and its opulence is now less stuffy and more welcoming than in the 1980s. The main section, around Prospect Street and Girard Avenue, has spotless sidewalks flanked by crisply trimmed grass, and the many upscale art galleries sit alongside chic cafés and swanky boutiques.

Although it's fairly expensive, La Jolla is worth a visit at least once to savor the town's unique (if contrived) elegance, which includes the ornate pink **La Valencia Hotel**, 1132 Prospect St, frequented by Hollywood's elite in the 1930s and 40s (see "Accommodation," p.232). On a quieter section of the same thoroughfare, the La Jolla site of the **Museum of Contemporary Art**, 700 Prospect St (daily 11am–5pm, Thurs closes 7pm; $6, free third Tues of month; Ⓦwww.mcasandiego.org), has a huge, rotating stock of works from 1955 onwards. Minimalism, Pop Art, and regional California work are in evidence, bolstered by a strong range of temporary shows, and there are fabulous views of the Pacific surf crashing against the rocks below the building's huge windows. Curiously, the museum building was once the home of **Ellen Scripps**, a local philanthropist who injected her seemingly endless wealth into La Jolla through the first half of the century. She commissioned early-modernist architect Irving Gill (who built several distinctive buildings in La Jolla, including the Marston House; see p.244) to design her house, and today the Scripps name is still almost everywhere, notably in the small, neat, and tasteful **Ellen Scripps Browning Park**, on the seaward side of the museum. Where the park meets the coast is the start of **La Jolla Cove**, much of it an ecological reserve, with an underwater park whose clear waters make it perfect for snorkeling (if you can ever find a parking space nearby).

Architecture fans inspired by the work of Gill will not want to miss a chance to tour the local citadel of high modernism, the **Salk Institute for Biological Studies**, 10010 N Torrey Pines Rd (daily 8.30am–5pm; tours by reservation at ☎858/453-4100 ext 1287, Ⓦwww.salk.edu), not only a respected institution for molecular biology and genetics, but also a considerably influential design by American architect Louis I. Kahn. A collection of spartan concrete blocks and walls, the complex features stark vistas that look out over the Pacific Ocean and a strange, austere serenity that's both welcome and unexpected. Although the site should be avoided by fans of, say, Horton Plaza, it nonetheless will appeal to anyone with a taste for Le Corbusier or any icon of the mid-twentieth-century International Style.

To find out more about the local heritage and various attractions in town, drop by the La Jolla Historical Society, 7846 Eads Ave (Tues & Thurs noon–4pm; Ⓦwww.lajolla.org/hist_soc), which can suggest some of the better old houses, hidden coves, and relevant sites to visit.

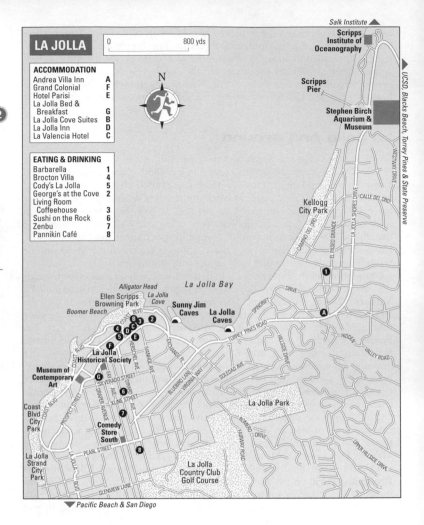

LA JOLLA

0   800 yds

ACCOMMODATION
Andrea Villa Inn   A
Grand Colonial   F
Hotel Parisi   E
La Jolla Bed &
  Breakfast   G
La Jolla Cove Suites   B
La Jolla Inn   D
La Valencia Hotel   C

EATING & DRINKING
Barbarella   1
Brocton Villa   4
Cody's La Jolla   5
George's at the Cove   2
Living Room
  Coffeehouse   3
Sushi on the Rock   6
Zenbu   7
Pannikin Café   8

N

Salk Institute

Scripps
Institute of
Oceanography

UCSD, Blacks Beach, Torrey Pines & State Preserve

Scripps
Pier

Stephen Birch
Aquarium &
Museum

WESTWAY DRIVE

Kellogg
City Park

CALLE DEL ORO

LA JOLLA SHORES DRIVE

CAMINO DEL ORO

EL PASEO GRANDE

La Jolla Bay

DRIVE

SPINDRIFT

Alligator Head   La Jolla
Ellen Scripps   Cove
Browning Park   Sunny Jim
Boomer Beach   Caves   La Jolla
  Caves

TORREY PINES ROAD

HILLSIDE DRIVE

HIDDEN

VALLEY ROAD

La Jolla
Historical Society

Museum of
Contemporary
Art

Coast
Blvd
City
Park

EXCHANGE PL

BLUEBIRD LANE

VIRGINIA WAY

SOLEDAD AVE

La Jolla Park

UPPER HILLSIDE DRIVE

COAST BLVD

PROSPECT STREET

DRAPER AVENUE

SILVERADO STREET

HERSCHEL AVE

IVANHOE AVE

GIRARD AVE

KLINE STREET

Comedy
Store
South

La Jolla
Strand
City
Park

LA JOLLA BLVD

PEARL STREET

GLENVIEW LANE

La Jolla
Country Club
Golf Course

ROMERO DRIVE

FAIRWAY ROAD

Pacific Beach & San Diego

North along the coast

North of La Jolla Cove, upmarket residential neighborhoods stretch from the cliff tops to the main route, Torrey Pines Road. Following this thoroughfare and then La Jolla Shores Drive, which soon branches left, several uneventful miles precede the **Stephen Birch Aquarium and Museum** (daily 9am–5pm; $10, kids $6.50; Ⓦaquarium.ucsd.edu), part of the Scripps Institute of Oceanography, which provides entertaining up-close views of captive marine life, informative displays on the earth's ecology, and exhibits detailing the marine exploration work carried out by the Institute. The highlights include the Hall of Fishes, a huge kelp forest home to countless sea creatures, and the Shark Reef, displaying a nice range of the fearsome creatures, including a few pint-sized versions. Altogether, the museum is a much more edifying experience than anything at SeaWorld, and a lot cheaper, too.

On a hillside setting above the museum and also reached from Torrey Pines Road, the **University of California at San Diego (UCSD)** campus is a huge, dull affair, only meriting a visit for its specially commissioned artworks scattered about the 1200-acre grounds. These pieces constitute the **Stuart Collection of Sculpture** (Ⓦstuartcollection.ucsd.edu), including works by Bruce Nauman, William Wegman, Nam June Paik, and Jenny Holzer. The first acquisition, from 1983, is still among the best: Niki de Saint Phalle's **Sun God**, a chunky, colorful bird whose outstretched wings welcome visitors to the parking lot opposite Peterson Hall. To find the rest, pick up a leaflet from the office in the Visual Arts Building or one of the campus's two visitor information booths (more information at Ⓣ858/534-2117). Without a car, you can reach the campus on bus #34 or #30 from Downtown, which terminate their routes a few miles away at the University Towne Square shopping mall.

As it leaves campus, La Jolla Shores Drive meets North Torrey Pines Road. A mile north of the junction, Torrey Pines Scenic Drive, branching left, provides the only access (via a steep path) to **Torrey Pines City Beach Park** – almost always called **Blacks Beach** – the region's premier clothing-optional, gay-friendly beach and one of the best surfing beaches in Southern California, known for its huge barreling waves during big swells. The beach lies within the southern part of the **Torrey Pines State Preserve** (daily 8am–sunset; parking $6; Ⓦwww.torreypine.org), best entered a few miles further north, which preserves the country's rarest species of pine, the Torrey Pine – one of two surviving stands. Thanks to salty conditions and stiff ocean breezes, the pines contort their ten-foot frames into a variety of tortured, twisted shapes best viewed at close quarters from the half-mile **Guy Fleming Trail**, a two-thirds mile loop that starts near the beachside parking lot. The small **museum and interpretive center** (daily 9am–5pm; free) will tell you all about pines, especially if your visit coincides with a guided nature tour (Sat & Sun 10am & 2pm). The less scenic and short **beach trail** leads from the center down to Flat Rock and a popular beach, great for sunbathing and picnics, though there is no picnicking allowed on the cliffs above the beach. Continuing beyond the preserve will lead you into the North County town of Del Mar (see p.263).

Eating

San Diego typically offers good **food** at reasonable prices, everything from old-time coffee shops to stylish ethnic restaurants. Although its range of culinary fare isn't quite as wide as LA's, San Diego still has a number of solid staples. Mexican food is much in evidence, especially in **Old Town**, while the **Gaslamp District** has the greatest concentration of tourist-friendly restaurants and bars, which are especially crazy on weekend nights. Ascendant **Little Italy**, on the northern fringes of Downtown, mainly appeals for its handful of decent restaurants, but is still too small to challenge the bohemian allure of **Hillcrest**, the most attractive area to simply hang out and chow down.

Downtown and Little Italy

Alambres 756 5th Ave, Downtown Ⓣ619/233-2838. Affordable Mexican food in a casual atmosphere, popular for its Speed Lunch – served within ten minutes or it's free – and its eponymous Alambres, fat tortillas stuffed to order.

Anthony's Fish Grotto 1360 Harbor Drive, Downtown Ⓣ619/232-5103. Fish-and-chips and other fish-related favorites are the draw at this longstanding bayside haunt. Lunch or dinner; one of several area locations.

Bandar 825 4th Ave, Downtown Ⓣ619/238-0101.

Tasty, top-shelf Persian cuisine that tempts the palate with staples like lamb kebabs and stuffed grape leaves, as well as more inventive items like black cherry rice. Even the eggplant stew's a winner.

Bella Luna 748 5th Ave, Downtown ☎619/239-3222. A romantic, moon-themed bistro with an artsy feel, serving up wonderful, mid-priced dishes from different regions of Italy, with hefty servings of pasta and succulent calamari. Pasta from $12–20; entrees run $10 more.

Café 222 222 Island Ave at 2nd, Downtown ☎619/236-9902. Hip café serving some of the city's best breakfasts and lunches, with excellent pancakes and waffles, and inventive twists on traditional sandwiches and burgers (including vegetarian), at reasonable prices. Open 7am–1:45pm; no credit cards.

Caffè Italia 1704 India St, Little Italy ☎619/234-6767. Sandwiches, salads, and great desserts served in a sleek modern interior or out on the sidewalk. Don't miss the Belgian-waffle bar on Sundays.

Candelas 416 3rd Ave, Downtown ☎619/702-4455. A Gaslamp District restaurant offering swank, pricey Mexican fare with inventive combinations of seafood and meat dishes – the California-cuisine influence is deliciously apparent in items like sea bass with grape sauce and wild mushrooms.

The Cheese Shop 627 4th Ave, Downtown ☎619/232-2303. Scrumptious deli sandwiches stuffed with different savory meats, with the roast beef a solid pick among many good choices, from lamb to salami to pork loin. Also offers filling breakfasts.

Chive 558 4th Ave, Downtown ☎619/232-4483. Chic and inventive are the buzzwords at this trendy eclectic joint. The prices can be steep, in the $20–30 range – worth it for the mean short ribs and curry pork chop, not so much so for the tofu falafel. Reservations required.

Croce's 802 5th Ave, Downtown ☎619/233-4355. Pricey but excellent range of pastas, desserts, and salads in the Gaslamp District. The Sunday jazz brunch is not to be missed. See also "Nightlife," p.258.

de' Medici 815 5th Ave, Downtown ☎619/702-7228. Upscale Italian fare that draws plenty of suits for the pseudo–Old World style; still, the food is scrumptious, with the gnocchi, beef filets, and *cioppino* rounding out a solid menu.

Dobson's 956 Broadway Circle, Downtown ☎619/231-6771. An upscale restaurant in an old two-tier building, loaded with business types in power-ties. The cuisine leans toward Continental, with puff pastries adding some zing to the fare,

which includes everything from pork loin and rib-eye steak to jerk chicken.

Filippi's Pizza Grotto 1747 India St, Little Italy ☎619/232-5094. Thick, chewy pizzas and a handful of pasta dishes served in a small room at the back of an Italian grocery. No-nonsense atmosphere, a good spot for devouring old favorites.

Grand Central Café 500 Broadway, Downtown ☎619/234-2233. Loaded with train decor, this cozy café serves inexpensive, gut-busting fare, mostly fat sandwiches and lip-smacking burgers. Breakfast-only on Sunday.

Olé Madrid 755 5th Ave, Downtown ☎619/557-0146. Enjoyable mid-priced Spanish restaurant with a wide range of tapas – anything from crab cakes to omelets – and some solid paella and pasta choices. Flamenco dancers at midweek; on weekends, it turns into a popular funk and dance venue – see "Clubs," p.257. Closed Mon.

Rei Do Gado 939 4th Ave, Downtown ☎619/702-8464. Barbeque Brazilian-style, delivered in a grand buffet atmosphere, where you pick what you want visually from an array of meat skewers, then out they come – piping hot and ready to stuff your gut.

Sammy's Woodfired Pizza 770 4th Ave, outside of Horton Plaza, Downtown ☎619/230-8888. Affordable California cuisine in a Mediterranean atmosphere. Pasta, salads, and seafood are the staples, but the eclectic pizzas, calzones, and "messy sundaes" are the real reasons to come. One in a local chain of eateries.

Taka 555 5th Ave, Downtown ☎619/338-0555. Good sushi and hot and cold appetizers – as well as the likes of sashimi and pasta – in a modern atmosphere stuffed to the gills with hipsters.

Hillcrest and Old Town

Berta's 3928 Twiggs St, Old Town ☎619/295-2343. A far cry from the area's many touristy Mexican restaurants, offering low-priced, authentic cooking from all over Latin America, with a range of hot and spicy concoctions to make you pound the table for more.

Café Pacifica 2414 San Diego Ave, Old Town ☎619/291-6666. A bit upper-end but worthwhile for its winning mix of California cuisine and lobster, lamb, and steak – plus a few tasty, if pricey, abalone offerings. The wine list is renowned for its quality and size.

Casa de Bandini 2600 Calhoun St, Old Town ☎619/297-8211. The crowds come in thick, ravenous packs to sample this restaurant's delicious combo plates, potent margaritas, and appealing (or annoying) mariachi musicians. Chow down on tostadas and the shrimp olé salad on the festive patio, and you're in the catbird seat.

Casa Guadalajara 4105 Taylor St, Old Town ☎619/295-5111. Festive Mexican fare that includes a wide range of savory combos, such as *chipotle* chicken and tequila-lime shrimp. Moderately priced and open on weekends until 1.30am.

Celadon 540 University Ave, Hillcrest ☎619/297-8424. Quality Thai eats at this solid favorite with a mix of staples and unique inventions – from spicy chili rice to Thai barbeque chicken to savory "jungle" curry.

Chilango's Mexico City Grill 142 University Ave, Hillcrest ☎619/294-8646. Gourmet Mexican food for under $10 is served in this tiny storefront locale that is packed to the rafters in the evenings. Try the savory south-of-the-border favorites such as *chile pasillo* and Red Snapper Veracruz.

City Delicatessen 535 University Ave, Hillcrest ☎619/295-2747. Huge New York–style deli menu – liver, brisket, and cabbage rolls make triumphant appearances – with belt-loosening portions to match and late hours (until 2am on weekends). An essential stop for the seriously ravenous.

Crest Café 425 Robinson Ave, Hillcrest ☎619/295-2510. Don't let the dumpy exterior fool you – this is solid, tasty American fare presented on the cheap. The salads, burgers, and pancakes will make your stomach happy, as will the delicious home-made desserts. Open 7am–midnight.

Ichiban 1449 University Ave, Hillcrest ☎619/299-7203. Altogether scrumptious Japanese cuisine, featuring a range of good rolls, *bentos*, soups, and sushi, in an unpretentious and popular restaurant. The combination platters are extremely well-priced. Also in Pacific Beach at 1441 Garnet Ave (☎858/270-5755).

Jack and Giulio's 2391 San Diego Ave, Old Town ☎619/294-2074. Although not too many diners come to this part of town expressly seeking Italian food, this comfy spot fits the bill for those who do. Take in the moderately priced lasagna or gnocchi, or splurge a little more for top-notch scampi and veal.

La Piñata 2836 Juan St, Old Town ☎619/297-1631. Affordable Mexican food with hefty portions of old-fashioned, fattening fare: steak-stuffed "fajitadillas" as well as the formidable Piñata Supreme. Pitchers of margaritas will give you a potent jolt to go with your combo plates.

Old Town Mexican Café 2489 San Diego Ave ☎619/297-4330. Lively and informal Mexican diner where the crowds expect to queue up before dining on Mexican ribs and Steak Azteca; only at breakfast are you unlikely to have to wait for a table.

Pizza Nova 3955 5th Ave, Hillcrest ☎619/296-6682. Trendy California-style pizzas with a range of savory toppings. Good, palatable fare draws a

sizeable contingent of locals and tourists. Also in Solana Beach (☎858/259-0666) and Point Loma (☎619/226-0268).

Taste of Thai 527 University Ave, Hillcrest ☎619/291-7525. Terrific Thai staples – spicy noodles, marinated shrimp, and pad thai – for reasonable prices in the center of Hillcrest; expect a wait on weekends.

Coronado, Ocean Beach, and Point Loma

Chez Loma 1132 Loma Ave, Coronado ☎619/435-0661. Intensely aromatic and delicious selection of French cuisine, especially strong on old-line favorites, though with nouvelle influences as well. Fixed-price menu ($38–45) focuses on steak and seafood entrees.

Eatopia 5001 Newport Ave, Ocean Beach ☎619/224-3237. Vegan central along the coast, where you can munch on raw foods and get your fix of wheatgrass smoothies, organic wraps, and soy milkshakes.

Humphrey's by the Bay 2241 Shelter Island Drive, Point Loma ☎619/224-3577. Eclectic California cuisine, heavy on inventive seafood platters – anything from crab cakes to miso salmon and wild mushrooms – but especially good for eye-catching bayside views, groovy weekend live music, and DJs who spin funk, dance, jazz, and rock.

Mexican Village 120 Orange Ave, Coronado ☎619/435-1822. Mexican diner of ballroom dimensions and fifty-year history, patronized as much for its lip-smacking margaritas and high-stepping music as for its cheap and serviceable food.

Miguel's Cocina 1351 Orange Ave, Coronado ☎619/437-4237. Savory fish tacos, lobster burritos, huevos rancheros, and a full range of other solid choices make this Mexican eatery worth seeking out.

Old Venice 2910 Canon Ave, Point Loma ☎619/222-5888. Upscale and hip atmosphere at moderately priced café and bar. Great for pizza, pasta, seafood, and salads – no real surprises here, just hearty favorites.

Point Loma Seafoods 2805 Emerson St ☎619/223-1109. Fast, inexpensive counter serving up San Diego's freshest fish in a basket, along with mean crabcake and squid sandwiches that make the locals cheer. Justly popular joint is packed on weekends; don't even try to find an adjacent parking spot.

Primavera 932 Orange Ave, Coronado ☎619/435-0454. Swank 'n' scrumptious Italian cuisine that's among the best in town – *carpaccio*, pasta, and risotto for those a little lighter in the wallets, steak and lamb chops for the big spenders.

Ranchos Cocina 1830-H Sunset Cliffs Blvd, Ocean Beach ☎619/226-7619. A healthy, affordable joint with tasty dishes like *mahi-mahi* tacos or eggplant burritos – many combine Tex-Mex, Spanish, and even Aztec fare. Try the daily seafood and veggie specials. One of several local eateries.

Stretch's 943 Orange Ave, Coronado ☎619/435-8886. Reasonably priced American cuisine; healthy salads and sandwiches made with fresh natural ingredients.

Theo's 4953 Newport Ave, Ocean Beach ☎619/225-9404. Hearty subs and pizza at cheap prices. A popular choice with the locals.

The Venetian 3663 Voltaire St, Ocean Beach ☎619/223-8197. Excellently priced pizzas and pasta, mostly Italian staples with big portions and affordable prices.

Mission Beach and Pacific Beach

The Eggery 4130 Mission Blvd, Mission Beach ☎858/274-3122. A coffee shop with imagination, serving breakfast – omelets, eggs benedict, pancakes, and other favorites – until 2pm. Be prepared to wait on weekends.

The Fishery 5040 Cass St, Pacific Beach ☎858/272-9985. Good range of seafood for varying prices at this straightforward fishhouse, where you can get your fill of oysters, sea bass, and the like, as well as cheaper swordfish sandwiches.

Karinya 825 Garnet Ave, Pacific Beach ☎858/270-5050. Hot and spicy soups, firecracker shrimp, and coconut curry to set your mouth ablaze, with a decent range of Thai staples such as noodle dishes and rolls as well. A solid, affordable bet.

Kono's 704 Garnet Ave, Pacific Beach ☎858/483-1669. A dependable choice for breakfast or lunch on the boardwalk, with inexpensive, sizeable portions of eggs, potatoes, toast, and sandwiches, and especially plump burgers and burritos. Beware the long line of hungry surfers. Adjacent to Crystal Pier.

Luigi's 3210 Mission Blvd, Mission Beach ☎858/488-2818. Sup on cheap and enormous pizzas while you take part in the rowdy beachside atmosphere, screaming at one of the sports games on competing TV sets.

Mission Café 3795 Mission Blvd, Mission Beach ☎858/488-9060. A wide range of choices, from French toast and tamales with eggs to tortillas with spicy seasonings to "roll-ups" stuffed with meat and pasta. Beer, specialty coffees, shakes, and smoothies all on tap. Also east of Hillcrest at 2801 University Ave (☎619/220-8992); both branches close at 3pm daily.

Sportsmen's Seafood 1617 Quivira Rd, Mission Beach ☎619/224-3551. For the serious fish-lover, a combo diner/market where the catch of the day is laid out before your eyes. A no-frills environment with cheap and delicious fare – the shrimp cocktails, squid steak, tuna burgers, fish'n'chips, crab or lobster platters, and fish tacos are all worth a try.

Zanzibar 976 Garnet Ave, Pacific Beach ☎858/272-4762. A great place to chill out, especially on the back patio, with inexpensive snacks, pizzas, sandwiches, smoothies, coffees, and desserts. As a major plus, breakfast is served all day. Open till 1am on weekends.

La Jolla

Barbarella 2171 Avenida de la Playa ☎858/454-7373. Eclectic Italian eatery that serves up a hearty range of pizza to pasta, risotto to ravioli, and even burgers to fries. Justifiably popular with the swells as well as the proles.

Brockton Villa 1235 Coast Blvd ☎858/454-7393. Superior American and California cuisine, featuring a nice range of rotating entrees, typically seafood, stews, and pasta – the paella, rack of lamb, and crab-stuffed lobster are signature dishes. Also features solid, somewhat familiar, choices for breakfast.

Cody's La Jolla 8030 Girard Ave ☎858/459-0040. Innovative, mid-priced California cuisine for lunch or breakfast; especially notable are the bouillabaise, ling cod, and scrumptious burgers. Sit on the patio and catch a glimpse of La Jolla Cove.

George's at the Cove 1250 Prospect St ☎858/454-4244. Although the downstairs level of this swank eatery offers delightful Cal-cuisine, the rooftop terrace has the unbeatable ocean views and somewhat cheaper fare.

Living Room Coffeehouse 1010 Prospect St ☎858/459-1187. One in a chain of five local coffee joints, with great sandwiches, soups, quiches, and pastries with fresh ingredients, in an antique-laden living room.

Sushi on the Rock 7734-A Girard Ave ☎858/456-1138. Tempting array of inexpensive sushi combination plates, many of them quite colorful and experimental – anything from a fiery 911 Roll to the fearsome-sounding Monkey Balls – throwing in different pan-Asian flavors and styles, and served to a soundtrack of rock and reggae.

Zenbu 7660 Fay Ave ☎858/454-4540. Another hip, swanky sushi bar in this upscale town, where you can enjoy delicious salmon rolls, sashimi, and other raw-fish fare to your heart's content.

Drinking: bars and coffeehouses

San Diego has a respectable range of appealing **bars** that can be found throughout much of the city, with the Gaslamp District being a good place to get dressed up for cocktails or for pure sports-bar swilling, while the beach communities offer a more rowdy atmosphere, abetted by plenty of beer and loud music. Pacific Beach boasts the best selection of the city's **coffeehouses**, which, aside from the usual espresso drinks and pastries, may also offer Internet access and quirky artworks.

Coffeehouses

Café Crema 1001 Garnet Ave, Pacific Beach ☎858/273-3558. Wake yourself up here before going to the bars, or sober up afterwards, with one of their large coffees. Features sidewalk seating, late hours (til 2am on weekends, 1am weekdays), on-site Internet access, and eclectic entertainment from oddball poets to avant-garde tunes.

Café Lulu 419 F St, Downtown ☎619/238-0114. Hipster joint with eye-catching, mildly freakish decor, as well as a good selection of coffees and late-night food orders until 2am on weekends, midnight on weekdays.

Claire de Lune 2906 University Ave, Hillcrest ☎619/688-9845. The prototypical coffeehouse, with steaming java, teas, and sandwiches, comfy seating, and entertainment that runs from smooth jazz to spoken-word to avant-garde.

Gelato Vero Caffe 3753 India St, at the southern end of Hillcrest ☎619/295-9269. Enjoy good espresso and tasty Italian gelato while getting clued in to local events by staff and regulars. Open until midnight weekdays, 1am on weekends.

Jungle Java 5047 Newport Ave, Ocean Beach ☎619/224-0249. If sipping on espresso and munching on pastries while shopping for plants sounds like a good idea, this is the place for you – another of this burg's quirky shops, with a good range of hot teas and coffee drinks to go with your ferns and creepers.

Pannikin Café 7467 Girard Ave, La Jolla ☎858/454-5453. Modest, friendly spot where you can knock back a java, read the paper, and dine on a sandwich, and deal with a bit less of the attitude you might find elsewhere in this upscale beachside community.

Upstart Crow 835 W Harbor Drive, Downtown ☎619/232-4855. Though located in dreary Seaport Village, this coffee bar fused with a bookstore makes for a lively cross-section of customers – and a surfeit of reading material.

Zanzibar 976 Garnet Ave, Pacific Beach ☎858/272-4762. Relatively serene retreat from the brash bars along this strip. Coffees, teas, sandwiches, and muffins served until 2am, or 4am on weekends. Also doubles as a restaurant (see opposite).

Bars

Callahan's 8111 Mira Mesa Blvd ☎858/578-7892. Located north of Downtown and east of the beach, in the middle of mini-mall nowhere, but worth the trip for its excellent combination of Irish food and style, and microbrewed faves like blueberry wheat beer and a "Nameless Nutbrown." Open until 1am weekends.

Coronado Brewing Company 170 Orange Ave ☎619/437-4452. Not as frenetic, quirky, or irreverent as some of the other microbreweries around town, but a solid choice if you want basic pasta, seafood, and burgers served with handcrafted brews, light and dark.

Dublin Square 554 4th Ave, Downtown ☎619/239-5818. Get your fill of chicken pot pie and lamb-shank stew as you quaff Irish beer and spirits at this Emerald Isle pub. Even the seafood

comes in a broth made from Guinness, and the chocolate cake is given a whiskey boost.

Henry's Pub 618 5th Ave, Downtown ☎619/238-2389. One of the more unusual brewpubs in town, where Scandinavian fare is doled out by the platter, house music pumps through the speakers, and the myriad European beers are on offer in bottles or on tap. A unique experience in the Gaslamp.

Karl Strauss Brewery & Grill 1157 Columbia St at B, Downtown ☎619/234-2739. Discerning beer hunters may enjoy ales and lagers – from the oatmeal stout to the Black's Beach Extra Dark – brewed here on the premises, or just quaff from a sampler tray, while the menu offers a solid assortment of hefty favorites like ribs and sausages. Four other area locations, and one in LA.

Kensington Club 4079 Adams Ave, Kensington District, north of Hillcrest ☎619/284-2848. Great joint for beer, wine, and cocktails, but also for wide-ranging live music selections from thumping-dance DJs to head-banging rockers to more sedate ambient groovers.

Live Wire 2103 El Cajon Blvd, just east of Hillcrest ☎619/291-7450. An impressive selection of imported beers, pinball, pool, and funky sub-bohemian atmosphere make this a fine choice for boozing, though it's no longer a live-music scene.

Martini Ranch 528 F St, Downtown ☎619/235-6100. Prime poseur bar where yuppies and dapper meat-marketeers go to swill fancy cocktails for upwards of $10 amid smooth and precious decor. Worth a go if you want to try your luck at the swank singles scene.

O'Hungry's 2547 San Diego Ave, Old Town ☎619/298-0133. Tall, dark beers and a boisterous crowd, enlivened by a cheesy nautical theme and cheap 'n' tasty comfort food.

Onyx Room 852 5th Ave, Gaslamp District ☎619/235-6699. Groovy underground bar with lush decor and comfortable seating, where you can listen to torch songs, knock back a few cocktails, and hit the back room for live jazz and dance tunes. The swanky lounge upstairs, *Thin*, has pricier drinks and bigger attitudes.

Red Fox Room 2223 El Cajon Blvd, just east of Hillcrest ☎619/297-1313. Makes a popular tandem nightcrawl with *Live Wire*, a block away. This old-style piano bar with good steaks draws nostalgia buffs of all ages.

Taylor's 721 Grand Ave, Pacific Beach ☎858/270-3596. Microbrews by the beach, boasting a prime location a short jump from the sands and prime selection of handcrafted ales, lagers, and the like. Freewheeling surfer-dude atmosphere as well.

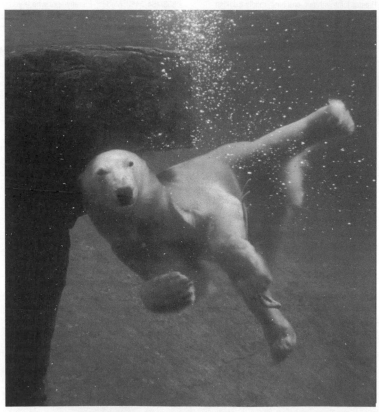

△ Polar bear swimming, San Diego Zoo

Nightlife: clubs and live music

When it comes to **live music**, San Diego has a number of top-notch venues that nearly rival those in LA, with good choices Downtown and in the Gaslamp (as well as a smattering along the coast). Decent **clubs**, though, are a bit harder to find – Hillcrest is notable for its gay-oriented spots (see p.261), while other clubs can be found mainly in the Gaslamp, predictably catering to the silk-shirt and leather-pants crowd.

For full listings, pick up the free *San Diego Reader* (Ⓦ www.sdreader.com), buy the Thursday edition of the *San Diego Union-Tribune* (Ⓦ www.signonsandiego.com), or seek out the youth-lifestyle-oriented *Slamm/San Diego CityBeat* (Ⓦ www.sdcitybeat.com) at some of the places listed below. **Cover charges** at live-music venues range from $3 to $15, unless a big-name act is playing, or a major DJ spinning.

Clubs

5ifth Quarter 600 5th Ave, Downtown ☎619/236-1616. Major-league meatmarket scene in the Gaslamp, where out-of-town trendoids mix with drunken locals to the head-pulsing sound of house and techno beats. Plenty of TVs tuned to sports if you get tired of dancing.

Bitter End 770 5th Ave, Downtown ☎619/338-9300. Two-story venue in the Gaslamp, complete with dancefloor, martini bar, and private lounge, for the sophisticated poseur who doesn't mind paying $9 for an appletini.

Blue Tattoo 835 5th Ave, Downtown ☎619/238-7191. Whether you want to indulge in a little foam dancing or just get nasty with the funk, disco, and rap, this is the place to come. There's often a long line at this prime dance venue, as well as a strict dress code, so leave your sneakers and jeans behind.

Café Sevilla 555 4th Ave, Downtown ☎619/233-5979. Traditional Spanish cuisine and tapas upstairs, hip Latin American–flavored club downstairs, with flamenco, house, and funk grooves to whet your musical appetite.

Olé Madrid 751 5th St, Downtown ☎619/557-0146. Spanish restaurant that becomes a very popular funk and dance club at night. Arrive before 11pm if you want to get in (see "Eating," p.252).

On Broadway 615 Broadway, Downtown ☎619/231-0111. The apotheosis of posing in San Diego, a velvet-rope scene that attracts the local celebrity elite (such as they are) and sends you into booty-shaking, roof-raising overdrive as you groove to national-league DJs and thunderous house and hip-hop beats.

Rosary Room 947 E St, Downtown ☎619/702-7160. With swank decor loaded with religious iconography and off-kilter designs, a good spot to indulge in scene-watching while grooving to dance DJs and knocking back an eclectic assortment of beer and wine.

Thrusters Lounge 4633 Mission Blvd, Pacific Beach ☎858/483-6334. Cozy bar and club where the hip-hop, dance, and reggae beats come hard and heavy, and jazz and rock make occasional appearances as well.

Live music venues

Rock and punk

4th and B 345 B St, Downtown ☎619/231-4343. Hard-thumping live rock music and dance club with two rooms and a hormone-fueled crowd of young bump 'n' grind enthusiasts. Despite the odor of testosterone, a high-spirited and funky place to shake your ass.

Brick by Brick 1130 Buenos Ave, Mission Bay ☎619/675-5483. Aggressively hip lounge that's one of the better known indie spots around town, attracting nationally known alternative, blues, and hard rock acts.

Canes Bar & Grill 3105 Ocean Front Walk, Mission Beach ☎858/488-1780. Mexican diner with pizza, burgers, and the rest, which also happens to host dance-music nights and a surprisingly solid array of touring rock and punk acts. Good for a bit of hardcore by the beach.

Casbah 2501 Kettner Blvd, Downtown ☎619/232-4355. Grungy joint that nevertheless hosts a solid, varying roster of blues, funk, reggae, rock, and indie bands. Local popularity contrasts with cramped environs.

Dick's Last Resort 345 4th Ave, Gaslamp District

☏619/231-9100. Old-fashioned seafood and chicken joint serving up gut-busting portions of meat to go with the fat, meaty sounds of nightly rockers with just the right snarl.

Epicentre 8450 Mira Mesa Blvd, north of Down-town ☏858/271-4000. Cozy haunt that draws a range of ages for its prime lineups, often of the punk tilt, but some nationally known rock and indie acts as well.

SOMA 3350 Sports Arena Blvd, west of Old Town ☏619/226-7662. Favorite all-ages spot for thrash-ing to punk acts or head-banging to rockers, set in a former moviehouse complex with two stages. No booze, but the frenetic atmosphere is more than enough to get you high.

Winston's Beach Club 1921 Bacon St, Ocean Beach ☏619/222-6822. A former bowling alley with rock bands most nights, along with reggae, blues, and indie, and an occasional 60s band to go with the matching decor. Close to the pier.

Pop, folk, and eclectic

Acoustic Music San Diego 4650 Mansfield St, south of Qualcomm Stadium ☏619/303-8176. Presenting performances in an actual church, a folk-and roots-music society putting on regular concerts of regional and national strummers and fiddlers.

Belly Up Tavern 143 S Cedros Ave, Solana Beach ☏858/481-9022. Mid-sized concert hall that plays host nightly to an eclectic range of live music – past acts include Buckwheat Zydeco, the Fugees, and Steel Pulse.

Humphrey's Concerts 2421 Shelter Island Drive, Point Loma ☏619/523-1010. Located near its eponymous restaurant (see p.253), this main-stream concert venue draws a range of mellow, agreeable pop, blues, folk, and lite-rock acts, often of national caliber.

Spreckels Theatre 121 Broadway, Downtown ☏619/235-9500. Former moviehouse since con-verted into elegant venue for pop and lite-rock acts, as well as comedy, world beat, jazz, and lecturers.

Jazz, blues, and reggae

Blind Melons 710 Garnet Ave, Pacific Beach ☏858/483-7844. Live blues, funk, and reggae bands play nightly to a crowd of beach and college hipsters in a spot right by the pier.

Croce's Jazz Bar 802 5th Ave, Downtown ☏619/233-4355. Classy jazz in the backroom of a pricey restaurant (see "Eating," p.252), with solid roster of traditional, cool, and smooth acts, and a jazz brunch on Sundays.

Dizzy's 344 7th Ave, Downtown ☏858/270-7467. As the name suggests, this joint is devoted to straight-up jazz and little else – literally, because the place is as spartan as they come, forcing you to focus on the music instead of chatting over cocktails.

Patrick's II 428 F St, Gaslamp District ☏619/233-3077. Fun, no-frills Irish bar with nice range of R&B, rock, jazz, and especially blues.

Performing arts and film

The **performing arts** in San Diego are represented by both provincial and national-quality venues, depending on the medium. **Theater** in town is variable, but can often be quite good, if not quite to the level of LA's scene. **Comedy**, however, rather pales in comparison here to the other major California cities, with just a few engaging options. **Classical music** and **opera**, by contrast, have much to recommend them, though prices are

Major concert venues

Coors Amphitheatre 2050 Entertainment Circle, Chula Vista ☏935/671-3600

Open Air Theatre 5500 Campanile Drive, San Diego State University ☏619/594-6947 or 619/220-TIXS

Palomar Starlight Theatre at Pala Casino Resort on Hwy 76 ☏760/510-4555.

Qualcomm Stadium 9449 Friars Rd, Mission Valley ☏619/641-3100 or 619/283-4494

San Diego Sports Arena 3500 Sports Arena Blvd, Mission Bay ☏619/224-4171 or 619/220-TIXS predictably steeper than for other performing-arts fare. Finally, San Diego has a handful of charming venues for classic, revival, and art **films**, with the first-run multiplexes thicker on the ground, devoted solely to the latest Hollywood product.

Depending on availability, **half-price tickets** for theater and classical music events for that evening can be purchased (for cash only) at Arts Tix, Broadway at Third Avenue, at Broadway Circle (Tues–Thurs 11am–6pm, Fri & Sat 10am–6pm, Sun 10am–5pm; ☎619/497-5000, ⓦwww.sandiegoperforms .com). Full-price advance sales are also available (credit cards accepted), and on Saturday, half-price tickets are issued for Sunday performances. Otherwise, tickets for all major shows can be purchased from the venue directly or through Ticketmaster (☎619/220-TIXS, ⓦwww.ticketmaster.com). The **SRH Info Hotline** (☎619/973-9269) has a list of alternative events; otherwise, check the local papers for times and venues.

Classical music and opera

The **San Diego Symphony** performs at a beautifully renovated 1929 movie palace, now called Copley Symphony Hall, Downtown at 750 B St (☎619/231-0938, ⓦwww.sandiegosymphony.com); the fare is usually Classical- and Romantic-era warhorses, with some lite-pops concerts to please the crowds. Other places where you can expect to see the odd soprano recital, violin sonata, or chamber-music concert include Escondido's California Center for the Arts, 340 N Escondido Blvd (☎760/839-4138, ⓦwww.artcenter.org), which also has jazz, comedy, and the like; and UCSD's Mandeville Center (☎858/534-3230, ⓦmandeville.ucsd.edu), which has jazz, classical, and world-music fare throughout the year. Other options include the jazz and classical music series held at the Museum of Contemporary Art's Sherwood Auditorium, 700 Prospect St in La Jolla (☎858/454-3541, ⓦwww.mcasd.org), and the chamber-oriented La Jolla Music Society (☎858/459-3728, ⓦwww.ljcms.org), which makes regular appearances at the Sherwood (among other venues) and also puts on the occasional sonata or jazz ensemble.

The **San Diego Opera**, based at the Civic Theatre, Downtown (☎619/570-1100, ⓦwww.sdopera.com), puts on the familiar big-ticket fare (Mozart, Puccini, Verdi, etc) and frequently boasts top international guest performers during its January–May season. For frothier fare, **San Diego Lyric Opera** (☎619/239-8836, ⓦwww.lyricoperasandiego.com), performs at Birch North Park Theatre, east of Hillcrest at 29th and University Avenue, presenting a bevy of toe-tapping operetta favorites from Strauss to Weill.

Theater

There's a thriving **theater** scene in San Diego, with several mid-sized venues and many smaller fringe venues putting on quality shows. Tickets are over $40 for a major production, $10–25 for a night on the fringe; the *San Diego Reader* (ⓦwww.sdreader.com) carries full listings. The main **venues** are the Lyceum Stage Theatre, 79 Horton Plaza (☎619/235-8025, ⓦwww .sandiegorep.com); the three Elizabethan-style Globe theaters in the Simon Edison Complex for the Performing Arts in Balboa Park, 1363 Old Globe Way (☎619/239-2255, ⓦwww.theglobetheatres.org); the Civic Theatre, Downtown at 202 C St (☎619/570-1100); and the La Jolla Playhouse at the Mandell Weiss Center on the UCSD campus at 2910 La Jolla Village Circle

(☎858/551-1010, ⓦwww.lajollaplayhouse.com), with the Playhouse's new complex – the Jacobs Center – opening nearby in 2005. Also up the road from San Diego is the estimable North Coast Repertory Theatre, 987 Lomas Sante Fe Drive in Solana Beach (☎858/481-1055, ⓦwww.northcoastrep. org), with raucous comedies and earnest dramas, and many local and world premier productions.

The **alternative** theatrics at Sushi Performance and Visual Art take place at rotating venues around town, but often St Cecilia's Playhouse, 1620 Sixth Ave, Downtown (☎619/235-8466, ⓦwww.sushiart.org); the shows are sometimes pretentious but rarely boring. Finally, 6th @ Penn, 3704 6th Ave, Hillcrest (☎619/688-9210, ⓦwww.sixthatpenn.com), is another solid alt-venue that puts on performances nightly – sometimes of varying quality, but often quite good and affordable.

Comedy

The **comedy** club scene in San Diego can barely be called a scene, with most jokes cracked (periodically) at venues like the Civic Theatre Downtown (see p.259) or at the restaurant and club *Humphrey's by the Bay*, in Point Loma (☎619/523-1010, ⓦwww.humphreysconcerts.com), or the Spreckels Theatre, 121 Broadway, Downtown (☎619/235-9500). If you want to catch some of the acts bound for the more glamorous venues in LA or New York, try the *Comedy Store South*, 916 Pearl St, La Jolla (☎858/454-9176, ⓦwww .thecomedystore.com/2000/lajolla.htm). For **improvisational** comedy – involving much audience participation and berserk antics – your best bets are the National Comedy Theatre, performing at the Marquis Theatre, 3717 India St, Mission Hills (☎619/295-4999, ⓦwww.nationalcomedy.com), and San Diego Theatresports, near SDSU at 6822 El Cajon Blvd (☎619/465-7469, ⓦwww.improvise.net).

Film

San Diego has many **cinemas**, most of them offering the usual Hollywood blockbusters. Scan the newspapers for full listings; admission is usually $6–9. For more adventurous programs – foreign-language films, monochrome classics, or cult favorites – look for the afternoon screenings (Mon–Sat) at the San Diego Public Library, 820 E St, Downtown, or the periodic showcases at the Museum of Photographic Arts, in Balboa Park (☎619/238-7559, ⓦwww.mopa.org). After dark, The Ken, 4061 Adams Ave (☎619/283-5909), in the Kensington area, is the most popular venue for **art** and **revival films**, changing its offerings regularly. The Hillcrest Cinemas, 3965 5th Ave (☎619/299-2100), and the La Jolla Village Cinemas, 8879 Villa La Jolla Drive (☎858/453-7831), can also be relied on to feature solid art-house fare. For an entirely different experience, the IMAX films at the Reuben H. Fleet Science Center (☎619/238-1233; see p.239) offer the kids an eye-popping selection of nature films and special-effects reels on a giant curved screen. Finally, as a nostalgic alternative, the South Bay Drive-Inn, 2170 Coronado Ave, in Imperial Beach (☎619/423-2727, ⓦwww .southbaydrivein.com), is one of the few venues of its kind left in Southern California, offering three outdoor screens showing mainstream flicks for $5 per person.

Gay and lesbian San Diego

Hillcrest is the heart of San Diego's **gay and lesbian** scene, and you can get information about it from a number of publications and resource centers, as well as the various gay bars and clubs. Although central San Diego is generally welcoming to visitors of all orientations, several hotels and bed and breakfasts are noted for their friendliness towards gay and lesbian travelers. For sun-worshippers, the most comfortable place to go is **Blacks Beach** (see p.251), north of La Jolla.

Publications and resource centers

The primary source of gay and lesbian news and upcoming events is the free weekly *Gay & Lesbian Times* (Ⓦ www.gaylesbiantimes.com), distributed through gay bars and clubs, many of the city's coffee bars, and gay-run businesses. Also useful is the newsy, free *Update* with its Etcetera insert full of personals, classifieds, and a "What's On" bulletin board. You can learn more by contacting the **Lesbian and Gay Men's Community Center**, 3916 Normal St, Hillcrest (Ⓣ 619/692-2077 or 760/744-0220, Ⓦ thecentersd.org), which has served the community for thirty years in several different locations.

Accommodation

Balboa Park Inn 3402 Park Blvd, Hillcrest Ⓣ 619/298-0823 or 1-800/938-8181, Ⓦ www .balboaparkinn.com. Elegant B&B in a Spanish Colonial building, within walking distance of Balboa Park and its museums. Fanciful, imaginative, or painfully themed rooms are the draw here; some have kitchenettes and there's also an onsite Jacuzzi. ❺–❼

Friendship Hotel 3942 8th Ave, Hillcrest Ⓣ 619/298-9898, Ⓦ www.friendshiphotel.net. One of the least expensive and most basic hotels in the area, but still offers clean rooms with TVs and refrigerators. Predominantly gay and lesbian. ❷

Harbor House Resort 642 W Hawthorn St, north of Downtown Ⓣ 619/338-9966, Ⓦ www.harbor houseresort.com. Serviceable rooms include refrigerators, ceiling fans, and some with harbor views. Also with complimentary breakfast, Jacuzzis, and sauna. ❺

Hillcrest Inn 3754 5th Ave, Hillcrest Ⓣ 619/293-7078 or 1-800/258-2280, Ⓦ www.bryx.com /hillcrestinn. Gay-oriented hotel in the heart of Hillcrest. The fairly basic, mostly non-smoking rooms all have baths, refrigerators, and microwaves. A bit drab but friendly. ❹

Park Manor Suites 525 Spruce St, near Balboa Park Ⓣ 619/291-0999 or 1-800/874-2649, Ⓦ www.parkmanorsuites.com. The tasteful rooms – all with kitchens and nice, large sitting areas – are not quite as swank as the lobby of this residential-style inn would suggest, but then prices are affordable for the area, and the atmosphere is quite relaxed. ❺

West Park Inn 1840 4th Ave Ⓣ 619/236-1600, Ⓕ 619/231-4734, Ⓦ www.westparkinn.com. Offers clean rooms, cable TV, refrigerators, and microwaves. Recently renovated, in a great location two blocks from the west entrance to Balboa Park. ❸

Bars and clubs

Bourbon Street 4612 Park Blvd, University Heights Ⓣ 619/291-0173. A chic gay crowd gathers nightly around the piano bar at this elegant New Orleans–style club north of Hillcrest, also featuring weekly karaoke and bingo, and $2–3 martinis during happy hour.

Brass Rail 3796 5th Ave, Hillcrest Ⓣ 619/298-2233. High-energy dancing every night at this longstanding neighborhood hangout, with male

go-go dancers on the weekends, periodic drag shows, and pool tables for a mellower scene.

Caliph 3102 5th Ave, Downtown Ⓣ 619/298-9495. Somewhat surreal piano bar with live music and kitschy, faux-Arabian decor, aimed mainly at an older male clientele.

Chee-Chee Club 929 Broadway, Downtown Ⓣ 619/234-4404. Comfortable, rumpled gay bar with casual atmosphere, grizzled crowd of regulars, and much less attitude than at some of the Hillcrest dance clubs.

Flicks 1017 University Ave, Hillcrest ☏619/297-2056. Popular drinking joint that plays music videos on four large screens and offers pinball, pool, and occasional comedy as well. Tuesday nights are reserved for lesbians.

Hamburger Mary's 308 University Ave, Hillcrest ☏619/491-0400. The epicenter for casual socializing and pre-party drinking in the area, a restaurant and bar which sports a mixed crowd for lunch but gets increasingly cruisey as darkness falls.

Lips 2770 5th Ave, Hillcrest ☏619/295-7900. Drag central in San Diego, with regular performances from smart-aleck queens and elegant divas alike. Signature events include drag karaoke (Mon) and bingo (Tues), and a curious Gospel Brunch as well (Sun 11am).

No. 1 Fifth Avenue 3845 5th Ave, Hillcrest ☏619/299-1911. Casual neighborhood bar with a pleasant patio. DJs play requests some nights, mainly Fifties through Seventies.

Rich's 1051 University Ave, Hillcrest ☏619/295-2195. Originally mainly a gay club, *Rich's* now attracts numerous straights for the heavy dance grooves on weekends, colorful drag queens, and "Hedonism" night on Thursday, when the hat check even accepts T-shirts and jeans. Cover charge most nights.

6 Degrees 3175 India St, south of Hillcrest ☏619/296-6789. Now that the *Flame* has gone under, this is San Diego's premier lesbian club, which offers a patio bar for casual boozing and inside dancing for a more frenetic vibe.

SRO Club 1807 5th Ave, Downtown ☏619/232-1886. Wild dancing and free-spirited atmosphere at this gay- and transgender-friendly club just a block from the south end of Balboa Park

Listings

American Express Two main branches are Downtown at 258 Broadway (☏619/234-4455, ⓦwww.americanexpress.com) and 1020 Prospect St in La Jolla (☏858/459-4161); both are open Mon–Fri 9am–5pm. Also at 7610 Hazard Center Drive in Mission Valley (Mon–Fri 9.30am–6pm, Sat 10am–3pm; ☏619/297-8101).

Amtrak based out of Santa Fe Depot, 1050 Kettner Blvd, Downtown; information at ☏619/239-9021 or 1-800/USA-RAIL.

Beach and surf conditions ☏619/221-8884

Car rental Alamo, 2942 Kettner Blvd (☏619/297-0311, ⓦwww.alamo.com); Avis, 3180 N Harbor Drive (☏619/688-5030, ⓦwww.avis.com); Bargain Auto, 3860 Rosecrans St (☏619/299-0009); Budget, 1904 Hotel Circle N (☏619/574-6975, ⓦwww.budget.com); Enterprise, 6330 Marindustry Dr (☏858/457-4909, ⓦwww.enterprise.com); Hertz, 333 W Harbor Drive (☏619/236-9771, ⓦwww.hertz.com); National, 3280 N Harbor Dr (☏619/497-6777, ⓦwww.nationalcar.com); Rent-a-Wreck, 3740 5th Ave (☏619/260-1673, ⓦwww.rentawreck.com); Thrifty, 1120 W Laurel St (☏619/515-0978, ⓦsandiego.thrifty.com).

Crime Victims Crisis Hotline ☏619/688-9200

Disabled assistance Accessible San Diego, 1010 2nd Ave, Suite 1630, San Diego 92101 (Mon–Fri 9am–4pm; ☏858/279-0704, ⓦwww.accessandiego.org); Access Center of San Diego, 1295 University Ave, Suite 10, San Diego 92013 (☏619/293-3500, TDD/293-7757, ⓦwww.accesscentersd.org).

Emergencies ☏911

Flea market The huge Kobey's Swap Meet takes place at the San Diego Sports Arena, 3500 Sports Arena Blvd (Fri–Sun 7am–3pm; 50¢ admission Fri, $1 weekends; ⓦwww.kobeyswap.com).

Hospitals For non-urgent treatment, the cheapest place is the Beach Area Family Health Center, 3705 Mission Blvd, Mission Beach (☏858/488-0644).

Information ☏411

Internet The Central Library, 820 E St, has free access, or try Web-friendly coffeehouses like *Café Crema*, 1001 Garnet Ave, Pacific Beach (☏858/273-3558, ⓦwww.cafecrema.com).

Left luggage At the Greyhound terminal and, for ticketed train and trolley travelers, at the Santa Fe Depot.

Pharmacy 24-hour pharmacy at Sharp Cabrillo Hospital, 3457 Kenyon St, between Downtown and Ocean Beach (☏619/221-3400, ⓦwww.sharp.com)

Post offices The Downtown post office is at 815 E St (Mon–Fri 8.30am–5pm; zip code 92101; ☏619/232-8612), but for poste restante (general delivery) use the main office at 2535 Midway Drive, between Downtown and Mission Beach (Mon 7am–5pm, Tues–Fri 8am–5pm, Sat 8am–4pm; zip code 92138; ☏619/758-7101 or 1-800/275-8777).

Rape Crisis Center/Hotline 4508 Mission Bay Drive ☏619/233-3088

Sports Baseball's San Diego Padres (☎619/283-4494, ⒲sandiego.padres.mlb.com) play at Petco Park, at the edge of the Gaslamp District, while football's Chargers (☎619/525-8282, ⒲www.chargers .com) play at Qualcomm Stadium in Mission Valley. Tickets are available at the stadiums' box offices.

Traveler's Aid At the airport (daily 9am–10pm; ☎619/231-7361) and at Santa Fe Railroad Depot Downtown (☎619/234-5191).
Western Union 135 Washington St, Downtown (☎619/291-8561), among other city locations (information at ☎1-800/325-6000, ⒲www .westernunion.com).

North San Diego County

Away from the city itself, **North San Diego County** runs from small bedroom communities to more rugged undeveloped country, where camping out and following forest and desert trails provide surprisingly appealing options for an area so close to a metropolis. **Transportation** around the region is straightforward. By car, I-5 skirts along the coast and I-15 runs a little deeper inland, while I-8 heads east from San Diego towards the southern part of the Anza–Borrego Desert State Park (see p.316). East of I-15, throughout the scattered rural communities, the main options involve a network of smaller, less improved roads. Public transit is no problem between San Diego and the North County coast, with the San Diego Coaster running from Downtown San Diego up to Oceanside, along with frequent Greyhound buses and Amtrak trains between LA and San Diego.

The North County coast

The towns of the **North County coast** stretch forty miles north from San Diego to the Camp Pendleton marine base, which divides the county from the outskirts of Los Angeles. As they get farther from the city and closer to military installations, the communities generally become more working class and less bourgeois, but by and large attract a mix of business commuters, beach bums, and crewcut-sporting tough guys. The main attraction is, of course, the coast itself: miles of excellent beaches with great opportunities for swimming and surfing.

Del Mar and Solana Beach

On the northern edge of the city of San Diego, the tall bluff that contains Torrey Pines State Preserve (see p.251) marks the southern boundary of **DEL MAR**, a town known mainly for its **Del Mar Racetrack**, which stages horse races between late July and early September (☎858/755-1141, ⒲www.dmtc .com), and for its **San Diego County fairgrounds**. Held for three weeks just before the racing season begins, the **Del Mar Fair** (☎858/755-1161, ⒲www .delmarfair.com) is an old-fashioned event with barbecues and livestock shows, though it's mixed with a fair amount of contemporary arts and music events, as well as cinema showings and the occasional haunted house. Otherwise, Del Mar is mainly a place to eat and shop well – at a price. Notable restaurants include *Pacifica Del Mar*, 1555 Camino Del Mar (☎858/792-0476), for its luscious combination of fresh seafood, California cuisine, and prime ocean views; and the top-notch but affordable offerings of the *Fish Market*, 640 Via de la Valle (☎858/755-2277), which also has a scrumptious oyster bar and primo location across from the racetrack. The town's train station is a short walk from its inviting beach.

SOLANA BEACH, the next town north from Del Mar, has some striking oceanside views from Solana Beach County Park and makes a reasonable place for an overnight stop. Standard-issue motels line the coastal road, and there's even some decent entertainment – the North Coast Repertory Theatre is up here (see p.260), as is the *Belly Up Tavern*, 143 S Cedros Ave (☎858/481-9022), one of the major mid-sized music venues in the area (see "Live music venues," p.258). For food, make sure to drop in on *Nobu*, 315 S Coast Hwy (☎858/755-7787), a singular spot for sushi and sashimi in a stretch dominated by more conventional seafood diners; and *Pizza Nova*, 945 Lomas Santa Fe Drive (☎858/259-0666), a North Coast outpost of the excellent regional chain. If you're driving, take a quick, four-mile detour inland along Hwy-8, passing the rolling town of **Fairbanks Ranch** (built by the film star Douglas Fairbanks Jr), to **Rancho Santa Fe**, a small but rich community with a distinctive Spanish architectural flavor from the 1920s and 1930s.

Encinitas and Leucadia

The major flower-growing center of **ENCINITAS** is at its best during the spring, when its blooms of floral color are most radiant. It's no surprise that an Indian guru chose the town as the headquarters of the Self-Realization Fellowship, near Sea Cliff Roadside Park, a popular surfing beach dubbed "Swami's" by the locals. The fellowship's serene **Meditation Gardens**, around the corner at 215 K St (Mon–Sat 9am–5pm; free; ☎760/753-1811, ⓦwww .yogananda-srf.org), are open to all, and nearby are the similarly relaxing **Quail Botanical Gardens**, 230 Quail Gardens Drive (daily 9am–5pm; $8; ☎760/436-3036, ⓦwww.qbgardens.com), rich with bamboo groves, variously themed gardens, and a pocket rainforest. Also compelling is **San Elijo Lagoon Ecological Reserve**, 2710 Manchester Ave (☎760/436-3944, ⓦwww .sanelijo.org), one of the biggest remaining coastal wetlands in the state, some 900 acres rich with endemic plants, fish, and birds, which you can explore on five miles of hiking trails. For more local information, call at the **visitor center**, 138 Encinitas Blvd (Mon–Fri 9am–5pm, Sat & Sun 10am–2pm; ☎760/753-6041, ⓦwww.encinitaschamber.org).

Encinitas and the adjoining community of **LEUCADIA**, three miles to the north, offer reasonably priced **accommodation**, such as the *Moonlight Beach Motel*, 233 2nd St, Encinitas (☎760/753-0623 or 1-800/323-1259; ❸), nicely located for beach access with kitchenettes in all rooms; and the *Ocean Inn*, 1444 N Coast Hwy, Encinitas (☎1-800/546-1598, ⓦwww.hoteloceaninn .com; ❹–❻), whose rather basic rooms do feature kitchenettes, microwaves, and fridges, and many have views of the ocean. Otherwise, there's the landscaped **campground** at San Elijo Beach State Park ($18; ☎1-800/444-7275, ⓦwww .reserveamerica.com), near **Cardiff-by-the-Sea** just to the south, whose name – the whim of its founder's British wife, which also explains the presence of Manchester and Birmingham avenues – is its only distinguishing feature. **Dining** options in the towns consist of the usual seafood eateries along the highway and a slew of basic breakfast-and-lunch diners; what stands out are places such as *I Trulli Trattoria*, 830 S Coast Hwy, Encinitas (☎760/943-6800), California-styled Italian cuisine with fresh and trendy ingredients jazzing up pizza and pasta dishes; and *Vigilucci's*, 505 S Coast Hwy, Encinitas (☎760/942-

7332), and 1933 San Elijo Ave, Cardiff (☎760/634-2334), another solid Italian entry with more straightforward pizza, pasta, and seafood, but still quite good.

Carlsbad

Surfers comprise the main visitors to **South Carlsbad State Beach** (with a busy cliff-top campground for RVs only; $12–18, day parking $5; ☎760/438-3143 or ☎1-800/444-7275, ⓦwww.reserveamerica.com), which also features swimming, fishing, and scuba diving. The beach marks the edge of **CARLSBAD**, whose cutesy, pseudo-Teutonic architecture derives from the early-1880s belief that water from a local spring had the same invigorating qualities as the waters of Karlsbad, a spa town in Bohemia (now part of the Czech Republic). "Carlsbad" thus became a health resort, promoted by pioneer-turned-entrepreneur John Frazier, whose bronze image overlooks the (now dry) original springs (near Carlsbad Blvd and Carlsbad Village Drive). The town's **visitor center**, 5934 Priestly Drive (Mon–Fri 9am–5pm, Sat 10am–4pm, Sun 10am–3pm; ☎760/434-6093 or 1-800/227-5722, ⓦwww.carlsbad.org), offers a look at this curious local history. Otherwise, the most popular attraction in Carlsbad these days is **Legoland California** (1 Lego Drive, exit Cannon Road off of I-5; $44, kids $37, parking $8; ☎760/918-5346, ⓦwww.legoland.com), where kids are encouraged to climb on larger-than-life Lego bricks, make their way through colorful mazes, ride the Coastersaurus rollercoaster, operate miniature cars and boats, and view assorted places built on a miniscule scale – among them Cape Canaveral, New Orleans, and Washington, DC.

Other than the campground, one of the better deals for **accommodation** is the *Surf Motel Carlsbad*, 3136 Carlsbad Blvd (☎760/729-7961, ⓦwww .surfmotelcarlsbad.com; ❹), whose renovated rooms offer continental breakfast, refrigerators, microwaves, and some kitchenettes. Good places to **eat** include *Pollos Maria*, 3055 Harding St (☎760/729-4858), for fast, tasty Mexican food; and *The Armenian Café*, 3126 Carlsbad Blvd (☎760/720-2233), where the American and Middle Eastern dishes are presented at very affordable prices. To really get into the spirit of the town, though, and stuff your ribs like you mean it, check out *Tip Top Meats*, 6118 Paseo del Norte (☎760/438-2620), a butchery and deli whose hefty German fare features the likes of bratwurst, stuffed cabbage, and smoked Polish sausages.

Oceanside

The most northerly town on the coast of San Diego County, **OCEANSIDE**, five miles north of Carlsbad, is dominated by the huge **Camp Pendleton** marine base, though its downtown is charming and its beaches are beautiful. It's also a major transit center (Amtrak, Greyhound, the Coaster, and Metrolink trains to LA all pass through) and the easiest place from which to reach Mission San Luis Rey (see p.266).

The town's prime attractions include the lagoon-centered **Buena Vista Audubon Nature Center**, 2202 S Coast Hwy (Tues–Sat 10am–4pm, Sun 1–4pm; free; ☎760/439-BIRD, ⓦwww.bvaudubon.org), especially good for spotting grebes, terns, coots, and pelicans, and for relaxing walks; the **California Surf Museum**, 223 N Coast Hwy (daily 10am–4pm; free; ☎760/721-6876, ⓦwww.surfmuseum.org), with displays on some of the top local surfers and boards that tackled the most wicked breaks; and the **Oceanside Museum of Art**, 704 Pier View Way (Tues–Sat 10am–4pm, Sun 1–4pm; $5; ☎760/721-2787, ⓦoma-online.org), housed in a spartan but elegant Irving Gill design from the early twentieth century, with a fine range of contemporary art from glassworks to photography to multimedia, typically shown in rotating exhibits during the year.

If you find yourself **staying** here, the *Beechwood Motel*, 210 Surfrider St (☎760/722-3866; ❷), is one of several decent motels in town. For **eating**, the *Hill Street Coffee House*, 524 S Coast Hwy (☎760/966-0985), is a rare worthwhile choice amid the fast-food joints, an old Victorian home offering great coffee, cakes, sandwiches, and salads, and weekend live music; and the classic *101 Café*, 631 S Coast Hwy (☎760/722-5220), is the town's oldest eatery and long a fixture for its 1950s decor and American diner fare.

Mission San Luis Rey and around

Four miles inland from Oceanside along Hwy-76 and accessible on local bus #313, **MISSION SAN LUIS REY**, 4050 Mission Ave (daily 10am–4.30pm; $5; ⓦwww.sanluisrey.org), founded in 1798 by Padre Laséun, was the largest of the California missions and once the center for three thousand Native American converts. Franciscan monks still inhabit the mission, and there's a **museum** and a serene candle-lit **chapel**. Even if you don't go inside, look around the foundations of the guards' barracks immediately outside the main building and, across the road, the remains of the mission's ornate **sunken gardens** (daily 10am–4.30pm; free), once *lavanderías*, where the mission's inhabitants did their washing.

Beyond the mission, push on another four miles to **Guajome County Park** (9.30am to an hour before dusk; $4 per vehicle, camping $18), whose centerpiece is a twenty-room adobe **rancho**, 2210 N Santa Fe Ave (guided tours Sat & Sun 11am, 12.30pm & 2pm; $2; ☎760/724-4082), erected in the mid-nineteenth century for newlyweds Cave Couts and Ysidora Bandini, socialites who later entertained celebrities like Helen Hunt Jackson – who, according to legend, based the title character of *Ramona*, her sentimental tale of Indian life in the mission era, on Ysidora's maid. After Couts' death in 1874, Ysidora tried to maintain the place but over the years it became dilapidated, until it was finally bought and restored by the county.

Hwy-76 continues inland to Mission San Antonio de Pala and Palomar Observatory (see p.268). Along the coast beyond Oceanside, the US military keeps its territory relatively undeveloped, creating a vivid impression of how stark the land was before commercialization took hold. The uncluttered **beach**, around the San Onofre Nuclear Plant, is popular with surfers, thanks to its slow-rolling, longboard-friendly waves, and very unpopular with environmentalists, who have been trying for decades to get the plant – built near a tectonic fault – shut down for good.

The North County inland

Unlike the coast, the **North County inland** has no sizeable towns and is mostly given over to farming, its terrain featuring dense forests, deep valleys, and mile-high mountain ranges. Besides a few reminders of the ancient indigenous cultures, remnants from the mission era, and a few tiny settlements – some of which may consume an hour or so of your time – it's best to make for the area's state parks and enjoy some leisurely countryside walks, or venture further east to the dramatic Anza-Borrego Desert (see p.316).

Escondido and around

About forty miles north of San Diego on I-15, and accessible via bus #20 from Downtown (connecting with bus #382 or #384), the little burg of **ESCONDIDO** is definitely worth a look for its **Heritage Walk** in Grape Day Park, offering a glimpse of several restored Victorian buildings (Thurs–Sat 1–4pm; free) and a 1925 railroad car with an elaborate scale model of the train that once linked Escondido to Oceanside, as well as an old-fashioned blacksmith shop, rustic barn, and windmill, and antique train depot. For more information, check out the **museum** devoted to the walk, 321 N Broadway (Thurs–Sat 1–4pm; $3; ☎760/743-8207). Nearby, the **California Center for the Arts**, 340 N Escondido Blvd (Tues–Sat 10am–4pm, Sun 1–4pm; $5; ⓦwww.artcenter.org), features a surprisingly good contemporary art museum, showcasing a range of traditional media as well as avant-garde video-art exhibitions, and two theaters that present comedy and dance performances, along with jazz, classical, and world music offerings. The other big draw is the new branch of the **Mingei International Museum** (based in Balboa Park; see p.238), at 155 W Grand Ave (Tues–Sat 10am–4pm; $5; ⓦwww.mingei.org), which displays a broad array of folk art, encompassing native artifacts, handcrafted art furniture, origami, woven garments, and ceremonial clothing, and just about anything else you can imagine. Finally, no trip to Escondido would be complete without a stop at the eye-opening **Queen Califia's Magical Circle**, Bear Valley Parkway at Mary Lane, in Kit Carson Park (daily dawn–dusk; free; ⓦwww.queencalifia.org), Niki de Saint Phalle's bizarre, strangely delightful art garden based around nine of her more fanciful mosaic sculptures, including such oddments as hissing snakeheads and gilded humans riding multicolored birds. The comprehensive **visitor center**, 360 N Escondido Blvd (Mon–Fri 9am–5pm, Sat 10am–3pm; ☎760/745-4741 or 1-800/848-3336, ⓦwww.sandiegonorth.com), provides information for the entire North County area.

Five miles south of Escondido amid stunning scenery, the **Orfila Winery**, 13455 San Pasqual Valley Rd (daily 10am–6pm; ⓦwww.orfila.com), offers wine tastings produced by a former Napa Valley vintner. Eight miles north of town off I-15 (no public transit) is Escondido's most renowned – or depressing – attraction, the **Lawrence Welk Resort**, 8860 Lawrence Welk Drive (☎760/749-3000 or 1-800/932-9355, ⓦwww.welkresort.com), a thousand-acre vacation complex of golf courses, guest villas, and the Welk Dinner Theater. Rising from accordion-playing unknown to musical juggernaut, TV bandleader Welk was the inventor of "champagne music" – basically waltzes and polkas with a touch of sanitized swing. Displayed around the theater lobby, the Welk hagiography is both fascinating and disturbing, and is in any case much less filling than the cheap lunch buffet laid out in the nearby restaurant.

The Welk Resort notwithstanding, Escondido is not really the ideal place to **stay**, with only a few reasonable options of the chain-motel variety. One exception is the pleasant *Zosa Gardens*, 9381 W Lilac Rd (☎760/723-9093, ⓦwww.zosagardens.com; ⑥–⑧), a bed and breakfast set in a replica Spanish hacienda on 22 acres, with thirteen somewhat precious rooms and onsite pool, Jacuzzi, and abundance of surrounding flowers and greenery. For **dining**, the *150 Grand Café*, 150 W Grand Ave (☎760/738-6868), is one of the bigger names in town for its succulent California cuisine, while the *Brigantine Escondido*, 421 W Felicita St (☎760/743-4718), doles out good, if pricey, surf 'n turf and has a good oyster bar, too.

North from Escondido

Hwy-S6 leads fifteen miles north from Escondido to **Mission San Antonio de Pala** (Wed–Sun 6am–6pm; donation; ℡760/742-3317), near the junction of Hwy-76 from Oceanside. Built as an outpost of Mission San Luis Rey in 1816, the mission lay in ruins until the Cupa Indians were ousted from their tribal home at the turn of the twentieth century (to make way for Warner Hot Springs) and moved to this site, where the mission was revived to serve as their church. Although the current buildings are just replicas of the originals, they do offer an eerie atmosphere, with an evocative cemetery, lovely gardens, and a single-room **museum**, which contains artifacts created by the Pala and dating back to the days of the original mission. There's also a small no-frills **campground** opposite the mission.

The enormous **Cleveland National Forest** (℡760/788-0250, ⓦwww.r5.fs.fed.us/cleveland), east from the mission on Hwy-76, is home to a good number of state and federal **campgrounds** and stretching south almost to the Mexican border. Less hearty backpackers tend to prefer the 1900-acre **Palomar Mountain State Park** (℡760/742-3462, ⓦwww.palomar.statepark.org), on Hwy-S7, for its cooler, higher altitude (some parts rise above 5000ft) and easy hiking trails. You can camp at the Doane Valley campground (℡1-800/444-7275, ⓦwww.reserveamerica.com) and pick up supplies from Palomar Mountain General Store at the junction of routes S6 and S7. Eight miles east of the park sits the two-hundred-inch Hale telescope of Cal Tech's **Palomar Observatory** on Hwy-S6 (daily 9am–4pm; free; ⓦwww.astro.caltech.edu/palomarpublic), capable of seeing a billion light years into the cosmos. As a visitor, it's not possible to view the distant galaxies directly, though you can look in on the observatory's impressive collection of deep-space photographs taken with the powerful lens.

East from Escondido

Ten miles east of Escondido on Hwy-78 (bus #307; Mon–Sat) and thirty miles north of San Diego (bus #878 or #879 from Grossmont Center; Tues–Sat), the San Diego Zoo's **San Diego Wild Animal Park**, 15500 San Pasqual Valley Rd (daily 9am–4pm, summer closes at 8pm; $26.50, kids $19.50, combined ticket with San Diego Zoo $56, parking $6; ⓦwww.sandiegozoo.org/wap), is the major tourist attraction in the area, a 2100-acre enclosure featuring a sizeable tropical-bird aviary, mock African

---

The North East Rural Bus System

The only daily bus service through sparsely populated northeastern San Diego County is the reliable but infrequent **North East Rural Bus System** (℡760/767-4287; calls answered daily 7am–noon and 2pm–5pm) that links San Diego with Escondido, Ramona, Santa Ysabel, Julian, and the Anza-Borrego Desert (see p.316). The departure point in San Diego is the Grossmont Center near El Cajon, roughly ten miles east of Downtown (accessed via city bus #15). Make sure to phone at least a day in advance to check schedules – especially if you want to be picked up from Cuyamaca State Park. Board the buses either at marked stops or, where there are none, simply flag the vehicle down. A consolation for the scarcity of buses are the low **fares**, typically $3. Bicycles are carried free of charge but, again, you must reserve in advance.

bush and Kilimanjaro hiking trail, elephant rides, and various films and exhibitions. The steep admission fee includes a fifty-minute ride on the **Wgasa Bush Line Monorail**, which skirts through the outer reaches of the park, where the animals – including lions, tigers, cheetahs, deer, and monkeys – roam about for your amusement. More historically minded visitors may, however, prefer a stop at the **San Pasqual Battlefield**, two miles away at 15808 San Pasqual Valley Rd (Sat & Sun 10am–5pm; free; ☎760/737-2201), whose visitor center provides the details of this 1846 battle in the Mexican–American War; an outlying historic trail also offers information on the region's ecosystem and native cultures predating the arrival of white colonists.

The terrain becomes increasingly sparse as you press further east along Hwy-78 into a region that's difficult to access without a car (see box opposite). If you're coming this way directly from San Diego, use Hwy-67 and join Hwy-78 at Ramona, eighteen miles from Escondido, and continue east for sixteen miles to **Santa Ysabel**. While unexceptional, this tiny crossroads is enlivened by **Dudley's Bakery**, 30218 Hwy-78, just before the junction with Hwy-79 (Wed–Sun 8am–5pm; ☎760/225-3348, ⓦwww.dudleysbakery.com), famous for its home-baked breads and pastries – the date, nut, and raisin loaf for one – at giveaway prices, and the small **Mission Santa Ysabel**, a mile and a half north of town at 23013 Hwy-79 (winter 8am–4pm; summer 8am–5.30pm; donation suggested; ☎760/765-0810), a 1924 replacement of an 1818 original structure. Sitting in moody isolation, the mission has a small chapel and, around the side, a one-room **museum** detailing the history of the site. Outside is an Indian burial ground, and the church continues to serve several local Native American communities.

Julian and around

Seven miles southeast of Santa Ysabel on Hwy-78A, the hamlet of **JULIAN** was amazingly once the second-biggest town in the San Diego area, thanks to an 1869 gold discovery here. Its population declined after that, and it faced a severe crisis in October 2003 when the devastating **Cedar wildfire** burned down much of the surrounding forest. Amazingly, the town itself was spared, thanks to some heroic, white-knuckle fire-fighting efforts – though some Californians mistakenly assume that the place was wiped out. Thus, business has been slow and many sites and retailers have had sparse crowds since then. Still, the town's formidable cider and apple pies can draw a fair crowd of weekend visitors, and at an elevation of 4000ft, this town provides a temperate base from which to make forays into the Anza-Borrego Desert (see p.316), less than ten miles to the east.

With its quaint buildings and rustic charm, Julian's appeal centers on its Main Street. For **accommodation**, the visitor center (see p.270) has details of the town's many appealing **B&Bs**. Among these, the *Julian Gold Rush Hotel*, 2032 Main St (☎760/765-0201 or 1-800/734-5854, ⓦwww .julianhotel.com; ❺), is the oldest functioning hotel in the state, opened in 1897 by a freed slave; rates include afternoon tea and a full breakfast. The *Julian Lodge*, 2720 C St (☎760/765-1420 or 1-800/542-1420, ⓦwww .julianlodge.com; ❺), is only a replica of a historic hotel, but has a similar country atmosphere, offering a buffet-style continental breakfast. **Eating** options include the *Julian Café*, 2112 Main St (☎760/765-2712), for the best old-time atmosphere and meals, including apple pie; *Bailey Woodpit Barbecue*, 2307 Main St (☎760/765-3757), featuring fine grilled meat served

fall-off-the-bone tender; and the *Julian Pie Company*, 2225 Main St
(☎760/765-2449, ⓦwww.julianpie.com), with three kinds of apple pies, and
dozens of wonderful fruit-pie combinations.

Julian has numerous old buildings in various states of preservation (the
majority saved from the wildfires). The most notable include the Gold
Rush–era mining equipment, antique buggies, stuffed animals, and assorted
Victoriana of the **Julian Pioneer Museum**, 2811 Washington St (April–
Nov Sat & Sun 10am–4pm; donation; ☎760/765-0227), and the creaky old
gold mine of the **Eagle Peak Mining Company**, at the end of C Street
(daily 10am–2pm; $8; ☎760/735-0036), where hour-long tours give a sense
of the subterranean perils faced by the town's early workers. To get a sense
of the full scope of history on display, drop by the **visitor center**, housed in
the hundred-year-old **Julian Town Hall**, 2129 Main St (daily 10am–4pm;
☎760/765-1857, ⓦwww.julianca.com), which has the usual photos and
displays, and offers a walking-tour guide of the local highlights.

North of Julian on Farmer Road, the **Volcan Mountain Wilderness
Preserve** (open 24hr; free; ☎760/765-2300, ⓦwww.volcanmt.org) also
makes for an interesting visit, whether on self-guided hikes or monthly guided
tours, with short trails passing through orchards, oak groves, and manzanitas,
leading to an excellent viewpoint of the area. For a natural experience of
a very different kind, visit the **California Wolf Center**, four miles south
of Julian at 18457 Hwy-79 ($8; by reservation only at ☎619/234-WOLF,
ⓦwww.californiawolfcenter.org), whose Saturday programs (at 2pm) provide
an introduction to all things lupine, giving you a 90min look at the steely-eyed
creatures in their packs and discussing the need and strategy to reintroduce
them to the wild.

Cuyamaca Rancho State Park

No area of San Diego County was more devastated by the autumn 2003
wildfires than the oaks, willows, sycamores, and pines of **CUYAMACA
RANCHO STATE PARK** (☎760/765-0755, ⓦwww.cuyamaca.statepark
.org), nine miles south of Julian and nine miles east of I-8 along Hwy-
79. From its lush subalpine meadows to stark mountain peaks, most of
the park's 25,000 acres, including its wilderness area, campgrounds, and
hundreds of miles of hiking trails, were damaged. In the year since then, an
army of volunteers has undertook the slow work of rebuilding the park's
facilities and reconstructing its trails. Beginning in the summer of 2004,
up to thirty percent of the trails have been reopened, along with Green
Valley **campground** ($5 day-use, $12–15 overnight). Pick up information
and maps from **park headquarters** (Mon–Fri 8am–5pm; general info
☎760/765-0755, park reconstruction ☎760/765-3020, ⓦwww.cuyamaca
.statepark.org), sixteen miles south of Julian, beside Hwy-79 in the heart
of the park. Make sure to visit the park's website or call its access numbers
before you come, though. With such an impressive amount of work in
store, it's unclear what may be open or closed in the coming years, and
at what price. Provided it's open when you come, the excellent **museum**
(Mon–Fri 10am–4pm, Sat & Sun 10am–2pm; free; ☎760/765-0755), in
the park headquarters, offers a good historical backdrop on how the local
Kumeyaay natives resisted Spanish attempts to cut down the area's forests,
strongly fought the arrival of white American settlers, and were one of the
last groups forced onto reservations.

Northern Baja California

Paradoxically, **NORTHERN BAJA CALIFORNIA** is one of the least culturally interesting areas in Mexico, but one of its most visited areas – a region where twenty million people annually cross the border (often stopping in Tijuana), most of them Californians and tourists on day-long shopping jags for blankets, pottery, cigarettes, tequila, dentistry, car repair, and even pharmaceutical drugs (see box, p.274). Since everything is lower-priced in Baja California than in the US (though more expensive than in the rest of Mexico), all of it is hawked with great vigor. **Tijuana** is obviously the main stop, for all of the above reasons, but coastal towns like **Rosarito** and **Ensenada** have their allure, too, for gringo visitors, with rolling beaches and plenty of freewheeling bars, diners, and other tourist enclaves in which to spend plenty of dollars.

Tijuana

What's most dramatic about **TIJUANA** ("tee-WAH-na") for first-time arrivals is the abrupt realization of the vast economic gulf separating the two countries. Crossing the **frontera**, or border, takes you past beggars crouched in corners and children scuffling for loose change thrown by tourists. It's both depressing and revealing, yet for regular visitors, it's a shock that soon fades. Tijuana is, in fact, one of the wealthiest Mexican cities, thanks to the influx of well-heeled residents from Mexico City and the large number of multinationals who operate **maquiladoras** (factories) here to get a cheaper workforce.

Keep in mind that while Tijuana can be an intriguing day-trip from San Diego, it's not typical Mexico, and if you want a proper taste of the country you'd do well to hurry on through. Things are much safer these days than decades ago when Tijuana lived up to its rough border-town image. Then, prostitution was rife and the streets extremely creepy after dark; these days the red-light area is limited to the easily avoided blocks around the junction of Avenida Artícula and Mutualismo. And while there's always a random incident of drunken frat-boys getting beaten and their wallets lifted after attending a grungy strip club, visitors with less taste for debauchery will find little danger in most parts of town.

Getting there

Getting to Tijuana from San Diego is straightforward enough. The San Diego Trolley's Blue Line (see p.225) ends its route close to the elevated concrete walkway which leads over the border, as does bus #932 from the Santa Fe Depot in Downtown San Diego. Though traffic and insurance problems make **public transportation** a better option, if you do decide to drive, make sure you invest in auto **insurance**, which you can procure for a nominal fee in San Ysidro (see p.276).

Crossing into Mexico, **border formalities** are minimal: simply walk through a turnstile and you're there. Customs and immigration checks are only carried out twenty miles or so inside the country, so you only need to be carrying a

Currency and information in Tijuana

Dollars are accepted as readily as pesos everywhere in Tijuana, but although you can **change money** at any of the banks along Avenida Revolución or at the **casas de cambio** on both sides of the border, it's only worth doing so if you're traveling further into Mexico. That said, you'll get marginally better prices if you do pay in pesos. Bánamex and the *casas de cambio* will also change travelers' checks.

To get more **information** on the city, contact the **Tijuana Tourism Board** (☎1-888/775-2417, ⓦwww.seetijuana.com), which can provide suggested itineraries, maps, and assorted material on some of the better places to stay, eat, and shop, along with the city's major attractions and lesser-known curiosities.

Mexican Tourist Card (and pay about $20) if you're going further south than Ensenada or staying in the country for more than 72 hours. Cards are available from any Mexican consulate in the US – the one in San Diego is Downtown at 1549 India St (Mon–Fri 8am–1pm; ☎619/231-8414, ⓦconsulmexsd.org) – and also at the Mexican customs office just inside the Tijuana side of the border. When returning to the US, however, the formalities are very stringent (see Basics, p.36), and even if you've just traveled down for the day, you'll need to satisfy rigorous entry requirements.

Accommodation

If you do want to stay overnight, Tijuana's **accommodation** options are fairly good, if basic. You'll spend much less here for a **hotel** room than you would north of the border, and many passable lodgings can be found close to the central streets. **Downtown** has a clutch of unexceptional spots, with the occasional worthwhile hotel here and there, while larger **resorts** are often scattered a few miles away from the central city.

Camino Real Tijuana Paseo de los Héroes 10305 ☎664/633-4000 or 1-800/7-CAMINO, ⓦwww.caminoreal.com/tijuana. A very nice and modern choice with plush rooms and two restaurants and bars. ❻

Cesar's Avenida Revolución 1079 ☎664/685-1606. Simple rooms with on-site cafeteria and pharmacy located Downtown. ❸

Corona Plaza Agua Caliente 1426 ☎664/681-8131. Serviceable choice with about a hundred plain rooms and restaurant, bar, spa, and pool. ❹

Fiesta Inn Tijuana Paseo de los Héroes 18818 ☎1-888/848-2928, ⓦwww.fiestainn.com. Located close to the border, with a good selection of rooms and a handful of nicer suites, both offering amenities like computer hook-ups, satellite TV, spa, and pool facilities. ❺

Grand Hotel Tijuana Agua Caliente 4500 ☎1-866/GRAND-TJ, ⓦwww.grandhoteltij.com.mx. One of the more prominent hotels in the area, housed in a pair of sleek towers two miles from the border, featuring gym, Jacuzzi, and elegant rooms and suites. ❻

Pueblo Amigo Paseo del Centenario 9211 ☎1-800/386-6985, ⓦwww.hotelpuebloamigo.com. Sleek modern complex with simple, tasteful rooms and suites, and on-site restaurant and bar, in a central location between the border and Zona Rio. ❺

La Villa de Zaragoza Avenida Madero 1120, between calles 7 and 8 ☎664/685-1837, ⓦwww.hotellavilla.biz. A good bargain, with clean rooms, a/c, and cable TV, in a fairly central location. ❸

The Town

The main streets and shopping areas in Tijuana are a few blocks west from the border in **Downtown**, where the major thoroughfare is **Avenida Revolución**, lined with street vendors, hustlers, and various shopping emporia, where you can

DOWNTOWN TIJUANA

SAN YSIDRO

Border Crossing

San Diego Trolley

USA

Greyhound Station

Pedestrian Crossing

INTERNATIONAL BORDER

MEXICO

BAJA CALIFORNIA

COAHUILA

NIÑOS HEROES

INTERNACIONAL

Market

Cathedral

Pedestrian Walkway

Central Vieja (Old Bus Station)

Footbridge

Viva Tijuana

Rio Tijuana

AV. PADRE KINO

Mexitlán

CONSTITUCION

4TH

5TH

6TH

7TH

8TH

9TH

10TH

MADERO

NEGRETE

OCAMPO

PTO. RICO

BLVD. SANCHEZ TABOADA

Pueblo Amigo

VIA ORIENTE

VIA PONIENTE

PASEO DE LOS HEROES

Palacio Fronton

Sanborn's

ACCOMMODATION

Camino Real Tijuana	F
Cesar's	B
Corona Plaza	D
Fiesta Inn Tijuana	G
Grand Hotel Tijuana	E
La Villa de Zaragoza	C
Pueblo Amigo	A

Centro Cultural

INDEPENDENCIA

Mercado Hidalgo

0   250 yds

N

▼ Post Office   **D**, **E**, **F**, Rosarito, ▼ Ensenada & **G**   Plaza Zapato ▼

Airport ►

pick up anything from a handwoven blanket to a pair of mounted bull horns to a creepy black-velvet painting for just a few bucks – even cheaper if you bargain for it. Stroll up and down for a while to get the mood and then retire to one of the plentiful bars and watch the tourists knocking back gallons of margaritas (the bigger bars charge $3 for a large one, $2 for a tequila shot, and about $1–2 for a beer). At night, the action mostly consists of drunken American and Mexican clubkids pounding the flesh in funky discos and rowdy rock'n'roll bars.

As a break from shopping or drinking, visit the **Centro Cultural**, or CECUT (daily 9am–8pm; 20 pesos or $2; ☏664/684-1111, ⓦwww.cecut.gob .mx), poised like a huge alien golf ball amid the office towers on the corner of Paseo de los Héroes y Mina and Avenida Independencia, in the Rio Tijuana area. The museum's exhibits give vivid accounts of Mexico's history and culture, along with the history and peoples of the California region, baja and alta; **films** in the Omnimax Theater ($5, including museum admission) focus on Mexican landscapes and cityscapes. Nearby, on Independencia at Avenida Taboada, is the **Mercado Hidalgo**, the city market, a freewheeling, colorful affair featuring everything from produce to piñatas, with a nice selection of chilis, chocolates, and spices, too. Also worth a visit is the **Plaza del Zapato**, Paseo de los Héroes at Plaza Río Tijuana, a tremendous shoe market where you can pick up anything from a pair of kick-ass boots to genteel loafers for much cheaper than in the States.

If you're really intrigued by the spectacle that is Tijuana, other notable attractions include **Mexitlán**, Avenida Ocampo between calles 2 and 3 (Wed–Sun 10am–5pm; $4), a miniature Mexican theme park with models of famous Mexican buildings, such as Baroque cathedrals and Mayan pyramids; and lively matches of **jai alai** – a Basque game similar to handball – at the Moorish-style Palacio Fronton on Avenida Revolución at Calle 8 (Tues–Sat 8pm; $5). Other sports are also famously on view in Tijuana, though your viewing appetite may waver depending on the event; greyhound-racing is always a big deal at the **Hipodromo Caliente Race Track**, Agua Caliente and Tapachula Ave (daily 7.45pm, also Sat & Sun 2pm; ☎664/681-7300), drawing a mix of locals and tourists, while bull-fighting is an irresistible magnet for bloodsport fans, though probably a minority of most US visitors these days. To check out the gory display, visit either the **Plaza El Toreo**, Downtown off Avenida Revolución (May–Sept Sun 4pm; ☎664/686-1510, ⓦwww.bullfights.org/tijuana), or the **Bullring-by-the-Sea**, on the Pacific shore near the border (see p.246). At either spot, it will cost from $20 to $50 per person to get in for a look at the sanguine spectacle.

Eating and nightlife

As you'd expect, most of the **eating** options in Tijuana are confined to cheaper, lower-end eateries, many of them little more than street vendors selling standard

Legal drug-buying in Tijuana

One of the top tourist draws in Tijuana – attracting an estimated third of all visitors, especially seniors – is the allure of cheap **pharmaceutical drugs**, available at Mexican pharmacies for a fraction of the cost of their obscenely overpriced US equivalents. Not surprisingly, this has opened up a whole new cottage industry, for local pharmacists (especially on Avenida Revolución), many of whom will gladly supply visitors with a sizeable quantity of different drugs – from Allegra to Zoloft – without a prescription from an American doctor. Note, however, that you should take **precautions** when purchasing something so important to your health. For one, if you're headed to Tijuana on a (legal) drug-buying mission, you'll still need to find a reputable **pharmacy** that won't sell you a product which does nothing or actively harms you. You can do the research on your own before you leave, or take your health in your own hands by relying on a Mexican cabbie to take you to one he recommends. Keep in mind, though, that there have been countless rumors of shady deals between cab drivers, or organized-crime syndicates, and certain pharmacies, and just because a particular pharmacist is well known does not mean he or she is reputable. Another problem is the difficulty of returning to the US with a hefty stack of pharmaceuticals in tow. Unless you're coming back with a large amount of prescription drugs, it's unlikely you'll end up in jail, though you could be detained by a US Customs agent and asked all manner of hostile questions and subjected to prison threats and other official browbeating. To save the trouble, you can always follow the official rules and bring back no more than a **three-month supply**; while anything more is out-of-bounds, most of the border guards' attention will doubtless be focused on looking for cocaine in your trunk, rather than Xanax in your shaving kit.

Mexican fare like tacos or enchiladas — both are excellent at *Sanborn's*, Calle 8 at Avenida Revolución — while a few more upscale restaurants cater to tourists looking for a more "refined" meal in Tijuana. The best choices include spots like *Cien Anos*, 1407 Jose Maria Velazco (☎664/685-8494), which offers an odd, but savory blend of Mexican and Aztec cuisine, with some fiery chili-seafood plates and rich soups (as well as some less than appealing sauteed grubs and ants); and *La Fonda Roberto*, 2800 Cuauhtemoc Blvd (☎664/686-4687), a longstanding favorite for its exotic combinations of ingredients and inventive menu including cactus salad and pumpkin *quesadillas* — also for inexpensive prices.

Apart from eating, many come to Tijuana to experience the **nightlife** — the legal drinking age is 18. Places like *Señor Frog's*, 60 Via Oriente (☎664/682-4964), offer plenty of hedonistic, bleary-eyed memories for drunken gringos, while *Baby Rock*, Diego Rivera 1482, Zona Rio (☎664/634-2404), is a very lively spot aimed at a younger crowd. The always enticing *Rodeo Santa Fe*, on Avenida Paseo Tijuana in Pueblo Amigo Plaza, Zona Rio ($8 cover; ☎664/682-4967), is a wild "rodeo" staged indoors with Tex-Mex and Latino music, a mechanical bull, lots of cowboy gear, and, if you need a break from the cowpoke scene, a frenetic upstairs disco. Whatever the venue, keep in mind that most clubs in Tijuana enforce a no-sandals, no-jeans dress code.

Further into Mexico

As for traveling **further into Mexico**, the northwest of the country has fewer cultural attractions than the mainland, and many people head straight for Mexico City and the regions to the south. A closer option is the more southerly peninsula of **Baja California**, which has miles of fairly pristine coast and a few moderately sized cities (as well as the tourist monolith of Cabo San Lucas). The only sensible destinations within easy reach of Tijuana are **Rosarito**, a laid-back party beach, and the sizeable burg of **Ensenada**. Go any further and you'll have to get a Mexican Tourist Card and pay $20 (see p.271).

Rosarito

Forty-five minutes south of Tijuana, on buses from the Central Vieja bus terminal at First and Madero, the old coastal road reaches the sea at **ROSARITO**, which boasts one of the best-looking beaches around, although the water is often polluted. While during the week it's much more relaxing here than in Tijuana, on weekends the town has a pervasive gringo frat-house atmosphere. Surfers are drawn here from across the border for the fine waves at beaches like **Calafia**, at km 35.5, and **Popotla**, at km 33. You can rent a board at Tony's Surf Shop, Blvd Juarez 312, and the area is also popular with golfers, who frequent the Real del Mar Golf Club (☎664/631-3401), among other such establishments.

As for **accommodation**, the town's landmark is the historic *Rosarito Beach Hotel* (☎661/612-0144, ⓦwww.rosaritohtl.com; ❺–❼), to which Hollywood's Prohibition refugees fled for a little of the hard stuff in the Thirties. These days, it offers elegant suites and apartments and blander, merely adequate rooms for a wide range of prices. For a cheaper option, try *Brisas del Mar*, 22 Blvd Juarez (☎661/612-2547; ❷–❸), just across the boulevard from the ocean, offering a pool and decent rooms with TV and air conditioning — and some suites on the second floor with hot tubs as well. The *Festival Plaza*, 1207 Blvd Juarez

(☎661/612-2950, ⊛www.festivalplaza.com; ❹), is a carnivalesque pile, with clean and basic rooms and beachside casitas with hot tubs – but its most notable feature is its El Museo, or **tequila museum** (daily 4pm–midnight, Fri–Sun noon–midnight; free), where you can sample some 150 different types of the renowned agave distillate.

For **dining**, the *Festival Plaza* has copious munching, drinking, and dancing in its *Rock & Roll Taco* hangout (same contact info), and there's no shortage of taco stands and cheap restaurants in town, many specializing in seafood. The weekend bonhomie is particularly frenzied at the beach-volleyball bar *Papas and Beer*, Boulevard Juarez near the *Rosarito Beach Hotel* (☎661/612-0444), while at *El Patio*, Boulevard Juarez in the *Festival Plaza* (☎661/612-2950), you can indulge in an upmarket taste of authentic Mexican food, featuring dishes like shrimp crêpes served in a pleasant, modern atmosphere. Finally, true lovers of tacos, tortillas, and *carnitas* will enjoy a stop at *La Flor de Michoacan*, 291 Blvd Juarez (☎661/612-1858), a longstanding treasure for its Mexican staples and convivial atmosphere.

Ensenada

Venturing to **ENSENADA**, two hours south from Tijuana's Central Vieja, brings a hint of the real Mexico, though somewhat obscured by waves of tourists. Cruise ships from San Diego dock here, and on weekends the bars are packed with American party animals. The place is laid out around **Parque Revolución**, the traditional public square off Avenida Obregon, while the **fish market**, at the north end of Boulevard Costero, sells locally caught tuna, shrimp, and other fare – though the safety of eating fish caught from these waters is debatable. On Avenida Mateos, you'll find the majority of the bars, restaurants, trinket shops, and **fishing-excursion** operators. As for the town's big attractions, at the *Bodegas de Santo Tomás* winery, Miramar 666 between Calle 6 and Calle 7 (tours Mon–Sat 11am, 1pm & 3pm, Sun 11am & 1pm; $2; ☎646/174-0836), the winery itself is unremarkable, but the restaurant therein is considered one of the best in Baja for its well-prepared local staples enlivened by fresh ingredients and creative presentation. Across the street, **La Esquina de Bodegas** (daily 8am–10pm; ☎646/178-3557) is a pleasant café/gallery and wine-shop annex. The other famous site is **La Bufadora**, a natural blowhole six miles south of Ensenada, which occasionally spouts up to eighty feet, though thirty is more common. **Buses** leave roughly hourly from the Tres Cabezas park on the coast road at the bottom of Avenida Riveroll.

The pick of the **accommodation** (book at weekends) is the *San Nicolas*, Mateos at Guadalupe (☎646/176-1901; ❺), which features a range of nice rooms, pool, Jacuzzi, fishing, whale-watching trips, and sports betting. As a

---

Getting around Northern Baja

Vehicle permits are not required in Baja, but most US rental agencies don't allow their vehicles into Mexico, so you'll need to approach companies such as California Baja Rent-a-Car, 9245 Jamacha Blvd, in the San Diego suburb of Spring Valley (☎619/470-RENT or 1-888/470-RENT, ⊛www.cabaja.com), which rents cars for use throughout Baja to drivers 21 and over. With your own vehicle, make sure you get **Mexican insurance**, easily obtainable from numerous companies whose fliers are all over San Ysidro: try Instant Mexico Insurance Services, 233 Via de San Ysidro (☎619/428-4714 or 1-800/345-4701, ⊛www.instant-mex-auto-insur.com). Ultimately, though, it's probably easier to take the bus.

budget alternative, the *Hotel del Valle*, 367 Avenida Riveroll (☎646/178-2224; ❶–❷), offers clean rooms with fans, TVs, and phones, while the alluring *Las Rosas*, north of town on Hwy-1 (☎646/174-4310, ⓦwww.lasrosas.com; ❻), is an oceanfront complex with a range of elegant rooms and suites and on-site pool and spa. For **eating**, *Hussongs Cantina*, Ruiz 113 (☎646/178-3210) – famous throughout Southern California – serves Western-friendly Mexican fare and has managed to maintain its rambunctious reputation as a loud party-spot on weekends. Soak up the beer with fish tacos from vendors near the fish market, or visit *Hacienda del Charro*, Lopez Mateos 454 (☎646/178-2114), which is worth a stop for its enticing heapings of tacos, enchiladas, and rotisserie chicken.

Travel details

Trains

San Diego to: Anaheim (10 daily; 2hr); Los Angeles Downtown (10 daily; 2hr 45min to 3hr 20min); Oceanside (10 daily; 45min to 1hr); San Juan Capistrano (10 daily; 1hr 15min to 2hr); Santa Barbara (4 daily; 5hr 30min to 6hr 30min); Solana Beach (10 daily; 40 min). For more information on the "Pacific Surfliner" route, call Amtrak (☎1-800/872-7245, ⓦwww.amtrak.com); Northern California cities require multiple transfers or bus connections.

US buses

San Diego, Downtown to: Anaheim (8 daily; 2hr 30min); Long Beach (8 daily; 2hr 30min–3hr); Los Angeles Downtown (25 daily; 2hr 30 min to 3hr); Oceanside (14 daily; 50min); San Clemente (5 daily; 1hr 20min); San Francisco (7 daily; 11–13hr); Santa Barbara (8 daily; 5–7hr). For more information, call Greyhound (☎1-800/231-2222, ⓦwww.greyhound.com).

San Diego, Grossmont Center to: Julian (1 daily; 2hr); Escondido (1 daily; 1hr 30min); Ramona (1 daily; 1hr); Santa Ysabel (1 daily; 1hr 30min). For more information, call the Northeast Rural Bus System (☎760/767-4287).

International buses

San Diego to: Tijuana (8am–9pm; 48 daily; 50min). Call Mexicoach for further details (☎619/232-5049, ⓦwww.mexicoach.com).

The deserts

CHAPTER 3 # Highlights

✳ **Palm Springs Aerial Tramway** Take a break from the scorching desert and ride the cable car up to the crisp pine forests and enjoy their stupendous panoramic views. See p.296

✳ **Living Desert** See the desert flora, fauna, and culture in complete safety at this combined zoo, botanic garden, and museum in swanky Palm Desert. See p.298

✳ **Joshua Tree National Park** The celebrated national park is resplendent with its unique freaky trees, gorgeous granite boulders, and coyotes that howl in the warm night air. See p.308

✳ **Salvation Mountain** Surviving on little more than religious devotion, one man has produced his personal monument to God, a bizarrely colorful synthesis of found objects, straw bales, and paint. See p.316

✳ **Borrego Palm Canyon** An hour's stroll across the Anza-Borrego Desert brings you to one of the largest natural oases left in the United States, a dense cluster of over a thousand mopheaded fan palms beside a crisp stream. See p.318

✳ **Historic Route 66** Trace a short stretch of the renowned Mother Road in search of classic Americana, such as Roy's gas station and café in Amboy. See p.329

△ Devil's Postpile National Monument

The deserts

The **deserts** of Southern California represent only a fraction of the half a million square miles of North American desert that stretch away eastward into another four states and cross the border into Mexico in the south. Contrary to the monotonous landscape you might expect, California's deserts are a varied and ever-changing kaleidoscope, dotted with everything from harsh settlements to posh resorts. The one thing you can rely on is that, for a large part of the year, they will be uniformly hot and dry. In fact, during the hottest summer months temperatures in the deserts can reach such dangerous heights that you'd be well advised to give them a miss altogether. And don't count on rain to cool things off – rainfall in this landscape is highly irregular and a whole year's average of three or four inches may fall in a single storm.

Most of the 25 million acres that make up the desert are protected in state and national parks, but not all are entirely unspoiled. Three million acres are used by the US Government as military bases for training and weapons testing, and when explosions aren't shaking up the desert's fragile ecosystem, the region's many fans flock here to do their own damage, many on off-road vehicles.

In spite of this, most of the desert remains a wilderness, and with a little foresight could be the undisputed highlight of your trip. Occupying a quarter of the state, California's desert divides into two distinct regions: the **Colorado** or **Low Desert** in the south, stretching down to the Mexican border and east into Arizona, where it's an extension of the Sonoran Desert; and the **Mojave** or **High Desert**, which covers the south-central part of the state. The Colorado is easily reached from LA, passing through the extravagantly wealthy Coachella Valley with **Palm Springs** serving as its gateway. It's the kind of town where it helps to have a bankroll for optimum enjoyment amid the plush resorts and swanky restaurants, but summer accommodation prices are remarkably low. And despite its glossy veneer, there's no shortage of moderately priced things to do – riding the **Palm Springs Aerial Tramway** to the cool of the San Jacinto Mountains, touring a microcosm of the desert in comfort at the **Living Desert**, and taking a **Celebrity Tour** of the homes of the rich and famous.

Serious desert enthusiasts should make a beeline for **Joshua Tree National Park**, which bridges the divide between the Colorado and Mojave deserts in a vast silent area of craggy trees. Hiking during the day then camping out amid the photogenic boulder stacks with the cry of coyotes on the night air is an experience not to be missed. In contrast, the undiluted Colorado Desert of the **Imperial Valley** to the south is mostly given over to agricultural land

Lake Mead

Hoover Dam

Colorado River

Needles

Lake Havasu City

Lake Havasu

Las Vegas

MOJAVE NATIONAL PRESERVE

Mitchell Caverns

Cima Dome

Cinder Cones

95

Shoshone

Tecopa

15

Baker

ZZYX & Soda Dry Lake

Kelso Dunes

40

Death Valley Junction

373

190

127

177

Afton Canyon

DEATH VALLEY NATIONAL PARK

Furnace Creek

Fort Irwin (Army)

Calico Early Man Site

Calico Ghost Town

Segs II

Searles Lake (dry)

China Lake Naval Weapons Center

MOJAVE DESERT

Stovepipe Wells

190

Panamint Springs

Trona Pinnacles

Rainbow Basin

Barstow

Victorville

Trona

178

China Lake Naval Weapons Center

Fossil Falls

Ridgecrest

395

136

190

Lone Pine

Johannesburg

Randsburg

Borax Visitor Center

Boron

58

Saddleback Butte State Park

14

395

Edwards Air Force Base

Lancaster

Palmdale

RED ROCK CANYON STATE PARK

Tehachapi

California Poppy Reserve

14

Vasquez Rocks County Park

Tehachapi Pass

Santa Clarita

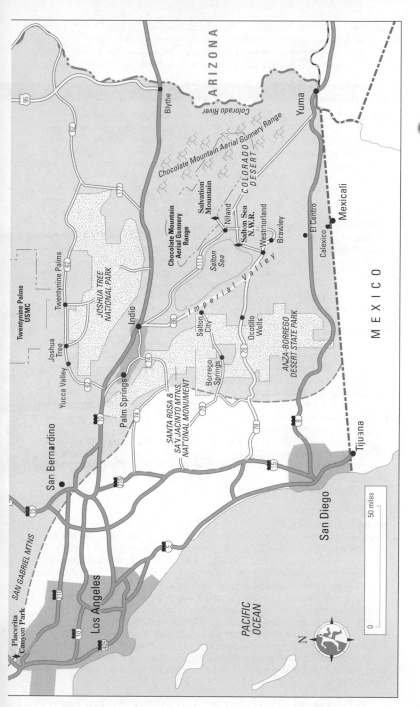

which you could pass through without realizing anyone lived there. Beyond is the **Salton Sea**, artificially created a century ago and now mostly a curiosity, though it is worth calling in at the bizarre **Salvation Mountain** and the migratory birds at the **Sonny Bono Salton Sea National Wildlife Refuge**.

Desert survival

To survive the rigors of the desert, you have to be cool in more ways than one. The desert is rarely conquered by pioneering spirit alone, and every year people die here. First and most obviously you're up against a pretty formidable **climate**. This varies from region to region, but the basic safety procedures remain the same: not only are you doing battle with incredible heat, but at high elevations at night you should be prepared for below-freezing temperatures too. Lots of visitors do come to the deserts in summer when daytime temperatures frequently exceed 120°F, but you'll appreciate the experience more if you time your desert travels during the **cooler months** from October to May when daytime temperatures range the mid-sixties and low nineties.

At any time of year, you'll stay coolest and best protected wearing loose, full-length clothing, and a wide-brimmed hat. That said, many people travel the deserts in shorts, T-shirt, and sunglasses, and get by quite happily.

Bear in mind too that while the desert may be a danger to man, man is also a danger to the desert. Smog from Los Angeles drifts quickly eastward, and you may notice patches of it obscuring vistas here. Use common sense: remove nothing from the land except your trash, and leave only footprints behind.

Driving through

Sticking to the main highways, desert travel doesn't generally pose much of a problem, and filling your water jugs and gas tank should be all the preparation you need. On steep grades, there is a chance of getting an **overheated engine**. If your car's temperature needle rises alarmingly, turn the air conditioning off and the heater on full-blast to cool the engine quickly. If this fails and the engine blows, stop with the car facing into the wind and the engine running, pour water over the radiator grille, and top up the water reservoir. Also consider taking along a windshield reflector to keep the car cool when parked.

On less well-traveled routes, surfaces may not be well maintained, and it could be a long time before anyone comes along. In these areas, be sure you have plenty of food and drink, and consider carrying an **emergency pack** with flares, a first-aid kit, matches, and a compass, a shovel, extra gas, and even a tire pump.

In an **emergency**, never leave the car: you'll be harder to find wandering around alone.

Hiking and camping

Going hiking requires much more forethought. If all you're doing is following a well-worn trail in a popular area of a national park, it is probably enough just to plan your hike for a cooler part of the day, take along a little food, and carry enough **water**. The body loses up to a gallon each day and even when you're not thirsty you are continually dehydrating and should keep drinking.

Only the well prepared can enjoy **longer hikes** in the desert with any sense of security. **Hydration** is even more important. Take two gallons of water per person per day (one is an absolute minimum), and don't save it for the walk back – drink it as you need it. Waiting for thirst, dizziness, nausea, or other signs of dehydration before doing anything can be dangerous. If you notice any of these symptoms, or feel weak and have stopped sweating, it's time to get to a doctor. Any activity in this heat can be exhausting so you also need to **eat** well, packing in the carbohydrates.

Both can be visited en route to the vast expanse of the **Anza-Borrego Desert**, the largest state park in the lower 48 states, boasting multifarious varieties of vegetation and geological quirks that can, with a little effort, be as rewarding as the better-known deserts to the north.

When hiking, try to cover most of your ground in the early morning: the midday heat is too debilitating, and you shouldn't even think about it when the mercury goes over 90°F. Almost all parks will require you to register with them – this is very wise, especially for those who are hiking alone. If you get lost, find some shade and wait. So long as you've registered, the rangers will eventually come and fetch you. In areas where registration is not required, tell somebody where you are going and your expected time of return.

In addition, you should carry an extra two days' food and water, and never go anywhere without a **map**.

In summer, **camping** ventures of more than one night are all but impossible, as you end up having to carry more water than is comfortable. In the valleys, you may also have to contend with **flash floods**, which can appear from nowhere: an innocent-looking dark cloud can turn a dry wash into a raging river. Never camp in a dry wash and don't attempt to cross flooded areas until the water has receded.

Desert wildlife

Most people's biggest fear of the desert is of encountering **poisonous creatures**. If you do, you'll be far better served by strong boots and long trousers than sport sandals and shorts. Not only do they offer some protection in case of attack, but firm footfalls send vibrations through the ground giving ample warning of your approach. Walk heavily and you're unlikely to see anything you don't want to.

Of all the **snakes** in the California desert, only the rattlesnake is poisonous. You might not be able to tell a rattler from any other kind of snake, so if in doubt, assume it is one. When it's hot, snakes lurk in shaded areas under bushes, around wood debris, old mining shafts, and piles of rocks. When it's cooler, they sun themselves out in the open, but they won't be expecting you and if disturbed may attack. While **black widow spiders** and **scorpions** are non-aggressive, they are extremely venomous and easily disturbed. A bite from any of the above is initially like a sharp pinprick, but within hours the pain becomes severe, usually accompanied by swelling and acute nausea. Forget any misconceptions you may harbor about sucking the poison out – it doesn't work and even tends to hasten the spread of venom. The best way of inhibiting the diffusion is to wrap the whole limb firmly, but not in a tourniquet, then contact a ranger or doctor as soon as possible. Do all you can to keep calm – a slower pulse rate limits the spread of the venom. Keep in mind that even if a snake does bite you, about fifty percent of the time it's a dry – or non-venomous – strike: snakes don't want to waste their venom on something too large to eat.

Tarantulas are not at all dangerous. A leg span of up to seven inches means they're pretty easy to spot, but if you're unlucky and get bitten, don't panic – cleansing with antiseptic is usually sufficient treatment once you've gotten over the initial pain.

Most **cacti** present few problems, but you should keep an eye out for the eight-foot **cholla** (pronounced "choy-uh") or jumping cholla as some are called, because of the way segments seem to jump off and attach themselves to you if you brush past. Don't use your hands to get them off, you'll just spear all your fingers; instead, use a stick or comb to flick off the largest piece and remove the remaining spines with tweezers. The large pancake pads of prickly pear cactus are also worth avoiding: as well as the larger spines they have thousands of tiny, hair-like stickers that are almost impossible to remove. You should expect a day of painful irritation before they begin to wear away. For more on the delights of desert flora and fauna, see Contexts, p.878.

Interstate 10 crosses the Colorado Desert from east to west and carries a considerable flow of traffic bound for Arizona. I-15 cuts north from I-40 at **Barstow**, often a first stop for those heading into the Mojave, where the **Mojave National Preserve** makes a rewarding natural detour en route to the unnatural neon oasis of **Las Vegas**, just across the border in Nevada (see Chapter 4, p.335).

Desert practicalities

Public transportation in the desert is poor to nonexistent: Los Angeles connects easily with the major points – Palm Springs, Barstow, Las Vegas – and the Anza-Borrego is marginally accessible from San Diego, but upon arrival you're stuck without your own vehicle. Amtrak runs two **trains** through the region. The *Southwest Chief* runs daily from LA to Chicago via San Bernardino, Victorville, Barstow, and Flagstaff, Arizona (for Thruway bus connection to the Grand Canyon), with LA departures at 6.45pm. The return train reaches LA daily at 8.20am. The *Sunset Limited* plies the southern route from LA to Orlando, Florida, with stops in Palm Springs and Tucson, Arizona. It departs LA at 10.30pm on Sunday, Wednesday, and Friday; and the return journey finishes in LA at 6.40am on the same days. For more regional public transportation information, see "Travel details," p.333.

If you do have a **car**, it will need to be in good working order. While the $500 Thunderbird you picked up in LA might be fine for the freeways, don't expect it to cope with the worst of the desert. Three major interstate highways cross the desert from east to west. I-15 cuts directly northeast through the middle of the Mojave on its way from Los Angeles to Las Vegas, passing through Barstow where I-40 cuts eastwards to the Grand Canyon. I-10 takes you from LA through the Palm Springs and Joshua Tree area, heading into southern Arizona.

Some fast, empty secondary roads can get you safely to all but the most remote areas of the desert, but be wary of using the lower-grade roads in between, which are likely to be unmaintained and are often only passable by four-wheel-drive. Other than in the Palm Springs area, **motels** in the California deserts are low in price, and you can generally budget for $40 to $50 per night. However, even if cost is no object, you'll get a greatly heightened sense of the desert experience by spending some time **camping** out.

The Colorado Desert

Despite the **Colorado Desert**'s hundreds of miles of beauty and empty highways, most visitors to the region have no intention of getting away from it all. They're heading for where it's at – **Palm Springs**, a few square miles overrun with the famous, the star-struck, the aging, and the aspirational. It is said, not completely in jest, that the average age and average temperature of Palm Springs are about the same – a steady 88. This is a town that fines homeowners who don't maintain their property to what local officials deem to be a suitable standard. However, you'll find it hard to avoid, as Palm Springs is the first stopping point east from LA on I-10. The town is the hub of the

Coachella Valley, a resort area that stretches out for miles to the east along Hwy-111. The valley's farming communities have the distinction of forming part of the most productive irrigated agricultural center in the world, growing dates, oranges, lemons, and grapefruit in vast quantities, though sadly they're steadily giving way to the condos and golf courses that comprise Palm Springs' ever-growing industry.

Fortunately you don't have to travel impossible distances to see the desert at its natural best. **Joshua Tree**, one of the most startling of California's national parks, lies less than one hour's drive east of Palm Springs, three from LA. A day-trip would give you a taste, but you really need a couple of days to fully appreciate Joshua Tree's sublime landscape, taking in the sunsets and the howl of coyotes at twilight. East of the park, towards the Colorado River and Nevada, and south towards the Mexican border, the desert is arid and uncomfortable, with only the highly saline **Salton Sea** to break the monotony. A drive in this direction is rewarded, however, by the **Anza-Borrego Desert**, southwest of Joshua Tree, whose starkly beautiful vistas are punctuated by several oases and unusual vegetation.

Palm Springs and the Coachella Valley

With its manicured golf courses, condominium complexes, and thousands of millionaires in residence, **PALM SPRINGS** does not conform to any typical image of the desert. Purpose-built for luxury and leisure, it tends to attract conspicuous consumers and comfort seekers rather than the scruffier desert rats and low-rent retirees of less geographically desirable areas. But though it may seem harder to find the natural attractions and reasonably priced essentials among the glitz, they do exist.

Palm Springs and the adjacent resort towns of the **Coachella Valley** – Cathedral City, Desert Hot Springs, Rancho Mirage, Palm Desert, Indio, Indian Wells, and La Quinta – sit in the lushest agricultural pocket of the Colorado Desert, with the massive bulk of the San Jacinto Mountains and neighboring ranges looming over its low-level buildings, casting an instantaneous and welcome shadow over the area in the late afternoon. Since Hollywood stars were spotted enjoying a bit of mineral rejuvenation out here in the 1930s, Palm Springs has taken on a celebrity status all its own, a symbol of good LA living away from the amorphous, smoggy city. In recent years it has also become a major **gay** resort (see box, p.289), with many exclusively gay – and generally expensive – hotels, bars, and restaurants.

For years, high-school kids arrived in the thousands, too, for the drunken revelry of Spring Break (around the end of March and beginning of April). Local antipathy finally persuaded the city council, under the leadership of the late Sonny Bono, to ban the annual invasion in 1993, and the inebriated youth promptly decamped east to Lake Havasu City. The alcoholically inclined still flock to the area, but not to get drunk – the **Betty Ford Center**, smack in the middle of the valley at Rancho Mirage, draws a star-studded patient list to its booze- and drug-free environment, attempting to undo a lifetime's behavioral disorders during a $16,000 month-long stay.

The town's setting is superb, surrounded by the beautiful Indian Canyons with the snow-capped **San Jacinto Mountains** behind. Meteorologists have noted changes in the humidity of the desert climate around the town, which they attribute to the moisture absorbed from the hundreds of swimming pools – the consummate condo accoutrement, and the only place you're likely to want to be during the day if you come in the hotter months. When scarce water supplies aren't being used to fill the pools or nourish the nearby orchards, each of the Coachella Valley's hundred-plus **golf courses** receives around a million gallons daily to maintain their rolling green fairways.

Palm Springs wasn't always like this. Before the wealthy settlers moved in, it was the domain of the **Cahuilla**, who lived and hunted around the San Jacinto Mountains, to escape the heat of the desert floor. They still own much of the town, and via an odd checkerboard system of land allotment, every other square mile of Palm Springs is theirs and forms part of the **Agua Caliente Indian Reservation** – a Spanish name which means "hot water," referring to the ancient mineral springs on which the town rests. The land was allocated to the tribe in the 1890s, but exact zoning was never settled until the 1940s, by which time the development of hotels and leisure complexes was well under way. The Cahuilla, finding their land built upon, were left with no option but to charge rent, a system that has made them one of the richest of the native tribes in America – and the money continues to pour in, thanks in part to revenue from their new **spa** and the **casinos** of Coachella Valley.

Arrival

Palm Springs lies 110 miles east of Los Angeles along the Hwy-111 turnoff from I-10. Arriving by **car**, you'll reach the town on North Palm Canyon Drive (Hwy-111), the main thoroughfare. Coming by **bus**, you'll alight downtown at the Greyhound terminus at 311 North Indian Canyon Drive (☎760/325-2053), linked with LA (6 daily; 3hr–3hr 30min) and Phoenix, Arizona (1 daily; 5hr 30min). You're unlikely to arrive by Amtrak **train** (ⓦwww.amtrak.com), as thrice-weekly services – from Los Angeles and Tucson, Arizona – all arrive in the middle of the night at a desolate platform three miles north of Palm Springs at North Indian Avenue, just south of I-10.

Alaska, American, Delta, Northwest, United, and a handful of regional carriers **fly** into Palm Springs International Airport, 3400 E Tahquitz Canyon Way (☎760/318-3800), where you can catch bus #21 into town. Tickets are often expensive, and if you're flying to California it is usually cheaper to fly into Los Angeles and rent a car from there.

Palm Springs now claims to have overtaken Key West as America's largest **gay resort**, with dozens of exclusively gay clothing-optional inns and hotels keeping the rainbow flag flying. With great weather almost all year round, it is hard to resist working on your tan by the pool all day while regaining your strength for another night around the clubs and bars.

The local gay press estimate that around forty percent of the town's residents are gay and you'll see evidence all over the place, but nowhere more so than along Arenas Road, near South Indian Canyon Drive, which has become something of a gay ghetto. Elsewhere businesses catering to a broader clientele are often gay run and there's a general sense that the gay and straight communities coexist happily. That said, in 2003, conservative city officials tried to shut down the White Party (see below), but the election of openly gay mayor Ron Oden, in November of that year, has brought a considerably warmer welcome.

The local tourist machine puts out a specialist version of its free semiannual brochure, the *Palm Springs Official Gay Visitors Guide*, though you'll get a better insight into the community from the free monthly *The Bottom Line* (Ⓦwww.psbottomline .com), or the *Desert Post Weekly* (also free), which has listings and discussions of current issues.

The single biggest draw is Easter weekend, when over fifteen thousand gay men flock here for **White Party** (☎1-888/777-8886, Ⓦwww.jeffreysanker.com), four days of hedonism throughout downtown Palm Springs, but centered on the *Wyndham Hotel*. It has been going since 1989 and has grown to the point where there are parties all the time (often in hotel pools). The big event, an all-nighter of epic proportions, is held Saturday at the Palm Springs Convention Center. A three-day weekend pass giving access to three dance parties and one after-party goes for around $250: get **tickets** from Ⓦwww.circuiticket.com.

Lesbians get their turn a couple of weeks earlier during what is still known as the **Dinah Shore Weekend** (☎1-888/44-DINAH). Officially it is now the LPGA Kraft Nabisco Championship golf tournament, held at Mission Hills Country Club in Rancho Mirage, where the 18th hole is named after Dinah Shore for her contribution to the game. The tournament ranks second only to the US Women's Open, but golf often plays second fiddle to the numerous hotel pool parties at what has become the nation's hottest lesbian vacation event.

Later in the year the **Palm Springs Pride** weekend (typically the first weekend in November; ☎760/416-8711, Ⓦwww.pspride.org) draws gay crowds for a couple of days of entertainment, a street parade, and more partying; and October brings the "Out on Film" **gay and lesbian film festival**.

Practicalities

Such is the power of the pink dollar in Palm Springs that virtually all hotels here are gay-friendly, though the Warm Sands district, half a mile southwest of downtown, contains around thirty exclusively **gay hotels**, most of them hedonistic fun palaces. More resorts populate the Deepwell neighborhood to the south along San Lorenzo Road and the Las Palmas area on North Palm Canyon Drive. Consult our listings on p.292, or check the town's website, Ⓦwww.palm-springs.org, for additional suggestions.

Hotel hosts are a mine of information about the hottest restaurants and bars, and will happily point you towards the sort of thing you're after, but **restaurants** with a strong gay following include: *El Gallito*, *Mykonos*, *Shame on the Moon*, *Red Tomato*, and *Tomboyz Café* (all listed on p.302). For predominantly gay bars and clubs, try *Blame It On Midnight* and *Heaven* (listed on p.303).

Information

On the approach to town from I-10 you can't miss the Palm Springs **visitor center**, 2901 N Palm Canyon Drive (Mon–Sat 9am–5pm, Sun 9am–4pm; ☎760/778-8418 or 1-800/347-7746, ⓦwww.palm-springs.org), recently installed in a revamped former gas station designed by Mid-Century Modern leading light Albert Frey. The sweeping roof over the forecourt shades the front of the center where helpful staff dispense an exhaustive selection of brochures including the Spring/Summer or Fall/Winter version of the *Palm Springs Official Visitors Guide*, and the *Palm Springs Official Gay Visitors Guide*, which is virtually the same but with more gay-oriented info. Ask too for local maps, including one that details the homes of the famous ($5), and another (also $5) guiding you past homes exemplifying the Mid-Century Palm Springs Modern style of architecture (see p.295). The subsidiary **Uptown Visitor Center**, 777 N Palm Canyon Drive (Mon–Sat 10am–5pm; ☎760/327-2828), is more convenient for downtown.

Getting around

Downtown Palm Springs is only a few blocks long and a couple of blocks wide and is manageable on foot. **Getting around** the rest of the Coachella Valley is possible with the natural-gas-powered fleet run by SunBus (☎1-800/347-8628, ⓦwww.sunline.org), which operates daily from 6am to 8pm (until 11pm on some routes) and charges $1 to get around town, plus an extra 25¢ for two transfers (good for two hours after purchase); a day pass costs $3. While the system is extensive and services fairly frequent, it is never a quick way to get about and you may prefer a **taxi**; call City Cab (☎760/322-4470).

To get the absolute best out of Palm Springs and the surrounding towns though, you should think about **car rental**. All the majors are at the airport, but there are usually cheaper deals with Aztec Car Rental, 477 S Palm Canyon Drive (☎760/325-2294, ⓦwww.azteccarrental.com).

If you're not planning to stray too far (or want to ride the Joshua Tree trails), **rent a bike** from Bighorn Bike Adventures, 302 N Palm Canyon Drive (☎760/325-3367), who charge $22–27 for half a day, $29–35 for a full day, and $65–70 for three days depending on the model.

The windmills of Palm Springs

After trawling through the dull eastern suburbs of Los Angeles, I-10 throws you a surprise at the San Gorgonio Pass just before Palm Springs. Over four thousand **wind turbines** dot the valley, their glinting steel arms sending shimmering patterns across the desert floor. Along with Tehachapi Pass (see p.325), this is one of the largest concentration of windmills in the country, generating enough electricity to service a small city, and the conditions are perfect. The sun beating down on the desert creates a low-pressure zone that sucks air up from the cooler coastal valleys, funneling it through the San Gorgonio Pass, the only break between two 10,000-foot-plus ranges of mountains. Strong winds often howl for days in spring and early summer, reaching an average speed of between fourteen and twenty miles per hour.

You can tour the wind turbines with **Windmill Tours** (Oct–April Wed–Sat 9am, 11am & 2pm; $23; ☎760/251-1997, ⓦwww.windmilltours.com; call for reservations) on ninety-minute trips around the fields of towers, which discuss the history and practice of wind generation.

Accommodation

Palm Springs was designed for the rich, and big luxury **resorts** and country clubs are abundant here. Comfort and style also come in large doses at smaller and very tasteful hotels in Palm Springs. Even if such places are outside your normal budget, you may find them surprisingly affordable if you **visit in summer** when temperatures rise and prices drop dramatically. Many of the

▲ (10) (8 miles) & (1) (16 miles)

CENTRAL PALM SPRINGS

0   1 mile

N

◄ Palm Springs Aerial Tramway (4 miles)

◄ Tahquitz Canyon (1 mile)

Palm Springs Visitor Center

LITTLE TUSCANY

SAN RAFAEL

FRANCIS DRIVE

RACQUET CLUB ROAD

NORTH PALM CANYON DRIVE

AVENIDA CABALLEROS

INDIAN CANYON DRIVE

A

111

WEST VEREDA SUR

Desert Regional Medical Center

VISTA CHINO

SUNRISE WAY

FARRELL DRIVE

GENE AUTRY TRAIL

TACHEVAH ROAD

Ruth Hardy Park

Palm Springs Air Museum

111

TAMARISK ROAD

Uptown Visitor Center
2

ALEJO ROAD

O'Donnell Golf Course

★ Greyhound Station

AMADO ROAD

PALM CANYON DRIVE

Palm Springs Desert Museum
B

Spa Hotel, Casino & Mineral Springs

Wyndham Hotel

TAHQUITZ CANYON WAY

Village Green Heritage Center

5

Palm Springs Mall

Palm Springs Regional Airport

D C 4
6 7
8
E
F

STROMBERG RD

BARISTO RD

ARENAS ROAD

CALLE SEGUNDO

CALLE ENCILIA

BARISTO ROAD

Library @

Palm Springs Swim Center

RAMON RD

9 H
G
WARM SANDS DRIVE
GRENFALL ROAD

SUNNY DUNES ROAD

I

MESQUITE AVENUE

10

SONORA ROAD

EL CIELO ROAD

11 J
M K
N

SOUTH INDIAN TRAIL

EAST PALM CANYON DRIVE

L

O

12

Moorten Botanical Garden

SOUTH PALM CANYON DRIVE

LAVERNE WAY

TOLEDO AVENUE

Canyon Golf Club

Smoke Tree Stables

Indian Canyons (1 mile)

Cathedral City ►

ACCOMMODATION

Calla Lily Inn	E
Casa Cody Inn	C
Casitas Laquita	M
Happy Traveler RV Park	I
Ingleside Inn	F
Motel 6	H
Orbit In	D
Palm Court Inn	A
Quality Inn	O
Queen of Hearts Resort	J
Terrazzo	L
Vagabond Inn	N
Villa Royale Inn	K
Warm Sands Villas	G
The Willows	B

RESTAURANTS

Cedar Creek Inn	10
The Deck	6
El Mirasol	11
Heaven	9
John Henry's	5
Las Casuelas Terraza	8
Le Vallauris	4
Melvyn's	F
Mykonos	3
Native Foods Café	12
Thai Smile	2
Tomboyz Café	7
Wheel-Inn Eat	1

bigger places slash their prices by up to seventy percent, and even the smaller concerns give twenty to thirty percent off. The visitor center (see p.290) also offers special deals. If you couldn't care less about cachet, *Motel 6* and other **low-priced chains** are liberally represented. Regardless of where you stay, no Palm Springs lodging is without a **pool**.

Bed and breakfasts are common, and with double-room rates at around $80 per night, they are a good bargain when you add up comfort, hospitality, and a nice breakfast. If you're traveling in a group, it may work out cheaper to rent an **apartment**: many of the homes in Palm Springs are used only for a brief spell and are let out for the rest of the year. Again summer is the best time to look, but there is generally a good supply throughout the year. The Coachella Valley's daily paper, the *Desert Sun* (Ⓦ www.thedesertsun.com), has rental information in its classified pages, and many rental agencies operate around town – the visitor center will be able to point you to the more affordable ones. **Camping** is not really a viable option, unless you have an **RV**; the only campground accommodating tents is Lake Cahuilla (see below); otherwise, tent-carriers will have a better time exploring Joshua Tree or Anza-Borrego.

Listed below are some of the more reasonable and/or appealing options, with weeknight high season rates quoted. Keep in mind that **high season** for Palm Springs runs from October to May; prices during the summer months will drop a price bracket or two. Weekend prices are a price bracket or two higher than weeknights throughout the year. In winter you should always **book in advance**: in summer this is rarely necessary and empty rooms make asking for a reduced rate worthwhile.

For an introduction to the exclusively **gay hotels** listed below, see our "Gay Palm Springs" box on p.289.

Hotels, resorts, and B&Bs

Calla Lily Inn 350 S Belardo Rd ☎760/323-4964 or 1-888/888-5787, Ⓦwww.callalilypalmsprings .com. Intimate place with just nine rooms and suites set around a pool of this restored 1950s inn. It is comfortable, welcoming, and summer deals offer the third night free. Winter ❼, summer ❺

Casa Cody Inn 175 S Cahuilla Rd ☎760/320-9346 or 1-800/231-2639, Ⓦwww.casacody.com. Built in the 1920s by glamorous Hollywood pioneer Harriet Cody, this historic B&B offers tastefully furnished Southwestern-style rooms, a shady garden, great pool, and tasty buffet breakfasts in a good location two blocks from downtown. All but the "rooms" have a kitchen. Families and small groups should go for the gorgeous two-bedroom adobe cottage (❼–❾). Winter: rooms and studios ❹–❺, suites ❼; Summer: rooms and studios ❸–❹, suites ❺

Ingleside Inn 200 W Ramon Rd ☎760/325-0046 or 1-800/772-6655, Ⓦwww.inglesideinn.com. Set in a serene enclave a couple of blocks from downtown, this loosely Spanish-style inn is the last of Palm Spring's original hotels, dating from 1935. It once drew the likes of Garbo, Dalí, and

Brando, and retains enough real class to lure the glitterati. Each room is different, but all have a restrained elegance, often with antiques. Of course there are private patios, a lovely pool, and the excellent *Melvyn's Restaurant* is on-site (see p.302). Off-peak rates are especially good. Winter: rooms ❺, villas ❼; Summer: rooms ❸, villas ❹

Orbit In 562 W Arenas Rd ☎760/323-3585 or 877/996-7248, Ⓦwww.orbitin.com. If you're on the mid-century architectural trail or just fancy hanging poolside in your impeccably decorated 1950s-retro studio with private patio, you can't go past this Modernist Nirvana, designed by Herbert Burns in 1957. Sip a complimentary Orbitini on arrival, cruise town on the free bikes, relax in rooms equipped with VCR and CD player, and languish over a continental breakfast. It is adults only, and a two-night stay is required (three nights for their slightly cheaper midweek-escape packages). Winter ❾, summer ❼

Villa Royale Inn 1620 S Indian Trail ☎760/327-2314 or 1-800/245-2314, Ⓦwww.villaroyale .com. Beautiful inn with individually designed and exquisitely furnished rooms and suites, most with Jacuzzi, situated around a pool. In the winter season, meals and drinks are served from the bougainvillea-draped restaurant. Winter: rooms ❼, villas ❾; Summer: rooms ❺, villas ❼ **The Willows** 412 W Tahquitz Canyon ☏760/320-0771 or 1-800/966-9597, ⊛www .thewillowspalmsprings.com. The former estate of a US Secretary of State, whose friends – among them Clark Gable, Carole Lombard, and Albert Einstein – holed up here during the 1930s. Opulently decorated rooms, gorgeous lush grounds, a stunning San Jacinto Mountain backdrop, sumptuous breakfasts, and an ideal downtown location make this well worth the splurge. Winter ❾, summer ❽

Motels and campgrounds

Happy Traveler RV Park 211 W Mesquite Drive, Palm Springs ☏760/325-8518, ✉happytrav@aol .com. RV-only campground with 130 full-hookup sites close to the center of Palm Springs. Couples-only in winter but families are welcome from mid-April to October. $35 per site.
Lake Cahuilla 58075 Jefferson St, La Quinta ☏760/564-4712. Large campground for tents and RVs located by a 135-acre stocked lake located roughly fifteen miles east of Palm Springs. There are showers, a dump station for RVs, a summer-only swimming pool, and provision for horses. RVs $18, tents $14.
Motel 6 660 S Palm Canyon Drive ☏760/327-4200, ⊛www.motel6.com. The most central of the budget motels, with a good pool. Winter ❸, summer ❷
Palm Court Inn 1983 N Palm Canyon Drive ☏760/416-2333 or 1-800/667-7918, ⊛www .palmsprings.com/hotels/palmcourtinn. On four nicely landscaped acres, so it doesn't feel like a faceless motel. There's a Jacuzzi as well as two pools and a fitness center, and continental breakfast is included in the room rate. Winter ❸, summer ❷
Quality Inn 1269 E Palm Canyon Drive ☏760/323-2775 or 1-877/474-6423, ⊛www .qualityinn.com. Modern motel with spacious grounds, including a nice pool, kids' wading pool, and restaurant. Winter ❹, summer ❷
Vagabond Inn 1699 S Palm Canyon Drive ☏760/325-7211 or 1-800/522-1555, ⊛www .vagabondinn.com. Well-run three-story motel with free continental breakfast and weekday newspaper, a good pool, coffee makers in each room, and refrigerators available. Winter ❸, summer ❷

Exclusively gay accommodation

Casitas Laquita 450 E Palm Canyon Drive, Palm Springs ☏760/416-9999, ⊛www .casitaslaquita.com. A private women's resort in a rustic Southwestern-style compound decorated with Native American crafts and motifs. All rooms have kitchen, private bathroom, and TV, and some come with a fireplace. Breakfast is taken in your room but there's plenty of opportunity to mingle over complimentary afternoon tapas. ❻
Queen of Hearts Resort 435 Avenida Olancha ☏760/322-5793 or 1-888/275-9903, ⊛www .queenofheartsps.com. On the site of Palm Springs' first lesbian hotel, this renovated resort has just nine rooms around a great pool, private mist-cooled patios, and gorgeous views of the Santa Rosa Mountains. ❺, rooms with kitchens ❻
Terrazzo 1600 E Palm Canyon Drive ☏760/778-5883 or 1-866/837-7996, ⊛www.terrazzo-ps.com. An intimate twelve-room, clothing-optional men's resort where comfort and service is such that you'll have trouble leaving the confines of the hotel. Sumptuous rooms around the pool, free airport transfer, on-site gym, fresh-baked goodies, and even complimentary sunscreen complete the deal. Winter ❼, summer ❺
Warm Sands Villas 555 Warm Sands Drive ☏760/323-3005 or 1-800/357-5695, ⊛www .warmsandsvillas.com. Recently renovated with marble floors and king beds throughout, this inn comes with a big welcome and a generous continental breakfast. Some rooms have kitchenettes. ❻

Palm Springs

Much of your time in the Coachella Valley is going to be spent in **Palm Springs**, home to the majority of the recognized sights. It is a sprawling place, but is focused in a fairly concentrated core.

Downtown Palm Springs stretches for about half a mile along Palm Canyon Drive, a wide, bright, and modern strip full of boutiques and restaurants that's engulfed the town's original Spanish-village-style structures. Despite the celebrity stars embedded in the sidewalk, the cooling misters around the better restaurants, and the neat rows of fan palms along Palm Canyon Drive, Palm Springs is looking decidedly downmarket. Only one block back from the main drag empty lots, broken asphalt, and low-rent shops clearly signal that the better shops and galleries (and their aspiring clientele) have moved east to Palm Desert and the other Coachella Valley towns. That said, Palm Springs is the only place with a strollable center and has the greatest concentration of places to eat. The departure of spring-breakers and civic regeneration efforts have seen a partial revival of its fortunes, though it is a far cry from the glitz you might be expecting with schlocky T-shirt emporia and bookstores devoted exclusively to Hollywood stars jockeying for position with retail art galleries, not all of them good.

Palm Springs isn't all rampant consumerism. It is worth spending time in the Palm Springs Desert Museum, and admiring the architecture of Little Tuscany (also known as the Heritage District and "the tennis club district"), just west of North Palm Canyon Drive, where some of the finest small hotels congregate. Further afield, cactus fans should spend an hour at **Moorten Botanical Garden**, while plane buffs are better served at the **Palm Springs Air Museum**.

You'll soon want to explore further, best done by spending half a day riding the **Palm Springs Aerial Tramway** into the San Jacinto Mountains and strolling the easy trails, then returning to explore the palm-filled **Indian Canyons**.

Downtown Palm Springs

Palm Springs owes its very existence to Hollywood, so it is no surprise to find yourself following a **Walk of Fame** as you stroll down South Palm Canyon Drive. Look up from the pavement stars to catch two life-sized bronze statues honoring local leading lights: former mayor Sonny Bono stands guard over the junction of Arenas Road, while long-time resident Lucille Ball graces the intersection with Tahquitz Canyon Way.

Star-struck visitors could easily miss the **Village Green Heritage Center**, 219 S Palm Canyon Drive, a small brick plaza around a fountain and surrounded by a handful of buildings including the 1884 McCallum Adobe, "Miss Cornelia's Little House" made of railroad ties, and the **Agua Caliente Cultural Museum** (June–Aug Fri–Sun 10am–4pm; Sept–April Wed–Sat 10am–4pm, Sun noon–4pm; free; ⓦwww.accmuseum.org), with its collection of basketry and pottery.

In any case, time is better spent seeking out the attractive **Palm Springs Desert Museum**, 101 Museum Drive (Tues, Wed, Fri & Sat 10am–5pm, Thurs noon–8pm, Sun noon–5pm; $7.50, but free Thurs 4–8pm & $1 first Sun of the month; ☎760/325-0189, ⓦwww.psmuseum.org), which has recently shed its natural history collection and focuses on traditional and contemporary art, principally from California, though with wider-ranging Native American and Southwestern art. The large, central space is dotted with works by major sculptors such as Henry Moore, Barbara Hepworth, and Alexander Calder, along with Duane Hanson's amazingly realistic *Old Couple on a Bench* – their watches even tell the time if the staff remember to change the batteries. Surrounding rooms highlight Western American art. Note especially the Romantic works of Albert Bierstadt, Thomas Moran, and William Keith, who all brought the soft tones of their European homelands to rugged Californian landscapes – Yosemite looks more like the Alps than the Sierra, and raging snowmelt rivers have an English pastoral quality to them.

The mezzanine is devoted to Meso-American artworks such as the turquoise-inlaid human skull from the Mixtec classical period (AD 550–950), and the subtly realized, 2000-year-old armadillo effigy from Colima in Mexico. The top floor is all contemporary work and ever changing.

Downtown's most anarchic piece of landscape gardening can be seen at **Moorten Botanical Garden**, 1701 S Palm Canyon Drive (Mon, Tues & Thurs–Sat 9am–4.30pm, Sun 10am–4pm; $2.50; ☎760/327-6555, ⓦwww .moplants.com/moorten), a bizarre and somewhat shambolic cornucopia of just about every desert plant – cacti, succulents, dwarf trees, etc – lumped together in no particular order, but interesting for those who won't be venturing beyond town to see them in their natural habitat.

Out by the airport, the **Palm Springs Air Museum**, 745 N Gene Autry Trail (daily: June–Sept 9am–3pm; Oct–May 10am–5pm; $8; ⓦwww .palmspringsairmuseum.org), contains an impressive collection of World War II European and US fighters and bombers, along with associated material on

Celebrity and architectural tours

Knowing that they're in the thick of a megastar refugee camp, few can resist the opportunity to see the homes and country clubs of the international elite on a **celebrity tour**. As tacky as they are, these tours have some voyeuristic appeal, allowing you to spy on places like Bob Hope's enormous house, and the star-studded area known as **Little Tuscany** – Palm Springs' prettiest quarter, where the famous keep their weekend homes. The tours only view the houses through the minibus window, but in the end it is not the houses that make the tours worthwhile but rather the fascinating trivia about the lives of those who live (or, most often, lived) in them. Most of the big names had their heyday fifty years ago so you'll need to be well up with your classic movies to really appreciate the fine detail.

Celebrity Tours, 4751 E Palm Canyon Drive (Oct–May daily; June–Sept on demand; ☎760/770-2700, ⓦwww.celebrity-tours.com), conduct one-hour jaunts around Palm Springs ($20) which drive past enough homes to satiate most people's celebrity craving. For the dedicated there are longer excursions (2.5hr; $25) around the country clubs and the Sinatra estate (where Frank used to bring Ava Gardner). Of course, if you've got a car, you can do it yourself with a $5 *Map of the Stars' Homes* from the visitor center (see p.290), but you'll miss the sharp anecdotal commentary that makes it such fun.

Palm Springs' popularity with the rich and famous during the Forties, Fifties, and Sixties saw a massive building boom. Many vulgar newcomers opted for ostentatious palaces, but the more discerning employed young, Modernist architects such as Richard Neutra, who was "governed by the goal of building environmental harmony, functional efficiency, and human enhancement into the experience of everyday living." His work, and that of contemporaries such as Albert Frey and R.M. Schindler, became known as **Mid-Century Modern**, with its expression in these parts often dubbed Desert Modern or even Palm Springs Modern. After several decades in the architectural wilderness, there has been a surge of interest in the soaring rooflines, glass walls, unity of form, and sympathy for the desert setting. All of a sudden Palm Springs has renewed cachet, and long-ignored houses by the movement's luminaries are now highly sought after. Many can be seen from the road by following the self-drive map ($5) from the visitor center, but you'll see a lot more (and learn fascinating details about the architects and their clients) by joining PS Modern Tours (☎760/318-6118, ⓔPSmoderntours@aol.com). Their two-and-a-half-hour minivan **tours** ($55) visit the exteriors of assorted residential, commercial, and civic buildings including: Richard Neutra's 1947 Kaufmann House (designed for Edgar Kaufmann, who commissioned Frank Lloyd Wright's Fallingwater in Pennsylvania); the 1968 Elrod Residence, with its spectacular living room used for scenes in the Bond flick *Diamonds are Forever*; and the 1962 House of Tomorrow, which later became Elvis and Priscilla's "Honeymoon Hideaway."

Tours run all year on demand, but less frequently in summer.

the campaigns they flew in and on the men who flew them. The museum is easily identified by the F-14 and F-16 "Top Gun" fighters proudly displayed outside.

Palm Springs Aerial Tramway and Mount San Jacinto State Park

When the desert heat becomes simply too much to bear, you can travel through five climatic zones from the arid desert floor to (sometimes) snow-covered alpine hiking trails on top of Mount San Jacinto by riding the **Palm Springs Aerial Tramway** (Mon–Fri 10am–8pm, Sat & Sun 8am–8pm; last car down 9.45pm; $20.80, $30 with dinner, downhill journey only $9; ⊕760/325-1391 or 1-888/515-TRAM, ⊛www.pstramway.com), located on Tramway Road, four miles southwest of Hwy-111 on the northern edge of Palm Springs. Every thirty minutes a large cable car sets off up the rocky Chino Canyon bound for the Mountain Station at 8516ft – almost six thousand feet above. Each car is fitted with a rotating floor that makes two full revolutions on the twelve-minute journey giving breathtaking 360-degree views only outdone by those from the top, some 75 miles all the way to the Salton Sea. There's a welcome drop of around 30°F from the temperature in the valley, so bring something to keep warm, or hide indoors at the cafeteria-style restaurant, bar, and a fine dining restaurant *Elevations*, obligatory gift shop, or watch a decent 23-minute video on the tramway's construction. Outside there are viewing decks, and access to a couple of forested **short trails**: the three-quarter-mile Discovery Trail loop and the mile-and-a-half Desert View Trail with views down onto the Coachella Valley way below. From November 15 through April 15, snow conditions permitting, the **Adventure Center** (Thurs & Fri 10am–4pm, Sat & Sun 9am–4pm; same contacts as Tramway office) offers cross-country **skiing** ($18 a day), and **snowshoeing** ($15 a day) high above the desert floor.

To stray further into the surrounding wilderness of the 13,000-acre **Mount San Jacinto State Park**, you'll need a permit from the State Park Visitor Center (Mon–Fri 1–5pm, Sat & Sun 9am–5pm) in the Mountain Station. This gives prepared hikers the freedom to summit the nearby peak of 10,834-foot Mount San Jacinto (six miles each way), trek down to Idyllwild (ten miles each way), or explore a number of other forest trails. See the Idyllwild account on p.304 for more details of the forest.

Exploring the canyons

Hard-core desert enthusiasts visit Palm Springs for the **hiking** and **riding** opportunities in the canyons that incise the San Jacinto Mountains immediately west of Palm Springs.

Indian Canyons

The best known and most accessible of the canyons are Palm Canyon, Andreas Canyon, and Murray Canyon, known collectively as **Indian Canyons** (daily 8am–5pm though sometimes closed summer weekdays, June–Sept Fri–Sun 8am–5pm, call to check; $6; ⊕760/325-3400 or 1-800/790-3398, ⊛www .indian-canyons.com), on part of the Agua Caliente Indian Reservation that lies to the south of downtown. Centuries ago, ancestors of the Cahuilla tribe settled in the canyons and developed extensive communities, made possible by the good water supply and animal stock. Crops of melons, squash, beans, and corn were grown, animals hunted, and plants and seeds gathered for food and medicines. Evidence of this remains, and despite the near extinction of some breeds, mountain sheep and wild ponies still roam the remoter areas. To reach the best of them, follow South Palm Canyon Drive about three miles south to the clearly signposted entrance, from where paved roads run to the entrances of each of the canyons.

The most popular is **Palm Canyon**, which comes choked with palms – some three thousand over seven miles – beside a seasonal stream along which runs the easy 1.5-mile Palm Canyon Trail. A one-mile loop visits the best of **Andreas Canyon**, noted for its rock formations and more popular than **Murray Canyon**, which is more difficult to reach but rewards those prepared to hike two miles with a twelve-foot waterfall.

A tiny trading post at Palm Canyon sells hiking maps, refreshments, and assorted native crafts. To indulge in real Wild West fantasy you should see things on **horseback**. Smoke Tree Stables, 2500 Toledo Ave (☎760/327-1372), offers scheduled one- and two-hour riding tours of the canyons at $30 per hour – well worth it, especially if you go early morning (tours start from 8am) to escape the midday heat. Longer rides are available by advance arrangement.

Tahquitz Canyon

After years of hippie colonization and subsequent abandonment, the local tribe have in recent years reopened **Tahquitz Canyon**, 500 W Mesquite Ave (daily 7.30am–5pm; $12.50; ☎760/416-7044, ⦿www.tahquitzcanyon.com), where the visitor center contains a small artifact-filled museum and a theater showing a video on the legend of the canyon. The palmless canyon itself can only be visited on a guided tour (at 8am, 10am, noon & 2pm) which spends around two and a half hours hiking through beautiful country past a sixty-foot waterfall.

Trips and tours

Sections of the canyons and surrounding land are set aside for the specific lunacy of **trailblazing** in jeeps and four-wheel-drives. For a taste, contact OffRoad Rentals, 59511 Hwy-111, about four miles north of the Palm Springs tram (☎760/325-0376, ⦿www.offroadrentals.com), who offer a range of guided quad-bike and dune-buggy tours (from $35), as well as rentals for those with appropriate skills. Alternatively, Desert Adventures, 67555 E Palm Canyon Drive, Cathedral City (☎760/324-5337 or 1-888/440-5337, ⦿www.red-jeep .com), runs excellent guided jeep adventures in the Santa Rosa Mountains from $80. One of the most popular tours takes you across the desert floor and two thousand feet up through bighorn sheep preserves, spectacular cliffs, and steep-walled canyons. It's a bit expensive, but brilliant fun for the fearless.

Swimming and spas

The desert sun will soon send you in search of a pool. In many cases you won't have to walk more than fifty feet from your room to the hotel pool, but these can be small and crowded and you may prefer the **Olympic-sized pool** at the Palm Springs Swim Center, Sunrise Way at Ramon Road (Mon, Wed, & Fri 11am–5pm, all other days 11am–3pm; open later in July & Aug; $3.50; ☎760/323-8278).

Lots more water gets used up at the 16-acre **Knott's Soak City USA**, 1500 Gene Autry Trail (March–Oct Mon–Fri 10am–5pm, Sat & Sun 9am–6pm; $24.95, kids $12.95, parking $6; ☎760/327-0499, ⦿www.knotts.com), where you can surf on its one-acre wavepool and mess around on its thirteen waterslides.

For a substantially more relaxing experience, visit one of Palm Springs' day spas, particularly the elaborate *Spa Resort Casino*, 401 Amado Rd (daily

8am–7pm; ☎1-888/293-0180, ⓦwww.sparesortcasino.com), based around the **mineral spring** that the Cahuilla discovered on the desert floor over a century ago. Here, the basic "Taking of the Waters" ($35) gives you a sauna, spa, steam, eucalyptus rooms, and as much time in the swimming pool and fitness center as you desire; though you're encouraged to spend a lot more on massages (from $65), assorted skin and body-care treatments (from $95), and of course at the on-site casino. A dozen more spas are listed in the *Palm Springs Visitors Guide*.

The other Coachella Valley towns

Palm Springs may have the prestige, but it is the other towns of the Coachella Valley that now have the bulk of the swanky resorts, big-name shops, and elegant expense-account restaurants. On initial acquaintance, it is hard to tell one town from another as they form an amorphous twenty-mile sprawl of gated communities, country clubs, and over a hundred golf courses. Not all the boundaries between them are clearly marked, and on their main drags they tend to share faceless, low-slung architecture – but differences become evident to those who have time to explore.

Hwy-111 runs the length of the valley through, or close to, most of the main points of interest, but if you've got a specific destination in mind and want to avoid endless stop lights, consider the faster **I-10** which runs parallel about four miles to the north.

Cathedral City and Rancho Mirage

Adjacent to Palm Springs, about five miles east along Hwy-111, **CATHE-DRAL CITY** ("Cat City") has no cathedral, but takes its name from the now-hidden Cathedral Canyon, which apparently reminded early explorers of some medieval minster. It boomed during Prohibition, when the absence of a police force encouraged bawdy establishments to set up shop. You may well come here to drink or dine, or to tap into the **gay scene** that's second only to the one in Palm Springs, but during the day there's not a lot to see except for the **Desert IMAX theater**, 68510 E Palm Canyon Drive (☎760/324-7333, ⓦwww.desertimax.com). In the same block, take a few minutes to admire Jennifer Johnson's richly-mosaiced *Fountain of Life* sculpture, complete with bighorn sheep, lizards, and tortoises. Poor Hispanic mothers who spend their week tending the houses and swimming pools of the wealthy bring their kids to play in the fountain here on Sunday afternoons.

Further east along the valley, the generally staid **RANCHO MIRAGE** tends to attract dignitaries – and high-profile substance abusers. This so-called "Playground of the Presidents" is home to former President Gerald Ford and his wife, and is also host to the latter's upscale drunk tank, the **Betty Ford Center**. Frank Sinatra was the first of the stars to move out this way in 1956 and others soon followed. The city now recognizes its more illustrious associations in its street names: Frank, Gerald, Bob Hope, and Dinah Shore all have drives named after them.

Palm Desert, Indian Wells, and La Quinta

PALM DESERT, directly east along Hwy-111, is the safest place to witness the desert wildlife that flourishes despite the inhospitable climate. Here, the ever-expanding **Living Desert**, 47900 Portola Ave (daily: mid-June to Aug 8am–1.30pm; Sept to mid June 9am–5pm; $10.50, summer $8; ☎760/346-5694, ⓦwww.livingdesert.org), is the area's only essential sight, now encompassing over 200 acres of land, all irrigated, manicured, and divided into sections representing different desert regions around the world. Stroll among the cacti of the Mojave or the Chihuahua gardens, through a garden specially designed to attract butterflies, or into a palm oasis. North American desert animals – coyotes, foxes, bighorn sheep, snakes, and mountain lions – have now been supplemented by sections devoted to African species, such as wild dogs, gazelles, zebras, cheetahs, and warthogs. There are shady *palapas* and cooling "mist stations" everywhere, but it is still best to arrive as the gates open for cool and fragrant morning air, particularly if you fancy the wilderness trail system, which penetrates the hill country behind the zoo. If you can't stand to walk around in the heat, hop on the non-narrated shuttle ($4 all day) which makes frequent circuits of the park.

You can glimpse a different species of local creature nearby on **El Paseo**. The wealthy and the wishful thinkers flock to this "Rodeo Drive of the Desert," a mile-long strip of fashionable stores and galleries which loops south off Hwy-111 and is one of the very few places in the whole Coachella Valley where you might leave your car and stroll.

Come November (usually the first Sunday), the non-indigenous but increasingly populous species *homo golfus* turns out en masse for the nation's only **golf cart parade** (℡760/346-6111, Ⓦwww.golfcartparade.com), with decorated buggies proceeding along El Paseo.

For more on local events and sights, call at the **Palm Desert Visitor Center**, 72990 Hwy-111 at Hwy-74 (Mon–Fri 9am–5pm, Sat & Sun 9am–4pm; ℡760-/568-1441 or 1-800/873-2428, Ⓦwww.palm-desert.org); for wilderness information, drive three miles south along Hwy-74 to the **Santa**

Golf in the Coachella Valley

With over 110 courses it is no surprise that the Coachella Valley has become synonymous with **golf**. Look at a detailed map of the valley and you could be forgiven for thinking that Rancho Mirage, Palm Desert, Indian Wells, and La Quinta are nothing but golf courses, and a home beside the fairway proclaims your arrival among the Coachella Valley elite. The top courses are among the finest anywhere, the barren mountains all around in spectacular contrast to the lush, green fairways and placid water traps. Of course, watering all those fairways is completely unsustainable, but no one seems too concerned about the gradually draining aquifer that underlies most of the valley, as long as places like Palm Desert's Bighorn and Indian Wells' Vintage Club Mountain Course continue to grace the pages of golfing magazines. Throughout the year, celebrities, pros, and amateurs flock to tournaments such as the Bob Hope Chrysler Classic (in late Jan), the Skins Game (in late Nov), and the Frank Sinatra Celebrity Invitational (in mid-Feb).

Many of the courses are **private**, with membership running up to $20,000 a year plus a $300,000 initial joining fee. Semi-private and **public courses** are more accessible, though green fees can still be steep in winter: for bargains go in summer and play in the less fashionable afternoon or evening. One of the best public courses is the 36-hole Desert Willow Golf Resort, 38995 Desert Willow Drive, Palm Desert (℡760/346-0015, Ⓦwww.desertwillow.com), where morning green fees run $130 in the popular winter season but drop as low as $45 in summer. The cheapest green fees in the Coachella Valley are around half that, at Tahquitz Creek Golf Resort, 1885 Golf Club Drive, Palm Springs (℡760/328-1005, Ⓦwww.tahquitzcreek.com). You can book directly with the course up to around a week in advance, or try one of the reservation agents who book **tee times** at a range of courses. Try Affordable Palm Springs Tee Times (℡760/324-5012, Ⓦwww.palmspringsteetimes.com), who have an online booking system that allows booking up to two months in advance.

Rosa and San Jacinto Mountains National Monument Visitor Center (generally daily 9am–4pm though reduced hours in summer).

The adjoining city of **INDIAN WELLS** has the largest per capita income in the US, as well as the largest concentration of the Coachella Valley's grand **resorts**. It's known for its four-day New Year **Jazz Festival**, its high-profile **tennis tournaments**, and its prestigious Desert Town Hall **lecture series** (Ⓦwww.deserttownhall.org), four talks from mid-February to mid-April with speakers of the caliber of Newt Gingrich, Margaret Thatcher, Rudi Giuliani, Garrison Keillor, and Jean-Michel Cousteau. Tickets start at around $150 for all four nights.

Next heading east comes **LA QUINTA**, named for the Valley's first exclusive resort – *Rancho La Quinta* – built in 1927 and thriving during the Depression, when Hollywood's escapist popularity rose as the country's income fell. Director Frank Capra wrote the script for multiple-Academy-Award-winner *It Happened One Night* at the resort in 1934 and considered the place so lucky he kept coming back, bringing the likes of Greta Garbo in his wake. It's still so posh that it's not marked on the main road (take Washington Street south to Eisenhower to find it). The Santa Rosa Mountain backdrop is stunning, and the rich no longer get very duded up, so you won't feel out of place if you come for a drink at the piano lounge.

Indio

In stark contrast is neighboring **INDIO**, a low-key town whose agricultural roots show in its many date and citrus outlets. Approaching from behind *Rancho La Quinta* along 50th Avenue east, you'll pass so many date groves you'll think you're in Saudi Arabia – in fact, the town of Mecca is not far away. Back on Hwy-111, stop in at the **Shields Date Gardens**, no. 80225 (daily: June–Aug 9am–5pm; Sept–May 8am–6pm; free; ⓣ346-0996 or 1-800/827-8017, Ⓦwww.shieldsdate.com), built in 1924 but renovated in the 1950s, for a date crystal shake ($3) at the original soda fountain. Wander out to see the date palms (all with ladders attached for harvesting the dates), and don't miss the kitschy free film, *The Romance and Sex Life of the Date*, with its cheesy commentary partly recorded in the 1950s by Floyd Shields who set the place up. The town's huge February **Date Festival** draws people from as far as LA to its wonderfully goofy camel and ostrich races.

More serious animal lovers might want to stop in at the **Coachella Valley Wild Bird Center**, 46-500 Van Buren St (10am–5pm daily; donations; ⓣ760/347-2647), where injured owls, hawks, and other desert avians are cared for and, if feasible, released back into the wild.

Desert Hot Springs

Isolated on the north side of I-10, **DESERT HOT SPRINGS**, twelve miles north of Palm Springs, was chosen in a national competition as having the best-tasting water in the country. The underground wells for which the town is named supply water for the multitude of swimming pools as well as for drinking. A good jumping-off point for visiting Joshua Tree, it's somewhat more casual than the other Coachella Valley communities. One exception to this is **Two Bunch Palms** (ⓣ1-800/472-4334, Ⓦwww.twobunchpalms.com; rooms ❼, suites around $500), a luxury resort nestled in between trailer parks and a favorite of celebrities from Los Angeles. Normal people are also welcome if they can pay the price – spa treatments run about $90 per hour. However, spending your days soaking in the hot-springs pool with a book and a cocktail, with intermittent breaks for mud baths and massages, is not a bad way to pass the time.

You might also want to call at **Cabot's Old Indian Pueblo Museum**, 67616 E Desert View Ave (Sept–June Sat 10am–4pm, Sun noon–4pm; July & Aug closed; donations; ☎760/329-7610, ☜www.cabotsmuseum.org), in a four-story Hopi-style structure built by one Cabot Yerxa over a twenty-year period. After a peripatetic adulthood in Alaska, Cuba, and all over California, Cabot became Desert Hot Springs' first resident in 1913, then laboriously hand-dug the first well. He returned in 1939 (when in his mid-fifties) and began construction of what was intended to be both his house and a monument to the Indian people he had grown to love. Without formal plans and using home-made adobe bricks, and any secondhand bits of wood he could get his hands on, he fashioned a wonderful, rambling structure with nothing symmetrical – adhering to the belief that symmetry retains evil spirits. Cabot died in 1965 having completed 35 rooms, four of which can now be visited on an entertaining guided tour.

Eating

Palm Springs **restaurants** run the gamut, from eminently posh to fast food, with some reasonable ethnic options in between. If you come in the offseason, the desert sun may squelch your appetite sufficiently that you go without eating most of the day and find yourself ravenous at dusk. Although most of the more famous restaurants in Palm Springs and Cat City are ultra-expensive, more affordable options can be found with a little effort. Dedicated diners might also want to sample what's on offer in the rest of the Coachella Valley; our recommendations only scrape the surface of the huge selection that's out there. Only at the finest places need you book in summer, but in winter places fill up quick and reservations are essential.

For the really budget-conscious, supermarket shopping is the best bet: try Von's in the Palm Springs Mall, Tahquitz Canyon Way, which is open from early morning until around 11pm.

Palm Springs restaurants

Cedar Creek Inn 1555 S Palm Canyon Drive ☎760/776-8888. Casual mid-range American dining with all sorts of under-$20 meal-plus-wine specials offered at less fashionable dining times such as late afternoons and midweek evenings. Everyone should find something from the huge range of pastas, steaks, seafood, and sandwiches.
The Deck 262 S Palm Canyon Drive ☎760/325-5200. Downtown restaurant with a popular deck overlooking Palm Canyon Drive with misters in summer and a fireplace in winter. Come for fish tacos ($17), steak in a sake, soy, and ginger sauce ($22), or just linger over a cocktail.
El Mirasol 140 E Palm Canyon Drive ☎760/323-0721. Both literally and figuratively a mile away from the somewhat touristy *Las Casuelas*, this Mexican restaurant is strong on regional dishes producing an excellent chicken *mole*, and *pollo en pipián*, a Zacatecan specialty made with ground pumpkin seeds and chilis. These, and more mainstream enchilada and tamale plates go for $9–11.

John Henry's 1785 Tahquitz Canyon Way at Sunrise Way, Palm Springs ☎760/327-7667. Large portions of eclectic American fare, from rack of lamb to imaginative fish dishes, perfectly served and at half the price you'd expect. Dinner is around $20; reserve after 2pm. Closed Sundays and June–Sept.
Las Casuelas Terraza 222 S Palm Canyon Drive ☎760/323-1003. *Las Casuelas* opened its original establishment in 1958 (still going strong at 368 N Palm Canyon Drive), but you can't beat this Spanish-Colonial–style sister restaurant with a bustling atmosphere, stacks of mist-cooled outdoor seating centered on a palm-roofed bar, and usually some live entertainment. The food suffers from south-of-the-border blanding but is still good and not too pricey.
Le Vallauris 385 W Tahquitz Canyon Way ☎760/325-5059, ☜www.levallauris.com. Palm Springs' best restaurant does not exactly hide its light under a bushel, describing itself as "*the* restaurant where the Stars entertain their friends"; you are indeed likely to run into one or two

once-renowned artistes. Even if star-gazing is not your style, the contemporary California-Mediterranean cuisine is excellent, the service impeccable, and the setting gorgeous. Main courses are in the $25–40 range. Open for lunch and dinner but closed July & Aug; reservations essential.

Melvyn's at the *Ingleside Inn* (see p.292). This classical Continental restaurant is old-fashioned in the best possible way – elegant, understated, and serving beautifully prepared dishes such as their signature veal dish with avocado and a mousseline sauce. Expect to part with $50 a head, or go for the four-course prix fixe dinner ($28). Book ahead, and leave time for a cocktail or two in the bar beforehand.

Mykonos 139 E Andreas Rd ☏760/322-0223. A family-run Greek place just off Palm Canyon Drive, with friendly service, large portions of excellent, unpretentious food, and low prices.

Native Foods Café 1775 E Palm Canyon Drive in the Smoke Tree Village Mall ☏760/318-1532. This totally vegan café puts a creative twist on traditional vegetarian fare. An eclectic menu, including tacos, pizzas, salads, and a variety of veggie burgers, and modest prices make this a worthwhile spot. The Jamaican jerk "steak" burger is highly recommended as is the Save the Chicken salad. Mon–Sat 11.30am–9.30pm.

Thai Smile 651 N Palm Canyon Drive ☏760/320-5503. Few points for decor or ambience but great, authentic Thai green curries and the occasional Szechwan dish for around $10. Lunch specials are often under $6 and takeouts are available.

Tomboyz Café 214 E Arenas Rd ☏760/322-9915. Popular gay and lesbian café that does perfectly good breakfasts, lunches, and dinners but is primarily a spot for people watching along Gay Central, Arenas Road.

The rest of the Coachella Valley

Daily Grill 73061 El Paseo, Palm Desert ☏760/779-9911. A bustling, elegant coffee shop–style restaurant with large portions at reasonable prices. The chicken pot pie is a favorite along with excellent steaks, fish, salads, and lemonade.

El Gallito 68820 Grove St, Cathedral City ☏760/328-7794. A busy Mexican cantina that has the best food for miles and lines to prove it – get there around 6pm to avoid the crowds.

Las Casuelas Nuevas 70050 Hwy-111, Rancho Mirage ☏328-8844. Down-valley sister restaurant of the famous *Las Casuelas Terraza*, this is a great spot for outdoor dining and serves a stupendous Sunday brunch. Live music nightly.

Red Tomato 68784 E Palm Canyon Drive, Cathedral City ☏760/328-7518. Patio and indoor dining on terrific thick-crust pizza, especially the garlicky "white" pies, plus Balkan-style lamb dishes, from 4pm nightly.

Shame on the Moon 69950 Frank Sinatra Drive at Hwy-111, Rancho Mirage ☏760/324-5515. Long-standing bistro with California cuisine and a dark, intimate bar, attracting a loyal, mature gay crowd. Drop in for an early-evening martini or stay to eat the likes of sesame-crusted seared *ahi* tuna steak ($20). There are often three-course specials under $20 in summer: reservations a must in winter. Closed Mon.

Wheel-Inn Eat 16 miles west on I-10 at the Cabazon exit (marked by two 50ft concrete dinosaurs built in the 1960s and 1970s). Humble, 24-hour desert truck stop with a burly clientele and enormous portions – so unpretentious you'd think they'd never heard of Palm Springs. One of the dinosaurs houses a wonderfully kitschy gift shop, run by creationists: check out the labels on the toy dinosaurs.

Nightlife, bars, and clubs

The scattered nature of the Coachella Valley and the predominance of staid, moneyed residents does little to promote a thriving **nightlife**. Unless you're a member of one of the exclusive country clubs, or disco-crazy, you'll have to work to find much at all (let along anything raucous) though you might stop in at one of the resort **piano lounges**, where, if you shell out for an over-priced drink, you can sometimes catch surprisingly good jazz.

The Palm Springs visitor center (see p.290) has details of **what's on** around town, and stocks the seasonal **Palm Springs Visitors Guide** and the gay *The Bottom Line*. Pick up the monthly *Desert Guide* (Ⓦwww.desertguide.com), a local publication, to find out the current nightlife situation. Unless you hear of something that warrants the journey you're best staying around Palm Springs, where nightlife tends to the retro side, or nearby Cathedral City which has some hipper options, especially for the gay crowd.

Palm Springs' main drag is particularly crowded on Thursday evenings (Oct–May 6–10pm; June–Sept 7–10pm), when the surprisingly funky **VillageFest street fair** draws equal numbers of tourists and young locals. Traffic is temporarily barred from half a dozen blocks of North Palm Canyon Drive, which sprouts booths selling everything from fresh baked bread to tacky souvenirs and local crafts, plus there's a kids' play zone.

For **theater**, the historic Plaza Theatre, 128 S Palm Canyon Drive, hosts the long-running **Fabulous Palm Springs Follies** (Nov–May daily at 1.30pm & 7pm; from $39; ☎760/327-0225, ⓦwww.psfollies.com), an enormously popular professional vaudeville show with artistes aged between 50 and 85. The **Annenberg Theater** (☎760/325-4490), inside the Palm Springs Desert Museum, has a seasonal program of shows, films, and classical concerts.

If you're around in January, don't miss out on the **Palm Springs International Film Festival** (ⓦwww.psfilmfest.org), which brings more nightlife to the city than the rest of the year combined. And in late March, the **La Quinta Arts Festival** (ⓦwww.la-quinta-arts-found.org) serves up fine art and entertainment.

Blame It On Midnight 777 E Tahquitz Canyon ☎760/323-1200. This predominantly gay establishment has a full restaurant but is best treated as a fun bar that draws a dressed-up crowd. Very much a place to be seen.

Blue Guitar 125 E Tahquitz Canyon Way ☎760/327-1549. Mainly a blues and old-school R&B bar, often with no cover, though frequently $5–10 at weekends and up to $25 when someone special is playing.

Heaven 611 S Palm Canyon Drive ☎760/416-0950. Large and lively gay venue with pool tables, a patio, karaoke on Thurs, cabaret on Fri and Sat, and dancing until late. Thurs–Sat only.

Peabody's Café, Bar and Coffee 134 S Palm Canyon Drive ☎760/322-1877. An eclectic crowd of patrons enjoy live jazz, poetry readings, karaoke, and extensive coffee selections.

Zeldaz Dance and Beachclub 169 N Indian Canyon Drive ☎760/325-2375. Lively and youthful, if a little cheesy, dance club with occasional theme nights. Thurs–Sat only.

Listings

Bank Bank of America, 588 S Palm Canyon Drive ☎760/340-1867.

Bookstore Barnes & Noble, corner Hwy-111 & Fred Waring Drive, Palm Desert, or more conveniently at Peppertree Bookstore, 622 N Palm Canyon Drive (☎760/325-4821, ⓦwww.peppertreebookstore.com), with a good stock for a fairly small shop.

Cinema Signature, 789 Tahquitz Canyon Way ☎760/322-3456; alternative and foreign films at Camelot, 2300 Baristo Rd, Palm Springs, ☎760/325-6565.

Hospital Desert Regional Medical Center, 1150 N Indian Canyon Drive ☎760/323-6511.

Internet access The Palm Springs Public Library (see below) offers free Internet access, and there's commercial access at Log-On, in the Smoke Tree Village mall at 1775 E Palm Canyon Drive (closed Sun).

Left luggage Greyhound station, 311 N Indian Canyon Drive.

Library Palm Springs Public Library, 300 S Sunrise Way (Mon & Tues 9am–8pm, Wed & Thurs 9am–5.30pm, Fri 10am–5.30pm, Sat 9am–5.30pm; ☎760/322-7323, ⓦwww.palmspringslibrary.org.

Pharmacy Rite Aid Drug Store, 366 S Palm Canyon Drive.

Police ☎760/323-8116 in Palm Springs; ☎760/770-0300 in Cathedral City.

Post office 333 E Amado Rd (Mon–Fri 8.30am–5pm; ☎1-800/275-8777), zip code 92262.

Around Palm Springs

As the largest desert community by far, the Coachella Valley towns, and Palm Springs in particular, make obvious bases for exploring the surrounding regions where urban comforts are often in short supply. They can, however, be found in **Idyllwild**, a small mountain resort set among the pines high above Palm Springs that's well set up for weekend retreats from LA. The real desert starts to the north, where the **Morongo Basin** provides access to Joshua Tree National Park via the small roadside communities of **Yucca Valley**, **Joshua Tree**, and **Twentynine Palms**.

Idyllwild

Five thousand feet up on the slopes of Mount San Jacinto, **IDYLLWILD** is the perfect antidote to the in-your-face success of Palm Springs, fifty road miles away. Pine-fresh, cool, and snow-covered in winter, this small alpine town of about two thousand inhabitants has only a few chalet-style restaurants and hotels, but it's a great place to slow up the cash drain inevitably incurred on a visit to Palm Springs. It is accessible by heading twenty miles west along I-10 to Banning, then taking the exit for Hwy-243, which sweeps you up the mountain on a good but sharply curving road.

The place is always busy at weekends when city escapees flood the town, but a more relaxed pace prevails midweek. At any time, there's considerable temptation to get active on the magnificent trails of the **Mount San Jacinto State Park**, either up towards Mount San Jacinto itself, or up to **Suicide Rock** and **Tahquitz**, two distinctive peaks which rise a couple of thousand feet above the town. Many of the local trails don't enter any designated wilderness and require no permits: ones worth trying include the gentle meander along beautiful **Strawberry Creek** to a more strenuous trek along **Deer Springs Trail** (six miles round-trip; 3–4hr; 1700ft ascent) to the stunning Suicide Rock. Overnight hiking and day-hikes along the popular and moderately difficult **Devil's Slide** to the top station of the Aerial Tramway (see p.296) do require a permit, available from the Forest Service's **Idyllwild Ranger Station**, 54270 Pine Crest Ave (daily 8am–4.30pm; ☏909/382-2921), which has stacks of information about hiking and camping in the area. Trail access is made more complex by the need to purchase an **Adventure Pass** ($5 per day, $30 a year; ⓦwww.fsadventurepass.org), which allows you to park at trailheads and can be obtained at sporting goods stores and the ranger station.

Practicalities

Places to stay are well scattered along the roads that fan out from Idyllwild's central shopping area. The cheapest rooms are the little red-and-white chalets of the recently renovated *Atipahato Lodge*, 25525 Hwy-243, half a mile north of the ranger station (☏909/659-2201 or 1-888/400-0071, ⓦwww.atipahato .com; luxury cabins ❻, standard cabins ❸), where tasteful rooms have forest-view balconies and kitchenettes. Also good is the woodsy *The Fireside Inn*, 54540 N Circle Drive, about half a mile east (☏909/659-2966 or 1-877/797-3473, ⓦwww.thefireside-inn.com; ❹), with cozy wood-paneled rooms, kitchens, and fireplaces; and for real luxury there's the B&B-style *Strawberry Creek Inn*, 26370 Hwy-243 (☏909/659-3202 or 1-800/262-8969, ⓦwww .strawberrycreekinn.com; weekends ❺, weekdays ❹), a few hundred yards south. You can set up **camp** anywhere over two hundred feet away from trails and streams, or in designated Yellow Post Sites (Adventure Pass needed) with fire rings but no water. There are also drive-in campgrounds run by the Forest Service (℡1-800/444-7275) and the county park (℡1-800/234-PARK) at a cost of $10–16 per night.

Plenty of decent **restaurants** vie for your custom, including the *Goodtimes Pub & Grill*, right in the center of town with steaks, barbecue ribs, and even fish and chips, all for around $9. On a sunny day sit out on the deck and dine at the *Bread Basket*, 54710 N Circle Drive (℡909/659-3506; closed Wed & Thurs evenings), a couple of miles from the center but worth the effort for French toast made with apple-nut loaf ($7), mushroom stroganoff ($10), or battered halibut ($10), all washed down with microbrews or espresso coffee.

There's **Internet access** at the library, 5485 Pinecrest Ave (℡909/659-2300), which has very sporadic opening hours.

The Morongo Basin

Driving from Palm Springs (or Los Angeles) to Joshua Tree National Park, the easiest access is through the **MORONGO BASIN**, a vast tract of high desert, almost a thousand square miles of which is taken up by the Marine Corps Air Ground Combat Center, the world's largest marine base, located just north of Twentynine Palms. Mostly useful as a supply and accommodation base, the Morongo Basin does have a couple of points of minor interest, principally the wildlife haven of the **Big Morongo Canyon Preserve**, the Western charms of **Pioneertown**, and the oddball **Desert Christ Park**.

While visiting Joshua Tree National Park using **public transportation** is not really an option, Morongo Basin Transit Authority (℡1-800/794-6282, ⓦwww.mbtabus.com) runs a regular bus service (4 daily) between Palm Springs and Yucca Valley with connections for the towns of Joshua Tree ($7.50 one way, $12 round trip) and Twentynine Palms ($10 one way, $16 round trip), but not into the park itself.

Yucca Valley and around

Heading north off I-10 along Twentynine Palms Highway (Hwy-62), the first point of interest is **Big Morongo Canyon Preserve**, 11055 East Drive (7 30am–sunset; donation suggested; ⓦwww.bigmorongo.org), a wildlife refuge based around the cottonwoods and willows of a vast oasis, which represents one of the largest bodies of natural surface water for miles around. Consequently, it is a big hit with both wildlife and keen birders, who might hope to spot vermilion and brown-crested flycatchers, Bell's vireo, summer tanager, and a whole lot more – the preserve host keeps a list of current sightings. The numerous boardwalks and trails meandering through the area can easily absorb a relaxing hour or two.

The Morongo Basin's largest settlement is **YUCCA VALLEY**, nine miles east, a typically unappealing string of malls running for a few miles beside Hwy-62. Between grabbing a feed or finding a place to stay (for both see p.306), you might call at the **Hi-Desert Nature Museum**, 57116 Hwy-62 (Tues–Sun 10am–5pm; free; ℡619/369-7212), which holds a largely poor collection of paintings and tacky souvenirs, but also some commendable catches of snakes, scorpions, and a pine cone from the world's oldest living tree.

There are greater rewards following Pioneertown Drive, which runs north off Hwy-62. After half a mile, turn right onto Sunnyslope Drive and continue half a mile to the **Desert Christ Park** (7am–dusk; free), which has 37 of local sculptor Antone Martin's massive fifteen-foot white concrete figures, erected in the 1950s and depicting tales from the Bible – a fittingly bizarre addition to the region. Return to Pioneertown Drive and continue 3.5 miles north to **Pioneertown**, an Old West town created in the 1940s for the filming of movies and TV serials – a nice bit of synthetic cowboy country when the real thing gets too much. It is nowhere near as tacky as it might sound, has a few places to stay, eat, and drink, and a bowling alley little changed since it was built.

For **tourist information** visit Yucca Valley's brand new California Welcome Center, 56711 Twentynine Palms Hwy (daily 8.30am–5.30pm; ☎760/365-5464, ⓦwww.yucca-valley.org), and you can surf the Net at the **library** (Mon, Wed & Fri 10am–6pm, Tues & Thurs noon–8pm, Sat 9am–5pm; ☎760/228-5455) next to the Hi-Desert Nature Museum. For **accommodation** try the *Desert View Motel*, 57471 Primrose Drive (☎760/365-2886; ❷), which is back off the highway and has a pool, or *Pioneertown Motel* at Pioneertown (☎760/365-4879, ⓦwww.pioneertown.com; ❸), where clean but ageing rooms are made more appealing by a full kitchen and a variety of decors: cowboy, madam, seascape, etc. There's good **food** and a great atmosphere at *Pappy & Harriet's*, also at Pioneertown (☎760/365-5956, ⓦwww.pappyandhariets.com), a Tex-Mex and mesquite barbecue, where there's an open-mike night on Sundays, and a band most Thursday to Saturday nights. Indeed, this place has become the area's main venue for touring bands, occasionally attracting the odd internationally recognized artist. On the main road through Yucca Valley there's reliable espresso and snacks at the *Water Canyon Coffee Co*, 55844 Twentynine Palms Hwy.

Joshua Tree

Six miles east of Yucca Valley, the town of **JOSHUA TREE** centers on the intersection of Twentynine Palms Highway and Park Boulevard, which runs south to the national park's West Entrance. There's not much to it, but several decent places to stay and eat make it perhaps the best base for the park if you're not camping.

General information is best sought at the privately-run **Park Center**, 6554 Park Blvd (June–Aug Mon–Fri 9am–6pm, Sat & Sun 10am–4pm; Sept–May daily 9am–6pm; ☎760/366-3448, ⓦjoshuatreeparkcerter.com), which also stocks books and has an attractive cactus garden outside.

The cheapest **place to stay** is the pool-equipped *High Desert Motel*, 61310 Twentynine Palms Hwy (☎760/366-1978 or 1-888/367-3898; ❸), but you might prefer the bed-and-breakfast-style *Joshua Tree Inn* (☎760/366-1188 or 1-800/366-1444, ⓦwww.joshuatreeinn.com; ❹), virtually opposite at 61259 Twentynine Palms Hwy, where comfortable rooms are set around a pool, and the convivial hosts contribute to a very relaxing atmosphere. Also consider *Spin and Margie's Desert Hideaway*, off Twentynine Palms Highway around three miles east of Joshua Tree (☎760/366-9124, ⓦwww.deserthideaway.com; ❺), with luxurious rooms vibrantly decorated in a desert style.

Several good **places to eat** huddle within a block or so of each other along Twentynine Palms Highway at its junction with Park Boulevard. Try *Crossroads Café and Tavern*, no. 61715 (☎760/366-5414), for good breakfasts, burgers, espresso, shakes, and microbrews; *Royal Siam*, no. 61599 (☎760/366-2923) for good low-cost Thai and $5–6 lunch specials (closed Tues); or the *Beatnik Café*, no. 61597 (☎760/366-2090), a hip coffeehouse with good food and drink, Internet access, and live music most weekends.

Climbers and hikers needing to buy or rent gear should stop by Nomad Ventures, 61795 Twentynine Palms Hwy (☎760/366-4684), or nip across the road to Coyote Corner, 6535 Park Blvd (☎760/366-9683), where you can fill up your water jugs before heading into the park or have a **shower** (coin-operated, from $1.50) after several days of dust and sand.

Safe at Home – Gram Parsons in Joshua Tree

A relatively minor star in his lifetime, **Gram Parsons**, the wild country outlaw of early Seventies rock, has since become one of the era's icons. His musical influence spreads wide, from ageing rockers like his old friend Keith Richards to Evan Dando, Beck, and the new breed of alt-country misfits, but his fame owes as much to his drug- and booze-fueled life and the bizarre circumstances surrounding his death, aged 27. It is a story embellished over the years by myth, fabrication, and gossip.

Joshua Tree was Gram's escape from the LA music pressure-cooker, and photos show him hanging out with Richards in pharmaceutically altered states, communing with nature and scanning the night sky for UFOs. On his final visit, Gram and three friends spent September 18, 1973, consuming as much heroin, morphine, marijuana, and Jack Daniels as possible, Gram finally ODing that night in Room 8 at the *Joshua Tree Inn*.

Parsons' stepfather stood to benefit from Gram's estate if he could get the body back to Louisiana for burial. However, Gram and his friend and tour manager, Phil Kaufman, had already agreed "the survivor would take the other guy's body out to Joshua Tree, have a few drinks and burn it." Three days after Gram's death, Kaufman persuaded an airline employee to release Gram's casket, drove out to Joshua Tree, doused his body in gasoline, and executed the wishes of his deceased friend. The body wasn't completely consumed, however, and Grams' remains now lie in a New Orleans cemetery. Kaufman was only charged with theft of a coffin and had to pay a $300 fine plus $708 for the coffin.

Fans come to stay in Room 8 at the *Joshua Tree Inn* (where you can inscribe your thoughts in a little black book and add your guitar pick to the collection), and to attend the annual Gramfest (ⓦwww.gramfest.com), a devotional music festival held each September. The principal **point of pilgrimage**, though, is a makeshift fans' shrine near where his body was cremated. From the Cap Rock parking lot at the start of the Keys View Road, follow a well-defined but unmarked trail around the west side of the rock to a point close to the road intersection. Here, a rock alcove is plastered with devotional graffiti. For many years the spot was marked by a small concrete plinth daubed with "Gram – Safe at Home," but this mysteriously disappeared sometime around 2003 to be replaced by a rough cross made of rocks. The Park Service is being pressured to officially recognize the site, though its literature currently makes no mention of Gram.

The **library**, by the crossroads at 6465 Park Blvd (Mon–Fri 10am–6pm; ☏760/366-8615), has free **Internet access**.

Twentynine Palms

Fifteen miles east of the town of Joshua Tree and just two minutes' drive from the park's north entrance, the small highway-side desert town of **TWENTYNINE PALMS** (locally known as "two-nine") is a pleasant enough little place despite the occasional artillery booms from the nearby marine base. The climate has been considered perfect for convalescents ever since physicians sent World War I poison-gas victims here for treatment of their respiratory illnesses; development of health spas and real estate offices has been considerable. The town is now billing itself as an "Oasis of Murals"; you can get a map of these hyperrealistic historical artworks – there's one of the Dirty Sock Camp (named for a method used by miners to filter out gold).

The town runs for almost five miles along the highway and is divided into two sections separated by a small hill. The only sights to speak of are the national park's **Oasis Visitor Center** (see p.311) on the eastern edge of town, and the nearby **Old Schoolhouse Museum**, 6760 National Park Drive (Oct–May Wed–Sun 1–4pm; June–Aug Sat & Sun 1–4pm; free; ☎760/367-2366), with a partly restored former schoolroom from 1927, and a collection of items of local interest: mining, the military, and desert wildlife.

Pick up **information** at the Twentynine Palms Chamber of Commerce, 6455 Mesquite Ave (Sept–May Mon–Fri 9am–5pm; June–Aug Mon–Fri 9am–3pm; ☎760/367-3445, ⓦwww.29palms.com), and get **Internet access** at the library, 6078 Adobe Rd (Mon & Tues noon–8pm, Wed–Fri 10am–6pm, Sat 9am–5pm).

The best place in town to **stay** is the *Twentynine Palms Inn*, 73950 Inn Ave off National Park Drive (☎760/367-3505, ⓦwww.29palmsinn.com), where an array of cozy adobe bungalows and wood-frame cabins are set around attractively arid grounds and gardens, while a central pool area contains a restaurant and bar. Owned by the same large family since 1928, the inn was built on the Oasis of Mara, the only privately owned oasis in the Mojave Desert, and (like the rest of the town) has several fault lines – including the Pinto Mountain Fault – running beneath it. Cabins (winter ❹, summer ❸) are comfortable but fairly basic, and it is worth stepping up to a bungalow (winter ❺, summer ❹) or even the lovely Irene's Historic Adobe (winter ❾, summer ❽), which sleeps four.

Among the cheaper options nearby are the large *Motel 6*, 71487 Twentynine Palms Hwy (☎760/367-2833; ❷), and the *El Rancho Dolores Motel*, along the same road at no. 73352 (☎760/367-3528; ❷). Both have perfectly acceptable pools and good rooms, but are nowhere near as much fun as the *Twentynine Palms Inn*.

There's low-cost lunch and early dinner **dining** at *Ramona's* (☎760/367-1929; closed Sun & Mon), an excellent, authentic Mexican at 72115 Twentynine Palms Hwy, but the best place to **eat** is the *Twentynine Palms Inn*, with excellent $10–15 meals including soup and salad, many of the ingredients grown in the oasis gardens. For good espresso, bagels, breakfast, wraps, and salads, try *WonderGarden Café*, 6257 Adobe Rd (☎760/367-1238), which has a health-food store on site.

Campers in need of a clean-up should head along to 29 Palms Family Fitness, 73782 Two Mile Rd at Adobe Road (☎760/361-8010), which has as-long-as-you-like **showers** with towels for $4.

Joshua Tree National Park

Sited in a singular transitional area where the high Mojave meets the lower Colorado Desert, **JOSHUA TREE NATIONAL PARK** is one of the most unusual and fascinating of California's national parks. Almost 800,000 acres have been set aside for these freaky trees, their branches ragged and gnarled, flourishing in an otherwise sparsely vegetated landscape. If you're staying in Palm Springs, there's no excuse not to visit; if you've further to come, make the effort anyway.

The startling Joshua trees (see box, p.310) are only found in the northwestern quarter of the park, where they form a perfect counterpoint to surreal clusters of monzogranite boulders, great rock piles pushed up from the earth by the movements of the Pinto Mountain Fault, running directly below. Often as high as a hundred feet or more, their edges are rounded and smooth from thousands of years of flash floods and winds, but there are enough nodules, fissures, and irregularities to make this superb **rock-climbing** territory.

JOSHUA TREE NATIONAL PARK

N

Lake Havasu City (100 miles)

Phoenix (200 miles)

Amboy (30 miles)

Barstow (80 miles)

Los Angeles (95 miles)

Anza-Borrego Desert (45 miles)

Salton Sea (20 miles)

EATING & DRINKING

Beatnik Café	2
Crossroads Café & Tavern	4
Pappy & Harriet's	1
Ramona's	5
Royal Siam	3
Twentynine Palms Inn	H
Water Canyon Coffee Co	7
WonderGarden Café	6

ACCOMMODATION

Desert View Motel	G
El Rancho Dolores Motel	B
High Desert Motel	B
Joshua Tree Inn	E
Motel 6	C
Pioneertown Motel	A
Spin and Margie's Desert Hideaway	F
Twentynine Palms Inn	H

MOJAVE DESERT

COLORADO DESERT

PINTO MOUNTAINS

OLD DALE MINING DISTRICT

PINTO MOUNTAINS

TRANSITION ZONE

PINTO BASIN

Old Dale Road

Black Eagle Mine Road

EAGLE MOUNTAINS

Mastodon Peak

Cottonwood Spring Oasis

Lost Palms Oasis

Bajada Nature Trail

Cottonwood Visitor Center

COTTONWOOD MOUNTAINS

Pinto Basin Road

Ocotillo Patch

Cholla Cactus Garden

HEXIE MOUNTAINS

MOJAVE DESERT

Pinkham Canyon Road

Berdoo Canyon Road

Twentynine Palms

Oasis Visitor Center

Utah Trail

Park Boulevard

Belle

White Tank

Skull Rock

Jumbo Rocks

Geology Tour Road

Indian Cove

Fortynine Palms

Barker Dam Desert Queen Ranch

Queen Valley

Sheep Pass (groups)

Lost Horse Mine

Ryan Mountain

Ke's View

Ryan

Park Boulevard

Lost Horse Valley

Boy Scout Trail

Wonderland of Rocks Area

Hidden Valley

Covington Flats

JOSHUA TREE NATIONAL PARK

LITTLE SAN BERNARDINO MOUNTAINS

TRANSITION ZONE

see Palm Springs & The Coachella Valley map

COLORADO DESERT

Indio

Coachella

Palm Desert

Joshua Tree

Von's

Hi-Desert Nature museum

Palm Wells

Black Rock Canyon

Desert Christ Park

Pioneertown

Yucca Valley

Big Morongo Canyon Preserve

Morongo Valley

Desert Hot Springs

Palm Springs

Legend

Rock Outcrops

Unpaved Road Surface

Suitable for 4WD only

0   5 miles

309

The Joshua tree

Unique to the Mojave Desert, the **Joshua tree** (*Yucca brevifolia*) is one of its oldest residents, with large examples probably over three hundred years old (the lack of growth rings makes their age difficult to determine). The Joshua tree isn't, in fact, a tree at all, but a type of yucca, itself a type of agave and therefore a giant member of the lily family.

Awkward-looking and ungainly, it got its unusual name from Mormons who traveled through the region in the 1850s and imagined the craggy branches to be the arms of Joshua leading them to the Promised Land. Of course, Native Americans had been familiar with Joshua trees for millennia, weaving the tough leaves into baskets and sandals, and eating the roasted seeds and flower buds. The trees became equally useful for homesteaders who arrived in the wake of the Mormons – the lack of better wood forced them to press the trunks of Joshua trees into use for fences and building material.

Joshua trees only grow at altitudes over two thousand feet and prefer extreme aridity and a bed of coarse sand and fine silt. By storing water in their spongy trunks, they can grow up to three inches a year, ultimately reaching heights of forty feet or more. To conserve energy, they only bloom when conditions are right, waiting for a crisp winter freeze, timely rains, and the pollinating attentions of the yucca moth before erupting in a springtime display of creamy white-green flowers, which cluster on long stalks at the tips of the branches. Successful young saplings start life as a single shoot, but eventually a terminal bud dies or is injured and the plant splits to form two branches, which in turn divide over time, producing the Joshua trees' distinctive shapes.

In all, it's a mystical, even unearthly, landscape, best appreciated at sunrise or sunset when the whole desert floor is bathed in red light. At noon, it can feel like an alien and threatening furnace, with temperatures often reaching 125°F in summer, though dropping to a more bearable 70°F in winter. If you're visiting between May and October, you must stick to the higher elevations to enjoy Joshua Tree with any semblance of comfort. In the Low Desert part of the park, the Joshua trees thin out and the temperature rises as you descend below three thousand feet.

Some history

"Joshua Tree" may be a familiar name today, thanks in part to U2's 1987 album of that name, but previously it was almost unknown. Unlike the vast bulk of the state, nobody, save a few Native Americans, prospectors, and cowboys, has had the chance to spoil it. Despite receiving only around four inches of annual rainfall, the area is surprisingly lush, and although craggy trees and rockpiles are what define Joshua Tree today, it was grass that attracted the first significant pioneers. Forty-niners hurrying through on their way to the Sierra Nevada gold fields told tales of good pastures, and early cattlemen were quick to follow. Rustlers discovered that the natural rocky corrals made perfect sites for branding their illegitimate herds before moving them out to the coast for sale. Ambushes and gunfights were common in the area. Seeking refuge in the mountains, rustlers discovered by chance small traces of gold and sparked vigorous mining operations that continued until the 1940s. In recognition of the uniqueness of the area, and the need for its preservation, the national park system took the land under its jurisdiction as a national monument in 1936 and has vigilantly maintained its beauty ever since. The park lost some of the original area to mining interests in the 1950s, but that was more than compensated for in 1994, when it was promoted to a national park, with the addition of 234,000 acres.

Park practicalities

Less than an hour's drive northeast from Palm Springs, Joshua Tree National Park (always open; $10 per vehicle for 7 days, $5 per cyclist or hiker; Ⓦ www.nps .gov/jotr) is best approached through the Morongo Basin (see p.305) along Hwy-62, which branches off I-10. Besides camping (see below), there is neither lodging nor anywhere to eat or buy supplies within the park, so the Morongo Basin towns of Yucca Valley, Joshua Tree, and Twentynine Palms are the main bases from which to explore. These are also the closest places served by public transportation, so visiting the park without your own wheels is not really an option: at best, you're looking at a ten-mile desert walk to get to anything of interest.

You can enter the park via the west entrance at the town of **Joshua Tree**, or the north entrance at **Twentynine Palms**, where you'll also find the **Oasis Visitor Center** (daily 8am–5pm; ☏760/367-5500). Alternatively, if you're coming from the south, there is an entrance and the **Cottonwood Visitor Center** (generally daily 8am–4pm; ☏760/367-5500), seven miles north of I-10. It's worth stopping at one of the visitor centers to collect the free national park **map** and *Joshua Tree Guide*, which are fine for most purposes, though hikers will want a more **detailed map**, the best being Trails Illustrated's *Joshua Tree National Park* map ($10).

Park staff are also at work running free, campground-based **ranger programs** (generally mid-Oct to mid-Dec and mid-Feb to May, but also summer weekends), which might include campfire talks, discovery walks, and geology hikes: check at visitor centers for the current schedule.

Camping

Joshua Tree National Park has nine **campgrounds**, all concentrated in the northwest except for one at Cottonwood by the southern entrance. All have wooden tables, places for fires (bring your own wood), and pit toilets, but only two (*Black Rock Canyon* and *Cottonwood*) have water supplies and flush toilets. The lack of showers and electrical and sewage hook-ups at any of the sites keeps the majority of RVers at bay, but in the popular winter months the place fills up quickly, especially at weekends. All campgrounds are first-come-first-served except *Black Rock Canyon* and *Indian Cove*. Each campsite is good for up to six people and two vehicles. **Winter** nights can be very cold, and campers here between November and March should come with warm jackets and sleeping bags or head for the lower (and warmer) *Cottonwood* campground.

Over eighty percent of the park is designated wilderness where **backcountry camping** is permitted provided you register before you head out. Twelve backcountry boards are dotted through the park at the start of most trails. Here you can self-register, leave your vehicle, and study the regulations that include prohibition of camping within a mile of a road, five hundred feet of a trail, and a quarter-mile of a water source.

The campgrounds are listed from southeast to northwest through the park.

Cottonwood 62 sites; 3000ft. Being lower down this is the pick for the cooler winter months. Water available. $10

White Tank 15 sites; 3800ft. Relatively small and quiet site with a short nature trail to Arch Rock. No water. $5

Belle 18 sites; 3800ft. Small, quiet site amid some lovely rocks. No water. $5

Jumbo Rocks 125 sites; 4400ft. The highest and largest site in the park, often busy and with regular ranger programs including a free Saturday-evening slide show. No water. $5

Sheep Pass 6 group sites; 4500ft. Campground only available to groups. Reserve on ☎1-800/365-2267. No water. $25–35

Ryan 31 sites; 4300ft. Medium-sized campground amid some lovely rocks and trees. No water. $5

Hidden Valley 45 sites; 4200ft. Popular campground that is almost entirely occupied by rock climbers in spring and fall. No water. $5

Indian Cove 101 sites; 3200ft. Large campground that's only accessible from outside the park. It is set among granite boulders and a trail from the eastern section of the campground road leads to Rattlesnake Canyon – its streams and waterfalls (depending on rainfall) breaking an otherwise eerie silence among the monoliths. Reservations on ☎1-800/365-2267. No water. $10

Black Rock Canyon 100 sites; 4000ft. Another large campground only accessible from outside the park. Reserve by calling ☎1-800/365-2267. Water available. $10

Exploring the park

The best way to enjoy the park is to be selective. As with any desert area, you'll find the heat punishing and an ambitious schedule impossible in the hotter months. Casual observers will find a day-trip plenty, most likely a leisurely drive along **Park Boulevard** and **Pinto Basin Road** – the paved roads which run right through the Park – perhaps joining a tour of the Desert Queen Ranch and driving up to Keys View. For desert-lovers a couple of nights camping out is a highlight that shouldn't be missed, and experienced hikers may want to take advantage of the park's excellent if strenuous trails and backcountry opportunities. The rangers and staff at the visitor centers will be able to recommend the most enjoyable itineraries, tailored to your requirements and abilities. And remember never to venture anywhere without a detailed **map** (see p.311).

Many of the roads are unmarked, hard to negotiate, and restricted to four-wheel-drive use. If a road is marked as such, don't even think about taking a normal car – you'll soon come to a grinding halt, and it could be quite a few panic-stricken hours before anybody finds you. Of course, maps are even more essential if you are planning to explore the park's **hiking trails** (see box opposite).

The northwest

Approaching from the township of Joshua Tree you enter in the park's north-western corner and immediately find yourself in the **Wonderland of Rocks** area comprising giant, rounded granite boulders that draw **rock climbers** from all over the world. The various clusters flank the road for about ten miles giving plenty of opportunity to stop for a little bouldering or, for those suitably equipped and skilled, to try more adventurous routes.

A little further on, close to the *Hidden Valley* campground, a well-signposted one-mile nature trails loops into **Hidden Valley**, a near-complete natural corral where cattle rustlers used to hide out. To the north, a side road leads past the entrance to the Desert Queen Ranch (see below) to the rain-fed **Barker Dam**, Joshua Tree's crucial water supply, built around the turn of the century by cattlemen (and rustlers) to prevent the poor beasts from expiring halfway across the park. The route back from the dam passes a number of petroglyphs.

Desert Queen Ranch

Just northeast of the *Hidden Valley* campground sits the **Desert Queen Ranch**, only accessible by joining the informative and entertaining ranger-led **guided walking tour** (Oct–May daily 10am & 1pm; June–Sept Wed & Fri 5.30pm; $5; reservations necessary March & April; ☎760/367-5555), which begins at

Nature trails and hikes in Joshua Tree National Park

To get a real feel for the majesty of the desert, you'll need to leave the main roads behind and hike, or at least follow one of the short (and mostly wheelchair-accessible) **nature trails** which have been set up throughout the park to help interpret something of desert ecology and plant life.

The more strenuous **hikes** outlined below are generally safe but be sure to **stick to the trails**: Joshua Tree is full of abandoned gold mines and although the rangers are fencing them as quickly as possible, they don't have the funds to take care of all of them.

Most of the listed trails are in the slightly cooler and higher Mojave Desert, but even on the easier trails allow around an hour per mile: there's very little shade and you'll tire quickly. There's tougher stuff on the eastern side of the park around **Pinto Basin**, though this is purely territory for experienced groups of hikers well armed with maps and water supplies. If you're thinking of heading out on anything more ambitious than the hikes described here be sure to discuss your plans with a ranger; and anyone planning to stay out overnight in the wilderness must **register** at one of the trailhead backcountry boards.

Nature trails

These are listed northwest to southeast through the park.

Bajada (400-yard loop). The plantlife of a naturally sloping drainage is explored half a mile north of the South Entrance.

Cholla Cactus Garden (400-yard loop). A beautiful stroll among these superbly photogenic cacti.

Oasis of Mara (800-yard loop). A series of explanatory panels around a significant fan-palm oasis right by the Oasis Visitor Center.

Some hikes

These are listed northwest to southeast through the park.

Fortynine Palms Oasis (3 miles; 2hr). Moderately strenuous, this leaves the badly signposted Canyon Road six miles west of the visitor center at Twentynine Palms. A barren rocky trail leads to this densely clustered and partly fire-blackened oasis which, since it was named, seems to have flourished on the seepage down the canyon. There's not enough water to swim in, nor are you allowed to camp (the oasis is officially closed 8pm–7am), but a late-afternoon or evening visit presents the best wildlife rewards.

Lost Horse Mine (4 miles; 3hr). Starting a mile east of Keys View Road, this moderately difficult trail climbs 450ft to the mine, which, in the 1890s, made an average of $20,000 a week. The hike takes you through abandoned mining sites, with building foundations and equipment still intact, to the top of Lost Horse Mountain.

Ryan Mountain (3 miles; 2hr). Some of the best views in the park are from the top of Ryan Mountain (5461ft), seven hundred strenuous feet above the desert floor. Start at the parking area near the Sheep Pass campground and follow the trail past the Indian Cave, which contains bedrock mortars once used by the Cahuilla and Serrano.

Mastodon Peak (3 miles; 2hr). Another peak climb, less strenuous than Ryan Mountain but with great views, especially south to the Salton Sea. Start from the Cottonwood campground.

Lost Palms Oasis (8 miles; 5hr). This moderate trail, starting from the Cottonwood campground, leads across desert washes, past palo verde, cottonwood, and ironwood trees to the largest stand of palms in the park. The trail offers possible scrambling side-trips to Victory Palms and Munsen Canyon. There's little surface water, but often enough to lure bighorn sheep.

the entrance to the ranch and takes around ninety minutes. Tickets can be bought in advance at the Oasis Visitor Center, or just turn up and hope there is space. The ranch was once home to tough desert rat and indefatigable miner Bill Keys, a Russian by birth who lived here (with his family) from 1910 until his death (aged 89) in 1969 – long after less-hardy men had abandoned the arid wasteland. He was briefly famous in 1943, when he was locked away for shooting one of his neighbors over a right-of-way argument, only to be paroled by the mystery writer Erle Stanley Gardner. Keys and family made a spartan but surprisingly comfortable living from growing vegetables, mining, ranching, and working as a farrier and general trader for just about everything a desert dweller could desire. The tour visits their ramshackle home, orchard site, workshop, and even a schoolhouse that operated for seven years from 1935.

The center and southeast

Bill Keys, of the Desert Queen Ranch, is further remembered at **Keys View**, eight miles south, a 5185-foot-high vista offering the best views in the whole park. On a good day, you can see as far as the Salton Sea and beyond into Mexico – a brilliant desert panorama of badlands and mountains. The trouble is, "good" days are increasingly rare. LA smog driven by prevailing winds is funneled between the mountains straight to Joshua Tree National Park with the result that **air pollution** is a significant issue. Campaigning organizations (such as the National Parks Conservation Association; Ⓦwww.npca.org) do what they can but with the inexorably expanding conurbation producing some

---

Biking and rock climbing in Joshua Tree National Park

While driving through Joshua Tree isolates you from the desert, and the need to carry all your water limits the scope for hiking, **biking** strikes a nice balance. With cyclists restricted to roads open to motor vehicles you shouldn't come expecting genuine off-road action, but there is an increasing number of bikeable and challenging dirt roads. Armed with your own set of wheels (there is no bike rental anywhere near the park), consider heading out on popular 15–20-mile routes like Geology Tour Road, Covington Flats Road, and Pinkham Canyon Road. These and more are listed in the *Joshua Tree Guide*.

Since the 1970s, the fractured lumps of golden rock that pepper the northwestern corner of the park have become fabulously popular and world renowned for **rock climbing** and **bouldering**. Climbers keen to find a springtime training ground while the Sierra crags were still under snow began putting up routes which now see sticky-rubber traffic from October to May – the summer months are generally way too hot. In spring and fall, rock climbers sometimes base themselves here for weeks, usually at the *Hidden Valley* campground. Climbers should pick up the *Climber Ethics* leaflet from one of the visitor centers, and may want to call at the climbing shops in the township of Joshua Tree to obtain guidebooks. The most comprehensive is Randy Vogel's *Rock Climbing: Joshua Tree* (Falcon), though his condensed, and much cheaper, *Joshua Tree National Park: Classic Rock* (Falcon) may suit short-term visitors. Boulderers will want *A Complete Bouldering Guide to Joshua Tree National Park* by Robert Miramontes (K Daniels). Beginners, or those after **instruction** and guiding should contact one of the rock-climbing schools that operate here. Both Joshua Tree Rock Climbing School (☎760/366-4745 or 1-800/890-4745, Ⓦwww .joshuatreerockclimbing.com) and Uprising (☎1-888/254-6266, Ⓦwww.uprising .com) offer a range of one-day courses for around $110 and a range of improvers' weekends for around $200. Check the websites for course dates, or go for private guiding, which costs around $225 a day for one person or $150 each for two.

of the nation's dirtiest air, it is going to be an epic and undoubtedly drawn-out struggle.

Park Boulevard then passes the start of the Ryan Mountain hike (see box, p.313) and the turnoff for **Geology Tour Road**, which leads down through the best of Joshua Tree's rock formations. A little further on, the *Jumbo Rocks* campground is the start of a hiking loop (1.7 miles) through boulders and desert washes to **Skull Rock**, which can also be easily seen from the road immediately east of the campground.

Continuing east, now on Pinto Basin Road, *White Tank* campground (see p.311) is worth a short stop to wander along a short trail through huge granite domes to a photogenic **rock arch**; the trail starts by site 9.

Almost at the transition zone between the Colorado and Mojave deserts and on the fringes of the Pinto Basin, the **Cholla Cactus Garden** is a quarter-mile loop through an astonishing concentration of the "jumping" **cholla** cactus (see box, pp.284–285), as well as creosote bushes, jojoba, and several other cactus species. It is a beautiful spot at any time, but come at dusk or dawn for the best chance of seeing the mainly nocturnal desert wood rat. Nearby, the near-barren desert at **Ocotillo Patch** comes stuffed with freakish spindly ocotillo plants, at their best when blooming scarlet in spring.

The Imperial Valley and the Salton Sea

The patch of the Colorado Desert **south** of Joshua Tree and Palm Springs is one of the least friendly of all the Californian desert regions and its foreboding aspect discourages exploration. It's best not to come between June and September, when intense heat makes journeys uncomfortable and services are greatly reduced; frankly, there's little reason to come here at all unless you're heading for the Anza-Borrego Desert State Park or the Mexican border.

Sandwiched between Hwy-111 and Hwy-86, which branch off I-10 soon after Palm Springs and the Coachella Valley, the area from the **Salton Sea** down to the furnace-like migrant-worker towns of the agricultural **Imperial Valley** lies in the two-thousand-square-mile Salton Basin: the largest area of dry land below sea level in the western hemisphere.

Created accidentally in 1905 (see box, p.316), the Salton Sea and its shores were once extremely toney, attracting the likes of Frank Sinatra and Dean Martin to its yacht clubs; in its 1940s heyday, the sea was actually a bigger tourist draw than Yosemite National Park. A series of mid-1970s storms caused the sea to rise and swallow shoreline developments, but gross pollution was already having a detrimental impact on tourism. Nestled 235 feet below sea level, the Salton Sea has no natural outlet and has, over the years, been plagued by agricultural runoff and toxic wastes carried in by two rivers from Mexico, and is now excessively saline. Local boosters are desperate to point out that the problems are exaggerated, but fish still carry a consumption warning, and people rarely swim and water-ski here these days.

Still, the Salton Sea remains an important wintering area for shore birds and waterfowl. Brown pelicans come by in summer, and terns and cormorants nest here. The best place to see them is the **Sonny Bono Salton Sea National Wildlife Refuge** (daily dawn–dusk; free; ⓦpacific.fws.gov/salton) at the sea's southern tip. By the informative **visitor center** (Mon–Fri 7am–3.30pm and some weekends; ☎760/393-3052) there's a viewing platform, or you can take the Rock Hill Trail for a closer look, a twenty-minute walk to the water's edge.

The accidental sea

At 35 miles long by up to 15 miles wide, the **Salton Sea** is California's largest lake, but one which only came into existence a century ago. Over the millennia, the shallow Salton Basin has repeatedly filled with floodwaters that spilled over from the Colorado River some fifty miles to the east, but each time the lake has dried up. When European Americans started pushing into the West, they recognized that the fertile Salton Basin and the surrounding Imperial Valley could be made super-productive by channeling water from the Colorado. In 1901, a development company did just that, but river silt soon blocked the channel and in 1905 almost the entire flow from the Colorado River was pouring into the Salton Basin. The deluge wasn't stanched for almost two years, by which time it had formed the Salton Sea – a huge freshwater lake up to fifty feet deep.

To get to the refuge, take the poorly signposted backroads off Hwy-111 south of **Niland** or off Hwy-86 at **Westmorland**; both run past fields of alfalfa, cantaloupe, tomatoes, and other crops – proof that just about anything will grow in this fertile land provided it is suitably irrigated.

If you've come this far it's worth turning east off Niland's Main Street and traveling three miles to see **Salvation Mountain**, a fantastic work of large-scale religious folk art built since 1985 by friendly eccentric, Leonard Knight. He has devoted his later life to this wildly colored mass of straw and adobe liberally painted with extracts from the Bible and exhortations to "Repent" – there's even an abandoned motorboat used to represent Noah's Ark. Leonard adds to his structure – already thirty feet high and a hundred feet wide – each morning, but spends much of the day guiding the trickle of visitors: a small donation is appreciated but never requested.

Salvation Mountain stands at the entrance to **Slab City**, a huge settlement of squatters that swells in size in winter when Canadian RVers come down for warmth – and free city water.

The only other reasons you might stop are to **camp** (primitive $7, developed sites $17, hook-ups $23) in the Salton Sea State Recreation Area, which encompasses a handful of lakeside sites along a fourteen-mile stretch of the eastern side of the Salton Sea from Bombay Beach to Mecca Beach. Agricultural work brings thousands of Mexicans north of the border, and the restaurants generally cater to them: practice your Spanish.

Anza-Borrego Desert State Park

Southwest of the Salton Sea, the **ANZA-BORREGO DESERT STATE PARK** is the largest state park in the country outside Alaska, covering 600,000 acres and, in contrast to the Imperial Valley, offering a diverse variety of plant and animal life as well as a legend-strewn history spanning Native American tribes, the first white trailfinders, and Gold Rush times. It takes its double-barreled name from Juan Baptista de Anza, a Spanish explorer who crossed the region in 1774, and the Spanish for the native bighorn sheep, **borrego cimarron**, which eats the brittlebrush and agave found here. Some of Anza-Borrego can be covered by car (confidence on gravel roads is handy), although you'll need four-wheel-drive for the more obscure – and most interesting – routes, and there are over five hundred miles of hiking trails where vehicles are not permitted at all.

N

PACIFIC CREST TRAIL

Sheep Canyon

Coyote Canyon

Desert Gardens Picnic Area

COYOTE MOUNTAIN

SANTA ROSA MOUNTAINS

Clark Dry Lake

Borrego Palm Canyon

BORREGO PALM CANYON TRAIL

Peg Leg Smith Monument

S22

(86) & Salton Sea (15 miles)

State Park Visitor Center

Chamber of Commerce

B ℹ
A
D C
E

Borrego Springs

Font's Point

Borrego Badlands

Culp Valley

S22

PINYON MOUNTAINS

S2

S3

F

The Slot

OCOTILLO WELLS STATE VEHICULAR RECREATION AREA

San Diego (60 miles)

Yaqui Well

Yaqui Pass

Tamarisk Grove

Ocotillo Wells

78

(86) & Salton Sea (15 miles)

Scissors Crossing

Julian

Banner

78

Harper Flat

VALLECITO MOUNTAINS

San Diego (40 miles)

Cuyamaca Reservoir

CUYAMACA RANCHO STATE PARK

79

S2

8

Box Canyon

Blair Valley

Vallecito Stage Station

Agua Caliente Regional Park

S1

Palm Spring

Carrizo Impact Area (Restricted Zone)

Mountain Palm Spring

IN-KO-PA MOUNTAINS

Bow Willow

S2

San Diego & Imperial Valley Railroad

Ocotillo

8

El Centro (25 miles)

— Anza-Borrego Boundary

⋯⋯ Southern Emigrant Trail Historic Route

ACCOMMODATION

Borrego Valley Inn	C
Hacienda Del Sol	B
La Casa Del Zorro	F
Palm Canyon Resort	D
The Palms at Indian Head	A
Stanlunds Resort Inn & Suites	E

0   5 miles

During the fiercely hot summer months, the place is best left to the lizards, although most campgrounds stay open all year. The desert **blooming season**, typically a couple of weeks somewhere between late February and early April, is popular, when scarlet ocotillo, orange poppies, white lilies, purple verbena, and other intensely colorful wildflowers are a memorable – and fragrant – sight. For the latest information call the 24hr Wildflower Hotline (℡760/767-4684). As well as taking the usual desert precautions (see box, pp.284–285), you should read the comments in Basics on p.70 – this is mountain-lion territory.

Though accessible from the Salton Sea along Hwy-178 or Hwy-S22, the Anza-Borrego is usually approached from San Diego, through Julian (see p.269). Approaching from Julian you'll hit the park at Scissors Crossing with most of the developed facilities to the north and much of the more interesting historical debris to the south.

Borrego Springs

Human activity in Anza-Borrego revolves around **BORREGO SPRINGS**, a tiny town in the heart of the park centered on a large traffic island known as Christmas Circle. There's usually not much happening in Borrego Springs, but it's one of the most pleasant of all the desert towns, self-contained and remarkably uncommercialized. On a short visit to the park it is probably best to base yourself in Borrego Springs or camp at *Borrego Palm Canyon* campground, just out of town, where there's an abundance of ranger-led walks and nature hikes, and a campfire program: check with the visitor center (see below) for the latest details. If you're camping out, it's the place to gather (expensive) supplies – but don't expect any big supermarket chains here.

Your first stop, two miles west of here, should be the excellent **State Park visitor center**, 200 Palm Canyon Drive (June–Sept Sat, Sun & holidays 9am–5pm; Oct–May daily 9am–5pm; ℡760/767-5311, ⒲www.anzaborrego.statepark.org), which is so well landscaped into the desert floor you barely notice it as you approach. Here you can also pick up an informative free newspaper, which contains a detailed map of the park along with numerous suggestions for hikes. Outside, the half-mile **All-Access Nature Trail** allows you to weave across the desert identifying the flora.

A mile to the north, the main *Borrego Palm Canyon* campground marks the start of the **Borrego Palm Canyon Trail** (3 miles round-trip; 2hr; 350ft ascent), the most popular trail in the park (day-use fee $4 per vehicle). It follows a detailed nature trail to one of the largest oases left in the US, with a quarter-mile of stream densely flanked by around a thousand mop-topped California fan palms (sometimes known as Washingtonia palms from their Latin name *Washingtonia filifera*) – the only palms native to the western United States.

Practicalities

Borrego Springs is accessible by **public transportation**: from San Diego, the Metropolitan Transit System (℡1-800/858-0291, ⒲www.sdcommute.com; see p.224) makes the trip with a change in Ramona (2–4 daily, except Sun or Mon). Most of the town's commercial activity goes on either in The Center or The Mall, opposite each other on Palm Drive. Here you'll find the bulk of the restaurants, shops, and accommodation, but you'll need to head half a mile east for the **Chamber of Commerce**, 786 Palm Canyon Drive (June–Sept Mon–Fri 10am–3pm; Oct–May Mon–Sat 10am–4pm; ℡760/767-5555 or 1-800/559-5524, ⒲www.borregospringschamber.com). There's **Internet access** at the library by The Mall (closed Sun & Mon).

There are some lovely primitive and developed campgrounds in the park (see box, p.320), but if you're not feeling adventurous enough, there's a handful of good **places to stay**. In season, even the basic motels seem quite expensive, though rates drop dramatically in summer. There are a few **places to eat**, some of which close or run reduced hours in summer.

Accommodation

Borrego Valley Inn 405 Palm Canyon Drive ☏760/767-03111 or 1-800/333-5810. Probably the pick of the local accommodation, this lovely and centrally-located cluster of Southwestern-style rooms is set in a cactus garden and comes with two heated pools, rooms with kitchenettes, afternoon snacks, and a hearty continental breakfast. Rooms are all tastefully decorated and well equipped, but step up to the deluxe rooms if you can. There's a two-night minimum stay at weekends. Closed June–Aug. Weeknights ⑤, weekends ⑥

Hacienda del Sol 610 Palm Canyon Drive ☏760/767-5442. Central, budget motel with some kitchenettes, and separate cottages. Rooms ④, kitchen units ⑤, cottages ⑥

La Casa del Zorro 3845 Yaqui Pass Rd ☏760/767-5323 or 1-800/824-1884, ⓦwww .lacasadelzorro.com. The place to go if you really want to live it up, a gorgeous hotel in a date-palm oasis with beautifully appointed rooms and assorted pools, gyms, and tennis courts. The hefty prices increase one code at weekends. Winter ⑧, summer ⑦

Palm Canyon Resort 221 Palm Canyon Drive ☏1-800/242-0044, ⓦwww.pcresort.com. Modern hotel a mile west of town done in ersatz Old West style with comfortable rooms and an RV site ($29) with water, electricity, cable TV, and high speed Internet access (extra $5). Winter ⑥, summer ⑤

The Palms at Indian Head 2220 Hoberg Rd ☏1-800/519-2624, ⓦwww.thepalmsatindianhead .com. Stylish 1950s Modernist hotel – once the domain of Monroe, Brando, and the like – with a great pool, all very tastefully done. It had seen better days but is improving all the time and the emphasis is very much on relaxation. Winter ⑥, summer ④

Stanlunds Resort Inn & Suites Borrego Springs Road ☏760/767-5501. About the cheapest rooms around (rooms with kitchenettes) and a nice pool, located three-quarters of a mile south along Borrego Springs Road. Continental breakfast is included. Winter ⑤, summer ④

Eating

Carlee's Place 660 Palm Canyon Drive ☏760/767-3262. Handy downtown restaurant and bar with a lively atmosphere and a menu extending to burgers, sandwiches, pizza ($13–15), and the likes of tequila chicken fettuccini ($14).

Kendall's Café The Mall, Palm Canyon Drive ☏760/767-3491. Combined diner and Mexican café that's always a favorite with locals. Most dishes $6–10. Daily, closes 8pm.

Krazy Coyote Saloon & Grill at *The Palms at Indian Head* (see above). The pick of the area's more upscale restaurants with a varied menu – steaks, pastas, salads – and patio dining overlooking the pool. Daily in winter and Wed–Sun dinner in summer.

Northern Anza-Borrego

Six miles east of Borrego Springs along Hwy-S22, there's a memorial marker to Peg Leg Smith, an infamous local spinner of yarns from Gold Rush days who is further celebrated by a festival of tall tales – the **Peg Leg Liars Contest** – which takes place at this spot on the first Saturday in April. Anybody can get up before the judges and fib their hearts out for five minutes, the most outrageous stories earning a modest prize. Roughly four miles further on, a fairly tough dirt road (check with the State Park visitor center or Chamber of Commerce for conditions) leads to **Font's Point** and a view over the **Borrego Badlands** – a long, sweeping plain devoid of vegetation whose strange, stark charms are oddly inspiring. Sunset is the best time to appreciate fully the layered alluvial banding.

If you want to be outside but shaded from the sun's fierce rays, make for **The Slot**, a narrow fifty-foot-deep canyon carved from the soft rock by infrequent flooding. You can walk down into the canyon then follow it downstream for

Camping in Anza-Borrego

Anza-Borrego Desert State Park manages two developed and nine primitive camp-grounds, but this is one of the few parks that allows **open camping**, giving you the freedom to pitch a tent pretty much anywhere without a permit, although it's advisable to let someone know your plans. The few provisos are that you don't drive off-road, don't camp near water holes, camp away from developed campgrounds, light fires only in fire rings or metal containers, collect no firewood, and leave the place as you found it, or cleaner.

The largest site, and the only one with RV hook-ups, is the *Borrego Palm Canyon* campground a mile from the visitor center (hook-ups $19, tents $13). *Tamarisk Grove*, thirteen miles south on Hwy-S3 ($13), is the only other developed site. Both charge $4 per vehicle for day-use of the facilities, which include water supply and coin-op **showers**. Both also organize **guided hikes** and have regular discussion and activity evenings led by a volunteer naturalist. Places can be reserved through ReserveAmerica.com on ☎1-800/444-7275 (essential for holidays and weekends, and in the March–April blooming season). The other primitive campgrounds fill on a first-come-first-served basis; those in the backcountry always have space. All are accessible by road vehicles and are free, except for *Bow Willow*, which charges $7 and is the only one with **drinking water**. Most sites are below 1500ft, which is fine in winter, but in the hotter months you might try *Culp Valley*, eight miles southwest of Borrego Springs, at a blissfully balmy 3400ft. In addition there's a commercial campground at the Agua Caliente Regional Park (see below).

five minutes to a quarter-mile-long section where it is only just wide enough for one person to squeeze through. To get there, travel 1.5 miles east from the junction of Borrego Springs Road and Hwy-78, then follow the very sandy Buttes Pass Road for 1.8 miles, keeping left at the only junction. The road is usually passable for ordinary cars but if you have any doubts about your or your vehicle's abilities, turn back.

Southern Anza-Borrego

At Scissors Crossing, Hwy-78 from Julian intersects Hwy-S2 which heads towards the park's southeast corner following the line of the old **Butterfield Stage Route**, which began service in 1857 and was the first regular line of communication between the eastern states and the newly settled West. Along the way you pass through **Blair Valley**, with its primitive campground, to **Box Canyon**, where the Mormon Battalion of 1847, following what is now known as the **Southern Emigrant Trail Historic Route**, forced a passage along the desert wash. It isn't especially spectacular, but makes for some safe desert walking, never more than a couple of hundred yards from the road. Nine miles further on, the **Vallecito Stage Station** (Sept–May 9am–sunset; June–Aug closed) is an old adobe stage rest-stop that gives a good indication of the comforts – or lack of them – of early desert travel. The building is in the grounds of a county-run **campground** ($12), which requires you to pay a day-use fee of $2 per vehicle to see it.

A further three miles south, the **Agua Caliente Regional Park** (Sept–May daily 9.30am–5pm; $5 per vehicle) contains a couple of naturally fed pools, one large outdoor affair kept at its natural 96°F, and one smaller indoor pool kept at a more modest temperature and fitted with water jets. Most visitors stay at the **campground** (tents $14, hook-ups $18; reservations ☎858/565-3600), which surrounds the pools and gives you longer access for evening soaking.

△ Joshua Tree, Joshua Tree National Park

To the south lies the least-visited portion of Anza-Borrego, good for isolated exploration and undisturbed views around Imperial Valley, where there's a vivid and spectacular clash as gray rock rises from the edges of the red desert floor, and a primitive **campground** close to the small oasis at Mountain Palm Spring.

Hiking, biking, and other recreational opportunities

Recreational opportunities in the park are strictly controlled to preserve the fragile ecosystem. **Hiking** is perhaps the most obvious pursuit, with the Borrego Palm Canyon Trail (see above) being the most popular. If you'd prefer the desert to yourself, consider one of the other hikes listed in the park's free annual newspaper: the Pena Spring Trail (0.6 miles round-trip) is good for spotting bird- and wildlife, or try the tougher Hellhole Canyon/Maidenhair Falls Trail (6 miles round-trip) which involves some rock scrambling and ends at a canyon oasis.

Mountain bikers are not allowed on hiking trails, but provided you bring your own set of wheels (there are no local rentals available) you've free rein on the dirt roads which cross the desert. If you'd rather have a larger saddle, try **desert horse-trekking** with Smoketree Arabian Horse Rental (℡760/767-5850, ⓦsmoketree.micronpcweb.com), who offers one-hour ($55) and two-hour ($95) rides, even in summer when they start at 7am.

Care for the fragile ecosystem is not paramount inside the **Ocotillo Wells State Vehicular Recreational Area**, a region to the east of the park mapped out for dune buggies and the like. Owners drive like demons in a maelstrom of tossed sand and engine noise; if you're tempted to join them, you'll need to bring along your own rig and contact the Recreation Headquarters (daily 8am–4pm; ℡760/767-5391) for information.

The Mojave Desert

Desolate, silent, and virtually lifeless, the **MOJAVE DESERT**, mythic badland of the West, has no equal when it comes to hardship. Called the **High Desert** because it averages a height of around two thousand feet above sea level, the Mojave is very dry and for the most part deadly flat, dotted here and there with the shaggy form of a Joshua tree and an occasional abandoned miner's shed. For most, it's the barrier between LA and Las Vegas, an obstacle to get over before they reach either city; and, short on attractions as it is, you may want to follow their example. However, you should linger a little just to see – and smell – what a desert is really like: a vast, impersonal, extreme environment, sharp with its own peculiar fragrance, and alive in spring with acres of fiery orange poppies – the state flower of California – and other brightly colored wildflowers.

You will have relatively little company. If LA is the home of the sports car, the Mojave is the land of huge dust-covered trucks, carrying goods across the state to Nevada and beyond. Other signs of life include the grim military subculture marooned on huge weapons-testing sites. There is also a hard-core group of desert fans: backdrop for the legion of road movies spawned by the underground film culture in the late 1960s and early 1970s, the Mojave is a favorite with bikers and neo-hippies drawn by the barren panorama of sand dunes and mountain ranges. Members of the California Sierra Club and other savvy in-state nature lovers light out for the less barren beauties of the Mojave National Preserve. But otherwise visitors are thin on the ground, and, for most of the year, you can rely on being in sparse company.

I-15 cuts through the heart of the Mojave, dividing it into two distinct regions. To the north lies the desolate **Western Mojave**, as well as **Death Valley** (covered in Chapter Five), and to the south lie Barstow and the Mojave National Preserve. **Barstow**, the lackluster capital of the Mojave, is redeemed only by its location halfway between LA and Las Vegas on I-15, which makes it both a potential stopover between the two points and a good base for the surrounding attractions.

If Barstow isn't exactly alluring, the huge **Mojave National Preserve**, which lies just south of the road to Las Vegas, is. Here you can see spectacular sand dunes, striking rock formations, and a huge variety of plant life, including large concentrations of Joshua trees. Much of the preserve rises to about 4000 feet, so it also offers respite from the harshest of the area's heat.

The Western Mojave

The **western expanse** of the Mojave Desert spreads out on the north side of the San Gabriel Mountains, fifty miles from Los Angeles via Hwy-14. It is a barren plain that drivers have to cross in order to reach the alpine peaks of the eastern Sierra Nevada Mountains or Death Valley, at the Mojave's northern edge. The few towns that have taken root in this stretch of desert over the past couple of decades are populated in the main by two sorts of people: retired couples who value the dry, clean air, and aerospace workers employed in one of the many military bases or aircraft factories. **Lancaster**, near Edwards Air Force Base, is the largest town and one of the few places to pick up supplies; **Mojave**, thirty miles north, is a desert crossroads that caters mainly to drive-by tourists. **Tehachapi**, twenty miles west and a few thousand feet higher, offers a cool retreat. Hwy-14 joins up with US-395 another forty miles north, just west of the huge naval air base at **China Lake** and the faceless town of **Ridgecrest**, good if only for its location as a jumping-off point for some interesting attractions.

Lancaster and the Antelope Valley

From the north end of LA's San Fernando Valley, Hwy-14 cuts off from I-5 and heads east around the foothills of the San Gabriel Mountains, passing the site of California's earliest gold discovery in 1842, now preserved within the **Placerita Canyon Park** nature reserve (daily 9am–5pm; free; ⓦwww .placerita.org), a mile and a half off Hwy-14 along Placerita Canyon Road. Eleven miles further along Hwy-14 stands the distinctive sandstone outcrop of the 745-acre **Vasquez Rocks County Park** (daily 8am–sunset; $3 per vehicle), once a hiding place for frontier bandits and bank robbers, and later used by Hollywood movie studios as the backdrop for a variety of TV shows and films including *The Flintstones*. Beyond here, Hwy-138 cuts off east, heading up to the ski resorts and lakes along the crest of the San Gabriel Mountains, while Hwy-14 runs north across the sparsely settled flatlands of the Mojave Desert.

Some twenty miles on you hit the biggest places for miles, the twin towns of **PALMDALE** and **LANCASTER**, two soulless side-by-side communities of retirees and RV parks whose economy is wholly based on designing, building, and testing airplanes, from B-1 bombers for the military to the *Voyager*, which made the first nonstop flight around the globe in 1987. The free **Blackbird Airpark** (Fri–Sun 11am–4pm), three miles east of Hwy-14 along Avenue P in Palmdale, can be recognized by the two sinister-looking black planes standing by the roadside. These are in fact the fastest and highest-flying planes ever created. The A-12 was designed in the 1950s as prototype for the SR-71 – the *Blackbird* – a reconnaissance plane that could reach 2100 miles per hour at 85,000ft. Unless you strike one of the infrequent "open cockpit" days, all you can do is circle the planes admiring the sleek lines and astonishing statistics. There are several other impressive aircraft in the park, and more are added regularly.

If you're not a military buff, there's little to draw you into Lancaster except the need of a bed or supplies. The **Chamber of Commerce**, at 554 W Lancaster Blvd (Mon–Fri 9am–5pm; ☎661/948-4518), has information on **accommodation** at motels such as *Motel 6* (☎661/948-0435; ❷) at 43540 W 17th St, just off Hwy-14, or the more salubrious *Desert Inn*, 44219 Sierra Hwy (☎661/948-8401 or 1-800/942-8401, ⓦwww.desert-inn.com; ❺): each has a pool.

To learn more of the desert sights, stop by the **Mojave Desert State Parks visitor center**, 43779 15th St West (Mon–Sat 10am–4pm; ☎661/942-0662, ⓦwww.calparksmojave.com), handily sited in a mall near the Avenue K exit off Hwy-14. This is the main contact point for the surrounding sights such as the **Antelope Valley California Poppy Reserve** (daily sunrise–sunset; in poppy season $5, otherwise free), fifteen miles west of Hwy-14 on Lancaster Road. You can come to stroll the easy desert trails at any time of year, but the main reason to come is to witness the place blanketed in the bright orange of California's state flower, the Golden Poppy. It is a temperamental and unpredictable plant but given enough rain it usually blooms between mid-March and late April; for details, call the visitor center or consult the Theodore Payne Foundation for Wildflowers and Native Plants (☎818/768-3533, ⓦwww.theodorepayne.org). During the blooming season you can also visit the excellent **interpretive center** (seasonal: Mon–Fri 9am–4pm, Sat & Sun 9am–5pm), which has displays of desert flora and fauna. The building itself is proof that passive-solar underground architecture works: built into the side of a hill, it keeps cool naturally and is powered entirely by an adjacent windmill generator.

Saddleback Butte State Park, seventeen miles east of Lancaster at the junction of Avenue J and 170th Street (daily dawn–dusk; $5 per vehicle), centers on a smallish hill whose slopes are home to a splendid collection of Joshua trees. It's also a likely spot to catch a glimpse of the desert tortoise, for whom the park provides a refuge from the motorcyclists and dune-buggy enthusiasts who tear around the region. There's a half-mile nature trail and a simple **campground** ($12), which is mostly under-used but is popular for star-gazing on summer weekends. Three miles southwest, the **Antelope Valley Indian Museum** on Avenue M (mid-Sept to mid-June Sat & Sun 11am–4pm; $2), housed in a mock Swiss chalet painted with Native American motifs, contains an extensive collection of ethnographic material from all over the state.

Mojave, Tehachapi, and Red Rock Canyon

MOJAVE, strung out along the highway thirty miles north of Lancaster, is a major junction on the interstate train network, though it's used solely by freight trains. The town itself – largely a mile-long highway strip of gas stations, $40-a-night motels, and franchised fast-food restaurants, open around the clock – is a good place to fill up on food and gas before continuing north into the Owens Valley or Death Valley.

The desert and dry lake beds east of Mojave make up **Edwards Air Force Base**, the US military testing ground for experimental, high-speed and high-altitude aircraft (such as the *Blackbird*; see opposite), which incorporates NASA's Dryden Flight Research Center, and back-up space-shuttle landing site. To visit the base's **Air Force Flight Test Center Museum** (Tues–Sat 9am–5pm; free; ☎ 661/277-3517, ⓦ www.edwards.af.mil) you must reserve in advance for admittance to the base: US citizens will have a better chance than foreigners.

Mojave's dry conditions not only suit the military, but make the Mojave Airport, a mile east of town, the perfect parking lot for **mothballed airplanes**. Commercial airliners that are surplus to requirements get pastured here, often for years, and you can see the rows of Airbus and 747 tailplanes still decked out in the livery of their owners.

Mojave also hit the headlines in October 2004 as the launch and landing site of **SpaceShipOne**, which became the first privately funded spaceship to achieve suborbital flight (around 62 miles above the earth) twice within 14 days, thereby claiming the $10 million X-prize.

Tehachapi

About twenty miles west from Mojave, Hwy-58 rises to the rolling hillsides of **TEHACHAPI**, an apple-growing center that, at an elevation of around 4000 feet, offers a nice respite from the Mojave's heat. In addition to its pretty setting, the town has a couple of minor claims to fame. Some 5100 **wind generators** – built here since the early 1980s – make the Tehachapi Wind Resource Area, ranked along Cameron Ridge to the east, one of the world's most productive renewable energy stations. They're very visible from Hwy-58, but there are few places to stop so you may prefer to follow Tehachapi Willow Springs Road, a minor road between Tehachapi and Mojave running just south of Hwy-58.

Train enthusiasts, meanwhile, cross states to see groaning Santa Fe diesels hauling their mile-long strings of boxcars around the **Tehachapi Loop**, eight miles west of town. Built in 1876 as the only means of scaling the steep slopes of the region, the tracks double back on themselves to make a complete 360° loop. It is an impressive sight seeing a train (anything over 85 boxcars long) twisting around a mountain, its front end 77ft above its tail. You can't see it properly from Hwy-58, so follow the signs three miles from the Keene exit to a roadside plaque commemorating the loop's engineers.

For **information** about these and other local attractions, ranging from pick-your-own-fruit orchards and antiques shops to ostrich farms, stop in at the **Chamber of Commerce**, 209 E Tehachapi Blvd (Mon–Fri 9am–5pm, Sat & Sun 9am–4pm; ☎ 661/822-4180), right by the train tracks in the older section of town.

Nearby you'll find **accommodation** at the *Santa Fe Motel*, 120 W Tehachapi Blvd (☎ 661/822-3184, ⓕ 822-7905; ❷), and the *Best Western Mountain Inn*, 418 W Tehachapi Blvd (☎ 661/822-5591; ❺). Eight miles southwest of town off Highline Road, there's **camping** (☎ 661/868-7000; $10) among the pines at a refreshing 6000 feet in the *Tehachapi Mountain Park*: there's toilets and water but no other facilities. Popular local **restaurants** include the daytime-only *Apple Shed*, 333 E Tehachapi Blvd (☏661/823-8333), good for country-style breakfasts or apple-pie breaks, and *Domingo's*, 20416 Valley Blvd (☏661/822-7611), a family-owned Mexican and seafood place in the newer section of town a mile or so west.

North of Mojave along Hwy-14

Following Hwy-14 northeast from Mojave the desert is virtually uninhabited, the landscape marked only by the bald ridges of the foothills of the Sierra Nevada Mountains that rise to the west, though you might see the odd ghostly sign of the prospectors who once roamed the region in search of gold and less precious minerals. Twenty-four miles north of Mojave, Hwy-14 passes through **Red Rock Canyon**, a brilliantly colored rocky badlands of wonderfully eroded formations.

The highway passes right through the center of the most impressive section, though if you walk just a hundred yards from the road you're more likely to see an eagle or a coyote than another visitor. Better still, call at **Red Rock Canyon State Park** (always open; $5), where the **visitor center** (open spring & fall Fri noon–8pm, Sat 9am–7pm, Sun 9am–3pm; closed summer and winter; ☏661/942-0662) can point you to a number of short trails and runs a weekend ranger program of nature walks and campfire talks, ranging from Native American visits to movie filming in the area. The adjacent *Ricardo* **campground** ($12) is fairly primitive but beautifully sited amid Joshua trees and colorful rocks.

Around 25 miles north of Red Rock Canyon, Hwy-14 meets US-395 which heads north to the Owens Valley and the western entrance to Death Valley, regions covered in depth in Chapter Five. A further twenty miles north of the junction, Cinder Rock Road leads east to **Fossil Falls**, another rather unearthly formation some 27 miles northwest of Ridgecrest. Relatively recent volcanic eruptions (about 20,000 years ago) drove lava through one of this region's dry river channels, creating what looks like a petrified cataract. Some remaining petroglyphs as well as various small artifacts and polished indentations in the rocks, used for grinding grain, attest to widespread human habitation in this area.

Boron, the Rand Mining District, and Ridgecrest

Busy Hwy-58 runs east from Mojave skirting the northern side of the Edwards Air Force Base for thirty miles to a signed exit for the **Borax Visitor Center** (daily 9am–5pm; $2 per vehicle; ⊛www.borax.com/borax6.html), a modern complex on a hill overlooking a processing plant and the vast open-cast borax mine – the largest mine in California. Borax is sodium borate, a crystalline mineral which was originally used as a flux to improve the working properties of gold and silver, but more recently has found applications in everything from washing detergents to heat-resistant glass and fiberglass. The center is primarily a promotional tool for the Borax Company, which owns the site, but call in if only to see the seventeen-minute video (complete with a 1960s snip of Ronald Reagan advertising hand cleaner), which finishes with curtains opening on a great view into the mile-wide, 650-foot-deep pit.

There's more of the history of boron extraction and the role of the twenty mule teams which hauled paired ten-ton wagons of borax out of Death Valley and elsewhere at the **Boron Twenty Mule Team Museum**, 26962 Twenty

Mule Team Rd (daily 10am–4pm; donation; ⓦrnrs.com/20MuleTeam), in the one-street town of **BORON** three miles further east. The museum also has coverage of movies filmed here – parts of *Erin Brockovich* for one – and has a video about the Solar Energy Generating Station (SEGS), which spreads across the desert six miles at the junction of Hwy-58 and US-395. This vast array of shiny panels produces around thirty megawatts of electricity and is part of five such installations across the Mojave Desert.

The Rand Mining District

Following US-395 north of Boron there's no reason to stop in the first thirty miles until you reach the **RAND MINING DISTRICT**, a close cluster of three virtually deserted towns, whose lifeblood is provided by the Yellow Aster and Baltic gold mines, the last to be commercially worked in California. **Red Mountain** and **Johannesburg** are a couple of miles apart on US-395, but the area's real interest lies a mile to the west on a loop road between the two towns. Here you'll find **Randsburg**, a near ghost town of scruffy-looking shacks surrounded by the detritus of ancient mines. The streets are very quiet midweek, but the tempo picks up a little at weekends when a couple of antique-cum-knick-knack shops open up. This mild gentrification aside, the place retains a certain Wild West charm to its 200-yard-long main street with its two bars, antique shops, and the **Desert Museum**, 161 Butte Ave (Sat & Sun 10am–5pm; free), which has displays on the glory days of the 1890s, when upwards of three thousand people lived in the town, mining gold, silver, and tungsten out of the arid, rocky hills. The nearby **General Store**, at no.35, is a fascinating slice of history with its embossed tin ceiling, 1904 soda fountain (the super-thick chocolate shakes are locally celebrated), and a small restaurant surrounded by shelves of groceries and mining supplies. It is open daily, and is a good source of local **information** (ⓣ760/374-2418).

You are free to wander off and explore the nearby hills and old mine workings, but land-use conflict between off-roaders and the Bureau of Land Management, which is seeking to protect desert-tortoise habitat, means you should ask locally about areas which may be closed.

Should you decide to **stay** overnight in Randsburg, the *Cottage Hotel*, 130 Butte Ave (ⓣ760/374-2285, ⓦwww.randsburg.com; ⑤), provides comfortable, Victorian-themed accommodation. **Eating** options in town are limited to the general store and the *Opera House Café*, also on Butte Avenue.

Ridgecrest

Twenty miles north of Randsburg, Hwy-178 cuts east towards Death Valley, reaching the sprawling desert community of **RIDGECREST**, dominated by the huge China Lake Naval Weapons Center. Jet fighters scream past overhead, taking target practice on land that's chock-full of ancient **petroglyphs** – the largest grouping in the western hemisphere. Though access to the sites is strictly controlled, you can get some idea of the native culture of the Mojave Desert by visiting the **Maturango Museum**, on the corner of China Lake Boulevard and East Las Flores Avenue (daily 10am–5pm; $3; ⓣ760/375-6900, ⓦwww.maturango.org), which as well as acting as **visitor center** (free), has exhibits on both the natural and cultural history of the region, including examples of the rock-art figures. To get out and see the figures and designs in their natural surroundings, join a full-day volunteer-led **tour** organized through the museum (mid-March to mid-June & mid-Sept to mid-Dec only; $35). The most concentrated collections of petroglyphs are on the military base and, in the security-conscious aftermath of September 11, visitors need access clearance which can take a few days, and may be refused to foreigners (though it is worth applying). For the latest information call the museum or check its website (where you can download an application form), and be prepared to reserve a place several weeks in advance.

Visitors interested in rockets, guided missiles, and the navy's role in the area can visit the **US Naval Museum of Armaments and Technology** (Mon–Fri 10am–4pm; free; ℡760/939-3140) on the China Lake base. Again, security checks are needed and some visitors may be denied entry.

It is perhaps more rewarding to stray four miles east of town to the Bureau of Land Management's **Wild Horse and Burro corrals**, where sometimes over a thousand animals are kept while waiting for adoption. Even if you're not prepared to take one home, you can call in (Mon–Fri 7.30am–4pm; free; ⓦwww.wildhorseandburro.blm.gov); to ensure an enthusiastic reception, bring along some apples or carrots.

Ridgecrest has an abundance of **accommodation**, the vast majority being chain motels such as the budget *Economy Inn & Suite*, 416 S China Lake Blvd (℡760/375-1591; ❶), and the upscale *Heritage Inn & Suites*, 1050 N Norma St (℡760/446-6543 or 1-800/843-0693; ❹). For something different, try the antique-furnished *BevLen Haus B&B*, 809 N Sanders St (℡760/375-1988, ⓦwww.bevlen.com; ❸), with en-suite rooms and a hearty breakfast.

Trona Pinnacles and Searles Valley

Hwy-178 runs northeast from Randsburg past the burro corrals and out into the dry and desolate **Searles Valley**, which offers a back road into Death Valley with access to Telescope Peak (see p.382). Some sixteen miles northeast of Randsburg, a five-mile dirt road (passable except after rain) leads to the **Trona Pinnacles National Natural Landmark** (unrestricted access; free) where over five hundred tufa spires stretch up to 140ft. Mostly conical and grouped in clusters, these soft-rock pinnacles were considered extraterrestrial enough-looking to form a backdrop for parts of *Star Trek V* and can be viewed best on the half-mile nature trail. The park's campground was washed out during an El Niño storm, but you are free to **camp** anyway: there are vault toilets but you'll have to bring water. There are basic supplies six miles north on Hwy-178 at the industrial and substantially run-down borax-processing town of **Trona**.

Victorville, Barstow, and around

The long desert drive from LA to Las Vegas takes you along I-15, part of which follows the original line of Route 66. You'll see little of the old road – or anything else of great interest – from the freeway, so you should definitely consider taking time out to explore a few minor attractions. **Victorville** warrants a brief detour to view the highwayside Americana in the Route 66 Museum. **Barstow** is better for what lies nearby, particularly the colored rocks of Rainbow Basin and the faux ghost town of Calico. Further east there are early human remains at the **Calico Dig**, and the etymological curiosity that is **Zzyzx**.

Victorville

I-15 heads north from San Bernardino slicing between the San Gabriel and San Bernardino mountains to reach the Mojave Desert. The first town of any size is **VICTORVILLE**, some eighty miles northeast of LA. There's all the

The advent of the interstates in the 1950s tolled the death knell on what John Stein-beck called The Mother Road in *Grapes of Wrath*. Route 66 was the umbilical cord between Chicago and Los Angeles, conceived in the 1920s when existing roads were stitched together to form a single 2400-mile route across eight states. It was just one of many such migration routes but is the one that most captured the public imagination – not least through Nat King Cole's 1946 hit *(Get your kicks on) Route 66* – and became America's most famous highway. As freeways obliterated the old road and franchise hotels and restaurants populated their flanks, the old diners and mom-and-pop motels gradually disappeared, further enhancing its iconic status.

Large sections of the old route vanished long ago, but it was the realization that some of the last vestiges were about to disappear that kickstarted a revival. Sections of the original route have since sprouted Route 66 signs, though these were promptly liberated by fans and you now tend to see "Historic Route 66" shields painted onto the asphalt. After considerable lobbying by Route 66 associations, Bill Clinton passed a National Preservation Bill benefiting the Route 66 Corridor in 1999, and the tourist machine now promotes the old road vigorously. Some 320 miles of the origi-nal route ran through California, and Kingman, Barstow, and San Bernardino all get name-checked in the famous song, but the best-preserved section is in the Mojave Desert east of Barstow. Fans will want to visit the small **museums** in Victorville (see below) and Barstow (see p.330), or even try to track down San Bernardino's classic *Wigwam Motel* (at 2728 W Foothill Blvd ☏909/875-3005), but for most it is enough to drive the desert section that loops south off I-40 from Ludlow to Essex. One essential stop is *Roy's* gas station and café at Amboy, a place that seems instantly familiar from dozens of road-trip movies and car commercials.

To delve deeper, check out websites such as Ⓦwww.national66.com and Ⓦwww.historic66.com.

motels, fast-food joints, and gas stations you could ask for along the freeway, but it is worth ducking off into the old town center for a quick look at the small **California Route 66 Museum**, 16825 D St at Fifth Street (Thurs–Mon 10am–4pm; free; ☏760/951-0436, Ⓦwww.califrt66museum.org). Dedicated to American myth, it has devotional displays relating to the westernmost strip of the Mother Road (see box above). Relics from an old roadside attraction called "Hulaville" are the museum's most interesting feature, but there are vari-ous old-time videos and a stack of nostalgic merchandise.

Barstow and around

Almost thirty miles northeast of Victorville along the thundering, seemingly endless I-15, **BARSTOW** looms up out of the desert, providing a welcome opportunity to get out of the car. Though situated at the crossroads of three major thoroughfares (I-40 and Hwy-58 also run through here), it's a small town, consisting of just one main road lined with a selection of motels and restaurants that make a budget overnight stop possible. This main street was once part of the famed **Route 66**, so fans of neon will enjoy some classic examples. There, however, the town's appeal ends. For many months of the year, the relentless sun manages to keep people in their air-conditioned homes for a good part of the day and Barstow can seem more like a ghost town than the capital of the Mojave.

Historical interest focuses on the grand 1911 **Harvey House**, also known as the Casa del Desierto (the "House of the Desert"), built as a train station with associated restaurant and lodging. Trains still stop here and the building remains striking, but is largely empty and has a forlorn air despite containing a couple of small museums. The **Western American Railroad Museum** (Fri–Sun 10am–4pm; donation suggested; ℡760/256-9276, Ⓦwww .barstowrailmuseum.org), is dedicated to preserving the history of Southwest railroading, while the **Route 66 "Mother Road" Museum**, 681 N 1st Ave (Fri–Sun 11am–4pm; free; Ⓦwww.barstow66museum.itgo.com), is full of highway Americana and some classic photos of yesteryear Barstow. For those with less specialized interests, there's the **Mojave River Valley Museum**, 270 E Virginia Way (daily 11am–4pm; free; Ⓦmvm.4t.com), containing material on the history and natural history of the area with a sizeable archeological collection including material from the Calico Dig (see opposite).

Getting out of town, your first stop should be **Rainbow Basin** (unrestricted access), eleven miles north along Irwin Road, which runs off First Street just north of the Harvey House, a rock formation which, after thirty million years of wind erosion, has been exposed as a myriad shades from vivid greens to deep reds, all best taken in around dawn or dusk. Most visitors will probably be content to weave the car along the winding four-mile loop road around the canyon and marvel at the prettiness of it all. You can camp here (see below) at minimally equipped sites.

Heading eight miles east on I-40, just past Dagget, the original Department of Energy's Solar One Power Plant has been replaced by the **SEGS II Solar Power Plant**, which, marked by a hundred-acre field of mirrors, is a surreal example of how California is putting its deserts to use. Anyone who has seen the film *Bagdad Café* will remember the light reflections the mirrors give off for miles around.

Practicalities

The **California Welcome Center** (daily 9am–6pm; ℡760/253-4782, Ⓦwww.californiadeserts.com), four miles west of Barstow in the Tanger Outlet Mall off I-15 at the Lenwood Road exit, has a good selection of maps of the surrounding area, lodging and restaurant guides, and various flyers on local attractions. There's also the **Chamber of Commerce**, 409 E Fredricks St (Mon–Fri 9am–5pm; ℡760/256-8617, Ⓦwww.barstowchamber.com), right in town.

Greyhound buses stop at 1611 E Main St, where it crosses I-15, a mile east of downtown, but arriving by **train**, you'll be dropped at the Amtrak station in the Casa del Desierto (see p.329), on First Street. Main Street is the best place to look for **motels**, generally only distinguished by the condition of the neon sign outside. Basically you get what you pay for, but good starting points are *Days Inn*, 1590 Coolwater Lane (℡760/256-1737; ❶), or for a little more comfort, the corporate-style *Ramada Inn*, 1511 E Main St (℡760/256-5673; ❸). You can **camp** eleven miles north of Barstow in the simple *Owl Canyon* campground ($6; no water) at Rainbow Basin (see above), or if you need more facilities, at **Calico**, a re-created ghost town (see opposite) with shaded canyons where you can pitch a tent for $18, hook up campers for $22 per night, or stay in one of the cabins (❶).

Food in Barstow, though far from exotic, is plentiful and cheap. Restaurants sit snugly between the many hotels on Main Street: visit your favorite franchise or try *Idle Spurs Steak House*, 290 Old Hwy-58, just north of town ℡760/256-8888), which does a good slab of meat; *Rosita's*, 540 W Main St (℡760/256-9218), for authentic Mexican; or *Carlos & Toto's*, 901 W Main (℡760/256-7513), for more Americanized but extremely good south-of-the-border fare. Evening **entertainment** comes in the form of a few grubby bars frequented by bike gangs, the least threatening of which is *Katz*, 127 W Main St at First, open from 6am to 2am.

East of Barstow: along I-15

Most people who stop in Barstow are not here to enjoy the desert, but to visit the contrived **Calico Ghost Town** (daily 9am–5pm; $6, admission free with camping; ☎1-800/863-2542, ⓦwww.calicotown.com), seven miles northeast along I-15 then three miles north. In the late nineteenth century, Calico produced millions of dollars' worth of silver and borax and supported a population of almost four thousand. Attractively set in the color-streaked Calico Hills, but subject to the extreme heat of the Mojave, the town was quickly deserted when the silver ran out. It's since been rather cynically – and insensitively – restored, with souvenir shops and hot-dog stands, and a main thoroughfare lined with ersatz saloons, an old schoolhouse, a vaudeville playhouse, and shops kitted out in period styles. However, should you so desire, there are miles of mining shafts and tunnels open to crawl around in – until claustrophobia forces you up for air.

Various festivals brighten up Calico, the best of which are May's **Spring Festival**, a family-oriented affair with a bluegrass hootenanny, and October's **Calico Days**, a celebration of early days with a Wild West parade, burro run, and assorted games and contests.

There's a more highbrow appeal to the **Calico Early Man Site** (visit by guided tour only Wed 12.30pm & 4.30pm, Thurs–Sun 9.30am, 11.30am, 1.30pm & 3.30pm; $2.50, minimum of two people; ⓦwww.ca.blm.gov /barstow/calico.html), at the Minneola Road exit off I-15, six miles northeast of the Calico exit then 2.5 miles north. More popularly known as the "Calico Dig," it has become one of the most important archeological sites in North America since Louis Leakey excavated it in 1964. Some of the old tools and primitive shelters found here have been dated at around 20,000 years old, controversially establishing mankind's presence here several thousand years earlier than was previously thought – debate rages on.

After driving 23 miles further east of the site, take the Afton Road turn-off from I-15 to get to **Afton Canyon**, dubbed the "Grand Canyon of the Mojave." At a couple of hundred feet deep it's far less impressive than the Arizona original, but it's only three miles off I-15 and is striking nevertheless, with multicolored strata formed by erosion from an extinct lake. The lake may be gone, but Afton Canyon is one of the three places where the Mojave River flows above ground throughout the year, making this a marshy mecca for almost two hundred types of desert creatures including rare bird species such as the vermillion flycatcher and summer tanager. There's camping here on a first-come-first-served basis (☎760/256-8313 or 252-6000; $10).

Back on I-15 there's little of interest for twenty miles until Zzyzx Road. This leads just over four miles south to the western edge of the preserve and the oasis of **Zzyzx** at the base of rocky hills and on the edge of the usually arid Soda Dry Lake. From 1905 to 1940, the site was on the Tonopah & Tidewater Railroad, and when the company decamped, the charismatic quack, preacher, and LA radio personality Curtis "Doc" Springer set up a mineral springs resort. He renamed the spot Zzyzx, correctly surmising that the odd name would draw custom. Unfortunately, he never actually owned the land, and in 1974 he was evicted and the resort closed. Some dilapidated buildings continue to rot away, but most have been transformed into California State University's Desert Studies Center. If there are no happy-to-be-distracted researchers around, you can just stroll around the artificial palm-fringed lake on what is effectively a nature trail, and search for evidence of the area's colorful history.

From the Zzyzx Road junction on I-15 it is six miles to Baker.

Baker and the Eastern Mojave

There's not much to **BAKER** – essentially a strip of fairly expensive gas stations and fast-food joints plus a couple of decent motels and restaurants – but it is a handy spot for refueling with body and rig, and as a base for exploring some of California's remoter corners. Death Valley lies immediately north, and it is in honor of the town's proximity to the country's hottest place that Baker has the **world's tallest functioning thermometer**, rising as high as 134 feet to commemorate the highest temperature ever recorded in the US – 134°F in 1913. Baker is also a springboard for the Mojave National Preserve, for which you can pick up information at the **Mojave National Preserve Desert Information Center** (daily 9am–5pm; ☎760/733-4040), at the base of the thermometer. Note that this information center may close sometime in 2005 when the park's new visitor center opens at Kelso.

One man's small empire along Baker Boulevard near the thermometer contains most of the best places to stay and eat. For **lodging**, try the functional *Bun Boy Motel* (☎760/733-4363; ❸) or the *Wills Fargo Motel* (☎760/733-4477; ❷), which has a heart-shaped pool and slightly more character to its rooms. The supplies at the town's **general store** aren't cheap, but this is your last chance to stock up. Standing out from the fast-food joints, the great-value *Mad Greek* (☎760/733-4354) serves a huge and eclectic range of cuisines from Greek and Middle Eastern such as gyros, kebabs, and falafel, to burgers, sandwiches, Mexican dishes, espresso coffees, pastries, and delicious fresh strawberry shakes.

Mojave National Preserve

In 1994, 1.4 million acres of undeveloped country wedged between I-15 and I-40 were set aside as the **MOJAVE NATIONAL PRESERVE** (Ⓦwww.nps .gov/moja), a perfect spot to take a break from the freeway and maybe camp out a night or two to prepare for the excesses of Las Vegas seventy miles ahead. It is a little higher than much of the desert hereabouts, making it a little cooler in summer but also subject to winter snows.

Immediately west of Baker, Kelbaker Road shoots past a series of dramatic black-red **cinder cones**, created relatively recently (a thousand years ago), before reaching the graceful Mission Revival–style **Kelso Depot**, built in 1924 for workers on the Union Pacific Railroad. Closed in 1985, the building is in the process of being restored as a visitor center for the preserve. Visible to the south of the depot are the spectacular **Kelso Dunes**, a golden five-mile stretch of sand reaching up as high as seven hundred feet. The faint booming sound you might hear is caused by dry sand cascading down the steep upper slopes.

Turn northeast at Kelso to get to the small town of **Cima** (there's a little store here, but no gas) and the adjacent **Cima Dome**, a perfectly formed batholith rising some 1500ft above the desert floor. Cloaked in Joshua trees, parts of it can be visited on foot. To the southeast, along Black Canyon Road, you'll see a turnoff for the *Mid Hills* **campground** (open all year; $12), beautifully sited at 5600ft in piñon-juniper woodland; from here a moderately difficult eight-mile trail winds through Wild Horse Canyon and ends up at the park's other developed campground, *Hole-in-the-Wall* (open all year; $12). Named by Bob Hollimon, a member of the Butch Cassidy gang, because it reminded him of his former hideout in Wyoming, *Hole-in-the-Wall* sits in at an elevation of 4500 feet among striking volcanic rock formations. If you've driven here and don't want to take a long hike, an interpreted nature trail leads from the seasonal **visitor center** (May–Sept Fri–Sun 9am–4pm; Oct–April Wed–Sun 9am–4pm).

In the offseason, you'll still find someone at the visitor center for the 5900-acre **Providence Mountain State Recreation Area**, a further ten miles south, then six miles west. Vegetation here changes from scrubby bushes at lower desert elevations to the piñon pines that grow along rocky Fountain Peak (6996ft) and Edgar Peak (7171ft). Some people come to camp at the small campground (six spaces only; $9), but most are here to tour **Mitchell Caverns** (late May–early Sept Sat & Sun at 1.30pm, early Sept–late May Mon–Fri 1.30pm, Sat & Sun 10am, 1.30pm & 3pm; $4; ☎760/928-2586), which were used by the Chemehuevi Indians for almost five hundred years. There's one brief claustrophobia-inducing part, but otherwise this ninety-minute walk through stalactites and stalagmites and rarer limestone formations is superb.

Travel details

Trains

LA to: Barstow (1 daily; 4hr); Flagstaff (1 daily; 10hr); Palm Springs (3 weekly; 2hr 30 min).

Buses

All buses are Greyhound unless otherwise stated.
Barstow to: Bakersfield (2 daily; 3hr); Las Vegas (11 daily; 3hr); Los Angeles (11 daily; 3–5hr).
Las Vegas to: Barstow (11 daily; 3hr).

Los Angeles to: Barstow (11 daily; 3–5hr); Las Vegas (10 daily & 3 Amtrak Thruway; 6–8hr); Palm Springs (6 daily; 3hr–3hr 30min).
Palm Springs to: Bakersfield (6 daily & 1 Amtrak Thruway daily; 5hr 30min–7hr); Joshua Tree (1 Morongo Basin Transit Authority daily; 55 min); Los Angeles (6 daily; 3hr–3hr 30min); Phoenix, Arizona (1 daily; 5hr 30min).
San Diego to: Borrego Springs (0–4 Northeast Rural Bus System buses daily; 2hr 50min).

Las Vegas and
the Grand Canyon

CHAPTER 4

Highlights

✳ **The Venetian** Las Vegas's most spectacular casino has to be seen to be believed; you can even ride a gondola on the Grand Canal. See p.344

✳ **Caesars Palace** With its ever-expanding Forum shops, great restaurants, and over-the-top entertainment, Las Vegas's best-known name is still a must-see attraction. See p.347

✳ **The Buffets of Las Vegas** Prices aren't quite what they were, but the all-you-care-to-eat buffets of Las Vegas still offer amazing value. See p.350

✳ **The Cirque de Soleil** The postmodern Canadian troupe rules the roost in Las Vegas; choose from six stunning shows. See p.352

✳ **The Havasupai Reservation** Swim in the turquoise waterfalls of this remote Native American reservation, one of the hidden jewels of the Grand Canyon. See p.361

✳ **Phantom Ranch** Whether you reach it by mule or on foot, spending a night at the bottom of the Grand Canyon is a once-in-a-lifetime experience. See p.361

△ The *Venetian* and its Grand Canal, Las Vegas

4

Las Vegas and the Grand Canyon

The glamorous neon oasis that is **Las Vegas**, Nevada, lies just across the state line from Southern California. Don't write it off without seeing it; even if you're not into gambling, Las Vegas offers great nightlife, dining, and entertainment, but above all the sheer spectacle of the place is breathtaking. Two or three days in Las Vegas is as long as most visitors can take, but love it or hate it they're certain to be among the most memorable days of your trip.

The 250-mile drive up to Las Vegas from Los Angeles – take I-15 via Barstow – takes at least four hours on a good day, and much longer on a Friday evening, when it seems as though half California is heading out for a lost weekend. Having come this far, you may well feel like pressing on into Arizona, to see the magnificent **Grand Canyon**. Las Vegas–based helicopter trips can take you to the canyon and back in an afternoon, but they're not cheap, and most in any case only go as far as a minor canyon overlook known as Grand Canyon West. To see the full majesty of the canyon, you have to drive four more hours from Las Vegas, following I-40 across northern Arizona, to the national park headquarters at the **South Rim**. In this chapter, we also describe how to reach the remote waterfalls of the Havasupai Reservation. Sadly, there's no space to detail the many other wonders within a day's drive east of Las Vegas; get hold of the Rough Guides to the *Grand Canyon* or *Southwest USA* for full descriptions.

Las Vegas and around

Little emphasis is placed on the gambling clubs and divorce facilities – though they are attractions to many visitors – and much is being done to build up the cultural attractions. No cheap and easily parodied slogans have been adopted to publicize the city, no attempt has been made to introduce pseudo-romantic architectural themes or to give artificial glamor or gaiety. Las Vegas is itself – natural and therefore very appealing to people with a wide variety of interests.

WPA Guidebook to Nevada, 1940

Shimmering from the desert haze of Nevada like a latter-day El Dorado, **LAS VEGAS** is one of the most dynamic, spectacular cities on earth. At the start of

Monument Valley

Lees Ferry
Navajo Bridge
Vermilion Cliffs Nat. Mon.
Marble Canyon
Point Imperial
Cape Royal
Desert View
SOUTH RIM
89
89A
64
San Francisco Peaks
Flagstaff
Sedona & Phoenix

DeMotte Park
NORTH RIM
Bright Angel Point
Phantom Ranch
Grand Canyon Village
Tusayan
180
64
Valle
Red Lake
Williams
Grand Canyon Railway
Prescott

UTAH
89
Kanab
Fredonia
67
Jacob Lake
67
Colorado River
GRAND CANYON NATIONAL PARK
Ash Fork
89

Kaibab-Paiute Indian Reservation
SUNSHINE ROUTE
Supai
Hualapai Hilltop
Havasupai Indian Reservation
ARIZONA
Seligman
HISTORIC ROUTE 66

Colorado City
Pipe Spring National Monument
CLAYHOLE ROUTE
Toroweap Overlook
18
66

Mount Trumbull
Mount Trumbull
Diamond Creek
40

St George
MAIN STREET ROUTE
Grand Canyon-Parashant National Monument
GRAND CANYON WEST
Grand Point
Hualapai Indian Reservation
Peach Springs
Truxton
Valentine
15

Mesquite
Pierce Ferry
DIAMOND BAR ROAD
BUCK AND DOE ROAD
ANTARES ROAD
Antares Point
STOCKTON HILL ROAD
Chloride
Kingman
68
Los Angeles
Phoenix

NEVADA
Temple Bar
Lake Mead
93
Bullhead City
169
167
Hoover Dam
Searchlight
Laughlin
163
169
147
93
582
146
Boulder City
95
164
Las Vegas
15

CALIFORNIA
Los Angeles
N
20 miles
0

the twentieth century, it didn't even exist; now it's home to over one million people, with enough newcomers arriving all the time for the city to need a new school every month. Boasting sixteen of the world's twenty largest hotels, it's a monument to architectural exuberance, whose flamboyant, no-expense-spared **casinos** lure in thirty-seven million tourists each year.

Las Vegas has been stockpiling superlatives since the 1950s, but never rests on its laurels for a moment. First-time visitors tend to expect the city to be a repository of **kitsch**, but the casino owners are far too canny to be sentimental. Yes, there are a few Elvis impersonators around, but what characterizes the city far more is its endless quest for **novelty**. Long before they lose their sparkle, yesterday's showpieces are blasted into rubble, to make way for ever more extravagant replacements. A few years ago, when the fashion was for fantasy, Arthurian castles and Egyptian pyramids mushroomed along the legendary Strip; now Vegas demands nothing less than entire cities, and boasts pocket versions of New York, Paris, Monte Carlo, and Venice.

While Las Vegas has certainly cleaned up its act since the early days of Mob domination, there's little truth in the notion that it's become a **family** destination. In fact, for kids, it's not a patch on Orlando. Only five percent of visitors bring children, and the crowds that cluster around the exploding volcanoes and pirate battles along the Strip remain almost exclusively adult. Nor is Vegas as consistently **cheap** as it used to be. It's still possible to find inexpensive rooms and cut-price buffets, but the casino owners have finally discovered that high-rollers happy to lose hundreds of dollars per night don't mind paying premium prices to eat at top-quality restaurants, and the latest developments budget on room rates of more like $300 than $30 per night.

When you arrive in Las Vegas, you have to learn a new set of rules: here the religion is luck, the language is money, and time is measured by the revolutions of a roulette wheel. Once you're acclimated, the whole spectacle can be absolutely exhilarating, assuming you haven't pinned your hopes – and your savings – on the pursuit of a fortune. Las Vegas is an unmissable destination, but one that palls for most visitors after a couple of (hectic) days.

If you've come solely to gamble, there's not much to say beyond the fact that all the casinos are free and open 24 hours per day, with acres of floor space packed with ways to lose money: **million-dollar slots**, **video poker**, **black-jack**, **craps**, and much more. The casinos love it if you try to play a system; with the odds stacked against you, your best hope of a large win is to bet your entire stake on one single play and then stop, win or lose.

Some history

Las Vegas has one of the shortest histories of any city in the world. The only US city founded in the twentieth century to boast over a million inhabitants, it's also perhaps the only one that has consistently prioritized the need to attract visitors over the quality of life of its own residents.

The name *Las Vegas* – Spanish for "the meadows" – originally applied to natural springs that from 1829 onwards replenished travelers on the Old Spanish Trail. For the rest of the nineteenth century, the Paiute Indians shared the region with Mormon ranchers, and the valley had a population of just thirty in 1900. Things changed in 1905, with the completion of the now-defunct rail link between Salt Lake City and Los Angeles. Las Vegas itself was founded on May 15 that year, when the railroads auctioned off lots around what's now Fremont Street.

Ironically, Nevada was the first state to outlaw gambling, in 1909, but it became legal once more in 1931, and the workers who built nearby Hoover

Perhaps the second most popular reason to visit Las Vegas – after making your fortune – is to **get married**. Well over a hundred thousand weddings are performed here each year, some so informal that bride and groom just wind down the window of their car during the ceremony. Long before the Britney Spears' fiasco, a Vegas wedding was a byword for tongue-in-cheek chic. What's surprising, however, is that in fact most marriages are deeply formal affairs. Both the casinos and a horde of independent wedding chapels compete to offer elaborate ceremonies with all the traditional trimmings, from white gowns and black limousines to garters and boutonnieres.

You don't have to be a local resident or take a blood test to get wed here. Assuming you're both at least 18 years old, carrying **picture ID**, and not already married, simply turn up at the Clark County Marriage Bureau, downtown at 200 S Third St (Mon–Thurs 8am–midnight, continuously from Fri 8am to Sun midnight; ☎702/445-4515, �🌐www.accessclarkcounty.com/clerk/Marriage_Information), and buy a marriage license for **$55 cash**. You can then walk over to the Clark County Court House at 309 S Third St (daily 8am–10pm), and be married by the Commissioner for Civil Marriages.

If you want a little more ceremony than that, wedding chapels claim to charge as little as $55 for basic ceremonies, but at that sort of rate even the minister is an "extra," costing an additional $45, while you can expect to pay another $50 or more for photos. Count on paying at least $150 for the bare minimum, which is liable to be as romantic a process as checking in at a hotel and to take about as long. The full deluxe service ranges up to whatever you can afford. Novelty options include plighting your troth on the deck of the USS *Enterprise* at the Hilton (☎702/697-8750); floating in a gondola in the *Venetian*'s Grand Canal (☎702/414-4253); cavorting in medieval costume at *Excalibur* (☎702/597-7278); or beside your helicopter at the bottom of the Grand Canyon (*Papillon*; ☎702/736-7243).

Chapels

Candlelight Wedding Chapel 2855 Las Vegas Blvd S ☎702/735-4179 or 1-800-962-1818, �🌐www.candlelightchapel.com. Busy little chapel across from *Circus Circus*, where you get a carnation bouquet with the $189 wedding package, or a garter with the $499 option.

Graceland Wedding Chapel 619 S Las Vegas Blvd ☎702/382-0091 or 1-800-824-5732, �🌐www.gracelandchapel.com. Home of the King – an Elvis impersonator will act as best man, give the bride away, or serenade you, but unfortunately he can't perform the service.

Little Church of the West 4617 Las Vegas Blvd S ☎702/739-7971 or 1-800-821-2452, �🌐www.littlechurchlv.com. Once part of the *Last Frontier* casino, this fifty-year-old chapel is on the National Register of Historic Places and has moved progressively down the Strip to its current site, south of *Mandalay Bay*. Among the more peaceful and quiet places to exchange your Vegas vows – if that's really what you want.

Little White Chapel 1301 S Las Vegas Blvd ☎702/382-5943 or 1-800-545-8111, �🌐www.alittlewhitechapel.com. Where Bruce Willis and Demi Moore married each other, and Michael Jordan and Joan Collins married other people. Open all day every day, with ceremonies in the roofed-over driveway (or "Tunnel of Love") for those in a major hurry.

Dam flocked to Vegas to bet away their pay-packets. Hotel–casinos such as the daringly large 65-room *El Rancho* began to appear in the early 1940s, but the Midwest Mafia was the first to appreciate the potential for profit. Mobster Bugsy Siegel raised $7 million to open the *Flamingo* on the Strip in December

1946; early losses forced him to close within a month, and although he swiftly managed to reopen, his erstwhile partners were dissatisfied enough to have him murdered in LA in June.

By the 1950s, Las Vegas was booming. The military had arrived – mushroom clouds from desert **A-bomb tests** were visible from the city, and visitors would drive out with picnics to get a better view – and so, too, had big guns like **Frank Sinatra**, who debuted at the *Desert Inn* in 1951, and **Liberace**, who received $50,000 to open the *Riviera* in 1955. As the stars gravitated towards the Vegas honeypot, nightclubs across America went out of business, and the city became the nation's undisputed live-entertainment capital.

The beginning of the end for Mob rule in Vegas came in 1966, after reclusive tycoon **Howard Hughes** moved into the *Desert Inn*. When the owners tired of his non-gambling ways, he simply bought the hotel, and his clean-cut image encouraged other entrepreneurs to follow suit. Another Las Vegas legend, **Elvis Presley**, arrived a little later; the young rock'n'roller had bombed at the *New Frontier* in 1956, but started a triumphant five-year stint as a karate-kicking lounge lizard at the *International* (now the *Las Vegas Hilton*) in 1969.

Endless federal swoops and stings drove the Mob out of sight by the 1980s, but just as the city appeared to be in terminal decline it managed to reinvent itself on a surge of junk-bond megadollars. The success of Steve Wynn's *Mirage* in enticing a new generation of visitors from 1989 onwards spawned a host of imitators. *Excalibur* and the *MGM Grand* were followed first by *Luxor* and *New York–New York* and then, as the millennium approached, by the opulent quartet of *Bellagio*, *Mandalay Bay*, the *Venetian*, and *Paris*. The twenty-first century, however, started with a bunch of shocks. Unsuccessful investments elsewhere forced Wynn to sell *Bellagio* and the *Mirage* to the MGM group; the new *Aladdin* swiftly went bankrupt; and the tragedy of September 11, 2001, hit the Las Vegas economy hard.

And yet, as ever, Las Vegas has bounced back, with the *Venetian* after an uncertain start going from strength to strength as the flagship for all that the city does best, and Wynn himself opening his biggest casino yet, his namesake *Wynn*, on the site of the old *Desert Inn*, in 2005. Wall Street's faith in the city's future has been reflected in a string of jaw-dropping billion-dollar mergers – 2004 saw *MGM Mirage* buy the Mandalay Resort Group, and *Harrah's* buy *Caesars* – though what the domination of the Strip by just a handful of mega-corporations will mean for visitors remains to be seen.

Arrival, information, and getting around

Las Vegas's busy **McCarran International Airport** (☎702/261-5211, ⓦ www.mccarran.com) is a mile east of the southern end of the Strip, and four miles from downtown. Some hotels run free shuttle buses, while Bell Trans (☎702/739-7990, ⓦ www.bell-trans.com) run **minibuses** from the airport to the Strip ($4.75) and downtown ($6); a **cab** to the Strip costs from $15 for the southern end up to $25 further north. Greyhound's long-distance **buses** use a terminal at 200 S Main St downtown, but Amtrak **trains** no longer serve Las Vegas.

Any number of free sheets and magazines provide local **information**, while the daily *Las Vegas Review-Journal* carries a four-page guide to the city every day. The **visitor center** at the vast Convention Center, 3150 Paradise Rd (daily 8am–5pm; ☎702/892-0711 or 1-877/VISIT-LV, ⓦ www.vegasfreedom .com), is, at half a mile east of the Strip, too far to reach on foot, and its brochures hold little that you can't find more easily elsewhere.

In 2004, the city finally unveiled the long-promised **Las Vegas Monorail**, which runs along the eastern side of the Strip from the *MGM Grand* to the *Sahara* (℡702/699-8200, ⓦwww.lvmonorail.com). Though plagued by repeated closures owing to mechanical faults in its first few months, it's expected to transform local traffic problems, especially if it's ever extended to the airport and downtown. Business travelers in particular appreciate its off-Strip detour via the Convention Center and the *Hilton*. A single trip costs $3, a ten-ride pass $25. Separate, free monorail systems also connect *Mandalay Bay* with *Excalibur* via *Luxor*; *Bellagio* with the *Monte Carlo*; and the *Mirage* with *TI*.

In addition, CAT **buses** (℡702/228-7433, ⓦwww.catride.com) serve the whole city; #301 and #302 connect the Strip to downtown ($2). The **Las Vegas Strip Trolley** (℡702/382-1404) plies the Strip between *Mandalay Bay* and the *Stratosphere*, for a flat fare of $1.50, while the similar **Downtown Trolley** (℡702/229-0624) loops between the *Stratosphere* and downtown for 50¢. Only if you plan to see more of Vegas than the Strip will you need a **car**.

Accommodation

Although Las Vegas has well over 130,000 motel and hotel rooms (almost all hitched to casinos), it's always best to book accommodation ahead. Whatever you may have heard, the casinos no longer offer incredibly cheap deals; with occupancy rates averaging ninety percent year-round, they don't need to. True, serious gamblers can get their accommodation free, but to count as "serious" you'd have to commit yourself to gambling several thousand dollars, which is a strange definition of "free."

Where you stay makes a real difference. The basic choice lies between the **Strip**, which holds all the largest casinos, plus the best restaurants, shows, and attractions, and **downtown**, which some visitors, especially serious gamblers, consider more "authentic," and is generally cheaper. Even on the Strip, it's worth choosing a hotel where you'll be happy to spend most of your time; it can take twenty minutes just to reach the open air from a room in the *MGM Grand* or *Caesars Palace*. The most popular areas are at its **southern** end, where *New York–New York* faces off against the *MGM Grand*, and the **mid-Strip** area near Flamingo Avenue, home to *Bellagio*, *Paris*, the *Venetian*, and *Caesars Palace* among others.

Room rates are entirely dictated by supply and demand. Even if you stay in the same room for several days, you'll be charged a different rate for each day, depending not only on the day of the week but also which conventions or events may be happening in town, as well as the general level of business. The one sure-fire way to get a cut-price room is to **visit during the week** rather than the weekend. Rates everywhere rise enormously on Friday or Saturday; expect to pay perhaps $30 to $50 extra per night in a lower-end property, such as *Circus Circus* or the *Stratosphere*, and $100 or more extra in the big-name casinos, like *Caesars Palace* or the *Venetian*. On top of that, many hotels won't accept Saturday arrivals. **Room taxes** add an additional eleven percent downtown, nine percent elsewhere.

The **Las Vegas Convention & Visitors Authority** offers a reservations hotline on ℡1-877/VISIT-LV. It's also worth trying both general **online reservations** websites such as ⓦwww.travelocitycom, www.expedia.com, or www.priceline.com (though be warned that Priceline specifies hotels as being in "Las Vegas Strip Area" rather than necessarily on the Strip itself), as well as local reservation specialists Las Vegas Hotels (℡1-800/715-7666, ⓦwww.vegashotel.com).

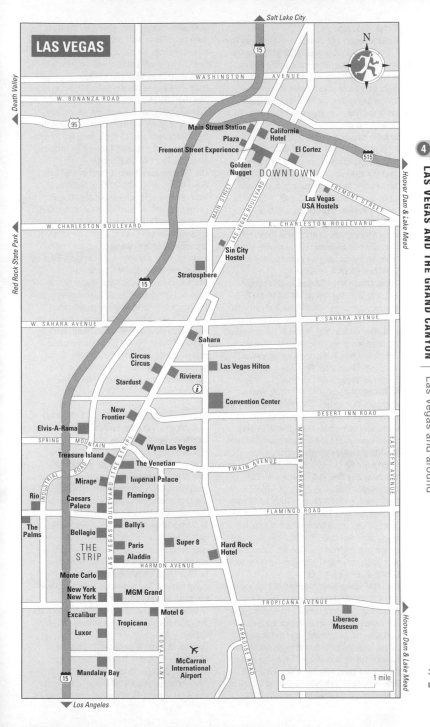

LAS VEGAS

Salt Lake City

N

Death Valley

W A S H I N G T O N   A V E N U E

W. BONANZA ROAD

95

Main Street Station
Plaza
Fremont Street Experience
California Hotel
El Cortez
Golden Nugget
DOWNTOWN
FREMONT STREET
Las Vegas USA Hostels

Hoover Dam & Lake Mead

515

W. CHARLESTON BOULEVARD
E. CHARLESTON BOULEVARD

Red Rock State Park

Sin City Hostel

Stratosphere

15

W. SAHARA AVENUE
E. SAHARA AVENUE

Sahara
Circus Circus
Las Vegas Hilton
Stardust
Riviera
Convention Center
New Frontier

DESERT INN ROAD

Elvis-A-Rama
SPRING   MOUNTAIN
Wynn Las Vegas

Treasure Island
The Venetian
TWAIN AVENUE

MARYLAND PARKWAY
EASTERN AVENUE

Mirage
Imperial Palace
Rio
Flamingo
Caesars Palace
FLAMINGO ROAD

The Palms
Bally's
Bellagio
Paris
Super 8
Hard Rock Hotel
THE STRIP
Aladdin
Monte Carlo
HARMON AVENUE
New York New York
MGM Grand
Excalibur
Motel 6
TROPICANA AVENUE
Tropicana
Liberace Museum
Luxor

KOVAL LANE
PARADISE ROAD

Hoover Dam & Lake Mead

15
Mandalay Bay
McCarran International Airport

0   1 mile

INDUSTRIAL   ROAD

LAS VEGAS BOULEVARD (THE STRIP)

MAIN STREET
LAS VEGAS BOULEVARD

Los Angeles

The Strip

Aladdin Resort and Casino 3667 Las Vegas Blvd S ☎702/785-5555 or 1-877/333-9474, ⓦwww .aladdincasino.com. More manageable than most of its giant neighbors, with each of its 2600 rooms within easy reach of an elevator. If short on Arabian Nights theming, the rooms are spacious, and dining and shopping are first class. Sun–Thurs ❹, Fri & Sat ❼

Bellagio Resort & Casino 3600 Las Vegas Blvd S ☎702/693-7111 or 1-888/987-6667, ⓦwww .bellagio.com. The very top end of the Vegas spectrum. Extremely luxurious rooms, superb pool complex, and the best restaurants in town (see p.349). Sun–Thurs ❼, Fri & Sat ❽

Caesars Palace 3570 Las Vegas Blvd S ☎702/731-7222 or 1-800/634-6661, ⓦwww .caesarspalace.com. *Caesars'* older rooms still burst with pseudo-Roman splendor, while those in the newer towers are more conventionally elegant. Sun–Thurs ❺, Fri & Sat ❽

Circus Circus Hotel/Casino 2880 Las Vegas Blvd S ☎702/734-0410 or 1-800/444-2472, ⓦwww.circuscircus.com. Still the best option for families: kids love the theme park and circus acts, adults love the low rates. Rooms in the motel-like Manor section at the back are pretty grim; pay a little more to stay in one of the towers instead. Sun–Thurs ❷, Fri & Sat ❹

Luxor Las Vegas 3900 Las Vegas Blvd S ☎702/262-4102 or 1-888/777-0188, ⓦwww .luxor.com. Vast smoked-glass pyramid, in which all the two thousand extra-large rooms face outwards, with tremendous views. Unlike the extra two thousand rooms in the newer tower next door, however, most have showers not baths. Sun–Thurs ❹, Fri & Sat ❻

Mandalay Bay Resort & Casino 3950 Las Vegas Blvd S ☎702/632-7777 or 1-888/632-7000, also 1-877/632-7700 for THEhotel, ⓦwww .mandalaybay.com. This upscale, young-adult playground is a long way from the central Strip, but all its rooms have both baths and walk-in showers, the new THEhotel extension has added even more luxury, and there's a spectacular wave pool. Sun–Thurs ❺, Fri & Sat ❼

The MGM Grand Hotel/Casino 3799 Las Vegas Blvd S ☎702/891-1111 or 1-800/929-1111, ⓦwww.mgmgrand.com. Waiting for any kind of service, especially check-in, at America's largest hotel – 5005 rooms and counting – can be horrendous, but you get a great standard of accommodation for the price. For the highest standard, ask for a room in the Grand Tower. Sun–Thurs ❹, Fri & Sat ❻

New York–New York Hotel & Casino 3790 Las Vegas Blvd S ☎702/740-6050 or 1-800/693-6763, ⓦwww.nynyhotelcasino.com. Thanks to sheer attention to detail, the most exuberantly enjoyable casino on the Strip. The rooms are very nice, if a bit small, and filled with Art Deco flourishes. Sun–Thurs ❹, Fri & Sat ❻

Paris–Las Vegas Casino-Resort 3655 Las Vegas Blvd S ☎702/946-7000 or 1-877/796-2096, ⓦwww.parislasvegas.com. If not the absolute pinnacle of luxury, the rooms and services at the flamboyant *Paris* are still pretty good, and for location, views, and ambience it more than holds its own. Sun–Thurs ❻, Fri & Sat ❼

The Stratosphere Hotel & Casino 2000 Las Vegas Blvd S ☎702/380-7777 or 1-800/998-6937, ⓦwww.stratospherehotel.com. Despite its unfashionable location at the far north end of the Strip, the *Stratosphere* survives thanks to low rates and a steady flow of budget tour groups. No accommodation is in the tower, so don't expect amazing views, just large, plain but good-value rooms. Sun–Thurs ❷, Fri & Sat ❹

The Venetian 3355 Las Vegas Blvd S ☎702/414-1000 or 1-877/883-6423, ⓦwww.venetian.com. The Strip's best-value luxury hotel will almost certainly become the world's largest hotel during this guide's lifetime. Even the standard rooms are split-level suites, offering gorgeous antique-style canopied beds, plus roomy living areas, marble bathrooms, and a mind-blowing array of shops and restaurants at hand (see p.349). Sun–Thurs ❽, Fri & Sat ❾

Downtown and off-Strip accommodation

California Hotel & Casino 12 Ogden Ave at First St ☎702/385-1222 or 1-800/634-6255, ⓦwww.thecal.com. Most of the guests in this low- to mid-range downtown casino are Hawaiian, and Hawaiian food and drink dominate the bars and restaurants. The actual rooms are plain but adequate. Sun–Thurs ❷, Fri & Sat ❸

El Cortez Hotel & Casino 600 E Fremont St ☎702/385-5200 or 1-800/634-6703, ⓦwww .elcortezhotelcasino.com. Veteran downtown casino, where the cut-price rooms in the main building are better than the dismal gaming area might suggest. The mini-suites in the new tower are good value at $44, while the bargain-basement accommodation in *Ogden House* across the street costs just $18 for a private room with bathroom. ❶

Hard Rock Hotel & Casino 4475 Paradise Rd ☎702/693-5000 or 1-800/473-7625, ⓦwww .hardrockhotel.com. Over a mile east of the Strip, "the world's only rock'n'roll casino" can't match Las Vegas's giants for size or splendor. Instead it's relatively intimate and even chic, with above-average rooms, high-class restaurants, a fabulous pool, and the odd big-name rock gig. Sun–Thurs ⑤, Fri & Sat ⑦

Las Vegas USA Hostels 1322 E Fremont St ☎702/385-1150 or 1-800/550-8958, ⓦwww .usahostels.com. Former *Best Western* motel, in a slightly forbidding neighborhood six blocks east of downtown, that's much the better of the city's two independent hostels, with dorm beds from $13 and private doubles from $38. Rates include free pancake breakfast, free BBQ and beer on Sundays, and free pick-up from Greyhound, and there's a heated swimming pool. The friendly staff arranges national-park and city tours, including a weekly clubbing night. ①–②

Main Street Station 200 N Main St at Ogden ☎702/387-1896 or 1-800/465-0711, ⓦwww .mainstreetcasino.com. Downtown's best-value option, two blocks from Fremont Street, with four hundred large guest rooms plus a brewpub and good restaurants. Ask for a room on the south side, not right next to the freeway. Sun–Thurs ②, Fri & Sat ③

Palms Resort & Casino 4321 W Flamingo Rd ☎702/942-7777 or 1-866/942-7777, ⓦwww

.palms.com. Very much the hottest new casino in town, thanks to some very fancy nightclubs and restaurants and a strong celebrity presence, the *Palms* is in other respects a presentable but rather dull "locals" casino, so while the rooms are very comfortable you may not feel it's worth paying premium rates for the inconvenient location a mile west of the Strip. Sun–Thurs ④, Fri & Sat ⑧

Rio Suite Hotel & Casino 3700 W Flamingo Rd ☎702/777-7777 or 1-877/752-9746, ⓦwww .playrio.com. Though west of the interstate, the *Rio* makes a serious attempt to rival the Strip giants. The restaurants, bars, and buffets are all excellent, the pool is great, and the rooms are large and luxurious. However, the prices are not cheap, and the Strip stands half a mile away, along a highway no one would dream of walking. Sun–Thurs ⑥, Fri & Sat ⑦

Sin City Hostel 1208 Las Vegas Blvd S ☎702/385-9955. Recently revamped independent hostel in a dilapidated former motel, in an insalubrious area on the fringes of downtown. A dorm bed, or a basic "semi-private" double, costs $17.50. Demand is heavy, especially in summer. Non-drivers won't enjoy walking in the immediate neighborhood, but the staff can fix up local tours. ①

The City

Though the Las Vegas sprawl measures fifteen miles wide by fifteen miles long, most tourists stick to the six-mile stretch of **Las Vegas Boulevard** that includes the **Strip**, home to the major casinos, and the **downtown** area, slightly southeast of the intersection of I-15 and US-95. In between lie two somewhat seedy miles of gas stations, fast-food drive-ins, and wedding chapels, while the rest of town is largely residential, and need barely concern you at all.

The Strip

For its razor-edge finesse in harnessing sheer excess to the serious business of making money, there's no place like the **Las Vegas Strip**. It's hard to imagine that Las Vegas was once an ordinary city, and **Las Vegas Boulevard** a dusty thoroughfare scattered with edge-of-town motels. After six decades of capitalism run riot, with every new casino-hotel setting out to surpass its neighbors, the Strip is locked into a hyperactive craving for thrills and glamour, forever discarding its latest toy in its frenzy for the next jackpot.

The southern Strip

As the Strip pushes deeper into the desert, a procession of new casinos continues to rise at its southern end, not far west of the airport. The procession north kicks off with the gilt tower of 1999's Burmese-themed **Mandalay Bay**. Financed through profits from *Luxor* and *Excalibur*, *Mandalay Bay* is more upmarket than either, and its excellent restaurants and the *House of Blues* (see p.351) keep it lively at night. During the day, all it has to offer sightseers is the **Shark Reef** aquarium (daily 10am–11pm; $16, under-12s $10), where crocodiles, jellyfish, and, of course, sharks lurk in a steamy, half-submerged temple complex, and the so-called "coral" is actually multicolored plastic.

Next door, connected by both a separate monorail system and a shopping mall-cum-footbridge, stands the 36-story smoked-glass pyramid of **Luxor**. From the palm-fringed avenue of sphinxes guarding the entrance, to the reconstruction of Tutankhamun's tomb inside, the whole building plays endless variations on Egyptian motifs and ranks as a real must-see. Upstairs on the "Attractions Level," paying a hefty $25 buys you unlimited IMAX simulator rides.

Luxor's architect, Veldon Simpson, had previously designed **Excalibur**, immediately north. A less sophisticated mock-up of a medieval castle, complete with drawbridge, crenellated towers, and a basement stuffed with sideshows for the kids, it's usually packed out with low-budget tour groups. Its brief reign as the world's largest hotel, from 1990 to 1993, ended when the five-thousand-room **MGM Grand** – another Simpson creation, itself since overtaken by a hotel complex in Thailand – opened across the street. Turnover here is so phenomenal that when crowds after the Holyfield–Tyson debacle in 1997 mistook popping champagne corks for gunfire, forcing the tables to close down for two hours, losses were estimated in the millions of dollars. Its **Lion Habitat** is a walk-through zoo where lions lounge around another ruined temple (daily 11am–11pm, free; $20 to have your photo taken with a lion cub).

The northwest corner of the intersection of Las Vegas Boulevard and Tropicana Avenue – reputedly the busiest traffic junction in the US – is occupied by an exuberant re-creation of the Big Apple, **New York–New York**. Twelve skyscrapers, fronted by a larger-than-life Statue of Liberty but mercifully not including the World Trade Center, form the skyline of this miniature Manhattan, built, like the original, in response to space limitations. Unusually, the interior is every bit as carefully realized, with a lovely rendition of Central Park at dusk. In one respect, it even surpasses New York; for $12.50 you can swoop around the whole thing at 65mph on the hair-raising Manhattan Express **rollercoaster**.

The central Strip

North of the *MGM Grand*, the **Aladdin** opened in 2000 as the first megacasino of the new millennium. Beset by funding difficulties, it was tipped into bankruptcy by the terrorist attacks of September 2001. The Middle Eastern theme didn't exactly help, and is expected to disappear as new owners Planet Hollywood remodel the entire property. Ironically the factors that held the *Aladdin* back financially – that you can explore its gigantic **Desert Passage** shopping mall, go to concerts at its 7000-seat auditorium, and get to and from your hotel room without ever crossing the casino floor – mean that it's actually quite a nice place.

Next door, **Paris** was the 1999 handiwork of the same team that created *New York–New York*. Straddled by a half-scale Eiffel Tower, it all feels a little compressed, but once again the attention to detail is a joy, and there's a fine assortment of top-notch French restaurants. Elevators soar through its roof and up to the summit of the Eiffel Tower, for stunning views (daily 10am–midnight; $9).

The Eiffel Tower was cheekily positioned to enjoy a perfect prospect of **Bellagio**, opposite, *Mirage*-owner Steve Wynn's 1998 attempt to build the best hotel in world history. *Bellagio's* main block, a stately curve of blue and cream pastels, stands aloof from the Strip behind an eight-acre artificial lake, in which hundreds of fountains erupt every half-hour in water-ballets, with booming music and colored lights. Inside, its proudest boasts are the **Via Bellagio**, a mall of glamorous designer boutiques, and the opulent **Conservatory** (free admission), where the flowerbeds beneath a Belle Epoque canopy of copper-framed glass are replanted every six weeks.

Across Flamingo Road from *Bellagio* – via the intersection where rapper Tupac Shakur was gunned down in 1996 – **Caesars Palace** still encapsulates Las Vegas at its best. Beyond a vast labyrinth of slots and green baize, peopled by strutting Roman centurions and Cleopatra-cropped waitresses, lies the extraordinary **Forum** mall, with its blue-domed ceiling endlessly cycling from dawn to dusk, and its ornate fountains, where animatronic statues come to life at regular intervals. Recent renovations, including an open-air **Roman Piazza** holding cafés and snack bars, have vastly improved its Strip frontage

Nighttime crowds jostle for space on the sidewalk outside the glittering **Mirage**, beyond *Caesars*, to watch a half-hearted volcano erupt every fifteen minutes, spewing water and fire into the lagoon below. Next door, the former **Treasure Island**, once the flagship of the new child-friendly Las Vegas, has stopped trying to please the kids, renaming itself **TI** and crassly re-jigging the "pirate battle" outside so it's now won by sexy showgirls known as the **Sirens of TI** (every ninety minutes after dark; free). Around the back, at 3401 Industrial Rd, you can admire (if not step on) the King's very own blue suede shoes at **Elvis-A-Rama** (Mon–Sat 10am–6pm, Sun 10am–5pm; $10). In addition to a stunning array of Elvis memorabilia, this small but enjoyable museum puts on hourly impersonator shows, included in the admission price.

Across the Strip, the facade of another 1999 newcomer, the **Venetian**, includes facsimiles of six major Venice buildings, as well as the Rialto Bridge and the Bridge of Sighs. The main emphasis within is on the **Grand Canal Shoppes**, reached via a stairwell topped by vivid frescoes. The ludicrous **Grand Canal** itself, complete with gondolas and singing gondoliers ($12.50 a ride), is quintessential Las Vegas, and as such utterly irresistible – it's *upstairs*, for goodness' sake.

Only one of the two ultramodern art museums unveiled by the *Venetian* in 2001, amid much talk of how Las Vegas was finally ready to appreciate fine art, remains open. The **Guggenheim Hermitage** (daily 9am–8.30pm; $15, under-13s $7; Ⓦwww.guggenheimlasvegas.org) provides much-needed funds for St Petersburg's State Hermitage Museum in return for displaying its finest treasures on rotation. Exhibitions so far have concentrated on Impressionism and Cubism, with Monet, Picasso, and Van Gogh well represented. The *Venetian* also holds the first (and ridiculously expensive) US outpost of **Madame Tussaud's** waxwork museum. This calls itself **Interactive Wax** (daily 10am–10pm; $20, under-13s $10), on the grounds that visitors can shoot hoops with Shaq, sink a putt with Tiger, or sing karaoke in front of Simon Cowell.

Immediately north of the *Venetian*, on the site of the former *Desert Inn*, stands the newest casino of them all, **Wynn Las Vegas**. It's so new, in fact, that the opening date of April 2005 was after this book went to press. Entrepreneur Steve Wynn, previously responsible for the *Mirage* and *Bellagio*, has enigmatically described it as being "designed from the inside out," in that it's concealed from the Strip behind an artificial mountain, and best seen instead from within. Boasting eighteen restaurants, at least two shows, and Ferrari and Maserati dealerships, it's aimed at the very top end of the market.

The northern Strip

The family-oriented **Circus Circus**, another mile north, uses live circus acts to pull in the punters – a trapeze artist here, a fire-eater there – and also has an indoor theme park, the **Adventuredome** (Mon–Thurs 11am–6pm, Fri & Sat 10am–midnight, Sun 10am–8pm; Ⓦwww.adventuredome.com), where you pay separately for each rollercoaster or river-ride. Half a mile east at 3000 Paradise Rd, the **Las Vegas Hilton** is home to the expensive **Star Trek Experience** (daily 11am–11pm; $30; ⦿www.startrekexp.com), featuring two dramatic simulator rides, Klingon Encounter and Borg Invasion 4-D. If you're lucky enough to arrive when the lines are short, it's still worth lingering over the glossy display panels that recount such historical highlights as World War III in 2053 and the birth of Spock in 2230.

Half a mile towards downtown from *Circus Circus* stands the 1149-foot-tall **Stratosphere**, whose outdoor deck and indoor viewing chamber near the summit offer amazing panoramas ($9). Three demented thrill rides can take you even closer to heaven; the world's highest rollercoaster ($4) swirls around the outside, the ludicrous Big Shot ($8) shunts you to the very top of an additional 160-foot spire, from which you free-fall back down again, and X-Scream ($8) tips you over the edge on a sliding bench.

Downtown and the Liberace Museum

As the Strip has gone from strength to strength, **downtown** Las Vegas, the city's original core, has by comparison been neglected. Long known as "Glitter Gulch," it consists of a few compact blocks of lower-key casinos, though Fremont Street, its principal thoroughfare, has been roofed with an open-air mesh to create the **Fremont Street Experience**. This self-styled "Celestial Vault" is studded with over two million colored light bulbs, choreographed by computer in dazzling nightly displays (hourly 8pm–midnight; free), but there's a long way to go before the district as a whole can compete with the Strip once again.

All Las Vegas's handful of museums are eminently missable, with one unarguable exception: the **Liberace Museum**, two miles east of the Strip at 1775 E Tropicana Ave (Mon–Sat 10am–5pm, Sun noon–4pm; $12, students aged 6 and over $8; ⦿www.liberace.org). Popularly remembered as a beaming buffoon who knocked out torpid toe-tappers, Liberace, who died in 1987, started out playing piano in the rough bars of Milwaukee during the 1940s. His story is recalled by a yellowing collection of cuttings and family photos, along with electric candelabra, bejeweled quail eggs with inlaid pianos, rhinestone-covered fur coats, glittering cars, and more.

Eating

As recently as the early 1990s, Las Vegas's **restaurant** scene was governed by the notion that visitors were not prepared to pay for gourmet food. All the casinos laid on pile-'em-high buffets and 24-hour coffee shops, but the only quality restaurants were upscale Italian places far from the Strip. Since then, the situation has reversed, as the major casinos lure culinary superstars to open Vegas outlets, and many tourists come specifically to eat at some of the best restaurants in the United States. The choice on the Strip in particular is overwhelming, and you'll almost certainly find a good restaurant to suit your tastes and budget in your own hotel. For that reason, the places reviewed here tend towards the higher end of the spectrum; they're the ones it's worth making a special effort to reach. Sadly, however, although when the boom first started, you could expect to pay less for a fine meal in Las Vegas than almost anywhere in the US, these days the top restaurants seem able to charge sky-high prices.

Almost every casino still features an all-you-care-to-eat **buffet**, open to guests and non-guests alike. Even at the worst, you're bound to find something you can keep down, while the best of the traditional buffets are like being granted unrestricted access to the food court in an upmarket mall; you'll find good fast food, but not great cooking. The best such buffets tend to be neither on the Strip nor downtown, but in casinos like the *Rio*, the *Palms*, and the *Stations* chain that depend on locals as well as tourists. By contrast, those at the largest Strip casinos, like *Excalibur* and the *MGM Grand*, are often poor. A more recent development, however, has been for high-end casinos like *Bellagio* and *Paris* to raise buffet prices to a level that makes it possible to provide true gourmet feasts.

Restaurants

America *New York–New York*, 3790 Las Vegas Blvd S ☎702/740-6451. Cavernous diner, featuring a vast 3-D "map" of the United States. Each menu item supposedly comes from some specific part of the country, with entrees including Texan barbecue ribs for $14 and New York–style pizza for $9–11. At any hour of day or night, there really is something for everyone. Daily 24hr.

Aureole *Mandalay Bay*, 3950 Las Vegas Blvd S ☎702/632-7401. A wine-lover's paradise, where harnessed "wine angels" swoop around a three-story "wine tower" that holds ten thousand bottles, and the "Progressive American Cuisine" is out of this world. So too are the prices; the $85 prix-fixe menu buys a substantial appetizer and entrée, while the $95 "Celebration Menu" features up to eight smaller courses, plus the odd "amuse-bouche" and "pre-dessert." Standout dishes include the curry-nut crusted tuna, the halibut topped with a black truffle foam, and the pork chop stuffed with prosciutto and gruyere. Daily 6–11pm.

Bouchon *The Venetian*, 3355 Las Vegas Blvd S ☎702/414-6200. Thomas Keller has been hailed as the world's best chef, but his re-creation of a classic French bistro is both friendly and affordable. Sitting outside, on the huge tenth-floor piazza of the *Venetian*'s Venezia Tower, is a real joy. Every dish is prepared with perfect precision, and the prices surprisingly reasonable, with a delicious French onion soup for $8.50 and a flavorful roast chicken with onions and garlic at $22.50. Breakfast is a Francophile's dream of croissants, pastries, yogurt, and coffee. Daily 6.30am–10.30am & 5.30–11pm.

The Coffee Shop *Binion's Horseshoe*, 128 E Fremont St ☎702/382-1600. Downtown's quintessential round-the-clock Las Vegas coffee shop, with excellent prices for a changing timetable of specials. Best bargains are at the dead of night, 11pm–7am, when a steak dinner, with two eggs and home fries, costs just $6. Breakfast, which works out better value than most buffets, is served 24hrs. Daily 24hr.

Commander's Palace *Desert Passage, Aladdin*, 3663 Las Vegas Blvd S ☎702/892-8272.

New Orleans' renowned haute-Creole restaurant – repeatedly voted the best restaurant in the US – is formal but friendly, though the prices can come as a shock. Classic appetizers like shrimp *remoulade* ($10.50); entrees such as pecan-crusted Gulf fish ($29) or veal chop Tchoupitoulas ($39); and bananas Foster for dessert ($7.50). $39 buys a three-course set dinner. Mon–Fri 9–11am, 11.30am–2pm & 5–10pm; Sat & Sun 10.30am–2.30pm & 5–10pm.

Fat Burger 3765 Las Vegas Blvd S ☎702/736-4733. There's no more to this gleaming, all-American burger joint than meets the eye; just walk or drive in from the Strip at any time and get a perfect burger, fries, and a shake. Daily 24hr.

Il Fornaio *New York–New York*, 3790 Las Vegas Blvd S ☎702/650-6500. Rural Italian restaurant that's the nicest place to enjoy *New York–New York*. Pizza for $12, or full meals like mixed antipasto ($9.50) followed by seafood linguini ($19) or rotisserie chicken ($16). The delicious olive breads, pastries, and coffees are also sold in a separate deli nearby from 6am daily. Mon–Thurs & Sun 7am–10pm, Fri & Sat 7am–midnight.

Mon Ami Gabi *Paris*, 3655 Las Vegas Blvd S ☎702/944-4224. Las Vegas life doesn't get much better than lunch at *Mon Ami Gabi*, with its open-air seating right on the Strip, and the feel of a French pavement bistro. At lunch, try the glorious onion soup ($7), mussels ($11), or thin-cut steak frites ($21). Dinner features more expensive steak cuts and fish entrees. Mon–Thurs & Sun 11.30am–3.30pm & 5–11pm, Fri & Sat 11.30am–3.30pm & 5pm–midnight.

Mr Lucky's 24/7 *Hard Rock Hotel*, 4455 Paradise Rd ☎702/693-5000. Very stylish 24-hour coffee shop, with open kitchen and faux-fur booths, where the food is well above average too. As well as the usual breakfast items, it serves burgers, sandwiches, pizza, and pasta dishes for $7–12, a 12oz steak for $17, and milkshakes or microbrews for $5.

Olives *Bellagio*, 3600 Las Vegas Blvd S ☎702/693-8181. *Bellagio*'s best-value gourmet restaurant, facing the Eiffel Tower across the lake, where the largely Mediterranean menu is uniformly fresh and superb. It's a great lunch spot, with $10–13 appetizers like tuna or beef *carpaccio* and slow-braised lamb ribs; $15 pizza (or "individual oven-baked flatbreads"); and specials such as barbecued yellow-fin tuna ($21.50). Dinner entrees are pricier, at $28–50. Daily 11am–2.30pm & 5–11.30pm.

Vialé Roman Plaza, *Caesars Palace*, 3500 Las Vegas Blvd S ☏702/731-7110. This inexpensive sidewalk Italian *trattoria*, right beside the Strip on *Caesars'* Roman Plaza, is an unexpected delight. A lunchtime burger or sandwich costs under $10, and a Caesar salad (well you would, wouldn't you?) $7, or $10 with chicken. The dinner menu adds pasta as both appetizer ($7–9) and entree ($12–17), and more substantial entrees like pan-seared halibut for $19. A takeout window sells pizza by the slice. Daily 11am–4pm & 5–11pm.

Zefferino Grand Canal Shoppes, *The Venetian*, 3355 Las Vegas Blvd S ☏702/414-3500. Very romantic, yet utterly playful high-class Italian restaurant, with ornate balconies overlooking the Grand Canal. Dinner entrees can be pricey, with a basic ravioli at $26 and fish dishes at $26–40, but the $20 three-course set lunch, served daily except Sundays, is exceptional value. Mon–Sat 11.30am–1am, Sun 10am–2.30pm & 5–11pm.

Buffets

The Buffet *Bellagio*, 3600 Las Vegas Blvd S ☏702/791-7111. Far and away Las Vegas's best buffet; the sheer range is extraordinary. For breakfast ($14), as well as bagels, pastries, and eggs, there's salmon smoked or baked, fruit fresh or in salads, and omelets cooked to order. Lunch offerings ($18) can include sushi, barbecued wild boar ribs, and lamb *osso buco*, plus fresh-baked focaccia and tasty fruit tarts. At dinner, costing $26 Mon–Fri & Sun and $32 on Sat, the stakes are raised again with lobster claws, fresh oysters, and venison.

Cravings Buffet *The Mirage*, 3400 Las Vegas Blvd S ☏702/792-7777. If not quite "the ultimate buffet dining experience," the new *Mirage* buffet is

certainly among the best around. The room itself is fabulous, all glitter and sparkle, and small-scale serving areas provide personalized service, with much of the food cooked to your own order. The wide spectrum includes sushi, stir-fries, dim sum dumplings, barbecue, rotisserie chicken, and a carvery, plus home-made ice cream and individually prepared salads; dinner sees extra seafood and meat dishes. Breakfast $12.50, lunch $17.50, dinner $22.50.

Fantasy Market Buffet *The Palms*, 4321 W Flamingo Rd ☏702/942-7777. Easy to find and easy to afford, The *Palms'* buffet has rapidly established itself as a local favorite. Food and decor alike are bright and appealing without being fancy, with offerings like salads, a little sushi, Mexican and Italian specialties, chicken teriyaki, barbecue beef, and a lot of lovely cakes and pies. Breakfast $6, lunch $7, dinner Sat–Thurs $12, Fri crab legs and prime rib, $16.

Garden Court Buffet *Main Street Station*, 200 N Main St ☏702/387-1896. Everything is clean and spruce, if not wildly exciting, at downtown's best-value buffet. Dishes range from fried chicken and corn, to tortillas and fajitas, or pork chow mein and oyster tofu. Breakfast $6, lunch $8, and dinner $11–16.

Le Village Buffet *Paris*, 3655 Las Vegas Blvd S ☏702/946-7000. *Paris's* buffet showcases only delicious French dishes, in a fun if distinctly Disney-esque setting. The seafood is superb, whether it's the scallops, shrimp, and crab in Sunday's brunch or the Dover sole and rich bouillabaisse midweek; roast chicken comes fricasseed, as *coq au vin*, or with mustard; vegetables are super-fresh; and there's a full cheese board. Breakfast is $13, lunch $18, and dinner $25.

Todai Seafood Buffet Desert Passage, *Aladdin*, 3663 Las Vegas Blvd S ☏702/892-0021. Magnificent all-you-care-to-eat Japanese spreads, with unlimited sushi and sashimi plus hot entrees, noodles, and barbecued and teriyaki meats. Lunch Mon–Fri $15, Sat & Sun $17; dinner Mon–Thurs $26, Fri–Sun $28.

Bars and clubs

As the perfect fuel to turn a dithering gawker into a diehard gambler, alcohol is very easy to come by in Las Vegas. If you want a drink in a casino, just wait for a tray-toting waitress to come and find you. All the casinos do have actual **bars** as well, and the old-fashioned Las Vegas **lounge** has also returned in force. Las Vegas has also come of age as a **clubbing** capital; the success of nightclubs at hipper casinos like the *Hard Rock* and *Mandalay Bay* has prompted their rivals to follow suit with their own clubs and "ultra-lounges," often with spectacular results.

As for **live music**, check newspapers like the *Las Vegas Review Journal* (Ⓦwww.lvrj.com) and the free *City Life* (Ⓦwww.lvcitylife.com) to see who's appearing when you're in town, or call the casinos directly.

The Beach 365 Convention Center Drive ☎702/731-1925, Ⓦwww.beachlv.com. Round-the-clock multiroom dance club that's a permanent Spring Break, attracting a very young crowd to the massive dancefloor downstairs and sports bar upstairs. Daily 24hr. Cover (men only) usually $10.

Gaudí Bar *Sunset Station*, 1301 W Sunset Rd, Henderson ☎702/547-7777. Las Vegas's most weird and wonderful casino lounge; a billowing mosaic-encrusted toadstool of a tribute to Spanish architect Gaudí, complete with faux sky-underbelly and best appreciated with the aid of a $4 specialty martini. Daily 24hr.

Gipsy 4605 Paradise Rd ☎702/731-1919. High-profile gay dance club, where apart from the free cruise nights on Wednesdays, there's normally live entertainment to justify the $5 cover charge, with go-go boys Friday and Saturday, and beer busts most nights. The elaborate lost-city decor attracts young ingenues and local celebs. Daily 9pm–5am.

House of Blues *Mandalay Bay*, 3950 Las Vegas Blvd S ☎702/632-7600. The Strip's premier live-music venue, the voodoo-tinged, folk-art-decorated *House of Blues* has a definite but not exclusive emphasis toward blues, R&B, and the like. Prices range from $25 up to over $100.

Rain *The Palms*, 4321 W Flamingo Rd ☎702/940-7246. This glitzy, water-themed dance club is currently the hottest celebrity hangout in town, so the likes of you and I can expect to wait an hour or more to be allowed in. Thurs 11pm–5am, Fri & Sat 10pm–5am; $20.

rumjungle *Mandalay Bay*, 3950 Las Vegas Blvd S ☎702/632-7777. Hybrid bar-restaurant-nightclub where you have to run a gauntlet of go-go dancers and volcanic gas jets just to get in. Leopardskin-clad staff serve well-priced cocktails, plus a vast menu of rums, and it's too loud to do anything more than watch the pole dancers above the bar, or join the Latin-tinged action on the (small-ish) dancefloor. Mon & Thurs–Sat 5.30pm–4am, Tues, Wed 5.30pm–2am; cover for non-diners only, $20.

Triple Seven Brewpub *Main Street Station*, 200 N Main St ☎702/386-4442. Roomy, high-ceilinged downtown brewpub with poor service but great beers and tasty food. Daily 11am–7am.

Venus Lounge *The Venetian*, 3265 Las Vegas Blvd S ☎702/414-4870. This gloriously kitsch retro-lounge, right by the Strip, features a lovingly re-created tiki bar, but turns into a run-of-the-mill dance club as the night wears on. Wed–Sun 5pm–5am. Cover weekends only, up to $20.

Entertainment

Only Celine Dion's long-term residency at *Caesars'* Colosseum (which she shares with Elton John for 25 nights a year) harks back to the days when Las Vegas represented the pinnacle of any show-business career, and Frank Sinatra's Rat Pack would sing the night away at the *Sands*. With the abrupt end of Sieg-fried and Roy's fourteen-year reign at the *Mirage* in 2003, following a near-fatal juxtaposition between Roy Horn and a white tiger, the city's **entertainment** industry is now less reliant on star names than ever, and dominated instead by the spectacular postmodernism of the Cirque du Soleil and the Blue Men. Five separate Cirque shows are currently playing, with typical ticket prices well in excess of $100, and a sixth is due to open at the *Mirage* in 2006, based on the music of the Beatles.

The Amazing Johnathan *Riviera*, 2901 Las Vegas Blvd S ☎702/794-9433. Barring the violence he directs against his ditzy blonde assistant "Psychic Tanya," the Amazing Johnathan's quite a lovable comedy magician, with the emphasis on comedy meaning that he barely completes a trick all evening (although you'll love his daft "foam magic"). Carefully honed patter and skits like "Bad Karate Theater" make this one of Las Vegas's fun-niest shows. Daily except Thurs 10pm. $47–58.

Blue Man Group *Luxor*, 3900 Las Vegas Blvd S ☎702/262-4400. Enter a strange and unfamiliar world, in which three bald, blue performance artists sell out a 1250-seat theater inside a giant pyramid every night of the week. Don't expect stars, or a plot, or even words; just be ready to laugh a lot at synchronized eating of breakfast cereal and live endoscopies on audience members, and to be blown away by deafening drumming and stunning special effects. Note that the Blue

Men are due to transfer to a new showroom at the *Venetian* in September 2005. Mon, Wed, Fri & Sun 7pm & 10pm; Tues & Thurs 7pm; Sat 4pm, 7pm & 10pm. $63–90.

Celine Dion in A New Day The Colosseum, *Caesars Palace*, 3500 Las Vegas Blvd S ☏702/731-7865. The best-selling female singer of all time stars in a show designed by Cirque du Soleil stalwart Franco Dragone, in the 4000-seat Roman Colosseum. If you're a fan, this will be the night of your life; if you're not, the sheer spectacle of the thing will keep you fascinated. The Cirque du Soleil touches don't gel that well – think bewildered bellboys, deadpan clowns, and lots of silly shuffly dancing – but the staging is downright awesome, with the live action brilliantly complemented by back projection on the world's largest LED screen. Seasonal, Wed–Sun 8.30pm. $87.50–225.

Lance Burton *The Monte Carlo*, 3770 Las Vegas Blvd S ☏702/730-7160. Las Vegas's best family show. Master magician Lance Burton kicks off with impressive stunts involving playing cards, hand-kerchiefs, and doves, then moves on to large-scale illusions like the disappearance of an airplane and a narrow escape from hanging. Tues & Sat 7pm & 10pm, Wed–Fri 7pm. $66 & $73.

Mystère *TI*, 3300 Las Vegas Blvd S ☏702/796-9999 or 1-800/963-9634, ⑩www.cirquedusoleil .com. The Cirque du Soleil's original Las Vegas show is such a visual feast that it barely matters if you see its dreamscape symbolism as profound or meaningless. Above all, it's a showcase of fabulous circus skills, with tumblers, acrobats, trapeze art-ists, pole climbers, clowns, and strong men, but no animals apart from fantastic costumed appari-tions. Wed–Sat 7.30pm & 10.30pm, Sun 4.30pm & 7.30pm. $95.

O *Bellagio*, 3600 Las Vegas Blvd S ☏702/796-9999 or 1-800/963-9634, ⑩www.cirquedusoleil .com. An astonishing testament to what's possible when the budget is barely an issue. Any part of the stage at any time may be submerged to any depth. One moment a performer walks across a particular spot, the next someone dives headfirst into it. From the synchronized swimmers onwards, the Cirque du Soleil displays its magnificent skills to maximum advantage. Highlights include a colossal trapeze frame, draped like a pirate ship, and flying footmen in swirls of velvet drapery. Wed–Sun 7.30 & 10.30pm. $99–150.

Penn & Teller Samba Theatre, *Rio*, 3700 W Flamingo Rd, ☏702/777-7776. Fans who enjoy Penn & Teller's schtick of deconstructing classic magic tricks to show how they're done will probably love seeing them in their own Las Vegas show; while they perform their set-piece stunts undeniably well, however, the pacing is frankly rather flat, and when not truculent Penn Jillette's endless patter seems merely complacent. Daily except Tues 9pm. $77.

Listings

American Express In the *MGM Grand* at 3799 Las Vegas Blvd S (☏702/739-8474).

Banks and exchange There's not a single bank on the Strip, but there can be no easier city in which to get cash or change money: the casinos gladly convert almost any currency, day and night, and their walls are festooned with every conceivable ATM machine, most of which impose a service charge of around $2. Bear in mind that withdrawing cash with a credit card can incur punitive interest.

Car rental All the major national chains have outlets at McCarran airport, while at least one is represented in each of the major casinos.

Conventions During large conventions, which can attract up to 200,000 visitors, room rates in Las Vegas can rise enormously. The biggest annual events include the Consumer Electronic Show, in the second week of January; the Men's Apparel Guild (or MAGIC) in both mid-February and early September; and Comdex com-puter show in mid-November.

Helicopters Helicopter tours are very big business in Las Vegas, with the most popular options being a ten-minute jaunt over the Strip, ideally at night, and the much longer trips via the Hoover Dam to the Grand Canyon, almost all of which go to the so-called Grand Canyon West, 80 miles east on the Hualapai Indian Reservation, rather than the 200 miles to the South Rim. Papillon Helicopters (☏702/736-7243 or 1-888/635-7272, ⑩www .papillon.com) charge from $55 for a Las Vegas night flight, and $239 for a tour to Grand Canyon West.

Hospitals 24-hour emergency rooms operate at the University Medical Center, 1800 W Charleston Blvd (☏702/383-2000), and Sunrise Hospital, 3186 Maryland Pkwy (☏702/731-8080).

Internet access *Cyber Stop Internet Café*, 3763 Las Vegas Blvd S (daily 7am–2.30am; ☏702/736-4782, ⑩www.cyberstopinc.com).

Kids Several casinos will look after your children while you gamble or simply explore; these include the *MGM Grand*, whose Youth Center costs $8.50 per hour for guests, or $10.50 for outsiders, and the various members of the *Stations* chain. Typi-cally, you can leave your kids for a maximum of

3hr 30min in any 24-hour period. For a babysitter, call Around The Clock Child Care (☎702/365-1040 or 1-800/798-6768).

Library 1401 E Flamingo Rd (Mon–Thurs 9am–9pm, Fri & Sat 9am–5pm, Sun 1–5pm; ☎702/733-7810).

Medical Help The independent, 24-hour Nevada Resort Medical Center is located on the eighth floor of the *Imperial Palace*, 3535 Las Vegas Blvd S (☎702/893-6767).

Pharmacy CVS Pharmacy, on the Strip next to the *Monte Carlo* at 3758 Las Vegas Blvd S (☎702/262-9284), stays open 24hr daily.

Photography The only casinos in Las Vegas that allow visitors to take photographs of the action on their slot machines and gaming tables are *Excalibur* on the Strip, and the *Four Queens* downtown.

Post office You'll be able to mail postcards, letters, and packages from your hotel, but the nearest post office to the Strip is behind the *Stardust* at 3100 Industrial Rd (Mon–Fri 8.30am–5pm).

Tipping You're supposed to tip dealers at the gaming tables a chip or two each time you win (you can also place bets on behalf of the dealer, if you choose). Bar staff, or cocktail waitresses bringing free drinks, normally expect $1–2 per drink.

Lake Mead and the Hoover Dam

LAKE MEAD, the vast reservoir created by the construction of the Hoover Dam in 1935, makes a bizarre spectacle thirty miles southeast of the city, its blue waters a vivid counterpoint to the surrounding desert. Even if you don't need details of how to sail, scuba dive, water ski, or fish from the marinas along the five-hundred-mile shoreline, call in at the Alan Bible visitor center (daily 8.30am–4.30pm; ☎702/293-8990, ⓦwww.nps.gov/lame), four miles northeast of Boulder City on US-93, to enjoy a sweeping prospect of the whole thing.

Eight miles further southeast, beyond the rocky ridges of the Black Mountains, US-93 reaches the **HOOVER DAM** itself. Designed to block the Colorado River and provide low-cost electricity for the cities of the Southwest, it's among the tallest dams ever built (760ft high), and used enough concrete to build a two-lane highway from the West Coast to New York. Quite how much access visitors are allowed to the internal workings of the dam has varied ever since September 11, 2001, but in principle regular half-hour guided tours ride the elevator to the turbine room at the bottom, leaving from the **Hoover Dam Visitor Center** on the Nevada side of the river (daily 9am–5pm; $10, $5 parking; ☎702/597-5970).

The Grand Canyon

The **GRAND CANYON OF THE COLORADO** in Arizona, three hundred long and featureless driving miles from Las Vegas, is one of those sights that you really have to see once in your life. Once you've ventured east of the California state line, it would be a real shame to exclude it from your itinerary.

Although almost five million people visit **Grand Canyon National Park** every year, the Canyon itself remains beyond the grasp of the human imagination. No photograph, no set of statistics, can prepare you for such vastness. At more than one mile deep, it's an inconceivable abyss; at from four to eighteen miles wide, it's a seemingly endless expanse of bewildering shapes and colors, glaring desert brightness and impenetrable shadow, stark promontories, and soaring never-to-be-climbed sandstone pinnacles.

Somehow it's so impassive, so remote – you could never call it a disappointment, but at the same time many visitors are left feeling peculiarly flat; in a sense, none of the available activities can quite live up to that first stunning sight of the chasm. The **overlooks** along the rim all offer views that shift and

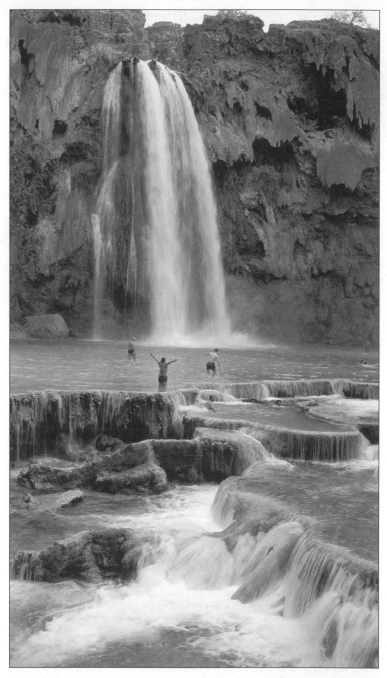

△ Havasu Falls, the Grand Canyon

change unceasingly from dawn to dusk; you can **hike** down into the depths on foot or by mule, hover above in a **helicopter**, or **raft** through the whitewater rapids of the river itself; you can spend a night at **Phantom Ranch** on the Canyon floor, or swim in the waterfalls of the idyllic **Havasupai Reservation**; and yet that distance always remains – the Grand Canyon stands apart.

The vast majority of visitors come to the **South Rim**, described in full on the next few pages – it's the most accessible part of the Canyon, there are far more facilities (mainly at **Grand Canyon Village**), and it's open year-round. There's another lodge and campground at the **North Rim**, which by virtue of its isolation can be a whole lot more evocative (for accommodation reservations, see box, p.358), but at one thousand feet higher this is usually closed by snow from mid-October until May. An even less eventful drive from Las Vegas will get you there, via St George in southern Utah. Few people visit both rims; to get from one to the other demands either a two-day hike down one side of the Canyon and up the other, or a 215-mile drive by road. Until the 1920s, the average visitor would stay for two or three weeks; these days, it's more like two or three hours – of which forty minutes are spent actually looking at the Canyon.

Finally, there's a definite risk that on the day you come the Grand Canyon will be invisible beneath a layer of fog; many people blame the 250 tons of sulphurous emissions pumped out every day by the Navajo Generating Station, seventy miles upriver at Page. Admission to the park, valid for seven days on either rim, costs $20 per vehicle, or $10 per pedestrian or cyclist.

Canyon practicalities

Most visitors enter from the south and base themselves – even if they're there just to do a quick hit of a few scenic overlooks – around the South Rim. That's where most trails begin from, as well as where the relatively few lodges and eating establishments are located.

Arrival

The most usual **approach** to the South Rim of the Grand Canyon is by road, turning north off I-40 at **Williams** to drive the last 56 miles on Hwy-64, or detouring further east via larger **Flagstaff** and then following Hwy-180 past the San Francisco Mountains. The two roads join twenty miles before the Canyon, at Valle. Most of this stretch is through thick ponderosa pine forests, so the ride up from Williams on the restored **steam trains** of the Grand Canyon Railway is not especially scenic, even if the crew keep you entertained with Western-style antics (departs Williams daily 10am; $58 round-trip, with higher fares for more luxurious carriages; ☎928/773-1976 or 1-800/843-8724, ⊛www.thetrain.com). Passengers who arrive on Flagstaff's two daily **Amtrak** trains can reach Grand Canyon Village on the Open Road Tours and Transportation buses ($20; ☎928/226-8060 or 1-877/226-8060, ⊛www.openroadtours.com); one leaves Flagstaff at 8.30am, calls at Williams at 9am, and arrives at the Canyon's Maswik Transportation Center at 10.15am, the other leaves Flagstaff at 3pm and Williams at 3.30pm, reaching the Canyon at 4.45pm. Return services leave Maswik at 11.45am and 5.45pm, arriving at Williams at 1pm and 7pm respectively, and Flagstaff at 1.30pm and 7.30pm. A full-day guided tour costs $69.

The small **airport** at Tusayan – six miles from the South Rim, and used primarily by "flight-seeing" tour companies (see box, p.360) – also welcomes scheduled services, especially from Las Vegas, with operators such as Scenic Airlines (☎702/638-3300 or 1-800/634-6801, ⊛www.scenic.com).

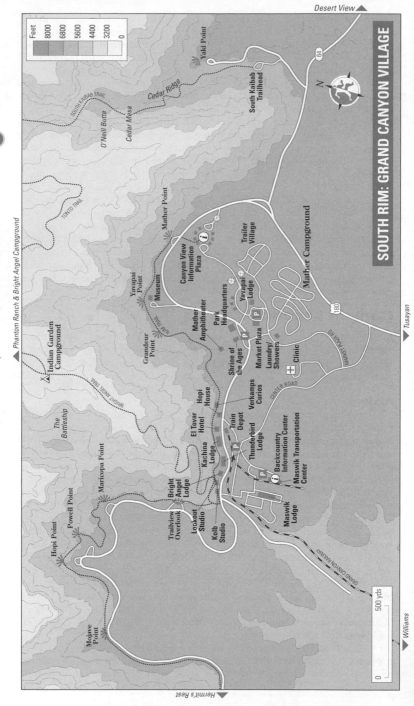

SOUTH RIM: GRAND CANYON VILLAGE

Desert View ▲

Yaki Point

SOUTH KAIBAB TRAIL

Cedar Ridge

Cedar Mesa

O'Neill Butte

South Kaibab Trailhead

64

N

Feet
8000
6800
5600
4400
3200
0

TONTO TRAIL

Mather Point

Canyon View Information Plaza

Trailer Village

Mather Campground

180

Tusayan ▶

▲ Phantom Ranch & Bright Angel Campground

Indian Garden Campground

Yavapai Point

Museum

RIM TRAIL

Grandeur Point

Mather Amphitheater

Park Headquarters

Yavapai Lodge

Shrine of the Ages

Market Plaza

Laundry/ Showers

Clinic

MARKET PLAZA RD

BRIGHT ANGEL TRAIL

The Battleship

Hopi House

El Tovar Hotel

Verkamps Curios

Train Depot

CENTER ROAD

Backcountry Information Center

Maswik Transportation Center

Maricopa Point

Trailview Overlook

Lookout Studio

Kolb Studio

Bright Angel Lodge

Kachina Lodge

Thunderbird Lodge

Maswik Lodge

GRAND CANYON TRAMWAY

Hopi Point

Powell Point

Mojave Point

▲ Hermit's Rest

Williams ▶

0

500 yds

Getting around

You arrive at a time when, to put it charitably, the park is in an ongoing state of flux. So far, a proposed new transportation scheme, under which private vehicles would be banned from the Canyon area, with visitors ferried around instead on a **light-rail** network, has been only minimally implemented, and it's looking as if it never will be. All that's happened so far is the construction of the large open-air **Canyon View Information Plaza**, located well short of the Grand Canyon Village center near Mather Point (daily: May to mid-Oct 8am–6pm; mid-Oct to April 8am–5pm; Ⓦwww.nps.gov/grca). It looks great, but as, ludicrously, there's no parking available, it's done nothing to relieve traffic congestion.

For the foreseeable future, **Grand Canyon Village** remains accessible to private vehicles, as is the road **east** from the village to **Desert View**. Both the road **west** from the village to **Hermit's Rest**, however, and the short access road to **Yaki Point** – the first overlook east of Mather Point, and the trailhead for the popular **South Kaibab Trail** – are only open to private vehicles during the months of December, January, and February. The park runs three free **shuttle-bus** routes: the ponderous **Village Route**, which loops laboriously between Grand Canyon Village and the information plaza; the **Kaibab Trail Route** between the plaza and Yaki Point; and the eight-mile **Hermit's Rest Route**, which heads west to eight Canyon overlooks.

Accommodation

All the **lodges** in the village charge similar prices, with no budget accommodation alternative. To see the Canyon, it makes little difference where in the village you stay; very few rooms in the "rim-edge" properties offer much of a view, though the older properties, the *El Tovar Hotel* (Ⓖ) and the *Bright Angel* (Ⓓ), are much more attractive in their own right than the motel-like *Thunderbird* and *Kachina* lodges (both Ⓖ). Both *Maswik Lodge* (cabins and rooms Ⓓ) and *Yavapai Lodge* (Ⓖ) are ten minutes' walk from the rim.

Camping facilities (and a laundry) are available at the year-round **Mather campground and RV park**, south of the main road through Grand Canyon Village. Sites for up to two vehicles and six people cost $15 per night between April and November, when reservations, which are strongly recommended, can be made up to five months in advance through Spherix (Ⓣ1-800/365-2267 or 301/722-1257 from outside the US, Ⓦreservations.nps.gov). No reservations are accepted between December and March, when sites are first-come-first-served, and the fee drops to $10 per night. The adjacent **Trailer Village** consists exclusively of RV sites with hook-ups, costing $25 per site per night for two people, plus $2 extra for each additional adult (reservations Ⓣ1-888/297-2757, Ⓦwww.grandcanyonlodges.com). The summer-only *Desert View* campground, 26 miles east, is first-come-first-served, costs $10, and has no hook-ups. It's also possible to camp inside the Canyon itself, if you first obtain a permit from the Backcountry Reservations Office near *Maswik Lodge* (daily 8am–noon & 1–5pm; Ⓣ928/638-7875; permits $10 + $5 per person per night).

If all the park accommodation is full, the nearest alternative is the underwhelming service village of **Tusayan**, just over a mile south of the park entrance. *Seven Mile Lodge* (Ⓣ928/638-2291; Ⓒ) offers the least expensive rooms; the newer *Grand Hotel* (Ⓣ928/638-3333 or 1-888/634-7263; Ⓦwww.visitgrandcanyon.com; Ⓖ) is more stylish. The most popular of the commercial campgrounds outside the park – with families, at least – is *Flintstone's Bedrock City* (mid-March to Oct; Ⓣ928/635-2600; $14–18), 22 miles south at the junction of Hwy-64 and Hwy-180, which has its own prehistoric theme park.

Eating

Thanks to the Canyon's remoteness and lack of water, **food** prices tend to be well above average; if you're on a tight budget, bring your own. However, *Yavapai* and *Maswik* lodges have reasonable basic cafeterias, open until 10pm. *Bright Angel Lodge* has its own restaurant, as well as the *Arizona Steakhouse*, both also open until 10pm, and both offering a wide range of standard American entrees for under $20. At *El Tovar* (reservations on ℡928/638-2631), where the dining room looks right out over the Canyon, the sumptuous menu, abounding in rich meat dishes, is enormously expensive. Breakfast is the most affordable meal; lunch and dinner can easily cost upwards of $40. In Tusayan, the *Canyon Star* in the *Grand Hotel* (℡928/638-3333) serves fairly ordinary food but features Native American dancers nightly, while *We Cook Pizza & Pasta* (℡928/638-2278) offers reasonably priced meals.

The geology and history of the Canyon

Layer upon layer of different rocks, readily distinguished by color and each with its own fossil record, recede down into the Grand Canyon and back through time, until the strata at the riverbed, which are among the oldest exposed rocks on earth. And yet the Canyon's **formation** remains a mystery. Satellite photos show that the Colorado actually runs through the heart of an enormous hill (what the Indians called the Kaibab, "the mountain with no peak"); experts cannot agree on how this could happen. Studies show that the Canyon still deepens, at the slow rate of 50ft per million years. Its fantastic sandstone and limestone formations were not literally carved by the river, however; they're the result of erosion by wind and extreme cycles of heat and cold. These features were named – **Brahma Temple**, **Vishnu Temple**, and so on – by Clarence Dutton, a student of comparative religion, who wrote the first Geological Survey report on the Canyon in 1881.

It may look forbidding, but the Grand Canyon is not a dead place. All sorts of desert **wildlife** survive here – sheep and rabbits, eagles and vultures, mountain lions and, of course, spiders, scorpions, and snakes. The **human** presence has never been on any great scale, but signs have been found of habitation as early as 2000 BC, and the **Ancestral Puebloans** were certainly here later on. A party of **Spaniards** passed through in 1540 – less than twenty years after Cortés conquered the Aztecs – searching for cities of gold, and one Father Garcés spent some time with the Havasupai in 1776. It was **John Wesley Powell**'s expeditions along the fearsome and uncharted waters of the Colorado in 1869 and 1871–72 that truly brought the Canyon to public attention. A few abortive attempts were made to mine different areas, but facilities for tourism were swiftly realized to be a far more lucrative investment. With the exception of the Indian reservations, the Grand Canyon is now run exclusively for the benefit of visitors; although even as recently as 1963 there were proposals to dam the Colorado and flood 150 miles of the Canyon, and the Glen Canyon dam has seriously affected the ecology downstream.

Grand Canyon Village

GRAND CANYON VILLAGE is not a very stimulating place to spend any time. However, in the absence of significantly cheaper accommodation within fifty miles (for example, in Tusayan at the park entrance), there's little option but to stay here. The centerpiece is the magnificent terrace that stretches in front of **Bright Angel Lodge** (usually the liveliest spot in town) and the black-beamed 1905 **El Tovar Hotel**, which gives many visitors their only look at the Canyon – though the Colorado itself is too deep in the Inner Gorge to be seen from here. Further back are more lodges and gift shops, and employee housing, with the post office, the general store, and the campground about a mile east through the woods.

Along the South Rim

It's possible to **walk** along the South Rim for several miles in either direction from the village, the first few of them on railed, concrete pathways. The most obvious short excursions are to see the sun rise and set. At or near the village, the giant wall that reaches out in the west overshadows much of the evening view. If, however, you walk right out to **Hopi Point** at its end, looking down as you go onto the Bright Angel Trail as it winds across the Tonto Plateau, you may well see a magical sunset, with the Colorado – 350ft wide at this point – visible way below.

The best place within walking distance to watch the dawn is **Mather Point**, close to the visitor center. Nearby, if you can tear your eyes away from its panoramic bay windows, the **Yavapai Observation Station** (daily: hours vary from 8am–8pm in summer down to 8am–5pm in winter; free) has illuminating displays on how the Canyon may have been formed.

Further dramatic views are available along the **East Rim Drive** – although unless you take an excursion you'll need your own vehicle to see them. **Desert View**, 23 miles out from the village, is at 7500ft the highest point on the South Rim. Visible to the east are the vast flatlands of the Navajo Nation; to the northeast, Vermillion and Echo Cliffs, and the gray bulk of Navajo Mountain ninety miles away; to the west, the gigantic peaks of the Vishnu and Buddha temples. Through the plains comes the narrow gorge of the Little Colorado; somewhere in the depths, before it meets the Colorado itself, is the *sipapu*, the hole through which the Hopi believe that men first entered this, the Third World. The odd-looking construction on the very lip of the Canyon is **Desert View Watchtower** (daily: summer 9am–5.30pm;winter 9am–4.30pm; free), designed by Mary Colter in 1932 in a conglomeration of Native American styles (though a steel frame props it all up) and decorated with Hopi pictographs. It contains a gift shop, as does the general store a few yards away. Groups of **tarantulas** are often seen in the evenings at Desert View, scuttling back into the warmth of the Canyon for the night.

Into the Canyon

Hiking any of the trails that descend into the Grand Canyon offers something more than just another view of the same thing. Instead you pass through a sequence of utterly different landscapes, each with its own distinct climate, wildlife, and topography. However, while the Canyon can offer a wonderful wilderness experience, it's essential to remember that it can be a hostile and very unforgiving environment, gruelling even for expert hikers.

Grand Canyon tours

As well as managing the park lodges, Xanterra (see p.358) operates guided **bus tours** along the South Rim, including the four-hour **Desert View Tour** to the east, timed to coincide with sunset at Desert View ($28.50); the two-hour **Hermit's Rest Tour** to the west ($16.25); and shorter **Sunrise** and **Sunset** tours ($12.50). It's also responsible for the famous **mule rides** down the Bright Angel Trail from Grand Canyon Village, for which reservations are accepted up to a year in advance. Riders must be at least four feet seven inches tall (1.38 meters), speak fluent English, and weigh not more than 200 pounds (91kg). All rides set off early in the morning, with one-day, seven-hour round-trips as far as Plateau Point costing $133. Overnight trips to **Phantom Ranch**, where you spend the rest of the day beside the river and sleep in two-person cabins, cost $361 for one person and $642 for two. **Two-night** rides, available between mid-November and March only, are $507 and $856 respectively. Reservations for both buses and mules are handled by the "transportation desk" in each lodge, or call ☏928/638-2631.

Airplane tours cost from around $75 for 30min ($45 child) up to as long as you like for as much as you've got. Operators include Air Grand Canyon (☏928/638-2686 or 1-800/247-4726, ⊛www.airgrandcanyon.com) and Grand Canyon Airlines (☏928/638-2359 or 1-866/235-9422, ⊛www.grandcanyonairlines.com). **Helicopter tours**, from $110 for 30min, are offered by AirStar Helicopters (☏928/638-2622 or 1-800/962-3869, ⊛www.airstar.com) and Papillon Helicopters (☏928/638-2419 or 1-800/528-2418, ⊛www.papillon.com), who also operate the $45 day-trips to the Havasupai Reservation, described opposite. All are based in Tusayan, at or near the airport.

The South Rim is 7000 feet above sea level, an altitude that for most people is fatiguing in itself. Furthermore, all hikes start with a long, steep descent – which can come as a shock to the knees – and unless you camp overnight you'll have to climb all the way back up again when you're hotter and wearier. If you're day-hiking, the golden rule is to keep track of how much time you spend hiking down and allow twice that much to get back up again. Average **summer temperatures** inside the Canyon exceed 100°F; to hike for eight hours in that sort of heat, you have to drink an incredible thirty pints of water. Always carry at least a quart per person, and much more if there are no water sources along your chosen trail. You must have food as well, as drinking large quantities without also eating can cause water intoxication.

There's only space here to detail the most popular trail, the **Bright Angel**. Many of the others, such as the **Hermit**, date from the days prior to 1928, when the obstreperous Ralph Cameron controlled access to the Bright Angel and many other rim-edge sites by means of spurious mining claims, and the Fred Harvey Company had to find other ways to get its customers down to the Colorado. These other trails tend to be overgrown now, or partially blocked by landslides; check before setting out.

Bright Angel Trail

The **BRIGHT ANGEL TRAIL**, followed on foot or mule by thousands of visitors each year, starts from the wooden shack in the village that was once a photographic studio. It takes 9.6 miles to switchback down to **Phantom Ranch** beside the river, but park rangers have a simple message for all would-be hikers: don't try to hike down and back in a single day. It might not look far on the map, but it's harder than running a marathon. The longest feasible day-hike is to go instead as far as **Plateau Point** on the edge of the arid Tonto

Plateau, an overlook above the Inner Gorge, from which it is not possible to descend any further – a twelve-mile round-trip that will probably take you at least eight hours. In summer, water can be obtained along the way.

The first section of the trail was laid out by miners a century ago, along an old Havasupai route, and has two short tunnels in its first mile. After another mile, the **wildlife** starts to increase (deer, rodents, and the ubiquitous ravens), and there are a few **pictographs**, which have been all but obscured by graffiti.

At the lush **Indian Gardens** almost five miles down, where you'll find a ranger station and campground with water, the trails split, to Plateau Point or down to the river via the Devil's Corkscrew. The latter route leads through sand dunes scattered with cacti and down beside **Garden Creek** to the Colorado, which you then follow for more than a mile to get to Phantom Ranch.

Phantom Ranch

It's a real thrill to spend a night at the very bottom of the Canyon, at the 1922 **PHANTOM RANCH**. The cabins are reserved exclusively for mule riders (see box, opposite), while beds in the four ten-bunk **dorms** ($27) are usually reserved way in advance, through Xanterra (see p.358), but it's worth checking for cancellations at the *Bright Angel Lodge* transportation desk as soon as you reach the South Rim. Do not hike down without a reservation, and even if you do have one, reconfirm it the day before you set off. All supplies reach Phantom Ranch the same way you do (an all-day hike on foot or mule), so **meals** are expensive, a minimum of $17 for breakfast and $20 for dinner.

The Havasupai Reservation

A 1930s anthropologist called the **HAVASUPAI RESERVATION** "the only spot in the United States where native culture has remained in anything like its pristine condition"; things have changed a little since then, but the sheer magic of its turquoise waterfalls and canyon scenery make this a very special place. Traditionally, the Havasupai would spend summer on the Canyon's floor and winter on the plateau above. However, when the reservation was created in 1882, they were only granted land at the bottom of the Canyon, and not until 1975 did the concession of another 251,000 acres up above make it possible for them to resume their ancient lifestyle.

Havasu Canyon is a side canyon of the Grand Canyon, about 35 miles west of Grand Canyon Village as the raven flies, but almost two hundred miles by road. Turn off the interstate at Seligman or Kingman, onto AZ-66, which curves north between the two, stock up with food, water, and gas, and then turn on to Arrowhead Hwy-18. Plans to build a road – or even a tramway – down into Havasu Canyon have always been rejected, in part because much of the income of the five or six hundred Havasupai comes from guiding visitors on foot, mule, or horseback. Instead, the road ends at Hualapai Hilltop, from where an eight-mile trail zigzags down a bluff and leads through the stunning waterless Hualapai Canyon to the village of **Supai**. Riding down costs $70 one way, $120 for a round-trip, while hiking is free; all visitors, however, pay a $20 entry fee on arrival at Supai.

Beyond Supai the trail leads to a succession of spectacular waterfalls. The first, **Havasu Falls**, spills over a broad lip of travertine limestone into a limpid pool that offers irresistible swimming. A mile further on, precipitous Mooney Falls is named after an unfortunate prospector who dangled here for three days in the 1890s, at the end of a snagged rope, before falling to his death. Hikers who brave the steep climb down the side, aided by tunnels and iron chains, reach another pristine pool, but it's still another seven very demanding miles to the Colorado River.

A **campground** (℡928/448-2141), charging $10 per night, stretches between Havasu and Mooney Falls, and Supai itself holds the motel-like *Havasupai Lodge* (℡928/448-2111; ❹), along with a café, a general store, and the only post office in the US that still receives its mail by pack train. Only visitors who have made definite advance arrangements at either the campground or lodge should set off from the trailhead; note also that from time to time Supai is hit by freak floods, which can result in the temporary closure of both.

If you don't have the time to make the long overland trek to the reservation, consider **flying** there from the South Rim with Papillon Helicopters (℡702/736-7243 or 1-888/635-7272, ⓦwww.papillon.com). Even a day-trip costs over $450, but it's an amazing Indiana Jones–style adventure, and you get to explore the canyon at your own pace.

Flagstaff

Northern Arizona's most attractive and characterful town, **FLAGSTAFF**, occupies a superbly dramatic location beneath the San Francisco Peaks, half-way between New Mexico and California. Straddling the I-40 and I-17 interstates, it's a major waystation for tourists en route to the Grand Canyon, just eighty miles northwest, but it's also a worthwhile destination in its own right.

Downtown, where barely a building rises more than three stories, oozes Wild West charm. Its main thoroughfare, Santa Fe Avenue, used to be **Route 66**, while before that it was the pioneer trail west. A stroll around its central few blocks is gloriously evocative of the past, though these days the diners and saloons are interspersed with outfitter stores and coffee bars, and the local cowboys and Indians share the sidewalks with students from Northern Arizona University.

The exceptional **Museum of Northern Arizona** (daily 9am–5pm; $5; ⓦwww.musnaz.org), three miles northwest on Hwy-180 (and not on a local bus route), provides a superbly detailed and well-illustrated introduction to Arizona's Native American cultures, past and present, as well as background on fascinating displays that explain the formation of the Grand Canyon.

Practicalities

Two Amtrak trains still pull in each day – the 5.27am to Albuquerque and the 9.01pm to Los Angeles – at the wooden stationhouse right in the heart of town, adjoining the helpful visitor center at 101 W Santa Fe Ave (Mon–Sat 7am–6pm, Sun 7am–5pm; ℡928/774-9541 or 1-800/842-7293, ⓦwww.flagstaffarizona.org). Open Road Tours and Transportation run twice-daily **bus services** via Williams to the Grand Canyon (daily 8.30am & 3pm; $20; ℡928/226-8060 or 1-877/226-8060, ⓦwww.openroadtours.com), while Greyhound, 399 S Malpais Lane (℡928/774-4573 or 1-800/231-2222), connects with Las Vegas, LA, San Diego, and San Francisco.

Two good central **hostels**, south of the tracks and run by the same management, offer dorm beds for around $16 and private rooms for more like $30. Both the *DuBeau International Hostel*, 19 W Phoenix Ave (℡928/773-1656 or 1-800/398-7112, ⓦwww.dubeau.com; ❶), and the *Grand Canyon International Hostel*, 19 S San Francisco St (℡928/779-9421 or 1-888/442-2696, ⓦwww.grandcanyonhostel.com; ❶), run excursions up to the Grand Canyon. The *Monte Vista*, 100 N San Francisco St (℡928/779-6971 or 1-800/545-3068, ⓦwww.hotelmontevista.com; ❸–❺), is a pleasant little hotel where the assorted restored rooms, with and without attached bathrooms, are named for celebrity guests from Bob Hope to Michael Stipe. Chain motels abound just off the interstate further east, with the smart, good-value *Super 8 West*, 602 W Route 66 (☎928/774-4581; ❷), closer at hand, less than a mile southwest of downtown. The best campground is three miles south on US-89A, at *Fort Tuthill County Park* (☎928/774-5139).

As for **food**, *Macy's European Coffee House & Bakery*, south of the tracks at 14 S Beaver St (☎928/774-2243), offers good breakfasts and substantial vegetarian dishes later on, plus free wireless **Internet access**, while *Pasto*, downtown at 19 E Aspen Ave (☎928/779-1937), serves well-priced Italian dinners. The *Mad Italian* at no. 101 S San Francisco St (☎928/779-1820) is a highly sociable bar with several pool tables, while the *Museum Club*, 3404 E Route 66 (☎928/526-9434), is a real oddity: a 1930s log-cabin taxidermy museum that somehow transmogrified into a classic Route 66 roadhouse, saloon, and country music venue, and became a second home to hordes of dancing cowboys.

Travel details

Trains

Flagstaff to: Los Angeles (1 daily; 10hr).

Buses

All buses are Greyhound unless otherwise stated. **Grand Canyon** to: Flagstaff (2 Open Road Tours daily; 2hr).

Las Vegas to: Flagstaff (2 daily; 5hr 40min); Los Angeles (14 daily; 5hr 30min–8hr 30min).

5

Death Valley, the Owens Valley, and the Eastern Sierra

CHAPTER 5

Highlights

✳ **Rhyolite** Assorted gold-rush ruins, a house made from bottles, a weird collection of fiberglass sculptures, and a location on the fringes of Death Valley make this an essential stop. See p.373

✳ **Furnace Creek Inn** This grand 1920s hotel is the perfect – in fact the only – place to experience Death Valley in luxury. See p.375

✳ **Scotty's Castle** More chateau than castle, the beautiful interiors of this folly of a Chicago millionaire make a cool respite from the Death Valley heat. See p.380

✳ **Mount Whitney** The highest point in the continental US has an iconic appeal, the stupendous summit views best appreciated as part of an overnight camping trip. See p.386

✳ **Bristlecone Pine Forest** The gnarled and wizened forms of the world's oldest living things – some nearly five millennia old – are on display in this alpine forest. See p.391

✳ **Mono Lake** Take a canoe or kayaking trip amid the lakeside tufa towers, which create an otherworldly – and highly photogenic – landscape. See p.406

✳ **Bodie Ghost Town** Bring a picnic, your camera, and leave half a day to explore the best-preserved ghost town in the West. See p.409

✳ **Whoa Nellie Deli** A casual restaurant at a gas station at the junction of US-395 and Hwy-120, the *Whoa Nellie* has justly gained a reputation for great food and a lively atmosphere. See p.409

△ Badwater, Death Valley National park

5

Death Valley, the Owens Valley, and the Eastern Sierra

The far eastern edge of California, rising up from the Mojave Desert and cleaving to the border with Nevada, is a long narrow strip as scenically dramatic as anywhere else in the state, veering from blistering desert to ski country, much of it in the lee of the mighty Sierra Nevada. It's a region devoid of interstates, scarcely populated, and, but for the scant reminders of gold-hungry pioneers, developed in only the most tentative way.

At the region's base, technically forming the Mojave's northern reach but more usually visited along with the Owens Valley, is **Death Valley**. With the highest average summer temperatures on earth and so remote that it's almost a region unto itself, this vast national park is a distillation of the classic desert landscape: an arid, otherworldly terrain of brilliantly colored, bizarrely eroded rocks, mountains, and sand dunes, a hundred miles from the nearest town.

Heading north, the towering **eastern** peaks of the Sierra Nevada drop abruptly to the largely desert – and deserted – landscape of the Owens Valley far below. Seen from the eastern side, the mountains are perfectly described by their Spanish name, **Sierra Nevada**, which literally translates as "snowcapped saw." Virtually the entire range is preserved as wilderness, and hikers and mountaineers can get to higher altitudes quicker here than almost anywhere else in California: well-maintained roads lead to trailheads at over eight thousand feet, providing swift access to spires, glaciers, and clear mountain lakes. **Mount Whitney**, the highest point in the continental US, marks the southernmost point of the chain, which continues north for an uninterrupted 150 miles to the backcountry of Yosemite National Park.

At the foot of Mount Whitney, the five-mile-wide **Owens Valley** starts, hemmed in to the east by the **White Mountains**, nearly as high but drier and less hospitable than the High Sierra, and home to the ancient, gnarled **bristle-cone pines**. In between the two mountain ranges, US-395 runs the length of the valley, which has few signs of settlement at all beyond the sporadic roadside towns and the larger **Bishop**.

▲ *Reno (100 miles)*

Buckeye Hot Springs

TOIYABE NATIONAL FOREST

Bridgeport
Travertine Hot Springs

YOSEMITE NATIONAL PARK

◆ **Bodie State Historic Park**

Black Point Fissures

Tuolumne Meadows

120

TOIYABE NATIONAL FOREST

361

0   40 miles

N

Mono Lake

Lee Vining

Yosemite Village

120

360

June Lake

Mono Craters

95

DEVIL'S POSTPILE NATIONAL MONUMENT

Crowley Lake

395

Mammoth Lakes

Benton

6

264

SIERRA NATIONAL FOREST

WHITE MOUNTAINS

INYO NATIONAL FOREST

N E V A D A

95

Laws Railroad Museum

ANCIENT BRISTLECONE PINE FOREST

Keough's Hot Springs

Bishop

168

SIERRA NEVADA

Palisade Glacier

Big Pine

266

Tinemaha Wildlife Viewpoint

KINGS CANYON & SEQUOIA NATIONAL PARKS

Onion Valley

Independence

Scotty's Junction

INYO MTNS.

Manzanar National Historic Site

Scotty's Castle

Whitney Portal

267

Lone Pine

Mt. Whitney

Saline Valley

Rhyolite Ghost Town

136

INYO NATIONAL FOREST

Leg Flat

Beatty

Stovepipe Wells

95

SEQUOIA NATIONAL FOREST

Olancha

Owens Lake (dry)

Panamint Springs

Skidoo

Death Valley

190

Lake Isabella

Darwin

190

Furnace Creek

Lathrop Wells

373

178

Telescope Peak

PANAMINT RANGE

US Naval Weapons Center

ARMAGOSA RANGE

395

Ballarat Ghost Town

Death Valley Junction

China Lake

178

Trona

DEATH VALLEY NATIONAL PARK

Pahrump

160

Ridgecrest

Red Rock Canyon

Shoshone
Tecopa Hot Springs

14

Randsburg ● Johannesburg

127

Tecopa

395

China Date Ranch

58

Four Corners

◀ *Bakersfield (40 miles)*

▶ *Las Vegas (50 miles)*

▼ *Barstow (28 miles)*

▼ *Baker (30 miles)*

An hour's drive further north, **Mammoth Lakes** is the Eastern Sierra's busiest resort, thick with skiers in winter, and with fishers and mountain bikers in summer. Finally, at the point where many turn west for Yosemite, bizarre rock formations rise from the placid blue waters of ancient **Mono Lake**, set in a dramatic desert basin of volcanoes and steaming-hot pools. Beyond, and far enough out of most people's way to deter the crowds, lies the wonderful ghost town of **Bodie**, which preserves a palpable sense of gold-town life eight thousand feet up in a parched, windswept valley.

Getting around

Getting around the region is best done by car, primarily using **US-395** – the lifeline of the Owens Valley and pretty much the only access to the area from within California. Once north of Mojave, where Hwy-58 branches west to Bakersfield, no road crosses the Sierra Nevada until Hwy-120, a spur over the 10,000-foot Tioga Pass into Yosemite. To the east Hwy-190 cuts through the Panamint Range into Death Valley.

Neither Amtrak nor Greyhound run any services in the region and the only long-distance **public transportation** is the bus service run by Carson Ridgecrest Eastern Sierra Transit or CREST (☎760/872-1901 or 1-800/922-1930), which runs along the Owens Valley linking Ridgecrest in the south (see p.327) and Reno, Nevada, in the north (see p.727). Both towns have onward connections. Buses generally have racks or space onboard to accommodate bikes.

In addition there are a number of small companies running minibuses up to mountain trailheads, but these are more like taxi services and have no regular schedule.

Death Valley National Park

Initially **DEATH VALLEY** seems an inhuman environment: burning hot, apparently lifeless and almost entirely without shade, much less water. If you just drive through in half a day, it can appear barren and monotonous, but

What makes Death Valley so hot and dry

As part of the northern Mojave Desert you'd expect **Death Valley** to be **hot and dry**, but certain factors combine to make this small patch of land hotter than anywhere else on earth, based on a year-round average.

Perhaps the biggest contributor to its unforgiving heat is its location: Death Valley sits at sea level in the **rain shadow** of four mountain ranges, receiving on average only an inch and a half of precipitation each year. Prevailing winds carry the Pacific Ocean's weather patterns into the Coast Ranges where the moisture is lost as rainfall. From there the air struggles over the 14,000-foot Sierra Nevada, leaving behind its burden as snowfall. By the time the air gets east of the Sierra it contains very little moisture, and the last of the precipitation is squeezed out as it climbs over the Angus Range and the 11,000-foot Panamint Range.

As this very dry air descends from these heights it compresses, causing it to heat up until it finds itself trapped in a narrow basin where the beating sun, the lack of shade-giving plants, and the low altitude allow the air temperature to reach unbearable levels. Even overnight the air doesn't get much chance to cool, as the surrounding mountains trap it in creating strong, hot winds – at times it can feel like you're standing in front of a hair dryer.

5

DEATH VALLEY AND THE EASTERN SIERRA | Death Valley National Park

369

longer acquaintance reveals multiple layers of interest. Death Valley itself is just the central portion (but very much the focal point) of the much larger **DEATH VALLEY NATIONAL PARK**, which extends a hundred miles from north to south and is almost as wide in some parts. Grand vistas sweep down from the subalpine slopes of the eleven-thousand-foot **Telescope Peak** to **Badwater**, the lowest point in the western hemisphere at 282 feet below sea level; sharply silhouetted hills are folded and eroded into deeply shadowed crevices, their exotic mineral content turning million-year-old mud flats into rainbows of sunlit phosphorescence; and stark hills harbor the bleached ruins of mining enterprises that briefly flourished against all odds.

On the face of it, it seems impossible that such a hot and dry landscape could support any kind of life, yet it is home to a great variety of creatures, from snakes and giant eagles to tiny fish and bighorn sheep. What little vegetation there is can be fascinating both for its adaptation to the rigors of the environment and the almost sculptural effect it has on the landscape.

Throughout the summer, the **air temperature** in Death Valley averages 112°F (44°C), and in 1913 the mercury topped 134°F (57°C), the highest temperature ever recorded in the US, and only ever beaten by two degrees in Libya in 1922. There are frequent periods when the temperature tops 120°F daily, and at such times the ground can reach near boiling point, so it's best to stay away. Visitors still come though, joining the car manufacturers who have been bringing their latest models out here for extreme testing ever since Dodge paved the way in 1913.

Unless you're a real glutton for scorching, potentially fatal punishment, it's better to come during the spring, especially March and early April, when wildflowers may be in bloom (though many years they refuse to play ball) and daytime temperatures average a manageable 83°F, dropping to the mid-fifties at night. Any time between October and May, it's generally mild and dry, with occasional rainfall on the surrounding mountains causing flash floods through otherwise bone-dry gullies and washes.

Throughout the park, roads and services are sparse, mostly concentrated in the central north–south valley, after which the park is named. Hwy-190 runs the length of the valley linking **Furnace Creek** and **Stovepipe Wells**, the park's two main outposts for provisions and accommodation. Forays from these bases give access to extensive **sand dunes**, intriguing **ghost towns**, cool high-country camping in the **Panamint Range**, and the incongruous mansion that is **Scotty's Castle**.

Geology and history

The sculpted rock layers exposed in Death Valley, tinted by oxidized traces of various **mineral deposits**, comprise a nearly complete record of the earth's past, from 500-million-year-old mountains to relatively young **fossils**, and deposits left on the valley floors by the Ice Age lakes, which covered most of the park's low-lying areas. There's also dramatic evidence of volcanic activity, as at the massive **Ubehebe Crater** on the north side of the park.

Humans have lived in and around Death Valley for thousands of years, beginning about ten thousand years ago, when the Valley was still filled by a massive lake; the climate was then quite mild and wildlife was more abundant than it is today. Later, wandering tribes of desert **Shoshone** wintered near perennial freshwater springs in the warm valley, spending the long, hot summers at cooler,

For advice on **desert survival**, see box, pp.284–285.

higher elevations in the surrounding mountains; some of their descendants still live at Furnace Creek.

The first non-natives passed through in 1849, looking for a shortcut to the Gold Rush towns on the other side of the Sierra Nevada; they ran out of food and water but most managed to survive, though the death of one of their number encouraged a survivor to dub the place Death Valley. For the next 75 years, the only people willing to brave the hardships of the desert were miners, who searched for and found deposits of gold, silver, and copper.

The most successful mining endeavors were centered on **borates**, a harsh alkaline used in detergent soaps (and, eventually, in a variety of industries – everything from cosmetics to nuclear reactors). In the late nineteenth century, borate miners developed twenty-mule-team wagons to haul the borate ore across the deserts to the railroad line at Mojave. In the 1920s, the first tourist facilities were developed, and in 1927 the *Furnace Creek Inn* was built on the site of the former Furnace Creek mining camp. Six years later, the two million acres of Death Valley and its environs were purchased by the US government, to be preserved as a national monument. In 1994, as part of the **California Desert Protection Act**, Congress accorded it national park status and added a further 1.3 million acres to its area, making Death Valley the largest national park in the country outside Alaska.

Getting to Death Valley

Death Valley is a long way from anywhere, with **Las Vegas** (see p.337) being the nearest city, over 130 miles away. There's **no scheduled public transportation** into the park, and though **Beatty**, forty miles north of Furnace Creek in Nevada, does have a bus service, it is of little use for getting to Death Valley unless you have a bicycle. The following are the main routes into the park; be sure to top up your **gas** tank before you head into the park as it is expensive here.

From the south: Tecopa Hot Springs and Shoshone

Hwy-127 branches off I-15 at Baker (see p.332) – the last stop for supplies on the southern route into Death Valley – and cuts across fifty miles of desolate Mojave landscape into the Armagosa Valley before reaching any civilization. A couple of miles east of Hwy-127 and fifty-odd miles north of Baker, two dilapidated settlements of scrappy trailer homes make unexpectedly decent places to stop off.

TECOPA HOT SPRINGS has become a popular winter retreat, thanks to its natural **hot springs** (always open except Mon & Fri 7am–noon; free), bequeathed in perpetuity by a local chief provided they remain gratis. Separate male and female clothing-free bathhouses are ugly and subject to a long list of largely commonsense rules, but are relaxing nonetheless. For a more intimate experience head for the nearby *Delight's Hot Springs Resort*, where you can soak in private, odor-free mineral pools ($12 for two people all day).

While in the area, drive seven miles southeast to **China Ranch Date Farm**, China Ranch Road (daily 9am–5pm; ☎760/852-4415, ⓦwww.chinaranch .com), where you are free to wander among the mostly young groves, follow a shady streamside nature trail, explore wider along the Old Spanish Trail (a pack route between old mission stations which ran nearby), then repair to the cactus garden for a refreshing date shake and, of course, buy some dates.

Many people **stay** across the road from the hot springs at the bleak campground (tents $10, hook-up $14), though the cabins at *Delight's Hot Springs Resort* (see p.376), the hostel in nearby **Tecopa** (see p.375), and the *Ranch House Inn*, by the China Ranch Date Farm, are all better bets.

The hamlet of **SHOSHONE**, eight miles north of Tecopa Hot Springs, wouldn't really rate a mention but for a gas station, a decent motel (see p.376) within striking distance of the park, and *C'est Si Bon* (closed Tues & Wed), the best **café** for miles around, located in a former railroad building now tastefully decorated with artworks and photos. Apart from good espresso and Internet access, the café sells Thai iced tea, smoothies, granola and yogurt breakfasts, cheese platters, crêpes, home-made cakes, and more.

While here, it is worth spending a few minutes at the small **Shoshone Museum** and Death Valley **Chamber of Commerce** (daily 9.30am–5pm; ☎760/852-4524, ⓦwww.deathvalleychamber.org) and ask them to direct you to **Doublin Gulch**, a series of hand-hewn cave homes once used by miners, and so named because early in the twentieth century the area was so popular it kept "doublin" in size. The last resident moved out in 1986.

The route into Death Valley continues north through Death Valley Junction (see below).

From the east: Death Valley Junction and Ash Meadows

For the most direct and interesting route from Las Vegas, take US-95 or Las Vegas Boulevard south to Blue Diamond Route (Hwy-160 west), which leads past the scenic **Red Rock Canyon Recreation Area** to the town of **Pahrump**; the Smith's supermarket there is a good spot to load up on last-minute supplies.

Some 25 miles on you reach the tiny and virtually abandoned settlement of **DEATH VALLEY JUNCTION**. It offers no fuel or supplies, but its *Amargosa Hotel* (see p.375) houses the **Amargosa Opera House**, the creation of Marta Becket, a New York dancer and artist who settled here in the late 1960s. The inside of the theater is painted with trompe l'oeil balconies peopled by sixteenth-century Spanish nobles and revelers, apparently a confidence-building gesture when audiences dwindled. Ballet-pantomimes, in which Ms Becket, now in her eighties, takes almost all the parts herself, are staged here through the winter (Oct to early May Sat only; $15; ☎760/852-4441, ⓦwww.amargosa-opera-house.com) with performances starting at 7.45pm. Come for the spirit of the enterprise rather than the show itself, and come soon, as there is sporadic talk of retirement.

From Death Valley Junction it is an easy thirty-mile drive to Furnace Creek, passing Zabriskie Point and the junction for Dante's View (see p.380 for both) along the way.

Also consider detouring nine miles north of Death Valley Junction (along Hwy-373 towards Lathrop Wells), then five miles east to reach the **ASH MEADOWS NATIONAL WILDLIFE REFUGE** (daily sunrise–sunset), a small desert oasis which contains the US's greatest concentration of endemic species – some 24 plants and animals found nowhere else in the world. Head for the visitor center and the adjacent **Crystal Spring Boardwalk Trail**, which runs a third of a mile beside a stream to its source, a beautiful clear spring that's quite at odds with the desert all around. Here the rare desert pupfish, a tiny silver-colored fish, dwell.

From the northeast: Rhyolite and Beatty

An alternative route into Death Valley from Las Vegas runs past the Nellis Air Force Base and the old US nuclear-weapons testing range beside US-95 to **BEATTY**, where there's a small **chamber of commerce**, at 119 Main St (Tues–Sat 9am–5pm; ☎775/553-2424), a few **places to stay** including an HI hostel (see p.376), a couple of casinos with 24hr diner-style restaurants, and the folksy **Beatty Museum**, 417 Main St (daily 10am–4pm; free; ☎775/553-2303), which tells tales of the local Bullfrog Mining District.

Don't pass up the opportunity to visit the appealing ghost town of **RHYO-LITE** (ⓦwww.rhyolitesite.com), up a side road three miles west of Beatty. Rhyolite was a gold-mining town whose mines were prematurely closed in 1912, after just six boom years. Mismanagement and a lack of technological know-how were largely to blame, and the working Bullfrog Mine just outside the town attests to the area's continuing mineral wealth. By then the town had spread over the hillside (made of the rock that gave the town its name) and had its own train station. The station is still the dominant structure, but the remains of other buildings, including a jail, schoolhouse, and bank, still stand, as does Tom Kelly's **bottle house**, built of some fifty thousand beer and spirit bottles in 1906. A more recent attraction is the roadside Goldwell Open Air Museum, a distinctly off-beam **sculpture garden** (unrestricted access; ⓦ www .goldwellmuseum.org) complete with structures built from car parts and an arresting series of white fiberglass figures arranged in imitation of *The Last Supper*. These are the work of Belgian artist Albert Szulalski, who died in 2000 after getting other artists to contribute: you can't help but notice the huge sheet-metal miner and similarly proportioned penguin that greet you as you enter town.

From Rhyolite, you'll coast down into the park on Hwy-374, watching Death Valley unfold from above. There's also the chance to explore the one-way **Titus Canyon** road, which winds past several crumbling lead mines on its way to Scotty's Castle (p.380). High-clearance or four-wheel-drive vehicles are recommended.

From the southwest: the Panamint Range and Ballarat

Probably the least used access road to Death Valley is from the southwest, leading from Ridgecrest past the Trona Pinnacles (see p.328) and the industrial borax town of **Trona** and into the park. This provides the quickest approach into the more mountainous backcountry of the national park on the western slopes of the **PANAMINT RANGE**.

Twenty miles north of Trona, a signposted road heads three miles east to the scant, eroded adobe ruins of the former gold-mining town of **BALLARAT**. Four-wheel-drive roads head further into the hills, where one fairly popular destination is Barker Ranch in Goler Wash where Charles Manson and his "family" holed up after the notorious Tate–LaBianca murders in 1969.

Almost ten miles north of the Ballarat junction the highway splits: left to Panamint Springs on a good road, or right along the winding **Emigrant Canyon Road** towards Telescope Peak (see p.382) in the park itself.

From the west: Owens Lake and Darwin

From the west, two routes (Hwy-138 and Hwy-190) spur off US-395 towards Death Valley. They run either side of the dry bed of what, until the 1920s, used to be **OWENS LAKE**, which for a time in the nineteenth century saw steamships carrying bullion bars. The water that would naturally flow into the lake has been diverted to Los Angeles via the aqueduct that parallels US-395, leaving a pan of toxic alkali dust. Schemes are now under way to control this by planting native vegetation and drip-feeding some water into the ecosystem.

Almost thirty miles east of US-395, and just before the Death Valley National Park boundary, a seven-mile paved side road leads to **DARWIN**, another virtual ghost town that once had a population of over forty thousand and is now just about hanging on with fifty residents and a small post office. Only tumbledown wooden ruins remain of the town, which was built in the 1870s by prospectors searching for seams of silver, inspired by tales of an Indian who repaired an explorer's rifle by fashioning a gunsight out of solid silver. Explore carefully, as residents are protective of their patch of desert.

Park information and orientation

Entrance to the park is $10 per vehicle, or $5 per person if you are mad enough to walk or cycle. For that, you get unrestricted entry for seven days, an excellent map, the park newspaper with up-to-date details on campgrounds and visitor services, and a glossy booklet on the national park. There are no staffed entrance stations, so pay at one of the self-serve machines near park entrances, or at one of the visitor centers and ranger stations.

Most visitor facilities are concentrated in Furnace Creek and Stovepipe Wells, neither of which are towns in the usual sense, just a resort with a motel, a restaurant or two, a gas station, and a grocery store. The busier of the two, **Furnace Creek**, is right in the center of the Valley and has an excellent **visitor center** (daily 8am–6pm; ☏760/786-3220, ⊛www.nps.gov/deva) with a small but interesting **museum** (same hours; free) and a twelve-minute orientational slide program. The only other significant source of information is at the ranger station at Scotty's Castle (see p.380).

There are **no banks** in the park but Furnace Creek and Stovepipe Wells both have ATMs.

Accommodation

While the main sights of Death Valley can be seen in a day, you really should try to stay the night. To get the full impact of a desert visit, **camping** out is the most rewarding option. For most of the year you don't even need a tent – it isn't going to rain – though a sleeping bag is a good idea. If camping isn't a possibility you are limited to fairly expensive **hotels** and **motels** inside the park, or lower-cost choices on the fringes.

Hotels and motels

Within the park, only the *Furnace Creek Inn* is worthy of special praise. Otherwise you have a choice of fairly overpriced **motel**-style accommodation at Furnace Creek, Stovepipe Wells, and Panamint Springs. Outside the park boundaries the range of options expands and prices come down, though you lose the chance to wake up with Death Valley all around you.

Reservations should be made as early as possible, especially during peak winter holiday periods. The following listings cover all the rooms in the park and the settlements nearby, but also see Lone Pine (p.383) for accommodation slightly further afield.

Inside the park

Furnace Creek Inn Furnace Creek ☏760/786-2345 or 1-800/236-7916, ⊛www.furnacecreekresort.com. A beautifully situated Mission-style hotel built of adobe in the 1920s amid date palms and tended lawns, this is the place to stay if you're in the Valley with money to burn. Rooms are modern but tastefully done, many with great views across the Valley of the Panamint Range. It is only open in the more fashionable cooler months when you can laze by the pool, which has bar service. The on-site restaurant (see p.382) is the best around. Closed mid-May to early Oct. Rooms ❼, suites ❾

Furnace Creek Ranch Furnace Creek ☏760/786-2345 or 1-800/236-7916, ⊛www.furnacecreekresort.com. Functional, family-oriented, and cheaper than the *Furnace Creek Inn*, but lacking atmosphere. The comfortable motel rooms are rather overpriced but at least you get free access to the chlorine-free mineral swimming pool fed by springs at a constant 84°F. Cabins ❺, rooms ❻

Panamint Springs Resort Panamint Springs ☏775/482-7680, ⊛www.deathvalley.com. Ageing and pretty basic motel rooms (and no pool) 35 miles west of Stovepipe Wells, that's made more appealing by its restaurant and bar where you can sit and lunch on the shady terrace or sip a beer in the warm night air. There's an adjacent campground (see p.376). ❸

Stovepipe Wells Motel Stovepipe Wells ☏760/786-2387, ⊛www.stovepipewells.com. The best-priced option inside the park, offering comfortable rooms, a mineral-water pool, a restaurant with buffet meals, and a bar. Non-guests can use the pool for $2. ❸

Just outside the park

Amargosa Hotel Death Valley Junction ☏760/852-4441, ✉amargosa@amargosa-opera-house.com. Pleasantly run-down adobe hotel built by the Pacific Coast Borax Company in 1924. It has no TVs or phones, but boasts an attached opera house (see p.373). Ask to see a few of local artist Marta's hand-painted rooms before choosing, as they vary enormously – there's a trompe l'oeil wardrobe in the Jezebel room and cherubs in the Baroque. ❷

Delight's Hot Springs Resort 368 Tecopa Hot Springs Rd ☎1-800/928-8808 or 760/852-4343, ⊛www.delightshotspringsresort.com. Dusty RV park with plain cabins with kitchenettes, which are gradually being substantially beautified. Guests have free 24hr access to private hot pools on site. Cabins ❸, RV hook-ups $25

HI-Desertaire Hostel 2000 Old Spanish Trail, Tecopa ☎760/852-4580 or 1-877/907-1265, ⊛www.desertairehostel.com. A relaxed hostel an hour south of Furnace Creek. There are only ten beds (members $15, non-members $18) and one family room ($40, non-members $50), but you can sleep outside in the warm desert air in a wooden tower with commanding views of the surrounding desert. ❶

Happy Burro Hostel 100 Main St, Beatty ☎775/553-9130, ✉happyburrro@pcweb.net. HI hostel centrally located in Beatty, but the dorms are a little cramped and lacking in atmosphere. One double available (❷). Members $15, non-members $18.

Motel 6 550 Main St, Beatty ☎775/ 553-9090 or 800/466-8356, ⊛www.motel6.com. Brand new motel, comfortable and clean, with phone and TV but otherwise fairly basic facilities. ❷

Phoenix Inn 350 First St, Beatty ☎775/553-2250 or 1-800/845-7401. On a quiet side street, and one of the few Beatty motels not in or attached to a casino. ❷

Ranch House Inn Tecopa ☎760/852-4358, ⊛www.ranchhouseinn.com. Attractive and welcoming B&B in a 1920s cottage on the China Ranch Date Farm (see p.372). It's imaginatively decorated, peaceful, and includes a full breakfast served on the screened porch. Dinner is also available ($15) and you can BYO wine. ❺

Shoshone Inn Shoshone ☎760/852-4335. Recently remodeled motel an hour south of Furnace Creek on Hwy-127 with access to local warm springs, and Tecopa Hot Springs eight miles south. ❷

Campgrounds and RV parks

Almost all the campgrounds in Death Valley National Park are operated by the National Park Service, most costing $10 a night, while sites without a water supply are free. The majority of National Park sites cannot be reserved and stays are limited to thirty days (so that people don't move in for the winter). Take note of the **altitude** listed for each, as this gives an idea of the temperatures you might expect, and remember that the only places with guaranteed shade are the canyons on the forested slopes of Telescope Peak, on the western edge of the park. There's also a commercial campground at Panamint Springs (see below).

RV drivers will only find hook-ups at Panamint Springs in the western reaches of the park and at sites outside the park, but there are several dump stations dotted around.

Free **backcountry camping** is allowed in most areas of the park provided you keep two miles away from any roads (paved or otherwise) and two hundred yards from water sources. No permits are required, but voluntary backcountry **registration** is strongly recommended.

In the lowlands

Emigrant Open all year; 2100ft. Located eight miles west of Stovepipe Wells, this is the only free lowland campground, and is tent-only. Fires are not allowed but there is water and flush toilets. Free

Furnace Creek Open all year and reservable up to five months in advance in the winter months; ☎1-800/365-2267; -196ft. With 136 sites this is one of the larger campgrounds in the park, but it still fills up very early on winter weekends. Comes equipped with water, flush toilets, and a dump station. Mid-Oct to mid-April $16, mid-April to mid-Oct $10

Mesquite Spring Open all year; 1800ft. Fairly small, pleasant, and relatively shady site near Scotty's Castle on the north side of the park. Has water, flush toilets, and a dump station. $10

Panamint Springs Resort Panamint Springs ☎775/482-7680, ⊛www.deathvalley.com. Restaurant and motel (see p.375) with adjacent campground which has tent sites ($12), water and electric hook-ups ($25), and $3 non-guest showers.

Stovepipe Wells Open mid-Oct to late April; sea level. Moderate-sized campground close to the Stovepipe Wells restaurant and pool. Comes with water, flush toilets, and a dump station. $10

Sunset Open mid-Oct to late April; 196ft. Conveniently sited at Furnace Creek, this enormous site is virtually an RV parking lot. Fires are not allowed but there's water, flush toilets, and a dump station. First-come-first-served. $10

Texas Spring Open mid-Oct to late April; sea level. Furnace Creek's "quiet" site with water, flush toilets, and fires permitted. First-come-first-served. $12

In the hills

Mahogany Flat Open March–Nov; 8200ft. The remotest and coolest campground in the park; virtually identical to *Thorndike* (below). Free

Thorndike Open March–Nov; 7400ft. Small site in the pines which is usually only accessible in high-clearance or four-wheel-drive vehicles. There are pit toilets but bring your own water. Free

Wildrose Open all year; 4100ft. Expect moderate temperatures at this site on the way to the charcoal kilns. There are pit toilets but drinking water is only available April–Nov. Free

Outside the park

Shoshone RV Park Shoshone ☎760/852-4524. Shady RV park and campground with sites from $12 and access to the local warm springs.

Exploring Death Valley

You can get an unforgettable feel for Death Valley just by passing through, and you could quite easily see almost all the essential sights in a day. If you have the time, though, aim to spend at least a night here, if possible camped out somewhere far from the main centers of activity. Even if you've got your own car, the best way to experience the huge, empty spaces and the unique landforms of Death Valley is to leave the roads (and virtually all other visitors) behind and wander off – taking care to remember the way back. Sunrise and sunset are the best times to experience the color that's bleached out by the midday sun, and they're also the most likely times for seeing the **wildlife**, mostly lizards, snakes, and small rodents, which hide out through the heat of the day.

Most of the park's recognized sights lie south of Furnace Creek **along the Badwater road** where colorful rocks line Artist's Drive and a small pond marks the lowest point in the western hemisphere. The hills immediately to the east offer a couple of great viewpoints – **Dante's View** and **Zabriskie Point** – but the bulk of visitors head swiftly north past the **Keane Wonder Mine** to the ever popular **Scotty's Castle**. It is out on a limb, so leave time to explore **Ubehebe Crater** and, perhaps, **Racetrack Valley** while you're up here. On Death Valley's western flank rises **Telescope Peak**, a much cooler place to go hiking or exploring the **Wildrose Charcoal Kilns**.

Furnace Creek

Though by no means a big place, **FURNACE CREEK** is the hub of Death Valley for most visitors, with the park's only significant **visitor center** (see p.375), three campgrounds, the *Furnace Creek Inn*, *Furnace Creek Ranch* (for both, see p.375), three restaurants, a couple of bars, a general store, a **post office** (Mon–Fri 8.30am–5pm), and a **gas station** (gas available 24hr with a credit card). Here you'll find the small **Borax Museum** (daily 10am–4pm; free), located in an 1883 wooden building, the Valley's oldest structure. The story of the mineral and its excavation is rather ploddingly told through geological exhibits, a diorama of a twenty-mule-team, and plenty of old photos, but don't overlook the fine collection of arrow points, some dating back 2000 years. Outside, heavy-wheeled borax wagons and an old steam locomotive are ranged around an 1880s arrastre used for grinding up gold ore. Armed with a little background knowledge, head two miles north to the old **Harmony Borax Works** (unrestricted entry), where a quarter-mile interpretive trail tells of the mine and processing plant.

Anything more than a short **hike** in the oppressive heat of Death Valley can become an ordeal. This is less true on the trails around Telescope Peak and Wildrose Peak in the Panamint Range, but you still need to carry all your **water** with you and will want a wide-brimmed hat.

While Death Valley National Park offers ample opportunities for **mountain biking**, only roads open to road vehicles are accessible to cyclists. Hiking trails are off limits. This still leaves plenty to go at for those who bring their wheels along: there are no rentals available. The map provided with your entry ticket shows the major four-wheel-drive routes: Echo Canyon into the Funeral Mountains and the Inyo Mine, Cottonwood Canyon from Stovepipe Wells, and the Warm Springs Canyon/Butte Valley road in the south of the park are all worthwhile.

Whatever you do, always register your intended route at the visitor center or any of the ranger stations, and for anything a little more adventurous than the walks listed here, get yourself a **topographic map** from the visitor center.

The pick of the hikes

Golden Canyon to Zabriskie Point (5 miles round-trip; 3hr; 500ft ascent). An unmaintained, moderately strenuous trail along ridges and through badlands to Zabriskie Point. Done in reverse, it is all downhill.

Gower Gulch Loop (4 miles round-trip; 2–3hr; 200ft ascent). Worthwhile loop walk starting at Golden Canyon and following the interpretive trail to marker #10. From there follow a trail back to the start down Gower Gulch including an easy scramble down a couple of dry falls. A leaflet on the hike is available from the visitor center.

Mosaic Canyon (1 mile round-trip; 30min; 100ft ascent). A rough three-mile access road just west of Stovepipe Wells leads to the trailhead for a relatively easy hike through this narrow canyon full of water-polished marble and mosaic-patterned canyon walls. Beyond this most heavily trafficked section, the canyon carries on for another mile and a half, with some scrambling at the upper end.

Telescope Peak (14 miles round-trip; 8hr; 3000ft ascent). The easy-to-follow but moderately strenuous trail climbs from the trailhead by *Mahogany Flat* campground, skirting a pair of 10,000-foot peaks, through bristlecone pines to the summit and its grand panorama of Death Valley and across to Mount Whitney and the eastern face of the Sierra Nevada. Sign the summit register while you admire the view. There's no water en route except for snowmelt (often well into June), which should be treated. Crampons and ice axes may be required in harsh winters, and at all times you should self-register in the book a short way along the trail.

Wildrose Peak (8 miles round-trip; 5hr; 2000ft ascent). If winter conditions or your own level of fitness rule out Telescope Peak, this hike makes a perfect, easier alternative. Start by the Charcoal Kilns on Wildrose Canyon Road and wind up through piñon pines and juniper to a stunning summit panorama.

The *Furnace Creek Ranch* is the only place in the national park offering organized **outdoor activities**. Palms and tamarisk trees line the fairways of the *Ranch*'s 18-hole **golf course** (℡760/786-2301) – at 214ft below sea level, the world's lowest grass course. It is open to anyone keen to pay the greens fees (Oct–May $55; June–Sept $30) and in the peak of summer when only the fanatical and foolhardy play, there are packages including greens fees, electric cart, and club rental for as little as $25. To check out the scenery and get a sense of how pioneers might have experienced Death Valley, join one of the walking-pace **horseback rides** offered at the *Ranch* (mid–Oct to early May; ℡760/786-3339) for $30 an hour. Even better, join one of the hour-long full-moon rides ($40) which take place several nights a month.

Perhaps best of all is the large **swimming pool** (guests free, others $3) which is constantly fed hot mineral-water and kept at a constant 85°C – a little warm for real swimming but great for wallowing.

Furnace Creek has the tenor of an extended resort, but there is still a small, inhabited **Timbisha Shoshone village** on a forty-acre patch of land just southwest of the *Furnace Creek Ranch*. Displaced then virtually ignored for decades, their tribe finally gained federal recognition in 1983, and in 2001 they were granted rights to 7000 acres of park and nearby land. They largely keep to themselves, but you may catch their Timbisha Free Radio broadcast on 91.1FM (generally Mon–Fri 8am–4pm, Sat & Sun noon–8pm).

The road to Badwater

Many of the park's most unusual sights are located south of Furnace Creek along the road to Badwater, which forks off Hwy-190 by the *Furnace Creek Inn*. A good first stop, two miles along, is **Golden Canyon**. Periodic rainstorms over the centuries have washed a fifty-foot-deep slot-shaped gully through the clay and silt here, revealing golden-hued walls that are particularly vibrant in the early evening. A three-quarter-mile-long interpretive trail winds into the U-shaped upper canyon, and a loop hike (see box, opposite) continues from there.

Five miles further on, signs point to **Artist's Drive**, a twisting one-way loop road, perhaps best left until the drive back, especially if this means catching the afternoon sun on the **Artist's Palette**, an evocatively eroded hillside covered in an intensely colored mosaic of reds, golds, blacks, and greens.

A couple of miles further south, a dirt road heading west leads a mile to the **Devil's Golf Course**, a weird field of salt pinnacles and hummocks protruding a couple of feet from the desert floor. Capillary action draws saline solutions from below the surface where alternate layers of salt and alluvial deposits from ancient lakes have been laid down over the millennia. As the occasional rainfall evaporates, the salt accretes to form a landscape as little like a golf course as you could imagine.

It is another four miles south to **Badwater**, an unpalatable but non-poisonous thirty-foot-wide pool of water, loaded with chloride and sulphates, that's also the only home of the endangered, soft-bodied Badwater Snail. Notice how much hotter it feels in the humid air beside the water, and take a look up on the hill behind where a sign marks sea level. From the pool, two rather uninteresting hikes, both around four miles long, lead across the hot, flat valley floor to the two **lowest points in the western hemisphere**, both at 282ft below sea level. Neither are marked and there's little satisfaction in being just two feet lower than

---

Badwater Ultramarathon

Driving through Death Valley in mid-July can seem like madness even in an air-conditioned vehicle, but an international field of almost a hundred masochists now choose this time of year to run the grueling **Badwater Ultramarathon** (Ⓦwww .badwaterultra.com), one of the most demanding, extreme, and prestigious in the world. Searing heat and draining dehydration are constant threats on this 135-mile road race which kicks off at Badwater 282 feet below sea level and, after a total elevation gain of around 14,000, finishes at the 8360ft Whitney Portal, the trailhead for ascents of Mount Whitney.

One Al Arnold was the first to run the course in 1977, but the race didn't actually get under way until 1988 and has been run every year since, with most competitors in the invitation-only field managing to finish. The current men's record, set in 2000 by the Russian Anatoli Kruglikov, is 25 hours and 9 minutes; while in the 2002 event, American Pam Reed knocked almost two hours off the women's record (and beat all the men in the field) to record a time of just under 27 hours 57 minutes.

you were at the roadside, though it is worth wandering half a mile out to where the salt deposits form polygonal shapes on the valley floor.

Zabriskie Point and Dante's View

The badlands around **ZABRISKIE POINT**, overlooking Badwater and the Artist's Palette, four miles south of Furnace Creek off Hwy-190, were the inspiration for Antonioni's eponymous 1970 movie. Proximity to Furnace Creek makes this a popular sunrise destination as photographers try to capture the early rays catching Manly Beacon, an eminence rising above the badlands.

The point's sculpted spires of banded rock are less interesting than **DANTE'S VIEW**, a further 21 miles south off Hwy-190 and then ten miles on a very steep (and very hot) road. At a point almost six thousand feet above the blinding white saltpan of Badwater, the valley floor does indeed look infernal. The view is best in the early morning, when the pink and gold Panamint Range across the Valley is highlighted by the rising sun.

North from Furnace Creek

Twelve miles to the north, the **Keane Wonder Mine** and **Keane Wonder Mill** (unrestricted entry to both) were indeed wonderful during their heyday. Between 1904, when the mine was discovered by Jack Keane, and 1916, gold and silver worth $1.1 million was extracted at the mountainside mine. The ore was then carried to the valley-floor mill using a three-quarter-mile-long aerial tramway which is still more or less intact. From the parking lot by the remains of the mill, a very steep path climbs (an ascent of 1500 feet) alongside the thirteen tramway towers to the lowest of the mineshafts. It is only a mile but seems a lot more in the noonday heat. Don't be tempted to seek shelter in the adits and shafts leading off the path; all are dangerous and most unfenced.

Just east of Stovepipe Wells and north of Hwy-190, the most extensive of the Valley's **Mesquite Flat Dunes** spread out, fifteen rippled and contoured square miles of ever-changing sand dunes, some over a hundred feet high. Most people are happy to photograph them from the road (best in late afternoon), but while there are no formal trails, it is easy enough to pick a route out to the nearest of the dunes (about half a mile away) or even to the top of the highest dune (3–4 miles round-trip).

On the opposite side of Hwy-190 stands the **Devil's Cornfield**, an expanse of tufted arrowweed grasses perched on mounds that make them look like corn shocks.

STOVEPIPE WELLS, a couple of miles on from the dunes, is really just a motel (see p.375) with associated restaurant, a campground, and a gas station. It is a good place to take a break with views of the dunes, and is handy for trips to **Mosaic Canyon** (see box, p.378). The *Stovepipe Wells Motel* **pool** is open to the public ($2).

Scotty's Castle

On the northern edge of the park, 45 miles from the visitor center, stands **SCOTTY'S CASTLE** (tours depart daily on the hour 9am–5pm; $9). It is well out of the way of most of the rest of the attractions but is nevertheless the most popular single stop in the park; hordes of overheated tourists wait in long lines for the chance to wander through this surreal and unfinished but still luxurious mansion. Executed in extravagant Spanish Revival style, the castle was built during the 1920s – at a cost of $2million – as the desert retreat of wealthy Chicago insurance broker Albert Johnson. He was seldom there, so local cowboy, prospector, and publicity hound, "Death Valley" Scotty, claimed the house was his own and financed by his hidden gold mine – a fantasy Johnson was happy to indulge. The house features intricately carved wooden ceilings, waterfalls in the living room, beautifully crafted tiled floors and, most entertaining of all, a remote-controlled 1121-pipe organ. In winter, it is best to arrive as the doors open to avoid long waits for the fifty-minute-long **tours** of the opulently furnished house, left pretty much as it was when Johnson died in 1948. Scotty himself lived here until 1954 and is buried on the hill just behind the house: a good place to wander while waiting for your tour.

To achieve city comforts in such an inhospitable environment, Johnson arranged for the latest conveniences to be installed: primitive air conditioning, a hydroelectric generating system, and other minor marvels can be seen on the one-hour **Technology Tour** (Oct–April 4–8 tours daily; May–Sept 11.15am & 3.15pm; $9).

Ubehebe Crater, Racetrack Valley, and the Eureka Sand Dunes

Eight miles southwest of Scotty's Castle – though it might as well be five hundred miles for all the people who venture here – gapes the half-mile-wide, 500-foot-deep **UBEHEBE CRATER**, the rust-colored result of a massive volcanic explosion some three thousand years ago; a half-mile south sits its thousand-year-old younger brother, **Little Hebe**. Beyond the craters the road (high-clearance vehicles recommended) continues south for another 27 dusty miles to **RACETRACK VALLEY**, a two-and-a-half-mile-long mud flat across which giant boulders seem slowly to be racing, leaving faint trails in their wake. Scientists believe that the boulders are pushed along the sometimes icy surface by very high winds; sit and watch (but don't hold your breath). Park two miles south of the **Grandstand**, then walk half a mile southeast for the best view of the rocks and their tracks.

The expansion of Death Valley when it became a national park claimed several features formerly outside its boundaries. The **EUREKA SAND DUNES**, forty miles northwest of Scotty's Castle, are the most exciting, but only accessible in a high-clearance vehicle. Far more extensive than the Mesquite Flat dunes around Stovepipe Wells, these stand up to seven hundred feet above the surrounding land, making them the highest dunes in California and a dramatic place to witness sunrise or sunset. While here, keep your eyes open for the Eureka Dunes grass and evening primrose, both indigenous to the area and federally protected.

Aguereberry Point, Wildrose Charcoal Kilns, and Telescope Peak

To escape the heat and dust of the desert floor, head south from Stovepipe Wells into the **Panamint Range** along Emigrant Canyon Road. Ten miles up the canyon, a nine-mile dirt track turns off to the east toward the very meager remains of **Skidoo Ghost Town**, a 1915 gold-mining camp of seven hundred people that was watered by snowmelt from Telescope Peak, 23 miles away, and kept informed by telegraph from Rhyolite. There's very little to see, so a better side trip is to **AGUEREBERRY POINT**, a wonderful viewpoint looking six thousand feet down into Death Valley, and reached along a six-mile dirt road off Emigrant Canyon Road.

Yet further south the *Wildrose* campground (see p.377) marks the start of a steep five-mile road up Wildrose Canyon to the **WILDROSE CHARCOAL KILNS**. This series of ten massive, beehive-shaped stone kilns some 25 feet high was used in the 1880s to make charcoal from piñon and juniper logs for use in the smelters of local silver mines. The road then deteriorates (high-clearance recommended) and climbs through juniper and pine forests past the free *Thorndike* campground to its end at *Mahogany Flat*, where there's another free campground and the trailhead for the strenuous hike up **TELESCOPE PEAK**, which at 11,049ft is the highest – and coolest – point in the park (see box, p.378). From the summit you can see both the highest (Mount Whitney) and the lowest (near Badwater) points in the continental United States.

Darwin Falls, Lee Flat, and Saline Valley

A mile west of Panamint Springs along Hwy-190, a two-mile dirt road south brings you to a trailhead from where a mile-long creekside trail up a small canyon leads to the thirty-foot, spring-fed **DARWIN FALLS**. It is hardly dramatic, but does feed a welcome and shady cottonwood oasis, though because it supplies Panamint Springs with water, swimming here is not allowed.

You might not expect to see Joshua trees in Death Valley, but **LEE FLAT**, a dozen miles west of Panamint Springs, has a whole forest of them on its higher slopes. At this point most visitors continue west towards US-395 (see p.369), but adventurous drivers with sturdy vehicles might fancy exploring the northwestern corner of the park. A dirt road leads north past more Joshua trees at Lower Lee Flat, then continues on a very rough and unsigned fifty-mile trek out to **SALINE VALLEY** – obtain the best map you can and ask for local advice about road conditions. Old mine workings and the remains of a dilapidated salt tramway can be seen along the way, but the highlights are the generally clothing-free **hot springs** at Saline Warm Spring and the adjacent Palm Hot Spring, both easily spotted by the palm trees. Other than hot water and a free, primitive campground there are no facilities, so take everything you might need. After a dip it is possible to continue north to meet US-395 at Big Pine.

Eating and drinking

There's not a great variety of **eating and drinking places** in Death Valley and you'll almost certainly find yourselves eating very close to where you sleep. Furnace Creek has easily the best selection, though there are restaurants at both Stovepipe Wells and Panamint Springs – all somewhat overpriced.

Beatty, with restaurants attached to all-night casinos, offers a couple of inexpensive diners, though it's quite a long drive back to the park after dark.

Expensive **grocery stores** with a limited supply are located at Furnace Creek and at Stovepipe Wells.

49er Café at *Furnace Creek Ranch*. Diner-style family restaurant with the likes of sandwiches and burgers ($9–11), pasta ($15), and steak and fish mains ($15–18). Open 7–9am in winter, and all year 10am–9pm.

Corkscrew Saloon at *Furnace Creek Ranch*. To quench a thirst after a day in the sun, join the few locals at this basic bar with pool table, juke box, draft beer, espresso, a limited selection of light meals, and pizza to go (2–9.30pm only). Open until around midnight.

Inn Dining Room at *Furnace Creek Inn*. For dinner reservations ☎760/786-2345. Gourmet dining in a beautiful room almost unchanged since the 1920s. Soups, salads, sandwiches, and pizza are available for lunch (when dress is casual), but at dinner expect the likes of tortilla lime soup ($6), rattlesnake empanada ($13), and New York steak ($27), and be prepared to dress up; shorts and T-shirts are banned and jeans are only permitted after 8.30pm. Open early Oct to mid-May.

Lobby Lounge at *Furnace Creek Inn*. Pop up to the *Inn* for afternoon tea (served daily in season) or call in for an evening cocktail. Open early Oct to mid-May.

Panamint Springs Resort Relaxing restaurant and bar serving daytime sandwiches and good pasta, salad, and steak dinners either inside or out on the terrace, which is cool enough for outdoor summer dining.

Stovepipe Wells Family restaurant and adjacent saloon serving three à la carte meals a day in winter, and buffet breakfast and dinner (but no lunch) in summer. Dinner might be chicken *taquitos* ($8) followed by pork medallions ($16). **Wrangler Buffet and Steakhouse** at *Furnace Creek Ranch*. The *Ranch*'s main restaurant, serving buffet breakfast (6–9am or 10am; $9), buffet lunch (10.45am–2pm; $11), and dinners (6.30–10pm), which extend to Caesar salad ($7), chicken pasta ($22), and assorted steaks ($23–27) served with peppercorn-brandy or mushroom-burgundy sauce.

The Owens Valley

Rising out of the northern reaches of the Mojave Desert, the Sierra Nevada mountains announce themselves with a bang two hundred miles north of Los Angeles at **Mount Whitney**, the highest point on a silver-gray knifelike ridge of pinnacles that forms a nearly sheer eleven-thousand-foot wall of granite. It provides a wonderful backdrop to the **OWENS VALLEY**, a hot, dry, and numinously thrilling stretch of desolate semi-desert landscape running from **Lone Pine** north beyond **Bishop**.

The small towns along its length don't really amount to much, and if you're intent on visiting California's more cultural sights, you could easily drive through in half a day. However, for scenic beauty and access to a range of outdoor activities the Owens Valley is hard to beat. Twisting mountain roads rise quickly from the hot valley floor to cool ten-thousand-foot-high trailheads ideal for **hiking** among Sierra lakes and forests or setting out for the summit of Mount Whitney or any of hundreds of other peaks.

The Owens Valley comes billed as the deepest valley in the US, and with its floor averaging 4000ft and the mountains either side topping out above 14,000ft that seems completely believable. Its eastern wall is formed by the contiguous **Inyo Mountains** and **White Mountains**; rounded and weathered in comparison with the Sierra and less dramatic, though with their own beauty, especially around the wonderful **Ancient Bristlecone Pine Forest**, which contains the world's oldest trees.

US-395 runs the length of the Owens Valley, a vital lifeline through a region that is almost entirely unpopulated outside of the handful of small towns, though a few solitary souls live in old sheds and caravans off the many dirt roads and tracks that cross the floor of the valley. Naturally a semi-desert with only around five inches of rain a year, the region relies on Sierra snow-melt which once made the area a prime spot for growing apples and pears. But since 1913, its plentiful natural water supply has been drained away to fill the swimming pools of Los Angeles (for more on this hot topic, read the box on p.408).

Lone Pine, Mount Whitney, and around

LONE PINE isn't much more than a single-street rural town strung with motels, gas stations, and restaurants, but it is lent a more vibrant air by being at the crossroads of desert and mountains. Any night of the week, there'll be desert rats mixing with Mount Whitney wilderness hikers and tourists recovering from the rigors of Death Valley. It also makes a good base and supply post for exploring the area, particularly if you're not prepared to camp out.

Part of what really makes it special is the unparalleled access it provides to the 14,497-foot summit of **MOUNT WHITNEY** – the highest point in the US outside Alaska. The view of the sharply pointed High Sierra peaks which

Sierra pass and trailhead closures

After coming through the Mojave or Death Valley, it seems hard to imagine that many of the passes across the Sierra Nevada can remain closed well into June. The authorities try to open **Tioga Pass** (from Mono Lake into Yosemite) by Memorial Day weekend (at the end of May), but harsh winters sometimes leave it closed until late June. Passes to the north of here, **Hwy-108** and **Hwy-4**, tend to open a couple of weeks earlier, in mid-May. All three close again with the first heavy snowfall, perhaps around late October or early November. **Hwy-88**, yet further north, stays open all year. For information on the state of the highways contact CalTrans (℡1-800/427-7623 or follow the "Road Conditions" link from ⓦwww.dot.ca.gov).

Eastern Sierra **trailheads** are equally affected by snow, with most only accessible from May until early November. Even in June and early July the trails leading from the trailheads can be impassable without ice axe and crampons.

---

dominate the town – captured by photographer Ansel Adams in a much-reproduced shot of the full moon suspended above stark cliffs – is fantastic.

Arrival and information

CREST **buses** stop outside Statham Hall, not far from the **Chamber of Commerce**, 126 S Main St (Mon–Sat 8am–5pm; ℡760/876-4444 or 1-877/253-8981, ⓦwww.lonepinechamber.org), which is fine for local information. For details of hiking, camping, and high-pass conditions in the whole of eastern California – including the High Sierra, Owens Valley, White Mountains, and Death Valley – you're better off visiting the excellent **Eastern Sierra Interagency Visitor Center** (daily 8am–5pm; ℡760/876-6222, ⓦwww.r5.fs.fed.us/inyo), a mile south of town on US-395 at the junction of Hwy-136, the Death Valley road. Most of the region is protected within the massive **Inyo National Forest**, and if you're planning to spend any amount of time in the area, pick up the very helpful **map** ($6), which covers everything between Mount Whitney and Yosemite National Park, including all hiking routes and campgrounds. Interestingly, this is the only map that makes clear the extent of the City of Los Angeles's holdings in the Owens Valley – basically the entire valley floor, bought in the early years of the twentieth century to slake the thirst of the expanding city (see box on p.408). Wilderness permits are issued at the **Mount Whitney Ranger Station**, 640 S Main St (daily: June–Oct 8am–6pm; Nov–May 8am–4.30pm; ℡760/876-6200), which should be moving to a new building beside the Eastern Sierra Interagency Visitor Center sometime in 2005.

In summer, the **swimming pool** at the high school on Muir Street south of town is open daily ($2); after a week in the mountains, you can get cleaned up at Kirk's Sierra Barber Shop, 104 N Main St, where you can take a **hot shower** for $4.

Accommodation

If you're looking for a **motel**, try the *Dow Villa Motel/Historic Dow Hotel*, 310 S Main St (℡760/876-5521 or 1-800/824-9317, ⓦwww.dowvillamotel.com; ❷–❺), the older section built in 1923 to house movie industry visitors (though John Wayne always requested Room 20 in the newer motel section). There's an impressive range of accommodation, from basic bathless rooms in the hotel ($42), rooms with bath ($56), and plush motel units ($82), some with VCR and whirlpool ($115). Moving slightly upscale, go for the *Best Western Frontier Motel*,

1008 S Main St (℡760/876-5571 or 1-800/231-4071; ❺), which offers a heated pool, basic continental breakfast, and some rooms with mountain views.

There are also plenty of **campgrounds** nearby, all off Whitney Portal Road, which heads west from town at the lights. The closest is the *Portagee Joe* campground ($10; 3800ft) on Tuttle Creek Road, though you can save a few dollars by driving a couple of miles further to the *Tuttle Creek* campground (free; no water; 4000ft) on Horseshoe Meadow Road. At the Mount Whitney trailhead, twelve miles west of Lone Pine, lie a couple more sites: the family-oriented *Whitney Portal* (mid-May to late Oct; $14; 8100ft; ℡1-877/444-6777), and the hikers' *Whitney Portal Trailhead* (mid-May to late Oct; $6; 8300ft; maximum one-night stay).

Eating

Lone Pine's range of **restaurants** isn't great, but the *Mt Whitney Restaurant*, 227 S Main St (℡760/876-5751), backs up its claim to serve "the best burgers in town" with over half a dozen types of patties – bean, ostrich, venison, veggie – on which to build your creation; *Pizza Factory*, 301 S Main St (℡760/876-4707), produces pretty decent pizza; and *Pepe's*, 104b N Main St (℡760/876-4768; closed Tues), serves basic but filling Mexican. There's **Internet access** and good coffee at *The Espresso Parlor*, 123 N Main St.

Alabama Hills

Between Lone Pine and the Sierra Nevada stand the **ALABAMA HILLS**, a rugged expanse of brown, tan, orange, and black granite and some metamorphic rock that's been sculpted into bizarre shapes by 160 million years of erosive winds and rains. Some of the oddest formations are linked by the **Picture Rocks Circle**, a paved road that loops around from Whitney Portal Road, passing rocks apparently shaped like bullfrogs, walruses, and baboons; it takes a degree of imagination and precise positioning to pick them all out, but it is an attractive drive nonetheless, especially at sunset. A map (free from the visitor centers) details the best spots and marks the sites used as backdrops for many early Westerns, including the 1939 epic *Gunga Din*.

There's also plenty of scope for exploration, either mountain biking along the dirt roads and narrow trails (the loose sand is firmest in fall after the first rains), or hiking and scrambling among the rocks. Dusk is particularly pleasant with the scent of sagebrush in the air. A couple of fairly unspectacular but photogenic natural **rock arches** act as a focus for your wanderings. The visitor centers have rough explanatory maps, but the best of the arches is off Movie Road, just west of Lone Pine, where a ten-minute walk should find you at an eight-foot span.

In celebration of its movie heritage, the town now hosts the **Lone Pine Film Festival** (Ⓦwww.lonepinefilmfestival.org), held over Columbus Day weekend (the second weekend in October), showing only films made in the area. There are also plans for a Museum of Film History at the corner of US-395 and Hopalong Cassidy Lane at the southern end of town, perhaps opening in 2006. In the meantime you'll have to make do with the movie room in the Chamber of Commerce.

Whitney Portal

Ten miles west of the Alabama Hills lies **Whitney Portal** (usually accessible May to early Nov), the eight-thousand-foot-high trailhead for hiking up Mount Whitney. Even if a full-on slog to the summit is furthest from your mind, you might appreciate a refreshing break from the valley frazzle in the

Hiking up to the 14,497-foot **summit** of Mount Whitney is a real challenge: it's a very strenuous, 22-mile round-trip, made especially difficult by the lack of oxygen in the rarefied air of what is the highest point in the 48 contiguous states (see advice on Acute Mountain Sickness in Basics, p.71). Vigorous hikers starting before dawn from the 8365-foot trailhead can be up and back before dark, but a couple of days spent acclimatizing up here is advisable, and the whole experience is enhanced by camping out at least one night along the route. The trail gains over a mile in elevation, cutting up past alpine lakes to boulder-strewn Trail Crest Pass – the southern end of the 211-mile John Muir Trail that heads north to Yosemite. From the pass it ascends along the clifftops, finally reaching the rounded hump of the summit itself, where there's a **stone cabin** – not a place you'd choose to be in during a lightning storm. Water is available along the first half of the route, but must be filtered or treated.

Ambitious hikers with experience of scrambling or technical rock climbing might like to tackle the "**Mountaineers' Route**," which follows the North Fork of Lone Pine Creek, taking a more direct and much steeper (though no quicker) route to the summit past the base of the numerous rock climbs on the mountain's east face. Ropes aren't generally needed, but a head for heights definitely is. Ask for directions and current advice at the ranger station and at the Whitney Portal store.

The **Inyo National Forest** also manages permits for various other sections of the 78,000-acre wilderness area detailed in this chapter. Except for the Whitney Trail, day-use permits are not required, but a permit (free; reservations $5) is needed if you want to spend the night; inquire at the Eastern Sierra Interagency Visitor Center (see p.384) for the ranger station nearest the region you'd like to hike. Sixty percent of permits can be reserved. Out of season (Nov–April), self-issue permits are available at local ranger stations and the Eastern Sierra Interagency Visitor Center.

Obtaining permits

Such is the popularity of Whitney, that from May to October **overnight and day hikers** must obtain a permit ($15 reservation fee) through the Whitney Zone **lottery**, which takes place in February. Dates in July, August, and September (the only time the trail is completely free of snow) fill up fast, so May (when you may need an ice axe), June, and October (when there may be some snow on the ground) are better bets. Day hikers also require a permit but a different quota is used and it may be easier to get a place, though you should seriously consider your ability and fitness.

Apply for an overnight or day-use **wilderness permit** by phone, fax, or mail through Inyo National Forest Wilderness Permit Office, 351 Pacu Lane, Suite 200, Bishop, CA 93514 (℗760/873-2483, ℱ760-/873-2484, ⊛www.r5.fs.fed.us/inyo), making sure it is postmarked or dated in February. Application forms can be downloaded from the website. If you're not that organized (or miss out) your best shot is to hope for a cancellation. Starting from May 1 you can apply for any spaces at least two days before your planned ascent; check availability on the website. Free **last-minute permits** can be obtained from the Mount Whitney Ranger Station (see p.384) a day in advance of your planned ascent at 11am: avoid weekends when demand is highest. Overnight hikers are also required to pack their food in a **bear-resistant food canister** which can be rented from the ranger station ($2.50 per day; minimum $5), the Whitney Portal Store (⊛www.whitneyportalstore.com), and local sporting goods stores.

Once armed with a permit, hikers should drive to Whitney Portal or catch the Lonesome Polecat shuttle-bus service (reserve on ℗760/876-8232). Day hikers will want to **camp** at the small, first-come-first-served *Whitney Portal Trailhead* campground ($6) ready for an early start. Overnight hikers have more leisure and can plan to hike to one of two designated campgrounds (both first-come-first-served and free): *Outpost Camp* at 3.8 miles and *Trail Camp* at 6.2 miles.

cool shade of the pines and hemlocks. What's more there's a small café and general store for when you need fortifying between strolls around the trout-stocked pond, along the cascading stream, or up the Mount Whitney Trail to Lone Pine Lake (five miles round-trip; no permit required).

Manzanar National Historic Site

Just west of US-395, twelve miles north of Lone Pine, on the former site of the most productive of the Owens Valley apple and pear orchards, stand the concrete foundations of the **MANZANAR NATIONAL HISTORIC SITE** (daytime access; free; ☏760/878-2194, ⓦwww.nps.gov/manz), where more than ten thousand Americans of Japanese descent were corralled during World War II. Considering them a threat to national security, the US government uprooted whole families, confiscated all their property and brought them to what was known as the Manzanar War Relocation Center. They were released at the end of the war, though claims for compensation were only settled in 1988, when President Reagan finally offered the 60,000 survivors an official apology and agreed to pay damages amounting to millions of dollars. Ringed by barbed wire, the one-square-mile camp was filled with row upon row of wooden barracks but, as part of an agreement with the landowner, everything was razed when the camp was closed in late 1945. Now only a couple of pagoda-like sentry posts, an auditorium, and a small cemetery remain among the sagebrush and scraggy cottonwoods. As the bronze plaque on the guardhouse says: "May the injustices and humiliation suffered here as a result of hysteria, racism and economic exploitation never emerge again." This was a sentiment shared by many at the time, and photographer **Ansel Adams** (see box, p.475) spent several weeks here in 1943 depicting the prisoners as industrious and loyal Americans. Some of the former internees return each year, on the last Saturday in April, in a kind of pilgrimage. They often leave mementoes on a kind of cenotaph in the cemetery, which is inscribed with Japanese characters meaning "soul-consoling tower."

Manzanar is now managed by the National Park Service which has turned the auditorium into an excellent **Interpretive Center** (8.30am–5pm; free) where the moving 22-minute film *Remembering Manzanar* runs every half-hour. Pick up a leaflet for the three-mile **auto tour** past 27 points of interest around the camp, including remaining examples of Japanese gardens. Thirty- to ninety-minute **walking tours** (year-round usually between 9–11am; check website for current times; free) stick closer to the interpretive center and may include a visit to a former mess hall which has been returned to the site and is in the process of being restored.

Independence and around

Six miles north of Manzanar, the sleepy town of **INDEPENDENCE** takes its heroic name not from any great libertarian tradition but from a Civil War fort that was founded north of the town on the Fourth of July, 1862. Every year on that day, there's a parade down Edwards Street (US-395) followed by a mass barbecue and fireworks show in **Dehy Park**, along tree-shaded Independence Creek on the north side of town. The park is marked by a large steam locomotive, which once ran from here to Nevada on narrow-gauge tracks.

The main reason to stop is to visit the **Eastern California Museum** at 155 N Grant St (daily except Tues 10am–4pm; donation suggested; ☏760/878-0364), three blocks west of the porticoed County Courthouse, which contains an evocative and affecting exhibit about Manzanar, detailing the experiences of many of the young children who were held there. In the absence of any remaining barracks at the site, the museum has reconstructed part of a family-sized unit, and also holds an extensive collection of evocative photos of camp life (not always on show) taken by Toyo Miyatake, who was interned at Manzanar and managed to smuggle in a lens and film holders.

The museum also has displays on the region's history, from native Paiute basketry to old mining and farming equipment, and on the natural environment of the Owens Valley, including the **California bighorn sheep**, a protected species which inhabits the mountains to the west of Independence. Nimble creatures that roam around the steep, rocky slopes and sport massive, curling horns, they now number only around a hundred and fifty, and efforts to establish new populations are thwarted by appreciative mountain lions who promptly eat them.

Outside the museum, there's a reconstructed pioneer village made up of old buildings from all over the Owens Valley that have been brought together and restored, and a fledgling Native Plant Garden, which makes a nice spot to rest for a few minutes beside Independence Creek.

Practicalities

Local information is available from the Independence **Chamber of Commerce**, 139 N Edwards St (US-395; Mon, Tues, Fri & Sat 9am–noon & 1–4pm; ☎760/878-0084, ⊛www.independence-ca.com). If you're in the anti-camping camp, Independence offers a few **places to stay** indoors. Try the inexpensive *Independence Courthouse Motel* at 157 N Edwards St (☎760/878-2732 or 1-800/801-0703; ❸), or the *Winnedumah Hotel*, 211 N Edwards St (☎760/878-2040, ⊛www.winnedumah.com; B&B ❹, hostel rooms ❷, room-share $25), once a film-star haven that has retained its 1920s atmosphere, especially in the comfy lounge, which comes decorated with native crafts. The hotel doubles as a backpacker **hostel** with fairly basic facilities and the option of a continental breakfast ($5), which is otherwise included. There's also the *Independence Creek* campground ($10) half a mile west of town on Onion Valley Road.

The choice of **restaurants** is limited, though there is the wonderful *Still Life Café*, 135 S Edwards St (Wed–Sun 11am–2pm & 5.30–9pm; ☎760/878-2555, ⊛www.stilllifecafe.com) which serves burgers and sandwiches for lunch, but excels with its evening French menu which might extend to entrecotes of pork with caramelized onions ($22), or a delicious tuna-packed pasta *putanesca* ($20). Wines are mostly French, many available by the glass. A typical diner is promised, but at the time of writing the only other places to eat are *Mair's Market*, 149 N Edwards St, which has a deli section, and *Subway* across the street.

Around Independence

West from Independence, the minor Onion Valley Road twists up the mountains to the pine-shrouded trailhead at **Onion Valley**, fifteen miles away. The Onion Valley **campground** (June–Sept; $11; 9200ft; ☎1-877/444-6777) marks the start of **hiking** trails across the Sierra Nevada into Kings Canyon National Park, a sixteen-mile journey over Kearsarge Pass to Cedar Grove (see p.447). This is the easiest and shortest route across the Sierra and you can get the required **wilderness permit** from the Inyo National Forest Wilderness Reservation Service (see box, p.392) or at local ranger stations in the off season.

On the opposite side of the Owens Valley, a small blip on the Inyo Mountains ridgeline turns out to be a seventy-foot-high granite monolith known as

Winnedumah. Sacred to the local Paiute, it is apparently the body of a brave who was turned to stone when an enemy warrior yelled "Winnedumah," or "stand right where you are." Legend has it that he awaits release by the Great Spirit. An exhausting full-day boulder-hopping hike will get you to the rock: pick up instructions from the Eastern California Museum (see p.387).

There's brief respite from the valley heat on the leafy margins of a picturesque pool where trout mature as part of the **Mt Whitney Fish Hatchery** (Mon–Fri 7.30am–5pm, Sat & Sun 8am–5pm; free), two miles north of Independence and a mile west along Fish Hatchery Road. A vending machine sells fish food, and for more information about the hatchery's operation you can wander into the lobby of the main 1916 building, artfully fashioned like some European country retreat.

A further eight miles north of Independence is the actual start of the **LA Aqueduct**, though the waters that flow into it have been channeled through a long pipe from around Mono Lake. Follow any of the dirt tracks that head east from US-395 and you can't fail to spot the traces of the railroads built to haul in the material needed to construct the great ditch – which Space Shuttle astronauts claim to have seen while orbiting the globe.

The **Tinemaha Wildlife Viewpoint**, a further twenty miles north, warrants a brief pause to see if you can spot any of the five-hundred-strong herd of **tule elk**, now-protected California natives which were nearly wiped out by the end of the nineteenth century. A few dozen were relocated here from the San Joaquin Valley in 1914, and they seem to be thriving.

Big Pine and around

The town of **BIG PINE**, 28 miles to the north of Independence, is slightly larger but doesn't have much more in the way of services. It does, however, act as a gateway to three of the most impressive natural phenomena in California: the **Palisade Glacier** in the Sierra Nevada to the west of town; the ancient Bristlecone Pine Forest in the barren **White Mountains** to the east; and the northern reaches of Death Valley, in particular the Eureka Sand Dunes (see p.381) and the hot springs of the Saline Valley (see p.382).

Just off US-395 some eight miles north of Big Pine, there's a worthwhile diversion to **Keough's Hot Springs**, Keough's Hot Springs Road (daily 9am–7pm or later; $7; ☎760/872-4670, ⊛www.keoughshotsprings.com), a mineral-water-fed swimming pool and hot soaking pool that was once the social center of the region and is being progressively restored. A couple of hundred yards before the springs' entrance a dirt road cuts north to some **natural hot springs** where locals have created a couple of clothing-optional bathing pools, their idyllic setting only slightly marred by the overhead power wires and indiscriminate littering.

Practicalities

Information about all these can be gleaned from the **visitor center**, 126 S Main St (daily 8am–4.30pm; ☎760/938-2114, ⊛www.bigpine.com). There are a couple of good-value **motels** along US-395 – the *Big Pine Motel*, 370 S Main St (☎760/938-2282; ❷), and the slightly nicer *Starlight Motel*, 511 S Main St (☎760/938-2011; ❷), which has HBO and a little patio. There is also the *Glacier View* **campground** (tents $10, hook-up $15) half a mile north of town at the junction of Hwy-168, and several more camping spots up Glacier Lodge Road (see p.391). Good diner **food** is available at the *Country Kitchen*, 181 S Main St, almost opposite the visitor center.

The White Mountains

Rising to the east of Big Pine, the intimidating **WHITE MOUNTAINS** are effectively an alpine desert: bald, dry, and little visited, yet almost as high as the Sierra. The range is made up of some of the oldest fossil-filled rock in California and geologically has more in common with the Great Basin to the

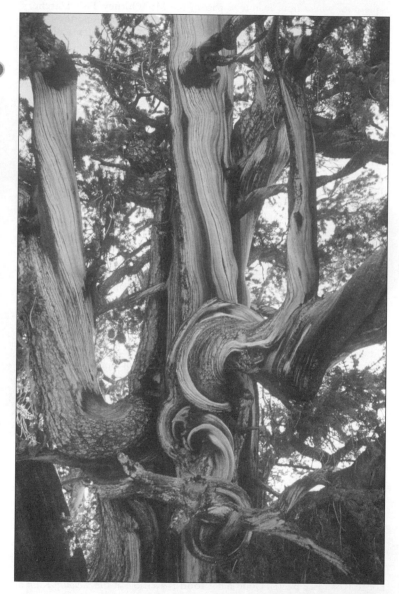

△ Bristlecone Pines, White Mountains

east than the spiky Sierra, which came into being several hundred million years later. It looks like it too: the scrubby, undulating high country appears more Scottish than Californian. The mountains are accessible only by car (or bike) via Hwy-168. Be sure to fill up on gas and **drinking water**, both of which are unavailable east of US-395.

The gnarled trees that are the prime reason for coming here stand on the lower slopes in the ancient **Bristlecone Pine Forest**, but snow renders them inaccessible for all but three or four months in the summer. **Schulman Grove** ($2.50 per person or $5 per car) is the most accessible collection, some 23 miles from Big Pine along a paved road that twists up from Hwy-168. The grove is split up into two self-guided nature trails. The mile-long Discovery Trail passes by a number of splendid examples, while the four-mile Methuselah Trail loops around past the oldest tree, the 4700-year-old Methuselah, though you'll have to guess which of the trees it is since it is unmarked due to fears of vandalism. These trails are at 10,000ft so are tougher than their length would indicate. Both trails start at the **visitor center** (mid-June–Sept daily 10am–5pm; early June & Oct call for hours; ℡760/873-2500), which explains the importance of the grove's namesake, Dr Edmund Schulman. An early practitioner of dendrochronology, he revealed the extreme age of these trees in the mid-1950s and applied the knowledge gained from core samples of the trees to correct a puzzling error in early carbon-dating techniques. It turned out that artifacts from the Balkans, previously thought of as stylistic variations on Middle Eastern wares, were in fact a thousand years older, so changing our perception of history. If you want to know more, show up at one of the free ranger talks scheduled frequently through July and August, plus there is usually a ranger-led walk on Saturdays.

Patriarch Grove, twelve miles further on, along a dusty dirt road that gives spectacular views of the Sierra Nevada to the west and the Great Basin ranges of the deserts to the east, contains the Patriarch Tree, the largest of the bristlecone pines. Four miles beyond here, a research station (closed to the public) studies the physiology of high-altitude plant and animal life, which is in many ways similar to that of the arctic regions. From here you can **hike to the summit of White Mountain** (15 miles round-trip; 6–8 hr; 2500ft ascent), the highest point in the range, and at 14,246 feet the third highest in California. A gate prevents unauthorized vehicles from getting to the research station, though all-terrain **mountain bikes** are permitted to continue. In fact, the canyons running down from the ridge between the bristlecone groves are tailor-made for thrill-seekers, who race down the steep washes at incredibly high speeds.

There is **camping** (but no water) at the 8600ft *Grandview* campground (all year; free), two miles south of Schulman Grove. Backcountry camping is not permitted in the ancient Bristlecone Pine Forest, but is allowed in the surrounding forest provided you have a campfire permit for your stove. The ranger station in Bishop can provide this and tell you which springs and small creeks (if any) are flowing.

The Palisade Glacier

The **PALISADE GLACIER** is the southernmost glacier in the US and the largest in California. It sits at the foot of the impressive Palisade Crest, center of one of the greatest concentrations of enjoyable alpine climbing in the Eastern Sierra: Norman Clyde Peak in the south is named after California's most prolific early mountaineer; the immense bulk of Temple Crag offers a range of routes unparalleled outside of Yosemite Valley; and, to the north, Thunderbolt

Bristlecone pines

Great Basin **bristlecone pines** (*pinus longaeva*) are the oldest-known living things on earth. Some of them have been alive for over 4500 years (1500 years more than any sequoia), earning them a place in the *Guinness Book of Records*. The oldest examples cling to thin alkaline soils (predominantly dolomite) between 10,000 and 11,000 feet, where the low precipitation keeps the growing season to only 45 days a year. But such conditions, which limit the trees' girth expansion to an inch every hundred years, promotes the dense resin-rich and rot-resistant wood that lasts for millennia. Battered and beaten by the harsh environment into bizarrely beautiful shapes and forms, they look like nothing so much as twenty-foot lumps of driftwood. The most photogenic examples comprise mostly **dead wood**, the live section often sustained by a thin ribbon of bark. Even when dead, the wind-scoured trunks and twisted limbs hang on without decaying for upwards of another thousand years, slowly being eroded by wind-driven ice and sand.

Bristlecones thrive at lower altitudes and in richer soils than those in the White Mountains, growing tall and wide. But they seldom live as long as specimens subjected to the harsher conditions and, in fact, they're hardly recognizable as bristlecone pines, only the five-needle bundles and the egg-shaped, barbed cone which lends the tree its name giving the game away.

For more information, consult the Inyo Forest website at Ⓦ www.r5.fs.fed.us/inyo or better still, the excellent Ⓦ www.sonic.net/bristlecone.

Peak and Mount Agassiz are highlights of the Inconsolable Range. The Palisade Glacier itself is an excellent introduction to snow and ice climbing.

Hikers not suitably equipped for (or skilled at) technical climbing can still get a sense of this wondrous area by hiking from the trailhead at Big Pine Canyon, ten miles west of Big Pine at the end of Glacier Lodge Road; follow Crocker Street in Big Pine. July, August, and September are the best (snow-free) months for hiking, best done along the trail to **First Lake** (9 miles round-trip; 5–7hr; 2300ft ascent). From here there is a network of shorter trails to six more lakes and one to the **base of the Palisade Glacier** (18 miles round-trip from the parking lot; 10–12hr; 4600ft ascent). Backcountry campers must obtain a **permit** (see box, p.386).

At the trailhead, you'll find three **campgrounds** (late April–Oct; $13) – *Sage Flat*, *Upper Sage Flat*, and *Big Pine Creek* – all above 7000ft and with water and toilets; and the free *First Falls* walk-in site at 8300ft, a mile beyond the trailhead. *Glacier Lodge* (☏760/938-2837, Ⓦwww.jewelofthesierra.com; $80–95), right at the end of the road, is a slightly more luxurious option, with cabins, RV parking ($20–25), overnight parking for hikers ($3), a limited general store, and showers ($4).

Bishop

BISHOP, fifteen miles north of Big Pine, rivals Mammoth Lakes as the **outdoor pursuits** capital of the Eastern Sierra. It may not have downhill skiing on its doorstep but its proximity to the wilderness makes it an excellent base from which to explore the surrounding mountains; if you want to try cross-country skiing, fly fishing, and especially rock climbing, there's no better place to be, with some of the world's best mountaineers offering their services through lessons and guided trips. With an urban population of 3500 and several thousand more in outlying districts, it is the largest town in the Owens Valley, yet maintains a laid-back ambience which makes it worth hanging around to enjoy. There's even a real town center, though the pleasure of strolling through it is mitigated by eighteen-wheelers thundering through.

Arrival and information

Almost everything of interest lies along or just off Main Street (US-395) where you'll find the CREST **bus stop** at 201 S Warren St (☎760/872-1901) and the main **visitor center**, 690 N Main St (Mon–Fri 9am–5pm, Sat & Sun 10am–4pm; ☎760/873-8405 or 1-888/395-3952, ⓦwww .bishopvisitor.com), which hands out a comprehensive town visitor guide. For specific information on **hiking** and **camping** in the area, and permission to visit the local petroglyphs, contact the **White Mountain Ranger Station**, 798 N Main St (June–Sept daily 8am–5pm; Oct–May Mon–Fri 8am–4.30pm; ☎760/873-2500), which also issues the first-come-first-served wilderness permits.

Accommodation

There's a reasonable range of **accommodation** for which booking in advance is advised on summer weekends (especially during **festivals**; see "Listings," p.395). There are campgrounds in town, and plenty of Inyo National Forest sites all around.

Best Western Creekside Inn 725 N Main St ☎760/872-3044 or 1-800/273-3550. Modern, upscale hotel in the center of town offering large rooms (some with kitchenette), complimentary breakfast, and an outdoor pool. ❼

Brown's Town Campground Schober Lane, off US-395, a mile south of town ☎760/873-8522. Large, Old West–themed RV and tent campground with a pool, kids' play area, and other facilities, and costing $17 for tents and $20 for water and electric hook-up.

Chalfant House 213 Academy St ☎760/872-1790 or 1-800/641-2996, ⓦwww.chalfanthouse .com. Antique-filled Victorian-era B&B just off the 200 block of North Main Street. Rooms all have private bath, ceiling fans, and a/c, and there's full gourmet breakfast. ❹

El Rancho Motel 274 W Lagoon St ☎760/872-9251 or 1-888/872-9251. Well-maintained budget motel on the south side of town with cable TV, ceiling fans, and some rooms with kitchenette (for which you pay $8 extra). Popular with fishers, so book well in advance for weekends. ❸

Joseph House Inn 376 W Yaney St ☎760/872-3389, ⓦwww.josephhouseinn.com. Upscale B&B in three acres of gardens with nicely decorated rooms, full gourmet breakfast, and wine and cheese on arrival. Two-night minimum on holiday weekends. ❼

The Village Motel 286 W Elm St ☎760/872-8155 or 1-888/668-5546, ⓦwww.bishopvillagemotel .com. Budget motel with ageing but decent rooms and heated outdoor pool, peacefully sited off the busy main drag. Rooms ❸, kitchen suites ❹

The Town

Specific sights in town are few, though anyone interested in gorgeous images of the Sierra, the Owens Valley, and beyond should pay a visit to **Mountain Light Gallery**, 106 S Main St at Line Street (Mon–Thurs & Sun 10am–6pm, Fri & Sat 10am–9pm; free; ☎760/873-7700, ⓦwww .mountainlight.com), which is lined with works by Galen Rowell, one of the world's foremost landscape photojournalists until his untimely death in a plane crash in 2002. Also a talented rock climber and mountaineer, Rowell photographed the region for over thirty years and extended his oeuvre to Patagonia, the Himalayas, northern Canada, Alaska, Antarctica, and elsewhere. You'll have to part with well over $500 to obtain one of the large-scale framed photos that line the walls, but it is well worth half an hour's browsing.

You should also drive a mile or so west to the **Paiute Shoshone Cultural Center**, 2301 W Line St (sporadic hours; call ☎760/873-9478; $4), run by local natives who mostly live on a reservation on the edge of town, similar to those found outside each of the valley settlements. Here, they put on displays of basketry and weaving, food gathering and processing, and of traditional ways of building; they also run a good bookstore. Their ancestors once roamed the area and left their mark all over the Owens Valley in the form of petroglyphs, the best examples of which are found a few miles outside town (see p.396).

Outdoor activities

Outdoor enthusiasts congregate in Bishop, their rigs laden with tents, sleeping bags, mountain bikes, rock-climbing gear, fishing tackle, crampons, and ice axes.

All year round there is somewhere to **rock climb**: in winter the sport climbs of the Owens River Gorge (see p.396) see a good deal of traffic, as do bouldering areas such as the nearby Happy Boulders and the Buttermilk Boulders (see opposite). As the daytime temperature pushes a hundred, climbers decamp to the High Sierra peaks, particularly Rock Creek, about twenty miles north of Bishop, and Tuolumne in Yosemite (see p.476). For more information, visit Wilson's Eastside Sports, 224 N Main St (☏760/873-7520, ⓦwww.eastsidesports.com), an excellent mountaineering and sporting-goods supply shop with gear rental and a climbers' notice board.

Much more of the money that flows into Bishop comes from the brigades of **fishing** enthusiasts, who spend their summer vacations angling for rainbow trout placed in the streams and lakes by the state government. When the high-country lakes and streams are still frozen or inaccessible there's still good fishing around Bishop, though the main trout season generally runs from late April to late October. As a taster of things to come, the Blake Jones Trout Derby takes place in mid-March at the Pleasant Valley Reservoir, six miles north along US-395; then there's a huge assembly of fisherfolk on the last Saturday in April around **Crowley Lake**, an artificial reservoir built to hold water diverted from Mono Lake, thirty miles north of town.

Eating and drinking

With a huge 24-hour Vons store at 1190 N Main St, and a number of good cafés and diners, Bishop is a good place to feast after a few days in the hills and to buy **food** and **supplies** for the next leg.

Amigo's Mexican Restaurant 285 N Main St ☏760/872-2189. Mainstream Mexican with a good range of Tex-Mex staples at good prices and $9 daily specials.

Erick Schat's Bakkery 736 N Main St ☏760/873-7156. Huge and bustling pseudo-Dutch bakery which has been making their "Original Sheepherder Bread" since early in the twentieth century. There are dozens of other varieties – such as multigrain and sourdough – tables for tucking into their sandwiches ($8), and a huge range of cakes and pastries.

Jack's Restaurant and Bakery 437 N Main St. Well-regarded diner that bakes its own bread, used in their extensive range of burgers and sandwiches. Leave space for a plate of their locally

famous waffles or a slice of fruit pie. Open from 6am for breakfast.

Kava Coffeehouse 206 N Main St ☏760/872-1010. Hip, central café serving some of Bishop's best coffee and muffins, and offering speedy Internet access and a wireless hot spot. Evenings are quiet in summer but in the cooler seasons might include live music or chess matches.

Whiskey Creek 524 N Main St ☏760/873-7174. Among Bishop's more upscale restaurants with a sunny deck and an attached bar (where you can also eat) serving Whiskey Creek microbrews. Maybe start with tempura shrimp ($10) and follow with ribs or halibut ($19–22) and a deep-dish boysenberry pie ($6).

Listings

Climbing and hiking guides For expert instruction or guided rock climbing, alpine climbing, and ski mountaineering contact: Sierra Mountain Guides (☎760/648-1122, ⓦwww .themountainguide.com); Sierra Mountain Center, 174 W Line St (☎760/873-8526, ⓦwww .sierramountaincenter.com); or Sierra Mountaineering International, 236 N Main St (☎760/872-4929, ⓦwww.sierramountaineering.com).

Festivals Bishop comes alive over Memorial Day weekend for Mule Days (☎760/872-4263, ⓦwww.muledays.org), with a huge parade, mule-drawn chariot racing, a county hoe-down, arts and crafts fair, and much more. The Tri-County Fair over Labor Day weekend includes a Wild West Rodeo.

Library 210 Academy St (☎760/873-5115) has speedy Internet access and is open Mon, Wed & Fri 10am–8pm, Tues & Thurs noon–8pm, Sat 10am–1pm.

Medical treatment Northern Inyo Hospital, 150 Pioneer Lane (☎760/873-5811), has 24hr emergency and intensive care.

Movies Bishop Twin Theatre, 237 N Main St, shows the latest Hollywood offerings.

Post office 595 W Line St (☎760/873-3526). For general delivery use zip code 93514.

Showers and laundry There are showers at the City of Bishop Park Pool, 688 N Main St, behind the visitor center (late May–early Sept Tues–Sun 7am–8pm; $2), and showers and laundry at the Wash Tub, 236 Warren St (daily 7am–9pm; $5).

Around Bishop and north towards Mammoth

You may well stay and eat in Bishop, but the main attractions lie outside town, either west along South Lake Road (Hwy-168), which runs to a Sierra trailhead, north onto the so-called volcanic tablelands to see native petroglyphs, north towards the Owens River Gorge.

If you don't have your own vehicle, you can still access the surrounding area using Kountry Korners Trailhead Shuttle Service (☎760/938-2650 or 1-888/656-0756, ⓔkountryks@aol.com). which effectively operate as trailhead taxi services and charge according to distance and numbers.

West along Hwy-168

Hwy-168 runs west from Bishop past the Paiute Shoshone Cultural Center and climbs some fifteen miles through aspens and cottonwoods to a cluster of alpine lakes and 10,000-foot trailheads.

Roughly six miles west of Bishop, small, dirt Buttermilk Road leads northwest off the highway into an arid land of lumpy hills and large, golden granite rocks known as the **Buttermilk Boulders**. Year-round, rock climbers travel the state to pit themselves against an almost limitless selection of low-lying boulder problems in a beautiful location. Visit Wilson's Eastside Sports (see p.394) for details and guidebooks.

Hwy-168 ends at the dammed **Lake Sabrina**, where there's a restaurant that sells fishing tackle and rents boats. Nearby, **South Lake**, also nineteen miles from Bishop, is flanked by *Bishop Creek Lodge* (☎760/873-4484, ⓦwww .bishopcreekresorts.com; ❺), with a general store, fishing shop, boat rentals, cabins, and $4 public showers. A number of **hiking routes** set off up into the High Sierra wilderness from trailheads at these lakes.

The trail from South Lake over Bishop Pass heads into Dusy Basin, where you can see the effects of centuries of glaciation in the bowl-like cirques and giant "erratic" boulders left by receding glaciers. Another path follows the northern fork of Bishop Creek under the rusty cliffs of the Paiute Crags, before climbing over Paiute Pass into the Desolation Lakes area of the John Muir Wilderness. There are a number of **campgrounds** between 7500 and 9000 feet up – almost all with water and costing $16 a night. The shady *Sabrina* site, right by the lake of the same name, is perhaps the best.

Laws and the Red Rock Canyon petroglyphs

On the northern edge of Bishop, US-395 divides from US-6, which runs north and east into Nevada. Four miles along US-6 is the **Laws Railroad Museum** (daily 10am–4pm; $3; Ⓦwww.thesierraweb.com/bishop/laws), a handful of relocated old buildings and a slender black train known as the "Slim Princess" arranged in the restored old town of **LAWS**. From 1883 to 1959 this was an important way station on the narrow-gauge Carson and Colorado Railroad, which ran along the eastern side of the Owens Valley from Carson City to the northern shores of Owens Lake, just south of Lone Pine.

Northwest of Laws a stark desert plateau harbors the **Red Rock Canyon Petroglyphs**, where ancient native peoples have carved mysterious designs – spirals, geometric forms, even spacey figures – onto the rocks. Many beautiful examples exist, but several have been vandalized (and even stolen) over the years, so to help protect them the Bureau of Lands Management, in conjunction with the native owners, require visitors to sign in at the White Mountain Ranger Station in Bishop (see p.393). There are no permits, fees, or gates to open, but they'll give you a map that pinpoints three petroglyph concentrations, the most interesting being Red Rock Canyon.

North along US-395

Around ten miles north of Bishop, US-395 starts climbing the **Sherwin Grade**, twelve miles of steady climbing which brings you from 4000 feet to the 6500-foot **Mono Basin**. As you climb the grade, Power Plant Road heads off on the right to the precipitously steep **Owens River Gorge**, another excellent rock-climbing spot in an area which until recently was completely dry. Since 1994, the Los Angeles Department of Water and Power has been forced to allow water to flow down the gorge, and the flora and fauna is slowly returning along with trout fishers and hikers.

Mammoth Lakes and around

MAMMOTH LAKES, forty miles north of Bishop, and the associated skiing, snowboarding, and mountain biking hot spot of **Mammoth Mountain**, jointly make up the Eastern Sierra's biggest resort, and one that is only challenged in California by those around Lake Tahoe. During the winter months, masses of weekend skiers speed through the Owens Valley on their way to some of the state's premiere pistes, which rise above this pine-shrouded town. It is for this and the summer fishing that Mammoth is traditionally known, although the town is now increasingly hyped for its accessible mountain-biking terrain and a number of on- and off-road bike races.

Despite its popularity with LA weekenders, Mammoth has always been a fairly low-key resort, but in recent years the involvement of corporate resort owner, Intrawest, has propelled Mammoth into the ranks of the winter sports mega-resorts like those at Vail in the Rockies, and Whistler/Blackcomb in Canada. Intrawest is now the majority owner of the ski operation and large chunks of Mammoth real estate, and is putting the final touches to its **Village at Mammoth** development, complete with pricey hotels, swanky stores, and linked to the mountain by the new Village Gondola. Lots of new lodging has

MAMMOTH LAKES
AND AROUND

0   2 miles

Chairlift

N

Bishop (30 miles)

Hot Creek Geological Site

Convict Lake
Convict Lake

JOHN MUIR
WILDERNESS

Laurel
Mountain
(11,812 ft)

Hot Creek
Fish Hatchery

HOT CREEK HATCHERY RD

395

CONVICT LAKE ROAD

Hartley Springs Campground (3 miles) & Mono Lake (20 miles)

INYO   NATIONAL   FOREST

MAMMOTH SCENIC LOOP ROAD

395

Shady Rest Park

Mammoth
Visitor Center
& Ranger Station

203

SHERWIN CREEK ROAD

see Central
Mammoth Lakes map

Tamarack Lodge & Resort
& Lakefront Restaurant

Emerald
Lake

Lake Mary

SKY MEADOWS TRAIL

PANORAMA
DOME TRAIL

Inyo Crater
Lakes

JOHN MUIR
WILDERNESS

Minaret
Vista

Climbing
Rock

Devil's Postpile
Main Lodge &
Panorama Gondola Station

Mammoth Mountain Inn

LAKE MARY ROAD

Twin Lakes
Twin Lakes

CRYSTAL LAKE TRAIL

Lake
George

Mammoth
Mountain
(11,053 ft)

Panorama Gondola

ANSEL ADAMS
WILDERNESS

JOHN MUIR
WILDERNESS

203

Mammoth
Mountain
Ski Area &
Bike Park

Entrance
Station

ROAD CLOSED
NOVEMBER
MID-JUNE

Agnews
Meadows

MAMMOTH SCENIC LOOP ROAD

San Joaquin Ridge

San Joaquin River

Red's Meadow

Red's Meadow

Red's Meadow
Pack Station

ANSEL ADAMS
WILDERNESS

Devil's
Postpile

Devils's
Postpile
National
Monument

Rainbow
Falls

San Joaquin River

been built along with Mammoth's second golf course, and Intrawest is lobbying hard for a much expanded airport with scheduled flights.

Residents are torn between enthusiasm for the new opportunities presented and nostalgia for the way things used to be, but for the moment Mammoth remains unbeatable for outdoor activities and is scenically as dramatic as just about anywhere in the Sierra. You may find the testosterone overload oppressive and the town overpriced, but it is easy to escape to the hills during the day and return each evening to good food, lively bars, and even a couple of movie theaters.

Arrival and information

Hwy-203 runs three miles west from US-395 into the town of Mammoth Lakes, from where it continues six miles to the Main Lodge for Mammoth Mountain, then ascends the San Joaquin Ridge and drops down to the Devil's Postpile National Monument.

Year-round **CREST buses** (see p.369) stop three times a week in the *McDonald's* parking lot on Hwy-203. There's also a seasonal **YARTS service** to Tuolumne Meadows and Yosemite Valley (July & Aug once daily; June & Sept Sat & Sun only; ⓦwww.yarts.com) which departs from *Mammoth Mountain Inn*, opposite the skifield Main Lodge, at 7am and returns that evening around 9pm. In the ski season, get around on the five-route **Mammoth Shuttle** which goes everywhere you'll want to. During the warmer months, **rent a bike** (see "Listings," p.404), and make use of the free summer **shuttle** which plies a route between the main ski lodge and Devil's Postpile National Monument, some fifteen miles west of town.

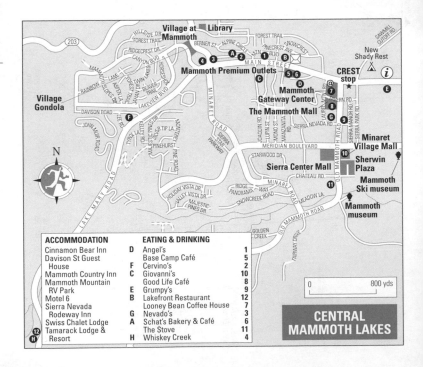

ACCOMMODATION		EATING & DRINKING	
Cinnamon Bear Inn	D	Angel's	1
Davison St Guest House		Base Camp Café	5
	F	Cervino's	2
Mammoth Country Inn	C	Giovanni's	10
Mammoth Mountain RV Park		Good Life Café	8
	E	Grumpy's	9
Motel 6	B	Lakefront Restaurant	12
Sierra Nevada Rodeway Inn		Looney Bean Coffee House	7
	G	Nevado's	3
Swiss Chalet Lodge	A	Schat's Bakery & Café	6
Tamarack Lodge & Resort	H	The Stove	11
		Whiskey Creek	4

CENTRAL MAMMOTH LAKES

The best source of practical information for the area is the combined US Forest Service and Mammoth Lakes **visitor center** (daily 8am–5pm; ☏760/924-5500, 🖰www.visitmammoth.com), on the main highway half a mile east of the town center.

Accommodation

About every second building in Mammoth is a condo, but there are numerous other **accommodation** opportunities (including a hostel and some welcoming B&Bs), so beds are at a premium only during ski-season weekends. Winter prices are highest, summer rates (quoted here, and still fairly high) come next, and in the months in between some relative bargains can be found. If you fancy staying in a **condo** try contacting Mammoth Mountain Reservations (☏760/934-5771 or 1-800/223-3032, 🖰www.mammothreservations.com).

There is also mile upon mile of backcountry (see box, p.401) in which to pitch a tent, and plenty of family sites with campers almost overwhelmed by choice. There are some twenty **campgrounds** within a ten-mile radius of town; the two main concentrations being around Twin Lakes and along the Devil's Postpile–Red's Meadow road. Almost all come with water, cost $15–16, and are let on a first-come-first-served basis. The Mammoth Lakes visitor guide (available free from the visitor center) has full details along with rules for free dispersed camping on national forest lands around about.

Motels, B&Bs, and condos

Cinnamon Bear Inn 113 Center St ☏760/934-2873 or 1-800/845-2873, 🖰www.cinnamon bearinn.com. Reasonably priced, 22-room B&B inn close to downtown with comfortable rooms, all with TV and phone (and some with VCR), use of hot tub, wine-and-nibbles happy hour on arrival, and a full breakfast. Midweek ❺, weekends ❻

Davison Street Guest House 19 Davison St ☏760/924-2188, 🖰www.mammoth-guest.com. Mammoth's only backpacker hostel is in a wooden A-frame chalet with mountain views from its deck. There's a spacious lounge, good communal cooking facilities, bunks in fairly compact dorms (summer $22, winter weekdays $30, winter weekends $35), two-bed rooms (summer ❷, winter weekdays ❸, winter weekends ❹), and one en-suite room for an extra $20.

Mammoth Country Inn 75 Joaquin Rd ☏760/934-2710 or 1-866/934-2710, 🖰www .mammothcountryinn.com. Welcoming and good-value B&B in a quiet neighborhood with seven modern and tastefully themed rooms, all with private baths and some with Jacuzzis. There's wine and hors d'oeuvres on arrival, and full and delicious breakfasts. Midweek ❹, weekend ❺

Mammoth Mountain RV Park Hwy-203 ☏760/934-3822 or 1-800/582-4603, 🖰www .gocampingamerica.com. Year-round fully featured RV park right in town opposite the visitor center, with indoor spas, kids' play areas, tent sites ($21), and a range of full hook-up sites ($29–34).

Motel 6 3372 Main St ☏760/934-6660 or 1-800/466-8356, 🖰www.motel6.com. Basic modern motel close to the town center with all you really need at an affordable price. ❸

Sierra Nevada Rodeway Inn 164 Old Mammoth Rd ☏760/934-2515 or 1-800/824-5132, 🖰www .mammothsnri.com. At the cheaper end of Mammoth motels but still with large comfy rooms, pool, spa and sauna, and on-site restaurant. Weekends ❺, midweek ❹

Swiss Chalet Lodge 3776 Viewpoint Rd ☏760/934-2403 or 1-800/937-9477, 🖰www .mammoth-swisschalet.com. Plain rooms with TV and phone in an ageing but recently remodeled place that's one of the few low-cost establishments in Mammoth with mountain views, especially from the upper floor. Also boasts a good sauna, a large indoor hot tub with views, and a reception desk full of cuckoo clocks. Weekends ❹, midweek ❸

Tamarack Lodge & Resort Lake Mary Rd ☏760/934-2442 or 1-800/626-6684, 🖰www .tamaracklodge.com. Away from the town and with a woodsy setting right by Twin Lake on the edge of a cross-country ski area, this luxurious lodge in rustic style offers lodge rooms (shared bath ❹, private bath ❼), rustic cabins (❻) with fully-equipped kitchens, and some gorgeous deluxe cabins (❾).

Camping and RVs

Convict Lake Open late April to Oct; 7600ft. Wooded, lakeside National Forest campground just west of US-395 around four miles south of the Mammoth turnoff, with the longest opening season in the area. Showers are available at the nearby *Convict Lake Resort* (℡760/934-3800, ⓦwww .convictlake.com; $2 for two minutes). $15

Devil's Postpile Open mid-June to mid-Oct; 7600ft. National Park Service campground half a mile from the rocks themselves along the Devil's Postpile–Red's Meadow road, and a good base for hikes to Rainbow Falls or along the John Muir Trail. $14

Hartley Springs Open early May–Oct; 8400ft. Just one of several primitive waterless campgrounds in the area, this one located 1.5 miles west of US-395 along Glass Flow Road around eleven miles north of the Mammoth turnoff. Free

New Shady Rest Open mid-May to Oct; 7800ft. Large and busy campground close to town with flush toilets and a dump station. Several sites can be reserved on ℡1-877/444-6777. $15

Red's Meadow Open mid-June to mid-Oct; 7600ft. National Forest campground along the Devil's Postpile–Red's Meadow road and within easy hiking distance of Devil's Postpile, Rainbow Falls, and a nice nature trail around Sotcher Lake. It also comes with a natural hot-spring bathhouse open to all (donations appreciated). $15

Twin Lakes Open mid-May–Oct; 8600ft. The longest-opening of five near-identical sites in this area of glacially scooped lake beds, a mile southwest of Mammoth Lakes township. Lakeside setting among the pines and plenty of hiking trails nearby. $16

Mammoth Mountain: biking, hiking, and fishing

Mammoth is all about getting into the outdoors. Aside from eating, drinking, and mooching around the sports shops and factory clothing outlets, you'll find little reason to spend much time in town, though anyone interested in Mammoth's gold-mining and timber-milling origins may fancy a visit to the small **Mammoth Museum**, 5489 Sherwin Creek Rd (June–Sept daily 10am–6pm; free), located in a 1920s log cabin. Winter sports fans will find more of interest in the **Mammoth Ski Museum**, 100 College Parkway (Tues–Sun 10am–5pm; $3; ℡760/934-6592, ⓦwww.mammothskimuseum.org), a small but well-presented collection of skiing-related paraphernalia, most of it amassed over sixty years by one Mason Beekley. There's the expected racks of old skis, a chair from the original Mammoth chairlift, and a 450-year-old book by a Swedish monk which illustrates skiing, but the museum's strength is in the graphic arts. The walls come lined with vintage ski posters, photos (some by Ansel Adams), and even woodcuts; many are reproduced and available at the gift shop. The little theater runs free movies on local ski history daily (typically 12.30pm, 2pm & 3.30pm).

There's more fun to be had four miles west of the center up on the slopes of the dormant volcano that is **Mammoth Mountain**, where the **Panorama Gondola** (late June–Sept daily 9am–4.30pm; $16 round-trip) will whisk you to the top of Mammoth Mountain in eight minutes, for fine mountain views all around.

If you'd rather work up a sweat there are a number of ways to do just that: mountain biking, hiking, plus stacks of people willing to get you mobile: **kayaking** and **rock climbing** are both covered in "Listings" on p.404, and **horseback riding** is discussed in the box on p.405.

Mountain biking

Once the ski runs have freed themselves of the winter snows, the slopes transform into the 3500-acre **Mammoth Mountain Bike Park** (late June–Sept daily 9am–4.30pm; ℡760/934-0706, ⓦwww.mammothmountain.com) with over eighty miles of groomed singletrack trails. Chairlifts quickly give you and your bike an altitude boost, allowing you to hurtle down the twisting sandy trails, brushing pines and negotiating small jumps and tree roots. The emphasis here is definitely on going downhill, and when you're transported to the rarefied eleven-thousand-foot air at the top of the chairlift you very quickly appreciate the logic of this. The bike park produces a color map of the mountain showing the lifts and trails in three grades of difficulty, and indicates X-Zones where they've created enhanced freeriding terrain for the more aggressive riders. Beginners often take the **Downtown** run into Mammoth (from where a bike shuttle bus returns you to the bike park), while those with a little more skill or ambition might opt for the **Beach Cruiser**, which carves its way down the western side of the mountain from near the summit. Experts and those with a death wish can tackle the **Kamikaze**, scene of the ultimate downhill race which has traditionally formed the centerpiece of the annual World Cup racing weekend (usually around late Sept), at which competitors hit speeds of sixty miles per hour.

The basic **park use fee** ($10) gives you access to the trails, and you can rent bikes for $36 a day. In addition there's a complex selection of deals such as the Park Pass (one day $31, two days $55), which gives all-day access to the Panorama Gondola to the summit and the bike shuttle from town. Gondola and bike rental combos include a half-day package ($50) giving four hours' bike rental and two gondola rides, and a full-day unlimited deal ($64).

If you don't fancy forking out for use of the bike park, or just prefer something a little gentler, there is plenty more **trail riding** around the resort, made comfortable by mid-summer temperatures reliably in the seventies. Several bike stores around town will point you in the right direction and rent bikes (see "Listings," p.404) which can also be taken to the bike park. Likely candidates include: the relatively gentle Shady Rest Park, close to central Mammoth; the Lakes Basin area near *Tamarack Resort*; and Inyo and Mono craters. The visitor center offers free trail maps and a brochure on route descriptions and trail ethics.

Hiking

Interwoven among the bike trails on Mammoth Mountain are a couple of **hiking paths** which top out at the summit. The views are stupendous but, in common with many volcanoes, the hiking isn't the best and you're better off riding the gondola to the summit (see opposite) and saving your legs for hikes elsewhere.

Listed in the box below are some of the best of the **short hikes** around Mammoth. No permits are required for these, though you'll need to obtain a free **wilderness permit** if you want to spend the night in the Ansel Adams

---

Hikes around Mammoth Lakes

Crystal Lake (3.5 miles round-trip; 2hr; 650ft ascent). From the Lake George trailhead the path skirts high above Lake George revealing increasingly dramatic views as you climb towards Crystal Lake, hunkered below Crystal Crag. Fit hikers can tack on the Mammoth Crest Trail (a further 2.5 miles round-trip; 2–3hr; 1000ft ascent).

Panorama Dome Trail (1 mile round-trip; 30min; 100ft ascent). Great views over the town and the Owens Valley reward this short sylvan trail from Twin Lakes on Lake Mary Road (see town map, p.398).

Sky Meadows Trail (4 miles; 1.5–2hr; 1200ft ascent). Starting at the southern end of Lake Mary, this delightful hike along the wildflower-flanked Coldwater Creek passes Emerald Lake on its way to Sky Meadow at the foot of the striking Blue Crag.

Rainbow Falls Trail (5 miles; 2hr; 300ft ascent). Moderate hike that combines the two key features of the Devil's Postpile National Monument. Start from the *Devil's Postpile* campground and stroll to the monument itself, then continue to the top of Rainbow Falls.

or John Muir wilderness areas to the south and west. On all trailheads into the wilderness there is an overnight quota season from May to October when the number of overnight hikers setting off from each trailhead is limited. Call the Wilderness Reservations Office in Bishop (℡760/873-2483, ℻873-2484, Ⓦwww.r5.fs.fed.us/inyo) up to six months and at least two days in advance; there is a $5 reservation fee.

Fishing
There is no Mammoth Lake, but the town of Mammoth Lakes makes a great base for reeling in brook, rainbow, and brown trout in the dozens of lakes all about. During the main summer season many anglers head for Mary Lake, the largest hereabouts, where you can rent boats and spend the day hooking fish in beautiful surroundings. You won't be alone, but with a little imagination it is easy enough to find a peaceful spot. Pick up information from one of the many fishing shops in town, such as Kittredge Sports, 3218 Main St (℡1-877/441-3331, Ⓦwww.kittredgesports.com), which has a board outside giving the latest on the region's fishing spots along with fly and spinner advice, and rents gear.

The artificial **Crowley Lake** (see p.394) is also a popular spot and is just twelve miles south along US-395. For **river fishing**, the San Joaquin, over the hill near the Devil's Postpile, is a winner for those in search of trout.

Along Minaret Road: Devil's Postpile National Monument

From the ski area, the narrow and winding **Minaret Road** (typically open mid-June to Oct) climbs briefly to a nine-thousand-foot pass in the San Joaquin Ridge, then plummets into the headwaters of the Middle Fork of the

---

Winter and spring in Mammoth

With one of the longest Californian seasons (from early November often until well into June), three thousand vertical feet of skiing, and more than its fair share of dreamy deep powder, **Mammoth Mountain** (daily 8.30am–4pm; ℡1-800/626-6684, lift and snow conditions ℡1-888/766-9778, Ⓦwww.mammothmountain.com) ranks as one of California's premier ski mountains. It is well balanced, too, with roughly equal areas of beginner, intermediate, and expert terrain plus snow parks and half-pipes. Add to that a cat's-cradle of intersecting gondolas and chairlifts – seemingly being added to each year and now numbering over thirty – bundles of snow-making equipment, and a whole resort of bars and restaurants designed with après-ski in mind, and you can hardly go wrong. As if this weren't enough, your lift ticket is also valid at June Lake (see p.405), a few miles north.

Pick up **lift tickets** ($57 weekdays, $62 weekends) from the Main Lodge on Minaret Road, where you can also rent **equipment** ($27 for basic skis, boots, and poles; $30 for snowboard and boots), and book **lessons** ($55–60 per half-day).

Off the mountain there are stacks of **cross-country skiing** trails; *Tamarack Lodge & Resort* (see "Accommodation," p.399) offers ski packages, including instruction, tours, and rentals, and charges $19 a day ($22 at weekends) for access to the trails.

If you prefer a motorized approach to the white stuff, you can rent gear and clothing from DJ's Snowmobile Adventures (℡760/935-4480, Ⓦwww .snowmobilemammoth.com), who have one-hour (single $60, double $78), two-hour ($104/142), and half-day ($208/284) rentals. Beyond that, there's **ice skating, bobsled riding**, and even shooting down the bobsled course on a giant inner tube.

San Joaquin River, ending some eight miles beyond at the Red's Meadow pack station. This is the only road access into the evocatively named **DEVIL'S POSTPILE NATIONAL MONUMENT** (day-pass $7, three-day pass $14, Golden Eagle Pass OK, National Park Pass not accepted; ⓦ www.nps .gov/depo), which centers on a collection of slender, blue-gray basalt columns ranged like hundreds of pencils stood on end. Some are as tall as sixty feet, others are twisted and warped, while vulnerable sections are shorter where the brittle rock has cracked and the upper sections have fallen forward to form a talus slope of shattered rubble. It was formed as lava from Mammoth Mountain cooled and fractured into multi-sided forms, a phenomenon best appreciated by skirting round to the top of the columns. The Postpile itself is a half-mile stroll from the *Devil's Postpile* campground where there is a small **visitor center** (mid-June to Oct daily 9am–4pm), from where rangers guide daily walks at 11am and lead evening campfire programs (Tues & Sat 8pm).

The second highlight of the National Monument is **Rainbow Falls**, where the Middle Fork of the San Joaquin River plunges 101 feet into a deep pool, the spray refracting to earn its name, especially at midday. It is two miles away through Red's Meadow, reached on a pleasant hike (see box, p.401).

Throughout the summer, Minaret Road is closed to private vehicles during the day and you must access Devil's Postpile by **shuttle bus** (daily 7am– 8.30pm, last bus leaves the Postpile 7.45pm; free with National Monument entry), which leaves every thirty minutes from the Mammoth Mountain Main Lodge Gondola Building. Campers are allowed vehicular access at all times, and in the early morning and evening (after 7.30pm) others can drive along Minaret Road; drive over before 7am and you can come back whenever you wish. During the day, the furthest you can drive without taking the shuttle bus is **Minaret Vista**, a parking lot high on the San Joaquin Ridge with wonderful views of the **Minaret Peaks**, a spiky volcanic ridge just south of pointed Mount Ritter – one of the Sierra's most enticing high peaks.

Eating, drinking, and nightlife

Mammoth offers by far the widest selection – and some of the best examples – of **restaurants**, **cafés**, and **bars** (some with live **music**) on this side of the Sierra. That may be reason enough to stick around for a while, but if you've got used to the relative austerity elsewhere in the mountains, the drain on your finances may come as something of a shock. If you're just after replenishing your cooler, pick up **groceries** at Von's, in the Minaret Village mall, and healthy goodies at Sierra Sundance Earth Foods in The Mammoth Mall.

Angel's Main St at Sierra Blvd ℡760/934-7427. The menu has a Southwestern kick at this broadly appealing and family-friendly restaurant. The Angel's salad ($4) and jalapeño corn fritters ($6) are very good and there is a decent selection of burgers ($8–9) and $10 mains such as spinach and mushroom lasagna, and chicken pot pie, all washed down with Mammoth Brewing Company microbrews.

Base Camp Café Main St ℡760/934-3900. Great low-cost café usually bustling with the outdoors and active set here for the hearty breakfasts ($4–7), tasty soups and sandwiches, bargain daily specials, organic espresso coffees, and microbrews. Also open for dinner (Thurs–Sat to around 8pm).

Cervino's 3752 Viewpoint Rd ℡760/934-4734. Excellent Northern Italian fine dining; try portobello mushrooms stuffed with goat's cheese and pecans ($11) followed by veal served with prosciutto in a sage-butter sauce ($24). Their three-course prix fixe menu goes for under $30. Closed Mon & Tues in summer.

Giovanni's Minaret Village Mall, Old Mammoth Rd ℡760/934-7563. The favorite local stop for low-cost dining; three out of ten for decor and ambience but very good pasta and pizza, and great lunchtime deals.

Good Life Café The Mammoth Mall ℡760/934- 1734. Doesn't cater to vegetarians and vegans as well as they'd like you to believe, but probably the best around with freshly made veggie burritos, good salads, and vegetable wraps as well as plenty of burgers and egg dishes at modest prices, all served inside or on the sunny deck. Daily 6.30am–3pm.

Grumpy's 361 Old Mammoth Rd ☏760/934-8587, Ⓦwww.grumpysmammoth.com. Sports bar with forty TVs, pool table, and a good grill serving the likes of the half-pound Grumpy Melt with ortega chilies and grilled onions ($10), and a fine halibut and chips ($11).

Lakefront Restaurant *Tamarack Lodge* ☏760/934-2442. Superb lake views accompany dishes from a menu with French-Californian leanings, which might include wild-mushroom strudel ($11), walnut-crusted chicken breast ($22), and a sumptuous selection of desserts and ports.

Looney Bean Coffee House The Mammoth Mall ☏760/934-1345. The most vibrant of Mammoth's coffee bars with good coffee, muffins, and the like, served up to dedicated regulars either inside (where there's a stack of magazines) or out front. Stays open late in the ski season.

Nevados Main St and Minaret Rd ☏760/934-4466. Another favorite with the foodies with an eclectic menu from crisp nori-wrapped shrimp with *wasabi* to hazelnut-crust rack of lamb and, a $35 prix fixe deal for an appetizer, main, and dessert.

Schat's Bakery & Café 3305 Main St ☏760/934-6055. Easily the best range of baked goods in town, either to take out or eat in with a coffee.

The Stove 644 Old Mammoth Rd ☏760/934-2821. Long-standing Mammoth favorite for its traditional country cooking, serving egg, waffle, and pancake breakfasts, sandwiches and full meals later on – all in massive portions.

Whiskey Creek Main St and Minaret Rd ☏760/934-2555. Traditional American dining in one of the town's better restaurants, which particularly excels with its seafood, Sierra Ranch salad, and meatloaf. Upstairs is one of the livelier bars in town, serving its own Mammoth Brewing Company beers (happy hour 5–6.30pm daily) and often putting on bands, especially at weekends.

Listings

Banks Several around town (all with ATMs) including the Bank of America, corner of Main Street and Old Mammoth Road.

Bookstores Booky Joint in the Minaret Village Mall (☏760/934-3240 or 934-2176) has the best all-round selection; Book Warehouse, 3399 Main St (☏760/924-3551), is stacked with remaindered books of all sorts at bargain prices.

Cinemas First-run Hollywood fare at the Plaza Theatre in the Sherwin Plaza Mall and Minaret Cinema in the Minaret Village Mall (both ☏760/934-3131).

Festivals During the annual Jazz Jubilee, held over four days around the second weekend in July (details on ☏760/934-2478, Ⓦwww .mammothjazz.org), bars, restaurants, and impromptu venues around town pack out with predominantly trad-jazz types. Blues fans should come later for Bluesapalooza (☏760/934-0606), held over the first weekend in August.

Internet access The library (see below) has free surfing for an hour at a time, and there's access and a hot spot at Abbey Road in the Mammoth Gateway Center.

Laundry Mill City Laundry, corner of Main Street and Old Mammoth Road. Also coin-op machines at *Mammoth Mountain Inn* (7am–9pm).

Library The public library is located at 960 Forest Trail (Mon–Fri 10am–7pm, Sat 9am–5.30pm) and has Internet access.

Mountain biking Footloose Sports, corner of Main Street and Old Mammoth Road (☏760/934-2400, Ⓦwww.footloosesports.com), rent front- and full-suspension bikes ($9/hr, $39/day), plus the latest demo models ($15/60) and organize weekly group rides; Mammoth Sporting Goods, Sierra Center Mall (☏760/934-3239, Ⓦwww.mammothsporting goods.com), offer slightly better rates for a similar range of machines and also run summer-only group rides (July–Oct Wed 5.30pm & Sat 9am) and a Friday-evening night ride starting at 9pm.

Photographic supplies Speed of Light Photo & Video, 1 Minaret Village Mall ☏760/934-8415.

Rock and alpine climbing Mammoth Zip & Climb (☏760/934-0706) run family-oriented sessions on a 32-foot artificial climbing rock (late June–Sept daily 10am–5pm; single climb $9, or $19 an hour, shoes $3) in front of the *Mammoth Mountain Inn*. To get out on the real stuff, contact Mammoth Mountaineering School (☏760/924-9100 or 1-800/239-7942, Ⓦwww .mammothweb.com/recreation/mountaineering), who run rock classes at all grades from $80 and are based at Sandy's Ski & Sports on Main Street; or Southern Yosemite Mountain Guides (☏1-800/231-4575, Ⓦwww.symg.com), who offer a rock and alpine guiding service at $345 a day for up to six people. The Bishop-based guide services (see p.395) also run trips in the Mammoth area.

Want to explore the High Sierra but don't fancy carrying all your food and camping gear? Help is at hand in the form of **pack stations** which offer **horseback trips** ranging from a single night to seven-, ten-, or even twenty-day trips over the Sierra Crest and into Yosemite or Kings Canyon national parks. Cheapest are custom **spot trips**, where you and your gear are taken to a suitable campsite then picked up at some pre-arranged time. Rates depend on numbers and distance traveled, but taking a group of four to a destination 4–6 hours away, you might expect to pay $350–550 each round-trip. Multi-night **trail rides** with a guide usually work to a schedule advertised in advance and are likely to cost close to $200 a day. For these you'll generally be teaming up with others. Most outfitters also rent stock for carrying gear and will even use horses to drop off gear for you at a specified location.

Below we've listed a few popular packers from south to north up the Owens Valley:

Sequoia Kings Pack Trains ☎760/387-2797 or 1-800/962-0775. Independence-based packers serving King's Canyon National Park and Mount Whitney.

Rainbow Pack Outfitters ☎760/873-8877. Located near South Lake, west of Bishop, with great rides into Dusy Basin and LeConte Canyon on the Middle Fork of the Kings River.

Mammoth Lakes Pack Outfit ☎760/934-2434 or 1-888/475-8748, ⓦwww .mammothpack.com. Mammoth-based, working a slightly different area to the Red's Meadow crowd.

Red's Meadow ☎760/934-2345 or 1-800/292-7758, ⓦwww .redsmeadowpackstation.com. Right by Devil's Postpile (see p.403), and four miles north at Agnew Meadow.

Showers In Mammoth township try Twin Lakes Store (daily 7am–7pm; $3; ☎760/934-7295) or *Mammoth Mountain Inn* (see "Accommodation"; daily 24hr; $5 with towel). In the Devil's Postpile area, head for the natural hot spring bathhouse at the Red's Meadow campground (donations appreciated).

Around Mammoth

Mammoth makes a good base for exploring a little of the **surrounding area**, even as far as Mono Lake and Bodie Ghost Town. Closer to hand, there's warm bathing at Hot Creek and a mass of fine alpine scenery around the June Lake Loop.

Hot Creek Geological Site

Three miles east of US-395 is one of the more easily accessible examples of the region's volcanic activity in the hot springs that bubble up at the **Hot Creek Geological Site** (daily dawn–dusk; free), on Hot Creek Hatchery Road three miles south of the exit for Mammoth Lakes. Jets of boiling water mix with the otherwise chilly, snowmelt water to form pools ranging from tepid to scalding; you have to search to find a happy medium, and it's a bit of a challenge since the flows are ever-changing. Note, too, that the US Forest Service discourages bathing, because of the risk of burns and the sometimes high chemical content – not that anyone takes much notice. Paths and wooden steps lead down to the most likely spots, but wear shoes or sport sandals as there may be broken glass underfoot. Unlike most of the region's hot springs, bathing suits are required. For more on the region's hot springs, see box, p.406.

June Lake Loop

The popularity of the Mammoth Mountain slopes sends some skiers and summer visitors a few miles further north to the relative solitude of **June Lake**

Vulcanism and hot springs in the Eastern Sierra

One of the pleasures of any extended visit to the Owens Valley is soaking your bones in one of the numerous **hot springs**. None is well signposted, and most are primarily used by locals who are welcoming enough if you are respectful. Most springs are tucked away miles down some rutted dirt road and often comprise little more than a ring of rocks or a hollowed-out tub into which people have diverted the waters to create pools of differing temperatures. Most are **clothing-optional**, but you'll stand out as a tourist if you don't strip off. We've mentioned several springs in the text – those in the Saline Valley (p.382), Keough's Hot Springs (p.389), Travertine Hot Springs, and Buckeye Hot Springs (both p.410) – but aficionados will want to get hold of *Hot Springs of the Eastern Sierra* by George Williams III, which has full descriptions and detailed directions.

The springs are all the result of groundwater being heated by magma, which rises close to the surface in these parts. In fact Mammoth Mountain stands on the edge of a geologically volatile region known as the **Long Valley Caldera**. A vast oval some eighteen miles by twelve, the caldera was formed 760,000 years ago when a massive eruption spread ash as far away as Nebraska. Vulcanism has continued with the creation of Mammoth Mountain around 50,000 years ago, the Mono Craters and, most recently, **Paoha Island** in Mono Lake only 300 years back.

In the last couple of decades, scientists have been alerted to ongoing activity manifest in swarms of earthquakes and measurable ground swelling which normally precedes eruptions. One cluster of earthquakes in 1989 is thought to have triggered the release of carbon dioxide from an underground gas reservoir, and since 1994 this gas seeping up through the soil has killed 120 acres of trees near Horseshoe Lake.

An eruption is not likely in the near future, but the United States Geological Survey continues to monitor the region extensively for ground temperature changes, land deformation, and frequency and amplitude of quakes. For more, visit the relevant section of the USGS website Ⓦlvo.wr.usgs.gov.

and its neighbors, Grant, Silver, and Gull lakes. Reached by way of the sixteen-mile **June Lake Loop** road, which branches off US-395 fifteen miles north of the Mammoth exit, this region of high-altitude lakes is one of the most striking in these parts, and offers Mammoth's attractions on a more manageable scale.

The small township of **June Lake**, two miles off US-395, is the most alpine-looking of any Sierra community and a place where imitation Swiss chalets don't look entirely out of place. There's a reasonable range of roofed accommodation here (Ⓦwww.junelake.com), but the region is primarily a place for **camping**, easily done at one of several $14 Forest Service campgrounds scattered beside the various lakes, including the relatively busy *June Lake* and *Oh! Ridge* locations (both reservable on ☎1-877/444-6777), and the more serene first-come-first-served *Grant Lake*, nine miles further on, where there is boat and fishing tackle rental.

When the June Lake Loop road hits US-395 at its northern end, turn left for Lee Vining or right to directly access Mono Lake's tufa formations at South Tufa.

Mono Lake and around

North of Mammoth, the landscapes become more open. The Sierra still provides the western backdrop but as the White Mountains drop away to the south you're entering the fringes of the Great Basin which stretches away across

Nevada towards Utah. Mostly sagebrush, semi–desert terrain, it is inhospitable territory but a fascinating area centered on the freakish **Mono Lake**. The few people who live hereabouts cluster in the lakeside **Lee Vining** or the peaceful town of **Bridgeport**, but a century ago the place to be was **Bodie**, now a fascinating ghost town.

Mono Lake

The blue expanse of **MONO LAKE** sits in the middle of a volcanic desert tableland, its sixty square miles reflecting the statuesque, snowcapped mass of the eastern Sierra Nevada. At over a million years old, it's an ancient lake with two large volcanic islands – the light-colored **Paoha** and the black **Negit** – surrounded by salty, alkaline water. It resembles nothing more than a science-fiction landscape, with great towers and spires formed by mineral deposits ringing the shores; hot springs surround the lake, and all around the basin are signs of lava flows and volcanic activity, especially in the cones of the Mono Craters, just to the south.

The lake's most distinctive feature, the strange, sandcastle-like **tufa** formations, were increasingly exposed from the early 1940s to the mid-1990s as the City of Los Angeles drained away the waters that flow into the lake (see box, p.408). The towers of tufa were formed underwater, where calcium-bearing freshwater springs well up through the carbonate-rich lake water; the calcium and carbonate combine and sink to the bottom as limestone, slowly growing into the weird formations you can see today. Before striking out for a close look at the lake and its tufa, call in at the excellent **Mono Basin Scenic Area Visitor Center**, a mile north of Lee Vining beside US-395 (daily May–Oct 9am–4.30pm; Nov–April generally weekends only 9am–4pm; ☎760/873-2408, ⓦwww.r5.fs.fed.us/inyo). Exhibits and a good short film detail the lake's geology, and rangers give talks on various aspects of its ecology; the center organizes ninety-minute **guided walks** (July to early Sept daily 10am, 1pm & 6pm) around the tufa formations.

The Mono Lake Committee (see p.409) runs regular hour-long **canoe trips** (mid-June–early Sept Sat & Sun 8am, 9.30am & 11am; $17; reservations recommended ☎760/647-6595), which give a closer look at what the lake has to offer. Otherwise, you can go by kayak with Mammoth Lakes–based Caldera Kayaks (☎760/934-1691, ⓦwww.calderakayak.com), who run natural-history tours on Mono Lake ($65) and rent kayaks for $40 a day (doubles $50). Both trips require reservations as far in advance as you can manage.

Under your own steam, visit **South Tufa**, five miles east of US-395 via Hwy-120 ($3; valid one week), the single best place to look at the tufa spires. Boardwalks and trails lead around and among these twenty-foot-high limestone cathedrals and along the lakeshore where photo ops turn up around every corner. About a mile to the east lies **Navy Beach** (free), where there are more (though less spectacular) spires, and the opportunity to float in water at least twice as buoyant as (and a thousand times more alkaline than) sea water. Adjacent to the south shore of the lake stands **Panum Crater**, a 700-year-old volcano riddled with deep fissures and fifty-foot towers of lava, visited on **Plug Trail** and **Rim Trail**, two short and fairly easy trails. This is the most recent of the **Mono Craters**, a series of volcanic cones that stretch twelve miles south from here towards Crowley Lake. This constitutes the youngest mountain range in North America, entirely formed over the last forty thousand years.

On the north shore of the lake, three miles along US-395, a side road leads to **Mono County Park**, where a guided boardwalk trail leads down to the lakefront and the best examples of mushroom-shaped tufa towers. A further five miles along this (mostly washboard gravel) side road is the trailhead for the **Black Point Fissures**, the result of a massive underwater eruption of molten lava some thirteen thousand years ago. As the lava cooled and contracted, cracks and fissures formed on the top, some only a few feet wide but as much as fifty feet deep. You can explore their depths, but pick up a directions sheet from the Visitor Center and be prepared for hot, dry, and sandy conditions.

A thirsty city and the battle for Mono Lake

Mono Lake is one of the oldest on the continent and has survived several ice ages and all the volcanic activity that the area can throw at it, but the lake's biggest threat has been the City of Los Angeles, which owns the riparian rights to Mono Lake's catchment.

From 1892 to 1904, the fledgling city of Los Angeles experienced a twelve-year drought and started looking to the Owens River as a reliable source of water that could be easily channeled to the city. Under the auspices of the Los Angeles Department of Water and Power, the city bought up almost the entire Owens Valley, then diverted the river and its tributaries into a 223-mile gravity-fed aqueduct to take this water to LA. Farms and orchards in the once-productive Owens Valley were rendered useless without water, and Owens Lake near Lone Pine was left to dry up entirely.

The aqueduct was completed in 1913 but the growing city demanded ever more water. Consequently, in 1941, LA diverted four of the five streams that fed Mono Lake through an eleven-mile tunnel into its Owens Valley Aqueduct. This was an engineering marvel, dug through the volcanically active Mono Craters, but it has been overshadowed by the legal battle surrounding the depletion of the lake itself, long one of the biggest **environmental controversies** raging in California.

Over the next fifty years, the **water level** in Mono Lake dropped over forty feet, a disaster not only because of the lake's unique beauty, but also because Mono Lake is the primary nesting ground for **California gulls** and a critical resting point for hundreds of thousands of migratory eared **grebes** and **phalaropes**. The lake was down to roughly half its natural size, and as the levels dropped, the islands in the middle of the lake where the gulls lay their eggs became peninsulas, and the colonies fell prey to coyotes and other mainland predators. Also, as less fresh water reached the lake, the landlocked water became increasingly saline, threatening the unique local ecosystem. About all that will thrive in the harsh conditions are brine shrimp and alkali flies, both essential food sources for the birdlife. Humans are not immune to the harmful effects – winds blowing across the salt pans left behind by the receding lake create alkaline clouds containing selenium and arsenic, both contributors to lung disease.

Seemingly oblivious to the plight of the lake, the City of Los Angeles built a second aqueduct in 1970 and the water level dropped even faster, sometimes falling eighteen inches in a single year. Prompted by scientific reports of an impending ecological disaster, a small group of activists set up the **Mono Lake Committee** (W www .monolake.org) in 1978, fighting for the preservation of this unique ecosystem partly through publicity campaigns – "Save Mono Lake" bumper stickers were once de rigueur for concerned citizens – and partly through the courts. Though the California Supreme Court declared in 1983 that Mono Lake must be saved, it wasn't until 1994 that emergency action was taken. A target water height of 6377ft above sea level (later raised to 6392ft) was grudgingly agreed to make Negit Island once again safe for nesting birds. Streams dry for decades are now flowing again, and warm springs formerly located by lakeside interpretive trails are now submerged. The target level – 18 feet higher than its recorded minimum, but still 25 feet below its pre-diversion level – won't be reached at least until 2014 when the agreement is up for renegotiation, something that concentrates the ongoing efforts of the Mono Lake Committee.

Lee Vining

Within easy walking distance of Mono Lake, the appealing small town of **LEE VINING** offers the usual range of visitor services along either side of US-395, but not a great deal more. The town's **Mono Lake Committee Information Center** (daily: July & Aug 9am–10pm; rest of year 9am–5pm; ☎760/647-6595, ⓦ www.leevining.com) is partly the showcase for the committee's battle for Mono Lake, featuring an excellent twenty-minute video presentation, but also has helpful staff and many books on the Eastern Sierra. There's even a tasteful gift shop and **Internet access**.

There are several **motels** all close together along US-395 including the well-presented *Murphey's* (☎760/647-6316 or 1-800/334-6316, ⓦwww .murpheysyosemite.com;), with a/c, satellite TV, and some units with kitchens, and the slightly cheaper but inferior *El Mono Motel* (☎760/647-6310; ❸). The *Mono Vista RV Park* (☎760/647-6401) caters to RVs ($25–28) and tents ($15), and has showers for non-guests ($2.25 for 5min; daily 9am–6pm); and there are a number of $7 Forest Service **campgrounds** along Lee Vining Creek off Tioga Pass Road, Hwy-120.

The best **dining** around these parts is at *Whoa Nellie Deli* (☎760/647-1088) in the unlikely setting of the Mobil gas station at the junction of US-395 and Hwy-120. There's always a lively atmosphere, and they dish up great tortilla soup, jambalaya ($9), fish tacos ($9), burgers and steaks, along with espresso coffees, microbrews, and margaritas. Sit in or out on the lawn where there is sometimes live music in summer. There's also the diner-style *Nicely's Restaurant* (☎760/647-6477) on US-395, a great Fifties vinyl palace that opens at 6am; and the dinner-only *Mono Inn Restaurant* (☎760/647-6581; closed Tues and Nov–April; ⓦ www.monoinn.com), almost five miles north along US-395, owned by Ansel Adams' granddaughter, which serves up lovingly prepared meals on the patio or inside, both with a superb lake view. Expect the likes of roasted artichoke and porcini mushroom risotto ($10) followed by salmon with lemon arugula pesto ($19).

Bodie Ghost Town

In the 1880s, the gold-mining town of **BODIE**, eighteen miles north of Lee Vining then thirteen miles (three of them dirt) east of US-395, boasted three breweries, some sixty saloons and dance halls, and a population of nearly ten thousand. It also had a well-earned reputation as the raunchiest and most law-less mining camp in the West. Contemporary accounts describe a town that ended each day with a shootout on Main Street, while the firehouse bell, rung once for every year of a murdered man's life, seemed never to stop sounding. The town boomed for just four years, starting in 1877, when a fairly poor existing mine collapsed, exposing an enormously rich vein. Within four years this was the second largest town in the state after San Francisco, even support-ing its own Chinatown. By 1885, gold and silver currently valued at around $1.2 billion had been extracted, but a drop in the gold price made mining largely unprofitable. The town dwindled and then was virtually destroyed by

Yosemite-bound?

Lee Vining is over two hours' drive from Yosemite Valley but makes an affordable base for exploring the eastern reaches of **Yosemite National Park**, particularly the Tuolumne Meadows area, around twenty miles distant.

two disastrous fires, the last in 1932. The school finally closed in 1942, but a few hardly souls stuck it out until the early 1960s when the site was taken over by the State of California.

What remains has been turned into the **Bodie State Historic Park** (daily: June to mid-Sept 8am–7pm; March–May & mid-Sept to Oct 8am–5pm; Nov–Feb 8am–4pm; $3; ☎760/647-6445, ⓦwww.bodie.com), where lack of theme-park tampering gives the place an authentically eerie atmosphere absent from other US ghost towns. Bodie is almost 8400 feet above sea level and, although the park is open throughout the year, snow often prevents vehicular access between December and April; call for road conditions. If you can get in during that time, bundle up: Bodie is often cited on the national weather report as having the lowest temperature in the US. Whenever you go, remember to bring all you need: there are no services at the site.

A good self-guided tour booklet ($1) leads you around many of the 150-odd wooden buildings – about six percent of the original town – surviving in a state of arrested decay around the intact town center. Some buildings have been re-roofed and others supported in some way, but it is by and large a faithful preservation: even the dirty dishes are much as they were in the 1940s, little damaged by sixty years of weathering. The **Miner's Union Building** on Main Street was the center of the town's social life; founded in 1877, the union was the first in California, organized by workers at the Standard and Midnight mines. The building now houses a small **museum** (daily: June–Aug 9am–6pm; May & Sept 9am–5pm; free), which paints a graphic picture of mining life. Various **tours** depart from here in the summer, particularly on weekends, though schedules are flexible and you should call ahead if you have specific interests.

The history talk is free, but there's also a fifty-minute tour of the **Standard Consolidated Stamp Mill** (generally June–Aug daily 11am & 2pm; $5), otherwise off limits, and one along a ridge ($5) which offers some of the best views of Bodie. Other highlights of the town include the **Methodist church** with its intact pipe organ, the **general store** with its beautiful pressed-steel ceiling, the **saloon**, and the **cemetery** on the hill where lie the remains of Bill Bodey, after whom the town was (sort of) named.

Bridgeport

Seven miles north of the Bodie road junction along US-395 is tiny **BRIDGE-PORT**, an isolated village in the middle of a mountain-girt plain that provided the new start in life for fugitive Robert Mitchum in the film noir masterpiece *Out of the Past*. The gas station he owned in the film is long gone, though the place is otherwise little changed; a pretty high-country ranching community typically full of **fishermen** through the summer. If you want to join their ranks, head to Ken's Sporting Goods, 258 Main St (☎760/9332-7707), for local information and all the tackle you could desire. Otherwise it is only worth stopping here to stroll Bridgeport's small and time-warped Main Street past the dainty white 1880 **County Courthouse**, and to visit the small local history **museum** (late May–Sept daily 10am–4pm; $1.50), behind the town park in a restored old schoolhouse.

Consider sticking around the region long enough to enjoy the local hot springs, one of the most popular ways to wind down after a day wrestling trout. The handiest are **Travertine Hot Springs**: follow US-395 half a mile south of town, turn left into Jack Sawyer Road then fork left at the first junction and keep right for just over a mile. Many prefer the streamside setting of the lovely **Buckeye Hot Springs**, reached by following US-395 four miles north of Bridgeport, turning left for *Buckeye Campground* and continuing 4.6 miles to where a rough track leads from a dirt parking area to three small pools.

With the lure of the springs, you may want to stay overnight, and **accommodation** ranges from a beautifully furnished B&B, *The Cain House*, 340 Main St (℡760/932-7040 or 1-800/433-2246, ⓦwww.cainhouse.com; closed Nov–May; ❺), through decent motels such as the *Silver Maple Inn*, 310 Main St (℡760/932-7383, ⓦwww.silvermapleinn.com; closed Nov–May; ❹), to the decidedly decrepit *Victoria House* across the street (℡760/932-7020; closed Nov–May; ❶), a building which, like several in Bridgeport, is said to have been transported here from Bodie. The *Best Western Ruby Inn*, 333 Main St (℡760/932-7241; ❻), is one of the only lodgings that stays open year round.

For **eating**, there are good breakfasts and lunches at *Hays Street Café*, 21 Hays St, on the southern approach to town; decent espresso at *The Pony Expresso Coffee Co.*, 157 Main St (℡760/932-7798); reasonably priced grills, sandwiches, and specialty pizzas at *Rhino's Bar & Grill*, 226 Main St (℡760/932-7345); and top-rated fine dining at *1881*, 362 Main St (℡760/932-1918; June–Oct daily, rest of year Thurs–Sun), where local trout ($23) might be followed by vanilla crème brûlée ($6). A drive six miles south along US-395 is rewarded by reliably excellent dining at *Virginia Creek Settlement* (℡760/932-7780, ⓦwww.VirginiaCrkSettlement.com; closed Mon), renowned in the region for its fresh and tasty steaks (from $18), pasta dishes ($10–12), and pizzas (from $10) – particularly the excellent gorgonzola.

From Bridgeport, US-395 continues north into Nevada, through the capital Carson City and the gambling city of Reno, both described fully in Chapter Nine.

Travel details

Neither Greyhound buses nor Amtrak trains run any services within this region. The only long-distance bus services are the CREST bus along the Owens Valley (see p.369) and the summer-only YARTS service from Mammoth Lakes to Yosemite (see p.398).

Buses

Bishop to: Big Pine (3 weekly; 15min); Bridgeport (3 weekly; 2hr); Independence (3 weekly; 45min); Lee Vining (3 weekly; 1hr 25min); Lone Pine (3 weekly; 1hr 10min); Mammoth Lakes (3 weekly; 50min); Reno (3 weekly; 4hr 45min); Ridgecrest (3 weekly; 2hr 30min).

Mammoth Lakes to: Bishop (3 weekly; 50min); Lee Vining (3–5 weekly; 30min); Tuolumne Meadows (summer 2–7 weekly; 1hr); Yosemite Valley (summer 2–7 weekly; 3hr).

Reno to: Bishop (3 weekly; 4hr 45min); Bridgeport (3 weekly; 2hr 50min); Lee Vining (3 weekly; 3hr 20min); Mammoth Lakes (3 weekly; 4hr).

Ridgecrest to: Big Pine (3 weekly; 2hr); Bishop (3 weekly; 2hr 20min); Independence (3 weekly; 1hr 35min); Lone Pine (3 weekly; 1hr 20min).

The San Joaquin Valley, Yosemite, and the Western Sierra

Highlights

✳ **Basque cuisine** Sample one of Bakersfield's Basque restaurants, notably the *Noriega Hotel*, where groaning dishes and jugs of wine are served at long, communal tables. **See p.421**

✳ **Kern River** Some of California's finest and most accessible whitewater rafting is available on this river, which emanates from the lofty slopes of Mount Whitney. **See p.423**

✳ **A&W Root Beer Drive-In** If you are passing through Modesto, be sure to stop at this classic 1950s diner known for its roller-skating waitresses. **See p.433**

✳ **Giant Forest** The densest collection of the world's largest trees, the mighty sequoias, can be found in this section of Sequoia National Park, accessible by a myriad of trails. **See p.443**

✳ **Ahwahnee Hotel** Stay at Yosemite's finest lodging, tastefully appointed with Native American motifs, or – for a little less money – come for a meal in the fabulous baronial dining room. **See p.465**

✳ **Hike Half Dome** Follow the wonderful Mist Trail to the summit of Yosemite's most famous peak, which forms the sheerest cliff in North America. **See p.471**

△ A&W Root Beer Drive-in, Modesto

6

The San Joaquin Valley, Yosemite, and the Western Sierra

The vast interior of California – stretching three hundred miles from the edges of the Mojave Desert in the south right up to the Gold Country and Northern California – comprises the wide floor of the agricultural **San Joaquin Valley**, flanked on the east by the massive Sierra Nevada mountains. It's a region that contains unparalleled beauty, yet the ninety percent of Californians who live on the coast are barely aware of the area, encountering it only while driving between LA and San Francisco on the admittedly tedious I-5, and consider it the height of hicksville.

The San Joaquin Valley is radically different from anywhere else in the state. During the 1940s, this arid land was made super-fertile by a massive program of aqueduct building, using water flowing from the mountains to irrigate the area. The valley, as flat as a pancake, now almost totally comprises farmland, periodically enlivened by scattered cities that offer a taste of ordinary Californian life away from the glitz of LA and San Francisco. More than anywhere else in the state, the abundance of low-paying agricultural jobs has encouraged decades of immigration from south of the border, and there are now towns in the San Joaquin Valley where Spanish is the first language and **taquerias** outnumber burger joints ten to one. Fertile land and cheap labor has brought relative wealth to large numbers of San Joaquin Valley residents who have responded by becoming increasingly mobile. This, and town planning, which dictates that everyone must drive everywhere, has led to a dense photochemical haze – trapped by mountains on both flanks – that is so thick the pristine peaks once visible throughout the year are now seldom seen.

If coastal Californians pass through the San Joaquin Valley, it is to reach the **national parks** that cover the foothills and upper reaches of the Sierra Nevada. From the valley, a gentle ascent through rolling, grassy foothills takes you into dense forests of huge pine and fir trees, interspersed with tranquil lakes and cut by deep rocky canyons. The most impressive sections are protected within three national parks. **Sequoia** is home to the last few stands of huge prehistoric trees, giant sequoias that form the centerpiece of a rich natural landscape. **Kings Canyon** shares a common border with Sequoia – together they make up one huge park – and presents a similar, slightly wilder array of Sierra wonders. **Yosemite**, with its towering walls of silvery granite artfully sculpted by Ice Age glaciers, is the most famous of the parks and one of the absolute must-sees in California. While only a few narrow, twisting roads penetrate the hundred miles of wilderness in between these three parks, the entire region is crisscrossed by hiking trails leading up into the pristine alpine backcountry of the **Sierra Nevada**, which contains the glistening summits of some of the highest mountains in the country.

Getting around

Drivers who aren't particularly interested in exploring the wilds can simply barrel through on I-5, an arrow-straight interstate through the western edge of the San Joaquin Valley that's the quickest route between LA and San Francisco. Four daily **trains** and frequent Greyhound **buses** run through the valley, stopping at the larger cities and towns along Hwy-99 – Merced being the most useful with its bus connections to Yosemite. Otherwise, getting to the mountains is all but impossible without your own vehicle, though with a bit of advance planning, you might be able to join one of the many camping trips organized by the Sierra Club, the California-based environmentalist group (see p.69).

The San Joaquin Valley

The **SAN JOAQUIN VALLEY** grows more fruit and vegetables than any other agricultural region of its size in the world – a fact that touches the lives, in one way or another, of every one of its inhabitants. The area is much more conservative and Midwestern in feel than the rest of California, but even if the nightlife begins and ends with the local ice cream parlor, it can all be refreshingly small-scale and enjoyable after visiting the big coastal cities. Admittedly, none of the towns have the energy to detain you long, and, between the settlements, the drab hundred-mile vistas of almond groves and vineyards can be sheer torture. The weather, too, can be a challenge – summers in the San Joaquin are frequently scorching and winters bring the cold and thick Tule fog, so aim to visit in spring or fall, particularly March when the fruit trees are in full bloom.

Bakersfield, the first town you come to across the rocky peaks north of Los Angeles, is hardly the most prepossessing destination, but in recent years its **country music** scene has burgeoned into the best in the state. And, surprisingly enough, there are few better places on this side of the Atlantic to sample **Basque cuisine**. Bakersfield also offers a museum recording the beginnings of the local population, and the chance to sample some of the state's finest **whitewater rafting** on the nearby Kern River. Further on lies **Visalia**, a likeable community, and the well-restored turn-of-the-century town of **Hanford**.

In many ways the region's linchpin, **Fresno** is the closest thing to a bustling urban center the valley has. Though economically thriving, it's frequently cited as one of the least desirable places to live in the US, and on arrival it's easy to see why. Its redeeming features, such as they are, take a bit of time to discover, though you shouldn't pass up the opportunity to visit the bizarre labyrinth of **Forestiere Underground Gardens**.

Beyond Fresno, in the northern reaches of the valley, lie sedate **Merced** and slightly more boisterous **Modesto**, the inspiration for George Lucas's movie *American Graffiti*. At the top end of the valley, **Stockton** is scenically improved by the delta that connects the city to the sea, but is otherwise a place of few pleasures, though you may pass through on your way from San Francisco to the Gold Country or the national parks.

Bakersfield and around

BAKERSFIELD's flat and featureless look, surrounded by oil derricks, does nothing to suggest that this is one of the nation's liveliest country music communities, with a batch of venues where locally and nationally rated musicians jam. It also has the country's largest community of Basque descent, making it *the* place to taste Basque cuisine, at its best in one of the specialist restaurants run by descendants of sheepherders who migrated to the San Joaquin Valley in the early twentieth century. Speed freaks will find entertainment in Bakersfield's assorted motorsports, all a far cry from the town's beginnings in 1851 when Colonel Thomas Baker made his field available as a stagecoach rest stop.

Racecars, country music, and Basque cuisine aside, there's not much reason to visit, though the moribund downtown area has seen something of a renaissance, with half a dozen new bars opening up, and on the outskirts of town a progressive small **zoo** warrants a visit. If the hills are calling out, it's only an hour's drive east to **Lake Isabella**, a reservoir in the Sierra foothills that's well geared to family camping and watersports. Without your own equipment, you're better off making for **Kernville**, a few miles up the Kern River, which provides the venue for a full range of springtime **whitewater rafting**.

Arrival, information, and accommodation

Bakersfield is an important public transportation hub and the downtown area – half a dozen blocks each way from the junction of 19th and J streets – is home to both the **Amtrak station**, 601 Truxton Ave, the southern terminus of Amtrak's San Joaquin route from San Francisco (connections to LA via Thruway bus), and the **bus station**, 1820 18th St (⊕661/327-5617). Traveling by Greyhound you may need to change routes here – although overnight stops are rarely necessary. The best source of information is the **Kern County Board of Trade**, 2101 Oak St (Mon–Fri 8am–5pm; ⊕661/861-2367 or 1-800/500-5376, ⊕www.visitkern.com), which has free **Internet access** on a single computer. The **Bakersfield Chamber of Commerce**, 1725 Eye St (Mon 9am–5pm, Tues–Fri 8am–5pm; ⊕661/327-4421), is slightly less useful but handier to downtown.

Bakersfield is dotted with clusters of cheap **motels**, though there is little else. Two handily placed a short stagger from *Buck Owens' Crystal Palace* are the *EZ-8*, 2604 Buck Owens Blvd (⊕661/322-1901, ⊕www.ez8motels .com; ❷), and the adjacent, and considerably smarter *La Quinta*, 3232 Riverside Drive (⊕661/325-7400 or 1-866/725-1661; ❹); both have pools. A couple of miles north around the Olive Drive exit, off Hwy-99, you get fractionally better value for money at the pool-equipped *Motel 6*, 5241 Olive Tree Court (⊕661/392-9700; ❷). The best bet in the center of town is the *Downtowner Inn*, 1301 Chester Ave (⊕661/327-7122, ⊕327-8350; ❷). **Campers** should head fifteen miles east to the shores of Lake Ming at the *Kern River County Park* (mid-March to mid-Oct $18 per vehicle; mid-Oct to mid-March $10 per vehicle), where there are grassy and reasonably shaded sites but no hook-ups.

The Town

Bakersfield owes its existence to the fertile soil around the Kern River – once the longest river in the state but now dammed to form Lake Isabella – and to the discovery of local oil and gas deposits. The **Kern County Museum**, a mile north of downtown at 3801 Chester Ave (Mon–Sat 10am–5pm, Sun noon–5pm, last admission 3pm; $8; ⊕www.kcmuseum.org), documents the town's petrochemical roots through Black Gold: The Oil Experience, a modern science, technology, and history exhibit complete with 1922 "nodding donkey" pump, a moderately enlightening 18-minute movie, and an unconvincing mock-up "undersea journey" in a diving bell. Leave a little time to browse the fifty-plus (mostly) restored rail wagons and assorted buildings, many of them dating from the late nineteenth or early twentieth century; and those needing to get kids out of the heat will want to visit the hands-on science exhibits in the site's **Lori Brock Children's Discovery Center**.

For something a little more highbrow, visit the **Bakersfield Museum of Art**, 1930 R St (Tues–Fri 10am–4pm, Sat & Sun noon–4pm; $5; ⊕www .bmoa.org), which usually has interesting touring exhibits, along with its own collection, which includes works by Georgia O'Keeffe and Diego Rivera.

Wildlife fans will have to stray a little further out, where the greatest interest is at the **California Living Museum (CALM)**, 10500 Alfred Harrell Way (Tues–Sun 9am–5pm; $4.50; ⊕www.calmzoo.org), some twelve miles east of town off the road to Kernville. It is effectively a small zoo, but one focusing solely on Californian native species and only those animals that have been injured and cannot be returned to the wild. Stroll around the landscaped grounds past the golden and bald eagles, pause to admire the black bears and bobcats, then repair to the reptile house with its array of snakes and lizards. The animals tend to hide from the heat of the day, so come early. A half an hour west of Bakersfield is the **Tule Elk Reserve State Park**, Morris Road (daily 8am–sunset; free), where around thirty of these beasts can be seen from a viewing platform, best at 3pm when they are fed nearby. Large herds used to roam hereabouts, but hunting and loss of habitat forced them to the brink of extinction early in the twentieth century; only projects like this and a major relocation to the Owens Valley (see p.383) have saved them. To get there, follow Stockdale Highway west for twenty miles, and then just after crossing I-5, follow the signs a mile or so south on Morris Road.

Country music in Bakersfield

The main reason to dally for more than a few hours in Bakersfield is to hear **country music** – on any weekend the town's numerous honky-tonks reverberate to the sounds of some of the best country musicians in the US, many of them local residents.

The roots of Bakersfield's country music scene are with the Dust Bowl Okies who arrived in the San Joaquin Valley during the Depression, bringing their hillbilly instruments and campfire songs with them. This rustic entertainment quickly broadened into more contemporary styles, developed in the bars and clubs that began to appear in the town, where future legends such as Merle Haggard and Buck Owens (long-time owner of country radio stations KUZZ 107.9 FM and the more traditional KCWR 107.1 FM) cut their teeth. A failed attempt to turn Bakersfield into "Nashville West" during the 1960s by bringing the major country music record labels here from their traditional base has left the town eager to promote the distinctive "**Bakersfield Sound**": a far less slick and commercial affair than its Tennessee counterpart. You can gain an inkling of the Bakersfield Sound from the 1988 hit *Streets of Bakersfield*, a duet by Buck Owens and Dwight Yoakam, but you really need to get out and listen to some live music.

Venues

To find out **what's on**, read the Friday Entertainment section of the *Bakersfield Californian* (ⓦwww.bakersfield.com), check the flyers at the tourist offices mentioned above, or phone one of the venues we've listed. Fridays and Saturdays are the liveliest nights, although there's often something to enjoy during the week, even if it's only the free **country dancing lessons** offered several nights a week at *Rockin' Rodeo* (see below). There's seldom a cover charge for someone spinning platters, and only a small one for live sets (perhaps $5), usually entailing one band playing for four or five hours from around 8pm and taking a fifteen-minute break every hour. Stetson hats and Nudie shirts are the sartorial order of the day, and audiences span generations.

Most venues are hotel lounges or restaurant backrooms, though there are a couple which don't fit the mold: one not to be missed is *Trouts*, 805 N Chester Ave (ⓣ661/399-6700), a country music bar a couple of miles north of downtown that's been in business for over forty years. Closer to town, the ersatz-Western *Buck Owens' Crystal Palace*, 2800 Buck Owens Blvd (ⓣ661/328-7560, ⓦwww.buckowens.com), is very much the showpiece for the master's ever-expanding empire: a cabaret-style set-up (entry $6 for the cheap seats, up to $12 for the front row) with burgers and grills available while local and touring bands perform on Wednesday and Thursday (generally free); Tuesday is karaoke night. Buck (now into his seventies) does a turn on Friday and Saturday nights at 7.30pm, playing numbers from his own back catalogue, classic country tunes, and beyond. Write your request on a napkin and he may play it. If you can't make Buck's set, it is broadcast live on KCWR 107.1 FM (and 550 AM). Cases around the walls make up a small **museum** (daily except Fri 11am–4pm and visible during any show; free) of knickknacks Buck has picked up over the years – promo photos, Buck Rogers bolo tie clasps, platinum records, red-white-and-blue guitars, and a glittering display of rhinestone jackets. The other hot spot to add to your itinerary is the younger and more clubby *Rockin' Rodeo*, 3745 Rosedale Hwy (ⓣ661/323-6617), with a New Country/Rock DJ every night and a Texas-style oval dancefloor. Thursday is karaoke night and Friday sees live bands.

In some circles Bakersfield is synonymous with **motorsport**, and for an oil town that's probably just as it should be. Speed freaks come for all manner of car racing and even drag boat racing on the Kern River's Lake Ming some fifteen miles east of town. There's drag racing at the Famoso Raceway (Ⓦwww.famosoraceway.com), twenty miles north of town, NASCAR at Mesa Marin Raceway (mid-March–Oct; Ⓦwww.mesamarin.com), ten miles east of town on Hwy-178, and all manner of racing around a highbanked oval at the Bakersfield Speedway (Ⓦwww.bakersfieldspeedway.com), eight miles north. Tickets for all can usually be bought at the gate.

Eating, drinking, and nightlife

Don't pass Bakersfield without **eating** Basque food. The most authentic experience is at the century-old *Noriega Hotel*, 525 Summer St (Ⓣ661/322-8419), where louvered shutters and ceiling fans cool diners communally sat at long tables and served an all-you-can-eat set menu of soup, salad, beans, pasta, a meat dish, and cheese to finish, along with jug wine to wash it all down. There are three sittings ($10 breakfast from 7–9am, $11 lunch at noon sharp, and $17 dinner at 7pm), and reservations are recommended for dinner which will include the Basque specialty of pickled tongue. There's similar fare at *Pyrenees*, 601 Sumner St (Ⓣ661/323-0053), where dining hours are more flexible, and at *Wool Growers*, 620 E 19th St (Ⓣ661/327-9584), where there's an *à la carte* menu.

If Basque doesn't appeal, the diner-style *24th Street Café*, 1415 24th St, does top-rate breakfasts; *Joseph's*, hidden back off the road at 3013 F St (Ⓣ661/322-7710), serves a huge, very impressive calzone to a band of dedicated regulars; while *The Garden Spot*, 3320 Truxton Ave (closed Sat), makes healthy eating a pleasure with an all-you-can-eat salad-bar buffet for around $8. To stay in tune with Bakersfield's country-music persona, eat at *Zingo's*, 3201 Buck Owens Blvd, a 24-hr truck stop whose frilly-aproned waitresses deliver plates of diner staples; or try the extensive Sunday brunch at the *Buck Owens' Crystal Palace* (9.30am–2pm; $18).

Nightlife now extends beyond slide-guitar and torch songs with a number of places downtown offering local rock bands several nights a week, usually with no cover charge. Stroll 19th Street and see what turns up, but you'll probably end up at *Guthrie's Alley Cat*, 1525 Wall St, tucked down an alley parallel to 18th and 19th streets.

Lake Isabella, Kernville, and the Kern River

After a night spent in Bakersfield's honky-tonks, you might like to clear your head by driving forty-five miles east to the mile-wide **LAKE ISABELLA**, typically alive with windsurfers, jet skiers, and anglers. Mountain biking and rock climbing are also popular activities here, and the place is heaving in the summer. Information on activities and rental outlets is available from the lakeside **visitor center** (mid-May to Oct daily 8am–5pm; Nov to mid-May Mon–Fri 8am–4.30pm; Ⓣ760/379-5646), half a mile north of Hwy-178 along Hwy-155. Developed, though barely shaded, **campsites** ring the dry, sage-brush lakeside, almost all costing $17 a pitch; you can reserve at least a week in advance with ReserveUSA (Ⓣ1-877/444-6777, Ⓦwww.reserveusa.com), but first-come-first-served sites are typically available. If the frenetic lake activity doesn't suit, backtrack to the riverside *Hobo* campground ($15) on Old Fern Canyon Road, parallel to Hwy-178.

Lake Isabella is fed by the **KERN RIVER**, which churns down from the slopes of Mount Whitney and spills into the lake at the small, appealing town of **KERNVILLE** on its northern shore. It is a peaceful retiree-dominated place, but come on a summer weekend, or anytime in July and August, and it is full of adrenaline junkies blasting mountain bikes along the local trails or negotiating the rapids in all manner of aquatic paraphernalia. Most people come to ride the Kern, which ranks as one of the steepest "navigable" rivers in the United States, dropping over 12,000ft in 150 miles, and producing some truly exhilarating **whitewater** opportunities, especially along a forty-mile section around Kernville. The tougher stuff is generally left to the experts, but during the season, which usually runs from May until early August (longer if there has been a heavy winter), commercial rafting operators vie for custom (see box, opposite). If you've got time to kill while friends raft, delve into the Native, gold mining, and lumbering history in the **Kern Valley Museum**, 49 Big Blue Rd (Thurs–Sun 10am–4pm; free), or take a look at their film room of movies shot in the area, mostly Westerns: John Wayne features prominently.

Kernville is big enough to have a bank, ATM, post office, and supermarket, but only campers will find ultra-cheap **accommodation**. Central motels start at around $75, the best value being *The Kernville Inn*, 11042 Kernville Rd (℡760/376-2206 or 1-877/393-7900; rooms ❹, with kitchen ❺), right in the center and with a pool and comfortable rooms, some with kitchens. Up the scale, there's the *Kern River Inn B&B*, 119 Kern River Drive (℡760/376-6750 or 1-800/986-4382, ⓦwww.kernriverinn.com; ❻), and the luxurious *Whispering Pines Lodge*, 13745 Sierra Way (℡760/376-3733 or 1-877/241-4100, ⓦwww.kernvalley.com/inns; ❼), a mile north of town, with a nice pool, balconies overlooking the river, and a delicious breakfast served on the terrace. *Falling Waters River Resort*, three miles north of town at 15729 Sierra Way (℡760/376-2242 or 1-888/376-2242, ⓦwww.chuckrichards.com; ❸, cottages ❺), has decent budget motel rooms and plusher self-catering cottages marred by overenthusiastic decor. Tent **campers** can stay in the various RV parks around town, but are better off in the string of riverside campgrounds to the north (see p.424).

There are several **restaurants** around town, including the reliable and authentic *That's Italian*, 9 Big Blue Rd (℡760/376-6020; closed Mon & weekday lunches), by the central park; the espresso haven of the *Big Blue Bear* gift shop, opposite; and *El Jacalita,* 11301 Kernville Rd (℡760/376-8613), a good Mexican option. If you are prepared to drive fifteen miles north, you'll find great steak at *McNally's*, Sierra Way (℡760/376-2430).

For general information contact the central **Chamber of Commerce**, 11447 Kernville Rd (Mon–Sat 9am–noon & 2–4pm; ℡760/376-2629, ⓦwww.kernvillechamber.org); for details on the wooded country to the north call in at the **Kernville Ranger Station**, 105 Whitney Rd (mid-May–Oct daily 8am–5pm, Nov–mid–May Mon–Fri 8am–4.30pm; ℡760/376-3781, ⓦwww.fs.fed.us/r5/sequoia), next to the museum.

Sequoia National Forest

Wedged between Lake Isabella and the Sequoia National Park lies the **SEQUOIA NATIONAL FOREST**, a vast canopy of pine trees punctuated by massive, glacier-polished domes and gleaming granite spires. Much of it is untouched wilderness that's barely less stunning than the national parks to the north, and in recognition of this a large section of this was redesignated the **Giant Sequioa National Monument** (unrestricted access) as one of Bill Clinton's final gestures before leaving office. True to its name, it's packed with

Three main sections of the Kern River are regularly rafted: the **Lower Kern**, downstream of Lake Isabella (generally June–Aug); the **Upper Kern**, immediately upstream of Kernville (early May to June); and **The Forks**, fifteen miles upstream of Kernville (early May to June), which drops an impressive sixty feet per mile.

By far the most popular section of the Upper Kern, the site for the **Lickety-Split** rafting trip – one for families and first-timers, with some long, bouncy rapids. This one-hour excursion (including the bus ride to the put-in) costs around $24, and with over half a dozen operators running trips throughout the day, there is little need to book ahead. Other trips run less frequently, and you should reserve in advance, though you've got a better chance mid-week when crowds are thinner and prices a few dollars lower. The pick of these are the day-trips on the Upper Kern, which run close to the $125 mark ($145 at weekends), the two-day Lower Kern trip ($270, weekends $320), and the three-day backcountry trips on The Forks which range around $700–800. Wetsuits (essential early in the season and for the longer trips) are extra. Within this basic framework there are any number of permutations: check with Chuck Richards' Whitewater (℡760/376-4444 or 1-800/624-5950, ⓦwww.chuckrichards.com) or Whitewater Voyages (℡1-800/488-7238, ⓦwww .whitewatervoyages.com).

As you'd expect, kayaking is also big here, and Sierra South, 11300 Kernville Rd (℡760/376-3745 or 1-800/457-2082, ⓦwww.sierrasouth.com), supplement their rafting operation with one of Southern California's top **kayaking** schools, offering Eskimo rolling sessions, instruction at all levels, and guided multiday river trips, all generally costing around $150 a day. They also offer full-day beginner **rock-climbing** lessons ($110) on the nearby Kernville Slab, as do Mountain & River Adventures, 11113 Kernville Rd (℡760/376-6553 or 1-800/861-6553, ⓦwww .mtnriver.com), who stretch up to intermediate grades and have their own outdoor climbing wall three miles north along Sierra Way.

If you have the equipment for private rafting or kayaking expeditions, you'll still need to grab a free **permit** from any of the area's Forest Service offices.

---

giant sequoias (in 38 small groves), and, as the forest is far less visited than the national parks, it is perfect for those seeking total solitude; hiking trails run virtually everywhere. Camping only requires a free permit for your stove or fire, available from the ranger stations dotted around the perimeter of the forest and which also have details of the scores of drive-in campsites which stud the forest – some free, others up to $17 a pitch.

There's **no public transportation** through here; the roads are in good shape though, if subject to **snow closure** in winter (mid-Nov to mid-May).

Sierra Way and the Western Divide Highway

The best access is along Sierra Way from Lake Isabella, which passes through Kernville and follows the Upper Kern River past numerous basic camping sites (free) and half a dozen shaded, waterside campgrounds ($15, $17 at weekends; reserve for summer weekends on ℡1-877/444-6777) to Johnsondale Bridge, twenty miles north of Kernville. From the bridge, hikers can follow the **River Trail** upstream passing the numerous rapids of The Forks section of the Kern, great for spotting rafters and kayakers on weekend afternoons and even for camping at one of several free walk-in sites along the river; the first is about ten minutes' hike.

The road splits at Johnsondale Bridge. The eastern branch follows the Sherman Pass Road which cuts through the Golden Trout Wilderness to Hwy-395 and the Owens Valley, passing numerous free "dispersed" **campgrounds**: essentially just designated sites with no toilets or piped water. Sticking with Sierra Way, you turn west and start climbing to tiny Johnsondale – just a seasonal store and restaurant – where a trail access road cuts 23 miles north to the Jerkey Meadow trailhead. Along the Jerkey Meadow road there are great views of The Needles, and abundant dispersed **camping**, best at Camping Area 4, four miles along, where the stream has sculpted a lovely series of **bathing pools** and smooth rocks for sunning yourself. The *Lower Peppermint* campground ($14), a few miles further along, has toilets and water.

Continuing along Sierra Way it is seven miles to a road junction where you join the twisting and narrow **Western Divide Highway** (Hwy-190) which, after a couple of miles, passes the **Trail of a Hundred Giants** ($5 per vehicle), an easy, shaded interpretive trail around a stand of giant trees which may or may not be open depending on trail funding. Among more sequoias across the road is the *Redwood Meadow* campground (early April to mid-Nov; $15; book through NRRS ☎1-877/444-6777).

Further north, you catch glimpses of magnificent Sierra vistas as the road climbs above the 7000-foot mark, but for the best views it is worth pressing on five miles to the 7200-foot exfoliated scalp of **Dome Rock**, just half a mile off the highway, or **The Needles**, a further three miles on. This series of tall pinnacles – the Magician, the Wizard, and the Warlock, among others – present some of America's most demanding crack climbs, and can be visited on the moderate, undulating hiking and biking **Needles Lookout Trail** (5 miles round-trip; 2hrs), which starts three miles off the highway up a dirt road. The final switchback leads to a fire-lookout station (sometimes open to visitors during the June–Oct fire season), precariously perched atop the Magician with supreme views over the Kern Valley and across to Mount Whitney. Nearby **accommodation** extends to the *Quaking Aspen* campsite (early April to mid-Nov; $15), half a mile to the north of the Needles, the woodsy *Mountain Top B&B*, half a mile to the south (☎559/542-2639 or 1-888/867-4784, ⓦwww.mountaintopbnb.com; ❺), and the adjacent *Ponderosa Lodge* (☎559/542-2579; ❹), with pleasant motel rooms, a restaurant, bar, grocery store, and expensive gas. The Western Divide Highway then executes endless twists and turns forty miles down to the valley town of Porterville, where you can turn right for Sequoia and Kings Canyon national parks or continue straight to rejoin Hwy-99 and head north to Visalia.

Visalia

Leaving Bakersfield northbound towards Fresno on Hwy-99, the oil wells fade into full-blown agricultural territory. Only a couple of towns warrant much of your time, the first and largest being **VISALIA**, seventy miles north of Bakersfield and just east of Hwy-99 on Hwy-198. As the closest substantial town to the southern entrance of Sequoia National Park – less than an hour's drive away along Hwy-198 – Visalia makes a comfortable base for exploring the surrouding untramelled wilderness.

Owing to a large oak forest that offered both shade and timber for home-building, Visalia was the first place in the San Joaquin Valley to be settled. Although the forest is gone, large numbers of oaks and sycamores are still planted around the city and locals put an extraordinary amount of care into the upkeep of parks and gardens. In short, it's a pretty place, with a compact and leafy town center that invites evening strolls in the relative cool of the evening.

Central Visalia is best seen on foot: self-guided walking tours of the grand old houses in its older parts can be obtained free from the **Chamber of Commerce** (see below). Further out, **Mooney Grove Park**, three miles down South Mooney Boulevard (nominally $5 per vehicle, though often free midweek), contains a huge slice of a giant sequoia which marks the **Tulare County Museum** (mid-May–mid-Sept Thurs–Sun 10am–4pm; free), packed with good Yokuts basketry and a collection of buildings and agricultural equipment brought here from around the region.

Close to the park's south entrance, and visible from South Mooney Boulevard, you'll find a bronze replica of the *End of the Trail* statue, which was made for the 1915 Panama–Pacific International Exposition in San Francisco and was intended to mark the closing of the western frontier. It portrays the defeat of Native Americans at the hands of advancing white settlers and is intentionally gloomy. The statue became well known throughout the West, and still inspires a host of copies; the original was situated here for fifty years before being given to the National Cowboy & Western Heritage Museum near Oklahoma City.

To get a sense of what the Visalia area was like before the city's founding, drive seven miles east along Hwy-198 and half a mile north along Road 182 to the **Kaweah Oaks Preserve** (Ⓦwww.kaweahoaks.com), over three hundred acres of oak and sycamore woodland threaded by easy trails, though a little too close to the highway to be genuinely peaceful.

Practicalities

Greyhound buses, along with Orange Belt Stages from Hanford, arrive at the **bus station** downtown at 425 E Oak St (Ⓣ559/734-3507), ten short blocks from the **Chamber of Commerce**, 720 W Mineral King Ave (Mon–Fri 8.30am–5pm; Ⓣ559/734-5876 or 1-877/847-2542, Ⓦwww.visaliatourism .com). There's free **Internet access** at the Tulare County Library, 200 W Oak Ave (Ⓣ559/733-6954).

The most sumptuous **accommodation** is at the pool- and spa-equipped *Ben Maddox House B&B*, 601 N Encina St (Ⓣ559/739-0721 or 1-800/401-9800, Ⓦwww.benmaddoxhouse.com; Ⓢ), a large redwood house built in 1876 for Ben Maddox, the man who brought hydroelectricity to the San Joaquin Valley. South Mooney Boulevard has the densest concentration of **motels** including the recently renovated *Econo Lodge*, no. 1400 (Ⓣ559/732-6641 or 1-800/242-4261; Ⓢ), with pool and breakfast; or step up to the *Lamp Liter Inn*, 3300 W Mineral King Ave (Ⓣ559/732-4511 or 1-800/662-6692, Ⓕ732-1840; Ⓢ), which has a very nice pool and a sports bar and grill restaurant on site.

Visalia also has some of the best places to **eat** for miles around, including *Merle's*, 604 S Mooney Blvd, a Fifties-style drive-in diner with semicircular vinyl booths and a reputation for its chocolate mudslide sundae. Alternatively, wander around downtown and choose from *Café 225*, 225 W Main St (Ⓣ559/733-2967), a modern bistro with an eclectic menu that features artichoke fritters ($7), baked red snapper ($16), and prosciutto and roasted garlic pizza ($11); *Tazzaria*, 208 W Main St (Ⓣ559/732-5282), for good espresso and tea drinking; and *Brewbakers*, 219 E Main St (Ⓣ559/627-2739), which serves its own microbrews with bar meals. Upscale diners are catered for at the *Vintage Press*, 216 N Willis St (Ⓣ559/733-3033), where you might ease down the likes of wild mushrooms sautéed in cognac followed by red snapper with toasted almonds and capers, a dessert, and coffee, for around $50 a head, much more if you explore the vast and wonderful wine list.

Hanford

HANFORD, twenty miles west of Visalia on Hwy-198, was named after James Hanford, a paymaster on the Southern Pacific Railroad who became popular with his employees when he took to paying them in gold. The town formed part of a spur on the railroad and remains a major stopover on the route between Los Angeles and San Francisco. Today it exhibits a calm and restful air – if you're seeking anything more active you'll be disappointed.

Hanford's visitor center (see opposite) can give you a map of the town detailing the now spotless and spruced-up buildings around Courthouse Square, once the core of local life at the beginning of the twentieth century. The honey-colored **Courthouse** retains many of its Neoclassical features – including a magnificent staircase – and has, more recently, been occupied by shops and galleries. It stays open long hours, not least to provide access to *Jerseys Sports Bar* on the upper floor. As you'd expect, the old Hanford jail, rather pretentiously modeled on the Paris Bastille, is only a ball-and-chain's throw away. It was used until 1968 and is now restored as a restaurant (*The Bastille*; see opposite), although you can wander through to see the old cells – now and again used for secluded dining.

Much less ostentatiously, rows of two-story porched dwellings, four blocks east of the square, mark the district that was home to most of the eight hundred or so Chinese families who came to Hanford to work on the railroad. At the center of the community was the **Taoist Temple** on China Alley (open for groups of 6–20 only and by appointment; more details from the visitor center or call ☎559/582-4508). Built in 1893, the temple served a social as well as a spiritual function, providing free lodging to work-seeking Chinese immigrants, and was used as a Chinese school during the early 1920s. Everything inside is original, from the teak burl figurines to the marble chairs, and it's a shame that entry is so restricted. You can, however, take a look at another institution of Hanford's Chinese community: the **Imperial Dynasty Restaurant**, 406 China Alley (Thurs–Sun dinner only; ☎559/582-0196), two doors on from the temple, still run by the family who opened it fifty years ago. The interior is rich with paper lanterns and painted screens, but the cooking, oddly, is mostly French rather than Chinese. Mains are in the $16–26 range.

Mildly absorbing oddments from Hanford's past are gathered at the **Hanford Carnegie Museum**, 108 E Eighth St (Tues–Fri noon–3pm, Sat noon–4pm; $1; ☎559/584-1367), filling part of the interior of the town's elegant 1905 library – one of many small-town libraries financed by altruistic millionaire industrialist Andrew Carnegie.

For something more diverting, head six miles south of town to the **Ruth & Sherman Lee Institute for Japanese Art**, 15770 Tenth Ave (Tues–Sat 1–5pm; closed Aug; free; ⓦwww.shermanleeinstitute.org), incongruously located on the walnut orchard of local cattle rancher Bill Clark. With the guidance of friends and mentors Ruth and Sherman Lee, Clark has been amassing Japanese scrolls, folding screens, lacquerware, and sculpture since the 1970s and even designed the institute's Japanese-inspired building and his adjacent house and garden. Slip off your shoes and admire the dragon-in-clouds temple ceiling before entering the main room where you can sit on tatami mats to view the works up close. Only a small portion of the collection is on show at one time but there are always outstanding pieces, some dating back to the tenth century and many from the Edo Period (1615–1868). In particular, look out for two superb thirteenth-century sculptural pieces: the *Bodhisattva of the Wish-granting Jewel* and the *Daiitoko Myoo* – the institute's signature piece – with its multi-limbed figure astride a kneeling ox. Docent-led tours (Sat 1pm; free) are particularly illuminating.

Practicalities

Orange Belt Stages (☎1-800/266-7433) provide twice-daily **bus** links to Visalia and the Greyhound station at Goshen Junction, near Visalia (for connections to Los Angeles and San Francisco), and also continue across to San Luis Obispo on the coast. The town's **visitor center** (Mon–Fri 9am–5pm; ☎559/582-5024, ⊛www.visithanford.com) is conveniently located inside the handsomely restored Amtrak depot at 200 Santa Fe Ave. Free **Internet access** is available at the library at 401 Douty St (Mon–Wed 10am–8pm, Sat noon–6pm).

If you decide to **stay**, your choice is limited to the Victorian-styled *Irwin Street Inn*, 522 N Irwin (☎559/583-8000 or 1-866/583-7378, ⊛www .irwinstreetinn.com; rooms ❹, suites ❻), and a couple of downtown motels: the budget *Downtown Motel*, 101 N Redington (☎559/582-9036; ❷), and the nearby *Comfort Inn*, 10 N Irwin St (☎559/584-9300 or 1-800/228-5150; ❺). For **eating**, the most atmospheric place is *The Bastille*, 113 Court St, a fine steakhouse also serving mountainous lean burgers and sandwiches until late, followed by *Art Works*, 120 W Sixth St, a good espresso café doing a great range of smoothies and sometimes putting on live music. During the day, don't miss the rich creaminess of the made-on-the-premises ice cream at *Superior Dairy*, 325 N Douty St, just across from *The Bastille*.

Fresno

FRESNO, with its population of 400,000, is the largest city between LA and San Francisco, and an increasingly Hispanic one. It is very much the hub of business in the San Joaquin Valley, though in some ways feels little more than an overgrown farming town. For many years, Fresno seemed to miss out on the restoration programs that improved similar communities elsewhere in California, but recently the business heart has been rejuvenated. Witness the stridently modern buildings like the delta-winged steel-and-glass form of the **Fresno City Hall** close to the Amtrak station, and the stadium for Fresno's Minor League baseball team, the Grizzlies, right downtown.

Still, there's an odd mix of civic pride and urban decay, the latter fueling Fresno's status as one of the US's crime hot spots: Fresno's residents once looked down their noses at Bakersfield, but the position is now largely reversed. For all that, Fresno does have its good points, and you might want to spend a night here to take in the fascinating **Forestiere Underground Gardens** in the northern suburbs and something of the nightlife in the vibrant **Tower District**.

If you're in the region in late February and early March you should also consider following at least part of the 62-mile **Blossom Trail** (free map from the visitor center; see p.428), which weaves among fruit orchards, citrus groves, and the vineyards that make Fresno the world's raisin capital.

FRESNO

0   800 yds

TOWER DISTRICT

ACCOMMODATION	
Motel 6	A
Parkside Inn	B
La Quinta Inn	C
Super 8	D

EATING & DRINKING	
Chicken Pie Shop	4
Daily Planet	2
Kern St Coffee Company	6
Roger Rocka's	3
Sequoia Brewing Company	1
Veni Vidi Vici	5

Roeding Park

Chaffee Zoological Gardens

African American Historical & Cultural Museum

Farmers Market

Arte Américas

Metropolitan Museum

Meux Home Museum

City Hall

Train Station

Library

Fulton Mall

City Airport

Greyhound Station

Visalia (40 miles) ▼

Forestiere Underground Gardens (4 miles) & Merced (55 miles)

Kearney Mansion (5 miles)

Kings Canyon & Sequoia National Parks (75 miles)

Arrival, information, and accommodation

The **bus** and **train** terminals are downtown – Greyhound at 1033 H St (℡559/268-1829) and Amtrak at 2650 Tulare St and Q – both an easy walk from the **visitor center**, on the corner of Fresno and O streets (Mon–Fri 10am–4pm, Sat 11am–3pm; ℡559/237-0988, ⒲www.fresnocvb.org), located in a distinctive, conical-roofed water tower that dates back to 1894. Here you can check details on everything in and around the city including the nearby Fresno County Library, 2420 Mariposa St (Mon–Thurs 9am–9pm, Fri & Sat 9am–6pm, Sun 1–6pm; ℡559/488-3195), where there is free **Internet access**.

Downtown is just about small enough to walk around if you don't mind the heat, but non-drivers will want to make use of the Fresno Area Express ($1, exact change; ℡559/498-1122), if only to reach Forestiere Underground Gardens. Route #20, picked up downtown on Van Ness (every 30–60min) comes within a mile, and you can transfer to the #9 for the last stretch. Routes #26 and #28 travel between Van Ness and the Tower District.

If you decide to **stay**, you'll appreciate the low prices at numerous **motels**, all with pools, clustered together near the junction of Olive Avenue (the Tower District's main drag) and Hwy-99. Some charge rock-bottom rates but the rooms are well below par and are best avoided: the best deals here are *Motel 6*, 1240 N Crystal Ave (℡559/237-0855, ⒻF497-5869; ❷), or *Parkside Inn*, 1415 W Olive Ave (℡559/237-2086 or 1-800/442-2284; ❸). **Downtown**, there's the budget *Super 8*, 2127 Inyo St at L Street (℡559/268-0621 or 1-800/800-8000, ⒲www.super8.com; ❸), and the more upscale *La Quinta Inn*, 2926 Tulare St (℡559/442-1110 or 1-800/725-1661; ❺). All the motels listed have pools.

6

THE SAN JOAQUIN VALLEY | Fresno

The Town and around

To get the best of Fresno, you'll have to leave the center, and if time is short, the place to start is Forestiere Underground Gardens, a one-of-a-kind warren of rooms hewn out of the hardpan to protect one man and his crops from the heat. The Kearney Mansion also warrants an hour of your time before you return to the lesser attractions of downtown.

Forestiere Underground Gardens and Kearney Mansion

The one place which turns Fresno into a destination in its own right is **Forestiere Underground Gardens**, 5021 W Shaw Ave (Easter–early Sept Wed–Sun tours at 10am, 11am & noon; early Sept–Easter some weekends; $9; ℡559/271-0734, ⓦwww.undergroundgardens.com), seven miles northwest of the center, a block east of the Shaw Avenue exit off Hwy-99. A subterranean labyrinth of over fifty rooms, the gardens were constructed by Sicilian émigré and former Boston and New York subway tunneler Baldasare Forestiere, who came to Fresno in 1905. In a fanatical attempt to stay cool and protect his crops, Forestiere put his digging know-how to work, building underground living quarters and skylit orchards with just a shovel and wheelbarrow. He gradually improved techniques for maximizing his yield but wasn't above playful twists like a glass-bottomed underground aquarium and a subterranean bathtub fed by water heated in the midday sun. He died in 1946, his forty years of work producing a vast earth honeycomb, part of which was destroyed by the construction of Hwy-99 next door, while another section awaits restoration. Wandering around the remainder of what he achieved is a fascinating way to pass an hour out of the heat of the day, enlivened by the tour guide's homespun anecdotes.

With more time to spare, head seven miles west from downtown along Kearney Boulevard, a long, straight, palm-lined avenue that was once the private driveway through the huge Kearney Park ($3 per car; free with Mansion entry) to the **Kearney Mansion** (Fri–Sun tours at 1pm, 2pm & 3pm; $4). It was built between 1900 and 1903 for M. Theo Kearney, an English-born agricultural pioneer and raisin mogul, who maintained it in the opulent French Renaissance style to which he seemed addicted. He had even grander plans to grace Fresno with a French chateau, the mind-boggling designs for which are displayed here. Regarded locally as something of a mystery man, Kearney apparently led a busy social life on both sides of the Atlantic, which may explain why he died during an ocean crossing following a heart attack.

Downtown Fresno

Once you've seen Forestiere Underground Gardens and the Kearney Mansion, you've seen the best of the town: downtown sights are limited to a quintet of minor museums. The **Meux Home Museum**, 1007 R St at Tulare St (guided tours Fri–Sun noon–3.30pm; $5; ℡559/233-8007, ⓦwww.meux.mus.ca.us), is Fresno's only surviving late-nineteenth-century house, built for what was then the staggering sum of $12,000. This was the home of a doctor who arrived from the Deep South, bringing with him the novelty of a two-story house and a plethora of trendy Victorian features. What isn't original is a convincing reconstruction, and the turrets, arches, and octagonal master bedroom help make the place stylish and absorbing – quite out of sync with the Fresno that has sprawled up around it.

Each of the three museums clustered a dozen blocks to the west helps illustrate the historic and continuing importance of immigration to the city.

The **Fresno Metropolitan Museum**, 1555 Van Ness Ave (Tues–Sun 11am–5pm $7; Thurs 5–8pm $1; ☎559/441-1444, ⓦwww.fresnomet.org), mainly hosts temporary exhibitions but has a small collection of jigsaw puzzles dating back a century and a half, and a delightful display of over two hundred mostly nineteenth-century Chinese snuffboxes arranged thematically – flowers, deities, mythological creatures, and so on. Fresno's most famous son, the novelist and scriptwriter **William Saroyan**, gets hagiographic treatment in the museum despite his early desire to leave Fresno and never come back. He did keep coming back, however, creating a fictional identity for Fresno in his writing and died here in 1981 at the age of 72. He is best known for his Pulitzer Prize–winning *The Time of Your Life*, and *The Human Comedy*, which he also wrote and adapted for the screen, earning himself an Academy Award. He refused to pick up his award after a tiff with Louis B. Mayer, but the Oscar is on display along with his Underwood typewriter and panels with telling quotes from his life. Along the street, **Arte Américas**, 1630 Van Ness Ave (Tues–Sun 11am–5pm; $3, free Thurs 5–8pm; ☎559/266-2623, ⓦwww.arteamericas.org), has several galleries exploring mostly Hispanic-American visual and performing arts along with Mexican and Central and South American contributions. Fresno's black history is told at the **African American Historical and Cultural Museum**, 1857 Fulton St (Mon–Fri 9am–4pm, Sat 10am–2pm; $4; ☎559/268-7102), though the hundreds of portraits and assorted newspaper clippings are unlikely to divert you long from the often impressive temporary exhibits and the African statuary for sale in the museum store.

A couple of miles north of downtown, the **Fresno Art Museum**, 2233 N First St at Clinton, in Radio Park (Tues, Wed & Fri–Sun 11am–5pm, Thurs 11am–8pm; $4, Tues free; ☎559/441-4221, ⓦwww.fresnoartmuseum.org), has a changing roster of high-quality modern art that is usually worth browsing, plus an attractive sculpture garden and rooms devoted to pre-Columbian Mexican art spanning Mesoamerican styles from 2500 years ago until the arrival of the Spanish in the early sixteenth century. There's also a relatively minor but beautiful 1926 Diego Rivera canvas, *El Dia de las Flores, Xochimilco*, along with an explanation of how it came to be here.

The Tower District

In a town with a tradition of almond growing and cattle rustling, Fresno's **Tower District**, three miles north of downtown, comes as a pleasant surprise. Proximity to the City College campus made the area something of a hippy hangout during the Sixties; today it has a well-scrubbed liberal feel, plus several blocks of antique shops, bookstores, ethnic restaurants, and coffeehouses to fill a few hours of idle browsing. On the Tower District's western edge at the end of Olive Avenue, the tree-filled **Roeding Park** (Feb–Oct $1 per car, Nov–Jan free) boasts the **Chaffee Zoological Gardens** (daily: Feb–Oct 9am–4pm; Nov–Jan 10am–3pm; $7), a couple of amusement parks, and a lake. This is where Fresnoites come to convince themselves that the city is a nice place to live, and when strolling here on a day that's not totally baking you could almost believe them.

Eating and drinking

To pick up fresh, good **food**, head for the **farmers market** at Fulton and San Joaquin (Tues, Thurs & Sat 7am–2pm), and downtown check out the *Kern St Coffee Company*, 2134 Kern St, for good java. Otherwise, the Tower District, centered on the Tower Theatre at the junction of Olive and Wishon avenues, is very much the place to eat and drink. You'll get decent diner food along with locally famed chicken (and fruit) pies at bargain prices at the *Chicken Pie Shop*,

861 E Olive Ave (☎559/237-5042), and good-value lunches and dinners, plus excellent home-brewed beers at the *Sequoia Brewing Company*, 777 E Olive Ave (☎559/264-5521). The *Daily Planet*, 1211 N Wishon Ave (☎559/266-4259), serves a fixed-price four-course dinner (usually under $20) in Art Deco surroundings, and for something special, visit the dinner-only *Veni Vidi Vici*, 1116 N Fulton St (☎559/266-5510; closed Mon), for the likes of grilled beef Thai rolls ($13) and chicken breast on bok choy with shiitake mushrooms ($20).

Dining and joining the boozy Tower District throng will probably suffice for your evening's **entertainment**, but you could always visit the 250-seat *Roger Rocka's Dinner Theater*, 1226 N Wishon (☎559/266-9494, ⓦ www.gcplayers .com; closed Mon & Tues), where Broadway-style shows are preceded either by a sumptuous buffet (Wed, Thurs & Sun matinee; $37 all up), or a table-service meal (Fri & Sat; $40).

Northern San Joaquin Valley

The towns of the northern San Joaquin Valley largely follow the pattern of those strung along Hwy-99 further south. Founded on agriculture, all had the hearts ripped out of them by suburban sprawl in the latter half of the twentieth century, leaving only winos, crazies, and a lot of poor Mexican immigrants. But in recent years the town centers have rebounded. There are enough of the old downtown streets left to evoke something out of an Edward Hopper painting, but the smartened-up cityscapes are all increasingly pleasant places to stroll, the ubiquitous *taquerias* now joined by java joints.

None of the three main towns warrant more than a few hours' exploration. You may spend the night in **Merced**, especially if **Yosemite-bound**; **Modesto** offers a couple of interesting sites and vestiges of the 1950s, and **Stockton** has a certain down-at-heel charm.

Merced

The best thing about sluggish **MERCED**, fifty miles north of Fresno, is its courthouse, a gem of a building in the main square that's maintained as the **County Courthouse Museum**, corner of N & W 20th Streets (Wed–Sun 1–4pm; free; ⓦ www.mercedmuseum.org). This striking Italian Renaissance–style structure, with columns, elaborately sculptured window frames, and a cupola topped by a statue of the Goddess of Justice (minus her customary blindfold), was raised in 1875 when it completely dominated the few dozen shacks that comprised the town. Impressively restored in period style, the courtroom retained a legal function until 1951, while the equally sumptuous offices were vacated in the 1970s, leaving the place to serve as storage space for local memorabilia – most exotic among which is an 1870s Taoist shrine, found by chance in a makeshift temple above a Chinese restaurant. You might also pass a pleasant half-hour in the mostly contemporary galleries in the **Merced Multicultural Arts Museum**, 645 W Main St (Mon–Fri 9am–5pm, Sat 10am–2pm; free; ⓦ www.artsmerced.org).

Six miles north of Merced, close to the dormitory community of **Atwater** – and signposted off Hwy-99 – lies the **Castle Air Museum** (June–Sept daily 9am–5pm; Oct–May daily except Tues 10am–4pm; $8; ⓦ www.elite .net/castle-air). Forty-odd military aircraft from WWII to Vietnam – mostly bulky bombers with a few fighters thrown in, including the world's fastest plane, the SR-71 – are scattered outdoors, while inside there's a static B52 simulator, assorted military paraphernalia, and a collection of some 120 model planes crafted by one enthusiast from redwood. Route #8 of Merced's transit system, "The Bus" (Mon–Sat only; ☎1-800/345-3111), runs out here about every ninety minutes for $2 each way.

Practicalities

None of these sights are much of a reason to visit Merced, though the convenient **bus links to Yosemite** are. Greyhounds from Bakersfield, Sacramento, and San Francisco stop downtown at the **Transpo Center** on W 16th Street at N Street, where you'll find **Merced California Welcome Center**, 710 W 16th St (daily: June–Sept 8.30am–7pm; Oct–May 8.30am–5pm; ☎209/384-7092 or 1-888/446-5353, ⓦwww.yosemite-gateway.org), which covers the region, and the **Chamber of Commerce**, 690 W 16th St (Mon–Fri 8.30am–5pm; ☎209/384-7092, ⓦwww.merced-chamber.com), which is good for local information. The **Amtrak station** is somewhat isolated at 24th and K streets, about ten blocks away on the opposite side of the town center: follow K Street off W 16th Street. Train and bus stations are both stops for the four daily **YARTS buses** (☎1-877/989-2787, ⓦwww.yarts.com) to Yosemite: see p.460 for more on getting to Yosemite.

If you are relying on public transportation, by far the best **place to stay** is the reservations-only *HI-Merced Home Hostel* (☎209/725-0407, ⓔmerced-hostel@juno.com; $16). Check-in hours and access hours are limited (7–9am & 5–10pm) but this is a small price to pay for a ride to and from the stations, an enthusiastic welcome, as much information as you can handle, and a free dessert every evening. It is a great place to hook up with Yosemite-bound travelers, who might wish to team up and rent a car from Aide Rent A Car, 1530 W 16th St (☎209/l722-8084), which usually has vehicles from as little as $35 a day.

Drivers in need of a motel should take the Mariposa/Yosemite exit from Hwy-99, as it leaves you right by two good places to stay: the *Holiday Inn Express*, 730 Motel Drive (☎209/383-0333 or 1-800/465-4329, ⓔhixmerced@hotmail .com; ❹), and the bargain *Happy Inn*, 740 Motel Drive (☎209/722-6291; ❶), both with pool and continental breakfast. Closer to the Transpo Center, try the extremely cheap *Slumber Motel*, 1315 W 16th St (☎209/722-5783; ❶), with a small pool and cable TV.

The **eating** scene downtown has picked up a little in recent years: *Wired* at 450 W 18th St does good espresso (made from fair-traded organic beans) and muffins and has fast **Internet access**, and the bustling, modern *Firehouse Brewpub*, 560 W 18th St at M (☎209/384-2337), offers a substantial range of burgers, pasta dishes and more, plus a dozen beers on tap. Eight blocks north, *La Nita's*, 1327 18th St at T (closed Mon), does authentic Mexican at modest prices, and further afield, the popular *Paul's Place*, 2991 G St at Alexander (☎209/723-1339), boasts a broad range of ethnic and American dishes at very reasonable prices; try the Portuguese *linguisa* sausage omelet.

Modesto

Forty miles north of Merced along Hwy-99 you reach **MODESTO**, a town which got its unusual name after prominent San Francisco banker William Ralston was too modest to accept the new town being named after him. Much later, it was the childhood home of movie director George Lucas, and became the inspiration (though not the location) for his movie *American Graffiti*, the classic portrayal of growing up in small-town America during the late

1950s. The movie contains a number of references to local people, particularly the teachers who rubbed Lucas the wrong way in his formative years. Sadly, local ordinances (enacted in 1992 after several years of bad behavior) put an end to the fine art of **cruising**, though in recent years The Car Show (middle weekend in June) has stepped in with dozens of classic cars from all over the state and beyond dusted off and cruised through the city. About the only other reminder of those heady days is the **Lucas Plaza Statue**, a rather token duck-tail, bobby-sox, and '57 Chevy affair at the corner of J Street and McHenry Avenue. A more evocative celebration of the era is the **A&W Root Beer Drive-In**, 1404 G St, which has roller-skating waitresses serving root beer floats ordered from illuminated car-side menus. Despite the ban, you'll still see the better-kept cruising rigs parked here on Friday and Saturday nights until 10pm.

It may seem hard to believe, but as a fairly typical valley town, Modesto does have a history stretching back beyond the Fifties. Its (comparatively) distant past is encapsulated by the shabbily grand **Modesto Arch** – erected in 1912 over Ninth and I to attract attention to the city's expanding economy. The slogan "Water, Wealth, Contentment, Health" clearly lays out the priorities of the city fathers in a time when the need for irrigation was paramount.

More imposingly, the Victorian **McHenry Mansion** at 906 15th St (daily except Sat 12.30–4pm; donations appreciated) is jam-packed with fixtures, fittings, and the personal features of a family whose fate was linked with Modesto's for years. Robert McHenry was a successful wheat rancher in the mid-nineteenth century who did much to bring about a general uplift in the agricultural wellbeing of the area. Surprisingly, his luxurious dwelling was still being rented out as apartments, at quite low rates, as recently as the early 1970s. Docent-led tours enhance appreciation of the house, its history, and restoration.

A block from the mansion, a fine Victorian building originally financed by the McHenry family as the fledgling city's library now operates as the **McHenry Museum**, 1402 I St (Tues–Sun noon–4pm; free), which sports mock-ups of a doctor's office, blacksmith's shop, dentist's surgery, and gathering of cattle brands, revealing something of bygone days, although lacking the period atmosphere of the mansion. Adjoining the museum, the **Central California Art League Gallery** (Mon–Sat 10am–4pm; free) displays a show of regional painting and sculpture that should consume no more than a few minutes.

Practicalities

There's not much reason to spend the night in Modesto, and if you're looking for a place to stop before diving into Yosemite for a day-trip, Merced is the better bet. Still, you can find out more about the town and pick up maps at Modesto's **visitor center**, 1150 9th St at L St (Mon–Fri 8am–5pm; ☎209/526-5588 or 1-888/640-8467, ⓦwww.visitmodesto.com). Greyhound **buses** stop downtown at the Modesto Transportation Center, 1001 9th St at J, handy for **accommodation** such as the huge, upscale *Doubletree Hotel*, 1150 9th St (☎209/526-6000 or 1-800/222-8733; ❻), which includes a pool, sauna, and exercise room, though slightly less handy than the *Chalet Motel*, 115 Downey St (☎209/529-4370, ⒻJ579-9545; ❷), a mile away at the junction with J Street, which also has a pool.

You'll find downtown liberally supplied with decent **places to eat**. *J Street Café*, 1030 J St (closed Sun), is a relaxing spot for good espresso, muffins, and sandwiches, and *DeVa*, 1202 J St, is an affordable café and coffeehouse that serves great sandwiches and coffee throughout the day. Beer drinkers should seek out *St Stan's Brewery, Pub and Restaurant*, 821 L St (☎209/524-2337), where you've a choice of a dozen draught beers to wash down a burger or more substantial meal.

Stockton and around

The immediately striking thing about **STOCKTON**, perched at the far northern limit of the San Joaquin Valley some thirty miles north of Modesto, is the occasional sight of ocean-going freighters so far inland. The San Joaquin and Sacramento rivers converge here, creating a vast delta with thousands of inlets and bays, and a sixty-mile deep-water canal (built in the early 1930s) enables vessels to carry the produce of the valley's farms (especially Japan-bound bagged rice) past San Francisco and directly out to sea. But the geography that aided commerce also saddled Stockton with the image of being a grim place to live and a tough city to work in. During the Gold Rush it was a supply stop on the route to the mines, and it became a gigantic flophouse for broken and dispirited ex-miners who gave up their dreams of fortune and returned here to toil on the waterfront. Though valiant efforts have been made to shed this reputation and beautify the less attractive quarters for this city of a quarter of a million, it's still primarily a hard-working, sleeves-rolled-up city.

A smattering of buildings downtown evoke the early decades of the twentieth century, thanks to which Stockton is often in demand as a film set. John Huston's downbeat boxing picture, *Fat City*, for example, was shot here. Marginally more appealing are the blocks bordered by Harding Way and Park Street, and El Dorado and California streets, a short way north of the center. This area has been preserved as the **Magnolia Historical District**, with sixteen intriguing specimens of domestic architecture spanning seven decades from the 1860s.

Roughly a mile west of the Magnolia District, in Victory Park, Stockton gathers totems of its past in the varied and large stock of the **Haggin Museum**, 1201 N Pershing Ave (Wed–Sun 1.30–5pm; $5; ℡209/940-6300, 🌐www .hagginmuseum.org). Not surprisingly, much is given over to agriculture, including the city's finest moment: the invention by local farmers of a caterpillar tread to enable tractors to travel over muddy ground, adapted by the British for use on tanks and standard use since for the military everywhere. In tremendous contrast, the museum also contains a batch of nineteenth-century French paintings, including works by Renoir and Gauguin, as well as Bouguereau's monumental 1878 painting of nymphs bathing, *The Nymphaeum*.

Practicalities

Stockton's **Greyhound station** is downtown at 121 S Center St, a third of a mile east of the **Chamber of Commerce**, Waterfront Warehouse, 445 W Weber Ave (Mon–Fri 8am–noon & 1–5pm; ℡209/547-2770, 🌐www .visitstockton.org), which has limited information but stocks a free leaflet on the Magnolia District. **Amtrak** has two stops: downtown at 735 S San Joaquin St, and half a mile northeast at the corner of N Aurora and E Weber streets. Even traveling by public transportation doesn't mean you have to stay overnight in Stockton; connections both onwards to San Francisco and south down the valley are plentiful – but it can be worth stopping here to **eat**, ethnic restaurants being in good supply. For Chinese, the essential stop near downtown is *On Lock Sam*, 333 S Sutter St (℡209/466-4561), run by the same family since 1898. A couple of blocks north, the *Sutter Street Café*, 544 Market St at S Sutter (closed Sun), serves good sandwiches, smoothies, and espresso; and at nearby *Yasoo Yani*, 326 E Main St (℡209/464-3108; closed Sat & Sun), Nick's Greek salad is more than enough for a meal. There's more choice along the so-called **Miracle Mile**, a stretch of Pacific Avenue starting around a mile north of downtown – follow Madison from downtown. Here, among the bookshops, espresso bars, and restaurants, you'll find the Mexican-Southwestern *Fernando's*

Santa Fe Café, 2311 Pacific Ave (closed Sun), which turns out tasty fajitas for $13. Afterwards, stroll across the road for a microbrew to the *Valley Brewing Company*, 157 W Adams St (☎209/948-2537). For entertainment, you may be able to catch stars of yesteryear performing downtown at the Fox Theater, 220 Main St, which at press time is closed for restoration.

If you're forced to stay over, you can stay in the city in one of the plentiful mid-range chain **hotels** and budget **motels**, mostly near the Waterloo Road exit off Hwy-99. Downtown, try the *Stockton Travelers Motel*, 631 N Center St (☎209/466-8554; ❷), or if this seems a little unsavory, go for the pool-equipped *Howard Johnson Express Inn*, 33 N Center St (☎209/948-6151 or 1-800/446-4656, ⓦwww.hojo.com; ❸), close to the Greyhound station.

Micke Grove Park and Lodi

If it's too nice a day to spend in a city, venture ten miles north to the Armstrong Road exit off Hwy-99 for the pastoral relief – at least outside weekends and holidays – of the **Micke Grove Park** (daily 8am–dusk; parking $5 at weekends, $2 midweek), an oak grove which holds a Rose Garden, a Japanese Garden, and a zoo. It also features the **San Joaquin Historical Museum** (Wed–Sun 10am–3pm; $2), recording the evolution of the local agricultural industry and, more revealingly, the social history that accompanied it. Don't miss the Stockton clamshell dredge bucket, a tool used in the reclamation of the delta and restored and displayed like a major work of art.

Just three miles north of the park sits **LODI**, a small country town immortalized in song by Credence Clearwater Revival ("Oh Lord, stuck in Lodi again"). Undoubtedly, it was no place to get stuck then, but in the last decade its downtown – centered on its ceremonial Mission Revival–style Lodi Arch – has been rejuvenated with brick paving, trees, and a liberal lick of paint. After an absence of thirty years, Amtrak trains once again call at the smart station, downtown on Sacramento Street, though departures are too infrequent to encourage getting off. Still, it is now a pleasant place to wander around aided by a map from the **Chamber of Commerce**, 35 S School St (Mon–Fri 8.30am–4.30pm; ☎209/367-7840, ⓦwww.visitlodi.com).

Lodi is best known for its **wineries**, mostly located in an area centered on the **Lodi Wine & Visitor Center**, 2545 W Turner Rd, three miles northwest of town (daily 10am–5pm; ☎209/365-0621, ⓦwww.lodiwine.com), where you can taste three flights of three wines ($3 per flight), one flight always concentrating on the region's famed red Zinfandel. They'll furnish you with a map of local boutique vineyards, most of whom offer free tastings.

Sequoia and Kings Canyon national parks

Separate parks but jointly run and with a long common border, **SEQUOIA AND KINGS CANYON NATIONAL PARKS** contain an immense variety of geology, flora, and fauna. **Sequoia National Park**, as you might expect from its name, contains the thickest concentration – and the biggest individual specimens – of giant sequoia trees to be found anywhere. These ancient trees tend to outshine (and certainly outgrow) the other features of the park – an assortment of meadows, peaks, canyons, and caves. Notwithstanding a few notable exceptions, **Kings Canyon National Park** doesn't have the

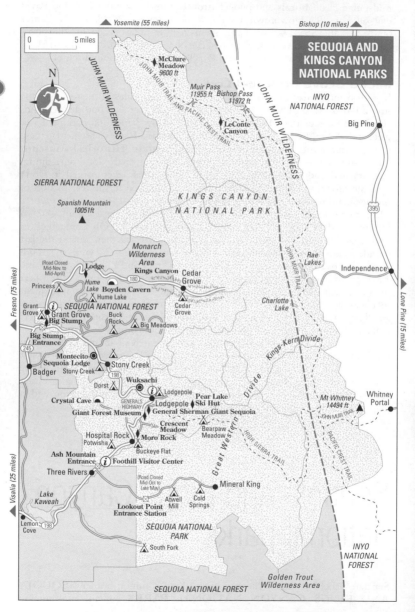

big trees but compensates with a gaping canyon gored out of the rock by the Kings River, which cascades in torrents down from the High Sierra during the spring snow-melt period. There's less of a packaged tourism feel here than in Yosemite: the few established sights (principally the big trees) are near the main roads and concentrate the crowds, leaving the vast majority of the landscape untrammeled and unspoiled, but well within reach for willing hikers. Through it all runs the **Generals Highway**, actually a fairly slow and winding paved road which links two of the biggest sequoias hereabouts, the General Sherman Tree and the General Grant Tree.

To the north of the parks lies the even more vast and almost equally spectacular **Giant Sequoia National Monument**, an enclave within the much larger **Sierra National Forest**, which is bound by fewer of the national-park-style restrictions on hunting and the use of motorized playthings. Consequently there is a greater potential for disturbance, though this is counteracted by the sheer immensity of the region.

The **best time to come** is in late summer and fall, when the days are still warm, the nights are getting chilly at altitude, the roads remain free of snow, and most visitors have left. Bear in mind that although most roads are kept open through the winter, snow blocks Hwy-180 into Kings Canyon and the road into Mineral King (see box, p.438). May and June can also be good, especially in Kings Canyon where snowmelt swells the Kings River dramatically and the canyonside yuccas are in bloom.

Some history

The land now encompassed by the Sequoia and Kings Canyon national parks was once the domain of **Yokuts sub-tribes** – the Monache, Potwisha, and Kaweah peoples – who made summer forays into the high country from their permanent settlements in the lowlands, especially along the Marble Fork of the Kaweah River. The first real European contact came with the 1849 California **Gold Rush**, when prospectors penetrated the area in search of pasture and a direct route through the mountains. Word of abundant lumber soon got out and loggers came to stake their claims in the lowlands. The high country was widely ignored until, in 1858, local natives led Hale Tharp, a cattleman from Three Rivers, up to the sequoias around Moro Rock. Tharp spent the next thirty summers up there in his log home where he was occasionally visited by John Muir, who wrote about the area and brought it to the attention of the general public and the loggers. Before long, narrow-gauge railways and log flumes littered the area, mainly for clearing fir and pine rather than the sequoias, which tended to shatter when felled. Nonetheless, Visalia conservationist George Stewart campaigned in Washington for some degree of **preservation** for the big trees and, in 1890, four square miles around Grant Grove became Sequoia National Park, the country's second national park after Yellowstone. In 1940 this was incorporated into the newly formed Kings Canyon National Park.

Arrival and information

There is no public transportation into Sequoia and Kings Canyon, but the twin parks are easy to reach by **car**. The fastest approach is along Hwy-180 from Fresno, though it is slightly shorter following Hwy-198 from Visalia, a fifty-mile drive with a tortuous ascent on which RVs longer than 22 feet and anything with a trailer are strongly discouraged. Those not bound by this limitation generally loop in one entrance and out the other. Visitors should prepare

The high country of both parks is covered in a blanket of **snow**, usually from November until April or May, and while this limits a great deal of sightseeing and walking, it also opens up opportunities for some superb cross-country skiing. With chains, **access** is seldom much of a problem. Both main roads into the parks – Hwy-198 to Giant Forest and Hwy-180 to Grant Grove – are kept open all year, except for extraordinary circumstances when they are still cleared quickly. The Generals Highway is also plowed after snowfall, but has the lowest priority and sometimes takes a few days to clear: it's best then to choose one section of the parks as a base. The Cedar Grove section of Kings Canyon is off limits to cars from mid-November to mid-April, but Grant Grove stays open all year. Facilities are restricted and camping is only available at snow-free lowland sites.

The big winter activities up here are **cross-country skiing** and **snowshoeing**. The northern highway gives access to two places at the hub of miles of marked trails: the Grant Grove Ski Touring Center at Grant Grove (Nov–April; call KCPS on ☎559/335-5500), where there's ski and snowshoe rental, guided naturalist snowshoe walks at weekends, restaurants, and accommodation; and the *Montecito-Sequoia Lodge* (see opposite), a resort with its own groomed trails, also open to visitors for around $25 a day. Nearby, the mile-long Big Meadows Nordic Ski Trail is perfect beginner's terrain. To the south, Sequoia Ski Touring works out of *Wuksachi Lodge* (see opposite), with no groomed trails but plenty of scope in the backcountry: skis and snowshoes can both be rented for $18 a day. Unless you are staying at *Wuksachi Lodge* or are a super-hardy camper, you'll need to return to Three Rivers for somewhere to stay.

Experienced skiers and snowshoers might want to spend the night 9200 feet up at the ten-berth **Pear Lake Ski Hut** (mid-Dec to April; $22 per person), beautifully sited at the end of a steep six-mile trail from Wolverton Meadow: contact the Sequoia Natural History Association (☎559/565-3759, ⊛www.sequoiahistory.org) for reservations.

Snowmobiles are banned in the national parks, but can be used on designated routes in the national forest, such as Big Meadows, Quail Flat, and Cherry Gap.

by stocking up with **cash** and **gas** before entering the parks, though some of both is available (see "Listings," p.450).

The parks are always open: **park entry** costs $10 per car, or $5 per hiker or biker, and is valid for seven days. This will be collected at the entrance stations, where you'll be given an excellent map and a copy of the free quarterly newspaper with the latest listings of ranger programs, **guided hikes**, and other interpretive activities, as well as general information on the parks.

For information, consult the parks' **website** (⊛www.nps.gov/seki), or call at one of the four **visitor centers**: the park headquarters at **Foothills**, a mile north of the southern (Hwy-198) entrance (daily: June–Aug 8am–5pm; Sept–May 8am–4.30pm); and others at Lodgepole, Grant Grove Village, and Cedar Grove Village (see the relevant accounts for details). There is also a useful **ranger station** at Mineral King. For details of hikes and campsites in the surrounding Sequoia National Forest, visit the **Hume Lake Ranger District Office**, 35860 Hwy-180 at Clingan's Junction, 17 miles west of the Big Stump entrance (Mon–Sat 8am–4.30pm; ☎559/338-2251, ⊛www.r5.fs.fed.us/sequoia). There is also a comprehensive 24-hour recorded **information line** (☎559/565-3341), with details on camping, lodging, road conditions, and the facility to order information by mail.

Accommodation

Inside the parks, all facilities, including accommodation, are managed by one of two concessionaires: Kings Canyon Park Services (KCPS ☎559/335-5500 or 1-866/522-6986, ⓦwww.sequoia-kingscanyon.com), who operate in Cedar Grove and Grant Grove; and Delaware North (DN ☎559/565-4070 or 1-888/252-5757, ⓦwww.visitsequoia.com), who cover Lodgepole and Wuksachi. In recent years, the opening of two new lodges to replace those removed from Giant Forest, has raised the standard of **accommodation**, shifting away from rustic towards greater luxury, though simple cabins are still available. You can occasionally pick up cancellations on the day, but space is at a premium during the summer when booking a couple of months in advance is advisable. Rates quoted are for the summer season, but huge savings can be had outside peak times, especially at the pricier places.

Heavy demand and the relatively high price of accommodation forces many to stay **outside the parks**, in the motels and B&Bs lining the approach roads a few miles from the entrances. The best selection is in the south at Three Rivers, where booking ahead is advised at **weekends** through the summer and holidays. Rates can also be up to one price code higher on Friday and Saturday nights, though this varies with demand.

Under the first two headings below, all available roofed accommodation has been included, with just a selection of the best places to stay listed under the final two headings. For **camping**, see the box on p.441.

In the parks

Bearpaw Meadow Camp mid-June to mid-Sept; call DN. Soft beds, fluffy towels, hot showers, and hearty meals served up in magnificent wilderness are the trump cards for this cluster of wooden-floored permanent tents (sleeping a total of twelve) at 7800 feet on the High Sierra Trail, 11 miles' walk east of Giant Forest Village: just follow the High Sierra Trail from Crescent Meadow. There's no electricity, everything is helicoptered in for the season, and all meals are included in the price tag. Bookings are accepted from January 2 when most weekends and holidays are taken, though you've a reasonable chance of an on-spec place on weeknights in June and September. $160 per person.

Cedar Grove May–Oct; call KCPS. Cozy lodge with private bathroom and air conditioning, right by the Kings River and in the same block as the restaurant and shops. ❺, kitchenette rooms ❻

Grant Grove and John Muir Lodge all year; call KCPS. The widest selection of ways to sleep under a roof, with most options accommodating up to four people. The most basic are the summer-only canvas-roofed cabins (❷) with cook stove, propane heater, and linen service. More solid rustic cabins (❹) were mostly built in the 1920s and many have been nicely restored and modernized; but for a private bath step up to deluxe cabins (❺), or the swanky, modern *John Muir Lodge* (rooms ❻, suites ❼) with very comfortable hotel rooms.

Wuksachi Lodge all year; call DN. Directly competing with the *John Muir Lodge* for the best rooms in the park, the *Wuksachi* consists of several blocks of rooms (ask for mountain views on the upper floor) widely scattered in the woods around an elegant central lounge and restaurant area. Rooms ❼, suites ❽

In Sequoia National Forest

Montecito-Sequoia Lodge for reservations ☎650/967-8612 or 1-800/227-9900, for the lodge ☎559/565-3388 or 1-800/843 8677, ⓦwww.mslodge.com. On the Generals Highway (Hwy-198) between Grant Grove Village and Giant Forest Village, this large but low-key family resort is tastefully set next to an artificial lake with all manner of activity programs: canoeing, swimming, horseback riding, wakeboarding, and volleyball in summer; and snowshoeing, skating, and cross-country skiing in winter. It is booked solid from mid-June to early Sept (except, curiously, Sat nights), but at other times you can almost always stay in rustic cabins ($79 per person) or lodge rooms with private bath ($99 per person). Rates include all meals, and they're pretty good too.

Stony Creek Generals Highway; late May to Oct; call KCPS. Plain, comfortable motel-style rooms with showers in a block with a good restaurant and a grocery store. A generous continental breakfast is included.

South of the parks: Lemon Cove, Three Rivers, and Mineral King

Buckeye Tree Lodge 46000 Hwy-198, Three Rivers, 0.3 miles south of the park entrance ☎559/561-5900, ⓦwww.buckeyetree.com. Small but comfortable modern rooms with TV, private bathrooms, and verandahs overlooking the foaming river, plus a five-berth cottage (❽), all located right by the park entrance and equipped with a nice pool. ❺

The Gateway 45978 Hwy-198, Three Rivers, 0.3 miles south of the park entrance ☎559/561-4133, ⓦwww.gateway-sequoia.com. Old but clean and perfectly functional cable-equipped motel-style rooms and a large house sleeping six with self-catering facilities ($265–325). It is located right beside the Kaweah River and the better rooms have a deck overlooking the water. ❺

Plantation B&B 33038 Hwy-198, Lemon Cove, 17 miles south of the park entrance ☎559/597-2555 or 1-800/240-1466, ⓦwww.theplantation .net. Luxurious B&B with comfortable en-suite rooms (some with balconies) and truly delicious breakfasts, located on a citrus orchard 17 miles from the park entrance. Rooms follow a *Gone With the Wind* theme to the extent that the Belle Watling room comes bordello-hued with a mirrored bedstead. Outside there's a heated pool, hot tub, and an acre of ageing orange trees and youthful palms that's ideal for relaxing. Rooms ❼, suites ❽

Sierra Lodge 43175 Hwy-198, Three Rivers, 4 miles south of the park entrance ☎559/561-3681 or 1-800/367-8879, ⓦwww.sierra-lodge.com. An older-style but spacious and clean lodge with pool and modernized rooms with bathrooms, many with decks, plus suites, some of which have cooking facilities. Rooms ❹, suites ❺

Silver City Mountain Resort Mineral King, 20 miles east of Three Rivers ☎559/561-3223, ⓦwww.silvercityresort.com. A bucolic bolt-hole in the woods that has been catering to committed regulars and casual visitors since the early 1930s. The rustic cabins are gorgeous, with potbelly

stoves, kitchen, and propane lighting, and some come with a toilet. The more modern chalets have full bathroom and electric lighting whenever the generator is running. Sheets and towels are provided for out-of-state guests (otherwise bring your own) and the chalets (but not cabins) have a two-night minimum stay. Bring food for self-catering, though there is a store with limited supplies, and the resort has a restaurant attached. Open June to mid-Oct. Deluxe chalets ❽, comfy cabins sleeping six ❼, rustic cabins sleeping four ❹

Three Rivers Hideaway 43365 Hwy-198, 3.7 miles south of the park entrance ☎559/561-4413, ⓦwww.threerivershideaway.com. Small RV and tent site with ageing but renovated cabins (some with kitchens) at the lowest prices in the district. Tents $20, RV hook-ups $25–29, cabins ❸, kitchen cabins ❺

Along Hwy-180

Sequoia View Vineyard B&B 1384 S Frankwood Ave, Sanger, just off Hwy-180, 35 miles west of the park entrance, 20 miles east of Fresno ☎559/787 9412 or 1-866/738 6420, ⓦwww .svbnb.com. One large and tastefully furnished room with king-sized sleigh bed and balcony is available above this small winery's tasting room, as is a similarly priced country cottage with its own living room and kitchenette. A full country breakfast is served. ❻

Sierra Inn Motel 37692 Hwy-180, Dunlap ☎559/338-0678. Small and functional motel rooms with TV and air conditioning, located 14 miles west of the Big Stump entrance and next to a sandwiches-and-steaks restaurant and bar. ❸

Snowline Lodge 44138 Hwy-180 ☎559/336-2300, ⓔsnowline lodge@aol.com. Just six old but clean and well-kept rooms with ceiling fans in a wayside lodge eight miles west of the park entrance. There are a couple of family rooms, and some have access to a wide verandah. No TV or phones but the owners hope to reopen the adjacent restaurant and bar soon. ❹

Eating

There are **food** markets and fairly basic cafeterias at Lodgepole (the most extensive), Stony Creek, and Cedar Grove Village, though none of them are spectacular and prices will be higher than places outside the park, such as Three Rivers. Much the same applies to restaurants, with Three Rivers offering the best local selection at reasonable prices. In the restaurants inside the parks, diner fare prevails, with the exception of the restaurant at *Wuksachi*.

Except during public holidays, there is always plenty of **camping space** in the parks and the surrounding National Forest. All sites operate on a first-come-first-served basis except for *Lodgepole* and *Dorst*, which can be reserved through the National Park Reservation System (NPRS: ☎301/722-1257 or 1-800/365-2267, Ⓦreservations.nps.gov), and *Princess* and *Hume Lake*, which are reserved through the Forest Service (☎1-877/444-6777, Ⓦwww.reserveusa.com). RV drivers won't find any hook-ups, but there are dump stations at *Potwisha*, *Lodgepole*, *Dorst*, and *Princess*. Collecting "dead and down" firewood is permitted in both the National Park and National Forest, but for cooking you really want to bring along a portable stove. For **backcountry** camping, see box on p.448. There are public **showers** at several locations (see "Listings," p.450).

Campsites are listed south to north, and the nighttime temperatures you can expect are indicated by the site's altitude. **Fees** are sometimes reduced or waived outside the main summer season and when piped water is disconnected, especially in winter.

South Fork (all year; $12; 3600ft). Trailer-free site a twisting thirteen miles east of Lake Kaweah on the very southwestern tip of the park. River water available.

Cold Springs Mineral King (late May–Oct; $12; 7500ft). Excellent shaded riverside site 25 miles west of Hwy-198, with some very quiet walk-in sites. River water available.

Atwell Mill Mineral King (late May–Oct; $12; 6650ft). Quiet and pleasant campground on the site of a former Potwisha summer camp. Slightly less appealing than *Cold Springs*, but five miles closer to the highway. Some tent-only sites. Water available.

Potwisha (all year; $18; 2100ft). Smallish, RV-dominated site close to Hwy-198 three miles northeast of the park's southern entrance and beside the Marble Fork of the Kaweah River. Water available.

Buckeye Flat (late-May to mid-Oct; $18; 2800ft). Peaceful, trailer-free site six miles east of Hwy-198, close to the park's southern entrance and beside the Middle Fork of the Kaweah River. Water available.

Lodgepole (all year; $18, or $20 if reserved; 6700ft). Largest and busiest of the sites, four miles north of Giant Forest Village and close to the highway. Reserve through NPRS in the high season, when pay showers, a camp store, water, and flush toilets are all made available.

Dorst (late May–early Sept; $20; 6700ft). Another large site, eight miles north of Lodgepole, with flush toilets and water during the season. Reserve through NPRS in summer.

Buck Rock (late May–Oct; free; 7500ft). Excellent and under-utilized National Forest site three miles west of the highway, midway between Lodgepole and Grant Grove Village. No water.

Big Meadows (late May–Oct; free; 7500ft). Similar site to *Buck Rock*, a mile further west among exfoliated granite domes. Mosquitoes in summer. Stream water.

Princess (late May–Sept; $15, or $17 if reserved; 5900ft). National Forest campground with water and toilets, handily sited on the way into Kings Canyon. Reserve through Forest Service.

Hume Lake (mid-May to Oct; $17, or $19 if reserved; 5200ft). Reservable National Forest site with water, toilets, and lake swimming for the brave.

Sunset, **Azalea**, and **Crystal Spring** Grant Grove Village. (*Azalea* year round, others as needed; $18; 6500ft). Comparable large sites all within a few hundred yards of the Grant Grove visitor center.

Sheep Creek, **Sentinel**, **Canyon View**, and **Moraine** Cedar Grove Village (early May to Oct; $18; 4600ft). A series of all-but-contiguous forest sites around the Cedar Grove visitor center. *Canyon View* is tents-only.

In the parks and surrounding National Forest

Grant Grove Restaurant Grant Grove. Basic diner fare – burgers, sandwiches, and breakfasts – plus fish, chicken, and steak dinners for $13–19 and pizza to stay or go ($14 for a 14-inch). There's also an espresso cart out on the umbrella-shaded terrace.

Lodgepole Deli Lodgepole. The best of the parks' budget eating places with respectable low-cost breakfasts, sandwiches, and coffee.

Montecito-Sequoia Lodge See p.439. Hearty breakfasts (8–9.30am; $10), lunches (noon–1.30pm; $10), and dinners (6–7.30pm; $17) are all served communally at large tables, and there's a bar operating until 9pm.

Stony Creek Generals Highway (late May to Oct; call KCPS). Fairly mainstream diner/restaurant serving decent burgers ($7) and the likes of grilled chicken ($15) and steak ($20). Open daily except Mon 11.30am–2pm & 5–8pm.

Wuksachi Lodge Dining Room Wuksachi ⊤559/565-4070. The finest dining in the twin parks, with the likes of Baja chicken sandwiches ($9), steaks ($25), and crusted mahi mahi ($20), plus a full buffet breakfast for $10, all served in a modern baronial-style room. The bar is open daily until 11pm; reserve for dinner.

Three Rivers

The Cabin 42251 Hwy-198, 5.3 miles south of the park entrance ⊤559/561-4785. The best espresso hereabouts.

Gateway Restaurant 45978 Hwy-198, 0.3 miles south of the park entrance. Superbly set restaurant with a shady deck hung out over the Kaweah River. Great for a lunch of perhaps chicken tostadas ($8), emu burgers ($8), or eggplant Parmigiana ($9), or their Sunday brunch ($13), but also open for meat and fish dinners ($16–25).

We Three Bakery 43368 Hwy-198, 3.7 miles south of the park entrance. A good and friendly stop for breakfast or lunch either inside or out, or drop by for their freshly baked cakes and pastries. Open Wed–Sun 7.30am–3pm.

Sequoia National Park

The two main centers in **SEQUOIA NATIONAL PARK** are **Giant Forest** and **Lodgepole**, the starting points for most of the hiking trails. To the south there's also the more isolated Mineral King area. While trees are seldom scarce – patches where the giant sequoias can't grow are thickly swathed with pine and fir – the scenery varies throughout the park: sometimes subtly, sometimes abruptly. Everywhere paths lead through deep forests and around meadows, and the longer treks rise above the tree line to reveal the barren peaks and superb sights of the High Sierra.

The history of the park is laced with political intrigue. In the 1880s, the Giant Forest area was bought by the Co-operative Land Purchase and Colonization Association, a group of individuals known as the **Kaweah Colony** that had the idea of forming a workers' colony here. They began what became the four-year task of building a road from the San Joaquin Valley up to Giant Forest, intending to start commercial logging of the huge trees there. Owing to legal technicalities, however, their rights to the area were disputed, and in 1890 a bill (probably instigated by a combination of agricultural and railroad interests) was passed by the Senate that effected the preservation of all sequoia groves. The colony lost everything and received no compensation for the road, which remained in use for thirty years – although decades later the ex-leader of the colony acknowledged that the eventual outcome was of far greater benefit to society as a whole than his own scheme would have been.

Three Rivers, Kaweah, and Mineral King

Approaching the park from the south, you pass through **THREE RIVERS**, a lowland community strung out for seven miles along Hwy-198 and providing the greatest concentration of accommodation and places to eat anywhere near the parks. As you approach the center of town, six miles south of the park entrance, a sign directs you three miles west to what remains of the Kaweah Colony, essentially just the **Kaweah Post Office**, the smallest still operating in California, with its original brass-and-glass private boxes.

A couple of miles north of Three Rivers, the twisting, early 1880s Mineral King Road branches 25 miles east into the southern section of the park to **MINERAL KING**, sitting in a scalloped bowl at 7800ft surrounded by snowy peaks and glacial lakes. This is the only part of the high country accessible by car (but not RVs, buses, or trailers) and makes a superb hiking base when you can reach it – essentially late May to mid-October, or a little longer if the snows hold off. Eager prospectors built the thoroughfare hoping the area would yield silver. It didn't, the mines were abandoned, and the region was left in peace until the mid-1960s when Disney threatened to build a huge ski resort here, only to be defeated by the conservation lobby which campaigned for the region's inclusion in the Sequoia National Park, something finally achieved in 1978. Now there's just a few small stands of sequoias, a couple of basic campgrounds, one quaint resort, and near-complete tranquility. Having negotiated the seven-hundred-odd twists and turns from the highway, you can relax by the river before hiking up over steep Sawtooth Pass and into the alpine bowls of the glaciated basins beyond. There's also a gentler introduction to the flora and fauna of Mineral King by way of a short **nature trail** from the Cold Springs campground.

Pick up practical information and wilderness permits from the **ranger station** (late May–Sept daily 8am–4.30pm; ℡559/565-3768) opposite the *Cold Springs* campground. No permits are required for day-walks but overnight permits ($15 per party) are issued until late September (and self-issued thereafter). They're in great demand in July and August: reservations can be made in advance from March 1, and some permits are offered on a first-come-first-served basis.

Unless you are committed to camping, the place to stay is the *Silver City Mountain Resort* (see p.440), five miles before the road end, which has a small, low-cost **restaurant** (daily except Tues & Wed) and excellent home-baked fruit pies. The *Atwell* campground is nearby.

Giant Forest

Entering the park on **Hwy-180 from Visalia**, you pass **Hospital Rock**, easily spotted by the side of the road and decorated with rock drawings and grain-grinding holes from an ancient Monache settlement. The rock got its name from a trapper who accidentally shot himself in the leg and was treated by the local tribe – who are further remembered by a small outdoor exhibition telling something of their evolution and culture. The road opposite leads to the small and appealing *Buckeye Flat* campground.

From Hospital Rock, the road soon becomes the **Generals Highway** and twists rapidly uphill into the densely forested section of the park, the aptly labeled **Giant Forest**. A major tourist draw, with the greatest accessible concentration of giant sequoias, Giant Forest contained a small village until 1998, but concerns over the health of the sequoias prompted the Park Service to raze the settlement. Almost three hundred hotel and restaurant structures built virtually on top of the sequoias' root systems have been removed, intrusive paths have been rerouted, and the whole area is in the process of being restored and re-seeded. The former shop, restaurant, and gas station have been transformed into the **Giant Forest Museum** (daily: July & Aug 8am–6pm; June & Sept 8am–5pm; Oct–May 9am–4.30pm; free), which admirably illustrates the life and times of the giant sequoias and shows some great footage of sequoia felling and early tourism. Outside, the fire-damaged Sentinel Tree is barricaded off to allow seedlings a chance to get established.

Various short hikes fan out from here through the trees, including the **Beetle Rock Trail** (5min round-trip), which affords a view down to the San Joaquin Valley, and the **Big Trees Trail** (0.6 mile loop; 30min–1hr), which follows a well-formed boardwalk along the perimeter of Round Meadow.

Along Crescent Meadow Road

The densest concentration of sights (many specifically engineered for that purpose) is along **CRESCENT MEADOW ROAD**, which spurs off the main highway just before the Giant Forest Museum and comes with abundant photo opportunities. The first attraction is the **Auto Log**, a fallen trunk originally chiseled flat enough for motorists to nose up onto it, though rot has now put an end to this practice. Beyond here, a side loop leads to the dramatic **Moro Rock**, a granite monolith streaking wildly upward from the green hillside. Views from its remarkably level top can stretch 150 miles across the San Joaquin Valley and, in the other direction, to the towering Sierra. Thanks to a concrete staircase, it's a comparatively easy climb to the summit (which is also reputed to make a good platform for feeling vibrations of distant earthquakes), although at nearly 7000ft the altitude can be a strain.

Back on the road, you pass under the **Tunnel Log**: a tree that fell across the road in 1937 and has since had a vehicle-sized hole cut through its lower half. Further on, **Crescent Meadow** is, like other grassy fields in the area, more accurately a marsh, and too wet for the sequoias that form an impressive boundary around. Looking across the meadow gives the best opportunity to appreciate the changing shape of the ageing sequoia. The trail circling its perimeter (1.5 miles; 1hr; mainly flat) leads to **Log Meadow**, to which a farmer, Hale Tharp, searching for a summer grazing ground for his sheep, was led by local Native Americans in 1856. He became one of the first white men to see the giant sequoias, and the first to actually live in one – a hollowed-out specimen which still exists, remembered as **Tharp's Log**. Peer inside to appreciate the hewn-out shelves. From here the loop presses on to the still living **Chimney Tree**, its center completely burnt out so that the sky is visible from its hollow base. Hardy backpackers can pick up the John Muir Trail here and hike the 74 miles to Mount Whitney (the tallest mountain in the continental US; see p.386).

The big trees and Crystal Cave

North of Crescent Meadow Road, the Generals Highway enters the thickest section of Giant Forest and the biggest sequoia of them all (reachable on foot by various connecting trails). The three-thousand-year-old **General Sherman Tree** is 275ft high, has a base diameter of 36ft, and was, for a time, renamed the Karl Marx Tree by the Kaweah Colony. While it's certainly a thrill to be face-to-bark with what is widely held to be the largest living thing on earth, its extraordinary dimensions are hard to grasp in the midst of all the almost equally monstrous sequoias around – not to mention the other tremendous batch that can be seen on the **Congress Trail** (2 miles; 1–2hr; negligible ascent), which starts from the General Sherman Tree itself.

When you've had your fill of the magnificent trees, consider a trip nine miles from Giant Forest along a minor road to **Crystal Cave** (45min guided tours mid-May–Sept daily 11am–4pm; $10) which has a mildly diverting batch of stalagmites and stalactites. The early-morning tours are not usually full, and whatever time you go, remember to take a jacket as the cave is at a constant 50°F. Those with a deeper interest in the cave's origins and features should join the two-hour **Discovery Tour** (mid-June–Aug daily except Sat 4.15pm; $18). Tickets for both trips cannot be bought at the cave, and must be purchased at the Lodgepole or Foothills visitor centers at least a couple of hours beforehand.

Lodgepole and around

Whatever your plans, you should stop at **LODGEPOLE VILLAGE** – three miles north of the General Sherman Tree – for the geological displays, film shows, and general information at the **visitor center** (July & Aug daily 8am–6pm; May, June & Sept daily 8am–5pm; Oct–April Fri–Mon 9am–4.30pm; ☎559/565-4436). With its grocery store, burger bar, showers, laundromat, and campground, Lodgepole is very much at the center of Sequoia's visitor activities, and its situation at one end of the Tokopah Valley, a glacially formed canyon (not unlike the much larger Yosemite Valley), makes it an ideal starting point to explore a number of hiking trails (see box, p.448). Foremost among them is the **Tokopah Valley Trail** – leading from Lodgepole through the valley to the base of Tokopah Falls, beneath **The Watchtower**, a 1600-foot cliff. The top of The Watchtower and its great view of the valley are accessible by way of the **Lakes Trail**, or try the sharpest ascent of all the Lodgepole hikes, the **Alta Peak and Alta Meadows Trail**, which rises four thousand feet over seven miles.

Beyond Lodgepole the Generals Highway turns west and runs four miles to **Wuksachi**, with a fancy modern lodge and restaurant, partly designed to replace

Giant Forest Village. The road soon swings north again and passes into the Giant Sequoia National Monument – where there is accommodation and food to be had at both **Stony Creek** and the *Montecito-Sequoia Lodge*, and free camping at a couple of primitive sites – before striking into the Kings Canyon National Park.

Kings Canyon National Park

KINGS CANYON NATIONAL PARK is wilder and less visited than Sequoia, with just two small settlements containing the park's main visitor facilities: **Grant Grove** lies close to the Big Stump entrance, and **Cedar Grove** huddles in the bottom of the canyon some 25 miles to the east, at the start of most of the marked hikes. The one real road (closed in winter; usually mid-Nov to mid-April) links the two, spectacularly skirting the colossal canyon. Away from these two places, you're on your own. The vast untamed park has a maze of canyons and a sprinkling of isolated lakes – the perfect environment for careful self-guided exploration.

Grant Grove and the Big Stump Area

Unless you're planning a major backcountry hike across the parks' boundaries you'll have to pass through **GRANT GROVE** to get to Kings Canyon. Indeed, this cluster of visitor facilities – including accommodation, post office, restaurant, and small supermarket – set amid concentrated stands of sequoias, sugar pines, incense cedar, black oak, and mountain dogwoods makes a good base for exploring Kings Canyon National Park. Grant Grove's useful **visitor center** (daily: June–Aug 8am–6pm; May & Sept daily 8am–5pm; Oct–April 9am–4.30pm; ☏559/565-4307) can supply all the background information you'll need, and contains a small **museum** (free entry) with old-time photos, logging paraphernalia, and a cross section of a tree, and a 24-foot-diameter room that would fit inside the base of many of the larger trees. It gives a sense of scale that is often absent when you are out in the forest. In the centre of the room a mounted sequoia seed seems way too small to grow into such monsters.

Grant Grove is home to a couple of trees that rival the General Sherman for bulk, the **Robert E. Lee Tree** and the **General Grant Tree**, after which the area is named. The General Grant is the world's third largest tree and was proclaimed as "The Nation's Christmas Tree" by President Coolidge in 1926. Every year on the second Sunday in December the people of the nearby town of Sanger hold a yuletide celebration with carols sung under its snow-weighted boughs. It is also the nation's only living shrine, dedicated to all those who have died in war. A half-mile trail wends its way among these and other giants, calling in at the **Fallen Monarch**, which you can walk through, and the **Gamlin Cabin**, where Israel and Thomas Gamlin lived while exploiting their timber claim until 1878. The massive stump of one of the trees' scalps remains after a slice was shipped to the 1876 Centennial Exhibition in Philadelphia – an attempt to convince cynical easterners that such enormous trees really existed.

Two miles south of Grant Grove, the **BIG STUMP AREA** unsurprisingly gets its name from the gargantuan stumps that litter the place – remnants from early logging of sequoias carried out during the 1880s. An easy trail (one to two miles depending on how many sad stumps you can bear to see) leads through this scene of devastation to the **Mark Twain Stump**, the headstone of another monster killed to impress: a sliver of this one resides in the American Museum of Natural History and another was sent to London's British Museum. Look too for pine boughs laid on the ground to break the fall of huge trees, and check out the meager foundations of the sawmill which once processed all the lumber.

Before leaving the area, consider a twisting, two-mile drive east from the visitor center up to **Panoramic Point** for long views over Kings Canyon.

Hume Lake

About eight miles north of Grant Grove, a minor road spurs off three miles to **HUME LAKE**, actually a reservoir built in 1908 to provide water for logging flumes, and now forming the heart of an underpopulated area of the Sequoia National Forest. Handily placed for local hiking trails, it's also a delightful spot to swim or launch your canoe and makes a good place to **spend a night** beside the lake at the comparatively large *Hume Lake* **campground** (see box, p.441). At the head of the lake, the facilities of the *Hume Lake Christian Camp* provide expensive gas, groceries, a post office, and a coffee shop.

Kings Canyon Highway

For most, Hume Lake doesn't even warrant a diversion from the northern park's main attraction, **Kings Canyon**, which some measurements make the deepest canyon in the US, at some 7900ft. Whatever the facts, its wall sections of granite and gleaming blue marble, and the white pockmarks of spectacularly blooming yucca plants (May and early June in particular) are visually outstanding: this is especially true from Junction View as Hwy-180 winds its way down to the riverside. A vast area of the wilderness beyond is drained by the South Fork of the Kings River, a raging torrent during the springtime snowmelt spate, and perilous for wading at any time: people have been swept away even when paddling close to the bank in a seemingly placid section.

The approach to the canyon leads through a section of the Giant Sequoia National Monument with two rewarding excursions. The first is a short drive to the **Chicago Stump**, yet another epitaph to a felled giant, this one carted in numbered sections to Chicago in 1893 where it was reassembled for the World's Columbian Exposition. A more alluring diversion leads past another sequoia graveyard, **Stump Meadow**, to a trailhead for the **Boole Tree**, the world's fattest sequoia and one that towers above the forest where all other sequoias were felled. No one seems to know why this one was spared. Despite this and some fine examples of fire scarring, it is seldom visited, perhaps on account of its position on a two-mile loop trail: take the gentler left-hand trail and you'll be there in around half an hour.

Near the foot of the canyon, the road passes the less diverting of the region's two show caves, the **Boyden Cavern** (daily: June–Aug 10am–5pm; late April–May & Sept–early Nov 11am–4pm; 45min tours on the hour; $10), whose interior has a number of bizarre formations grown out of the forty-thousand-year-old rock, their impact intensified by the stillness and cool inside. The cave stays at a constant 55°F, causing the numerous small animals who tumble in through the hole in the roof to enter instant hibernation.

Cedar Grove

Once properly into the national park, the canyon sheds its V-shape and gains a floor, where the settlement of **CEDAR GROVE** sprawls among

The **trails** in Kings Canyon and Sequoia see far less traffic than those in Yosemite, but can still get busy in high summer. Almost all those leaving from Mineral King and Kings Canyon climb very steeply, so if you're looking for easy and moderate hikes, jump to the second sub-heading below.

There are **no restrictions on day-walks**, but a quota system (operational late May–late Sept) applies if you are planning to camp in the backcountry. Numbers are limited, but around a quarter of the places are offered on a first-come-first-served basis and, provided you are fairly flexible, you should be able to land something by turning up at the ranger station nearest your proposed trailhead early in the afternoon on the day before you wish to start. **Wilderness permits** cost $15 per party per entry into the wilderness, and there is no extra charge if you make an advance reservation. These can be obtained from Wilderness Permit Reservations, Sequoia & Kings Canyon National Park, HCR 89 Box 60, Three Rivers, CA 93271 (☎559/565-3766, ℗565-4239), stating entry and exit dates, desired route with an alternative, number of people, and estimated camping spots. Reservations are accepted after March 1 and at least three weeks before your start date, and outside the quota period, permits can be self-issued at trailheads. More details are available on the park website and in the free *Backcountry Basics* newspaper available from park visitor centers. The visitor centers also sell localized hiking maps ($2.50 each) and more detailed topographical maps.

Remember that this is **bear country**: read the box on p.463. Bear canisters can be rented ($3 per day and $75 deposit) at Mineral King, Foothills, Lodgepole, Grant Grove, and Cedar Grove; and bought ($75) at the Lodgepole store and most visitor centers.

From Mineral King, Sequoia

Eagle Lake Trail (7 miles round-trip; 4–6hr; 2200ft ascent). Starting from the parking area a mile beyond the ranger station, this trail begins gently but gets tougher towards the lovely Eagle Lake. Highlights include the Eagle Sink Hole (where the river vanishes) and some fantastic views.

Mosquito Lakes No. 1 Trail (7 miles round-trip; 4–5hr; 1150ft ascent). Follows the first half of the Eagle Lake Trail, then branches left to the lowest of the Mosquito Lakes at 9000ft.

Mosquito Lakes No. 5 Trail (10 miles round-trip; 6–8hr; 2300ft ascent). As above plus a bit, bringing you to the uppermost lake at over 10,000ft. Some tough hiking is rewarded by stupendous views.

Paradise Peak via Paradise Ridge Trail (9 miles round-trip; 9hr; 2800ft ascent). Superb walk starting opposite the *Atwell Mill* campground and climbing steeply to Paradise Ridge, which affords views of Moro Rock. From there it is a fairly flat stroll to the 9300-foot Paradise Peak.

White Chief Canyon Trail (6–8 miles round-trip; 4–6hr; 1800–2200ft ascent). Steady trail following a creek up to a band of marble where prospectors established White Chief Mine, where a tunnel burrows into the rock. Continue up to the head of the valley to reach a pretty alpine bowl surrounded by jagged mountains.

incense cedars. With a lodge, a food store and snack bar, several campgrounds, and, across the river, a **visitor center** (mid-June to Aug daily 9am–5pm; ☎559/565-3793), this is as close to a built-up area as the park gets.

Three miles east are the **Roaring River Falls** which, when in spate, undoubtedly merit their name. Apart from the obvious appeal of the scenery, the main things to see around here are the **flowers** – leopard lilies, shooting

From Giant Forest, Wolverton, and Lodgepole

Alta Peak and Alta Meadows Trail (14 miles round-trip; 8–10hr; 4000ft ascent). Strenuous but rewarding trail rising four thousand feet over seven miles. The trail starts at the Wolverton trailhead and splits after three miles: there's an easy, level walk to Alta Meadow and its fine views of the surrounding peaks (and a four-mile trail to the desolate Moose Lake), or the daunting near-vertical hike to the stunning Alta Peak.

Little Baldy Trail (3.5 miles round-trip; 2–3hr; 700ft ascent). Starting from Little Baldy Saddle, six miles north of Lodgepole, this loop trail leads to this rocky summit with spectacular views.

Tokopah Falls Trail (3 miles round-trip; 2–3hr; 500ft ascent). Fairly easy valley walk beside the Marble Fork of the Kaweah River and leading to impressive granite cliffs and the Tokopah Falls, which cascades into a cool pool, perfect for a bracing dip. Starts at the eastern end of the *Lodgepole* campground.

The Watchtower and Lakes Trail (13 miles round-trip; 6–8hr; 2300ft ascent). A popular if fatiguing trail leading up from the Wolverton trailhead to The Watchtower (3–5hr round-trip), an exposed tower of granite overlooking Tokapah Falls far below. From there the path leads past three lakes in increasingly gorgeous and stark glacial cirques. The two furthest lakes, Emerald Lake (9200ft) and Pear Lake (9500ft), have campgrounds that, for the adventurous and experienced, make good starting points for self-guided trekking into the mountains.

From Kings Canyon

Cedar Grove Overlook Trail (5 miles round-trip; 3–4hr; 1200ft ascent). Starting half a mile north of Cedar Grove Village on Pack Station Road, this trail switchbacks steeply through forest and chaparral to a viewpoint overlooking Kings Canyon.

Don Cecil Trail to Lookout Peak (13 miles round-trip; 7–9hr; 4000ft ascent). Starting 400 yards east of Cedar Grove Village, a strenuous trail that largely follows the pre-highway route into King's Canyon. After two miles you reach the shady glen of Sheep Creek Cascade before pressing on up the canyon to the wonderfully panoramic summit.

Hotel Creek-Lewis Creek Loop Trail (8 miles round-trip; 5hr; 1200ft ascent). Follows the first two miles of the Cedar Grove Overlook Trail, before branching downhill and returning to Cedar Grove through some extensively fire-damaged forest.

Mist Falls Trail (9 miles round-trip; 3–5hr; 600ft ascent). An easy sandy trail starts from Road's End, eventually climbing steeply past numerous thundering cataracts to Mist Falls, one of the largest waterfalls in the twin parks.

Rae Lakes Loop (4–5 days round-trip). One of the best of the multi-day hikes in these parts following the Kings River up past Mist Falls and beyond, through Paradise Valley and Castle Domes Meadow to Woods Creek Crossing, where it meets the John Muir Trail. It follows this for eight miles, passing Rae Lakes before returning to Kings Canyon along Bubbs Creek and the South Fork of the Kings River. Trail maps ($4.50) are available from the Grant Grove visitor center. Permits are available from the Road's End ranger station.

stars, violets, Indian paintbrush, lupines, and others – and a variety of birdlife. The longer hikes through the creeks, many of them seven or eight miles long (see box above), are fairly stiff challenges and you should carry drinking water. An easy alternative is to potter along the **nature trail** (1.5 miles; 1–2hr; flat) around the edge of **Zumwalt Meadow**, a beckoning green carpet a mile beyond the falls and a short walk from the road, beneath the forbidding gray walls of Grand Sentinel and North Dome mountains. The meadow boasts a collection of big-leaf maple, cat's-tails, and creek dogwood, and there's often a chance for an eyeful of animal life.

Just a mile further, Kings Canyon Road comes to an end at **Copper Creek**, from where a network of hiking trails penetrates the multitude of canyons and peaks that constitute the Kings River Sierra. Almost all are best enjoyed armed with a tent and some provisions. To obtain **wilderness permits** in this area, call at the Road's End Wilderness Permit Station (June to mid-Sept daily 7am–4pm; rest of Sept Fri & Sat 7am–2pm) at the end of Hwy-180. The less ambitious only need to venture a hundred yards riverward to **Muir Rock**, to see where John Muir (see box, p.460) conducted early meetings of the Sierra Club. On the way back down the valley, cut right just before the road crosses the Kings River and follow the unmarked **River Road** (westbound only) along the north side of the river back to Cedar Grove.

Listings

Banks There are no banks in either park, but credit cards and travelers' checks are widely accepted. Lodgepole, Stony Creek, Grant Grove, and Cedar Grove have ATMs.

Cycling Within the parks, bikes are not permitted on trails, limiting you to park roads, many of which are very steep and with limited space for passing. A better bet is the network of trails in the surrounding national forest.

Gas There is no gas available in the parks, so drivers should fill up in Visalia or Fresno, or with slightly pricier stuff at Three Rivers. In desperation, you can get expensive gas at Stony Creek Village, the *Hume Lake Christian Camp* (see p.447), or at *Kings Canyon Lodge* on Hwy-180, which claims to have the oldest gravity-fed pumps in the country, dating back to the 1920s.

Horseback riding Stables and pack stations exist in four locations through the national parks and surrounding forest mostly open from mid- or late May to early September: Mineral King (℡559/561-3106), the Horse Corral between Lodgepole and Grant Grove (℡559/565-3404), Grant Grove (℡559/335-9292), and Cedar Grove (℡559/565-3464). All offer anything from an hour or two in the saddle (roughly $45 for two hours) to multi-day backcountry excursions.

Internet access No public facilities in the parks. The closest is Three Rivers Library, 42052 Eggers Drive (Tues & Thurs 10am–1pm & 2–6pm), five miles south of the park entrance.

Laundry Lodgepole (summer daily 8am–8pm) and Cedar Grove Village (daily 8am–8pm) both have coin-operated laundries.

Phones Many public phones in the two parks don't accept coins; make sure you have some kind of phonecard.

Post offices Both post offices accept General Delivery mail: at Lodgepole (Mon–Fri 8.30am–1pm & 2–4pm) write to c/o General Delivery, Sequoia National Park, CA 93262; and at Grant Grove (Mon–Fri 9am–3.30pm, Sat 9–11.30am) write to Kings Canyon National Park, CA 93633.

Rafting From mid-April to the end of June, Kaweah Whitewater Adventures, 42323 Hwy-198, Three Rivers (℡559/561-1000 or 1-800/229-8658, ✆www.kaweahwhitewater.com), run a series of rafting trips on the Kaweah River between Three Rivers and Lake Kaweah. Trips range from a relatively gentle two hours ($45) to serious Class IV and V full-day trips for $130.

Roads For road conditions call ℡559/565-3341.

Showers There are showers at Lodgepole (summer daily 8am–1pm & 3–8pm; coin-op, min $2), Stony Creek (mid-May to Sept daily 8am–7.30pm; $4), Grant Grove Village (all year daily 11am–4pm; $4), and Cedar Grove Village (summer daily 9am–5pm; $4).

The Sierra National Forest

Consuming the entire gaping tract of land between Kings Canyon and Yosemite, the **SIERRA NATIONAL FOREST** boasts some of the California interior's most beautiful mountain scenery, though it is less well known than either of its national park neighbors. Lacking the environmental protection given to the parks, many of the rivers within the federally run area have been dammed and much of the forest developed into resort areas that are better for fishing and boating than hiking. Residents of the San Joaquin Valley are well aware of this, and stream up here throughout the summer for week-end get-aways. That said, there are far fewer people and any number of remote corners to explore, not least the rugged, unspoilt terrain of the vast **John Muir Wilderness**, and the neighboring **Ansel Adams Wilderness**, which contain some of the starkest peaks and lushest alpine meadows of the High Sierra. If you want to discover complete solitude and hike and camp in isolation, this is the place to do it – the sheer challenge of the environment can make the national parks look like holiday camps. But don't try any lone exploration without thorough planning aided by accurate maps, and don't expect buses to pick you up if you're tired. Public transportation is virtually nonexistent. We haven't highlighted any walks in this area: there are hundreds of them and any of the **ranger stations** can suggest suitable hikes, supply free permits (necessary for any overnight hikes into most of the forest), and sell you the detailed *Sierra National Forest Map* ($12), useful even if you are only driving.

The paltry network of roads effectively divides the forest into three main areas: the more southerly **Pineridge District**, accessible by way of Hwy-168; the **Bass Lake and Mariposa districts**, just off Hwy-41 between Fresno and Yosemite; and the **Sierra Vista National Scenic Byway**, which reaches out into the Sierra to the southeast of Yosemite. Call ☏559/855-5360 for road information.

The Pineridge District and the John Muir Wilderness

A forty-mile drive from Fresno along Hwy-168 through a parched and knobbly landscape dotted with blue, live, and scrub oak soon brings you to the best place for adventurous hiking, the **PINERIDGE DISTRICT**. Around **Kaiser Pass**, which scrapes 9200ft, you'll find isolated alpine landscapes, served by decent campgrounds, a couple of minor resorts, and even some relaxing hot springs. The western section of the district is dominated by the weekend boating and fishing playgrounds of Huntington and Shaver lakes, while the east, up and over Kaiser Pass and around three hours' drive from Fresno, is big-time hiking territory. The region is swamped by **reservoirs** – Edison, Florence, Mammoth Pool, Redinger, and others – built as part of the "Big Creek" project that, more than anything else, made the San Joaquin the agricultural heart of California. With only modest hyperbole, the Sierra meltwater in these parts is touted as "the hardest-working water in the world."

Hwy-168 – aka **The Sierra Heritage National Scenic Byway** – penetrates seventy miles into the forest among the snow-capped peaks of the **JOHN MUIR WILDERNESS**. It's a drive of at least four hours, even in good weather – and this is an area prone to bad weather and road closure, although you can always get to the lakes. The best-placed source of information is the **High Sierra Ranger District** office (April–Nov daily 8am–4.30pm; Dec–March Mon–Sat 8am–4.30pm; ☏559/855-5355), located along Hwy-168 at Prather, five miles west of the forest entrance.

Shaver and Huntington lakes

From the ranger station, the good and fast Hwy-168 climbs rapidly over eighteen miles from undulating foothills studded with oaks to **SHAVER LAKE**, a mile-high community scattered among the pines, where Dinkey Creek Road (see opposite) cuts deep into the forests to the south. If you fancy an afternoon dodging the jet skiers out on the lake, drop in at Shaver Lake Watersports (☏559/841-8222), on the highway in Shaver, to rent windsurfers, canoes, and double kayaks (all $45 a day). Otherwise, there's little reason to stop except for groceries, gas, and meals at one of the half-dozen restaurants, notably the ever-popular *Village Restaurant and Bakery*, Hwy-168. Non-campers may choose to **stay** at one of several lodges and cabins, all of which charge around twenty percent more at weekends. Try the fully self-contained lodging at *Knotty Pine Vacation Cabins*, 41851 Hwy-168 (☏559/779-8426, ⓦwww.knottypinecabins .com; ❹), or the wide range of cabins three miles east at *Shaver Lake Lodge*, 44185 Hwy-168 (☏559/811-3326; basic rooms ❹, luxury rooms ❻), where

Many campgrounds in the Sierra National Forest can be booked between Memorial Day and Labor Day through **ReserveUSA** (☏1-877/444-6777, ⓦwww.reserveusa .com) for $10 per booking.

some units come with queen-sized beds, a kitchenette, and lake views. The *Lodge* serves burger-and-fries-type **meals** in the bar or on the sunny deck overlooking Shaver Lake. There are a couple of decent **campsites** hereabouts: *Dorabelle*, near the lake on Dorabelle Road (mid-May to mid-Sept; reservable; $17), which has water; and *Swanson Meadow*, three miles east on Dinkey Creek Road ($13) beside some gorgeous meadows.

Beyond Shaver Lake, Hwy-168 heads twenty miles east over the 7500-foot Tamarack Ridge to **HUNTINGTON LAKE**. Effectively separated from the San Joaquin Valley, Huntington Lake feels more isolated than its neighbor over the hill, but is almost equally popular; again watersports and angling are the pastimes of choice. Just before the lake, the *Rancheria* campground (open all year; reservable; $17) marks the turnoff to **Rancheria Falls**. A side road, east off Hwy-168, leads a mile to a trailhead from where the mile-long **Rancheria Falls Trail** (350ft ascent) heads off through broadleaf woods to the 150-foot falls. A mile beyond the turnoff, Hwy-168 reaches the lake by the **Eastwood Visitor Center** (daily except Tues & Wed 8am–4.30pm; ☎559/893-6611), where the Kaiser Pass Road splits east over Kaiser Pass (see below). Continuing west around Huntington Lake you soon hit the 1920s *Lakeshore Resort* (☎559/893-3193, ⓦwww.lakeshoreresort.com; RV parking $30; rooms ❹, suites ❺), with rustic knotty-pine **cabins**, most sleeping four or five. There's a great **restaurant**, a lively bar, a gas station, post office, and general store all a few yards from the lake. From here on, the lakeshore is almost entirely taken up by $17 campsites. If you crave solitude, head to the lake's western end, where a winding forty-mile, partly-gravel road skirts the whole of the Kaiser Wilderness, passing a couple of free, primitive campgrounds, before rejoining Kaiser Pass Road on the east side. It's a trek, but once you're here you'll feel a million miles from anywhere.

Beyond Kaiser Pass: Mono Hot Springs and around

Beyond the Eastwood Visitor Center, you're into true wild country, climbing Kaiser Pass on a rapidly deteriorating road up to 9200 feet, passing the *Badger Flat* campground (free; no water) along the way. Eight miles from Eastwood, a mile-long side road (passable in a high-clearance vehicle) leads to **White Bark Vista**, one of the best mountain views in these parts. Over the pass is a vast basin, draining the south fork of the San Joaquin River. The lumpy single-lane road drops past the beautifully situated *Portal Forebay* campground ($12; lake water), and the **High Sierra Visitor Center** (late May–early Sept Thurs–Sun 8am–4.30pm; ☎559/877-7173) heralds a fork from where two very narrow and winding seven-mile roads split: north to Lake Edison, its approach marred by a huge earth dam, and west to Florence Lake.

MONO HOT SPRINGS, two miles north of the junction on the road to Lake Edison, is the best thing about the region and a great place to relax and clean up after hikes. For the full hot-springs experience, head for the *Mono Hot Springs Resort* (mid-May to Oct; ☎559/325-1710, ⓦwww.monohotsprings .com; RV parking $25; tent cabins sleeping up to five ❸, rustic cabins ❷ for up to four, modern cabins ❹). Located on the banks of the San Joaquin River, the *Resort* is a modest affair with individual mineral baths ($5), showers ($4), and massages for $40 per half-hour. Outside, there's a chlorinated spa filled with spring water, costing $5 for an all-day pass. Accommodation at the resort ranges from simple cabins with communal ablutions and no linen, to more commodious affairs with toilets and kitchen. Typically there is a three-night minimum but you may be able to slot into a shorter gap, especially at the ends of the season.

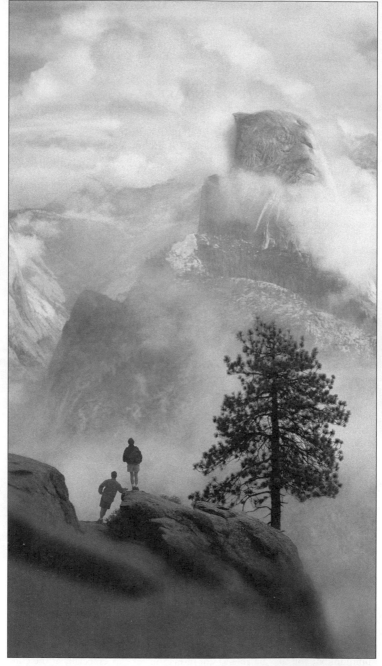

△ Hikers looking at Half Dome, Yosemite National Park

The resort also has a small restaurant, a limited general store, the *Mono Hot Springs* campground (early June–late Sept; Ⓦwww.reserveusa.com; $15), and a post office used for mail and food pick-ups by hikers on the nearby John Muir and Pacific Crest trails. Better still, across the river there's a five-foot-deep concrete **bathing tank** (unrestricted access) that's perfect for soaking your bones while stargazing. This is just one of many pools on this side of the river; ask around.

Beyond Mono Hot Springs, the road continues past several more campgrounds amid wonderful mountain scenery to **Lake Edison** and the *Vermillion Valley Resort* (Ⓣ559/259-4000, Ⓦwww.edisonlake.com; tent cabins ❷, motel units ❹), mainly geared towards boaters and anglers but also useful for folk heading out into the John Muir Wilderness. Save yourself a dull seven-mile hike by taking the small **ferry** (June–Sept twice daily; $9 each way) across the lake.

Florence Lake is more immediately appealing than Lake Edison: there's a greater sense of being hemmed in by mountains, and it is reached through an unearthly landscape of wrinkled granite shattered over the centuries by contorted junipers. There's a small store, the *Jackass Meadow* campground (late May–Sept; reservable; $15), located unnervingly below the dam, and another **ferry** across the lake (late May–late Sept; 5 daily; $9 each way). This ferry trip opens up multi-day hikes along the John Muir and Pacific Crest trails, and to the northern end of Kings Canyon National Park. If you can't face being totally self-sufficient, you can sometimes stay at the *Muir Trail Ranch* (from mid-June to Sept; Ⓣ209/966-3195, Ⓦwww.muirtrailranch.com), a cabin and tent retreat with hot pools and horses located in magical scenery five miles beyond the far end of Florence Lake. When not taken over by groups, it is open for short stays (usually the middle two weeks in June and the third week in Sept) at $125 a night for room, breakfast, sack lunch, and dinner, but not including horses, charged at $65 a day. Access is by the cross-lake ferry, and then you either hike or arrange to be met with a horse ($40 each way).

Dinkey Creek Road and McKinley Grove

The region to the southeast of Shaver Lake is accessible along **Dinkey Creek Road**, which threads its way through thirty miles of thick forests and around lush meadows to the Wishon Reservoir. It is altogether less alpine than the regions farther east, but no less impressive and a good deal warmer. Deep in the forest almost twenty miles southeast of Shaver Lake lies **McKinley Grove**, a less impressive stand of giant sequoias than others in the Sierra, though it is always an honor to be among these giants. The adjacent *Gigantea* campground (May–Oct $13) makes a nice place to stop. Beyond lies Wishon Reservoir from where tracks penetrate the Woodchuck and Red River Basin portions of the John Muir Wilderness.

Bass Lake

The northern reaches of the Sierra National Forest are most easily reached from **Oakhurst** (see "Approaching Yosemite," p.460), the center of the Mariposa District and just seven miles west of much the biggest tourist attraction in the area – the pine-fringed **BASS LAKE**. A stamping ground of Hell's Angels in the 1960s – the leather and licentiousness memorably described in Hunter S. Thompson's *Hell's Angels* – Bass Lake is nowadays a family resort, crowded with boaters and anglers in summer, but a good spot to rest for a day or two. For detailed campground and hiking information, consult the Bass Lake Ranger District office (see p.456).

Road 222 runs right around the lake, though not always within sight of it. At the main settlement, **Pines Village**, you can buy groceries, eat well, and **spend the night** at *The Pines Resort* (☎559/642-3121 or 1-800/350-7463, 🖰www.basslake.com; **❼**) in luxurious two-story chalets with kitchens or even more palatial lakeside suites. By the southwestern tip of the lake, *Miller's Landing Resort*, 37976 Rd 222 (☎559/642-3633 or 1-866/657-4386, 🖰www .millerslanding; **❷–❾**), offers cabins without bathrooms right up to fancy chalets and suites. *Miller's Landing* is also the best place to rent aquatic equipment – including fishing boats ($60 a day) and jet skis ($90 an hour) – and they have public showers and laundry.

The western side of Bass Lake is slung with $19-a-night family **campgrounds**, most oriented towards long stays beside your camper. In summer, book well in advance (see box, p.452), though no-shows are sometimes available at the Bass Lake Recreation Area office, 39900 Rd 222, on the southwest side of the lake (late May to early Sept Mon–Fri 8am–8pm, Sat & Sun 8am–9pm; ☎559/642-3212). For tent campers, the best site is *Lupine* ($19), just north of Miller's Landing.

Sierra Vista Scenic Byway

If Bass Lake is too commercial and overcrowded for you, the antidote starts immediately to the north. The **SIERRA VISTA SCENIC BYWAY** makes a ninety-mile circuit east of Hwy-41, topping out at the Clover Meadow Station (7000ft), which is the trailhead for much of the magnificent **Ansel Adams Wilderness**. Apart from a lot of trailheads and campgrounds, there's not a great deal to it, though the views are fantastic and people are scarce. A straight circuit (snow-free July–Oct at best) takes five hours, and is especially slow going on the rough dirt roads of the north side. Stock up on supplies before you start: there are a couple of stores and gas stations dotted along its length but they're not cheap and the range is limited. Accommodation on the circuit is largely limited to campgrounds, all (except two free sites) costing $12–14.

The best source of information on the circuit is the **Bass Lake Ranger District** office (Mon–Fri 8am–4.30pm; ☎559/877-2218) in the hamlet of North Fork at the southern end of Bass Lake, where you can pick up a **map** – important, as there are numerous confusing forestry roads and few signposts.

The south side

Before setting out from North Fork, check out the **Sierra Mono Indian Museum** (Tues–Sat 9am–4pm; $3), with some good examples of local Native American basketry and beadwork, as well as a lot of stuffed animals in glass cases. Once on your way, there's little to stop for on the first 25 miles until **Mile High Vista**, which reveals endless views of muscle-bound mountain ranges and bursting granite domes stretching back to Mammoth Mountain (see p.400). A little further on, an eight-mile side road cuts south to the dammed **Mammoth Pool**, where anglers boat on the lake and smoke their catch at one of the four **campgrounds**. The quietest of them are *Sweetwater* ($14; 3800ft) and *Placer* ($14; 4100ft), away from the pool but by streams.

Back on the Scenic Byway, you'll pass the rather disappointing **Arch Rock**, where the earth under a slab of granite has been undermined to leave a kind of bridge, and continue climbing to a small ranger outpost (late June–Sept occasionally staffed daily; ☎559/877-2218), and the Minarets Pack Station (mid-June to Sept; ☎559/868-3405, 🖰www.highsierrapackers.org/min.htm). Apart from a general store and reasonable meals, the station offers simple

6

lodging and horseback trips from $55 a day. It's a great base for wilderness trips, many of which start by the **Clover Meadow Wilderness Station**, a couple of miles up a spur road (late June to mid-Sept daily 9am–5pm; permits available). Nearby are two free and wonderfully sited campgrounds, *Clover Meadow* and *Granite Creek*, both at 7000 feet, the former with potable water.

The north side

The Minarets Pack Station marks the start of the descent from the backcountry and the end of the asphalt; for the next few miles you're on rough dirt, generally passable in ordinary vehicles when clear of snow. The hulking form of **Globe Rock** heralds the return to asphalt, which runs down to **Beasore Meadow**, where the summer-only Jones Store (open mid-June to mid-Oct) has supplied groceries, gas, and basic meals (8am–8pm) for the best part of a century, and offers showers to hikers. A short distance further on you reach Cold Springs Meadow, the junction with Sky Ranch Road (follow it left to continue the loop) and a spur to the wonderful *Fresno Dome* campground ($14; no water; 6400ft), a great base for a moderately strenuous walk to the top of the exfoliated granite namesake.

The Scenic Byway then passes several $12 campgrounds, most without running water, en route to the **Nelder Grove Historical Area** (unrestricted entry), a couple of miles north along a dirt road. Over a hundred giant sequoias are scattered through the forest here, though the overall impression is of devastation evidenced by the number of enormous stumps among the second-growth sugar pine, white fir, and cedar. The mile-long "Shadow of the Giants" interpretive walk explains the logging activities which took place here in the 1880s and early 1890s and, with its low visitor count, offers a more serene communion with these majestic trees than in any of the national parks. A second interpretive trail leads from the nearby, wooded *Nelder Grove* campground (free; 3500ft; stream water) to **Bull Buck Tree**, once a serious contender for the world's largest tree. From here it is only seven twisting miles back to Hwy-41, reached at a point around four miles north of Oakhurst.

Yosemite National Park

No temple made with hands can compare with the Yosemite. Every rock in its walls seems to glow with life. Some lean back in majestic repose; others, absolutely sheer or nearly so for thousands of feet, advance beyond their companions in thoughtful attitudes, giving welcome to storms and calms alike, seemingly aware, yet heedless, of everything going on about them.

John Muir, *The Yosemite*

More gushing adjectives have been thrown at **YOSEMITE NATIONAL PARK** than at any other part of California. But however excessive the hyperbole may seem, once you enter the park and turn the corner that reveals Yosemite Valley – only a small part of the park but the one at which most of the verbiage is aimed – you realize it's actually an understatement. For many,

Yosemite Valley is, very simply, the single most dramatic piece of geology to be found anywhere in the world. Just seven miles long and one mile across at its widest point, the valley is walled by near vertical, three-thousand-foot-high cliffs whose sides are streaked by cascading waterfalls and whose tops, a variety of domes and pinnacles, form a jagged silhouette against the sky. At ground level, too, the sights can be staggeringly impressive. Grassy meadows are framed by oak, cedar, maple, and fir trees, with a variety of wild flowers and wildlife in attendance – deer, coyotes, and even black bears are not uncommon. As if that wasn't enough, in the southern reaches of the park near **Wawona**, sequoias grow almost as densely and to as vast dimensions as those in the Sequoia National Park.

Understandably, you're not the first to appreciate Yosemite's appeal. Each year Yosemite has to cope with three and a half million visitors, and if you're looking for peace it's advisable to avoid Yosemite Valley and Wawona on weekends and holidays. That said, the whole park is diverse and massive enough to endure the crowds: you can visit at any time of year, even in winter when the waterfalls turn to ice and the trails are blocked by snow, and out of high summer even the valley itself resists getting crammed. Further-flung reaches of the park, especially around the crisp alpine **Tuolumne** (pronounced Too-ool-uh-me) **Meadows**, and the completely wild backcountry accessible beyond them, are much less busy all year round – nature in just about the most peaceful and elemental setting you could imagine.

Yosemite has had more than its fair share of negative press in the past few years. There have been BASE jumping deaths and a series of brutal murders, though *Outside* magazine claims that the chances of being killed in an American national park are around two million to one, about the same as drowning in your own bath. Yosemite Valley has also experienced severe flooding and rockfall close to visitor accommodation, two major considerations in the drafting of the **Yosemite Valley Plan**, which aims to improve safety and enhance the park's appeal for visitors. Due to be implemented over the next ten to fifteen years, the plan calls for constructing buildings away from hazardous areas, removing some valley roads to allow meadow restoration, extending the valley shuttle-bus system and, most contentious of all, reducing day-use parking in the valley and requiring visitors to bus in from outlying parking lots. Small modifications are already under way, but you can still drive into Yosemite Valley, a situation unlikely to change for many years, if ever.

Some history

Yosemite Valley was created over thousands of years by glaciers gouging through and enlarging the canyon of the Merced River; the ice scraped away much of the softer portions of granite but only scarred the harder sections, which became the present cliffs. As the glaciers melted a lake formed, filling the valley, and eventually silting up to create the present valley floor. The **Awahneechee** people occupied the area quite peaceably for some 4000 years until the mid-nineteenth century when the increasingly threatening presence of white Gold Rush settlers in the San Joaquin Valley led the tribes here to launch raiding parties against the nearest encampments. In 1851, Major James Savage led a force, the **Mariposa Battalion**, in pursuit of the Native Americans, trailing them into the foothills and beyond, and becoming the first white men to set foot in Yosemite Valley. It wasn't long before the two groups clashed properly, and the original population was moved out to white settlements to make way for farmers, foresters, and, soon after, tourists (the first group of sightseers arriving in 1855). Moves were quickly afoot to conserve the natural beauty of the area: in 1864 Yosemite Valley and the Mariposa Grove were preserved as the Yosemite Land Grant, the nation's first region specifically set aside to protect the wilderness. In 1890 it became America's third national park, thanks in great part to the campaigning work of Scottish naturalist **John Muir** (see box, p.460).

John Muir was one of nature's most eloquent advocates, a champion of all things wild who spent ten years living in Yosemite Valley in the 1870s, and the rest of his life campaigning for its preservation. Born in Scotland in 1838, he grew up in Wisconsin, became a mechanical inventor, and embarked on his first journey at the age of 27, noting in his diary, "All drawbacks overcome ... joyful and free... I chose to become a tramp."

After walking a thousand miles to Florida with little more than a volume of Keats' poems and a plant press for company, he wound up in California in 1868 and asked for "anywhere that is wild." Working in Yosemite Valley as a sheepherder, mill worker, and hotel clerk, he spent every waking moment exploring the mountains and waterfalls, traveling light, and usually going to sleep hungry under the stars.

He dubbed the Sierra Nevada the "Range of Light," and spent years developing his theory of how glaciers shaped the range. His articles gradually won him academic acceptance, and the general public was soon devouring his journal-based books, such as *My First Summer in the Sierra* and *The Yosemite*, which became classics.

Muir was desperate to protect his beloved landscape from the depredations of sheep grazing, timber cutting, and homesteading, and through magazine articles and influential contacts goaded Congress into creating Yosemite National Park in 1890. Two years later, he set up the **Sierra Club**, an organization whose motto "take only photographs; leave only footprints" has become a model for like-minded groups around the world. Despite his successes, in 1913 Muir failed to save the Hetch Hetchy Valley from being dammed (see p.474), a blow that hastened his death a year later.

The publicity actually aided the formation of the present National Park Service in 1916, which promised – and has since provided – greater protection. Muir's name crops up throughout California as a memorial to this inspirational figure, not least in the 211-mile John Muir Trail which twists through his favorite scenery from Yosemite Valley south to Mount Whitney.

Approaching Yosemite

Getting to Yosemite by car is straightforward, though on summer weekends parking can be a problem. Three roads enter the park from the west: Hwy-41 from Fresno, Hwy-140 from Merced, and Hwy-120 from Stockton and the San Francisco Bay area. All are generally kept open throughout the year as far as the valley, though in extreme circumstances Hwy-120 is the first to close. The only road into the eastern side of the park is Hwy-120, the 10,000-foot Tioga Road, which branches off US-395 close to Lee Vining – though this is usually closed from late October to late May and in bad weather. **Gas** (see "Listings," p.482) is not available in Yosemite Valley, and though Crane Flat, some fifteen miles away, has 24-hour pumps, it is fairly expensive; fill up before heading into the park.

In an effort to encourage visitors to arrive by **public transportation**, the Park Service and local authorities maintain the YARTS bus system (☎209/388-9589 or 1-877/989-2787, ⓦwww.yarts.com), which runs a useful service along Hwy-140 from Merced (see p.431), which in turn has Amtrak and Greyhound connections. There are four departures daily picking up at both the Merced Transpo Center and the Amtrak station and arriving (after brief stops en route at all towns and significant accommodation) in the valley almost three hours later. A couple more services run into the valley from Mariposa along the same route, and there is a limited summer service from Mammoth Lakes (see p.396) and Lee Vining, over Tioga Pass and through Tuolumne Meadows to Yosemite Valley. **Timetables** are available on the YARTS website and from visitor centers in the area. **Tickets** can be bought on board, and the round-trip **fare** (which includes the park entrance fee) to Yosemite from Merced is $20, from Mariposa and Midpines $10, and from El Portal just $7.

Generally speaking, anything called a **sightseeing tour** that begins outside the park will involve you in an unsatisfying race through the valley. Alternatives which don't fit this pattern include San Francisco–based tours in converted "communal" buses run by **Green Tortoise** (T 415/956-7500 or 1-800/867-8647, W www.greentortoise.com). These are geared towards active, outdoorsy types who enjoy camping out and pitching in. Their **weekend trip** (April–Sept; departs 9pm Fri returns 7am Mon; $99, plus $36 food fund) heads to the valley and the Mariposa Grove; a slightly more expensive **three-day trip** (Jun–mid-Oct; $139, plus $46 food fund: Mon & Fri evening departures) also allows half a day in Tuolumne Meadows and time around nearby Mono Lake as well as some hot springs. **Incredible Adventures** (T 415/642-7378 or 1-800/777-8464, W www.incadventures.com) offer enjoyable minibus tours from San Francisco. The **one-day trip** ($115) includes a quick jaunt around the main Yosemite Valley sights and three hours to explore and hike. The more satisfying **two-day** ($150) and **three-day camping-based tour** ($200) includes high-country hiking around Tuolumne and visiting the sequoias.

The gateway towns

The heavy demand for accommodation within the park drives many to consider staying in one of the small, mostly former gold-mining towns along the main access roads. These are increasingly gearing themselves to park-bound tourists and do a reasonable job offering both lodging and food (for both of which see the following pages), though they are a poor substitute for actually staying in the park.

Approaching from the east: Lee Vining

From sometime around late May or early June until late October you can approach Yosemite from the east over the ten-thousand-foot Tioga Pass from US-395 and the town of **LEE VINING** (see p.409). You are almost two hours' drive from the Yosemite Valley heartland, but this area provides unparalleled access to the Tuolumne Meadows high country. Unless you want to stay in Lee Vining, or at *Tuolumne Meadows Lodge* (see p.465), your best bet is to **camp** just outside the park at the *Sawmill Walk-in* campground or the campgrounds in Lee Vining Canyon (see p.409 for all).

Approaching from the west: Groveland, Coulterville, and Mariposa

Better bets for bases outside of the park are the western towns, particularly tiny **GROVELAND**, forty miles from the valley on Hwy-120, which retains verandahed wooden sidewalks and exudes a liberal air. South of here, and slightly off the main routes into the park, lies **COULTERVILLE**, the entirety of its diminutive heart listed as a State Historical Site. Most of the buildings and covered boardwalks date back to the mid-nineteenth century when this was on the main stage route into Yosemite. Travelers often stayed at **George Coulter's Hotel**, now transformed into a small local **museum** (Wed–Sun 10am–4pm; donations suggested), while others – John Muir and Theodore Roosevelt among them – stayed across the road at *Hotel Jeffery* (see "Accommodation" on p.465). Built in 1854, it remains the centerpiece of the town, and after a few minutes following the self-guided tour around the old town you should definitely repair to the long wooden bar of the hotel's swing-door *Magnolia Saloon*. Horse tack and mining paraphernalia hang from the ceiling, old aquatints and prints cover the walls, and there might even be someone bashing away at the honky-tonk piano in the corner.

Further south, Hwy-140 runs through the bustling Gold Rush town of **MARIPOSA**, 45 miles from the valley, which, in the **Mariposa Country Courthouse**, corner of Jones and 10th streets (free tours by arrangement ☎209/966-3685), boasts the oldest law-enforcement establishment west of the Mississippi still in continuous use. Built without nails, the lumber was rough-cut from a nearby stand of white pine, and you can still see the saw marks on the hand-planed spectator benches. The town's heritage is further celebrated at the **Museum and History Center**, corner of Jesse and 12th streets (March–Oct daily 10am–4.30pm; Feb, Nov & Dec daily 10am–4pm; Jan Sat & Sun only; $3; ☎209/966-2924), mildly diverting for its mock-up of a Gold Rush–era store and the large-scale mining paraphernalia scattered outside. In truth, you're better off at the **California State Mining and Mineral Museum**, two miles south on Hwy-49 (May–Sept daily 10am–6pm; Oct–April daily except Tues 10am–4pm; $3; ☎209/742-7625, @www.parks.ca.gov), which revels in the glory days of the mid-nineteenth century with realistic reconstructions of a mine and stamp mill plus a vault where, among the assorted treasures, lies the largest existing nugget ever uncovered in California, a thirteen-pound chunk valued at over $1 million. There's the very helpful **Mariposa County Visitor Centre** at 5158 Hwy-140 (mid-May–mid-Sept Mon–Sat 7am–8pm, Sun 8am–5pm; mid-Sept–mid-May Mon–Sat 8am–5pm, Sun closed; ☎209/966-7081, recorded info ☎1-800/208-2434, @www.mariposa.org), with all you need to know about Yosemite and around. Free **Internet access** is available at the library, beside the courthouse at Jones and 10th (Mon & Sat 10am–2pm, Tues & Thurs 9.30am–6pm, Wed & Fri 9.30am–5pm).

Further east along Hwy-140, on the way to Yosemite, the small towns of **Midpines** and **El Portal** also offer affordable lodging outside of the park (see "Accommodation," p.465).

Approaching from the south: Oakhurst and Fish Camp

Yosemite visitors arriving from the south will come through **OAKHURST**, fifteen miles south of the southern park entrance, a booming sprawl of malls and sky-high signs for chain hotels and fast-food joints. Nonetheless, it makes a handy base for the southern section of the park and, with your own transport, day-trips into Yosemite Valley, fifty miles away, are quite feasible. The relocated buildings of the **Fresno Flats Historical Park**, almost a mile from the center on Road 427 (unrestricted access), won't detain you for long, though you should make use of the **Yosemite Sierra Visitors Bureau**, 41969 Hwy-41 (Mon–Sat 8.30am–5pm, Sun 9am–1pm; ☎559/683-4636, @www.go2yosemite.net), which stocks armloads of information on Yosemite. The tiny huddle of hotels which makes up **FISH CAMP** lies ten miles north of Oakhurst, handy for Wawona, the Mariposa Grove, and something to keep the kids quiet – *The Logger*, 56001 Hwy-41 (March–Oct daily; $14; ☎559/683-7273, @www.ymsprr.com), an oil-burning train that plies a two-mile track into the forest from where hewn timber was once carted. In the height of summer, several trains run each day giving you the option of spending some time at the picnic area in the woods at the far end.

Smarter than the average bear

You may never see a **bear** anywhere else in California, but spend a couple of days in Yosemite Valley and you've a good chance of spotting one, probably breaking into a car or roaming the campgrounds looking for a free meal. Banging pans and yelling – from a safe distance, of course – will probably drive them off, but their dependence on human food has led to several bears being shot each year. Safe **food storage** is now mandatory in the park and, as they say, "a fed bear is a dead bear," so do them and yourself a favor by keeping all food and smelly items – deodorant, sun screen, toothpaste, etc – either inside your room or in the metal lockers in campgrounds, parking lots, and at trailheads. There is greater risk at night, but it is sensible to use bear boxes 24/7 unless you are actually preparing the food. Bring a padlock if you are concerned about your groceries being stolen.

Yosemite bears are not deterred by tent walls or car panels. They have learnt to recognize coolers, bags of groceries, food wrappers, and even empty soda cans inside vehicles, and once on the scent all the bear needs to do is pop a window by leaning on it or peel back a door with one paw.

You are encouraged to **report bear-related problems** (and even sightings) on ☏209/372-0322.

Arrival, information, and park transport

Yosemite is always open: **park entry** costs $20 per vehicle including passengers, $10 for each cyclist and hiker, and is valid for seven days. Pay at the ranger stations when you enter, or if they're closed, at the visitor center in the valley, or when you leave. To encourage use of public transportation, bus passengers pay no entry fees.

On arrival at any of the park entrances, you'll be given an excellent map of the park, the glossy annual *Yosemite* booklet, and the current *Yosemite Today*

Winter in Yosemite

From December to April, those prepared to cope with blocked roads – the Tioga Pass is always closed in winter – and below-freezing temperatures are amply rewarded at Yosemite; thick snow, frozen waterfalls, and far fewer people make for almost unimaginable beauty and silence. **Accommodation** is cheaper at these times too (check the website for special deals), and much easier to obtain, though weekends can still get pretty full. Many low-country **campgrounds** are open, and restrictions on backcountry camping are eased – you'll want a good sleeping bag and tent.

Much of Yosemite is fabulous **skiing** territory. Lessons, equipment rental, tows, and 25 miles of groomed cross-country trails are available at the **Badger Pass Ski Area** (ⓦwww.badgerpass.com) on the road to Glacier Point, accessible via a free shuttle from the valley. All-day lift tickets for the modest downhill ski area cost $31, daily equipment rental will set you back $22.50 for downhill, $17 for cross-country, and $32.50 for snowboards. Lessons start from $42. If you want someone to take you out on Badger Pass's groomed trails, contact the Cross Country Ski Center (☏209/372-8444), who run all manner of beginners, improvers, and Telemark and skating lessons, and lead overnight ski tours. In Yosemite Valley there's **ice skating** at the open-air Curry Village rink (normally $6.50, plus $3.25 skate rental).

Be aware if driving into the park that **tire chains** are recommended from November to April and can be rented in towns approaching the park. Inside the park, they are only available for sale.

Delaware North Companies Parks & Resorts at Yosemite (DNC) 6771 N Palm Avenue, Fresno CA 93704; Lodging reservations ☎559/252-4848; Tour reservations ☎209/372-1240; Guest facilities and services ☎209/372-1000, ⓦwww .yosemitepark.com. DNC runs virtually all park lodging, restaurants, tours, activities, and shuttle buses. Reservations can be made up to a year and a day in advance, Mon–Fri 7am–pm, Sat & Sun 7am–6pm PST.

National Park Reservation Service (NPRS) PO Box 1600, Cumberland, MD 21502 ☎301/722-1257 or 1-800/436-7275, ⓦreservations.nps.gov. Advance campground reservations by mail, website, or phone (7am–7pm PST).

Wilderness Permits and Information Yosemite Association, PO Box 545, Yosemite, CA 95389 ☎209/372-0740, ⓦwww.nps.gov/yose/wilderness. Park Service contact for obtaining wilderness permits for overnight stays in the backcountry.

Yosemite National Park ☎209/372-0200, ⓦwww.nps.gov/yose. Detailed website and recorded info covering everything about the park including weather and road conditions.

listings paper which comes out every week or two and covers current events and the extensive range of (mostly free) ranger programs. If you have more specific inquiries, try the park's most useful **visitor center** at **Yosemite Village** (daily: June–Sept 9am–7pm, Oct–May 8.30am–5pm; ☎209/372-0299), where you can pick up information and maps, including a topographic map ($9) essential for any adventurous hikes. There are other visitor centers at **Tuolumne Meadows** (mid-June–Sept daily 9am–5pm, later in mid-season; ☎209/372-0263), at the **Big Oak Flat** entrance (Easter–Sept daily 9am–5pm; Oct & Nov Fri–Mon 9am–noon & 1–5pm; Dec–Easter open occasional weekends; ☎209/379-1899), and **Wawona** (mid–May to mid–Sept daily 8.30am–4.30pm; ☎209/375-9501). For **free** hiking permits and all the route-planning help you could ask for, pop next door to the **Wilderness Center** (mid-May–June & early Sept–mid-Oct daily 8am–5pm; July–early Sept daily 7.30am–6pm; closed in winter; ☎209/372-0745).

Useful **phone numbers** and **websites** are covered in the box above, and all manner of other services are included in the "Listings" section (see p.481).

Park transport

Three roads from the San Joaquin Valley end up at **Yosemite Valley**, roughly in the center of the park's 1200 square miles, and home to its most dramatic scenery. At the southern edge of the park, Hwy-41 passes the **Mariposa Grove** and **Wawona**; from here it's 27 miles further to the valley. **Tuolumne Meadows** is in the high country, sixty-odd miles northeast of the valley, close to the Tioga Pass entrance (Hwy-120) on the eastern side of the park.

While having your own vehicle is a boon for exploring the wider park, traffic congestion spoils everyone's fun on the valley floor, and if you're driving in just for the day, leave your vehicle in the day-use parking lots at Yosemite and Curry villages. You can then use the free and frequent **shuttle buses** that operate on the valley floor, running anticlockwise on a loop that passes through, or close to, all the main points of interest, trailheads, and accommodation areas. In high season, they run roughly every twenty minutes between 7am and 10pm to most sections of the valley, with slightly reduced hours at other times.

Although bicycles are not allowed off paved surfaces, **cycling** is an excellent way to get around the valley with twelve miles of dedicated bike paths along the valley floor. Yosemite Lodge and Curry Village (April–Nov only) both rent city bikes for $7.50 per hour or $24 per day.

For straying further afield use the hikers' buses, which call at roadside trailheads on the way to Tuolumne Meadows and Glacier Point, and double as round-trip narrated tours for those on a tighter schedule. The **Tuolumne Meadows Hikers' Bus** (mid-June–early Sept; $14.50 one way, $23 round-trip) makes the two-and-a-half-hour run to Tuolumne Meadows, leaving hotels around Yosemite Valley around 8.20am and departing Tuolumne at 2.35pm, giving just over three hours at the Meadows. The **Glacier Point Hikers' Bus** (June–Oct; 2 daily; $15 each way) runs up to Glacier Point three times a day, where it stays for around an hour.

Failing that, there are always **guided tours** (℡209/372-1240), which range from the rather dull two-hour valley-floor spin, costing $20.50, to the all-day Mariposa and Glacier Point Grand Tour (June–Oct) at $55; all bookable through accommodation reception areas.

Accommodation

Once in the park, **accommodation** can be a problem; it's almost essential to book well in advance and anything other than camping can be expensive. Even canvas tents cost what you would pay for a reasonable motel elsewhere. All accommodation in the national park – the majority of it right in the valley – is operated by **DNC** (see box, opposite) and should be booked a few weeks ahead, longer for holiday weekends. Places generally reduce their charges in winter, though weekend prices remain close to high-season levels. One solution to the problem is to stay just outside the park (see "Approaching Yosemite," p.460) and commute into it daily.

If you are really well organized you might also want to consider the High Sierra camp vacations (see "Listings," p.482).

In the valley

The Ahwahnee a short distance from Yosemite Village at shuttle stop 3 (call DNC). Undoubtedly the finest place to stay in Yosemite, with rooms decorated in the hotel's Native American motif. Usually booked months in advance despite room rates starting close to $400, but worth visiting to view the wonderfully grand public areas, or for a drink or a meal. **9**

Curry Village a mile from Yosemite Village at shuttle stops 14 and 20 (call DNC). A large family-oriented area dotted mostly with canvas tent cabins each fitted with four beds on a wooden plinth. There are also cramped solid-walled cabins and spacious motel-style rooms and some attractive cottages. Cottages **7**, rooms **5**, cabins with bath **5**, cabins without bath **4**, tent cabins **3**

Housekeeping Camp half a mile from Yosemite Village at shuttle stop 12 (call DNC). Ranks of simple concrete-walled plastic-roofed cabins with beds on sleeping platforms and the use of a fire grate and picnic table. April to late Oct only. **3**

Yosemite Lodge half a mile west of Yosemite Village at shuttle stop 8 (call DNC). Sprawling middle-market accommodation popular with tour groups, its proximity to half-decent restaurants, grocery stores, and a pool making it perhaps the most convenient accommodation in the valley. Rooms are motel-style, all with private bath and phone but no TV or a/c. Deluxe rooms **7**, standard rooms **5**

The rest of the park

Tuolumne Meadows Lodge Tuolumne Meadows (call DNC). A large cluster of canvas tent cabins each with four beds and a wood-burning stove, but no electricity, located at nearly 9000ft and perfect for the first or last night of a long hiking trip. Only available mid-June to mid-Sept. Meals served. **4**

Wawona Hotel Wawona (call DNC; front desk ℡209/375-6556). An elegant New England–style hotel, parts of which date from 1879, with attractive public areas, distinctive wooden verandahs dotted with white wicker chairs, and

Rock climbers the world over flock to Yosemite, drawn by the challenge of inching up three-thousand-foot walls of sheer granite that soar skyward under the California sun. Quite simply, the valley is seen as the pinnacle of climbing aspirations, with acres of superb, clean rock, easily accessible world-class routes, and reliable summer weather drawing a vibrant climbing community bubbling over with campfire tales.

Wander near the base of most of the valley's cliffs and you'll hear the (sometimes) gentle banter of climbers and telltale chink of climbing hardware. But the best place to marvel at climbers' antics is from the roadside next to **El Cap Meadows**, always dotted with tourists craning their necks and training binoculars on the biggest slab of granite of them all, **El Capitan**. The apparently featureless face hides hairline crack systems a thousand feet long, seemingly insurmountable overhangs, and gargantuan towers topped off with narrow ledges only given any sense of scale by the flea-like figures of climbers. The routes are highly convoluted, but what is probably the world's most famous climb, **The Nose**, lies straight ahead, tracing a line up the prow of the El Capitan past the relative luxury of El Cap Towers. This twenty-foot by six-foot patio, over 1500 feet above the valley floor, is used as a bivouac spot by climbers who typically spend three to five nights on the route. "In-a-day" attempts usually involve 24 hours of continuous climbing, though the current record (set in 2001) stands at an astounding three hours and twenty-four minutes. The renowned **North American Wall** route lies to the right passing directly through a massive stain on the rock, which looks remarkably like a map of North America.

Big Wall climbing

Many of the most celebrated routes in Yosemite are what's known as "Big Wall" routes, tackled by **aid climbing**, where bits of metal are hammered into cracks and hauled on to achieve upward movement. The scale of Yosemite's walls is such that few cracks can be followed from bottom to top and to get from one crack to another, climbers employ death-defying **pendulums**, and repeatedly sweep across the face gaining momentum until they can lunge out at a tiny flake or fingertip hold. All this "nailing" and swinging takes time and most Big Wallers are forced to spend nights slung in a kind of lightweight camp bed known as a **portaledge**. Food, gallons of water, sleeping bags, warm clothing, and wet-weather gear must all be lugged up in haul sacks, along with a boombox and a rack of CDs deviously strapped and arranged so they can't be dropped – after all, it can get a bit tedious hammering away up there for hours on end. As Yosemite veteran John Long writes: "Climbing a wall can be a monumental pain in the ass. No one could pay you enough to do it. A thousand dollars would be too little by far. But you wouldn't sell the least of the memories for ten times that sum."

Some history

Yosemite has long captured the imagination of climbers but technical rock climbing didn't kick off here until 1933, when four Bay Area climbers reached what is now known as the Lunch Ledge, 1000 feet up Washington Column – the tower opposite Half Dome. With the aid of heavy steel **pitons** for driving into cracks, and equally weighty **karabiners** for attaching the ropes to the pitons, climbers began to knock off climbs such as the fifteen-pitch **Royal Arches** route, which weaves its way up the ledges and slabs behind *The Ahwahnee*.

After World War II, demobbed climbers employed newly developed, tough nylon ropes and lightweight safety equipment to push standards to new levels, and pipe dreams became realistic propositions. An early conquest, in 1947, was **Lost Arrow Spire**, which rises to the right of Yosemite Falls and is easy to spot in the early morning and late afternoon light when the spire casts a shadow on the wall nearby. This was the first route intentionally approached as a multi-day ascent, much of the groundwork being laid by Swiss-born blacksmith **John Salathé**. He was at the cutting edge of climbing, putting up technically demanding aid routes through the late 1940s and early 1950s, and even fashioning his own tougher carbon-steel pitons from the axles of a Model A Ford.

For the next twenty years Salathé's mantle was assumed by classical purist **Royal Robbins**, and **Warren Harding**, who was prepared to place a protection bolt just about anywhere if it would help him get up something new. Little love was lost between them but when Robbins' team first scaled the face of **Half Dome** in 1957, Harding was on the summit to congratulate them. It was a magnificent effort and ranked as the hardest climb in North America at the time. Yosemite became an international forcing ground for aid climbing, and Americans were suddenly matching, and even surpassing, the achievements of previously dominant Europeans.

Now even the mighty El Cap seemed possible. **The Nose** was the most obvious line but refused to submit for seventeen months, even after Warren Harding used four massive pitons fashioned from stove legs scavenged from the Berkeley city dump and drove them into what are still known as the Stoveleg Cracks. Harding and two colleagues finally topped out in 1958 after a single thirteen-day push, the culmination of 47 days' work on the route.

With these critical ascents completed, climbers' aspirations broadened and the 1960s became the **Golden Age** of climbing in the Yosemite Valley, when it drew a motley collection of dropouts and misfits, many ranking among the world's finest climbers. Almost all the major walls and hundreds of minor routes were completed at this time. Purists at the top of their sport became disenchanted with the artificiality of aid ascents and began to "free" pitches: not hauling up on all the hardware, but using it only for protection in case of a fall. The culmination of years of cutting-edge climbing, and months of route-specific training was Lynn Hill's ground-breaking free ascent of The Nose in 1993, praised and admired by all, if ruefully by some in Yosemite's traditionally macho climbing community.

Practicalities

The **best months** for climbing in Yosemite Valley are April, May, September, and October. In summer, the climbs on the domes around Tuolumne Meadows are cooler and usually considered a better bet. Some areas, notably the southeast face of El Capitan, are occasionally off limits to protect the nesting sites of peregrine falcons. Whatever type of climbing you do, follow the guidelines for "**minimum impact climbing**" – never chip holds or add bolts to existing routes, and remove all litter, including human waste.

Everyone stays at the bohemian **Camp 4**, near *Yosemite Lodge*, a trampled, dusty, and noisy site often entirely taken over by climbers. It is relatively cheap, with a great sense of camaraderie, and an excellent **bulletin board** for teaming up with climbing partners, selling gear, organizing a ride, or just meeting friends.

For a more organized introduction to the climber's craft or to brush up on a few skills, engage the services of the Yosemite Mountaineering School (℡209/372-8344), which is based at Tuolumne Meadows in summer (June–Aug) and in Yosemite Valley for the rest of the year. Experts run daily courses ranging from the one-day beginners' classes ($120–160) through various intermediate classes to private full-day guided climbs (one person $285, two people $210 each).

Rock-climbing **gear** is available from the Mountain Shop in Tuolumne Meadows (summer only), and the well-stocked and competitively priced Mountain Shop in *Curry Village* (daily 8am–6pm).

The essential **guidebooks** to local climbs are Don Reid's *Yosemite: Free Climbs* and *Yosemite: Big Walls*, published by Falcon Guides (ⓦwww.globepequot.com), and Chris McNamara's selection of *Supertopos*, which are available in bookstores and downloadable at ⓦwww.supertopos.com.

grounds that include a pool, tennis courts, and a nine-hole golf course. Rooms all lack phone, TV, and a/c, but have been gracefully restored with old-style furniture, Victoria-patterned wallpaper, and ceiling fans – though those in the main lodge are fairly small and lack bathrooms. Rooms with bath ➐, without bath ➎

White Wolf Lodge about halfway from the valley to Tuolumne Meadows (call DNC). Spacious four-berth tent cabins with wood-burning stove and candles perfectly sited for day-hikes to Lukens and Harden lakes, and the Grand Canyon of the Tuolumne River. Late June–early Sept only. Cabins ➎, tent cabins ➍

Yosemite Peregrine 7509 Henness Circle, Yosemite West ☎209/372-8517 or 1-800/396-3639, ⓦwww.yosemiteperegrine.com. Well-appointed B&B midway between the valley and Wawona, tastefully decorated in Southwestern or woodsy themes, and with a hot tub. Home-cooked breakfast is served on the deck if the weather cooperates. The adjacent *Falcon's Nest* (same contact details) has a couple of more budget-oriented rooms and a two-night minimum (➎). ➐

Hwy-120: Groveland and Coulterville

The following are listed by increasing distance from Yosemite.

Yosemite Lakes 31191 Hwy-120, five miles from the Big Oak Flat entrance ☎209/962-0100 or 1-800/533-1001, ⓦwww.stayatyosemite.com. Reasonable family-oriented resort that benefits from being close to the park. Tent sites are well spaced ($27.50; full hook-up $38), there are rustic shared-bath bunkhouse cabins (➍), and conical canvas-walled yurts – with polished wood floors, a deck, cooking facilities, shower, and toilet – which sleep four in considerable comfort. ➏

Yosemite Westgate Lodge 7633 Hwy-120, 15 miles from the Big Oak Flat entrance ☎209/962-5281 or 1-800/253-9673, ⓦwww.insight.com. The closest standard motel to the park on Hwy-120 is comfortable and has all the expected facilities including satellite TV, phone, pool, and spa. There's a decent restaurant next door and two kids under 12 stay free with two adults; rates drop dramatically in winter. ➍

Groveland Motel & Indian Village 18933 Hwy-120, Groveland, 25 miles from the Big Oak Flat entrance ☎209/962-7865 or 1-888/849-3529. Some fairly basic a/c cabins with cable TV (➍), an assortment of mobile homes, mostly with small kitchens (➍), and a three-bedroom house that

sleeps six (➐) scattered around wooded grounds, plus concrete-floored teepees (➊), each with a double bed.

Hotel Charlotte 18959 Hwy-120, Groveland, 25 miles from the Big Oak Flat entrance ☎209/962-6455 or 1-800/961-7799. Basic but full of character, this warm and no-nonsense ten-room hotel dates back to 1921. Rooms are mostly small and without phone or TV, and some share beautiful old-fashioned bathrooms. Rates include a good continental breakfast, and there's a common TV room. ➍

Groveland Hotel 18767 Hwy-120, Groveland, 25 miles from the Big Oak Flat Entrance ☎209/962-4000 or 1-800/273-3314, ⓦwww.groveland.com. Gorgeous mining-era hotel with luxurious individually styled antique-filled rooms, mostly with deep baths. Suites (➑) feature spa tubs and real fires. ➏

Hotel Jeffrey junction of Hwy-49 & Hwy-132, Coulterville, 30 miles from the Big Oak Flat entrance ☎209/878-3471 or 1-800/464-3471, ⓦwww.yosemitegold.com/jefferyhotel. Classic Gold Rush–era hotel used by original Yosemite sightseers, as well as John Muir and Theodore Roosevelt. Rooms are mostly old-fashioned and smallish, but there are also some two-room suites. All have access to a communal lounge and sunny deck. Suites ➏, en-suite rooms ➎, rooms ➍

Yosemite Gold Country Motel 10407 Hwy-49, Coulterville ☎209/878 3400 or 1-800/247-9884, ⓦwww.yosemitegoldcountry.com. This excellent-value motel, half a mile north of Coulterville, has ageing, but well-kept and nicely appointed a/c motel rooms each with VCR/TV, fridge, and microwave.

Hwy-140: Mariposa, Midpines, and El Portal

The following are listed by increasing distance from Yosemite.

Yosemite View Lodge 11136 Hwy-140, El Portal, two miles west of the Arch Rock entrance ☎209/379-2681 or 1-888/742-4371, ⓦwww.yosemite-motels.com. Vast and luxurious – though slightly soulless – complex beside the tumbling Merced River, hard against the park boundary. The modern rooms all have a/c, phone, cable TV, but you pay a premium to get river view, fireplace, in-room spa, and kitchenette. Often booked out but worth trying for no-shows. ➐

Yosemite Bug Hostel & Lodge 6979 Hwy-140, Midpines, 23 miles west of the Arch Rock entrance ☎209/966 6666, ⓦwww.yosemitebug.com. Set in twenty acres of woodland, this low-cost to mid-range lodge, HI-USA hostel and campground is the handiest budget lodging near Yosemite. Basic self-catering facilities exist for those staying in dorms, but there's also the excellent *Café at the Bug* (see p.481) on site. Comfortable mixed and single-sex dorms ($14.30, non-members $17.60) are supplemented by tent cabins (❷), shared-bath private rooms (❸), and very comfortable and distinctively decorated en-suite rooms with decks but no phone or TV (❺, weekends ❻). Pitching your own tent costs $17 per site. There's Internet access, a lounge with books and games, access to a good summer swimming hole, and a YARTS bus stop outside. Reservations essential June–Sept. ❷–❻

Muir Lodge 6833 Hwy-140, Midpines, 8.6 miles east of Mariposa, 23.2 miles west of the Arch Rock entrance ⊕209/966-2468, ⓦyosemitemuirlodge .com. Old and fairly basic motel units (with TV and microwave) that haven't been upgraded for years, but are at least clean and cheap. ❸

EC Yosemite Motel 5180 Jones St, Mariposa, 35 miles from the Arch Rock entrance ⊕209/742-6800, ⓦwww.eclodgeyosemite.com. Pleasant and good-value motel with some new, large a/c rooms mostly with two beds; all rooms have shower/tub combos and cable TV. There's a heated pool and spa, and rates may drop to as little as $55 a night in winter. ❹

Sierra View Motel 4993 7th St, Mariposa, 35 miles from the Arch Rock entrance ⊕209/966-5793 or 1-800/627-843. Peaceful, welcoming, and good-value budget motel just off Mariposa's main drag, offering continental breakfast with smallish rooms and larger suites, all equipped with a/c. ❸

Highland House B&B 3125 Wild Dove Lane, Mariposa, 35 miles from the Arch Rock entrance ⊕209/966-3737 or 1-888/477-5089, ⓦwww .highlandhousebandb.com. Tucked away amid ponderosa pines and incense cedars over six miles off Hwy-140, it is worth the effort to reach this superb and tranquil B&B. Its three elegantly furnished rooms all have private bathroom with tub and shower, and the suite (❻) has a four-poster bed, fireplace, and VCR. The breakfasts are gorgeous, and the common area even comes with a pool table. ❺

Sierra House B&B 4981 Indian Peak Rd, Mariposa, 40 miles from the Arch Rock entrance ⊕209/966-3515 or 1-800/496-3515, ⓦwww .sierrahousebnb.com. Welcoming rural B&B right beside Hwy-49, four miles southeast of Mariposa, where the three rooms all have private facilities,

though you'll need to go for the Middle East Room (❻) to get a clawfoot bath. A full breakfast is served and you can plan your day in the lounge or out on the sunny porch. ❺

Hwy-41: Oakhurst and Fish Camp

The following are listed by increasing distance from Yosemite.

Owl's Nest Lodging 1235 Hwy-41, Fish Camp ⊕559/683-3484, ⓦwww.owlsnestlodging.com. Perhaps the best deal on the southern side of the park, with large guest rooms for two (❺) and self-contained chalets (❼) that sleep up to six. Nicely decorated, friendly, and right by a stream. Closed Nov–March. ❺–❼

Narrow Gauge Inn 48571 Hwy-41, Fish Camp ⊕559/683-7720 or 1-888/644-9050, ⓦwww .narrowgaugeinn.com. Attractive lodge with a wide selection of rooms, many with a balcony and views over the forest, and a fine on-site restaurant (see p.481). All rooms come with phone, TV, and continental breakfast, and the inn has a pool and spa. ❻

Sierra Sky Ranch 50552 Rd 632, Oakhurst, 12 miles from the South entrance ⊕559/683-8040, ⓦwww.geocities.com/sierraskyranch. This woodsy lodge was started in 1875 on what was the largest ranch in the state. It still has a spacious feel with a verandah-girt main lodge and large lounge plus a pool, creek swimming, and fishing on-site. Ageing rooms come without TV or phone but a continental breakfast is included. ❺

Hounds Tooth Inn 42071 Hwy-41, 3 miles north of Oakhurst ⊕559/642-6600 or 1-888/642-6610, ⓦwww.houndstoothinn.com. Modern B&B with a dozen individually decorated rooms, most with either a fireplace or spa bath (or both) and all with a/c. Complimentary wine served each evening, and the buffet breakfasts are delicious. Rooms ❻, deluxe ❼

Days Inn 40662 Hwy-41, Oakhurst ⊕559/642-2525 or 1-800/329-7644, ⓦwww.daysinn.com. The cheapest of Oakhurst's franchise motels, but still done to a high standard with comfortable rooms and HBO. ❹

The Homestead 41110 Rd 600, 2.5 miles off Hwy-49 in Ahwahnee, near Oakhurst ⊕559/683-0495, ⓦwww.homesteadcottages.com. Just a handful of very attractive and beautifully outfitted adobe cottages – a/c, TV, gas grill – each with full self-catering facilities, comfortable lounge area, and a nice deck. Two-night minimum stay at weekends. ❼

Camping

As with any national park, **camping** is the best way to really feel part of your surroundings, though this is perhaps less true in Yosemite Valley where the campgrounds are large and crowded. In summer it is almost essential to book beforehand (see "Useful Yosemite contacts" box, p.464): reservations open in one-month chunks, four months in advance, so to book for the month beginning July 15 you can, and should, call from March 15. Otherwise you'll need to show up at the Curry Village Reservations Office very early in the morning and hope for cancellations. Other than *Camp 4*, all valley sites cost $18 and none have **showers** or **laundry** facilities (see "Listings," p.481). Camping in the valley is restricted to a month in any calendar year but between May and mid-September a week is the maximum stay. Camping outside recognized sites in the valley is strictly forbidden.

In addition to the main campgrounds there are **backpacker campgrounds** in Yosemite Valley, Tuolumne Meadows, and Hetch Hetchy, designed for hikers about to start (or just finishing) a wilderness trip and costing $5 per night – you must have a wilderness permit to use these.

Finally, with enough time you really should get out to one of several **primitive campgrounds** in the backcountry. Designed specifically for hikers, these have fire rings and some form of water source, which must be treated. To use them, or to camp elsewhere in the backcountry, you must get a **free wilderness permit** (see box, pp.478–479) – as ever, you must camp a mile from any road, four miles from a populated area, and at least a hundred yards from water sources and trails. Remember to carry a stove and fuel as indiscriminate use of trees could jeopardize future freedom to camp in the backcountry. Camping on the summit of Half Dome is not permitted.

In the valley

Camp 4 Walk-in (all year; $5 per person; 4000ft). First-come-first-served campground west of and away from the other valley sites, popular with rock climbers. It is a fairly bohemian (some would say squalid) place with six-person sites just a few yards from a dusty parking lot. It is often full by 9am, especially in spring and fall, so join the line early.

North Pines, Upper Pines, Lower Pines (March–Oct, Upper Pines all year; $18; 4000ft). Largely indistinguishable, pine-shrouded sites, all with toilets, water, and fire rings. Popular with RV users. Reservations essential.

Outside the valley

Bridalveil Creek (July–early Sept; $12; 7200ft). High country, first-come-first-served campground off Glacier Point Road with good access to wilderness trails.

Crane Flat (June–Sept; $18; 6200ft). Large campground northwest of the valley, at the start of Hwy-120 and close to a stand of sequoias. Reservations required.

Hodgdon Meadow (all year; $18; 4900ft). Relatively quiet campground right on the park's western boundary just off Hwy-120. Take Old Big Oak Flat Road for half a mile. Reservations required May–Sept, first-come-first-served ($12) at other times.

Porcupine Flat (July–early Sept; $8; 8100ft). Attractive and small first-come-first-served campground near the road to Tuolumne Meadows, nearly forty miles from the valley. Stream water available.

Tamarack Flat (June–Sept; $8; 6300ft). Small campground two miles off the Hwy-120 Tioga Road, 23 miles from the valley and with only limited RV access. Stream water available.

Tuolumne Meadows (July–Sept; $18; 8600ft). Large and popular streamside campground beside a subalpine meadow that is effectively three campgrounds in one. Half the sites are available by advance reservation, half by same-day reservation, and a further 25 sites ($5 per person) are available for backpackers with wilderness permits. There are flush toilets, piped water, and showers ($3) nearby at *Tuolumne Meadows Lodge*.

Wawona (all year; $18; 4000ft). The only site in the southern sector of the park, approximately a mile north of the *Wawona Hotel*. Some walk-in sites are reserved for car-free campers. Reservations required May–Sept; rest of year $12.

White Wolf (July–early Sept; $12; 8000ft). First-come-first-served tent and RV site a mile north of Hwy-120 midway between the valley and Tuolumne Meadows.

Yosemite Creek (July–early Sept; $8; 7600ft). First-come-first-served tent-only site ideal for escaping the crowds, though it can fill up very quickly in the summer. Inconveniently sited five miles off Hwy-120, but almost equidistant between the valley and Tuolumne Meadows. Stream water available.

Outside the park

Dimond O Evergreen Road, off Hwy-120 West (late April–mid-Oct; $16; 4400ft). National Forest campground one mile west of the Big Oak Flat entrance, with tent and RV sites, piped water, and pit toilets.

Lee Vining Creek off Hwy-120 East (late April–Oct; $8; 7800ft). A series of almost identical streamside National Forest campgrounds along Poole Power Plant Road, 9 miles west of the Tioga Pass entrance.

Sawmill Walk-in Mile 1.5 Saddlebag Lake Road, 3.7 miles east of the Tioga Pass entrance (June–mid-Oct; $9; 9800ft). Primitive walk-in campground around four hundred yards from its parking lot, superbly sited amid jagged peaks that feel a world away from the glaciated domes around Tuolumne.

Summerdale Hwy-41 (May–Oct; $17; 5000ft). National Forest campground 1.5 miles south of the park's South entrance and handy for both Wawona and the Mariposa Grove.

Yosemite Valley

Even the most evocative photography can only hint at the pleasure to be found in simply gazing at **YOSEMITE VALLEY**. From massive hunks of granite rising three thousand feet up from the four-thousand-foot valley floor to the subtle colorings of wild flowers, the variations in the valley can be both enormous and discreet. Aside from just looking, there are many easy walks around the lush fields to waterfalls and lakes, and much tougher treks up the enormous cliffs (see box, pp.478–479).

The valley's defining features are its enormous cliffs and thundering waterfalls; in fact nowhere else in the world is there such an array of cascades concentrated in such a small area, though a mild winter can cause many of these falls to dry up as early as July.

If there is any drawback, it's that this part of Yosemite is the busiest, and you're rarely far from other visitors or the park's commercial trappings, notably in **Yosemite Village** and **Curry Village**, the two main concentrations of shops and restaurants. Most of the crowds can be easily left behind by taking any path which contains much of a slope, but a couple of days exploring the valley leaves you more than ready to press on to the park's less populated regions.

The big cliffs

However you approach the valley, your view will be partially blocked by **El Capitan**, a vast monolith jutting forward from the adjacent cliffs and looming 3593ft above the valley floor. One of the largest pieces of exposed granite in the world, "The Captain" is a full 320 acres of gray-tan granite seemingly devoid of vegetation and almost vertical. El Cap's enormous size isn't really apparent until you join the slack-jawed tourists craning their necks and training binoculars and cameras on rock climbers on the face. Eventually you'll pick out flea-sized specks inching up what appears to be a flawless wall, though closer inspection reveals a pattern of flakes, fissures, and small ledges. The most accessible sequence of these comprises what is probably the most famous rock-climbing route in the world, **The Nose** (see box, pp.466–467).

Impressive though El Capitan is, for most people it is the arching **Half Dome** that instantly grabs their attention. A stunning sight topping out at 8842 feet, it rises almost 5000 feet above the valley floor, with its two-thousand-foot northwest face only seven degrees off the vertical, making it the **sheerest cliff in North America**. Though impressive from the valley, the best views of Half Dome are from Glacier Point (see p.477), especially around sunset.

Ambitious day-hikers (see pp.478–479) wanting to get up close and personal can make it to the shallow saddle of the dome's thirteen-acre summit, tackling the final 400 feet by way of a steep steel-cable staircase hooked on to the rock's curving back. Once at the almost flat summit, the brave (or foolish) can inch out towards the edge of the projecting lip for a vertiginous look straight down the near-vertical face. While the cables remain all year, the cable supports and wooden slats only stay in place from late May to mid-October, making a winter ascent very difficult (though not impossible). Keep clear of the summit if there are any signs of impending storms; lightning strikes during almost every thunderstorm, which can occur at any time of year.

The major waterfalls

At 2425 feet, **Yosemite Falls** is widely claimed to be the fifth highest water-fall in the world, and the highest in North America. It is a somewhat spurious assertion, since it is actually two falls separated by 675 feet of churning rapids and chutes known as **Middle Cascade**. Nonetheless, the 1430-foot **Upper Yosemite Fall** and the 320-foot **Lower Yosemite Fall** are magnificent, especially in May and early June when runoff from melting snow turns them into a foaming torrent. The flow typically dries up by mid-August, leaving a dark stain of algae and lichen to mark the spot. A flat, quarter-mile asphalt trail (from shuttle-bus stop 6) leads along an avenue of incense cedars and ponderosa pines that frame Upper Yosemite Fall, which appears to be stacked directly above Lower Yosemite Fall, creating a perfect photo op.

Perhaps the most sensual waterfall in the park is the 620-foot **Bridalveil Fall**, a slender ribbon at the valley's western end, which in Ahwahneechee goes by the name of *Pohono* or "spirit of the puffing wind." While Bridalveil seldom completely dries up, it is best seen from April to June when winds blow the cascade outward up to twenty feet away from its base, drawing the spray out into a delicate lacy veil. The quarter-mile trail from the parking lot is four miles west of the village and not accessible by shuttle bus.

Two of the park's most striking falls are guaranteed to still be active year-round, but are sequestered away from the road up the Merced River canyon, near Happy Isles (see p.474). It is a relatively easy walk to get a glimpse of the distant 317-foot **Vernal Fall**, a curtain of water about eighty feet wide that casts bright rainbows as you walk along the wonderful Mist Trail (see box, p.478). It requires much more commitment to hike steeply upstream as far as the 594-foot **Nevada Fall**, but it is worth the effort for a close look at this sweeping cascade that drops for half its height then fans out onto the apron below.

Yosemite Village

Very much the heart of the valley, **YOSEMITE VILLAGE** is not really a cohesive "village" at all, but a settlement of scattered low buildings where mule deer wander freely. You'll find yourself returning time and again to visit shops, restaurants, banking facilities, Internet access, the post office (see "Listings" on pp.481–482 for the last three), and one of the park's **main visitor centers** (see p.464 for hours). Here, you can watch the 23-minute *Spirit of Yosemite* (every 30min), which has great footage of Yosemite through the seasons. For more great images of the park walk a few steps east to the **Ansel Adams Gallery**, which is full of fine-art prints, posters, and postcards.

Immediately west of the visitor center a hefty nine-foot **slice of a giant sequoia** trunk marks the **Yosemite Museum** (daily: July & Aug 9am–5pm; Sept–June 10am–4pm; free), home to a small selection of artifacts focusing on Native American heritage, specifically the local Ahwahneechee and the neighboring Mono Lake Paiute, with whom they traded and intermarried. One of the few crafts to flourish after contact with whites was **basketwork**: fine examples on display include a superbly detailed 1930s Mono Lake Paiute basket almost three feet in diameter, and its even larger Miwok/Paiute equivalent, painstakingly created by famed basket maker Lucy Telles. Basket-making demonstrations are given by Ahwahneechee practitioners throughout the day. A couple of **feather-trimmed dance capes** warrant a look, as does the buckskin dress worn by natives in the 1920s and 1930s during tourist demonstrations of basket weaving and dance. Though completely alien to the Miwok tradition, the Plains-style buckskin clothing and feather headdresses fulfilled the expectations of the whites who came to watch. Outside, a self-guided trail weaves around the **Indian Village of Ahwahneechee** (always open; free) with its cluster of reconstructed Indian buildings.

Fifty yards west of the museum, the **Yosemite Cemetery** (always open; free) holds just three dozen graves of early white settlers. Among the simple headstones are the graves of early orchardist **James Lamon**, and park guardian **Galen Clark**, both marked with century-old sequoias.

Worth a quick look even if you don't intend to stay or eat there is **The Ahwahnee**, a short signposted walk or shuttle-bus ride from Yosemite Village. It was built in grand style in 1927 from local rock, and is decorated with Native American motifs and some wonderful oriental rugs and carpets. It was intended to blend into its surroundings and attract the richer type of tourist, and still does both fairly effortlessly – pop in for a few minutes to sink into the deep sofas, view the collection of paintings of Yosemite's early days, or browse the skiing exhibitions in the Winter Club Room off the Great Hall.

Curry Village and the eastern valley

At some point, almost everyone finds themselves at the eastern end of the valley, which has the densest concentration of accommodation: all the main campgrounds are here along with the permanent cabins of *Housekeeping Camp* and the tent cabin complex of **CURRY VILLAGE**. This is a direct descendant of **Camp Curry**, which was started in 1899 by David and Jeannie Curry, who were keen to share their adopted home in the valley and charged just $12 a week for a "good bed, and a clean napkin every meal." It is now a rambling area of tent cabins and wooden chalets centered on a small complex of restaurants, shops, pay showers, a post office, and an outdoor amphitheater hosting ranger programs and evening shows. There's also a winter ice rink, bike rental, and a kiosk that rents rafts for use on the nearby Merced River.

The western end of Curry Village is marked by the **LeConte Memorial Lodge** (May–Sept Wed–Sun 10am–4pm; free; shuttle stop 12), a small rough-hewn granite-block structure where the **Sierra Club** maintains displays on its history, runs a conservation library, and has a fascinating relief map of the valley dating back to around 1885. The Lodge itself was built by the Sierra Club in 1903 to commemorate the eminent geologist and early supporter of John Muir, **Joseph LeConte** (1823–1901), and as the Sierra Club's Yosemite headquarters, it was managed for a couple of summers in the early 1920s by **Ansel Adams**, who was happy to do anything if it meant he could spend more time in the valley. Their evening programs (usually Fri–Sun; free) are a little more highbrow than those elsewhere in the park and might include a slide show or talk by some luminary; check *Yosemite Today* for details.

Shuttle buses head east from Curry Village to the **Nature Center at Happy Isles** (early May to mid-Sept daily 10am–4pm; free; shuttle stop 16), containing a most **family-friendly** set of displays on flora and fauna plus a hands-on exhibit allowing you to feel how hunks of rough granite get weathered down to sand, and an exhibit on a year in the life of a bear. At the rear of the Nature Center, be sure to check out the **rockfall exhibit** where a number of explanatory panels highlight the pulverized rock and flattened trees that resulted from the 1996 rockfall.

Perhaps one of the most rewarding of the easy trails leads from shuttle stop 17 around the edge of the valley floor to **Mirror Lake** (2 miles; 1hr; 100ft ascent). This compellingly calm lake (typically dry in late summer) lies beneath the great bulk of Half Dome, the rising cliff reflected on the lake's surface, and is best seen in the early morning, before too many others arrive. Most visitors to Mirror Lake follow the traffic-free paved road from the shuttle stop, but several easily found diversions steer you clear of the asphalt and the crowds.

Northern Yosemite

From the valley, Big Oak Flat Road climbs rapidly to Crane Flat, where there's a store and the closest gas station to the valley. From here Hwy-120 West runs to the Big Oak Flat entrance and **Hetch Hetchy**, once a scenic rival for Yosemite Valley, though now partially filled with a water supply for San Francisco.

East of Crane Flat, **Tioga Road** (Hwy-120 East) climbs through dense forests into the Yosemite high country around Tenaya Lake, Tuolumne Meadows, and Tioga Pass – open grasslands pocked by polished granite domes and with a southern horizon delineated by the sawtooth crest of the **Cathedral Range**.

Hetch Hetchy

John Muir's passion for Yosemite Valley was matched, if not exceeded, by his desire to preserve the beauty of **HETCH HETCHY**, eighteen miles north of the valley, and close to the Oak Flat entrance. Once a near replica of Yosemite Valley with grassy, oak-filled meadows and soaring granite walls, it is now largely under the dammed waters of the slender Hetch Hetchy reservoir. When it came under threat from power- and water-supply interests in San Francisco in 1901, Muir battled for twelve years, instigating the first environmental letter-writing campaign to Congress. Eventually, in 1913, the cause was lost to a federal bill that paved the way for the Tuolumne River to be blocked by the **O'Shaughnessey Dam**. Hetch Hetchy is no longer a match for its southern kin, but the view of granite domes and waterfalls from the path crossing the dam gives some sense of what it must have been like. It is barely worth the trip though, unless you plan on using the backpacker campground (wilderness permit required) as a base for trekking through the little-visited northern reaches of the park. A short and mostly flat alternative crosses the dam, passes through a short tunnel, and follows the north bank of the reservoir to **Wapama Falls** (five miles round-trip) and on to **Rancheria Falls** (a further four miles each way); both are at their best in May and June but are dry by August.

Tioga Road and Tuolumne Meadows

From Crane Flat, the eastbound **TIOGA ROAD** soon passes a parking lot from where there's a mile-long walking trail to the **Tuolumne Grove** of

Few photographers have stamped their vision as unforgettably as **Ansel Adams** has done with Yosemite Valley. While he worked all over the American West, Yosemite was Adams' home and the site of his most celebrated works, icons of American landscape photography such as 1940's *Jeffrey Pine – Sentinel Dome*; *Clearing Winter Storm* from 1944; and *Moon and Half Dome* from 1960.

Born in 1902 into a moderately wealthy San Francisco family, Adams was given his first camera – a Box Brownie – when he was fourteen, on his first trip to Yosemite. Though classically trained as a concert pianist, he claimed that he knew his "destiny" on that first visit to Yosemite, and soon turned his attentions to the mountains, returning every year and taking up a job as custodian of the Sierra Club headquarters.

He first made a mark in 1927 with *Monolith, The Face of Half Dome*, his first successful **visualization**: Adams believed that, before pressing the shutter, the photographer should have a clear idea of the final image and think through the entire photographic process, considering how lenses, filters, exposure, development, and printing need to be used to achieve that visualization. This approach may seem obvious today, but compared to the hit-and-miss methods of the time, it was little short of revolutionary. Visualization was made easier by applying the **zone system** of exposure calculation, which, though not new, was codified and promoted by Adams as the basis for his teaching. This blend of art and science divides the range of possible tones into ten zones from velvet black (I) through middle gray (V) to pure white (X), and allows precise tone control, something Adams felt was the key to full expression through photography.

As Adams fine-tuned his artistic theories through the 1930s, the idea of photography as fine art was still considered novel, and Adams spent much of his time lobbying for more respect for his craft. Adams was therefore delighted when, in 1940, he was made vice-chairman of the newly established **Department of Photography** at the Museum of Modern Art (MoMA) in New York City. Even so, there was still very little money in photography, and Adams continued to take commercial assignments, including shooting menu photos for *The Ahwahnee*. Commercial and personal work through the 1940s and 1950s earned Adams a wider audience. While still demanding the highest standard of reproduction, the artist had tempered his perfectionism, and allowed his work to appear on postcards, calendars, and posters. By now, he was virtually a household name, and for the first time in his life he began making money to match his status as the grand old man of Western photography. His final triumph came in 1979, when MoMA put on the huge "Yosemite and the Range of Light" exhibition. That same year, he was asked to make an official portrait of President Jimmy Carter – the first time a photographer had been assigned an official presidential portrait – and was subsequently awarded the nation's highest civilian honor, the Medal of Freedom.

Throughout his life, Adams had another great passion, one that he pursued with the same fervor as photography: **conservation**. Back in 1932, the artist had a direct hand in creating Kings Canyon National Park. Two years later, he became a director of the **Sierra Club**, a position he held until 1971, overseeing several successful environmental campaigns. He never quit campaigning for the cause of conservation, and, after an interview in which he suggested he'd like to drown Ronald Reagan in his own martini, agreed to meet the president to promote the environmental cause.

Since Adams' death on April 22, 1984, aged 82, he has become even more honored. The mountain that had been widely known as Mount Ansel Adams since 1933 now bears that name officially, and a huge chunk of the High Sierra south of Yosemite National Park is known as the Ansel Adams Wilderness.

giant sequoias, which is nowhere near as spectacular as the Mariposa Grove (see opposite), but more convenient. The road then climbs steadily through deep pine forests past the *White Wolf* and *Porcupine* campgrounds rising above 8000 feet just before **Olmsted Point**, which is up there with Glacier Point as one of the finest views on Yosemite's roads, looking down Tenaya Creek towards Half Dome. In the late 1950s, when the Tioga Road was being upgraded, Ansel Adams fruitlessly fought against its re-routing past here and along the gorgeous shores of **Tenaya Lake** to Tuolumne.

The alpine area around **TUOLUMNE MEADOWS** (literally "meadow in the sky") has an atmosphere quite different from the valley, 55 miles (about a ninety-minute drive) away. Here, at 8600ft, it is much more open; the light is more intense, and the air always has a fresh, crisp bite. That said, there can still be good-sized blasts of carbon monoxide at peak times in the vicinity of the campground and *Tuolumne Meadows Lodge* (see p.465) – the only accommodation base in the area.

Its location almost five thousand feet higher than Yosemite Valley makes Tuolumne Meadows a better starting point for **hiking** into the surrounding High Sierra wilderness, though you can expect to still find snow on the trails in June and into July. We've covered a number of hikes in the area (see box, pp.478–479). The meadows themselves are the largest in all of the Sierra: twelve miles long, between a quarter and half a mile wide, and threaded by the meandering Tuolumne River. Snow usually lingers here until the end of June, forcing the **wildflowers** to contend with a short growing season. They respond with a glorious burst of color in July, a wonderful time for a wander.

The distinctive glaciated granite form of **Lembert Dome** squats at the eastern end of the meadows gazing across the grasslands towards its western twin, **Pothole Dome**, which makes for a great sunset destination. The mountain scenery is particularly striking to the south, where the **Cathedral Range** offers a horizon of slender spires and knife-blade ridges. Look out for the appropriately named **Unicorn Peak**, and **Cathedral Peak**, textbook example of a glaciated "Matterhorn," where glaciers have carved away the rock on all sides leaving a sharp pointed summit. Some of the best views are from the naturally carbonated **Soda Springs** (see box, pp.478–479), described in 1863 as "pungent and delightful to the taste." And so it is, though the Park Service discourages drinking it.

Tuolumne Meadows Hikers' Bus (mid-June–early Sept; $14.50 one-way, $23 round-trip) runs up here once a day from Yosemite Valley stopping at trailheads along the journey, and at various points around Tuolumne Meadows including the **visitor center** (see p.464). There's also a **free shuttle** service linking Tuolumne to Olmsted Point, just west of Tenaya Lake (mid-June–mid-Sept daily 7am–7pm).

Southern Yosemite

Lying south of Yosemite Valley, **SOUTHERN YOSEMITE**'s broad swathe of sharply peaked mountains extends from the foothills in the west twenty miles to the Sierra crest in the east. In summer, visitors congregate at **Wawona**, where the hotel and campground provide most services, or at the nearby **Mariposa Grove**, the most impressive of the park's stands of giant sequoias. Roughly midway between Yosemite Valley and Wawona, Glacier Point Road carves its way to the park's **viewpoint** *par excellence* at **Glacier Point**, right on the rim of Yosemite Valley and on a level with the face of Half Dome.

Glacier Point, Sentinel Dome, and Taft Point

The most spectacular views of Yosemite Valley are from **GLACIER POINT**, the top of a 3200-foot almost sheer cliff, 32 miles by road (usually open mid-May to late Oct) from Yosemite Valley. The valley floor lies directly beneath the viewing point, and there are tremendous views across to Half Dome (easy from here to see how it got its name) and to the distant snow-capped summits of the High Sierra. It's possible to get there on foot using the very steep Four-Mile Trail (see box, pp.478–479), though you may prefer to use the **Glacier Point Hikers' Bus** (June–Oct 2 daily; $15 each way) to get here from the valley then hike down.

The road to Glacier Point passes the **Badger Pass Ski Area** (generally open mid-Dec to early April; ☏209/372-8430, ⓦwww.badgerpass.com), which has a few short tows and a ski school that runs excellent **cross-country ski** trips eleven miles to Glacier Point. You'll also pass a number of signposted trailheads for easy and longer hikes. One of the best is to the 8122-foot summit of **SENTINEL DOME** (two miles round-trip), a gleaming granite scalp topped by the rotting remains of a Jeffrey pine made famous by Ansel Adams photos from the 1940s. From the Sentinel Dome parking lot, a second dusty, undulating trail leads west to **TAFT POINT** (2 miles round-trip), which trades Glacier Point's Half Dome vista for a view across the valley to the top of El Capitan and Yosemite Falls. Far fewer people follow this trail, perhaps because of the vertiginous drops all around, only protected by the flimsiest of barriers in one spot. Here, the granite edges have been deeply incised to form what is known as the **Taft Point Fissures**.

Wawona and the Mariposa Grove

There's a decidedly relaxed pace at **WAWONA**, 27 miles (or an hour's drive) south of Yosemite Village on Hwy-41. Most people spend their time here strolling the grounds of the landmark *Wawona Hotel* (see p.465), surrounded by a nine-hole golf course where $25 will get you a full eighteen-hole round (plus $10 for club rental, if needed), on the Sierra's oldest course. There are also tennis courts ($2 per hour). Close by is the **Pioneer Yosemite History Center**, a collection of buildings culled from the early times of white habitation, which can be visited on a self-guided walking tour (free). The jail, homesteads, covered bridge, and the like are good for a scoot around, and through the summer months (particularly weekends) the buildings are open and interpreted by attendant rangers. Once away from the main road, the area makes a quiet spot for a picnic.

The **Mariposa Grove**, three miles east of Hwy-41 on a small road that cuts off just past the park's southern entrance, is the biggest and best of Yosemite's groves of giant sequoia trees. To get to the towering growths, walk the two-and-a-half-mile loop trail from the parking lot at the end of the road, or take the narrated **Big Trees Tour** around the grove (June–Oct 9am–5pm; $11), which follows a paved road to the major sights. There is also a free shuttle to the parking area from Wawona.

Trails around the sequoia groves call first at the **Fallen Monarch**, familiar from the 1899 photo, widely reproduced on postcards, in which cavalry officers and their horses stand atop the prostrate tree. The most renowned of the grouping, well marked along the route, is the **Grizzly Giant**, thought to be 2700 years old and with a lower branch thicker than the trunk of any non-sequoia in the grove. Other highlights include the **Wawona Tunnel Tree** through which people drove their cars until it fell in 1969, the similarly bored **California Tunnel Tree**, which you can walk through, and all manner of trees which have grown together, split apart, been struck by lightning, or are simply staggeringly large.

There are no restrictions on **day hiking** in Yosemite, so for all the following hikes you need only equip yourselves properly – map, raingear, food, etc – get to the trailhead and set off. Unless otherwise noted, the following distances and times are for a round-trip.

Day-hikes from Yosemite Valley

Mist Trail to the top of Vernal Fall (3 miles; 2–3hr; 1100ft ascent). If you only do one hike in Yosemite, this should be it, especially during the spring snowmelt when Vernal Fall is often framed by a rainbow, and hikers get drenched in spray; bring a raincoat or plan to get wet. Start at shuttle stop 16 and head uphill crossing a footbridge with great views of Vernal Fall. Then follow the Mist Trail along a narrow path which, though hardly dangerous, demands sure footing and a head for heights. At the top of the fall, either retrace your steps to the trailhead, or return via the John Muir Trail.

Half Dome (17 miles; 9–12hr; 4800ft ascent). This is one of the valley's finest and most arduous walks, initially following the Mist Trail (see above) and continuing around the back of Half Dome. The final 400ft ascent is over the huge, smooth, humped back aided by a pair of steel cables and wooden steps which are partly removed in winter (mid-Nov to late May) to discourage ascent: there's usually a pile of free-use gloves at the base of the cables to protect tender hands. Once at the summit, anyone concerned about their outdoor credibility will want to edge out to the very lip of the abyss and peer down the sheer 2000ft northwest face. If you plan a one-day assault, you'll need to start at the crack of dawn.

Four-mile Trail to Glacier Point (10 miles; 5–6hr; 3200ft ascent). The steep asphalt path from the valley floor to Glacier Point doesn't give much of a sense of being in the wilderness, but the magnificent views make this one of the valley's more popular day walks. Generally open mid-May to Oct.

Upper Yosemite Fall (7 miles; 4–7hr; 2700ft ascent). This perennially popular, energy-sapping hike climbs steeply to the north rim of the valley with great views of Upper Yosemite Fall for much of the way, and the opportunity to sit virtually on the edge of the fall and gaze down at the Lilliputian activity below in Yosemite Village. Its northern aspect keeps the trail open longer than most (April–Dec) but is best done during the spring snowmelt: start before 7am to avoid the worst of the midday heat. The trailhead is just by the *Camp 4* campground (shuttle stop 7).

Day hikes from Tuolumne Meadows

Soda Springs and Parsons Lodge (4-mile loop; 2hr; negligible ascent). An easy meander around some of Tuolumne Meadows' best and most accessible features: especially good in the late June and July wildflower season. Cross the meadow from a trailhead 300 yards east of the visitor center to reach the *Soda Springs* and *Parsons Lodge*, then follow a broad trail to the base of Lembert Dome; finally either walk back along Tioga Road or use the shuttle bus.

It's also worth dropping into the **Mariposa Grove Museum** (daily 9am–4pm; free), towards the top end of the trail, which has modest displays and photos of the mighty trees. For more on the life of the sequoia, see the box on p.444.

Eating, drinking, and entertainment

With a couple of notable exceptions, **eating** in Yosemite is more a function than a pleasure. Food, whether in restaurants or in the grocery stores around

Lembert Dome (3.7-mile loop; 2–3hr; 850ft ascent). This hike up the Meadows' most prominent feature offers expansive views from the summit and examples of glacially polished rock and "erratic" boulders left behind by retreating glaciers. Start at the parking lot at the dome's base and follow signs for Dog Lake, then head right to ascend via the bare rock of the dome's northeast corner. Descend, then turn right to complete a loop around the dome.

Cathedral Lakes (8 miles; 4–6hr; 1000ft ascent). A candidate for the best Tuolumne day-hike, this route follows several miles of the John Muir Trail as far as a pair of gorgeous tarns in open alpine country with long views to a serrated skyline. Hike from the trailhead just west of the Tuolumne Meadows visitor center, gradually getting improved views of the twin spires of Cathedral Peak. Near its base are Upper Cathedral Lake (where there is excellent camping) and Lower Cathedral Lake, a divine spot lodged in a cirque now partly filled with lush meadows and split by a ridge of hard rock polished smooth by ancient glaciers.

Overnight hiking

Camping out overnight opens up the majority of Yosemite's eight hundred miles of backcountry trails. Choosing from the enormous range of trails is almost impossible, though some of the most popular are those which run between Yosemite Valley and Tuolumne Meadows, a two-day hike for anyone with reasonable fitness. Further suggestions are outlined in the dedicated *Rough Guide to Yosemite*.

To camp out overnight you need a **wilderness permit** which is available free of charge from ranger stations – at Wawona, Big Oak Flat, Hetch Hetchy, and Tuolumne – and the Wilderness Center in Yosemite Village (mid-May to June and early Sept to mid-Oct daily 8am–5pm; July to early Sept daily 7.30am–6pm; closed in winter). Numbers are limited by a quota system, but with a little flexibility you'll often find you can get a permit the day before you wish to start your hike. Large groups, people with tight schedules, and anyone hiking at busy times should **reserve in advance** ($5 per person) from 24 weeks to two days ahead of your trip. Book either by phone (℡209/372-0740), or by writing to Wilderness Permits, PO Box 545, Yosemite, CA 95389, and stating your name, address, daytime phone number, the number in your party, method of travel (foot, ski, horse, etc), start and finish dates, entry and exit trailheads, and main destination. Suggesting alternate dates and trailheads are a good idea too. Checks should be made payable to the Yosemite Association and credit-card bookings should include the number and expiry date. For more details see ⓦwww.nps.gov/yose/wilderness.

Don't despair if you have trouble landing the trail you want: paths are so numerous that you may start at a less popular trailhead but end up doing largely the same hike. From November to April when demand is lowest, permits are issued at nearby visitor centers. When obtaining your permit you'll be instructed in **backcountry etiquette**, especially water purification and waste disposal, and you must rent a **bear-resistant food canister** (unless you have your own). **Camping gear** can be rented quite reasonably from Yosemite Mountaineering School (see box, p.467).

Yosemite Village (where there's a well-stocked supermarket), Curry Village, Wawona, and Tuolumne Meadows, is at least twenty percent more expensive inside the park than out. **Outside the park**, the choice is considerably better, with plenty of good restaurants and a smattering of bars in the gateway towns of Groveland, Mariposa, and Oakhurst. The park's restaurants serve beer and wine, plus there's a lively **bar** at *Yosemite Lodge*, a swankier affair at *The Ahwahnee*, and a lounge with occasional piano entertainment at the *Wawona Hotel*.

To help visitors interpret Yosemite, the Park Service and related organizations run a number of **ranger programs** – nature hikes, photo walks, talks about bears, etc – most of which are free. In addition there is **evening entertainment** in the form of ranger-led campfire talks at most of the campgrounds, occasional star-gazing sessions, natural-history slide shows, and music shows. The *Yosemite Today* newspaper carries a full catalog of events, along with listings of the *Yosemite Theater* program ($8), which presents two ninety-minute one-man shows featuring the talents of actor Lee Stetson, who has been impersonating John Muir since 1982.

In the valley

Ahwahnee Bar *Ahwahnee Hotel* (11am–11pm). Intimate piano bar perfect for indulging in something from their selection of Armagnacs, ports, classic martinis and other cocktails ($8–14). There's also light food such as a Caesar salad ($9) or wild boar chili con carne ($9), plus there's espresso coffee and live music most Friday and Saturday nights, usually something subdued.

Ahwahnee Dining Room *The Ahwahnee* ☏209/372-1489. One of the most beautiful restaurants in the US, built in baronial style with 34-foot-high ceilings of exposed beams, rustic iron chandeliers, and floor-to-ceiling leaded windows. The food is by far the best in Yosemite, and dinner might consist of a salmon terrine or an endive and watercress salad ($11) followed by seared *ahi* tuna with *shoyu* butter and *wasabi* ($30). Dishes are simpler earlier in the day with items like a three-egg frittata ($14) or an apple crêpe ($14) for breakfast, then a portobello mushroom and sun-dried tomato roll ($11) or a smoked-duck Caesar salad ($15) for lunch. The Sunday brunch ($32) is particularly stupendous. Casual dress is permitted during the day, but formal wear is expected for dinner (sports coats are available free of charge).

Degnan's Café, Deli & Loft Yosemite Village. Three eating spots in one building. There's a daytime café serving reasonable espressos and specialty teas plus a selection of Danishes and cin-namon rolls (both around $2), served inside or out; a takeout deli with bowls of soup ($2.50–3.25) and chili ($4–5), and massive sandwiches, burritos, and salads at under $6.50; and a gourmet pizza restau-rant ($14–18 for medium, $17–22 for a large).

Pavilion Buffet Curry Village. Lively cafeteria serving great value all-you-can-eat breakfasts ($10) with plenty of fresh fruit, juices, eggs, bacon, hash browns, waffles, yogurt, and the like. Dinner ($12) suffers a little from over-cooked vegetables and sloppy preparation, but you can still fill up on salads, build-your-own tacos, chicken-fried steak, simple pasta dishes, cakes, and sodas. Alcoholic drinks are not available.

Pizza Patio and Pavilion Bar Curry Village. Very much the place to repair on balmy evenings after a hard day in the hills. Fight for an outdoor table while you wait for a pretty decent build-your-own pizza (from $14 for twelve slices), and maybe a pint of good draft beer ($4.50) or a margarita ($6.50).

Yosemite Lodge Food Court *Yosemite Lodge*. Bright and cheerful self-serve café/restaurant serving a full range of cold and cooked breakfasts ($5–9), muffins, Danishes, and coffee, plus lunches and dinners that range from a grilled chicken sandwich, pizza or gyro platter (all $6) to pasta and meatballs ($9) or chicken, vegetables, and rice ($9). There is some outdoor seating.

The rest of the park

Tuolumne Meadows Grill Tuolumne Meadows. Basically a burger joint, also serving small and pricey breakfasts and sandwich lunches.

Tuolumne Meadows Lodge ☏209/372-8413. Family-style breakfasts ($5–10) and burgers, steak, chicken, and fish dinners ($13–23) served in a large tent beside the Tuolumne River.

Wawona Hotel Dining Room Semi-formal dining off white linen tablecloths, though the food is neither very expensive nor particularly special. Still, you can lunch on the likes of chicken alfredo, ratatouille, or a club sandwich ($9), then dress smart for dinner, such as pan-fried trout ($17) and a raspberry nut cake ($4). There's also a wonderful Sunday brunch buffet (Easter–Thanksgiving 7.30am–1.30pm; $19) and a Saturday Barbecue (late May–early Sept 5–7pm).

White Wolf Lodge just off Hwy-120 ☏209/252-4848. Large portions of good-value American food in rustic surroundings for $16–20. Breakfast and dinner only.

Hwy-120: Groveland

Cocina Michoacana 13955 Hwy-120, Groveland. Authentic and low-priced Mexican spot; six bucks will get you a great breakfast of scrambled eggs with strips of steak, and later they serve a full range of favorites including great fajitas ($19–21 for two) and melt-in-the-mouth breaded shrimps.

Iron Door 18761 Main St, Groveland. With its grill and soda fountain, the *Iron Door* is a fine place to eat, with a locally famous garlic soup, fine New

York steak ($20), buffalo and black bean burgers, and a host of other dishes all beautifully prepared and presented. But what makes it special is the atmospheric bar, reliably claimed to be the oldest saloon in California. It comes with pool table and all manner of paraphernalia on the walls plus a live band most weekends.

Victorian Room *Groveland Hotel*, 18767 Hwy-120 ℡209/962-4000. The best restaurant in town with a seasonally changing menu and nightly chef's specials that might run to crab cakes with cilantro and caper sauce, and honey-glazed baby back pork ribs. Expect to pay $45–50 for three courses including a glass or two from their extensive wine list.

Hwy-140: Mariposa, Midpines, and El Portal

Café at the Bug *Yosemite Bug Hostel & Lodge*, Midpines. Superb-value licensed café with quality food at a good price. Wholesome breakfasts ($4.50–6.50), packed lunches ($6), and dinners ($8–14) are served to all comers. If you don't mind the slightly frenetic hostel atmosphere, it's definitely worth the drive out for the likes of slow-roasted Cajun pork or baked trout filet with butter-pecan sauce. Good microbrews on tap as well.

Charles Street Dinner House 5043 Hwy-140, Mariposa ℡209/966-2366. Mariposa's premiere fine-dining establishment. Discerning diners might kick off with a Portobello ravioli parmesan ($14) and follow with a scallop and abalone blend served with toasted almonds and lemon butter ($19), though the wise will leave space for the mocha ice-cream pie ($5). There's a full wine list, and all dishes are cooked to order, so set the evening aside. Closed Mon, Tues & Jan.

High Country Café Hwy-140 & Hwy-49, Mariposa. Daytime health-food café with sandwiches ($5–6) along with salads, enchiladas, and carrot cake. There's also a health-food store next door offering good bread, organic fruit, and goodies in bulk bins that are perfect for trail mix. Closed Sun.

Savoury's 5027 Hwy-140, Mariposa ℡209/966-7677. Excellent dinner-only restaurant offering a relaxed atmosphere with a touch of class: modern decor, black linen tablecloths, and a secluded patio out back for those warm summer evenings. Choose from the likes of chicken picatta ($14), lemon chive scallops ($19), and spinach and pine-nut pasta ($15), perhaps followed by chocolate bread pudding ($4). Wine is available by the glass. Closed Mon & Tues.

Hwy-41: Oakhurst and Fish Camp

Mountain House junction of Hwy-41 & Bass Lake Road, 3 miles north of Oakhurst. Reliable, friendly, and efficient diner that's the best place around for burgers, sandwiches, and pasta dishes, along with a locally renowned New York steak ($17) and charbroiled trout ($12).

The Narrow Gauge Inn 48571 Hwy-41, Fish Camp ℡559/683-6446. Fine dining in an Old World setting with candlelight and a warming fire. Start by dipping sourdough into a rich fondue and continue with charbroiled swordfish or filet mignon. Expect to pay $40 each, more with wine. Mid-April to mid-Oct only, daily except Tues 5.30–9pm.

Three Sisters Café 40291 Junction Drive, off Hwy-49 behind Raley's supermarket, Oakhurst ℡559/642-2253, ⊛www.threesisterscafe.com. It is worth planning around the Quixotic opening hours at this small restaurant with European influences where breakfast ($7–8) might consist of chicken quesedilla, salmon omelet, or bratwurst, potato pancake, and eggs. Dinner mains range from penne prawns with asparagus ($16) to Navajo buffalo stew ($19), and several vegetarian and vegan dishes are offered. In the evening there's a fixed-price menu from two courses ($25) up to five ($36). BYO wine. Only open for brunch Wed–Fri & Sun 9am–1.15pm; and dinner Wed & Thurs 5–7.15pm, Fri & Sat 5–9pm.

Yosemite Coffee & Roasting Company 40879 Hwy-41, a mile north of Oakhurst. Relaxed java joint with mismatched chairs and newspapers, ideal for breakfast burritos, toothsome muffins, sandwiches, cakes, and good espresso at modest prices.

Listings

Banks There are no banks in Yosemite, though there are several 24hr ATMs all charging a transaction fee of $2 on US accounts: try Yosemite Village Store, outside the Art Activity Center, in the lobby of *Yosemite Lodge*, inside the Curry Village Store, inside the Wawona Store, and just outside the park at the *Yosemite View Lodge* in El Portal.

DNC has a check-cashing service (Mon & Fri 8am–4pm, Tues–Thurs, Sat & Sun 8am–2pm) in Yosemite Village in the lobby of the Art Activity Center ($5 for cashing each check), but there is no provision for foreign-currency exchange.

Bike rental Bikes are only allowed on the valley's flat, paved roads and bikeways, so the basic single-speed bikes ($7.50/hr, $24/day) available at Yosemite Lodge (all year) and Curry Village (summer only) are quite adequate.

Books The Yosemite Village Visitor Center has a good selection of Yosemite-related books and maps; the Ansel Adams Gallery specializes in photography and nature publications; and the Mountain Shop at Curry Village stocks climbing guides.

Campfires Summertime air-quality restrictions exist limiting campfires from 5pm to 10pm from May to mid-October. For ecological reasons, firewood must not be gathered in the valley or above 9600 feet, but is available for sale at stores throughout the park.

Camping equipment Camping gear can be rented from the Yosemite Mountaineering School at Curry Village – expect to pay $13 for a sleeping bag and $15 for an overnight pack, and comparable rates for tents, bear canisters, snowshoes, etc – and bought from the Village Sport Shop in Yosemite Village, or better from the Mountain Shop in *Curry Village*. The store in Tuolumne Meadows also stocks camping equipment, climbing gear, and lightweight food.

Gas Available at good prices in Oakhurst, moderate prices in Mariposa and Groveland, and expensively in the park, year-round at Wawona and Crane Flat, and seasonally at Tuolumne Meadows. There are no gas stations in Yosemite Valley.

Guided trips The Yosemite Mountaineering School (⊤209/372-8344, ⊛www.yosemitemountaineering .com) runs guided backpacking, rock-climbing, and alpine trips from around $125 each per day for groups of four or more.

High Sierra camp vacations Visitors organized enough to enter a lottery (Nov to mid-Dec) can apply for July to mid-September stays in a series of five dormitory-style tent cabin complexes – complete with proper beds, hot showers, and meals cooked for you – dotted around the Yosemite high country. Most combine them in a circuit, either the seven-day guided hike with one rest day, the six-day mule-back saddle trip, or the four-day saddle trip. Prices are around $135 a night per person and include a delicious breakfast and dinner. *Merced Lake*, the largest of the camps, sometimes has spare short-notice spaces for those willing to hike the thirteen miles from Yosemite Valley or the fifteen miles from Tuolumne Meadows. Obtain a lottery application form either by calling ⊤559/253-5674 (Mon–Fri 7am–9pm, Sat & Sun 7am–6pm PST) or downloading one from the accommodation section of the ⊛www .yosemitepark.com website.

Horseback riding Saddle trips accommodating riders of all standards are run from stables in

Yosemite Valley (April–Oct; ⊤209/372-8348), Tuolumne Meadows (early June–Sept; ⊤209/372-8427), and Wawona (May–Sept; ⊤209/372-8427): scenic rides cost $51 for two hours, $94 for the day. There are also multi-day High Sierra Saddle Trips starting at $744 for four days.

Internet access Limited facilities at the Yosemite Village Public Library (see below) and at the libraries and copy centers in the hinterland towns.

Laundry There's a coin-op affair at *Housekeeping Camp* (8am–8pm).

Library A public research library (Tues–Fri 8am–noon & 1–5pm) is situated upstairs from the museum entrance in Yosemite Village and contains all manner of Yosemite, backcountry, and climbing information, including recent magazines and daily papers. There is also a public library which opens for three or four hours a day (Mon 11am–2pm, Tues & Wed 10am–2pm, Thurs 3–6pm) and is located close to the Yosemite Village Visitor Center in a building signed "Girls Club."

Lost and found ⊤209/372-4357 for items lost at hotels and restaurants; ⊤209/379-1001 for stuff lost elsewhere.

Medical assistance Yosemite Medical Clinic, between Yosemite Village and *The Ahwahnee* (⊤209/372-4637) has 24-hour emergency care, drop-in and urgent care (daily 8am–7pm), and accepts appointments (Mon–Fri 8am–5pm, Sat 9am–noon). Dental treatment (⊤209/372-4200) is also available.

Photography The Ansel Adams Gallery in Yosemite Village stocks slide, professional, and ordinary print film at reasonable prices, and run free two-hour guided photography walks. There are also year-round photography walks run by the park concessionaire in Yosemite Valley: check *Yosemite Today* for all times.

Post office Located in Yosemite Village (Mon–Fri 8.30am–5pm, Sat 10am–noon) and accepting general delivery (aka poste restante). Also year-round services at *Yosemite Lodge* (Mon–Thurs 11.30am–2.45pm, Fri 1.30–4.30pm) and Wawona (Mon–Fri 9am–5pm, Sat 9am–1pm), and summer-only service at Curry Village (Mon–Fri 2.30–4pm) and Tuolumne Meadows (Mon–Fri 9am–5pm, Sat 9am–1pm). The park's zip code is 95389.

Rafting Inside the park itself, Curry Village rents six-berth rafts ($13.50 per person; minimum 2; June and July only) allowing you to float gently along the placid and relatively gentle section of the Merced River – the cost includes a return bus ride. Outside the park, from April to June, far more rugged (Class III–IV) one-day stretches are run in the traditional guided fashion by Mariah Wilderness Expeditions (⊤1-800/462-7424, ⊛www.mariahwe

.com), Ahwahnee Whitewater (☎1-800/359-9790, ⓦwww.ahwahnee.com), Whitewater Voyages (☎1-800/ 400-RAFT, ⓦwww.whitewatervoyages .com) and others, all charging around $140 midweek and $155 at weekends.

Recycling Glass, aluminum, newspapers, and plastic are recycled at Yosemite Village, and beverage containers may be returned for a small deposit at all retail outlets.

RVs Campers can use all the main campgrounds, but there are no hook-ups in Yosemite. Dump stations are in Yosemite Valley, Wawona, and Tuolumne Meadows (summer only).

Showers In Yosemite Valley at Curry Village (24 hours; $2) where outside the peak summer season there is often nobody to either provide a towel or take your money. Outside the valley the only public showers are at *Tuolumne Meadows Lodge* (see "Accommodation," p.465; $3).

Swimming There are pools in the valley at Yosemite Lodge and Curry Village (both free to hotel guests and $2 for others), the *Wawona Hotel* and *The Ahwahnee* both have pools for guests, and there numerous small river beaches throughout the valley and at Wawona.

Travel details

Trains

The **San Joaquin** service runs four times daily between Bakersfield and Emeryville, near Oakland, from where Amtrak Thruway buses run into San Francisco. Amtrak Thruway bus connections from San Diego, Orange County, and Los Angeles link with the train at Bakersfield; and there are also Amtrak Thruway bus links between Merced and Yosemite National Park.

Bakersfield to: Fresno (1hr 45min); Hanford (1hr 15min); Merced (3hr); Emeryville (6hr); Stockton (4hr).

Buses

Buses are either Greyhound, Amtrak Thruway, or Orange Belt Stages (☎1-800/266-7433, ⓦwww .orangebelt.com), which often use Amtrak and Greyhound stations as hubs for their network.

Bakersfield to: Barstow (2 daily; 3hr); Merced (12 daily; 3hr 30min–4hr 30min).

Fresno to: Merced (10 daily; 1hr 10min); Modesto (9 daily; 2hr); Stockton (9 daily; 3hr).

Hanford to: San Luis Obispo (2 daily; 3hr); Visalia (2 daily; 1hr).

Los Angeles to: Bakersfield (14 daily; 2hr 30min–3hr); Fresno (13 daily; 4–6hr); Merced (6 daily; 6–7hr); Modesto (6 daily; 6–8hr); Stockton (7 daily; 6hr 30min–8hr 30min); Visalia (5 daily; 4–5hr).

Merced to: Bakersfield (12 daily; 3hr 30min–4hr 30min); Los Angeles (6 daily; 6–7hr); Fresno (10 daily; 1hr 10min); Modesto (9 daily; 1hr); Sacramento (7 daily; 3hr); San Francisco (6 daily; 4–5hr); Stockton (7 daily; 1hr 30min–2hr); Yosemite (3–5 daily; 2hr 45min).

Modesto to: Fresno (9 daily; 2hr); Merced (9 daily; 1hr).

San Francisco to: Bakersfield (5 daily; 7hr 30min–9hr); Fresno (7 daily; 5–6hr); Merced (4 daily; 4hr 15min); Modesto (6 daily; 3–5hr); Stockton (5 daily; 3–6hr); Visalia (2 daily; 7–8hr).

Stockton to: Fresno (6 daily; 3hr); Lodi (5 daily; 30min); Merced (7 daily; 1hr 30min–2hr); Sacramento (10 daily; 1hr); San Francisco (5 daily; 3–6hr).

Visalia to: Hanford (2 daily; 1hr); San Francisco (2 daily; 7–8hr).

Flights

Fresno to: Los Angeles (hourly or better; 1hr 10min); San Francisco (7 daily; 50min).

The Central Coast

Highlights

✳ **Channel Islands National Park** This beguiling chain of desert islands off the coast of Los Angeles offers spectacular hiking and the chance to spot passing whales. See p.491

✳ **Hearst Castle** Unquestionably, one of the most intriguing sights in America: a palatial monument to the life and ego of William Randolph Hearst. See p.512

✳ **Mission San Antonio de Padua** The best conserved of all the missions, and an evocative place to imagine the past. See p.517

✳ **Big Sur** Boasting a rugged, eye-popping coastline and, in the interior, some of the most stunning waterfalls in the state, this is still very much a wild and eminently rewarding region. See p.521

✳ **Monterey Bay Aquarium** A world-class museum in a small Californian town – the Jellies exhibit is freakish, stylish, and informative. See p.535

✳ **Santa Cruz boardwalk** A classic Californian seaside boardwalk, filled with old rides and an amusement arcade – irresistible, cheesy fun. See p.547

△ Leopard shark, Monterey Bay Aquarium

The Central Coast

The four hundred miles of coastline in between LA and San Francisco is arguably one of the most beautiful oceanside stretches of land anywhere in the world. From sandy beaches to rocky cliffs and from rural charm to upscale sophistication, the allure of the **CENTRAL COAST** is wide in range. Sparsely populated outside a few medium-sized towns, much of the area is barely disturbed by modern life. Indeed, first-time visitors may be surprised to find just how much of the region survives in its natural state, despite nestling snugly between two of America's largest and richest cities. The mountain ranges that separate the shore from the farmlands of the inland valleys are for the most part pristine wilderness, sometimes covered in thick forests of tall and slender redwood trees, while, in winter especially, fast-flowing rivers and streams course down valleys to the sea. All along the shore, sea otters and seals play in the waves, and endangered gray whales pass close by on their annual migration from Alaska to Mexico.

Big Sur, where the brooding Santa Lucia Mountains rise steeply out of the thundering Pacific surf, is the heart of the region, and **Point Lobos**, at its northern tip, is the best place to experience this untouched environment at its most dramatic. Nature aside, though, the Central Coast also marks the gradual transition from Southern to Northern California. The two largest towns here, **Santa Barbara** and **Santa Cruz**, are poles apart: Santa Barbara, a hundred miles north of Los Angeles, is a conservative, wealthy resort; in Santa Cruz, 75 miles south of San Francisco, long hair and tie-dyes are very much the order of the day. What the two towns have in common is miles of broad, clean **beaches**, with chilly waters but excellent surf, and a branch of the University of California energizing the local nightlife. In between, the small town of **San Luis Obispo** provides a languorous contrast to them both, and is a feasible base for the Central Coast's biggest tourist attraction, **Hearst Castle**, the opulent hilltop palace of publishing magnate William Randolph "Citizen Kane" Hearst.

The Central Coast also contains the bulk and the best of the late eighteenth-century Spanish Colonial **missions** – the first European settlements on the West Coast, set up to convert the natives to Christianity while co-opting their labor. Almost all of the towns that exist here today grew up around the adobe walls and red-tiled roofs of these Catholic colonies, strung out along the Pacific. Each was deliberately situated a long day's walk from the next and typically composed of a church and a cloistered monastery, enclosed within thick walls to prevent attack by native tribes. **Monterey**, a hundred miles south of San Francisco, was the capital of California under Spain, and later Mexico, and today retains more of its early nineteenth-century architecture than any other city

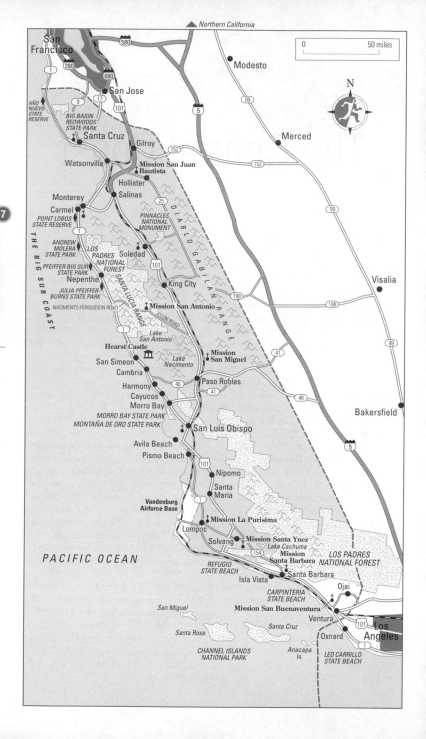

in the state; it's also a good base for one of the most beautiful of the missions, which stands three miles south in the uppercrust seaside resort of **Carmel**.

Practicalities

Getting around the Central Coast is easy by Californian standards: some of the best views in the state can be had from Amtrak's Coast Starlight train, which runs right along the coast up to San Luis Obispo before cutting inland north to San Francisco. Greyhound buses stop at most of the towns, particularly those along the main highway, US-101 – though the best route, if you've got a car, is the smaller Hwy-1, which follows the coast all the way but takes twice as long. Places to stay are relatively easy to find, at least outside summer weekends when otherwise quiet towns and beaches are packed solid with vacationing families. Opportunities for camping are plentiful, too, in a string of state parks, beaches, and forests.

Ventura

Suburban Los Angeles meets the Pacific Ocean at **VENTURA**, an agricultural town now being submerged beneath fast-food joints and mini-malls, many spilling over from the larger industrial city of **Oxnard** to the south (useful mainly for its Metrolink train connections to downtown LA; see p.93). Ventura offers a few good reasons to stop if you're in the area, including buying fresh strawberries and other seasonal produce from the roadside stalls, and catching a boat out to the offshore Channel Islands (see p.490) from the harbor four miles southwest of town. The most compelling sight in town, though, is just north of the US-101 and Hwy-1 intersection, where the restored **Mission San Buenaventura**, 211 E Main St (Mon–Fri 10am–5pm, Sat 9am–5pm, Sun 10am–4pm; $1; ⓦ www.sanbuenaventuramission.org), was raised in 1782 as the ninth of the 21 California missions and the last founded by Junípero Serra. Although it's been repeatedly damaged by neglect or earthquakes and then restored – not always for the better – it still retains a quaint parochial charm that makes it a worthwhile stop for passers-by or more intrepid "mission tourists" – though if you're looking for truly inspired church architecture, this unassuming Spanish Colonial relic probably won't fit the bill.

Main Street is also home to two small but engaging museums. The **Albinger Archaeological Museum**, at no. 113 (Tues–Fri 10am–2pm, Sat & Sun 10am–4pm; free; ⓣ 805/648-5823), has exhibits on 3500 years of local history, from ancient Native American cultures to the Spanish era – including parts of the nearby mission's original foundation dating from the 1780s. Across the street, the **Ventura County Museum of History and Art**, 100 E Main St (Tues–Sun 10am–5pm; $4; ⓦ www.venturamuseum.org), takes up where the former leaves off, with exhibits on local pioneer families and antique agricultural machinery, plus preserved old saddles, Catholic devotional paintings, and more contemporary native artifacts. Another glimpse of early life in California can be found at **Olivas Adobe Historical Park**, further out at 4200 Olivas Park Drive (tours Sat & Sun 10am–4pm; donation suggested; ⓦ www.geocities.com/olivasadobe), where the titular adobe was once the centerpiece of land baron Jose Olivas's estate in the 1840s, before the Mexican–American War altered the balance of power in the region. Still, Olivas, his wife, and their 21 kids lived out the century there, and today it's decorated in the rustic style of the mid-nineteenth-century, with antique tools and a family chapel on display, as well as decor appropriate to the era.

Amtrak **trains** (Pacific Surfliner only) pull in near Harbor Boulevard and Figueroa Street, three blocks from the Greyhound **bus** stop at 291 E Thompson Blvd at Palm Street. The **visitor center**, 89 S California St, Suite C (Mon–Fri 8.30am–5pm, Sat 9am–5pm, Sun 10am–4pm; ☎805/648-2075 or 1-800/333-2989, ⊛www.ventura-usa.com), can help with accommodation and has local bus maps. As Ventura is a base for visiting the Channel Islands, there is a **Channel Islands National Park visitor center** (daily 8.30am–5pm; ☎805/658-5730, ⊛www.nps.gov/chis) next to the ferry landing in Ventura Harbor, which covers the geology and plant and animal life of the islands, including seals, sea lions, pelicans, and giant kelp forests. It also has current information on arranging trips, and an **observation tower** from which, on fine days, you can view the islands.

Ojai

Nestled in the hills above Ventura, the hamlet of **OJAI** (pronounced "O-hi") is a wealthy resort community frequented by weekend jet-setters from LA, shown in the many exclusive health spas and tennis clubs that dot the surrounding countryside. Perhaps appropriately, it's also a New Age hub that's the headquarters of the Krishnamurti Society, honoring the theosophist who, in the 1920s, lived and lectured in the Ojai Valley, which he considered "a vessel of comprehension, intelligence and truth." The **Krishnamurti Library and Archives**, four miles northeast of town at 1070 McAndrew Rd (Wed–Sun 1–5pm; free; ☎805/646-4948, ⊛www.kfa.org), details his progressive ideas on spirituality, while a mellow **retreat** in a classic ranch house, nearby at no. 1130 ($55, $85 double), lets you get into the holistic spirit by taking nature walks in a shaded glade and reading up on the master's teachings. In town, the **Ojai Valley Museum**, 130 W Ojai Ave (Wed–Fri 1–4pm, Sat 10am–4pm, Sun noon–4pm; $3; ⊛www.ojaivalleymuseum.org), housed in a former Mission Revival church built in 1919, has ambitious exhibits on history, agriculture, oil prospecting, and art, highlighted by a Chumash garden that recalls the local peoples who predated the American settlers.

Given its location in a historic chapel, the **visitor center** next door, at no. 150 (Mon & Wed–Fri 9.30am–4.30pm, Sat & Sun 10am–4pm; ☎805/646-8126, ⊛www.the-ojai.org), is the best place for information on the town's historical attractions and numerous old-fashioned **B&Bs**. On a country farm ten minutes from downtown, the friendly *Farm Hostel* (☎805/646-0311, ⊛www.hostelhandbook.com/farmhostel) offers free pick-up from the Greyhound and Amtrak stations in nearby Ventura and dorm beds for $15, but you must have an international air-travel ticket or current visa (3–6-month period) to stay there. For both domestic and foreign visitors, the cushy, Mission-flavored *Ojai Valley Inn & Spa*, 905 Country Club Rd (☎805/646-5511 or 1-800/422-6524, ⊛www.ojairesort.com; **❼**), is a luxurious resort aimed at golfers; while the more central *Rose Garden Inn*, at 615 W Ojai Ave (☎1-800/799-1881, ⊛www.rosegardeninnofojai.com; **❹**), offers nice rooms with fridges, microwaves, and kitchenettes, as well as cottages with fireplaces and pool and spa access. If you'd prefer to rough it, near Ojai is the massive **Los Padres National Forest**, with good hiking and decent campgrounds ($5 pass required; reservations at ☎1-800/280-2267); the area ranger station, 1190 E Ojai Ave (daily 8.30am–4pm; ☎805/646-4348, ⊛www.fs.fed.us/r5/lospadres), provides information and maps.

Channel Islands National Park

Stretching north from Santa Catalina Island off the coast of Los Angeles, a chain of fascinating desert islands is preserved as the 250,000-acre **CHANNEL ISLANDS NATIONAL PARK**, offering excellent hiking trails and splendid views of marine life (with two thousand species present), as well as fishing and scuba- and skin-diving through the many caves, coves, and shipwrecks in the crystal-clear Pacific waters. All five of the main islands are accessible, though the closest, Anacapa, some fourteen miles south of Ventura, sees the most eco-tourist traffic. The best time to visit is between February and April, when you have the opportunity of **whale watching**. Inland **hiking** requires a permit (☎805/658-5711, ⓦwww.nps.gov/chis for information) and **divers** can explore the two exposed wrecks on either side of the island.

Park practicalities

If you're considering visiting the Channel Islands, the best introduction to their unique geology, flora, and fauna can be found in Ventura at the park's **visitor center**, 1901 Spinnaker Drive (daily 8.30am–5pm; free; ☎805/658-5730), which also offers models, films, and telescopes to view the islands at a distance.

The Nature Conservancy acquired ninety percent of the islands in 1988 and has made them accessible to the public on **day-trip tours** – the only way to visit the park is by boat, through operators that run from Ventura Harbor. Anacapa is served by several tours run by Island Packers, 1867 Spinnaker Drive, three miles west of US-101 and a mile south of town (☎805/642-7688 for 24hr recorded information, ☎805/642-1393 for reservations 9am–5pm, ⓦwww.islandpackers.com). Packages include all-day trips ($42–62, depending on the island), half-day cruises without landings ($25), two-day camping excursions ($54–90), and whale-watching excursions that last about three hours and start at $25. The trip over takes ninety minutes to three hours each way (or four to five hours for San Miguel), and boats don't run every day and often fill up, so reserve ahead. Truth Aquatics, 301 W Cabrillo Blvd (☎805/962-1127 or 805/963-3564, ⓦwww.truthaquatics.com), has alternative itineraries to all the islands on smaller vessels at higher prices, including two-day hiking, diving, and kayaking excursions.

Another way to reach Santa Rosa is to take a half-hour **flight** from Channel Islands Aviation (☎805/987-1301, ⓦwww.flycia.com), which runs four-hour day-trips and weekend excursions ($130 & $200, respectively) from Camarillo (off US-101, twenty miles south of Ventura) and Santa Barbara airports. Santa Cruz is also the destination for kayak trips from Ventura and Santa Barbara (see p.492).

There are a number of free, primitive **campgrounds** (permits $7.35) on each island if you want to rough it. Bring plenty of food and especially water, as none is available on the island.

The islands

Tiny **Anacapa** is actually two islets: **West Anacapa** is largely a refuge for nesting brown pelicans and much of it is off limits to the public – with the exception of **Frenchy's Cove**, a pristine beach and good base for scuba or snorkeling expeditions; **East Anacapa** has a small visitor center and a mile-and-a-half-long nature trail. There are no beaches here, but swimming in the cove where the boats dock is allowed. West of Anacapa, **Santa Cruz** is the largest and highest of the islands, with three-quarters of it owned by the Nature Conservancy; throughout the island, you can hike or even camp in remote landscapes – a visitor center on the eastern end can provide more information. Almost as big as Santa Cruz, **Santa Rosa** has many grasslands, canyons, and steep ravines, but is less rugged overall. Especially interesting are its archeological sites, some of which date back 11,000 years and are still being investigated. The most distant island – windswept **San Miguel**, fifty miles offshore – is alive with numerous seals and sea lions, and is thought to be the burial place of sixteenth-century Spanish explorer Juan Cabrillo. No grave has been found, but a monument has been erected at Cuyler Harbor on the island's eastern end. Seasoned hikers may also wish to make the rugged cross-island trip to Point Bennett to spy on the plentiful wildlife. South of the main islands lies the smallest of the Channel group, **Santa Barbara**, named by Sebastian Vizcaíno, who dropped by on St Barbara's Day, December 4, 1602. The island's appeal these days is largely due to its kestrels, larks, and meadowlarks, which can be seen on land gradually recovering its native flora after years of destruction by now-extinct rabbits.

Santa Barbara

The speedy US-101 that whips along the coast above Ventura slows to a more leisurely pace a hundred miles north of Los Angeles at **SANTA BARBARA**, a seaside resort beautifully situated on the gently sloping hills above the Pacific – though oddly named after the patron saint of firefighters and artillerymen. Despite a vast shopping mall in the center of town and a growing number of motels and fast-food joints on its outskirts, Santa Barbara has managed to preserve the character of its charming architecture. The town's low-rise Spanish Colonial Revival buildings feature red-tiled roofs and white stucco walls, a lovely background to the golden, palm-lined **beaches** below, winding along a gently curving bay.

Once home to Ronald Reagan, and a weekend escape for much of the old money of Los Angeles, Santa Barbara has both a traditional conservative side, as well as a more relaxed libertarian character among the younger set. Still, it's a fairly provincial place; local culture is confined to playing volleyball, surfing, cycling, sipping coffee, or cruising in expensive convertibles along the shore. After an essential visit to **Mission Santa Barbara**, a quiet lunch, and a leisurely walk along the pier, it shouldn't take much longer than half a day to get a sense of the place and move on.

Arrival, information, and transportation

Greyhound **buses** arrive from LA and San Francisco every few hours, stopping downtown at 34 W Carrillo St, while Amtrak **trains** stop at 209 State St, a block west of US-101. Santa Barbara **airport** (☏805/683-4011, ⓦwww .flysba.com), eight miles north of the town center (near UC Santa Barbara), at 500 Fowler Rd, has a limited and often expensive scheduled service to other cities in the Western US.

For more information on Santa Barbara, or for help with finding a place to stay, contact the **visitor center**, 1 Garden St (Mon–Sat 9am–5pm, Sun 10am–5pm; ☏805/965-3021, ⓦwww.santabarbara.com). For information on **hiking** in the area, the US Forest Service office, 3505 Paradise Rd (Mon–Sat

8am–4.30pm; ☎805/967-3481, ⓦwww.r5.fs.fed.us/lospadres), can steer you toward the many trails accessible from town.

Getting around Santa Barbara mainly involves walking, though there's the 25¢ **shuttle** that loops between downtown and the beach on a ten-minute "State Street" schedule, and from the harbor to the zoo every thirty minutes on the "Waterfront" line (daily 10.15am–5.45pm; ☎805/683-3702). Other areas are covered by Santa Barbara Metropolitan Transit District **buses** (fares $1.25; ☎805/683-3702, ⓦwww.sbmtd.gov). If you want to **rent a car**, the best value is U-Save Auto Rental, in town at 510 Anacapa St (☎805/963-3499, ⓦwww.usavesantabarbara.com), and at the airport at 310 S Fairview Ave (☎805/964-5436), which rents late-model cars for as little as $26 a day. Major operators Budget (☎805/963-6651) and Hertz (☎805/967-0411) have offices at the airport, too.

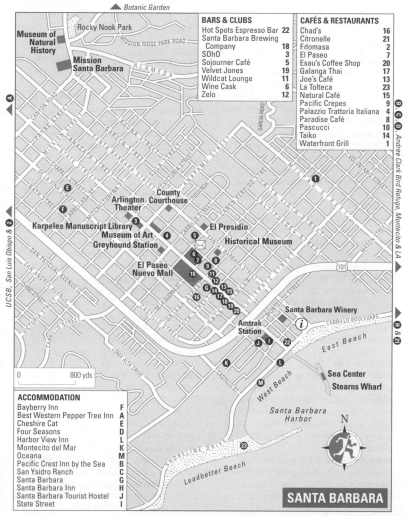

BARS & CLUBS

Hot Spots Espresso Bar	22
Santa Barbara Brewing Company	18
SOhO	3
Sojourner Café	5
Velvet Jones	19
Wildcat Lounge	11
Wine Cask	6
Zelo	12

CAFÉS & RESTAURANTS

Chad's	16
Citronelle	21
Edomasa	2
El Paseo	7
Esau's Coffee Shop	20
Galanga Thai	17
Joe's Café	13
La Tolteca	23
Natural Café	15
Pacific Crepes	9
Palazzio Trattoria Italiana	8
Paradise Café	4
Pascucci	10
Taiko	14
Waterfront Grill	1

ACCOMMODATION

Bayberry Inn	F
Best Western Pepper Tree Inn	A
Cheshire Cat	E
Four Seasons	D
Harbor View Inn	L
Montecito del Mar	K
Oceana	M
Pacific Crest Inn by the Sea	B
San Ysidro Ranch	C
Santa Barbara	G
Santa Barbara Inn	H
Santa Barbara Tourist Hostel	J
State Street	I

SANTA BARBARA

493

Accommodation

Home to some of the West Coast's most deluxe resorts, Santa Barbara is among California's most expensive places to **stay**, with many rooms averaging over $150 a night. However, with a bit of advance planning, finding somewhere reasonable shouldn't take too big a bite out of your budget. The least expensive, as well as most of the more moderate, places are usually booked throughout the summer, but if you get stuck, enlist the assistance of *Hot Spots*, a 24-hour hotel-reservation center and espresso bar at 36 State St (☎805/564-1637 or 1-800/793-7666, ⓦwww.hotspotsusa.com), which offers specials on lodging.

There is a **hostel**, and, while there are no **campgrounds** in Santa Barbara proper, there are several spots along the coast to the north, including El Capitan and Refugio state beaches (both at ☎805/968-1033 or 1-800/444-7275; $16–21), and to the south, Carpinteria State Beach (☎805/684-2811 or 1-800/444-7275; $16–25); all are accessible through ⓦwww.reserveamerica.com. In the mountains of the Santa Ynez Valley, there are a number of other options, including sites around Lake Cachuma (☎805/688-4658; $16–21).

Bayberry Inn 111 W Valerio St ☎805/569-3398, ⓦwww.bayberryinnsantabarbara.com. Lovely little spot offering nine comfortable B&B rooms themed around various berries and color schemes, and with comfortable canopy beds and tasteful period furnishings. ❼

Best Western Pepper Tree Inn 3850 State St ☎805/687-5511 or 1-800/338-0030, ⓦwww.bestwestern.com. Three miles from the city center, a comfortable inn that offers slightly better rates than most accommodation of the same type along the beach, with two pools, hot tubs, and a gym. ❼

Cheshire Cat 36 W Valerio St ☎805/569-1610, ⓦwww.cheshirecat.com. Loaded with precious Victorian decor, this B&B features a hot tub, bikes for guests' use, and Alice in Wonderland theme. Complimentary wine on arrival and breakfast under a palm tree. ❾

Four Seasons 1260 Channel Drive ☎805/969-2261, ⓦwww.fourseasons.com/santabarbara. The apex of swanky resort style in the area, where the opulent rooms boast such amenities as fireplaces and wrought-iron balconies, the suites have two to four bedrooms, and the site has a spa, pool, and fitness center. ❾

Harbor View Inn 28 W Cabrillo Blvd ☎805/963-0780 or 1-800/755-0222, ⓦwww.harborviewinnsb.com. One of the more appealing luxury hotels around, offering on-site restaurant and bar, pool and Jacuzzis, and elegant rooms (and ten even better suites) with oceanfront views and refrigerators. ❾

Montecito del Mar 316 W Montecito St ☎1-888/464-1690, ⓦwww.santabarbarahotel316.com. One of the city's best deals, a Spanish Revival inn with a wide range of room styles and rates, offering quaint basic rooms up to more elaborate suites, plus three spas, complimentary breakfast, and excellent location three blocks from the sands. ❹–❼

Oceana 202 W Cabrillo Blvd ☎1-800/965-9776, ⓦwww.hoteloceanasantabarbara.com. Mission-style resort with splendid architecture, striking and well-decorated rooms loaded with amenities, several pools, spa, fitness center, and nice ocean-side views. ❼

Pacific Crest Inn by the Sea 433 Corona Del Mar ☎805/966-3103, ⓦwww.pacificcrestinn.com. Basic lodging with a motel atmosphere, but it offers clean and modern rooms. A good alternative to its pricier neighbors along the beach. ❹

San Ysidro Ranch 900 San Ysidro Lane ☎805/969-5046 or 1-800/368-6788, ⓦwww.sanysidroranch.com. Jackie and JFK spent their honeymoon at this gorgeous, ultra-posh resort with private cottages, fireplaces, and terraces set in lovely gardens, in the hills a ten-minute drive south of town. ❾

Sandpiper Lodge 3525 State St ☎805/687-5326. Comfortable, motel lodging in uptown part of the city, with basic and clean rooms, pool, spa, and complimentary breakfast. ❸

Santa Barbara 533 State St ☎805/957-9300 or 1-888/259-7700, ⓦwww.hotelsantabarbara.com. Surprisingly good rates for comfortable, well-decorated rooms, Web access, complimentary breakfast, and a prime downtown location. ❻

Santa Barbara Inn 901 E Cabrillo Blvd ☎805/966-2285 or 1-800/231-0431, ⓦwww.santabarbarainn.com. Upscale oceanfront rooms with large pool, lovely views from private balconies, Internet access, and tasteful modern decor in the rooms. But while luxurious –

especially with the swank *Citronelle* restaurant (see p.498) – the inn still has the odd look of a fancy motel. **❼**

Santa Barbara Tourist Hostel 134 Chapala St ☏805/963-0154, ⓦwww.sbhostel.com. Centrally located hostel near the beach and State Street, with bicycle and surfboard rentals, complimentary breakfast, and Internet access. Dorm rooms start at $21, doubles for $45–55, and nearby cottages available May–Nov for $59.

State Street 121 State St ☏805/966-6586. Near the wharf and beach in a colorful old Mission-style building, though it is subject to some noise from the nearby railway and only offers communal bathrooms. Cheap rates include breakfast. **❸**

The Town

Up until the 1920s, Santa Barbara was a fairly typical California beachside community, with lingering bits of Victoriana and historic-revival styles mixed with a handful of Spanish Colonial castoffs from the nineteenth century – with the Presidio and Mission among the more conspicuous examples. Somewhat ironically, Santa Barbara owes its current Mission-era atmosphere – with its attendant quaintness and historical "authenticity" - to a devastating **earthquake** in 1925, after which the city authorities decided to rebuild virtually the entire town as an apocryphal Mission-era village – even the massive "historic" El Paseo shopping mall has a whitewashed adobe facade – with charming arcades linking shops, offices, and restaurants. Despite its dubious origins, the planning scheme has become surprisingly successful, and the square-mile town center, squeezed between the south-facing **beaches** and the foothills of the Santa Ynez Mountains, has one of the region's liveliest street scenes. The main drag, **State Street**, is home to an assortment of diners, bookstores, coffee bars, and nightclubs catering as much to the needs of locals – among them twenty thousand UC Santa Barbara students – as to visitors.

The historic center

What can be called the **historic center** of Santa Barbara, lying mostly along State Street a few blocks inland from the highway, is an obvious place to start exploring, where the town's few genuine Mission-era structures are preserved as **El Presidio de Santa Barbara** (daily 10.30am–4.30pm; $4; ⓦwww.sbthp .org/presidio), built around the fourth and last of the Spanish military garrisons in the region, though only the living quarters of the soldiers who once guarded the site remain. One of these structures, the modest **El Cuartel**, two blocks east of State Street at 123 Canon Perdido St, is the second-oldest building in California, dating from 1782, and now houses historical exhibits and a scale model of the small Spanish colony. A block away, at 136 E De la Guerra St, the **Santa Barbara Historical Museum** (Tues–Sat 10am–5pm, Sun noon–5pm; donation suggested; ☏805/966-1601, ⓦwww.santabarbaramuseum.com), built around an 1817 adobe, contains displays on Spanish- and Mexican-era life, and presents other aspects of the city's past, too, from Ice Age geology to artifacts from native settlements to photographs from modern times. Nearby, where De la Guerra Street meets State Street, the **Casa de la Guerra** (Thurs–Sun noon–4pm; donation suggested; ⓦwww.sbthp.org/casa) preserves what was, in the 1820s, one of the more upscale residences in town (though still built in the spartan Spanish Colonial style), home to one of the Presidio's commanders. These days, it holds spurs, saddles, toys, and weapons, plus exhibits of antique tools, furniture, and religious icons.

On the corner of State and Anapamu, at 1130 State St, the fine if small **Santa Barbara Museum of Art** (Tues–Sun 11am–5pm; $9; ⓦwww.sbmuseart.org) features some classical Greek and Egyptian statuary, a smattering of French

Impressionists, an Asian collection of some note, and interesting modern photography. Its main features, though, come from its **American collection**, which is particularly strong in nineteenth-century landscape painters such as Albert Bierstadt and in postwar California modernists such as Richard Diebenkorn, Larry Bell, and John McLaughlin. Just east, the still-functioning **County Courthouse**, at 1100 Anacapa St (Mon–Fri 8.30am–4.30pm, Sat & Sun 10am–4.30pm; free tours Mon–Sat 2pm, also Mon, Tues & Fri 10.30am; info at ☎805/962-6464), is a Spanish Revival gem, an idiosyncratic 1929 variation on the Mission theme that is widely known as one of the finest public buildings in the US, with striking murals, tilework, and fountain. Take a break in the sunken gardens, explore the quirky staircases, or climb the seventy-foot-high "**El Mirador**" clocktower for a nice view out over the town. Two blocks up State Street, at no. 1317, the landmark 1930s **Arlington Theater** (☎805/963-4408) is an intact and functional movie palace and performance arts venue, with a trompe l'oeil interior modeled after an atmospheric Spanish village plaza. It is also home to the modest but respected Santa Barbara Symphony (tickets $20–50; ☎805/898-9526, ⓦ www.thesymphony.org). Nearby, at 21 Anapamu St, the beautifully decorated **Karpeles Manuscript Library** (daily 10am–4pm; free; ☎805/962-5322, ⓦ www.rain.org/~karpeles) is home to a diverse array of original documents such as the Constitution of the Confederate States of America, Napoleon's battle plans for his Russian invasion, and the manuscripts of famous figures such as Mark Twain, Thomas Edison, John Locke, and Jorge Luis Borges.

The beaches and around

Half a mile down State Street from the town center, Cabrillo Boulevard runs along the south-facing shore, a long, clean strip stretching from the yacht and fishing harbor beyond palm-lined **West Beach** to the volleyball courts and golden sands of **East Beach**. In the vicinity of Chase Palm Park, an outdoor **arts and crafts market** (Sun 10am–dusk; free) presents the work of local artisans every week. At the foot of State Street, take a stroll among the pelicans on the 1872 **Stearns Wharf**, the oldest wooden pier in the state. It was nearly destroyed in November 1998, when a third of it was engulfed in flames, but it

---

Santa Barbara County wineries

Wine fanatics – doubtless inspired by the 2004 film *Sideways* (see p.888) – may desire a visit into Santa Barbara County's copious vineyards, of which there are more than seventy. Although it's not the Napa Valley per se, the area does offer plenty of **wineries** with the requisite tastings and merchandise for sale – though their relative quality depends on your own palate and level of pedantry. Falling slightly out of the town's center, not far from US–101, the **Santa Barbara Winery**, 202 Anacapa St at Yanonali Street (daily 10am–5pm; tastings $5; ☎805/963-3646, ⓦ www .sbwinery.com), is worth a detour from the historic center of town to see one of the oldest commercial wineries in the county, built in 1964. You can get more information on this and other of the county's wineries by contacting the Santa Barbara Vintners' Association (ⓦ www.sbcountywines.com), or the similar WineCountry site (ⓦ santabarbara.winecountry.com), which also has information on winery-related lodging, restaurants, and so on. True vino fanatics may also enjoy a trip further out into the area's wine country courtesy of **Cloud Climbers** (by reservation only at ☎805/965-6654, ⓦ www.ccjeeps.com), who for $95 will take you on a six-hour jeep tour of any ten local wineries, with lunch and four tasting fees included.

has since been restored to its former glory. The wharf is lined with knickknack shops, seafood restaurants, ice-cream stands, and the **Sea Center** (daily 10am–5pm; $3; ☎805/962-0885), an annex of the Museum of Natural History (see below), which offers a selection of whale bones and tot-friendly tide pools.

Just west of the pier, athletes keep in shape in the fifty-meter **Los Baños del Mar** swimming pool, 401 Shoreline Drive (☎805/966-6110), an open-air, year-round facility; **windsurfers** can be rented from beachfront stalls, and **kayaks** are available from Paddle Sports, 117 Harbor Way (☎805/899-4925, ⓦwww.paddlesportsantabarbara.com), starting at $20 for two hours and $40 for a full day; they can also arrange trips to the Channel Islands via Island Packers (see p.491). For **bicycles**, Wheel Fun Rentals, 22 State St (☎805/966-6733, ⓦwww.wheelfunrentals.com), and 101 State St (☎805/963-0353), has models for around $20–35 a day, and provides a map of Santa Barbara's extensive system of bike paths. The longest and most satisfying path leads west along the bluffs to Isla Vista and UC Santa Barbara, and passes a mile or so back from the rarely crowded, creekside **Arroyo Burro Beach** (locally known as "Hendry's"), four miles west of the wharf at the end of Las Positas Road. Alternatively, head along the beachfront bike path two miles east past the small-but-worthwhile **Santa Barbara Zoo**, 500 Ninos Drive (daily 10am–5pm; $9; ☎805/962-6310, ⓦwww.santabarbarazoo.org) – notable for its sharks, stingrays, and turtles, plus a handful of monkeys and excellent display of sea lions – and cycle around the **Andree Clark Bird Refuge**, 1400 E Cabrillo Blvd (unrestricted access), an enclosed, 42-acre saltwater marsh where you can see many interesting seabirds, including egrets, herons, and cormorants.

Mission Santa Barbara and beyond

The mission from which the city takes its name, **Mission Santa Barbara** (daily 9am–5pm; donation suggested; ⓦwww.sbmission.org), is located in the hills above town at 2201 Laguna St. Known as the "Queen of the Missions," its imposing twin-towered facade – facing out over a perfectly manicured garden towards the sea – combines Romanesque and Mission styles, giving it a formidable character lacking in some of the prettier outposts in the chain. The present structure, built to replace a series of three adobe churches that had been destroyed by earthquakes, was finished and dedicated in 1820, but the huge 1925 earthquake damaged the mission, and the ensuing restoration cost nearly $400,000. Today, a small **museum** displays artifacts from the mission archives, and the cemetery contains remains of some four thousand Native Americans, many of whom helped build the original complex, which once included aqueducts, waterworks, a grist mill, a pottery kiln, and two reservoirs. To get to the mission, take SBMTD bus #22 from the Courthouse, along Anapamu Street downtown, or walk or drive the half-mile from State Street up Mission Street and Mission Canyon.

Just beyond the mission at 2559 Puerta del Sol Rd, the **Museum of Natural History** (daily 10am–5pm; $7; ⓦwww.sbnature.org) has intriguing and informative displays on the plants and animals of Southern California. It can be viewed after walking through an entrance constructed out of the skeleton of a blue whale. For a closer glimpse of nature, if you continue on into the hills from the mission, you come to the splendid **Botanic Gardens**, 1212 Mission Canyon Rd (Mon–Fri 9am–4pm, Sat & Sun 9am–5pm, closes an hour later in summer; $6; ⓦwww.santabarbarabotanicgarden.org), whose 65 acres feature pleasant hiking trails amid endemic cacti, manzanita, trees, and wild flowers - a relaxing respite through hillside meadows and glades.

Eating

Santa Barbara has a number of very good and very expensive **restaurants**, but it also has many more affordable options that offer a range of cuisines. Since it's right on the Pacific, you'll find a lot of seafood and sushi; Mexican places are also numerous, and smoothies – blended fruit-and-yoghurt – are everywhere, a welcome snack on a hot summer day.

Chad's 625 Chapala St ☏805/568-1876. A popular local favorite, serving modern American cuisine – with the orange and cinnamon steak as one of the highlights – in the intimate atmosphere of a historic Victorian home. Prices are relatively modest, considering the quality.

Citronelle 901 E Cabrillo Blvd, in the *Santa Barbara Inn* ☏805/963-4717. Stylish big-name restaurant with a range of delicious entrees like the lamb shank and porcupine shrimp, sweeping coastal views, and unsurprisingly exorbitant prices.

Edomasa 2710 De la Vina ☏805/687–0210. Affordable, cozy sushi joint with a good menu and nice presentation – the salmon and marina rolls are top-notch. Frequented more by locals than tourist interlopers. Open till 11pm.

El Paseo 10 El Paseo ☏805/962–6050. Upscale Mexican restaurant serving mainly the familiar staples, though in a historic home with a colorful fountain courtyard.

Esau's Coffee Shop 403 State St ☏805/965-4416. Ancient-looking café serving Santa Barbara's most popular greasy-spoon breakfasts, namely the omelets and corned-beef hash. Open until 1pm daily.

Galanga Thai 507 State St ☏ 805/963-6799. Not much in the way of atmosphere, but still a good spot to drop in for well-prepared and tasty dishes of coconut soup, eggplant curry, and pad Thai.

Joe's Café 536 State St ☏805/966-4638. Long-established bar and grill. A great place to stop off for a burger and a beer, more or less midway between the beach and the downtown museums.

La Tolteca 600 N Milpas St ☏805/899-4857. Fine Mexican food in a casual atmosphere for lunch or dinner, at a longstanding neighborhood fave that's been serving authentic tacos and *rellenos* for many decades.

Natural Café 508 State St ☏805/962-9494. Scrumptious, cheap veggie meals – with pasta, sandwiches, salads, falafel, and desserts – in a prime spot for people watching.

Pacific Crêpes 705 Anacapa St ☏805/882-1123. About as close to a decent crêpe as you're going to get between San Francisco and LA, in this case authentically prepared by real French cooks, and especially good for the dessert crêpes. Expect to wait for service.

Palazzio Trattoria Italiana 1026 State St ☏805/564-1985. One of the better Italian restaurants in town, with old-fashioned sauce-heavy cuisine, gut-buster-sized portions, moderate prices, and one mean *tiramisu*.

Paradise Café 702 Anacapa St ☏805/962-4416. Stylish, slightly upmarket 1940s-era indoor/outdoor grill, with good steaks, fresh seafood, solid pies, and burgers. Service can be marginal at times.

Pascucci 729 State St ☏805/963-8123. Somewhat snooty but worth it for cheap and delicious pastas, gourmet pizzas, and panini served in a small, elegant dining room or al fresco among the shoppers.

Taiko 511 State St ☏805/564-8875. Drop in for a well-prepared salmon teriyaki, tuna sashimi, triple eel roll, or various other rolls and tempura on offer, at this prime sushi restaurant in the heart of the action.

Waterfront Grill 113 Harbor Way ☏805/564-1200. Specializing in seafood and views. Downstairs is casual fine dining. Escape the higher prices by heading upstairs to the *Endless Summer Bar and Café* (☏805/564-4666) – good for its scrumptious burgers, mussels, oysters, and fish'n'chips fare – and enjoy the surfing-inspired decor.

Bars and clubs

There are quite a few **bars** and **clubs** along State Street, especially downtown; for the most up-to-date **nightlife** listings, check out a copy of the free weekly *Santa Barbara Independent* (ⓦ www.independent.com), available at area bookstores, record stores, and convenience marts.

Hot Spots Espresso Bar 36 State St ☏ 805/963-4233. A block from the beach, this

cozy spot is open 24hr for java, smoothies, pastries, and sandwiches. It also offers one of

the city's better information and hotel-
reservation services.

Santa Barbara Brewing Company 501 State
St ☎805/730-1040. Serviceable American fare
– burgers, seafood, and sandwiches – with solid
microbrewed beers and live music on weekends.
The Santa Barbara Blonde and State Street Stout
are both worth a swig.

SOhO 1221 State St ☎805/962-7776, ⓦwww
.sohosb.com. Favorite local place to catch a jazz
show, with nightly performances and the occasional big name. Mixes the vibe with frequent rock,
acoustic, and world-beat artists and bands.

Sojourner Café 134 E Cañon Perdido ☎805/965-
7922. Coffee, beer, wine, and a range of vegetarian
food in a friendly bohemian setting, with increasing
crowds and live music some nights.

Velvet Jones 423 State St ☎805/965-8676,
ⓦwww.velvet-jones.com. One of the few decent

places in town to catch a rock show, typically of
the indie variety, and drawing the usual crowd of
students and would-be hellraisers.

Wildcat Lounge 15 W Ortega St ☎805/962-7970,
ⓦwww.wildcatlounge.com. Renovated dive bar
that now hosts DJs and bands, and offers a mix of
locals, students, and out-of-towners.

Wine Cask 813 Anacapa St ☎805/966-9463.
Darkly elegant spot with many different international varieties of vino and tasty desserts,
especially good for after-hours romancing, when
smart locals plop down on one of the comfortable
couches or luxuriate by the fireplace.

Zelo 630 State St ☎805/966-5792, ⓦwww.zelo
.net. One of Santa Barbara's more fashionable bars
and restaurants, the *Zelo* evolves into a dance club
as the night wears on, offering alternative dance,
Latin, retro, and other eclectic fare throughout
the week.

On from Santa Barbara

Continuing north from Santa Barbara you can either cut inland through the
wine region of the Santa Ynez Valley (see below) or continue along the coast
where you'll pass **Goleta Beach** – popular with families – as well as the
characterless town of **Isla Vista**, which borders the forty-year-old campus of
the **University of California at Santa Barbara**. Isla Vista Beach has some
good tide pools and, at the west end, a popular surfing area at **Coal Oil Point**
("Devereux" to locals); the estuary nearby has been preserved as a botanical
study center and nature refuge, where birdwatchers will find much of interest.

All along this part of the coast **the beaches** face almost due south, so the surf
is very lively, and in winter the sun both rises and sets over the Pacific. About
twenty miles out from Santa Barbara, **El Capitan State Beach** is a popular surfing beach, while **Refugio State Beach**, another three miles along, is one of the
prettiest in California, with palm trees dotting the sands at the mouth of a small
creek, giving the area a tropical feel. Inland on Refugio Road, up the canyon
high in the hills, stands Rancho El Cielo, the one-time Western White House
of retired President Ronald Reagan. Ten miles west, **Gaviota State Beach** is
not as pretty, but there's a fishing pier and a large wooden railway viaduct that
bridges the mouth of the canyon. All the state beaches have **campgrounds**, and
reservations can be made through ParkNet (☎1-800/444-7275; $12).

Just beyond Gaviota, the highways split, US-101 heading inland and the more
spectacular Hwy-1 branching off nearer the coast. Half a mile off the highway,
but a world away from the speeding traffic, is the small **Las Cruces hot spring**
(daylight hours; parking $2), a pool of 95°F mineral water set in a shady, peaceful
ravine. To get there, take the turnoff for Hwy-1, but stay on the east side of the
freeway and double back onto a small road a quarter of a mile to the parking lot
at the end. Walk half a mile or so up the trail until you smell the sulfur.

The Santa Ynez Valley

An alternative to the coastal route out of Santa Barbara is to take Hwy-154
up and over the very steep **San Marcos Pass** through the **Santa Ynez**

Valley, a pleasant route through a prime wine-growing region that's popular with leather-clad bikers and masochistic cyclists.

Three miles out of Santa Barbara, the walls of the **Chumash Painted Cave**, on the narrow Painted Caves Road, are daubed with pre-conquest Native American art. You can't actually enter the sandstone cave as it has been closed off to protect against vandalism. But peering through the bars will give you a good look at the colorful paintings inside.

Several miles further, beyond the San Marcos Pass, Paradise Road follows the Santa Ynez River up to **Red Rocks**, an excellent swimming area amidst the stony outcrops. **Lake Cachuma**, six miles further along Hwy-154, is a popular recreation area with a large **campground** ($16; ☎805/686-5054, ⊛www .sbparks.org/docs/cachuma); it's not actually a lake but a massive reservoir that holds the over-stretched water supply for Santa Barbara.

Beyond the lake, Hwy-246 cuts off to Solvang, while Hwy-154 continues on through the vineyards around **Los Olivos**, where wineries like Fess Parker, Firestone, and Bridlewood are clustered. The Santa Barbara County Vintners' Association (☎805/688-0881 or 1-800/218-0881, ⊛www.sbcountywines .com) publishes a handy wine-touring map of the area which includes each winery's address and hours.

Solvang and around

It is difficult to imagine anyone falling for the sham windmills and plastic storks that fill the saccharine-sweet town of **SOLVANG**, but people come by the busloads to see the community, established in 1911 by expat Danish teachers from the Midwest looking for a place to found a Danish folk school. Nowadays, the town, three miles off US-101 on Hwy-246, lives on tourism, and locals dress in "traditional" costume to entertain visitors. There are **visitor information** stands around the little town run by the local CVB (daily 10am–4pm; ☎805/688-6144 or 1-800/468-6745, ⊛www.solvangusa.com), but the only things that make the town worth a stop are the fresh coffee and pastries sold in one of the many Danish bakeries in town.

While Solvang may mean "Sunny Fields" in Danish, life wasn't so bright for the thousands of Native Americans buried in the cemetery at the **Mission Santa Ines**, 1760 Mission Drive (daily: June–Sept 9am–7pm; Oct–May 9am–5.30pm; $3; ☎805/688-4815, ⊛www.missionsantaines.org), hidden away behind the rows of gingerbread buildings on the eastern edge of town. A century before the Danes tried to make the place look like home, the Spanish were here doing the same, and in 1804 they erected the nineteenth Spanish mission in their chain here. Though the structure has undergone numerous restorations, the buildings are original, and the trompe l'oeil green-marble trim on the church's interior walls is one of the best surviving examples of mission-era decorative art. There is also one of the better mission museums, displaying period furnishings and church documents, including a set of plaques thanking the Franciscan fathers for improving the lives of the native Chumash.

If you'd like to see for yourself how the natives fared, head over to **Santa Ynez**, three miles east of Solvang, where the **Chumash Casino** (24 hours; ☎1-877/CHUMASH, ⊛www.chumashcasino.com) has been trying its best to suck in whatever money tourists haven't blown on Danish pastries. In recent years, there have been attempts by California lawmakers to make slot machines, even on Native American lands, illegal: they haven't succeeded thus far, so you can still shake hands with the one-armed bandit all you like. Passing through the town proper, it's hard to imagine a town that serves as a sharper contrast to prosperous Solvang, or what another blow to the local economy would do.

If the whole spectacle makes you weary of humanity, you can always escape to the **Nojoqui** (pronounced No-ho-kee) **Falls County Park** (daily 8am–sunset; free; ☎805/934-6123, ⊛www.sbparks.org), six miles from Solvang off US-101, where a gentle ten-minute walk brings you to a 75-foot waterfall. The route to the park is gorgeous, winding along Alisal Road under thick garlands of Spanish moss that dangle from a canopy of oak trees.

Lompoc

Hwy-1 splits off US-101 near Gaviota on a marvelous route through the inland valleys of the Santa Ynez Mountains. **LOMPOC** (pronounced Lom-POKE), the only town for miles, calls itself the "flower seed-growing capital of the world" and claims to produce as much as three-quarters of the flower seeds sold on earth. In summer, you'll see a thick carpet of color over the gently rolling landscape of the surrounding countryside. For a leaflet detailing where particular species have been planted this season, contact the **Lompoc Valley Chamber of Commerce**, 111 South I St (Mon–Fri 9am–5pm; ☎805/736-4567 or 1-800/240-0999, ⊛www.lompoc.com), where you can also find out about the folksy **murals** which, in recent years, have sprung up to beautify an otherwise faceless downtown.

For tourist information at weekends, head to **Lompoc Museum**, 200 South H St (Tues–Fri 1–5pm, Sat & Sun 1–4pm; $1; ☎805/736-3888, ⊛store.yahoo.com/lompoc/lompocmuseum). As for the collection here, it's strong on Chumash and other Native American artifacts. It also has material on the town's **original mission site**, the scant remains of which can be found three blocks to the south on F Street off Locust Avenue.

Lompoc is also the home of **Vandenberg Air Force Base**, sprawled along the western side of town, where various new missiles and guidance systems get put through their paces over the Pacific Ocean. Their vapor trails are visible for miles, particularly at sunset, though the only way to see any of it up close is by the Amtrak Coast Starlight train (see p.489), which runs along the coast. The route was **Jack Kerouac**'s favorite rail journey – he worked for a while as a brakeman on the train and subsequently used the "Midnight Ghost" for a free ride between LA and the Bay Area. Aerospace enthusiasts who plan at least a week ahead can visit the air base on four-hour **tours** (2nd and 4th Wed of each month 10am–2pm; free; reservations essential; ☎805/606-3595, ⊛www.vandenberg.af.mil) that visit launch pads and a missile silo.

The **beaches** along this section of coast are secluded, undeveloped, and nearly inaccessible much of the year, either because of bad weather or impending missile launches. **Jalama Beach** (daily 8am–sunset; $6; ☎805/736-6316 or 805/736-3504, ⊛www.sbparks.org) at the end of Jalama Road, twisting fourteen miles off Hwy-1, spreads beneath coastal bluffs, where you can camp overnight ($18). If you're only planning on stopping by during the day, head to the large sand dunes of **Ocean Beach** (free), a broad strand at the mouth of the Santa Ynez River ten miles west of Lompoc, the nesting grounds of many sea birds.

La Purísima Mission State Park

Four miles east of Lompoc and signposted off Hwy-246, **La Purísima Mission State Park** (daily 9am–5pm; $4 per family vehicle, up to nine people; ☎805/733-3713, ⊛www.lapurisimamission.org) is the most complete and authentic reconstruction of any of the 21 Spanish missions in California and one of the best places to get an idea of what life might have been like in these early settlements. La Mission la Purísima Concepción de Maria Santisima was founded in 1787 on a site three miles north of here, and by 1804 had converted around 1500 Chumash, five hundred of whom died in a smallpox epidemic over the next two years. In 1812, an earthquake destroyed all the buildings, and the fathers decided to move to the present site. This new design was the only mission in the chain to be built in a linear fashion rather than in the defensive quadrangle style, used both to confine Native Americans and to keep them out – an especially important detail as the number of able-bodied residents had been slashed by the epidemic. The complex did not last long, however, after the missions were secularized in 1834; like all the rest, it was soon abandoned and gradually fell into disrepair.

The buildings that stand here today were rebuilt on the ruins of the mission as part of a Depression-era project for the unemployed. From 1933 to 1940 over two hundred men lived and worked on the site, studying the remaining ruins and rebuilding the church and outbuildings using period tools and methods. Workers made adobe bricks from straw and mud, shaped roof timbers with handtools, and even took the colors of their paints from native plants.

The heart of the mission is a narrow church, decorated as it would have been in the 1820s; nearby, at the entrance, small but engaging displays of documents and artifacts from the mission era and photographs of the reconstruction are housed in the old wagon house that serves as a **museum** and gift shop. On summer weekends you might catch a "living history day," when volunteers dress up as padres and natives and hold a traditional Mass, along with craft demonstrations that are evocative, if hokey, fun. Call ☎805/733-1303 or check ⓦwww.lapurisimamission.org for more information.

Pismo Beach and Avila Beach

Most of the land along the Santa Maria River, 75 miles north of Santa Barbara, is given over to farming, and both Hwy-1 and US-101 pass through a number of agriculture-based towns and villages. **Santa Maria** is the largest and most developed, though it's hardly worth stopping except to refuel or for a peek at the historic planes on display at the **Museum of Flight**, 3015 Airpark Drive (Fri–Sun 10am–4pm; $5; ☎805/922-8758, ⓦwww.smmof .org). Other towns seem hardly to have changed since the 1930s, when thousands of Okies, as they were known, fled to the region from the Dust Bowl of the Midwest – an era portrayed in John Steinbeck's novel and John Ford's movie, *The Grapes of Wrath* (see p.519 for the National Steinbeck Center in Salinas).

Twenty-five miles north of Lompoc, Hwy-1 passes through the center of **Guadalupe**, a small farming village where Spanish signs and advertisements far outnumber those in English, and ramshackle saloons, cafés, and vegetable stalls line the dusty streets. Along the coast, just several miles west, lies the **Guadalupe/Nipomo Dunes Preserve** (daily 8am–sunset, visitor center Tues–Sun 10am–4pm; free; ☎805/343-2455, ⓦwww.dunescenter.org), where you can look for whales out at sea or climb the 500ft sand dunes. The highest on the California coast, the dunes surround wetlands that are an essential habitat for endangered sea birds.

Pismo Beach

The dunes stretch ten miles up the coast, reaching as far as two miles inland and ending just south of **PISMO BEACH**, where the two highways merge. The southern portion of the dunes, three miles south of the town, is open to off-road-vehicle enthusiasts, who excite themselves flying up and over the sandpiles of the **Pismo Dunes State Vehicle Recreation Area** in dune buggies and four-wheel-drives, motoring along the beach to reach them. Recently, the State Coastal Commission voted to allow even greater vehicle access to California's only drive-on beach, bringing some four million dollars in tourist revenue to the area. Thankfully, the northern portion of the dunes inland is protected as a **nature reserve**.

North of the nature reserve, between the town and the dune-buggy area, a number of beachfront **campgrounds** line Hwy-1; mostly RV-packed, they all charge around $20 a site. The **Pismo Beach State Park** has hot showers and beach camping for $18 (call ParkNet ☎ 1-800/444-7275), and is a good place to see the black-and-orange Monarch butterflies that winter in the eucalyptus trees here from October to February and leave before the summer crowds. However, the once-plentiful **Pismo clams** that gave the town its name (from the local Indian word *pismu*, or "blobs of tar" that the shells resemble) have been so depleted that any you might dig up nowadays are probably under the four-and-a-half-inch legal minimum size.

Most of the town's commercial activity happens at the junction where Pomeroy Avenue crosses Hwy-1. If you have no interest in dunes or watersports, you're in the wrong place, as the dozens of surf shops around you will attest. You can, however, walk out on the gigantic pier for views back to town over the heads of surfers riding the waves.

Practicalities

The **Chamber of Commerce**, 581 Dolliver St (Mon–Sat 9am–5pm, Sun 10am–4pm; ☎ 805/773-4382 or 1-800/443-7778, ⓦ www.pismochamber .com), will help with accommodation, and there are a number of affordable **motels**, including the *Ocean Palms*, 390 Ocean View Ave (☎ 1-805/773-4669 or 1-800/776-3983; ❸), or the *Sea Gypsy*, 1020 Cypress St (☎ 805/773-1801 or 1-800/592-5923, ⓦ www.seagypsymotel.com; ❷) – both have standard, floral motel decor, but the *Sea Gypsy* also offers natty studio apartments with kitchens and balconies for a small premium. For something right on the beach, try the *Edgewater*, 280 Wadsworth Ave (☎ 805/773-4811 or 1-888/248-1354, ⓦ www .edgewater-inn.com; ❹), which has a heated pool, hot tubs, and some rooms with kitchens. If you have a little more to spend, *The Best Western Shorecliff Lodge*, 2555 Price St (☎ 805/773-4671, ⓦ www.shorecliff.com; ❺), is dramatically situated, with a cliff-hugging swimming pool, gazebo, and excellent views.

For **dining** options, people have been known to drive to Pismo Beach just to sample the clam chowder at the fun but touristy *Splash Café*, 197 Pomeroy Ave (☎ 805/773-4653). For fancier dining, try *Giuseppe's*, an old-world Italian restaurant with hearty, simple food, 891 Price St (☎ 805/773-2870). The only **public transportation** is Greyhound, which stops downtown five times a day in each direction.

Avila Beach

North of Pismo Beach the coastline becomes more rugged, with caves and tide pools below ever-eroding bluffs, and sea lions in the many coves. The three-mile-long strand in front of the summer resort town of **AVILA BEACH**, the last outpost of Southern California beach life, is finally recovering from a devastating ecological disaster brought on by a spill from the nearby Unocal Refinery. The ambitious clean-up and reconstruction project that began soon after the spill has helped restore much of the area to its pre-disaster status.

The area has a high concentration of burger stands and one good budget **motel**, the *Inn at Avila Beach*, 256 Front St (☎805/595-2300, ⓦwww .avilabeachca.com; ❹). On the road into town, *Sycamore Mineral Springs*, at 1215 Avila Rd (☎805/595-7302 or 1-800/234-5831, ⓦwww.sycamoresprings .com; ❺), boasts rooms with their own private mineral baths. The *Olde Port Inn* (☎805/595-2515), dramatically situated out on Port San Luis, is *the* spot to **eat** in Avila and has magnificent views: of course, the menu's mostly fish – try the fish tacos ($10) for lunch or the soupy, spicy cioppino stew of fish and shellfish for dinner ($27).

On the beach, you'll find teenagers on the loose from their families cruising the boardwalk, while anyone old enough takes refuge in the loud, local **bars**. The party atmosphere continues all summer long, and no one seems to mind the presence of the **Diablo Canyon Nuclear Plant**, which straddles an earthquake fault six miles up the coast (for what it's worth, three long bursts of a loud siren indicate catastrophe). The scenic route north from here to San Luis Obispo, **See Canyon Road**, cuts off north a mile from US-101, climbing gradually up the narrow, overgrown canyon between sharply profiled volcanic cones, with great views out over the Pacific.

San Luis Obispo

Almost exactly halfway between LA and San Francisco, **SAN LUIS OBISPO** is a main stopoff for both Amtrak and Greyhound. It's an underappreciated gem: primarily an agricultural town, the influx of students from adjacent Cal Poly have perked up the town's nightlife considerably and it's a pleasant place to dawdle and browse. The town center boasts well-preserved architecture, from turreted Victorian residences along **Buchon Street** to the south of the town center to the Art Deco Fremont Theater on Monterey Street. There are a number of good places to eat, a couple of pubs and nightclubs, and – outside summer holiday weekends – affordable accommodation. All these factors make it a smart base from which to explore Hearst Castle, too (see p.512).

Arrival and information

The Greyhound terminal is at 150 South St (☎805/543-2121), half a mile down Higuera Street from the center of town near US-101; and there are regular **bus connections** with both LA and San Francisco. Amtrak trains and Thruway buses stop several times each day in each direction at the end of Santa Rosa Street, half a mile south of the business district. You can pick up a free walking-tour map highlighting much of the town's best architecture from the **Chamber of Commerce** at 1039 Chorro St (Sun 11am–5pm, Mon 10am–5pm, Tues–Wed 8am–5pm, Thurs 8am–8pm, Fri 8am–7pm, Sat 10am–7pm; ⓦwww.visitslo.com), which will also help with finding accommodation. The **Visitors and Conference Bureau** at 1037 Mill St (Mon–Fri 8am–noon & 1–5pm; ☎805/781-2531 or 1-800/634-1414, ⓦwww.sanluisobispocounty.com) may also come in handy. To

find out what's on and where, check out the free weekly *New Times* (Ⓦwww
.newtimeslo.com) or check out the "Ticket" supplement every Friday in the
local *San Luis Obispo Tribune* (50¢).

Accommodation

Monterey Street was the site of the world's first (and long gone) **motel** – the
Motel Inn (see box, p.506). Rates in its modern counterparts are generally low.
The best **camping** nearby is south of town beyond Pismo Beach, or north off
Hwy-1 in Morro Bay.

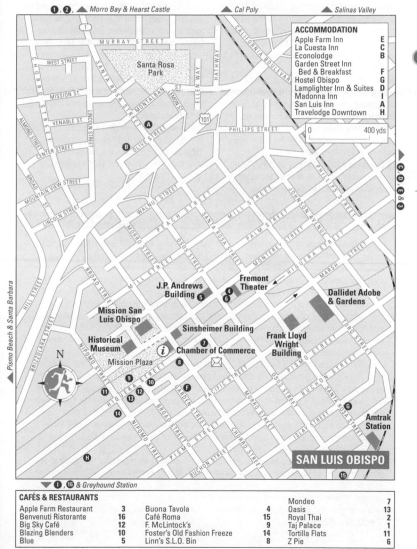

❶, ❷, ▲ Morro Bay & Hearst Castle   ▲ Cal Poly   ▲ Salinas Valley

ACCOMMODATION	
Apple Farm Inn	E
La Cuesta Inn	C
Econolodge	B
Garden Street Inn	
Bed & Breakfast	F
Hostel Obispo	G
Lamplighter Inn & Suites	D
Madonna Inn	I
San Luis Inn	A
Travelodge Downtown	H

0   400 yds

SAN LUIS OBISPO

◀ Pismo Beach & Santa Barbara

▼ ❶, ⓰ & Greyhound Station

CAFÉS & RESTAURANTS					
				Mondeo	7
Apple Farm Restaurant	3	Buona Tavola	4	Oasis	13
Benvenuti Ristorante	16	Café Roma	15	Royal Thai	2
Big Sky Café	12	F. McLintock's	9	Taj Palace	1
Blazing Blenders	10	Foster's Old Fashion Freeze	14	Tortilla Flats	11
Blue	5	Linn's S.L.O. Bin	8	Z Pie	6

7

Apple Farm Inn 2015 Monterey St ☎805/544-2040 or 1-800/255-2040, ⓦwww.applefarm.com. Charming inn with homely Victoriana furnishings including canopy beds, excellent B&B-style breakfasts, and an affable staff. Rates are lower in the Court building than the Inn proper. ④–⑥

Econolodge 950 Olive St ☎805/544-8886, ⓦwww.econolodge.com. Part of a national chain, this branch offers a good standard of accommodation at a great price. ④

Garden Street Inn Bed & Breakfast 1212 Garden St ☎805/545-9802 or 1-800/488-2045, ⓦwww.gardenstreetinn.com. Very central B&B in a restored 1880s house with comfortable rooms (some with TV, all with phone). There is complimentary wine on arrival and gourmet cooked breakfasts. ⑥

Hostel Obispo 1617 Santa Rosa St ☎805/544-4678 ⓦwww.hostelobispo.com. Recently relocated to a handier, more central spot, this comfortable hostel has dorm beds at $18 for HI members, $20 for others. There are a small number of private rooms also available ($45–70). Office open 8–10am, 4.30–10pm. ①

La Cuesta Inn 2074 Monterey St ☎805/543-2777 or 1-800/543-2777, ⓦwww.lacuestainn .com. As popular with businesspeople as

vacationers, with spacious modern rooms and a good-sized swimming pool and spa. ④

Lamplighter Inn & Suites 1604 Monterey St ☎805/547-7777 or 1-866/756-7378, ⓦwww .lamplighterinn.com. Older but comfortable motel with a pool and usual amenities (fridges, microwaves, free in-room hi-speed Internet access). Popular with families. ③–④

Madonna Inn 100 Madonna Rd ☎805/543-3000 or 1-800/543-9666, ⓦwww.madonnainn.com. Local landmark (see opposite) set in over 2000 acres, but the very standard "theme" rooms in this shocking kitsch monstrosity are a big disappointment at such inflated rates, especially after touring the imposingly pink, chalet-style lobby. More last days of Elvis in Vegas than the hip-swiveling hound-dog. ⑥–⑦ rooms, ⑧ suites

San Luis Inn 404 Santa Rosa St ☎805/544-0881 or 1-800/447-8080, ⓦwww.sanluisinn.com. Clean, standard rooms, free continental breakfasts, and a heated pool. ②

Travelodge Downtown 345 Marsh St ☎805/543-6443 or 1-800/458-8848. Simple motel but excellent value and location. There is another chain location at 1825 Monterey St (☎805/543-5110). ②

The world's first motel

The Milestone Motel opened in San Luis Obispo in 1925, designed to take advantage of the postwar mushrooming of car ownership among Americans. Initially, enthusiastic Model–T drivers had used automobile "campgrounds" for overnight stays, pitching tents alongside their cars, and since San Luis Obispo is almost exactly between San Francisco and Los Angeles, it became an especially popular place to stop. Savvy architect **Arthur Heineman**, who'd recently overseen the development of a series of residential bungalows, recognized the potential of adapting the bungalow concept for the travel industry, combining the convenience of a campground with the comfort and respectability (not to mention, higher prices) of a hotel.

Heineman and his brother Alfred opened the first motel in the auto nexus of San Luis Obispo but envisaged a chain stretching from San Diego to Seattle, each one-day's journey from the next, much like the first European settlements along the Camino Real – hence the Mission-style architecture of the existing *Milestone* building. Unfortunately, only one motel was built, and Heineman didn't even manage to copyright the word he'd formed as a contraction of "motor" and "hotel." It entered the dictionary in 1950, long after hundreds of copycats had sprung up across America.

The *Milestone*, then known as the *Motel Inn*, closed in the early 1990s and fell into ten years of disrepair until its new owners launched an ambitious restoration plan in 2000, which included linking it with the nearby *Apple Farm Inn* (see review above). Work is progressing extremely slowly, and there's still no firm date for its reopening – for up-to-date information, call *Apple Farm* at ☎805/544-2040 or 1-800/374-3705.

The Town

San Luis is eminently walkable, with a compact core centered on the late eighteenth-century **Mission San Luis Obispo de Tolosa**, 751 Palm St (daily: June–Dec 9am–5pm; Jan–May 9am–4pm; free; ☎805/543-6850, ⓦwww .oldmissionslo.org). A fairly plain and unremarkable church, it was the fifth structure in the mission trail and the prototype for the now ubiquitous red-tiled roof – developed as a replacement for the original, flammable thatch, which caught fire here in 1776 during attack by Native Americans. Between the mission and the tourist office, **Mission Plaza**'s terraces step down along San Luis Creek. It's a leafy, restful spot, along which footpaths meander, criss-crossed by bridges every hundred feet and overlooked by a number of stores and outdoor restaurants on the south bank; it's a delightful place to dawdle with a book.

Downstream, across a small park, the **San Luis Obispo County Historical Museum**, 696 Monterey St (Wed–Sun 10am–4pm; free; ☎805/543-0638, ⓦwww.slochs.org), holds a low-key collection of local artifacts tending toward the domestic and housed in a richly detailed 1904 Carnegie Library building. The main drag, **Higuera Street** (pronounced "Hi-GEAR-a"), a block south of Mission Plaza, springs to life every Thursday afternoon and evening for the **Farmers' Market**, when the street is closed to cars and filled with vegetable stalls, mobile barbecues, and street-corner musicians. All of San Luis (and a fair smattering of tourists) comes out to sample the foods and entertainment of this weekly county fair.

Though a number of commercial buildings of minor architectural note are detailed on the Chamber of Commerce's **self-guided walking tour**, the only one not to be missed is the doctor's surgery designed by Frank Lloyd Wright at Santa Rosa and Pacific streets, although there's no admittance except for patients. Close by, at the end of Pacific Street, stands the **Dallidet Adobe and Gardens**, at no. 1185 (gardens open year-round Thurs 2.30–5.30pm & Memorial Day–Labor Day Sun 1–4pm, docent-led tours of house Sun 1–4pm; donation suggested; ☎805/543-6762), one of the county's oldest buildings, which was constructed by a disillusioned French forty-niner who, eluded by a fortune in the Mother Lode, ended up living in town. It's set among manicured grounds with two redwoods that are more than 125 feet tall.

If you have neither the time nor the inclination to sample the small-town charms of San Luis, at least stop to look at the now-famous **Madonna Inn** (see opposite). Featured in the cult classic film *Aria*, the *Inn* has rooms decorated in a variety of themes from fairy-tale princesses to Stone Age cavemen; its signature shocking-pink has even been registered as an official color in the PMS printing system. A very different sort of place is the **Shakespeare Press Museum** on the Cal Poly campus (Mon–Fri by appointment; free; ☎805/756-2495, ⓦwww.grc.calpoly.edu/pages/spm) – nothing to do with the Bard (Shakespeare was the nickname given by his friends to Charles Palmer, owner of the donated collection, for his obsessive book-loving habits), but a great collection of old printing presses and lead typefaces collected mainly from the frontier newspapers of California's Gold Rush towns.

Eating

Higuera Street is the place to head to **eat**, especially during the Thursday afternoon Farmers' Market, when barbecues and food stalls are set up amidst the jostling crowds.

Apple Farm Restaurant 2015 Monterey St ☎805/544-6100. In the *Apple Farm Inn*, this casual, family-style restaurant serves up traditional American dishes (try the chicken and dumplings) and is a surprisingly good value.

Benvenuti Ristorante 457 Marsh St ☎805/541-5393. Slightly upscale Italian food in an almost painfully cute restored Victorian house. Good wine list and lots of patio seating.

Big Sky Café 1121 Broad St ☎805/545-5401. An airy, modern place with an emphasis on Cajun and Creole food. $7 dishes and an assortment of coffees.

Blazing Blenders 1108 Broad St ☎805/546-8122. A small, studenty juice bar, with limited seating, massive fish tank, and meal-sized smoothies ($3.50).

Blue 988 Monterey St ☎805/783-1135. Swanky lounge/bar/restaurant, with bare brick walls, dark wood fixtures, and a trendier, dressier crowd than most spots in town. Graze on snacks like *ahi* grilled tuna or pork tenderloin in the lounge ($10–11) or opt for larger, dinner portions in the restaurant ($19–22).

Buona Tavola 1037 Monterey St ☎805/545-8000. Small and stylish bistro with good range of moderately priced Northern Italian food and wine.

Café Roma 1020 Railroad Ave ☎805/541-6800. Extremely popular family-owned Italian restaurant with excellent pasta dishes served in a romantic setting for around $10.

F. McLintock's 686 Higuera St ☎805/541-0686. Mainstream bar-restaurant that's always reassuringly busy: standard burgers, pasta, and sandwiches in an Old West atmosphere for around $8 each – try the taco salad in a crispy shell or the gooey French dip.

Foster's Old Fashion Freeze 590 Marsh St ☎805/543-7639. Old-time ice cream parlor, a Swiss chalet-like building painted blue and white with ample tables outside. Order a shake, malt, sundae, or parfait in flavors like vanilla and hot fudge; if you're brave enough, sample a treacle-thick freeze that's almost too stiff to suck through a straw ($2.10–2.73).

Linn's S.L.O. Bin 1141 Chorro St ☎805/546-8444. Casual restaurant featuring a large variety of salads, soups, and sandwiches.

Mondeo 893 Higuera St #D4 ☎805/544-2956. Asian-inflected fast-food joint, with an inventive made-to-order menu. Every recipe can be served as a wrap or carb-skipping bowl ($6–9): try an Americana with swordfish or a Mediterraneo with basil scampi. The home-made ginger ale's also delicious.

Oasis 675 Higuera St ☎805/543-1155. Unexpectedly delicious Middle Eastern cuisine in a souk-like setting: try the chicken delight with sweet potatoes and raisins. Excellent-value set lunches.

Royal Thai 777 E Foothill Blvd in Foothill Plaza ☎805/544-9777. Extensive Thai menu – stick with chicken and beef to keep costs down. The lunch express menu is hearty, quick, and cheap.

Taj Palace 795 E Foothill Blvd ☎805/543-0722. The city's one Indian choice is slightly pricier than what you might find in a city with more competition, but good: the $5.95 buffet lunch, including staples like chicken tikka and *aloo gobi* (spicy cauliflower and potatoes) is the cheapest way to eat here.

Tortilla Flats 1051 Nipomo St ☎805/544-7575. Raucous, neon-lit Mexican restaurant, better known for copious margaritas than great food, but with free happy-hour nachos and dancing from 9pm.

Z Pie 1060 Osos St ☎805/544-9743. Eccentric and tasty modern takes on the pot pie, with fillings including steak and cabernet or shrimp and roasted garlic, all for around $5. Filling and fun.

Bars and nightlife

San Luis Obispo's sizeable student population keeps **nightlife** edgier than you might expect for a small Californian town. Stop by the superb Boo Boo Records, 978 Monterey St (☎805/541-0657), one of the true holdouts in the tradition of great, independent record stores; their stock of music is vast, and you can also pick up CDs by, and tickets for, local bands. Reliable venues include the Performing Arts Center at Cal Poly (☎805/756-2787 or 1-888/233-2787, ⓦwww.pacslo.org) and the *Avila Beach Resort* in nearby Avila Beach (☎805/595-4000, ⓦwww.avilabeachresort.com).

You'll also find a couple of popular **bars** and **cafés** on and just off Higuera, around the Mission Plaza area. The café *Linnaea's*, 1110 Garden Street (☎805/541-5888, ⓦwww.linnaeas.com), serves good espresso and offers live music on Thursday, Friday, and Saturday nights. Otherwise, stop by *SLO*

Brewing Company opposite, 1119 Garden St (☎805/543-1943, ⓦwww.slobrew.com), which also hosts regular music and live performances. *Blue* (see opposite) has live jazz Wednesday to Friday and a mainstream, down-tempo DJ every Saturday.

Morro Bay and the coast to San Simeon

North of San Luis Obispo the highways diverge again: US-101 – favored by trains and buses – speeds up through the Salinas Valley (see p.515), while Hwy-1 takes the more scenic route along the coast. The first dozen miles of Hwy-1 follow the line of a ridgeback string of hills, a series of plugs from extinct volcanoes, the most prominent of which have been dubbed the **Seven Sisters**. Two more continue the chain; the ninth is invisible under the sea, while the eighth is the **Morro Rock** in the sea close to the coast. According to local lore, it was named by the sixteenth-century explorer Juan Cabrillo, who thought it looked like the Moorish turbans in southern Spain. Nowadays, it's off limits to the public in order to protect the nesting areas of the endangered peregrine falcons; in any case it's most impressive from a distance, dominating the fine harbor at **MORRO BAY**, where the local fishing boats unload their catches to sell in the many fish markets along the waterfront.

This easy-paced resort town is accessible from San Luis Obispo via CCAT **buses** #11 or 12 (12–14 departures weekdays, fewer at weekends; $1.25–1.50, day-pass $4; ☎805/781-4472, ⓦwww.slorta.org), though apart from the many seafood restaurants the only places worth coming here for are spread around the bay, miles from public transportation. You get one of the best views of the rock and surrounding coastline from the top of **Cerro Alto**, a 2620-foot volcanic cone with good hiking and camping, eight miles east of Morro Bay off Hwy-41.

Closer in, on a point above the bay a mile south of town at the end of Main Street, but providing a good view of Morro Rock, there's the **Museum of Natural History** (daily 10am–5pm; $2; ☎805/772-2694, ⓦwww.mbspmuseum.org). Recently renovated, this formerly fusty spot's now a state-of-the-art interactive ecology museum, aimed squarely at curious kids – the best display's the chance for any visitor to build his or her own sand dune. Otherwise, the **campground** across the street in **Morro Bay State Park** (reserve through ParkNet ☎1-800/444-7275) costs $18 a night and has hot showers. Across the bay, the thin sandy peninsula that protects the harbor is hard to reach except by boat – it's entirely undeveloped and about the only place where you stand a chance of finding any Pismo clams. You can rent **kayaks**, which cost about $9 per hour and $22 half-day, from the likes of Kayak Horizons, 551 Embarcadero (☎805/772-6444, ⓦwww.kayakhorizons.com), or hike the two miles out there from Los Osos Valley Road.

Montaña de Oro State Park (daily dawn–dusk; free; ☎805/528-0513 or 805/772-7434, ⓦwww.parks.ca.gov), four miles south at the end of Los Osos Valley Road, is much more primitive than Morro Bay State Park, and has some excellent tide pools as well as a good beach at Spooner's Cove. The windswept promontory stands solidly against the crashing sea, offering excellent hiking along the shore and through the sagebrush and eucalyptus trees of the upland hillsides, which in spring are covered in golden poppies.

There are $18 **campgrounds** in the park (call ParkNet ☎1-800/444-7275), and numerous reasonably priced **motels** in town, including a *Motel 6*, 298 Atascadero Rd (☎805/772-5641 or 1-800/466-8356; ❷), close to the beach, and the cozier *El Morro Masterpiece Motel*, 1206 Main St (☎805/772-5633, ⓦwww.masterpiecemotels.com; ③). For **eating** try *Hofbrau Der Albatross*, 901 Embarcadero (☎805/772-2411), a deluxe burger joint with bratwurst on the menu; *Lolo's*, 2848 Main St (☎805/772-5686), for authentic Mexican cuisine; and *The Coffee Pot Restaurant*, 1001 Front St (open daily 7.30am–1.30pm; ☎805/772-3176), for hearty breakfasts and lunches. The **Chamber of Commerce** is at 880 Main St (Mon–Fri 10–5pm, Sat 10am–4pm, Sun 10am–3pm; ☎805/772-4467 or 1-800/231-0592, ⓦwww.morrobay.org).

The next town north is **Cayucos**, four miles along Hwy-1, originally a small port built by Englishman James Cass in the 1870s, and now a sleepy place ranged along sandy beaches with a nice pier: it's a pleasant enough pit

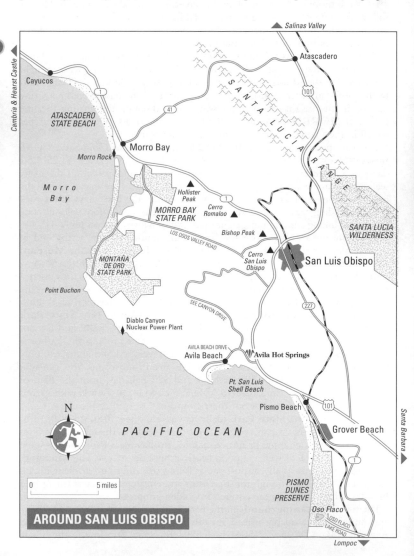

AROUND SAN LUIS OBISPO

stop on a journey along the coast. *The Cypress Tree Inn*, 125 S Ocean Ave (☎805/995-3917, ⓦwww.cypresstreemotel.com; $39), is just one block from the beach. For coffee, muffins, and pastries, you can't beat *Kelley's*, 155 N Ocean Ave (☎805/995-2980). Surprisingly, the town also has some of the area's best **nightlife** in *Ye Olde Cayucos Tavern and Card Room*, 130 N Ocean Ave (☎805/995-3209), in the heart of the two-block-long ramshackle center, with live bands on weekends and late-night poker games. The **Chamber of Commerce** is at 767 Main St (Mon–Fri 9am–5pm, Sat & Sun noon–4pm; ☎805/927-3624, ⓦwww.cambriachamber.org).

Cambria

About six miles to the north, you could drive right past **Harmony** without even noticing it. This tiny hamlet has a population of 18, yet manages to operate several gift shops and offer wine tastings at Harmony Cellars (daily 9.30am–5pm; ☎805/927-1625). **CAMBRIA**, a few miles further, is a rather twee, self-conscious town, glutted with pricey amenities thanks in part to everything it's done to cash in on its proximity to San Simeon and Hearst Castle, seven miles north. Hidden away in a wooded valley half a mile off Hwy-1, Cambria was an established town serving the local ranchers and fishermen long before Hearst Castle became the region's prime tourist attraction. Still, it manages to keep its growing pains to a minimum, perhaps because its residents have enacted ordinances that make any view-blocking development illegal. The older section of town, known as Main Village, is half a mile east of Hwy-1 on Main Street, while the newer part with most of the cheaper hotels is referred to as East Village. It's a comfortable enough place to stretch your legs or kill some time till your scheduled tour at the castle begins, and holds one acknowledged oddity: **Nit Wit Ridge**, 881 Hillcrest Drive (tours daily by appointment; donation; ☎805/927-2690). This weird, whimsical folly was the brainchild of one Art Beal, who came to Cambria from San Francisco in the 1920s and bought a plot of land where, over a fifty-year period, he built a Baroque castle out of trash. Recycling old toilet seats as picture frames or waterpipes as handrails, this eccentric misfit's glorious folly lay abandoned for ten years after his death in 1989. Now, though, it's gradually being restored, and a tour of the labyrinthine house is an offbeat counterpoint to the luxuries of Hearst Castle.

The **Chamber of Commerce**, 767 Main St (Mon–Fri 9am–5pm, Sat & Sun 10am–2pm; ☎805/927-3624, ⓦwww.cambriachamber.org), can help with **accommodation**. Back across Hwy-1, picturesque, seafront Moonstone Beach Drive has plenty of places to stay, but you'll pay for the views. The most reasonable beachfront rates are at *Castle Inn*, at no. 6620 (☎805/927-8605, ⓦwww.cambria-online.com/CastleInnByTheSea/; ➎). More affordable, though less dramatically situated are the *Cambria Palms Motel*, 2662 Main St (☎805/927-4485 or 1-866/489-4485; ➊), or the *Bluebird Inn* at 1880 Main St (☎805/927-4634 or 1-800/552-5434, ⓦwww.bluebirdmotel.com; ➋). **Camping** is available at San Simeon State Park (☎805/927-2020 ext 2 or 1-800/444-7275), two miles north along the coast; there are two sites here – San Simeon Creek has facilities including showers ($15 low season, $20 high season), while Washburn is a primitive pitch-only area ($11 low season, $15 high season). You'll need to reserve a spot here from March through September; rest of the year it's first come, first served.

You'll find good **food** at *Linn's*, 2277 Main St (☎805/927-0371), which serves a good selection of brunch staples along with cakes, salads, and sandwiches; *Robin's*, 4095 Burton Drive (☎805/927-5007), which features internationally influenced California meals at moderate prices (entrees $16–19); for lunch, grab a doorstop sandwich ($6–8) at the *Cambria Courtyard Deli*, 604 Main St (☎805/927-3833), so crammed with filling it's almost impossible to eat whole. The *West End Bar & Grille*, 774 Main St (☎805/927-5521), is a friendly neighborhood pub with a large selection of beers, good meals, and live music.

Hearst Castle and San Simeon

Forty-five miles northwest of San Luis Obispo, **HEARST CASTLE** sits on a hilltop overlooking rolling ranchlands and the Pacific Ocean. Far and away the biggest single attraction for miles, the former holiday home of publishing magnate **William Randolph Hearst** is one of the most opulent and extravagant houses in the world. Its interior combines walls, floors, and ceilings torn from European churches and castles with Gothic fireplaces and Moorish tiles. Nearly every room is bursting with Greek vases and medieval tapestries, and even the many pools are lined with works of art. Ironically, the same financial power and lust for collecting that allowed Hearst to hoard these artifacts to himself have made them viewable to more people than ever would have seen them had they stayed in their respective lands. The castle may once have been a weekend retreat for only the most famous politicians and movie stars of the 1920s and 1930s – Hearst's highly selective range of guests included Winston Churchill, Walt Disney, and Charles Lindbergh, while the most frequent weekenders were Cary Grant and Charlie Chaplin (known here as "the Court Jester"); but it now brings in more than a million visitors a year, and it would be unthinkable to visit the region without stopping off here.

Note that, remarkably, the devastating earthquake in nearby Paso Robles left the castle largely untouched, thanks to its location on a rocky ridge; a few antiques inside were damaged, as well as some planters in the gardens, but all have now been restored.

The Castle

Hearst Castle, which Hearst himself referred to as "the ranch" (the official name is now "Hearst San Simeon State Historic Monument"), is the extravagant palace one would expect from the man whose domination of the national media inspired Orson Welles's classic film *Citizen Kane*. The structure is actually more of a complex of buildings than a "castle." Three guesthouses circle the hundred-room main **Casa Grande**, in which Hearst himself held court. What may come as a surprise is the harmony with which the many diverse art treasures that he collected were brought together by his mother's favorite architect Julia Morgan. Morgan designed each room and building in the spirit of the masterpieces destined to be housed inside (and received only $80,000 for her efforts); her role was more like architectural seamstress than designer, effectively stitching together ready-made elements into a cohesive whole.

After the death of Hearst's mother Phoebe in 1919, construction began on the southern edge of the inherited 250,000-acre ranch that became Hearst's own private free-roaming zoo with lions, tigers, zebras, and bears. The work was never truly completed: rooms would often be torn out as soon as they were finished in order to accommodate more acquired treasure. It's no wonder that the castle looks more like a church than a mansion: the main facade is a

William Randolph Hearst, the real life of Citizen Kane

It would be quite easy to portray **William Randolph Hearst** (or "W.R.") as a power-mad monster, but in retrospect he seems more like a very rich, overindulged little boy. Born in 1863, the only son of a multimillionaire mining engineer, he was avidly devoted to his mother, Phoebe Apperson Hearst, one of California's most sincere and generous philanthropists, a founder of the University of California and the Traveler's Aid society.

Hearst learned his trade in New York City working for the inventor of inflammatory **"Yellow Journalism,"** Joseph Pulitzer, who had four rules for how to sell newspapers: emphasize the sensational; elaborate the facts; manufacture the news; and use games and contests. When he published his own newspaper, Hearst took this advice to heart, his *Morning Journal* fanning the flames of American imperialism to help ignite the **Spanish–American War** of 1898. As he told his correspondents in Cuba: "You provide the pictures, and I'll provide the war." Hearst eventually controlled an empire that, at its peak during the 1930s, sold 25 percent of the newspapers in the entire country, including two other New York papers, the *Washington Times*, and the *Detroit News* – as well as *Cosmopolitan* and *Good Housekeeping* magazines. In California, Hearst's power was even more pronounced, with his San Francisco and Los Angeles papers controlling over sixty percent of the total market. Besides his many newspapers, Hearst owned eleven radio stations and two movie studios.

Somewhat surprisingly, considering his warmongering and extreme nationalism, Hearst was fairly middle-of-the-road politically, a lifelong Democrat who served two terms in the House of Representatives but failed in bids to be elected mayor of New York and president of the US.

It was through his movie studio proprietorship that he made his mistress **Marion Davies** – Hollywood's Golden Era answer to Pia Zadora – a star. Although Hearst was married, his estranged wife Millicent disliked Hearst Castle, so Marion was queen-consort there; the only time Mrs Hearst spent here was as hostess whenever a head of state, like Churchill or Coolidge, was a visitor (while Davies was invariably billeted at a mansion in LA). Her relationship with Hearst endured despite constant accusations of gold-digging and swirling rumors around a mysterious death onboard Hearst's boat (allegedly, Hearst murdered the man who was Davies' lover, and covered it up, a story recently featured in the movie *The Cat's Meow*). When the Depression hit, Hearst was forced to sell off most of his holdings but remained a wealthy man; he continued to exert power and influence until his death, aged 88, at Marion Davies' ranch in 1951. She stuck by him until the end, despite the private sniggers of his upper-crust cohorts; in explanation, Davies is said to have shrugged "My mother raised me to be a gold-digger, but I fell in love."

twin-towered copy of a Mudejar cathedral in Ronda, Spain, while the main door was pilfered from a convent there. Casa Grande stands at the top of steps that curve up from an expansive **swimming pool** (one of the most photographed in the world), which is filled with pure spring water and lined by a Greek colonnade and marble statues. Indoors there is another pool, lined with blue Venetian glass and gold tiles, its soft lights reflecting in the water's steamy surface.

Highlights inside the castle include the **Refectory**, lined with choir stalls from Spanish and Italian churches, and the **Gothic Suite**, where Hearst conducted his daily business in medieval splendor. The **private cinema** shouldn't be missed either – inside, Hearst saw first cuts of leading Hollywood films of the day before they were released to the general public. The one disappointing element of the interior is its art collection: there are plenty of cherry-cheeked Madonnas and musty Old Masters, but not a single standout work – clearly,

Hearst's taste was more decorative than artistic (the one exception's a so-so ceiling in a duplex suite by Simon Vouet).

Outside the castle proper there are several other major buildings, including the seventeen Neptune Pool dressing rooms, still hung with period swimwear and sports equipment; the Casa del Mar, an elaborate guesthouse with a largely Eastern theme that Marion Davies claimed to be Hearst's favorite spot on the whole estate; and the Casa del Monte, a smaller guesthouse with fully furnished rooms overlooking the Santa Lucia Mountains. The estate's extensive Italian- and Spanish-influenced gardens, terraces, and walkways require a full tour in themselves as they feature hundreds of species of rare and imported flowers, bushes, and trees.

Castle practicalities

To see Hearst Castle, you must take one of the guided **tours** (daily: June–Aug 8am–4pm; Sept–May 8am–3.20pm; $12–24; ☎916/414-8400 ext 4100 or 1-800/444-4445, ⓦwww.hearstcastle.com). The Experience Tour, or Tour #1 ($18), which includes a lush, slushy film on the building's construction plus an introductory spin around the guesthouse and the main rooms of the Casa Grande, is usually recommended for the first visit – to guarantee a spot on the tour, make a **reservation**. However, it's worth skipping this and opting for Tour #2 ($12): instead of groups of forty or more, you'll be ambling around with only a handful (maximum 12) of other visitors; the docent's information on Hearst is just as in-depth; while visiting the upper floors of the main house (including Hearst's library and bedroom) suite gives a more personal insight into the man than gawping at the staterooms seen on Tour #1 (the only difference is that you won't be able to catch that so-so biopic). If you're fascinated enough to stay for the whole day, there are two other tours ($12 each): Tour #3 is strictly for aficionados, concentrating as it does on the Casa del Monte guesthouse; while Tour #4 (spring and summer only) focuses on the grounds, gardens, and wine cellar. Tour #5 only runs from April through October on selected evenings: docents in period dress take visitors through the castle on a visit that combines elements of Tours #1, 2, and 4 ($24). They speak of Hearst in the present tense, ending the visit at the lamplit Neptune Pool, with stories of the legends who frolicked with each other there after dark. For details of schedules, call the recorded information line at ☎805/927-2020; book online or via ☎1-800/444-4445.

For each tour, budget around two hours including the trundling ride via bus from the visitor center to the hilltop; all tours leave from the same depot at the rear of the center, through double doors past the ticket office. Make sure to collect your tickets before lining up for the tour. If you've arrived early, you can find out more about Hearst and his castle from the mildly diverting **museum** (daily 9am–5pm; free) in the rear half of the visitor center, beyond the point where you board the buses.

Finally, try and visit the castle first thing in the morning, when coastal fogs often hide the castle from the world below. After a long bus ride from the visitor center to the top of the steep hill on which the mansion rests, you poke through the clouds into sunlight, as if entering Heaven. The cherubic white statues seem to lift off the icy blue pool along with the last misty vapors of the morning.

San Simeon and north

The boarded-up pier of **SAN SIMEON**, an all-but-abandoned harbor town along the coast just north of Hearst Castle, is where all of Hearst's treasures were unloaded, as were the many tons of concrete and steel that went into the building of the house. Before the Hearsts bought up the land, San Simeon was a whaling and shipping port, of which all that remains is a one-room schoolhouse and the 1852 *Sebastian's Store*, a combination post office, café, and souvenir shop. The beach south of the pier is protected by San Simeon Point, which hooks out into the Pacific, making it safe for swimming. Along the highway three miles south there's a concentrated blot of gas stations, fast-food restaurants, and **motels**, mostly overpriced with the exception of a few along Castillo Drive, such as the *Motel 6 Premiere*, no. 9070 (☎805/927-8691 or 1-800/4-MOTEL6, ⓦwww.motel6.com; ❷), and the *Inns of California-San Simeon*, no. 9280 (☎805/927-8659 or 1-800/556-0400, ⓦwww.innsofcal .com; ❷), both with heated pools and rates that tend to double on weekends in summer. There's **camping** four miles south along the beach at San Simeon State Park (see p.511).

North of Hearst Castle the **coastline** is mostly rolling grasslands and cattle ranches, still owned and run by the Hearst family, with few buildings on the distant hills. About three miles past San Simeon, a small strip of sand provides a resting point for a large colony of **seals** in the fall and early winter; trails – officially off limits to the public, though easily negotiated by the brave and healthy – lead past a gate near the car park down to the beach, where you can watch the huge piles of blubber cuddle one another and frolic in the waves. Beyond here the highway seems to drop off in mid-air, marking the southern edge of Big Sur (see p.521), one of the most dramatic stretches of coastline in America.

The Salinas Valley and Steinbeck Country

If you're in a hurry, US-101 through the **Salinas Valley** takes four hours to cover the 220 miles between San Luis Obispo and San Francisco, compared to the full day it takes to drive the more scenic coast along Hwy-1 through Big Sur. In any case, as both Greyhound and Amtrak take the inland route, you may not have the choice; Amtrak's Thruways service barrels through the area, while Greyhound's local buses stop at all the small rural towns. The four-lane freeway closely follows the path of El Camino Real, the trail that linked the 21 Spanish **missions** through the miles of farmland along the Salinas River that are some of the most fertile in the nation and earned it the nickname of the "Salad Bowl of the World," thanks to the millions of lettuces (known as green gold) produced here each summer.

This region is also popularly known as **Steinbeck Country** for having nurtured the imagination of Nobel Prize–winning author John Steinbeck, whose naturalistic stories and novels, including the epic *East of Eden*, were set in and around the valley.

The Salinas Valley

North of San Luis Obispo over the steep Cuesta Pass, US-101 drops down into the **SALINAS VALLEY** and, before long, **Atascadero**: a small town laid out to a curiously grand plan in 1914 that centers on its Palladian City Hall, 6500 Palma Ave, a huge redbrick edifice whose domed rotunda now houses a small **museum** (Mon–Sat 1–4pm; free; ☎805/466-8341, ⓦwww .atascaderochamber.org) describing the area's history. A few miles north, **Templeton** has a strip of historic Wild West buildings along Main Street, among them the town's information center inside the **Templeton Historical Museum** (Fri–Sun 1–4pm; free; ⊤805/434-0807, ⓦwww.templetonmuseum .org). Down the block at no. 424, chocolate is a science at Herrmann's Chocolate Lab (Mon–Thurs 11.30am–7pm, Fri & Sat 11.30am–8pm, Sun 11.30am–6.30pm; ⊤805/434-3007), which sells chocolate-dipped everything and can custom shape chocolate with some advance notice; while local favorite *McPhee's Grill* at no. 416 (⊤805/434-3204) is a surprisingly impressive restaurant, serving broiled twists on modern American food – think pork chops with chili-apricot glaze or oak-grilled sirloin – alongside local produce for around $25 an entree.

Paso Robles (pronounced "ROBE-ulls"), a few more miles north, is a thriving little town surrounded by horse ranches, nut farms, and a number of **wineries** that are among the finest in the state; remarkably, despite a 6.5 magnitude earthquake on December 22, 2003, the town has rebounded quickly and there's little day-to-day evidence of destruction other than a large pit just off the town square (casualties were limited to two women killed when the nineteenth-century clocktower collapsed downtown). The Paso Robles Vintners and Growers (⊤805/239-8463, ⓦwww.pasowine.com) publish a free map to their wine country, which can also be picked up at the town's Chamber of Commerce, 1225 Park St (Mon–Fri 8.30am–5pm, Sat 10am–4pm; ⊤805/238-0506, ⓦwww.pasorobleschamber.com). The pick of the many vineyards include three situated just east of town on Hwy-46: Eberle (daily: Sept–March 10am–5pm; April–Aug 10am–6pm; ⊤805/238-9607, ⓦwww .eberlewinery.com), Meridian (daily 10am–5pm; ⊤805/237-6000, ⓦwww .meridianvineyards.com), and the lively Tobin James Cellars (daily 10am–6pm; ⊤805/239-2204, ⓦwww.tobinjames.com). In town, there are a number of **accommodation options** of much better value than anything you'll find closer to Hearst's former abode. The *Holiday Inn Express Hotel*, 2455 Riverside Ave (⊤805/238-6500 or 1-800/465-4329, ⓦwww.holidayinnpaso .com; ❺), is a reasonable mid-range option; for more luxury, stay at the *Paso Robles Inn*, 1103 Spring St (⊤805/238-2660 or 1-800/676-1713, ⓦwww .pasoroblesinn.com; ❺), which has rooms with two-person tubs on the balconies, with water fed from local hot springs.

In the center of town, **restaurants** cluster on and around the town square: try *Lombardi's*, 836 11th St (⊤805/237-7786), which serves tasty pasta and pizza, many with lashings of gorgonzola, for around $10 in a casual setting. For breakfast there's nowhere better than *Joe's Place*, 608 12th St (Mon–Sat 6am–2pm, Sun 7am–2pm; ⊤805/238-5637), for sloppy, hearty servings of bacon and home fries. About thirty miles east of town, on Hwy-46 past the junction of Hwy-41 near Cholame, you can pay your respects at the stainless-steel monument near the site where **James Dean** crashed in a silver Porsche Speedster on September 30, 1955.

Even if you're racing up US-101, it's only a thirty-minute break from your journey for an essential peek at one of the least visited yet the most intact and authentic of California's Spanish missions, **Mission San Miguel Arcangel**, 801 Mission St (daily 9.30am–4.30pm; free; ⊤805/469-3256), just off the freeway in the small town of **San Miguel**. Founded in 1797 as the sixteenth mission in the chain, the current building dates from 1816; it's the only mission not to have suffered from improvement-minded restorationists. It was actually used for a while as a saloon and dancehall, though the chapel was left pretty much unscathed, with colorful painted decoration and a marvelous sunburst reredos, complete with a striking *Eye of God*, all painted by Native Americans. The other buildings are notable, too, for their rough imprecision, with irregularly arched openings and unplastered walls forming a courtyard around a cactus garden. Note that this mission was the most high-profile casualty of Paso Robles' 2003 earthquake; it didn't topple, but the building's infrastructure was severely damaged. At time of writing, both main chapel and quadrangle are closed to the public until at least $20m can be found to shore up the place. The *Western States Inn*, right off Hwy-101 at 1099 K St (℡805/467-3674, Ⓦwww.westernstatesinn.com; ❸), is the only hotel in town and has surprisingly comfortable rooms.

Another mission, accessible only by car, lies twenty miles west of US-101 along the Jolon Road (G-18), which splits off the highway twelve miles north of San Miguel near the town of Jolon. The **Mission San Antonio de Padua** (daily: summer 8am–6pm; winter 8am–5pm; $1; ℡831/385-4478) is a rarely visited restoration of the 1771 original settlement. Less sanitized than some of the other California missions, it gives a very good idea of what life might have been like for the missionaries and their converts. Third to be founded, this mission was among the most prosperous of the entire chain, and around the extensive grounds, in a wide valley of oak trees and tall grasses, a number of scattered exhibits describe the work that went on in the long-abandoned vineyard, tannery, and gristmill. There's a monastic peace to Mission San Antonio these days, and the brown-robed Franciscan friars who live here are rarely disturbed, despite being eerily situated inside Hunter Liggett Army Base. Indeed, the only sign of the military is at the gates of the base, five miles east of the mission, where you'll have to show your passport or some other form of ID. The large house across the valley from the mission used to belong to Hearst, who sold it and most of the land between here and Hearst Castle to the government in 1940 to help clear a $120-million debt. Today, the *Hacienda Guest Lodge* (℡831/386-2900, Ⓦwww.usawines.com/hacienda; ❶ without bath, ❷ with bath), as it's now called, offers basic, if rather monastic, **accommodation**.

Nearby **Jolon** has a market and gas station, and the washed-out ruins of an 1840s stagecoach stop at the *Old Dutton Hotel*. **Lake San Antonio** (open 24hr, visitor center Mon–Fri 8am–4pm; $7 per vehicle; ℡805/472-2311, Ⓦwww.lakesanantonio.net), five miles southeast, has swimming, **camping** (reservations ℡831/588-2267 or 831/755-4899; $22 summer, $20 winter), and showers along the west shore, as does the Nacimiento Reservoir further south. There are normally more campsites along the Nacimiento–Fergusson Road, which leads west from Jolon on a tortuous but picturesque journey over the mountains to Big Sur (see p.521); in 1999, 80,000 acres of the **Ventana Wilderness** burned in a tragic fire – started by a particularly violent lightning storm – that took months to be contained. Though things are nearly back to normal, it's not uncommon for natural disasters to befall this area, and visitors should call ahead for the latest updates before planning any excursions in the area. The **US Forest Service office**, off the freeway at 406 S Mildred Ave (Mon–Fri 8am–4.30pm; ℡831/385-5434, Ⓦwww.r5.fs.fed.us/lospadres), handles questions about the area and issues backpacking permits for the **Santa Lucia Mountains**, which divide the Salinas Valley from the Big Sur coast.

The Jolon Road loops back to US-101 at **King City**: "the most metropolitan cow town in the West," as it likes to be known. On the town's western edge, just off US-101, San Lorenzo Park is the site of the **Agricultural and Rural Life Museum** (daily 10am–4pm; free, parking weekdays $3, weekends $5; ℡831/385-8020, Ⓦwww.mcarlm.org), a collection of old barns, farmhouses, and a one-room schoolhouse, all gathered here from various sites in Monterey County. The park also has a campground along the Salinas River.

The Pinnacles National Monument and around

From King City, you have a choice of approaches to the bizarre rock formations of the **PINNACLES NATIONAL MONUMENT**. One choice is to follow G-13 and Hwy-25 to the eastern entrance and the visitor center (park daily 7.30am–9pm, visitor center daily 9am–5pm; $5 per vehicle, good for seven days; ☎831/389-4485, ⓦwww.nps.gov/pinn); the better option is to continue up Hwy-101 to Soledad, from where it's a 30-minute drive through windy roads (stick to Hwy-146 as it turns into East Street and then Metz Boulevard) to the more spectacular western side. Contrary to what appears on some maps, no road goes right through the monument, but the place is small and it is quite possible to hike from one side to the other and back in a day.

This region of startling volcanic spires, brilliant reds and golds against the blue sky, is best visited in the spring, when the air is still cool and the chaparral hillsides are lushly sprinkled with wild flowers, in particular the orange California poppy and deep-lilac owl's clover. Its many **trails** include a popular two-mile loop around the high peaks on the **Juniper Canyon Trail**, and the two-mile **Balconies Trail** to the multicolored, 600-foot face of the Balconies outcrop – good for rock climbing (register at the visitor center and use only brown chalk when climbing) – and a nearby series of talus **caves** (take a flashlight) formed by huge boulders that have become wedged between the walls of the narrow canyons. These dark caves were popular with bandits who would hide out here after robbing stagecoaches. Rangers at both the east and west entrances can set you up with information and permits if you're interested in trying out some of the more advanced trails or if you'd like to do **climbing**, **top-roping**, or **bouldering**. The trails are exposed so avoid hiking in the middle of the day in summer, and remember to carry plenty of water. There are several private and state-run **campgrounds** on either side of the park, the largest of which is the swimming-pool-equipped *Pinnacles Campground Inc.* (reservations office open Tues–Thurs 4–6pm, Fri 4–9pm, Sat & Sun 9am–5pm; $7 per person; ☎831/389-4462, ⓦwww.pinncamp.com) – reservations are essential in summer.

Soledad and Mission Soledad

The nearest town to the Pinnacles is **SOLEDAD**, a quiet farming community twelve miles west of the western entrance, best known as the site of the Soledad State Penitentiary – a grim building looming alongside US-101 two miles north of town, where black militant "Soledad Brother" George Jackson was imprisoned for many years. The town itself has a definite Mexican flavor, its *panaderias* selling cakes and fresh tortillas – a good place to stock up on food and drink for a trip to the monument. But the main reason to stop is **Mission Nuestra Señora de la Soledad** (daily 10am–4pm; free; ☎831/678-2586), three miles west of US-101 on the south side of town. The thirteenth mission in the chain lay neglected for over a hundred years until it was little more than a pile of mud. Never a great success (perhaps because of its full name, which translates as the "most sorrowful mystery of the solitude"), the mission suffered through a history of epidemics, floods, and crop failures. Parts have been dutifully restored and now contain a museum on mission life, but the ruins adjacent to the rebuilt church are the most evocative section.

Salinas and around

The second-largest city between LA and San Francisco, and the seat of Monterey County, **SALINAS**, twenty miles north of Soledad and Paraiso, is a sprawling agricultural town of 120,000 people. It's best known as the birthplace of **John Steinbeck**, and for the **California Rodeo** (tickets $19–76; ☎1-800/549-4989 or 831/775-3100, ⓦwww.carodeo.com), held during the third week in July and the biggest in the state. These attractions aside, you may well find yourself here anyway – Salinas is a main stop for Greyhound buses and the Coast Starlight train, and makes an inexpensive base for exploring the perhaps more obvious attractions of the **Monterey Peninsula**, twenty miles away over the Santa Lucia Mountains, with the MST bus #21 making the 55-minute trip every hour from the Transit Center on Salinas Street.

Salinas and the agricultural valley to the south are often bracketed together as Steinbeck Country. The writer John Steinbeck was born in 1902 and raised in Salinas, but left the town in his mid-twenties to live in Monterey and later in New York City. His childhood home at 132 Central Ave (daily 11.30am–2pm, closed Dec and Jan; ☎831/424-2735) has been turned into an English-style tearoom called the *Steinbeck House*. Diehard fans can sign up for a tour (every 15min; Sundays Memorial Day–Labor Day; $3), though since these sweep simply through the restaurant and gift shop rather than the upstairs living quarters, there isn't much memorable to see.

A much better introduction, the gigantic new **National Steinbeck Center**, at 1 Main St (daily 10am 5pm; $10.95; ☎831/796 3833, ⓦwww .steinbeck.org), takes you on a sprightly, interactive journey through the author's life and work. A fifteen-minute **biographical film** shown in a constant loop at the museum's entrance offers an informative and lively approach to Steinbeck, and sets the tone for the rest of the museum. If you knew very little of the author, then you will find the exhibits throughout engaging

The novels of John Steinbeck

John Steinbeck's novels and short stories are remarkable for their historical content as for their narratives; he had a newspaperman's eye for the hardships of working-class life. **The Grapes of Wrath**, his best-known work, was made into a film starring Henry Fonda while still at the top of the bestseller lists, having captured the popular imagination for its portrayal of the Depression Era–miseries of the Joad family on their migration to California from the Oklahoma Dust Bowl. *Cannery Row* followed in 1945, a nostalgic portrait of the Monterey fisheries, which ironically went into steep decline the year the book was published. Steinbeck spent the next four years writing *East of Eden*, an allegorical retelling of the biblical story of Cain and Abel against the landscape of the Salinas Valley; in this book, which he saw as his masterpiece, Steinbeck expresses many of the values that underlie the rest of his work.

Much of Steinbeck's writing is concerned with the dignity of labor, and with the inequalities of an economic system that "allows children to go hungry in the midst of rotting plenty." Although he was circumspect about his own political stance, when *The Grapes of Wrath* became a bestseller in 1939 there was a violent backlash against Steinbeck in Salinas for what were seen as his Communist sympathies. Later, he was so wounded at the outcry over his worthiness of the Nobel Prize for Literature in 1962 that he never wrote another word. He died in New York City in 1968; today his ashes are buried in Salinas in the **Garden of Memories Cemetery**, 768 Abbott St.

enough and might even be inspired to purchase a novel or two from the center's large supply. However, if you're already well versed in Steinbeck and his oeuvre, your time will be better spent using the center's informative **map** to cruise by all the actual places in the surrounding area that were influential in the writer's life.

Today, as much as in Steinbeck's day, Salinas is a hotbed of labor disputes, with the gap between the low-paid manual laborers who pick the produce and the wealthy owners of agribusiness empires who run the giant farms still unbridged. In the 1960s and early 1970s, the United Farm Workers union, under the leadership of Cesar Chavez and Dolores Huerta, had great success in organizing and demanding better pay and working conditions for the almost exclusively Latino workforce, masterminding a very effective boycott of the valley's main product, lettuce. But workers are once again under siege, with wages less than half of what they were two decades ago amidst increasing worries about the dangers of exposure to pesticides and agricultural chemicals.

Main Street downtown has finally been spruced up and is a pleasant strip to wander along: it's tree-lined and full of prettified Victorian buildings, home to clothing boutiques and craft stores, as well as the 1921 Art Deco **Fox Theater** at no. 239. The other notable attraction is at the end of West Laurel Drive, a mile west of US-101, the **Boronda Adobe**; it's worth a visit only if you have an afternoon to spare. Located in the middle of a beautiful drive through rich farmland, the simple, Old California–style building has been virtually unaltered since its construction in 1848, and rests alongside other historic structures that have been brought to the site as part of an expanding regional-history center.

Between Salinas and the Monterey Peninsula, twenty miles distant via Hwy-68, are a couple of other places of divergent interest. **Spreckels**, five miles southwest, is a small factory town built in 1898 for employees of the Spreckels sugar factory (whose scion was Adolph, husband of the wild, art-loving beauty Alma – see p.594). When built, it was at the time the largest in the world: the small, torchlike wooden objects on the gable ends of the many workers' cottages are supposed to represent sugar beets. Parts of the movie *East of Eden* were filmed here, including the famous scene when James Dean – playing Cal – hurls blocks of ice down a chute to get his father's attention.

Practicalities

Hourly Greyhound buses between LA and San Francisco stop in the center of town at 19 W Gabilan St (☎831/424-4418) near Salinas Street, while Amtrak trains leave once a day in each direction, two blocks away at 40 Railroad Ave. For a handy **place to stay**, try the *Traveler's Hotel* at 16 E Gabilan St (☎831/758-1198; ❷), which is more convenient than pleasant; frankly, if you're driving, choose from the many $45-a-night motels along Main Street on either side of US-101. For help with finding a place to stay, and for a free map and guide to the places that Steinbeck wrote about, contact the **Chamber of Commerce** at 119 E Alisal St (Mon 9.30am–5pm, Tues–Fri 8.30am–5pm; ☎831/424-7611, ⓦwww.salinaschamber.com). There are quite a few good Mexican **restaurants** around the city, the best, oldest, and most central being *Rosita's Armory Café*, 231 Salinas St (☎831/424-7039): settle into one of the big brown melamine booths here alongside the old men chowing down on the super-cheap but delicious food – lunch specials are $4.50, entrees around $8.

The Big Sur Coast

The nebulous name used to describe the ninety miles of rocky cliffs and crashing seas along the California coast just south of the Monterey Peninsula, **BIG SUR** is not an official designation, and there are no marked boundaries. You'll know you're in Big Sur, however, when the estuaries and beaches of the Central Coast give way to craggy rock faces and distant redwood groves. Named by the Spanish *El Pais Grande del Sur* (the "big country to the south" of their colony at Monterey), it's still a wild and undeveloped region that's breathtakingly unspoilt given its proximity to San Francisco and other cities.

Before Hwy-1 was completed in 1937, the few inhabitants of Big Sur had to be almost entirely self-sufficient, farming, raising cattle, and trapping sea otters for their furs. The only connections with the rest of the world were by infrequent steamship to Monterey, or by a nearly impassable trail over the mountains to the Salinas Valley. Despite the better transport links, the area's growing more remote as each year passes, with fewer people living here today than a hundred years ago; most of the land is still owned by a handful of families, many of whom are descendants of Big Sur's original pioneers. Locals have banded together to protect the land from obtrusive development and to fight government plans to allow offshore oil drilling, and their ornery determination seems to be paying off.

The Big Sur Coast is also the protected habitat of the **sea otter**, and **gray whales** pass by close to the shore on their annual winter migration. Visit in April or May to see the vibrant **wildflowers** and lilac-colored *ceanothus* bushes, though the sun shines longest, without the morning coastal fog, in early autumn through until November. Hardly anyone braves the turbulent winters, when violent storms drop most of the eighty inches of rain that fall each year in the region, often taking sections of the highway with it into the sea. Summer weekends, however, see the roads and campgrounds packed to overflowing and the wildness of the area is dampened by the hundreds of people you'll see.

Resist the temptation to try and see Big Sur in a single day: the best way to enjoy its isolation and beauty is slowly. Leave the car behind as often as you can and wander through parks and wilderness preserves, where a ten-minute walk takes you from any sign of the rest of the world.

Arrival, information, and getting around

The only public transportation through Big Sur is the summer-only (May–Oct) MST bus #22 from Monterey (see p.537), which runs as far south as Nepenthe, four times a day in each direction. Whether coming from San Francisco to the north or San Luis Obispo to the south, it's always a good idea to stop by the local tourism offices at either end of the long coastal road to check on the current weather and driving conditions.

There is no Big Sur Village as such, and facilities like gas stations and grocery stores are surprisingly scarce – expect those you do find to be premium priced, so it's best to fill your gas tank and go shopping before you hit the deserted coastline. Note, too, that cellphone coverage here is patchy at best, so buy a phonecard if you have calls to make; as for Internet access, at time of writing, the only public terminals are at the Henry Miller Library (donation). Pick up a copy of the free *El Sur Grande* newspaper (Ⓦwww.bigsurcalifornia.org) as soon as you can, since its comprehensive listings are an invaluable resource: you can find it at park information offices and some stores along the route. Otherwise, call the **Chamber of Commerce** (Mon, Wed, Fri 9am–1pm; ☎831/667-2100,

@ www.bigsurcalifornia.org) or stop by the Pfeiffer Big Sur State Park head-quarters (@831/667-2315).

While the narrow Hwy-1 is a perennial favorite with cyclists despite its precipitous curves, most visitors will need a car to travel through the area, following the dramatic coast road as it winds a tortuous, exhilarating route through bedrock cliffs five hundred feet above the Pacific Ocean. The three main inhabited areas are at Big Sur's northern end, close to the **Pfeiffer Big Sur State Park**: around the post office two miles south of the park; at Fern-wood, a mile north past the main entrance; and at The Village, a further mile and a half north. It's the northern end of Big Sur around Hwy-1 that's both most developed and most interesting for first-time visitors. Pfeiffer Big Sur State Park is a fantastic base for exploring: you can swim among giant boulders, hike up redwood canyons to a waterfall, or sunbathe on a fine sandy beach. If you're feeling more intrepid, venture into the **Ventana Wilderness** or the **Santa Lucia Mountains**, although note that both have recently suffered great damage due to wildfires.

There's no official notation for addresses in Big Sur, so we've used the distance from major landmarks as an approximate guide for listings along Hwy-1.

Accommodation

In keeping with Big Sur's backwoodsy qualities, most of the available **accommodation** is in rustic (but rarely inexpensive) mountain lodges, and the very few rooms on offer are full most nights throughout the summer, especially on weekends. Mid-range accommodation is limited to a few cabins and motels, usually adjoining a privately operated campground or right along the highway, and not really ideal for getting the total Big Sur experience.

Big Sur Campgrounds and Cabins a mile north of Pfeiffer Big Sur State Park on Hwy-1 @831/667-2322, @www.bigsurcamp.com. Swanky campground with the best of the cabins: wooden tent affairs sleeping up to three for $59 and fancier places from $109. ❸–❺
Big Sur Lodge in Pfeiffer Big Sur State Park @831/667-3100 or 1-800/424-4787, @www .bigsurlodge.com. These plushly furnished rooms have porches and enormous sit-down showers but no phones, TVs, alarm clocks, or radios; the park entrance fee's included in the rate. There's also a pricey café on site (around $25 per entree). ❺
Big Sur River Inn Resort two and a half miles north of Pfeiffer Big Sur State Park on Hwy-1 @831/667-2700 or 1-800/548-3610, @www .bigsurriverinn.com. Woodsy lodge with a handful of very nice rooms with bright tropical bedspreads and verandas, overlooking the river. There are

cheaper, more basic motel-style rooms across Hwy-1; there's also a handy on-site grocery store and reasonable restaurant. Recommended. ❹
Deetjen's Big Sur Inn on Hwy-1 seven miles north of Julia Pfeiffer Burns State Park @831/667-2377, @www.deetjens.com. Built by Norwegian immigrant "Grandpa" Deetjen, this compound is now a nonprofit organization, offering lodging in ski-lodge-style log cabins, with fire-places, rocking chairs, and old-fashioned leaded windows. ❹ shared bath, ❺ private
Glen Oaks Motel just over a mile north of Pfeiffer Big Sur State Park on Hwy-1 @831/667-2105, @www.glenoaksbigsur.com. Simple rooms, friend-ly staff, and one of the best bargains in the area. There are two separate cottages that can make a smart option for groups of 4. No credit cards. ❸ rooms, ❻ cottage

Southern Big Sur

The southern coastline of Big Sur is the region at its most gentle – with sandy beaches hidden away below eroding yellow-ochre cliffs. The landscape grows more extreme the further north you go. Twenty miles north of Hearst Castle, a steep trail leads down along Salmon Creek to a coastal waterfall, while the chaparral–covered hills above were booming during the 1880s with the gold mines of the **Los Burros Mining District**.

Another ten miles north, the cliffs get steeper and the road more perilous around the vista point at **Willow Creek**, where you can watch the surfers and the sea otters playing in the waves. **Jade Cove**, a mile north, takes its name from the translucent California jade stones that are sometimes found here, mainly by scuba divers offshore. The rocky cove is a ten-minute walk from the highway, along a brambly trail marked by a wooden stile in the cattle fence: the close-up views of the crashing waves reinforce the awesome power of the sea.

Just beyond the Plaskett Creek **campground**, half a mile to the north, **Sand Dollar Beach** is a good place to enjoy the surf or watch for **hang-gliders**, launched from sites in the mountains off the one-lane Plaskett Ridge Road. This steep road is good fun on a mountain bike, and passes by a number of free, basic campgrounds along the ridge, ending at the paved Nacimiento–

Camping in Big Sur

Public campgrounds are dotted all along **the Big Sur Coast**, in addition to a few less-developed ones in the **Santa Lucia Mountains** above, where you can also see deer, bobcats, and (rarely) mountain lions. Sites along the coast are popular year-round, and all, unless otherwise stated, are available for around $16 a night on a first-come-first-served basis, so get there early in the day to ensure a space. Reservations are, however, taken at the **State Park** sites (call ParkNet ☏1-800/444-7275, or log onto ⓦwww.parks.ca.gov): most cost $18, other than *Andrew Molera*, which is a bargain at $9 per site. For further **information** on camping in Big Sur, phone the park directly (☏831/667-2315). The following campgrounds are listed south to north.

Plaskett Creek ☏877/444-6677 or 805/434-1996, ⓦwww.parksman.com. Thirty miles north of Hearst Castle and a mile south of Pacific Valley. Across the highway from the ocean with some hiker/biker sites. $18

Kirk Creek ☏805/434-1996, ⓦwww.parksman.com. Three miles north of Pacific Valley and more exposed, but right on the ocean and with hiker/biker sites. $18

Limekiln State Park ☏831/667-2403. Two miles south of Lucia, with hot showers, general store, and developed trail to the limekilns. $18

Julia Pfeiffer Burns State Park ☏831/667-2315. This has two campgrounds, beautifully situated overlooking the Pacific at the end of the Overlook Trail. Note that there's no water, the toilets are primitive, and the area is often windy and chilly even in summer. $18

Pfeiffer Big Sur State Park This is the main campground in the area, with spacious and well-shaded sites, many among the redwoods. Hot showers, a well-stocked store, a laundrette, and some (officially) biker-only sites. $18

Andrew Molera State Park The only walk-in site around. A vast ten-acre meadow, half a mile from the beach, with water and latrines. First-come-first-served basis, so show up early. Camping payment waives day-use fee. $9

There are also four commercially operated **campgrounds** in the Big Sur Valley: *Ventana* (☏831/667-2712, ⓦwww.ventanawildernesscampground.com; $27 per car weekdays, $35 per car weekends), *Fernwood* (☏831/667-2422, ⓦwww.fernwoodbigsur.com; $24), *Riverside* (☏831/667-2414, ⓦwww.riversidecampground.com; $28), and *Big Sur* (☏831/667-2322, ⓦwww.bigsurcamp.com; weekdays $25, weekends $27). All charge about $28 a night for two people, offer deluxe facilities, and accept reservations; they also rent out **cabins** (see "Accommodation," opposite). By Californian standards, all are fairly crowded, and all but *Riverside* mix tents with RVs.

Fergusson Road. Check at the **Pacific Valley ranger station** (irregular hours; ☎805/927-4211) for up-to-date information on backcountry camping, since some areas may be closed in summer during the peak of the fire season. The station also handles the 25 permits a day allowed to people wanting to hang-glide, ten of which are given out on a first-come-first-served basis on the day. **Pacific Valley Center**, a mile north, has an expensive gas station, a grocery store, and a good coffee shop, open from 8am until dark.

Kirk Creek to Julia Pfeiffer Burns State Park

The coastal **campground** at **KIRK CREEK** (see p.523) sits at the foot of the Nacimiento–Fergusson Road, which twists over the Santa Lucia Mountains to the Salinas Valley. The road passes the excellent Mission San Antonio de Padua (see p.517), but it would be a shame to break the continuity of the drive up the coast, and in any case the views are better coming over the hills in the other direction. Two miles north of here, **Limekiln Creek** is named after the hundred-year-old kilns that survive in good condition along the creek behind the privately owned **campground**. In the 1880s local limestone was burned in these kilns to extract lime powder for use as cement, then carried on a complex aerial tramway to be loaded onto ships at Rockland Landing. The ships that carried the lime to Monterey brought in most of the supplies to this isolated area.

Esalen (ESS-allun), ten miles further north, is named after the local Native Americans, the first tribe in California to be made extinct. Before they were wiped out, they frequented the healing waters of the natural **hot spring** here, at the top of a cliff two hundred feet above the raging Pacific surf – now owned and operated by the Esalen Institute (information ☎831/667-3000, reservations ☎831/667-3005, ⓦwww.esalen.org). Since the 1960s, when all sorts of people came to Big Sur to smoke dope and get back to nature, Esalen has been at the forefront of the "New Age" human-potential movement. Today's devotees tend to arrive in BMWs on Friday nights for the expensive, reservation-only massage treatments, yoga workshops, and seminars on "potentialities and values of human existence" – if you want to join them, make sure to reserve a place well in advance.

JULIA PFEIFFER BURNS STATE PARK (daily dawn–dusk; free; ☎831/667-2315, ⓦwww.parks.ca.gov), three miles north of Esalen along McWay Creek, has some of the best day-hikes in the Big Sur area: a ten-minute walk from the parking area leads under the highway along the edge of the cliff to an overlook of McWay Falls, which crash onto a beach below Saddle Rock. A less-traveled path leads down from Hwy-1 two miles north of the waterfall (at milepost 37.85) through a two-hundred-foot-long tunnel to the wave-washed remains of a small wharf at **Partington Cove**, one of the few places in Big Sur where you can get to the sea.

Nepenthe and Pfeiffer Beach

Just before you reach **NEPENTHE**, you'll pass the Henry Miller Library across Hwy-1 (Sept–May Thurs–Sun 11am–6pm, Memorial Day–Labor Day Wed–Mon 11am–6pm; ☎831/667-2574, ⓦwww.henrymiller .org). Miller's own home, further south on the Big Sur Coast, is now a private residence, but this house was owned by his old friend Emil White, and stands as a ramshackle bookshop-cum-monument to the work of the author who lived in the area on and off until the 1960s. There's little Millerabilia, but the secluded front lawn is a pleasant place to grab a free coffee; there's also

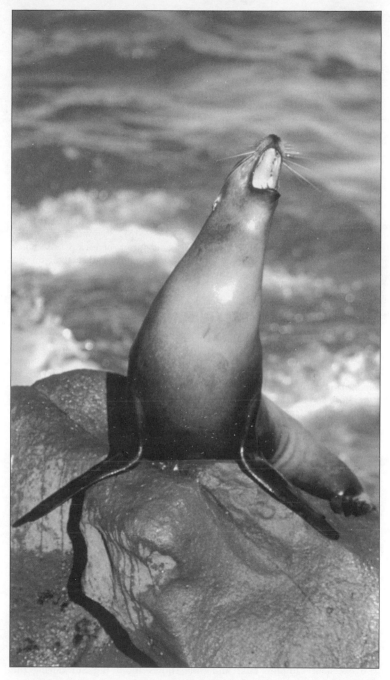

525

△ Sea lion

first-come-first-served, free Internet access – it works on an honor system where most leave a donation ($1–5) and spend no more than 15 minutes on the single terminal at a time. It's with Nepenthe (☎831/667-2345, ⊛www .nepenthebigsur.com) that Big Sur's commercial development starts in earnest: it's not a town proper, but rather a complex of expensive restaurants and stores that's named after the mythical drug that induces forgetfulness. The one point of interest is its location: this is the hilltop site where star-crossed lovers Orson Welles and Rita Hayworth once shared a cabin. The terribly overpriced restaurants here have been emptying the pockets of reflective visitors in search of upscale romance since the 1960s, though *Café Kevah* (see "Eating and drinking," opposite), on a terrace on the middle level of the building, is more affordable and has better views (although a coffee still costs $3). Downstairs there's an outdoor sculpture gallery and a decent bookstore, including a wide selection of works by Miller.

Two miles north along Hwy-1, the unmarked Sycamore Canyon Road leads a mile west to Big Sur's best beach, finally reopened after years of renovation and now boasting a paved access road rather than a dirt track: **PFEIFFER BEACH** (dawn–dusk; $5 per car; ☎831/667-2315) – a sometimes windy, white-sand stretch dominated by a charismatic hump of rock whose color varies from brown to red to orange in the changing light. Park where you can at the end of the road and walk through an archway of cypress trees along the lagoon to the sands.

The Big Sur River Valley

Two miles north of Pfeiffer Beach, Hwy-1 drops down behind a coastal ridge into the valley of the Big Sur River, where most of the accommodation and eating options are located. The first stop should be the Big Sur Ranger Station (daily: summer 8am–6pm; winter 8am–4.30pm; ☎831/667-2315), which handles the camping permits for the Ventana Wilderness in the mountains above and is the center for information on all the other parks in the area. A popular hike leads steeply up from the Pine Ridge trailhead behind the station, ten miles into the mountains to **Sykes Hot Springs** (unrestricted entry), just downstream from the free campground at *Sykes Camp* along the Big Sur River. This is an overnight expedition, at least five hours' walk each way; don't forget to pick up a fire permit, if you plan to cook.

Plumb in the middle of the valley, the **Pfeiffer Big Sur State Park** (daily dawn–dusk; $5 per vehicle; ☎831/667-2315, ⊛www.parks.ca.gov) is one of the most beautiful and enjoyable parks in California, with miles of hiking trails and excellent swimming along the Big Sur River. In late spring and summer, the river has deep swimming holes among the large boulders in the bottom of the narrow steep-walled gorge, and the water is clean and clear. Nude sunbathing is tolerated (except on national holidays, when the park tends to be overrun with swarms of screaming children) and, since it's sheltered a mile or so inland, the weather is warmer and sunnier than elsewhere along the coast. This is also the main **campground** ($24) in the Big Sur region.

The most popular hiking trail in the park leads to the sixty-foot **Pfeiffer Falls**, half a mile up a narrow canyon shaded by redwood trees, from a trailhead opposite the entrance. The thoroughly functional bridges over the river have an understated grace, as does the nearby amphitheater – built by the Civilian Conservation Corps during the Depression – where rangers give excellent campfire talks and slide shows about Big Sur during the summer season.

Eating and drinking

Most of the places to **eat and drink** in Big Sur are attached to the inns and resorts listed below. Many of these are fairly basic burger-and-beer bars right along the highway, but there are a few special ones worth searching out, some for their good food and others for their views of the Pacific. Because of its isolation, prices anywhere in Big Sur are around 25 percent higher than you'd pay in town.

Big Sur Bakery Hwy-1 at the south end of The Village next to the post office ☎831/667-0520. Rather than just churning out cakes and pastries, this moderately priced café has an on-site rotisserie where all the meats are cooked: lunch is largely pizza (try the five-onion with onion sauce) and sandwiches, while the dinner menu's fancier, with grilled steak and pork from well-known Niman Ranch nearby.

Big Sur River Inn Resort at the north end of The Village ☎831/667-2700. The slightly upscale restaurant features a creative range of sautéed and grilled seafood starters and hearty main dishes served in a spacious, redwood-log dining room. In summer, you can linger over lunch and cocktails on the sunny terrace or in the riverside garden; in winter, the fireplace attracts locals and visitors alike. Live entertainment on the weekend.

Café Kevah Nepenthe ☎831/667-2344. Tasty, if slightly overpriced, organic concoctions served up café-style on a sunny, outdoor terrace: some of the best views around, but stick to the snacks. March–Dec 9am–4pm.

Deetjen's Big Sur Inn on Hwy-1 seven miles north of Julia Pfeiffer Burns State Park ☎831/667-2378. Excellent, unhurried breakfasts ($8) and a variety of top-quality fish and vegetarian dinners ($13–25) in a snug, redwood-paneled room.

Fernwood Hwy-1 a mile north of Pfeiffer Big Sur State Park ☎831/667-2422. For burgers or fish-and-chips, this budget diner is the place. There's a small grocery store/deli in the same building if you want to pick up supplies for a picnic.

Habanero Burrito Bar Inside the Big Sur River Inn General Store, two and a half miles north of Pfeiffer Big Sur State Park on Hwy-1 ☎831/667-2700, ⓦwww.bigsurriverinn.com. New sandwich-bar stashed in the rear of the store that's one of the scant few places to pick up dinner for under $10 – just make sure to eat early as it's only open 11am–7pm. Order an overstuffed Mexican burrito to go – the choices and ingredients are standard chilis and cheeses – then eat it by the river on the grounds of the inn.

Nepenthe Nepenthe ☎831/667-2345. Above the *Café Kevah*, this overpriced steak-and-seafood place has raging fires, an amazing view, and a James Bond-ish après-ski atmosphere.

The Roadhouse Hwy-1 in The Village ☎831/667-2264. Cal-Mex cuisine – think tortillas, burritos, and spicy salads – served in a cozy, flower-filled cottage: make sure to order some of the chunky guacamole ($4.95). Closed Tues.

North to Monterey

Though it's rarely visited, **Andrew Molera State Park** (daily dawn–dusk; parking $2; ☎831/667-2315, ⓦwww.parks.ca.gov), five miles north of Pfeiffer Big Sur State Park, is the largest park in Big Sur with two and a half miles of rocky oceanfront reached by a mile-long trail. It occupies the site of what was the El Sur Ranch. This was one of the earliest and most successful Big Sur cattle ranches, initially run in the early nineteenth century by Juan Bautista Alvarado, who became California governor in 1836; later, it was overseen by English sea captain Roger Cooper, whose cabin is preserved here. Although the cabin itself isn't open to the public, you can reach the site on some of the fifteen miles of hiking trails also used for guided two-hour **horseback rides** from the stables ($25–59 weather permitting; ☎831/625-5486 or 1-800/942-5486, ⓦwww.molerahorsebacktours.com). There is also walk-in **camping** (see box, p.523).

From the north end of the park the Old Coast Road takes off inland from Hwy-1 up over the steep hills, affording panoramic views out over miles of coastline. The part-paved, roughly ten-mile road winds over wide-open ranch lands and through deep, slender canyons until it rejoins the main highway at **Bixby Creek Bridge**, fifteen miles south of Carmel. When constructed in 1932, this was the longest single-span concrete bridge in the world, and it is the most impressive (and photogenic) engineering feat of the Coast Road project, a local construction program sponsored by the WPA during the Depression.

A mile and a half north, beyond the **Point Sur Light Station** (weather permitting tours Sat 10am & 2pm, Sun 10am, additional tours July & Aug Wed 10am & 2pm, Thurs 10am; $5; ℡831/625-4419, ⓦwww.pointsur.org), a paved road turns off up **Palo Colorado Canyon**, past a number of houses and the remains of an old lumber mill obscured behind the redwood trees, finishing up eventually at *Bottcher's Gap* campground on the edge of the Ventana Wilderness. On the coast at the foot of the road, the derelict buildings at **Notley's Landing** were once part of a bustling port community. The northernmost stop on the wild Big Sur Coast is at the wild-flower-crammed **Garrapata State Park** (daily dawn–dusk; free; ⓦwww.parks.ca.gov), three miles south of Point Lobos and the Monterey Peninsula. A mile-long trail leads from Hwy-1 out to the tip of **Soberanes Point**, about ten miles south of Carmel – a good place to watch for sea otters and gray whales.

The Monterey Peninsula

The dramatic headlands of the **MONTEREY PENINSULA** mark the northern edge of the spectacular Big Sur Coast, a rocky promontory where gnarled cypress trees amplify the collision between the cliffs and the thundering sea. The manicured towns of the Peninsula thrive now thanks to the regular flow of tourists, but still retain individual characters. **Carmel-by-the-Sea** is by far the toniest: it's secluded, unshowy, and a little sniffy, though the election of Clint Eastwood twenty years ago in 1986 showed its starstruck side: Oscar-winner or not, you'll need a cool million or so to snap up a home here. To the west, **Pebble Beach** is a small village, similar to Carmel in its self-conscious refinement, while at the tip of the Peninsula, with spectacular views out across the ocean, stands **Pacific Grove**, known for its butterflies and Victorian architecture, a pleasant if rather sleepy place. The most convenient and practical base on the Peninsula is **Monterey** itself: the largest town, it was the capital of California under the Spanish and the Mexicans, and retains many old adobe houses and places of genuine historic appeal. The local population is a little younger on average than in the other towns, and this also means Monterey has the liveliest nightlife and restaurant scene.

Arrival, information, and getting around

The Monterey Peninsula juts out into the Pacific to form the Monterey Bay, a hundred miles south of San Francisco; coastal Hwy-1 cuts across its neck, and Hwy-68 links up with US-101 at Salinas, twenty miles east. Greyhound **buses** (three daily in each direction between LA and San Francisco) stop at the Monterey Bay Mini Mart gas station, 1042 Del Monte Ave (℡831/373-4735), along the waterfront. Amtrak trains stop in Salinas, connecting with local bus #21 for the 55-minute trip (every hour) to Monterey.

Monterey's **visitor center**, 401 Camino El Estero at Franklin Street (April–Oct Mon–Sat 9am–6pm, Sun 9am–5pm; Nov–March Mon–Sat 9am–5pm,

Sun 10am–4pm; ☎831/649-1770 or 1-888/221-1010, ⓦwww.montereyinfo
.org), has free parking, lots of advertiser-based brochures, and hotlines to local
hotels. Both it and the less busy Chamber of Commerce **tourist office** at 380
Alvarado St (Mon–Fri 8.30am–5pm; ☎831/648-5360, ⓦwww.mpcc.com) can
help with accommodation. The **Pacific Grove Chamber of Commerce**
(Mon–Fri 9.30am–5pm, Sat 11am–3pm; ☎831/373-3304 or 1-800/656-
6650, ⓦwww.pacificgrove.org), across from the Natural History Museum at
Forest and Central, has walking-tour maps of Pacific Grove's historic buildings and can help find a room in the many local bed-and-breakfast inns. In
Carmel Valley, call the Chamber of Commerce (☎831/659-4000, ⓦwww
.carmelvalleychamber.com) for local information, notably on the raft of
wineries. The best guide to **what's on** in the area is the widely available freebie
Monterey County Weekly (ⓦwww.coastweekly.com), with listings of movies,
music, and art galleries.

Getting around is surprisingly easy. Monterey-Salinas Transit (MST) buses
(☎831/899-2555, ⓦwww.mst.org) run between 7am and 6pm (11pm on
some routes), radiating out from Transit Plaza in the historic core of Monterey,
and covering the entire region from Nepenthe on the Big Sur Coast north to
Watsonville near Santa Cruz and inland to the agricultural heartland of the
Salinas Valley. The region is divided into seven zones: the Peninsula, Salinas,

Gonzales, King City, Big Sur and Carmel Valley, North County and Watsonville, and Gilroy; and fares are $1.75 per zone. Passes are available on board, costing $3.50 for an all-day, single-zone pass, and $7 for an all-routes, all-zones day-pass. The most useful routes are buses #4 and #5, which link Monterey with Carmel; #21, which runs between Monterey and Salinas; and #1, which runs along Lighthouse Avenue past the main sights and out to Pacific Grove; there's also the WAVE trolley which runs every ten minutes from downtown to the Monterey Bay Aquarium on Cannery Row, and from Cannery Row to Pacific Grove (Memorial Day–Labor Day daily 10am–7pm; ℡831/899-2555, Ⓦwww.mst .org). The only way to get to the Big Sur Coast on public transportation is on bus #22, which leaves eight times a day from Memorial Day through Labor Day.

Another option is to **rent a bike**: in Monterey, try Adventures by the Sea, 299 Cannery Row or 201 Alvarado St ($6/hour, $24/day or $30/two days; ℡831/372-1807, Ⓦwww.adventuresbythesea.com), or Bay Bikes, 585 Cannery Row or 99 Pacific St ($10/2hr, $22/day; ℡831/655-2453, Ⓦwww .baybikes.com).

Accommodation

What Santa Barbara is to Southern California, the Monterey Peninsula is to the north, meaning the area is among the most exclusive and expensive resort areas in California, with **hotel** and **bed-and-breakfast** room rates averaging $120 a night. This may tempt you to stay elsewhere – in Santa Cruz, or in agricultural Salinas – and come here on day-trips; the other budget option is to avail yourself of one of the many motels along North Fremont Street (also a good place for cheap eats) or Munras Avenue, about one mile from the center.

The only **camping** within walking distance is in Veteran's Memorial Park (℡831/646-3865), site of Steinbeck's fictional Tortilla Flat, at the top of Jefferson Street in the hills above town. It's only $3 a night if you're on foot or bike (though it's a steep two miles or so uphill), or $15 per car, and is operated on a first-come-first-served basis.

Hotels and inns

Carmel Resort Inn Carpenter and 2nd Ave, Carmel ℡831/624-3113 or 1-800/454-3700. One of the least expensive properties in Carmel; cottage rooms have fireplaces. ❸

Green Gables Inn 104 5th St, Pacific Grove ℡831/375-2095 or 1-800/722-1774, Ⓦwww .foursisters.com. Plush doubles in one of the prettiest houses in a town of fine homes, on the waterfront just a few blocks from the Monterey Bay Aquarium. ❺

Horizon Inn 3rd St and Junípero, Carmel ℡831/624-5327 or 1-800/350-7723, Ⓦwww .horizoninncarmel.com. Comfy bed-and-breakfast place with a pool. ❻

Mariposa Inn 1386 Munras Ave, Monterey ℡831/6491414 or 1-800/824-2295. The best deal in town, offering cozy rooms with fireplaces and full amenities including balconies and a heated pool at reasonable rates. Larger groups should opt for one of the stand-alone townhouses which are great value. ❹

Monterey Hilton 1000 Aguajito Rd, Monterey ℡831/373-6141 or 1-800/HILTONS, Ⓦwww .hilton.com. Plush hotel on the outskirts of town, set around a rambling garden, with extensive amenities, including swimming pool and ample parking. ❺

Pacific Grove Inn 581 Pine Ave at Forest, Pacific Grove ℡831/375-2825 or 1-800/732-2825, Ⓦwww.pacificgrove-inn.com. Thoughtfully modernized 1904 mansion with 17 spacious rooms, the *Pacific Grove Inn* is five blocks from the shore. ❺

Rosedale Inn 775 Asilomar Blvd, Pacific Grove ℡831/655-1000 or 1-800 /822-5606, Ⓦwww .rosedaleinn.com. These log-cabin-style rooms are refreshingly modern, with ceiling fans and pine furniture, as well as fireplaces and Jacuzzi baths; what makes the real difference is the affable, easygoing staff. ❻

Seven Gables Inn 555 Ocean View Blvd, Pacific Grove ℡831/372-4341, Ⓦwww.7gables -grandview.com. You'll enter this restored Victorian house through the gloriously overdone Rococo parlor, dripping with gold fixtures; then continue to the plumply furnished mini-suites. Afternoon snacks are a meal in themselves and breakfast is enormous. The same management also runs the equally sumptuous *Grandview Inn* nearby (☎831/372-4341; $175–290). **❼–❾**

Motels and hostels

Bide-a-Wee Inn & Cottages 221 Asilomar Blvd, Pacific Grove ☎831/372-2330 ⊛www .bideaweemotel.com. Nicely spruced-up rooms with modern, homely furnishings including fridge and microwave. Rates more than double at weekends. **❸**

Borg's Ocean Front Motel 635 Ocean View Blvd, Pacific Grove ☎831/375-2406. Good value for basic rooms, some with great views from Lovers Point: be aware that the oceanfront rooms are almost double the others in cost. **❸** without view, **❺** with view

Cypress Gardens Resort Inn 1150 Munras Ave, Monterey ☎831/373-2761 or 1-877/922-1150, ⊛www.cypressgardensinn.com. One of the better Munras motels, with a leafy garden and a large pool. **❸**

Econolodge 2042 Fremont St, Monterey ☎831/372-5851. Comfortable, standard rooms with free local calls and continental breakfasts. **❷**

El Dorado Inn 900 Munras Ave, Monterey ☎831/373-2921 or 1-800/722-1836. Cheap, basic accommodation at budget rates in a motel-style, two-story building. **❷**

HI-Monterey 778 Hawthorne St, Monterey ☎831/649-0375, ⊛www.montereyhostel.org. Standard hostel in downtown Monterey near Cannery Row, with dorm beds costing $20 members, $23 non-members. There's a three-day maximum stay and an 11pm curfew. **❶**

Lovers Point Inn 625 Ocean View Blvd, Pacific Grove ☎831/373-4771, ⊛www.loverspointinn .com. Rooms here are fine, though bland; the exterior makes up for the interior's ordinary decor, though – from kitsch oddities like heart-shaped numbers on each room door to the salmon-and-turquoise color scheme. **❸**

Pacific Grove Motel Lighthouse Ave at Grove Acre, Pacific Grove ☎831/372-3218 or 1-800/525-3373. Simple, small motel in marvelous setting, 100 yards from the sea. Rates rise in summer and at weekends. **❶**

Monterey

The town of **MONTEREY** rests in a quiet niche along the bay formed by the forested Monterey Peninsula, proudly proclaiming itself the most historic city in California, a boast that, for once, may be true. Its compact town center features some of the best vernacular **buildings** of California's Spanish and Mexican colonial past, most of which stand unassumingly within a few blocks of the tourist-thronged waterfront. The single best stop – and one of the unmissable highlights of the region – is the **Monterey Bay Aquarium**, a mile west of town at the end of Cannery Row.

Monterey was named by the Spanish merchant and explorer Vizcaíno, who landed in 1602 to find an abundant supply of fresh water and wild game after a seven-month voyage from Mexico. Despite Vizcaíno's enthusiasm for the site, the area was not colonized until 1770, when the second mission in the chain – the headquarters of the whole operation – was built in Monterey before being moved to its permanent site in Carmel. Under the Spanish, the Presidio de Monterey was also the military headquarters for the whole of Alta California, and thereafter Monterey continued to be the leading administrative and commercial center of a territory that extended east to the Rocky Mountains and north to Canada, but had a total population, excluding Native Americans, of less than seven thousand.

American interest in Monterey was purely commercial until 1842, when an American naval commodore received a false report that the US and Mexico were at war, and that the English were poised to take California. Commodore Catesby Jones anchored at Monterey and demanded the peaceful surrender of the port, and two days later, the American flag was raised. The armed but cordial US occupation lasted only until Jones examined the official documents closely and realized he'd got it all wrong (and his exuberance cost him his job). When the Mexican–American War began in earnest in 1846, the United States took possession of Monterey without resistance. The discovery of gold in the Sierra Nevada foothills soon focused attention upon San Francisco, and Monterey became something of a backwater, hardly affected by the waves of immigration that followed.

The waterfront and Old Monterey

More than half a century ago, when Monterey first tried to pass itself off to wealthy visitors from San Francisco and beyond as an upscale resort, there was

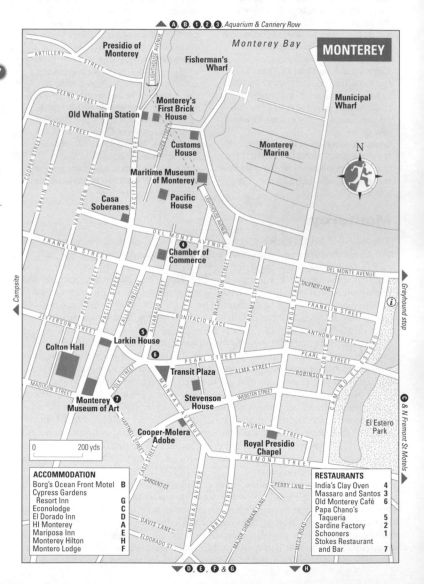

▲ Ⓐ, Ⓑ, ❶, ❷, ❸, *Aquarium & Cannery Row*

MONTEREY

Monterey Bay

Presidio of Monterey

ARTILLERY STREET

Fisherman's Wharf

Municipal Wharf

Monterey's First Brick House

Old Whaling Station

SEENO STREET

SCOTT STREET

Customs House

Monterey Marina

N

Maritime Museum of Monterey

Casa Soberanes

Pacific House

COOPER STREET

LARKIN STREET

VAN BUREN STREET

PACIFIC STREET

DEL MONTE AVENUE

FRANKLIN STREET

❹ Chamber of Commerce

DEL MONTE AVENUE

◄ *Campsite*

► *Greyhound stop*

PIERCE STREET

PACIFIC STREET

CALLE PRINCIPAL

ALVARADO STREET

BONIFACIO PLACE

TYLER STREET

WASHINGTON STREET

ADAMS STREET

FIGUEROA STREET

FRANKLIN STREET

ⓘ

JEFFERSON STREET

ANTHONY STREET

❺ Larkin House

❻

PEARL STREET

ALMA STREET

PEARL STREET

ROBINSON ST.

CORTES STREET

CAMINO EL ESTERO

Colton Hall

POLK STREET

Transit Plaza

MADISON STREET

Stevenson House

WEBSTER STREET

❼

Monterey Museum of Art

HARTNELL STREET

MUNRAS AVENUE

CHURCH STREET

El Estero Park

Cooper-Molera Adobe

CASS STREET

Royal Presidio Chapel

FREMONT STREET

► Ⓖ & N *Fremont St Motels*

0   200 yds

SARGENT CT.

PERRY LANE

MESA ROAD

DAVIS LANE

MUGRAS AVENUE

ABREGO STREET

MAJOR SHERMAN LANE

ELDORADO ST.

▼ Ⓓ, Ⓔ, Ⓕ & Ⓖ   ▼ Ⓗ

a great deal of doubt whether or not the demand would ever match the supply. Today, those worries have been put neatly to bed along with the visiting mass that stays here nightly, and tourism is now Monterey's main livelihood. A good deal of the trade is concentrated along the waterfront around the tacky **Fisherman's Wharf**, where the catch-of-the-day is more likely to be families from San Jose than the formerly abundant sardines. Most of the commercial fishermen moved out long ago, leaving the old wharves and canneries as relics of a once-prosperous industry; fat sea lions float by under the piers.

The most prominent building near the wharf, at the foot of Pacific Street, is the modern **Maritime Museum of Monterey** (daily 10am–5pm; $8; ☎831/372-2608 ext 22) with well-displayed but essentially mundane collections of ships in glass cases enlivened by interesting background on the town's defunct sardine industry. If none of this appeals, you should still pop in for the free, fourteen-minute film on Monterey history in preparation for a stroll on the **Path of History**. This loosely organized, roughly mile-and-a-half-long trail connects 37 sites in the **Monterey State Historic Park** scattered throughout the quarter-mile square of the modern city. The path is marked with small yellow discs at regular intervals on the sidewalk, and a free companion booklet giving detailed information on each site is available from most local tourist offices. Many of Monterey's historic buildings have survived in pristine condition: if you want to see inside, the best option is to join one of the 45-minute guided **walking tours** of the Path of History (Mon–Wed, Fri & Sat 10.30am; free; ☎831/649-7118, Ⓦwww.parks.ca.gov), which leave from the Pacific House Museum.

Among the essential buildings to visit, the **Pacific House** (Tues–Wed, Fri–Sun 10am–3pm; free; ☎831/649-2907) stands on the east side of the plaza outside the Maritime Museum; since its construction in 1847, it has been a courthouse, a rooming house, and a dance hall. It is now the best of the local **museums**, with displays on Monterey history and a fair collection of Native American artifacts; the lobby is an informal information center for the whole of the Monterey State Historic Park. While in the area, be sure to wander by the **Customs House** (Thurs–Mon 10am–3pm; free; ☎831/649-2909), the oldest governmental building on the West Coast, portions of which were built by Spain in 1814, Mexico in 1827, and the US in 1846. The balconied building has been restored and now displays 150-year-old crates of confiscated coffee and liquor in a small museum inside. A block west, outside the **Old Whaling Station**, don't miss the battered, diamond-shaped paving stones made by enterprising locals from whalebone vertebrae, which have lasted surprisingly well. Next door stands Monterey's **First Brick House** (daily 10am–3pm; free), which was built in 1847 and has a small display on the area's buildings.

But the best place to get a feel for life in Old Monterey is at the **Larkin House** (45-minute tours on Wed, Sat & Sun at 2pm; free; ☎831/649-7118, Ⓦwww.parks.ca.gov), on Jefferson Street a block south of Alvarado, home of the first and only American Consul to California and successful entrepreneur, Thomas Larkin. New England–born Larkin, the wealthy owner of a general store and a redwood lumber business, was one of the most important and influential figures in early California. He was actively involved in efforts to attract American settlers to California and lobbied the Californians to turn towards the United States and away from the erratic government of Mexico. Through his designs for his own house, and the Customs House near Fisherman's Wharf, Larkin is credited with developing the now-familiar Monterey style of architecture, combining local adobe walls and the balconies of Southern plantation homes with a puritan Yankee's taste in ornament. The house, the first two-story adobe in California, is filled with many millions of dollars' worth of antiques and is surrounded by gorgeous gardens.

As unhappy with the American military government as he had been with the Mexicans, Larkin helped to organize the Constitutional Convention that convened in Monterey in 1849 to draft the terms by which California could be admitted to the US as the 31st state – which happened in 1850. The meetings were held in the grand white stone building just down the street from his house, the then newly completed **Colton Hall**, built by William Colton, the first American *alcalde* (mayor-judge) of Monterey. It's now an engaging **museum** (daily 10am–4pm; free; ☎831/646-5648, ⓦwww.monterey .org/museum/), furnished as it was during the convention, with quill pens on the tables and an early map of the West Coast, which was used to draw up the boundaries of the nascent state. The **Monterey Museum of Art** at 559 Pacific St (Wed–Sat 11am–5pm, Sun 1–4pm; $5, free third Thurs and first Sun each month; ☎831/372-5477, ⓦwww.montereyart.org), presents a strong case for its much-touted title of "best small-town museum in the US." The museum's four galleries – featuring a rotating collection of mostly local art as well as temporary exhibits – are housed in a two-room adobe surrounded by splendid rose and rhododendron gardens and surrounded in turn by stone walls inlaid with painted tiles.

Stevenson House, at 530 Houston St (closed for earthquake retrofitting, call ☎831/649-1770 for further information), is an old rooming house filled with Robert Louis Stevenson memorabilia. The writer collected much of it on his travels round the South Sea Islands, and his family bequeathed the ephemera to the museum after his death: at the moment, the place is going through a major refit, and there's no confirmed date for its reopening, though the gardens are open (daily 10am–4pm). Two blocks east, on Church Street at the top of Figueroa, stands the oldest building in Monterey, the **San Carlos Cathedral**, also known as the **Royal Presidio Chapel** (daily 7.30am– 4.30pm; free; ☎831/373-2628, ⓦwww.sancarloscathedral.com). This small and much-restored Spanish Colonial church was built in 1795 as part of a mission founded here by Junípero Serra in 1770, the rest of which was soon removed to a better site along the Carmel River. In the rear garden is a fragment of the ancient oak tree under which explorer Vizcaíno said Mass back in 1602.

There are two other notable historic buildings in Monterey: the best preserved historic home is the **Cooper–Molera Adobe**, at 525 Polk St (45-minute tours Wed, Fri–Sun 1pm; free; ☎831/649-7109, ⓦwww.parks .ca.gov), which illustrates architecturally the evolution of Monterey. This housing complex was built by New England sea captain John Rogers Cooper, who settled locally and married a Mexican woman. Cooper and co lived in two buildings: the first, a squat, old-fashioned Mexican-style house, known as the Diaz Adobe, with simple, whitewashed walls, no closets, and thick adobe bricks to serve as primitive air-conditioning. The second was a more formal, fashionable home that Cooper himself constructed in the early 1850s and follows an East Coast design, with a double parlor, decorative printed wallpaper, and fitted carpeting.

A few blocks north, at the corner of Pacific and Del Monte, stands **Casa Soberanes** (30-minute tours Tues 1pm, Fri 11.30am; free; ☎831/649-7118, ⓦwww.parks.ca.gov). This is a classic California-style adobe building built in the 1830s, with its floating balconies supported only by heavy floor beams, red tiling, and symmetrical doors and windows. The interior of the house has been somewhat modernized, but the low ceilings and boxy rooms of its original construction have been preserved.

Cannery Row and the Monterey Bay Aquarium

A waterfront **bike path** runs from the wharf along the disused railroad two miles out to Pacific Grove, following the one-time Ocean View Avenue, renamed **CANNERY ROW** after John Steinbeck's evocative portrait of the rough-and-ready men and women who worked in and around the thirty-odd fish canneries here. During World War II, Monterey was the sardine capital of the Western world, catching and canning some 200,000 tons of the fish each year. However, overfishing ensured that by 1945 the fish were more or less all gone, and the canneries were abandoned, falling into disrepair until the 1970s, when they were rebuilt, redecorated, and converted into shopping malls and flashy restaurants, many with names adopted from Steinbeck's tales.

Ride, walk, or take the WAVE trolley from Fisherman's Wharf to visit the engaging **MONTEREY BAY AQUARIUM**, a mile west of town at the end of Cannery Row (daily 10am–6pm; last ticket 5.30pm; $19.95, $3 audio tour; ☎831/648-4888 or 1-800/756-3737, ⓦwww.montereybayaquarium.org). **Reservations** at Monterey's single most popular attraction are essential in any season. Built upon the foundations of an old sardine cannery and housed in modernist buildings that blend a sense of adventure with pleasant promenades along the Bay, the aquarium is one of the largest, most stunning displays of underwater life in the world. The new temporary exhibit, Sharks: Myth and Mystery, is frankly a little disappointing, especially for adults; the whole display's firmly aimed at grade schoolers, swooping round the world to highlight different sharks and local cultures surrounding them. There's a climb-inside Mayan temple to explore in the Central American section, and shark masks to wear in the Pacific; one campy highlight is the looped video of Quint's tales from *Jaws* shown alongside the cutesy cartoons of *Finding Nemo*. Aside from this display, head for the gigantic Outer Bay room, outlining the ecosystem of the deep waters just beyond the Bay; the enormous tank here is a highlight, featuring lazy hammerhead sharks and foul-tempered tuna among others. Upstairs, there's the kid-friendly Splash Zone plus petting pools; the museum also opens directly onto the Bay, so you can wander out and peer into wild tide pools after wandering round the captive tanks. Try not to miss the sea otters at feeding

Robert Louis Stevenson and Monterey

The Gold Rush of 1849 bypassed Monterey for San Francisco, leaving the community little more than a somnolent Mexican fishing village – which was pretty much how the town looked in the fall of 1879, when a 29-year-old, feverishly ill Scotsman arrived by stagecoach, flat broke, and desperately in love with a married woman. **Robert Louis Stevenson** came to Monterey for fresh air and looking for **Fanny Osbourne**, whom he had met while traveling in France two years before. He stayed here for three months, writing occasional articles for the local newspaper and telling stories in exchange for his meals at the saloon-restaurant run by Frenchman Jules Simoneau, behind what is now the **Stevenson House**, halfway between the Larkin House and the Royal Presidio Chapel (see opposite). It's said that he started *Treasure Island* here and used Point Lobos (see p.539) as inspiration for Spyglass Hill.

Stevenson witnessed Monterey (no longer politically important but not yet a tourist attraction) in transition, something he wrote about in his essay *The Old and New Pacific Capitals*. He foresaw that the lifestyle that had endured since the Mexican era was no match for the "Yankee craft" of the "millionaire vulgarians of the Big Bonanza," such as Charles Crocker, whose lavish Hotel Del Monte, which opened a year later (the site is now the Naval Postgraduate School, east of downtown), turned the sleepy town into a seaside resort of international renown almost overnight.

time (usually 10.30am, 1.30pm, & 3.30pm); the playful critters were hunted nearly to extinction for their fur – said, with some one million hairs per square inch, to be the softest in the world. Otherwise, stop off at the 335,000-gallon Kelp Forest for a fish feeding frenzy (11.30am & 4pm).

Pacific Grove

PACIFIC GROVE – or "Butterfly Town USA," as it likes to call itself – stands curiously apart from the rest of the Peninsula, less known but more impressively situated than its two famous neighbors. The town began as a campground and Methodist retreat in 1875, a summertime tent city for revivalist Christians in which strong drink, naked flesh, and reading the Sunday papers were firmly prohibited. The Methodists have long since gone, but otherwise the town is little changed. Its quiet streets, lined by pine trees and grand old Victorian wooden houses, are enlivened each year by hundreds of thousands of golden **monarch butterflies**, which come here each winter from all over the western US and Canada to escape the cold and have become the town's main tourist attraction. In fact, the migration of these little orange-and-black butterflies is so important to the local economy that they're protected by local law; there's a $1000 fine for molesting a monarch.

Downtown Pacific Grove centers upon the intersection of Forest Street and Lighthouse Avenue, two miles northwest of central Monterey. Two blocks north, at 667 Lighthouse Ave, the **Bookworks** bookstore and café (Sun & Mon 9.30am–6pm, Tues–Thurs 9.30am–8pm, Fri & Sat 9.30am–9pm; ℡831/372-2242) is the place to pick up more detailed guides to the local area, or just stop for a cup of coffee and a pastry. A block down Forest Street, on the corner of Central Avenue, the **Pacific Grove Museum of Natural History** (Tues–Sat 10am–5pm; free; ℡831/648-5716, Ⓦwww.pgmuseum.org) has an informative collection of local wildlife, including lots of butterflies, over four hundred stuffed birds, a relief model of the undersea topography, and exhibits on the ways of life of the native Costanoan and Salinan peoples. Across the park, the **Chautauqua Hall** was for a time in the 1880s the focus of town life as the West Coast headquarters of the instructional and populist Chautauqua Movement, a left-leaning, traveling university that reached thousands of Americans long before there was any accessible form of higher education. Nowadays, the plain white building is used as a dance hall, with a three-piece band playing favorites from the Thirties and Forties every Saturday night, and square dancing on Thursday.

About the only reminder of the fundamentalist camp meetings are the intricately detailed, tiny wooden **cottages**, along 16th and 17th streets, which date from the revival days; in some cases wooden boards were simply nailed over the frames of canvas tents to make them habitable year-round. Down Central Avenue at 12th Street, at the top of a small wooded park overlooking the ocean, stands the deep-red Gothic wooden church of **Saint Mary's By-The-Sea**, Pacific Grove's first substantial church, built in 1887, with a simple interior of redwood beams polished to a shimmering glow, and an authentic signed Tiffany stained-glass window, nearest the altar on the left.

Ocean View Boulevard, which runs between the church and the ocean, circles along the coast around the town, passing the headland of **Lovers Point** – originally called Lovers of Jesus Point – where preachers used to hold sunrise services. Surrounded in early summer by the colorful red and purple blankets of blooming ice plants, it's one of the peninsula's best **beaches**, where you can lounge around and swim from the intimate, protected strand – if you're lucky enough to have arrived on one of the rare fog-free days in summer – or rent a glass-bottomed boat and explore the sheltered cove. Ocean View Boulevard runs another mile along the coast out to the tip of the Peninsula, where the 150-year-old **Point Piños Lighthouse** (Thurs–Sun 1–4pm; free; ☎831/648-5716, ⓦwww.pgmuseum.org) is the oldest continuously operating lighthouse on the California coast.

Around Pacific Grove, there are two worthwhile detours. One follows the coastal road as it changes from Ocean View Boulevard to Sunset Drive, leading on to **Asilomar State Beach**, a wild stretch with dramatic surf, too dangerous for swimming, though the rocky shore provides homes for all sorts of tide-pool life. The second tracks the **Butterfly Trees** on Ridge Road, a quarter of a mile inland along Lighthouse Avenue: this is where you should be able to spot giant brown clumps of monarchs discretely congregating high up in the treetops during season (Nov–early March). The quickest way out of town is to follow Hwy-68 from the end of Sunset Drive inland over the hills: it joins Hwy-1 just north of Carmel. But if you've time, the **Seventeen Mile Drive** (daily dawn–dusk; $8.25 per car; ☎831/649-8500) is a privately owned, scenic toll road which loops from Pacific Grove along the coast south to Carmel and back again; on the way, it swoops past the golf courses and country clubs of Pebble Beach. Don't miss the trussed-up figure of the **Lone Cypress** halfway along the route, as it's the subject of many a postcard; there are enough beautiful vistas of the rugged coastline to make it almost worth braving the hordes that pack the roads on holiday weekends.

Carmel

Set on gently rising headlands above a sculpted rocky shore, **CARMEL** is confined to a few neat rows of quaint shops and miniature homes running along either side of Ocean Avenue towards the largely untouched coastline. Besides all the rampant cuteness, Carmel's only real crime is its ridiculously inflated price scale; with its posh seaside mansions and moneyed locals, think of it as the West Coast's middle-aged answer to New York's Hamptons.

The town's reputation as a rich resort belies its origins: there was nothing much here until the San Francisco earthquake and fire of 1906 led a number of artists and writers from the city to take refuge in the area, forming a bohemian colony on the wild and uninhabited slopes that soon became notorious throughout the state. The figurehead of the group was the poet George Sterling, and part-time members included Jack London, Mary Austin, and the young Sinclair Lewis. But it was a short-lived alliance, and by the 1920s the group had broken up, and an influx of wealthy San Franciscans had put Carmel well on its way to becoming the exclusive corner it is today.

Despite continued growth of tourism to the area, Carmel still seems the epitome of parochial snobbishness. Franchise businesses are banned outright within the city limits, while there's an array of laws enacted to stringently maintain the gingerbread charm of the town's central district: parking meters and street addresses are prohibited, for instance. One long-term byproduct of this bizarre rebellion against street numbers was that all mail had to be picked up in person from the post office – at least until recently, when a local resident sued for home delivery and was rewarded with the chance to pay a premium to have mail delivered.

Carmel's center, fifteen minutes south of Monterey on MST bus #4 or #5, doesn't have much to recommend it. Indeed, it is largely designer-shopping territory: Carmel Plaza Mall at Ocean Avenue and Mission Street holds branches of Saks Fifth Avenue and Louis Vuitton, and there are a number of tacky, overpriced art **galleries** along Dolores Street (there's even a clothing store for pampered lap dogs on Ocean Avenue). The Weston Gallery on Sixth Street between Dolores and Lincoln (summer daily 10.30am–5.30pm, winter closed Mon; ☎831/624-4453, ⊛www.westongallery.com) is worth a look, however, hosting regular shows of the best contemporary photographers and featuring a permanent display of works by Fox Talbot, Ansel Adams, and Edward Weston – who lived in Carmel for most of his life. To get the lowdown on the other galleries, check out the free, widely available *Carmel Gallery Guide*.

The town's best feature, however, is the largely untouched nearby coastline, among the most beautiful in California. **Carmel Beach** is a tranquil cove of emerald blue water bordered by soft white sand and cypress-covered cliffs; the tides are deceptively strong and dangerous, so be careful if you chance a swim. A mile south from Carmel Beach along Carmel Bay, **Tor House** was, when built in 1919, the only building on a then treeless headland. The poet Robinson Jeffers (whose very long, starkly tragic narrative poems were far more popular in his time than they are today) built the small cottage and adjacent tower by hand, out of granite boulders he carried up from the cove below. There are hourly guided tours of the house and gardens (Fri & Sat 10am–3pm; $7; ⊛www.torhouse.org); to make a reservation in advance call ☎831/624-1813 (Mon–Thurs 10am–3pm), or for same-day bookings call ☎831/624-1840 (Fri & Sat 10am–4pm). The tours overload visitors with an obsequious account of the now-forgotten writer's life and work, but the house itself is pleasant enough. Note that the entrance is at 26304 Ocean View Ave, one block back from the clifftop; note, too, that's there's little parking, since this is a residential neighborhood, so allow ample time to find a spot.

Another quarter of a mile along Scenic Road, around the tip of Carmel Point, you'll find the idyllic, mile-long **Carmel River State Beach** (☎831/649-2836, ⊛www.parks.ca.gov). It's less visited than the city beach, and includes a bird sanctuary on a freshwater lagoon that offers safe and sometimes warm swimming. Again, if you brave the waves, beware of the strong tides and currents, especially at the south end of the beach, where the sand falls away at a very steep angle, causing big and potentially hazardous surf.

The Carmel Mission

Half a mile or so up the Carmel River from the beach, also reachable by following Junípero Avenue from downtown, **Carmel Mission Basilica** (Sept–May Mon–Sat 9.30am–4.30pm, Sun 10.30am–4.30pm; $4; ☎831/624-3600, ⊛www.carmelmission.org) – San Carlos Borromeo de Carmelo – was founded in 1770 by Junípero Serra as the second of the California missions and the headquarters of the chain. Father Serra never got to see the finished church – he died before its completion and is buried under the floor in front of the altar. Finally completed by Father Lasuen in 1797, the sandstone church has undergone one of the most painstakingly authentic restorations in the entire mission chain, a process well detailed in one of the three excellent **museums** in the mission compound. By 1937, when the reconstruction began, the mission had lain derelict for more than eighty years and was little more than its foundations and a few feet of wall; but today the whimsically ornate structure stands firmly as the most romantic mission in the chain. The dainty building has a dark side too: three thousand local Native Americans are buried in the adjacent **cemetery**.

Point Lobos State Reserve

Two miles south of the mission along Hwy-1, accessible in summer on MST bus #22, the **POINT LOBOS STATE RESERVE** (summer daily 9am–7pm, last entry 6.30pm; winter daily 9am–5pm, last entry 4.30pm; $8 parking; ☏831/624-4909, ⓦwww.parks.ca.gov) has plenty of natural justifications to support its claim of being "the greatest meeting of land and water in the world." There are over 250 bird and animal species along the **hiking trails** in the area, and the sea here is one of the richest underwater habitats in California. Because the point juts so far out into the ocean, there are some of the earth's best undisturbed views of the ocean: craggy granite pinnacles, landforms that inspired Robert Louis Stevenson's *Treasure Island*, reach out of jagged blue coves. Sea lions and otters frolic in the crashing surf, just below the many vantage points along the park's coastal trail. Gray whales are often seen offshore – sometimes as close as a hundred yards away – migrating south in January and returning with young calves in April and early May. The park, named after the *lobos marinos* – the noisy, barking sea lions that group on the rocks off the reserve's tip – protects some of the few remaining Monterey cypress trees on its knife-edged headland, despite being buffeted by relentless winds.

Except for a small parking lot, the reserve is closed to cars, so lines sometimes form along the highway to wait for a parking space. A worthwhile guide and map is included in the admission fee.

Carmel Valley

About fifteen miles inland, east along route G16, lies **Carmel Valley Village**, where the weather is warmer and more predictable than the coast: that's one of the reasons this country hamlet can bill itself as the epicenter of the Monterey County's wine country, a cluster of vineyards encompassing an area as far afield as King City to the south on Hwy-101. In the **CARMEL VALLEY** that surrounds the village, you'll find a number of vineyards in a quiet pastoral setting – a big breath of relief after crowded, coastal Carmel: most are known for their red wines, since the searing summer heat (up to 105°F) suits hardier varietals better. The Monterey County Vintners and Growers Association (☏831/375-9400, ⓦwww.montereywines.org) publishes a map to the area, and the **Chamber of Commerce** (Mon–Fri 10am–4pm; ☏831/659-4000, ⓦwww.carmelvalleychamber.com) lures visitors from Carmel with a new local map – available from most any visitor center in Monterey County – crammed with shopping and dining possibilities. One of the most pleasant wineries for tastings is Joullian, 2 Village Drive (daily 11am–5pm; ☏831/659-8100, ⓦwww.joullian.com), where the friendly, knowledgeable staff will be happy to talk at length about the region's history and current winemaking strengths.

Eating

There are many excellent **places to eat** all over the Peninsula, and though prices tend to float near resort prices, the competition for tourist dollars insures quality. For a full list of the hundreds of eating options in the area, check out a copy of the free, weekly, and widely available *Go!* or *Coast Weekly*. If you're on anything like a tight budget, the best eats are on the north side of Monterey along North Fremont Street, on and around Lighthouse Avenue (just south of Cannery Row), and in the shopping malls along Hwy-1 south of Carmel.

Cafés

Bay Books 316 Alvarado St, Monterey
℡831/375-1855. Sip coffee until 10pm (11pm at weekends) while browsing in one of Monterey's better bookshops.

Carmel Bakery Ocean Ave between Lincoln and Dolores, Carmel ℡831/626-8885. Refreshing low-key café on the main drag serving old-fashioned gooey cakes and coffee to browsing locals.

Old Monterey Café 489 Alvarado St, Monterey ℡831/646-1021. Reasonable more-than-you-can-eat breakfasts, with great omelets and buckwheat pancakes, plus tasty sandwiches; breakfast and lunch only.

Patisserie Boissière Mission St between Ocean and 7th, Carmel ℡831/624-5008. With savory quiches, salads, and even Coquille Saint Jacques on the menu, this mid-range restaurant also serves the pastries you'd expect from the name and prepares picnic lunches with advance notice.

Tuck Box Tearoom Dolores St between Ocean and 7th,Carmel ℡831/624-6365. Breakfast, lunch, and afternoon tea in half-timbered mock-Tudor Old England cottage; costly, kitschy, and fun.

Wildberries 667 Lighthouse Ave, Monterey ℡831/644-9836. Café adjoining the Bookworks bookstore (see p.536) that features live music some nights and light lunch fare at reasonable prices, although it usually closes around 8pm.

Restaurants

Fishwife at Asilomar Beach, 1996 Sunset Drive at Asilomar, Pacific Grove ℡831/375-7107. Long-standing local favorite, serving great food at reasonable prices in cozy, unpretentious surroundings. Try the king prawns sautéed in red peppers and lime juice with rice and steamed vegetables for $15.

India's Clay Oven 150 Del Monte Ave, 2nd floor, Monterey ℡831/373-2529. If you're overcome by the sudden desire for papadums and *saag paneer*, you now know where to go for slightly upscale versions of the same – the best local Indian option. Expensive.

La Bohème Dolores St between Ocean and 7th sts, Carmel ℡831/624-7500. A worthwhile splurge, Carmel-style, this French-inspired bistro offers a single, multi-course *menu fixe* that changes daily for $31 plus wine and service. Charming if a little chintzy.

Little Napoli Dolores St between Ocean and 7th sts, Carmel ℡831/626-6335. One of the town's many excellent mid-range Italian restaurants, this tiny eatery serves oversized portions of fresh pasta with original sauces in an atmosphere with all the romantic charm you'd expect from a Carmel address.

Massaro and Santos 32 Cannery Row #H-1, Coast Guard Pier, Monterey ℡831/649-6700. Dine here for views out across the Bay and meaty, fish-crammed stews like *bouillabaisse*, not to mention dozens of daily specials – entrees are around $15 but save room for the gooey, gorgeous desserts.

Paolina's San Carlos between Ocean and 7th sts, Carmel ℡831/624-5599 Fresh home-made pastas are served up in a casual courtyard setting at half the price of other Carmel dining.

Papa Chano's Taqueria 462 Alvarado St, Monterey ℡831/646-9587. One of the few bargain eateries in town, this fast-food-style *taqueria* nevertheless serves juicy, authentic Mexican specialties – the *chorizo* (spicy sausage) is particularly tender.

Pasta Mia Trattoria 481 Lighthouse Ave, Pacific Grove ℡831/375-7709. Family-owned restaurant offering tasty home-made pastas, grilled seafood, and veal in a rustic, homely setting. The pasta entrees run for about $12.

Pepper's Mexicali Café 170 Forest Ave, Pacific Grove ℡831/373-6892. Gigantic plates of Mexican food for around $10 per person, piled high with fresh, local produce: less healthful than it sounds but guaranteed to fill even the biggest stomach – try the chicken slathered in rich *mole* sauce ($11.50)

Porta Bella Ocean Ave between Lincoln and Monte Verde, Carmel ℡831/624-4395. Upscale, flower-filled bistro, serving fancy French food in a pleasant setting, with crisp white tablecloths and a charming garden tucked away beneath a vine-filled trellis at the back. Watch the local ladies who lunch, lunch.

Robata Grill & Sake Bar 3658 The Barnyard, Carmel ℡831/624-2643. Local favorite for sushi and tempura in a warm, wood-paneled setting. Not cheap, but tasty and unpretentious for its locale.

Sardine Factory 701 Wave St, Monterey ℡831/373-3775. California seafood cuisine served in French château splendor at less-than-expected prices, although it's still pretty wallet walloping.

Schooners in the *Monterey Plaza Hotel*, 400 Cannery Row, Monterey ℡831/372-2628. Colorful upscale California bistro in a historic hotel with views over the bay. Try a grilled, local Castroville artichoke, served with herbed mayonnaise.

Stokes Restaurant and Bar 500 Hartnell St, Monterey ℡831/373-1110. Built in 1833, the historic former home is now an elegant restaurant serving Mediterranean cuisine with a Californian flare.

Bars and nightlife

The Peninsula has always been better known as a sleepy, romantic getaway than as a hub of hip nightlife. However, the best selection of bars is in Monterey, and the local **Jazz Festival** in mid-September (℡1-800/307-3378, ⓦwww .montereyjazzfestival.org) is the oldest continuous festival in the world, drawing crowds from afar. Check out the widely available *Monterey County Weekly* for the most current listings.

Britannia Arms Pub & Restaurant 444 Alvarado St, Monterey ℡831/656-9543, ⓦwww .britanniaarms.com. This authentic-feeling British pub is oddly incongruous in the heart of Monterey; it's filled with a largely local, laid-back crowd and serves greasily tasty traditional pub grub.
Club Octane 321d Alvarado St, Monterey ℡831/646-9244, ⓦwww.cluboctane.com. Lively downtown club with three dancefloors and a youngish, collegiate crowd – more fun than hip. Closed Tues & Wed.
Lallapalooza 474 Alvarado St, Monterey ℡831/645-9036. Martini bar with poppy, olive-themed art on the walls, a small sidewalk terrace and stylish oval bar – the dressiest place to drink in town. There's a reasonable restaurant attached, too.
Lighthouse Bar & Grill 281 Lighthouse Ave, Monterey ℡831/373-4488, ⓦwww .lighthousebarandgrill281.com. Rather dilapidated gay bar with a low-key, pub atmosphere, pool tables, and an older crowd.
The Mucky Duck 479 Alvarado St, Monterey ℡831/655-3031. The menu at this friendly and popular Tudor-style bar/restaurant features British food with a California flair. Occasional live music; DJ dancing on back patio.

North from Monterey

The landscape around the **Monterey Bay**, between the Peninsula and the beach town of Santa Cruz, 45 miles north, is almost entirely given over to agriculture. **Castroville**, ten miles north along Hwy-1, has two claims to fame, one more glamorous than the other. Today, surrounded by farmland, it produces more than 85 percent of the nation's artichokes (try them deep-fried in one of the local cafés); more than fifty years ago in 1947, the first woman to be crowned Artichoke Queen was one Norma Jean Baker, later known as Marilyn Monroe. The wide **Pajaro Valley**, five miles further north, is covered with apple orchards, blossoming white in the spring. The marshlands that ring the bay at the mouths of the Salinas and Pajaro rivers are habitats for many of California's endangered species of coastal wildlife and migratory birds. **Moss Landing** is an excellent place to stop for seafood – try dramatically situated *Phil's Fish Market*, 7600 Sandholt Rd (℡831/633-2152), on the small island linked by a short bridge to the mainland, where you can pick from the catch of the day, then fish a bottle of white wine for yourself from the cooler. At the nearby **Elkhorn Slough Estuarine Sanctuary** (Wed–Sun 9am–5pm, free guided tours Sat & Sun 10am, 1pm; $2.50; ℡831/728-2822, ⓦwww.elkhornslough.org) you may spot a falcon or an eagle among the 250 species of bird that call it home. Guided nature boat tours can be booked through Elkhorn Slough Safari on the harbor ($26; ℡831/633-5555, ⓦwww .elkhornslough.com). The beaches along the bay to Santa Cruz are often windy and not very exciting, though they're lined by sand dunes into which you can disappear for hours on end.

    Sunset State Beach, fifteen miles south of Santa Cruz, has **campgrounds** (book through ParkNet ℡1-800/444-7275; information only ℡831/763-7062; $18) along a seven-mile strand. Four miles inland, east of Hwy-1, the earthquake-devastated town of **Watsonville** was more or less the epicenter of the October 1989 Loma Prieta tremor that rattled San Francisco. Its once-quaint downtown of ornate Victorian houses and 1930s brick structures was virtually flattened, and more recently the area economy has been hard hit by closure of its Green Giant vegetable-packing plant, once one of the largest in the country. Like many American cities, the place is saturated with fast-food restaurants and outlet malls and there isn't a lot of interest for travelers, but Watsonville is still the main transfer point between the Monterey and Santa Cruz **bus** systems, so you may well have to pass through.

San Juan Bautista and Gilroy

Inland from the Monterey Bay area, on US-101 between Salinas and San Francisco, tiny **SAN JUAN BAUTISTA** is an old Mexican town that, but for a modest scattering of craft shops, has hardly changed since it was bypassed by the railroad in 1876. The early nineteenth-century **Mission San Juan Bautista** (daily 9.30am–4.45pm; $3; ☎831/623-4528, ⓦwww.oldmissionsjb .org), largest of the Californian mission churches – and still the parish church of San Juan Bautista – stands on the north side of the town's central plaza, its original bells still ringing out from the bell tower. The arcaded monastery wing that stretches out to the left of the church contains relics and historical exhibits, including a vast collection of ceremonial robes. If it all looks a bit familiar, you may have seen it before – the climactic stairway chase scene in Alfred Hitchcock's *Vertigo* was filmed here. Note that the **San Andreas Fault** runs just a few yards in front of the church.

The town that grew up around the mission was once the largest in central California and has been preserved as a **state park** (daily 10am–4.30pm; $2; ☎831/623-4881, ⓦwww.parks.ca.gov) with exhibits around the evocative central square interpreting the restored buildings. On the west side of the plaza, the two-story, balconied adobe Plaza Hotel was a popular stopping place on the stagecoach route between San Francisco and Los Angeles; next door, the 1840 **Castro-Breen Adobe**, administrative headquarters of Mexican California, later belonged to the Breen family – survivors of the ill-fated Donner Party (see box, p.755) – who made a small fortune in the Gold Rush.

Across from the mission, the large **Plaza Hall** was built to serve as the seat of the emergent county government, but when the county seat was awarded instead to Hollister – a small farming community eight miles east, and scene of a motorcycle gang's rampage that inspired the movie *The Wild One* – the building was turned into a dance hall and saloon. The adjacent stables display a range of old stagecoaches and wagons, and explain how to decipher an array of cattle brands, from "lazy H" to "rockin' double B."

The commercial center of San Juan Bautista, a block south of the plaza, lines Third Street in a row of evocatively decaying facades. If you're hungry, the best of the half-dozen **places to eat** is the unfussy *Mission Café* at 300 3rd St, on the corner of Mariposa (☎831/623-2635), which serves breakfast and lunch and is especially notable for its friendly staff; for dinner, try *Joan & Peter's German Restaurant*, 322 3rd St (☎831/623-4521), with its hearty specials of *bratwurst* and *wurstteller* for around $10. For **information** contact the Chamber of Commerce, 410 3rd St (Mon–Thurs 9am–4pm, Fri 9–11am; ☎831/623-2454, ⓦwww.san-juan-bautista.ca.us).

A bit further north, you'll know you've come to **GILROY** by the smell, for this farming community is best known for its garlic. For information on the annual summer Garlic Festival, which features everything from vampire-chasing garlands to garlic ice cream (not nearly as bad as it sounds), stop by the Gilroy Visitors Bureau, a small Swiss-chalet-like building stashed hidden by huge trees at 7780 Monterey St (Mon–Fri 9am–5pm, Sat 10am–3pm; ☎408/842-6436, ⓦwww.gilroyvisitor.org).

Santa Cruz

Seventy-five miles south of San Francisco, the unassuming yet edgy community of **SANTA CRUZ** is a hard place to pin down. In many ways it's the quintessential Californian coastal town with miles of beaches for sunning and superb surfing, thousands of acres of mountaintop forests for hiking, and a lively historic boardwalk amusement park – complete with a wild wooden rollercoaster – for strolling. It's also home to a great number of homeless people who've spilled over from San Francisco and neighboring communities to benefit from the town's numerous liberal resources, joining with its hippie past to bring out the crustier side of local life. Santa Cruz enjoyed – or, rather, endured – a growth spurt in the late 1990s: it was commandeered as a dormitory suburb for San Jose and Silicon Valley during the dot-com boom, which pushed up its property prices significantly and drove some long-term locals away; that boom's stabilized but prices have yet to drop. Even so, some of its suburbs still have a conservative, almost redneck feel more akin to the Central Valley than the laid-back languid coast. All this means that you rarely get an impression of a resort totally at ease with itself: the underlying conflicts are one of the many reasons why the town is so slow to change and makes an intriguingly schizophrenic place to visit. In 2002, when the town council, eager to buff up downtown's shopping strip, shelled out more than $200,000 on a gaudy, neon sign marking the entrance to "River Street," locals protested fiercely after its erection – camping out around the sign and even urinating on it – and eventually officials were forced to look into its removal. The cost of tearing down the sign proved prohibitive, so it was offered for sale on eBay; that it's still standing at the time of writing is proof that Santa Cruz could find no buyers.

The town's enduring reputation as a holdout from the 1960s is only fitting since this is where it all began. Ken Kesey and his Merry Pranksters turned the local youth on to the wonders of LSD years before it defined a generation, a mission recorded by Tom Wolfe in *The Electric Koolaid Acid Test*. The area is still considered among the most politically and socially progressive in California – one reason that Santa Cruz has become known, in recent years, as a lesbian mecca (see p.552) – and there are still a few freaky holdouts from its hippie heyday. The town is also surprisingly untouristy: no hotels spoil the miles of wave-beaten coastline – in fact, most of the surrounding land is used for growing fruit and vegetables, and roadside stalls are more likely to be selling apples or sprouts than postcards and souvenirs. Places to stay are for once good-value and easy to find, and the town sports a range of bookstores and coffeehouses, as well as some lively bars and nightclubs where the music varies from hard-core surf-punk to long-time local Neil Young and friends.

Arrival, information, and city transportation

By **car**, Santa Cruz is on Hwy-1, 45 miles north of Monterey; Hwy-17 runs over the mountains, 33 miles from San Jose and US-101. **Greyhound buses** (T831/423-1800 or 1-800/231-2222) stop five times a day in each direction at 425 Front St in the center of town, with connecting services to all the major cities in the state. Amtrak Thruway buses connect the town with San Jose four times daily; there's also a weekly Green Tortoise. Coming from the Monterey Peninsula, local MST and SCMTD buses link up in Watsonville.

The **Santa Cruz Conference and Visitors Center** at 1211 Ocean St (Mon–Sat 9am–5pm, Sun 10am–4pm; T831/425-1234 or 1-800/833-3494, Wwww.santacruz.org) has lots of handy information on places to stay, and sells

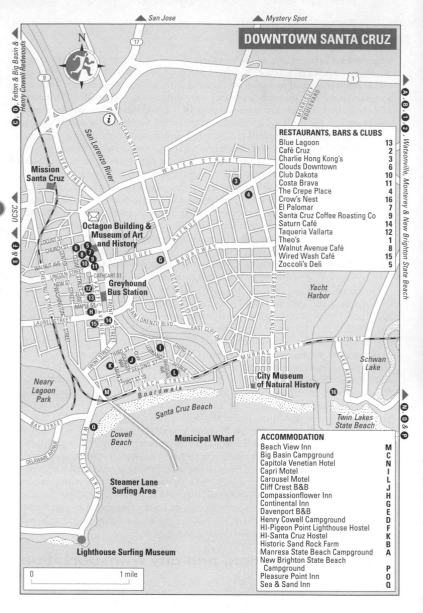

San Jose

Mystery Spot

Felton & Big Basin & Henry Cowell Redwoods

UCSC

THE CENTRAL COAST | Santa Cruz

A, B, C, Watsonville, Monterey & New Brighton State Beach

N, O & P

Mission Santa Cruz

Octagon Building & Museum of Art and History

Greyhound Bus Station

Neary Lagoon Park

Steamer Lane Surfing Area

Lighthouse Surfing Museum

Cowell Beach

Municipal Wharf

Santa Cruz Beach

Boardwalk

City Museum of Natural History

Yacht Harbor

Schwan Lake

Twin Lakes State Beach

RESTAURANTS, BARS & CLUBS

Blue Lagoon	13
Café Cruz	2
Charlie Hong Kong's	3
Clouds Downtown	6
Club Dakota	10
Costa Brava	11
The Crepe Place	4
Crow's Nest	16
El Palomar	7
Santa Cruz Coffee Roasting Co	9
Saturn Café	14
Taqueria Vallarta	12
Theo's	1
Walnut Avenue Café	8
Wired Wash Café	15
Zoccoli's Deli	5

ACCOMMODATION

Beach View Inn	M
Big Basin Campground	C
Capitola Venetian Hotel	N
Capri Motel	I
Carousel Motel	L
Cliff Crest B&B	J
Compassionflower Inn	H
Continental Inn	G
Davenport B&B	E
Henry Cowell Campground	D
HI-Pigeon Point Lighthouse Hostel	F
HI-Santa Cruz Hostel	K
Historic Sand Rock Farm	B
Manresa State Beach Campground	A
New Brighton State Beach Campground	P
Pleasure Point Inn	O
Sea & Sand Inn	Q

0   1 mile

a detailed map of the entire county for \$1.50. To find out what's on in the area, check out the free magazine rack at the **Bookshop Santa Cruz**, 1520 Pacific Ave (☎831/423-0900), where you'll find generally useful weeklies like *Good Times* and the *Metro Santa Cruz*; another option is to pick up a copy of the local newspaper, *The Santa Cruz Sentinel*.

Santa Cruz has an excellent **public transportation system**, based around the Metro Center wedged between Front Street and Pacific Avenue, and operated by the Santa Cruz Metropolitan Transit District or SCMTD (information Mon–Fri 8am–4pm; ☎831/425-8600, ⊛www.scmtd.com), which publishes *Headways*, a free bilingual guide to getting around the area. The basic fare is $1.50 and an all-day pass costs $4.50. Some of the most useful routes are the University Service, which runs up the hill to UCSC; #71 to Watsonville; and #7 along the western beaches to the lighthouse. Route #35, which runs up Hwy-9 into the mountains to Big Basin Redwoods State Park (March–Dec only), is equipped with bike racks.

Though there are buses to most of the beaches, you might find it easier to get around by **bicycle** – in fact, Santa Cruz is a bike-crazy town. Options for rental (all around $25 per day) include Another Bike Shop, 2361 Mission St (☎831/427-2232, ⊛www.anotherbikeshop.com), Dave's Recycled Bikes, 318 Pacific Ave (closed Mon; ☎831/423-1169, ⊛www.davrecbikes.forabike.com), or Electric Sierra Cycles, 302 Pacific Ave (☎831/425-1593 or 1-877/372-8773, ⊛www.electricrecbikes.com). You can get ocean-going **kayaks** for $20 for 2 hours or $35 a day from Venture Quest on the wharf at 125 Beach St (daily 10am–6pm; ☎831/427-2267, ⊛www.kayaksantacruz.com); and Santa Cruz Sport Fishing, Dock X in the north harbour (☎831/426-4690, ⊛www.santacruzsportfishing.com; from $100 per person), rent skiffs and fishing equipment along with bait and tackle.

Accommodation

Compared to most California beach resorts, **accommodation** in Santa Cruz is inexpensive and easy to come by, especially during the week or outside of summer: most of the establishments we've listed offer good-value weekly rates and there's a clump of inexpensive motels along Ocean Street. **Camping** opportunities in and around Santa Cruz are abundant and varied, from beaches to forests and points in between; **reservations** for all state park campgrounds are handled through ParkNet (☎1-800/444-7275).

Hotels, motels, and B&Bs

Beach View Inn 50 Front St ☎831/426-3575 or 1-800/946-0614, ⊛www.beach-viewinn.com. Clean budget motel near the boardwalk; the rooms are basic but have microwaves and fridges, while the laidback, helpful staff is a major plus. Rooms are rented weekly Dec–March. ❶

Capitola Venetian Hotel 1500 Wharf Rd, Capitola ☎831/476-6471 or 1-800/332-2780, ⊛www.capitolavenetian.com. Quirky, ageing beachfront hotel just across the bridge from Capitola's lively esplanade. All rooms have kitchens, some are two-bedroom suites; rates increase at weekends when there's a two-night minimum. ❸

Capri Motel 337 Riverside Ave ☎831/426-4611. The cheapest of a dozen or so budget motels near the beach and the boardwalk: it's clean, with air conditioning, a pool, and free on-site parking, but don't expect lavish facilities. ❶

Carousel Motel 110 Riverside Ave ☎831/425-7090 or 1-800/214-7400, ⊛www.santacruzmotels.com. Sparklingly clean bargain, its simple rooms fitted out with blond wood furniture and loud,

1980s-inspired bedcovers; each room has a large TV and microwave, and there's free continental breakfast included. Even better, it's directly across from the boardwalk. Winter rates are rock bottom, but double in summer. Rates double in summer. ❷

Cliff Crest B&B Inn 407 Cliff St ☎831/427-2609, ⊛www.cliffcrestinn.com. Plushly furnished 1887 Queen Anne–style Victorian home with only five guestrooms, set in lovely gardens at the top of Beach Hill. It's within walking distance of the boardwalk and rates include a full breakfast served in the conservatory, and afternoon sherry. ❺

Continental Inn 414 Ocean St ☎831/429-1221 or 1-800/343-6941, ⊛www.continentalinn.net. Top value for an off-the-bottom-rung motel. Comfortable if basic rooms and an easy walk to everything. ❷

Davenport Bed and Breakfast Inn 31 Davenport Ave, Davenport ☎831/425-1818 or 1-800/870-1817, ⊛www.swanton.com/BnB. This is the only accommodation in Davenport, and it's a funky inn, with slightly run-down ethnic decor, and rooms filled with brightly colored throws and mirrored pillows. ❺

Historic Sand Rock Farm 6901 Freedom Blvd, Aptos ☎831/688-8005, ⓦwww.sandrockfarm .com. Owned by a local chef, this five-room guesthouse has been lovingly restored (look for details like rare panels of curly redwood) and filled with arts and crafts antiques; the multi-course made-to-order breakfasts are lavish and filling. A secluded bolthole away from the beach and highly recommended. ❼

Pleasure Point Inn 2-3665 E Cliff Drive ☎408/469-6161 or 1-877/557-2567, ⓦwww .pleasurepointinn.com. A well-designed, hip B&B with clifftop views, a roof sundeck, and hot tub: rooms have built-in stereos, Jacuzzi baths, and all amenities. Highly recommended for those allergic to chintz. ❼

Sea and Sand Inn 201 W Cliff Drive ☎831/427-3400, ⓦwww.santacruzmotels.com. This small, upscale motel is well situated on the wharf, with great views over the bay; flowerboxes burst with color under every window and the subtle, floral rooms are lushly decorated. Larger groups can opt for one of the individual cottages with private patio and outdoor Jacuzzi. Complimentary breakfast. ❺

Hostels

HI-Pigeon Point Lighthouse Hostel Pescadero ☎650/879-0633, ⓦwww.norcalhostels .org/pigeon/. Located some 25 miles north of town, near Año Nuevo State Park, but well worth the effort for a chance to bunk down in the old lighthouse-keeper's quarters right on the point. Dorm beds $18 per person, plus $3 for non-HI members; more expensive private doubles or triples ($23–26 per person), and there's an excellent hot tub ($7 per person per half-hour, with two person minimum) hanging out over

the thundering surf. Office open 7.30–10am, 4.30–11pm.

HI-Santa Cruz Hostel 321 Main St ☎831/423-8304, ⓦwww.hi-santacruz.org. Well-situated hostel in a set of 1870s cottages just a couple of blocks from the beach. The atmosphere is informal but the place is closed during the day and is often booked up in advance. Members $18, non-members $21; office open 8–10am, 5–10pm for reservations.

Campgrounds

Big Basin Redwoods State Park 21600 Big Basin Way on Hwy-236, Boulder Creek ☎1-800/444-7275 or 831/338-8860, ⓦwww .santacruzstateparks.org. High up in the hills; sites with showers for $12, and numerous back-country sites for hikers and mountain bikers.

Henry Cowell Redwoods State Park 101 N Big Trees Park Rd, Felton ☎831/335-4598 or 1-800/444-7275, ⓦwww.santacruzstateparks .org. In the hills above town and UC Santa Cruz, in a redwood grove along the San Lorenzo River. Bus #35 serves the park, and sites cost $12 a night.

Manresa State Beach Campground 205 Manresa Rd, La Selva Beach ☎831/761-1795 or 1-800/444-7275, ⓦwww.santacruzstateparks.org. Isolated, tent-only site by a forested ravine that runs into the sand. Sites with showers $12.

New Brighton State Beach 1500 Park Ave, Capitola ☎831/464-6330 or 1-800/444-7275, ⓦwww.santacruzstateparks.org Three miles south of Santa Cruz on the edge of the beach-front village of Capitola, set on bluffs above a lengthy strand. Sites cost $12 a night, including hot showers.

The Town

Santa Cruz provides a sharp contrast to the upscale resort sophistication of Monterey Peninsula across the bay. This sleepy community of 45,000 residents, along with 10,000 students, is spread out at the foot of thickly wooded mountains along a clean, sandy shore. There's not a lot to see in the town, almost all of which is within a ten-minute walk of the beach, apart from the many blocks of Victorian wooden houses.

The sluggish San Lorenzo River wraps around the town center, two blocks east of **Pacific Garden Mall**, a landscaped, prettified, and pedestrianized stretch of Pacific Avenue that is Santa Cruz's main street, lined with bookstores, record and beachwear shops, and cafés. Disheveled hippies, trapped forever in their favorite decade, wander ceaselessly along the mall's length, brushing shoulders with wealthy shoppers who dodge occasionally into clothing and furniture stores. The homeless and the practically homeless cluster around park benches in the area, playing instruments, distributing literature, or simply dozing off.

One place that survived the massive 1989 earthquake which damaged a large portion of the town is the ornate brick-and-stone **Octagon Building**, 118 Cooper St, at the north end of Pacific Avenue. Completed in 1882 as the Santa Cruz Hall of Records, it now houses the museum store along with an exhibit or two from the adjacent **Museum of Art and History** at 705 Front St (Tues, Wed, Fri–Sun 11am–5pm, Thurs 11pm–7pm; $5; ☎831/429-1964, Ⓦwww .santacruzmah.org), which has a sprightly display on the region's checkered history. Several blocks away, past the clocktower fountain on Pacific and up the hill at 126 High St, fragments dating from the region's earlier Spanish colonial days are shown off in a restored army barracks, next to a scaled-down replica of **Mission Santa Cruz** (daily 9am–5pm; free; ☎831/426-5686, Ⓦwww.geocities .com/athens/aegean/7151/). The original adobe church, the sixteenth in the mission chain, was destroyed by an earthquake in 1857; the half-scale replica that stands on its site today was built in the twentieth century and is dwarfed by a large Gothic Revival church next door.

Between the town center and the beach, **Beach Hill** rises at the foot of Pacific Avenue, its slopes lined with some of Santa Cruz's finest turn-of-the-century homes, such as the striking Queen Anne–style house at 417 Cliff St, and the slightly odd structure around the corner at 912 3rd St, constructed out of the remains of a shipwreck.

The boardwalk and around

Standing out at the foot of the low-rise town in a slightly run-down neighborhood, the **Santa Cruz Boardwalk**, 40 Beach St (June–Aug open daily, fall and spring open Sat & Sun only, call for hours; closed Dec; $1.95–3.90 per ride, unlimited rides $25.95; ☎831/426-7433 or 831/423-5590, Ⓦwww .beachboardwalk.com), stretches half a mile along the sands, one of the last surviving beachfront amusement parks on the West Coast. Packed solid on weekends with teenagers on the prowl, most of the time it's a friendly funfair where barefoot hippies mix with farmers and their families. First opened in 1907 as a gambling casino, the elegant *Coconut Grove* at the west end recently underwent a $10million restoration, and the grand ballroom now hosts 1940s swing bands plus salsa and R&B combos, offering a change of pace from the raucous string of bumper cars, shooting galleries, log flume rides, and Ferris wheels that line up beside the wide beach, filled in with every sort of arcade game and test of skill. The newest ride is the 125-foot-tall Double Shot, which shoots riders in seconds from the ground to the top of its tower; but the star attraction is still the 80-year-old **Giant Dipper**, a wild wooden rollercoaster that's been ridden by more than 45 million people and is listed on the National Register of Historic Places; it often doubles for a Coney Island attraction in the movies.

Half a mile west of the boardwalk, the hundred-year-old wooden **Municipal Pier** juts out into the bay, crammed with fresh-fish shops, burger joints, and seafood restaurants, at the end of which people fish for crabs. You don't need a license and can rent tackle from one of the many bait shops. Just east of the boardwalk, across the river, the small **Santa Cruz City Museum of Natural History**, 1305 E Cliff Drive (Tues–Sun 10am–5pm; $2.50; ☎831/420-6115, Ⓦwww.santacruzmuseums.org), marked by a concrete whale, has concise displays describing local animals and sea creatures, and a brief description of the local Native American culture.

The beaches

The **beach** closest to town, along the boardwalk, is wide and sandy, with lots of volleyball courts and water that is warm enough for swimming in summer.

Not surprisingly, it can get crowded, rowdy, and dirty, so for a bit more peace and quiet, or to catch the largest waves, simply follow the coastline east or west of town to one of the smaller beaches hidden away at the foot of the cliffs: most are undeveloped and easily accessible.

From the City Museum, **East Cliff Drive** winds along the top of the bluffs, past many coves and estuaries. The nearest of the two coastal lagoons that border the volleyball courts of **Twin Lakes State Beach** half a mile east at Seventh Avenue (℡831/429-2850), was dredged and converted into a marina in the 1960s. The other, **Schwann Lake**, is still intact, its marshy wetlands serving as a refuge for sea birds and migrating waterfowl. Twin Lakes is often warmer than the surrounding area, thanks to its proximity to Schwann Lagoon; beyond here, you'll come to **Lincoln Beach** and good tide pools at **Corcoran Lagoon**, a half-mile on.

East Cliff Drive continues past popular surfing spots off rocky **Pleasure Point**, to the small beachfront resort of **Capitola**, its quiet conservativeness a sharp contrast with the alt-rock vibe of Santa Cruz. The town, three miles east of central Santa Cruz, began as a fishing village, living off the many giant tuna that populated the Monterey Bay, but soon became popular as a holiday spot, with its own railway line. The large wooden trestle of the now-disused railroad still dominates what is now a moneyed town, rising over the soft and peaceful sands of **Hooper Beach**, west of the small fishing pier. Capitola is especially attractive in late summer, when the hundreds of begonias – the town's main produce – are in bloom; at any time of year, the town is a relaxing escape from the rowdier Santa Cruz crowd. The **Chamber of Commerce**, 716G Capitola Ave (Mon–Fri 10am–4pm; ℡831/475-6522, ⓦwww.capitolachamber.com), has all the usual information.

A bit further east you'll come upon **Aptos** – originally named Awatos, meaning "where the waters meet," by Native Americans. It's the most conservative settlement in the area, even more so than Capitola, and was devastated in 1989 by the earthquake whose epicenter was close by in the forest of Nisene Marks. Otherwise, it's best known for the shortest parade on earth every Fourth of July and the remains of the *Palo Alto*, an experimental concrete ship which dropped anchor in 1919 to become a long-defunct restaurant and dance hall. The **Chamber of Commerce**, at 7605A Old Dominion Court (Mon–Fri 9am–5pm, Sat 10am–5pm, Sun 10am–4pm; ℡831/688-1467, ⓦwww .aptoschamber.com), has plenty of information and can help with accommodation reservations.

The beaches west of the Santa Cruz Boardwalk, along **West Cliff Drive**, see some of the biggest waves in California, not least at **Steamer Lane**, off the tip of Lighthouse Point beyond the Municipal Pier. Cowell Beach, just north of the municipal pier, is the best place to give surfing a try; Club Ed (℡831/464-0177, ⓦwww.club-ed.com), in the parking lot, will rent boards and assist with lessons. Otherwise, plenty of surfers also gather just off Pleasure Point Beach. The ghosts of surfers past are animated at the tiny redbrick **Surfing Museum** (Wed–Mon noon–4pm; $1 donation suggested; ℡831/420-6289, ⓦwww .santacruzsurfingmuseum.org), attached to the old lighthouse on the point; there are surfboards ranging from the twelve-foot redwood planks used by the early pioneers to modern, high-tech, multi-finned cutters. The best time to stop by is on a Friday, when Harry Mayo, a local surf pioneer, staffs the store and will happily reminisce about the early days of the California surf scene. A clifftop bicycle path runs two miles out from here to **Natural Bridges State Beach** (8am–dusk; $6 per car; ℡831/423-4609, ⓦwww .santsacruzstateparks.org), where waves have cut holes through the coastal cliffs, forming delicate arches in the remaining stone; three of the four bridges after which the park was named have since collapsed, leaving large stacks of stone sticking out of the surf. The park is also famous – like Pacific Grove further south – for its annual gathering of monarch butterflies, thousands of whom return each winter.

Above Santa Cruz: UCSC and the mountains

The **University of California at Santa Cruz**, on the hills above the town (served by SCMTD bus #1), is very much a product of the 1960s: students don't take exams or get grades, and the academic program stresses individual exploration of topics rather than rote learning. Architecturally, too, it's deliberately different. Its 2000-acre park-like campus is divided into small, autonomous colleges, where deer stroll among the redwood trees overlooking Monterey Bay – a decentralized plan drawn up under the then-governor Ronald Reagan, which cynics claim was intended as much to diffuse protests as to provide a peaceful backdrop for study. You can judge for yourself by taking one of the guided tours that start from the **visitor center** at the foot of campus (☎831/459-0111, ⓦadmissions.ucsc.edu/see/campusTour). If you don't have time to visit the entire campus, at least stop by the **UCSC Arboretum** (daily 9am–5pm; free; ☎831/427-2998, ⓦwww2.ucsc.edu/arboretum), world famous for its experimental cultivation techniques and its collections of plants from New Zealand, South Africa, Australia, and South America, all landscaped as they would be in their original habitats.

On the south side of the San Lorenzo River, three miles up Branciforte Drive from the center of town, there's a point within the woods where normal laws of gravity no longer apply. Here, trees grow at odd angles, pendulums swing counterclockwise and balls roll uphill – and it's all thanks to the **Mystery Spot** (frequent 30min tours; Memorial Day–Labor Day daily 9am–7pm; Sept–May daily 9am–5pm; $5; ☎831/423-8897, ⓦwww.mysteryspot.com). The tours of this freaky, inexplicable place are hokey, but amusing; guides lead groups up and down the hill, via a small toolshed that teeters on the edge of the hill, with seven different demonstrations of how the laws of physics seem not to apply here. Much of the amusement's down more to canny perspective tricks set up by the owners than metaphysical skullduggery; it's a diverting treat even so, as guides posit the various theories about what caused the Mystery Spot, including everything from extraterrestrial interference to excess carbon dioxide seeping up from the earth.

High up in the mountains that separate Santa Cruz from Silicon Valley and the San Francisco Bay Area, SCMTD bus #35 runs to the village of **Felton**, six miles north of Santa Cruz on Hwy-9, where the hundred-year-old **Roaring Camp and Big Trees Narrow Gauge Railroad** (summer daily 11am–3pm; rest of year departures on most weekdays at 11am, Sat & Sun at 10.30am, 11am, 12.15pm, 2pm & 2.30pm; parking $5, steam-train ride $18, beach-train ride $20; ☎831/335-4484, ⓦwww.roaringcamp.com), steams on a six-mile loop among the massive trees that cover the slopes of the **Henry Cowell Redwoods State Park** (dawn–dusk; $6 per car; ☎831/335-4598, ⓦwww.santacruzstateparks.org) along the San Lorenzo River gorge. From the same station the 1920s-era **Santa Cruz Big Trees and Pacific Railway Company** (see above) powers down to the boardwalk and back (or you can board there and ride up) in around two and a half hours.

Buses continue further up the mountains to the **Big Basin Redwoods State Park** (dawn–dusk; $6 per vehicle; ☎831/338-8860, ⓦwww.santacruzstateparks.org), an hour's ride from Santa Cruz, where acres of three-hundred-foot-tall redwood trees cover some 25 square miles of untouched wilderness, with excellent hiking and camping. A popular "Skyline-to-the-Sea" backpacking **trail** steps down through cool, moist canyons ten miles to the coast – fifteen miles north of Santa Cruz and less than ten from the former whaling town of **Davenport** – at **Waddell Creek Beach**, a favorite spot for watching world-class windsurfers negotiate the waves. From here, SCMTD bus #40 (twice daily) can take you back to town.

Eating

Restaurants in and around Santa Cruz are surprisingly diverse: from vegetarian cafés and all-American burger-and-beer bars to elegant dining options including a number of good seafood establishments on the wharf. The Wednesday-afternoon **Farmers' Market** downtown, popular with local hippies, is a good place to pick up fresh produce.

Bittersweet Bistro 787 Rio Del Mar Blvd, Rio Del Mar ☎831/662-9799. Delicately prepared gourmet fish and pasta dishes for $15–20. Don't miss the beautifully presented desserts. A few miles east of Santa Cruz along Hwy-1, but worth the trip.
Café Cruz 2621 41st Ave ☎831/476-3801. Tasty, reasonably priced Italian food in a Tuscan-inspired courtyard setting, inauspiciously located across from K-Mart. Delicious smoked chicken specials.
Charlie Hong Kong's 1141 Soquel Ave ☎831/426-5664. Small, pagoda-like hut with limited outdoor seating serving tasty, mostly vegetarian noodle dishes for under $5.
Ciao Bella 9127 Hwy-9, Ben Lomond ☎831/336-9221. A shrine to everything outlandish, this bar/restaurant a few miles from downtown is known more for its campily outrageous atmosphere than for its Italian-American food: the walls are covered with dolls' heads and there's a stripper-worthy pole on the cabaret stage. Great fun, even so, especially when the leather-short-sporting owner is holding court. Reservations essential.
Clouds Downtown 110 Church St ☎831/429-2000. Well-seasoned meats and Cal-Italian dishes in a pleasantly upbeat environment. The stuffed portobello mushrooms are especially good. Entrees go for $10–20.
Costa Brava 1222 Pacific Ave ☎831/425-7871. Innovative Latin American food with Italian and Californian influences. Exceptional atmosphere and portions for the price. There's another location at 505 Seabright Ave ☎831/423-8190.
The Crêpe Place 1134 Soquel Ave ☎831/429-6994. Thirty-year local institution that serves bargain stuffed crêpes with savory and sweet fillings – try the Crêpe Gatsby, stuffed with pesto, mushrooms, feta, mozzarella, and chicken. The flower-filled, tumbleweed back garden is a groovy place to lounge on a warm summer evening. Highly recommended.

Crow's Nest Santa Cruz Yacht Harbor, 2218 E Cliff Drive ☎831/476-4560. The modern American, fish-dominated menu here's tasty, if a little overpriced, but the real reason to come is for the spectacular views across the bay: eat dinner early and catch a fiery sunset. There's also a standard pub-style bar upstairs.
Davenport Restaurant and Cash Store in the *Davenport Inn*, 31 Davenport Ave, Davenport ☎831/426-4122. Rustic atmosphere in a peaceful coastal inn with undisturbed views of the coast and notoriously decadent cinnamon rolls.
El Palomar 1336 Pacific Ave ☎831/425-7575. Don't be put off by the location (on the ground floor of a historic building that was once a resort hotel and now houses government-subsidized apartments). This mid-range Mexican serves standard dishes, most with a fishy twist, for between $11–15 per entree.
Santa Cruz Coffee Roasting Co 1330 Pacific Ave ☎831/459-0100. Just the place to start the day, with an excellent range of coffees, by the bean or by the cup.
Saturn Café 145 Laurel St ☎831/429-8505. Wacky vegetarian diner – diners who wear wigs on Wed night receive 20 percent off their checks and there's a temporary tattoo vending machine next to the bar – set in a round building and decorated with red vinyl banquettes and Formica tables. There are burgers and sandwiches for $6.50–8, as well as specialties like vegan nachos with tofu ($6.95). It's open until 3am Sun–Thurs and until 4am Fri & Sat, so is a terrific option for late-night eats. Recommended.
Shadowbrook 1750 Wharf Rd, Capitola ☎831/475-1511. Very romantic, very upscale steak and seafood place, stepping down along the banks of a creek.
Taqueria Vallarta 1101A Pacific Ave ☎831/471-2655. It looks like a fast-food joint, but the food

is cooked to order and authentic, and they even serve rice and tangy tamarind drinks. Don't be shy to ask for plenty of tortilla chips with your order – the self-service salsa bar has a delicious range to try.

Theo's 3101 N Main St, Soquel ☎831/462-3657. Upscale, anniversary-friendly restaurant with an all-organic menu, crisp white tablecloths, and hushed but attentive staff. In summer, much of the ingredients come from the owner's garden out back, while all fish and meats are from sustainable sources. A guilt-free gourmet treat (entrees hover around $30) – just make sure to dress up.

Walnut Avenue Café 106 Walnut Ave ☎831/457-2307.This diner is a hearty local favorite serving massive, cheap breakfasts, and lunches (sandwiches $6.95–8), only a block from Pacific Avenue Mall.

Wired Wash Café 135 Laurel St ☎831/429-9473. Handy laundromat-cum-café open until midnight daily; the brushed-steel decor's industrial chic and the large noticeboard's a handy place to pick up information on mostly student-run nightlife or events.

Zoccoli's Deli 1534 Pacific Ave at Water St ☎831/423-1711. Old Italian deli serving up hearty food, including a minestrone that's a meal in itself: find it by the wafting smells of garlic and basil that snake down the sidewalk from its outdoor café. Mon–Sat 10am–6pm, longer hours in summer.

Bars and nightlife

Santa Cruz has the Central Coast's rowdiest **nightlife**, ranging from coffeehouses to bars and nightclubs where the music varies from surf-thrash to reggae to the rowdy rock of local resident Neil Young – sometimes all on the same dancefloor. Residents may wear tie-dye, but that doesn't mean they're not capable of breaking into fistfights. For hanging out, your best bet is the range of espresso bars and coffeehouses lining Pacific Avenue; otherwise, we've listed a range of nightlife options – check with *Good Times* for the latest listings or pick up flyers at Streetlight Records, 939 Pacific Ave (☎831/421-9200). The Rio Theatre, 1205 Soquel Ave (☎831/423-8209, ⓦwww.riotheatre.com), is a performance venue that now focuses on an eclectic selection of live bands rather than movies; for first-run foreign and indie films, head to the Del Mar (1124 Pacific Ave, ☎831/469-3220, ⓦwww .thenick.com) or Nickelodeon cinemas (210 Lincoln St ☎831/426-7500, ⓦwww.thenick.com).

99 Bottles of Beer 110 Walnut Ave ☎831/459-9999. This airy pub-style bar offers more than 40 beers on tap: the crowd's friendly and more mainstream than in many other local drinking holes.

Asti 715 Pacific Ave ☎831/423-7337. Divey, old-timers' cocktail lounge that now attracts a sizeable crowd of postmodern artsy types who enjoy its retro grittiness.

Caffè Pergolesi 418A Cedar St ☎831/426-1775. Fun, friendly coffeehouse in an old wooden house with a garden. Open until around midnight.

The Catalyst 1011 Pacific Ave ☎831/423-1336. The main venue for big-name touring artists and up-and-coming locals, this medium-sized club has something happening nearly every night. Usually 21 and over only; cover varies.

Henfling's Firehouse Taven 9450 Hwy-9, Ben Lomond ☎831/336-8811, ⓦwww.henflings.com. Softcore biker bar with good live blues and classic rock most nights – call or check online for performance schedules.

Kuumbwa Jazz Center 320 Cedar St ☎831/427-2227. The Santa Cruz showcase for traditional and modern jazz, in a friendly and intimate garden setting tucked back in a small alley. Mondays are usually the big-name nights, as performers like Chick Corea stop off on their way to San Francisco. Cover ranges from $1–15.

Lulu Carpenter's 1545 Pacific Ave ☎831/429-9804. Stylish yet cozy café, serving gooey cakes, coffees, and drinks, open from 6.30am until midnight. Housed in one of the few downtown buildings to survive the 1989 earthquake, it has a bar/lounge vibe, an open courtyard out back, and is lively most evenings.

Soif 105 Walnut Ave ☎831/423-2020. Newly opened young-professional hot spot, bathed in warm light with varnished wooden tables, serving small plates alongside more than fifty different wines by the glass.

Gay and lesbian Santa Cruz

Santa Cruz has now established itself as one of the country's hippest lesbian hangouts, and there's also a sizeable local gay population – local wags have taken to calling it Santa Cruise. For information, stop by the well-connected LGBT Diversity Center, 177 Walnut Ave (☎831/425-5422, ⓦwww .diversitycenter.org), or check in at Herland, 1014 Cedar St (☎831/429-6636, ⓦwww.herland.50megs.com), a lesbian/feminist store selling books and CDs that also has a large message board for events. Otherwise, grab one of the monthly free **newspapers** – either *La Gazette* for girls or *Manifesto*, which has listings for boys too.

Most local **accommodation** is gay-friendly, although the *Compassionflower Inn*, 216 Laurel St (☎831/466-0420, ⓦwww.compassionflowerinn.com; ⑤), in a gorgeously restored Victorian mansion is especially lovely; it's a self-proclaimed "Bed, Bud & Breakfast" that allows those with doctors' approval to light up on the premises. As for **nightlife**, there are two main options: *Blue Lagoon*, 923 Pacific Ave (☎831/423-7117, ⓦwww.thebluelagoon.com), for boys, where good DJs spin techno and hip-hop on weekends, and *Club Dakota*, 1209 Pacific Ave (☎831/454-9030), for girls and a few guys, which is open Monday to Friday 4pm to 2am, Saturday to Sunday 2pm to 2am (21 and over, and bring ID); *Saturn Café* (see p.550) is also a popular gay and lesbian hangout. Further afield, the camp disco extravaganza and drag show at *Franco's Norma Jean Club*, 10639 Merritt St in Castroville (☎831/633-2090 or 831/758-9266, ⓦwww .francosbar.com), named in honor of Marilyn Monroe, also attracts gay locals and visitors from around the area.

The coast north to San Francisco

The **Año Nuevo State Reserve**, New Year's Creek Road (8am–sunset; $6 per car; recorded info ☎650/879-0227 or office 650/879-2025, ⓦwww.parks .ca.gov), 25 miles north of Santa Cruz, was named by the explorer Vizcaíno, who sailed past on New Year's Day 1603. It's a beautiful spot to visit at any time of year, and in winter you shouldn't miss the chance to see one of nature's most bizarre spectacles – the mating rituals of the Northern Elephant Seal. These massive, ungainly creatures, fifteen feet long and weighing up to three tons, gather on the rocks and sand dunes to fight for a mate. The male's distinctive, pendulous nostrils aid him in his noisy honking, which is how he attracts the females; their blubbery forms are capable of diving deeper than any other mammal, to depths of over 4500ft. Obligatory three-hour **tours** (reservation line Mon–Fri 9am–5pm, Sat & Sun 9am–3pm ☎1-800/444-4445; $5) are organized during the breeding season (Dec 15–Mar 31); throughout the year you're likely to see at least a few, dozing in the sands; note, too, that the abundance of seals also attracts a hefty chunk of hungry great-white sharks so you might spot them, too. See "Contexts", p.873, for more on the elephant seal's mating habits, and on other coastal creatures.

Five miles north of Año Nuevo, Gazos Creek Road heads inland three miles to **Butano State Park** (8am–sunset; $6 per car; ☎650/879-2040, ⓦwww .parks.ca.gov), which has five square miles of redwood trees, views out over the Pacific, and **camping** among the redwoods for $18 (reserve through ParkNet ☎1-800/444-7275). Another two miles north along Hwy-1, and fifty miles south of the Golden Gate Bridge, the beginning of the San Francisco Peninsula

is marked by the **Pigeon Point Lighthouse** (℡650/879-2120, Ⓦwww.parks
.ca.gov) and the adjacent **hostel** (see p.546), where you can spend the night
in the old lighthouse-keeper's quarters and relax in a hot tub, cantilevered out
over the rocks. Pigeon Point took its name from the clipper ship *Carrier Pigeon*
that broke up on the rocks off the point, one of many shipwrecks that led to
the construction of the lighthouse in the late nineteenth century; note that
the lighthouse itself is currently closed due to structural problems, but the surrounding park and facilities are still accessible.

The cargo of one of these wrecked ships inspired residents of the nearby fishing village of **Pescadero**, a mile inland on Pescadero Road, literally to "paint
the town," using the hundreds of pots of white paint that were washed up on
the shore. The two streets of the small village are still lined with white wooden
buildings, and the descendants of the Portuguese whalers who founded the
town keep up another tradition, celebrating the **Festival of the Holy Ghost**
every year, six weeks after Easter, with a lively and highly ritualized parade.
Pescadero is also well known as one of the better places to **eat** on the entire
coast, with the excellent *Duarte's* restaurant, 202 Stage Rd (℡650/879-0464),
serving staples like deep-fried calamari and Pacific oysters; and, at the other
end of the price scale, *Los Amigos* (℡650/879-0232), a celebrated fast-food
Mexican restaurant in the gas station on the corner.

Half Moon Bay is really the next place of note north along the coast, and is
covered in the following chapter.

Travel details

Trains

LA to: Amtrak's Coast Starlight leaves at 9.30am
for Oakland (1 daily; 10hr 45min; a shuttle bus
connects to San Francisco); Salinas (1 daily; 8hr
15min); San Jose (1 daily; 9hr 50min); San Luis
Obispo (3 daily; 5hr 20min); Santa Barbara
(1 daily; 2hr 30min); and continues on through
Sacramento, Chico, Redding, through Oregon to
Seattle.
One train a day leaves Oakland at 9.30am on the
return route.

Buses

All buses are Greyhound unless otherwise stated.
LA to: Salinas (8 daily; 8hr); San Francisco

(19 daily; 8–12hr; also one Green Tortoise per
week in each direction along the coast); San
Luis Obispo (7 daily; 4hr 45min); Santa Barbara
(11 daily; 3hr 10min); Santa Cruz (6 daily; 10hr
30min).
Oakland to: Santa Cruz (4 daily; 2 hr).
San Francisco to: LA (19 daily; 8–12hr); Monterey
(6 daily; 4hr); Sacramento (21 daily; 2hr 20min);
Salinas (10 daily; 2hr 45min); San Luis Obispo
(6 daily; 6hr); Santa Barbara (6 daily; 7hr); Santa
Cruz (4 daily; 2hr 40min); San Jose (16 daily; 1hr
30min).
San Jose to: Santa Cruz (4 daily; 1hr).

8

San Francisco and the Bay Area

Highlights

✳ **Cable cars** Famous for a good reason, these glorious old trams offer both irresistible photo opportunities and a leisurely way to avoid climbing downtown San Francisco's heftiest hills. See p.576

✳ **Jackson Square** Time-travel back to see how San Francisco looked before the devastating fire and earthquake of 1906. See p.581

✳ **Tien Hou temple, Chinatown** Festooned with gold and red lanterns, cloudy with heady incense, this temple is a precious relic of old Chinatown. See p.584

✳ **Valencia Street** Check out the hipster artery of the Mission, where Anglo and Latino cultures collide. See p.602

✳ **Telegraph Avenue, Berkeley** This lively strip gives you the chance to check out a dazzling array of politically subversive stalls, book and music stores, and cafés. See p.659

✳ **Whale watching, Point Reyes** The lighthouse at the westernmost point of the Point Reyes National Seashore is a great spot to glimpse migrating gray whales. See p.701

△ Victorian house, Haight-Ashbury

San Francisco and the Bay Area

One of the prettiest and most liberal cities in the US – it certainly has had more platitudes heaped upon it than any other – **SAN FRAN-CISCO** is in serious danger of being clichéd to death. In the last twenty-five years, though, the city has undergone a steady transition: the iconoclasm that made it famous has been glossed with a palpable air of widespread affluence that's created a swanky, high-end town. One by one, the central neighborhoods have been smartened up, with poorer families edged out into the suburbs, leaving only a couple of areas that could still be considered transitional. Ironically, some of the groups who began on the margins, like the gay and lesbian community, are now wealthy and influential – even a little conservative.

For all the change, however, San Francisco remains an outdoorsy, surprisingly small city whose people pride themselves on being the cultured counterparts to their cousins in LA, as if this place were the last bastion of civilization on the lunatic fringe of America. A steadfast rivalry exists between the two cities: San Franciscans like to think of themselves as less obsessed with money, less riddled with status than those in the south – a rare kind of inverted snobbery, which Angelenos sniffily dismiss and which you'll encounter almost immediately. But San Francisco has its own narcissism, rooted in the sheer physical aspect of the place. Downtown streets lean upwards on impossible gradients to reveal stunning views of the city, the Bay, and beyond. It has a romantic weather pattern, as blanket fogs roll in unexpectedly to envelop the city in mist, adding a surreal quality to an already unique appearance.

This is not, however, the California of monotonous blue skies – the temperatures rarely exceed the seventies, and even during summer they can drop much lower, when consistent and heavy fogs muscle in on the city and the area as a whole. Autumn is the best time to visit, as warm temperatures and cloudless skies fill the days of September and October.

San Francisco proper occupies just 48 hilly square miles at the tip of a slender peninsula, almost perfectly centered on the California coast. But its metropolitan area sprawls out far beyond these narrow confines, east and north across to the far sides of the Bay, and south back down the coastal strip. This is the **BAY AREA**, one of the most rapidly growing regions in the US: less than 750,000 people live in the actual city, but there are nearly seven million in the Bay Area as a whole. It's something of a mixed bag. In the East Bay, across one of the two great bridges that connect San Francisco with its hinterland, are industrial **Oakland** and the radical locus of **Berkeley**; while to the south lies the gloating new wealth of **the Peninsula**, which has earned the tag of "Silicon Valley" thanks to its multi-billion-dollar computer industries, wiping out the agriculture which still predominated as recently as thirty years ago. Across the Golden Gate Bridge to the north, **Marin County** contains some of the Bay Area's

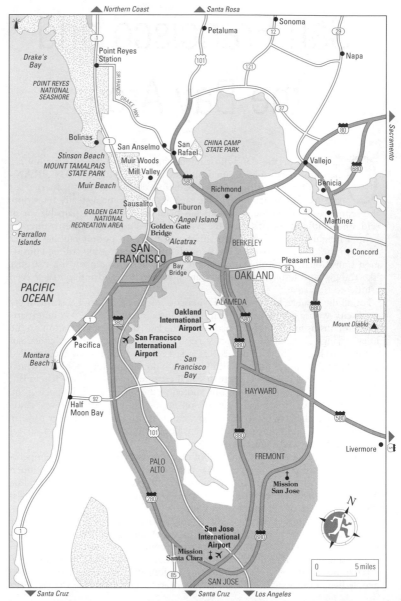

wealthiest suburbs, its woody, leafy landscape and rugged coastline a bucolic – though in places very chic – harbinger of the delights of California's earthy northern coast. Specific practical information on the different Bay Area locales is given within the various regional accounts.

San Francisco

A compact and highly approachable place of some four dozen or so hills by the Bay, San Francisco is one of the few US cities in which you can survive comfortably without a car. Indeed, given how expensive and time-consuming parking can be – not to mention how agreeable its year-round climate – walking is the ideal daytime mode for taking in the city's world-renowned museums, stately Victorian homes, sophisticated and historic neighborhoods, and stirring hilltop vistas. After dark, San Francisco is quite safe for visitors exercising reasonable caution; it's best known for its astonishing assortment of first-class restaurants and its vibrant nightlife, both gay and straight.

Some history

The original inhabitants of San Francisco were **Ohlone Indians**, who lived in some 35 villages spread out around the Bay. In 1776, **Mission Dolores**, the sixth in the chain of Spanish Catholic missions that ran the length of California, was established and harsh mission life, combined with the spread of European diseases, killed off the natives within a few generations. Mexicans took over from the Spanish in the early 1820s, but their hold was tenuous, and the area finally came under American rule after the **Bear Flag Revolt** of 1846, which took place a few miles north in Sonoma. The bloodless coup was supported by local land-owning *alcaldes* (a hybrid of judge and mayor), who recognized the potential of huge profits. The coup brought US Marines, sailing on the *USS Portsmouth*, into the San Francisco Bay that year, prompting one soldier, John Fremont, to christen its spectacular entrance the "**Golden Gate**." The Marines docked their boat at the tiny town plaza founded in 1835 by British sailor William Richardson and renamed it **Portsmouth Square**, raising an American flag and claiming the city for the United States. The following year, the hamlet known as Yerba Buena was rechristened San Francisco, honoring the dying wish of Father Junípero Serra, the Franciscan founder of Mission Dolores.

Just over ten years later, in 1848, San Francisco's population exploded when pioneer Sam Brannan bounded across Portsmouth Square waving bottles of gold dust he claimed came from the Sierra foothills and ignited the **Gold Rush**. Within a year, fifty thousand pioneers had arrived from all over the country as well as overseas, especially China, turning San Francisco from a muddy village and wasteland of dunes into a thriving supply center and transit town. By the time the **transcontinental railroad** was completed in 1869, San Francisco was a lawless, rowdy boomtown of bordellos and drinking dens, something the monied elite – who hit it big on the much more dependable

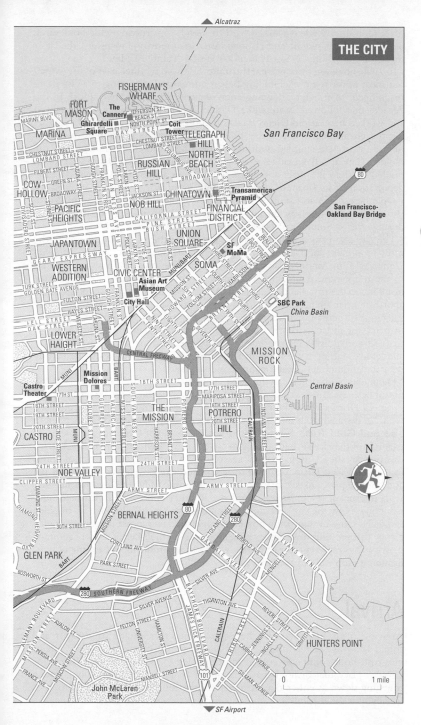

▲ Alcatraz

THE CITY

San Francisco Bay

FISHERMAN'S
WHARF

FORT
MASON
The Cannery
Ghirardelli
Square
MARINA

JEFFERSON ST
BEACH ST
NORTH POINT ST
BAY STREET
Coit
Tower
TELEGRAPH
HILL
CHESTNUT STREET
LOMBARD STREET
NORTH
BEACH
RUSSIAN
HILL

MARINE BLVD
CHESTNUT STREET
FILBERT STREET
COW
HOLLOW
GREEN ST
BROADWAY
PACIFIC
HEIGHTS
JACKSON ST
NOB HILL
CHINATOWN
Transamerica
Pyramid
CALIFORNIA STREET
PINE STREET
BUSH STREET

San Francisco–
Oakland Bay Bridge

8

JAPANTOWN
UNION
SQUARE
SF
MoMa
GEARY EXPRESSWAY
WESTERN
ADDITION
SOMA
CIVIC CENTER
Asian Art
Museum
City Hall

TURK STREET
GOLDEN GATE AVENUE
FULTON STREET
HAYES STREET
FELL STREET
OAK STREET
LOWER
HAIGHT

SBC Park
China Basin

Central Basin

Castro
Theater
Mission
Dolores
CENTRAL FREEWAY
16TH STREET
17TH STREET
MARIPOSA STREET
18TH STREET
THE
MISSION
POTRERO
HILL
MISSION
ROCK

CASTRO
19TH STREET
20TH STREET
NOE VALLEY
24TH STREET
CLIPPER STREET
ARMY STREET

N

BERNAL HEIGHTS
GLEN PARK
30TH STREET
CORTLAND AVE
PARK STREET
BOSWORTH ST
280 SOUTHERN FREEWAY

HUNTERS POINT

John McLaren
Park

0   1 mile

▼ *SF Airport*

silver Comstock Lode – worked hard to mend, constructing wide boulevards, parks, a cable-car system, and elaborate Victorian redwood mansions, the latter replacing the whores as San Francisco's famed "Painted Ladies."

In 1906, however, a massive **earthquake**, followed by three days of fire, wiped out most of the town. Rebuilding began immediately, resulting in a city more magnificent than before, drawing anew writers, artists, and free spirits. In the decades that followed, writers like Dashiell Hammett and Jack London lived and worked here, as did Diego Rivera and other WPA-sponsored artists. During the Great Depression of the 1930s, San Francisco's position as the nexus of trade with Asia, coupled with its engineering projects – including both the Golden Gate and Bay bridges – lessened the agonies of the Depression for its residents. While the strict anti-immigration laws against the Chinese and the deportation of its Japanese citizens during World War II remains in memory, people here prefer to canonize the exploits of the Beat Generation in North Beach and Cow Hollow during the Fifties and the message of the Hippies during 1967's "Summer of Love" in the Haight-Ashbury district.

The city also prides itself on being the **gay capital** of the world: one of the most prominent local Democratic politicians is openly gay former stand-up comedian Tom Ammiano, who narrowly lost the last local mayoral election to the toothy and photogenic Gavin Newsom (Newsom himself then made headlines as the first elected official in America to legalize gay weddings, albeit abortively). San Francisco basks in its reputation as a liberal oasis and a model of tolerance – there's nowhere you won't see gay couples walking proudly hand in hand, for instance. But it also struggles with a certain smugness thanks to that self-consciously open-minded attitude: the local mantra seems to be "live and let live" rather than "live with and let live," and different groups are tribally separated along lines of race, gender, and sexuality.

Despite its boldface fame as the hub of counterculture, San Francisco has always meant business and wealth, evinced today by a walk through the skyscraper-filled Financial District. Exquisite restaurants, new art museums, "shopping-entertainment" in designer malls, and the further gentrification of neighborhoods point to a **second Gold Rush**. San Francisco was the cradle of Internet mania, another example of the city's eye for the main chance – for a while many locals worried that one day they'd live in "SanFrancisco.com," a bedroom community of bistros for Silicon Valley. Tenancy rates throughout the city hovered at 99 percent full and housing prices rocketed: the once shabby South of Market area was bursting with Internet start-ups, at least until the Internet bubble itself burst and most went bust. Now, the city's reclaiming a calmer sense of self, although it's troubled more and more by a growing homeless population and local bureaucratic inefficiency that prevents much progress being made on their behalf. Newly anointed mayor Newsom has promised to battle both these problems, but at time of publication it's too early to tell what progress he'll make.

Arrival

Arriving in San Francisco isn't the trafficky mess that finding your way in and round Los Angeles for the first time can prove. Of course, as in every major city, rush-hour commuter congestion does clog local roadways, but San Francisco's a place that firmly believes in public transport; and especially if you're touching down at either Bay Area airport, the journey into the city proper is usually quick and painless.

By plane

All international and most domestic flights arrive at **San Francisco International Airport** (SFO), located about fifteen miles south of the city (☎1-800/435-9736 or 650/821-8211, ⊛www.flysfo.com). There are several ways of getting into town from here, each of which is clearly signed from the baggage-reclaim areas. The best option's the newly completed BART link: the effortless thirty-minute journey whisks you from the airport to the heart of downtown for only $4.95 (⊛www.bart.gov) and leaves every 15–20 minutes. The cheapest option into town, though, is to take a San Mateo County Transit (SamTrans) **bus** (☎1-800/660-4287 or 510/817-1717), which leave every half-hour from the upper level of the airport: the #KX express ($3.50) takes around 25 minutes to reach the Transbay Terminal downtown, while the slower #292 ($1.25) stops frequently and takes nearly an hour. On the #KX, you're allowed only one small carry-on bag; on the #292, you can bring as much as you want provided you can carry it onto the bus yourself. Otherwise, the SFO Airporter bus ($10) makes pick-ups outside each baggage-claim area every fifteen minutes; the only snag is that it just serves major hotels downtown – look for signs saying 'Airporter' on the lower Arrivals level. The Supershuttle, American Airporter Shuttle, and Yellow Airport Shuttle **minibuses** depart every five minutes from the upper level of the circular road and take passengers to any city-center destination for around $12 a head. Be ruthless – competition for these and the several other companies running shuttle services is fierce and lines nonexistent. They're signposted on the lower Arrivals level as 'Door to Door Vans'. **Taxis** from the airport cost $25–30 (plus tip) for any downtown location, more for East Bay and Marin County – definitely worth it if you're in a group or too tired to care. If you're planning to drive, take the AirTrain's Blue line shuttle train (operates 24 hours; free) to the **car rental** agencies' depots. Driving from SFO, head north on gritty US-101 or northwest on prettier I-280 for the 20–30-minute drive downtown.

Several domestic airlines fly into **Oakland International Airport** (OAK; see p.643 for details), across the Bay. As close to downtown San Francisco as SFO, OAK is efficiently connected with the city by the $2 AirBART shuttle bus, which drops you at the Coliseum BART station. Get on BART and San Francisco's downtown stops are fifteen minutes away ($2.75). The third regional airport, **San Jose International** (SJO), also serves the Bay Area, but should only be considered if you plan to begin your stay in Silicon Valley. Fares in and out of SJO are comparable to the airports north and public transportation to the city is inconvenient.

By bus, train, and car

All of San Francisco's **Greyhound** services use the Transbay Terminal at 425 Mission St, near the Embarcadero BART station in the South of Market (SoMa) district. Green Tortoise buses stop behind the Transbay Terminal on First and Natoma. Amtrak **trains** stop across the Bay in Oakland, from where free shuttle buses run across the Bay Bridge to the Transbay Terminal, or you can take BART. A more efficient route is to get off the train at Richmond, where a transfer to the nearby BART can get you into San Francisco more quickly. Although technically closer to San Francisco, don't get off at the stop before Oakland, Emeryville, as consistent public transportation to the city doesn't exist (though you can hail a cab here).

From the east, the main route **by car** into San Francisco is I-80, which runs via Sacramento all the way from Chicago. I-5, fifty miles east of San Francisco, serves as the main north–south route, connecting Los Angeles with Seattle. From I-5, I-580 takes you to the Bay Area. US-101 also runs the length of California from north to south, but if you have time and a tolerance of winding roads, take Hwy-1, the Pacific Coast Highway, which traces the edge of California.

Information

The **San Francisco Visitor Information Center**, on the lower level of Hallidie Plaza at the end of the cable-car line on Market Street (Mon–Fri 9am–5pm, Sat & Sun 9am–3pm, closed Sun Nov–April; ☎415/283-0177 or recorded information line ☎415/283-0177, ⊛www.sfvisitor.org), has free maps of the city and the Bay Area, oodles of pamphlets on hotels and restaurants, and can help with lodging and travel plans. Its free *San Francisco Book* and *Visitors Planning Guide* provide detailed, if somewhat selective, information about accommodation, entertainment, exhibitions, and stores. The center also sells the **City Pass** ($40; ⊛www.citypass.net), a half-price ticket valid for entry to the Exploratorium, California Palace of the Legion of Honor, Steinhart Aquarium and Academy of Sciences, Asian Art Museum, Museum of Modern Art, and passage on a Blue and Gold Fleet San Francisco Bay cruise – all that, plus a free week's pass on MUNI transit (see opposite).

The city's several **newspapers** are indispensable sources of information. Two dailies have competed for decades – the *Chronicle* (⊛www.sfgate.com; 50¢) and *Examiner* (free). Their recent history has been turbulent: the Hearst Corporation wanted to buy the *Chronicle* but was only allowed to do so by divesting itself of the long-held *Examiner*, which was sold to an unpopular local family, the Fangs, who had little experience running a high-profile daily. The paper sputtered on for months, eventually morphing into a thin freesheet with a

---

Festivals in San Francisco

Like most major cities, San Francisco has a huge range of special festivals – the biggest of which are detailed below (for gay-and-lesbian-geared events, see box, p.635). Note that hotels and hostels will book up quickly during most of these festivals, especially Pride, so plan ahead.

Chinese New Year (end of Jan or early Feb) A week-long celebration around the lunar New Year, which culminates in the Golden Dragon Parade headed by the namesake 75-foot-long dragon (☎415/982-3000, ⊛www.chineseparade.com).

Cherry Blossom Festival (Late April) The normally sedate Japantown's transformed into a riot of life and rowdy parades for two consecutive weekends; it culminates in a parade from Civic Center (☎415/563-2313, ⊛www.nccbs.org).

Bay to Breakers (Third Sun in May) Only in San Francisco: this kooky, campy fun-run is a 12km footrace from the Embarcadero to Ocean Beach. But it's the costumes, not the contest, that really count here – it's also known for a sizeable contingent of nude joggers (☎415/359-2800).

Hallowe'en (Oct 31) Wild fun is guaranteed during this holiday, despite attempts by the powers-that-be to calm down its riotous edge; dress up and watch the parade along Market Street – or better still, just hang out in the Castro for the evening to catch the best of the stuff-strutting (☎415/826-1401).

tabloid sensibility sniffed at by many locals. It's recently been sold yet again, this time to financier Philip Anschutz who – against most locals' expectations – has pumped money into the paper to try to return it to its former glories. Only time will tell if he'll be successful; in the meanwhile, for the most comprehensive arts and food listings, check the *Chronicle*'s Sunday edition supplement, *Datebook* (also known as the "Pink Pages") which contains previews and reviews for the coming week. The city's alternative press picks up the slack the more conservative dailies leave behind, resulting in two fine free weekly papers, *The Bay Guardian* (ⓦwww.sfbg.com) and *SF Weekly* (ⓦwww.sfweekly.com), available from racks around town. Both offer more in-depth features on local life and better music and club listings than the dailies. Another reliable source is the free monthly *Paper City* – great for trendier types and also available from streetside boxes. **Online**, check out ⓦwww.sfstation.com for the best of the many websites that cover the Bay Area.

City transportation

San Francisco is a rare American city where you don't need a car to see everything. In fact, given the chronic shortage of parking downtown, horrible traffic, and zealous meter maids, going without one makes more sense. The **public transportation** system, MUNI, though much maligned by locals for its unpredictable schedule, covers every neighborhood inexpensively via a system of cable cars, buses, and trolleys. **Cycling** is a good option, though you'll need stout legs to tackle those hills. **Walking** the compact metropolis is still the best bet, with each turn revealing surprises.

MUNI

The city's public transportation is run by the San Francisco Municipal Railway, or **MUNI** (☏415/673-6864, ⓦwww.sfmuni.com). A comprehensive network of buses, trolley buses, and cable cars run up and over the city's hills, while the underground trains become streetcars when they emerge from the downtown metro system to split off and serve the suburbs. On buses and trains the flat fare (correct change only) is $1.25; with each ticket you buy, ask for a free transfer – good for another two rides on a train or bus in any direction within ninety minutes to two hours of purchase. Note that cable cars cost $3 one way, and do not accept transfers. The best option if you're in town for a while is to buy a MUNI passport pass, available in one-day, three-day, and seven-day denominations ($9, $15, $20). It's valid for unlimited travel on the MUNI system and BART stations (see below) within the city limits. A fast pass costs $45 for a full calendar month and also offers unlimited travel within the city limits. MUNI trains run throughout the night on a limited service, except those on the M-Ocean View line, which stop around 1am. Most buses run all night, but services are greatly reduced after midnight. For more information, pick up the handy MUNI map ($2) from the Visitor Information Center or bookstores.

BART and other train services

Along Market Street downtown, MUNI shares station concourses with **BART** (Bay Area Rapid Transit; ☏415/817-1717 or 510/465-BART, ⓦwww.bart.gov),

Main MUNI routes

Useful bus routes

#5 From the Transbay Terminal, west alongside Haight-Ashbury and Golden Gate Park to the ocean.

#7 From the Ferry Terminal (Market Street) to the end of Haight Street and to Golden Gate Park.

#15 From Third Street (SoMa) to Pier 39, Fisherman's Wharf, via the Financial District and North Beach.

#20 (Golden Gate Transit) From Civic Center to the Golden Gate Bridge.

#22 From the Marina up Pacific Heights and north on Fillmore.

#28 & #29 From the Marina through the Presidio, north through Golden Gate Park, the Richmond, and Sunset.

#30 From the CalTrain depot on Third Street, north to Ghirardelli Square, via Chinatown and North Beach, and out to Chestnut Street in the Marina district.

#38 From Geary Street via Civic Center, west to the ocean along Geary Boulevard through Japantown and the Richmond, ending at Cliff House.

MUNI train lines

MUNI F-Market Line Restored vintage trolleys from around the world run downtown from the Transbay Terminal up Market Street and into the heart of the Castro. The new extension along the refurbished Embarcadero to Fisherman's Wharf is one of MUNI's most popular routes.

MUNI J-Church Line From downtown to Mission and the edge of the Castro.

MUNI K-Ingleside Line From downtown through the Castro to Balboa Park.

MUNI L-Taraval Line From downtown west through the Sunset to the zoo and Ocean Beach.

MUNI M-Ocean View From downtown west by the Stonestown Galleria shopping center and San Francisco State University.

MUNI N-Judah Line From the Caltrain station, past the new baseball stadium, along South Beach to downtown west through the Inner Sunset to Ocean Beach.

Cable car routes

Powell-Hyde From Powell Street/Market along Hyde through Russian Hill to Fisherman's Wharf.

Powell-Mason From Powell Street/Market along Mason via Chinatown and North Beach to Fisherman's Wharf.

California Street From the foot of California Street at Robert Frost Plaza in the Financial District through Nob Hill to Polk Street.

which is the fastest way to get to the East Bay – including downtown Oakland and Berkeley – and outer suburbs east and south of San Francisco. Tickets aren't cheap ($1.10–4.70 depending on how far you ride), but the trains feature four routes that follow a fixed schedule, usually arriving every ten minutes. Trains run from 4am weekdays, 6am Saturdays, 8am Sundays until midnight, and tickets can be purchased on the station concourse; save your ticket after entering the station, as it is also needed when exiting the train. Free schedules are available at BART stations.

The CalTrain commuter railway (depot at Fourth and Townsend, South of Market) links San Francisco south to San Jose; call ☏ 1-800/660-4287 or log onto ⊛www.caltrain.com for schedules and fares.

Driving: taxis and cars

Taxis ply the streets and, while you can flag them down (especially downtown), finding one can be difficult. The granting of more taxi licenses is a contentious issue in San Francisco, with many arguing that the streets are clogged enough. Phoning around, try Veterans (℡415/552-1300) or Yellow Cab (℡415/626-2345, ✆www.yellowcabsf.com). Fares (within the city) begin with a fee of $1.70 to start the meter and $1.80 per mile thereafter, plus the customary fifteen-percent tip.

The only reason to **rent a car** in San Francisco is if you want to explore the Bay Area, the Wine Country, or the landscape north or south along the coast. Driving in town, pay attention to San Francisco's attempts to control downtown traffic: the posted speed limit is 30mph, speeding through a yellow light is illegal, and pedestrians waiting in a crosswalk have the right-of-way. In addition, it's almost impossible to make a left turn anywhere in the city center, meaning you'll have to get used to looping the block, making three rights instead of one left. Cheap, available parking is even rarer than a left-turn signal, but it's worth playing by the rules: police issue multiple tickets for illegally parked vehicles and won't hesitate to tow your car if it's violating any posted laws. Downtown, plenty of garages exist, most advertising rates beginning at $2.50 per fifteen minutes. Take care to observe the San Francisco law of curbing wheels – turn wheels into the curb if the car points downhill and away from the curb if it points up; violators are subject to a $20 ticket. Bridge tolls are collected only when entering San Francisco by car: the Golden Gate Bridge toll costs $5, while the Bay Bridge runs $3.

Cycling and rollerblading

Cycling is a great way to experience San Francisco. Golden Gate Park, the Marina and Presidio, and Ocean Beach all have great, paved trails and some off-road routes. And throughout the city, marked bike routes – with lanes – direct riders to all major points of interest, but note that officials picked the routes for their lack of car traffic, not for the easiest ride. Blazing Saddles, which rents bicycles, has several locations (℡415/202-8888, ✆www.blazingsaddlessanfrancisco.com or ✆www.bikethebridge.com) – two of the most convenient are 1095 Columbus Ave at Francisco, North Beach, and Pier 41. Rental for bikes is $7 an hour, $28 a day. Another option, with similar rates, is Bike & Roll, 734 Lombard St at Columbus Avenue (℡415/771-8735, ✆www.bikerental.com). For a tranquil trek through undeveloped nature, head north over the Golden Gate Bridge (the western side is reserved solely for bikes) to either Angel Island (see p.699) or into the Marin Headlands for a series of off-road trails along cliffs, ocean, and into valleys (see p.693).

San Francisco's roads and pathways aren't rollerblade-ready, but there are a few good **places to skate** around the Marina and, to a lesser extent, in Golden Gate Park. On Sunday, most of Golden Gate Park's roads are closed to autos, bringing out hordes of bladers. Skaters also use the flat sidewalk along Ocean Beach, and the good trails around Lake Merced, although both are away from the action of downtown. Skates on Haight, 1818 Haight St at Stanyan, Haight-Ashbury (℡415/752-8375, ✆www.skatesonhaight.com), rents both rollerblades and rollerskates for $6 an hour and $24 overnight. San Francisco's many plazas are more welcoming to **skateboarding**, even if local law conspires to ban thrashers from city limits.

Organized tours

One way to orient yourself is an **organized tour**. Gray Line Tours (☎415/558-9400 or 1-888/428-6937, ⓦwww.graylinesanfrancisco.com), takes three-and-a-half fairly tedious hours to tour the city for $38 a head; there are also deals that combine city stops with Muir Woods, Alcatraz, or even Monterey, the Wine Country, or Yosemite in a day. Considerably more exciting is the El Camión Mexicano, the Mexican Bus Tour (call for itineraries and reservations; ☎415/546-3747, ⓦwww.mexicanbus.com) through the Mission district, which takes in local Mexican restaurants and salsa clubs for drinking and dancing, for $38.

Walking tours

A great way to get to know the quieter, historical side of San Francisco is to take a **walking tour**. The better ones keep group size small and are run by natives who truly love their subject matter and jobs. Some, like those sponsored by the library, are free. Reservations are recommended for all walks. The Visitor Information Center can give you a full list of available walks – every neighborhood has at least one – but among those you should consider are:

City Guides (☎415/557-4266, ⓦwww.sfcityguides.com). A terrific free series sponsored by the library covering every San Francisco neighborhood, as well as themed walks on topics ranging from the Gold Rush to the Beat Generation; its wide-ranging subject matter means you'll often be trekking alongside locals instead of fellow tourists. Schedule varies – call for details.

Cruisin' the Castro (☎415/550-8110, ⓦwww.webcastro.com/castrotour). The Grand Dame of San Francisco walks, Ms. Trevor Hailey, leads you through her beloved neighborhood and explains how and why San Francisco became the gay capital of the world. It's as much a history lesson as a sightseeing tour. $45 per person, including lunch at *Firewood* restaurant.

Haight-Ashbury Flower Power Walking Tour (Tues & Sat 9.30am; ☎415/863-1621, ⓦwww.hippiegourmet.com). Learn about the Human Be-in, Grateful Dead, Summer of Love, and also the Haight's distant past as a Victorian resort destination. $15 per person.

HobNob Tours (Mon–Fri 10am & 1.30pm; ☎650/851-1123; ⓦwww.hobnobtours.com). Terrific, information-crammed ramble round the haunts of Silver Kings and Robber Barons, mostly in and around Grace Cathedral. Highly recommended. $30 per person.

Mangia! North Beach (Sat 10am; ☎415/925-9013, ✉gaw@sbcglobal.net). Culinary tour of North Beach's Italian nooks, run by larger-than-life local food writer Grace-Ann Walden. $70 including lunch.

Mission Mural Walk (Sat & Sun 1.30pm; ☎415/285-2287, ⓦwww.precitaeyes.org). Two-hour presentation by mural artists leads around the Mission district's outdoor paintings. Includes a slide presentation on the history and process of mural art. $12 per person; call for schedule of walks.

Victorian Home Walk (daily 11am; ☎415/252-9485, ⓦwww.victorianwalk.com). Leisurely tour through Pacific Heights and Cow Hollow where you'll learn to tell the difference between a Queen Anne, Italianate, and Stick-Style Vic. $20 per person for a two-hour tour. Meet by the clock in the lobby of the *Westin St Francis Hotel*.

Wok Wiz Tours (daily 10am; ☎415/981-8989, ⓦwww.wokwiz.com). A walk through Chinatown run by chef-writer Shirley Fong-Torres and her team. Plenty of anecdotes but a little thin on historical information. $28 per person, $40 per person including lunch.

For breathtaking views of the Bay, take a chilly 75-minute Bay cruise with the Blue & Gold Fleet (☎415/705-5555, ⊛www.blueandgoldfleet.com) from Pier 39 and Pier 41 – though be warned that everything may be shrouded in fog, making the price less than worth it ($20). Undoubtedly the most impressive – and expensive – tours are aerial: the best operator's San Francisco Helicopter Tours (☎650/635-4500 or 1-800/400-2404, ⊛www.sfhelicoptertours.com), which offer a variety of spectacular flights over the Bay Area beginning at $120 per passenger for a twenty-minute flight.

For information on guided walking tours, see box opposite.

Accommodation

Full-time residents of San Francisco complain constantly about skyrocketing rents, and it's no different for the visitor. Expect accommodation to cost around $100 per night in a reasonable hotel or motel, slightly less out of season. We've listed some smart bargains below (some as cheap as $50 a night offseason) but if you want to snag one of these cheaper rooms, it's essential to call around and book ahead. You'll also normally find significantly better rates in rooms that share baths. In all cases, bear in mind that all quoted room rates are subject to a **fourteen percent room tax**.

The **Visitor Information Center** (☎1-888/782-9673, ⊛www.sfvisitor.org) can provide the latest accommodation options; and **San Francisco Reservations** (Mon–Fri 6am–11pm, Sat & Sun 8am–11pm; ☎510/628-4450 or 1-800/677-1500, ⊛www.hotelres.com) will find you a room from around $100 a double.

For **B&Bs**, the city's fastest-growing source of accommodation, contact a specialist agency such as Bed and Breakfast San Francisco (Mon–Fri 9am–5.30pm; ☎415/899-0060, ⊛www.bbsf.com). If funds are tight, look into one of the many excellent **hostels** (listed below), where beds start at around $22. Specifically gay and lesbian accommodation is listed on p.633; there are some mixed gay-straight places, too, which we've included in the listings below.

Downtown and Chinatown

See map on pp.578–579.

Adagio 550 Geary St at Jones ☎415/775-5000, ⊛www.jdvhospitality.com. The decor at this hotel echoes its ornate Spanish Revival facade with deep reds and ochres, and the large rooms are well appointed with all mod cons. The *Adagio* also provides free computers with high-speed Internet access and even free printing facilities. ❺

Baldwin Hotel 321 Grant Ave at Bush, Chinatown ☎415/781-2220 or 1-800/6-BALDWIN, ⊛www.baldwinhotel.com. Surprisingly quiet, given its hub location in the heart of Chinatown, the *Baldwin's* rooms are oatmeal and taupe, outfitted in neutral colors with simple furnishings and ceiling fans. Rooms are rented weekly offseason so negotiate hard if you're staying fewer than seven nights. ❾ per week / ❹ per night

Clarion Hotel Cosmo 761 Post St at Jones ☎415/673-6040 or 1-800/252-7466, ⊛www.hotel-cosmo.com. A high-rise hotel aiming for a funkier feel than most chains, with its lavender and lilac lobby and jaunty elevator muzak, though the white formica-filled rooms feel a little cheap. Try to snag a room on the upper floors so you can enjoy the views across downtown and the Theater District. ❻

Clift 495 Geary St at Taylor, Theater District ☎415/775-4700 or 1-800/658-5492, ⊛www.morganshotelgroup.com. The old-school *Clift Hotel* is yet another postmodern Ian Schrager–Philippe Starck conversion. The rooms are vaguely oriental and vintage Starck, with quirky touches like the Louis XIV–style chairs with mirrors on the seat and back, and sleigh beds – pity the bathrooms are so small and the walls so thin (bring earplugs). ❼

Commodore International 825 Sutter St at Jones, Theater District ☎415/923-6800 or 1-800/338-6848, ⊛www.jdvhospitality.com. Each room is named after a different area attraction (such as the Haas-Lilienthal house or Mission murals), which is then glossed on a plaque by the door. They are decorated in warm, earthy colors offset by shiny steel neo-Deco fixtures. If you're traveling in a group of four or more, ask about the funky, airy Panoramic Suite where rates start at only $200. **⑤**

Gates Hotel 140 Ellis St at Powell, Union Square ☎415/956-4186. The large, salmon-pink rooms here are spartan and a little frayed, but clean. The rock-bottom rates for its Union Square location make up for the lack of luxuries. **②**

Grant Hotel 753 Bush St at Mason, Chinatown ☎415/421-7540 or 1-800/522-0979, ⊛granthotel.citysearch.com. Good value for its location, this hotel has small but clean rooms, overpowered a little by the relentlessly maroon carpets. Basic but convenient. **②**

Hotel Astoria 510 Bush St at Grant, Chinatown ☎415/434-8889 or 1-800/666-6696, ⊛www.hotelastoria-sf.com. Located right next to the arch at the entrance to Chinatown, the *Hotel Astoria*'s decor is friskier than many other budget hotels, with TV and full in-room amenities; continental breakfast is included in the rate and there's discounted parking nearby ($20/24 hr). **②**

Monaco 501 Geary St at Taylor, Union Square ☎415/292-0100 or 1-800/214-4220, ⊛www.monaco-sf.com. Quirky boutique hotel, part of a small national chain, that's housed in a historic Beaux Arts building. There are canopied beds in each room, and the rest of the decor's equally riotous, colorful, and a little over the top. Ask about the complimentary goldfish. **⑧**

Orchard Hotel, 665 Bush St at Powell, Union Square ☎415/362-8878, ⊛www.theorchardhotel.com. A little-known gem, this hotel's rates are lower than its ample amenities would suggest: every room has a DVD player with free movies on loan, free breakfast, and larger-than-average rooms, decorated like a clubby study in dark teak woods and striped fabrics. **⑧**

Sir Francis Drake 450 Powell St at Sutter, Union Square ☎415/392-7755 or 1-800/227-5480, ⊛www.sirfrancisdrake.com. The lobby here's a hallucinogenic evocation of all things heraldic: it's crammed with faux British memorabilia, chandeliers, and drippingly ornate gold plasterwork. Thankfully, the rooms are calmer, with a gentle apple-green color scheme and full facilities. The hotel's known for its classic bar *Harry Denton's Starlight Room* on the 21st floor. **⑦**

Triton 342 Grant Ave at Bush, Chinatown ☎415/394-0500 or 1-888/364-2622, ⊛www.hotel-tritonsf.com. Trippy, eccentric hotel that offers modern amenities like a 24hr gym and in-room fax, as well as weirder services like nightly tarot-card readings and an eco-floor of environmentally sensitive rooms. The rooms themselves are stylish but gaudy, painted in rich, clashing colors and plenty of gold. **⑦**

Westin St Francis 335 Powell St at Sutter, Union Square ☎415/397-7000 or 1-800/WESTIN1, ⊛www.westinstfrancis.com. This completely renovated landmark hotel has a sumptuous lobby, four restaurants and lounges, a fitness center, and a spa. Yet aside from the views across downtown, the rooms are disappointingly plain. Worth entering the lobby to see the famous clock, ornate ceiling, painting of Queen Elizabeth amidst American celebs, and the steps where President Gerald Ford almost met his end from a would-be assassin's bullet. **⑦**

North Beach and Nob Hill

See map on pp.578–579 for locations.

Boheme 444 Columbus Ave at Vallejo, North Beach ☎415/433-9111, ⊛www.hotelboheme.com. Smack in the middle of Beat heartland, this small, 15-room hotel has tiny but dramatic rooms, with canopied beds and Art Deco-ish bathrooms, all done in rich, dark colors plus free Wi-Fi. Columbus Avenue can be noisy, so if you're a light sleeper, ask for a room at the back. **⑦**

Mark Hopkins InterContinental One Nob Hill, 999 California St at Mason, Nob Hill ☎415/392-3434, ⊛www.markhopkins.net. Grand, castle-like hotel that was once the chic choice of writers and movie stars: it's more corporate these days in both clientele and design, thanks to a massive recent renovation. All rooms are identical, but rates rise as the floors do. The *Top of the Mark* rooftop bar is popular with tourists. **⑨**

San Remo 2237 Mason St at Chestnut, North Beach ☎415/776-8688 or 1-800/352-7366, ⊛www.sanremohotel.com Quirky option close to Fisherman's Wharf. Rooms in this warren-like converted house are cozy and chintzy: all share spotless bathrooms and a few have sinks. Bear in mind that there are no phones or TVs in the bedrooms and no elevator. **②**

SW Hotel 615 Broadway at Grant, North Beach ☎415/362-2999, @www.swhotelsf.com. Well-located hotel on the boundary between Chinatown and Little Italy. The decor in the large rooms is modern Asian with carved armoires and headboards and bright yellow bedspreads. ❺

Washington Square Inn 1660 Stockton St at Union, North Beach ☎415/981-4220 or 1-800/388-0220, @www.washingtonsquareinnsf.com. This B&B-style hotel overlooking Washington Square has large, airy rooms, decorated in modern shades of taupe and cream, and friendly, amenable staff. ❻

The northern waterfront and Pacific Heights

See map on pp.578–579 for locations.

Argonaut 495 Jefferson St at Hyde ☎415-397-5572 or 1-800/790-1415, @www.argonauthotel.com. This brand new nautical-themed hotel (there's an anchor motif running through much of the decoration) in the Cannery complex has large, lush rooms that feature DVD players, stereos, and impressive views. Surprisingly quiet for its location. ❾
Best Western Tuscan Inn 425 North Point at Mason ☎415/561-1100 or 1-800/648-4626, @www.tuscaninn.com. Despite its name, this waterfront hotel is more English country manor than Tuscan farmhouse, with cozy rooms decorated in warm colors. It has attentive touches like an afternoon wine reception and a free limo to downtown in the mornings. ❼
Cow Hollow Motor Inn 2190 Lombard St at Steiner, Cow Hollow ☎415/921-5800, @www.cowhollowmotorinn.com. Swiss-chalet-style inn, with plentiful parking and charmingly retro common areas. The rooms, though, are utterly modern, recently refurbished and enormous. ❺
Del Sol 3100 Webster St at Lombard, Cow Hollow ☎415/921-5520 or 1-877/433-5765, @www.thehoteldelsol.com. Funky, offbeat, updated motor lodge with a tropical theme, plus a swimming

pool. The color scheme combines zesty walls with chunky mosaics and palm trees wrapped in fairy lights: the best place for budget cool in the city. ❺
Greenwich Inn 3201 Steiner St at Greenwich, Cow Hollow ☎415/921-5162 or 1-800/280-3242, @www.greenwichinn.com. Formerly a *Travelodge*, this sprightly, good-value option in the Marina offers 32 rooms, each recently refurbished, if a little dark, but the friendly owners make up for it. There's free on-site parking, too. ❸
Laurel Inn 444 Presidio Ave at California, Laurel Heights ☎415/567-8467 or 1-800/552-8735, @www.thelaurelinn.com. This Laurel Heights hotel is steps from Sacramento Street's antique shops and near the bustling Fillmore strip of cafés and stores. All rooms come with a VCR and CD player; the decor's stylish update of 1950s Americana, with muted graphic prints and simple fixtures. ❻
Surf Motel 2265 Lombard St at Pierce, Cow Hollow ☎415/922-1950. This old-school motel has two tiers of bright, simple rooms that are sparklingly clean. Ask for a room at the back, since the busy Lombard Street thoroughfare roars past the main entrance. ❷

SoMa, the Tenderloin, and the Civic Center

See map on pp.578–579 for locations.

Best Western Carriage Inn 140 7th St at Mission, SoMa ☎415/552-8600 @www.renesonhotels.com. Enormous, elegant rooms with sofas and working fireplaces. There's free room-service breakfast each morning and shuttle to Union Square: the only downside is its location, on a slightly sketchy block of SoMa. ❺
Four Seasons 757 Market St at 3rd, SoMa ☎415/633-3000, @www.fourseasons.com. Sparkling hotel on Market Street with spectacular views across the city: its plush rooms are the ultimate indulgence, from the soft, luxurious comforters to the stand-alone two-person shower

stocked with Bulgari beauty products. There's an enormous on-site health club with a pool and vast gym that's free to guests. The place to stay if you win the lottery or someone else is paying. ❾
Hotel Griffon 155 Steuart St at Mission, SoMa ☎415/495-2100 or 1-800/321-2201, @www.hotelgriffon.com. Secluded hotel close to the waterfront: rooms are elegant and understated, with exposed brick walls, window seats, CD player, and refrigerator. ❼
The Mosser 54 4th St at Market, SoMa ☎415/986-4400, @www.themosser.com. This hotel is a recent funky conversion fusing

Victorian touches like ornamental molding with mod leather sofas. The chocolate-and-olive rooms may be tiny but each is artfully crammed with amenities including multi-disc CD players. Highly recommended – one of the best values in town, especially for its central location. ❷ (shared bath), ❺ (private bath)

Palace Hotel 2 New Montgomery St at Market, SoMa ☏415/512-1111, ⊛www.sfpalace.com. Hushed, opulent landmark building, known for its fabulous, historic Garden Court tearoom: the grand lobby and corridors are mismatched with rooms that are small for the sky-high prices, decorated in lush golds and greens like an English country house. Stay here for snob value rather than good value. ❾

The Phoenix 601 Eddy St at Larkin, Tenderloin ☏415/776-1380 or 1-800/248-9466, ⊛www

jdvhospitality.com. This raucous retro motel conversion is a favorite with up-and-coming bands when they're in town. There's a small pool, and the 44 rooms are eclectically decorated in tropical colors with changing local artwork on the walls – ask for the "Tour Manager Room," which has a fridge, fax, and microwave. ❺

The Renoir 45 McAllister St at 7th, Civic Center ☏415/626-5200 or 1-800/576-3388, ⊛www .renoirhotel.com. This wedge-shaped building is a historic landmark. The superior rooms cost $20 more than standard – worth the extra if you can snag one of the oddly shaped large rooms at the building's apex. Especially popular during Gay Pride for its Market Street views along the parade route. ❹

The Mission and the Castro

See map on p.601 for locations.

Beck's Motor Lodge 2222 Market St at Sanchez, Castro ☏415/621-8212 or 1-800/227-4360. This is one of only two accommodation options in the area that isn't a B&B. The clientele's more mixed than you'd expect from its location, and the soft, bluish rooms are plusher than the gaudy yellow motel exterior might suggest. If you're a light sleeper, ask for a room well away from the road, as it can be noisy. ❺

Dolores Park Inn 3641 17th St at Dolores, Mission ☏415/621-0482, ⊛www.doloresparkinn.net. Housed in an artfully restored Italianate Victorian, this sumptuous B&B offers only four rooms, one of which has an en-suite bath. They're all large, though, and crammed with a Baroque assortment of ornate European antiques; the owner even keeps a photo book of past guests. Its seclusion close to the park is a major plus. ❻

Travelodge Central 1707 Market at Valencia, Mission ☏415/621-6775 or 1-800/578-7878.

Very basic motel-style lodging, but couldn't be more conveniently located – the free on-site parking makes up for the slightly worn, floral motel rooms. ❹

Twin Peaks Hotel 2160 Market St at Dolores, Castro ☏415/863-2909. This hotel's basic and very spartan: the small, simply furnished rooms have vanities and large TVs, but almost all share bathrooms. A bit like a brusque boarding house, but the prices make up for the lack of amenities. ❷ (shared), ❸ (private bath)

Village House 4080 18th St at Castro, Castro ☏415/864-0994 or 1-800/900-5686, ⊛www.24henry.com. Oddly, given its location, this newish B&B is mixed gay-straight and popular with visiting parents. The rooms are grand and a little gaudy, with primary colored walls and plenty of closet space. For camp Eastern extravagance, ask for room 2; or take a trip back to the 1980s in room 4. ❹

Haight-Ashbury and west of Civic Center

See map on p.606 for locations.

Archbishop's Mansion 1000 Fulton St at Steiner, Fillmore ☏415/563-7872 or 1-800/543-5820, ⊛www.thearchbishopsmansion.com. The last word in camp elegance, this B&B stands on the corner of Alamo Square and is crammed with $1m worth of antiques, including the very chandelier that featured in the ballroom of *Gone With the Wind* and Noël Coward's baby grand piano. Built to house an archbishop, it's also served as a school for wayward

Catholic boys; now it caters to wayward boys of a different kind, attracting plenty of gay travelers. ❼

Best Western Miyako 1800 Sutter St at Buchanan, Japantown ☏415/921-4000 or 1-800/528-1234, ⊛www.bestwestern.com/miyakoinn. Recently renovated, this standard corporate hotel is one of the few options in Japantown and around that isn't a B&B. Nothing special, but there can be great price deals offseason. ❺

The Carl 198 Carl St at Stanyan, Haight-Ashbury
☎415/661-5679 or 1-888/661-5679, ⌨carlhotel
.citysearch.com. Plainer than many of the surrounding B&Bs, this hotel is a bargain for its
Golden Gate Park location. Small but florally pretty
rooms, with microwaves and fridges; the six with
shared bath are especially well-priced. ❹
(private), ❸ (shared)
Château Tivoli 1057 Steiner St at Fulton, Fillmore
☎415/776-5462 or 1-800/228-1647, ⌨www
.chateautivoli.com. Rooms in this lavishly furnished
Victorian mansion are named after artists like
Isadora Duncan and Mark Twain: there's history
everywhere, whether in the building itself (built
for an early local lumber baron) or the furniture
(one of the beds was owned by Charles de Gaulle).
Grand, and very serious, but a luxurious alternative
to many of the cozy B&Bs elsewhere. ❻ (shared
bath), ❼ (private) $99 to $265
Hayes Valley Inn 417 Gough St at Hayes, Hayes
Valley ☎415/431-9131 or 1-800/930-7999,
⌨www.hayesvalleyinn.com. Homely, apple-green
rooms in a secluded location: furnishings are minimal, and baths are shared, but the friendly, well-
stocked kitchen/breakfast room is a major plus. ❸
Queen Anne 1590 Sutter St at Octavia, Fillmore
☎415/441-2828 or 1-800/227-3970, ⌨www

.queenanne.com. Gloriously excessive restored
Victorian, that began as a girls' school before
becoming a bordello. Each room is stuffed with
gold-accented Rococo furniture and bunches of
silk flowers: the parlor (where afternoon sherry is
served) is over-filled with museum-quality period
furniture. Miss Mary Lake, former principal of the
school, is said to still make periodic, supernatural
appearances in Room 410. ❻
The Red Victorian Bed, Breakfast and Art
1665 Haight St at Cole, Haight-Ashbury ☎415/
864-1978, ⌨www.redvic.com. Quirky B&B and
Peace Center, owned by Sami Sunchild and decorated with her ethnic arts. Rooms vary from simple
to opulent: the best feature is the shared bathrooms,
including a goldfish-filled toilet cistern. Breakfast's a
lavish but highly communal affair, so be prepared to
chat with your neighbors while you eat. ❹
Stanyan Park Hotel 750 Stanyan St at Waller,
Haight-Ashbury ☎415/751-1000, ⌨www
.stanyanpark.com. Overlooking Golden Gate
Park, this small hotel has 35 sumptuous rooms
that are oddly incongruous in its counter-culture
neighborhood, busily decorated in country florals
with heavy drapes and junior four-poster beds.
Continental breakfast and an ample, cookie-filled
afternoon tea are included. ❻

The Richmond and the Sunset

Ocean Park Motel 2690 46th Ave at
Wawona, Ocean Beach ☎415/566-7020,
⌨oceanparkmotel.citysearch.com. A fair way
from downtown (25min by MUNI), this is
nonetheless a great Art Deco motel (San
Francisco's first) and an outstanding example
of Streamline Moderne architecture. It's
convenient for the beach and the zoo, plus

there's a kids' play area and an outdoor hot tub
and Jacuzzi for adults. ❹
Oceanview Motel 4340 Judah St at LaPlaya,
Ocean Beach ☎415/661-2300, ⌨oceanviewmotel
.citysearch.com. No-frills lodging out in the Sunset
District, with smallish, simply furnished rooms.
There's free on-site parking and convenient MUNI
access. ❸

Hostels

Green Tortoise 494 Broadway at Montgomery,
North Beach ☎415/834-1000 or 1-800/867-8647,
⌨www.greentortoise.com. This laid-back hostel is
the choicest option if money's tight: there's room
for 130 people in dorm beds and double rooms
(with shared bath). Both options include free Internet access, use of the small on-site sauna, and
complimentary breakfast. There's no curfew, and
the front desk is staffed 24hr: there's a ten-night
maximum stay. $19 dorms, $48 rooms.
HI-San Francisco City Center 685 Ellis St at
Larkin, Tenderloin ☎415/474-5721, ⌨www
.norcalhostels.org. Recent conversion from the old
Atherton Hotel, this is a spiffy new hostel; its 272

beds are divided into four-person dorms, each with
en-suite bath. There's no curfew, and overall it's
friendly, funky, and California cool: good for meeting other travelers, since there are plenty of
activities laid on (nightly movies, communal
pancake breakfast); its only downside is the
location in a sketchier part of the Tenderloin. $22
members, $25 non-members; private rooms $66
members, $69 non-members.
HI-San Francisco Downtown 312 Mason St
at Geary, Union Square ☎415/788-5604. With
almost 300 beds, this downtown hostel still fills
up quickly in peak season: four-person dorms are
spotless, sharing bathroom facilities between eight

people. The private rooms are pricier and sleep two people. Open 24 hours, there's a kitchen with microwave and vending machines, a funky little reading room and Internet access ($1 for 10 min). Dorms $22 members, $25 non-members; private rooms $60 members, $66 non-members.

HI-San Francisco Fort Mason Building 240, Fort Mason ☎415/771-7277, ⊛www.norcalhostels.org. On the waterfront between the Golden Gate Bridge and Fisherman's Wharf, this is a choice option for the outdoorsy traveler, mostly thanks to its location, housed in a historic former Civil War barracks in a rolling park. Be aware that although public transport connects the hostel with the main sights, it's a little out of the way on the federal complex at Fort Mason. The upside of its federal land location is that it can't require a membership fee so it's even cheaper than the other HI hostels. $23.

Interclub/Globe Hostel 10 Hallam Place, SoMa ☎415/431-0540. Lively South of Market hostel with young clientele and 33 rooms, split between dorms and private rooms. There's free coffee and, best of all, no curfew. Note, though, you'll need to provide a passport or similar proof that you're a traveler from overseas as it's only for foreigners. $15 per person; doubles $40.

Pacific Tradewinds Guesthouse 680 Sacramento St at Kearny, Chinatown ☎415/433-7970 or (May–Oct only) 1-800/486-7975, ⊛www.pactradewinds.com. The best budget option in the center of town, this small hostel offers free, high-speed Internet access, a clean kitchen, plus a large, communal dining table that's an easy way to get to know fellow travelers. It's certainly an international hub – house rules are posted in almost forty languages, including Afrikaans and Catalan. There are only 38 beds so book ahead in high season. $15–20 per person, depending on season.

YMCA Central Branch 220 Golden Gate Ave at Leavenworth, Tenderloin ☎415/885-0460, ⊛www.centralymcasf.org. Rooms may be simple, but this is one of the best deals in the city center: $12 overnight parking, free breakfast, free use of YMCA fitness center, Internet access at a nominal fee, and on-site laundry. There are private rooms with both private and shared baths, as well as a few dorms (only available in winter) so book ahead. Be aware of the YMCA's location in a grimy part of the Tenderloin. $25.95 incl tax (dorm), $43.62 incl tax (shared bath) $73.56 incl tax (private bath).

The City

The first thing that strikes visitors to San Francisco is that it is a city of hills and distinct neighborhoods. Here, as a general rule, geographical elevation is a stout indicator of wealth – the higher you live, the better off you are. Commercial square-footage is surprisingly small and mostly confined to the downtown area, and the rest of the city is made up of primarily residential neighborhoods with street-level shopping districts, easily explored on foot. Armed with a good map and strong legs, you could plough through much of the city in a couple of days, but frankly the best way to get to know San Francisco is to dawdle, unbound by itineraries; the most interesting districts merit – at the very least – half a day each of just hanging out.

Most of the forty-odd hills that rise above the town serve as geographic barriers between neighborhoods. The flattest stretch of land, created by landfill and bulldozing, at the top right-hand corner of the Peninsula, bordered by I-80 to the south, US-101 to the west, and the water, comprises **downtown**. The city center is bisected by the wide, diagonal thoroughfare of **Market Street**, which is the main reference point for your wanderings. Lined with stores and office buildings, Market Street begins at the water's edge of the **Embarcadero** and runs southwest along the corporate high-rises of the **Financial District**; the cable-car and shopping quarter of **Union Square**; beside the scruffy **Tenderloin** district and chic **Hayes Valley**; and reaches the primarily gay district of the **Castro**. It then spirals around **Twin Peaks**, the most prominent of San Francisco's heights.

South and east of Market Street stands **SoMa**, which used to be one of the city center's few industrial enclaves, until the artsy, nightclubbing crowd discovered it. It was at the heart of the dot-com boom when Internet start-ups paid sky-high rents to stake their claim in SoMa's warehouses and lofts. Commercial development poured in, from Sony's laughable **Metreon** mall to the glorious waterfalls at **Yerba Buena Gardens** and the new **San Francisco Museum of Modern Art**. SoMa has suffered since the collapse of the Internet industry, and more than four years later, many of its sparkling new office buildings still lie empty, vacated by vanished companies. SoMa's waterfront, long-neglected **South Beach** has been re-zoned for housing and businesses, and is anchored by **Pac Bell Ballpark**, the waterfront stadium built for baseball's San Francisco Giants.

South of SoMa sits San Francisco's largest, and one of its most interesting, neighborhoods, the **Mission**. Built around the wedding cake-like Mission Dolores and, thanks to fog-blocking hills, almost always sunny, the largely Hispanic Mission district offers enough food, cinema, nightclubs, and shops to fill a separate vacation – or at least a day off the well-trodden tourist path around downtown.

North and west of Market Street, the land rises dramatically, and with it, property values, as evinced by the stunning mansions atop the province of robber barons: **Nob Hill**. Beside this posh residential quarter, a short cable car ride or walk away down the hill, rests cluttered **Chinatown**, a thriving neighborhood of apartments, restaurants, temples, and stores built around **Portsmouth Square**, the spiritual heart of San Francisco. The land east of the square, towards the Bay, used to be entirely water before hundreds of sailors heading for the Gold Rush abandoned their ships, resulting in an unnatural extension of the waterfront. The beached boats rapidly piled up along the shore of Portsmouth Square, until merchants began using the dry-docked vessels as hotels, bars, and shops. Now it's filled by the towering Transamerica Pyramid, which shadows the **Jackson Square** historical neighborhood of restored redbrick businesses. The diagonal artery **Columbus Avenue**, which separates Portsmouth from Jackson Square, is the spine of the Italian enclave of **North Beach**, much loved by Beat writers and espresso drinkers. North Beach extends to the northernmost tip of the city, the tourist-trap waterfront known as **Fisherman's Wharf**, but not before passing the peaks of **Russian Hill**, home to the famously curvy Lombard Street, and **Telegraph Hill**, perch of the celebrated Coit Tower.

New paved trails along the northern water's edge lead west towards the **Golden Gate Bridge**, but not before passing the expansive green parkland of **Fort Mason** and through the ritzy **Marina** district, home to the Palace of Fine Arts and some of the city's best shopping. High above, the mansions and Victorians of **Pacific Heights** snuggle up against neighborhood cafés and designer boutiques, along with spectacular views of the bridges and Bay. The Heights slope down to the south to workaday **Japantown** and suburban **Western Addition** districts. Directly west of here, you'll come to **Haight-Ashbury**, once San Francisco's Victorian resort quarter before hippies and flower children took over. Today it's a rag-tag collection of used-clothing stores and hippies squeezing as much money as they can out of their fading past.

The western and southern sides of San Francisco are where most of the city's residents live, and – much to their dismay – the area is experiencing skyrocketing rents. **Geary Boulevard**, the main east–west passage, begins in the Financial District and ends at the Pacific Ocean in the **Richmond** district. Geary's lined with some of the city's best Asian and Russian restaurants, while a block north, the Clement Street area is known as "New Chinatown" for its collection of Chinese groceries, hot-pot restaurants, and dumpling cafeterias. The

Richmond is hugged by nature on three of its sides: the beaches, the Golden Gate Bridge, and **Presidio** to the north; Land's End and Ocean Beach to the west; and the expansive Golden Gate Park to the south. On the other side of Golden Gate Park, the **Sunset** district stretches on in suburban sameness south, though the district's Ninth Avenue and Irving Street strip of restaurants is worth a detour for a fine selection of boutique eateries.

Union Square

The focus of downtown San Francisco, **UNION SQUARE** is a sixteen-block area filled with stores, hotels, and flocks of tourists. Thanks to a grueling and lengthy refit which finished in 2003, the plaza itself, on the block north of Geary between Powell and Stockton streets, is more welcoming and much less shabby than it once was. The benches here are a good place to take a break from trekking round, and there's a handy café on its eastern rim. In the center of the square, the 97-foot-tall Corinthian column commemorates Admiral Dewey's success in the Spanish–American War: the voluptuous female figure on top of the monument was modeled on **Alma de Bretteville Spreckels,** who founded the California Palace of the Legion of Honor art museum (see p.611). Though the site takes its name from its role as gathering place for pro-Unionist speechmakers on the eve of the Civil War, these days it's remembered more for the attempted assassination of President Gerald Ford outside the bordering *Westin St Francis* hotel in 1975. The opulent hotel also featured prominently in many of Dashiell Hammett's detective stories, including *The Maltese Falcon* – in fact, during the 1920s Hammett worked there as a Pinkerton detective, investigating the notorious rape and murder case against silent film star Fatty Arbuckle.

The southern side of the plaza is dominated by a gigantic **Macy's** department store, but if you're looking for more interesting, albeit pricier, browsing, head east to **Maiden Lane,** ground zero for designer-label chasers. Before the 1906 earthquake and fire, it was known as Morton Street, one of San Francisco's lowest-class red-light districts; an average of around ten homicides a month occurred here, and prostitutes used to lean out low-hung windows of "cribs" that bore signs that read "Men taken in and done for." Now other than shopping, though, there's one major sight: the only **Frank Lloyd Wright–designed building** in San Francisco, at no. 140. From the outside, it's a squat orange-brick building, oddly lacking in Wright's usual obsession with horizontal lines; the interior, though, is extraordinary, a swooping, sweeping, curved ramp that links the floors and is a clear ancestor of the famed Guggenheim in New York. The building's now occupied by the Xanadu ethnic art gallery – if it's open, feel free to wander inside, but don't expect a warm welcome from the gallery's staff.

Around the corner, marooned on a traffic island at the intersection of Kearney and Market, lies **Lotta's Fountain**, one of the city's most beloved landmarks. Restored and repainted in 1999, this ornate caramel-colored fountain served as the legendary message center after the 1906 earthquake, where distraught locals gathered to hear the latest damage reports. Named in honor of actress Lotta Crabtree, the fountain enjoyed its greatest moment when world-renowned opera diva Luisa Tetrazinni sang a free Christmas Eve performance atop it in 1910.

If you're heading back up to the waterfront, **cable cars** run beside Union Square along Powell Street but are usually too packed to board at the **Hallidie Plaza** terminus. There are three line-dodging tips for cable car riders. First, come late in the day – by 7pm or so, the line should be much shorter; second, if you're here during peak hours, head a block north along Powell Street since drivers usually leave a bit of extra room on board at the start of the journey. Finally, if the Powell Street lines are just too busy, the California Street line (terminus at California and Market streets) crawling up Nob Hill is less popular and normally line-free.

Theater District

The area between tourist-heavy Union Square and the grubby Tenderloin is known as the **THEATER DISTRICT**, although most of the playhouses lack the grandeur of many old theaters in New York or London (the one exception's the Geary – see below). Despite its proximity to a number of tourist attractions, this neighborhood is a convenient bolthole from the crowds and a secluded place to stay in the city center. The district's anchored by the American Conservatory Theater's **Geary Theater**, 415 Geary St (☎415/742-2228), whose Neoclassical colonnaded facade is a nod to its Beaux Arts–era origins. The Geary was rebuilt in 1909 after the earthquake catastrophe three years earlier; the 1989 earthquake damaged the structure again, and it was closed for several years in the early 1990s for retrofitting and upgrading of its facilities. The ACT company usually performs major plays five nights a week – for details, see p.630.

The blocks of Post and Sutter streets, which cut through this area, are home to some of downtown's least visible landmarks: some fourteen **private clubs** hidden behind discreet facades. Money isn't the only criteria for membership to these highly esteemed institutions, though being *somebody* usually is. Most notorious is the **Bohemian Club**, at 624 Taylor St, whose Bohemian Grove retreat at the Russian River (see p.793) is where ex-presidents and corporate giants assemble for Masonic rituals and schoolboy larks; the San Francisco chapter is housed in a Lewis Hobart Moderne-style building. Organized in 1872 as a breakfast club for newspapermen, it evolved into a businessmen's club with an artsy slant, counting Ambrose Bierce, Jack London, Bret Harte, and Frank Norris among its members.

The Financial District

From Hallidie Plaza to the waterfront, Market Street traces the southern edge of the **FINANCIAL DISTRICT**, San Francisco's business hub clogged with banks, including the famous **Bank of America**, founded here by Italian immigrant A.P. Giannini in 1901 (and used by disaster-minded 70s filmmakers for the exterior shots of camp classic *The Towering Inferno*). As with most central business districts, this isn't a place that hums at the weekends: to see it at its liveliest, wander through on a weekday lunchtime.

At the western end of the Financial District stands the **Wells Fargo History Museum**, in the Wells Fargo Bank, 420 Montgomery St (Mon–Fri 9am–5pm; free; ☎415/396-2619, ⓦwww.wellsfargo.com), a pleasant but toothless exhibition space. The glowing accounts of the bank's contributions to the Old West tarnish are unintentionally humorous, and include a wall of 150 employee luminaries, although the display of old letters upstairs is more intriguing.

Another notable Financial District museum further east on the edge of Chinatown is the tiny **Pacific Heritage Museum**, 608 Commercial St (Tues–Sat 10am–4pm; free; ☎415/362-4100, ⓦwww.citysearch.com/sfo/pacificheritage). The rolling exhibits of Asian art are fine, but the real draw is the structure itself – a late nineteenth-century US Subtreasury building, now neatly incorporated into a modern skyscraper.

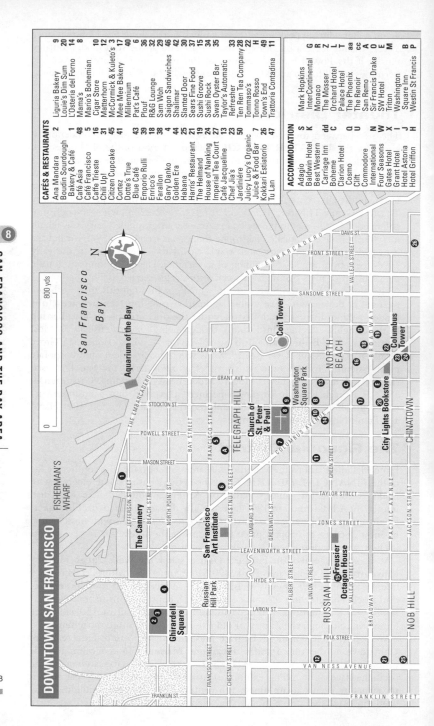

DOWNTOWN SAN FRANCISCO

N

San Francisco Bay

FISHERMAN'S WHARF

Aquarium of the Bay

The Cannery

Ghirardelli Square

San Francisco Art Institute

Russian Hill Park

Freusier Octagon House

Washington Square Park

Church of St. Peter & Paul

Telegraph Hill

Coit Tower

NORTH BEACH

Columbus Tower

City Lights Bookstore

CHINATOWN

RUSSIAN HILL

NOB HILL

0   800 yds

CAFÉS & RESTAURANTS

Ana Mandara	2
Boudin Sourdough	1
Bakery & Café	1
Café Asia	48
Café Francisco	16
Caffe Trieste	31
Chili Up!	41
Citizen Cupcake	45
Cortez	40
Dotte's True	43
Blue Café	43
Emporio Rulli	39
Enrico's	18
Farallon	38
Gary Danko	4
Golden Era	44
Habana	25
Harris' Restaurant	21
The Helmand	19
House of Nanking	24
Imperial Tea Court	27
Café Jacqueline	13
Chef Jia's	50
Jardinière	23
Juicy Lucy's Organic	
Juice & Food Bar	7
Kokkari Estiatorio	26
Tu Lan	47

Liguria Bakery	9
Louie's Dim Sum	20
L'Osteria del Forno	14
Mama's	8
Mario's Bohemian	
Cigar Store	10
Matterhorn	12
McCormick & Kuleto's	3
Mee Mee Bakery	17
Millennium	40
Pat's Café	6
Plouf	36
R&G Lounge	32
Sam Woh	29
Saigon Sandwiches	46
Shalimar	42
Slanted Door	30
Sears Fine Food	37
Sushi Groove	15
Sushi Rock	34
Swan Oyster Bar	35
Taylor's Automatic	
Refresher	33
Ten Ren Tea Company	28
Tommaso's	22
Tonno Rosso	H
Town's End	49
Trattoria Contadina	11

ACCOMMODATION

Adagio	S
Baldwin Hotel	K
Best Western	
Carriage Inn	dd
Boheme	C
Clarion Hotel	
Clift	Q
Cosmo	U
Commodore	
International	N
Four Seasons	W
Gates Hotel	X
Grant Hotel	I
Hotel Astoria	J
Hotel Griffon	H

Mark Hopkins	G
InterContinental	R
Monaco	Z
The Mosser	L
Orchard Hotel	T
Palace Hotel	
The Phoenix	aa
The Renoir	cc
San Remo	A
Sir Francis Drake	O
SW Hotel	E
Triton	M
Washington	
Square Inn	B
Westin St Francis	P

HOSTELS

Green Tortoise Hostel   D
Hi-San Francisco City Centre   Y
Hi-San Francisco Downtown   V
Interclub/Globe   ee
Pacific Tradewinds Guesthouse F
YMCA Central Branch   bb

THE EMBARCADERO

Ferry Building

Jewish Museum

Embarcadero Center

FINANCIAL DISTRICT

Federal Reserve Bank

Transbay Terminal

Museum of Modern Art

Trans-america Pyramid

Bank of Canton

Bank of America

Moscone Convention Center

Yerba Buena Gardens

Portsmouth Square

Pacific Union Club

Sony Metreon

SOUTH OF MARKET

Union Square

Grace Cathedral

CIVIC CENTER

Civic Plaza

VAN NESS AVENUE

FRANKLIN STREET

8

The cable cars

San Francisco's **cable cars** first appeared in 1873, the brainchild of Andrew Hallidie, an enterprising engineer with an eye for the main chance. Scots-born Hallidie is said to have been inspired to find an alternative to horse-drawn carriages when he saw a team of horses badly injured while trying to pull a dray up a steep hill in the rain. More than equine welfare was under threat – his father had patented a strong wire rope that had been extensively used in the mines of eastern California but, as the Gold Rush there slowed, Hallidie needed a new application for his family's signature product and a privately owned transit system like the cable cars was the ideal solution.

The cable-car **pulley system** was dubbed "Hallidie's Folly" by unconvinced locals, but doubters were soon proved wrong as high sections of San Francisco like Nob Hill suddenly became accessible, and businesses and homes were constructed along cable-car routes. At their peak, just before the 1906 earthquake, more than six hundred cable cars traveled on eight lines and 112 miles of track throughout the city, traveling a maximum 9.5 mph.

Unfortunately, though, the cable system was vulnerable to the onset of the automobile thanks to the devastation after the earthquake, when large chunks of the tracks were wrecked. However, when it was rumored in 1947 that the ailing system would be phased out altogether, a local activist organized a citizens' committee to save them. The protests worked, and seventeen years later the cars were put on the National Register of Historic Places and the remaining seventeen miles (now down to ten) was saved. Now there are 44 cars in use – each unique – and around 23 miles of moving cable underground. Since the mid-1980s, MUNI has been rebuilding the cars by hand: the process has taken far longer than the ten years originally estimated, requiring as much as 3000 hours and $275,000 per car.

The Embarcadero

At the northeastern edge of the Financial District, the thin, long waterfront district known as **THE EMBARCADERO** is centered on the **Ferry Building** (Mon–Fri 10am–6pm, Sat 9am–6pm, Sun 11am–5pm; ☎415/693-0996, ⓦwww.ferrybuildingmarketplace.com). Once cut off from the rest of San Francisco by the double-decker Embarcadero Freeway – damaged in the 1989 earthquake and torn down in 1991 – this structure, at the foot of Market Street, was modeled on the cathedral tower in Seville, Spain. Before the bridges were built in the 1930s, it was the arrival point for fifty thousand cross-Bay daily commuters, and a few ferries still dock here. But it's just undergone a multi-year, multi-million-dollar facelift to turn it into a foodie mall, filled with artisanal cheese shops and vintners – for details, see "Eating," p.612, and "Drinking," p.621. It's also home to the **Ferry Plaza Farmers' Market** (Tues 10am–2pm, Thurs 10am–2pm, Sat 8am–2pm, Sun 10am–2pm, ☎415/291-3276, ⓦwww .ferryplazafarmersmarket.com), a good place for local produce. San Francisco foodies make pilgrimages here to sample snacks from the city's pricey restaurants, which often set up temporary stalls among the fruit and vegetables.

Nearby **Justin Herman Plaza** was named in honor of the pasha of urban renewal who tore down acres of historic buildings in the Western Addition in the 1960s. It's perhaps fitting that it should be home to one of the ugliest modernist sights in the city, the **Vaillancourt Fountain**, a tangled mass of concrete tubing clearly inspired by air-conditioning ducts. The water was turned off here in a money-saving gesture in 2000, but is finally flowing again, which softens the brutalist ugliness of the sculpture. The fountain's best known, though, as the meeting place for Critical Mass, the bike rally which convenes here on the last Friday of each month and then rides around the city en masse to help gum up car traffic and in the process promote cycling as a more environmentally friendly alternative. The five-mile **waterfront**, which stretches north and south from the foot of Market Street, was teeming during the first half of the twentieth century with ships loading and unloading cargo. The area experienced something of a slump after World War II, but recent development, including the building of a new MUNI station, the extension of the cable-car lines, and the Ferry Building's refit, has brought San Franciscans back here to jog, bike, and skate.

Inland from the waterfront, the area's dominated by the four massive modern skyscrapers known collectively as the **Embarcadero Center**. It's packed with stores, restaurants, and, oddly, dozens of doctors, all geared to filling the lunch times of the thousands of local office workers; there's little to detain a visitor other than a couple of fine hotels (see "Accommodation", p.569).

Two blocks west, at the corner of Washington and Montgomery streets, stands San Francisco's tallest building, the **Transamerica Pyramid**, 600 Montgomery St (☎415/983-4100, ⊛www.tapyramid.com), a glossy, controversial landmark designed by LA-based architect William Pereira in 1972. Nicknamed "Pereira's Prick" thanks to its phallic shape, it's so tall and thin it looks more like a squared-off rocket than a pyramid. The building does have four triangular sides, rising from a square city block to a lofty point high above; it's fully earthquake-proof and was unscathed by the earthquake of 1989, although there's no longer public access to the viewing platform on the 27th floor. Rudyard Kipling, Robert Louis Stevenson, Mark Twain, and William Randolph Hearst all rented office space in the building that once stood at the corner of Montgomery and Washington streets, and regularly hung around the famous *Bank Exchange* bar within. Legend also has it that Dr Sun Yat-Sen – whose statue is in Chinatown, three blocks away – wrote the Chinese constitution and orchestrated the successful overthrow of the Manchu dynasty from his second-floor office here.

Jackson Square historic district

Confusingly, there's no plaza in **JACKSON SQUARE**. The area bordered by Washington, Columbus, Sansome, and Pacific streets wasn't known by that name until the 1960s, when interior designers who'd recently opened showrooms here decided on a suitably artsy yet old-fashioned tag to replace the notorious **Barbary Coast**, the district of San Francisco where vice flourished during the nineteenth century. The constant stream of sailors provided an endless supply of customers looking for illicit entertainment, and the area was nicknamed "Baghdad by the Bay" for its unsavory reputation as a nexus for shanghai'ing: hapless young males were given Mickey Finns and, unconscious, taken aboard sailing ships into involuntary servitude. Though buildings here remarkably survived the 1906 disaster, the rowdy, raunchy businesses were hugely affected as nearby poor, residential areas were leveled. The double whammy of fire and fury (chiefly, the relentless campaigning from William Randolph Hearst's *Examiner* newspaper against the district) soon put an end to most illicit fun here.

Remains of San Francisco's earliest days can be seen today in the restored redbrick buildings of Jackson Square's **historic district**, bordered by Washington, Columbus, Sansome, and Pacific streets. Standing on **Jackson Street** is the one place in the city where you can hope to imagine what early San Francisco looked like. Here you'll find the only cluster of downtown buildings that escaped the great fire of 1906 unharmed. The **Hotaling Building** (pronounced hote-UH-ling), at nos. 451–455, was a distillery that was saved by a savvy manager at the height of the fire. Afterward, local wags came up with the doggerel: "If as they say God spanked the town for being so over frisky, why did he burn the churches down and spare Hotaling's whiskey?"

Montgomery Street, on the district's western flank, has retained much of its historic character, and several of the buildings have interesting pasts. **No. 732** was the home of San Francisco's first literary magazine, the *Golden Era*, founded in the 1850s; it helped launch the careers of Bret Harte and Mark Twain. Later, John Steinbeck and William Saroyan spent many a night drinking in the vanished *Black Cat Café* down the street. In the middle of the block, **nos. 722–728** (the Belli and Genella buildings) have been stripped of their original stucco and done up in overwrought Victorian mode. The building was at one time a theater, but has also been a Turkish bath, a tobacco warehouse, and an auction room. The building was bought by the flamboyant San Francisco lawyer Melvin Belli, but his widow's plans to turn the site into a museum have come to nothing. Today, the building has fallen into disuse, hidden from view by shuttered windows, encroaching ivy, and gnarled tree branches, and has a sadly ruined feel.

As the district merges with North Beach and Chinatown, at the intersection of Jackson Street and Columbus Avenue stands the distinctive green-copper siding of the **Columbus Tower**, 906 Kearney St. It's now owned by director and San Francisco native Francis Ford Coppola, and his office, with doubtless spectacular views, is in the rounded tower that gives the building its name. Unfortunately, it's not open to the public.

Portsmouth Square

One block south of Columbus Tower, **PORTSMOUTH SQUARE** was San Francisco's original city center and the first port of entry. Today, it's hard to imagine the city springing up from this once dusty patch of land nestled between Nob, Telegraph, and Rincon hills, but it was here that Englishman William Richardson received permission from Mexican rulers to begin a trading post on the coast of the Bay. John Montgomery came ashore in 1846 to claim the hamlet for the United States, raising a flag whose location is marked by the Stars and Stripes that flies in the square today. A small settlement was built on the edges of the square, but it was Sam Brannan's 1848 cry of "Gold!" here (see p.559) that sent property prices and development skyrocketing to levels from which they still haven't returned.

There are four points of interest in Portsmouth Square aside from the American flag. The first is a monument to writer **Robert Louis Stevenson**, featuring a replica of the galleon *Hispaniola* from his novel, *Treasure Island*: Stevenson spent much time observing the locals in Portsmouth Square during his brief sojourn in San Francisco and the Monterey Peninsula in the late 1870s. The plaque nearby honors **California's first public school**, built here in 1848; while the third monument is a tribute to cable-car poobah **Andrew Hallidie**, whose first line ran on Clay Street down the steps. The most recent addition to the square recognizes its role in the modern Chinatown: Thomas Marsh's bronze *Goddess of Democracy*, erected in memory of the 1989 Tian'anmen Square protests. Indeed, Portsmouth Square now marks the beginning of Chinatown, and whatever the time of day, it is filled with elderly Chinese practising *t'ai chi*, playing chess, or watching their grandchildren climb the new playground equipment.

Chinatown

CHINATOWN's twenty-four square blocks smack in the middle of San Francisco make up the second-largest (after New York City) Chinese community outside Asia. Its roots lie in the migration of Chinese laborers to the city after the completion of the transcontinental railroad, and the arrival of Chinese sailors keen to benefit from the Gold Rush. San Francisco is still known in China as "Old Gold Mountain," its storied moniker from the nineteenth century. The city didn't extend much of a welcome to Chinese immigrants: they were met by a tide of vicious racial attacks and the 1882 Chinese Exclusion Act that banned new immigration, a law that resulted in thousands of single Chinese men being forbidden from both dating local women and bringing wives from China. A rip-roaring prostitution and gambling quarter developed, controlled by gangs known as tongs. With the loosening of immigration rules due to China's partnership with the US during World War II, and decades of hard work by its residents, Chinatown has grown into a self-made success.

Many visitors assume that the neighborhood remains autonomous – cut off from San Francisco by language and cultural barriers. But Chinatown's residents are as American as the rest of the city's citizens, and the district has one of its highest voter turnouts come election day. Nowadays the population of Chinatown, descendants of Cantonese- and Fujianese-speaking southern mainlanders, as well as Taiwanese, have been joined by Mandarin-speaking northerners, Vietnamese, Koreans, Thais, and Laotians, turning the area into **Asiatown**. By day the area bustles with activity, by night it's a blaze of neon. Overcrowding is compounded by a brisk tourist trade – sadly, however, Chinatown boasts some of the tackiest stores and facades in the city, more like shopping in a cheesy part of Hong Kong than in Beijing. Indeed, Chinese visitors are often disappointed in the neighborhood's disorder and pandering to tourists – for a truer sense of everyday Chinese life in San Francisco, you're better off heading to the Richmond district (see p.610).

One major improvement to Chinatown – an attempt to keep tourists coming – is the new night market that happens under the stars every Saturday evening from 6pm to 11pm in Portsmouth Square, June to October (☎415/397-8000 for more information). Stalls pitching everything from fresh honey to leather jackets surround free performances of classical opera and traditional music.

The best way to approach Chinatown is through the dramatic **Chinatown Gate**, on the southern end of Grant Avenue at Bush. Facing south, per *feng shui* precepts, it's a large dragon-clad arch, with a four-character inscription that reads *Xia tian wei gong* or "The reason to exist is to serve the public good," given by the People's Republic of China to the city in 1969. It's hard to see how that idea is carried out on the blocks ahead: Grant's sidewalks are paved with plastic Buddhas, cloisonné "health balls", noisemakers, and chirping mechanical crickets that assault the ear and eye from every doorway. One of the oldest thoroughfares in the city, **Grant Avenue** – originally called Dupont Street – was a wicked ensemble of opium dens, bordellos, and gambling huts policed, if not terrorized, by tong hatchet-men. After the 1906 fire, though, the city decided to rename it in honor of president and Civil War hero Ulysses S. Grant and so in the process excise the seedy excesses for which it had been famous. Note the two pagoda-topped buildings on the corner of Grant and California streets, the Sing Fat and Sing Chong, important because they were the first to be constructed after the 1906 fire, signaling Chinese resolve to remain on the much-coveted land.

A few blocks west, running parallel to Grant Avenue, **Stockton Street** is refreshingly undertouristed, the commercial artery of the area for locals, packed with grocery stores and dim sum shops, as well as herbalists and fishmongers. Between Stockton Street and Grant Avenue, narrow Waverly Place also runs north–south and holds two opulent but skillfully hidden temples: **Norras** on the third floor of no. 109, and **Tien Hou** (pronounced TEE-en How) on the fourth floor of no. 125. This latter is especially impressive, a Taoist temple dedicated to the Goddess of Heaven, its ornate interior splashed with gold and vermilion, and its ceiling dripping with tassels and red lanterns. Both temples are still in use and open to visitors (daily 10am–5pm): note the pyramids of oranges, considered lucky because the Cantonese pronunciation of orange sounds similar to the word for wealth. Although the temples don't charge admission, it's respectful to leave a donation and not use cameras or camcorders inside. Note, too, the tiny mirrors fastened to the balcony of 829 Sacramento Street at the eastern end of Waverley Place: they're intended to ward off evil spirits.

Detour east along Washington Street from Grant Avenue to find the eye-catching **Bank of Canton**, no. 743, a small red pagoda-like structure built in 1909 for the Chinese American Telephone Exchange: note how the roof curves out and then back on itself, since evil spirits travel in a straight line. It stands on the original site of the offices of Sam Brannan's *California Star* newspaper, which carried the news of the earliest ore discoveries back to the East Coast in 1848 and so played a major role in creating the Gold Rush. Visitors interested in Buddhism should head to Buddha's Universal Church (☎415/982-6116) at no. 720, where America's largest Zen sect gives free tours on the second and fourth Sunday of each month, the only time it's open to the public. This five-story building was painstakingly constructed by the sect's members from an exotic collection of polished woods, adorned everywhere by the mosaic images of Buddha.

North Beach

Bordering Chinatown at the junction of Grant Avenue and Broadway, and Fisherman's Wharf to the south, bustling **NORTH BEACH** has always been a gateway for immigrants. Italian immigration to San Francisco was ignited, unsurprisingly, by the Gold Rush, although it gained momentum at the end of the nineteenth century, when this area began to develop the characteristics – delis, wine bars, salami grocers – of a true "Little Italy." The freewheeling European flavor here, coupled with a robust nightlife and wide availability of housing, attracted rebel writers like Lawrence Ferlinghetti, Allen Ginsberg, and Jack Kerouac in the 1950s, making North Beach the nexus of the **Beat movement** (see box opposite).

The main drag of North Beach is **Columbus Avenue**, proudly tagged as Little Italy by the flags painted on each lamppost, and now one of San Francisco's liveliest nighttime drags. At its southern end at the crossroads of **Columbus and Broadway**, you'll find the former site of many old bars and comedy clubs from the 1950s, where politically conscious comedians like Mort Sahl and Lenny Bruce performed. Many of the venues are now porno stores, which took over spaces here during the death throes of the Beat movement. It's ironic, given San Francisco's penchant for political correctness, that one of the city's legacies is the topless waitress phenomenon: at the *Condor Club* in 1964, Carol "44 inches" Doda slipped out of her top one night and into the history books. The club's now reincarnated as the (fully clothed) *Condor Sports Bar* at

The Beats in North Beach

Beat literature didn't begin in San Francisco, but emerged a decade earlier in New York, where bohemian Jack Kerouac had joined with the Ivy League–educated Allen Ginsberg, as well as William Burroughs, to bemoan the conservative political climate there. The group quickly grew frustrated with New York and moved out West, most of them settling in North Beach and securing jobs at the docks to help longshoremen unload the fishing boats. The first rumblings of interest in the movement were signaled by the opening, in 1953, of the first bookstore in America dedicated solely to paperbacks: Lawrence Ferlinghetti's City Lights Bookstore (see p.660) drew attention to the area as the latest literary capital of California.

But it wasn't until the publication four years later of Ginsberg's pornographic protest poem *Howl* – originally written simply for his own pleasure rather than for printing – that mainstream America took notice. Police moved in on City Lights to prevent the sale of the book, inadvertently catapulting the Beats to a national notoriety – assisted by press hysteria over their hedonistic antics, including heavy drinking and an immense fondness for pot – that matched what fame was based on the literary merits of their work. Ginsberg's case went all the way to the Supreme Court, which eventually ruled that so long as a work has "redeeming social value" it could not be considered pornographic. Within six months, Jack Kerouac's *On the Road*, inspired by his friend Neal Cassady's benzedrine monologues and several cross-country trips, had shot to the top of the bestseller lists, cementing the Beats' fame.

It's said that the word *Beatnik* was coined by legendary local newspaper columnist Herb Caen, who noted that the writers were as far out as the recently launched Soviet rocket, Sputnik, and so jokily christened them Beatniks. Soon, North Beach was synonymous across America with a wild and subversive lifestyle, an image that soon drove away the original artsy intelligentsia, many of whom ended up in Haight-Ashbury. Instead heat-seeking libertines swamped the area, accompanied by tourists on "Beatnik Tours," who were promised sidewalks clogged with black-bereted, goateed trendsetters banging bongos. (The more enterprising fringes of bohemia responded in kind with "The Squaresville Tour" of the Financial District, dressed in Bermuda shorts and carrying plaques that read "Hi, Squares.") It wasn't long before the Italians who'd once dominated North Beach moved back in and reclaimed it from the dwindling Beat movement.

Almost singlehandedly, Ferlinghetti has kept the Beat legend alive in North Beach. He successfully petitioned City Hall for streets to be renamed as a tribute to the famous figures who have graced the neighborhood; indeed, the small alley that runs down the side of the City Lights store has been called "Jack Kerouac Lane." Enamored of the way Paris honors its writers with street names, Ferlinghetti also campaigned for the inclusion of local non-Beat writers and artists. Accordingly, San Francisco now has streets bearing the names of many authors, including Mark Twain, Jack London, and Dashiell Hammett.

300 Columbus Ave. However, the current owners have preserved photos and clippings from the *Condor Club*'s heyday: one of the choicest stories is the sad tale of a randy bouncer and a waitress, who climbed on top of the club's rising piano together. In the throes of passion, they accidentally hit the lever, sending the piano up to the ceiling: the man was crushed to death, but he cushioned the woman beneath him and she survived. The only other notable sex joint, *The Lusty Lady*, 1033 Kearney St at Columbus (box office ☏415/391-3991), is a female-owned-and-operated strip club with unionized workers, successful enough to be opening satellite branches around the country.

Most people don't make a pilgrimage here for the porn, though; rather, they want to visit a beacon of San Francisco culture, **City Lights Bookstore**, 261

Columbus Ave at Broadway (Mon–Thurs & Sun 10am–11.30pm, Fri & Sat 10am–12.30am; ☎415/362-8193, ⊛www.citylights.com). This was the heart of Beat North Beach and struggles on as an independent bookstore, despite the encroachment of big-name chains and a surfeit of surly, Beat-inspired staff. The place is still owned by Ferlinghetti, who's now in his eighties: aside from its kooky section dividers – books filed under "Anarchism" and "Muckraking," for instance – the best reason to come here is the upstairs poetry room, where you'll find everything from $1 mini-books and poster-sized poems from Beatnik legends to various collections and anthologies.

The area grows more Italian as you head north along Columbus Avenue: from Vallejo Street to the waterfront, expect plenty of cafés, delis, and restaurants selling strong coffee and salami. One exception is the section of **Grant Avenue** north of Vallejo, where you'll find one of the best emerging shopping streets in the city, lined with clothing stores and divey cafés. It's also the site of San Francisco's oldest bar, *The Saloon*, at no. 1232 (☎415/989-7666) – a rare North Beach survivor of the 1906 fire, now little more than a hole in the wall.

The soul of North Beach is **Washington Square Park**, a grassy plaza that plays host to dozens of older, local Chinese each morning, clumped in groups across the lawn to practice *t'ai chi*. Delightfully loopy local legend Lillie Coit's not-so-subtle fascination with firefighters (see opposite) can be seen on the Columbus side in the form of a big, bronze macho monument with men holding hoses. On the north side of the park, the white lacy spires of the **Church of St Peter and Paul** look like a pair of fairytale castles rising beneath the shadow of Telegraph Hill's Coit Tower: unfortunately, the interior's an unremarkable nineteenth-century confection with little to recommend it. In 1954, local baseball phenom Joe DiMaggio and Marilyn Monroe had their wedding pictures taken here (though the actual marriage took place earlier at City Hall since both were divorced). Note how masses here are celebrated in three languages: Italian, English, and Cantonese, reflecting the shift in the neighborhood's population.

Telegraph Hill

Dominated by Coit Tower, **TELEGRAPH HILL** is a quiet cluster of hill-hugging homes. The most direct path up its slope is Filbert Street, but be aware that the gradient east of Grant Avenue is very steep. The ten-minute walk's pleasant enough, though, past clapboard houses and flowery gardens on a terraced sidewalk – don't hurry and keep turning round to catch the breathtaking views. Since there are few parking spots at the tower, non-walkers are better holding out for the (infallibly infrequent) MUNI bus #39 to the top. Once you reach the summit, it's easy to see why it was used as a signal tower for ships entering the Golden Gate. A watchman on the hill would identify the boat's origin and name by the flags flying on the mast, and relay the information via telegraph to the docks along Fisherman's Wharf. A plaque in front of a statue honoring Christopher Columbus in **Pioneer Park**, which lies at the foot of the tower, marks the watchman's spot.

The park, which was donated to the city by private citizens in 1875, contains the best viewpoint in all of Telegraph Hill, **Coit Tower** (daily 10am–5pm; $3; ☎415/362-0808, ⊛www.coittower.org). Built with money bequeathed by Lillie Coit in 1929 as a tribute to the city's firemen, the tower is an attractive component of the city's skyline, and rewards those who trudge uphill with sweeping views from its observation deck. Legend has it that as a young girl,

Lillie answered the cries of "Help!" and assisted the Knickerbocker Engine Company No. 5 of the Volunteer Fire Department as they towed their engine up Telegraph Hill. Grateful firefighters made her their mascot, and even after she married wealthy Easterner Howard Coit in 1868, Lillie continued attending firemen's balls and playing poker over cigars with "her" men of Company No. 5. Local stories abound of her character and exploits, including scenes of dashing away from society balls and chasing clanging fire engines. Upon her death, she left behind $125,000 "to be expended in an appropriate manner for the purpose of adding to the beauty of the city, which I have always loved." The result is the 212-foot pillar that looks alarmingly like a firehose nozzle. Coit's rumored liaisons with firemen add fuel to the speculation that the tower was actually her parting memorial to another part of a fireman's equipment.

While waiting to ascend to the top, take some time to admire the frescoes at the interior's base. They were an early project overseen by the Public Works of Art Authority, a predecessor of the WPA that employed artists to decorate public and government buildings during the Depression. Those chosen for this project were students of the famous Mexican artist, **Diego Rivera**, who was both artistically and politically influenced by Russian Communism. As in his work, the figures are typically muscular and somber, emphasizing the glory of labor, although there's a wide variation in style and quality between panels, despite their thematic cohesion. You can take a free tour of the murals Saturday at 11am as part of the City Guides series (ⓦwww.sfcityguides.com).

The best way down Telegraph Hill is on the eastern side, where the Greenwich Steps cling to the hill at a 45-degree angle, one of several walkways and pedestrian streets. Another, equally lovely walkway is the **Filbert Steps**, dropping down even more steeply before plateauing at Montgomery Street in a leafy garden surrounded by simple cottages. These single-story houses were built in the 1850s by Gold Rush immigrants, who needed quick, temporary homes while they found their fortunes. At the foot of Telegraph Hill, between Battery Street and the Embarcadero stands **Levi Strauss Plaza** (Mon–Fri 9am–6pm, Sat & Sun 10am–5pm; free; ☏415/501-6000, ⓦwww.levistrauss .com), current headquarters of blue-jean inventors Levi Strauss & Co. (hence the "SF" on the pocket rivets). It's a grim, unappealing place, constructed entirely out of red brick, with looming buildings and little life on the terraces. The company recently upgraded its forlorn museum in the lobby into a state-of-the-art visitors center to showcase its history and product; the result's inevitably rather breathless and uncritical, but the displays of consumers' letters to the company is intriguing.

Russian Hill

West of North Beach, elegant **RUSSIAN HILL**, named for six unknown Russian sailors who died on an expedition here in the early 1800s and were buried on its southeastern tip, has the odd point of interest. The modest high-rises that you see at the top of the hill were fiercely contested when they were first built in the 1920s, prompting many of San Francisco's stringent zoning laws. Most people, though, come here for the white-knuckle drive down Lombard Street, a terracotta-tiled waterchute for cars. Its tight, narrow curves swoop down one block, and there's a 5mph speed limit here – not that you'll be able to drive much faster given the usual lines to enjoy the drive. Wealthy owners of the manicured houses along its edges have petitioned numerous times to close the road, but given how often this cutesy block is featured in San Francisco publicity shots – not to mention the city's supine bureaucracy – they're unlikely to succeed. The best time to enjoy it is early morning or, better still, late at night when the city lights twinkle below and the tourists have gone.

It's easy to get your bearings in the neighborhood, as the cable-car tracks along **Hyde Street** neatly divide the district in two. Two blocks east down the hill, the low-rise Mission-style building of the **San Francisco Art Institute**, 800 Chestnut St at Leavenworth (gallery hours Mon–Sat 11am–6pm; free; ☎415/771-7020, ⊛www.sanfranciscoart.edu), clings to the side of a steep street. It's easy to miss this place, which is in fact the oldest art school in the West (past students include Jerry Garcia and Lawrence Ferlinghetti; Ansel Adams started its photography department). Unfortunately, many of its galleries are often closed, since it's still a working school. The one unmissable sight is the **Diego Rivera Gallery**, with an outstanding mural called *The Making of a Fresco Showing the Building of a City*, executed by the painter in 1931 at the height of his fame.

Nob Hill

The posh hotels and Masonic institutions of **NOB HILL**, south of Russian Hill and west of Chinatown, exemplify San Francisco's old wealth: it was here that the four men who transformed California through railroads all built their houses. Once you've made the stiff climb up (or taken the California line cable car), there are very few real sights as such, apart from the astounding views over the city and beyond. Indeed, the streets are oddly deserted, and despite its dense population, there's a definite sense of isolation and privacy that exists in few other parts of the city.

Originally called California Street Hill, the 376-foot-high hill used to be scrubland occupied by sheep. The invention of the cable car made it accessible to Gold Rush millionaires, and the area became known as Nob Hill (from "nabob" a Moghul prince, or "snob," or "knob" as in rounded hill) after **The Big Four** – Leland Stanford, Collis P. Huntington, Mark Hopkins, and Charles Crocker – came to the area to construct the Central Pacific Railroad, and built their mansions here.

Ostentatious designs created out of Marin-headlands redwood were the fashion: unfortunately, after the earthquake and fire of 1906, every one of the mansions on Nob Hill had burned to the ground, with a single exception. James C. Flood had bucked local fashions and instead emulated the brownstone style popular on New York's Fifth Avenue: the stone weathered the fire, as did the burnt-out shell of the as-yet-uncompleted *Fairmont Hotel*. Flood's mansion, constructed in 1886 at the cost of a cool $1 million, is now the private **Pacific Union Club**, a retreat for the rich, closed to the public. Across California Street, you'll find another jaw-dropping view and even more startling prices at San Francisco's most famous vista-bar, *The Top of the Mark*, in the grand, castle-like **Mark Hopkins Hotel** (supposedly where Tony Bennett found his inspiration for *I Left My Heart in San Francisco*).

Overlooking Huntington Park, the manicured green space at the summit of Nob Hill, is one of the biggest hunks of sham-Gothic architecture in the US, **Grace Cathedral**, 1100 California St (Mon–Fri & Sun 7am–6pm, Sat 8am–6pm, Sun 7am–7pm; free tours available Mon–Fri 1–3pm, Sat 11.30am–1.30pm, Sun 12.30–2pm; ☎415/749-6300, ⊛www.gracecathedral .org). Although this pale copy of Notre Dame in Paris was begun after the 1906 fire on land donated by the wealthy Crocker family, it took until the early 1960s to finish – and it suffers from a hodgepodge of styles as a result. The cathedral gives an impression of unloved hugeness, despite florid touches

San Francisco's steepest streets

Though no street can match Lombard for its fabled curves, the wait to go down them may force you to consider another itinerary if pressed for time. The city's second-twistiest street lies coiled in the outer Potrero Hill neighborhood, on Vermont Street between McKinley and 22nd streets: it has five full and two half-turns (compared with Lombard's eight), and its location keeps traffic flowing. Another San Francisco thrill that'll test the brakes of your car is to take a ride down any of the city's steepest streets. Since most locals prefer not to brave the steeper streets – even if that forces them to make an elaborate detour – you won't normally have to wait to freewheel down one of the following. We've included the hill's neighborhood to help find it on a map.

	degree
1) Filbert between Leavenworth and Hyde, Russian Hill	31.5
2) 22nd Street between Church and Vicksburg, Castro/Noe Valley	31.5
3) Jones between Union and Filbert, Russian Hill	29.0
4) Duboce between Buena Vista and Alpine, Lower Haight	27.9
5) Jones between Green and Union, Russian Hill	26.0
6) Webster between Vallejo and Broadway, Pacific Heights	26.0
7) Duboce between Alpine and Divisadero, Lower Haight	25.0
8) Jones between Pine and California, Nob Hill	24.8
9) Fillmore between Vallejo and Broadway, Pacific Heights	24.0

like the faithful replicas of Ghiberti's Renaissance doors from the Florence Baptistry adorning the main entrance. Utterly out of place, they're included simply because they were available: during construction, the first commercial copies of the fifteenth-century masterpiece were produced, and the supervising architect snapped them up. Inside, check out the AIDS Interfaith Chapel to the right of the main entrance with a bronze altar designed by the late pop artist Keith Haring.

Fisherman's Wharf

San Francisco doesn't go dramatically out of its way to court and fleece the tourist, but with **FISHERMAN'S WHARF** it makes a rare exception (ⓦwww.fishermanswharf.org). This is the one place in town guaranteed to produce shudders of embarrassment from most locals and, even for visitors with kids, there are better places (like Golden Gate Park; see p.608) to dawdle for an afternoon. Despite its tacky reputation, though, the wharf is massively popular: a creative use of statistics allows the area to proclaim itself the most visited attraction in the entire country. If you want to enjoy the waterfront, a better option is a stroll through the parks in the Marina; but if you're determined to see the wharf, avoid weekends and try to get there as early as possible before the crowds descend.

Hard as it might be to believe now, Fisherman's Wharf was once a serious fishing port. The few fishermen that can afford the exorbitant mooring charges these days are usually finished by early morning and are gone before visitors arrive. You can still find some decent seafood here at some of the better restaurants (see "Eating," p.612), but worthwhile sights or remnants of the fishing trade are few and far between. The most endearing sight at the wharf is a large colony of boisterous sea lions (no feeding allowed) that have taken over a number of floating platforms at sea level between piers 39 and 41. To see more aquatic life, check out Aquarium of the Bay at Pier 39 (summer daily

9am–8pm; rest of year Mon–Fri 10am–6pm, Sat & Sun 10am–7pm; $12.95, $6.50 kids; ⊕1-888/732-3483, �ⓦwww.aquariumofthebay.com). Here, you'll get spectacular close-up views of fish and crustaceans that surround you as you trundle slowly along a 400ft acrylic viewing tunnel – it's just a pity about the throbbing muzak. It isn't a patch on the Monterey Bay Aquarium, though (see p.535), so if you have time, you're better off heading down the coast instead of spending money here. Close by at Pier 45 is the eccentric Musée Mécanique (Mon–Fri 11am–7pm, Sat & Sun 10am–8pm; ⊕415/346-2000, ⓦwww .museemecanique.com).It's an appealing collection of historic arcade games; if you want to play, bring plenty of quarters. The games range from retro classics like a 1980s Pac Man to a freakish, gap-toothed clown who'll cackle forever in return for 25¢.

Where once the wharf focused on catching fish, now it is disposable tourist dollars it's after – there are dozens of tacky souvenir shops as well as bland malls. An exception is the sensitively converted **Ghirardelli Square**, 900 N Point St at Larkin (⊕415/775-5500, ⓦwww.ghirardellisq.com): originally a woollen mill, it was purchased by Domenico Ghirardelli to house his expanding chocolate empire. Ghirardelli was a gold prospecter-turned-grocer who in 1865 discovered the Broma process, which sweats butter out of raw cocoa, and made a fortune. There are a few pricey shops here, and some fine restaurants, although there's no manufacturing on site now (Ghirardelli's has moved across the Bay to cheaper premises in Oakland).

Bay cruises depart from piers 39, 41, and 431/2 several times a day; they're run by various operators, including the firm that ships tourists out to Alcatraz (see below) and usually cost $20 per person. Provided the fogs aren't too heavy (which, even in summer, is often an issue), they give worthwhile city views.

Alcatraz

The rocky little islet of **ALCATRAZ**, rising out of San Francisco Bay north of Fisherman's Wharf, was originally home to nothing more than the odd pelican. In the mid-nineteenth century, the island became a military fortress, first to help defend the coastline of the newly created state of California; and later, during the Civil War, to protect the state from falling into confederate hands. But military technology soon improved enough that fortresses such as this became obsolete; eventually, in 1934, the rock was put to use again and converted into one of America's most **dreaded high-security prisons**. Surrounded by freezing, impassable water, Alcatraz was an ideal place for a jail: this is where many of America's brand-name criminals like Al Capone and Machine Gun Kelly were held. Although conditions were softened as time passed – look for the radio jacks installed in each cell in the 1950s – a stay in one of the tiny, lonely rooms must have been psychologically grueling, especially given the islet's proximity to the glittering lights of San Francisco. Escape, of course, was impossible, thanks to the violent currents that churn constantly in the icy bay: in all, nine men managed to get off "The Rock," but no one managed to swim to freedom.

Note that The Rock's curious name is part corruption, part mistake. An early explorer christened one island in the Bay *Isla de Alcatraces* (Island of Pelicans) in honor of the hundreds of birds who lived on it; however, the island he was referring to is not the one we now know as Alcatraz. The pelicans' old home is currently called Yerba Buena Island because a clumsy English sea captain got confused when mapping the Bay in 1826. He assumed (wrongly) that the rock he saw covered with guano must be the birds' home; so he marked that in mangled Spanglish as Alcatraz, then assigned the name Yerba Buena to the other penguin-dotted islet.

These days the island's only function is as a tourist attraction, and at least 750,000 visitors each year take the excellent hour-long, self-guided audio **tours** ($4) of the abandoned prison. These include some sharp anecdotal commentary as well as campy re-enactments of prison life featuring improvised voices of characters like Capone and Kelly. Skip the dull twelve-minute introductory film at the dock – you're far better joining one of the lively, free ranger talks on a variety of themes, which run five times daily (check the schedule when you arrive or call ☎415/705-5555, ⊛www.nps.gov/alcatraz). Blue and Gold Fleet runs enormous **boats** to Alcatraz, leaving from Pier 41 (frequent departures from 9.30am, last boat back at 4.30pm, 6.30pm in summer, also evening cruises, times and prices vary; $16 including audio tour, $11.50 without; information ☎415/773-1188, advance booking ☎415/705-5555, ⊛www .blueandgoldfleet.com). Advance reservations are essential: expect a two-week wait in peak season. In summer, the company also runs a day-tour that combines a visit to Alcatraz with a stop at Angel Island ($41.50).

The western waterfront and around

A little way west of the wharf, beyond Ghirardelli Square, the **Golden Gate National Recreation Area** was established in 1972 to protect much-needed central park space for the city, and now encompasses almost seventy square miles of waterfront property, from the beaches to the south right up to the cliffs of Marin County across the Golden Gate Bridge. Closest to the wharf, the **Aquatic Park** complex of buildings groups around the foot of Hyde Street, at its center the "bathhouse" – a bold, Art Deco piece of architecture now home to the **Maritime Museum**, 900 Beach St (daily 10am–5pm; free; ☎415/556-3002, ⊛www.maritime.org). Sadly, few of the exhibits hold much interest other than the trippy **mural** in the main room, painted by Hilaire Hiller in 1939 and symbolizing the lost continent of Atlantis in 37 individual panels; the rest of the complex includes a maritime library and a forgettable collection of ocean-going memorabilia. Better, in fact, is the small selection of naval knickknacks at the Visitor Center inside the nearby Cannery complex (499 Jefferson St, June–Sept 9.30am–7pm; Oct–May 9.30am–5pm; free; ⊛www.nps.gov/safr). There's a relief map of the treacherous ridges along the

Native Americans and Alcatraz

For all its usefulness as a jail, **Alcatraz** turned out to be a fiscal disaster, and, after years of operating at massive costs, it finally closed in 1963. The remaining prisoners were distributed among decidedly less horrific detention centers, and the island remained abandoned until 1969, when a group of **Native Americans** staged an occupation as part of a peaceful attempt to claim the island for their people – citing treaties which designated all federal land not in use as automatically reverting to their ownership. The government, using all the bureaucratic trickery it could muster, finally ousted the floundering movement in 1971 by claiming the operative lighthouse on The Rock qualified it as active. The occupation may have seemed a failure, but in marking the 25th anniversary of the event, participant Fortunate Eagle noted that it acted as a huge bargaining chip for American Indians, citing President Nixon's **return of contested lands** back to Native American tribes as a victory made possible by the precedent action.

seabed around San Francisco showing where dozens of ships have wrecked over the years, as well as the original lamp from the Farrallon Island lighthouse in the bay. At the adjacent **Hyde Street Pier** (mid-May to mid-Sept daily 9am–5.30pm; mid-Sept to mid-May daily 9am–5pm; $5; ☎415/561-7100, ⓦwww.maritime.org), the museum has restored a number of old wooden ships that are worth clamoring around on to get a sense of the boats that voyagers like Richard Henry Dana entrusted with their lives. The best is the square-rigger *Balclutha*, built in 1886 and the sole survivor of the great sailing ships that journeyed around Cape Horn in the 1800s. Of course, being that it's now in California, the boat also had a second career in the movies, playing bit parts in 1930s films like *Mutiny on the Bounty*.

Fort Mason

Half a mile west along the waterfront, **Fort Mason** (ⓦwww.fortmason.org) sits behind a lovely open park giving great views of the Golden Gate Bridge. The area can be reached by walking along the Golden Gate Promenade, a stretch of pavement popular with joggers and in-line skaters. Originally a Civil War defense installation, now turned over to public use, the old buildings of Fort Mason are occupied by around fifty non-profit groups including theaters, galleries, and museums, plus a youth hostel (see p.574).

The centerpiece of the complex's museums is the **Museum of Craft and Folk Art** in Building A (Tues–Fri & Sun 11am–5pm, Sat 10am–5pm; $3, free Sat 10am–noon; ☎415/775-0991, ⓦwww.mocfa.org), which features up to ten different exhibitions each year, including both local and international work. Of the other museums here, the two best are in the large waterfront Building C at the heart of the complex: the **Museo Italo-Americano** (Wed–Sun noon–5pm; $3; ☎415/673-2200, ⓦwww.museoitaloamericano.org), with displays relating to the culture and history of the Italian community in the US; the **African-American Historical and Cultural Society** (Wed–Sun noon–5pm; $2; ☎415/441-0640), meanwhile, commemorates local black leaders and historical figures. The best time to visit is on the first Wednesday of every month, when every museum is not only free, but open until 7pm too.

San Francisco's most theatrical piece of architecture lies a few hundred yards further west at Marina Boulevard and Baker Street. **The Palace of Fine Arts**, 3301 Lyon St (☎415/563-6504, ⓦwww.palaceoffinearts.org), is not the museum its name suggests, but a huge, freely interpreted classical ruin by Bernard Maybeck that anyone can wander around. It was erected for the Panama Pacific International Exhibition in 1915 and, when all the other buildings were torn down, the palace was saved simply because locals thought it too beautiful to destroy. Unfortunately, since it was built of wood, plaster, and burlap, it crumbled with dignity until the late 1950s when a wealthy resident put up money for the structure to be recast in reinforced concrete. To a modern eye, the palace is a moody and mournfully sentimental piece of Victoriana, complete with weeping figures on the colonnade by sculptor Ulric Ellerhusen, said to represent the melancholy of life without art (the originals are now in the Exploratorium nearby).

Next door, the **Exploratorium**, 3601 Lyon Street at Baker, is the best kids' museum in San Francisco (Tues–Sun 10am–5pm; $12, free first Wed of the month; information ☎415/563-7337, Tactile Dome reservations ☎415/561-0362, ⓦwww.exploratorium.edu). It crams in more than 650 hands-on exhibits, including the famous Tactile Dome, a total sensory-deprivation dome, explored on hands and knees, which is not for the claustrophobic (reservations essential). Plan to visit as early as possible since it can get very busy later in the day, especially during school holidays. From here, the waterfront stretches west through the Presidio National Park and the quirky Presidio pet cemetery on Crissy Field Avenue, to Fort Point, the Golden Gate Bridge, and the beach area close to Golden Gate Park (see p.608).

The Marina
The area around the Palace of Fine Arts, the **MARINA**, is one of the city's greenest districts, enjoying a prime waterfront location and lots of open space. Homogeneously young, white, professional, and straight, it prompts derision from artier locals, who pinpoint the Marina, with its swanky yacht clubs and jogger-laden paths, as the local yuppie mother lode. Ironically, though it was built specifically to celebrate the rebirth of the city after the massive earthquake of 1906, the Marina was the worst casualty of the earthquake in 1989 – tremors tore through fragile landfill and a good number of homes collapsed into smoldering heaps. The neighborhood's commercial center runs along Chestnut Street between Broderick and Fillmore, and most of the amenities are geared to swinging singles. The local watering holes are known as "high intensity breeder bars" and there's a massive branch of Safeway, the heterosexual answer to the frenzied gay cruising that takes place in the Market Street outpost near the Castro. In fact, so prevalent is the pick-up scene that the Marina location has even been dubbed, without a trace of irony, "The Body Shop."

Cow Hollow
Originally a small valley of pastures and dairies in the post–Gold Rush years, **COW HOLLOW** languished until the 1950s, when problems with open sewage and complaints from neighbors up on prestigious Pacific Heights about the smell of the cows allowed enterprising merchants to transform the area. The gorgeous old Victorian houses have since been refitted, especially around Filbert and Green streets, and the stretch of Union between Van Ness and Divisadero now holds one of the city's densest concentrations of boutiques and cafés. This street is alive with neighborhood shoppers and the dearth of tourist sights is what keeps it appealing.

The one sight that's worth seeking out is the oddball **Octagon House Museum** on the corner of Union and Gough streets (second Sun, second and fourth Thurs of each month noon–3pm; closed Jan; donation suggested; ☎415/441-7512). It's worth a peek if you happen to be there during its very limited hours of operation, thanks in part to the knowledgeable and enthusiastic docents. Built in 1861, when it was believed increased exposure to sunlight benefited one's health, the house remains in excellent, and sunny, condition. A time capsule stashed under the stairs by its first owner was discovered during recent renovations, and is a captivating glimpse of late nineteenth-century local life including a letter, a newspaper, and photographs of his family. Next door, leafy **Allyne Park** is named after the sisters who donated the land for both the house and garden: it feels more like someone's backyard than a public space, but its redwood trees and comfy benches are an idyllic place to rest.

Pacific Heights
Perched on steep hills between Cow Hollow and Japantown, wealthy **PACIFIC HEIGHTS** is home to some of the city's most monumental Victorian piles and stone mansions – a millionaires' ghetto, beautifully poised around two windswept parks. The lavishly proportioned mansions that teeter precipitously atop these hills today are the chosen domains of stockbrokers, business magnates, and the odd best-selling novelist, like Danielle Steel (see p.594), who lives in one of the largest houses in the city.

The neighborhood is neatly divided by Fillmore Street: to the west are the large dwellings that earned the neighborhood its reputation; to the east, swanky Art Deco apartment buildings that do little to damage it. West of Fillmore Street, lower Pacific Heights is centered on restful **Alta Plaza Park**, at Clay and Steiner streets, where local dog-walkers earn their keep by exercising pampered pooches. East of Fillmore, facing the cypress-dotted peak of **Lafayette Park** are several noteworthy mansions: the squat brownstone at 2150 Washington St at Laguna is known as the **Phelan Mansion** and was built by former mayor James Phelan. He's famous both as an anti-Asian protectionist and the senator who pushed to bring a poet laureateship to California. Not far away stands the **Spreckels Mansion**, 2080 Washington St at Octavia: this gaudily decadent white-stone palace was constructed for sugar magnate Adolph Spreckels and his wayward wife, Alma, a former nude model who posed for the statue at the center of Union Square (see p.576). Auguste Rodin's first US patron, Alma donated her spectacular collection of his work to the California Palace of the Legion of Honor, a museum she built (see p.611). The home she and Adolph shared is now owned by romance pulpist Danielle Steel, who pumped a not-so-small fortune into the structure's restoration and upkeep. Neither of these houses is open to the public – for admission to a Pacific Heights mansion, you'll have to head two blocks east to the ornate **Haas–Lilienthal House** at 2007 Franklin St at Washington (compulsory 1hr tours leave every 20–30min, Wed noon–3pm, Sun 11am–4pm; $5; ☎415/441-3004, ⊛www.sfheritage.org). This double-sized Queen Anne Victorian was built for his growing family by a wealthy merchant, William Haas; and the talky tours are more illuminating about the family's day-to-day life than about the architecture of the building. Even so, it's a grand symbol of old wealth, with intricate wooden towers outside, and Tiffany art-glass and stenciled leather paneling inside.

SoMa, the Tenderloin, and the Civic Center

While parts of San Francisco can almost seem to be an urban utopia, the adjoining districts of the **Tenderloin** and the **Civic Center** reveal harsher realities. Particularly in the Tenderloin, the homeless and disaffected are very much in evidence – the flipside of California's low-tax prosperity is alive and unwell – and their constant presence in front of City Hall is an ironic reminder of governmental failures. Thus far, sporadic attempts to improve the areas have been at best well-meaning hit-and-misses or, at worst, patently cosmetic gestures bound to fail; Gavin Newsom, who took office as mayor in 2004, guaranteed that this problem would be one of his priorities if elected, though so far he's made little visible headway. In contrast, the once shabby **SoMa** took an unimaginable upswing in recent years, thanks in part to Internet start-up companies attracted to the district's low rents. Once the dot-com crash came, the techies fled and the neighborhood slowly sank back into its grimier former appearance. Slowly once more, the district's reviving; at night, it booms with the muffled reverberations of underground dance clubs, but nearer to downtown, **Yerba Buena**, a new museum and entertainment complex, draws daytime visitors, as does the new baseball stadium along the waterfront to the east.

South of Market

SOMA, the distinctly urban district **So**uth of **Ma**rket Street, stretches diagonally from the Mission in the southwest to the waterfront in the northeast. While the western sections have always been a working-class community, it's

Constructed from redwood culled from the Marin Headlands across the Golden Gate, San Francisco's **Victorians** enjoyed their greatest popularity in the late nineteenth century, preferred by homeowners who could use "signature details" in crafting the facade to differentiate their house from every other. This ostentation came at a price: unlike many of the stone-built homes, the earthquake and fire of 1906 easily destroyed most of the city's grandest Victorians on Nob Hill, and the axe-ravaged hillsides of Marin County made replacing them difficult. Also, a post-1906 trend made embellishment embarrassing, ushering in an era of muted stone or stucco designs still seen around town today.

Nostalgia coupled with tourism and a thriving economy, plus thousands of new homebuyers, resurrected the Victorian style in San Francisco. A 1976 survey by the National Endowment for the Arts found 13,487 Victorians in the city, and restoration efforts were undertaken to save the crumbling edifices in the Haight-Ashbury, Western Addition, Noe Valley, and other southern neighborhoods. Today, Victorian restoration is a lucrative – and grueling – profession for city engineering firms, and a "saved" home rarely sells for less than $500,000, no matter how seedy the neighborhood.

ironic, given the area's grubby recent history, that the waterfront **Rincon Hill** – not to mention the South Park district – were home to the first of the city's banking elite. By the 1870s, they were drawn away to Nob Hill by the newly invented cable car and within thirty years, South of Market had been turned over to industrial development and warehouses. The poorer community that remained was largely driven out by fires following the 1906 earthquake, and Rincon Hill was eventually cleared in 1930 to make way for the new Bay Bridge. By the 1990s factories and warehouses were relentlessly converted to offices for the fledgling Internet industry, instantly creating a bustling, lively neighborhood filled with young people. Sadly, when the Internet excesses crashed, so did SoMa, and the acres of empty office spaces are testament to its renewed struggle for economic prosperity. Despite the Web boom and bust, there are still parts of SoMa that are downright dangerous: the most notorious is Sixth Street (where you're quite likely to see drug deals go down in broad daylight). Stay accordingly alert and keep valuables hidden.

The big new attraction here is temporary: the **California Academy of Sciences** has decamped from Golden Gate Park until late 2008 while its original site is radically rebuilt (there's a model of the Renzo Piano–designed replacement – an eco-friendly modernist building – in the lobby). The two-level current location showcases a smaller collection in a rugged, industrial setting that's unlikely to captivate adults but is a delight for kids – and expect it to be clogged with school groups during the week (875 Howard St at 5th; daily 10am–5pm, docent tours available Wed & Thurs 10am–2pm, Fri 10am–noon; $7; ☎415/321-8000, @www.calacademy.org). There are rotating science exhibits spread across both floors plus Nature's Nest, a themed playroom for the under-5s; while the **Steinhart Aquarium** has a permanent, if tiny, home here until 2008. Among the clearly labeled modular tanks, each holding a different species, look for the garishly furry pink and white anemones and the shy, oddly unscary piranhas which lurk at the bottom of their tank.

Along the SoMa's bayfront, meanwhile, an array of new upscale condominium complexes have sprung up in the nascent **South Beach** district, aided by public works aimed at improving transportation and beautifying a waterfront long hidden in the shadows of the thankfully departed freeway. A block inland from the waterfront is the **Rincon Center** at 101 Spear St and Mission. Originally a US Post Office, it was constructed in 1939, and the building is a fine example of Depression Moderne architecture, with its smooth, imposing lines, outer simplicity, and ornamented interior. The lobby of the old post office is lavishly decorated with murals about California history, the largest commission ever by the WPA, painted by Russian expat artist Anton Refregier in 1941. It became a yuppified shopping center in the 1980s and still has a few good lunch spots.

Unfortunately, the area of SoMa around Second Street was especially doomed by the dot-com bust, and many of the companies that energized the local real-estate market are gone, leaving nothing but chic office furniture and "For Rent" signs in their wake. There are two noteworthy attractions, though, that make a detour here worthwhile: firstly, the **California Historical Society**, at 678 Mission St at Second (Wed–Sat noon–4.30pm; $3; ☎415/357-1848, ◉www.californiahistoricalsociety.org). A tiny, offbeat gem, it showcases ephemera from the state's history, including maps and photographs, and is especially strong on the cultural and political fallout from early Spanish settlement. Opposite stands another appealing but overlooked attraction: the **Cartoon Art Museum**, 655 Mission St at New Montgomery (Tues–Sun 11am–5pm; $6, first Tues of the month voluntary donation; ☎415/227-8669, ◉www.cartoonart.org). In its enormous slab-concrete gallery space, the museum curates rotating exhibits of cells and drawings, usually a sprightly mix of high concept "art-oons" by the likes of French illustrator Möebius and populist strips like *Peanuts*.

Until it was finally, socially fumigated a decade or so ago, Third Street symbolized San Francisco's urban issues: a crime-ridden strip minutes from the tourist trail along Market Street. The new wave of development, centered on Yerba Buena Gardens, is an indication of how seriously San Francisco has tried to spiff up the neighborhood. **Yerba Buena Gardens** has inviting lawns that are often packed with office workers on warm weekday lunchtimes: don't miss the fifty-foot granite waterfall memorial to Martin Luther King Jr, inscribed with extracts from his speeches, which stretches along its eastern edge. On the terrace above the waterfall, a Sister Cities garden features flora from each of the thirteen cities worldwide that are twinned with San Francisco: look for camellias from Shanghai and cyclamen from Haifa, among others.

New attractions radiate from the gardens on each side: to the east stands the **Yerba Buena Center for the Arts**, 701 Mission St at Third (Thurs–Sat noon–8pm, Sun, Tues & Wed noon–5pm, first Thurs of every month 11am–8pm; $6; ☎415/978-2787, ◉www.ybca.org). The center was initially conceived as a forum for community art projects but has recently expanded its repertoire, hosting international touring exhibitions and performances in its two main spaces. The small second-floor screening room shows works by local experimental filmmakers, as well as themed programs of cult and underground films – call or check the center's website for the latest schedules.

Opposite the Center for the Arts is the area's – perhaps the city's – marquee museum: the **SF Museum of Modern Art** at 151 3rd St (June–Aug Fri–Tues 10am–6pm, Thurs 10am–9pm, closed Wed; $10, free first Tues of every month, half price Thurs 6–9pm; ☎415/357-4000, ◉www.sfmoma.org), an attraction so adored that it risks suffocating under the weight of superlatives piled on it since its construction in 1995. Certainly, it's a striking structure. Designed by Swiss architect Mario Botta at a reported cost of $62 million, SFMoMA vies to be the West Coast's premier exhibition space. It hosts touring shows from New York and Europe while struggling to assemble a collection worthy of its housing. Frankly, the traveling exhibits are more impressive than the patchy permanent work: head to the upper floors for temporary exhibits and make sure to stop by the fine outdoor sculpture garden on the fourth floor. The best permanent holdings are of the **California school**, with works by Richard Diebenkorn as well as Frida Kahlo and her husband Diego Rivera, plus a notable collection of **abstract expressionist** works by Mark Rothko, Jackson Pollock, and Robert Rauschenberg. Whatever the quality of work within, the building steals the show and is itself worth visiting: a huge central skylight floods the space with light, while the upper galleries are connected by a vertigo-inducing metal catwalk made up of tiny slats that challenges the definition of "adventurous" art.

Next to the glorious gardens stands one of the least appealing sights in the city: the **Sony Metreon**, 101 4th St at Mission (daily 10am–10pm; ☎415/369-6000, ⓦwww.metreon.com). If Sony made food, you could buy it here: as it is, you'll have to settle for a *Starbucks* coffee while wandering through this enormous, 3-D advert for the electronics giant. Thanks to its blatant and relentless shill on behalf of the company's products, and the fact it's jammed with arcade games, as a mall, the Metreon's empty and rather dull: the one upside, according to locals, is that there's now a large cinema within convenient reach of downtown, as well as an **IMAX** theater (check ⓦwww.metreon.com for schedule and prices).

Walking further down the entirely unscenic Third Street might not seem to promise much, but hidden down a short alley next to a gas station is the surprising sanctuary of **South Park**, a picturesque European-style common. The park was the nexus of SoMa's multimedia community and locals have been able to gauge the health of the ailing industry by the diminishing numbers of office workers eating lunches in the park. Its shops and cafés are pricey, but it's still an extremely pleasant place to get a meal or lounge for the afternoon. Along with Jackson Square (see p.581), this is also one of the only spots in the city that truly feels like a window into another time – it's not hard to imagine horse-drawn carriages leisurely passing the park's slender oval.

The name may not be pretty, but **SBC Park**, the San Francisco Giants' new stadium south of South Park, is undoubtedly a major improvement over their much-maligned old home at Candlestick Park. Prone to gusts of brutally cold wind, the "Stick" (as it was semi-affectionately known) was everything you didn't want in a baseball stadium, making an afternoon at the ballgame feel like leisure time in a meat locker. The new stadium, in one of the sunniest parts of town, has an outfield that opens onto the Bay; special permission was required from the league to allow the design, since the short rightfield fence allows superstar Barry Bonds to hit home runs more easily. (Bonds is a stalwart of the team, who's shattered the season home-run record – he hit 73 out of the park – as well as leading the Giants to victory in the World Series 1992, their first triumph since the 1980s.) If you want to see the stadium but not the team, terrific tours leave from the dugout store on Third Street (daily except on home-game days 10.30am & 12.30pm). Tickets cost $10 – more than the price of a cheap seat and you'll not only get to sit in the padded dugout and wander on the turf, but you'll also snag some superb views out across the city to the Bay Bridge from the upper balconies (☎415/972-2000, ⓦwww.sfgiants .com). For info on catching a game, see "Listings," p.641.

Farther southeast, the strip of **Folsom Street** centered on Eleventh Street isn't much to look at during the day, but comes alive at night. Longtime home to the city's leather community, the area now hosts a range of bars, clubs, and restaurants serving every subculture under the stars. Eleventh Street is the kernel of activity and an obvious destination for a night out, provided you don't mind waiting in a line or two. If you happen to be here during daytime hours, wander back east to 214 Sixth St at the corner of Mission to look at **Defenestration**, a Quixotic piece of public art by local artist Brian Goggin, involving furniture that has been bolted to the outside of an abandoned building. Just don't linger too long – it's one of the nastier corners in town.

The Tenderloin

The **TENDERLOIN**, sandwiched between Civic Center and Union Square on the north side of Market Street, is one of the poorest, most dangerous places in San Francisco, just minutes from its tourist center. This small, uninviting area – no more than four blocks by five – remains a blight on the heart of the city though you should be safe as long as you keep your wits about you and don't mind vagrants asking you for money. Exercise extra caution at night, and the vicinity of Taylor Street, particularly around Turk and Eddy, is best avoided altogether.

The area's oddball name has never been definitively explained. One tale is that nineteenth-century police were rewarded with choice cuts of steak for serving a particularly perilous tour of duty here. A less flattering version is that, thanks to the constant bribes they collected from the gambling houses and brothels, those same policemen were able to dine in the city's finest restaurants. Yet others say that the name is based on the district's shank shape or even its notoriety for flesh-flashing brothels: whatever the answer, it's always been the seediest part of town and the heart of San Francisco's vigorous sex industry. Recent waves of Pakistani and South Asian immigrants have begun transforming the neighborhood, establishing numerous spots for a cheap bowl of curry or Vietnamese *pho* soup. If you're not too busy hurrying to your destination, there are a few sights worth seeing tucked into the neighborhood's dark corners, the best of which is the **Glide Memorial Church** at 330 Ellis St at Taylor (☎415/674-6000, ⊚www.glide.org). The church provides a wide range of social services for the neighborhood's downtrodden but it's best known for its rollicking Sunday service, which attracts a gloriously diverse crowd ranging from pious locals to drag queens (Sun 9am & 11am; be sure to arrive at least an hour ahead if you want a seat in the main church – the overflow usually has to make do with watching the proceedings via CCTV in a smaller room nearby). If you're not stopping by on a Sunday, step inside to see the AIDS Memorial Chapel – the altarpiece triptych was the last work artist Keith Haring completed before his death from the disease.

At the western limits of the Tenderloin, on Polk Street, between Farrell and California, lies **Polk Gulch**; it's a congregating point for the city's transgender community, and a hub for the flesh trade. This area inherited many of the displaced residents and merchants who fled Haight-Ashbury in the early 1970s; and it's now best known for the famous gay bars that once lined the street (most of which are now shuttered), not to mention a lingering smatter of young hustlers. The intersection of O'Farrell and Polk is home to a neighborhood landmark of sorts, the strip club known as **Mitchell Brother's O'Farrell Theater** (11.30am–2am; $15–40; ☎415/776-6686, ⊚www.ofarrell .com). The Mitchell boys achieved considerable notoriety in the 1970s when they persuaded a young Ivory Soap model named Marilyn Chambers to star in their porno film *Behind the Green Door*, which they debuted at the Cannes Film Festival. While the pair slowly slipped back into obscurity over the ensuing decades, they made a tragic return to tabloid fame when Jim Mitchell shot and killed his brother Artie in 1991.

The Civic Center

To the immediate southwest of the grubby Tenderloin stands San Francisco's grandest architectural gesture: the complex of Beaux Arts buildings known as the **CIVIC CENTER**. This cluster was the brainchild of brilliant urban planner Daniel Burnham: even before 1906, he planned to level San Francisco and build boulevard-like traffic arteries fanning out like spokes across the city, extensive subways, and a grand civic plaza. Unfortunately, after the earthquake, the city was choked in bureaucracy, and his plan was heavily diluted until only the civic plaza was approved. Even then, it wasn't finished until several years after his death. Despite Burnham's beliefs that grand architectural answers would silence social questions, the Civic Center today is simply the Tenderloin with better buildings.

Most people arrive at the Civic Center MUNI and BART station at the corner of Market and Leavenworth streets and are immediately disgorged into the **United Nations Plaza**, built to commemorate the founding of the UN here in 1945 – look for the UN Charter etched on a black stone shard. It's filled with fountains and homeless people: not somewhere to dawdle, other than on Wednesdays and Sundays when, from dawn to dusk, the square's transformed into a **Farmers Market**, a convenient place to pick up a cheap lunch (though produce can be hit and miss, so choose carefully).

The first building you'll see is the **San Francisco Public Library**, 100 Larkin St at Grove (Mon & Sat 10am–6pm, Tues–Thurs 9am–8pm, Fri noon–6pm, Sun noon–5pm; free; ☎415/557-4400, ⊛www.sfpl.lib.ca.us), which moved into its current location in 1996 from its original site, now the Asian Art Museum (see below). This move was controversial since the sleek new headquarters – which included a large, light-filled central atrium and plenty of space for lounging readers – didn't incorporate much space for books, and portions of the library's holdings have repeatedly been sold off in order to squeeze everything into the new stacks. It contains the James C. Hormel Gay and Lesbian Center (named in honor of the gay activist and meat magnate), the first of its kind in the nation, topped by a dome with a mural depicting leading figures in gay rights and literary movements.

Next door stands the **Asian Art Museum**, 200 Larkin St at McAllister (Tues, Wed, Fri–Sun 10am–5pm, Thurs 10am–9pm; $10, $5 after 5pm Thurs, free first Tues of every month; ☎415/581-3500, ⊛www.asianart.org), freshly relocated from its original, earthquake-crippled quarters next to the M.H. de Young Museum in Golden Gate Park (see p.608). The building conversion was masterminded by Gae Aulenti, the same woman who whipped up the fabulous Musée d'Orsay in Paris from a dingy old train station; here, Aulenti opened up the musty, bookstack-crammed interior and created a welcoming, airy space that's ideal for the massive collection on show. With more than 10,000 paintings, sculptures, ceramics, and textiles from all over Asia, this museum is almost overwhelming in its size, so it's well worth picking up an audio guide to navigate the highlights (the docent tours are less satisfying, and tend to career around at breakneck speed). The museum's most precious holding is undoubtedly the oldest known Chinese Buddha image, dating back to 338 AD. There's also a superb, well-priced café accessible to both visitors and passers-by – see p.613.

The central plaza in front of these buildings is usually filled with a combination of political protesters and the homeless. Grand **City Hall** stands on the other side of the plaza (Mon–Fri 8am–8pm, Sat noon–4pm; ☎415/554-4799, ⊛www.ci.sf.ca.us/cityhall). After the first city hall was destroyed in 1906, a contest with a prize of $25,000 was announced for local architectural firms to design a new building. The winning design was by Bakewell and Brown, former students of the Ecole des Beaux Arts in Paris, who wanted to create a structure inspired by the haughty, gilded dome of Les Invalides there. City Hall cost an astonishing $3.5m to build, and includes more than ten acres of marble, shipped in from Vermont, New Hampshire, and Italy. It was here in 1978 that conservative ex-Supervisor Dan White got past security and assassinated Mayor George Moscone and gay City Supervisor Harvey Milk; later, when White was found guilty of manslaughter (not murder), it was the scene of violent demonstrations as protesters set fire to police vehicles and stormed the doors of the building (see box, p.604). The best way to see the interior of the building is on one of the frequent, free tours (Mon–Fri 10am, noon, 2pm, Sat 12.30pm) – sign up at the Docent Tour Kiosk on the Van Ness Avenue side of the main building.

Directly behind City Hall on Van Ness Avenue are San Francisco's cultural mainstays, most elegant of which is the **War Memorial Opera House**, where the United Nations Charter was signed in 1945. Today, it's home to the San Francisco Opera and Ballet, and its understated grandeur is a sharp contrast to the giant modernist fishbowl of the **Louise M. Davies Symphony Hall** one block down. Built in 1980, at a cost of almost $35 million, the hall has some fans in the progressive architecture camp, though the general consensus is that it's an aberration of the otherwise tastefully harmonious scheme of the Civic Center. Both buildings enjoy a healthy patronage, and San Francisco's hidden elite gather here regularly: unfortunately, few performances are subsidized, so don't expect budget ticket prices. (For full details of ballet and opera schedules, see p.629).

The Mission

San Franciscans often speak of the **MISSION** today as a "neighborhood in transition," but the phrase could easily be applied throughout much of the district's 200-year history. After California's annexation, the area became home to succeeding waves of immigrants: first Scandinavians, followed by a significant Irish influx, and then a sizeable Latin American settlement. Though long heavily Spanish, this tangled melting pot is now a trendy destination for local Anglos; they're headed to the hip bars and restaurants, notably along Valencia Street, that jostle for space with old *taquerias* and grocery stores (and, of course, crowd them out); rising rents have engendered a certain amount of ill will toward newcomers. Still, at various points in its history the Mission has been one of the city's richest neighborhoods and one of its poorest, making this latest transformation but one in a long line of facelifts. What doesn't change is the Mission's gloriously sunny skies: the mass of Twin Peaks acts as a giant windbreak and even when the rest of the city is cold and foggy, the Mission is bright and (relatively) warm. Be aware that there's often gang activity on Mission Street between 14th and 19th streets and it's best not to wander around map in hand whatever the time of day.

The area gets its name from the oldest building in the city, the **Misión San Francisco de Asis**, more commonly known as **Mission Dolores**, 3321 16th St at Dolores (daily 9am–4pm; free; ☎415/621-8203, ⊛www .graphicmode.com/missiondolores). Its moniker dates back to the first European camp here, for the Spanish arrived on the Friday before Palm Sunday – the Friday of Sorrows – and finding an ample freshwater supply, decided to pitch their tents here, naming the site *Laguna de los Dolores*. The first mass celebrated at Mission Dolores on June 29, 1776, marks the official founding of the city, though the community was then known as Yerba Buena. The evolution

DUBOCE AVENUE

Levi Strauss Building

Mission Dolores

Castro Theater

THE CASTRO

Dolores Park

Women's Building

THE MISSION

NOE VALLEY

Bernal Heights Park

Twin Peaks

CAFÉS & RESTAURANTS

2223	4
Andalu	7
Baobab	13
Blue	10
Boogaloo's	17
Bruno's	14
Chow	3
Emmy's Spaghetti Shack	23
El Farolito	18
Café Flora	6
Foreign Cinema	16
Home	1
Luna Park	11
Miss Millie's	20
Mitchell's	22
La Rondalla	15
Samovar Tea Lounge	12
Suriya	21
Thai House	4
Ti Couz	8
El Trébol	19
Truly Mediterranean	9
World Sausage Grill	2

ACCOMMODATION

Beck's Motor Lodge	C
Dolores Park Inn	D
Travelodge Central	A
Twin Peaks Hotel	B
Village House	E

0   300 yds

of San Francisco is reflected in the mission's architecture: the original building, dating from 1782, is squat and relatively spare, while the more prominent basilica next door, built in 1913, is a riot of ornate design. Aside from periodic tour-bus herds, the building can be quite serene, with a stained-glass-lit interior offering a pleasant opportunity to gaze into the city's long-erased past. The backyard cemetery (made famous in Hitchcock's *Vertigo*) holds the graves of the mission's founders, as well as hundreds of "converted" Native Americans. Far removed from the plastic gimmickry of Fisherman's Wharf, this is one of the city's best historical icons, and is well worth a visit.

A short walk from the mission down the stately, palm-tree-lined Dolores Street, arguably the most attractive stretch of asphalt in the city, brings you to the sunbather-covered slope of Dolores Park. Though during the week much of the park is little more than a glorified dog run, on weekends the southwest corner transforms into "Dolores Beach," where members of the Castro gay community come to bronze their gym-toned muscles. Aside from the mission itself, the other best known local landmark is much more recent: the **Women's Building**, 3543 18th St at Guerrero (☏415/431-1180, ⊕www .womensbuilding.org), is a community space, housing workshops, drop-in daycare and resource center, all with a feminist slant. The building is tattooed with an enormous, sprawling mural, known by the horrifically self-conscious name of *Maestrapeace*. Big and awkward, it was designed by seven female designers and executed by a team of 100 muralists: on one side, there's an enormous mother-goddess figure, while on the other, there's a gigantic portrait of Rigoberta Menchú, the Guatemalan woman who won the Nobel Peace Prize in 1992.

Heading east into the heart of the neighborhood, you'll hit **Valencia Street**, one of the best shopping and dining strips in the city, packed with upscale boutiques sitting next to thrift stores and *taquerias* alongside chic new restaurants. Browsing down this strip between 16th and 24th streets is one of the delights of San Francisco. At its northern end is the original **Levi's factory building**, 250 Valencia St, a huge lemon-yellow structure set back from the road. While the pants Levi's makes today bear only a remote resemblance to the original item, invented during the Gold Rush, the jeans have outlasted countless trends, though recently the company's finances have been so rocky that it's laid off a significant portion of its local staff. After the sole guide who led groups around the building retired a few years ago, there are unfortunately no longer tours of the building's interior and Levi's has no plans to open it to the public again; rather, if you're looking for information on Levi's history, you now need to head to the visitors center on the Embarcadero (see p.580).

If Valencia Street is the hipster heart of the Mission, then **Mission Street** is the commercial hub of the **Latino community**: it's lined with five-and-dime shops selling a virtually identical stock of kitschy religious items, along with dozens of *taquerias*. It's mostly untouched by the gentrification that has bled into the northern edge of the district: there are a few groovy bars here, but this strip still primarily caters to the needs of local Latin families. The 200-odd **murals** you'll see everywhere underscore a strong sense of community pride and Hispanic heritage. The greatest concentration of work can be found on **Balmy Alley**, an unassuming back way between Treat and Harrison streets, where's there barely an inch of wall unadorned. The murals here are painted on wooden fences, rather than stucco walls, and consequently are regularly refreshed and replaced. The project began during a small community-organizing event in 1973, but the tiny street has become the spiritual center of a burgeoning Latino arts movement that has grown out of both the US civil rights struggle and pro-democracy movements in South America. Frankly, many of the murals are more heartfelt than either skilled or beautiful; it's worth stopping by for a peek, although the heavy-handed political imagery can be wearing. For a tour of the artwork, call the **Precita Eyes Mural Arts Center**, 2981 24th St at Harrison (tours Sat & Sun 1.30pm; $12; ☏415/285-2287, ⊕www.precitaeyes.org), which has sponsored most of the paintings since its founding in 1971.

The Castro and Twin Peaks

The next area west of the Mission district, the **CASTRO** was formerly a wild frontier, though it's settled down considerably in recent years, mellowing into middle age. Gentrified by the city's gay community during the 1970s as a primarily residential quarter, the Castro was part of the bacchanalian atmosphere that prevailed in San Francisco's gay culture during that decade. The assassination of gay City Supervisor Harvey Milk in 1978 (see box, p.604), which sparked the most intense rioting in the city's history, and the onset of the AIDS epidemic motivated many in the community to focus their energy on political organizing instead of the wild life. As a result the community now finds itself increasingly wealthy and politically influential – adopting the self-consciously enlightened demeanor of what is probably the world's most prominent gay community. But with this comfort has come a certain conservatism, and while activists argue that residents must still lead the fight on human rights issues such as AIDS funding and legal recognition of gay couples, many in the area seem increasingly concerned about more immediate quality-of-life issues such as chain stores and rising rents.

Oddly enough, for a neighborhood bursting with energy, there's not an awful lot to do in the Castro and the best way to while away an afternoon or evening here is to wander around. The heart of the Castro is filled with stores, restaurants, and bars all flying the rainbow flag and it's usually packed with people whatever the time of day: it's especially throbbing on a Sunday afternoon, crammed with men strolling, cruising, and sipping a coffee on the sidewalk. If you're lucky, you might spot one of the **Sisters of Perpetual Indulgence**, volunteers who dress as white-faced nuns to promote safe-sex and HIV awareness in a camp parody of Catholic pageantry. If the crowds of people are too much, head for the neighborhood's side streets, scrupulously manicured and lined with neat rows of brightly painted Victorians – a world away from the stores and bars crammed along the Castro. With its lovely Art Deco neon sign rising high above the street, the **Castro Theater**, 429 Castro St at Market, is a landmark that shines brightly in a neighborhood where people, not places, are the star attractions. Screening a well-curated schedule of classic film revivals and unusual premieres, the unofficial "Castro Cathedral" manages to find quality cinema that's more than a match for the theater's ambience. The ornate balconies, wall-mounted busts of heroic figures, and massive ceiling ornament would provide ample visual stimulation, even without a film showing on the gigantic screen. Come early for an extra treat: before each evening screening a Wurlitzer organ rises from the stage for a pre-showtime serenade. The musical medley always draws to a close with *San Francisco*, as the crowd merrily claps along.

After leaving the Castro, make an effort to go to **TWIN PEAKS**, about a mile and a half along Market from the Harvey Milk Plaza. (Travel west until you hit Twin Peaks Boulevard; the #37 Corbett bus will take you to Park Ridge.) The highest point in the city, Twin Peaks gives a 360-degree view of the Peninsula. Real-estate prices in the city are gauged in part by the quality of the views, so it's no surprise that the curving streets that wind around the slopes of Twin Peaks hold some of the city's most outrageously unaffordable homes. During the day, busloads of tourists arrive to point their cameras, and during the summer crowds often build up waiting for the fog to lift. It's better to go at night, picking out landmarks from either side of the shimmering artery of Market Street. If you want to avoid the crowds, Tank Hill, a small promontory just beneath Twin Peaks – where you'll need a map to find your way through the maze of small streets – is alternative, though sometimes sketchy after dusk.

You might also consider a quick visit to **Noe Valley**. Despite being just a couple of blocks from both the Castro and the Mission, the quiet bedroom community feels worlds apart, thanks to some very steep hills that help keep the area isolated. The neighborhood's heart is 24th Street, where baby strollers often seem to outnumber cars. Frankly, there's not much to do once here besides sipping cappuccinos or shopping for cardigans.

Haight-Ashbury, the Western Addition, and Japantown

Two miles west of downtown San Francisco, the **HAIGHT-ASHBURY** neighborhood lent its name to an entire era, giving it a fame on which it has traded mercilessly ever since. Originally part of the Western Addition, it was unofficially carved off following the widespread publication of a picture of the Grateful Dead, posing at the sign for the intersection of Haight and Ashbury streets – where now, with breathtaking irony, there's a branch of the Gap. For all its fame, 'The Haight' proper is tiny, spanning no more than eight blocks of attractive Edwardian and Victorian buildings. Despite some locals' nostalgia, it's changed dramatically since it emerged in the 1960s as the focus of the countercultural scene. Haight-Ashbury in the 21st century is theme-park boho, crammed with shops offering hippie-themed souvenirs or trendy boutiques selling designer clothes. Look hard enough, though, and you can still unearth the embers of its radical past: a handful of stores selling leftist literature and

The assassination of Harvey Milk

In 1977, eight years after New York's Stonewall riots brought gay political activism into the spotlight, Castro camera-shop owner Harvey Milk won election as the city's first openly gay supervisor (or councilor), and quickly became one of the most prominent gay officials in the country. Milk was a celebrated figure for the city's gay community, nicknamed the "Mayor of Castro Street," so it came as a horrifying shock when, in 1978, former Supervisor Dan White walked into City Hall and shot both Milk and Mayor George Moscone dead. White was an ex-cop who had resigned from the board, claiming he couldn't live on the small salary. In fact, he was angered that the liberal policies of Moscone and Milk didn't accord with his conservative views: a staunch Catholic, White saw himself as a spokesman for San Francisco's many blue-collar Irish families and, as an ex-policeman, saw himself as the defender of the family values he believed gay rights were damaging. At his trial, White claimed that harmful additives in his fast-food-laden diet had driven him temporarily insane – a plea which came to be known as the "Twinkie defense" (Twinkies being synthetic-cream cakes) – and was sentenced to five years' imprisonment for manslaughter. The gay community exploded when the news of White's light sentence was announced and the "White Night" riots that followed were among the most violent San Francisco has ever witnessed, as protesters stormed City Hall, turning over and burning police cars as they went. White was released from prison in 1985 and moved to Los Angeles, where he committed suicide shortly after. In a happier coda, current City Supervisor Tom Ammiano, a former stand-up comedian, who has said that he found the courage to come out publicly as gay through Milk's activism, is now one of the most powerful political figures in the city. (He recently lost the mayoral election to local businessman-cum-media-darling Gavin Newsom, himself a heterosexual champion of gay causes.)

vintage clothing, cafés filled with dawdling intellectuals, and a few surviving hippies.

Roughly divided into half by **Divisadero Street**, the Haight consists of the Upper and Lower Haight districts, with the **Upper Haight** stretching west to the park and the **Lower Haight** running east up to Buchanan Street. Though less famous, the Lower Haight is currently the more vibrant neighborhood. Long an African-American neighborhood, the Lower Haight has been transformed over the past decade by youthful immigrants from Britain into the center of the city's rave culture. DJ shops line Haight Street between Webster and Divisadero, while bars blatantly capitalize on Old World nostalgia (even for the food). Though the Mission has stolen much of the Lower Haight's trend-hopping spotlight, the neighborhood remains very much torn between its older and newer identities – a conflicted identity that has led to some tensions. It's best to exercise caution at night, particularly in the vicinity of Webster Street.

In much the same way that the Lower Haight tends to be overshadowed by its flashier neighbor up the hill, longtime resident **Kenneth Rexroth** (1905–1982) has largely been overshadowed by the writers he inspired. As a poet, novelist, and translator of Chinese literature, Rexroth lived a wildly adventurous life that was an inspiration for Kerouac and crew. While not open to the public, you can take a walk past Rexroth's old apartment at 250 Scott St, a place where several of the early Beats crashed upon first arriving in San Francisco.

Continuing uphill toward the heart of the Haight will bring you to **Buena Vista Park**, a mountainous forest of Monterey pines and California redwoods. Used by dog walkers in the daylight hours, come nightfall the park plays host to much sex-in-the-shrubbery; walk here accompanied by day and not at all at night, unless you're male and looking for some action. Continue past here along Haight Street, and the sidewalks become crowded by an increasing number of musicians, panhandlers, and hardcore hippie burnouts. Two blocks west, the **Grateful Dead House**, 710 Ashbury at Haight, was once ground zero for the counterculture. A 1967 drug bust only added to the band's myth, which survived countless tours and a rotating cast of keyboard players. Even the 1995 death of guitarist Jerry Garcia has done little to quell fans' devotion.

To the north of Haight Street, the **Panhandle** is a rivulet of greenery that runs like a tributary into Golden Gate Park. Though the grass is noticeably scraggly these days, it was once a ritzy thoroughfare catering to horse-drawn carriages and the lovely houses speak of wealthier times; it's now one of the trendier areas to live in the city.

The Western Addition

Spreading north and east of the Haight, the **WESTERN ADDITION** is one of the central city's few predominantly black neighborhoods and almost relentlessly poor – dangerous in parts and, but for one standout sight, certainly not tourist territory. The nadir for the neighborhood was in the 1960s, when the dual forces of urban renewal and blunderheaded civic planner **Justin Herman** – honored with a public park along the Embarcadero (see p.580) – led to the demolishing of blocks of precious Victorian housing. They were replaced with acres of monolithic concrete apartment blocks, leaving few vestiges of the Western Addition's history or character. The exception that proves the rule is a small area surrounding **Alamo Square Park**, at Hayes and Scott – just uphill from the Lower Haight. A staple of every tour bus company in town, the park's southeast slope is home to small flocks of amateur photographers eager to snap a picture of "the Painted Ladies." These six Victorian houses, originally built in

⑧

HAIGHT-ASHBURY &
WEST OF CIVIC CENTER

◀ Golden Gate Park

Civic Center ▶

CAFÉS & RESTAURANTS						ACCOMMODATION	
Absinthe	6	Kate's Kitchen	14	Suppenküche	7	Archbishop's Mansion	D
Asqew Grill	10	Mifune	3	Thep Phanom	15	Best Western Miyako	A
Brother-in-Laws		On the Bridge	3	Zona Rosa	11	The Carl	H
Bar-B-Q	4	Quince	2	Zuni	9	Château Tivoli	C
Chez Nous	1	Rosamunde				Hayes Valley Inn	E
EOS	16	Sausage Grille	12			Queen Anne	B
Escape from New York	13	Sapporo-Ya	3			Red Victorian	F
Frijtz	8	Stelline	5			Stanyan Park Hotel	G

1894, and colorfully and attractively restored, have been a postcard staple for years. Even if you've forgotten your camera, it's still worth the steep climb up here for the brilliant **views** across the city – on a clear day you can see over the city and across the Bay all the way to the hills of North Berkeley.

Be sure to detour downhill east from here to reach **Hayes Valley**, reborn when the freeway that once overshadowed it was demolished after the 1989 earthquake. The heart of the neighborhood is **Hayes Street** between Franklin and Octavia streets, although the district is swelling daily as new shops open. Hayes Valley is more racially integrated than many older neighborhoods, and the chichi boutiques sit alongside earthy remnants of the area's past. It's one of the best places to wander aimlessly and browse, and Hayes Street is lined with

Hippies

The first hippies were an offshoot of the Beats, many of whom had moved out of their increasingly expensive North Beach homes to take advantage of the low rents and large spaces in the Victorian houses of the Haight. The post-Beat bohemia that subsequently began to develop here in the early 1960s was initially a small affair, involving drug use and the embrace of Eastern religion and philosophy, together with a marked anti-American political stance and a desire for world peace. Where Beat philosophy had emphasized self-indulgence, the hippies, on the face of it at least, attempted to be more embracing, focusing on self-coined concepts such as "universal truth" and "cosmic awareness." Naturally it took a few big names to get the ball rolling, and characters like Ken Kesey and his Merry Pranksters soon set a precedent of wild living, challenging authority, and dropping (as they saw it) out of the established norms of society. Drugs were particularly important, and seen as an integral – and positive – part of the movement. LSD especially, the affects of which were just being discovered and which at the time was not actually illegal, was claimed as an avant-garde art form. It was pumped out in private laboratories and distributed by Timothy Leary and his network of supporters with a prescription ("Turn on, tune in, drop out") that galvanized a generation into inactivity. An important group in the Haight at the time was The Diggers, who, famed for their parties and antics, truly believed LSD could be used to increase creativity.

Before long, life in the Haight began to take on a theatrical quality: Pop Art found mass appeal, light shows became legion, dress flamboyant, and the Grateful Dead, Jefferson Airplane, and Janis Joplin made names for themselves. Backed by the business weight of promoter Bill Graham, the psychedelic music scene became a genuine force nationwide, and it wasn't long before kids from all over America started turning up in Haight-Ashbury for the free food, free drugs, and free love. Money became a dirty word, the hip became "heads," and the rest of the world were "straights."

Other illustrious tenants of the Haight in the Sixties included Kenneth Rexroth, who hosted a popular radio show and wrote for the *San Francisco Examiner*. Hunter S. Thompson, too, spent time here researching and writing his book *Hell's Angels*, and was notorious for inviting Angels round to his apartment on Parnassus Street for noisy, long, and occasionally dangerous drinking and drug-taking sessions.

Things inevitably turned sour towards the end of the decade, but during the heady days of the massive "be-in" in Golden Gate Park in 1966 and the so-called Summer of Love the following year, this busy little intersection became home to no less than 75,000 transitory pilgrims who saw it as the mecca of alternative culture.

shady trees and sidewalk cafés, not to mention some of the funkiest galleries, homeware, and clothing stores around.

Japantown

The determinedly thorough can continue north on a dismal strip of Fillmore Street to reach **JAPANTOWN**, something of a misnomer for what is basically a shopping mall with an eastern flavor – the Japan Center – around which only a small percentage of San Francisco's Japanese Americans actually live. Its one notable sight is the 100-foot **Peace Pagoda**, standing in the central plaza like a stack of poured-concrete space-age mushrooms. Nearby are the **Kabuki Hot Springs**, 1750 Geary St at Fillmore (daily 10am–9.45pm; $15 weekdays before 5pm, $18 weekends and weekday evenings; ☎415/922-6000, ⓦwww.kabuki-springs.com), recently refurbished and funked up, but retaining at least some of the original spa's eccentricity. If you're in the area, jump over a few blocks to where Geary Street meets Gough and look at the elaborately modern **St Mary's**

Cathedral, 1111 Gough St (Mon–Fri 7am–4.30pm, Sat 7am–6.30pm, Sun 7am–4.45pm; free; ☎415/567-2020, ⊛www.stmarycathedralsf.org). Built in 1971 to replace a fire-damaged predecessor, this stunning piece of modernist architecture has been derided by local wags for its supposed resemblance to a washing-machine agitator (earning it the nickname "Our Lady of the Maytag"). Make sure to step inside for the swooping, vaulted interior that swirls with movement.

Golden Gate Park

Unlike most American cities, San Francisco is not short on green space, and **GOLDEN GATE PARK** is its largest, simultaneously full of the bustle of urban living and hidden natural environments offering welcome respite to city residents. The park was designed in 1871 by Park Commissioner William Hall in the style of Frederick Law Olmsted, who was the man behind Central Park in New York. Spreading three miles or so west from the Haight as far as the Pacific shore, Golden Gate Park was constructed – on what was then an area of wild sand dunes buffeted by the spray of the nearby ocean – with the help of a dyke to protect the western side from the sea. Even so, the landscape still undergoes a natural transition as it approaches the ocean and, in contrast to the relatively placid Bay, the strong winds blowing through the Park and gusting up streets in the surrounding neighborhoods are a constant reminder of the sea's more turbulent temperament. It's generally best to visit in late morning or early afternoon – even on seemingly sunny days, a chilly fog often rolls in before dusk. Although the original planners intended to keep the park free of buildings, that proved impossible and its eastern half is now dotted with city sights like the California Academy of Sciences. Most of them date from the 1894 World's Fair, the first held in California, which was designed as a recession-busting sideshow by local newspaperman M.H. de Young. It was so successful that de Young was honored with a permanent museum in his name (see below).

Exploration of the whole place could take days of footwork. Among its more obvious attractions, there's a Japanese Tea Garden, a giant greenhouse (allegedly modeled on the Palm House at Kew Gardens in London), a Shakespeare Garden with every flower or plant mentioned in the writer's plays, not to mention the usual contingent of serious joggers, cyclists, and in-line skaters. At the moment, though, the park's in a state of flux since the museums clustered in a hub together at its heart are all closed for renovation. The **California Academy of Sciences** and **Steinhart Aquarium** (☎415/750-7145, ⊛www.calacademy.org) are in a much smaller temporary site in SoMA (see p.595) until their refurbished digs debut here in 2008. The **M.H. de Young Museum** opposite (☎415/863-3330, ⊛www.thinker.org) is closed at time of writing; its old quarters, horribly cramped and dated, have been leveled and replaced by a new futuristic design that will provide the museum twice the exhibition space in a smaller structure, as well as a viewing platform across the Golden Gate Park. It's scheduled to open in October 2005, with galleries specially designed to showcase the varied collection, from wide open spaces holding African and Pacific objects to smaller, more intimate galleries housing American paintings and antique furniture. Until then, though, the museum's holdings have partially been transferred to its sister site, the California Palace of the Legion of Honor (see p.611).

The one sight close by that is still open is the ever-crowded **Japanese Tea Garden** (daily 9am–6pm; $3.50; ☎415/751-1171). Built in 1894 for the

SAN FRANCISCO AND THE BAY AREA

△ Downtown San Francisco

California Midwinter Exposition, the garden was beautifully landscaped by the Hagiwara family, who were also responsible for the invention of the fortune cookie during the Pan-Pacific Exposition of 1915 (despite the prevalent belief that fortune cookies are Chinese). The Hagiwaras looked after the garden until World War II, when, along with other Japanese Americans, they were sent to internment camps. A massive bronze Buddha dominates the garden, which is much larger than it at first appears; it's soothing to spend time exploring among the bridges, footpaths, pools filled with shiny oversized carp, as well as bonsai and cherry trees – as long as you can ignore the busloads of tourists that pour in regularly throughout the day. The best way to enjoy the garden is to get there around 9am when it first opens and have a breakfast of tea and fortune cookies in the teahouse.

Perhaps the most unusual thing about Golden Gate Park is its small herd of a dozen or so bison, roaming around the **Buffalo Paddock,** the sunken field north of JFK Drive near 38th Avenue. They're fenced in with hefty metal railings, and the closest you can get to the animals is in their feeding area at the far west end. Moving towards the edge of the park at Ocean Beach, passing a tulip garden and two crumbling windmills donated by the Queen of Holland, you'll come to the **Beach Chalet** (daily 8am–midnight; free; ⊕415/386-8439, ⓦwww.beachchalet.com). This two-story, white-pillared building was designed by Willis Polk and houses a series of 1930s frescoes depicting the growth of San Francisco as a city and the creation of Golden Gate Park. It also holds a small visitor center that provides information about the park's numerous guided walking tours. Upstairs there's a lively brewery/restaurant, great for late weekend brunches.

Sunset, Richmond, and the beaches

Golden Gate Park is hugged by the large, residential neighborhoods of **RICHMOND** to the north and **SUNSET** to the south. As late as the 1940s, much of what comprises these two districts was still mile after mile of sand dunes, stretching to the ocean. And while residents of the city's more intensely urban eastern half might turn up their noses and say that, in terms of liveliness, not much has changed in the half-century since, the truth is that both neighborhoods – the multiethnic Richmond in particular – offer some rewarding oases of activity. More than the tourist-saturated downtown neighborhoods, this area is a window into the less seen side of San Francisco: a comfortable, though occasionally lethargic, blend of cultures. Numerous good, cheap restaurants, serving food from around the world, and the California Palace of the Legion of Honor's remote cultural outpost will reward those who stop here en route to the breathtaking (but often fog-bound) coastline at the city's edge.

Partly due to the weather and partly due to the coldness of the ocean water, beach culture doesn't exist in San Francisco the way it does in Southern California, and people here tend to watch the surf rather than ride it. Powerful currents and crashing waves dissuade all but the most fearless swimmers, and as a result the city's beaches remain blissfully uncrowded. Stretching south a mile from the Golden Gate Bridge, **Baker Beach** is San Francisco's prettiest and most popular, drawing a mixed crowd of fishermen and nude sunbathers, and giving some great views of the soaring red bridge. It's also easy to reach: stairways drop down from Lincoln Avenue, and MUNI bus #29 stops at the main parking lot every thirty minutes. A half-mile further southwest at the foot of the ritzy Sea Cliff district, **China Beach** is more protected and better for swimming, and also offers free showers and changing rooms; you can reach it via a cluster of rocks at low tide. Rising to the west from the beaches, paths curl south around the Peninsula to **Land's End**: it takes about thirty minutes to get round the cliffs, tricky to negotiate but worth it for the brilliant views of the ocean. A small beach in a rocky cove beneath the cliffside walk known as **Golden Gate Beach** is a favorite spot for gay and/or nude sunbathers.

The stately **California Palace of the Legion of Honor** (Tues–Sun 9.30am–5pm; $8; free Tuesday, $2 reduction with valid MUNI transfer; ☎415/750-3600 for switchboard, 415/863-3330 for recorded information, ⊛www.legionofhonor.org) is one of the best museums in San Francisco. The building itself is no less staggering than its setting, built in 1920 by Alma de Bretteville Spreckels (see p.576), with a cast of Rodin's *The Thinker* set dramatically on a pedestal in the center of the museum's front courtyard.

The museum's Rodin holdings are breathtaking in their depth and range, although there are more bronzes than marble sculptures: with over 80 pieces, it's one of the best collections of its kind in the world and the Rodin rooms alone make this museum unmissable. Sadly, the magnificent museum is somewhat let down by its lackluster collection of Old Masters – many of the artworks, including those by Giambologna, Cellini, and Cranach, are "attributed to" or "the workshop of," rather than *bona fide* masterpieces. However, while the de Young museum is closed (see p.608), its fine-art collection has been transplanted here featuring magnificent work by El Greco, Gainsborough, and David. The museum's most easily reached by taking the #38 bus from Geary Boulevard and transferring to the #18 at the Lincoln Park Golf Course; fitter types can skip the second bus and walk 10 minutes uphill to the main entrance.

Rounding the Peninsula, a rather bigger stop for the tour buses is **Cliff House**, 1090 Point Lobos Rd (☎415/386-3300, ⊛www.cliffhouse.com), precipitously balanced on the western tip of the Peninsula above the head of Ocean Beach. The complex – today, mostly just restaurants – underwent a radical renovation in early 2004 to upgrade its rather faded interior, though most travelers would do better to skip the food and come only for the views or the small visitor center (daily 10am–5pm). It has information on the surrounding area and an exhibit on the original Cliff House built by Prussian immigrant Adolph Sutro in the late nineteenth century as an exclusive resort for the leisured classes, which burned down long ago. On the lower landing is a rare **Camera Obscura** (11am–sunset, weather permitting; $2; ☎415/750-0415). Using a rotating mirror – and a trick of light – the camera allows entrants to see a panoramic view of the surrounding area. Unfortunately, the camera is mostly surrounded by water, making the view less interesting than the presentation.

Down by the water you'll find the remains of other bygone amusements – the **Sutro Baths**. This collection of opulent recreational pools, gardens, and elegant sculptures, all covered with 100,000 feet of stained glass, was sadly destroyed by fire in the 1960s. From here you can explore the ramparts and tunnels of the fortified coastline – a bit frightening at night, when the surf really starts crashing, but there's a certain romance too, and on a rare warm evening it becomes one of the city's favorite making-out spots.

Stretching to the city's southern border, buffeted by sea breezes and fog, the thin strip of **Ocean Beach** seems to constantly be on the brink of either being washed out to shore or blown into locals' backyards. Aside from a small community of particularly hearty surfers (most notably country-rock crooner Chris Isaak), the beach is the almost exclusive territory of joggers and dog walkers.

The Golden Gate Bridge

The orange towers of the **GOLDEN GATE BRIDGE** – arguably the most photographed bridge in the world – are visible from almost every point of elevation in San Francisco. As much an architectural as an engineering feat, the Golden Gate was begun in January 1933 and took only 52 months to build, opening in May 1937. Overseen by Chicago-born Joseph Strauss, the final design was in fact the brainchild of his local-born assistant, Irving Morrow. The first massive suspension bridge in the world, with a span of 4200ft, it ranked until 1959 as the world's longest. Connecting the Peninsula's northwesterly point to Marin County and Northern California, the bridge rendered the hitherto essential ferry crossing redundant, and was designed to stand winds of up to a hundred miles an hour. Handsome on a clear day, the bridge takes on an eerie quality when the thick white fogs pour in and hide it almost completely. Note that its ruddy color was originally intended as a temporary undercoat before the grey topcoat was applied, but locals liked it so much, the bridge has stayed orange ever since – and it takes more than 5000 gallons of paint annually to keep it that way.

You can either drive, bike, or walk across. The toll for southbound cars is $5, although biking is more thrilling since you teeter along under the bridge's towers. Note that cyclists headed south across the bridge are always routed along the east side, while northbound cyclists must take the west side Monday to Friday, and the east side on weekends. The half-hour walk across, though, really gives you time to take in its enormous size and absorb the views of the city behind you and the headlands of Northern California straight ahead. Pause at the midway point and consider the seven or so suicides a month who choose this spot, 260ft up, as their jumping-off spot. Monitors of such events speculate that victims always face the city before they leap – perhaps because the western walkway is closed to pedestrians. In fact, ten years ago in 1995, when the suicide toll from the bridge had reached almost 1000, police kept the figures quiet to avoid a rush of would-be suicides going for the dubious distinction of being the thousandth person to leap (25-year-old Eric Atkinson, who jumped that July, is pegged as the unofficial 1000th suicide); there's no word on where that number stands today.

Standing beneath the bridge is almost as memorable as traveling over it. **The Fort Point National Historic Site** (Fri–Sun 10am–5pm; free; ☎415/556-1693, ⑩www.nps.gov/fopo), a brick fortress built to guard the Bay in the 1850s on the initial landing place of the city's first Spanish settlers, gives a good sense of the place as the westernmost outpost of the nation. Formerly part of the Presidio Army Base (now a National Park), it was to have been demolished to make way for the bridge above, but the redesign of the southern approach – note the additional arch which spans overhead – left it intact. It's a dramatic site reachable via Marine Drive in the Presidio, the surf pounding away beneath the great span of the bridge high above – a view made famous by Kim Novak's suicide attempt in Alfred Hitchcock's *Vertigo*.

Eating

Only surpassed by Paris in number of restaurants per capita, San Francisco fully lives up to its hype as a food-crazed city. With so much agricultural land nearby it's not surprising that locals are ingredient snobs; indeed, menus regularly boast of their steak coming from the Niman Ranch or of serving only Hoffman chicken. San Francisco's obsession with restaurants dates back to the Gold Rush days, when the city was overrun with single men staying in boardinghouses, who had to find somewhere to eat every evening. Dozens of diners sprung up in response, and the city's been restaurant-crazy ever since.

At the lower end of the scale, the **dim sum** houses of Chinatown and the **Mexican** places of the Mission are not only cheap, but cook up some of the best food in town. There are, inevitably, dozens of **Italian** restaurants in North Beach (though quality varies wildly); **French** food is a perennial favorite, at least with the power-brokering crowd, although nouvelle cuisine is finally beginning to loosen its grip on San Franciscan menus. **California cuisine** nowadays has grown away from its minimalist roots, but still features the freshest food, beautifully presented. **Japanese** food is massively popular as are an increasing number of **Thai**, **Korean**, and **Indonesian** eateries. Not surprisingly, health-conscious San Francisco also has a wide range of **vegetarian** and **wholefood** restaurants, and it's rare to find anywhere that doesn't have at least one meat-free item on the menu. It's also very worthwhile to plan on one splurge meal while in town – the high price you'll pay for a world-class meal here is still far below the big-city average.

Be warned: San Francisco closes up early and you'll be struggling to find places that will serve you much after 10 or 11pm, unless they're of the 24-hour diner variety. As well, you cannot smoke in any restaurant in the city.

We've divided San Francisco's restaurant scene into two sections: the first, "**Cafés and light meals**," lists inexpensive places to grab a snack or a light meal. The second, "**Restaurants**," is divided by neighborhood and offers a range of eateries in every conceivable price range across a wide variety of cuisines. We've also provided a rundown of some of the better round-the-clock places to eat.

Cafés and light meals

Asqew Grill 1607 Haight St at Clayton, Haight-Ashbury ☎415/701-9301. This café, with its wooden beams and knicknack-crammed surfaces, is a refreshing alternative to most fast food: it serves more than a dozen different kinds of grilled skewers, from pork apple and pear to shrimp, tomato, and squash. Save room for the grilled brownie hot-fudge sundae.

Betty's Café 167 11th St at Howard, SoMa ☎415/431-2525. Known for its hearty $2.65 breakfast specials, including choice of meat, eggs, hash browns, and toast. No frills, but who'd expect them at prices like these?

Boogaloo's 3296 22nd St at Valencia, Mission ☎415/824-3211. Breakfast's the big draw here: black beans and chorizo (spicy sausage) feature heavily on the Latinized versions of American diner classics, costing $5–7 per dish. The decor's basic, but perked up with bright orange and yellow tables. Daily 8am–3.30pm.

Boudin Sourdough Bakery & Cafe 156 Jefferson St at Mason, Fisherman's Wharf ☎415/928-1849. The sourdough bread at this chain is the best around, made from a 150-year-old recipe and yeast that's descended from the first batch.

Brother in Laws Bar-B-Q 705 Divisadero St at Grove, Western Addition ☎415/931-7427. The service and atmosphere here are dreadful, but it still packs people in thanks to delicious, crunchy short-end ribs and smokey brisket – just get them to go.

Café Asia Asian Art Museum, 200 Larkin St at McAllister, Civic Center ☎415/581-3630. This bright, airy canteen-style café's a superb addition to the neighborhood and a superior museum eatery: try the chicken salad with Asian pear and crispy rice noodles ($6.50) or BBQ sesame beef ($8.95). If you're not browsing the museum, pick up a special ticket from the main desk that allows free access to the restaurant; it's open Tues, Wed, Fri–Sun 10am–5pm, Thurs 10am–9pm.

Café Flore 2298 Noe St at Market, Castro ☎415/621-8579. Wedged into the triangle at the corner of Market and Noe streets, this café has a sunny, plant-filled courtyard that's a great place to grab a coffee and a gooey cake; be aware that it can be very cruisey, especially during the early evening.

Café Francisco 2161 Powell St at Francisco, Fisherman's Wharf ☎415/397-2602. Cheap neighborhood café that's great for a lazy breakfast lounging with the newspapers or a quiet lunchtime sandwich only blocks from the wharf.

Caffe Trieste 601 Vallejo St at Grant, North Beach ☎415/392-6739. Small, crowded Italian coffeehouse. Its real attraction is the Saturday-afternoon amateur opera hour, when old Italian ladies from the neighborhood come to gossip over a coffee and listen to charmingly off-key live singers.

The Canvas 12000 9th Ave at Lincoln Way, Sunset ☎415/504-0060. Massive café-cum-gallery-cum-performance-space cluttered with mismatched mod furniture. There are performances each night: Mon is poetry, Wed open mic and Sun live jazz (free–$5). Try one of the sake cocktails or juicy sandwiches for around $7.50 – the shrimp curry's a standout. It's open until 2am Friday and Saturday.

Chili Up! 4 Embarcadero Center, Embarcadero ☎415/576-0811. Its mall-based location may be unappealing, but this local chainlet is a top-notch lunch option downtown – the gourmet chilli comes in seven different varieties, from Ballpark (dark beer, beef, and three kinds of beans) to a veggie option called Hoofless. Branch: Levi Plaza, Battery and Greenwich sts ☎415/397-1230.

Citizen Cupcake Virgin Megastore, 3rd floor, 2 Stockton St at Market, Union Square ☎415/399-1565. Downtown offshoot of the popular Civic Center café stashed inside a record store: there's coffee, tea, sake, and Asian-inflected sandwiches and salads as well as the namesake cupcakes. Try a Joe Cool (chocolate cake, chocolate cream and mint frosting).

Cool Beans 4342 California St at 6th Ave, Richmond ☎415/750-1955. Neighborhood coffee spot where the locals go to meet and greet over a game of backgammon or chess.

Dottie's True Blue Café 522 Jones St at O'Farrell, Tenderloin ☎415/885-2767. Hefty portions of home-made cakes, eggs, and other breakfast favorites are the draw at this inexpensive diner – along with quirky owner Kurt, who's always good for a gab. Breakfast and lunch only. Try the cinnamon-ginger pancakes with grilled sausage.

El Farolito 2779 Mission St at 24th, Mission ☎415/824-7877. A scruffy local institution, this 24-hour *taqueria* is pretty basic but the food is outstanding and cheap. Go for a quesadilla suiza (creamy swiss with chicken) and don't miss the delicious, tangy green salsa.

Emporio Rulli Stockton Street Pavilion, 333 Post St, Union Square ☎415/433-112. Café on Union Square's plaza that serves bracingly strong coffee and Italian pastries (try the cheesecake) and provides the best pit-stop from the nearby shopping. There are tables outside if you want to lounge.

Escape from New York 1737 Haight St at Shrader, Haight-Ashbury ☎415/668-5577. Low-key pizzeria selling both whole pies and warmed-to-order slices with traditional toppings as well as California-style pesto or feta-spinach-artichoke. Branches at 508 Castro St at 18th, Castro ☎415/252-1515, and 333 Bush St at Kearny, Financial District ☎415/421-0700.

Frjtz 579 Hayes St at Laguna, Hayes Valley ☎415/864-7654. Trendy, tiny *friterie*, serving cones of crunchy Belgian-style fries with dips like tabasco-chive ketchup or spicy yoghurt peanut. The overstuffed sofa in the tiny window is a great place to hunker down and listen to live DJs playing at the decks next to the main counter.

Imperial Tea Court 1411 Powell St at Broadway ☎415/788-6080. Dart into this wood-paneled hideaway in the heart of downtown to sit and sip a hot cup of tea – there are 32 different varieties to choose from. Plan to linger.

Juicy Lucy's Organic Juice & Food Bar 703 Columbus Ave at Filbert, North Beach ☎415/786-1285. Don't let the overgrown hippie decor (clashing, vivid colors and cod-Eastern Buddha statues) put you off – this juice bar is a gem. The smoothies and elixirs here are blended from in-season fruits, served in earthenware bowls, and feature tangy touches like mint and ginger.

Kate's Kitchen 471 Haight St at Fillmore, Lower Haight ☎415/626-3984. Monstrously huge portions of hearty breakfast food and crunchy hushpuppies are the pluses at this small diner; the massive crowds at weekends the minus.

Liguria Bakery 1700 Stockton St at Filbert, North Beach ☎415/421-3786. Marvelous old-world Italian bakery overlooking Washington Square Park, with deliciously fresh focaccia – the raisin's delicious if rather inauthentic. Get there early, as it simply closes when sold out.

Louie's Dim Sum 1236 Stockton St at Broadway, Chinatown ☎415/989-8380. The glistening, pearly dumplings are ranged in vast metal trays in front of you, and although variety is limited, they're all delicious and cheap ($1 for two).

Mama's 1701 Stockton St at Washington Square, North Beach ☎415/362-6421. There are cheery bright yellow tablecloths and sunny staff at this homely diner: try the crab benedict or one of the gooey, cakey French toast specials. Expect gargantuan lines at the weekend, whatever the time, so bring a book. Tues–Sun 8am–3pm.

Mario's Bohemian Cigar Store 566 Columbus Ave at Union, North Beach ☎415/362-0536. The "bohemian" in the name is dead-on even if there are no cigars now. Try one of the chunky, cheap house-made focaccia sandwiches or a pungent, fresh shot of espresso.

Mee Mee Bakery 1328 Stockton St at Broadway, Chinatown ☎415/362-3204. Little-known

Chinatown gem that sells delicate almondy treats as well as a variety (Biblical, Adult) of fortune cookies starting at $2 per pound.

Mitchell's 688 San Jose Ave at 29th, Mission ☏415/648-2300. In a fairly desolate southern corner of the neighborhood is the perfect spot for an after-dinner treat. *Mitchell's* serves home-made ice cream in an array of exotic tropical flavors – try the buko (baby coconut), avocado, or sweet bean.

Patisserie Delanghe 1890 Fillmore St at Bush, Pacific Heights ☏415/923-0711. Gourmet French bakery, run by two expats, who make flaky, buttery croissants and glistening fruit tarts for $2 or so – the fruit brioche is a good choice. There are a few tables in the window if you want to linger.

Pat's Café 2330 Taylor St at Columbus, Fisherman's Wharf ☏415/776-8735. Bright and basic with simple formica and a short menu of burgers and sandwiches, starting at $6.

Pizzetta 211 211 23rd Ave at California, Richmond ☏415/379-9880. You can rely on inventive and unusual pizza here: there's a different menu each week, offering whatever's fresh and seasonal as a pizza topping (although you'll usually find eggs as one option).

Rosamunde Sausage Grille 545 Haight St at Fillmore, Lower Haight ☏415/437-6851. Tiny storefront grill with a few stools at the bar, just serving grilled sausages on a sesame roll. Choose from a cherry-laced chicken sausage to the light flavors of a shrimp, scallop, and snapper sausage.

Saigon Sandwiches 560 Larkin St at Eddy, Tenderloin ☏415/474-5698. Hole-in-the-wall store selling outstanding made-to-order Vietnamese sandwiches for $2 each: choose between BBQ chicken, BBQ pork, and meatballs, then add lashings of fresh greens and tongue-curling hot pickles. Highly recommended.

St Francis Fountain, 2801 24th St at York, Mission ☏415/826-4200. Old-school soda fountain founded in 1918 that's just been overhauled by the same team behind *Boogaloo's* (see p.613): the decor's still retro (white formica, candy jars), but the menu now offers burgers any way you want (even vegan) alongside grand traditions like a strawberry double-dip sundae, cooked up from vanilla ice cream, strawberry syrup, and soda.

Samovar Tea Lounge 498 Sanchez St at 18th, Castro ☏415/626-4700. Earthy, cushion-filled café that serves more than 100 varieties of tea as well as tasty Asian snacks; the overstuffed wicker chairs are a great place to curl up with a book for the afternoon.

Sears Fine Food 439 Powell St at Post, Union Square ☏415/986-1160. This old-fashioned breakfast joint, founded in 1938, recently changed owners but has fortunately undergone only minimal changes (the largest that it's now open for dinner). Try the dollar-sized Swedish pancakes, or a hefty Denver omelet served all day.

Swan Oyster Depot 1517 Polk at California, Polk Gulch ☏415/673-1101. No frills – and officially, no full meals – at this cheap seafood counter. Grab a stool and hang onto it (it gets crowded and competitive here) and suck down some cheap shellfish and seafood.

Taylor's Automatic Refresher 1 Ferry Building, Embarcadero ☏1-866/EAT-FOOD. Casual café serving a Mex-American menu of burgers and fish tacos, as well as offbeat offerings like fish and chips. All are made from fresh ingredients, though most people come for one of the super-thick milkshakes – try a "black and white" made from chocolate sauce and pure vanilla ice cream.

Ten Ren Tea Company 949 Grant Ave at Washington, Chinatown ☏415/362-0656. Large, well-stocked tea emporium where you can stop in for tea-by-the-pound or a fresh brew to go; the scented iced teas, thick with gloopy tapioca balls, are delicious.

Ton Kiang 5821 Geary Blvd at 22nd Ave, Richmond ☏415/387-8273. Huge dim sum eatery sprawling across two floors in the heart of New Chinatown and catering to a mixed Asian and Caucasian crowd. Try the pork buns or *sin lung bao,* Shanghai-style steamed dumplings.

Town's End 2 Townsend St at Embarcadero ☏415/512-0749. Gourmet brunch spot, famed for its tasty basket of baked goods that's served instead of bread. The food's modern American (smoked-chicken hash and the like) and most entrees cost around $10.

Truly Mediterranean 3109 16th St at Valencia, Mission ☏415/252-7482. *Truly Mediterranean's* version of the falafel is wrapped in thin, crispy *lavash* bread rather than a pita, though once you get it, you'll find barely anywhere to sit in the tiny windowfront restaurant. The busy staff's spontaneous singing and dancing comes free of charge.

World Sausage Grill 2073 Market St at 14th, Mission ☏415/621-7488. Open till midnight every day, this brightly painted café is a fresh fast-food option: all the wieners are preservative-free, and alongside standard sauces and toppings there are more unusual combos like pork sausage with southwestern salsa and cilantro or seafood sausage made from minced scallops, shrimp, and red snapper. Most cost around $5.

Late-night eating

Bagdad Café 2295 Market St at 16th, Castro ☎415/621-4434. The best-priced 24-hr option in the neighborhood.

Bruno's 2389 Mission St at 20th, Mission ☎415/648-7701. Jazz lounge serving modern American food until 2am.

Caffè Greco 423 Columbus Ave at Vallejo, North Beach ☎415/397-6261. Coffee and light meals at this old-fashioned Italian snack bar.

El Farolito Mission. See p.614.

La Rondalla 901 Valencia St at 20th, Mission ☎415/647-7474. Christmas-themed (yes, really) Mexican restaurant serving a full menu until 2am.

Mario's Bohemian Cigar Store North Beach. See p.614.

Yuet Lee 1300 Stockton St at Broadway, Chinatown ☎415/982-6020. Terrific Chinese seafood until 3am; daily except Tuesday.

Restaurants

Downtown and Chinatown

Chef Jia's 925 Kearny St at Columbus, Chinatown ☎415/398-1626. Just a couple of doors down from the ultra-popular *House of Nanking* (see below), they serve quick, tasty, and cheap specialties that, if not quite equal to the offerings of its famous neighbor, are a decent stand-in.

Cortez *Adagio Hotel*, 550 Geary St at Jones, Theater District ☎415/292-6360. This new restaurant from audacious Bay Area chef Pascal Rigo is one of the buzziest places in town: the menu's mostly Mediterranean tapas, sharing plates of succulent treats like pan-fried soft-shell crab ($12) and foie gras terrine ($14). If only the portions were a little bigger and the staff a little less snotty.

Farallon 450 Post St at Powell, Union Square ☎415/956-6969. Come for seafood prepared and served with great fanfare: the champagne-steamed clams are light and tender, while mackerel tartare and tuna carpaccio are delicious, flavor-packed appetizers. It's a pity that the jelly-fish-inspired decor with its dangling luminescent mobiles is so offputting.

House of Nanking 919 Kearny at Jackson, Chinatown ☎415/421-1429. This tiny spot has become a legend: expect a long but rapidly moving line, curt service, and a fabulous, underpriced meal. Those in the know let the waiters do the ordering for them.

Kokkari Estiatorio 200 Jackson St at Front, Financial District ☎415/981-0983. By far, the best Greek restaurant in town. Though the decor is purely Northern California, the cuisine is classic Greek, relying on staples such as lamb and eggplant, served both separately and cooked together as moussaka.

Plouf 40 Belden Lane at Bush, Chinatown ☎415/986-6491. French seafood bistro, usually packed out with a yuppie crowd: the atmosphere's airy and the food is rustic and southern, with most entrees costing $12–16. Plouf, incidentally, is the French answer to "Splash!"

R&G Lounge 631 Kearny St at Clay, Chinatown ☎415/982-7877. This enormous Hong Kong–style restaurant is popular with both Chinese and Westerners. Dishes come family style, and there's a heavy bias towards seafood; if you plan 24 hours ahead, though, you can order the house special, a whole chicken hollowed out, stuffed with rice, and deep fried.

Sam Woh 813 Washington St at Grant, Chinatown ☎415/982-0596. Cheap and popular late-night spot where Kerouac, Ginsberg, and others used to hold court – just don't expect smiley service. Walk through the kitchen and up the cramped stairs to reach the dining room.

Slanted Door Ferry Building Marketplace, Financial District ☎415/861-8032. This understated restaurant has plenty of buzz and so fills up quickly: book ahead or eat early. The menu, which changes daily, is light, French-Vietnamese; there are several deliciously fragrant chicken dishes, and the tea list is impressive and eclectic. Recommended. The original space, 584 Valencia St at 17th, Mission, has been shuttered for some time, but the owners say it should open some time in 2005 as a more casual (read: cheaper) street-food restaurant: call for updates.

North Beach and Nob Hill

Café Jacqueline 1454 Grant Ave at Union, North Beach ☎415/981-5565. A romantic, candlelit gourmet experience, this restaurant serves only chef-owner Jacqueline Margulis's signature soufflés, both savory and sweet (crab and chocolate are top picks). Since every dish is made to order, don't plan on a quick bite here – and though it's pricey (around $40 per entree), the food's more than worth it.

Enrico's 504 Broadway at Kearny, North Beach ☎415/982-6223. The fine, streetside patio (a good option for smokers) and plenty of tables inside means that you'll rarely have to wait. The Cal-Italian food is tasty, if a little overambitious: stick with simpler dishes for a delicious meal. $17–23 entrees.

Harris' Restaurant 2100 Van Ness at Pacific, Pacific Heights ☎415/673-1888. Clubby and proudly old-fashioned, *Harris'* is one of the premier steakhouses in the city: the staff is warm and welcoming (if a little over-assiduous at times), as is the decor, heavy on padded chairs and comfy booths. There's every cut of beef imaginable – from a $35 filet to a $65 Kobe rib-eye – and all are buttery sweet and tender.

The Helmand 430 Broadway at Kearny, North Beach ☎415/362-0641. The decor here is simple and unassuming – unlike the food, which is unforgettable. The menu's filled with tangy and spicy Afghani staples: try the *kaddo borwani* (caramelized pumpkin) or the grilled beef tenderloin. Highly recommended.

L'Osteria del Forno 519 Columbus Ave at Green, North Beach ☎415/982-1124. Tiny, authentic North Italian eatery on the main drag of Little Italy that's a glorious refuge from the nearby tourist traps. The menu's small, and driven by whatever's freshest at the market: *focaccine* sandwiches (made with springy, fluffy Italian bread) are only $6. Try one of the bean salads.

Sushi Groove 1916 Hyde St at Union, Russian Hill ☎415/440-1905. Groovy, throbbing modern sushi restaurant that serves inventive and original maki rolls as well as a sprinkling of Pan-Asian fusion dishes (delicious sake martinis, too). The two downsides are the sloppy service and its tiny size, which usually means you'll have to wait for a table. The SoMa branch, which often hosts local DJs, is bigger and just as hip but hard to find, since there's no sign: *Sushi Groove South*,1516 Folsom St at 11th, SoMa ☎415/503-1950.

Tommaso's 1042 Kearny St at Broadway, North Beach ☎415/398-9696. This restaurant claims to be home to the first pizza oven installed on the West Coast (in 1935). Whatever the origins, the crispy pizzas are delicious: ask for one topped with clams in the shell. The space is cavelike and homely, decorated with splashy murals.

Trattoria Contadina 1800 Mason St at Union, North Beach ☎415/982-5728. This tiny, family-owned *trattoria* still caters primarily to the local Italian community: the food's outstanding if traditional, like rigatoni with eggplant and smoked mozzarella.

The northern waterfront and Pacific Heights

Ana Mandara Inside Ghirardelli Square, 891 Beach St at Polk, Fisherman's Wharf ☎415/771-6800. Yes, it's co-owned by washed-up Eighties stars Don Johnson and Cheech Marin, but the modern Vietnamese and Thai menu is delicious (if pricey). If you're on a tighter budget, go for drinks and appetizers in the beautiful, bamboo-decorated lounge area and listen to the fine live jazz.

Baker Street Bistro 2953 Baker St at Lombard, Cow Hollow ☎415/931-1475. Cramped but charming café with a few outdoor tables: the slightly older, neighborhood crowd enjoys simple food served by French staff. Wines are well-priced and the $14.50 prix fixe dinner is a bargain.

Betelnut 2026 Union St at Buchanan, Cow Hollow ☎415/929-8855. Sceney local hangout, known for its offbeat Asian menu served in smaller portions in a hybrid of the dim sum and tapas traditions. Not cheap (around $8–10 per plate) but exotic pairings such as lychee tea-smoked quail, not to mention delicious green beans, are well worth sampling.

Bistro Yoffi 2231 Chestnut St at Pierce, Marina ☎415/885-5133. Chef Sarah Lewington serves eclectic modern American dishes at this refreshingly quirky (given its location) bistro, packed with potted ferns and mismatched chairs. Try to snag a table for brunch in the lush garden out back.

Ella's 500 Presidio Ave at California, Pacific Heights ☎415/441-5669. Perhaps the most famous breakfast wait in town, so put on some comfortable shoes before braving the line that forms outside for scrumptious Californian interpretations of American classics, like the mandarin pancakes with mango syrup.

Gary Danko 800 North Point at Hyde, Fisherman's Wharf ☎415/749-2060. Don't let the location put you off – this understated eatery regularly vies for the title of best restaurant in this foodie city. Granted, it's performance food, served with a self-conscious flourish but it's utterly splurgeworthy. The menu changes seasonally, but expect dishes like horseradish-crusted salmon or lemon herb duck breast; order individually or splash out on the five-course tasting menu for $79 per person.

Greens Fort Mason Center, Building A, Marina ⊤415/771-6222. The queen of San Francisco's vegetarian restaurants, this pricey gourmet spot boasts a picturesque setting on a pier at Fort Mason Center that offers spectacular views of the Bay.

Habana 2080 Van Ness Ave at Pacific, Russian Hill ⊤415/441-CUBA. The decor at this upscale Cuban eatery is meant to bring back memories of pre-Castro Havana, though the menu's more modern, serving twists on staples like *ropa nueva*, where a juicy chunk of steak sits on top of a traditional shredded beef stew. Make sure to order one of the minty mojitos.

Matterhorn 2323 Van Ness Ave at Green, Russian Hill ⊤415/885-6116. Hidden in an apartment building, this authentically Swiss restaurant (the kitschy ski-lodge-style decor was shipped here in pieces from the motherland and reassembled on site) is known for its fondues, whether cheese, beef, or chocolate. The standout's undeniably the Fondue Ticinese, a thick and spicy blend of cheeses, pepperoncini, and tomatoes.

McCormick & Kuleto's 900 North Point St at Larkin, Ghirardelli Square, Fisherman's Wharf ⊤415/929-1730. Despite its size (it's enormous) and location (within seconds of Fisherman's Wharf), *McCormick & Kuleto's* serves reliable, sometimes even exceptional, seafood: the salmon gravlax is delicious, as are the coconut prawns with papaya mango salsa. Save room for an enormous slab of banana cream pie, big enough for three.

Neecha 2100 Sutter St at Steiner, Pacific Heights ⊤415/922-9419. Good, cheap Thai option, given its location: the pad thai is especially succulent and nutty.

Sociale 3665 Sacramento St at Locust, Laurel Heights ⊤415/921-3200. This intimate Italian bistro, nestled in a small courtyard at the end of a tiny alleyway, is worth seeking out for the warm atmosphere and friendly staff, not to mention the food, which is mostly light, Cal-Italian – the mozzarella-crammed deep-fried olives are worth splurging for.

SoMa, the Tenderloin, and the Civic Center

Acme Chop House 24 Willie Mays Plaza at King and 3rd, SoMa ⊤415/644-0240. Vegetarian Hell, this resoundingly old-style restaurant is another brainchild of local chef wunderkind, Traci Des Jardins (see *Jardinière*, below). This place is enormous and usually packed with businessmen chowing down on chunky, choice cuts of steak – try the filet or the butcher steak.

Asia SF 201 9th St at Howard, SoMa ⊤415/255-2742. Glorious gender illusion bar/restaurant – don't you dare call them drag queens – where the waitresses perform cheeky, campy burlesque on the bar throughout the evening. The sake martinis are delicious and deadly, while the Cal-Pacific food (sushi rolls and funky salads) is inventive, if beside the point.

Bacar Restaurant and Wine Salon 448 Brannan St at 4th, SoMa ⊤415/904-4100. This enormous three-level restaurant was white hot when it opened a few years back but has settled into a mellower spot. The menu, primarily Modern American, changes seasonally (expect duck, *osso buco*, and thin-crust pizzas) and there's a live, three-piece house band most nights. The loungey downstairs bar is groovier, filled with overstuffed chairs where you can linger over appetizers and sample one of the 100-plus wines served by the glass.

Citizen Cake 399 Grove St at Franklin, Hayes Valley/Civic Center ⊤415/861-2228. Stylish, pricey bakery-cum-restaurant with a soft jazz soundtrack serving delectable, delicate pastries: its signature cake, unsurprisingly also a nod to Orson Welles, is the "Rosebud," a rose-scented crème brûlée tart. Weekend brunches are a standout – try the soufflé pancake with home-made jam for $9.50.

Fringale 570 4th St at Brannan, SoMa ⊤415/543-0573. Delightful, low-key charmer on a quiet SoMa block. The service is as exceptional as the food, predominantly French but with Basque touches like serrano ham. The decor is simple and romantic – just the place to feed your date one of the sumptuous after-dinner truffles. Highly recommended.

Golden Era 572 O'Farrell St at Leavenworth, Tenderloin ⊤415/673-3136. Subterranean vegan eatery with a pan-Asian menu that swerves through Thai, Chinese, and Japanese: try the crispy mint-cilantro rolls and Thousand Layers Eggplant in pepper sauce.

Jardinière 300 Grove St at Franklin, Civic Center ⊤415/861-5555. Run by big-name chef Traci Des Jardins, this boxy brick space caters to a pre-theater crowd with valet parking and plenty of pizzazz. The French-Cal food's a splurge ($27–30 an entree), but you'll get what you pay for; there's an emphasis on indulgence from beginning (foie gras) to end (aged cheese platter). Try the gnocchi with oxtail sauce and make sure to ask for a table upstairs away from the bar where it's quieter.

Lulu 816 Folsom St at 4th, SoMa ⊤415/495-5775. Famed Californian restaurant with a rustic, rather cramped dining room: the shared, family-style dishes are hit and miss, although the pearl-sized gnocchi are meltingly fluffy; the spectacular wine list – many by the glass – is also impressive.

Millennium *Savoy Hotel*, 580 Geary St at Hyde, Theater District ☎415/345-3900. Legendary vegetarian restaurant, offering flavor-packed entrees ($18–21) like fried portobello mushrooms, robust enough to please even avid meat eaters. The dark wood-paneled decor's gauzy and romantic, and the crowd's as much opera buff as eco-warrior.

The Public Restaurant and Bar 1489 Folsom St at 11th ☎415/552-3065. This newish eatery is decked out in mismatched thrift-store decor, and serves midprice modern American food. The two bars, thanks to live DJs and cheap happy-hour martinis, make it a good choice for a hip, heavy-drinking date.

The Ramp 855 China Basin St at Illinois, China Basin ☎415/621-2378. American restaurant right on the water at the southern tip of SoMa. The crowd and the place are both super casual and there's a refreshingly diverse selection of people. The best time to come is for brunch or breakfast on the patio overlooking the water – the corned-beef hash is outstanding, as are the Bloody Marys.

Shalimar 532 Jones St at Geary, Tenderloin ☎415/928-0333. This hole-in-the-wall serves delicious, cheap Pakistani food, all of it made to order before your eyes in the *kulcha* oven: the chicken tikka is fantastic value at only $3.50 for an enormous portion. There are a few tables if you want to linger.

Sushi Rock 1508 Polk St at Sacramento, Polk Gulch ☎415/345-1690. Reliable sushi restaurant in Polk Gulch, large enough that you should always be able to snag a table whatever the time of day. There's free seaweed salad and miso soup in front of you as soon as you've sat down; stick with the sushi, as some maki rolls are rather bland.

Tonno Rosso *Hotel Griffon*, 155 Steuart St at Mission, SoMa ☎415/495-6500. Rustic Italian dishes are the staples at this understated but homely hotel restaurant: order the medium-rare *ahi* tuna with capers ($20) or the veal ravioli ($14), and don't leave without trying a piled-high plate of truffle-oil-drizzled house-made potato chips. Try to snag a table at the rear for the spectacular views of the Bay Bridge.

Tu Lan 8 6th St at Market, SoMa ☎415/626-0927. A legend ever since Julia Child first sampled the Vietnamese cooking in this cramped, dingy space on one of the seediest blocks in town. Should you sit at the sticky counter, you'll be nearly singed by the flames from the stove. Nevertheless, the food is consistently fresh, authentic, and flavorful – just don't look up at the grubby ceiling!

The Mission, the Castro, and south

2223 2223 Market St at Noe, Castro ☎415/431-0692. This restaurant is one of the most mixed gay/straight venues in the neighborhood – likely both because of its friendly, chatty vibe and because everyone wants to sample the sumptuous, simple interpretations of California cuisine like lightly roast chicken topped with onion rings. The setting's a soft, pale yellow room with high ceilings and low lighting.

Andalu 3198 16th St at Guerrero, Mission ☎415/621-2211. Airy, upscale tapas bar with high ceilings, deep green walls, and huge paper chandeliers, serving an inventive blend of Californian, European, and comfort food – think *ahi* tartare tacos ($11) or mac'n'cheese ($5). Make sure to try one of the cocktails made from *soju* (Korean potato vodka) and a serving of donut holes for dessert.

Baobab 2323 Mission St at 19th, Castro ☎415/826-9287. Covering a lot of bases: all-American egg and French toast breakfasts in the morning; Senegalese food, such as fried bananas and fish stew in the evening, and a popular bar later at night.

Blue 2337 Market St at Castro, Castro ☎415/863-2583. Small, retro diner/restaurant that's decked out in industrial chromes and blacks, but serves deliciously simple comfort food like chicken pot pie and chili, to the early hours. Thanks to a restrictive liquor license, *Blue* also mixes up inventive, original martinis and cocktails with a sake base and even a selection of root beers.

Chow 215 Church St at Market, Castro ☎415/552-2469. Unfussy comfort food, like bargain pastas and wood-fired pizzas, some with an Asian twist. Spaghetti and meatballs is great value for $6 and most dishes cost no more than $10. No reservations accepted, and the wait can be long. There's a branch called *Park Chow* in the Sunset (see p.621).

El Trébol 3324 24th St at Mission, Mission ☎415/285-6298. Run by a husband-and-wife team, this café serves excellent versions of Nicaraguan standards like *churrasco* (grilled beef) and *chancho con yucca* (fried pork), in haphazard atmosphere washed with Latin music. The mouth-puckering tamarindo drink is an experience; just don't plan on enjoying the menu to its full if you're dieting.

Emmy's Spaghetti Shack 18 Virginia St at Mission, Bernal Heights ☎415/206-2086. This funky café is filled day and night with local hipsters who give it a laid-back, neighborhoody vibe and the chunky, tasty food makes it even more appealing: try the house meatballs and spaghetti for around $8.

Foreign Cinema 2534 Mission St at 21st, Mission ☎415/648-7600. Originally, the dominant gimmick at this upscale Cal-French restaurant was its hybrid nature: part bistro, part drive-in with movies projected onto the large outdoor wall and speakers on each table. Now, the movies are secondary to the food, including an excellent oyster/raw bar selection and grilled Meyer Ranch steak. The *Laszlo* martini bar is on the same site.

Home 2100 Market St at Church, Castro ☎415/503-0333. The menu at this upscale diner offers dishes that a chef might cook at home for his friends (hence the name) – expect comfort food like moules frites for around $10–12 per entree; the two-course meal deal for $10.99 including a glass of wine is especially good value. It's popular with a mixed crowd of guppies and yuppies, and there's a groovy patio bar with DJs at the weekend.

Luna Park 694 Valencia St at 18th, Mission ☎415/553-8584. Outstanding restaurant, with a groovy local vibe no matter what day of the week. It's decked out like a lush bordello with deep red walls and ornamental chandeliers, and menus come in little black books. Most of the entrees, like a tuna salad niçoise or moules frites, hover around $15. Don't miss the offbeat but excellent goat cheese fondue with grilled bread and sliced apples as an appetizer, or the excellent cocktails.

Miss Millie's 4123 24th St at Church, Noe Valley ☎415/285-5598. A weekend brunch institution, thanks to fresh home-baked goods and deliciously light French toast. Expect a wait of close to an hour and be prepared to have your conversation interrupted by the dozens of yuppie babies around you; snag a table on the patio if you can.

Moki's Sushi and Pacific Grill 830 Cortland Ave at Gates, Bernal Heights ☎415/970-9336. Japanese food with a liberal dash of Hawaiian favorites, heavy on fruit and seafood. There's seating in the main room and at the sushi bar, where you can also order sashimi and maki rolls, but the choicest tables are on the tiny, hidden patio out back.

Suriya 1432 Valencia St at 25th, Mission ☎415/824-6655. You'll feel like you're in Bangkok at this tiny restaurant, which is crammed with antiques and palms. The flamboyant food rarely disappoints – try the emerald noodles, the pumpkin curry, or the deep-fried green papaya wedges in shredded coconut butter. Recommended.

Thai House 151 Noe St at Henry, Castro ☎415/863-0374. Warm, intimate neighborhood eatery that looks incongruously like a Swiss chalet and is widely regarded as a contender for best Thai food in town: the corn cakes are delicious, and the menu always offers quirky, tasty daily

specials. There's a new satellite branch at 599 Castro St ☎415/864-5000.

Ti Couz 3108 16th St at Valencia, Mission ☎415/252-7373. Friendly, hip, and gracious, this crêperie was one of the pioneers of the newly groovy Mission scene on Valencia. It still holds its place as one of the best cheaper restaurants around, serving savory buckwheat pancakes for $6 or so, and lighter, fluffier dessert crêpes.

Haight-Ashbury and west of Civic Center

Absinthe 398 Hayes St at Gough, Hayes Valley ☎415/551-1590. Brasserie-cum-bistro, with two separate dining areas, both serving robust French food in an authentic, if trendy, atmosphere. The bar's a good option round here for drinks, since it's open until 2am and does smallish snacks for $6 or so per plate.

Chez Nous 1911 Fillmore St at Pine, Fillmore ☎415/441-8044. This pan-Mediterranean tapas bar draws huge crowds to Fillmore – hence the usual long wait and loud noise inside. It's worth it, though, since the menu's fresh and wide-ranging, and offers dishes in both large and tapas sizes: the lamb chops and spinach gnocchi are both excellent.

EOS 901 Cole St at Carl, Cole Valley ☎415/566-3063. Visually spectacular East–West fusion cooking, including ginger Caesar salad and lemongrass risotto, as well as sumptuous desserts, plus an extensive wine bar. This is one of the neighborhood's favorite hangouts, so it can get busy at weekends; not cheap, but worth it.

Mifune Japan Center, 1737 Post St at Fillmore, Japantown ☎415/922-0337. Everything at this noodle house on the bridge of the Japan Center is just the right temperature – the beer's ice cold, and the tangy noodles piping hot. More elegant than most neighbors, with a large array of soup toppings and a small selection of sushi.

On the Bridge Japan Center, 1581 Webster St at Post, Japantown ☎415/922-7765. Smallish cafeteria serving *yoshoko*, or westernized Japanese food, such as spaghetti with *kim chi* (pickled cabbage).

Quince 1701 Octavia St at Bush, Japantown ☎415/775-8500. New rustic Italian restaurant nestled in the Western Addition that's caught attention from local foodies thanks both to the pedigree of its chef (he trained under Alice Waters, the guru of California cuisine) and its ever-changing, seasonal menu. Try a housemade pasta (the roasted chicken cannelloni is a standout) or roasted lamb. Expensive, but worth it.

Sapporo-Ya Japan Center, 1581 Webster St at Bush, Japantown ☎415/563-7400. Come here for a $10 dinner: this eatery specializes in soupy, slurpy bowls of ramen (try the barbecued pork floating with noodles in a glassy, jewel-like liquid) or even *okonomiyaki*, a meat-topped frittata-like pancake.

Stelline 330 Gough St at Hayes, Hayes Valley ☎415/626-4292. Red-checkered tablecloths, a handwritten and photocopied menu plus affable, chatty staff make this a cheap, easy place to grab a pasta lunch.

Suppenküche 601 Hayes St at Laguna, Hayes Valley ☎415/252-9289. Here, you can pair traditional beer-garden fare, such as spaetzle, sausages, and sauerkraut, with a good selection of lagers and lemony wheat beers. There's a beer-hall atmosphere, complete with bare walls, stark pine chairs, and tables.

Thep Phanom 400 Waller St at Fillmore, Lower Haight ☎415/431-2526. One of the best Thai restaurants in the city, catering to both hippie holdouts and yuppies: the curries are fragrant, pungent, and cheap, and the spinach with peanut sauce is sweet and sharp. Try the Three's Company seafood medley in coconut sauce.

Zona Rosa 1797 Haight St at Shrader, Haight-Ashbury ☎415/668-7717. By no means an "authentic" burrito – they use too many vegetables for that – but with a good and flavorful selection of *mole* and *verde* sauce-smothered fillings.

Zuni 1658 Market St at Gough, Hayes Valley ☎415/552-2522. Once nouveau and now a staple, *Zuni* features the most famous Caesar salad in town – made with home-cured anchovies – and an equally legendary focaccia hamburger, which is rustic Californian in style. The decor's heavy on brick and glass, and the restaurant's light and airy with large glass windows opening onto the street; most entrees are in the $18–22 range.

The Richmond and the Sunset

Aziza 5800 Geary Blvd at 22nd, Richmond ☎415/752-2222. Classy Moroccan eatery with opulent decor and fun touches, including a pewter ewer and basin that's passed around so you can wash your hands, plus live belly dancing Thursday to Sunday. Try the $35 tasters' menu, which boasts Middle Eastern specialties like hummus and *baba ghanoush*, or the tagines of rabbit spiced with paprika.

Chapeau! 1408 Clement St at 15th, Richmond ☎415/750-9787. Downtown-quality French food at foggy Richmond prices, packed with locals enjoying a relaxed provincial atmosphere.

Fountain Court 354 Clement St at 5th Ave, Richmond ☎415/668-1100. Unusual Chinese restaurant serving authentic Shanghainese food – the stews and long-cooked dishes may be less familiar than stir-fry-heavy Cantonese staples, perhaps, but they're just as delicious. Try the lion's-head soup or aromatic chicken poached in five-spice broth.

Park Chow 1240 9th Ave at Lincoln, Sunset ☎415/665-9912. The sequel to popular *Chow* near the Castro. Reliable renditions of pizza, pasta, and the like, perfect for a post-park lunch.

PJ's Oyster Bed 737 Irving at 9th, Sunset ☎415/566-7775. From Tuesday to Thursday this rowdy, unpretentious restaurant offers spicy, tangy Cajun dishes like blackened catfish and alligator fillets. On weekends, it broadens the menu to offer fish specials like delicious Peruvian stew, with prawns, scallops, and mussels in a chili cream sauce. Watch out for the free Jello vodka shots the owner periodically passes around.

Q 225 Clement St at 3rd, Richmond ☎415/752-2298. There's over-the-top decor – like a table with a tree growing through it – and outlandish portions of comfort food (think fish tacos and mac'n'cheese) at this hip outpost.

Thanh Long 4101 Judah St at 46th Ave, Sunset ☎415/665-1146. The original restaurant by the owners of the (over) hyped *Crustacean* in Polk Gulch serves upscale French-Vietnamese food in a low-key atmosphere. Try the catfish claypot or one of the soft-shell crab dishes.

White Caps Café 3738 Geary Blvd at Arguello, Richmond ☎415/221-1613. This casual café is known for its extensive list of British favorites: sample the likes of shepherd's pie or Cornish pasties and pick up some salt and vinegar crisps to go from the on-site grocery. There's a small patio area out back.

Drinking

While famous for its restaurants, San Francisco also has a huge number of **drinking** establishments, ranging from comfortably scruffy jukebox joints to the chic watering holes of social climbers. Though spread fairly evenly over the city, happening bars are particularly numerous in North Beach and the Mission, where they line up one after the other. Some of the more colorful (and seedy) are to be found in the Tenderloin and the Haight, while yuppie cruising zones populate the Marina and slick lounges speckle downtown and have begun to spread into SoMa. According to new California law, there is **no smoking** allowed in any bar unless its sole employees are the owners, though the debate still rages and enforcement has been spotty.

The city is also dotted with excellent **cafés** serving first-rate coffees, teas, and soft drinks in addition to beer and wine. More social than utilitarian, people hang out in these generally lively venues to pass time as much as refresh themselves. Other non-drinkers looking for social alternatives to bars are opting for the old English tradition of afternoon tea. So far it has only taken root in the big hotels, but neighborhood cafés are catching on fast.

Unsurprisingly, the city has many specifically **gay bars** (see p.634), most plentifully in the Castro, Polk Street, and the Mission – although few bars are at all threatening for either gay men or lesbians, or women on their own.

Downtown and Chinatown

Bix 56 Gold St at Montgomery, Jackson Square ☎415/433-6300. Hidden on a tiny side street, this bar-restaurant has a touch of 1940s glamour to its decor: the bar's packed after work with an office crowd, while music fans slip in later for the supper club for dinner. It's famed for its gin martinis.

The Bubble Lounge 714 Montgomery St at Jackson, Financial District ☎415/434-4204. Champagne bar that attracts a young, label-touting crowd – surprisingly, the prices here are very reasonable.

Cathay House 718 California St at Grant, Chinatown ☎415/982-3388. Don't be put off by the diners in the window – sitting smack in the middle of a run-of-the-mill restaurant is an inviting circular bar, centered on a large Buddha.

Li Po's Bar 916 Grant Ave at Jackson, Chinatown ☎415/982-0072. Named after the Chinese poet, *Li Po's* is a little grotty, although that's part of its charm. One of the few places to drink in Chinatown.

The London Wine Bar 415 Sansome St at Sacramento, Financial District ☎415/788-4811.

Claiming to be America's first wine bar, this clubby place has a worn mahogany bar and cozy paneled booths, and caters to an older crowd.

Maxfield's *Palace Hotel*, 2 New Montgomery St at Market, SoMa ☎415/392-8600. Named after the artist Maxfield Parrish, whose famous mural of the Pied Piper decorates the bar, this mahogany-paneled room is a secluded, elegant place for a martini.

Red Room *Commodore International Hotel*, 827 Sutter St at Jones, Theater District ☎415/346-7666. This trendy, sexy bar is – as its name implies – completely red: walls, furniture, glasses, and even many of the drinks. The clientele's young and mixed gay-straight, and it can get crowded at weekends.

The Redwood Room *Clift Hotel*, 495 Geary St at Taylor, Theater District ☎415/775-4700. This clubby, landmark bar was made over by Starck & Schrager, who added lightboxes on the wall displaying paintings that shift and fade. It's fun and hip – just don't choke on the drink prices.

North Beach, Nob Hill, and the northern waterfront

A16 2355 Chestnut St at Division, Marina ☎415/771-2216. This Southern Italian restaurant (named for the freeway that bisects the region around Naples) serves terrific, thin-crust pizzas in the room at the rear, but the real draw is the extensive wine list – more than forty different options, mostly Southern Italian and Californian, by the glass. Try the Red Flight of five tasting wines for $22.

Balboa Café 3199 Fillmore St at Greenwich, Marina ☎415/921-3944. Marina singles on the prowl pack this dark-wood bar with its high ceilings and excellent wine list most nights of the week.

The Crow Bar 401 Broadway at Montgomery, North Beach ☎415/788-2769. This hole-in-the-wall is an appealing escape on a club-saturated strip, with a pool table out back and an unpretentious crowd.

Gino and Carlo 548 Green St at Grant, North Beach ☎415/421-0896. Visitors wanting to stop by to play pinball or pool won't feel unwelcome at this, the classic drunken pressman's bar, filled with regulars and old-school locals all day.

Hawaii West 729 Vallejo St at Stockton, North Beach ☎415/362-3220. Come here for the cursing parrot, drag-queen owner, and a pool table you don't have to wait in line for. If you're lucky, the owner will serenade the crowd with some karaoke.

Liverpool Lil's 2942 Lyon St at Greenwich, on the edge of the Presidio ☎415/921-6664. Brit-centric, eccentric old-fashioned pub that's refreshingly rough-edged amid the Marina's hordes of wine bars. Come to drink pints of Bass ale and chow down on steak and kidney pie until 1am most nights; for some reason, it's popular with local windsurfers at weekends.

Matrix 3138 Fillmore St at Greenwich, Marina ☎415/563-4180. Inspired by the original *Matrix* that opened on the same spot in 1965 and hosted big-name rock acts, this bar couldn't be more different now. It's glamorous and a little posey, with a Marina crowd sipping wine by the glass and dancing to mainstream house and disco.

Pier 23 Pier 23, Telegraph Hill ☎415/362-5125. Sit out on the bayside deck under the heatlamps and enjoy cocktails to the sound of a live band, not to mention a gorgeous view of the Bay Bridge.

Rosewood 732 Broadway at Powell, North Beach ☎415/951-4886. Deliberately hidden bolthole, that doesn't even have a sign outside. The interior's retro groovy, and complemented by great lounge-core DJs: the downside is the pricey drinks and the out-of-towners who pour in at weekends. Best on weeknights by far.

San Francisco Brewing Company 155 Columbus Ave at Pacific, North Beach ☎415/434-3344. Probably the most touristy of the various micro-brewpubs around town, with a bland crowd of non-locals and big shining tanks of beer. Still, great happy-hour deals from 4 to 6pm.

Silver Clouds 1994 Lombard St at Webster, Marina ☎415/922-1977. Brash mainstream bar notable mostly for its raucous karaoke sessions and amusingly abrasive staff: avoid on weekends when it's clogged with out-of-towners.

Spec's 12 Saroyan Place at Columbus, North Beach ☎415/421-4112. Friendly dive bar in the heart of North Beach, packed with an older, eccentric local crowd. It's known for its chatty barstaff who'll often serve up cheese and crackers to regulars.

Tonga Room *Fairmont Hotel*, 950 Mason St at California, Nob Hill ☎415/772-5278. This basement Tiki lounge has grass huts and a floating band at night, not to mention an indoor rainstorm every fifteen minutes. Come for happy hour when there's a terrific all-you-care-to-eat $6 buffet, as long as you buy a (pricey) drink. Recommended.

Tunnel Top 601 Bush St at Stockton, Union Square ☎415/986-8900. This grimy but groovy bar is hidden behind a seedy storefront on top of the Stockton Street tunnel. Inside is arty-industrial – check out the chandelier festooned with empty wine bottles – and there are movies projected on the walls. One of the few tobacco-friendly places downtown.

SoMa, the Civic Center, and the Tenderloin

Bambuddha *Phoenix Hotel*, 601 Eddy St at Larkin, Tenderloin ☎415/885-5088. Relaxed, groovy lounge, with a New Age-meets-Asian vibe (think swirling, elemental decor and *feng shui*–favorable fountains).

Bigfoot Lodge 1750 Polk St at Washington, Polk Gulch ☎415/440-2355. San Francisco outpost of a campy bar from LA, themed as a 1950s ski lodge. Expect plenty of faux wood, hunting trophies, antlers – as well as an enormous papier mâché statue of Bigfoot himself.

Bobby's Owl Tree 601 Post St at Taylor, Tenderloin ☎415/776-9344. A true local oddity, this bar is crammed with owls – from clocks to statues to paintings – without a trace of hip irony. For that reason alone, it's worth a visit for a freaky, off-kilter experience.

Butter 354 11th St at Folsom, SoMa ☎415/863-5964. Stylized "white trash" bar and diner featuring imitation trailer-park decor, like a bar covered with shingles. The serving window to one side serves only microwaveable junk food. Hip, fun, and ironic, if a little less supercool than it once was.

Edinburgh Castle 950 Geary St at Polk, Tenderloin ☎415/885-4074. Just your average Scottish bar, filled with heraldic Highland memorabilia (although it's actually run by Koreans); the bartender, Alan, is a local legend for his impenetrable Scottish accent and impeccable literary taste – he brought the play version of *Trainspotting* to the bar for its US premiere. The room upstairs regularly hosts comedy and live music.

Gordon Biersch Brewery 2 Harrison St at Embarcadero, SoMa ☎415/243-8246. Bayfront

While the surrounding countryside may be devoted to winemaking, the city of San Francisco is renowned for its beer, specifically its **microbreweries**: the best-known local product is so-called **steam** beer, a hybrid lager-bitter. It was invented when early local brewers, finding the ice needed for lager production too expensive, instead fermented their yeast at room temperature like an ale: the result was a beer with the lower ABV of lager but the hearty flavor of bitter. (The precise origin of the odd name, unfortunately, has never been established.) To find out more head over to the **Anchor Steam Brewery**, 1705 Mariposa St at Carolina, Potrero Hill, for a **tour** (free; reservations essential ⊤415/863-8350, ⊛www.anchorbrewing.com), though the product is universally available at bars and stores. The pick of the local microbrewpubs are:

Gordon Biersch Brewery SoMa. See p.623.
San Francisco Brewing Company North Beach. See p.623.
Thirsty Bear Brewing Company SoMa. See below.

outpost of the successful Peninsula microbrewery housed in a converted Hills Brothers coffee warehouse with a lovely view of the bridge, good bar food, and some of the best beers in San Francisco.
Hemlock Tavern 1131 Polk St at Post, Polk Gulch ⊤415/923-0923. Neighborhood bar that hosts regular live gigs from jobbing bands ($7–10) but is most beloved by smokers for its handy, enclosed patio where you can puff and sip in peace.
House of Shields 39 New Montgomery St at Mission, SoMa ⊤415/495-5436. This is a schizophrenic space: after work, it's an old-school clubby piano bar, opened in 1908, that has preserved its longterm decor (dark wood paneling) and longterm regulars (slightly crumpled businessmen). But late nights, it's been turned over to a promoting team who've brought in avant-garde DJs and a punkier crowd – Thursday is the best night to stop by.

Julip 839 Geary St at Larkin, Tenderloin ⊤415/474-3216. Owned by the same team as the divey *Dalva* (see below), this bar looks like Salvador Dalí was its head designer: there are tree trunks protruding from walls and weird religious icons dotted round the candlelit room. Live DJs every night, and a small Spanish-tapas-style menu of nibbles.
The Ramp 855 China Basin St at Illinois, China Basin ⊤415/621-2378. Way out on the old docks, this is well worth the half-mile trek from downtown to sit out on the patio and sip beers overlooking the abandoned piers and new boatyards.
Thirsty Bear Brewing Company 661 Howard St at 2nd, SoMa ⊤415/974-0905. A combination brewpub and tapas bar, packed in the evenings with local office workers; the food's well-priced ($6–8 a plate) and tasty (try the fried calamari).

The Mission, the Castro, and south

The Beauty Bar 2299 Mission St at 19th, Mission ⊤415/285-0323. Campy and tongue-in-cheek, this San Francisco import of New York's *Beauty Bar* is outfitted like a 1950s hair salon. Sip on a cocktail while enjoying a manicure, but come during the week if you want to avoid the crowds.
Blondie's Bar & No Grill 540 Valencia St at 16th, Mission ⊤415/864-2419. Always packed, this fun bar with a good-sized patio serves huge cocktails and often hosts live music. As a bonus, the Wetspot back room is also smoker-friendly.
Dalva 3121 16th St at Valencia, Mission ⊤415/252-7740. *Dalva's* divey and dark, and though the wafer-thin space is easy to miss, that doesn't stop a diverse, artsy crowd from packing in to lean against one of the narrow tables.

Doc's Clock 2575 Mission St at 21st, Mission ⊤415/824-3627. Easy-to-spot Deco-style bar, thanks to the hot-pink neon sign blazing out front; it attracts an artsy and alternative crowd.
La Rondalla 901 Valencia St at 20th, Mission ⊤415/647-7474. It's always Christmas at this festive Mexican dive, decorated year-round with an orgy of tinsel and trinkets. There's a live mariachi band most nights.
Lazslo Foreign Cinema, 2532 Mission St at 21st, Mission ⊤415/648-7600. This industrial-chic bar, attached to the film-themed restaurant, is unsurprisingly named in homage to the movies – Jean-Paul Belmondo's character in *A Bout de Souffle*; there's a DJ every night except Monday and the cocktails, especially the *mojitos*, are outstanding.

The Lone Palm 3394 22nd St at Guerrero, Mission ☎415/648-0109. Like a forgotten Vegas review bar from the 1950s, this dim, candlelit cocktail lounge is a secret gem. The namesake palm is actually metal and there's a TV above the bar playing classic American movies.

Lucky 13 2140 Market St at Church, Castro ☎415/487-1313. A primarily hetero, divey rocker bar on the border between the Castro and the Lower Haight, filled with frat boys playing pool and listening to the Sex Pistols on the jukebox.

Luna Park 694 Valencia St at 17th, Mission ☎415/553-8584. The smallish bar at the front of this outstanding new restaurant has a groovy local vibe but the inventive cocktails are the real draw: try an appletini, made from Granny Smith–infused vodka.

Mecca 2029 Market at 14th, Castro ☎415/621-7000, ⊛www.sfmecca.com. Impressive, if pricey, nightspot serving a range of fruity cocktails (the vodka *mojitos* are oddly delicious); try to stop by on Wed when there's live jazz – if you're a fan, try to snag one of the dinner tables that overlook the small performance area by the massive central bar. There's also a restaurant on site.

Odeon Bar 3223 Mission St at Valencia, Bernal Heights ☎415/550-6994, ⊛www.odeonbar.com. Creepy, intriguing dive bar, run by wacky performance artist "Chicken John": the bar's stage often hosts bizarre performers and the general vibe is bohemian and eccentric.

Sublounge 620 20th St at 3rd, Mission ☎415/552-3603. Futuristic jetset decor (airplane seats and video games) make this new lounge one of the city's hot spots – not to mention the fact that it's smoker-friendly. Come to drink and dance: the upstair's bar is jammed against the dancefloor, and the soundtrack's mostly house and hip-hop – call for dates of the unmissable monthly "Bikini Wax" party.

Haight-Ashbury and west of Civic Center

An Bodhran 688 Haight St at Pierce, Lower Haight ☎415/431-4724. Not quite on a par with the *Mad Dog* up the block, but occasional live Irish folk music makes this a popular spot. (Incidentally, it's pronounced "an bau-rawn").

Mad Dog in the Fog 530 Haight St at Fillmore, Lower Haight ☎415/626-7279. Aptly named by the two lads from Birmingham, England, who own the joint, this is one of the Lower Haight's most loyally patronized bars, with darts, English beer, copies of the *Sun* tabloid, and a typical pub menu that includes bangers'n'mash and ploughman's lunch.

Martin Macks 1568 Haight St at Ashbury, Haight-Ashbury ☎415/864-0124. This neighborhood pub is popular for its simple, tasty food, but you can still grab a pint of Guinness by the bar – if you can squeeze past the crowds that usually pack in by lunchtime.

Noc Noc 557 Haight St at Steiner, Lower Haight ☎415/861-5811. Decor straight out of an Orwellian sci-fi film, with static-filled TVs in every corner. The bar doesn't have a license to sell hard alcohol, so all cocktails are made from sake: it's supergroovy, extra dark, and worth the trip.

Persian Aub Zam Zam 1663 Haight St at Clayton, Haight-Ashbury ☎415/861-2545. There's a retro jazz jukebox at this Casbah-style cocktail lounge. Bar regulars purchased the place after the death of its ornery owner, Bruno, and have just about managed to retain the surly but warm vibe.

The Rickshaw Stop 155 Fell St at Van Ness, Hayes Valley ☎415/861-2011. Newbie neighborhood bar in gentrified Hayes Valley known for its offbeat music programming and unusual themed parties like "Tots'n'Tonic," a cocktail bash where you can bring the kids. Recommended. Wed–Sat only.

Golden Gate Park, the beaches, and outlying areas

The Abbey 4100 Geary Blvd at 5th, Richmond ☎415/221-7767. Quintessentially Irish, this sports bar is friendly and upscale, often hosting live Irish folk music when there aren't any important games on TV.

Pig & Whistle Pub 2801 Geary Blvd at Wood, Richmond ☎415/885-4779. Thoroughly British pub, serving a good selection of English and California microbrews, with a pool table and dartboards, and excellent pub food.

Trad'r Sam's 6150 Geary Blvd at 26th, Richmond ☎415/221-0773. Open since 1939, this is a classic tiki bar, complete with flaming bowls of exotically named cocktails: it's groovier and less student-dominated during the week.

Yancy's Saloon 734 Irving St at 8th, Sunset ☎415/665-6551. Mellow, plant-festooned collegiate bar with free darts and cheap drinks.

Nightlife

Compared to Los Angeles, where you need money and attitude in equal amounts, San Francisco's **nightlife** demands little of either. This is no 24-hour city, and the approach to socializing is often surprisingly low-key, with little of the pandering to fads and fashions that goes on elsewhere. The casualness is contagious, and manifests in a **club scene** that, far as it is from the cutting edge of hip, is encouragingly inexpensive compared to other cities. Forty dollars or so can buy you a decent night out, including cover charges and a few drinks, and maybe even a taxi home. The live music scene is similarly economical – and, frankly, what the city does best. San Franciscans may be relatively unconcerned with fashion, but there are some excellent rock, jazz, and folk venues all over town, many entertaining you for no more than the price of a drink. Be sure to always bring a **picture ID** with you to get past the bouncers.

San Francisco has a great reputation for **opera and classical music**; its orchestra and opera company are among the most highly regarded in the country. **Theater** is accessible and much less costly than elsewhere, with discount tickets available, but most of the mainstream downtown venues – barring a couple of exceptions – are mediocre, forever staging Broadway reruns, and you'd do better to take some time to explore the infinitely more interesting fringe circuit.

Cabaret and **comedy** are also lively, and **film**, too, is almost as big an obsession as eating in San Francisco; you may well be surprised by the sheer number of movie theaters – repertory and current release – that flourish in this city.

Clubs

Still trading on a reputation for hedonism earned decades ago, San Francisco's **nightclubs** in fact trail light years behind those of other large American cities. That said, the compensations are manifold – it is rare to encounter high cover charges, ridiculously priced drinks, feverish posing, or long lines, though a few of the cavernous dance clubs in SoMa do have lines on weekends. Instead you'll find a diverse range of small- to medium-sized, affordable clubs in which leather-clad goths rub shoulders with the bearded and beaded, alongside a number of gay hangouts (listed on p.632) still rocking to the sounds of high-energy funk and Motown. You'll find the occasional DJ hangout, which plays two-step and drum'n'bass, but what San Francisco does best is all the old favorites – songs you know the words to; clubbing is more of a party than a pose in this city. The greatest concentration of clubs is in **SoMa**, especially the area around 11th Street and Folsom, though the **Mission** is similarly well provided with bars (plus small live-music venues) – not to mention a couple of outrageous drag bars – of almost exclusively Latino origin. There are a few places in North Beach too, so just pick a neighborhood and explore.

Unlike most other cities, where the action never gets going until after midnight, many San Francisco clubs have to **close at 2am during the week**, so you can usually be sure of finding things well under way by 11.30pm. At weekends, most places stay open until 3 or 4am. Very few venues operate any kind of dress code or restrictive admission policy, and only on very busy nights are you likely to have to wait. Unfortunately, most live music and dancing opportunities are restricted to those 21-and-over, forcing underage revellers to be more creative when it comes to late-night entertainment.

12 Galaxies 2365 Mission St at 21st, Mission ☎415/970-9777. This huge, ultra-hip club with industrial decor centers on a low-rise stage where there are live performances most nights ($6–16); best views are from the mezzanine. If you don't want to dance, there's a pool table and a small snack menu.

26 Mix 3024 Mission St at 26th, Mission ☎415/826-7378, ⓦwww.26mix.com. Low-key Mission spot to catch top DJs, a self-proclaimed "Sound Bar" that's halfway between a large bar and smallish club. Closed Sun and Wed. $3–5.

330 Ritch St 330 Ritch St at Townsend, SoMa ☎415/541-9574. The only constant at this small, out-of-the-way club is its location: different nights attract wildly varied crowds, but it's best known for the "Thursday Popscene" party, ground zero for Modish Britpoppers in San Francisco. $5–15.

1015 Folsom 1015 Folsom St at 6th, SoMa ☎415/431-1200, ⓦwww.1015.com. Multi-level superclub, popular across-the-board for late-night dancing: the music's largely house and garage, and expect marquee names like Sasha and Digweed on the main floor. $10–15.

Cat Club 1190 Folsom St at 8th, SoMa ☎415/431-3332. Predominantly lesbian club often mixing live entertainment with dancing: this is a serious late-night spot, so don't plan on arriving before the early hours. $5–10.

DNA Lounge 375 11th St at Harrison, SoMa ☎415/626-1409, ⓦwww.dnalounge.com Changes its music style nightly, but draws the same young hipsters, a mixed gay-straight crowd. Downstairs is a large dancefloor, while the mezzanine is a comfy, sofa-packed lounge where you can chill. $15–20.

Fluid 662 Mission St at 3rd, SoMa ☎415/615-6888. Pricey, dressy bar-club, playing mostly hip-hop and mainstream house. The first, large room is the lounge, its mirrored walls illuminated by the neon, flashing floor – cocktails hover around $10 – while the rear room is home to a tiny dancefloor.

Hush Hush Lounge 496 14th St at Guerrero, Mission ☎415/241-9944. A great place to hang out and dance, this hidden bar has no sign outside. Inside, expect a slightly older crowd, playing pool or dancing to nu-disco and classic 1970s funk (Wed to Sat). On Sunday nights, at "Smile," the playlist switches to 1960s and 1970s rock. Free–$5.

Mezzanine 444 Jessie St at 5th, SoMa ☎415/820-9669, ⓦwww.mezzaninesf.com. Massive megaclub with mainstream, brand-name DJs – make a reservation for the VIP Ultra Lounge if you're feeling flush and flash. The music programming is more eclectic than most, taking in disco, electroclash, and even the occasional live rock show. $15 and up.

Mighty 119 Utah St at 15th, Potrero Hill ☎415/626-7001, ⓦwww.mighty119.com. Massive converted warehouse space huddled close to the freeway in Potrero Hill: it's a combination art gallery, performance venue, club, and lounge – check out the frozen vodka bar. As for the music, it's mostly live funk or DJs spinning old-school classic house. $10 and up.

Pink 2925 16th St at Capp, Mission ☎415/431-8889, ⓦwww.pinksf.com. You could walk right on by without noticing it, but this tiny, fun club is a rare place for serious dancing in the Mission's otherwise loungey bar district; it's a friendly, mixed gay-straight place. $5–10.

Skylark Bar 3089 16th St at Valencia, Mission ☎415/621-9294. Club-bar hybrid, with low lighting and plenty of booths, marred slightly by its yuppified clientele: during the week, it's more geared to drinking, while at weekends it's a full-scale dancehall. No cover.

Sno-drift 1830 3rd St at 16th, Potrero Hill ☎415/431-4766. Alpine ski lodge-themed club, designed by the team behind the *Red Room* (see p.622). Almost everything here is igloo-white, including an enormous padded vinyl bar. The restaurant attached serves pricey food: if you eat there, though, you'll be excused the cover charge. Music varies, but is mainly house. $15.

Space 550 550 Barneveld Ave at Oakdale, Hunter's Point ☎415/289-2001, ⓦwww.space550.com. This enormous warehouse club is known for its trancey, industrial dance programming: although it's a long way out, in an iffy part of town, serious clubbers will find it's worth the trek. $5–15.

Live music: rock, jazz, blues, and folk

San Francisco's music scene reflects the character of the city as a whole: laid back and not a little nostalgic. The options for catching **live music** are wide and the scene is consistently progressive, characterized by the frequent emergence of good young bands. San Francisco has never recaptured its crucial 1960s role, though in more recent years the city has helped launch acid jazz (beat-heavy jazz that's become *de rigueur* dinner-party music across the country), a classic swing revival, and the East Bay pop-punk sound.

Bands are extremely easy to catch. Many restaurants offer live music, so you can eat, drink, and dance all at once and often with no cover charge; ordinary neighborhood bars regularly host groups, often for free, and there are any number of good and inexpensive small venues spread out across the city. Few fall into any particular camp, with most varying their bill throughout the week, and it can be hard to specify which of them cater to a certain music style.

What follows is a pretty comprehensive list of established **venues**, but be sure to check the weeklies or the local websites ⓦwww.sfstation.com or sanfrancisco.citysearch.com. Between the lot you should be able to find exhaustive listings of events in the city and Bay Area as a whole.

Large performance venues

Although San Francisco has a couple of major-league concert halls, bear in mind that some of the Bay Area's best large-scale venues, where the big names tend to play, are actually across the Bay in Oakland and Berkeley.

Bimbo's 365 Club 1025 Columbus at Chestnut, North Beach ☎415/474-0365, ⓦwww.bimbos365.com. Don't let the strange name put you off: the savvy booker here schedules underground European acts, kitschy tribute bands, and big-name rock acts in equal proportion – check for the latest listings. $15 and up.

The Fillmore Auditorium 1805 Geary St at Fillmore, Japantown ☎415/346-6000, ⓦwww.thefillmore.com. A local landmark, the Fillmore was at the heart of the 1960s counterculture, masterminded by the legendary Bill Graham. It reopened a decade ago after several years' hiatus and is home now to rock and alt-rock touring acts. Cover varies.

The Great American Music Hall 859 O'Farrell St at Polk, Tenderloin ☎415/885-0750, ⓦwww.musichallsf.com. Starting out as a bordello in the 1900s, the Music Hall's fortunes soon went into decline. It was resuscitated in the 1970s and now the gorgeous venue plays host to a wide variety of rock, country, and world music acts. $10–30.

The Warfield 982 Market St at 6th, SoMa ☎415/775-7722, ⓦwww.thefillmore.com/warfield.asp. Smaller than its sister venue the Fillmore, with seating, and so better suited to more intimate shows. $25 and up.

Rock, blues, folk, and country

Biscuits and Blues 401 Mason St at Geary, Union Square ☎415/292-2583, ⓦwww.biscuitandblue.citysearch.com. Certainly a tourist trap, but this is still one of the best spots in town to catch classic New Orleans jazz and delta blues, accompanied by delicious, if overpriced, soul food. Show times vary. $5–15.

Boom Boom Room 1601 Fillmore St at Geary, Japantown ☎415/673-8000,ⓦwww.boomboomblues.com Gritty venue in the Fillmore close to the Japan Center, that was owned by the late bluesman John Lee Hooker until he died in 2001: the dark low-rise building plays host to a fine selection of touring blues and funk artists. $5–12.

Bottom of the Hill 1233 17th St at Missouri, Mission ☎415/621-4455, ⓦwww.bottomofthehill.com. The best place in town to catch up-and-coming or determinedly obscure rock acts. Frequently packed for shows, there's a small patio out back to catch a breath of fresh air or, on Sundays, have a bite of barbecue. $6–10.

Hotel Utah Saloon 500 4th St at Bryant, SoMa ☎415/421-8308, ⓦwww.thehotelutahsaloon.com. Singer-songwriters take the stage at this small South of Market bar, dating back to 1908. $5–8.

The Independent, 628 Divisadero St at Hayes, Lower Haight ☎415/771-1421, ⓦwww.theindependentsf.com. New indie venue in the space that once housed the *Justice League* nightclub, with strong sightlines, an impressive sound system, and eclectic booking policy, ranging from rock to rap. $8–20.

Last Day Saloon 406 Clement St at 5th, Richmond ☎415/387-6343, ⓦwww.lastdaysaloon.com. A must for live music in the otherwise sleepy Richmond district, popular with nearby students. The line-up varies, with over-dependence on jangly pop and hippie rock, but it's always worth checking out. $5–10.

The Make-Out Room 3225 22nd at Mission, Mission ☎415/647-2888, ⓦwww.makeoutroom.com. This small dark space is primarily a place to drink at the enormous mahogany bar, but there are regular performances by local indie bands on Sundays and Mondays. $6–10.

Paradise Lounge 308 11th St at Folsom, SoMa ☎415/621-1911. Three stages vie for your attention at this enormous cornerstone of the 11th Street club district. If rock, punk, and country aren't your thing, duck upstairs to play pool by the bar. $5–10.

Slim's 333 11th St at Folsom, SoMa ☎415/522-0333, ⓦwww.slims-sf.com. Owned by local (and once popular rocker) Boz Skaggs, this is a prime venue to catch an array of punk, alternative, and world music, played mostly by local bands. $12–20.

Tongue & Groove 2513 Van Ness Ave at Union, Cow Hollow ☎415/928-0404, ⓦwww .tongueandgroovesf.com. This large venue has two spaces: the front is dominated by a stage, while the back room is loungier and more geared to drinking. Expect smart, edgy bands and unusual performers. $8–10.

Jazz and Latin

Blue Lamp 561 Geary St at Jones, Tenderloin ☎415/885-1464. Rather unfriendly looking hole-in-the-wall offers live blues, funk, and jam rock just a short walk from the hotel district. No cover.

Bruno's 2389 Mission St at 20th, Mission ☎415/648-7701, ⓦwww.brunoslive.com. Like something from a Scorsese movie, this retro restaurant has an intimate live venue attached, filled with 1960s-style white-vinyl furniture surrounding a tiny stage. The music's a mixture of jazz and nu-school R&B – the Monday-night open mic jam session is a standout. If you eat in the (rather average) restaurant, there's no cover charge. $5–7.

Café du Nord 2170 Market St at Sanchez, Castro ☎415/861-5016, ⓦwww.cafedunord.com. Primarily a jazz club, this subterranean club (formerly a speakeasy) is a great place to enjoy cocktails: the varied booking provides constant surprises. It's recently been overhauled to improve sight lines and facilities. $3–8.

Elbo Room 647 Valencia St at 17th, Mission ☎415/552-7788, ⓦwww.elbo.com. The birthplace of acid jazz, a popular local variant that emphasizes a danceable groove over complex improvisation. Also hosts world-music performers. $5–8.

The Plough and Stars 116 Clement St at 2nd, Richmond ☎415/751-1122. The Irish expat community crams into this terrific pub for hearty pints of Guinness, games of pool and darts, and live music six nights a week at 8.30pm. No cover.

The Ramp 855 China Basin at Illinois, China Basin ☎415/621-2378. A bayside restaurant serving up live salsa on summer Sunday afternoons: it closes at 10pm weeknights, 8.30pm weekends.

Red Devil Lounge 1695 Polk St at Clay, Polk Gulch ☎415/921-1695, ⓦwww.reddevillounge .com. Competing with the *Elbo Room* for fans of acid jazz and funk, this neo-Goth lounge is kitschily decorated with gargoyles. The music, though, is mainstream cool and it's a reliable option if you want to dance. $6–20.

Roccapulco 3140 Mission St at Cesar Chavez, Outer Mission ☎415/648-6611. Catering to the Mission's Latino population, this large club books salsa and Tejano music, including performers rarely heard in the US and big names like Celia Cruz. Wednesdays there are salsa lessons, Thursdays are Latino hip-hop nights, while the live acts dominate Fridays and Saturdays. $8–15.

Classical music, opera, and dance

San Francisco has an excellent reputation for the **performing arts** – there are five major symphonies based in the Bay Area, for example. It's also the only city on the West Coast to have its own professional **opera** and **ballet** companies – even if some observers sniff that quantity doesn't always guarantee quality. During the summer months, look out for the free concerts in Stern Grove (at 19th Avenue and Sloat Boulevard), where the symphony orchestra, opera, and ballet give open-air performances for ten successive Sundays beginning in June.

Companies and concert halls

San Francisco Ballet War Memorial Opera House, 301 Van Ness Ave at Grove, Civic Center ☎415/864-3330, ⓦwww.sfballet.org. The city's ballet company, the oldest and third largest in the US, puts on an ambitious annual program (Feb–May) of both classical and contemporary dance, and a Christmas production of *Nutcracker*. Founded in 1933, the ballet was the first American company to stage full-length productions of *Swan Lake* and *Nutcracker*. Tickets range upward from $30.

San Francisco Opera War Memorial Opera House, 301 Van Ness Ave at Grove, Civic Center ☏415/864-3330, ⊛www.sfopera.org. The Opera House, designed by architect Arthur Brown Jr, the creator of City Hall and Coit Tower, makes a very opulent venue for the San Francisco Opera Association, which has been performing here since the building opened in 1932. Still probably the strongest of San Francisco's cultural trio, the Opera Association has a main season that runs Sept to Jan plus a brief summer session in June; and its opening night is one of the principal social events on the West Coast. Tickets cost upwards of $20 – for which you do at least get supertitles. Standing room begins at a bargain $15, and 250 tickets are available (one per person) at 10.30am on the day of performance.

San Francisco Symphony Louise M. Davies Symphony Hall, 201 Van Ness Ave at Hayes, Civic Center ☏415/864-6000, ⊛www.sfsymphony.org. The permanent home of the San Francisco Symphony Orchestra, which offers a year-round season of classical music and sometimes performances by other, often offbeat, musical and touring groups. Established in 1909 as a small musical group, the orchestra rose to international prominence in the 1950s when it started touring and recording. Although not quite on a par with the New York Philharmonic or Chicago Symphony, the tenure of conductor Michael Tilson Thomas has catapulted it into the top half-dozen US orchestras. Prices obviously depend on the performance, but are marginally lower than either the opera or ballet, with the least expensive seats going for around $20 and bargain standby tickets available 2hr before performances.

Theater

The majority of the city's **theaters** congregate downtown around the Theater District. Most aren't especially innovative (although a handful of more inventive fringe places are scattered in other parts of town, notably SoMa), but tickets are reasonably cheap – up to $30 a seat – and there's usually good availability. Check out the *Sunday Chronicle*'s "Pink Pages" to read up on the latest productions around town.

Most tickets can be purchased either through the individual theater's box offices or by calling **Tickets.com** (☏415/776-1999, ⊛www.tickets.com). For last-minute bargains try the **Tix Bay Area** booth on the western rim of Union Square, between Stockton and Powell streets (Tues–Thurs 11am–6pm, Fri & Sat 11am–7pm; ☏415/433-7827).

Downtown

450 Post Street Theatre 450 Post St at Powell, Union Square ☏415/433-9500, ⊛www.poststreettheatre.com. Converted Gothic theater with drama, musicals, comedy, and mainstream theater pieces. Tickets from $50.

American Conservatory Theater (ACT) Geary Theater, 415 Geary St at Taylor, Theater District ☏415/742-2228, ⊛www.act-sfbay.org. San Francisco's flagship theater company, the Tony Award–winning ACT puts on eight major plays each season. The city's best serious theater venue often has rush tickets available ninety minutes before the show. Tickets start at $20.

Golden Gate Theater 1 Taylor St at Golden Gate Ave and Market St, Tenderloin ☏415/551-2000, ⊛www.bestofbroadway-sf.com. Originally constructed during the 1920s and recently restored to its former splendor, the Golden Gate's marble flooring, rococo ceilings, and gilt trimmings make it one of San Francisco's most elegant theaters. It's a pity the programs don't live up to the surroundings – generally a mainstream diet of Broadway musicals.

Lorraine Hansberry Theater 620 Sutter St at Mason, Theater District ☏415/474-8800, ⊛www.lorrainehansberrytheatre.com. The impressive mainstay of African-American theater in San Francisco. Traditional theater as well as contemporary political pieces and jazz/blues musical revues.

Orpheum Theater 11192 Market St at Hyde, Tenderloin ☏415/551-2000, ⊛www.bestofbroadway-sf.com. Arguably the top local space, in terms of seating capacity and glitz, hosting big-name Broadway productions.

Yerba Buena Center for the Arts 701 Mission St at 3rd, SoMa. ☏415/978-2787, ⊛www.yerbabuenaarts.org. Modern 750-seat performance space that hosts a wide-ranging mix of touring companies – the programming's unpredictable but always high quality.

The rest of the city

Beach Blanket Babylon *Club Fugazi*, 678 Green St at Powell, North Beach ☎415/421-4222, ⊛www.beachblanketbabylon.com. A 30-year local institution, this revue, based loosely on the story of Little Red Riding Hood, is a riotous evening, thanks to the spot-on celebrity pastiches and quick-fire wit of the mostly veteran cast. Camp, tacky, and highly recommended. Tickets $20–70.

Intersection for the Arts 446 Valencia St at 16th, Mission ☎415/626-3311, ⊛www.theintersection.org. Well-meaning, community-based group that tackles interesting productions in inadequate, rather outdated facilities. Tickets from $5.

Magic Theatre Fort Mason Center, Building D, Fort Mason ☎415/441-8822, ⊛www.magictheatre.org. The busiest and largest company after the ACT, and probably the most exciting, the Magic Theater specializes in the works of contemporary playwrights and emerging new talent; Sam Shepard traditionally premieres his work here.

The Marsh 1062 Valencia St at 22nd, Mission ☎415/826-5750, ⊛www.themarsh.org. Small space known for its highly experimental, hit-and-miss productions from raw, personal monologues to impenetrable playlets. Worth a gamble if you're a true theater buff.

New Conservatory Theater Center 25 Van Ness Ave at Market, Civic Center ☎415/861-8972, ⊛www.nctcsf.org. This mid-size theater is known for its Pride season of gay-themed plays, as well as performances of musicals in concert. Tickets start at $20.

Project Artaud Theater 450 Florida St at Mariposa, Mission ☎415/621-7797, ⊛www.artaud.org. Modern theater in a converted warehouse offering dance and theater performances, many less obscure than the theater's artsy name might imply. Tickets from $15. Recommended.

Theater Rhinoceros 2926 16th St at S Van Ness, Mission ☎415/861-5079, ⊛www.therhino.org. The city's prime gay-oriented theater space actually has two spaces, hosting everything from raunchy revues to issues-based dramas. Tickets start at $15, though the two performances before each play's opening night are designated "pay what you can."

Comedy

Comedians have always found a welcoming audience in San Francisco – after all, local political bigwig Tom Ammiano started out as a stand-up performer. Few of the comedians are likely to be familiar: as with any cabaret you take your chances, and whether you consider a particular club to be good will depend on who happens to be playing the week you go. You can expect to pay roughly the same kind of cover in most of the clubs ($7–15), and two-drink minimums are common. There are usually two shows per night, the first kicking off around 8pm and a late show starting at around 11pm. For bargains, check the press for "Open Mike" nights when unknowns and members of the audience get up and have a go; there's rarely a cover charge for these evenings and, even if the acts are diabolical, it can be a fun night out.

Venues

Cobb's Comedy Club The Cannery, 915 Columbus Ave at Lombard, North Beach ☎415/928-4320, ⊛www.cobbscomedy.com. Pricey and usually full of tourists, but the standard of the acts is fairly consistent. Worth a look if everything else is booked up. $10–35 with two-drink minimum.

The Marsh 1062 Valencia at 21st, Mission ☎415/641-0235, ⊛www.themarsh.org. Successful alternative space hosting solo shows, many with a political bent. $15–25.

The Punch Line 444 Battery St at Washington, Jackson Square ☎415/397-7573, ⊛www.punchlinecomedyclub.com. Frontrunner of the city's "polished" cabaret venues, this place has an intimate, smoky feel that's ideal for downing expensive cocktails and laughing your head off. The club usually hosts the bigger names in the world of stand-up and is always packed. $5–30.

Film

San Franciscans attend more **movies** than residents of any other city in America and there's a staggering assortment of current-release and repertory film houses,

The **San Francisco Film Festival**, specializing in political and short films you wouldn't normally see, is held at the Kabuki eight-screen cinema, the Castro Theater, and the Pacific Film Archive in Berkeley (see p.659), at the end of April and first week or so of May. Tickets sell extremely fast and you'll need to book well in advance for all but the most obscure movies. If you know you're going to be in town, call ☏415/931-FILM or buy tickets on the Web at 🌐www.sfiff.org. Just as popular is the **Lesbian, Gay, and Transgender Film Festival**, held in June at the Castro and other theaters. Call ☏415/703-8650 or check 🌐www.frameline.org for program and ticket information.

with programs that range from the latest general-release films to Hollywood classics, iconoclastic Sixties pieces, and a selection of foreign and art films. For screening times and locations of current-run films, call ☏415/777-FILM.

Cinemas

AMC Kabuki 8 Japan Center, 1881 Post St at Fillmore, Japantown ☏415/922-4AMC. Part of the Japan Center complex, this multiplex screens a mixture of indie and big-budget titles. Validated parking at the underground parking lot.

Artists' Television Access (ATA) 992 Valencia St at 21st, Mission ☏415/824-3890, 🌐www.atasite.org. Nonprofit media center that puts on the city's most challenging barrage of film, video, and performance art, often with a political or psychosexual bent; or sometimes just trashy entertainment. Screenings Thurs–Sat.

The Castro Theatre 429 Castro St at Market, Castro ☏415/621-6120, 🌐www.thecastrotheatre.com. San Francisco's most beautiful movie house, offering a steady stream of reruns, art films, Hollywood classics, and (best of all) a Wurlitzer organ played between films by a man who rises up from below the stage.

Four Star 2200 Clement St at 23rd, Richmond ☏415/666-3488, 🌐www.hkinsf.com. Way out in the fog belt, but worth a visit for the interesting mix of Asian, international, and American culture films; two screens.

Landmark's Embarcadero Cinema 1 Embarcadero Center at Sansome, Financial District ☏415/267-4893. A good choice for American, international, and some art films. Five screens, two with digital sound; free parking on weekends and evenings with validation, or just take the BART.

Landmark's Lumière 1572 California St at Polk, Polk Gulch ☏415/267-4893. Another opulent Spanish Revival art house, a bit run down but often with an interesting program of obscure art films as well as a select choice of current-release films.

The Red Vic 1727 Haight St at Cole, Haight-Ashbury ☏415/668-3994, 🌐www.redvicmoviehouse.com. Friendly collective, housed in a room full of ancient couches where you can put your feet up and munch on organic popcorn.

The Roxie 3117 16th St at Valencia, Mission ☏415/863-1087, 🌐www.roxie.com. An adventurous rep house and film distributor, the Roxie is one of the few theaters in the country willing to take a risk on documentaries and little-known foreign directors – and usually the risk pays off. For even less mainstream fare, check out the satellite space, Little Roxie, next door.

Gay and lesbian San Francisco

San Francisco's reputation as a city of **gay celebration** is not new – in fact it may be a bit outdated. Though still considered by many to be the gay capital of the world, the gay community here has made a definite move from the outrageous to the mainstream, a measure of its political success. The exuberant energy that went into the posturing and parading of the 1970s has taken on a much more sober, down-to-business attitude, and these days you'll find more political activists organizing conferences than drag queens throwing parties.

Nowadays San Franciscans appreciate and recognize the huge economic and cultural impact of gays on the city, and to be an openly gay politician or businessperson is not as much of an issue to locals as it would be anywhere else in the United States, making it easy to forget things were not always this way.

Socially, San Francisco's gay scene has also mellowed, though in what is an increasingly conservative climate in the city generally, gay parties, parades, and street fairs still swing better than most. Like any well-organized section of society, the gay scene definitely has its social season – see the events listing below for highlights. **Lesbian culture** flowered in the 1980s, but today, though women's club nights do exist, the scene is more in evidence in bookstores than bars. Many have claimed Oakland for their own, though Bernal Heights and some areas of the Mission continue to be girl-friendly.

Details of gay accommodation, bars, and clubs appear below; mention of gay bookstores and theater and film venues are under the relevant headings throughout this chapter.

Information and resources

The **LGBT Community Center**, 1800 Market St at Octavia, Hayes Valley (Mon–Fri noon–10pm, Sat 9am–10pm; free; ☎415/865-5555, ⊛www .sfcenter.org), not only has plenty of resources at the first-floor information desk, but also regularly hosts performances by comedy and theater groups on site – check the website or call for details. The **Golden Gate Business Association** promotes gay-owned businesses   check ⊛www.ggba.com for a list of members.

The *Lavender Pages*, a telephone-cum-resource book, is available at A Different Light (see p.637) and other gay bookstores, as is the newly republished, but still opinionated, *Betty and Pansy's Severe Queer Review*, an offbeat guide to everything gay. Otherwise, there are plenty of freesheets that provide entertainment and bar listings. For newspapers, check out the *San Francisco Spectrum*, a monthly community newsletter, as well as the better-known *Bay Times* and the *Bay Area Reporter*, which has a thorough entertainment and reviews supplement. For nightlife, check the biweekly *Gloss*, or the weekly *Frontiers* (also online at ⊛www.frontiersnewsmagazine.com). Alternatively, the website ⊛www.scum -online.com provides quirkier, more underground information.

Accommodation

Choose any hotel in San Francisco and a single-sex couple won't raise an eyebrow at check-in: some, like the *Queen Anne* and the *Archbishop's Mansion* attract equal numbers of gay and straight visitors. There are, however, a few places that especially cater to gay and lesbian travelers that we've singled out below.

24 Henry 24 Henry St at Sanchez, Castro ☎415/864-5686 or 1-800/900-5686, ⊛www.24henry.com. This small blue-and-white home tucked away on a leafy residential street north of Market is a predominantly gay male guest house with five simple rooms, one with private bath. It makes a friendly bolthole from the cruisey Castro scene nearby. ❹

Inn on Castro 321 Castro St at Market, Castro ☎415/861-0321, ⊛www.innoncastro.com. This

luxurious B&B is spread across two nearby houses. It has eight rooms and three apartments available, all of which are brightly decorated in individual styles and have private baths and phones. There's a funky lounge where you can meet other guests. Two-night minimum at weekends, three-night minimum on holidays, but good midweek discounts. ❺

Monarch 1015 Geary St at Polk, Polk Gulch ☎415/673-5232 or 1-800/777-3210, ⊛www.themonarchhotel.com. Large converted motel with nondescript, floral rooms that are clean if basic: a good base for exploring the bars of Polk Gulch. ❹

Noe's Nest 3973 23rd St, Noe Valley ☏415/821-0751, ⓦnoesnest.citysearch.com. Seven-room bed and breakfast (six with private bath) on a quiet street in Noe Valley: all rooms have TV, VCR, and a private phone line. Lavish breakfasts are served each morning, and there's a hot tub, too. ❺

The Parker House 520 Church St at 18th, Castro ☏415/621-3222 or 1-888/520-7275, ⓦwww.parkerguesthouse.com. This converted Edwardian mansion is set in beautiful gardens and has a

friendly vibe, thanks to its ample, large common areas: there's a sunny breakfast room and on-site sauna. ❻, ❺ without bath

The Renoir 45 McAllister St at 7th, Civic Center ☏415/626-5200 or 1-800/576-3388, ⓦwww.renoirhotel.com. This wedge-shaped building is a historic landmark with 135 rooms that have recently been unexcitingly, if florally, refurbished. The superior rooms cost $20 more than standard – worth the extra if you can snag one of the oddly shaped rooms at the building's apex which are much larger. Popular during Gay Pride for its Market Street views along the parade route. ❺

Bars

San Francisco's **gay bars** are many and varied, ranging from cozy cocktail bars to no-holds-barred leather-and-chain hangouts. In the last few years, nearly every single lesbian bar has disappeared, with the notable exception of *Lexington Club* (see below). Otherwise, if you want exclusively female company you'll have to check out clubs that have lesbian nights. Many of the places in this section may turn up the music later and transform into mini-clubs: for hardcore dancing, though, check out "Clubs" below.

Badlands 4131 18th St at Castro, Castro ☏415/626-9320, ⓦwww.sfbadlands.com. Decked out in distressed brick and shiny chrome, this video bar attracts a pretty, thirtysomething crowd and is usually packed at weekends. There's a wide selection of imported beer, and overall it's one of the less sceney places in the neighborhood.

Detour 2348 Market St at Castro, Castro ☏415/861-6053. The crowd here is young, buff, and cruisey, and oddly, the main floor is bisected by a chain link fence. There are go-go boys on Saturday and throbbing house DJs every night.

The Eagle Tavern 398 12th St at Harrison, SoMa ☏415/626-0880. This good, old-fashioned leather bar is particularly popular on Sundays, when it holds a late-afternoon "beer bust" for charity: all you can down for $8.

Esta Noche 3079 16th St at Valencia, Mission ☏415/861-5757. A gay Latin drag bar, that's great fun and attracts a youngish, racially mixed clientele: there are shows nightly at 11.30pm, except on Sundays (7pm, 10.30pm, midnight).

Ginger's Trois 246 Kearny St at Bush, Financial District ☏415/989-0282. A charming, low-rent bar smack in the heart of downtown, with a group of diehard regulars who'll happily sing along with the showtunes occasionally played by the bartenders.

Hole in the Wall Saloon 289 8th St at Folsom, SoMa ☏415/431-4695. Formerly a rock'n'roll paradise, this divey bar is now part of the biker scene, and attracts hardcore, punky leather boys

who want to play pool and pinball or hook up. Remember to dress accordingly, and don't be surprised to see an old man in diapers.

Lexington Club 3464 19th St at Lexington, Mission ☏415/863-2052, ⓦwww.lexingtonclub.com. The only place in the city where the girls outnumber the boys (men must be accompanied by a woman to enter), this bustling lesbian bar attracts all sorts with its no-nonsense decor, friendly atmosphere, and excellent jukebox.

The Lone Star 1354 Harrison St at 10th, SoMa ☏415/863-9999. One of the tamer biker bars in SoMa, the *Lone Star* attracts leather daddies, bears, cubs, and those who love them. It's large, friendly, and welcoming.

Martuni's 4 Valencia St at Market, Mission ☏415/241-0205, ⓦwww.martunis.citysearch.com. This piano bar attracts a well-heeled, middle-aged crowd, all keen to sing along to classics from Judy, Liza, and Edith. There are regular open-mike evenings as well as a singles evening on Wed. Try a martuni, the signature cocktail, made from Bombay Sapphire gin and dry vermouth with a lemon twist.

Midnight Sun 4067 18th St at Castro, Castro ☏415/861-4186, ⓦwww.midnightsunsf.com. Long, narrow video bar, always busy with well-dressed white boys checking out the movies shown on the monitors, as well as each other: it's not a place to strike up a casual conversation. The weekly showings of popular television programs are a big draw.

AIDS Candlelight Memorial March & Vigil (May) Procession from the Castro to Civic Center, commemorating all those who've died of AIDS (☎415/863-4676, Ⓦwww.actupgg.org).

Frameline 28 (June) Short films and features from amateurs and auteurs – usually at either the Castro or Roxie cinemas – at the Gay and Lesbian Film Festival (☎415/703-8650, Ⓦwww.frameline.org).

San Francisco LGBT Pride Parade (Late June) One of the largest Pride parades in the world – and also one of the longest (it can last up to four hours). Don't miss Pink Night, the evening when the Castro is virtually pedestrianized by thousands of revelers or the Dyke March that takes place on Friday night (☎415/864-3733, Ⓦwww.sfpride.org).

Up Your Alley Fair (Late July) Folsom Street Fair's little brother takes place on nearby Doré Alley: it's a more sex-driven event with fewer onlookers and plenty of S&M (Ⓦwww.folsomstreetfair.com/alley).

Folsom Street Fair (Late Sept) Hardcore leather fair, full of hairy-chested men in chaps. Surprisingly friendly and fun (☎415/861-3247, Ⓦwww.folsomstreetfair.com).

Castro Street Fair (Oct) Food and craft stalls take over the Castro (☎415/467-3354, Ⓦwww.castrostreetfair.org).

My Place 1225 Folsom St at 8th, SoMa ☎415/863-2329. Hardcore leather bar, sleazy and cruisey, known for its cheap drinks and anything-goes vibe. There's a dark, smoky backroom.
Pendulum 4146 18th St at Castro, Castro ☎415/863-4441. Famous as the one place in the Castro that's popular among the black gay community, and there's a groovy, friendly atmosphere here. The women's night on Thursday, "Alley Catz", is funky and great fun – plus there's no cover.
Pilsner Inn 225 Church St at Market, Castro ☎415/621-7058. The best neighborhood gay bar in the Castro, filled with a diverse, slightly older crowd playing pool and darts. There's a large, smoker-friendly patio out back, and a generally welcoming, open vibe.

Powerhouse 1347 Folsom St at Doré Alley, SoMa ☎415/861-1790. One of the prime pick-up joints in the city, this very cruisey old-school leather bar has plenty of convenient dark corners. The dress code (uniform, leather) is strictly enforced except on Thursday, which is underwear night.
Trax 1437 Haight St at Ashbury, Haight-Ashbury ☎415/864-4213, Ⓦwww.traxsf.com. The only gay bar in the Haight is a smoker's paradise, although it's been spiffed up slightly from its grungy heyday. There's a good mix of gays and straights, meaning it's much less cruisey than other bars.
Wild Side West 424 Cortland Ave at Wool, Bernal Heights ☎415/647-3099. Unpretentious, friendly lesbian pick-up joint, with a huge outdoor terrace – there are no heat lamps, though, so stay inside on a cold evening.

Clubs

There's currently a relative void of gay-centric places to dance; aside from the old favorites listed below, check local listings for up-to-date information and new venues for nights like "Pleasuredome" and "Club Universe".

The Café 2367 Market St at Castro, Castro ☎415/861-3846. There's a DJ here seven nights a week, and for a long time, it was one of the few places to dance in the Castro, despite its postage-stamp-sized dancefloor. The music's mainstream Hi-NRG and house, while the crowd is dominated by lesbians and their swishy gay male friends. There's still usually a long line at weekends, inspired no doubt by the free entrance.

Cat Club 1190 Folsom St at 8th, SoMa ☎415/431-3332. This dark, loud club is one of the lesbian hot spots of the city, mixing dancing and live performances. It's livelier the later you arrive. $5–10.
The EndUp 401 6th St at Harrison, SoMa ☎415/357-0827, Ⓦwww.theendup.com. Open all night (though you can only drink until 2am), and attracting hardcore clubbers for after-hours dancing on its cramped dancefloor. If you want a break from

the Beats, there's an outdoor patio with plenty of seating. Club nights vary, but it's especially known for "Fag Fridays" (@www.fagfridays.com). $5.
Pink 2925 16th St at Capp, Mission ☎415/431-8889. This tiny, fun club is easy to miss as you walk by, but it's one of the city's best places to dance with a mixed, social gay-lesbian-straight crowd. Be aware that this is a grottier part of the Mission, so take care on the street. $2–10.

The Stud 399 Folsom St at 9th, SoMa ☎415/252-7883, @www.studsf.com. Legendary gay club that's still as popular as ever, attracting a diverse, energetic, and uninhibited crowd. Check out the fabulously freaky drag-queen cabaret at "Trannyshack" (Tues) – an unmissable legend in local nightlife. "Sugar" on Saturday, meanwhile, is one of the best underground gay dance nights in the city. $5–8.

Sex clubs

There are plenty of underground sex clubs and backrooms in bars across the city: those listed below are clean, secure, and promote safe sex.

Eros 2051 Market St at Church, Castro ☎415/864-3767, @www.erossf.com. This clean, all-male sex club has a sauna and steam room and is open late most nights. Mon–Thurs 4pm–midnight, Fri 4pm–4am, Sat 2pm–4am, Sun 2pm–midnight. $13.
Osento 955 Valencia St at 20th, Mission ☎415/282-6333, @www.osento.com. Women-only spa that's the closest the city comes to a lesbian bathhouse. There's an indoor hot tub, as well as

saunas and massages. Daily noon to midnight. Cover varies.
The Power Exchange 74 Otis St at Gough, Civic Center; ☎415/487-9944, @www.powerexchange.com. Four-floor sexual playland, with themed rooms (leather, forest with tents, dancefloor). The top two floors are gay men only, the rest for men and women of every sexual orientation. Thurs & Sun 9pm–4am, Fri & Sat 9pm–6am. $12.

Shopping

Aside from the retail palaces around **Union Square** (including Macy's, Saks, and practically every major designer label), San Francisco's shopping scene is refreshingly edgy, peppered with one-off boutiques selling locally designed clothes and stylish homeware stores. There's also a brilliantly varied selection of **independent booksellers** (including the world-famous Beat poet favorite, City Lights) as well as terrific **music stores**, some focusing solely on rarities and others jammed with DJs rifling through the latest import 12" records from Europe. It's worth remembering that, unlike many other American cities, stores in San Francisco close relatively early – 6pm Monday to Saturday and 5pm on Sunday isn't unusual – so start a major shopping expedition early in the day.

Shopping streets

Below we've given San Francisco's prime **shopping streets**, alphabetized according to the neighborhood in which each is situated – it's not an exhaustive list, as there are many other great places to browse, but should be useful for any shopaholic planning a day of retail therapy.

The Castro Castro Street, between 17th and 19th sts; Market Street, between Castro and Church. Gay-oriented boutiques, clubwear, and shoes.
Cow Hollow Union Street, between Steiner and Gough. Sweet if rather conservative boutiques (mostly for women), shoe stores, and cute homewares.

Haight-Ashbury Haight Street, between Stanyan and Masonic. Clothing, especially vintage and secondhand.
Hayes Valley Hayes Street, between Franklin and Laguna. Trendy but upscale, with edgy boutiques for men and women, as well as jewelry galleries and other gorgeous, high-end goodies.

Laurel Heights Sacramento Street, between Arguello and Divisadero. Antique magnet of San Francisco, with vintage used clothes for women.
The Marina Chestnut Street, between Broderick and Fillmore. Yuppified strip of health foods, wine shops, and women's clothing boutiques.
The Mission Valencia Street, between 14th and 21st. The best choice for urban hipsters, with lots of used furniture and clothing stores, bookshops, and avant-garde designer gear.
North Beach/Telegraph Hill Grant Avenue between Filbert and Vallejo. Groovy boutiques, homewares, and divey cafés: one of the newest and freshest places to find cool clothes.

Bookstores

Unsurprisingly, for a city with such a rich literary history, San Francisco excels in terrific **specialty bookstores**: from the legendary City Lights in North Beach to the new literary hub in the Mission, home to some of the city's more energized – and politicized – bookstores. As for **secondhand booksellers**, there's a fine selection in the city, but rabid old book buyers should head across the Bay to Oakland and Berkeley for richer pickings. Most bookstores tend to open every day, roughly 10am to 8pm, though City Lights is open daily until midnight.

General

Borders Books and Music 400 Post St at Powell, Union Square ☏415/399-1633. Massive, emporium-style bookstore with some 160,000 books to chose from as well as CDs, videos, and software on four floors. There's also a café, popular with cruising singles, and a stage for performances and readings.
City Lights Bookstore 261 Columbus Ave at Broadway, North Beach ☏415/362-8193. Legendary bookstore, renowned as the first place in the country to stock only paperbacks and ground zero for the Beat era. Oddball and thoroughly browsable, where else could you find books filed under sections like "Stolen Continents" and "Anarchism"? Pity about the belligerent staff.
A Clean, Well Lighted Place for Books Opera Plaza, 601 Van Ness Ave at Golden Gate, Civic Center ☏415/441-6670. The stock here is now more mainstream and less impressively exhaustive than it once was, but it's worth checking out for the regular readings by authors.
Green Apple 506 Clement St at 6th Ave, Richmond ☏415/387-2272. Funky store with deft, eccentric touches like the regular section of "Books that will never be Oprah's picks." Not bargain prices, but a pleasure to rummage through the shelves. There's a smaller, less impressive music annex nearby.

Specialist and secondhand

Abandoned Planet Bookstore 518 Valencia at 16th, Mission ☏415/861-4695. Encouraging its customers to "Break the TV habit!" this eccentric and utterly San Francisco bookstore crams its black shelves with left-wing and anarchist volumes. A rebellious, oddball hold-out against the gentrification elsewhere on Valencia.
Argonaut Bookshop 786 Sutter St at Jones, Theater District ☏415/474-9067. Best bookshop by far for local history: it specializes in volumes on California and the West, from Gold Rush era to the dot-com bomb. The knowledgeable staff are a major plus.
A Different Light 489 Castro St at 18th, Castro ☏415/431-0891, ⊛www.adlbooks.com. This is a well-stocked bookshop featuring gay and lesbian titles, with an especially strong fiction section. Readings and events are held here regularly – check the website for up-to-date information. Daily 10am–10pm.
Dog Eared Books 900 Valencia St at 20th, Mission ☏415/282-1901. Smallish corner bookstore with a snappy selection of budget-priced remainders as well as an eclectic range of secondhand titles, all in terrific condition. There's even one rack of low-priced secondhand CDs.
Get Lost 1825 Market St at Valencia, Hayes Valley/Mission ☏415/437-0529. Tiny triangular travel bookstore, crammed with unusual titles alongside the standard guidebooks. It also stocks a decent assortment of maps and gear for the adventure traveler; the staff is especially helpful.
The Great Overland Bookstore Company 2848 Webster St at Union, Cow Hollow ☏415/351-1538. Cluttered with piles of books, this is a first-rate, old-fashioned store with mint-condition first editions as well as cheap paperbacks. You can browse for hours listening to protest rock on the store's loudspeakers.
Kayo 814 Post St at Leavenworth, Theater District ☏415/749-0554. Glorious vintage paperback

store, crammed with bargain classics including pulpy mysteries, sci-fi, and campy 1950s sleaze fiction. Closed Mon and Tues.

McDonald's Bookshop 48 Turk St at Mason, Tenderloin ☏415/673-2235. Massive and messy, this store's the place to come for a vintage magazine or ten – it's piled high with ramshackle stacks of any title imaginable. There's little or no filing system, so expect to rummage. There's also a selection of used books and music.

Modern Times 888 Valencia St at 20th, Mission ☏415/282-9246. Hefty stock of Latin American literature and progressive political publications as well as small, but well-chosen selection of gay and lesbian literature and radical feminist magazines. Stages regular readings of authors' works.

Smoke Signals 2223 Polk St at Green, Polk Gulch ☏415/292-6025. Enormous newsstand stocking close to any magazine, domestic or foreign, that you can ask for.

Food and drink

Be sure to try such **local specialties** such as Boudin's sourdough bread (see p.613), Gallo salami, and Anchor steam beer – all of which are gourmet treats. If you're looking for everyday essentials, there are supermarkets across the city, including several branches of Safeway – the large, cruisey outpost on Market Street in the Castro is the most convenient for downtown. California alcohol laws are liberal: most stores carrying food sell alcohol too, provided you show ID proving you're at least 21 years of age.

Andronico's Market 1200 Irving St at Funston, Sunset ☏415/753-0403. The California gourmet's answer to Safeway. Pricey but gorgeous produce: microbrews, good wine, craft breads, fancy cheeses, an olive bar, and a pretty good deli. Not the cheapest, but way better quality than your average supermarket.

Castro Village Wine Co. 4121 19th St at Castro, Castro ☏416 /864-4411. Low-key, laid-back neighborhood winery at the heart of the Castro: prices are reasonable and the selection (especially of local wines) is enormous.

D & M Wine & Liquor Co. 2200 Fillmore St at Sacramento, Pacific Heights ☏415/346-1325. Great selection of Californian wines, but located as it is in Pacific Heights, the house specialty is champagne. Despite its swanky locale, though, bargains abound.

Good Life Grocery 488 Cortland Ave at Andover, Bernal Heights ☏415/648-3221. There's a vast selection of organic or locally grown produce at this Bernal Heights gourmet grocery. Branch at 1524 20th St at Missouri, Potrero Hill ☏415/282-9204.

The Jug Shop 1567 Pacific Ave at Polk, Pacific Heights ☏415/885-2922. The Jug Shop is famous for its cheap Californian wines – and stocks an interesting range of New World vintages – but it also has more than 200 varieties of beer that are similarly well-priced.

Molinari's 373 Columbus Ave at Vallejo, North Beach ☏415/421-2337. Bustling veteran North Beach deli, jammed to the rafters with Italian goodies both familiar and exotic. Pick the bread of your choice and order a sandwich to go.

PlumpJack Wines 3201 Fillmore St at Greenwich, Cow Hollow ☏415/346-9870. If you're looking for an obscure Californian vintage for an oenophile relative, this is the place to come – it has an enormous, exhaustive selection of wines from across the state.

The Real Food Company 3060 Fillmore St at Filbert, Cow Hollow ☏415/567-6900. Smallish, artsy grocery store selling potions and vitamins alongside health foods. Excellent gourmet meat counter and whole-wheat pastries: grab a sandwich and sit outside on the terrace at one of the wrought-iron picnic tables.

Yum 1750 Market St at Gough, Hayes Valley ☏415/626-9001. Irresistible and fun hangarlike grocery store, whose slogan is "Have you played with your food today?" Gourmet selections of cookies are especially delicious and the friendly staff will let you sample most items before you buy. Head to the back of the store for its best feature: refrigerators filled with a vast selection of sodas from across the world.

Record stores

There are outposts of all the major **record stores** like Tower and Virgin in San Francisco but it's with its specialty stores that the city really shines: from old-school soul on vinyl to European 12" imports for local DJs, there are some superb **independent** and **collectors'** stores. And in Amoeba Records, Haight-Ashbury can lay claim to one of the best places to browse and buy music anywhere in the country.

Amoeba Records 1855 Haight St at Stanyan, Haight-Ashbury ☎415/831-1200. This big sister to Berkeley's renowned emporium is one of the largest used-music retailers in America. Divided between new and used CDs, this massive warehouse space hums with bargain hunters rifling through an encyclopedic selection of modern music. Don't be put off by its rip-off location in the heart of the Haight: this is a treasure trove for any music fan. Branch at 2455 Telegraph, Berkeley ☎510/549-1125.

Aquarius Records 1055 Valencia St at 21st, Mission ☎415/647-2272. Friendly, ramshackle record store with hip, friendly staff: there's an emphasis on less mainstream music, including experimental, folk, and world. Store devotees can even buy underwear with the Aquarius logo.

BPM 573 Hayes St at Laguna, Hayes Valley ☎415/487-8680. One of the top DJ record stores in the city, with the latest UK imports from top-name British DJs and masses of flyers for upcoming events.

Groove Merchant Records 687 Haight St at Pierce, Lower Haight ☎415/252-5766. Come here for secondhand soul, funk, and jazz: the owner's passionate and knowledgeable, so don't be afraid to ask questions.

Medium Rare 2310 Market St at Noe, Castro ☎415/255-7273. Tiny store is crammed with CDs, ranging from camp classics like Peggy Lee and other Fifties cocktail lounge singers to throbbing hi-NRG stars like Donna Summer.

Mikado 1737 Post St (Japan Center), Japantown ☎415/922-9450. Enormous Japanese record store sprawled across three units of the Japan Center. The staff will let you watch DVDs before you buy on the instore TV set and headphones.

Open Mind Music 342 Divisadero at Oak St, Lower Haight ☎415/621-2244. Slightly more peaceful alternative to the hordes of bargain hunters who throng to Amoeba nearby: it offers mainly vinyl (both new and used, rock and jazz) but the stock's well-chosen and not picked over.

Record Collector 3170 21st St at Mission, Mission ☎415/970-8400. Don't come looking for CDs here: this is strictly for vinyl snobs, who will find a snooty, unhelpful staff, a rundown store, and a stock of high-priced, rare gems.

Recycled Records 1377 Haight St at Masonic, Haight-Ashbury ☎415/626-4075. Good all-round store, with a decent selection of music publications, American and imported.

Taiyodo Record Shop 1737 Post St (Japan Center), Japantown ☎415/885-2818. One of several record stores in the mall selling the latest releases by Japanese singers, whether bubblegum pop or Asian alt rock. Also great for hard-to-find anime DVDs.

Virgin Megastore 2 Stockton at Market St, Union Square ☎415/397-4525. Three floors packed with music in a wide variety of styles. The third floor has a good stock of current, popular books, videos, and a café with windows overlooking Market Street.

Specialty stores and local labels

Flight 001 525 Hayes St at Octavia, Hayes Valley ☎415/487-1001. This sleek, futuristic travel store sells books, funky accessories (including chunky, dayglo luggage tags and all-in-one shaving kits), and dapper carry-on bags. The place to stock up on sundries if you only travel first-class – or want to act like it.

Good Vibrations 603 Valencia St at 17th, Mission ☎415/522-5460, ⊛www.goodvibes.com. Gloriously sexy store, run by a co-op of men and women, that's designed to destigmatize sex shops and make browsing fun and comfortable. It's packed with every imaginable sex toy, plus racks of erotica and candy-store-style jars of condoms. The co-op recently branched out into producing its own erotic videos in addition to the books it already publishes

under the Down There Press imprint; all that, plus an on-site vibrator museum. Branch at 1620 Polk St at Sacramento, Polk Gulch ☎415/345-0400.

Levi's 300 Post St at Stockton, Union Square ☎415/501-0100. Four levels of jeans, tops, and jackets set against a thumping backdrop of club music. This flagship offers the Levi's "Original Spin" service, where customers can order customized denim, although many of the funkier offerings here (like a bath in which you could sit until your jeans had shrunk to fit) have been removed. Since this stocks the entire Levi's line, it carries edgier pieces in the Red line as well as retro-inspired Western wear.

Oui, Three Queens 225 Gough St at Oak, Hayes Valley ☎415/621-6877. This tiny, cartoonish store produces custom-blended cosmetics, including lipsticks, at reasonable prices. The larger-than-life staff will make the process as well as the product utterly memorable, and the baroque, bejeweled space is glorious.

Paolo Iantorno 524 Hayes St at Laguna, Hayes Valley ☎415/552-4580. Don't tell anyone but your best friends about this gem: designer Iantorno produces a limited edition (20–25 pairs) of his own men's and women's shoe designs in Italy, then sells them from his two stores here. Prices hover around $200, and every style is edgy but wearable. Branch at 1971 Sutter St, Fillmore ☎415/885-5701.

Retro Fit Vintage 910 Valencia St at 20th, Mission ☎415/550-1530. Poppy, kitschy selection of smart vintage clothes: don't expect bargains, but

well worth it for a spot-on shirt or just-right jacket. Check out the DIY vintage tees: pick a style then flick through an enormous binder filled with retro transfers to customize the shirt, starting at $18.

Wasteland 1660 Haight St at Belvedere, Haight-Ashbury ☎415/863-3150. Smart, high-end vintage selection, sorted by style and color: you'll pay for the ease of browsing, but it's one of the best places to find top condition, fashionable vintage. Notable, too, for being housed in the only building that still stands from the Haight's first incarnation as an amusement park.

Worn Out West 582 Castro St at 19th, Castro ☎1-800/556-0311. Gay secondhand fetish gear. Feel free to browse: there's plenty of Western wear, as well as leather-studded collars, cuffs, and even bow ties, plus a smattering of sex toys.

Listings

American Express 455 Market St at 1st, Financial District (Mon–Fri 9am–5.30pm, Sat 10am–2pm; ☎415/536-2600). Also at 311 9th Ave at Clement, Richmond (Mon–Fri 9am–5pm; ☎415/221-6760).

Babysitting Bay Area Child Care (9 months and under $12/hr, 4hr minimum plus $15 agency fee; over 9 months $11/hr, 4hr minimum plus $15 agency fee, additional siblings $1 each per hr). Booking line ☎415/309-5662, staffed 24hr.

Car rental All the major firms have branches in the airport. Here we've listed their offices in town: Alamo, 687 Folsom St at 3rd, SoMa ☎415/882-9440; Avis, 675 Post St at Jones, Theater District ☎415/885-5011; Dollar, 364 O'Farrell St at Taylor, Theater District ☎415/771-5300; Enterprise, 1133 Van Ness Ave at Post, Tenderloin ☎415/441-3369; Hertz, 433 Mason St at Post, Union Square ☎415/771-2200; Reliable, 349 Mason St at Geary, Union Square ☎415/928-4414.

Children San Francisco is very much a place for adults – more so than, say, LA, where Disneyland and Universal Studios are major attractions. However, if you do have children with you, good options include the educational Exploratorium in the Marina as well as the Steinhart Aquarium in Golden Gate Park. There's also a merry-go-round and children's play area in Golden Gate Park – a pleasant place to spend a sunny afternoon.

Consulates UK, 1 Sansome St at Market, Financial District (Mon–Fri 8.30am–5pm; ☎415/617-1300); Ireland, 100 Pine St at Front, Financial District (Mon–Fri 10am–noon, 2–3.30pm; ☎415/392-4214); Australia, 625 Market St at Montgomery,

Financial District (Mon–Fri 8.45am–1pm & 2–4.45pm; ☎415/536-1970); New Zealand, One Maritime Plaza, Suite 400, Embarcadero (appointment only; ☎415/399-1255); Germany, 1960 Jackson St at Gough, Pacific Heights (Mon–Fri 9am–noon; ☎415/353-0300).

Dental treatment For a free referral to the nearest dentist, call the national Dental Society Referral Service (☎415/421-1435 or 1-800/511-8663).

Disabled visitors Steep hills aside, the Bay Area is generally considered to be one of the most barrier-free cities around, and physically challenged travelers are well catered for. Most public buildings have been modified for disabled access, all BART stations are wheelchair-accessible, and most buses have lowering platforms for wheelchairs – and, usually, understanding drivers. For more information, check ⓦwww.accessnca.com.

Drugstores Walgreens 24hr pharmacies 498 Castro St at 18th, Castro ☎415/861-6276, or 3201 Divisadero St at Lombard, Marina ☎415/931-6415.

Ferries Golden Gate Ferry, commute-hours to Sausalito and Larkspur in Marin County, leaves from the Ferry Building, east end of Market Street (☎415/923-2000, ⓦwww.goldengate.org); Blue and Gold Fleet bay ferries to Sausalito, Tiburon, Vallejo, and the Alcatraz Island tour, from piers 41 and 39, Fisherman's Wharf (info ☎415/773-1188, tickets ☎415/705-5555, ⓦwww.blueandgoldfleet.com).

Hospitals The San Francisco General Hospital, 1001 Potrero Ave at 23rd, Potrero Hill (☎415/206-8000 or 206-8111 emergency), has a 2hr emergency walk-in service. Castro-Mission

Health Center, 3850 17th St at Prosper, Mission (☎415/487-7500), offers a drop-in medical service with charges on a sliding scale depending on income, plus free contraception and pregnancy testing. California Pacific (formerly Davies) Medical Center, Castro and Duboce sts, Lower Haight (☎415/565-6060), has 24hr emergency care and a doctors' referral service. Haight-Ashbury Free Clinic, 558 Clayton St at Haight, provides a general health-care service with special services for women and detoxification, by appointment only (☎415/487-5632, phones answered Mon–Wed 9am–9pm, Thurs 1–9pm, Fri 1–5pm except from 12.30–1pm & 5.30–6pm).

Internet There's usually access at the hostels listed in the "Accommodation" section, but there's often a wait to get on a machine; likewise, the Public Library has 15min free access, often with a long wait; there are six terminals on the main floor – sign up for first come, first served. Wi-Fi's becoming a citywide standard, here, though – most travelers with laptops should be able to find a café with free or low cost access in any neighborhood. If you want a cup of coffee while surfing, there's free access with a purchase at *701 Café*, Yerba Buena Center for the Arts, 701 Mission St at 3rd, SoMa (☎415/243-0930). Otherwise, the following places all offer $3/per 20min and $7 per hr rates: *Blue Danube*, 306 Clement St at 5th, Richmond ☎415/221-9041, *Pendragon Bakery*, 400 Hayes St at Gough, Hayes Valley ☎415/552-7017, and *Yakkety Yak*, 679 Sutter St at Mason, Theater District ☎415/351-2090.

Legal advice Lawyer Referral Service, 465 California St at Montgomery, Financial District (Mon–Fri 8.30am–5.30pm; ☎415/989-1616).

Library Civic Center, 100 Larkin St at Grove ☎415/557-4400, ⊛www.sfpl.lib.ca.us. Mon & Sat 10am–6pm, Tues–Thurs 9am–8pm, Fri noon–6pm, Sun noon–5pm.

Passport and visa office US Dept of Immigration, 630 Sansome St at Washington, Jackson Square ☎1-800/375-5283.

Post office You can collect general delivery mail (bring your ID) from the main post office, 101 Hyde St at Fulton, Civic Center (Mon–Fri 8.30am–5.30pm, Sat 10am–2pm; ☎1-800/275-8777), but letters will only be held for ten days before being returned to sender, so make sure there's a return address on the envelope. San Francisco's two main post offices, with telephone and general delivery facilities, are at Sutter Street Station, 150 Sutter St at Montgomery, Financial District (Mon–Fri 8.30am–5pm), and Rincon Finance Station, 180 Steuart St at Mission, SoMa (Mon–Fri 7am–6pm, Sat 9am–2pm).

Rape Crisis Center and Hotline 24hr switchboard ☎415/647-7273, ⊛www.sfwar.org.

Religious services Grace Cathedral on Nob Hill at 1051 Taylor St has an Episcopalian (Anglican) congregation (☎415/749-6300, ⊛www.gracecathedral.org). Catholics can worship at St Mary's Cathedral, 600 California St at Grant (☎415/288-3800, ⊛www.oldsaintmarys.org). The grandest synagogue is Congregation Emanu-El, 2 Lake St at Arguello Blvd, at the eastern edge of the Richmond district by the Presidio (☎415/751-2535).

Sports Advance tickets for all Bay Area sports events are available through Tickets.com (☎510/762-2277, ⊛www.tickets.com) as well as from the teams themselves. **Baseball** The San Francisco Giants play in the new SBC Ballpark where the easy homeruns over the rightfield fence splash into the Bay (☎415/972-2000, ⊛www.sfgiants.com). The Giants' East Bay counterparts, the Oakland A's, play at the usually sunny Oakland Coliseum (☎510/638-0500, ⊛www.oaklandathletics.com). Manageable ticket prices ranging from $10 standing-room-only seats to $70 for a field-side box – combined with the policy of keeping 500 bleacher seats for sale 4hr before each home game (call for schedule) – make baseball one of the best ways of catching a major sports event in town. **Basketball** The Golden State Warriors play at the Oakland Arena (☎510/986-2222, ⊛www.nba.com/warriors/). **Football** The San Francisco 49ers appear at blustery 3COM Park on Candlestick Point, south of town (☎415/656-4900, ⊛www.sf49ers.com). Tickets start at $60 or so and are almost impossible to come by. Meanwhile, the boisterous Oakland fans don silver and black to root on their Raiders, who knock helmets at the Coliseum. Tickets are also around $60, but are almost always available – call Tickets.com or check ⊛www.raiders.com. **Ice hockey** The San Jose Sharks (☎1-800/888-2736, ⊛www.sjsharks.com), based at their own arena in the South Bay; tickets start at $19. **Fitness** If you're feeling active and want to work out instead of watch, check out Boot Camp SF, an outdoor workout session held four times a week in Golden Gate Park near the Kezar Stadium in the early morning: exhilarating, exhausting, and utterly unique ($20 per session; ☎415/921-8537, ⊛www.bootcampsf.com).

Suicide Crisis Hotline 24hr ☎415/781-0500.

Tax Sales tax, added to virtually everything you buy in a store save for food, is 8.5 percent; hotel tax will add 14 percent to your bill.

Telegrams Western Union has numerous locations around the Bay Area; call ☎1-800/325-6000 or check ⊛www.westernunion.com to find the nearest.

The Bay Area

Of the near seven million people who make their home in the San Francisco **Bay Area**, barely more than one in ten lives in the actual city of San Francisco. Everyone else is spread around one of the many less-renowned cities and suburbs that ring the Bay, either down the Peninsula or across one of the two impressively engineered bridges that span the chilly waters of the world's most exquisite natural harbor. There's no doubt about the supporting role these places play in relation to San Francisco – always "the city" – but each has a distinctive character and contributes to the range of people and landscapes that makes the Bay Area one of the most desirable places in the US to live or to visit.

Across the steel Bay Bridge, eight miles from downtown San Francisco, the **East Bay** is home to the lively, left-leaning cities of **Oakland** and **Berkeley**, which together have some of the best bookstores and restaurants, and a good proportion of the live music venues, in the greater Bay Area. The weather's generally much sunnier and warmer here too, and it's easy to reach by way of the BART trains that race under the Bay. The remainder of the East Bay is contained in Contra Costa County, which includes the short-lived early state capital of California, **Benicia**, as well as the former homes of writers John Muir and Eugene O'Neill.

South of the city, the **Peninsula** holds some of San Francisco's oldest and most upscale suburbs, spreading down through the computer-rich **Silicon Valley** and into **San Jose** – still California's fastest-growing city, and now a larger one in both square mileage and population than San Francisco – though apart from a few excellent museums, there's not a lot to see. To the west, however, the **beaches** are excellent – sandy, clean, and uncrowded – and there's a couple of youth hostels in old lighthouses perched on the edge of the Pacific.

For some of the most beautiful land- and seascapes in California, cross the Golden Gate Bridge or ride a ferry across the Bay to **Marin County**, a mountainous peninsula that's half wealthy suburbia and half unspoiled hiking country, with **redwood forests** rising sheer out of the thundering Pacific Ocean. A range of 2500-foot peaks divides the county down the middle, separating the yacht clubs and plush bay-view houses of **Sausalito** and **Tiburon** from the nearly untouched wilderness that runs along the Pacific Coast, through Muir Woods and the **Point Reyes National Seashore**. North of Marin County, at the top of the Bay, and still within an hour's drive of San Francisco, the Wine Country regions of the Sonoma and Napa valleys make an excellent day-trip; they're detailed in "Northern California," beginning on p.765.

The East Bay

The largest and most-traveled bridge in California, the **Bay Bridge** connects downtown San Francisco to the **East Bay**, part graceful suspension bridge and part heavy-duty steel truss. Built in 1933 as an economic booster during the Depression, the bridge is made from enough steel cable to wrap around the earth three times. Completed just seven months before the more famous (and better-loved) Golden Gate, it works a lot harder for a lot less respect: a hundred million vehicles cross the bridge each year, though you'd have to search hard to find a postcard of it. Local scribe Herb Caen dubbed it "the car-strangled spanner," a reflection of its often-clogged lanes. Indeed, the bridge's only claim to fame – apart from the much-broadcast videotape of its partial collapse during the 1989 earthquake – is that **Treasure Island**, where the two halves of the bridge meet, hosted the 1939 World's Fair. During World War II, the island became a Navy base but since the end of the Cold War it has been undergoing a gradual transfer to the city of San Francisco. As the island offers great views of San Francisco and the Golden Gate, the development authority has various plans to make it a tourist destination, including the reopening of its museum, closed since 1997.

The Bay Bridge eventually empties into **Oakland**, a hard-working, blue-collar city that is at the heart of the East Bay. The city traditionally earned its livelihood from shipping and transportation services, as evidenced by the enormous cranes in the massive Port of Oakland, but is in the beginning stages of a renaissance as it lobbies to attract businesses and workers from the information technology industry. Oakland spreads north along wooded foothills to **Berkeley**, an image-conscious university town that looks out across to the Golden Gate and collects a mixed bag of earnest young students, much-pierced dropouts, ageing 1960s radicals, and Nobel Prize–winning nuclear physicists in its cafés and bookstores.

Berkeley and Oakland blend together so much as to be virtually the same city, and the hills above them are topped by a twenty-mile string of **regional parks**, providing much-needed fresh air and quick relief from the concrete grids below. The rest of the East Bay is filled out by Contra Costa County, a huge area that contains some intriguing, historically important waterfront towns – well worth a stop if you're passing through on the way to the Wine Country region of the Napa and Sonoma valleys – as well as some of the Bay Area's most inward-looking suburban sprawl. Curving around the **North Bay** from the oil-refinery landscape of Richmond, and facing each other across the narrow **Carquinez Strait**, both **Benicia** and **Port Costa** were vitally important during California's first twenty years of existence after the 1849 Gold Rush; they're now strikingly sited but little-visited ghost towns. In contrast, standing out from the soulless dormitory communities that fill up the often baking-hot **inland valleys**, are the preserved homes of an unlikely pair of influential writers: the naturalist John Muir, who, when not out hiking around Yosemite and the High Sierra, lived most of his life near **Martinez**, and playwright Eugene O'Neill, who wrote many of his angst-ridden works at the foot of **Mount Diablo**, the Bay Area's most impressive peak.

Arrival

You're most likely to be staying in San Francisco when you visit the East Bay, though it is as convenient and sometimes better value to fly direct to **Oakland International Airport** (☏510/563-2984, automated flight info ☏1-800/992-7433, @www.oaklandairport.com), particularly if you're coming from elsewhere in the US. Most major domestic airlines serve the facility, which is less crowded and more desirable than its San Francisco counterpart. It's an easy trip from the airport into town. The **AirBART** shuttle van (every 15min; $2; ☏510/577-4294) runs to the Coliseum BART station, from where you can hop on **BART** to Berkeley, Oakland, or San Francisco. There are numerous door-to-door **shuttle buses** that run from the airport to East Bay stops and into the city, such as California Airporter Inc. (☏1-800/225-6316);

the fare to Oakland is $16 and expect to pay around $30 into San Francisco. **Taxis** run about $20 into Oakland and $40 into San Francisco.

The **Greyhound** station is in a dodgy part of northern Oakland alongside the I-980 freeway on San Pablo Avenue at 21st Street. **Amtrak** terminates at Second Street near Jack London Square, where a free shuttle bus heads across the Bay Bridge to the Transbay Terminal. A better option for heading into San Francisco is to get off at Richmond and change onto the nearby BART trains. The most enjoyable way to arrive in the East Bay is aboard an Alameda–Oakland **ferry** ($5.50 each way; ☎510/522-3300, ⓦwww.eastbayferry.com), which sails every hour from San Francisco's Ferry Building and Pier 39 to Oakland's Jack London Square. The fleet also runs a service to Angel Island via Pier 41, departing from Oakland (Sat & Sun mid-May–late Oct 9am, returning at 3.10pm; $12.50 round-trip, including park admission).

Information

The **Oakland CVB**, located next to the enormous *Marriot Hotel* at 463 11th St (Mon–Fri 8.30am–5pm; ☎510/839-9000, ⓦwww.oaklandcvb.com), is the best source of maps, brochures, and information on lodging and activities in the metropolitan area. In Berkeley, check in at the **Berkeley CVB**, 2015 Center St (Mon–Fri 9am–noon & 2–5pm; ☎510/549-7040, ⓦwww.visitberkeley.com). The **University of California's Visitor Services**, 101 University Hall (Mon–Fri 8.30am–4.30pm; ☎510/642-5215, ⓦwww.berkeley.edu), at the corner of Oxford and University, has plenty of info on the Berkeley campus, hands out free self-guided tour brochures, and conducts ninety-minute tours (see p.658). For information on hiking or horseriding in the many parks that top the Oakland and Berkeley hills, contact the **East Bay Regional Parks District**, 2950 Peralta Oaks Court, Oakland (☎510/562-7275, ⓦwww.ebparks.org). The widely available *East Bay Express* (issued every Wed; free) has the most comprehensive listings of what's on in the vibrant East Bay music and arts scene. The daily *Oakland Tribune* (50¢) is also worth a look for its coverage of local politics and sporting events.

Getting around

The East Bay is linked to San Francisco via the underground BART Transbay **subway** (Mon–Sat 6am–midnight, Sun 9am–midnight). Four lines (one of which starts at Millbrae and stops at San Francisco airport) run from Daly City through San Francisco and on to downtown Oakland, before diverging to service East Oakland out to Fremont, north to Berkeley and Richmond, and northeast into Contra Costa County as far as Concord and Pittsburg/Bay Point. A fifth line operates its entire length in the East Bay between Richmond and Fremont. Fares range from $1.25 to $7.45, and the cost of each ride is deducted from the total value of the ticket, purchased from machines on the station concourse. If you're relying on BART to get around a lot, buy a **high-value ticket** ($10 or $20) to avoid having to stand in line to buy a new ticket quite so often. For $4.40, you can tour the entire system and get off at any of the 43 station platforms for up to three hours, so long as you enter and exit at the same station; the same charge is made for lost tickets. To phone BART from San Francisco, dial ☎415/989-BART; from the East Bay ☎510/465-BART, or check ⓦwww.bart.gov. Bikes are allowed on most trains.

From East Bay BART stations, pick up a **free transfer**, saving you 25¢ on the $1.50 fares of the revamped AC Transit (☎510/817-1717 ext 1111,

@www.actransit.org), which provides a good **bus service** around the entire East Bay, especially Oakland and Berkeley. AC Transit also runs buses on a number of routes to Oakland and Berkeley from the Transbay Terminal in San Francisco. These operate all night and are the only way of getting across the Bay by public transit once BART has shut down. You can pick up excellent free maps of both BART and the bus system from any station. A smaller-scale bus company that can also prove useful, the Contra Costa County Connection (☎925/676-7500) runs buses to most of the inland areas, including the John Muir and Eugene O'Neill historic houses.

One of the best ways to get around the East Bay is by **bike**. A fine cycle route follows Skyline and Grizzly Peak boulevards along the wooded crest of the hills between Berkeley and Lake Chabot. Within Berkeley itself, the Ohlone Greenway makes for a pleasant cycling or walking route up through North Berkeley to El Cerrito. Not many places rent bikes in the East Bay but one exception is Solano Avenue Cyclery, 1554 Solano Ave, Berkeley (☎510/524-1094, @www.solanoavenuecyclery.com), whose rates are $35 for 24 hours or $150 per week. For those interested in **walking tours**, the City of Oakland sponsors free "discovery tours" (☎510/238-3234) of various neighborhoods; a popular excursion is the Oakland Historical Landmark Tour (Sun 1–3.30pm; free), beginning in front of the Oakland Museum at 10th and Fallon, and covering areas like Chinatown, Lake Merritt, Preservation Park, and Jack London Square.

If you're **driving**, allow yourself plenty of time to get there: the East Bay has some of California's worst traffic, with the Bay Bridge and I-80 in particular jam-packed sixteen hours a day. Car-pool lanes are becoming increasingly popular, so having three or more people in your vehicle can speed things up, slightly at least.

Accommodation

The East Bay's **motels** and **hotels** are barely any better value for money than their San Francisco equivalents. However, they give visitors the chance to stay just outside of the city's hubbub whilst affording easy access to it. **Bed and breakfasts** often represent the best value, tucked away as they are in Berkeley's leafy hills. Check with the Berkeley & Oakland Bed and Breakfast Network (☎510/547-6380, @www.bbonline.com/ca/berkeley-oakland) for a complete list, or get their brochure from the Berkeley CVB or UC's Visitor Services office. A few **campgrounds** and **dorm beds** are available in summertime.

Berkeley

Bancroft Hotel 2680 Bancroft Way, Berkeley ☎510/549-1000 or 1-800/549-1002, @www.bancrofthotel.com. Small hotel with 22 queen-bedded rooms, a good location right by the campus, and fine service. Breakfast included. ❺

Berkeley City Club 2315 Durant Ave, Berkeley ☎510/848-7800, @www.berkeleycityclub.com. Two blocks from the UC campus, this B&B was designed by Hearst Castle architect Julia Morgan, with an indoor swimming pool and exercise room. Each of the spacious rooms has a private bath. ❻

Berkeley YMCA 2001 Allston Way at Milvia St, a block from Berkeley BART ☎510/848-6400, @www.baymca.com. Berkeley's best

bargain accommodation; rates, starting at $39 for a single, include use of gym and pool. No dorms. ❷

Campus Motel 1619 University Ave, Berkeley ☎510/841-3844. No-frills motel but clean, and the cheapest one within easy walking distance of downtown. ❸

The Claremont Resort & Spa 41 Tunnel Rd, Berkeley ☎510/843-3000 or 1-800/551-7266, @www.claremontresort.com. Built in 1915, *The Claremont* is the lap of luxury among Berkeley hotels. Lavish rooms come with data ports for your laptop, hairdryers, cable TV, and big windows, some overlooking the large outdoor pool; spa sessions begin around $100 per hour for facials or massages. ❾

Elmwood House 2609 College Ave, Berkeley
℡510/540-5123, ⓦwww.elmwoodhouse.com.
Attractive 1902 house with small and sunny B&B
rooms, not far from UC Berkeley. ❹

French 1538 Shattuck Ave, North Berkeley
℡510/548-9930. Small and comfortable hotel
with 18 standard rooms in the heart of Berkeley's
Gourmet Ghetto. ❺

Golden Bear Inn 1620 San Pablo Ave, West
Berkeley ℡510/525-6770 or 1-800/525-6770,
ⓦwww.goldenbearinn.com. The most pleasant of
the many motels in the "flatlands" of West Berkeley, with smart furnishings, though somewhat out
of the way. ❹

Hotel Durant 2600 Durant Ave, Berkeley
℡510/845-8981 or 1-800/238-7268, ⓦwww
.hoteldurant.com. Upscale hotel at the heart of UC
Berkeley, featuring large, airy rooms with refrigerators. Best location to stay if you can afford it. ❼

Hotel Shattuck Plaza 2086 Allston Way, Berkeley
℡510/845-730, ⓦwww.hotelshattuckplaza.com.
A vast number of comfortable good-value rooms in
a central and well-restored older hotel, now under
new management. ❹

Rose Garden Inn 2740 Telegraph Ave, Berkeley
℡510/549-2145 or 1-800/992-9005, ⓦwww
.rosegardeninn.com. Pleasant, stylishly decorated
rooms with fireplaces in a pretty mock-Tudor
mansion half a mile south of UC Berkeley. ❺

Summer Visitor Housing 2601 Warring St,
Berkeley ℡510/642-4444, ⓦwww.housing
.berkeley.edu/conference/summervis. Agency that
can arrange summer-only rooms – singles cost
$50 – in university accommodation such as Stern
Hall. ❸

Oakland

Dean's Bed and Breakfast 480 Pedestrian Way,
Rockridge ℡510/652-5024. A hidden gem with
heated swimming pool (May–Oct) and Japanese
garden, near a trendy shopping strip and the
Rockridge BART stop. Currently only one fully-
operating room with kitchenette, cable TV, and
private phone line with answering machine. Highly
recommended. ❹

Howard Johnson Express Inn 423 7th St,
Oakland ℡510/451-6316 or 1-800/754-1115,
ⓦwww.oaklandhj.com. Spruced up, comfortable
ex-*Travelodge* providing one of the best deals
downtown. ❸

Jack London Inn 444 Embarcadero West, Oakland ℡510/444-2032 or 1-800/549-8780. Nicely
revamped hotel/motel with a 1950s feel; located
next to Jack London Square. ❹

Maya Motel 4715 Telegraph Ave, North Oakland
℡510/654-5850. Basic motel but tidy enough
and better than most of those on nearby
Macarthur Boulevard to the south. The trendy
Rockridge shops and eateries are within walking
distance. ❷

Waterfront Plaza Hotel Jack London Square,
Oakland ℡510/836-3800 or 1-800/729-3638,
ⓦwww.waterfrontplaza.com. Plush, modern
hotel located on the best stretch of the
Oakland waterfront, right among the square's
amenities. ❼

Further out

East Brother Light Station 117 Park Place, Point
Richmond ℡510/233-2385, ⓦwww.ebls.org. A
handful of rooms in a converted lighthouse, on
an island in the straits linking the San Francisco
and San Pablo bays. Not a handy base for seeing
the sights, this is a retreat and adventure for an
evening. Prices include highly rated gourmet dinners with wine as well as breakfast. Thursday to
Sunday nights only. ❽

Holiday Inn Bay Bridge 1800 Powell St, Emeryville ℡510/658-9300 or 1-800/HOLIDAY, ⓦwww
.holidayinn.com. Not outrageously pricey considering the great views of the bay to be had from the
upper floors. Free parking. ❻

Hotel Mac 10 Cottage Ave, Point Richmond
℡510/235-0010, ⓦwww.hotelmachotel.bigstep
.com. Built in 1907 and refurbished a few years
ago, *Hotel Mac* boasts luxurious rooms at reasonable prices. This was supposedly John Rockefeller's
favorite place to stay when visiting his Standard
Oil enterprise. ❺

Union Hotel and Gardens 401 First St, Benicia
℡707/746-0100, ⓦwww.unionhotelbenicia.com.
Historical hotel and once a bordello, now converted
into a classy bed and breakfast with twelve rooms,
all featuring a Jacuzzi. ❺

Campgrounds

Chabot Family Campground off I-580 in East
Oakland ℡510/562-2267, ⓦwww.ebparks.org.
Tent-only places, with hot showers and lots
of good hiking nearby; reservations wise in
summer; $16 for one vehicle and up to ten
people.

Mount Diablo State Park 20 miles east of
Oakland off I-680 in Contra Costa County
℡510/837-2525. RV and tent places in three
separate sites; book through ReserveAmerica
℡1-800/444-7275, ⓦwww.reserveamerica.com
in summer; $19.

Oakland

What was the use of me having come from Oakland, it was not natural for me to have come from there yes write about it if I like or anything if I like but not there, there is no there there.

Gertrude Stein, *Everybody's Autobiography*

As the workhorse of the Bay Area, **OAKLAND** is commonly known as a place of little or no play. One of the busiest ports on the West Coast and the western terminal of the rail network, it's also the spawning ground of some of America's most unabashedly revolutionary **political movements**, such as the militant **Black Panthers**, who gave a radical voice to the African-American population, and the **Symbionese Liberation Army**, who demanded a ransom for kidnapped heiress Patty Hearst in the form of free food distribution to the poor.

The city is also the birthplace of literary legends **Gertrude Stein** and **Jack London**, who grew up here at approximately the same time, though in entirely different circumstances – Stein was a stockbroker's daughter, while London was an orphaned delinquent. Most of the waterfront where London used to steal oysters and lobsters is now named in his memory, while Stein, who was actually born in East Oakland, is all but ignored here, not surprising given her unflattering quote above. Still, until very recently, locals found it hard to come up with anything better. Oakland businesses have a long history of deserting the place once the going gets good, and even the city's iconic football team, the Raiders, defected to Los Angeles for thirteen years before returning in 1995.

But residents who've stuck by the city through its duller and darker days are pleased overall with the efforts of the mayor, former California governor and one-time presidential candidate **Jerry "Moonbeam" Brown**, to revitalize (some residents say gentrify) the town and slash its infamous crime rate. Advertising his city's lower rents and always sunny climate – consistently rated the best in the US – Brown is well on his way to meeting his promise of bringing 10,000 new residents to Oakland before his second term expires in 2006. Already, rents in the increasingly popular **Rockridge** and **Lake Merrit** districts are approaching San Francisco prices. The city has also attracted a significant number of lesbians, who've left San Francisco's Castro and Mission, as well as a great number of artists pushed from their SoMa lofts by sky-high rents into the warehouses of West Oakland. Nor is the city devoid of cultural attractions, the outstanding one being the spacious and comprehensive Oakland Museum.

Perhaps, though, "Oaktown" (the local name for Oakland) is a better place in which to live than to visit. Locals call San Francisco "the city" and will point visitors to its myriad attractions before recommending those in the East Bay. But given it's a short hop on BART or quick drive across the Bay Bridge, a day-trip to Oakland is worth it to get a feel for the East Bay's diversity and changing times.

Downtown Oakland

Coming by BART from San Francisco, get off at the Twelfth Street–Civic Center station and you're at the new, open-air shopping and office space of **City Center** in the heart of **Downtown Oakland**. Oddly, the area can seem eerily deserted outside of rush hours. Downtown's compact district of spruced-up Victorian storefronts overlooked by modern hotels and office buildings has undergone an ambitious program of restoration and redevelopment for well over a decade. Fraught with allegations of illegal dealings and incompetent planning, the program has not been an unqualified success. One of the more controversial projects was the moat-like I-980 freeway, the main route through Oakland since the collapse of the Cypress Freeway in the 1989 earthquake. Entire blocks were cleared of houses. Yet some efforts were made to maintain the city's architectural heritage, most noticeably in the collection of character-ful properties of **Preservation Park** at 12th Street and Martin Luther King Jr Way. The late nineteenth-century commercial center along Ninth Street west of Broadway, now tagged **Old Oakland**, also underwent a major restoration some years ago, and nearly all premises are now occupied by tenants such as architect and design firms, much like San Francisco's Jackson Square. By way of contrast with the subdued Old Oakland area, stroll a block east of Broadway, between Seventh and Ninth, to Oakland's **Chinatown**, whose bakeries and restaurants are neither as lively nor picturesque as those of its more famous cousin across the Bay.

The city experienced its greatest period of growth in the early twentieth century, and many of the grand buildings of this era survive a few blocks north along Broadway, centered on the gigantic grass triangle of **Frank Ogawa Plaza** and the awkwardly imposing 1914 **City Hall** on 14th Street. This area hosts the annual **Art and Soul Festival** over Labor Day weekend, featuring live music and art displays ($5). Two blocks away at 13th and Franklin stands Oakland's most unmistakable landmark, the chateauesque lantern of the **Trib-une Tower**, the 1920s-era former home of the *Oakland Tribune* newspaper. A few blocks west at 659 14th St, the **African American Museum & Library** (Tues–Sat noon–5.30pm; free; ☎510/238-6716) is housed in an elegant Neo-classical building whose upper floor has a permanent display on the history of African Americans in California from 1775 to 1900, and revolving art and photo exhibitions. Several blocks further on, the **Ebony Museum of Art**, 1034 14th St (Tues–Sat 11am–6pm, Sun noon–6pm; free; ☎510/763-0141), is another showcase for black artists and promotes greater appreciation of the African American heritage.

Further north, around the 19th Street BART station, are some of the Bay Area's finest early twentieth-century buildings, highlighted by the outstand-ing Art Deco interior of the 1931 **Paramount Theater** at 2025 Broadway (tours 10am first and third Sat of the month; $1; ☎510/465-6400, ⊛www .paramounttheatre.com). The West Coast's answer to New York's Radio City Music Hall, the Paramount shows Hollywood classics, and hosts occasional concerts by the likes of Tom Waits and Neil Young, and performances by stand-up comedians, ballet troupes, and the Oakland Symphony. Nearby buildings are equally flamboyant, ranging from the wafer-thin Gothic "flati-ron" office tower of the **Cathedral Building** at Broadway and Telegraph, to the Hindu-temple-like facade of the magnificent 3500-seat **Fox Oak-land** (now closed) on Telegraph at 19th – the largest moviehouse west of Chicago at the time it was built in 1928 – and, across the street, the 1931 **Floral Depot**, a group of small modern storefronts faced in black-and-blue terracotta tiles with shiny silver highlights. If you want to get your skates on, lace up at the nearby **Oakland Ice Center**, 519 18th St (Mon–Fri noon–5pm, Sat & Sun 1–5pm, also Tues 7–8.30pm, Thurs 7–9pm, Fri & Sat 7–10pm; $7.50 plus $2.50 skate rental; ☎510/268-9000, ⊛www.oaklandice .com). The facility is the finest in the Bay Area, with a number of world-class instructors providing lessons here.

West of Broadway, the area around the Greyhound bus station on San Pablo Avenue is fairly seedy. San Pablo used to be the main route in and out of

CAFÉS, RESTAURANTS, & BARS

Adam's Burger	22
The Alley	23
Barney's	7 & 18
Bay Wolf Café	19
Ben and Nick's	10
Café Rustica	12
Cato's Ale House	17
Citron	11
Coffee Mill	21
Dreyer's	6
Fenton's	16
Garibaldi's on College	13
Genova Delicatessen	15
Grand Oaks Grill	28
Heinhold's First and	
Last Chance Saloon	34
Holy Land Kosher Food	24
Jade Villa	29
La Furia Chalaca (Chalaca)	32
Le Cheval	25
Lois the Pie Queen	14
Mama Bear's	3
Nan Yang	5
Oliveto	9

Pacific Coast Brewery	27
Royal Ground	4
Stork Club	26
Taqueria Moralia	
Los Caporales	30
Tijuana Restaurant	31
Tropix	20
White Horse, The	2
Your Black Muslim	
Bakery	1
Yoshi's	33
Zachary's Pizza	8

ACCOMMODATION

Dean's B&B	A
Jack London Inn	D
Howard Johnson	
Express Inn	C
Maya Motel	B
Waterfront	
Plaza Hotel	E

Oakland before the freeways were built, but many of the roadside businesses are now derelict, although gentrification is well under way in the district of **Emeryville**. Some of the old warehouses have been converted into artists' lofts and studios in an attempt to transform the area into a glitzy design centerpiece. Most intriguing is the new city hall, the **Civic Center**, at Park Avenue and Hollis Street, for which the 1902 town hall has been wrapped in a sheer glass box of 15,000 additional square feet of office space. Any gentrification here is diffused by the scenes on the street – prostitutes and drug dealers hang out under the neon signs of the dingy bars and gambling halls, such as the *Oaks Card Club*, where Oaktown rapper M.C. Hammer, who once made the city proud, used to work.

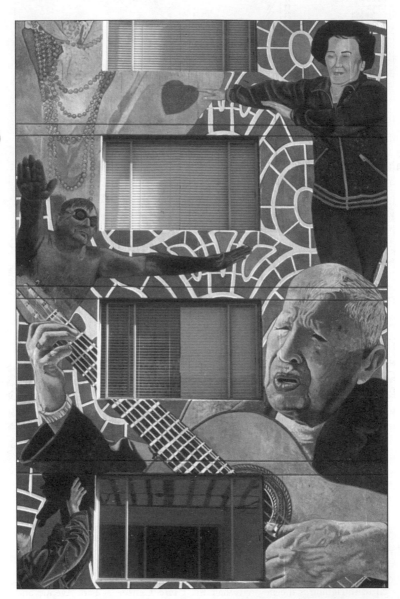

△ Mural, San Francisco

Lake Merritt and the Oakland Museum

Five blocks east of Broadway, the eastern third of downtown Oakland comprises **Lake Merritt**, a three-mile-circumference tidal lagoon that was bridged and dammed in the 1860s to become the centerpiece of Oakland's most desirable neighborhood. All that remains of the many fine houses that once circled the lake is the elegant **Camron-Stanford House**, on the southwest shore at 1418 Lakeside Drive, a graceful Italianate mansion whose sumptuous interior is open for visits (Wed 11am–4pm, Sun 1–5pm; $5; ☎510/444-1876, ⓦwww.cshouse.org). The lake is also the nation's oldest wildlife refuge, and migrating flocks of ducks, geese, and herons break their journeys here. **Lakeside Park** lines the north shore, where you can rent canoes, rowboats, kayaks, pedal boats, and a range of sailing boats and catamarans ($6–12 per hour) from the **Sailboat House** (summer Mon–Fri 9am–6pm, Sat & Sun 10am–6pm; winter daily 10.30am–3.30pm; ☎510/238-2196, ⓦwww.oaklandnet.com/parks) – provided you can convince the staff you know how to sail. A miniature Mississippi riverboat makes thirty-minute lake **cruises** ($1.50) on weekend afternoons, or you can splash out to be serenaded on the overpriced but romantic Gondola Servizio (from $45 for 30min; ☎510/663-6603, ⓦwww.gondolaservizio.com). Kids will like the puppet shows and pony rides at the **Children's Fairyland** (Wed–Sun 10am–4pm; $6; ☎510/452-2259, ⓦwww.fairyland.org), along Grand Avenue on the northwest edge of the park. At night, the lake's lit up by the "Necklace of Lights," an elegant source of local pride. Once you reach the north side of the lake, be sure to stroll under the MacArthur Freeway to soak up the relaxed atmosphere of the cafés and shops along gradually diverging Grand and Lakeshore avenues. Note the huge Art Deco-cum-mock-Classical facade of the still-functioning **Grand Lake Movie Theater**, a bastion of subversive political films.

Two blocks south of the lake, or a block up Oak Street from the Lake Merritt BART station, the **Oakland Museum**, 1000 Oak St (Wed–Sat 10am–5pm, Sun noon–5pm; $8, free every second Sun of month; ☎510/238-2200, ⓦwww.museumca.org), is undoubtedly Oakland's most worthwhile stop, not only for the exhibits but also for the superb modern building in which it's housed, topped by a terraced rooftop sculpture garden that gives great views out over the water and the city. The museum covers many diverse areas: displays on the **ecology** of California, including a simulated walk from the seaside through various natural habitats up to the 14,000-foot summits of the Sierra Nevada Mountains; state history, ranging from old mining equipment to the guitar that Berkeley-born Country Joe MacDonald played at the Woodstock Festival in 1969; and a broad survey of works by California artists and craftspeople, some highlights of which are pieces of turn-of-the-twentieth century **arts and crafts furniture**. You'll also see excellent **photography** by Edward Muybridge, Dorothea Lange, Imogen Cunningham, and many others. Additionally, the museum also has a collector's gallery that rents and sells works by California artists.

Jack London Square, Alameda, and West Oakland

Half a mile down from downtown Oakland on AC Transit bus #51, at the foot of Broadway on the waterfront, **Jack London Square** is Oakland's sole concession to the tourist trade. An erratic voluntarily-manned information booth on Broadway between Water and Embarcadero streets can supply maps detailing what the square has to offer, if you find it open. Also accessible by direct ferry from San Francisco (see "Arrival," p.643), this somewhat anesthetic complex of harborfront boutiques and restaurants, anchored by a huge Barnes and Noble bookstore, was named after the self-taught writer who grew up pirating shellfish around here, but is about as distant from the spirit of the man as it's possible to get. Jack London's best story, *The Call of the Wild*, was written about his adventures in the Alaskan Yukon, where he carved his initials in a small cabin that has been reconstructed here. The one sight worth stopping at is **Heinold's First and Last Chance Saloon**, a slanting tiny bar at the eastern end of the promenade, built in 1883 from the hull of a whaling ship. Jack London really did drink here, and the collection of yellowed portraits of him on the wall are the only genuine thing about the writer you'll find on the square. Massive redevelopment plans, to the tune of $200 million, are afoot to revamp the square into a top-notch entertainment venue by 2007.

If you're not a keen fan of London (and if you are, you'd be better off visiting his Sonoma Valley ranch – see p.782), there are still a few interesting things to do here. At the western end of the square you can visit a couple of **historical vessels**; dockside tours are available for both the *Light Ship Relief* (Thurs & Fri 10am–3pm, Sat & Sun 11am–4pm; $3) and the *USS Potomac* (Wed 10.30am–3.30pm, Fri & Sun noon–3.30pm; $7; ☏510/627-1215, ⊛www.usspotomac .org), Franklin D. Roosevelt's famous "floating White House." On Sunday, the square bustles with the weekly farmers' market, where you can pick up all sorts of bargains and stock up on food. Otherwise, walk a few short blocks inland to the **Produce Market**, along Third and Fourth streets, where a couple of good places to eat and drink lurk among the rail tracks (see "East Bay eating," p.668). This bustling warehouse district has fruit and vegetables by the fork-lift load, and is at its most lively early in the morning, from about 5am. On the Embarcadero between Clay and Washington, **Yoshi's World Class Jazz House** is the Bay Area's, if not the West Coast's, premier jazz club (see "East Bay Nightlife," p.673), as well as being a classy Japanese restaurant.

AC Transit bus #51 continues from Broadway under the inner harbor to **Alameda**, a quiet and conservative island of middle America dominated by a large, empty naval air station, one of the first to be closed by Bill Clinton in 1995. Alameda, which has been hit very hard by such post–Cold War military cutbacks, was severed from the Oakland mainland as part of a harbor improvement program in 1902. The fine houses along the original shoreline on, ironically, Clinton Street were part of the summer resort colony that flocked here to the *contra costa* or "opposite shore" from San Francisco, near the now demolished Neptune Beach amusement park. The island has since been much enlarged by dredging and landfill, and 1960s apartment buildings now line the long, narrow shore of **Robert Crown Memorial Beach** along the Bay – a quiet, attractive spot.

West Oakland – an industrial district of warehouses, rail tracks, 1960s housing projects, and decaying Victorian houses – may be the nearest East Bay BART stop to San Francisco, but it's light years away from that city's prosperity. Despite the obvious poverty, it's quite a safe and settled place, but the only time anyone pays any attention to it is when something dramatic happens – in the double-whammy year of 1989, for example, when former Black Panther Huey Newton was gunned down here in a drugs-related revenge attack, and the double-decker I-880 freeway, which divided the neighborhood from the rest of the city, collapsed in on itself during the earthquake, killing dozens of commuters. Now the neighborhood is a magnet for artists and skate punks from across the Bay, who revel in its dirt-cheap rents and open spaces, as its surprisingly tardy gentrification is still only progressing at snail's pace.

Local African-American leaders successfully resisted government plans to rebuild I-880, the old concrete eyesore which they asserted created an unsightly barrier within their community; the broad and less obtrusive **Nelson**

Mandela Parkway has replaced it. Otherwise, this remains one of the Bay Area's poorest and most neglected neighborhoods, and apart from a marvelous stock of turn-of-the-century houses, there's little here to tempt tourists. But locals – and Mayor Jerry Brown – say take a long look and buy now; given the district's proximity to San Francisco, West Oakland is bound to smarten up unrecognizably before too long.

East Oakland

The bulk of Oakland spreads along foothills and flatlands to the east of downtown, in neighborhoods obviously stratified along the main thoroughfares of Foothill and MacArthur boulevards. Gertrude Stein grew up here, though when she returned years later in search of her childhood home it had been torn down and replaced by a dozen Craftsman-style bungalows – the simple 1920s wooden houses that cover most of **East Oakland**, each fronted by a patch of lawn and divided from its neighbor by a narrow concrete driveway.

A quick way out from the gridded streets and sidewalks of the city is to take AC Transit bus #64 from downtown east up into the hills to **Joaquin Miller Park**, the most easily accessible of Oakland's hilltop parks. It stands on the former grounds of "The Hights," the misspelled home of the "Poet of the Sierras," Joaquin Miller, who made his name playing the eccentric frontier American in the literary salons of 1870s London. His poems weren't exactly acclaimed (his greatest poetic achievement was rhyming "teeth" with "Goethe"), although his prose account, *Life Amongst the Modocs*, documenting time spent with the Modoc people near Mount Shasta, does stand the test of time. It was more for his outrageous behavior that he became famous, wearing bizarre clothes and biting debutantes on the ankle. For years, Japanese poet Yone Noguchi also lived here, working the sprinkler as Miller impressed lady visitors with a rain dance he claimed to have learned from Native Americans.

Perched in the hills at the foot of the park, the pointed towers of the **Mormon Temple**, 4766 Lincoln Ave, look like missile-launchers designed by the Wizard of Oz – unmissable by day or floodlit night. In December, speakers hidden in the landscaping make it seem as if the plants are singing Christmas carols. Though you can't go inside the main temple unless you're a confirmed Mormon, there are great views from its courtyard out over the entire Bay Area, and a small museum explains the tenets of the faith (daily 9am–9pm; free); expect to be greeted and offered a free personalized tour of the museum by one of the faithful upon entering. Several miles up in the hills behind the temple, the new **Chabot Space & Science Center**, 10000 Skyline Blvd (summer Tues–Sun 10am–5pm, Fri & Sat 10am–10pm, Sun 11am–5pm; winter Wed & Thurs 2–5pm, Fri 2–10pm, Sat 10am–10pm, Sun 11am–5pm; $13; ☎510/336-7300, ⊛www.chabotspace.org), is a state-of-the-art museum with interactive displays and a fine **planetarium** – daytime shows are included in the admission but the evening Sky Tonight costs extra (Fri & Sat 7.30pm; $6), as do screenings at the impressive **Megadome Theater** (various times; $6); the museum can be reached on AC Transit bus #53 from the Fruitvale BART station.

Out past the airport in the suburb of San Leandro, **Oakland Zoo** (daily: summer 9am–5pm; winter 10am–4pm; $9; ☎510/632-9525, ⊛www.oaklandzoo.org) is home to over 300 species of animals, comfortably situated in the rolling hills of 525-acre Knowland Park; AC Transit bus #56 heads out there from Oakland, or it costs $5 to park. This is the only place of interest in the twenty miles of suburbs that stretch along the Bay southeast towards San Jose, apart from **Fremont**, at the end of the BART line, where the short-lived

Essanay movie studios were based. Essanay, the first studios on the West Coast, made over 700 films in three years, including Charlie Chaplin's *The Tramp* in 1914. Not much remains from these pre-Hollywood days, however, and the only real sight is the peaceful and leafy **Mission San Jose de Guadalupe** on Mission Boulevard south of the I-680 freeway (daily 10am–5pm; donation), which, in the best traditions of Hollywood set design, was completely rebuilt in Mission style some years ago.

North Oakland and Rockridge

The horrific October 1991 Oakland **fire**, which destroyed 3000 homes and killed 26 people, did most of its damage in the high-priced hills of **North Oakland**. It took the better part of two years, but most of the half-million - dollar houses have been rebuilt, and though the lush vegetation that made the area so attractive will never be allowed to grow back in order to prevent any more fires, things are pretty much back to normal. Which is to say that segregation is still in place: these bay-view homes, some of the Bay Area's most valuable real estate, look out across some of its poorest – the neglected flatlands below that in the 1960s were the proving grounds of Black Panthers Bobby Seale and Huey Newton.

Broadway is the dividing line between the two halves of North Oakland, and also gives access (via the handy AC Transit #51 bus) to most of what there is to see and do. One of Oakland's most neighborly streets, **Piedmont Avenue**, is lined by a number of small bookstores and cafés, and it makes for a nice stroll or relaxing day out. At the north end of Piedmont Avenue, the **Mountain View Cemetery** was laid out in 1863 by Frederick Law Olmsted (designer of New York's Central Park) and holds the elaborate dynastic tombs of San Francisco's most powerful families – the Crockers, the Bechtels, and the Ghirardellis. You can jog or ride a bike around the well-tended grounds, or just wonder at the enormous turtles in the pond. Next door, the columbarium, known as the **Chapel of the Chimes**, 4499 Piedmont Ave (daily 9am–5pm; free; ☎510/654-0123), was designed by Julia Morgan of Hearst Castle fame during her decade-long involvement with the chapel beginning in 1921. The structure is remarkable for its seemingly endless series of urn-filled rooms, grouped together around sky-lit courtyards, bubbling fountains, and intimate chapels – all connected by ornate staircases of every conceivable length. Morgan wanted the space to sing of life, not death, and she's succeeded – there's no better place in Oakland to wander about in peace, or even plop down with a book. Try and visit during one of the regular concerts held here for a completely unique – and distinctly Californian – experience.

Back on Broadway, just past College Avenue, Broadway Terrace climbs up along the edge of the fire area to small **Lake Temescal** – where you can swim in summer – and continues on up to the forested ridge at the **Robert Sibley Regional Preserve**. This includes the 1761-foot volcanic cone of Round Top Peak and offers panoramas of the entire Bay Area. The peak has been dubbed the "Volcanic Witch Project" by the local media due to the five mysterious mazes, carved into the dirt and lined with stones, located in the canyons around the crater. Nobody knows where they came from, but navigating the designs leads to their center, where visitors add to the pile of diverse offerings ranging from trinkets to cigarettes to poetry. Skyline Boulevard runs through the park and is popular with cyclists, who ride the twelve miles south to Lake Chabot or follow Grizzly Peak Boulevard five miles north to Tilden Park through the Berkeley Hills.

The majority of the Broadway traffic, and the AC Transit #51 bus, cuts off onto College Avenue through Oakland's most upscale shopping district, **ROCKRIDGE**, whose upper reaches merge into Berkeley. Spreading for half a mile on either side of the Rockridge BART station, the quirky stores and restaurants here, despite their undeniable yuppie overtones, are better than Piedmont's in variety and volume, and make for a pleasant afternoon's wander or night out.

Berkeley

This Berkeley was like no somnolent Siwash out of her own past at all, but more akin to those Far Eastern or Latin American universities you read about, those autonomous culture media where the most beloved of folklores may be brought into doubt, cataclysmic of dissents voiced, suicidal of commitments chosen – the sort that bring governments down.

Thomas Pynchon, *The Crying of Lot 49*

More than any other American city, **BERKELEY** conjures up an image of 1960s student dissent. When college campuses across the nation were **protesting** against the Vietnam War, it was the students of the University of California, Berkeley, who led the charge – gaining a name as the vanguard of what was increasingly seen as a challenge to the authority of the state. Full-scale battles were fought almost daily here at one point, on the campus and on its surrounding streets, and there were times when Berkeley looked almost on the brink of revolution itself: students (and others) throwing stones and gas bombs were met with tear-gas volleys and truncheons by National Guard troops under the nominal command of then-Governor Ronald Reagan.

Such action was inspired by the mood of the time and continued well into the 1970s, while during the conservative eighties and Clinton-dominated nineties, Berkeley politics became far less confrontational. But despite an influx of more conformist students, a surge in the number of exclusive restaurants, and the dismantling of the city's rent-control program, the progressive legacy has remained in the city's independent **bookstores** (see box, p.660) and at sporadic political demonstrations, such as when the owners of a local leftist radio station tried, unsuccessfully in the end, to remove its subversive staff from the premises in 1999. Unsurprisingly, the increasing national political polarisation caused by George W. Bush's uncompromising policies are particularly reflected in a town with such a strong radical heritage. Consequently, Berkeley has of late returned to being a bastion of the **anti-war movement** and streets like Telegraph Avenue are festooned with posters, stickers, badges, and T-shirts questioning the occupation of Iraq and the war against terrorism, or lampooning the "dunce-in-chief" in other ways.

The **University of California**, right in the center of town, completely dominates Berkeley and makes a logical starting point for a visit. Its many grand buildings and 30,000 students give off a definite energy, which spills down the raucous stretch of Telegraph Avenue that runs south from the campus and holds most of the student hangouts, including a dozen or so lively cafés, as well as a number of fine bookstores. Older students, and a good percentage of the faculty, congregate in the **Northside** area, the part of **North Berkeley** just above the campus, popping down from their woodsy hillside homes to partake of goodies from the **Gourmet Ghetto**, a stretch of Shattuck Avenue crammed with restaurants, delis, and bakeries. Of quite distinct character are the flatlands that spread through **West Berkeley** down to the Bay, a poorer but increasingly gentrified district that mixes old Victorian houses with builders' yards and light-industrial premises. Along the Bay itself is the **Berkeley Marina**, where you can rent sailboards and sailboats or just watch the sun set behind the Golden Gate.

The University of California

Caught up in the frantic crush of students who pack the **University of California** campus during the semesters, it's nearly impossible to imagine the bucolic learning environment envisaged by its high-minded founders. When the Reverend Henry Durant and other East Coast academics decided to set up shop here in the 1860s, these rolling foothills were still largely given over to dairy herds and wheatfields, the last remnants of the Peralta family's Spanish land-grant rancho, which once stretched over most of the East Bay. In 1866,

RESTAURANTS, BARS, & CLUBS

Ajanta	6	Café Strada	36	Long Life Vegi House	25
Albatross Pub	24	Cancún Taqueria	33	Mario's La Fiesta	41
Anna's	26	Cesar	12	Naan 'n' Curry	38 & 47
Barney's	3 & 16	Cha Am	15	O' Chame	23
Bette's Oceanview Diner	22	Cheese Board Pizza	14	Picante	9
Blue Nile	44	Chez Panisse	13	Pub	5
Breads of India	40	Fatapple's	10	Pyramid Alehouse	7
Brennan's	30	Homemade Cafe	43	Rick & Ann's	49
Brewed Awakenings	20	Juan's Place	45	Rivoli	2
Britt-Marie's	1	Jupiter	31	Saul's Deli	11
Café de la Paz	17	Kirala	46	Shattuck Avenue Spats	27
Café Fanny	18	Lalime's	8	Spenger's	29
Café Intermezzo	41	La Note	37	Steve's Barbeque	35
Café Mediterraneum	42	La Val's Pizza	19	Top Dog	39
Café Milano	34	Liu's Kitchen	4	Triple Rock Brewery	28
Café Rouge	21	Locanda Olmo	48	Vik's Chaat Corner	32

while surveying the land, a trustee recited "Westward the course of the empire takes its way," from a poem by George Berkeley. Moved by the moment, all assembled agreed to name their school after the bishop. Construction work on the two campus buildings – imaginatively named North Hall and South Hall – was still going on when the first 200 students, including 22 women, moved here from Oakland in 1873. Since then an increasing number of buildings have been squeezed into the half-mile-square main campus, and the state-funded university has become one of America's most prestigious, with so many Nobel laureates on the faculty that it's said you have to win one just to get a parking permit. University physicists built the first cyclotron, and plutonium was discovered here in 1941, along with thirteen other synthetic elements (including berkelium and californium). As such, sketches for the first atomic bomb

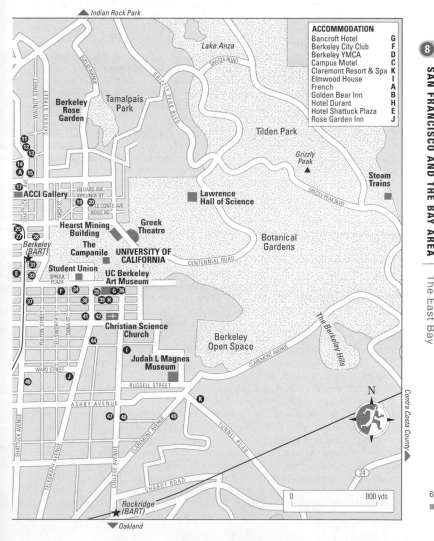

ACCOMMODATION
Bancroft Hotel	G
Berkeley City Club	F
Berkeley YMCA	D
Campus Motel	C
Claremont Resort & Spa	K
Elmwood House	I
French	A
Golden Bear Inn	B
Hotel Durant	H
Hotel Shattuck Plaza	E
Rose Garden Inn	J

began here. Nuclear weaponry and overcrowding aside, the beautifully land-scaped campus, stepping down from the eucalyptus-covered Berkeley Hills toward the Golden Gate, is eminently strollable. With maps posted everywhere, you'd have to try hard to get lost – though enthusiastic students will show you around on a free ninety-minute **tour** (Mon–Sat 10am, Sun 1pm; ☎510/642-5215), explaining the campus's history, architecture, and flavor. Be sure to take one if you want a fuller picture of Berkeley beyond looking at facades and the faces of passing students.

A number of footpaths climb the hill from the Berkeley BART station on Shattuck Avenue, but the best way to get a feel for the place is to follow Strawberry Creek from the top of Center Street across the southeast corner of the campus, emerging from the groves of redwood and eucalyptus trees at **Sproul Plaza**. It's the newest and largest public space on campus, often enlivened by street musicians playing for change on the steps of the **Student Union** build-ing and conga drummers pounding away in the echoing courtyard below. Sather Gate, which bridges Strawberry Creek at the north end of Sproul Plaza, marks the entrance to the older part of the campus. Up the hill, past the imposing facade of Wheeler Hall, the 1914 landmark **Campanile** (Mon–Fri 10am–4pm; $2) is modeled after the one in the Piazza San Marco in Venice; take an elevator to the top for a great view of the campus and the entire Bay Area. At the foot of the tower stands the redbrick **South Hall**, the sole survivor of the original pair of buildings.

Inside the plain white building next door, the **Bancroft Library** (Mon–Fri 9am–5pm, Sat 1–5pm; ☎510/642-3781) displays odds and ends from its exhaustive accumulation of artifacts and documents tracing the history of California, including a fake brass plaque supposedly left by Sir Francis Drake when he claimed all of the West Coast for Queen Elizabeth I. It also contains an internationally important collection of manuscripts and rare books, from the works of Mark Twain to James Joyce – though to see any of these you have to show some academic credentials. Around the corner and down the hill, just inside the arched main entrance to Doe Library, you'll find the **Morrison Reading Room**, a great place to sit for a while and read foreign magazines and newspapers.

Also worth a quick look is the **Museum of Paleontology** (Mon–Sat 8am–5pm; free; ☎510/642-1821, ⓦwww.ucmp.berkeley.edu) in the nearby Valley Life Sciences Building, although only a Tyrannosaurus Rex skeleton and some other bones and fossils are on general display in the atrium – you need to be on an academic mission to view the wealth of finds within. From here it's a quick walk to the collection of cafés and restaurants lining Euclid and Hearst avenues, and the beginning of the Northside.

The Hearst family name appears with disturbing regularity around the Berkeley campus, though in most instances this is due not to the notorious newspaper baron William Randolph but to his altruistic mother, Phoebe Apper-son Hearst. Besides inviting the entire senior class to her home every spring for a giant picnic, she sponsored the architectural competition that came up with the original campus plan and donated a good number of the campus buildings, including many that have since been destroyed. One of the finest survivors, the 1907 **Hearst Mining Building** (daily 8am–5pm; free), on the northeast edge of the campus, conceals a delicate metalwork lobby topped by three glass domes, above ageing exhibits on geology and mining – which is how the Hearst family fortune was originally made, long before scion W.R. took up publishing. Another Hearst legacy is the **Greek Theatre**, which hosts a summer season of rock concerts and is modeled after the amphitheater at Epidauros, Greece.

Higher up in the hills, above the 80,000-seat Memorial Stadium, the lushly landscaped **Botanical Garden** (daily 9am–5pm, closed first Tues; $3, free on Thurs) defeats on-campus claustrophobia with its thirty acres of plants and cacti. Near the crest, with great views out over the Bay, a full-sized fiberglass sculpture of a whale stretches out in front of the space-age **Lawrence Hall of Science** (daily 10am–5pm; $8.50; ☎510/642-5132, ⊛www.lawrencehallofscience.org), an excellent museum and learning center that features earthquake simulations, model dinosaurs, and a planetarium, plus hands-on exhibits for kids in the Wizard's Lab. Both the gardens and the Lawrence Hall of Science are accessible on weekdays via the free UC Berkeley Shuttle bus from the campus or the Berkeley BART station.

In the southeast corner of the campus, the **Phoebe Hearst Museum of Anthropology** in Kroeber Hall (Wed–Sat 10am–4.30pm, Sun noon–4pm; $2, free Thurs; ☎510/642-3682, ⊛www.hearstmuseum.berkeley.edu) holds a variety of changing exhibits as well as an intriguing display of artifacts made by Ishi, the last surviving Yahi Indian who was found near Mount Lassen in Northern California in 1911. Anthropologist (and father of writer Ursula Le Guin) Alfred Kroeber brought Ishi to the museum (then located on the UC San Francisco campus), where he lived under the scrutiny of scientists and journalists – in effect, in a state of captivity – until his death from tuberculosis a few years later.

The brutally modern, angular concrete of the **Berkeley Art Museum** at 2626 Bancroft Way (Wed 11am–7pm, Fri–Sun 11am–5pm; $8, free on first Thurs; ☎510/642-0808, ⊛www.bampfa.berkeley.edu) is a stark contrast to the campus's older buildings. Its skylit, open-plan galleries hold works by Picasso, Cézanne, Rubens, and other notables, but the star of the show is the collection of Fifties American painter Hans Hofmann's energetic and colorful abstract paintings on the top floor. The museum is renowned for its cutting-edge, changing exhibitions: the main space hosts a range of major shows – such as Robert Mapplethorpe's controversial photographs – while the Matrix Gallery focuses on lesser-known, generally local artists. The new quarters of the **Pacific Film Archive**, diagonally opposite at 2575 Bancroft, feature nightly showings ($7) of classics, Third World, and experimental films. Call for listings (☎510/642-5249), or pick up a free monthly calendar around campus. Other artistic fare can be found at **Zellerbach Hall** (☎510/642-9988), which showcases classical music, dance, and performances by modernists like Laurie Anderson and Philip Glass.

Telegraph Avenue

Downtown Berkeley – basically two department stores, a few banks, a post office, and the City Hall building – lies west of the university campus around the Berkeley BART station on Shattuck Avenue, but the real activity centers on **Telegraph Avenue**, which runs south of the university from Sproul Plaza. This thoroughfare saw some of the worst of the Sixties riots and is still a frenetic bustle, especially the four short blocks closest to the university, which are packed with cafés and secondhand bookstores. Sidewalk vendors hawk handmade jewelry and brilliantly colored T-shirts, while down-and-outs hustle for spare change and spout psychotic poetry. At no. 2455 the original Amoeba Records (☎530/549-1125), whose vast younger sister is across the Bay in Haight-Ashbury, still houses the East Bay's widest selection of used and new music.

People's Park, now a seedy and partly overgrown plot of land half a block up from Telegraph between Haste Street and Dwight Way, was another

Not surprising for a university town, Berkeley's **bookstores** are as exhaustive as they are exhausting. Perfect for browsing and taking your time, you won't be made to feel guilty or obliged to buy a book you've been poring over for ages. The CVB has a useful list of over fifty shops, of which the following are a representative selection:

Black Oak Books 1491 Shattuck Ave ☎510/486-0698. Huge selection of second-hand and new books for every interest; also holds regular evening readings by internationally acclaimed authors.

Cody's Books 2454 Telegraph Ave ☎510/845-7852. The flagship of Berkeley booksellers, with an excellent selection of fiction, poetry, and literary criticism. There's a newer branch at 1730 4th St at Virginia (☎510/559-9500).

Comic Relief 2138 University Ave ☎510/843-5002. All the mainstream stuff, plus self-published mini-comics by locals.

Comics and Comix 2502 Telegraph Ave ☎510/845-4091. Great selection of comic books, especially fantasy and science fiction, both current and classic.

Easy Going Travel Shop & Bookstore 1385 Shattuck Ave ☎510/843-3533. The essential bookstore for every traveler. Packed with travel paraphernalia, it offers a wide selection of guidebooks and maps for local, countrywide, and international exploration. Talks and slide shows by travel writers are also held on a regular basis.

Lewin's Metaphysical Books 2644 Ashby Ave ☎510/843-4491. The place to come for the best selection on spirituality, religions, astrology, and other esoteric subjects.

Moe's Bookstore 2476 Telegraph Ave ☎510/849-2087. An enormous selection of new and used books on four floors with esoteric surprises in every field of study; for academics, book collectors, and browsers. There's also an excellent art section on the top floor (☎510/849-2133).

Revolution Books 2425c Channing Way ☎510/848-1196. Wide range of books on political themes with, as you might expect, an emphasis on leftist and anarchist thought.

Serendipity Books 1201 University Ave ☎510/841-7455. This vast garage-like bookstore is off the loop of Berkeley bookstores, but an absolute must for collectors of first edition and/or obscure fiction and poetry, as well as black American writers. The prices are fair, and the owner – incredibly, given the towers of unshelved books – knows exactly where everything is to be found.

Shakespeare and Company 2499 Telegraph Ave ☎510/841-8916. Crammed with quality secondhand books at reasonable prices, Shakespeare and Company is the best place to linger and scour the shelves for finds, especially literature.

Signal Books 1816 Euclid Ave ☎510/843-1816. A variety of quality books to choose from on graphics, art, and music, as well as a good stock of magazines.

battleground in the late Sixties, when organized and spirited resistance to the university's plans to develop the site into dormitories brought out the troops, who shot dead an onlooker by mistake. To many, the fact that the park is still a community-controlled open space (and outdoor flophouse for Berkeley's legions of pushers and homeless) symbolizes a small victory in the battle against the Establishment, though it's not a pleasant or particularly safe place to hang about, especially after dark. A mural along Haste Street recalls some of the reasons why the battles were fought, in the words of student leader Mario Savio: "There's a time when the operation of the machine becomes so odious, makes you so sick at heart, that you can't take part, you can't even tacitly take part. And you've got to put your bodies upon the gears and upon the wheels, upon the levers, upon all the apparatus, and you've got to make it stop" – ideals that can't help but be undermined by the state of the place these days. Efforts by the university to reclaim the space with volleyball and basketball courts in 1991 were met with violent protests: rioters trashed Telegraph Avenue storefronts, and a 19-year-old woman enraged at the university's plans for the park was shot dead by the police while trying to assassinate the chancellor with a knife in his home.

Directly across Bowditch Street from People's Park stands one of the finest buildings in the Bay Area, Bernard Maybeck's **Christian Science Church**. Built in 1910, it's an eclectic and thoroughly modern structure, laid out in a simple Greek Cross floor plan and spanned by a massive redwood truss with carved Gothic tracery and Byzantine painted decoration. The interior is only open on Sundays for worship and for tours at 11am, but the outside is worth lingering over, its cascade of gently pitched roofs and porticoes carrying the eye from one handcrafted detail to another. It's a clever building in many ways: while the overall image is one of tradition and craftsmanship, Maybeck also succeeded in inconspicuously incorporating such materials as industrial metal windows, concrete walls, and asbestos tiles into the structure – thereby cutting costs.

North Berkeley

North Berkeley is a subdued neighborhood of professors and postgraduate students, spreading from the flat leafy blocks around the BART lines to the steep, twisting streets that climb up the lushly overgrown hills north of the campus. At the foot of the hills, some of the Bay Area's finest **restaurants** and **delis** – most famously *Chez Panisse*, started and run by Alice Waters, the acclaimed inventor of California cuisine – have sprung up along **Shattuck Avenue** to form the so-called Gourmet Ghetto, a great place to pick up the makings of a tasty alfresco lunch. There are also a few **galleries**, most notably ACCI, 1652 Shattuck Ave (Tues–Thurs 11am–6pm, Fri 11am–7pm, Sat 10am–6pm, Sun noon–5pm; free; ☎530/843-2527), an arts-and-crafts co-operative designed to exhibit and sell the work of local artists. Over a mile further northwest, where Berkeley meets Albany, **Solano Avenue** is fast catching up as a trendy shopping and dining area with a dazzling array of outlets, such as Tibetan craft shops, draped along its curved length.

Euclid Avenue, off Hearst and next to the north gate of the university, is a sort of antidote to Telegraph Avenue, a quiet grove of coffee joints and pizza parlors frequented by grad students, the focal point of the largely academic enclave known as **Northside**. Above Euclid (if you want to avoid the fairly steep walk, take the daily #65 bus or the weekdays-only #8), there are few more pleasant places for a picnic than the **Berkeley Rose Garden** at the corner of Euclid Avenue and Bayview Place (daily dawn–dusk; free), a terraced amphitheater filled with some three thousand varieties of roses and looking out across the Bay to San Francisco. Built as part of a WPA job-creation scheme during the Depression, a wooden pergola rings the top, stepping down to a small spring.

Tucked among the ridges of Berkeley Hills, a number of enticing parks give great views over the Bay. The largest and highest of them, **Tilden Park**, spreads along the crest of the hills, encompassing some 2065 acres of near wilderness. Kids can enjoy a ride on the carved wooden horses of the carousel or the 1950s mini-steam train through the redwood trees. In the warmer months, don't miss a swim in soothing **Lake Anza** (lifeguard on duty May–Oct daily 11am–6pm; $3).

Nearer to town, between the north end of Shattuck Avenue and east end of Solano Avenue, the gray basalt knob of **Indian Rock** stands out from the foothills, challenging rock climbers who hone their skills on its forty-foot vertical faces. Carved into similarly hard volcanic stone across the street are the mortar holes used by the Ohlone to grind acorns into flour. In between, and in stark contrast, stands the rusting hulk of a Cold War–era air-raid siren. Those who just want to appreciate the extraordinary view from the rock can take the steps around its back.

West Berkeley and the Waterfront

From downtown Berkeley and the UC campus, **University Avenue** runs in an almost imperceptible gradient downhill toward the Bay, lined by increasingly shabby frontages of motels and massage parlors. The liveliest part of this **West Berkeley** area is around the intersection of University and San Pablo avenues – the pre-freeway main highway north – where a community of recent immigrants from India and Pakistan have set up stores and restaurants that serve some of the best of the Bay Area's curries.

The area between San Pablo Avenue and the Bay is the oldest part of Berkeley, and a handful of hundred-year-old houses and churches – such as the two white-spired Gothic Revival structures on Hearst Avenue – survive from the time when this district was a separate city, known as Ocean View. The neighborhood also holds remnants of Berkeley's industrial past, and many of the old warehouses and factory premises have been converted into living and working spaces for artists, craftspeople, and computer software companies. The newly polished and yuppified stretch of **Fourth Street** between Gilman and University features upscale furniture outlets and quaint gourmet delis, as well as some outstanding restaurants (see "East Bay eating," p.668). Just to the south of here at 708 Addison St, you can take a tour of the huge Takara Sake USA Inc. brewery, whose tasting room and museum grant the opportunity to sample the company's products in elegant Japanese surroundings and learn about the process of sake-making (daily noon–6pm; free; ℡530/540-8250).

The I-80 freeway, and the still-used rail tracks that run alongside it, pretty well manage to cut Berkeley off from its **Waterfront**. The best way to get there is to take AC Transit bus #51, which runs regularly down University Avenue. Once a major hub for the transbay ferry services – to shorten journey times a three-mile-long pier was constructed, much of which still sticks out into the Bay – the **Berkeley Marina** (⊛www. ci.berkeley.ca.us/marina) is now one of the prime spots on the Bay for leisure activities, especially windsurfing and kayaking. People also stretch their own and their dogs' legs in the green confines of **Cesar Chavez Park**, north of the marina.

The North Bay and inland valleys

Compared to the urbanized bayfront cities of Oakland and Berkeley, the rest of the East Bay is sparsely populated, and places of interest are few and far between. The **North Bay** is home to some of the Bay Area's heaviest industry – oil refineries and chemical plants dominate the landscape – but also holds a few remarkably unchanged waterfront towns that merit a side-trip if you're passing by. Away from the Bay, the **inland valleys** are a whole other world of dry rolling hills dominated by the towering peak of **Mount Diablo**. Dozens of tract-house developments have made commuter suburbs out of what were once cattle ranches and farms, but so far the region has been able to absorb the numbers and still feels rural, despite having doubled in population in the past quarter-century.

The North Bay

North of Berkeley there's not a whole lot to see or do. Off the Eastshore Freeway in mostly mundane **Albany**, Golden Gate Fields has **horse racing** from October to June, and beyond it, the **Albany Mud Flats** are a fascinating place to stroll; impromptu works of art made from discarded materials vie with wild irises to attract the passer-by's eye in this reclaimed landfill jutting out into the Bay. Back inland, San Pablo Avenue's strip of bars and clubs, including *Club Mallard* (no. 752), *The Ivy Room* (no. 858), and *The Hotsy-Totsy* (no. 601), are some of the best in the East Bay – that is, if you're looking for authentic, gritty saloons featuring live rock'n'roll on weekends, well-stocked jukeboxes, and pool tables reminiscent of San Francisco's Mission district. About a mile from Albany, **El Cerrito**'s main contribution to world culture was the band Creedence Clearwater Revival, who staged most of their *Born on the Bayou* publicity photographs in the wilds of Tilden Park in the hills above. The town is still home to one of the best record stores in California, Down Home Music, at 10341 San Pablo Ave, which stocks an eclectic array of blues, gospel, Cajun, Tex-Mex, old time, jazz, world, and rock.

Depressing and rough **Richmond**, at the top of the Bay, was once a boom-town, building ships during World War II at the Kaiser Shipyards, which employed 100,000 workers between 1940 and its closure in 1945. Now it's the proud home to the gigantic Standard Oil refinery, the center of which you drive through before crossing the **Richmond–San Rafael Bridge** ($3) to Marin County. About the only reason to stop in Richmond is that it marks the north end of the BART line, and the adjacent Amtrak station is a better terminal for journeys to and from San Francisco than the end of the line in West Oakland.

Though not really worth a trip in itself, if you're heading from the East Bay to Marin County, **Point Richmond** merits a look. A cozy little town tucked away at the foot of the bridge between the refinery and the Bay, its many Victorian houses are rapidly becoming commuter territory for upwardly mobile professionals from San Francisco. Through the narrow tunnel that cuts under the hill stands the most obvious sign of this potential gentrifica-tion: "Brickyard Landing," an East Bay docklands development with modern bay-view condos, a private yacht harbor, and a token gesture to the area's industrial past – disused brick kilns, hulking next to the tennis courts on the front lawn. The rest of the waterfront is taken up by the broad and usually deserted strand of **Keller Beach**, which stretches for half a mile along the sometimes windy shoreline.

The Carquinez Straits

At the top of the Bay some 25 miles north of Oakland, the land along the **Carquinez Straits** is a bit off the beaten track, but it's an area of some natural beauty and much historic interest. The still-small towns along the waterfront seem worlds away from the bustle of the rest of the Bay Area, but how long they'll be able to resist the pressure of the expanding commuter belt is any-body's guess. AC Transit #74 runs every hour from Richmond BART north to **Crockett** at the west end of the narrow straits. This tiny town cut into the steep hillsides above the water seems entirely dependent upon the massive C&H Sugar factory at its foot, whose giant neon sign lights up the town and the adjacent Carquinez Bridge ($3).

From Crockett, the narrow Carquinez Straits Scenic Drive, an excellent cycling route, heads east along the Sacramento River. A turn two miles along drops down to **Port Costa**, a small town that was dependent upon ferry traffic across the straits to Benicia until it lost its livelihood when the bridge was built at Crockett. It's still a nice enough place to watch the huge ships pass by on their way to and from the inland ports of Sacramento and Stockton. If you don't have a bike (or a car), you can enjoy the view while riding on one of the Amtrak trains that run alongside the water from Oakland and Richmond, not stopping until Martinez at the eastern end of the straits, two miles north of John Muir's house (see p.666).

Benicia

On the north side of the straits, and hard to get to without a car (turn right onto I-780 after the bridge), **Benicia** is the most substantial of the historic waterfront towns, but one that has definitely seen better days. Founded in 1847, it initially rivaled San Francisco as the major Bay Area port and was even the state capital for a time. Despite Benicia's better weather and fine deep-water harbor, San Francisco, which is closer to the ocean, eventually became the main transportation point for the fortunes of the Gold Rush, and the town very nearly faded away altogether. Examples of Benicia's efforts to become a major city stand poignantly around the very compact downtown area, most conspicuously the 1852 Greek Revival structure that was used as the **first State Capitol** for just thirteen months. The building has been restored as a **museum** (Wed–Sun 10am–5pm; $2), furnished in the legislative style of the time, complete with top hats on the tables and shining spittoons every few feet.

A walking-tour map of Benicia's many intact Victorian houses and churches is available from the **CVB**, 601 First St (Mon–Fri 8.30am–5pm, Sat & Sun 11am–3pm; ☎707/745-2120, ⓦwww.beniciachamber.com). Included on the itinerary are the steeply pitched roofs and gingerbread eaves of the **Frisbie-Walsh house** at 235 East L St, a prefabricated Gothic Revival building shipped here in pieces from Boston in 1849. Across the City Hall park, the arched ceiling beams of **St Paul's Episcopal Church** look like an upturned ship's hull; it was built by shipwrights from the Pacific Mail Steamship Company, one of Benicia's many successful nineteenth-century shipyards. Half a dozen former brothels and saloons stand in various stages of decay and restoration along First Street down near the waterfront, from where the world's largest train ferries used to ply the waters between Benicia and Port Costa until 1930. These days the only time this spot draws large crowds is during the annual **Waterfront Celebration** festival on the last weekend of July.

In the last decade, Benicia has attracted a number of artists and craftspeople, and you can watch glassblowers and furniture makers at work in the **Benicia Glass Studios** at 675 East H St (Mon–Sat 10am–4pm, Sun in summer noon–5pm; free). Ceramic artist Judy Chicago and sculptor Robert Arneson are among those who have worked in the converted studios and modern light-industrial parks around the sprawling fortifications of the old **Benicia Arsenal**, whose thickly walled sandstone buildings east of the downtown area formed the main Army storage facility for weapons and ammunition from 1851 up to and including the Korean Conflict. One of the oddest parts of the complex is the **Camel Barn** in the **Benicia Historical Museum** (Wed–Sun 1–4pm; free; ☎707/745-5435, ⓦwww.beniciahistoricalmuseum. org): the structure used to house camels that the Army imported in 1856 to transport supplies across the deserts of the Southwestern US. The experiment failed, and the camels were kept here until they were sold off in 1864.

Vallejo and Six Flags Marine World

Directly across the Carquinez Bridge from Crockett, the biggest and dullest of the North Bay towns – **Vallejo** – was, like Benicia, an early capital of California, though it now lacks any sign of its historical significance. In contrast to most of the other Gold Rush–era towns that line the Straits, Vallejo remained economically vital, largely because of the massive military presence here at the **Mare Island Naval Shipyard**, a sprawling, relentlessly gray complex that covers an area twice the size of Golden Gate Park. Closed in late 1997, Mare Island was once Vallejo's largest employer, and its less than glamorous history – the yard built and maintained supply ships and submarines, not carriers or battleships – is recounted in a small **museum** in the old city hall building at 734 Marin St (Tues–Sat 10am–4.30pm; $2; ☎707/643-0077, ⓦwww.vallejomuseum.org), where the highlight is a working periscope that looks out across the Bay. Though no great thrill, it's worth a quick stop, situated in the center of a block to the west of Hwy-29, the main route from the East Bay to the Wine Country (see Chapter Ten).

The best reason to come to Vallejo, however, is the recently renovated **Six Flags Marine World** (daily June–Aug 10am–7pm or later, Fri–Sun & school holidays mid-March–May & Sept–early Nov; $46, $65 season pass; ☎707/643-6721, ⓦwww.sixflags.com), five miles north of central Vallejo off I-80 at the Marine World Parkway (Hwy-37) exit. Billing itself as the nation's only wildlife park, oceanarium, and theme park, it offers a well-above-average range of performing sea lions, dolphins, and killer whales kept in approximations of their natural habitats. It also features water-ski stunt shows and several newly constructed roller coasters, including the floorless Medusa, on which your legs dangle as you zoom through inversions at 65mph. The animals in the park seem very well cared for, their quarters are clean and spacious, and the shows are fun for all but the most jaded. The shark exhibit lets you walk through a transparent tunnel alongside twenty-foot Great Whites, and the tropical butterfly house is truly amazing. It is worth noting that standard discounts and regular specials are offered if you buy and print your tickets online. The most enjoyable way to get here from San Francisco is on the Blue and Gold Fleet **ferry** from Fisherman's Wharf, which takes an hour each way ($9.50 one way; ☎415/773-1188 or ⓦwww.blueandgoldfleet.com). You can also take BART to the El Cerrito Del Norte stop, where you transfer onto the Vallejo BARTlink bus (☎707/648-4666) to the park.

The inland valleys

BART tunnels from Oakland through the Berkeley Hills to the leafy-green stockbroker settlement of **Orinda**, continuing east through the increasingly hot and dry landscape to **Concord**, site of a controversial nuclear-weapons depot. In the mid-Nineties, a civilly disobedient blockade here ended in protester Brian Wilson losing his legs under the wheels of a slow-moving munitions train. The event raised public awareness – before it happened few people knew of the depot's existence – and earned Wilson a place in the Lawrence Ferlinghetti poem *A Buddha in the Woodpile*; but these days it's business as usual. Concord is also home to one of Six Flags' latest theme parks, **Waterworld USA** (daily June–Aug 11am–5pm or longer, Sat & Sun May & Sept same hours; $26; ☎925/609-1364, ⓦwww.sixflags.com), located near the Willow Pass exit from I-680 at 1950 Waterworld Parkway. The impressive range of aquatic slides and rides is broadly divided into "Thrills" and "Family" categories according to their rank on the white-knuckle scale.

From the Pleasant Hill BART station, one stop before the end of the line, Contra Costa County Connection buses leave every thirty minutes for **Martinez**, the seat of county government and a major Amtrak depot, passing the preserved home of naturalist **John Muir**, at 4202 Alhambra Ave (Wed–Sun 10am–5pm; $3; ☎925/228-8860), just off Hwy-4 two miles south of Martinez. Muir, an articulate, persuasive Scot whose writings and political activism were of vital importance in the preservation of America's wilderness, spent much of his life exploring and writing about the majestic Sierra Nevada, particularly Yosemite. He was also one of the founders of the **Sierra Club** – a wilderness lobby and education organization still with a strong presence today (see p.460 for more). Anyone familiar with the image of this thin, bearded man wandering the mountains with his knapsack, notebook, and packet of tea might be surprised to see his very conventional, upper-class Victorian home, now restored to its appearance when Muir died in 1914. Built by Muir's father-in-law, only those parts of the house Muir added himself reflect much of the personality of the man, not least the massive, rustic fireplace he had built in the East Parlor so he could have a "real mountain campfire." The bulk of Muir's personal belongings and artifacts are displayed in his study on the upper floor, and in the adjacent room an exhibition documents the history of the Sierra Club and Muir's battles to protect America's wilderness.

Behind the bell-towered main house is a large, still-productive orchard where Muir cultivated grapes, pears, and cherries to earn the money to finance his explorations (you can sample the fruits free of charge, pre-picked by staff gardeners). Beyond the orchard is the 1849 **Martinez Adobe**, homestead of the original Spanish land-grant settlers and now a small **museum** (same info as Muir House) of Mexican colonial culture. The contrast between Mexican and American cultures in early California is fascinating and, as a bonus, the building's two-foot-thick walls keep it refreshingly cool on a typically hot summer day.

At the foot of Mount Diablo, fifteen miles south, playwright **Eugene O'Neill** used the money he got for winning the Nobel Prize for Literature in 1936 to build a home and sanctuary for himself, which he named **Tao House**. It was here, before 1944 when he was struck down with Parkinson's disease, that he wrote many of his best-known plays: *The Iceman Cometh*, *A Moon for the Misbegotten*, and *Long Day's Journey into Night*. Readings and performances of his works are sometimes given in the house, which is open to visitors, though you must reserve a place on one of the free guided **tours** (Wed–Sun 10am & 12.30pm; ☎925/838-0249, ⓦwww.nps.gov/euon). As it's now protected National Park Service land, there's no parking on site, so the tours pick you up in the tony town of **Danville**, at a location given when you book. Danville's richest neighborhood, Blackhawk, is the home of the **Blackhawk Automotive Museum**, 3700 Blackhawk Plaza Circle (Wed–Sun 10am–5pm; $8; ☎925/736-2277). Here you will find an impressive collection of classic cars from Britain, Germany, Italy, and the US, along with artwork inspired by them.

Majestic **Mount Diablo** rises up from the rolling ranchlands at its foot to a height of nearly four thousand feet, its summit and flanks preserved within **Mount Diablo State Park** (daily 8am–sunset; $6 per vehicle). North Gate, the main road through the park, reaches within three hundred feet of the top, so it's a popular place for an outing and you're unlikely to be alone to enjoy the marvelous view: on a clear day you can see over two hundred miles in every direction. There's no public transportation, though the Sierra Club sometimes organizes day-trips: see "Basics," p.69.

Two main entrances lead into the park, both well-marked off I-680. The one from the southwest by way of Danville passes by the **ranger station**, where you can pick up a trail map ($5) which lists the best day-hikes. The other runs from the northwest by way of Walnut Creek, and the routes join together five miles from the summit. March and April, when the wild flowers are out, are the best times to come, and since mornings are ideal for getting the clearest view, you should drive to the top first and then head back down to a trailhead for a hike, or to one of the many picnic spots for a leisurely lunch. In summer it can get desperately hot and dry, and parts of the park are closed because of fire danger.

Livermore and Altamont Speedway

Fifteen miles southeast of Mount Diablo on the main road out of the Bay Area (I-580) or via WHEELS #1 from the Dublin/Pleasanton BART, the rolling hills around sleepy **Livermore** are covered with thousands of shining, spinning, high-tech **windmills**, placed here by a private power company to take advantage of the nearly constant gusts. The largest wind farm in the world, you'll probably have seen it used in a number of TV ads as a space-age backdrop to hype flashy new cars or sexy perfumes. Though the federal government provides no funding for this non-polluting, renewable source of energy, it spends billions of dollars every year designing and building nuclear weapons and other sinister applications of modern technology at the nearby **Lawrence Livermore National Laboratory**, where most of the research and development of the nuclear arsenal takes place. Atomic fans can arrange to take one of the in-depth two-and-a-half-hour laboratory tours (Tues & Thurs 9am; free) but you have to register well in advance – sixty days in the case of non-US citizens. Most folk, however, will be satisfied by peeking into the small **Discovery Center** (Mon–Fri 1–4pm; free; ☎925/423-3272, ⓦwww.llnl.gov), one mile south of I-580 on Greenville Road, which holds hands-on exhibits showing off various scientific phenomena and devices.

Nemesis at Altamont

Uncannily timed at the dying embers of the Sixties and often referred to as "the nemesis of the Woodstock generation," the concert headlined by the **Rolling Stones** at the **Altamont Speedway** on December 6, 1969, ended in total disaster. The free event was conceived to be a sort of second Woodstock, staged in order to counter allegations that the Stones had ripped off their fans during a long US tour. The band, however, inadvisably hired a chapter of Hell's Angels instead of professional security to maintain order and the result, predictably enough, was chaos. Three people ended up dead, one kicked and stabbed to death by the Hell's Angels themselves.

The whole sorry tale was captured remarkably on film by brothers David and Albert Maysles (plus co-director Charlotte Zerwin) in their documentary *Gimme Shelter*, released the following year. The footage of the concert clearly shows the deteriorating mood and atmosphere of growing menace in the crowd, exemplified by the scene when Jefferson Airplane vocalist Marty Balin jumped down into the crowd to break up a fight, an intervention which earned him a broken jaw. By the time the Stones came on stage matters were patently out of hand, and after several interruptions and pleas for sanity by Mick Jagger, all hell broke loose during, ironically, *Sympathy for the Devil*. Back in the studio during filming, Jagger, Richards, and company watch with numb looks as the glint of a knife signals the fatal stabbing.

Up and over the hills to the east near the town of Tracy, before I-580 joins I-5 for the four-hundred-mile route south through the Central Valley to Los Angeles, stands the still-functioning **Altamont Speedway**, officially known as the Altamont Raceway Park, site of the nightmarish Rolling Stones concert in December 1969 (see box, p.667). Needless to say, no historical plaque marks the site, yet if you wish to make the pilgrimage, the easiest way is by taking the Grant Line Road exit from I-580, then turning right after a mile or so onto Midway Road and continuing for a further mile and a half, crossing back over the freeway in the process.

East Bay eating

Official home of **California cuisine** and with some of the best restaurants in the state, Berkeley is an upmarket diner's paradise. But it's also a college town, and you can eat cheaply and well, especially around the southern end of the campus, along and around Telegraph Avenue. The rest of the East Bay is less remarkable, except when it comes to plain **American food** such as barbecued ribs, grilled steaks, or deli sandwiches, for which it's unbeatable.

Budget food: diners and delis

Adam's Burger 3401 Lakeshore Ave, North Oakland ☏510/834-5796. Cheap burgers, fries, and a few dishes like steak teriyaki in a simple down-home setting north of Lake Merritt.

Barney's 4162 Piedmont Ave, North Oakland ☏510/655-7180; 5819 College Ave, Rockridge ☏510/601-0444; and 1591 Solano Ave, Berkeley ☏510/526-8185. The East Bay's most popular burgers – including meatless ones – smothered in dozens of different toppings.

Bette's Ocean View Diner 1807 4th St, West Berkeley ☏510/644-3932. Named after the neighborhood, not after the vista, but serving up some of the Bay Area's best breakfasts and lunches. Very popular on weekends, when you may have to wait an hour for a table, so plan accordingly.

Genova Delicatessen 5095 Telegraph Ave, North Oakland ☏510/652-7401. Friendly deli, complete with hanging sausages, serves up superb sandwiches for around $5. Located in small off-road mall.

Holy Land 677 Rand Ave, North Oakland ☏510/272-0535. Casual diner-style kosher restaurant just beyond the freeway north of Lake Merritt, serving moderately priced Israeli food, including excellent falafel.

Homemade Café 2454 Sacramento St, Berkeley ☏510/845-1940. Non-traditional inexpensive California-style Mexican and Jewish food served for breakfast and lunch at shared tables when crowded.

Lois the Pie Queen 851 60th St at Adeline, North Oakland ☏510/658-5616. Famous around the

Bay for its Southern-style sweet potato and fresh fruit pies, this cozy diner also serves massive, down-home breakfasts and Sunday dinners, all for around $10 or less.

Rick & Ann's 2922 Domingo Ave, Berkeley ☏510/649-8538. Even in Berkeley sometimes folks want meatloaf and mashed potatoes instead of arugula, and to get their fill of both the crowds line up outside this neighborhood diner every weekend.

Saul's Deli 1475 Shattuck Ave, North Berkeley ☏510/848-3354. For pastrami, corned beef, kreplach, or knishes, this is the place. Great sandwiches and picnic fixings to take away, plus a full range of sit-down evening meals.

Top Dog 2534 Durant Ave, Berkeley ☏510/843-7450. OK, so the competition isn't exactly stiff, but when locals and starving college kids get a craving for the all-American treat, this dog always has its day.

Your Black Muslim Bakery 5836 San Pablo Ave, North Oakland ☏510/658-7080 and 365 17th St, Oakland ☏510/839-1313. Pastries and pamphlets bringing together Oakland's diverse denizens over some awesome sweet rolls.

American and California cuisine

Bay Wolf 3853 Piedmont Ave, North Oakland ☏510/655-6004. Comfortable restaurant serving grilled meat, fish dishes, and specialties such as duck-liver flan on an ever-changing, expensive menu.

Café Fanny 1603 San Pablo, West Berkeley ☏510/524-5447. Delicious and relatively cheap breakfasts and lunches (until 3pm, 4pm on Sat) in a small and unlikely space with a sparse industrial decor. Owned by Alice Waters of *Chez Panisse* fame (see below).

Café Rouge 1782 4th St, West Berkeley ☏510/525-1440. Located along a short cul-de-sac, their specialty is delicately prepared organic meats; they have their own butcher shop. Also serves vegetarian pasta dishes for the less carnivorous.

Chez Panisse 1517 Shattuck Ave, North Berkeley ☏510/548-5525. The California restaurant to which all others are compared, its chef Alice Waters is widely credited for inventing California cuisine. Expect to pay in excess of $100 for a meal for two with delights like Monterey Bay sardine toast with arugula and fennel, or Sonoma County duck with roasted butternut squash, beets, and tatsoi, plus wine.

Fatapple's 1346 Martin Luther King Jr Way, North Berkeley ☏510/526-2260. Crowded but pleasant family-oriented restaurant with excellent cheap American breakfasts and an assortment of sandwiches and burgers for lunch or dinner.

Grand Oaks Grill 736 Washington St, Oakland ☏510/452-1258. Moderately priced meat and seafood dishes, such as chicken marsala and calamari dore, cooked in a mixture of European and Asian sauces.

Lalime's 1329 Gilman St, North Berkeley ☏510/527-9838. A culinary dissertation on irony, as rich leftist Berkeley professors chow down on rich veal, pâté de foie gras, and other distinctly un-PC fare, in a casual setting. Expect to pay at least $40 per person.

Rivoli 1539 Solano Ave, North Berkeley ☏510/526-2542. Delivering all that is wonderful about Berkeley dining: first-rate fresh food based on Italian and French cuisine, courteous service, and a casual, friendly atmosphere. All followed by a steep bill: entrees are around $20.

Spenger's 1919 4th St, West Berkeley ☏510/845-7771. With a spacious sit-down restaurant and cheap takeout counter, this is a local institution. As one of the largest chains in the Bay Area, *Spenger's* serves up literally tons of simple, but well-cooked seafood dishes to thousands of customers daily.

Asian, African, and Indian

Ajanta 1888 Solano Ave, North Berkeley ☏510/526-4373. Pretty upmarket curry house featuring an interesting array of dishes, such as duck curry Kerala and Dhaniwal murg korma from different parts of India and Pakistan, not found in many other establishments.

Blue Nile 2525 Telegraph Ave, Berkeley ☏510/540-6777. Filling Ethiopian food, with an adequate range of meat and vegetarian choices all around $10, served with a smile amidst cosy African decor.

Breads of India 2448 Sacramento St, Berkeley ☏510/848-7648. This gourmet curry house turns out delicious fresh daily specials for under $10.

Cha Am 1543 Shattuck Ave, North Berkeley ☏510/848-9664. Climb the stairs up to this unlikely, always crowded small restaurant for deliciously spicy Thai food at moderate prices.

Jade Villa 800 Broadway, Oakland ☏510/839-1688. For endless dim sum lunches or traditional Cantonese meals, this is one of the best places in Oakland's Chinatown.

Kirala 2100 Ward St, Berkeley ☏510/549-3486. Many argue that *Kirala* serves the best sushi in the Bay Area; others argue that it's simply the best in the world. Moderate pricing, too – expect to pay $15–20 to get your fill.

Le Cheval 1007 Clay St, Oakland ☏510/763-8495. Serving exquisite Vietnamese the way it was meant to be in ample portions; the chic, spacious surroundings and moderate prices here won't let you down either.

Liu's Kitchen 1593 Solano Ave, North Berkeley ☏510/525-8766. Huge helpings of tasty Chinese fare at very reasonable prices – the filling pot stickers (meat-filled dumplings) are a meal in themselves.

Long Life Vegi House 2129 University Ave, Berkeley ☏510/845-6072. Cheap vegetarian cooking (no surprises there) that's perpetually popular with Cal students, although the dishes' good value often exceeds their quality.

Naan'n'Curry 2366 Telegraph Avenue, Berkeley ☏510/841-6226. Brightly decorated canteen serving a cross-section of curries and biryanis at low prices – help yourself to the free Indian-style tea after placing your order at the counter. A newer branch is located at 2986 College Ave (☏510/841-1668).

Nan Yang 6048 College Ave, Rockridge ☏510/655-3298. Burmese food served in colorful, large, palate-exciting portions. The political refugee owner/chef is willing to discuss all his esoteric delicacies.

O'Chamé 1830 4th St, West Berkeley ☏510/841-8783. One of the very best Japanese restaurants in the US, with beautifully prepared sashimi and sushi as well as a full range of authentic Japanese specialties. A treat, in the $15–25 range.

Sala Thai 807 1st St, Benicia ☏707/745-4331. Small-town, moderately priced Thai food can be just as delicious here as in any big city. Check out the enormous fish tank as your feet dangle in foot caves under the tables.

Steve's Barbeque in the Durant Center, 2521 Durant Ave, Berkeley ⊕510/848-6166. Excellent, low-priced Korean food (*kimchee* to die for); other cafés in the center sell Mexican food, healthy sandwiches, deep-fried donuts, and slices of pizza – not to mention bargain pitchers of beer.

Vik's Chaat Corner 726 Allston Way at 4th St, West Berkeley ⊕510/644-4412. A terrific lunchtime destination offering a wide array of Indian snacks – expect long queues at weekends. The ambience is minimal, leaving nothing to distract you from the delights of *masala dosa* or *bhel puri*. Open until 6pm.

Italian

Angelina's 485 E 14th St, San Leandro ⊕510/586-8646. Actually owned by a Greek, this friendly place serves up delicious pizza you can wash down with half-yards of ale. Not far from the airport or zoo.

Café Rustica 5422 College Ave, Rockridge ⊕510/654-1601. Intimate adobe-style, upscale eatery for designer pizza with a pesto and sun-dried tomatoes motif. If it's too expensive, try the tapas bar upstairs.

Cheese Board Pizza 1512 Shattuck Ave, North Berkeley ⊕510/549-3055. Tiny storefront selling some of the world's best and most unique pizza at very reasonable prices: $2.50 a slice, with a different topping every day. Well worth searching out, but keeps irregular hours: usually Tues–Sat 11.30am–2pm & 4.30–7pm.

Garibaldi's on College 5356 College Ave, Rockridge ⊕510/595-4000. Quality upmarket Italian with delicious pasta dishes and an emphasis on fine wines. Some of the sauces have a spicy Arabic and Middle Eastern element.

LaVal's Pizza 1834 Euclid Ave, Berkeley ⊕510/843-5617. Lively graduate-student hangout near the North Gate of campus. Pool table, widescreen TV broadcasting sports, wide selection of microbrewed beers, and great pizza. Lunch specials often a feature.

Locanda Olmo 2985 College Ave, Berkeley ⊕510/848-5544. Simple but discriminating menu at this tiny, intimate *trattoria* in the charming Elmwood neighborhood with not too outrageous prices – main courses run $15–20.

Oliveto 5655 College Ave, Rockridge ⊕510/547-5356. Chef Paul Bertolli creates appetizing gourmet Italian cuisine by using creative recipes and home-grown ingredients. The main dining room is very expensive but there's a less pricey basement section with more stolid fare on offer.

Zachary's 5801 College Ave, Rockridge ⊕510/655-6385 and 1853 Solano Ave, North Berkeley ⊕510/525-5950. Zealously defended as the best pizza in the Bay Area, *Zachary's* is also one of the only places offering the rich, deep-dish Chicago-style pizza.

Latin American and Caribbean

Café de la Paz 1600 Shattuck Ave, North Berkeley ⊕510/843-0662. Authentic versions of cuisine from throughout South America, especially Brazil, can be found in this large, attractive restaurant. Reasonable prices for such style appeal to the new-agey and leftist clientele.

Cancun Taqueria 2134 Allston Way, Berkeley ⊕510/549-0964. Popular and cheap downtown burrito joint. Self-service but huge portions of tasty food in lively and colorful surroundings.

Juan's Place 941 Carleton St, West Berkeley ⊕510/845-6904. One of Berkeley's oldest Mexican restaurants, serving heaps of great food to an interesting mix of people at moderate prices – meat dishes cost around $10.

La Furia Chalaca 310 Broadway, Oakland ⊕510/451-4206. Impressive range of seafood with pasta and various Peruvian sauces, as well as some meat dishes like the excellent braised pork.

Los Caporales 4481 E 14th St, East Oakland ⊕510/434-9017. Worth the long trip from downtown for the excellent burritos and other authentic dishes. Bar attached if you fancy a drink or game of pool while here.

Mario's La Fiesta 2444 Telegraph Ave, Berkeley ⊕510/486-0151. Always crowded with students and other budget-minded souls who flock here for the heaped portions of good, inexpensive Mexican food.

Picante 1328 6th St, West Berkeley ⊕510/525-3121. Fine and very reasonably priced tacos with fresh salsa, plus live jazz on weekends. Nicely decorated with an outdoor patio for fine weather.

Tijuana Restaurant 1308 E 14th St, East Oakland ⊕510/532-5575. Excellent and authentic Mexican food; famed for its *mariscada* – a plate piled high with garlicky seafood and fresh vegetables.

Tropix 3814 Piedmont Ave, North Oakland ⊕510/653-2444. Large portions of fruity Caribbean delicacies at reasonable prices, with authentic jerk sauce and thirst-quenching mango juice.

French and Spanish

Britt-Marie's Cafe and Wine Bar 1369 Solano Ave, Albany ⊕510/527-1314. Along with a fine selection of mostly Californian wines by the glass, well-priced eclectic home cooking, plus outstanding chocolate cake, is also served.

César 1515 Shattuck Ave, North Berkeley ☎510/883-0222. Perpetually crowded tapas bar serving small portions overflowing with taste. Loosely affiliated with *Chez Panisse*, the combination of quality and a relaxed atmosphere has made it a cultish destination for locals, though be mindful of the diminutive dishes which can add up. Gets expensive if you order too many.

Citron 5484 College Ave, Rockridge ☎510/653-5484. Neighborhood gem of a bistro that rivals San Francisco's best restaurants. Warm, unpretentious service and exquisite French-influenced food, but expensive.

La Note 2377 Shattuck Ave, Berkeley ☎510/843-1535. The appropriately sunny, light cuisine of Provence isn't the only flavor you'll find in this petite dining room: students and teachers from the Jazzschool (sic) next door routinely stop in for casual jam sessions.

Ice cream and desserts

Dreyers Grand Ice Cream Parlor 5925 College Ave, Rockridge ☎510/658-0502. Oakland's own rich ice cream, which is distributed throughout California, is served at this small, slightly dull Rockridge café.

Fenton's Creamery 4226 Piedmont Ave, North Oakland ☎510/658-7000. A brightly lit 1950s ice-cream and sandwich shop, open until 11pm on weeknights, midnight on weekends.

Yogurt Park 2433a Durant Ave, Berkeley ☎510/549-0570. Frozen yogurt is the specialty here; open until midnight for the student throngs.

Specialty shops and markets

Acme Bread 1601 San Pablo Ave, West Berkeley ☎510/524-1327. Small bakery that supplies most of Berkeley's better restaurants; the house specialty is delicious sourdough baguettes.

Berkeley Bowl 2777 Shattuck Ave, Berkeley ☎510/841-6346. A converted bowling alley now an enormous produce, bulk, and health-food market. The least expensive grocery in town, with the largest selection of fresh food.

Cheese Board 1504 Shattuck Ave, North Berkeley ☎510/549-3183. Collectively owned and operated since 1967, this was one of the first outposts in Berkeley's Gourmet Ghetto and is still going strong, offering over 200 varieties of cheese and a range of delicious breads. Great pizzas a few doors down, too; see opposite.

La Farine 6323 College Ave, Rockridge ☎510/654-0338. Small but extremely popular French-style bakery, with excellent *pain au chocolat*.

Monterey Foods 1550 Hopkins St, North Berkeley ☎510/526-6042. The main supplier of exotic produce to Berkeley's gourmet restaurants, this boisterous market also has the highest quality fresh fruit and vegetables available.

East Bay cafés and bars

One of the best things about visiting the East Bay is the opportunity to enjoy its many **cafés**. Concentrated most densely around the UC Berkeley campus, they're on a par with the best of San Francisco's North Beach for bohemian atmosphere – heady with the smell of coffee, and from dawn to near midnight full of earnest characters wearing their intellects on their sleeves. If you're not after a caffeine fix, you can generally also get a glass of beer, wine, or fresh fruit juice, though for serious drinking you'll be better off in one of the many **bars**, particularly in rough-hewn Oakland. Grittier versions of what you'd find in San Francisco, they're mostly blue-collar, convivial, and almost always cheaper. Not surprisingly, Berkeley's bars are brimming with students and academics.

Cafés and coffeehouses

Brewed Awakenings 1807 Euclid Ave, North Berkeley ☎510/540-8865. Spacious coffee- and teahouse near the North Gate of campus frequented by professors and grad students. Friendly staff, plenty of seating, and lovely artwork on the redbrick walls serve to explain how this is annually rated as the "Best Café to Study In" by the student press.

Café Intermezzo 2442 Telegraph Ave, Berkeley ☎510/849-4592. Huge sandwiches on homemade sliced bread, even bigger salads, and great coffee – all very fresh and cheap.

Café Mediterraneum 2475 Telegraph Ave, Berkeley ☎510/841-5634. Berkeley's oldest café featuring sidewalk seating. Straight out of the Beat archives: beards and berets optional, battered paperbacks de rigueur.

Café Milano 2522 Bancroft Ave, Berkeley
℡510/644-3100. Airy and artsy coffeehouse
directly across the way from the south side of
campus.

Café Strada 2300 College Ave, Berkeley
℡510/843-5282. Upmarket, open-air café where
art and architecture students cross paths with
would-be lawyers and chess wizards.

Coffee Mill 3363 Grand Ave, North Oakland
℡510/465-4224. Spacious room that doubles as
an art gallery, and often hosts poetry readings.

Royal 6255 College Ave, Rockridge ℡510/653-
5458. Bright, modern, and relaxing spot in the
Rockridge area, with outdoor seating. Perfect for a
leisurely afternoon with the newspaper.

Bars

Albatross Pub 1822 San Pablo Ave, West Berkeley
℡510/843-2473. Popular student super-bar, replete
with darts, pool, board games, and fireplace. Serves
a large selection of ales from around the world,
including a pretty good pint of Guinness. Live jazz,
flamenco, and blues music on weekends (free–$5).

Ben'n'Nick's 5612 College Ave, Rockridge
℡510/933-0327. Lively bar with good taped rock
music and tasty food, if you're hungry.

Cato's Alehouse 3891 Piedmont, North Oakland
℡510/655-3349. Very local and casual alehouse
with a decent beer selection. Relax with a couple
of beers and a pizza or sandwich.

Heinold's First and Last Chance Saloon 56
Jack London Square, Oakland ℡510/839-6761.
Authentic waterfront bar that's hardly changed
since the turn of the century, when Jack London
was a regular. They still haven't bothered to fix the
slanted floor caused by the 1906 earthquake.

Jupiter 2181 Shattuck Ave, Berkeley ℡510/843-
8277. Many types of lager, ale, and cider to select
from at this local favorite, which offers wood-fired
pizza and an outdoor beer garden. There's a real
buzz here, especially for the loud disco nights or
live jazz at weekends.

Pacific Coast Brewing Co 906 Washington
St, Oakland ℡510/836-2739. Oaktown's only
real microbrewery, which conjures up a range of
decent brews and offers quite an extensive menu
too. Attracts downtown office workers as well as a
younger crowd later on.

Pub (Schmidt's Tobacco & Trading Co) 1492
Solano Ave, Albany ℡510/525-1900. Just past the
official Berkeley limit, this small, relaxed bar lures
a mixture of bookworms and game players with a
good selection of beers. They even get away with
a semi-open smoking area out back, perhaps 'cos
their other specialty is selling the evil weed.

Pyramid Alehouse 901 Gilman St, West Berkeley
℡510/528-9880. Huge post-industrial space
makes a surprisingly casual spot to sip the suds.
Outdoor film screenings on weekend nights during
summer.

Rickey's Sports Lounge 15028 Hesperian Blvd,
San Leandro, near Bayfair BART ℡510/352-0200.
With seven giant-screen TVs and 35 others spread
around the cavernous room, this bar-cum-restaurant in a working suburb is the place to go to
watch sports.

Triple Rock Brewery 1920 Shattuck Ave, Berkeley ℡510/843-2739. Buzzing, all-American
microbrewery with decent food: the decor is
Edward Hopper–era retro, and the beers (brewed
on the premises) are a bit fizzy unless you ask for
one of the fine cask-conditioned ales at the end
of the bar.

Warehouse Café 5 Canyon Lake Drive, Porta
Costa ℡510/787-1827. Huge converted warehouse beside the water that is the prime nightspot
for this side of the Carquinez Straits. Odd decor
of Wild West elements and maps of English counties. Cheap snacks at the bar or a pricier sit-down
menu.

The White Horse 6560 Telegraph Ave at 66th St,
Oakland ℡510/652-3820. Oakland's oldest gay
bar – a smallish, friendly place, with mixed nightly
dancing for men and women.

East Bay nightlife

Nightlife is where the East Bay really comes into its own. Traditionally, dancing to canned music and paying high prices for flashy decor is not the thing
to do, although more venues have at least one dance/trance night these days,
often Thursday. On the other hand, there are still dozens of **live music** venues,
covering a range of musical tastes and styles – from small, unpretentious jazz
clubs to buzzing R&B venues – of which Oakland's hot spots are unsurpassed.
Berkeley's clubs tend more towards folk and world music, with other places
dedicated to underground rock, and the university itself holds two of the best
medium-sized venues in the entire Bay Area, both of which attract touring
big-name stars. **Tickets** for most venues are available at their box office or, for
a service charge, through BASS (℡510/762-2277).

Though not bad by US standards, the East Bay **theater** scene isn't exactly thriving, and shows tend to be politically worthy rather than dramatically innovative. By contrast, the range of **films** is first-class, with over a dozen movie theaters showing new releases and Berkeley's revamped Pacific Film Archive, one of the world's finest film libraries, filling its screens with obscure but brilliant art flicks. Check the free *East Bay Express* (ⓦwww.eastbayexpress.com) or the *SF Weekly* (ⓦwww.sfweekly.com) for details of who and what's on.

The large performance venues

Berkeley Community Theater 1930 Allston Way, Berkeley ⓣ510/845-2308. Jimi Hendrix played here, and the 3500-seat theater still hosts major rock concerts (Oasis to Joni Mitchell) and community events.

Center for Contemporary Music Mills College, 5000 MacArthur Blvd, Oakland ⓣ510/430-2191. One of the prime centers in the world for experimental music.

Oakland Coliseum Complex Coliseum BART, near the airport ⓣ510/639-7700, ⓦwww .oaklandcoliseum.com. Mostly stadium shows, inside the 18,000-seat arena or outdoors in the adjacent 55,000-seat coliseum. Used to be a favourite gig of the Grateful Dead's.

Paramount Theater 2025 Broadway, downtown Oakland ⓣ510/465-6400, ⓦwww .paramounttheater.com. Beautifully restored Art Deco masterpiece, hosting classical concerts, big-name crooners, ballets, operas, and a growing roster of rap and rock shows. Tickets $10–50. Some nights they play old Hollywood classics for $7.

Zellerbach Hall and the outdoor **Greek Theatre** on the UC Berkeley campus ⓣ510/642-9988, ⓦwww.calperfs.berkeley.edu. Two of the prime spots for catching touring big names in the Bay Area. Zellerbach showcases drama, classical music, and dance, while the Greek welcomes popular acts like the Indigo Girls or Ben Harper. Tickets $20–50.

Live-music venues

The Alley 3325 Grand Ave, North Oakland ⓣ510/444-8505. Ramshackle black-timber piano bar, decorated with business cards and with live old-time blues merchants on the keyboards. No cover.

Ashkenaz 1317 San Pablo Ave, West Berkeley ⓣ510/525-5054, ⓦwww.ashkenaz.com. World-music and dance café. Acts range from modern Afro-beat to the best of the Balkans. Kids and under-21s welcome. Cover $5–10.

Blakes 2367 Telegraph Ave, Berkeley ⓣ510/848-0886, ⓦwww.blakesontelegraph.com. Student-patroned saloon with a funky roster of live music most nights of the week. Latin, funk, soul, hip-hop, roots, rock, reggae, blues, and more. $3–8.

Freight and Salvage 1111 Addison St, West Berkeley ⓣ510/548-1761, ⓦwww.freightandsalvage .org. Singer-songwriters in a coffeehouse setting. Cover averages $15.

Gilman 924 Gilman St, West Berkeley ⓣ510/525-9926, ⓦwww.924gilman.org. Part social project, part outer edge of the hard-core punk scene in a bare, squat-like old warehouse. Weekends only; cover $5–10.

Jimmie's 1731 San Pablo Ave, Oakland ⓣ510/268-8445. Live blues, disco, ballads, and the occasional comedy act and fashion show at this lively bar. $5–30.

Kimball's East 4800 Shellmound St, Emeryville ⓣ510/658-2555, ⓦwww.kimballs.com. Fairly slick, high-style jazz, soul, and dancing venue. Cover $15–30.

La Peña Cultural Center 3105 Shattuck Ave, Berkeley, near Ashby BART ⓣ510/849-2568, ⓦwww.lapena.org. More folk than rock, and some Latin, often politically charged – the website encourages cultural activism for social change. $10–25.

Maiko Dance Club 1629 San Pablo Ave, Berkeley ⓣ510/527-8226, ⓦwww.411.salsafrenzy.com/ maiko's. Salsa and ballroom dance set to a live band in very chic environs. Lessons available for around $20. $12–25.

Mile High Club 3629 Martin Luther King Jr Way, North Oakland ⓣ510/655-6661. The best of the Bay Area blues clubs. Waitresses balance pitchers of beer on their heads to facilitate a safer passage through the rocking crowds. Cover $7–20.

Starry Plough 3101 Shattuck Ave, Berkeley, near Ashby BART ⓣ510/841-2082, ⓦwww .starryploughpub.com. Music ranges from noisy punk to alternative pop to country to traditional Irish folk, and the crowd is just as varied. Doubles as a friendly saloon and restaurant in the afternoon and early evening. Free to $5.

Yoshi's World Class Jazz House 510 Embarcadero West, Oakland ⓣ510/238-9200, ⓦwww .yoshis.com. If you only have time or money to visit one music venue, let it be this one. The

West Coast's premier jazz club near Jack London Square regularly attracts an impressive roster of performers nightly. The place is almost always full. $10–50.

Cinemas

Act One and Act Two 2128 Center St, Berkeley ☎510/548-7200. Foreign films and non-mainstream American ones.

Grand Lake Movie Theater 3200 Grand Ave, Oakland ☎510/452-3556. The grand dame of East Bay picture palaces, just above Lake Merritt, showing the best of the current major releases, with special emphasis on politically alternative works.

Oaks Theater 1875 Solano Ave, Berkeley ☎510/526-1836, ⊛www.renaissancerialto.com/current/oaks. A mixture of mainstream and political fims are shown at this cozy renovated Art Deco cinema, built in 1925.

Pacific Film Archive 2575 Bancroft at Bowditch St, Berkeley ☎510/642-5249, ⊛www.bampfa.berkeley.edu. The archive's splendid new digs plays the West Coast's best selection of cinema. It features nightly showings of classics, Third World, and experimental films, plus revivals of otherwise forgotten favorites. Call for listings or pick up a free monthly calendar around campus. Two films a night; tickets $7.

UC Theater 2036 University Ave, Berkeley ☎510/843-6267. Popular revival house, with a huge auditorium and a daily double-feature show-casing funky theme-weeks of noir, melodrama, and other genres. Tickets $5 matinee, $7 thereafter.

Theater

Berkeley Repertory Theater 2025 Addison St, Berkeley ☎510/845-4700, ⊛www.berkeleyrep.org. One of the West Coast's most highly respected theater companies, presenting updated classics and contemporary plays in an intimate modern theater. Tickets $10–30.

Black Repertory Group 3201 Adeline St, Berkeley ☎510/652-2120. After years of struggling, this politically conscious company moved into its own specially built home near Ashby BART in 1987, since when they've encouraged new talent with great success. Tickets $10–30.

California Shakespeare Festival Siesta Valley, Orinda ☎510/548-3422, ⊛www.calshakes.org. After fifteen seasons in a North Berkeley park, this summer-long outdoor festival was forced to move to a larger home in the East Bay Hills. Tickets $20–50.

Julia Morgan Center for the Arts 2640 College Ave, Berkeley ☎510/84-JULIA, ⊛www.juliamorgan.org. A variety of touring shows stop off in this cunningly converted old church. Tickets $10–30.

The Peninsula

The city of San Francisco sits at the tip of a five-mile-wide neck of land commonly referred to as the **Peninsula**. Home to old money and new technology, the Peninsula stretches for fifty miles of relentless suburbia south from San Francisco along the Bay, past the wealthy enclaves of Hillsborough and Atherton, winding up in the futuristic roadside landscape of the **"Silicon Valley"** near **San Jose**, the fastest-growing city in California and now eleventh-largest in the USA.

There was a time when the region was largely agricultural, but the computer boom – spurred by Stanford University in **Palo Alto** – has replaced orange groves and fig trees with office complexes and parking lots. Surprisingly, however, most of the land along the **coast** – separated from the bayfront sprawl by a spur of redwood-covered ridges – remains rural and largely undeveloped; it also contains some excellent **beaches** and a couple of affably down-to-earth communities, all well-served by public transportation.

Information

The **Palo Alto Chamber of Commerce**, 122 Hamilton Ave (Mon–Fri 9am–5pm; ☎650/324-3121, ⊛www.paloaltochamber.com), has lists of local restaurants and cycle routes; for information on Stanford University, contact its visitor center (Mon–Fri 8am–5pm, Sat & Sun 9am–5pm; ☎650/723-2560,

8

@www.stanford.edu) in the Memorial Auditorium opposite Hoover Tow
get a copy of the free *Stanford Daily*, published weekdays. To find out w
on in the area and where, pick up a free copy of the *Palo Alto Weekly*, availa
at most local shops or log onto the paper's @www.paloaltoonline.com, a wel
organized, rich databank of everything from local bike shops and restaurants
to history and movie times.

At the southern end of the Bay, the **San Jose Visitor Center** is at 125 S
Market St (Mon–Fri 8am–5pm, Sat & Sun 11am–5pm; ☏408/295-9600 or
1-888/726-5673, @www.sanjose.org), or you can call in at their new **V.I.B.C.**,
on the ground floor of the Convention Center at 150 W San Carlos St (same
hours; ☏408/977-0900); both locations are more geared towards helping visiting businesspeople than the casual traveler though. For a better idea of local
news and events pick up a copy of the excellent *San Jose Mercury* daily newspaper (@www.mercurynews.com) or the free weekly *Metro* (@www.metroactive
.com), although the latter usually lists as many events for San Francisco as it
does for the South Bay. The website @www.siliconvalley.citysearch.com also
holds a treasure of reviews and features on the area.

Along the coast, **Pacifica's Chamber of Commerce**, 225 Rockaway Beach
Ave (Mon–Fri 9am–5pm, Sat & Sun 10am–4.30pm; ☏650/355-4122, @www
.pacificachamber.com), is the nearest to San Francisco on the Peninsula. Further south, the **Half Moon Bay Chamber of Commerce**, at 520 Kelly Ave
(Mon–Fri 9am–4pm; ☏650/726-8380, @www.hmbchamber.org), gives out
walking-tour maps and information on accommodation. There is also a small
kiosk under the clocktower at the corner of Kelly Avenue and Main Street that
opens at weekends (Sat & Sun 10am–3pm).

Getting around

BART only travels down the Peninsula as far as Daly City, from where you
can catch SamTrans (☏1-800/660-4287, @www.samtrans.com) **buses** south
to Palo Alto or along the coast to Half Moon Bay. For longer distances, **Caltrain** (☏650/817-1717 or 1-800/660-4287, @www.caltrain.com) offers a rail
service at least every half-hour from its terminal at Fourth and King streets
in downtown San Francisco, stopping at most bayside towns between the city
and Gilroy via San Jose ($1.75–6.75); Greyhound runs regular buses along
US-101 to and from their San Jose terminal at 70 S Almaden, on the corner of
Santa Clara Street. Santa Clara Valley Transit Authority (VTA) ($1.50, day-pass
$4.50; ☏408/321-2300, @www.vta.org) runs buses and modern trolleys around
metropolitan San Jose. If you're going to be spending most of your time there,
most major domestic airlines fly direct into the recently renamed **Norman
J. Mineta San Jose International Airport** (☏408/501-7600, @www.sjc
.org), very close to downtown San Jose; the VTA SJC Airport Flyer bus runs
to downtown San Jose and Santa Clara for $3 and there is the usual choice of
taxis, limos, and shuttles for fancier rides to your destination.

Accommodation

Many visitors to San Francisco choose to stay on the Peninsula rather than in
the city. Dozens of $60-a-night motels line Hwy-82 – "El Camino Real," the
old main highway – and, with a bit of advanced planning (and a car), sleeping
here can save a lot of money. Also, if you're arriving late or departing on an
early flight from SFO you might want to avail yourself of one of the many airport hotels. Perhaps the best reasons to spend the night down on the Peninsula

low–priced, pleasant **hostels**, two of which are housed in old lighthouses along the Pacific Coast. San Jose's **hotels** are largely overpriced during week, catering more to the conventioneering corporate world than the urist or traveler, though it's possible to find decent deals at weekends.

Hotels and motels

Bay Landing Hotel 1550 Bayshore Highway, Burlingame ⊤650/259-9000, ⓦwww.baylandinghotel.com. One of the best options at the north of the peninsula with views of the Bay and planes taking off from SFO. Refreshingly, it's a family owned place with quality rooms and service. ❸

Cardinal Hotel 235 Hamilton Ave, Palo Alto ⊤650/323-5101, ⓦwww.cardinalhotel.com. Affordable rates and comfortable rooms in the heart of downtown Palo Alto. The cheaper rooms have shared bathrooms. ❸

Craig Hotel 164 Hamilton Ave, Palo Alto ⊤650/853-1133. Dumpy and threadbare, but right downtown and dirt cheap. Weekly rates work out around $30 a night. ❷

Fairmont Hotel 170 S Market St, San Jose ⊤408/998-1900 or 1-800/441-1414, ⓦwww.fairmont.com. San Jose's finest hotel and part of the luxury chain which began in San Francisco is located in the heart of downtown, on the Plaza. All the expected amenities, such as room service, swimming pool, lounge, and sparkling rooms. ❺

Hotel De Anza 233 W Santa Clara St, San Jose ⊤408/286-0500 or 1-800/843-3700, ⓦwww.hoteldeanza.com. Plush business and conference orientated hotel with full amenities in one of the livelier sections of town. Look out for special weekend packages. ❺

Howard Johnson Express 1215 S 1st St, San Jose ⊤408/280-5300 or 1-800/509-7666, ⓦwww.hojo.com. Adequate if characterless rooms downtown near the main nightspots in the city. ❸

Pacifica Motor Inn 200 Rockaway Beach Ave, Pacifica ⊤650/359-7700 or 1-800/522-3772, ⓦwww.pacificamotorinn.com. Large rooms just a block off the beach in a hamlet alongside Hwy-1. ❸

Ramada Inn 455 S 2nd St, San Jose ⊤408/298-3500 or 1-888/298-2054, ⓦwww.ramada.com. Right in downtown San Jose, with pool and sauna and comfortable, but characterless rooms. ❹

Sea Breeze Motel 100 Rockaway Beach Ave, Pacifica ⊤650/359-3903, ⓦwww.nicksrestaurant.net. Beachfront hotel with attached restaurant, *Nick's*. Rooms are well kept, but standard motel style. ❹

Stanford Park Hotel 100 El Camino Real, Menlo Park ⊤650/322-1234 or 1-800/368-2468, ⓦwww.stanfordparkhotel.com. Very pleasant and luxurious five-star hotel in extensive grounds near Stanford University. ❼

Valley Inn 2155 The Alameda, San Jose ⊤408/241-8500, ⓦwww.valleyinnsanjose.com. Above-average motel not far from the Rosicrucian Museum with special online rates. ❸

Bed and breakfasts

Cowper Inn 705 Cowper St, Palo Alto ⊤650/327-4475, ⓔcowper-inn@sbcglobal.com. Restored Victorian house with pleasant parlor and attractive rooms close to University Avenue. The cheaper rooms have shared baths. ❹

Old Thyme Inn 779 Main St, Half Moon Bay ⊤650/726-1616 or 1-800/720-4277, ⓦwww.oldthymeinn.com. Half a dozen incredibly quaint rooms, each with a private bath, in a lovely Victorian house surrounded by luxuriant herb and flower gardens. ❻

San Benito House 356 Main St, Half Moon Bay ⊤650/726-3425, ⓦwww.sanbenitohouse.com. Twelve restful B&B rooms in a hundred-year-old building, just a mile from the beach. Excellent restaurant downstairs. ❹

Hostels

HI-Pigeon Point Lighthouse Hwy-1, just south of Pescadero ⊤650/879-0633, ⓦwww.norcalhostels.org. Worth planning a trip around, this beautifully situated hostel, fifty miles south of San Francisco, is ideally placed for exploring the redwood forests in the hills above or for watching the wildlife in nearby Año Nuevo State Reserve. Outdoor hot tub. Office hours 7.30–10am & 5.30–10pm; check-in from 4.30pm, doors locked at 11pm. Members $18 per night, non-members $21; reservations essential in summer. Private rooms $48–55, minimum two people.

HI-Point Montara Lighthouse 16th St/Hwy-1, Montara ⊤650/728-7177, ⓦwww.norcalhostels.org. Dorm rooms in a converted 1875 lighthouse, 25 miles south of San Francisco and accessible by bike or SamTrans bus #1L or #1C (Mon–Fri until 5.50pm, Sat until 6.15pm). Outdoor hot tub. Office hours 7.30–10am & 4.30–9.30pm; doors locked 11pm. Members $18 per night, non-members $21; reservations essential in summer.

Hidden Villa 26807 Moody Rd, Los Altos Hills ⊤650/949-8650, ⓦwww.hiddenvilla.org.

Located on an 1800-acre ranch in the foothills above Silicon Valley with plenty of wilderness trails; closed June–Aug for eco summer camp; members $17 per night, non-members $20. Private cabins $35–50.
Sanborn Park Hostel 15808 Sanborn Rd, Saratoga ☎408/741-0166 ⓦwww .sanbornparkhostel.org. Comfortable rooms in a beautiful wooded area fifteen minutes southwest of San Jose. Call from downtown Saratoga and they will arrange to pick you up. Open 7–9am &

5–11pm (curfew); members $14 per night, non-members $16.

Campgrounds
Butano State Park Pescadero ☎650/879-2040. RV and tent spaces in a beautiful redwood forest; reserve through ReserveAmerica ☎1-800/444-7275; $20, $15 in winter.
Half Moon Bay State Beach Half Moon Bay ☎650/726-8820. Tent sites in the woods behind the beach for $20.

South along the Bay

US-101 runs south from San Francisco along the Bay through over fifty miles of unmitigated sprawl lined by light-industrial estates and shopping malls to San Jose. One place along the freeway in **San Mateo** worth a visit is the **Coyote Point Museum**, 1651 Coyote Point Drive (Tues–Sat 10am–5pm, Sun noon–5pm; $6; ☎650/342-7755, ⓦwww.coyoteptmuseum.org), four miles south of the airport off Poplar Avenue. Situated in a large bayfront park, the museum showcases examples of the natural life of the San Francisco Bay, from tidal insects to birds of prey, which are exhibited in engaging and informative displays, enhanced by interactive computers and documentary films.

Six-lane freeways don't usually qualify as a scenic route, but an exception is **I-280**, one of the newest and most expensive freeways in California. It runs parallel to US-101 but avoids the worst of the bayside mess by cutting through wooded valleys down the center of the Peninsula. Just beyond the San Francisco city limits the road passes through **Colma**, a unique place filled with cemeteries, which, other than the military burial grounds in the presidio, are prohibited within San Francisco. Besides the expected roll call of deceased San Francisco luminaries like Levi Strauss and William Hearst, are a few surprises, such as Wild West gunman Wyatt Earp. If you're interested, contact the Colma Historical Association (☎650/757-1676) for free graveyard tour information.

Beyond Colma, the scenery improves quickly as I-280 continues past the **Crystal Springs Reservoir**, an artificial lake that holds the water supply for San Francisco – pumped here all the way from Yosemite. Surrounded by twenty square miles of parkland, hiking trails lead up to the ridge from which San Francisco Bay was first spotted by eighteenth-century Spanish explorers; it now overlooks the airport to the east, but there are good views out over the Pacific Coast, two miles distant.

At the south end of the reservoir, just off I-280 on Canada Road near the well-heeled town of **Woodside**, luscious gardens surround the palatial **Filoli Estate** (mid-Feb–late Oct Tues–Sat 10am–3.30pm, last admission 2.30pm; tours by reservation only; $10; ☎650/364-8300 ext 507, ⓦwww.filoli.org). The 45-room mansion, designed in 1915 in neo-Palladian style by architect Willis Polk, may look familiar – it was used in the TV series *Dynasty* as the Denver home of the Carrington clan. It's the only one of the many huge houses around here that you can visit, although the gardens are what make it worth coming, especially in the spring when everything's in bloom.

Palo Alto and Stanford University

Palo Alto, just south and three miles east of Woodside between I-280 and US-101, is a small, leafy community, and despite its proximity to Stanford, retains little of the college-town vigor of its northern rival, Berkeley. In recent years, Palo Alto has become somewhat of a social center for Silicon Valley's nouveau riche, as evidenced by the trendy cafés and chic new restaurants that have popped up along its main drag, **University Avenue**. The computer industry boom job market made more than a few people rich, and this is where many of them came to spend their cash; small houses in the quaint neighborhoods surrounding the downtown area can cost close to a million dollars.

The town doesn't have a lot to offer in terms of sights other than Spanish Colonial homes, but it's a great place for a lazy stroll and a gourmet meal. Monthly historic tours of Palo Alto's neighborhoods take place during summer (☎650/299-8878), otherwise the best of the city's designs can be seen along **Ramona Street**. If you're feeling particularly energetic, or are tired of browsing in overpriced designer furniture stores, try cycling around the town's many well-marked bike routes; bikes are available for $20–30 a day from Action Sports Limited at 1047 El Camino Real (☎650/328-3180). Be aware, however, that **East Palo Alto**, on the Bay side of US-101, has a well-deserved reputation for gang- and drug-related violence, with one of the highest per capita murder rates of any US city. The area was founded in the 1920s as the utopian Runnymeade Colony, an agricultural, poultry-raising co-operative, and the local preservation society (☎650/329-0294) can point out the surviving sites. East Palo Alto, where Grateful Dead guitarist Jerry Garcia grew up, is about as far as you can get off the San Francisco tourist trail.

Stanford University, spreading out from the west end of University Avenue, is by contrast one of the tamest places you could hope for. The university is among the top – and most expensive – in the US, though when it opened in 1891, founded by railroad magnate Leland Stanford in memory of his dead son, it offered free tuition. Ridiculed by East Coast academics, who felt that there was as much need for a second West Coast university (after UC Berkeley) as there was for "an asylum for decayed sea captains in Switzerland," Stanford was defiantly built anyway, in a hybrid of Mission and Romanesque buildings on a huge arid campus that covers an area larger than the whole of downtown San Francisco.

Stanford, whose reputation as an arch-conservative think-tank was enhanced by Ronald Reagan's offer to donate his video library to the school (though Stanford politely declined), hasn't always been an entirely boring place, though you wouldn't know it to walk among the preppy future-lawyers-of-America that seem to comprise the majority of the student body. Ken Kesey came here from Oregon in 1958 on a writing fellowship, working nights as an orderly on the psychiatric ward of one local hospital, and getting paid $75 a day to test experimental drugs (LSD among them) in another. Drawing on both experiences, Kesey wrote *One Flew over the Cuckoo's Nest* in 1960 and quickly became a counterculture hero. The period is admirably chronicled by Tom Wolfe in *The Electric Kool-aid Acid Test*.

Approaching from the Palo Alto Caltrain and SamTrans bus station, which acts as a buffer between the town and the university, you enter the campus via a half-mile-long, palm-tree-lined boulevard which deposits you at its heart, the **Quadrangle**, bordered by the phallic **Hoover Tower**, whose observation platform (daily 10am–4.30pm; $2) is worth ascending for the view, and the colorful gold-leaf mosaics of the **Memorial Church**. Free hour-long walking tours of the campus leave from here daily at 11am and 3.15pm, though it's fairly big and best seen by car or bike. Indeed, driving tours in a golf cart are offered daily at 1pm during term ($5) from Memorial Auditorium.

Visitors should seek out the area if only to experience one of the finest museums in the Bay Area. The **Iris and B. Gerald Cantor Center for Visual Arts**

comprises 27 galleries (spread over 120,000 square feet) of treasures from six continents, dating from 500 BC to the present (Wed–Sun 11am–5pm, Thurs 11am–8pm; free; ☎650/723-4177). Housed in the old Stanford Museum of Art at the intersection of Lomita Drive and Museum Way, the Cantor Center is the result of a decade-long refurbishing effort undertaken to repair damage caused by the Loma Prieta earthquake in 1989. The enchanting result incorporates the former structure with a new wing, including a bookshop and café. Visiting exhibitions have featured the work of such artists as Duchamp, Oldenburg, and Lucien Freud. One of the finest pieces in the permanent collection is the stunning *Plum Garden, Kameido*, by Japanese artist Hiroshige. Be sure to have a look at its distinguished collection of over 200 **Rodin sculptures**, including a *Gates of Hell* flanked by a shamed *Adam and Eve*, displayed in an attractive outdoor setting on the museum's south side. There's a version of *The Thinker* here as well, forming a sort of bookend with the rendition that fronts the Palace of the Legion of Honor Museum in San Francisco.

History buffs will enjoy the **Herbert Hoover Memorial Exhibit Pavilion** (Tues–Sat 11am–4pm; free), which displays changing exhibits from the vast Hoover collection of posters, photographs, letters, and other documents. Meanwhile, science buffs interested in keeping up on the latest trends in subatomic behavior won't want to miss the **Stanford Linear Accelerator** (visitor center Mon–Fri 9am–4pm; tours by appointment only; free; ☎650/926-2204, ⊛www.slac.stanford.edu), a mile west of the central campus at 2575 Sand Hill Rd, where infinitesimally small particles are crashed into one another at very high speeds to see what happens. For a bird's-eye view of the campus and the rest of the Bay Area, head up one of the **hiking trails** that leads from the gate along Junípero Serra Boulevard at Stanford Avenue to Stanford's giant communications dish atop the foothills to the west of the campus.

San Jose

Burt Bacharach could easily find the way to **SAN JOSE** today – heading south from San Francisco, it should take under an hour (avoiding peak times) to reach the heart of the heat and smog that collects below the Bay. Sitting at the southern end of the Peninsula, San Jose has in the past 25 years emerged as the civic heart of Silicon Valley, spurred by the growth of local behemoths Apple, Cisco, Intel, and Hewlett-Packard. San Jose's current priority is the development of a culture outside the computer labs that surround the city, and new museums, shopping centers, restaurants, clubs, and performing-arts companies have mushroomed throughout the compact downtown area. However, the recent downturn in the economy has led to various ambitious downtown renewal plans being put on hold by the city council. Still, while the nightlife and cultural scene here can't begin to compete with San Francisco, there are enough attractions around the city's clean and sunny streets to warrant a day-trip.

Downtown San Jose

Though now rooted in the modern hi-tech world, San Jose's 1777 founding actually makes it one of the oldest settlements – and the oldest city – in California. The only sign of that downtown is the 1797 **Peralta Adobe**, at 184 W St John St (Sat & Sun noon–5pm; $6; ☎408/993-8182, ⊛www.historysanjose .org), notable more for its having survived the encroaching suburbia than anything on display in its sparse, whitewashed interior. Admission includes a tour of the **Fallon House**, a Victorian mansion across the street, built by the city's seventh mayor in 1855, a one-time frontiersman in the Fremont expedition.

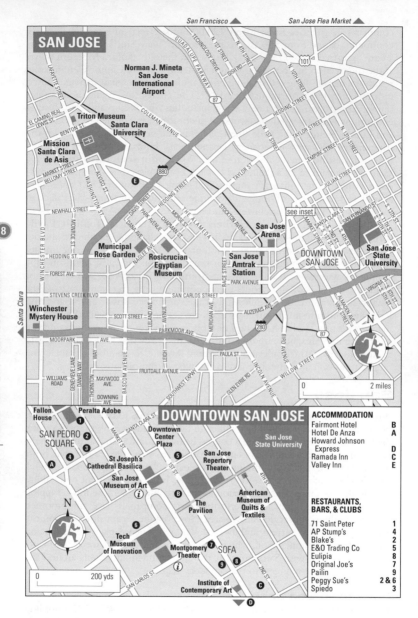

SAN JOSE

San Francisco ▲   San Jose Flea Market ▲

Norman J. Mineta
San Jose
International
Airport

Triton Museum
Santa Clara
University

Mission
Santa Clara
de Asis

Municipal
Rose Garden

Rosicrucian
Egyptian
Museum

San Jose
Arena

San Jose
Amtrak
Station

DOWNTOWN
SAN JOSE

see inset

San Jose
State
University

Winchester
Mystery House

N

0   2 miles

DOWNTOWN SAN JOSE

Fallon
House

Peralta Adobe

SAN PEDRO
SQUARE

Downtown
Center
Plaza

San Jose
State University

San Jose
Arena

St Joseph's
Cathedral Basilica

San Jose
Repertory
Theater

San Jose
Museum of Art

The
Pavilion

American
Museum of
Quilts &
Textiles

Tech
Museum
of Innovation

Montgomery
Theater

SOFA

Institute of
Contemporary Art

N

0   200 yds

ACCOMMODATION

Fairmont Hotel	**B**
Hotel De Anza	**A**
Howard Johnson Express	**D**
Ramada Inn	**C**
Valley Inn	**E**

RESTAURANTS, BARS, & CLUBS

71 Saint Peter	1
AP Stump's	4
Blake's	2
E&O Trading Co	5
Eulipia	8
Original Joe's	7
Pailin	9
Peggy Sue's	2 & 6
Spiedo	3

The guided tours through the fifteen rooms furnished from the period also include a comprehensive video presentation on the home and adobe's relationship to the development of the cityscape.

The two blocks of San Pedro Street that run south of the adobe form a restaurant row known as **San Pedro Square**. There's no central plaza as such, just a collection of some of San Jose's best eateries (see p.685). Further south, down

Market Street, lies the pleasant and palm-dotted **Plaza de Cesar Chavez**. The Plaza is San Jose's town square and there is no better place to catch some rays on the grass, read while sitting on one of the many wooden benches, or play in the unique **fountain** whose shooting spumes are a favorite hangout for kids in the summer.

A block north of the plaza, the **Cathedral Basilica of St Joseph** stands on the site of the first Catholic parish in California, circa 1803. The present building was dedicated in 1997, and you should duck inside to see its painted cupola, stained-glass windows, and Stations of the Cross. Masses are held daily, often in Spanish. Next door to the church at 110 S Market the fantastic **San Jose Museum of Art** (Tues–Sun 11am–5pm; free; ☎408/294-2787, ⓦwww.sjmusart.org) is set in the old post office building built in 1892 (a new wing was added in 1991). The museum contains more than one thousand twentieth-century works, with the spotlight falling on post-1980 Bay Area artists. A relationship with New York's Whitney Museum of American Art has recently been formed, allowing the museum to exhibit works from the Whitney's vast permanent collection. The sweeping, open galleries are flooded with light, as is the attached café, including its outdoor patio facing the plaza. On Sundays there are special workshops and activities to help make the art accessible to kids.

Facing the southwest corner of the plaza, downtown's biggest draw is the **Tech Museum of Innovation**, at 201 S Market St (daily 10am–5pm; $9.50; ☎408/294-8324, ⓦwww.thetech.org), with its hands-on displays of high-tech engineering. There are three floors of exhibits, as well as the inevitable IMAX theater ($9.50; combo ticket with museum entry $16). Highlights include a program that allows you to design a virtual roller coaster, regular demonstrations of state-of-the-art surgical instruments, and the chance to communicate with interactive robots. Unfortunately, the lines to access many of the best exhibits can seem like a virtual hell, and, unless you're a computer junkie, you may leave the museum feeling more like you've attempted to read an impervious software manual than visited a popular museum.

Aside from the attractions around the plaza, San Jose's other area worth walking through is the buzzing **"SoFA"** entertainment district, short for South First Street. To get here from the southern tip of the plaza, turn east on San Carlos Street and walk one block to First Street. SoFA forms the heart of San Jose's nightlife, with half a dozen clubs and discos along with a popular wine bar (see p.687). There's plenty to see during the day as well, including the **Institute of Contemporary Art** (Tues–Sat noon–5pm; free; ☎408/283-8155) at 451 S First St. The ICA's large, sunny room exhibits modern art, mainly Bay Area artists, but also work by international painters and sculptors. On the same street is downtown San Jose's **art cinema** house, the Camera 1, no. 366 (☎408/998-3300), and at no. 490, one of its performing-arts companies, **The Stage** (☎408/283-7142, ⓦwww.sanjosestage.com). Performances of contemporary work, like Steve Martin's *Picasso at the Lapin Agile*, regularly run Wednesday to Saturday, with tickets available for $20–42.

Walking north on First Avenue leads past the **Pavilion** shopping center, which has undergone a major renovation to become the anchor of commercial San Jose. The area needed it, having laid stagnant for decades as locals shopped at suburban malls. To combat this flight, city planners have zoned all of First and Second streets for the redevelopment mentioned earlier.

Around San Jose

Head four miles northwest of downtown and you'll come across two of San Jose's more intriguing, and relaxing, places to hang out. The first is the

Rosicrucian Egyptian Museum, 1342 Naglee Ave (Tues–Fri 10am–5pm, Sat & Sun 11am–6pm; $9; ☎408/947-3636, ⊛www.egyptianmuseum.org), a grand structure that contains a brilliant collection of Assyrian and Babylonian artifacts, with displays of mummies, amulets, a replica of a tomb, and ancient jewelry. The museum consists of a dark and musty room befitting its contents; don't miss the mummies of baboons, birds, and fish on the left-hand side of the tomb wing. There is also a **planetarium**, whose shows (Tues–Sun 2pm, Sat & Sun also 3.30pm; free) cover such esoteric subjects as "The Mithraic Mysteries". Aside from fascinating exhibits within, the best part about the Rosicrucian is its garden grounds, featuring a replica of the Akhenaten Temple from Luxor. You can find out more about the Rosicrucians' spiritual beliefs at ⊛www .rosicrucian.org. Across the street and two blocks west of the museum is the second peaceful locale, San Jose's **Municipal Rose Garden** (daily 8am–sunset; free). This beautiful expanse of green and rows of rose bushes is perfect for a picnic, and the fountain in the garden's center is a popular wading pool for local kids. Roll up your pants, soak your feet, and take in a nice view of the Santa Cruz Mountains to the west amidst the sweet scents.

Engulfed in the sprawl of northwestern San Jose, the small community of **Santa Clara** holds a few tourist attractions of its own. The late eighteenth-century **Mission Santa Clara de Asis** (daily sunrise–sunset; free), just south of The Alameda (Route 82) at 500 El Camino Real, is one of the least impressive structures in the mission chain that runs along the California coast on the traces of the El Camino Real. Hidden on the grounds of the Jesuit-run **University of Santa Clara**, there's not a lot to see of the original mission-era buildings here, though it is interesting to note how their remnants have been subtly preserved, integrated into the overall campus design. The **de Saisset Museum** (Tues–Sun 11am–4pm; $1 donation suggested; ☎408/554-4528, ⊛www.scu.edu/desaisset) within the complex traces the history of the mission through a permanent display of objects recovered from its ruins – the mission burned in a 1926 fire – along with changing shows of contemporary art. The bell in the belfry is original, a gift from King Carlos IV of Spain in 1798. Overall, the university is a green, quiet place to stroll around and pass an afternoon.

A few miles south of Santa Clara is a true American tourist trap, unmissable if you're into a good yarn. The **Winchester Mystery House**, 525 S Winchester Blvd, just off I-280 near Hwy-17 (daily 9am–5pm; $19.95; ☎408/247-1313, ⊛www.winchestermysteryhouse.com), belonged to Sarah Winchester, heiress to the Winchester rifle fortune, who was convinced upon her husband's death in 1884 that he had been taken by the spirits of men killed with his weapons. The ghosts told her that unless a room was built for each of them, the same fate would befall her. She took them so literally that the sound of hammers never ceased – 24 hours a day for the next thirty years. Now, unfinished, the house is a hodgepodge of extensions and styles: extravagant staircases lead nowhere and windows open onto solid brick walls. Today, the ghosts can't be much happier seeing that construction has stopped and the place has been converted into a shameless money-maker, where visitors have to run a gauntlet of ghastly gift stores and soda stands to get in or out. If you're a real sucker for punishment you can take the extra Behind the Scenes tour for $16.95 (combo with admission $24.95).

The only other spot on the Peninsula that might exercise a certain attraction, particularly to those fond of roller coasters, log rides, and all-American family fun is **Paramount's Great America** (summer daily 10am–10pm; rest of year Sat & Sun 10am–dusk; $48 at gate, $30 online, $26 three days in advance; ☎408/988-1776, ⓦwww.pgathrills.com). This hundred-acre amusement park on the edge of San Francisco Bay, just off US-101 north of San Jose, may not be in the same league as Disneyland, but the range of high-speed thrills and chills available – from the looping Top Gun Jetcoaster and Stealth, which zooms over the rails at 65mph, to the fierce Delirium ride, unveiled in 2002 – should satisfy even the most hardcore adrenaline junkies.

The coast

The largely undeveloped **coastline** of the Peninsula south of San Francisco is worlds away from the inland valleys. A few small towns, countless beaches, and sea lions trace the way 75 miles south to the mellow summer fun of Santa Cruz and Capitola. Bluffs protect the many **nudist beaches** from prying eyes and make a popular launching pad for hang-glider pilots, particularly at **Fort Funston**, a mile south of the San Francisco Zoo – also the point where the earthquake-causing San Andreas Fault enters the sea, not to surface again until Point Reyes. **Skyline Boulevard** follows the coast from here past the repetitious tracts of proverbial ticky-tacky houses that make up Daly City, before heading inland toward Woodside at its intersection with Hwy-1, which continues south along the coast. Driving **Hwy-1** can be a relaxing jaunt providing jaw-dropping views of the ocean, as long as you avoid the masses. Summer and weekend afternoons find the route clogged with campers creeping along at 30mph and few opportunities to pass. Try hitting the road at sunrise if you can manage it and, provided the fog isn't obscuring everything, expect a magical ride.

Pacifica and around

San Pedro Point, a popular surfing beach fifteen miles south of San Francisco proper, and the town of **PACIFICA**, mark the southern extent of the city's suburban sprawl. Pacifica is a pleasant stop-off for lunch and wave-gazing around Rockaway Beach. Visit the ultra-friendly **Chamber of Commerce** (see p.675 for details) for free maps of the area, including trail guides for **Sweeney Ridge**, from where Spanish explorer Gaspar de Portola discovered the San Francisco Bay in 1769. Pacifica's old **Ocean Shore Railroad Depot** here, now a private residence, is one of the few surviving remnants of an ill-advised train line between San Francisco and Santa Cruz. Wiped out during the 1906 earthquake, the line was in any case never more than a third complete. Its few patrons had to transfer back and forth by ferry to connect the stretches of track that were built, the traces of which you can still see scarring the face of the bluffs. The continually eroding cliffs make construction of any route along the coast difficult, as evidenced a mile south by the **Devil's Slide**, where a new cement support has been added to lessen the regularity with which the highway is washed away by winter storms. The slide area was also a popular dumping spot for corpses of those who fell foul of rum-runners during Prohibition, and is featured under various names in many of Dashiell Hammett's detective stories.

Just south of the Devil's Slide, the sands of **Gray Whale Cove State Beach** (daily 8am–sunset; free) are clothing-optional. Despite the name, it's not an especially great place to look for migrating gray whales, but the stairway at the bus stop does lead down to a fine strand. Two miles south and a good half-mile off Hwy-1, the red-roofed buildings of the 1875 **Montara Lighthouse**, set among the windswept Monterey pine trees at the top of a steep cliff, have been converted into a youth hostel (see p.676). Just south of the turning to the hostel, at the end of California Street, the **Fitzgerald Marine Reserve**

(☎650/728-3584; free) has three miles of diverse oceanic habitat, peaceful trails, and, at low tide, the best tidal pools in the Bay Area. The ranger often gives free guided interpretive walks through the reserve at low tide, the best time to explore, so call ahead or ask at one of the coast's tourist offices for low-tide times. At the south end of the reserve, Pillar Point juts out into the Pacific; just to the east, fishing boats dock at Pillar Point Harbor. Captured in all its raging glory in the surfing documentary *Riding Giants*, **Mavericks Beach**, just off Pillar Point beyond the enormous communications dish, boasts the largest waves in North America and attracts some of the world's best (and craziest) surfers when conditions are right. Just watching them can be an exhilarating way to spend an hour or so, and hundreds of people do every day. There's a long breakwater you can walk out on, too, but remember never to turn your back to the ocean – rogue waves have crashed in and swept unsuspecting tourists to their deaths. The surrounding villages of **Princeton-By-The-Sea**, whose main drag beside the marina is becoming increasingly trendy, and **El Grenada** both have good restaurants serving freshly caught fish and hamburgers. Further along, surfers also frequent the waters just offshore from the splendid long stretch of **Miramar Beach**. After a day in the water or on the beach, the place to head for is the beachfront *Douglass Beach House* (see p.687), an informal jazz club and beer bar that faces the sands.

Half Moon Bay

HALF MOON BAY, twenty miles south of the city and the only town of any size along the coast between San Francisco and Santa Cruz, takes its name from the crescent-shaped bay formed by Pillar Point. Lined by miles of sandy beaches, the town is surprisingly rural considering its proximity to San Francisco and Silicon Valley, and sports a number of ornate Victorian wooden houses clustered around its center. The oldest of these, at the north end of Main Street, was built in 1849 just across a little stone bridge over Pillarcitos Creek. The **Chamber of Commerce** (see p.675 for details) on Hwy-1 has free walking-tour maps of the town and information on the two annual festivals for which the place is well known. The first is the **Holy Ghost and Pentecost Festival**, a parade and barbecue held on the sixth Sunday after Easter, while the other, the **Pumpkin Festival**, celebrates the harvest of the area's many pumpkin farms, just in time for Halloween when the fields around town are full of families searching for the perfect jack-o'-lantern to greet the hordes of trick-or-treaters. If you fancy an equine experience, the combined Sea Horse and Friendly Acres ranches, one mile north of town at 2150 N Cabrillo Hwy (☎650/726-9903, ⊛www.friendlyacresinc.com), have trail **rides** for $30 per hour and ninety-minute beach rides for $40. Free, basic campgrounds line the coast in **Half Moon Bay State Park**, half a mile west of the town, although there is a parking fee for day-use (daily 8am–sunset; $6). The town is a good place to stop if you're low on gas, as the fifty-mile stretch of Hwy-1 to Santa Cruz doesn't offer many places to fill up.

SamTrans bus #294 route ends in Half Moon Bay; to continue south, transfer here to route #15, which runs every three hours to Waddell Creek, twenty miles away. **San Gregorio State Beach** (daily 8am–sunset; $6), ten miles south of Half Moon Bay, is at its best in the spring, after the winter storms, when flotsam architects construct a range of driftwood shelters along the wide beach south of the parking area. On hot summer days, the beach is packed with well-oiled bodies, but the sands around the bluffs to the north are quieter. Just north of Half Moon Bay off Hwy-1, Dunes Beach and Venice Beach are also beautiful expanses of sand and ocean.

The Butano redwoods and the Año Nuevo State Reserve

If you've got a car and it's not a great day for the beach, head up into the hills above the coast, where the thousands of acres of the **Butano Redwood Forest** feel at their most ancient and primeval in the greyest, gloomiest weather. About half the land between San Jose and the coast is protected from development in a variety of state and county parks, all of which are virtually deserted despite being within a thirty-minute drive of the Silicon Valley sprawl. Any one of a dozen roads heads through endless stands of untouched forest, and even the briefest of walks will take you seemingly miles from any sign of civilization. Hwy-84 climbs up from San Gregorio through the Sam McDonald County Park to the hamlet of **La Honda**, where Ken Kesey had his ranch during the Sixties and once notoriously invited the Hell's Angels to a party. From here, you can continue on to Palo Alto, or, better, loop back to the coast via Pescadero Road. A mile before you reach the quaint town of **Pescadero**, Cloverdale Road heads south to **Butano State Park**, where you can hike and camp overlooking the Pacific. Tiny Pescadero itself has one of the best places to eat on the Peninsula – *Duarte's* (see p.686), as well as a gas station. Just north of the turning to the village from Hwy-1, Pescadero State Beach is yet another fine spot for a dip, with no time restrictions or parking fee.

Five miles south of Pescadero, you can stay the night in the old lighthouse keeper's quarters and soak your bones in a marvelous hot tub at the *HI-Pigeon Point Lighthouse Hostel* (see p.676). The grounds of the light station are open to visitors (daily 8am–sunset; free; ☏650/879-2120) and you can call to see if one of the occasional tours is imminent. The calmest, most pleasant beach in which to wade is at **Bean Hollow State Beach**, a mile north of the hostel; it's free but has very limited parking.

If you're here between December and March, continue south another five miles to the **AÑO NUEVO STATE RESERVE** for a chance to see one of nature's most bizarre spectacles – the mating rituals of the **northern elephant seals**. These massive, ungainly creatures, fifteen feet long and weighing up to three tons, were once found all along the coast, though they were nearly hunted to extinction by whalers in the nineteenth century. During the mating season, the beach is literally a seething mass of blubbery bodies, with the trunk-nosed males fighting it out for the right to sire as many as fifty pups in a season. At any time of the year, you're likely to see a half dozen or so dozing in the sands. The reserve is also good for birdwatching, and in March you might even catch sight of migrating gray whales.

The slowly resurgent Año Nuevo seal population is still carefully protected, and during the breeding season the obligatory guided tours – designed to protect spectators as much as to give the seals some privacy – begin booking in October (hourly 8am–4pm; $4 per person, $2 parking; ☏650/879-2025 or 1-800/444-4445, ✆www.anonuevo.org). Otherwise tickets are usually made available to people staying at the *Pigeon Point Hostel*, and SamTrans (see p.563 for details) sometimes runs charter bus tours for $12.50 per person from the town of **San Mateo** on the Bay side of the Peninsula. (See "The Central Coast" chapter for an account of the area from Año Nuevo south to Santa Cruz and Monterey.)

Peninsula eating

The **restaurants** on the Peninsula, particularly in pseudo-ritzy Palo Alto and newly yuppified Burlingame, on the east side of the Peninsula about four miles south of San Francisco airport, are increasingly on a par with their San Franciscan counterparts. Many, filled with wealthy young computer executives, require dinner reservations every night of the week. In San Jose, consider dining around San Pedro Square for a good choice of cuisine. If you're in the mood for quiet conversation, check out one of the **cafés** listed, many of which feature fresh sandwiches and salads along with the requisite microbrewed beers (Gordon Biersch originated in San Jose) and gourmet coffees. The following list concentrates primarily on establishments centrally located in the downtown areas of the main Peninsula cities and towns, with a few others that are worth almost any effort to get to.

Restaurants

AP Stump's 163 W Santa Clara St, San Jose ☎408/292-9928. Best place to go if you have an unlimited expense account. Pricey (entrees all over $20) California cuisine, but one of the places to be seen in Silicon Valley. Great wine list.

Barbara's Fish Trap 281 Capistrano Rd, off Hwy-1, Princeton-by-the-Sea ☎650/728-7049. Oceanfront seafood restaurant with good-value fish dinners and an unbeatable view.

Bistro Elan 448 S California Ave, Palo Alto ☎650/327-0284. Serving spiffy Cal cuisine like duck confit and pan-seared Maine scallops to the cyber-elite. Prices are rather steep at over $20 per dinner entree, so consider a lunchtime visit.

Bistro Vida 641 Santa Cruz Ave, Menlo Park ☎650/462-1686. Giving Silicon Valley a much-needed style infusion by serving delicious Left Bank Parisian bistro fare at the rather inflated prices you might expect.

Blake's Steakhouse and Bar 17 N San Pedro St, San Jose ☎408/298-9221. Craving a New York strip or a steamed lobster, washed down with a fine martini? *Blake's* is the place. Entrees around $20, sandwiches also available.

Château des Fleurs 523 Church St, Half Moon Bay ☎650/712-8837. An exquisite flower garden in front welcomes you to this small, reasonably priced French restaurant.

Duarte's 202 Stage Rd, Pescadero ☎650/879-0464. Platefuls of traditional American food (especially fish) for around $10 are served in this down-home find connected to a bar full of locals in cowboy hats. Famous for their artichoke soup.

E&O Trading Company 96 S First St, San Jose ☎408/938-4100. Upscale Southeast Asian grill featuring curried fish and other Vietnamese/Indonesian fare. Entrees approaching $20.

El Amigo Burrito 4485 Stevens Creek Blvd, Santa Clara ☎408/248-3113. Relaxed place serving huge portions of authentic Mexican food at very reasonable prices.

Eulipia 374 S First St, San Jose ☎408/280-6161.

Stylish dinner spot boasting well-prepared versions of California cuisine staples like grilled fish and fresh pastas. Entrees from $12–28. Closed Mondays.

Evvia 420 Emerson St, Palo Alto ☎650/326-0983. Rather pricey California/Greek lamb dishes such as *paidakia arnisia* and *arni kapama*, as well as baked fish and other Hellenic faves, served in a cozy yet elegant dining room. Full bar.

Gin Wan 2810 Cabrillo Hwy, Half Moon Bay ☎650/726-6028. Copious portions of delicious Taiwanese and Szechuan cuisine at very reasonable prices in a simple dining room right on Hwy-1.

Il Forniao 327 Lorton Ave, Burlingame ☎650/375-8000. Part of an upscale chain serving reliably well-prepared Italian staple entrees and baked goods. Other branches at 520 Cowper St, Palo Alto (☎650/853-3888), and inside the *Hyatt Saint Claire* at 302 S Market St, San Jose (☎408/271-3366).

Joanie's Cafe 447 California Ave, Palo Alto ☎650/326-6505. Home-style breakfasts and lunches in a comfortable neighborhood restaurant.

John's Market Town and Country Village, Embarcadero at El Camino, Palo Alto ☎650/321-8438. Steer past the high-school kids on lunch break to get one of the best (and biggest) deli sandwiches around. Located across the street from Stanford Stadium.

Krung Siam 423 University Ave, Palo Alto ☎650/322-5900. Classy but not too expensive restaurant serving beautifully presented traditional Thai fare.

La Cheminée 530 Bryant St, Palo Alto ☎650/329-0695. Quality fare such as lavender-encrusted halibut or pork dijon are among the delights at this French bistro. The prices, mostly under $20 per entree, are not too outrageous either.

Los Gallos Taqueria 3726 Florence St, Redwood City ☎650/369-1864. Simply put, they make the best burritos on the Peninsula. Take the Marsh Road exit from Hwy-101 and look for the Marsh Manor shopping center.

Marigold 448 University Ave, Palo Alto ⊤650/327-3455. Moderate to expensive North Indian restaurant with an emphasis on ginger dishes – has gained acclaim since changing ownership and name.

Mike's Cafe, Etc. 2680 Middlefield Rd, Palo Alto ⊤650/473-6453. Unpretentious neighborhood restaurant hidden behind a hardware store. Excellent fresh salads, pastas, and simple meat dishes are sometimes brought to your table by Mike himself.

Nick's Seashore Restaurant 101 Rockaway Beach, Pacifica ⊤650/359-3903. Beloved enough to reel folks in from the city regularly, this all-purpose joint provides cheap brekky, moderate pasta, and pricier steak/seafood dishes.

Original Joe's 301 S First St, San Jose ⊤408/292-7030. Grab a stool at the counter or settle into one of the comfy vinyl booths and enjoy a burger and fries or a plate of pasta at this San Jose institution, where $10 goes a long way. Open 11am–1am.

Pailin 325 S First St, San Jose ⊤408/998-3306. Good inexpensive Chinese and Cambodian cuisine with authentic dishes from the southern Trieu Chau region that borders the two countries.

Peggy Sue's 29 N San Pedro St, San Jose ⊤408/298-6750. Inexpensive milkshakes, burgers, and fries served in a 1950s setting. Also has a vegetarian and kids' menu. Popular with Sharks' fans before ice hockey games. There's another outlet a few blocks away at 183 Park Ave ⊤408/294-0252.

Rock'n'Rob's 450 Dundee Way, Rockaway Beach, Pacifica ⊤650/359-3663. This new diner decorated in the old style churns out tons of burgers and fries all day, but no breakfast.

Saint Peter 71 N San Pedro St, San Jose ⊤408/971-8523. Patio dining and oyster bar centered on a menu of filet mignon, pork loin, chicken, and salads. Extremely hot with the in-crowd. Lunch Monday to Friday, dinner nightly.

Spiedo 151 W Santa Clara St, San Jose ⊤408/971-6096. Handmade pasta, pizza, calamari, salmon, and more delight the tastebuds at lunch and dinner daily. Entrees begin at $10.

St Michael's Alley 806 Emerson St, Palo Alto ⊤650/326-2530. This former student café hangout has transformed itself into one of Palo Alto's hottest bistros and the "casual California" cuisine served at lunch and dinner couldn't be farther from the old fare of bagels and coffee. A fine wine list and weekend brunch ($10) keeps guests coming back for seconds.

Cafés

Caffé Verona 236 Hamilton Ave, Palo Alto ⊤650/326-9942. Relaxing hangout for Palo Alto's intellectual crowd.

Global Village Café 172 N Main St, Sebastopol ⊤650/829-4765. A popular breakfast gathering-spot for techie types – when they make time for breakfast, that is.

Hookah Nites Café 371 S First St, San Jose ⊤408/286-0800. Avant garde art is showcased in this spacious and trendy venue, which serves fresh coffee and pastries.

M Coffee 522 Main St, Half Moon Bay ⊤650/726-6241. Coffees, teas, sandwiches, and ice cream in a small, homely eatery.

Printer's Inc Cafe 320 California Ave, Palo Alto ⊤650/323-3347. Good snacks, sandwiches, pastries, and coffees served adjacent to Palo Alto's best bookstore.

Peninsula drinking and nightlife

For a serious night out on the town, you're better off heading up to San Francisco, though many San Jose residents may try to convince you otherwise. Nevertheless, there are a number of good **bars** and **clubs** on the Peninsula – particularly in San Jose's SoFA district, but also in the studenty environs of Palo Alto.

Bars and clubs

Agenda 399 S First St, San Jose ⊤408/287-3991. A bar/restaurant/lounge in SoFA that heralded the arrival of nightlife in San Jose. DJ, dancing, and live jazz nightly.

B-Hive 372 S First St, San Jose ⊤408/298-2529. Upstairs dance club spinning hip-hop, R&B, and reggae. Rhythm Records, below, keeps them supplied with loops. Over-21s only.

Blue Chalk Café 630 Ramona St, Palo Alto ⊤650/326-1020. Yuppies and other young Silicon-ites have been flocking to this wildly successful bar/pool-hall/restaurant ever since it opened in 1993.

Brittania Arms Downtown 173 W Santa Clara St, San Jose ⊤408/266-0550. Latest addition to the growing chain of British-themed pubs with fish'n'chips, real ale, footie (meaning soccer) on TV, and a trivia quiz night.

Douglass Beach House Miramar Beach, two and a half miles north of Half Moon Bay on Hwy-1, go west down Medio Ave ⊤650/726-4143, ⓦwww .bachddsoc.org. Two-story country beach house with fireplace and outside deck; international jazz performers are frequently hosted by the Bach Dancing & Dynamite Society. The quieter *Ebb Tide Café* below is open Thurs–Sun.

Emma's Club Miami 177 W Santa Clara St, San Jose ☎408/279-3670. Huge San Pedro Square bar/ Mexican restaurant with Latin music and dancing in the upstairs club at weekends. Great patio.

Glo 394 S First St, San Jose ☎408/280-1977. Dance music from light hip-hop to heavy disco is featured at this club, which imports top DJs from SF, LA, and Vegas on Saturday nights.

Gordon Biersch Brewery 640 Emerson St, Palo Alto ☎650/323-7723. Among the first and still the best of the Bay Area's microbrewery-cum-restaurants. Also in San Francisco (see p.623) and in downtown San Jose at 33 E San Fernando St ☎408/294-6785.

Half Moon Bay Brewing Co. 390 Capistrano Rd, Princeton-by-the-Sea ☎650/728-2739. Lively watering hole with a rock soundtrack, where you can get your kisser round a range of decent brews from blond through amber to brown ale. Also has a popular restaurant serving Californian and American cuisine.

Kleidon's Cocktails 152 Post St, San Jose ☎408/293-2461. Old downtown San Jose dive bar that's perfect if you get tired of drinking amongst the beautiful people.

Moss Beach Distillery Beach and Ocean, Moss Beach ☎650/728-0220. If you don't feel like paying out $20 per entree at the popular restaurant, snuggle up under a wool blanket, order a drink and an appetizer, and watch the sunset from the patio overlooking the ocean.

Pete Escovedo's 400 S First St, San Jose ☎408/947-7500. Snazzy Latin and Jazz club with a dress code and $12–18 cover. On Sundays you can join in the salsa lessons for $10.

Tied House 65 N San Pedro St, San Jose ☎408/295-2739. Gigantic San Pedro Square sports bar and brewery that also serves burgers and the like.

Toon's S Second St at Santa Clara, San Jose ☎408/292-7464. Downtown San Jose's hip-hop dance club and pool bar. Sister club the *Voodoo Lounge*, next door, is for 21-and-over only and enforces a strict dress code of no hats, baggies, or tennis shoes.

Waves Smokehouse and Saloon 65 Post St, San Jose ☎408/885-9283. Huge sports screens dominate this spacious bar. Live country music on the first Tuesday of each month.

Wine Galleria 377 S First St, San Jose ☎408/298-1386. Large wine bar with plush sofas next to *Café Matisse*. Huge array of vintages for sale by the glass, with specials such as five for $20.

Zoe 417 S First St, San Jose ☎408/971-6647. One of SoFA's prime hip-shaking techno/disco spots, where silicon implants are a popular fashion accessory.

Marin County

Across the Golden Gate from San Francisco, **Marin County** (pronounced "Ma-RINN") is an unabashed introduction to Californian self-indulgence: an elitist pleasure zone of conspicuous luxury and abundant natural beauty, with sunshine, sandy beaches, high mountains, and thick redwood forests. Often ranked as the wealthiest county in the US, Marin has attracted a sizeable contingent of Northern California's wealthiest young professionals, many of whom grew up during the Flower Power years of the 1960s and lend the place its New Age feel and reputation. Though many of the cocaine-and-hot-tub devotees who seemed to populate the swanky waterside towns in the 1970s have traded in their drug habits for mountain bikes – which were invented here – in Marin still centers on personal pleasure, and the throngs you see hiking and cycling at weekends, not to mention the hundreds of esoteric self-help practitioners – rolfing, rebirthing, and soul-travel therapists fill up the classified ads of the local papers – prove that Marinites work hard to maintain their easy air of physical and mental well-being. Indeed, early in 2002, George Bush Sr came in for some flak and had to back down after criticising the wealthy residents of Marin for having so many hot tubs and yet still voting Democrat.

Flashy modern ferries, appointed with fully stocked bars, sail across the Bay from San Francisco and present a marvelous initial view of the county. As you head past desolate Alcatraz Island, curvaceous **Mount Tamalpais** looms larger until you land at its foot in one of the chic bayside settlements of **Sausalito** or **Tiburon**. **Angel Island**, in the middle of the Bay but accessible most easily from Tiburon, provides relief from the excessive style-consciousness of both towns, retaining a wild, untouched feeling among the eerie ruins of derelict military fortifications.

Sausalito and Tiburon (and the lifestyles that go with them) are only a small part of Marin. The bulk of the county rests on the slopes of the ridge of peaks that divides the Peninsula down the middle, separating the sophisticated harborside towns in the east from the untrammeled wilderness of the Pacific Coast to the west. The **Marin Headlands**, just across the Golden Gate Bridge, hold time-warped old battlements and gun emplacements that once protected San Francisco's harbor from would-be invaders, and now overlook hikers and cyclists enjoying the acres of open space and wildlife. Along the coastline that spreads north, the broad shore of **Stinson Beach** is the Bay Area's finest and widest stretch of sand, beyond which Hwy-1 clings to the coast past the rural village of **Bolinas** to seascapes around **Point Reyes**, where it is thought Sir Francis Drake may have landed in 1579 and claimed all of what is now California for England. Whale and seal watchers congregate here year-round for glimpses of migrations and matings.

Inland, the heights of Mount Tamalpais, and specifically **Muir Woods**, are a magnet to sightseers and nature lovers, who come to wander through one of the few surviving stands of the native coastal redwood trees. Such trees covered most of Marin before they were chopped down to build and rebuild the wooden houses of San Francisco. The long-vanished lumber mills of the rustic town of **Mill Valley**, overlooking the Bay from the slopes of Mount Tam, as it's locally known, bear the guilt for much of this destruction; the oldest town in Marin County is now home to an eclectic bunch of art galleries and cafés. Further north, Marin's largest town, **San Rafael**, is best left alone, though its outskirts contain two of the most unusual attractions in the county: **Frank Lloyd Wright**'s peculiar Civic Center complex and the preserved remnants of an old Chinese fishing village in **China Camp State Park**. The northern reaches of Marin County border the bountiful wine-growing regions of the Sonoma and Napa valleys, detailed in Chapter 10, "Northern California."

Arrival

Just getting to Marin County can be a great start to a day out from San Francisco. Golden Gate Transit **ferries** (☎415/923-2000 in SF, ☎415/455-2000 in Marin, ✪www.goldengate.org) leave from the Ferry Building on the Embarcadero, crossing the Bay past Alcatraz Island to **Sausalito** (Mon–Fri 7.40am–7.55pm, Sat & Sun 10.40am–6.30pm) and **Larkspur** (Mon–Fri 6.30am–9.35pm, Sat & Sun 12.30–7pm); they run every thirty to forty minutes during the rush hour, roughly hourly during the rest of the day, and about every ninety minutes to two hours on weekends and holidays. Tickets cost $6.15 one way to both destinations and refreshments are served on board. The slightly more expensive and less frequent Blue and Gold Fleet ($7.25 one way; ☎415/773-1188, ✪www.blueandgoldfleet.com) sail from Pier 41 at Fisherman's Wharf to Sausalito (Mon–Fri 11am–5pm, Sat & Sun 10.40am–6.30pm) and **Tiburon** (Mon–Fri 11am–5pm, Sat & Sun 9.45am–6.30pm) – from where the Angel Island ferry ($7 round-trip, $1 per bicycle; ☎415/435-2131) nips back and forth to **Angel Island State Park** daily in summer, weekends only in the winter. Blue and Gold Fleet provides additional weekday rush-hour crossings to Tiburon from the Ferry Building and an excursion service direct to Angel Island ($13 round-trip) from Pier 41, twice daily on weekdays, thrice at weekends. Note that the ferry timetables change quarterly, so it is best to check in advance.

Information

Three main on-the-spot sources can provide further information on Marin County: the **Marin County Visitors Bureau**, 1013 Larkspur Landing Circle, Larkspur (Mon–Fri 9am–5pm; ☏415/499-5000, ⊛www.visitmarin.org), the **Sausalito Visitor Center**, occupying a modest hut at 780 Bridgeway Ave (Tues–Sun 11.30am–4pm; ☏415/332-0505), and the **Mill Valley Chamber of Commerce**, 85 Throckmorton Ave (Mon–Fri 10am–noon & 1–4pm; ☏415/388-9700, ⊛www.millvalley.org), in the center of the town.

For information on hiking and camping in the wilderness and beach areas, depending on where you're heading, contact the **Golden Gate National Recreation Area**, Building 201, Fort Mason Center, San Francisco (Mon–Fri 9.30am–4.30pm; ☏415/561-3000), or the **Marin Headlands Visitor Center** (daily 9am–4.30pm; ☏415/331-1540); other outlets are the **Mount Tamalpais State Park Visitor Center**, 801 Panoramic Hwy, Mill Valley (daily 8am–5.30pm; ☏415/388-2070), and the Point Reyes National Seashore's **Bear Valley Visitors Center**, Point Reyes (Mon–Fri 9am–5pm, Sat & Sun 8am–5pm; ☏415/464-5100, ⊛www.nps.gov/pore). Information on what's on in Marin can be found in the widely available local freesheets, such as the down-to-earth *Coastal Post* (⊛www.coastalpost.com), or the New-Agey *Pacific Sun* (⊛www.pacificsun.com).

Getting around

Golden Gate Transit also runs a comprehensive **bus service** around Marin County and across the Golden Gate Bridge from the Transbay Terminal in San Francisco (same contacts as ferries above), and publishes a helpful and free system map and timetable, including all ferry services. Bus fares range from $1.85 to $7.25, with routes running every thirty minutes throughout the day, and once an hour late at night. Some areas can only be reached by GGT commuter services, which run only during the morning and evening rush hours (call ahead to check schedule). Also, San Francisco's MUNI bus #76 runs hourly from San Francisco direct to the Marin Headlands on Sundays only. Golden Gate Transit bus route #40, the only service available between Marin County and the East Bay, runs from the San Rafael Transit Center to the Del Norte BART station in El Cerrito ($3.10 each way).

If you'd rather avoid the hassle of bus connections, Gray Line (☏415/558-9400, ⊛www.grayline.com) offers four-hour guided **bus tours** from the Transbay Terminal in San Francisco, taking in Sausalito and Muir Woods (daily year-round 9am, check for increased services in summer; $41, $55 with Bay cruise); the Blue and Gold Fleet ferry also has a boat-and-bus trip to Muir Woods, via Tiburon (daily 9.15am & 2.15pm; 4–5hr; $47) from Pier 43 in the city.

One of the best ways to get around Marin is by **bike**, particularly using a mountain bike to cruise the many trails that crisscross the county, especially in the Marin Headlands. If you want to ride on the road, Sir Francis Drake Highway – from Larkspur to Point Reyes – makes a good route, though it's best to avoid weekends, when the roads can get clogged up with cars. All ferry services (except Alcatraz) allow bicycles.

#2: San Francisco–Marin Headlands–Marin City–Sausalito; weekdays.

#4: San Francisco–Mill Valley; weekdays.

#8: San Francisco–Tiburon–Sausalito; weekdays.

#10: Sausalito–Marin City–Mill Valley–Tiburon; daily.

#18: San Francisco–Corte Madera–College of Marin–Larkspur–San Anselmo; weekdays.

#20: San Francisco–Sausalito–Corte Madera–San Anselmo–San Rafael; daily.

#24: San Francisco–Greenbrea–San Anselmo–Fairfax–Lagunitas; weekdays.

#26: San Francisco–San Rafael–San Anselmo–Sleepy Hollow; weekdays.

#29: Larkspur Ferry–San Rafael; daily.

#30: San Francisco–Larkspur Ferry–San Rafael; weekdays.

#50: San Francisco–Sausalito–San Rafael–Novato–San Marin; daily.

#63: Marin City–Stinson Beach; weekends only.

#65: San Rafael–Point Reyes Station–Inverness; weekends only.

#80: San Francisco–San Rafael–Novato–Petaluma–Santa Rosa; daily.

#90: San Francisco–San Rafael–Sonoma Valley; weekdays.

#93: San Francisco Civic Center–Golden Gate Bridge; weekdays.

Accommodation

You might prefer simply to dip into Marin County using San Francisco as a base, and if you've got a car or manage to time the bus connections right it's certainly possible, at least for the southernmost parts of the county. However, it can be nicer to take a more leisurely look at Marin, staying over for a couple of nights in some well-chosen spots. Sadly, there are few **hotels**, and those that there are often charge well in excess of $100 a night; **motels** tend to be the same as anywhere, though there are a couple of attractively faded ones along the coast. If you want to stay in a B&B, contact the Bed and Breakfast Exchange, 45 Entrata Drive, San Anselmo (℡415/485-1971), which can fix you up with rooms in comfortable private homes all over Marin County from $60 a night for two, ranging from courtyard hideaways on the beach in Tiburon to houseboats in Sausalito. The best bet for budget accommodation is a dorm bed in one of the beautifully situated **hostels** along the western beaches.

Hotels and motels

Casa Madrona 801 Bridgeway Ave, Sausalito ℡415/332-0502 or 1-800/567-9524, ⓦwww
.casamadrona.com. Deluxe, European-style hotel with a new extension spreading up the hill above the Bay. Spa facilities available and the *Mikayla* restaurant is highly rated. ❽

Colonial Motel 1735 Lincoln Ave, San Rafael ℡415/453-9188 or 1-800/554-9118, Ⓔsdarbar@aol.com. Quiet, well-furnished, and friendly motel with decent rates in a residential neighborhood. ❸

Grand Hotel 15 Brighton Ave, Bolinas ℡415/868-1757. Just two budget rooms in a funky, run-down old hotel above a secondhand shop. ❷

Hotel Sausalito 16 El Portal, Sausalito ℡415/332-0700 or 1-888/442-0700, ⓦwww.hotelsausalito.com. Sixteen stylish rooms with views across the park and harbor. Owned and run by an entertaining Scot. ❻

Mill Valley Inn 165 Throckmorton Ave, Mill Valley ℡415/389-6608 or 1-800/595-2100, ⓦwww
.millvalleyinn.com. By far the best hotel in Marin County, this gorgeous European-style inn boasts elegant rooms, two private cottages, and a central location. ❼

Ocean Court Motel 18 Arenal St, Stinson Beach ℡415/868-0212, ⓦwww.oceancourt.ws. Large simple rooms with kitchens, just a block from the beach and west of Hwy-1; you pay for the location though. ⑤

Stinson Beach Motel 3416 Shoreline Hwy, Stinson Beach ℡415/868-1712, ⓦwww .stinsonbeachmotel.com. Average, slightly over-priced roadside motel right on Hwy-1, with tiny rooms. Five minutes' walk to the beach. ④

Bed and breakfasts

Blue Heron Inn 11 Wharf Rd, Bolinas ℡415/868-1102. Lovely double rooms in an unbeatable locale with ocean view. A friendly welcome, and its own restaurant serving good seafood and steaks help make this an excellent choice. ⑥

Lindisfarne Guest House Green Gulch Farm Zen Center, Muir Beach ℡415/383-3134, ⓦwww.sfzc .org. Restful rooms in a meditation retreat set in a secluded valley above Muir Beach. Price includes excellent vegetarian meals. ⑥

Mountain Home Inn 810 Panoramic Hwy, Mill Valley ℡415/381-9000 or 1-877/381-9001, ⓦwww.mtnhomeinn.com. Romantically located on Mount Tamalpais' crest, this B&B offers great views and endless hiking opportunities. Some rooms with hot tubs. ⑦

Olema Inn 10000 Sir Francis Drake Blvd, Olema ℡415/663-9559 or 1-800/532-9252, ⓦwww .theolemainn.com. Wonderful little B&B near the entrance to Point Reyes National Seashore, on a site that's been a hotel since 1876. Features a gourmet restaurant serving seafood and a full bar with heady wine list. Comfy rooms and absolutely no nightlife or traffic noise to speak of; perfect if you want to really take a break from the city. ⑥

Pelican Inn 10 Pacific Way, Muir Beach ℡415/383-6000, ⓦwww.pelicaninn.com. Very comfortable rooms in a romantic pseudo-English country inn, with good bar and restaurant down-stairs, ten minutes' walk from beautiful Muir Beach. ⑧

Ten Inverness Way 10 Inverness Way, Inverness ℡415/669-1648, ⓦwww.teninvernessway.com. Quiet and restful, with a hot tub and compli-mentary evening wine, in a small village of good restaurants and bakeries on the fringes of Point Reyes. ⑥

Hostels

HI-Marin Headlands Building 941, Fort Barry, Marin Headlands ℡415/331-2777 or 1-800/909-4776, ⓦwww.norcalhostels.org. Hard to get to without a car – it's near Rodeo Lagoon just off Bunker Road, five miles west of Sausalito – but worth the effort for its setting, in a cozy old army barracks near the ocean. On Sundays and holidays

only, MUNI bus #76 from San Francisco stops right outside. Closed 10am–3.30pm, except for registra-tion. Dorm beds $18 a night, double rooms $54.

HI-Point Reyes in the Point Reyes National Sea-shore; closed 10am–4.30pm; ℡415/663-8811, ⓦwww.norcalhostels.org. Also hard to reach without your own transportation: just off Limantour Road six miles west of the visitor center and two miles from the beach, it's located in an old ranch house and surrounded by meadows and forests. Dorm beds $14–16 a night.

Campgrounds

Angel Island State Park Angel Island ℡415/435-5390, ⓦwww.angelisland.org. Nine primitive walk-in (and one kayak-in) sites with great views of San Francisco, which explains why they cost as much ($20) per night as more developed sites elsewhere. In summer it's essential to book through ReserveAmerica ℡1-800/444-7275.

China Camp State Park off N San Pedro Rd, north of San Rafael ℡415/456-0766. Walk-in plots (just 600ft from the parking lot) overlooking a lovely meadow. First-come-first-camped for $20 a night. April–Oct reserve through ReserveAmerica ℡1-800/444-7275.

Marin Headlands just across the Golden Gate Bridge ℡415/331-1540, ⓦwww.nps.gov/goga. Five campgrounds, the best of which is very popular *Kirby Cove* (open April–Oct only), at the northern foot of the Golden Gate Bridge (reserva-tions Tues–Thurs 10am–2pm; $20; ℡415/561-4304). Of the remaining sites, one is a group camp ($20), and the other three are free.

Mount Tamalpais State Park above Mill Valley ℡415/388-2070. Two separate campgrounds ($15) for backpackers, one on the slopes of the mountain ($15), and the other towards the coast at Steep Ravine, which also has a few rustic cabins ($60 a night). Reserve through ReserveAmerica ℡1-800/444-7275.

Point Reyes National Seashore forty miles northwest of San Francisco ℡415/663-1092. A wide range of hike-in sites for backpackers, near the beach or in the forest. Reserve sites up to two months in advance (weekdays 9am–2pm; $12; ℡415/663-8054).

Samuel P. Taylor State Park on Sir Francis Drake Blvd, fifteen miles west of San Rafael ℡415/488-9897. Deluxe, car-accessible plots with hot show-ers, spread along a river for $20 a night, basic hiker/biker sites for $5. Don't miss the swimming hole or bat caves. In summer, reserve a place through ReserveAmerica ℡1-800/444-7275.

Across the Golden Gate: the Marin Headlands and Sausalito

The largely undeveloped **Marin Headlands** of the Golden Gate National Recreation Area, across the Golden Gate Bridge from San Francisco, afford some of the most impressive views of the bridge and the city behind. As the regular fog rolls in, the breathtaking image of the bridge's stanchions tantalisingly drifting in and out of sight and the fleeting glimpses of downtown skyscrapers will abide long in the memory. Take the first turn as you exit the bridge (Alexander Avenue) and follow the sign back to San Francisco – the one-way circle trip back to the bridge heads first to the west along Conzelman Road and up a steep hill. You'll pass through a largely undeveloped land, dotted by the concrete remains of old forts and gun emplacements standing guard over the entrance to the Bay, dating from as far back as the Civil War and as recent as World War II. The coastline here is much more rugged than it is on the San Francisco side, making it a great place for an aimless cliff-top hike or a stroll along one of the beaches dramatically situated near the crashing waves at the bottom of treacherous footpaths.

The first installation as you climb the steep hill up the headlands is **Battery Wallace**, the largest and most impressive of the artillery sites along the rocky coast here, cut through a hillside above the southwestern tip of the peninsula. The clean-cut military geometry survives, framing views of the Pacific Ocean and the Golden Gate Bridge. If you're interested in such things, come along on the first Sunday of the month and take a guided tour of an abandoned 1950s ballistic-missile launchpad, complete with disarmed nuclear missiles. Otherwise, continue along Conzelman for incredible views of the city from any of the many turnouts. For birdwatching, walk from the Battery Wallace parking lot through tunnels that lead 500 yards to the opposite bluff, overlooking **Rodeo Beach** and **Point Bonita Lighthouse** far below. To reach Point Bonita by vehicle, drive down the one-way lane that Conzelman becomes and keep winding down to the lighthouse. It stands sentry at the very end of the headlands and is often open for tours (Sat–Mon 12.30–3.30pm; free). Conzelman comes to a "T" in the road at the YMCA camp bunkhouse; turn left and park your car on the side of the road or at the parking lot 300 yards west, at the end of the drive. To reach the lighthouse, you have to walk the half mile pathway down, a beautiful stroll that takes you through a tunnel cut into the cliff, and across a precarious suspension bridge.

Looping back around, you'll be heading northeast on Bunker Road. Stop off at the **Marin Headlands Visitor Center** (see p.690 for details), alongside Rodeo Lagoon, for free maps of popular hiking trails in the area. Across the road and a bit further along, the largest of **Fort Barry**'s old buildings has been converted into the spacious but homely *HI-Marin Headlands* hostel (see opposite), an excellent base for more extended explorations of the inland ridges and valleys.

Turn off to the left where Bunker Road snakes down to wide, sandy Rodeo Beach (#76 MUNI bus from San Francisco: Sun & holidays only). The beach separates the chilly ocean from the marshy warm water of **Rodeo Lagoon**, where swimming is prohibited to protect nesting sea birds. North of the lagoon, the **Marine Mammal Center** (ⓦwww.tmmc .org) rescues and rehabilitates injured and orphaned sea creatures, such as dolphins and sea otters, which you can visit while they recover; there's also a series of displays on the marine ecosystem and a bookstore that sells T-shirts and posters.

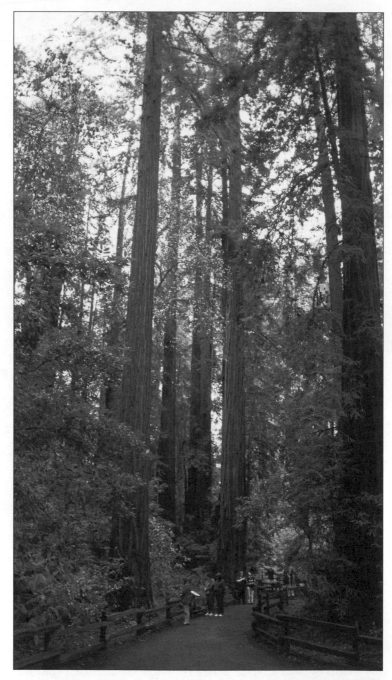

△ Muir Woods

Sausalito

Sausalito, fronting the Bay below US-101, is a picturesque, snug little town of exclusive restaurants and pricey boutiques along a pretty water-front promenade. Expensive, quirkily designed houses climb the overgrown cliffs above **Bridgeway Avenue**, the main route through town. Sausalito used to be a fairly gritty community of fishermen and sea-traders, full of bars and bordellos, and despite its upscale modern face it still makes a fun day out from San Francisco by ferry, the boats arriving next to the Sausalito Yacht Club in the center of town. Hang out in one of the waterfront bars and watch the crowds strolling along the esplanade, or climb the stairways above Bridgeway Avenue and amble around the leafy hills. If you have sailing experience, split the $127–199 daily rental fee of a four- to ten-person sailboat at Cass's Marina, 1702 Bridgeway Ave (☎415/332-6789, ⊛www.cassmarina .com). The other main diversion is sea kayaking, and Sea Trek (☎415/488-1000, ⊛www.seatrekkayak.com) rents single or double sea kayaks beginning at $15 for one hour's worth of superb paddling around the Bay. They offer sit-on-top kayaks, lessons, and safe routes for first-timers, or closed kayaks and directions around Angel Island for more experienced paddlers.

The old working wharves and warehouses that made Sausalito a haven for smugglers and Prohibition-era rum-runners are long gone; most have been taken over by dull steakhouses. However, some stretches of it have, for the moment at least, survived the tourist onslaught. A mile north of the town center along Bridgeway Avenue, an ad hoc community of exotic **barges** and **houseboats**, some of which have been moored here since the 1950s, are still staving off eviction to make room for yet another luxury marina. In the meantime, many of the boats – one looks like a South Pacific island, another like the Taj Mahal – can be viewed at Waldo Point, half a mile beyond the cavernous concrete **Bay Model Visitor Center**, 2100 Bridgeway Ave (Tues–Sat 9am–4pm; free; ☎415/332-3870, ⊛www.baymodel.org). Inside the huge building, elevated walkways lead you around a scale model of the Bay, surrounding deltas and its aquatic inhabitants, offering insight on the enormity and diversity of this area.

Sausalito's newest attraction, situated back towards the Golden Gate Bridge at 557 McReynolds Rd, is the **Bay Area Discovery Museum** (Tues–Fri 9am–4pm, Sat & Sun 10am–5pm; $8.50, free every second Sat 1–5pm; ☎415/339-3900, ⊛www.baykidsmuseum.org). Located in the remodelled barracks of **Fort Baker**, it comprises a series of activities and workshops for youngsters from tots to 10 or so, including art and media rooms as well as the outdoor Lookout Cove area, where kids can play in a mini-tidepool, on a shipwreck, or on the model of the Golden Gate Bridge as it was during construction – pretty cool, as the real one is visible in the distance if it's clear.

The Marin County Coast to Bolinas

The **Shoreline Highway**, Hwy-1, cuts off west from US-101 just north of Sausalito, following the old main highway towards Mill Valley (see p.698). The first turn on the left, Tennessee Valley Road, leads up to the less-visited northern expanses of the Golden Gate National Recreation Area. You can take a beautiful three-mile hike from the parking lot at the end of the road, heading down along the secluded and lushly green **Tennessee Valley** to a small beach along a rocky cove, or you can take a trail-ride lesson on horseback from Miwok Livery at 701 Tennessee Valley Rd ($50 for 90min; ☎415/383-8048, ⊛www.miwokstables.com).

Hwy-1 twists up the canyon to a crest, where **Panoramic Highway** spears off to the right, following the ridge north to Muir Woods and Mount Tamalpais; Golden Gate Transit bus #63 to Stinson Beach follows this route every hour on weekends and holidays only. Be warned, however, that the hillsides are usually choked with fog until 11am, making the approach from San Francisco to Stinson Beach/Bolinas via Hwy-1 both dangerous and uninteresting. Two miles before you reach the crest, a small paved lane cuts off to the left, dropping down to the bottom of the broad canyon to the **Green Gulch Farm Zen Center** (☎415/383-3134, ⊛www.sfzc.org), an organic farm and Buddhist retreat, with an authentic Japanese teahouse and a simple but refined prayer hall. On Sunday mornings the center is open from 8.15am for a public meditation period and an informal lecture on Zen Buddhism at 10.15am, after which you can stroll down to Muir Beach. If you are interested in learning more about Zen, inquire about the center's Guest Student Program, which enables initiates to stay from three days to several weeks at a time (it costs about $15 a night). Residents rise well before dawn for meditation and prayer, then work much of the day in the gardens, tending the vegetables that are eventually served in many of the Bay Area's finest restaurants (notably *Greens* in San Francisco – see p.618). If you just want a weekend retreat, you can also stay overnight in the far more upmarket *Lindisfarne Guest House* (see p.692) on the grounds.

Beyond the Zen Center, the road down from Muir Woods rejoins Hwy-1 at **Muir Beach**, usually uncrowded and beautifully secluded in a semicircular cove. Three miles north, **Steep Ravine** drops sharply down the cliffs to a small beach, past very rustic cabins and a campground, bookable through Mount Tamalpais State Park (see p.692). A mile on is the small and lovely **Red Rocks** nudist beach, down a steep trail from a parking area along the highway. **Stinson Beach**, which is bigger, and more popular despite the rather cold water (it's packed on weekends in summer, when the traffic can be nightmarish), is a mile further. You can rent kayaks at Off the Beach Boats, 15 Cal del Mar ($22 for two hours, $90 all weekend, cheaper in winter; ☎415/868-9445).

Bolinas and southern Point Reyes

At the tip of the headland, due west from Stinson Beach, is the laid-back village of **BOLINAS**, though you may have a hard time finding it – road signs marking the turnoff from Hwy-1 are removed as soon as they're put up, by locals hoping to keep the place to themselves. The campaign may have backfired, though, since press coverage of the "sign war" has done more to publicize the town than any road sign ever did; to get there, take the first left beyond the estuary and follow the road to the end. Another example of local eccentricity is the refusal to switch to Daylight Saving Time. Bolinas is completely surrounded by federal property: the Golden Gate National Recreation Area and Point Reyes National Seashore. Even the lagoon was recently declared a National Bird Sanctuary. Known for its leftist hippy culture, the village itself has been home at different times to Grace Slick and Paul Kantner, and a regular colony of artists, bearded handymen, writers (the late trout-fishing author Richard Brautigan and basketball diarist Jim Carroll among them), and stray dogs. There's not a lot to see apart from the small **Bolinas Museum**, 48 Wharf Rd (Fri 1–5pm, Sat & Sun noon–5pm; free; ☎415/868-0330, ⊛www .bolinasmuseum.org), which has a few historical displays and works by local artists in a set of converted cottages around a courtyard. Mostly, it's just a case of people watching and taking in the laid-back atmosphere.

Beyond Bolinas, there's a rocky beach at the end of Wharf Road west of the village and, half a mile west at the end of Elm Road, **Duxbury Reef Nature Reserve** lures visitors to its tidal pools, full of sea stars, crabs, and sea anemones. Otherwise, Mesa Road heads north from Bolinas past the **Point Reyes Bird Observatory** (☎415/868-1221, ⊛www.prbo.org) – open for informal tours all day, though best visited in the morning. The first bird observatory in the US, this is still an important research and study center, and if you time it right you may be able to watch, or even help, the staff as they put colored bands on the birds, such as puffins, cormorants, and sandpipers, to keep track of them. Beyond here, the unpaved road leads onto the **Palomarin Trailhead**, the southern access into the Point Reyes National Seashore (see p.701). The best of the many beautiful hikes around the area leads past a number of small lakes and meadows for three miles to **Alamere Falls**, which throughout the winter and spring cascade down the cliffs onto Wildcat Beach. **Bass Lake**, the first along the trail, is a great spot for a swim and is best entered from one of the two rope-swings that hang above its shore.

At the junction of Bolinas Road and Hwy-1, cross the highway and head due east. If there's no sign warning the road is closed (landslides and washouts are common), continue up this route, the **Bolinas–Fairfax Road**, for a superb, winding drive through redwoods and grassy hillsides. When you reach the "T" in the road, turn left to get to Fairfax, or right to scale Mount Tamalpais.

Mount Tamalpais and Muir Woods National Monument

MOUNT TAMALPAIS, fondly known as Mount Tam, dominates the skyline of Marin County, hulking over the cool canyons of the rest of the county and dividing it into two distinct parts: the wild western slopes above the Pacific Coast and the increasingly suburban communities along the calmer Bay frontage. Panoramic Highway branches off from Hwy-1 along the crest through the center of **Mount Tamalpais State Park** (☎415/388-2070), which has some thirty miles of hiking trails and many campgrounds, though most of the redwoods which once covered its slopes have long since been chopped down to form the posts and beams of San Francisco's Victorian houses. One grove of these towering trees does remain, however, protected as the **MUIR WOODS NATIONAL MONUMENT** (daily 8am–sunset; $3; ☎415/388-2595, ⊛www.nps.gov/muwo), a mile down Muir Woods Road from Panoramic Highway. It's a tranquil and majestic spot, with sunlight filtering through the 300-foot trees down to the laurel- and fern-covered canyon below. The canyon's steep sides are what saved it from Mill Valley's lumbermen, and today it's one of the few first-growth redwood groves between San Francisco and the fantastic forests of Redwood National Park (see p.816), up the coast near the Oregon border.

Its proximity to San Francisco makes Muir Woods a popular day-trip, and the paved trails nearest the parking lot are often packed with bus-tour hordes. However, if you visit during the week, or outside midsummer, it's easy enough to leave the crowds behind, especially if you're willing to head off up the steep trails that climb the canyon sides. Winter is a particularly good time to come, as the streams are gurgling – the main creek flows down to Muir Beach, and salmon have been known to spawn in it – and the forest's inhabitants, including the colonies of ladybugs that spend their winter incubating in the rich undergrowth, are more likely to be seen going about their business. Keep an eye out for the various species of salamanders and newts that thrive in this damp environment; be warned, though, that some are poisonous and will bite if harassed.

One way to avoid the crowds, and the only way to get here on public transportation, is to enter the woods from the top by way of a two-mile hike from the **Pan Toll Ranger Station** (☎415/388-2070) on Panoramic Highway – which is a stop on the Golden Gate Transit #63 bus route. As the state park headquarters, the station has maps and information on hiking and camping, and rangers can suggest hikes to suit your mood and interests. From here the **Pan Toll Road** turns off to the right along the ridge to within a hundred yards of the 2571-foot summit of Mount Tamalpais, where there are breathtaking views of the distant Sierra Nevada, and red-necked turkey vultures listlessly circle.

Mill Valley

From the east peak of Mount Tamalpais, a quick two-mile hike downhill follows the **Temelpa Trail** through velvety shrubs of chaparral to **MILL VALLEY**, the oldest and most enticing of Marin County's inland towns – also accessible every thirty minutes by Golden Gate Transit bus #10 from San Francisco and Sausalito. Originally a logging center, it was from here that the destruction of the surrounding redwoods was organized, though for many years the town has made a healthy living out of tourism. The **Mill Valley and Mount Tamalpais Scenic Railroad** – according to the blurb, "the crookedest railroad in the world" – was cut into the slopes above the town in 1896, twisting up through nearly three hundred tight curves in under eight miles. The trip proved so popular with tourists that the line was extended down into Muir Woods in 1907, though road-building and fire combined to put an end to the railroad by 1930. You can, however, follow its old route from the end of Summit Avenue in Mill Valley, a popular trip with daredevils on mountain bikes, which were, incidentally, invented here.

Though much of Mill Valley's attraction lies in its easy access to hiking and mountain-bike trails up Mount Tam, its compact yet relaxed center has a number of cafés and some good shops and galleries. The *Depot Bookstore and Café* (Mon–Sat 7am–10pm, Sun 8am–10pm; ☎415/383-2665) is a popular bookshop, café, and meeting place at 87 Throckmorton Ave, next door to the Chamber of Commerce (see p.690), which has free maps of Mount Tam and area hiking trails. Across the street, the **Pleasure Principle** is a reminder of the Northern California eclecticism hidden beneath a posh surface – the store, the self-declared UFO headquarters of Mill Valley, is also the proud purveyor of a large vintage porn collection. If in the area in early October, don't miss the **Mill Valley Film Festival**, a world-class event that draws a host of up-and-coming directors, as well as Bay Area stars like Robin Williams and Sharon Stone; for program information, call ☎415/383-5346, or check ⓦwww.mvff.com.

Tiburon

TIBURON, at the tip of a narrow peninsula three miles east of US-101 and five miles from Mill Valley, is, like Sausalito, a ritzy harborside village to which hundreds of people come each weekend, many of them via direct Blue and Gold Fleet **ferries** from Pier 41 in San Francisco's Fisherman's Wharf. It's a relaxed place, less touristy than Sausalito, and if you're in the mood to take it easy and watch the boats sail across the Bay, sitting out on the sunny deck of one of the many cafés and bars can be idyllic. There are few specific sights to look out for here, but it's pleasant enough to simply wander around, browsing the galleries and antique shops. The best of these are grouped together in **Ark Row**, at the west end of Main Street, where the quirky buildings are actually old houseboats that were beached here early in the century. Further along, you can get a taste of the Wine Country at the Windsor Vineyards tasting room, 72 Main St (daily 10am–6pm; ☎415/435-3113, ⊛www.windsorvineyards .com). On a hill above the town stands **Old St Hilary's Church** (April–Oct Wed–Sun 1–4pm; ☎415/789-0066), a Carpenter Gothic beauty that is best seen in the spring, when the surrounding fields are covered with multicolored buckwheat, flax, and paintbrush.

Cyclists can cruise around the many plush houses of **Belvedere Island**, just across the Beach Road Bridge from the west end of Main Street, enjoying the fine views of the Bay and Golden Gate Bridge. More ambitious bikers can continue along the waterfront bike path, which winds from the bijou shops and galleries three miles west along undeveloped Richardson Bay frontage to a bird sanctuary at **Greenwood Cove**. The pristine Victorian house here is now the western headquarters of the National Audubon Society and open for tours on Sundays (10am–4pm; free); a small interpretive center has displays on local and migratory birds and wildlife.

Angel Island

However appealing, the pleasures of Tiburon are soon exhausted, and you'd be well advised to take the Angel Island Ferry (hourly 10am–4pm; $10 round-trip, plus $1 per bicycle; ☎415/435-2131, ⊛www.angelislandferry.com) a mile offshore to the largest island in the San Francisco Bay, ten times the size of Alcatraz. **ANGEL ISLAND** is officially a state park, but over the years it has served a variety of purposes, everything from a home for Miwok Native Americans to a World War II prisoner-of-war camp. It's full of ghostly ruins of old military installations but it's the nature of the place that lures people to Angel Island nowadays, with its oak and eucalyptus trees and sagebrush covering the hills above rocky coves and sandy beaches, giving the island a feel quite apart from the mainland. It offers some pleasant biking opportunities as well: a five-mile road rings the island, and an unpaved track, along with a number of hiking trails, leads up to the 800-foot hump of **Mount Livermore**, with panoramic views of the Bay Area.

The ferry arrives at **Ayala Cove**, where a small snack bar selling hot dogs and cold drinks provides the only sustenance available on the island – bring a picnic if you plan to spend the day here. The nearby **visitor center** (daily 9am–4pm; ☎415/435-1915), in an old building that was built as a quarantine facility for soldiers returning from the Philippines after the Spanish–American War, has displays on the island's history. Around the point on the northwest corner of the island the **North Garrison**, built in 1905, was the site of a prisoner-of-war camp during World War II; while the larger **East Garrison**, on the Bay half a mile beyond, was the major transfer point for soldiers bound for the South Pacific.

Quarry Beach around the point is the best on the island, a clean sandy shore that's protected from the winds blowing in through the Golden Gate; it's also a popular landing spot for kayakers and canoeists who paddle across the Bay from Berkeley. **Camping** on Angel Island (see p.692 for details) is well worth considering for the view of San Francisco and the East Bay at night; the nine sites fill up fast, so make reservations well ahead. For **tours** of Angel Island, contact Angel Island TramTours (☎415/897-0715, ⊛www .angelisland.com), which rents mountain bikes ($10/hour, $30/day), gives tram tours ($12.50), and leads all-day kayak trips around the island (May–Oct weekends; $130).

Sir Francis Drake Boulevard and Central Marin County

The quickest route to the wilds of the Point Reyes National Seashore, and the only way to get there on public transportation, is by way of **SIR FRANCIS DRAKE BOULEVARD**, which cuts across central Marin County through the inland towns of **San Anselmo** and **Fairfax**, reaching the coast thirty miles west at a crescent-shaped bay where, in 1579, Drake supposedly landed and claimed all of what he called Nova Albion for England. The route makes an excellent day-long cycling tour, with the reward of good beaches, a youth hostel, and some tasty restaurants at the end of the road.

The Larkspur Golden Gate Transit **ferry**, which leaves from the Ferry Building in San Francisco, is the longest and, surprisingly, least expensive of the Bay crossings. Primarily a commuter route, it docks at the modern space-frame terminal at Larkspur Landing. The monolithic, red-tile-roofed complex you see on the bayfront a mile east is the maximum-security **San Quentin State Prison**, which houses the state's most violent and notorious criminals, and of which Johnny Cash sang so resonantly "I hate every stone of you." If you arrive by car over the Richmond–San Rafael Bridge, follow road signs off Hwy-101 for the **San Quentin Prison Museum**, Building 106, Dolores Way (Mon–Fri 10am–4pm, Sat 11.45am–3.15pm; $2).

San Anselmo, Fairfax, and Point Reyes Station

SAN ANSELMO, set in a broad valley two miles north of Mount Tam, calls itself "the antiques capital of Northern California" and sports a tiny center of specialty shops, furniture stores, and cafés that draws many San Francisco shoppers on weekends. The ivy-covered **San Francisco Theological Seminary** off Bolinas Avenue, which dominates the town from the hill above, is worth a quick visit for the view and mission-styled architecture. At serene **Robson-Harrington Park** on Crescent Avenue you can picnic among well-tended gardens, and the very green and leafy **Creek Park** follows the creek that winds through the town center, but otherwise there's not a lot to do but stop in at a restaurant or café or browse through fine bookstores, such as Oliver's Books, at 645 San Anselmo Ave (☎415/454-4421).

Center Boulevard follows the tree-lined creek west for a mile to **FAIRFAX**, a much less ostentatiously hedonistic community than the harborside towns, though in many ways it still typifies Marin lifestyles, with an array of wholefood stores and bookstores geared to a thoughtfully mellow crowd. From Fairfax, the narrow Bolinas Road twists up and over the mountains to the coast at Stinson Beach, while Sir Francis Drake Boulevard winds through a pastoral landscape of ranch houses hidden away up oak-covered valleys.

Ten miles west of Fairfax along Sir Francis Drake Boulevard, **Samuel Taylor State Park** has excellent camping (see p.692 for details); five miles more brings you to the coastal Hwy-1 and the hamlet of **Olema**, at the entrance to the park, which has good food and lodging. A mile north of Olema sits the tourist town of **POINT REYES STATION**, another good place to stop off for a bite to eat or to pick up picnic supplies before heading off to enjoy the wide open spaces of the Point Reyes National Seashore just beyond.

The Point Reyes National Seashore

From Point Reyes Station, Sir Francis Drake Boulevard heads out to the westernmost tip of Marin County at Point Reyes through the **POINT REYES NATIONAL SEASHORE**, a near-island of wilderness surrounded on three sides by more than fifty miles of isolated coastline – pine forests and sunny meadows bordered by rocky cliffs and sandy, windswept beaches. This wing-shaped landmass, something of an aberration along the generally straight coastline north of San Francisco, is in fact a rogue piece of the earth's crust that has been drifting slowly and steadily northward along the San Andreas Fault, having started some six million years ago as a suburb of Los Angeles. When the great earthquake of 1906 shattered San Francisco, the land here – the quake's epicenter – shifted over sixteen feet in an instant, though damage was confined to a few skewed cattle fences.

The park's **visitor center** (see p.690 for details), two miles southwest of Point Reyes Station near Olema, just off Hwy-1 on Bear Valley Road, holds engaging displays on the geology and natural history of the region. Rangers dish out excellent hiking and cycling itineraries, and have up-to-date information on the weather, which can change quickly and be cold and windy along the coast even when it's hot and sunny here, three miles inland. They also handle permits and reservations for the various hike-in **campgrounds** within the park. Nearby, a replica of a native Miwok village has an authentic religious **roundhouse**, and a popular hike follows the Bear Valley Trail along Coast Creek four miles to **Arch Rock**, a large tunnel in the seaside cliffs that you can walk through at low tide.

North of the visitor center, Limantour Road heads west six miles to the *HI-Point Reyes Hostel* (see p.692), continuing on another two miles to the coast at **Limantour Beach**, one of the best protected swimming beaches and a good place to watch the sea birds in the adjacent estuary. Bear Valley Road rejoins Sir Francis Drake Boulevard just past Limantour Road, leading north along Tomales Bay through the village of **Inverness**, so named because the landscape reminded an early settler of his home in the Scottish Highlands. Eight miles west of Inverness, a turn leads down past **Johnson's Oyster Farm** (Tues–Sun 8am–4pm; ☎415/669-1149) – which sells the bivalves for around $7–9 a dozen, less than half the price you'd pay in San Francisco – to **Drake's Beach**, the presumed landing spot of Sir Francis in 1579 (his voyage journal makes the exact location unclear). Appropriately, the coastline here resembles the southern coast of England, often cold, wet, and windy, with chalk-white cliffs rising above the wide, sandy beach. The road continues southwest another four miles to the very tip of Point Reyes. A precarious-looking **lighthouse** (Thurs–Sun 10am–4.30pm; free) stands firm against the crashing surf, and the bluffs are excellent for watching migrating **gray whales** from mid-March to April and late December to early February. Just over a mile back from the lighthouse a narrow road leads to **Chimney Rock**, where you can often see basking **elephant seals** or **sea lions** from the overlook. Keep in mind the distance and slow speeds it takes to reach these spots, which is hard to judge on a map. From the visitor center, it's 15 miles to Drakes Beach and 23 miles to the lighthouse. Check with the rangers on weather conditions before setting out.

The northern tip of the Point Reyes National Seashore, **Tomales Point**, is accessible via Pierce Point Road, which turns off Sir Francis Drake Boulevard two miles north of Inverness. Jutting out into Tomales Bay, it's the least-visited section of the park and a refuge for hefty **tule elk**; it's also a great place to admire the lupins, poppies, and other wildflowers that appear in the spring. The best swimming (at least the warmest water) is at **Heart's Desire Beach**, just before the end of the road. Down the bluffs from where the road comes to a dead end, there are excellent tidal pools at rocky **McClure's Beach**. North of Point Reyes Station, Hwy-1 continues past the famed oyster beds of Tomales Bay north along the crashing surf and up the Northern California coast.

San Rafael and Northern Marin County

You may pass through **SAN RAFAEL** on your way north from San Francisco on US-101, but there's little to detain you. The county seat and the only sizeable city in Marin County, it has none of the woodsy qualities that make the other towns special, though you'll come across a couple of good restaurants and bars along Fourth Street, the main drag. Its lone attraction is the old **Mission San Rafael Arcangel** (daily 11am–4pm; free), in fact a 1949 replica that was built near the site of the 1817 original on Fifth Avenue at A Street. The real points of interest, however, are well on the outskirts: the Marin County Civic Center to the north and the little-known China Camp State Park along the Bay to the east.

The **Marin County Civic Center** (Mon–Fri 9am–5pm; tours Wed 10.30am; free; ☏415/499-6646), spanning the hills just east of US-101 a mile north of central San Rafael, is a strange, otherworldly complex of administrative offices, plus an excellent performance space that resembles a giant viaduct capped by a bright-blue-tiled roof. These buildings were architect **Frank Lloyd Wright**'s one and only government project, and although the huge circus tents and amusement park at the core of the designer's conception were never built, it does have some interesting touches, such as the atrium lobbies that open directly to the outdoors.

From the Civic Center, North San Pedro Road loops around the headlands through **China Camp State Park** (☏415/456-0766), an expansive area of pastures and open spaces that's hard to reach without your own transportation. It takes its name from the intact but long-abandoned Chinese shrimp-fishing village at the far eastern tip of the park, the sole survivor of the many small Chinese communities that once dotted the California coast. The ramshackle buildings, small wooden pier, and old boats lying on the sand are pure John Steinbeck; the only recent addition is a chain-link fence to protect the site from vandals. On the weekend you can get beer and sandwiches from the old shack at the foot of the pier, but the atmosphere is best during the week at sunset, when there's often no one around at all. There's a **campground** (see p.692) at the northern end of the park, about two miles from the end of the Golden Gate Transit bus #23 route.

Six miles north of San Rafael, the **Lucas Valley Road** turns off west, twisting across Marin to Point Reyes. Although he lives and works here, it was not named after Star Wars filmmaker George Lucas, whose sprawling **Skywalker Ranch** studios are well hidden off the road. Hwy-37 cuts off east, eight miles north of San Rafael, heading around the top of the Bay into the Wine Country of the Sonoma and Napa valleys (see p.770).

Marin County eating

Marin's **restaurants** are as varied in personality as the people who inhabit the county – homely neighborhood **cafés** dish out nutritious portions to healthy mountain-bikers, well-appointed waterside restaurants cater to tourists, and gourmet establishments serve delicate concoctions to affluent executives. We have listed the best of the options below.

Broken Drum 1132 Fourth St, San Rafael ☎415/456-4677. Lively brewery/grill with pavement seating, where you can tuck into cheapish fish tacos with mango salsa or mesquite grilled ribs.
Bubba's Diner 566 San Anselmo Ave, San Anselmo ☎415/459-6862. Hip little old-fashioned diner with a friendly and casual atmosphere; be sure to try a delicious biscuit with your meal.
Cactus Café 393 Miller Ave, Mill Valley ☎415/388-8226. Reasonably priced, small, and friendly restaurant, tucked in an off-street mall, serving fun Cal-Mex food flavored with homemade hot sauce.
Caffè Trieste 1000 Bridgeway Ave, Sausalito ☎415/332-7770. This distant relative of San Francisco's North Beach institution serves good coffee, a wide menu of pastas and salads, and great *gelati*.
Deer Park Villa 367 Bolinas Rd, Fairfax ☎415/456-8084. Moderate to expensive Italian/ Californian-style cuisine, ranging from pastas to meat in adventurous sauces, dished up indoors or in the leafy garden.
Dipsea Café 200 Shoreline Hwy, Mill Valley ☎415/381-0298. Hearty pancakes, omelets, sandwiches, and salads, especially good before a day out hiking on Mount Tamalpais. Breakfast and lunch only.
Guaymas 5 Main St, Tiburon ☎415/435-6300. Some of the most unique, inventive Cal-Mex cuisine in the Bay Area (and priced accordingly), paired with a spectacular view of the city.
Hilda's 639 San Anselmo Ave, San Anselmo ☎415/457-9266. Great breakfasts and lunches in this down-home, cozy café.
The Lark Creek Inn 234 Magnolia Ave, Larkspur ☎415/924-7766. The place to go in Marin for fine dining. The contemporary American food at this classy restored Victorian is expensive, but not without reason: the food, such as pan-fried sweetbreads and gorgonzola soufflé is exquisite, the service first-rate, and the atmosphere charming.
Mountain Home Inn 810 Panoramic Hwy, above Mill Valley ☎415/381-9000. A place that's as good for the view of the surrounding valleys as for the food, with broiled meat and fish dishes served up in a rustic lodge on the slopes of Mount Tamalpais.

New Morning Café 1696 Tiburon Blvd, Tiburon ☎415/435-4315. Lots of healthy wholegrain sandwiches, plus salads and omelets.
Piazza D'Angelo 22 Miller Ave, Mill Valley ☎415/388-2000. Good salads, tasty pasta, and affordable pizzas, served up in a lively but comfortable room right off the downtown plaza.
Rice Table 1617 Fourth St, San Rafael ☎415/456-1808. From the shrimp chips through the crab pancakes and noodles on to the fried plantain desserts, these fragrant and spicy Indonesian dishes are an excellent value and worth planning a day around. Dinners only.
Sam's Anchor Café 27 Main St, Tiburon ☎415/435-4527. This rough-hewn, amiable waterfront café and bar has been around for more than 75 years. Good burgers, sandwiches, and very popular Sunday brunches are best enjoyed on the outdoor deck.
Sartaj India Cafe 43 Caledonia St, Sausalito ☎415/332-7103. Great, inexpensive Indian place that does a selection of meat and veggie dishes, including *thalis*, and, oddly enough, bagels for those who can't stomach a spicy breakfast.
Station House Café 11180 Hwy-1 (Main Street), Point Reyes Station ☎415/663-1515. Serving three meals daily, this friendly local favorite entices diners from miles around to sample their grilled seafood and top-notch steaks.
Stinson Beach Grill 3465 Shoreline Hwy, Stinson Beach ☎415/868-2002. Somewhat pricey, but relaxed, with outdoor dining – look out for the bright-blue building right in the heart of town. Mainly steaks and seafood, but leave room for the glorious puddings.
Sweet Ginger 400 Caledonia St, Sausalito ☎415/332-1683. Moderately-priced small Japanese restaurant that serves sushi, sashimi, and main courses like tempura and teriyaki.
Thai Orchid 726 San Anselmo Ave, San Anselmo ☎415/457-9470. Family restaurant dishing up spicy Thai fare, including a fine range of curries and zesty salads.
Tommy's Wok 3001 Bridgeway, Sausalito ☎415/332-5818. This Chinese specializes in organic vegetables, free-range meats, and fresh seafood, cooked in Mandarin, Hunan, and Szechuan recipes.

Marin County cafés, drinking, and nightlife

While the Marin County **nightlife** is never as charged as it gets in San Francisco, almost every town has at least a couple of **cafés** that are open long hours for a jolt of caffeine, and any number of saloon-like **bars** where you'll feel at home immediately. In addition, since most of the honchos of the Bay Area music scene and dozens of lesser-known but no less brilliant session musicians and songwriters live here, Marin's nightclubs are unsurpassed for catching big names in intimate locales.

Cafés

Bridgeway Café 633 Bridgeway, Sausalito ☎415/332-3426. A good place to relax over a coffee or grab a gourmet egg breakfast at reasonable prices by local standards.

Depot Bookstore and Café 87 Throckmorton Ave, Mill Valley ☎415/383-2665. Lively café in an old train station, sharing space with a bookstore and newsstand. Weekly readings from local and nationally recognized authors.

Fairfax Café 33 Broadway, Fairfax ☎415/459-6404. Excellent Mediterranean food with occasional evening poetry readings.

Java Rama 546 San Anselmo Ave, San Anselmo ☎415/453-5282. Specialty coffees and pastries along with modern rock on the stereo attracts a young crowd.

Sweden House 35 Main St, Tiburon ☎415/435-9767. Great coffee and marvelous pastries on a jetty overlooking the yacht harbor, all for surprisingly reasonable prices.

Bars

The Bar With No Name 757 Bridgeway Ave, Sausalito ☎415/332-1392. An ex-haunt of the Beats, which hosts live jazz several times per week beginning at 8pm and on Sundays from 3–7pm.

Broadway 19 Broadway, Fairfax ☎415/459-0293. Live music every night, featuring a wide range of acts, some quite well known, others local or up-and-coming talent.

Café Amsterdam 23 Broadway, Fairfax ☎415/256-8020. Live alternative folk-rock nightly with an outdoor patio, microbrews, espresso drinks, and an extensive menu.

Fourth Street Tavern 711 Fourth St, San Rafael ☎415/454-4044. Gutsy, no-frills beer bar with free, bluesy music most nights.

Marin Brewing Company 1809 Larkspur Landing, Larkspur ☎415/461-4677. Lively pub opposite the Larkspur ferry terminal, with half a dozen tasty ales – try the malty Albion Amber or the Marin Hefe Weiss – all brewed on the premises.

Pelican Inn Hwy-1, Muir Beach ☎415/383-6000. Fair selection of traditional English and modern Californian ales, plus fish'n'chips (and rooms to rent in case you overdo it).

Smiley's Schooner Saloon 41 Wharf Rd, Bolinas ☎415/868-1311. The bartender calls the customers by name here at one of the oldest continually operating bars in the state.

Sweetwater 153 Throckmorton Ave, Mill Valley ☎415/388-3820. Large, open room full of beer-drinking locals that after dark evolves into Marin's prime live-music venue, bringing in some of the biggest names in music, from jazz and blues all-stars to Jefferson Airplane survivors.

Travel details

Trains

A daily Amtrak shuttle bus departs from San Francisco from the San Francisco Shopping Center, 835 Market St (8am & 8.25pm); Pier 39 at Fisherman's Wharf (8.15am & 8.35pm); and the Ferry Building (8.40am & 8.55pm) to the Emeryville depot, from where the Coast Starlight train departs at 10.15pm northeast to Sacramento, Portland, and Seattle, and 8.20am south to San Jose, Santa Barbara, Los Angeles, and San Diego. The San Joaquin route operates four times daily to Stockton, Modesto, Fresno, and Bakersfield, where there are Amtrak Thruway bus connections to Los Angeles. Amtrak's Capitol Corridor route links Oakland with San Jose (four daily; 1hr). San Francisco–San Jose commuters rely more on Caltrain (☎1-800/660-

4287). Forty trains make the trip each way daily, taking 1hr 30min or a little more ($5.25 each way). The San Francisco station is at 4th and King streets.

Buses

Greyhound unless specified otherwise; note the number of services can vary during the course of the year:

San Francisco to: Eureka (2 daily; 7hr–7hr 45min); Los Angeles (18 daily; 7hr 25min–12hr 45min; or 1 Green Tortoise weekly; 12hr); Redding (6 daily; 5hr 30min–10hr); Reno (19 daily; 5–7hr); Sacramento (22 daily; 2–3hr); San Diego (7 daily; 10hr 30min–14hr 40min); San Jose (13 daily; 1hr–1hr 45min); San Rafael (2 daily; 1hr); Santa Rosa (3 daily; 1hr 50min–3hr 10min).

9

The Gold Country and Lake Tahoe

Highlights

* **Sacramento Capitol building**
The elegant Classical Revival building has some spectacular architectural detailing, and the comprehensive tours provide a glimpse of California's government innards. See p.715

* **The Empire Mine State Park**
Now retired among thick stands of pine, the impressive array of mining equipment here opens an atmospheric window onto California's Gold Rush heyday. See p.726

* **Indian Grinding Rock** In this national park nine miles from Jackson, the Miwok Indians once carved hundreds of small cups into the limestone. See p.735

* **Jamestown's Railtown 1897 State Historic Park** Even if you're not a trainspotter, it's worth stopping by to see the old engines, thanks to the enthusiastic, endlessly knowledgeable docents. See p.741

* **Lake Tahoe** Beautiful scenery is guaranteed at any time of year around Lake Tahoe, whether you're skiing the slopes or paddling on the lake itself. See p.742

* **Virginia City, Nevada** A more obvious Wild West feel than most of its California contemporaries can be enjoyed in this mining town. See p.761

△ Lake Tahoe

The Gold Country and Lake Tahoe

> The gold of California is a touchstone which has betrayed the rottenness, the baseness, of mankind. Satan, from one of his elevations, showed mankind the kingdom of California, and they entered into a compact with him at once.
>
> Henry David Thoreau, *Journal*, 1 February 1852

About 150 years before techies from all over the world rushed to California in search of Silicon Valley gold, the rough-and-ready forty-niners invaded the **GOLD COUNTRY** of the Sierra Nevada to pan for the real thing. The first prospectors on the scene – about 150 miles east of San Francisco – sometimes found large nuggets of solid gold sitting along the riverbanks. While the dot-commers spent hours tied to computer screens, the miners worked all day in the hot sun, wading through fast-flowing, ice-cold rivers to recover trace amounts of the precious metal that had been eroded out of the hard-rock veins of the Mother Lode – the name given by miners to the rich sources of gold at the heart of the mining district.

The region ranges from the foothills near Yosemite National Park to the deep gorge of the Yuba River, two hundred miles north. In many parts throughout this area, little seems to have changed since the argonauts began their digging, and even in the air-conditioned comfort of your rental car – without one it's nearly impossible to navigate the area – distances from one town to the next may seem exponentially greater than they appear on the map: count on plenty of switchbacks and steep climbs.

The **Mother Lode** was first discovered in 1848 at Sutter's Mill in **Coloma**, forty miles east of **Sacramento**, the largest city in the Gold Country, and the state capital. Sacramento was once a tiny military outpost and farming community that boomed as a supply town for miners. The mining areas spread to the north and south of Sacramento and preserve distinct identities. The **northern mines**, around the twin towns of **Grass Valley** and **Nevada City**, were the richest fields, and today retain most of their Gold Rush buildings in an unspoiled, near-alpine setting halfway up the towering peaks of the Sierra Nevada. The hot and dusty **southern mines**, on the other hand, became depopulated faster than their northern neighbors. These towns were the rowdiest and wildest of all, and it's not too hard to imagine that many of

Although plenty of people come through the area to see the Gold Rush sights, at least as many come to enjoy the thrills and spills of **whitewater rafting** and **kayaking** on the various forks of the American, Stanislaus, Tuolumne, and Merced rivers, which wind down through the region from the Sierra crest towards Sacramento. Whether you just want to float in a leisurely manner downstream, or fancy careening through five-foot walls of water, contact one of the many river-trip operators, among them American River Recreation (☏1-800/333-7238, ⓦwww.arrafting.com), CBOC Whitewater Raft Adventures (☏1-800/356-2262, ⓦwww.cbocwhitewater.com), O.A.R.S., Inc. (☏1-800/346-6277, ⓦwww.oars.com), Tributary Whitewater Tours (☏1-800/672-3846, ⓦwww.whitewatertours.com), and Whitewater Adventures (☏1-800/977-4837, ⓦwww.whitewater-adv.com). Trips run from late spring through early fall and start at about $75 per person.

the abandoned towns sprinkled over the area once supported upwards of fifty saloons and gambling parlors, each with its own cast of cardsharps and thieves, as immortalized by writers like Bret Harte and Mark Twain.

Most of the mountainous forest along the Sierra crest is preserved as near-pristine wilderness, with excellent hiking, camping, and backpacking. There's great skiing in winter around the mountainous rim of **Lake Tahoe** – "Lake of the Sky" to the native Washoe – on the border between California and Nevada, aglow under the bright lights of the casinos that line its southeastern shore. East of the mountains, in the dry Nevada desert, sit the highway towns of **Reno**, famed for low-budget weddings and speedy divorces, and **Carson City**, the Nevada state capital and one-time boomtown of the Comstock silver mines.

Getting around

Hwy-49 runs north to south, linking most of the sights of the Gold Country; two main highways, US-50 and I-80, along with the transcontinental **railroad**, cross the Sierra Nevada through the heart of the region, and there is frequent Greyhound **bus** service to most of the major towns. To get a real feel for the Gold Country, however, and to reach the most evocative ghost towns, you'll need a **car**. Also, though it's all very scenic, **cycling** throughout the region is not a viable option: the distances between the sights are long, and the roads are far too hilly and narrow for comfort.

Sacramento and the Central Mother Lode

Roughly midway between San Francisco and the crest of the Sierra Nevada, and well connected by Greyhound, Amtrak, and the arterial I-5 highway, **Sacramento** is likely to be your first stop in the Gold Country.

It's the quintessential American state capital, with sleepy tree-lined streets fanning out from the elegant State Capitol building. The city's waterfront quarter, restored to the style of Pony Express days, contains the region's largest collection of Gold Rush–era buildings. From Sacramento, two main routes climb east through the gentle foothills of the Mother Lode: US-50 passes through the old supply town of **Placerville** on its way to Lake Tahoe, while I-80 zooms by **Auburn** over the Donner Pass into Nevada. Both towns have retained enough of their Gold Rush past to merit at least a brief look if you're passing through, and both make good bases for the more picturesque towns of the northern mines.

Sacramento

Until recently, **SACRAMENTO** had the reputation of being decidedly dull, a suburban enclave of politicians and bureaucrats surrounded by miles of marshes and farmland. Little wonder: the government has long loomed large over the city, filling its streets on weekdays and emptying the center at weekends; but now residential neighborhoods are slowly reawakening, especially around the Midtown area, thanks to the cafés and restaurants that have mushroomed on many of the leafier blocks. The election of Arnold "the Governator" Schwarzenegger in a 2003 election didn't hurt either: his dash of Hollywood pizzazz (and Kennedy-grade connections courtesy of his wife, TV anchor Maria Shriver) has energized the city far more than his predecessor, the aptly named Gray Davis. Arnold has also proved a surprisingly popular and moderate governor, failing to fulfil many locals' early fears that he would turn state government into a media circus. Schwarzenegger aside, there's increasing local pride in the city's Gold Rush history, which has led to important historic preservation and restoration projects, injecting a hefty, bludgeoning dose of tourist dollars into the local economy.

Some history

Before gold was discovered in 1848, the area around Sacramento belonged entirely to one man, **John Sutter**. He came here from Switzerland in 1839 to farm the flat, marshy lands at the foot of the Sierra Nevada, which were then within Mexican California. Sacramento, the prosperous community he founded, became a main stopping place for the few trappers and travelers who made their way inland or across the range of peaks. Yet it was after the discovery of flakes of **gold** in the foothills forty miles east that things really took off and the small trading post was transformed.

Sutter's 50,000-acre settlement, set at the confluence of the Sacramento and American rivers in the flatlands of the northern Central Valley, was granted to him by the Mexican government and he worked hard to build the colony into a busy trading center and cattle ranch. He was poised to become a wealthy man when his hopes were thwarted by the discovery of gold at a nearby sawmill. His workers quit their jobs to go prospecting, and many thousands more flocked to the goldfields, trampling over Sutter's lands: he was left a broken man. The small colony was soon overrun: since ships could sail upriver from the San Francisco Bay, Sacramento quickly became the main supply point for miners bound for the isolated camps in the foothills above. The city prospered, and in 1854 Sacramento snagged the title of **California state capital**, thanks to its equidistance between the gold mines, the rich farmlands of the Central Valley, and the financial center of San Francisco. As the Gold Rush faded, Sacramento remained important as a transportation center, first as the western terminus of the Pony Express and later as the western headquarters of the Transcontinental Railroad. Although its administrative role saved the city when mining dollars dwindled, it also smothered much of its rough, pioneer edges and, even now, it's only slowly developing a distinct, urban personality.

Arrival, information, and city transportation

At the intersection of the I–5, I–80, US–50, and Hwy–99 freeways, Sacramento is the hub for many long-distance transportation networks. Sacramento International **airport** (℡916/874–0700, ⓦwww.sacairports.org), twelve miles northwest of downtown, is served by most major domestic airlines. SuperShuttle Sacramento vans (℡1–800/BLUEVAN, ⓦwww.supershuttle.com) can take you directly to any downtown destination for $13. Thanks to its status as a governmental hub, public transport links are plentiful: **trains** from Los Angeles and Chicago stop at the Amtrak station at Fourth and I streets, near Old Sacramento (℡1–800/872–7245, ⓦwww.amtrak.com), while the Capitol Corridor route has almost twenty daily services linking Sacramento with the Bay Area (℡1–800/872–7245, ⓦwww.amtrakcapitols.com). From here, it's easy to catch a Thruway bus into the main Gold Country towns and the Lake Tahoe area. An almost continuous stream of Greyhound **buses** pulls into the bus depot at 715 L St, a block from the K Street Mall (℡1–800/231–2222).

There are two **visitor centers**: one in the heart of tourist-clogged Old Sacramento at 1004 2nd St (daily 10am–5pm; ℡916/442–7644, ⓦwww.discovergold.org) and another close to K Street Mall downtown at 1608 I St (Mon–Fri 8am–5pm; ℡916/808–7777, ⓦwww.discovergold.org). Pick up a copy of the handy *Sacramento Visitors' Guide* (with maps and listings of accommodation and places to eat and drink in the city) at these offices or almost everywhere tourists congregate; the CVB also publishes an exhaustively informative self-guided walking tour of Sacramento's historic architecture. For the latest on **events and entertainment** in Sacramento, the best option is to check out the free *Sacramento News & Review*; otherwise, there's *Ticket*, the Friday supplement to the *Sacramento Bee* newspaper (50¢) or the free music listings publication *Alive and Kicking*. The city's gay and lesbian scene is lively enough to spawn two freesheets, *MGW* and *Outword*, which also contain general restaurant and events listings.

The city is compact, flat, and somewhat **walkable**, though many locals get around (especially along the 25-mile cycle path along the American River to Folsom Lake) by **bike** – rentals are available at Bike Sacramento, 1050 Front St, Suite 110, in Old Sacramento (℡916/444–0200), renting bikes starting around $15 an hour. The city center is criss-crossed with an extensive **bus and light rail** network – timetables and maps are available from the visitor centers and the main transportation office, 1400 29th St at N Street (Mon–Fri 8am–5pm; ℡916/321–2877). The service you're most likely to use is the DASH shuttle (Rte-30) connecting the Amtrak Station, K Street Mall, and Old Sacramento (50¢; ℡916/321–2877, ⓦwww.sacrt.com). The **riverboat tours** leaving from the L Street landing in Old Sacramento are popular if hokey: the paddle-wheel steamboats *Matthew McKinley* and *Spirit of Sacramento* offer varied trips along the Sacramento River ($10–35; ℡916/552–2933 or 1–800/433–0263, ⓦwww.spiritofsacramento.com). **Car rental agencies** include Budget, 6420 McNair Circle (℡1–800/527–0700), Enterprise, 1409 16th St (℡1–800/736–8222), and Hertz, 1025 16th St (℡916/448–2228).

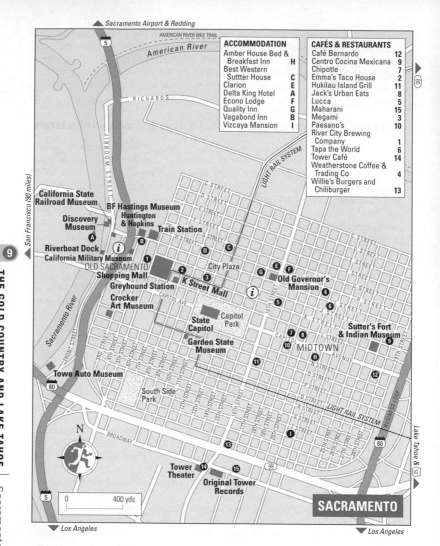

Sacramento Airport & Redding

AMERICAN RIVER BIKE TRAIL

American River

RICHARDS

ACCOMMODATION	
Amber House Bed &	
Breakfast Inn	H
Best Western	
Suttter House	C
Clarion	E
Delta King Hotel	A
Econo Lodge	F
Quality Inn	G
Vagabond Inn	B
Vizcaya Mansion	I

CAFÉS & RESTAURANTS	
Café Bernardo	12
Centro Cocina Mexicana	9
Chipotle	7
Emma's Taco House	2
Hukilau Island Grill	11
Jack's Urban Eats	8
Lucca	5
Maharani	15
Megami	3
Paesano's	10
River City Brewing	
Company	1
Tapa the World	6
Tower Café	14
Weatherstone Coffee &	
Trading Co	4
Willie's Burgers and	
Chiliburger	13

LIGHT RAIL SYSTEM

San Francisco (90 miles)

California State Railroad Museum
BF Hastings Museum
Discovery Museum
Huntington & Hopkins
Train Station
Riverboat Dock
California Military Museum
OLD SACRAMENTO
Shopping Mall
Greyhound Station
Crocker Art Museum

City Plaza
K Street Mall
Old Governor's Mansion

Sacramento River

FRONT STREET

State Capitol
Capitol Park
Garden State Museum

Sutter's Fort & Indian Museum

MIDTOWN

CAPITOL AVE.

Towe Auto Museum

South Side Park

Lake Tahoe & (50)

BROADWAY

LIGHT RAIL SYSTEM

BUSINESS LOOP

N

Tower Theater
Original Tower Records

SACRAMENTO

0   400 yds

Los Angeles   Los Angeles

Accommodation

Sacramento has plenty of reasonably priced places to stay, all within easy walking distance of the center. A number of **motels** cluster around the old Governor's Mansion on the north side of town around 16th and H streets, a convenient walk to the trendy **Midtown** area, where much of the city's night-life is centered. Dozens of other accommodation options line the highways on the outskirts, particularly Richards Boulevard, just off I-5. **Downtown**, choices are limited primarily to unexciting chains with a few B&Bs nearby – rates at weekends are often steeply discounted thanks to the exodus of government workers. There's no good **camping** anywhere within easy reach of Sacramento, though KOA runs the RV-heavy *Sacramento Metro* site, 3951

Lake Rd, West Sacramento (☏916/371-6771 or 1-800/562-2747, ⊛www
.sacramentokoa.com; ❶), four miles west of the center.

Amber House Bed & Breakfast Inn 1315 22nd
St at N, Midtown ☏916/444-8085 or 1-800/755-
6526, ⊛www.amberhouse.com. The pick of the
city's B&Bs, with luxurious rooms including marble
baths, *Amber House* offers sumptuous breakfasts
– with rates to match. A worthwhile treat to avoid
the endless chain motels nearby. ❻

Best Western Sutter House 1100 H St, Downtown ☏916/441-1314 or 1-800/830-1314,
⊛www.thesutterhouse.com. Low-rise hotel well
located in the center of town, with large, comfy
rooms set around an open-air pool and sun-baked
courtyard. ❺

Clarion 700 16th St at H, Downtown ☏916/444-
8000 or 1-800/443-0880, ⊛www.choicehotels
.com. Better than you might expect for a large
chain motel thanks to its central location, excellent
facilities (free parking, pool), and modern rooms
– the weekend rates are especially low if you book
ahead. ❺

Delta King Hotel 1000 Front St, Old Sacramento
☏916/444-5464 or 1-800/825-5464, ⊛www
.deltaking.com. A 1926 paddle-wheel river boat
now permanently moored on the waterfront:
although the rooms fail to justify their "stateroom"
advertising, the vessel makes an enjoyably
unusual place to stay. Be aware the area is
usually throbbing with visitors at weekends, and
prices rise accordingly. ❺–❼

Econo Lodge 711 16th St at H, Downtown
☏916/443-6631 or 1-800/553-2666,
⊛www.econolodge.com. Best deal in town, with
basic but comfortable rooms and complimentary
continental breakfast. ❷

HI-Sacramento 925 H St at 10th, Downtown
☏916/443-1691, ⊛www.norcalhostels.org. This
hostel is housed in a rambling 1885 mansion
that was recently shipped wholesale across the
street from its original location. It has all the
usual facilities, plus free bike rental, but there's
a daytime lockout and 11pm curfew. $23.50
for members, $26.50 for others. There's a very
limited number of private rooms ranging from
$40–75, depending on size and private vs.
shared bath. ❶

Quality Inn 818 15th St at I, Downtown
☏916/444-3980 or 1-800/228-5151, ⊛www
.qualityinn.com/hotel/ca505. Refurbished rooms
near the old Governor's Mansion, equipped with
a pool. ❸

Vagabond Inn 909 3rd St at J, Old Town
☏916/446-1481 or 1-800/522-1555, ⊛www
.vagabondinns.com. Motor-lodge-style
accommodation near the river and Old
Sacramento: there's a pool and free shuttle to
public transport hubs, plus free continental
breakfast. ❺

Vizcaya Mansion 2019 21st St at T, Midtown
☏916/455-5243 or 1-800/456-2019, ⊛www
.sterlinghotels.com. A lavish, historic property
with elegantly furnished rooms and marble-tiled
bathrooms. ❻

The Town

Most of the local attractions in Sacramento are close together, in one of the
three main areas that comprise the city center: the I-5 highway quarantines
Old Sacramento from the commercial hub of **Downtown**, centered on K
Street Mall, as well as the funkier, residential **Midtown** district further east.

Old Sacramento and the riverfront

Sacramento grew up **along the riverfront**, where the wharves, warehouses,
saloons, and stores of the city's historic core have been restored and converted into
the novelty shops and theme restaurants of **Old Sacramento** (☏916/558-3912,
⊛www.oldsacramento.com). It's a shame that such a large collection of authentic
Gold Rush–era architecture should be choked with such relentless fakery as the
costumed sales staff hawking souvenirs, and tourist-chasing bars dressed up as faux
Wild West saloons. In fact, although most of the buildings are original, some stood
elsewhere until they were forcibly relocated here in the 1960s to make way for
the massive I-5 highway that carves this area off from the rest of the city center.
To avoid the stampede of tourists in search of taffy and souvenirs, it's best to avoid
Old Sacramento completely at weekends, since that's when the place seems most
inauthentic, its streets more like a Hollywood backlot than the real thing.

Three of the area's main historical attractions stand in a row along **I Street**: the smallest is the Huntington & Hopkins hardware store at no. 113. Here, the **Big Four** – Leland Stanford, Mark Hopkins, Collis P. Huntington, and Charles Crocker – held their first meeting to mastermind the Central Pacific and later Southern Pacific railroads (see box, p.716). It's now a **museum** (Tues–Sun 10am–5pm; free; ☎916/323-7234) decked out as a spartan, 1840s supply store, highlighting the humble beginnings of the ruthless Huntington and the hen-pecked Hopkins, a meeker man who joined him as partner in his grocery store and later in the railroad. Upstairs there's a low-key homage to the men, with a re-creation of their boardroom and an archive of rail history.

One of the city's highlights is the **California State Railroad Museum** at 111 I St (daily 10am–5pm; $6; ☎916/445-7387, ⓦwww.californiastate railroadmuseum.org), which brings together a range of lavishly restored 1860s locomotives with "cow-catcher" front grilles and huge bulbous smokestacks. Frankly, despite its exhaustive exhibits on early railroad technology, it's still a place for dedicated trainspotters rather than the casual tourist. Instead, catch a leisurely taste of railroad life by heading across to the old passenger station and freight depot a block south, which is also part of the museum. There, you can take a seven-mile, 45-minute jaunt beside the river on a vintage train (April–Sept Sat & Sun hourly 11am–5pm; $6).

For a broader view of the area's history, the **Discovery Museum of History, Science and Technology** at 101 I St (Sept–May Tues–Sun 10am–5pm; June–Aug daily 10am–5pm; $5; ☎916/264-7057, ⓦwww.thediscovery.org) features a hands-on display about the early newspapers in California (including the *Sacramento Bee*, founded in 1857) as well as more recent history, like the Depression-era diner run by the pioneering African-American Dunlap family. The exhibits are hit and miss, but a better bet than the over-touted Railroad Museum.

Two smaller museums are really only worth a look if you're desperate to escape the souvenir shops. The **California Military Museum**, 1119 2nd St (Tues–Sun 10am–4pm; $3; ☎916/442-2883, ⓦwww.militarymuseum.org), provides an uninspiring chronicle – with documents, weaponry, and uniforms – of California's involvement in armed struggles from pre-statehood days to the present; there's even a section, albeit skimpy, on the 1992 race riots in Los Angeles. The **Wells Fargo Historical Museum**, 1000 2nd St at J (daily 10am–5pm; free; ☎916/440-4263), is one of the many corporate museums run by the bank across California. Unfortunately, it's not one of the best, with a tiny collection of unremarkable ephemera. In fact, most people only pass through to use the ATMs inside this 1853 bank building, which also held the first State Supreme Court, the unassuming old chambers of which are sometimes open for public view on the top floor.

Pass over the highway to reach the nearby **Crocker Art Museum** at 216 O St between Second and Third (Tues, Wed, Fri–Sun 10am–5pm, Thurs 10am–9pm; $6; ☎916/264-5423, ⓦwww.crockerartmuseum.org). Here, in an odd complex of Renaissance Revival and modern buildings, exhibits of paintings collected by Supreme Court judge Edwin Crocker, brother of railroad baron Charles, are on display. Although there are a few pictures of early Californian life, its Eurocentric collection (mainly old-master drawings by Dürer, Rembrandt, Boucher, and Fragonard, as well as some second-tier canvases from the likes of Henry Raeburn) seems oddly incongruous in this city. More appropriate to its setting, in the shadow of the massive I-5 and I-80 interchange at 2200 Front St, the **Towe Auto Museum** (daily 10am–6pm; $7; ☎916/442-6802, ⓦwww .toweautomuseum.org) offers an impressive collection of antique cars and trucks, from Model Ts and As to classic '57 T-birds and "woody" station wagons.

Downtown

Running east from the riverfront and the Old Sacramento development, past the Greyhound and Amtrak stations, the **K Street Mall** is the commercial heart of **Downtown Sacramento**, with the end of the modern suburban tramway running through the center of a pedestrianized shopping precinct. While its western reaches are rather forlorn, with plenty of empty storefronts, the street grows livelier the closer it gets to the massive, open-air **Downtown Plaza** shopping complex. There, you'll find every major retail name, a food court, plus an enormous cinema; at its western end, there's a time-warping tunnel that takes pedestrians under the highway to connect with Old Sacramento.

Northeast of the mall, at 16th and H, stands the old **Governor's Mansion** (tours daily on the hour 10am–4pm; $1; ⓦwww.parks.ca.gov). Although built in 1877 as a private home, this enormous and elaborate Victorian house was home to California's governors for more than sixty years, until 1967, when then-governor Ronald Reagan abandoned its high ceilings and narrow staircases in favor of a ranch-style house on the outskirts of town. His excuse was that the structure had been condemned as a firetrap, although it's likely that he simply craved better creature comforts than the traditional building could offer. Today, the meringue-like mansion has been restored to its former glory, and is a perfect place to begin a self-guided **walking tour** of Sacramento's historic architecture with one of the detailed free brochures published by the Sacramento CVB. And no, the Governator doesn't live here – in fact he hasn't even bought a house yet: instead, he bunks at the *Hyatt* hotel during the week then commutes home to Maria in LA at weekends.

The main building of the **State Capitol**, with its Classical Revival dome, was built in the 1860s, although there have been several significant, if insensitive, additions since then. It was restored to nineteenth-century opulence in 1976 in what was then the largest such project in US history; it underwent another heavy restoration following a catastrophic incident in early 2001 when a mentally unstable truck driver ploughed his milk tanker into the southern facade and caused almost $15 million in damage, most of it smoke related. Unsurprisingly, security has been tightened, and you'll need a photo ID to enter the Capitol building; once inside, you're free to ramble around the main floor using the self-guided leaflets on offer in the rotunda. You'll see more, though, if you take one of the free **tours** (daily 9am–5pm, last tour 4pm; ☏916/324-0333, ⓦwww.parks.ca.gov or www.capitolmuseum.ca.gov) that leave hourly from Room B-27 on the lower ground floor. These tours will take you through administrative rooms set up as if it were April 1906, when the devastating San Francisco earthquake occurred. You'll also visit the salmon-pink Senate Gallery and lush green Assembly Room. Note the gargoyle's face in the egg-and-dart molding of the Assembly Room ceiling, sticking its tongue out at the speaker (illicitly added, it's claimed, by disgruntled artisans during construction). The park around the Capitol is delightful, filled with rowdy flowerbeds, enormous trees, and a plague of friendly squirrels; it's often crowded on weekday lunchtimes with office workers snacking in the sun.

The **California State History Museum**, 1020 O St (Tues–Sat 10am–5pm, Sun noon–5pm; $5; ☏916/653-7524, ⓦwww.goldenstatemuseum.org), is an enormous, cutting-edge facility that focuses on both the state's physical history and the development of the often ridiculed "California-ness" in its settlers. The layout's rather confusing, since each exhibit bleeds into the next, but don't miss the eye-catching re-creation of an early Chinese herbalist store or the perky TV montage showing Californians' own, often amusing, reflections on their home state.

Midtown

Sacramento's trendiest district is **Midtown**, a pleasant neighborhood for a leisurely, leafy stroll – city planners planted trees on almost every street, so there's ample shade from the relentless sunshine. Here, although there are few actual attractions, you'll find dozens of funky restaurants and cafés (see opposite) dotted among the old Victorian mansions, not to mention one of the city's best sights, **Sutter's Fort State Historic Park**. This re-creation of Sacramento's original settlement stands at 27th and L streets: the main entrance is on the south side (daily 10am–5pm; $3; free entry after 4.30pm; ⊤916/445-4422, ⊚www.parks .ca.gov). With its low, starkly whitewashed walls, the fort is strikingly simple amid the residential frippery of the many Victorians nearby. Inside, motion-triggered audio commentary describes each room, like the Blacksmith's and the Bakery, and an adobe house exhibits relics from the Gold Rush; its empty stillness gives a vivid sense of early European life in California.

One block north, the small **Indian Museum** at 2618 K St (daily 10am–5pm; $1; ⊤916/324-0971) displays tools, handicrafts, and ceremonial objects of the Native Americans of the Central Valley and the Sierra Nevada, as well as recounting the story of Ishi, the last of the Yahi Indians, who was paraded around towns as a curiosity in the early twentieth century. Frankly, it's dark, a little threadbare and disappointing – the display on the Miwoks at Indian Grinding Rock (see p.735) is much more impressive.

A short walk from the main city center, on the corner of 16th Street and Broadway, stands the original **Tower Records**. Technically, it's the second location, as the chain started in what's now the *Tower Café* (see opposite), where local entrepreneur Russ Solomon owned a drugstore in the 1940s and started selling used jukebox records for 10¢ each. The current location opened in 1965, and the chain began to spread in earnest, first across America and then around the world.

The Big Four and California's early railroads

Starting in 1861, the **Central Pacific** and **Southern Pacific railroads** monopolized transportation and dominated the economy and politics of California and the western US for over twenty years. These companies were the creation of just four men – Leland Stanford, Mark Hopkins, Collis P. Huntington, and Charles Crocker – known collectively as the **Big Four**.

For an initial investment of $15,000, the four financiers, along with the railroad designer and engineer Theodore Judah who died before its completion in 1883, received federal subsidies of $50,000 per mile of track laid – twice what it actually cost. On top of this, they were granted half the land in a forty-mile strip bordering the railroad: as the network expanded, the Southern Pacific became the largest landowner in California, owning over twenty percent of the state. An unregulated monopoly – caricatured in the liberal press as a grasping **octopus** – the railroad had the power to make or break farmers and manufacturers dependent upon it for the transportation of goods. In the cities, particularly Oakland and Los Angeles, it was able to demand massive concessions from local government as an inducement for rail connections. By the end of the nineteenth century, the Big Four had extracted and extorted a fortune worth over $200 million each and ran a network that stretched across the country to New Orleans.

Although they all built fabulous mansions on San Francisco's swanky Nob Hill (see p.588), those palaces were destroyed soon after the men's deaths by the 1906 earthquake and fire. Perhaps the four's most enduring monument, though, is the prestigious university that vain Leland Stanford endowed in the honor of his namesake and only son after the boy's early death.

Eating

Dozens of fast-food stands, ice-cream shops, and overpriced Western-themed **restaurants** fill Old Sacramento, but you'd do better to steer clear of these and search out the places we've listed below. Many of the restaurants Downtown cater primarily to office workers and are therefore closed in the evening; for dinner, it's better to stroll over to Midtown, around 20th Street and Capitol Avenue, where you'll also find the odd good bar.

Café Bernardo 28th St and Capitol Ave, Midtown ℗916/443-1180. Large, refectory-style restaurant, where you can order huge portions of healthy, cheap food from the walk-up counter and eat in the casual dining room reminiscent of a Tuscan farmhouse. The menu's mainly Italian, with pastas, salads, and small pizzas; it's also open for breakfast, when the fare's more American, with French toast and pancakes.

Centro Cocina Mexicana 2730 J St, Midtown ℗916/442-2552. This innovative upscale Mexican restaurant offers regional cooking like delicious chicken and *mole* enchiladas from Oaxaca Province. Lunch prices and dishes are lighter; the bar's especially impressive, since it stocks more than fifty aged tequilas.

Chipotle 1831 Capitol Ave, Midtown ℗916/444-8940. This funky chain café has a simple menu offering three kinds of burritos, including the deliciously tangy *barbacoa* (shredded spicy beef) for around $5.

Emma's Taco House 723 K St, Downtown ℗916/446-2122. One of the better choices on the patchy K Street Mall, this is a friendly, rather dilapidated restaurant that offers lavish portions of Cal-Mex food at budget prices.

Hukilau Island Grill 1501 16th St at O, Midtown ℗916/444-5850. Loud, garish, but fun restaurant, complete with cartoonish Hawaiian decor and an eclectic, Pacific Rim menu: the simpler dishes, like grilled fish kebabs, are the most successful.

Jack's Urban Eats 1230 20th St at Capitol Ave, Midtown ℗916/444-0307. Groovy bargain rotisserie, serving slab-like sandwiches of juicy herb chicken or steak for $5, with stylish, stark decor and a few canvases by local artists on the walls. The urban-style fries, with blue cheese and spicy chili oil, are knockout.

Lucca 1615 J St at 16th, Midtown ℗916/669-5300. If you're hoping to spot the Governator, your best chance is here – he's a regular. The space is surprisingly low-key – bare brick walls, no tablecloths – as is the rustic, Tuscan food. Try the chicken, mushroom, and fontina risotto for $10 or a lavish fish stew for $15.

Maharani 1728 Broadway at 18th St, Downtown ℗916/441-2172. Slightly pricey Californian-style Indian that's light on oil, but still heavy on all the traditional spices – try the tandoori chicken.

Megami 1010 10th St at J St, Downtown ℗916/448-4512. A functional, bargain Japanese restaurant with lunch and combination sushi plates for under $5. You can also try the sesame chicken. Mon–Fri only.

Paesano's 1806 Capitol Ave at 18th St, Midtown ℗916/447-8646. Brick-walled pizzeria, serving hearty portions of pasta and oven-baked sandwiches at reasonable prices.

River City Brewing Company 545 Downtown Plaza ℗916/447-2745. One of the few acceptable places to stop off near Old Sacramento, this slick modern brewpub at the west end of the shopping mall serves standard food at regular prices, enhanced by tasty beers (some brewed on site).

Tapa the World 2115 J St at 20th St, Midtown ℗916/442-4353. Choose from twenty different tapas, or have a full meal of paella, lamb, or fresh fish, all while being serenaded by flamenco guitar.

Tower Café 1518 Broadway at 15th, Downtown ℗916/441-0222. The decor at this casual restaurant's as eclectic as the food – expect walls covered in masks and tapestries and a Caribbean-influenced menu. Try the jerk chicken or swing by for brunch for gooey and crispy French toast, soaked overnight in vanilla custard.

Weatherstone Coffee & Trading Co 812 21st St at H, Midtown ℗916/443-6340. Sacramento's oldest coffeehouse has a massive courtyard that's pleasant on a sunny afternoon; the interior's a little dilapidated, but it's unpretentious and easygoing. Note that it can be hard to find, tucked away on a largely residential block.

Willie's Burgers and Chiliburger 2415 16th St at X St, Downtown ℗916/444-2006. Old-school burger joint serving up sloppy, unmissable cooked-to-order burgers and fries ($3), as well as tamales and – best of all – hot, sweet *beignets* at breakfast time.

Drinking and nightlife

Sacramento's **nightlife** can be rather flat, especially in the center of the city once the office workers have headed home to the suburbs. The best place to catch off-beat, live music is *Old Ironsides*, 1901 10th St (T916/443-9751, W www.theoldironsides.com); another option is the *Capitol Garage*, 1427 L St at 14th (T916/444-3633, W www.capitolgarage.com): this coffee bar-cum-performance space features local bands with a nominal cover. For bigger touring names, try the *Crest Theater*, a refurbished Art Deco gem in the K Street Mall at no. 1013, which also hosts short runs of edgy indie **movies** (T916/442-7378, W www.thecrest.com). Otherwise, for art-house films, try the Tower Theater at Broadway and 16th (T916/442-4700).

The funky *Monkey Bar* adjacent to *Café Bernardo* (see p.717) (T916/442-8490), with its mosaic decor and mixed preppy-indie crowd, is the best place to drink and serves bargain cocktails for around $3. The biggest dance club in the city center is *Faces*, on the corner of K and 20th streets (T916/448-7798, W www.facesnightclub.com), with two dancefloors and nine bars; the cover hovers around $6, and there's a mixed gay/straight crowd. Opposite *Faces*, at 2001 K St, *The Depot* (T916/441-6823, W www.thedepot.net) is a friendly gay video bar.

The Central Mother Lode

From Sacramento, US-50 and I-80 head east through the heart of the Gold Country, up and over the mountains past Lake Tahoe and into the state of Nevada. The roads closely follow the old stagecoach routes over the Donner Pass, named in honor of the gruesomely tragic exploration (see box, p.755). In the mid-1860s, local citizens, seeking to improve dwindling fortunes after the Gold Rush subsided, joined forces with railroad engineer Theodore Judah to finance and build the first railroad crossing of the Sierra Nevada over much the same route – even along much of the same track – that Amtrak uses today. The area's less touristed than the northern or southern mines: either **Placerville** or **Auburn** make good bases, with affordable accommodation and some local points of interest in each. Placerville's especially handy if you want to cruise round and sample some of the vintages produced locally in the El Dorado wine country. And while the area's towns may not be nearly as postcard perfect as those elsewhere in the region, **Coloma** and **Folsom**, in between the two highways on the American River, are both worth exploring.

Folsom

In 1995, just as the **FOLSOM** powerhouse was gearing up for the centennial celebration of its pioneering efforts in long-distance electricity transmission, one of the sluice gates on the Folsom Dam gave way, sending millions of gallons of water down the American River towards Sacramento, twenty miles downstream. The levees held, but Folsom Lake had to be almost completely drained before repairs could be undertaken.

The event sent shockwaves through California's extensive hydroelectric industry and brought a fame to Folsom unknown since Johnny Cash sang of being "stuck in Folsom Prison" after having "shot a man in Reno, just to watch him die." The stone-faced **Folsom State Prison**, two miles north of town on Green Valley Road, has an arts-and-crafts gallery (daily 8am–5pm) selling works by prisoners, who get the proceeds when released. It's more worthwhile stopping at the small **museum** across the road (daily 10am–4pm; donation; ⓣ916/985-2561), which is filled with grisly photographs, the medical records of murderers and thieves who were hanged for their crimes, and a whole arsenal of handmade escape tools recovered from prisoners over the years.

Folsom itself is attractive enough, with a single main street, Sutter Street, of restored homes and buildings that date from the days of the Pony Express. A reconstruction of the 1860 Wells Fargo office makes an imposing setting for the **Folsom History Museum**, no. 823 (Tues–Sun 11am–4pm; $2; ⓣ916/985-2707, ⓦ www.folsomhistorymuseum.org), whose prized posses-sions include a working scale-model of a steam-powered gold dredge, artifacts from the Chinese community that settled here in the 1850s, and a huge mural depicting the area's main Native American people, the Maidu.

El Dorado wine country

In the 1860s, when the now-famous Napa and Sonoma valleys were growing potatoes, **vineyards** flourished in El Dorado County. However, the fields were neglected after the Gold Rush and killed off by phylloxera, a nasty yellow aphid that gorges itself on vine roots; it wasn't until 1972 that vineyards were systematically re-established. Since then, however, the **wineries** in El Dorado County, especially around Placerville, have rapidly gained a reputation that belies their diminutive size. Most are low-key affairs where no charge is made for tasting or tours, and you're encouraged to enjoy a bottle out on the veranda. At quiet times, you may even be shown around by the winemaker, a far cry from the organized tours and rampant commercialism of Napa and Sonoma (see p.776 and p.781).

The differences in altitude and soil types throughout the region lend themselves to a broad range of grape varieties, and the producers here are often criticized for being unfocused; either way, in recent years local wineries have regularly snagged awards. Zinfandel and Sauvignon Blanc are big, but it's the Syrah/Merlot blends that attract the attention, and the Barbera (from a Piedmontese grape) is said to be one of the best in the world.

If you're out for a relaxed day's tasting, avoid the one of the two **Passport Weekends** (ⓣ1-800/306-3956, ⓦ www.eldoradowines.org; $65), usually the last weekend in March plus the first in April and booked out months in advance, when the purchase of this passport entitles you to all manner of foodie extravagances to complement the tastings. Better to pick up the **El Dorado Wine Country Tour** leaflet from the El Dorado Chamber of Commerce (see p.720) and make your way to the Boeger Vineyard, 1709 Carson Rd (daily 10am–5pm; ⓣ530/622-8094, ⓦ www .boegerwinery.com), less than a mile from the Greyhound stop (see p.720), where you can sit in an arbor of apples and pears, or the Lava Cap Vineyard, 2221 Fruit-ridge Rd (daily 11am–5pm; ⓣ530/621-0175, ⓦ www.lavacap.com), which in recent years has produced some excellent Chardonnay and Muscat Canelli.

The quality of the local produce – not only grapes, but also apples, pears, peaches, cherries, and more – is widely celebrated around the district, especially during the **Apple Hill Festival** (ⓣ530/644-7692, ⓦ www.applehill.com) in October, when a shuttle bus runs from Placerville to the majority of the orchards and wineries situated in the Apple Hill region, along the winding country roads just north of I-50 and east of town. At other times, you'll have to make your own way. The Chamber of Commerce can also supply you with a *Cider Press Guide to Apple Hill* and a *Farm Trails Harvest & Recreation Guide*, which has detailed information and maps leading to farms, ranches, wineries, and historic country inns in the most remote areas of the county.

In town, the Folsom **Chamber of Commerce**, 200 Wool St (Mon–Fri 9am–5pm, Sat 11am–4pm; ☏916/985-5555 or 1-800/377-1414, ⓦwww .folsomchamber.com), has plenty of the usual brochures. There are plenty of chain **eateries** around town; otherwise, a good choice is the *Balcony Restaurant*, 801 Sutter St (☏916/985-2605), where you can have a hearty meal while enjoying the view of the historic downtown. For **accommodation**, you'd do better heading back to Sacramento, though if you're particularly tired and on a roomy budget, you might try the *Lake Natoma Inn*, 702 Gold Lake Drive (☏916/351-1500 or 1-800/808-5253, ⓦwww.lakenatomainn.com; ❺), with full amenities, restaurant, and a spa.

Placerville

PLACERVILLE, twenty miles east of Folsom, takes a perverse delight in having been known originally as Hangtown for its practice of lynching alleged criminals in pairs and stringing them up from a tree in the center of town. Despite these gruesome beginnings, Placerville has always been more of a market than a mining town and is now a major crossroads, halfway between Sacramento and Lake Tahoe at the junction of US-50 and Hwy-49. For a time in the mid-1850s, it was the third-largest city in California, and many of the men who went on to become the most powerful in the state got their start here: railroad magnates Mark Hopkins and Collis P. Huntington were local merchants, while car mogul John Studebaker made wheelbarrows for the miners.

The modern town spreads out along the highways in a string of fast-food restaurants, gas stations, and motels. The old Main Street, running parallel to US-50, retains some of the Gold Rush architecture, with an effigy dangling by the neck in front of the *Hangman's Tree* bar, which is built over the site where the town's infamous tree once grew. You'll also see many fine old houses scattered among the pine trees in the steep valleys to the north and south of the center. Nearby, one of the best of the Gold Country museums is in the sprawling El Dorado County Fairgrounds, just north of US-50. This, the **El Dorado County Historical Museum**, 104 Placerville Drive (Wed–Sat 10am–4pm, Sun noon–4pm; free; ☏530/621-5865, ⓦwww.co.el-dorado.ca.us/museum/), gives a broad historical overview of the county from the Miwok to the modern day, including logging trains and a mock-up of a general store, plus pioneer wagons and Native American handicrafts. There's also a library and research center which is crammed with archival photographs of the area's golden era. For more on the days of the argonauts, head across US-50 to the **Gold Bug Mine Park** on Bedford Avenue (Nov–March Sat & Sun noon–4pm, weather permitting; April–Oct daily 10am–4pm; $3, $1 audio tour; ☏530/642-5207, ⓦwww .goldbugpark.org), for a self-guided tour of a typical Mother Lode mine, including a hard-rock mining site as well as a stamp mill showing the ore extraction process. If you want to try your luck hunting for gold, you can rent a pan for $2 an hour – though don't expect to find anything.

Practicalities

Amtrak Thruway **buses** pull up twice daily outside the *Buttercup Pantry*, 222 Main St; while Greyhound buses on their way to South Lake Tahoe stop twice a day at 1750 Broadway, a mile and a half east of town. El Dorado Transit buses provide local transit service. Near the Greyhound stop are a number of **motels**, such as the *Mother Lode Motel*, 1940 Broadway (☏530/622-0895, ⓔlodgegoldcountry@aol.com; ❷), and *National 9 Inn*, 1500 Broadway (☏530/622-3884; ❸), with slightly larger, more modern rooms. With more money, you're far better off at the *Chichester-McKee House*, 800 Spring St (☎530/626-1882 or 1-800/831-4008, Ⓦwww.innlover.com; ⑤), a historic B&B and a landmark in its own right, offering guestrooms with period furnishings and home-made baked breakfasts, and reached by turning north off US-50 onto Hwy-49 at the traffic lights in town. The El Dorado County **Chamber of Commerce** office, 542 Main St (Mon–Fri 9am–5pm; ☎530/621-5885, Ⓦwww.eldoradocounty.org), has local information and can help set up **river-rafting** trips in Coloma (see below).

For **eating**, try the local concoction, "the Hangtown Fry," an omelet-like mix-up of bacon, eggs, and breaded oysters. It's said to have been whipped up using ingredients that were scarce at the height of the Gold Rush for a wealthy miner who wanted the priciest dish on the menu: try one at *Chuck's Pancake House*, 1318 Broadway (☎530/622-2858). *Sweetie Pies*, at 577 Main St (☎530/642-0128), serves great breakfasts and what could be the best cinnamon rolls on the planet. Grab an organic coffee or an authentic *chai* at the natural foods eatery *Cosmic Café*, housed inside the remnants of an actual gold mine, 594 Main St (☎530/642-8481). Not to be missed if you've got a car, *Poor Red's Barbeque* (☎530/622-2901) is housed in the old Adams and Co. stagecoach office on Hwy-49 three miles south of Placerville, which serves the Gold Country's best barbecued dinners for under $6, with $1 beers and two-fisted margaritas. If none of these appeal, *Lil' Mama D. Carlos*, 482 Main St (☎530/626-1612), serves up fine, affordable Italian food.

Coloma

Sights along Hwy-49 north of Placerville are few and far between, but it was here that gold fever began, when on January 24, 1848, James Marshall discovered flakes of gold in the tailrace of a mill he was building for John Sutter, along the south fork of the American River at **COLOMA**. By the summer of that year, thousands had flocked to the area, and by the following year Coloma was a town of ten thousand – though most left quickly following news of richer strikes elsewhere in the region, and the town all but disappeared within a few years. The few surviving buildings, including the cabin where Marshall lived and two Chinese stores, have been preserved as the **Marshall Gold Discovery State Historic Park** (daily 8am–sunset, museum daily 10am–4.30pm; $2 per car; ☎530/622-3470, Ⓦwww.parks.ca.gov). A reconstruction of **Sutter's Mill** stands along the river within the park and working demonstrations are held on most weekends at 10am and 1pm. There's a small historical museum across the road, and on a hill overlooking the town a statue marks the spot where Marshall is buried. Marshall never profited from his discovery, and in fact it came to haunt him. At first, he tried to charge miners for access to what he said was his land along the river (it wasn't), and he spent most of his later years in poverty, claiming supernatural powers had helped him to find gold.

Whether or not you believe in ghosts, Coloma certainly has one attraction that will still turn your knuckles white: it's the best place to begin a **whitewater rafting** journey on the American River. Tours can be booked with Mariah Wilderness Expeditions (☎530/626-6049 or 1-800/462-7424, Ⓦwww.mariahwe.com) or Rapid Descent Adventures (☎1-877/GO-RAFTN or 530/642-2370, Ⓔrapidd@pacbell.net): expect to pay around $100 for a half-day excursion; overnight trips start around $220. If you decide to stay for the night, the choicest **accommodation** is at the *Coloma Country Inn*, 345 High St (☎530/622-6919, Ⓦwww.colomacountryinn.com; ⑤), adjacent to the state park, with its antique-crammed rooms.

Auburn and Dutch Flat

Heading north thirty miles or so, the town of **AUBURN**, built into a hillside on three levels, manages to preserve its Gold Rush–era charm, even though it's right at the crossroads of Hwy-49 and I-80. Greyhound **buses** heading from Sacramento to Reno stop at 246 Palm Ave, and Amtrak **trains** depart from Nevada and Fulleiler streets. The outskirts are sprawling and modern, but the Old Town, on Auburn's lowest level just off Hwy-49, is one of the best preserved and most picturesque of the Gold Rush sights, with antique stores and saloons clustered around a Spanish-style plaza. You'll also find California's oldest post office, in continuous use since 1848, and the unmissable red-and-white tower of the 1891 **firehouse**. There are also a number of undervisited museums like the **Gold Country Museum**, 1273 High St (Tues–Sun 11am–4pm; free; ☎530/889-6500, ⓦwww.placer.ca.gov/museum/local-museums/goldctry). Of course, it's another mine of information with an authentic tunnel on site, and a replica of a miners' camp. More offbeat and unusual is the **Bernhard Museum Complex** at 291 Auburn-Folsom Rd (Tues–Sun 11am–4pm; free; ☎530/889-6500, ⓦwww.placer.ca.gov/museum/local-museums/bernhard), mostly since its former owner was looking for liquid, rather than nugget, gold. Come here for guided tours of an amateur viticulturist's 1851 home, as well as his carriage barn and modest winery.

For a free map and information on places to stay, stop by the **California Welcome Center**, north of town at 13464 Lincoln Way (Mon–Sat 9am–3pm, Sun 11am–3pm; ☎530/887-2111, ⓦwww.visitplacer.com). Affordable **accommodation** is available at the *Super 8 Motel* at 140 E Hillcrest Drive in Auburn, which offers comfort without the frills (☎530/888-8808 or 1-800/800-8000, ⓦwww.super8.com; ❸). If you're looking for a good **meal**, try either *Bootlegger's Old Town Tavern and Grill*, 210 Washington St (☎530/889-2229), where hearty fare is served in a stately brick building, or *Latitudes*, 130 Maple St (☎530/885-9535), for Californian interpretations of multicultural cuisines like East Indian curried tofu or teriyaki tempeh.

The twenty or so miles of Hwy-49 north of Auburn are a dull but fast stretch of freeway to one of the best parts of the Gold Country – the twin cities of Grass Valley and Nevada City (see opposite). For an interesting side trip on the way there, or if you're heading for Lake Tahoe, take I-80 from Auburn 27 miles east to the small town of **DUTCH FLAT**, where old tin-roofed cottages are sprinkled among the pine- and aspen-covered slopes. Miners here used the profitable, but very destructive, method of hydraulic mining (see p.729) to get at the gold buried under the surface – with highly visible consequences.

The northern mines

The **northern section** of the Gold Country includes some of the most spectacularly beautiful scenery in California. Fast-flowing rivers cascade along the bottom of steeply-walled canyons, whose slopes are covered in the fall with the flaming reds and golds of poplars and sugar maples, highlighted against an evergreen background of pine and fir trees. Unlike the freelance placer mines of the south, where wandering prospectors picked nuggets of gold out of the streams and rivers, the gold here was (and is) buried deep underground and had, therefore, to be pounded out of hard-rock ore. In spite of that, the **northern mines** were the most profitable of the Mother Lode – more than half the gold that came out of California came from the mines of **Nevada County**, and most of that from **Grass Valley**'s Empire Mine, now preserved as one of the region's many excellent museums. Just north, the quaint Victorian houses of **Nevada City** make it the most alluring Gold Rush town.

A few miles away, at the end of a steep and twisting backroad, the scarred yet curiously beautiful landforms of the **Malakoff Diggins** stand as an exotic reminder of the destruction wrought by overzealous miners, who, as gold became harder to find, washed away entire hillsides to get at the precious metal. Hwy-49 winds up further into the mountains from Nevada City, along the Yuba River to the High Sierra hamlet of **Downieville**, at the foot of the towering Sierra Buttes, and even smaller **Sierra City** further along. From here you're within striking distance of the northernmost Gold Rush ghost town of **Johnsville**, which stands in an evocative state of arrested decay in the middle of the forests of Plumas-Eureka State Park, on the crest of the Sierra Nevada.

You'll need a **car** to get to any of the outlying sights, but there is limited public transportation to Grass Valley and Nevada City in the form of four daily Amtrak Thruway **buses**. You'll find a few inexpensive motels and a handful of B&Bs, but there are no youth hostels; **camping** is an option too, often in unspoiled sites in gorgeous mountain scenery.

Grass Valley and Nevada City

Twenty-five miles north of Auburn and I-80, the neighboring towns of **GRASS VALLEY** and **NEVADA CITY** were the most prosperous and substantial of the gold-mining towns and are still thriving communities, four miles apart in beautiful surroundings in the lower reaches of the Sierra Nevada. Together they make one of the better Gold Country destinations, with museums evocative of the era and many balconied, elaborately detailed buildings staggering up hills and hanging out over steep gorges.

Gold was the lifeblood of the area as recently as the mid-1950s, and both towns look largely unchanged since the Gold Rush. The locals have retained a bit of the fiery determination of their rough-and-ready ancestors, as evidenced by the booming downtown businesses that combine the Old West with big-city sophistication. Since the 1960s, a number of artists and craftspeople have also settled in the old houses in the hills around the area, tempering the rugged regional culture with a vaguely alternative feel that's reflected in the free weekly *Community Endeavor* newspaper, the non-commercial community radio station KVMR (99.3FM), the disproportionate number of bookshops, and in the friendly throngs that turn out for the annual Bluegrass Festival in the middle of June. For a detailed rundown on the whole of Nevada County, including the mines, check out Ⓦwww.ncgold.com.

Both towns are very compact and connected every thirty minutes by the Gold Country Stage **minibus** (Mon–Fri 7am–6pm, Sat 10am–5pm; $1, $3 for a day-pass; ☏530/477-0103 or 1-888/660-7433), which follows the same stretch of road that burro trains and stagecoaches frequented in the twin towns' heyday, when it was the busiest four-mile route in California. The four daily Amtrak Thruway **buses** from Sacramento and Auburn stop on Sacramento Street in Nevada City and on West Main Street in Grass Valley.

Accommodation

There is a scattering of cheapish **motels** around but if you can afford to fork out more for a **bed and breakfast**, Nevada City in particular has some excellent options. Otherwise, there are a couple of revamped old Gold Rush **hotels**. See box, opposite, for **camping** options.

Coach 'N' Four Motel 628 S Auburn St, Grass Valley ☎530/273-8009, ⓕ530/273-0827. Handy for Empire State Park, this clean and comfortable motel offers the best rates around. ❸

Flume's End 317 S Pine St, Nevada City ☎530/265-9665, ⓦwww.flumesend.com. Across the Pine Creek Bridge from the center of town, this small inn overlooks a pretty waterfall and features lovely gardens ranged along Deer Creek. ❺

Grandmere's Inn 449 Broad St, Nevada City ☎530/265-4660, ⓦwww.grandmeresinn.com. Nice, friendly B&B with beautifully furnished rooms and a pleasant garden just up the hill from the center of town. ❼

Holbrooke Hotel 212 W Main St, Grass Valley ☎530/273-1353 or 1-800/933-7077, ⓦwww .holbrooke.com. Right in the center of town, this historic hotel, where Mark Twain once stayed, has great rooms and an opulent bar-cum-restaurant. ❹

Holiday Lodge 1221 E Main St, Grass Valley ☎530/2734406 or 1-800/742-7125. Comfortable, no-frills rooms in a lodge featuring a swimming pool, free breakfast, and free local calls. ❸

National Hotel 211 Broad St, Nevada City ☎530/265-4551. The oldest continuously operated hotel in the West and a state historic landmark, so plenty of character in the rooms and lobby, which boasts original photographs, musty wallpaper, and a grand staircase. ❹

Northern Queen Inn 400 Railroad Ave, Nevada City ☎530/265-5824 or 1-800/226-3090, ⓦwww .northernqueeninn.com. Good-value hotel with a heated pool. Attractive woodland cottages and chalets, along with simpler rooms in another building. ❹

Outside Inn 575 E Broad St, Nevada City ☎530/265-2233, ⓦwww.outsideinn.com. Quiet, 1940s motel with swimming pool, a 10min walk from the center of town. Credit cards not accepted. ❸

Piety Hill Cottages 523 Sacramento St, Nevada City ☎530/265-2245 or 1-800/443-2245, ⓦwww .pietyhillcottages.com. Cottages decorated in period furnishings with kitchenettes in a garden setting; the smaller ones are an especially good deal. ❹

Shady Rest Motel 10845 Rough and Ready Hwy, Grass Valley ☎530/273-4232. Ramshackle place a little way out of town, but a pleasant walk; cheap weekly rates available. ❷

Stagecoach Motel 405 S Auburn St, Grass Valley ☎530/272-3701. Decent rates and all the basic amenities, handily placed for the Empire Mine. ❸

Swan-Levine House 328 S Church St, Grass Valley ☎530/272-1873, ⓦwww.swanlevinehouse .com. Accommodation with the artist in mind – there is original artwork on display; the friendly owners also give instruction in printmaking. Attractively decorated, sunny en-suite rooms in an old Victorian hospital. ❹

Grass Valley

There's nothing Gold Country folk love better than telling a long tale about their town's toughest days, making it virtually impossible to pass through **GRASS VALLEY** without getting at least one rendition of the **Lola Montez** story. This Irish dancer and entertainer – the former mistress of Ludwig of Bavaria, and friend of Victor Hugo and Franz Liszt – embarked on a highly successful tour of America in the 1850s, playing to packed houses from New York to San Francisco. Her provocative "Spider Dance," in which she wriggled about the stage shaking cork spiders out of her dress, didn't much impress the miners, but she liked the wild lifestyle of the town, gave up dancing, and retired to Grass Valley with her pet grizzly bear, which she kept tied up in the front yard. Max Ophüls' 1955 *Lola Montes*, which had the largest budget of any film in the history of French cinema at the time of its release, tells a surreal, fictionalized version of her life story.

A few mementoes, such as clothes and accessories, of Lola's life are displayed in the **Grass Valley Museum**, in the Old St Mary's Academy at the corner of Church and Chapel streets (Tues–Fri 12.30–3.30pm; donation; ℗530/273-5509). The town's **tourist office** (Mon–Fri 9.30am–5pm, Sat 10am–3pm; ℗530/273-4667 or 1-800/655-4667, ⓦwww.grassvalleychamber .org) is housed in a replica of her home, on the south side of town at 248 Mill St. It also has reams of historical information, lists of accommodation, and a walking-tour map of the town, pointing out the oldest hardware store in California (which, sadly, closed in 1990 and has been converted into a tacky art gallery) among the wooden awnings and storefronts of the gas-lighted business district.

The North Star Mining Museum

The **North Star Mining Museum**, at the south end of Mill Street (early May–mid-Oct daily 10am–5pm; donation; ☎530/273-4255), is one of the best of all the Gold Country museums, with enthusiastic guides and interesting exhibits, illustrating the days when Grass Valley was the richest and most important of all the California mining towns. Housed in what used to be the power station for the North Star Mine, the centerpiece is the giant **Pelton wheel**. Patented in 1878 and resembling nothing so much as a thirty-foot-diameter bicycle wheel, the wheel became one of the most important inventions to come out of the Gold Country. Many Pelton wheels were used to generate electricity, though the one here drove an air compressor that powered the drills and hoists of the mine.

A series of dioramas in the museum describe the day-to-day working life of the miners, three-quarters of whom had emigrated here from the depressed tin mines of Cornwall in England. Besides their expertise at working deep underground, the "Cousin Jacks," as they were called by the non-Cornish miners, introduced the **Cornish pump** (not to mention the Cornish pastie, a traditional pastry pie) to the mines. You can see a mock-up of one of these mammoth beasts here, as well as a replica of the old surface mechanism.

The great machines are now at peace, but when they were in action the racket could be heard for miles around. The noisiest offenders were the thundering stamp mills – a scaled-down version of which is operated upon request – which once mashed and pulverized the gold-bearing quartz ore.

The Empire Mine State Park

The largest and richest gold mine in the state was the **Empire Mine**, now preserved as a state park a mile southeast of Grass Valley, just off Hwy-174 at the top of Empire Street. The 800-acre **park** (daily: Sept–April 10am–5pm; May–Aug 9am–6pm; $3; ☎530/273-8522, ⓦwww.empiremine.org) is surrounded by pines, amongst which are vast quantities of mining equipment and machinery, much of it only recently reinstated here after having been sold off for scrap after the mine closed in 1956. When standing among the machines, it is easy to imagine the din that shook the ground 24 hours a day, or the skips of fifty men descending the now-desolate shaft into the 350 miles of underground tunnels. After more than six million ounces of gold had been recovered, the cost of getting the gold out of the ground exceeded $35 an ounce – the government-controlled price at the time – and production ceased. Most of the mine has been dismantled, but there's a small, very informative **museum** at the entrance with a superb model of the whole underground system, built secretly to help predict the location of lucrative veins of gold. You can get some sense of the mine's prosperity by visiting the owner's house, the **Empire Cottage** at the north end of the park – a stone-and-brick, vaguely English manor house, with a glowing, redwood-paneled interior overlooking a formal garden.

Nevada City

Towns don't get much quainter than **NEVADA CITY**, four miles north of Grass Valley, with its crooked rows of elaborate Victorian homes set on the winding, narrow, maple-tree-lined streets, which rise up from Hwy-49. It gets away with all the quaintness, however, as it is one of the least changed of all the Gold Country towns with a cluster of excellent shops and restaurants in the town center – all in all, a good, if pricey, base for following the many steep streets up into the surrounding forest.

A good first stop is at the **tourist office** (Mon–Fri 9am–5pm, Sat 11am–4pm; ☎530/265-2692 or 1-800/655-6569, ⒲www.nevadacitychamber.com) at 132 Main St, a block north of Hwy-49, where you can pick up a free walking-tour **map** of the town. There are not many specific points of interest, but one place to start is the restored, lacy-balconied and bell-towered **Old Firehouse**, at 214 Main St, one block up from the tourist office, which houses a small **museum** (daily: May–Oct 11am–4pm; Nov–April Thurs–Sun 11.30am–4pm; donation) describing the social history of the region. The heart of town is Broad Street, which climbs up from the highway past the imposing 1854 **National Hotel** (see "Accommodation," p.724) and a number of antique shops and restaurants, all decked out in Gold Country balconies and wooden awnings. Almost the only exception to the rule of picturesque nostalgia is the Art Deco 1937 **City Hall**, near the top of Broad Street.

The **Miner's Foundry Cultural Center** (Mon–Fri 10am–4pm; free), close to the Deer Creek canyon at 325 Spring St, is an old tool foundry converted

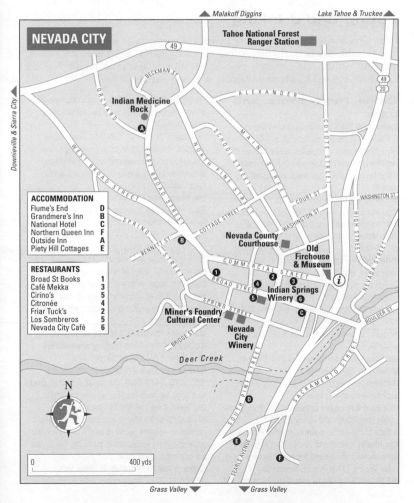

into a multi-use cultural center, art gallery, performance space, and KVMR radio studios. Immediately next door stands the **Nevada City Winery**, 321 Spring St (Mon–Sat 11am–5pm, Sun noon–5pm; ☎530/265-9463), where you can taste the produce of one of the state's oldest vineyards and take a free tour at 11.30am every Saturday. If you'd like to sample a different glass, stop by the **Indian Springs Winery**, which has its tasting room at 303 Broad St (Sun–Thurs 11.30am–4.30pm, Fri & Sat 11.30am–6pm; ☎530/478-1068 or 1-800/273-2550). Both wineries sell their product at very modest prices in comparison to those of the Wine Country.

Above the town at the top of Pine Street, a small plaque marks **Indian Medicine Stone**, a granite boulder with sunbeds worn into the hollows of the rock by Native Americans who valued the healing power of sunshine. Broad Street intersects Hwy-49 a block further on, and continues up into the mountains as the North Bloomfield Road, which twists up the hills to the Malakoff Diggins (see p.730).

Eating and drinking

Both Grass Valley and Nevada City have some surprisingly sophisticated places to **eat and drink**, including a few excellent **cafés**. Look out for pasties, brought to the Gold Country by Cornish miners, and crisp-tasting Nevada City beer, brewed locally and available at better establishments.

Cafés, restaurants, and bars

Bears Café 115 S Church St, Grass Valley ☎530/477-7873. The plethora of coffees and other beverages is complemented by a range of sweet and savoury snacks, but the main reason many people come is the wireless Internet connection.

Broad Street Books 426 Broad St, Nevada City ☎530/265-4204. Pastries, light fare, and espresso with wonderful tree-shaded outdoor seating.

Café Mekka 237 Commercial St, Nevada City ☎530/478-1517. Relaxed, fabulously decorated coffee shop – from exposed piping to *trompe l'oeil* wallpaper – popular with teenagers, trendies, and ex-hippies. Open 8am–11pm weekdays, and until 1.30am on weekends.

Cirino's 309 Broad St, Nevada City ☎530/265-2246. Good deli sandwiches for lunch and modestly priced Italian specialties at dinner, plus a full bar.

Citronée Bistro and Wine Bar 320 Broad St, Nevada City ☎530/265-5697. Upscale American-Mediterranean fusion cuisine in an elegant, yet unpretentious atmosphere.

Didi Bhai Himalayan Cuisine 12820 Rough and Ready Hwy, Rough and Ready ☎530/272-6229. A taste of the east in a surprising western locale; fine Tibetan *momos* and curries from Nepal and northern India are among the select items on offer.

Friar Tuck's 111 N Pine St, Nevada City ☎530/265-9093. Quality American, European, and Pacific Rim cuisine, including rare fondue dinners, are on the menu at this large and rather pricey establishment.

La Cucina Cirino 491 E Main St, Grass Valley ☎530/274-1337. Doubling as a cooking school, this Italian delicatessen prepares home-baked Italian breads and quality cold cuts, and serves Italian wines.

Los Sombreros 311 Broad St, Nevada City ☎530/478-0275. Huge portions of tasty Mexican favorites in cheerful, colorful surroundings.

Main Street Café 213 W Main St, Grass Valley ☎530/477-6000. The best bet in the area for a really good meal, this casual but refined restaurant has an eclectic range of dishes – from pastas to Cajun specialties – as well as fine grilled meats and fresh fish, all at moderate prices. Also has a full wine and cocktail bar next door with live local musicians Thurs & Fri.

Marshall's Pasties 203 Mill St, Grass Valley ☎530/272-2844. Mind-boggling array of fresh filled Cornish pasties, for takeout only.

Nevada City Café 216 Broad St, Nevada City ☎530/265-9440. Plain-looking, all-American diner with eggs for breakfast and burgers for lunch.

Old Town Café 110 Mill St, Grass Valley ☎530/273-4303. Classic modern diner in sharp renovation of what claims to be the oldest continuously operating restaurant in town. The breakfasts are especially good value.

Railroad Café 111 W Main St, Grass Valley ☎530/274-2233. Decent diner food accompanied

by the clatter of a model railroad continuously operating overhead. Breakfast & lunch only Sun–Thurs, all three meals Fri & Sat.
Sergio's Caffe 154 Mill St, Grass Valley ☎530/274-2600. Gourmet sandwiches, salads, and more substantial Italian entrees comprise the menu at this lively café/restaurant.

Swiss House 535 Mill St, Grass Valley ☎530/273-8272. The Central European decor in the heart of the Sierra foothills warrants at least a grin, and you might even be tempted to stay for one of the hearty, reasonably priced Swiss-German meals – try their *schnitzel* or apple strudel.

Nevada County

Grass Valley, Nevada City, and the foothills of **NEVADA COUNTY** yielded more than half the gold that came out of California. Before the deep, hard-rock mines were established in the late 1860s, there were mining camps spread all over the northern Gold Country, with evocative names like "Red Dog" and "You Bet," that disappeared as soon as the easily recovered surface deposits gave out. **Rough and Ready**, five miles west of Grass Valley, survives on the tourist trade alone – visitors come to take a look at the only mining town ever to secede from the United States, which Rough and Ready did in 1850. The band of veterans who founded the town, fresh from the Mexican–American War, opted to quit the Union in protest against unfair taxation by the federal government, and although they declared their renewed allegiance in time for that summer's Fourth of July celebrations, the conflict was not officially resolved until 1948. Now the place – little more than a handful of ramshackle buildings, including a gas station and a general store – isn't really worth visiting, except perhaps for the old-time singalong with the Fruit Jar Pickers band that takes place every Sunday from 10am to noon in the town's tiny square. If you do pass through, the **Chamber of Commerce** (☎530/272-4320) publishes a well-written brochure on the town's history that's about as long as the town's entire length; you can usually find one at the post office or general store.

Six miles northwest of Rough and Ready, off the winding Bitney Springs Road in the **South Yuba River State Park**, stands the **Bridgeport covered bridge**, the longest single-span, wood-truss covered bridge in the world, spanning the Yuba River. The swimming spot underneath offers some relief from a hot summer's day, and the nearby visitor center (☎530/432-2546) has plenty of information on the area's hiking trails, as well as guided wildflower, history, and birdwatching tours, as well as the inevitable gold-panning demonstrations.

Malakoff Diggins State Park

The waters of the Yuba River are now crisp and clear, but when the bridge was completed in 1862 they were being choked with mud and residue from the many **hydraulic mining** – or "hydraulicking" – operations upstream. Hydraulic mining was used here in the late 1850s to get at the trace deposits of gold that were not worth recovering by orthodox methods. It was an unsophisticated way of retrieving the precious metal: giant nozzles or monitors sprayed powerful jets of water against the gold-bearing hillsides, washing away tons of gravel, mud, and trees just to recover a few ounces of gold. It also required an elaborate system of flumes and canals – some still used to supply water to local communities – to collect the water, which was sprayed at a rate of over thirty thousand gallons a minute. Worst of all, apart from the obvious destruction of the landscape, was the waste it caused, silting up rivers, causing floods, impairing navigation, and eventually turning the San Francisco Bay, nearly 150 miles away, a muddy brown.

Site of the worst offense, whose excesses caused hydraulic mining to be outlawed in 1884, was the **MALAKOFF DIGGINS**, sixteen miles up steep and winding North Bloomfield Road from Nevada City (or reachable via the sixteen-mile Tyler Foote Crossing Road, which turns off Hwy-49 twelve miles northwest of Nevada City). Here, a canyon more than a mile long, half a mile wide, and over six hundred feet deep was carved out of the red and gold earthen slopes. Natural erosion has softened the scars somewhat, sculpting pinnacles and towers into a miniature Grand Canyon, now preserved as a 3000-acre **state park** (summer daily, winter Sat & Sun 9am–5pm; $6 per vehicle; ☎530/265-2740). While the park may seem just a short detour from Hwy-49 on your map, its interminable unmarked gravel roads and snaking bends may give you an eerie feeling. Inside the park, old buildings from ghost towns around the Gold Country have been moved to the restored town of **North Bloomfield**, where a small museum (June–Aug daily 10am–4pm; Sept–May Sat & Sun only; call ☎530/265-2740 for winter hours; free with park entry) shows a twenty-minute film on hydraulicking; there's a campground (ReserveAmerica ☎1-800/444-7275; $20) near the eerie cliffs.

Downieville and the High Sierra towns

From Nevada City, Hwy-49 climbs up along the Yuba River Gorge into some of the highest and most marvelous scenery in the Gold Country, where waterfalls tumble over sharp, black rocks bordered by tall pines and maple trees. In the middle of this wilderness, an hour's drive from Nevada City, **DOWNIEVILLE**, the most picturesquely situated of the Gold Rush towns, spreads out along both banks of the river, crisscrossed by an assortment of narrow bridges. Hwy-49 runs right through the center of town, slowing to a near-stop to negotiate tight curves that have not been widened since stagecoaches passed through. Thick stone buildings, some enhanced with delicate wooden balconies and porches, others with heavy iron doors and shutters, face on to raised wooden sidewalks, as their backs dangle precipitously over the steep banks of the river.

For what is now a peaceful and quiet little hamlet of three hundred people, Downieville seems strangely proud of its fairly nasty history. It has the distinction of being the only mining camp ever to have hanged a woman, Juanita, "a fiery Mexican dancehall girl," who stabbed a miner in self-defense. A restored wooden gallows, last used in 1885, still stands next to the County Jail on the south bank of the river, to mark the ghastly heritage. Across the river and two blocks north, at the end of a row of 1850s storefronts, the Downieville Museum (May–Oct daily 11am–4pm; donation; ☎530/289-3423) is packed full of odd bits and historical artifacts, including a set of snowshoes for horses and a scaleddown model of the local stamp mill, "made by the boys of the shop classes 1947–8." To ensure your visit is complete, pick up a walking-tour map of the town, which celebrated its 150th anniversary in the summer of 2002, from the phoneless and erratically opening **tourist kiosk** (May–Sept Sat & Sun only), which stands on a prime grassy spot by the river.

For such a diminutive town there are several very decent **accommodation** options, including the *Riverside Inn* (☎530/289-1000 or 1-888/883-5100, Ⓦwww.riversideinndv.com; ❸) and the nicely refurbished *Carriage House Inn* (☎530/289-3573, Ⓦwww.downievillecarriagehouse.com; ❹), on opposite sides of the Yuba River where Hwy-49 crosses it, and the *Sierra Shangri-La*

(☎530/289-3455, ⓦwww.sierrashangrila.com; ❹) two-and-a-half miles further northeast in thick woods above the river, which has B&B rooms and fully fixtured cottages, the latter available weekly in summer. If the quainter places are full, try the decent motel lodgings at *Downieville Inn*, 117 Main St (☎530/289-3242, ⓦwww.downievilleinn.com; ❸).

Eating and **drinking** options can be found on Main Street at the family-style *Downieville Diner* (☎530/289-3616) or the *Riverview Pizzeria* (☎530/289-3540), and have your favorite café drink at the *Downieville Bakery & Café* (☎530/289-0108) on the corner of Commercial and Main streets.

The full-sized original of the stamp mill is maintained in working order at the **Kentucky Mine Museum** (summer Wed–Sun 10am–5pm; $2; ☎530/862-1310), a mile east of **Sierra City** further up Hwy-49, where a guided tour (11am & 2pm; $5) takes you inside a reconstructed miner's cabin, down a mineshaft, and gives you a look at various pieces of equipment used for retrieving the gold-bearing ore. Until the mine was shut down during World War II, the ore was dug out from tunnels under the massive **Sierra Buttes**, the craggy granite peaks that dominate the surrounding landscape.

Sierra City is full of rustic charm and can be a useful base for visiting the surrounding area. Adequate **accommodation** is available year-round at *The Yuba River Inn* (☎530/862-1122, ⓦwww.yubariverinn.com; ❸), a rustic inn east on Hwy-49 by the river, and in town at the *Old Sierra City Hotel*, 212 Main St (☎530/862-1300, Ⓔoschotel@inreach.com; ❷). Seasonal places include the *Busch & Heringlake Inn* B&B, 231 Main St (☎530/862-1501; ❸), and *Herrington's Sierra Pines* resort (☎530/862-1151, ⓦwww.herringtonssierrapines.com; ❸), a little west of town. In the area you will also find some of the most remote and attractive **campgrounds** in the Gold Country, including the *Sierra Campground*, seven miles beyond Sierra City, and *Chapman Creek*, another mile upstream on the Yuba River. All sites are $18 and can be reserved by calling High Sierra Campgrounds (☎530/993-1410). The best **place to eat** is the English-run *Red Moose Inn*, 224 Main St (☎530/862-1990), which serves genuine fish'n'chips and filling sandwiches.

Hwy-49 continues east through the **Tahoe National Forest**, passing over the 6700ft **Yuba Pass** on its way to join forces with Hwy-89 just north of Sattley at Bassett Junction. Here Hwy-89 heads north to Johnsville and south to Truckee and the Lake Tahoe area. Five miles south of the junction, there are basic facilities at **Sierraville**: at a pinch you could stay at the *Sierraville Motel & RV Park* (☎530/994-3751; ❸) or stop for a quick meal or drink at the *Stagecoach Café & Branding Iron Saloon* (☎530/994-3013), both by the right-angle turn where the two highways separate again in the middle of the tiny town.

Johnsville

Founded in 1870, **JOHNSVILLE** is, after Bodie (see p.409), the best-preserved and most isolated old mining town in California. Located 25 miles north of Bassett Junction and five miles off Hwy-89, the ghost town is surrounded by over seven thousand acres of pine forest and magnificent scenery and lies at the center of the **Plumas-Eureka State Park** – which has $20 **camping** sites (reserve through ReserveAmerica ☎1-800/444-7275) and miles of **hiking** trails. Johnsville's huge stamp mill and mine buildings are being restored; in the meantime, a small museum (June–Aug daily 9am–4pm; $3) describes the difficult task of digging for gold in the High Sierra winters. Right in the center of the town's main road, the *Iron Door* (☎530/836-2376) serves up multinational cuisine, with an emphasis on steaks, schnitzel, and pasta, in the premises of the old general store. For the rest of Plumas County and the Hwy-89 route northwest to Lassen Volcanic National Park, see p.829.

The southern mines

Though never as rich or successful as the diggings further north, the camps of the **southern mines** had a reputation for being the liveliest and most uproarious of all the Gold Rush settlements and inspired most of the popular images of the era: Wild West towns full of gambling halls, saloons, and gunfights in the streets. Certainly, the southern settlements were more ethnically varied than those further north, even if most groups firmly stuck together – Sonora, for instance, was established by Mexican immigrants and Chinese Camp was almost exclusively Asian. The mining methods here were also very different from those used further north. Instead of digging out gold-bearing ore from deep underground, claims here were more often worked by itinerant, roving prospectors searching for bits of gold washed out of rocks by rivers and streams, known as **placer** gold (from the Spanish word meaning both "sand bar," where much of the gold was found, and – appropriately – "pleasure"). Nuggets were sometimes found sitting on the riverbanks, though most of the gold had to be laboriously separated from mud and gravel using handheld pans or larger sluices.

Mining wasn't a particularly lucrative existence: freelance miners roamed the countryside until they found a likely spot, and if and when they struck it rich quickly spent most of the earnings, either in celebration or buying the expensive supplies needed to carry on digging. Unsurprisingly, the boom towns that sprang up around the richest deposits were abandoned as soon as the gold ran out, but a few slowly decaying ghost towns have managed to survive more or less intact to the present day, hidden among the forests and rolling ranchland. Other sites were buried under the many **reservoirs** – built in the 1960s to provide a stable source of water for the agricultural Central Valley – that cover much of the lower elevations.

During spring, the hillsides are covered in fresh green grasses and brightly colored wild flowers, though by the end of summer the hot sun has baked everything a dusty golden brown. Higher up, the free-flowing rivers rush through steep canyons lined by oak trees and cottonwoods, and the ten-thousand-foot granite peaks in the Sierra Nevada above offer excellent skiing in winter, and hiking and camping in the pine and redwood forests all year round. South from Placerville, Hwy-49 passes through **Jackson**, which makes a convenient, if unattractive, base for exploring the many dainty villages scattered around the wine-growing countryside of **Amador County**, continuing on through the mining towns of **Calaveras County**. The center of the southern mining district, then as now, is **Sonora**, a small, prosperous town of ornate Victorian houses set on ridges above steep gorges. Once an archrival but now a ghost town, neighboring **Columbia** has a carefully restored Gold Rush–era Main Street. The gold-mining district actually extended as far south as **Mariposa**, but the mines here were comparatively worthless and little remains to make it worth the trip, except perhaps as a quick stop on the way to Yosemite National Park (see p.457).

You'll need your own **transportation** to see much of the southern Gold Country. Trains steer well clear of the hilly terrain and buses only pass through Mariposa on their way from Fresno and Merced to Yosemite. Drivers be warned – **speed traps** are rampant around the southern mines, particularly in Amador County and on any roads leading to Yosemite, where the speed limits tend to be a bit unrealistic and regional traffic police eagerly await to rake in some of that speedy tourist revenue.

Amador County

South from Placerville and US-50, the old mining landscape of **AMADOR COUNTY** has been given over to the vineyards of one of California's up-and-coming **wine-growing** regions, best known for its robust Zinfandel, a full-flavored vintage that thrives in the sun-baked soil. Most of the wineries are located above Hwy-49 in the Shenandoah Valley, near Plymouth on the north edge of the county. For a detailed map to all the local establishments, contact Amador Vintners in Plymouth (℡209/267-2297 or 1-888/655-8614, ⓦwww .amadorwine.com).

Amador City and Sutter Creek

About thirty miles east of Sacramento, Hwy-16 joins Hwy-49 at **AMADOR CITY**, whose short strip of antique shops gives it a cutesy, Old West look. The landmark *Imperial Hotel* at the northern edge dominates the town, its four-foot-thick brick walls standing at a sharp bend in Hwy-49. The hotel has recently been renovated, with sunny double **rooms** (℡209/267-9172, ⓦwww .imperialamador.com; ❹). Another option is the *Mine House Inn*, on the way to Sutter Creek (℡209/267-5900 or 1-800/646-3473, ⓦwww.minehouseinn .com; ❺) – as its name suggests, this place is a fancy conversion of an old 1870s mining office and now boasts luxury rooms and a solar-heated pool; while the secluded *Rancho Cicada Retreat*, at 10001 Bell Rd near Plymouth (May–Oct only; ℡209/245-4841 or 1-877/553-9481, ⓦwww.ranchocicadaretreat.com; tents ❶, cabins ❻), offers clothing-optional weekend retreats.

SUTTER CREEK, two miles south, is much larger than Amador City, but still little more than a row of tidy antique shops and restaurants catering to tourists along Hwy-49. Though there are a number of surprisingly large Victorian wooden houses – many styled after Puritan New England farm-houses – the town lacks the disheveled spontaneity that animates many of the other Gold Rush towns, perhaps because its livelihood was never based on independent prospectors panning for placer gold, but on hired hands working underground in the more organized and capital-intensive hard-rock mines. It was a lucrative business for the mine owners. The **Eureka Mine** operated until 1958: it was owned by one Hetty Green, the Warren Buffet of her day and at one time the richest woman in the world; at her death in 1916, her estate was worth $100m. She, however, was notorious for her cheapness, wearing old shabby clothes and giving nothing to charity. Hetty earned her nickname "The Witch of Wall Street" from fellow investors who envied her savvy ruthless-ness. Leland Stanford was more generous with the money he made from the **Lincoln Mine**, if no more personally endearing: he become a railroad magnate and governor of California, but used a chunk of his fortune to endow Stanford University (for more on Stanford and his cronies, see box on p.716).

Sutter Creek holds the bulk of Amador County's **accommodation** and **eating** places, with two central and very comfortable B&Bs: *The Foxes*, 77 Main St (℡209/267-5822 or 1-800/987-3344, ⓦwww.foxesinn.com; ❻), with well-appointed rooms and claw-foot baths; and the larger, more communally minded *Sutter Creek Inn*, 75 Main St (℡209/267-5606, ⓦwww.suttercreekinn.com; ❹), with no TVs, no phones, and no fake Victoriana, but a nice garden with hammocks and a welcoming atmosphere. The *Bellotti Inn*, 53 Main St (℡209/267-5211; ❷), has the cheapest accommodation in town and a decent **restaurant** serving full meals for $15 and pasta dishes for $7. *Susan's Place*, in the Eureka Street Courtyard, a half-block east of Hwy-49 (lunch only Thurs–Sun, dinner Fri & Sat; ℡209/267-0945), serves sandwiches, soups, and salads under a shaded gazebo and, across the street, the *Sutter Creek Coffee Roasting Co.* (℡209/267-5550) serves the best coffee in town. For dessert, don't miss the *Sutter Creek Ice Cream Emporium*, 51 Main St (℡209/267-0543), where the friendly owner will play Scott Joplin tunes on the piano while you sip a milkshake.

Jackson

After Sutter Creek, the town of **JACKSON**, four miles south, can seem distinctly blue collar, mainly because of the huge Georgia Pacific lumber mill that serves as its northern gateway. Nevertheless, it serves as a more affordable base for exploring the surrounding countryside. Most of the well-preserved buildings in the small historic downtown area were erected after a large fire in 1862, and today are a bit drowned out by the encroaching modern businesses that surround it. Note the lovely, if architecturally inappropriate, 1939 Art Deco front on the **County Courthouse** at the top of the hill, while further along the crest, the **Amador County Museum**, 225 Church St (Wed–Sun 10am–4pm; donation; ℡209/223-6386), has displays of all the usual Gold Rush artifacts, but is worth a look most of all for its detailed models of the local hard-rock mines – with shafts over a mile deep – that were in use up until World War II. The headframes and some of the mining machinery are still standing a mile north of the museum on Jackson Gate Road, where two sixty-foot-diameter **tailing wheels** (8am–dusk; free), which carried away the waste from the Kennedy Mine, are accessible by way of short trails that lead up from a well-signposted parking area. The headframe of the six-thousand-foot shaft, the deepest in North America, stands out at the top of the slope, along Hwy-49. The other major mine in Jackson, the **Argonaut Mine** (of which nothing remains), was the scene of a tragedy in 1922, when 47 men were killed in an underground fire.

The **Amador County Chamber of Commerce**, 125 Peek St (daily 9am–4pm; ℡209/223-0350 or for lodging info 1-800/726-INNS, ⓦwww.amadorcountychamber.com), is rather awkwardly situated at the junction of Hwy-49 and Hwy-88, but offers a *Visitors Guide to Amador County*, full of the usual maps and historical information. The best place to stay is the friendly, if slightly run-down, *National Hotel*, 2 Water St (℡209/223-0500, ⓔnationalhotel@volcano.net; ❹), an 1860s hotel with individually decorated rooms, such as the "Bordello Room" with flock wallpaper, a four-poster bed and a free-standing bathtub on iron claw feet. If the *National* is full, try the *Amador Motel* (℡209/223-0970; ❶) on Hwy-49 north of town, or the nearby *Jackson Lodge* (℡209/223-0486 or 1-888/333-0486,

Ⓦwww.jacksonlodge.com; ❷). *Mel and Faye's Diner*, 211 Mountain View Drive (℡209/223-0835), on Hwy-49 near the town center, is open all day for **breakfasts and burgers**, while *Café Max Swiss Bakery*, 140 Main St (℡209/223-0174), serves pastries and a mean cup of coffee until 6pm Monday to Saturday. For **drinking**, the *Fargo Club*, 2 Main St (℡209/223-3859), is the modern equivalent of a Wild West saloon, with cheap beers and all-night poker games.

Indian Grinding Rock and Volcano

Hwy-88 heads east from Jackson up the Sierra Crest, through hills that contain one of the most fitting memorials to the Native Americans who lived here for thousands of years before the Gold Rush all but wiped them out. Nine miles from Jackson, off Hwy-88, a side road passes by the **INDIAN GRINDING ROCK STATE HISTORIC PARK** (daily dawn–dusk; $6 per car; ℡209/296-7488, Ⓦwww.parks.ca.gov), where eleven hundred small cups – *Chaw'Se* in Miwok – were carved into the marbleized limestone outcropping to be used as mortars for grinding acorns into flour. It's the largest collection of bedrock mortar in North America, and if you arrive near dawn or dusk and look closely from the small elevated platform next to the biggest of the flat rocks, you can just detect the faint outline of some of the 360 **petroglyphs**. The state has developed the site into an interpretive center and has constructed replicas of Miwok dwellings and religious buildings with the close participation of tribal elders and community leaders. Descendants of the Miwok gather here during the weekend following the fourth Friday in September for **Big Time**, a celebration of the survival of their culture with traditional arts, crafts, and games. At the entrance to the site, the **Chaw'Se Regional Indian Museum** (Mon–Fri 11am–3pm, Sat & Sun 10am–4pm; ℡209/296-7488) explores the past and present state of the ten Sierra Nevada Native groups in a building said to simulate a Miwok roundhouse. The full process of producing acorn flour is covered, but the lack of information on modern Miwok life is a sad testament to the extent of the devastation done to Miwok culture. If you'd like to spend the night, a **campground** in the surrounding woods costs $18 per pitch; space is not reservable and is on a first-come-first-served basis. Note that the campground is closed for Native American gatherings on the third weekend in May, third weekend in June, and last weekend in September.

Named after the crater-like bowl in which it sits, **VOLCANO**, a tiny village a mile and a half north, once boasted over thirty saloons and dance halls. Today, it claims nearly as many historic sites as Jackson but has been mercifully bypassed by all the latter's development and traffic. The densely forested countryside around the village makes it well worth a visit, especially during spring (particularly mid-March to mid-April) when **Daffodil Hill**, three miles north of Volcano, is carpeted with more than 300,000 of the bobbing heads. Signs directing you there are only displayed when the flowers are in bloom. Its other notable attraction is the creaky cannon known as "Old Abe": locals threatened to fire it at a rebellious band of Southern sympathizers during the Civil War – this was the sole skirmish to take place in California, even though not a single shot was actually exchanged. The only **accommodation** in the immediate area is the friendly *St George Hotel* on Main Street (℡209/296-4458, Ⓦwww.stgeorgehotel.com; ❹), offering bed and breakfast without the comforts of televisions, phones, or private bathrooms. Guests congregate in the restaurant and bar, whose walls are decked with every office poster and wisecrack bumper sticker imaginable.

Highway-88

HIGHWAY-88 heads east beyond the Volcano turnoff to Pioneer, where it meets Hwy-26 from Mokelumne Hill (see below). Three miles east, the **Forest Ranger Station** (Mon–Fri 8am–4.30pm; ☎209/295-4251) supplies wilderness permits for overnighting in the **Mokelumne Wilderness**, a segment of the Stanislaus and Toiabe national forests south of Hwy-88, which closely follows the route of many early settlers. The ranger station also has details of camping and hiking in the **Eldorado National Forest**, beautiful in the fall, just before the winter snows turn the Sierra Nevada around the 8500-foot Carson Pass into *Kirkwood*, one of California's best cross-country ski resorts (see box, p.749). For more off-the-beaten-path recreation, try the **Bear River Lake Resort** (☎209/295-4868, ⓦwww.bearriverlake.com; rooms $94, campsite $25), just south of Hwy-88 on the way to Kirkwood and Tahoe, which offers camping, hiking, fishing, swimming, and boating, without all the hype of the better-known resorts.

Calaveras County

CALAVERAS COUNTY lies across the Mokelumne River, eight miles south of Jackson, and is best known for being the setting of Mark Twain's first published story, *The Celebrated Jumping Frog of Calaveras County*. Today, precious few sights of historic interest remain, though there are plenty of options in the country for rugged outdoor recreation. The most northerly town in the county, **Mokelumne Hill**, or "Moke Hill," was as action packed in its time as any of the southern Gold Rush towns, but tourism has been slower to take hold here, and today the town is an all-but-abandoned cluster of ruined and half-restored buildings, not without a certain melancholy appeal. The **Mokelumne Hill History Society**, 8367 East Center (Tues & Wed 10am–5pm, Thurs 1–5pm, Fri & Sat 10am–2pm; summer Sat & Sun 11am–3pm; donation suggested; ☎209/286-0507), has a modest exhibit on the history of the immediate area, once home to almost 10,000 people. The range of names and languages on the headstones of the **Protestant Cemetery**, on a hill a hundred yards west of town, gives a good idea of the mix of people who came from all over the world to the California mines.

San Andreas

Eight miles south, **SAN ANDREAS** hardly seems to warrant a second look: the biggest town for miles, it's now the Calaveras County seat, and has sacrificed historic character for commercial sprawl. The Calaveras County **Chamber of Commerce** (☎209/736-0049 or 1-800/225-3764, ⓦwww.visitcalaveras.org) publishes a handy map to the county that includes recreational activities in the area; it's available from the visitor center in Angels Camp (see opposite). What remains of old San Andreas survives along narrow Main Street, on a steep hill just east of the highway, where the 1893 granite-and-brick County Courthouse has been restored and now houses an interesting collection of Gold Rush memorabilia in the **Calaveras County Museum**, 30 N Main St (daily 10am–4pm; $2; ☎209/754-4658). Local history buffs have put together a detailed and diverse show: there are gold nuggets and miners' tools, like sluice boxes and baskets, as well as Miwok artifacts and a replica of an 1880s general store. Local **nightlife** revolves around the *Black Bart Inn*, 35 N Main St (☎209/754-3808,

The mysterious man known as Black Bart made an unlikely highwayman: Charles E. Bowles – sometimes Bolton – was a prominent and respectable San Francisco citizen in his 50s who claimed to be a wealthy mining engineer. In fact, Charles' background was rather more checkered: born to a farmer father in England, he'd emigrated to America as a child and moved to California to try his luck in the Gold Rush. His luck failed and – now married with children – Bowles enlisted in the Union Army, fighting through the Civil War.

Unsurprisingly, it left him a changed man; and once discharged, he drifted around the West Coast, losing contact with his family and trying his hand at silver mining. Finally, in 1875, Charlie turned to crime: over the next eight years, he'd commit almost thirty stagecoach robberies and yield a then-staggering income of $6000 a year. But what set Bart apart wasn't his money but his manners. No brutal thug, rather he always addressed his victims as "Sir" and "Madam," never shot them, and in a waggish touch, sometimes recited fragments of poetry before escaping with the loot (his name was pinched from a fictional story published in a local paper that mythologised a merciless criminal known as Black Bart).

But Bart's luck only held so long: he was finally discovered after dropping a hand-kerchief at the scene of a hold-up – the police got him by tracing the laundry mark back to a San Francisco laundry and from there to Bowles. He spent four years of a six-year sentence in San Quentin (of course, it was commuted for good behavior) and, after his release, disappeared without trace.

ⓦwww.blackbartinn.com), across the street, which hosts bands on weekends. It is named after the gentleman stagecoach robber, who was captured and convicted here (see box above).

Angels Camp and Carson Hill

The mining camps of southern Calaveras County were some of the richest in the Gold Country, both for the size of their nuggets and for the imaginations of their residents. The author Bret Harte spent an unhappy few years teaching in and around the mines in the mid-1850s and based his short story, *The Luck of Roaring Camp*, on his stay in **ANGELS CAMP**, thirty miles south of Jackson. There isn't much to see here these days, though the downtown feels mildly authentic. The **visitor center** is in a single-story clapboard building with a wide veranda at 1211 S Main St (Mon–Sat 9am–5pm, Sun 11am-3pm; ☎209/736-0049 or 1-800/225-3764, ⓦwww.visitcalaveras.org) and has plenty of information on the surrounding area as well as copious frog-related memorabilia in honor of **Mark Twain**. The saloon in the *Angels Hotel* on Main Street is where 29-year-old Twain was told a tale that inspired him to write his famous story, *The Celebrated Jumping Frog of Calaveras County*, about a frog-jumping competition. It's now a discount tire store. Aside from the relentless onslaught of frog-themed souvenirs, the most unfortunate legacy of Twain's story is the **Jumping Frog Jubilee**; it's held with the local state fair on the third weekend in May each year and inexplicably attended by thousands of people who come to watch as pet amphibians compete to see who can jump farthest. On the north side of town, the **Angels Camp Museum**, 753 Main St (winter Weds–Sun 10am–3pm; summer daily 10am–3pm; $1; ☎209/736-2963), presents a cornucopia of gold-excavating equipment and memorabilia, as well as a carriage barn filled with historic horse-drawn vehicles.

CARSON HILL, now a ghost town along Hwy-49 four miles south of Angels Camp, boasted the largest single nugget ever unearthed in California:

The limestone caverns in the Gold Country

Limestone caverns abound in the southern Gold Country: three have been developed expressly for public tours, the largest of which is the **Moaning Caverns** in Vallecito, just south of Hwy-4 and five miles east of Angels Camp off Parrots Ferry Road (May–Oct daily 9am–6pm; Nov–April Mon–Fri 10–5pm, Sat & Sun 9am–5pm; $12 walking tour, $45 rappel tour; ☏209/736-2708, ⓦwww.caverntours.com). Although discovered by gold-miners in 1851, bones have been found here dating back 13,000 years. It didn't take long for locals to recognize the lucrative potential of the eerie, lacy rock formations here, and the caves were opened as a tourist attraction in 1919. The owners first inserted a 234-step spiral staircase to facilitate access and then corked the cavern's opening by building a gift shop on top of it: ironically, these renovations wrecked the cave's natural acoustics and muted the moaning sounds after which it's named.

The same company oversees **California Caverns** in Calaveras (May–Oct daily 10am–5pm; Nov–Dec & Apr 10am–4pm; closed Jan–March; $12; ☏209/736-2708 or 1-866/732-2837, ⓦwww.caverntours.com), a horizontal network of caves that's a better choice for vertigo sufferers unwilling to brave the precipitous stairs at Moaning Caverns. Here, you can even take a four-hour Middle Earth Expedition ($99, reservations essential) wearing coveralls and a lighted helmet, and following a professional guide through miles of craggy recesses. The last of the local commercially developed sites, **Mercer Caverns**, a mile north of Murphys on Sheep Ranch Road, is known for the spectacular stalagmite and stalactite formations in its 800-foot-long gallery, resembling swooping angels' wings and giant flowers (Memorial Day–Sept Sun–Thurs 9am–5pm, Fri & Sat 9am–6pm; Oct–April daily 10am–4.30pm; $11; ☏209/728-2101, ⓦwww.mercercaverns.com).

195 pounds of solid gold fifteen inches long and six inches thick, worth $43,000 when it was discovered in 1854 and well over a million dollars today. Nearby, **New Melones Reservoir** is the third largest reservoir in California and has all the camping ($12 for tent-only, $16 for RV and tent site; reservations ☏1-877/444-6777 or ⓦwww.reserveusa.com), swimming, hiking, boating, and other recreational possibilities you could hope for, not to mention spectacular, if man-made, views. It's seldom visited by the throngs who fly through the Gold Country on their way to pricier recreational areas: for more information, stop at the **visitor center** (daily 10am–4pm; ☏209/536-9094 ext 22), just past Carson Hill on Hwy-49.

Murphys

Nine miles east of Angels Camp, up the fairly steep Hwy-4, **MURPHYS'** one and only street is shaded by locust trees and graced by rows of decaying monumental buildings. One of the Gold Country's few surviving wooden water flumes still stands on Murphys' northern edge, while the oldest structure in town now houses the **Oldtimer's Museum** (Fri–Sun 11am–4pm; donation suggested; ☏209/728-1160), a small gathering of documents with a wall-full of rifles. If you want to **stay** in town, head across the street to the old *Murphys Hotel*, 457 Main St (☏209/728-3444 or 1-800/532-7684, ⓦwww.murphyshotel.com; ❹), which hosted some of the leading lights of the boom days in its rustic double rooms. The **Calaveras Big Trees State Park** (visitor center open winter weekends only 11am–3pm, rest of year daily 11am–3pm; park dawn–dusk; $6 per car; ☏209/795-3840, ⓦwww.parks .ca.gov), fifteen miles east, covers six thousand acres of gigantic sequoia trees, threaded with trails. It makes for fine ski touring in winter, with **hiking** and **camping** (no reservations; $16) the rest of the year.

Sonora, Columbia, Jamestown, and Chinese Camp

SONORA, fifteen miles southeast of Angels Camp, is the center of the southern mining district: it was the site of the **Bonanza Mine**, one of the most lucrative Gold Rush digs. Now a logging town, set on steep ravines, the town makes a good base for exploring the southern region: there are two settlement clusters, Historic Sonora and the commercial district, known as East Sonora. There's little to see beyond the false-fronted buildings and Victorian houses on the main **Washington Street** and the Gothic **St James Episcopal Church** at its far end, but it's a friendly, animated place, worth spending an afternoon. The small **Tuolumne County Museum**, in the old County Jail at 158 W Bradford Ave (Mon–Fri & Sun 10am–4pm, Sat 10am–3.30pm; free; ℡209/532-1317, ⓦwww.tchistory.org), is worth a look for the restored cellblock, if not for the collection of old clothes and photographs. There's also a superb bookstore, Sonora Used Books, at 21 S Washington St (℡209/532-1884), with a vast selection of cheap paperbacks in good condition. Pick up architectural and historical walking-tour **maps** ($1) from the **Tuolumne** (rhymes with "you follow me") **County Visitors Bureau**, 542 W Stockton St (April–Sept Mon–Fri 9am–7pm, Sat 10am–6pm, Sun 10am–5pm; Oct–March Mon–Fri 9am–6pm, Sat 10am–6pm; ℡209/533-4420 or 1-800/446-1333, ⓦwww.thegreatunfenced.com), or check in with the Tuolumne Chamber of Commerce, 22 S Shepherd St (Mon–Fri 8am–noon & 1–5pm; ℡209/532-4212, ⓦwww.tcchamber.com).

One of the best-value **hotel** options in Sonora is the old adobe *Gunn House* at 286 S Washington St (℡209/532-3421, ⓦwww.gunnhousehotel .com; ❸), which has large, slightly dark rooms; for a few dollars more, the *Sonora Days Inn*, 160 S Washington St, is more central, although its decor has seen better days (℡209/532-2400, ⓦwww.sonoradaysinn.com; ❹). Otherwise, try the *Miner's Motel* (℡209/532-7850 or 1-800/451-4176; ❷) on Hwy-108, halfway to Jamestown. For **lunch** on Washington Street, try *Café Soma*, at no. 230 (℡209/532-8858), which serves organic goodies including sandwiches and pancakes, plus a wide range of freshly squeezed juices and smoothies. After dark, there are several good options along Washington Street. *Alfredo's*, at no. 123 (℡209/532-8332), is widely regarded as the best reasonably priced Mexican restaurant in these parts, serving standard burritos and enchiladas for $8 or so. Otherwise, the *Sonora Grill's* a reliable option for hefty portions of steaks and Italian food for around $16 (℡209/588-2090). Of several **bars** on Washington, *The Brass Rail* at no. 131, and the retro *Iron Horse Lounge* at no. 97 (℡209/532-4482) are the best places to find a hint of the Wild West.

Columbia

Sonora's one-time archrival, tourist-loving **COLUMBIA**, three miles north on Parrots Ferry Road, now passes itself off as a ghost town with a carefully restored Main Street that gives an excellent – if contrived – idea of what Gold

Rush life might have been like, complete with period costumed staff in the local hotels and restaurants. The town experienced a brief burst of riches after a Dr Thaddeus Hildreth and his party picked up thirty pounds of gold in just two days in March 1850. Within a month, over five thousand miners were working claims limited by local law to ten square feet, and by 1854 Columbia was California's second-largest city, with fifteen thousand inhabitants supporting some forty saloons, eight hotels, and one school. The town missed becoming the state capital by two votes – just as well, since by 1870 the gold had run out and Columbia was abandoned, but only after over two and a half million ounces of gold (worth nearly a billion dollars at today's prices) had been taken out of the surrounding area.

Thanks to agitation from locals, the entire town of Columbia is now preserved as a **State Historic Park** (daily 9am–5pm; ℡209/532-0150, Ⓦwww.parks.ca.gov), though it's also a genuine town with an active Main Street and year-round residents. Most of the buildings that survive date from the late 1850s, rebuilt in brick after fire destroyed the town a second time. Roughly half of them house historical exhibits – including a dramatized visit to the frontier dentist's office, complete with a two-hundred-proof anesthetic and tape-recorded screams. The rest have been converted into shops, restaurants, and saloons, where you can sip a sarsaparilla or munch on a hot dog. Two notable structures are the **Claverie Mason Building**, once the heart of Columbia's Chinatown, and the atmospheric ruins of the **Bixel Brewery**, a mile or so north along Main Street from downtown: although there's little to see now, it's an evocative change from the staged Victoriana in the center of town. As you might imagine, the park/town can be nightmarishly crowded, especially on **Living History Days** (early June), when volunteers dress up and act out scenes from the old days. If you want to escape the crowds, the hokey but fun stagecoach ride (April–Sept Tues–Sun, Oct–March Wed–Sun 10am–4.45pm; $5–6.50; ℡209/588-0808) leaves hourly from the Wells Fargo Building and zips along the old mining trails around the town. Alternatively, take a trip to the **Matelot Gulch gold mine**, where nuggets are still occasionally found: ninety-minute tours ($12; call for tour schedule ℡209/532-9693, Ⓔhiddengoldmine@mlode .com) start from the shack at the south end of Main Street and are hosted by amusingly crabby former miners.

At time of writing, the local visitor center is undergoing major renovations; it's scheduled to reopen in the Cheap Cash Store on Main Street as a full-scale museum and educational facility. In the interim, contact the local Chamber of Commerce about accommodation (℡209/536-1672, Ⓦwww.columbia california.com).

If you want to **stay**, the *Columbia City Hotel* on Main Street (℡209/532-1479 or 1-800/532-1479, Ⓦwww.cityhotel.com; ❺) is luxurious and central with a gourmet restaurant, while the *Columbia Inn Motel*, 22646 Broadway (℡209/533-0446, Ⓦwww.columbiainnmotel.com; ❷), is basic but spotless, with a small pool and cheery staff. Alternatively, a mile south of town, the *Columbia Gem Motel*, 22131 Parrots Ferry Rd (℡209/532-4508 or 1-866/436-6685, Ⓦwww.columbiagem.com; ❷), offers basic accommodation in rustic cabins.

Jamestown

Three miles south of Sonora on Hwy-49, **JAMESTOWN** serves as the southern gateway to the Gold Country for drivers entering on Hwy-120 from the San Francisco Bay Area. Before 1966, when much of James-town burned down in a fire, it was used as location for many well-known Westerns: the classic TV series *Little House on the Prairie* spent several seasons filming in town, and Clint Eastwood shot scenes for his Oscar-winning *Unforgiven* here. The train from that movie – also used forty years earlier in *High Noon*, starring Gary Cooper – can be found among many other steam giants in the **Railtown 1897 State Historic Park**, Jamestown's biggest attraction, five blocks east of Main Street at Fifth and Reservoir (daily: Nov–March 10am–3pm; April–Oct 9.30am–4.30pm; $3; ☎209/984-3953, ⓦwww.railtown1897.org). On weekends from April to October, you can ride one of the vintage trains for an additional fee (hourly 11am–3pm; $6). Along with its train collection, Jamestown is one of the few Gold Country towns that still has a **working mine** – the huge open-pit Sonora Mining Corporation west of town on Hwy-49 – and a number of outfits take visitors on gold-mining expeditions. Among them, Gold Prospecting Expeditions ($30 for 2hr; ☎209/984-4653 or 1-800/596-0009, ⓦwww .goldprospecting.com) gives brief instruction in the arts of panning, sluicing, and sniping, and allows you two hours to pan what you can from its local stream – although don't expect to strike it rich. Main Street is the town's central thoroughfare, with a few **accommodation** choices: the *National Hotel*, 77 Main St (☎209/984-3446 or 1-800/252-8299, ⓦwww .national-hotel.com; ❺), has nine rooms and a casually elegant restaurant with a small bar. Nearby is the plush and historic *Palm Hotel B&B* at 10382 Willow St (☎209/984-3429 or 1-888/551-1849, ⓦwww.palmhotel.com; ❺): its antiquey rooms are a riot of Victoriana, most with claw-footed tubs and stained-glass windows.

For **food** on Main Street, try the popular diner, *Mother Lode Coffee Shop*, at no. 18169, which is open for breakfast or lunch (☎209/984-3386), or grab a gooey sundae at the old-fashioned *Here's the Scoop* ice-cream parlor, no. 18242 (☎209/984-4583). Nearby, there's also the *Smoke Café* (☎209/984-3733), which serves tasty Southwestern-style Mexican food and huge margaritas in a touristy atmosphere; lunch specials hover around $6, and there's live music most nights.

Chinese Camp

Hwy-49 winds south from Sonora through some sixty miles of the sparsely populated, rolling foothills of **Mariposa County**, but first it passes the scant remains of the town of **CHINESE CAMP**. It was here that the worst of the Tong Wars between rival factions of Chinese miners took place in 1856, after the Chinese had been excluded from other mining camps in the area by white miners. Racism was rampant in the southern Gold Rush camps, something which also accounts for its most enduring legend, that of the so-called Robin Hood of the Mother Lode, **Joaquin Murieta**. Murieta was an archetype representing the dispossessed Mexican miners driven to banditry by violent racist abuse at the hands of newly arrived white Americans and likely never existed. Now there's little evidence of this rural village's violent past amid the run-down shacks and trailers other than a historic marker on the main road.

Further south on Hwy-49 lie the southern Gold Rush towns of **Groveland**, **Coulterville**, and **Mariposa**. Owing to their proximity to Yosemite National Park, all three are covered in detail in Chapter Six.

Lake Tahoe, Truckee, and into Nevada

High above the Gold Country, just east of the Sierra ridge, **Lake Tahoe** sits placidly in a dramatic alpine bowl, surrounded by high granite peaks and miles of thickly wooded forest. It's a big tourist area; the sandy beaches and surrounding pine-tree wilderness are overrun with thousands of fun-lovers (predominantly families) throughout the summer, and in winter, the snow-covered slopes of the nearby peaks are packed with skiers. The eastern third of the lake lies in Nevada and glows with light from the neon signs of the inevitable **Stateline casinos**.

Little visited beyond an influx of winter skiers, **Truckee**, fifteen miles north of Lake Tahoe, ranges along the Truckee River, which flows out of Lake Tahoe down into the desert of Nevada's Great Basin. **Donner Pass**, just west of town, was named in memory of the pioneer Donner family, many of whom lost their lives when trapped here by heavy winter snows.

Across the border in **Nevada**, **Reno**, at the eastern foot of the Sierra Nevada, is a downmarket version of Las Vegas, popular with slot-machine junkies and elderly gamblers; others come to take advantage of Nevada's lax marriage and divorce laws. Though far smaller than Reno, **Carson City**, thirty miles south, is the Nevada state capital, with a couple of engaging museums that recount the town's frontier history. Heading deeper into Nevada, and up into the arid mountains to the east, the silver mines of the **Comstock Lode**, whose wealth paid for the building of much of San Francisco, are buried deep below the evocative, if touristy, **Virginia City**.

Lake Tahoe

Fault-formed **LAKE TAHOE** is one of the highest, deepest, cleanest, coldest, and most beautiful lakes in the world. More than sixteen hundred feet deep, it is so cold – or so the story goes – that at its depths cowboys who drowned over a century ago have been recovered in perfectly preserved condition, gun holsters and all. The lake's position, straddling the border between California and Nevada, lends it a schizophrenic air, the dichotomy most evident at **South Lake Tahoe**, the lakeside's largest community, where ranks of restaurants, modest motels, and pine-bound cottages stand cheek by jowl with the high-rise gambling dens of **Stateline**, just across the border. **Tahoe City**, the hub of the lake's northwestern shore, does not escape the tourists but manages to retain a more relaxed – if somewhat exclusive – attitude. Expensive vacation homes and shabby family-oriented mini-resorts line much of the remainder of the lake. Tahoe is never truly offseason, luring weekenders from the Bay Area and beyond with clear, cool waters in the summer, snow-covered slopes in the winter, and slot machines all year round. On holiday weekends, expect traffic to reach maddening levels; convoys of cars and trucks spilling over with ski equipment and mountain bikes stretch throughout the area. To take advantage of the natural resources and still avoid at least some of the crowds, you might

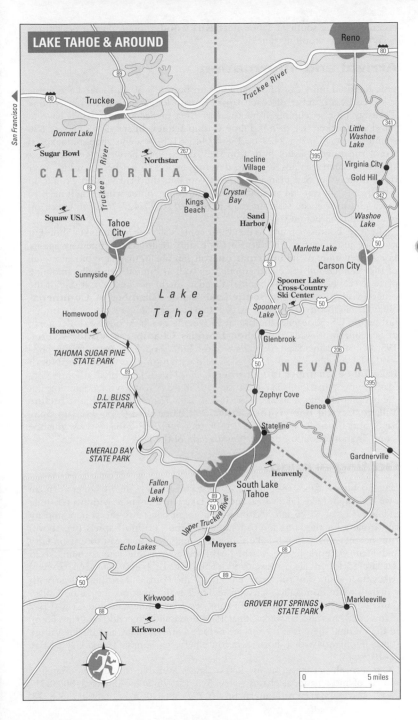

LAKE TAHOE & AROUND

San Francisco

Reno

80

Truckee

Truckee River

Donner Lake

Truckee River

Sugar Bowl

Northstar

267

Little
Washoe
Lake

341

CALIFORNIA

89

Incline
Village

395

Virginia City

Gold Hill

342

28

Kings
Beach

Crystal
Bay

Squaw USA

Tahoe
City

Sand
Harbor

Washoe
Lake

50

Marlette Lake

Sunnyside

Lake
Tahoe

28

Carson City

Homewood

Spooner Lake
Cross-Country
Ski Center

Homewood

Spooner
Lake

50

TAHOMA SUGAR PINE
STATE PARK

89

Glenbrook

206

D.L. BLISS
STATE PARK

50

NEVADA

395

EMERALD BAY
STATE PARK

Zephyr Cove

Genoa

Stateline

Gardnerville

Fallen
Leaf
Lake

Heavenly

89
50

South Lake
Tahoe

Upper Truckee River

Echo Lakes

Meyers

88

50

89

Kirkwood

GROVER HOT SPRINGS
STATE PARK

Markleeville

88

Kirkwood

N

0   5 miles

consider staying south of Tahoe near **Kirkwood**, though during peak times even that area can fill up quickly.

Arrival and information

One hundred miles east of Sacramento on both US-50 and I-80, Lake Tahoe is served by a number of coach **tours** but no longer Greyhound or Amtrak Thruway buses – coming from the Bay Area or Sacramento, you'll have to travel via Truckee (see p.753). Tahoe Casino Express **buses** ($20 one way, $36 round-trip; ☎775/785-2424 or 1-800/446-6128, ⓦwww.tahoecasinoexpress .com) run roughly every hour from 5.30am to 9pm between Reno Airport and the Stateline casinos. If you're **driving**, expect to get here in a little over three hours from San Francisco, unless you join the Friday-night exodus, in which case you can add an hour or two, more in winter when you'll need to carry **chains**; call the Caltrans road phone (☎1-800/427-7623) to check on road conditions before you depart.

There are booths claiming to be visitor centers all over South Lake Tahoe, but most are just advertising outlets for the casinos or fronts for timeshare agents. For slightly more useful **information**, you can obtain maps and brochures (all of them chock-full of advertisements), as well as limited help with finding a place to stay (if you haven't booked ahead, it might not be easy), at one of the official visitor centers. The **South Lake Tahoe Chamber of Commerce**, 3066 US-50 (Mon–Sat 9am–5pm; ☎530/541-5255, ⓦwww.tahoeinfo.com), is just before US-50 reaches the lake at El Dorado beach. About two miles north of Stateline in Nevada, the **Tahoe-Douglas Chamber & Visitor Center**, 195 US-50 (daily: Sept–May 9am–5pm; June–Aug 9am–6pm; ☎775/588-4591, ⓦwww.tahoechamber.org), will help with room reservations. The **North Lake Tahoe Chamber of Commerce**, 300 North Lake Blvd in Tahoe City (daily 9am–5pm; ☎530/581-6900 or 530/583-3494, ⓦwww.tahoefun.org), is the best bet for information on the North Lake region. And lastly, the **Incline Village/Crystal Bay Visitor Center**, 969 Tahoe Blvd (Mon–Fri 8am–5pm, Sat & Sun 10am–4pm; ☎775/832-1606 or 1-800/468-2463, ⓦwww.gotahoe .com), is another option on the Nevada side of the lake.

Getting around

BlueGo **buses** (☎530/541-6328, ⓦwww.bluego.org) run 24 hours a day all over the South Lake Tahoe area, and will take you anywhere within a ten-mile radius for a flat $1.75 fare ($3 buys you an all-day pass); the same company run trolleys for the same fares in summer. Tahoe Casino Express (see above) runs northeast from South Lake Tahoe to Glenbrook, then east to Carson City and Reno Airport. In the north, TART buses (roughly 6am to 6pm; $1.25 flat fare, $3 for an all-day pass; ☎530/550-1212 or 1-800/736-6365, ⓦwww .laketahoetransit.com) run between Sugar Pine Point and Incline Village, with a branch route from Tahoe City up to Truckee. In addition, the Tahoe Trolley (same contacts and fares as TART) runs between Tahoe City and Crystal Bay (6am–6pm), and also between Sugar Pine Point and Emerald Bay (9am–6pm); in the evening there is a free service between Squaw Valley and Incline Village (6pm–midnight), with a short extra route between Sunnyside and Crystal Bay (7–10.30pm).

Car rental, starting at about $30 a day, is available through the Stateline outlets of most national chains – try Avis (☎775/588-4450 or 1-800/831-2847, ⓦwww.avis.com), Enterprise (☎775/586-1077 or 1-800/736-8222,

@www.enterprise.com), and Hertz (☎775/586-0041 or 1-800/654-3131, @www.hertz.com). You could also **rent a bicycle** for around $20–25 a day from any of over a dozen lakeside shops in South Lake Tahoe – some of them offering a full range of **sports equipment rentals** – such as the Mountain Sports Center, Hwy-89 near the "Y" junction (☎530/542-6584), and Lakeview Sports, 3131 S Lake Blvd (☎530/544-0183), or the welter of outlets lining Ski Run Boulevard on the way to Heavenly. In Tahoe City on North Lake Boulevard, try Olympic Bike Shop, no. 620 (☎530/581-2500), or The Back Country, no. 255 (☎530/581-5861).

Accommodation

Most of the hundred or so **motels** that circle the lake are collected together along US-50 in South Lake Tahoe. During the week, except in summer, many have bargain rates, from around $40 for a double; however, these rates can easily double on weekends or in summer, so be sure to confirm – bear in mind the price codes below are based on the lowest high-season rates. Don't expect great deals at the **casinos**; there are fewer than in Las Vegas or Reno, and the casino hotels charge whatever the busy market will bear. If you're having trouble finding a room, **Lake Tahoe Central Reservations**, 3000 North Lake Blvd (☎530/434-1262 or 1-888/358-7461, @www.mytahoevacation .com), can book you a room anywhere on the lake for no fee.

Tahoe City lacks the range and competition of its southerly neighbor, South Lake Tahoe, so you can expect to pay slightly more for a room there, although the reprieve from the Stateline bustle may just make the extra cost worth it if you're looking for peace and quiet. There are also a few other pleasant options dotted around the lake. **Camping** (see box, p.751) is only an option during summer – Tahoe gets upwards of 20ft of snow every winter.

South shore

The Block 4143 Cedar Ave, South Lake Tahoe ☎530/544-2936 or 1-888/544-4055, @www .theblockattahoe.com. Just off US-50, between the casinos and the lakeshore, this is the trendiest if not the cheapest motel in the area with futuristic decor, a cybercafé and games room. ❹

Caesars Tahoe Resort/Casino US-50, Stateline, Nevada ☎775/588-3515 or 1-800/648-3353, @www.caesars.com. Deluxe resort and upmarket casino; the best rooms overlook the lake. Packages include buffet brunches and spa discounts. ❹

Camp Richardson Resort Hwy-89 between Emerald Bay and South Lake Tahoe ☎530/541-1801 or 1-800/544-1801, @www.camprichard-son.com. Hotel-style rooms and comfortable cabins with full kitchens on a 150-acre resort that also has campsites from $18. Cabins available by the week-only in summer from $865. ❸

Doug's Mellow Mountain Retreat 3787 Forest Ave, South Lake Tahoe ☎530/544-8065, @hostelguy@hotmail.com. Essentially Doug's home, operating as a relaxed, if cramped, hostel with cooking facilities and occasional barbecues.

Beds are $15 a night and double rooms are available. ❷

Driftwood Lodge 4115 Laurel Ave at Poplar, South Lake Tahoe ☎530/541-7400, @www .tahoedriftwood.com. The heated pool and private beach access make this otherwise very basic accommodation particularly appealing in summer; very close to Stateline. ❷

Inn by the Lake 3300 Lake Tahoe Blvd, South Lake Tahoe ☎530/542-0330 or 1-800/877-1466, @www.innbythelake.com. Nicely furnished rooms, a heated swimming pool and Jacuzzi, free breakfast, and use of bicycles render this relaxing spot good value for money. Free shuttle bus to the casinos. ❺

Pine Cone Acre 735 Emerald Bay Rd, between Emerald Bay and South Lake Tahoe ☎530/541-0375. Set in wooded grounds with a quieter location than most, pleasant and recently refurbished *Pine Cone Acre* offers a fridge and microwave in each room. ❷

Royal Valhalla 4104 Lakeshore Blvd, South Lake Tahoe ☎530/544-2233 or 1-800/999-4104, @www.tahoeroyalvalhalla.com. Balconied suites with kitchenettes overlooking the lake, right opposite the beach. ❸

Super 8 3600 Lake Tahoe Blvd ☎530/544-3476 or 1-800/800-8000, ⊛www.super8.com. National chain outlet with simple rooms and two miles from the main action, but reliable level of comfort and service, not always found in other cheapies. ❸

Zephyr Cove Resort 760 US-50, Zephyr Cove, Nevada ☎775/589-4907, ⊛www.zephyrcove.com. Run by the same management as the *MS Dixie II* (see opposite), its simple lodge rooms and smarter cabins are away from the hubbub in a quiet pine-clad nook. Smart camping sites are also available from $25. ❸

North shore

Ferrari's Crown Motel 8200 N Lake Blvd, Kings Beach ☎530/546-2583 or 1-800/541-4631. Relatively smart budget motel right by the lake, though you'll pay double for a room with a view. ❸

Franciscan Lakeside Lodge 6944 N Lake Blvd, Tahoe Vista ☎530/546-6300, ⊛www .franciscanlodge.com. Cozy cabins and some larger units, right by one of north shore's best beaches. ❸

Inn at Incline 1003 Tahoe Blvd, Incline Village ☎775/831-1025, ⊛www.innatincline.com. Nestled in a secluded forest setting, with private beach access, indoor pool, spa, and sauna. ❹

Lake of the Sky Motor Inn 955 N Lake Blvd, Tahoe City ☎530/583-3305, ⊛www .lakeoftheskyinn.com. Better value than the slightly more expensive *Tahoe City Inn* opposite, with greater comfort and more pleasant decor. ❹

Mayfield House 236 Grove St, Tahoe City 530/583-1001 or ☎1-888/518-8898, ⊛www .mayfieldhouse.com. Quality B&B with plush rooms in the converted mansion and the quaint cottage behind. ❻

Pepper Tree Inn 645 N Lake Blvd, Tahoe City ☎530/583-3711 or 1-800/624-8580, ⊛www .peppertreetahoe.com. Heated pool and standard hotel accommodation in an otherwise rather characterless high-rise. ❹

Resort at Squaw Creek 400 Squaw Creek Rd, Olympic Valley ☎530/583-6300 or 1-800/327-3353, ⊛www.squawcreek.com The area's most lavish resort with sweeping mountain views and

luxurious accommodations, though rather a stilted atmosphere. There's a golf course, private ski lift, and shopping mall thrown in too. ❼

River Ranch Lodge Hwy-89 & Alpine Meadows Road, Alpine Meadows ☎530/583-4264 or 1-800/535-9900, ⊛www.riverranchlodge.com. Historic and casual lodge on the Truckee River with one of the lake's best restaurants. ❹

Sunnyside 1850 W Lake Blvd, 1 mile south of Tahoe City ☎530/583-7200 or 1-800/822-2SKI, ⊛www.sunnysideresort.com. Large, comfortable mountain lodge right on the lakeshore. Unbeatable views of the lake from many rooms, and a popular restaurant on the ground floor. ❺

Tahoe City Inn 790 N Lake Blvd, Tahoe City ☎530/581-3333 or 1-800/800-8246, ⊛www .tahoecityinn.com. These basic facilities are centrally located and one of the better deals in the area. ❹

Tahoma Meadows B&B 6821 W Lake Blvd, Tahoma ☎530/525-1553 or 1-866/525-1553, ⊛www.tahomameadows.com. Well-furnished rooms in a lovely setting on the west shore, 7 miles south of Tahoe City. ❺

Tamarack Lodge 2311 N Lake Blvd, 1 mile northeast of Tahoe City ☎530/583-3350 or 1-888/824-6323, ⊛www.tamarackattahoe.com. Comfortable and clean lodging, nestled on a pleasant wooded knoll, that is one of the best deals anywhere on the lake. ❷

Further out

Sierrawood Guest House 12 miles from the south shore, Tahoe Paradise ☎530/577-6073 or 1-800/700-3802, ⊛www.sierrawoodbb.com. For that romantic getaway, a secluded chalet in the woods within a few minutes' drive of the casinos' glitter. Jacuzzi, exercise room, fireplace, and free snowmobiling on premises. Popular with gay and lesbian couples. ❺

Sorensen's 14255 Hwy-88, Hope Valley ☎530/694-2203 or 1-800/423-9949, ⊛www .sorensensresort.com. Nestled in the aspens of Hope Valley about a half-hour drive away from the south shore on the west fork of the Carson River, *Sorensen's* features kitsch and cozy cabins with a Bavarian ski-lodge theme. ❺

South Lake Tahoe and Stateline

Almost all of Tahoe's lakeshore is developed in some way or another, but nowhere is it as concentrated and overbearing as at the contiguous settlements of **SOUTH LAKE TAHOE** and **STATELINE**. The latter is compact, a clutch of gambling houses huddled, as you might expect, along the Nevada–California border.

The half-dozen or so casinos compete for the attentions of tourists, almost all of whom base themselves in the much larger South Lake Tahoe on the California side. This is the best place to organize one of the many **outdoor activities** the lake has to offer. Power boating, water skiing, surfing, parasailing, scuba diving, canoeing, and mountain biking are just a few of the proposed activities on the menu of local sporting-equipment rental offices (see p.745). If you happen to lose your vacation allowance at the tables and slot machines, you can always explore the beautiful hiking trails, parks, and beaches that adorn the surrounding area.

Though many stretches of the route around Lake Tahoe are stunning, the 72-mile **drive** is perhaps not the most beautiful in America, as at least one locally produced brochure touts. A better way to see the lake is to take a **paddlewheel boat cruise** on the *Tahoe Queen* from South Lake Tahoe or the *MS Dixie II* from Zephyr Cove, reached on a free shuttle from South Lake Tahoe; both offer three to four cruises daily, the more expensive ones including dinner (call for times; $26–55; ☎775/589-4906 or 1-800/238-2463, ⊛www .laketahoecruises.com). Perhaps most impressive is the view of the lake from above. For those with no athletic ambition, the lazy way to ascend is in one of the neighboring ski resort's **aerial trams**; the most convenient and popular is Heavenly's *Gondola* (see p.748 for details), which now runs from a new terminal only a couple of blocks from Stateline. Finally, in lousy weather you can always visit the modest **Lake Tahoe Historical Museum**, next to the Chamber of Commerce at 3058 US-50 (Tues–Sat 10am–4pm; $2; ☎530/541-5458), which has a small collection of local artifacts and historical displays.

West around the lake

In summer, many enjoyable music and arts events take place at the **Tallac Historic Site** (mid-June–mid-Sept daily; times and prices vary; ☎530/544-7383, ⊛www.tahoeheritage.org), beside Hwy-89 on the western side of the lake just northwest of the "Y" (where Hwy-89 and US-50 separate to the west and east of the lake). Even when there's nothing special going on, the historic site's sumptuous wooden homes – constructed by wealthy San Franciscans as lakeside vacation retreats in the late 1800s – are well worth a look; the grounds are open from dawn to dusk in summer. You can also see the remains of the lavish casino-hotel erected by Elias "Lucky" Baldwin, which brought the rich and famous to Lake Tahoe's shores until it was destroyed by fire in 1914. Inside the former Baldwin house, the **Tallac Museum** (daily 10am–4pm; free) records the family's impact on the region.

The prettiest part of the lake, however, is along the southwest shore, where **Emerald Bay State Park**, ten miles from South Lake Tahoe (daily 8am–dusk; $6 per vehicle; ☎530/541-3030), surrounds a narrow, rock-strewn inlet. In the park, at the end of a steep, mile-long trail from the parking lot, is **Vikingsholm**, an authentic reproduction of a Viking castle, believe it or not, built as a summer home in 1929 and open for half-hourly **tours** (summer daily 10am–4pm; $5). A short way out in the bay, diminutive **Fanette**, Lake Tahoe's only island, pokes pine-clad above the water. Its only structure is the defunct 1929 teahouse, built by Vikingsholm's original owner, Lara Knight. From Vikingsholm, the stunning **Rubicon Trail** runs two miles north along the lakeside to **Rubicon Bay**, flanked by other grand old mansions, dating from the days when Lake Tahoe was accessible only to the most well-heeled of travelers. You can also drive here on Hwy-89 and enter through the **D.L. Bliss State Park** (daily 8am–dusk; extremely limited parking $6; ☎530/525-7277), just to the north. Just under five miles further north, thickly pined **Sugar Pine Point**

Lake Tahoe has some of the best **downhill skiing** in North America, and its larger resorts rival their Rocky Mountain counterparts. The slopes are usually open by mid-November through April or later, with peak season January through March. Although skiing is certainly not cheap – the largest ski areas charge over $50 for the privilege of using their mountain for a single day at peak times – many resorts offer decent-value rental/lift ticket/lesson packages or multi-day discounts. There are also advance deals online and lower prices on either side of peak season. **Snowboarding** has, of course, caught on in a big way, and most resorts have now installed massive snow parks with radical half-pipes and jumps. The following list of ski resorts is not exhaustive, but highlights the best options for skiers of varying ability and financial standing. Skis can be rented at the resorts for about $28–32, and snowboards go for $35–40, but better deals for both can be found in the rental stores dotted around town. Pick up the *Reno–Tahoe Winter Vacation Guide for Skiers and Boarders* at any of the tourism information offices for a complete listing of resorts, along with prices and amenities. Rates below are for high season. For more detailed coverage of the area's wealth of wintertime diversions, consult *The Rough Guide to Skiing and Snowboarding in North America*.

Downhill skiing and snowboarding

Heavenly reachable by shuttle from Southshore, two miles from the casinos (☎775/586-7000 or 1-800/243-2836, ⓦwww.skiheavenly.com). Prime location and sheer scale (82 runs, 27 lifts, 3500 vertical feet) make this one of the lake's most frequented resorts. Those not seeking to ski or snowboard can take the *Gondola* aerial tram for the view from the 8200-foot summit ($22). Lift tickets are $65.

Homewood 6 miles north of Tahoe City on Hw y-89 (☎530/525-2992 or 1-800/824-6348, ⓦwww.skihomewood.com). Smaller and more relaxed than its massive neighbors, Homewood boasts some surprisingly good skiing with unbeatable views of the lake and reasonable prices. Lift tickets go for $44 with $25 "value days." Beginner package ($55) includes equipment, lesson, and beginner lift ticket.

State Park (daily 8am–dusk; $6 per vehicle; ☎530/525-7982) offers more lakeside relaxation potential and has one of only two year-round campgrounds (see box, p.751). It also attracts crowds to see the 15,000-square-foot **Hellman–Ehrman Mansion** (guided tours daily 11am–4pm on the hour; $2), which is decorated in a happy blend of 1930s opulence and backcountry rustic, as well as being surrounded by extensive lakefront grounds.

Lake Kirkwood and Grover Hot Springs State Park

About two dozen miles southwest of Tahoe, a dozen west of where Hwy-89 joins Hwy-88, **LAKE KIRKWOOD** is home to a popular ski resort (see box above), and a destination in its own right, with plenty of **outdoor recreation** possibilities without all the Tahoe hype. Stop by the adventure center in Kirkwood Village (Mon–Fri 9am–5pm, Sat & Sun 9am–6pm; ☎209/258-6000) for information on accommodation, equipment rentals, and hiking in the surrounding area, which includes nearly a dozen lakes, such as Winnemucca and Woods. For accommodation, try the *Lodge at Kirkwood* in the Village, which must be booked through Kirkwood Central Reservations (☎209/258-7000 or 1-800/967-7500, ⓦwww.kirkwood.com/lodging; ❺).

If you head a dozen miles southeast from the junction of Hwy-89 and Hwy-88, you'll come to **Markleeville**, a town of two hundred people on the Sierra Crest.

Kirkwood Ski Resort south of Lake Tahoe on Hwy-88 (☎209/258-6000 or 1-877/547-5966, ⓦwww.kirkwood.com). Kirkwood manages to escape the over-developed feel of many of the Tahoe resorts while still providing some amazing skiing. Lift tickets are $59.

Squaw Valley USA Squaw Valley Road, halfway between Truckee and Tahoe City (☎530/583-6955 or 1-800/766-9321, ⓦwww.squaw.com). Thirty-one lifts service over 4000 acres of unbeatable terrain at the site of the 1960 Winter Olympics. Non-skiers can take the aerial tram ($19) and use the ice-skating/swimming pool complex ($27 including tram). Lift tickets including night skiing are $62, beginner packages from $62 include equipment and 2hr lesson.

Sugar Bowl ten miles west of Truckee at the Soda Springs–Norden exit (☎530/426-9000, ⓦwww.sugarbowl.com). The closest ski area to San Francisco has ten lifts and newly expanded terrain. Inexplicably, this excellent mountain is often less crowded than others in the area. Lift tickets cost $59.

Cross-country skiing

Kirkwood Cross Country Center south of Lake Tahoe on Hwy-88 (☎209/258-7248, ⓦwww.kirkwood.com). More than 50 miles of groomed track and skating lanes for cross-country enthusiasts. Trail fee is $18.

Royal Gorge in Soda Springs, ten miles west of Truckee (☎530/426-3871 or 1-800/500-3871, ⓦwww.royalgorge.com). The largest and best of Tahoe's cross-country resorts has 204 miles of groomed trails. $28 trail fee, $19.50 rental fee, and $25–40 for lessons; good midweek discounts.

Spooner Lake in Nevada at the intersection of US-50 and Hwy-28 (☎775/749-5349, ⓦwww.spoonerlake.com). The closest cross-country resort to South Lake Tahoe has lake views and 63 miles of groomed trails. Trail fees are $20, rentals $18.50, and lessons $42.50, including pass and rental.

The major attraction here is the **GROVER HOT SPRINGS STATE PARK**, four miles west (May to mid-Sept daily 9am–9pm; closed last two weeks in Sept; reduced hours through winter; $6 per vehicle; ☎530/694-2248), with two concrete, spring-filled tubs – one hot, one tepid – in which the water appears yellow-green due to mineral deposits on the pool bottom. There's a $20-a-night **campground** (book through ReserveAmerica ☎1-800/444-7275) on site.

Tahoe City and around

TAHOE CITY, on the north shore, is less developed and more compact than South Lake Tahoe, and a close-knit population of permanent residents coupled with a family-oriented atmosphere give it a more relaxed, peaceful disposition. Still, you're never far from the maddening tourist crowds who flock here all year long.

At the western end of town, Hwy-89 meets Hwy-28 at Fanny Bridge, named for the body part that greets drivers as people lean over the edge to view the giant trout in the **Truckee River**. Flow-regulating sluice gates at the mouth of the river are remotely controlled from Reno, but were once operated by a gatekeeper who lived in what is now the **Gatekeeper's Museum** (mid-June–early Sept daily 11am–5pm; May–mid-June & early–late Sept Wed–Sun 11am–5pm; $2), containing a well-presented hodgepodge of artifacts from the nineteenth century, and a good collection of native basketware. Nearby, the **Truckee River Bike**

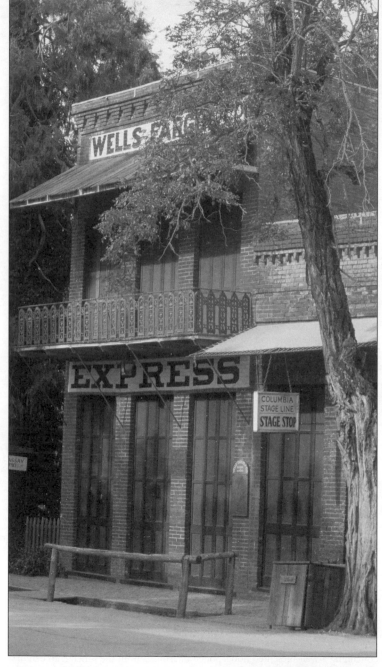

△ Columbia State Historic Park

Trail begins its three-mile waterside meander west to the River Ranch, which is also the end of a popular river-rafting route. **Rafting** down the Truckee is the thing to do on warm summer days, though it's really more of a relaxing social affair than a serious or challenging adventure. Several well-advertised boat-rental stands congregate along the river across from the Chevron station, or call Tahoe Whitewater Tours (☎530/581-2441 or 1-800/442-7238, ⓦwww.gowhitewater .com) for advance reservations. For an even more relaxed excursion on the lake

---

Hiking, biking, and camping around Lake Tahoe

Of the many wonderful hikes in the Lake Tahoe area, only one – the 150-mile **Tahoe Rim Trail** – makes the circuit of the lake, some of it on the **Pacific Crest Trail**, which follows the Sierra ridge from Canada to the Mexican border. Most people tackle only a tiny section of it, such as **Kingsbury Grade** to **Big Meadows** (22 miles), starting off Hwy-207 northwest of South Lake Tahoe and finishing on US-50, south of Lake Tahoe.

There are also many **mountain-biking** trails around the lake: **Meiss County**, between Hwy-89 and Hwy-88 twenty miles south of South Lake Tahoe, is a favored area, where several beautiful lakes that escape most tourist itineraries are located. **Fallen Leaf Lake**, **Echo Lakes**, and **Angora Lake** are all pleasant, somewhat remote alternatives to the big T. Biking trails near the south shore include the three-mile loop of the **Pope-Baldwin Trail**, and you can pick up the popular **Marlett Lake/Flume Trail** in the Nevada State Park.

Ask at the **US Forest Service Visitor Center**, 870 Emerald Bay Rd (summer Mon–Thurs, Sat & Sun 8am–5.30pm, Fri 8am–7pm; ☎530/573-2674), three miles northwest of the junction where Hwy-89 and US-50 separate to the west and east of the lake, for recommendations, free maps, and brochures on the entire area.

Camping

For overall range and quality of facilities, Lake Tahoe's best **campground** is *Camp-ground by the Lake*, on the lakeshore three miles west of Stateline (☎530/542-6096; $21–29). Other south-shore sites include *Fallen Leaf* (☎530/573-2600, reserve through NRRS ☎1-877/444-6777; $20) and *Eagle Point* (☎530/541-3030, reserve through ReserveAmerica ☎1-800/444-7275; $20), which is in Emerald Bay State Park. Details for sites at the *Camp Richardson* and *Zephyr Cove* resorts can be found in the accommodation listings on pp.745–746. The north shore has several sites within striking distance of Tahoe City, including nicely located *Tahoe State Rec-reation Area* (☎530/583-3074, reserve through ReserveAmerica ☎1-800/444-7275; $20) right in the center, and as crowded as you would expect. A mile and a half east, *Lake Forest* (☎530/583-3796; $15) is cheaper though further from the beach and cannot be reserved, and two miles southwest along Hwy-89, there's the large *William Kent* site (☎530/583-3642, reserve through NRRS ☎1-877/444-6777; $16). Halfway down the west shore, *Sugar Pine Point* (☎530/525-7982, reserve through ReserveAmerica ☎1-800/444-7275; $20) has lovely sites in thick pine forest.

Along the western side of the lake, the Tahoe Rim Trail follows the Pacific Crest Trail through the glaciated valleys and granite peaks of the **Desolation Wilderness**. Here, **wilderness permits** ($5) are required by all users, though for day-users these are self-issued. For overnighters, a quota system operates in summer: fifty percent of these are first-come-first-served on the day of entry from the Forest Service visitor center, the remainder are reservable up to ninety days in advance (☎530/644-6048). Among the most strenuous trails here is the five-mile Bayview Trail to Fontanillis Lake. The other wilderness areas around Tahoe – Granite Chief to the northwest and Mount Rose to the northeast – are used much less and consequently no wilderness permits are needed, though campfire permits are.

itself, you can take a **cruise** with the *Tahoe Gal* ($15–30; ☏530/583-0141 or 1-800/218-2464, ⓦ www.tahoegal.com) from the jetty at 850 N Lake Blvd.

A couple of miles south along Hwy-89, 500 yards past the Kaspian picnic grounds, it's well worth **hiking** ten minutes up the unmarked trail to the top of **Eagle Rock** (see box, p.751, for more ambitious hiking suggestions). The amazing panoramic views that surround you as you look down on the expansive royal-blue lake make this one of the world's greatest picnic spots. Several miles further south along Hwy-89 is **Chamber's Beach**, which, in summer, is as popular for sunning and **swimming** as it is for socializing.

You could also visit **Squaw Valley**, the site of the 1960 Winter Olympics, situated five miles west of Tahoe City off Hwy-89, although the original facilities (except the flame and the Olympic rings) are now swamped by the rampant development that has made this California's largest ski resort (see box, p.749). In the valley below, **hiking**, **horseback riding**, and **mountain biking** are all popular summertime activities.

East from Tahoe City are some unremarkable settlements but decent stretches of beach at **Tahoe Vista** and **King's Beach** on Carnelian Bay. As soon as you cross the Nevada state line from King's Beach into **Incline Village**, you are greeted by the predictable huddle of **casinos**, though they are not as numerous or in-your-face as at the south end of the lake. Consequently, the casual visitor might find having a flutter at the likes of the *Crystal Bay* or *Cal-Neva* somewhat less sordid and garish. Unfortunately the beaches here only open to guests at the casino hotels, but better swimming options are close at hand. Once you leave the buildings behind at the northeast corner of the lake and bear south, you enter one of the most appealing and quietest stretches. **Lake Tahoe Nevada State Park** boasts a great beach at **Sand Harbor**, though the water is always prohibitively cold, and has trails winding up through the backcountry to the Tahoe Rim Trail. Just south, **Secret Harbor** is an appropriate location for an idyllic nudist beach where gawkers are not tolerated.

Eating and drinking

South Lake Tahoe has few exceptional **restaurants**; average burger-and-steak places, rustic in decor with raging fireplaces, are commonplace. Far better are the **buffets** at the Nevada **casinos**, though they are not as cheap as in Reno or Vegas: *Harrah's*, for example, serves a wonderful spread, with tasty all-you-can-eat food. The casinos are also good places to **drink** and hold most of the region's entertainment options as well: low-budget Vegas-style revues, by and large. For its size, Tahoe City has a fair range of moderately priced places to eat as well as a couple of happening **bars**, all within a few minutes of each other.

South shore

The Brewery at Lake Tahoe 3542 Lake Tahoe Blvd, South Lake Tahoe ☏530/544-2739. Micro-brewery with decent ales ranging from pale to porter, and food specials such as beer-steamed shrimp and quality steaks.

Café Fiore 1169 Ski Run Blvd, South Lake Tahoe ☏530/541-2908. Small and intimate, *Café Fiore* serves innovative, upscale Italian meals, accompanied by an extensive list of top-notch wines.

Faces 270 Kingsbury Grade, Stateline ☏775/588-2333. The lake's main gay and lesbian bar – a bit frozen in time but friendly, with live DJs.

Nephele's 1169 Ski Run Blvd, South Lake Tahoe ☏530/544-8130. Long-standing restaurant at the foot of the *Heavenly* ski resort, with a great selection of fairly expensive California cuisine: grilled meat, fish, and pasta dishes.

Red Hut Waffle Shop 2723 US-50, South Lake Tahoe ☏530/541-9024. Ever-popular coffeeshop, justifiably crowded early winter mornings with skiers looking to load up on tasty carbs.

Rockwater Bar & Grill 787 Emerald Bay Rd ☏530/544-8004. Big portions of appetizers, followed by a variety of Tex-Mex and seafood dishes at moderate to expensive prices, plus a decent bar.

Scusa! 1142 Ski Run Blvd ☏530/542-0100. Subtly colorful decor and good service complement the fine seafood, steaks, and pasta at this well-respected Italian restaurant.

Six Bridges Bar & Grill 2500 Emerald Bay Rd, between South Lake Tahoe and the Emerald Bay ☏530/577-0788. Standard grill serving large portions of meaty fare in a quiet, woody location.

Sprouts 3123 US-50 near Alameda Ave, South Lake Tahoe ☏530/541-6969. Almost, but not completely vegetarian, with excellent organic sandwiches, burritos, and smoothies.

Taj Mahal 3838 Lake Tahoe Blvd, South Lake Tahoe ☏530/541-6495. Standard Indian fare with a cheap daily eleven-course lunch buffet.

Tep's Villa Roma 3450 Lake Tahoe Blvd, South Lake Tahoe ☏530/541-8227. South shore institution that serves large portions of hearty Italian food, including several simple yet tasty vegetarian pasta dishes for about $10.

North shore

Bridgetender Bar & Grill 30 W Lake Blvd, Tahoe City ☏530/583-3342. Friendly rustic bar with good music, a fine range of beers, and huge portions of ribs, burgers, and the like.

Hacienda del Lago 760 N Lake Blvd, Tahoe City ☏530/583-0358. Tasty Mexican fare at moderate prices on the upper level of the Boatworks Mall; great lake views from the open deck. Margaritas and Latin or jazz music on many evenings.

Jasons' Beachside Grille 8338 N Lake Blvd, Kings Beach ☏530/546-3315. Classic American fare with an emphasis on huge plates of meat plus a twelve-foot salad bar and great desserts. Outside deck with lake views.

Lakehouse Pizza 120 Grove St, Tahoe City ☏530/583-2222. In the Lakehouse Mall, Tahoe's best place for pizza is also a popular spot for

cocktails on the lake at sundown. Be prepared to wait in winter.

Pierce Street Annex in the back of the Safeway complex, Tahoe City ☏530/583-5800. The place for drinking and dancing on the north shore. Packed with sunburned skiers or drunk beach-goers, depending on the season.

River Ranch Hwy-89 and Alpine Meadows Road, Tahoe City ☏530/583-4264. A trendy place to watch whitewater rafters return from their adventure on the Truckee River as you kick back on the deck nibbling mid-range Californian cuisine.

Soule Domain just before the state line and casinos at 9983 Cove Ave, Crystal Bay ☏530/546-7529. Typical Tahoe "elegance" in unexpected surroundings: upscale cuisine in the cozy comfort of a real log cabin. Rather like finding some Parisian chic in Davy Crockett territory.

Spindleshanks 6873 N Lake Blvd, Tahoe Vista ☏530/546-2191. American bistro and wine bar, serving imaginative dishes like pan-roasted artichokes and *chipotle* lime-marinated brick chicken at moderate prices.

Sunnyside 1850 W Lake Blvd, Tahoe City ☏530/583-7200. One of the most popular places to have cocktails at sunset, on the deck overlooking the lake.

Tahoe House Bakery Hwy-89, half a mile south of Tahoe City ☏530/5831377. Family-style bakery with lots of deli items for picnics and the likes. Popular with locals.

Yama Sushi and Robata Grill 950 North Lake Blvd, Tahoe City ☏530/583-9262. Excellent range of tempura, sushi, and grilled *robata* dishes, all expertly prepared, makes this Lake Tahoe's top Japanese restaurant.

Za's 395 North Lake Blvd, Tahoe City ☏530/583-1812. At the back of the friendly *Pete and Peter's* bar, this pizzeria also has a selection of pastas and a wide variety of sauces.

Truckee and around

Just off I-80, along the main transcontinental Amtrak train route, **TRUCKEE**, 15 miles north of Lake Tahoe, makes a refreshing change from the tourist dependent towns around the lake. A small town mostly lined up along the north bank of the Truckee River, it retains a fair amount of its late nineteenth-century wooden architecture along the main section of Donner Pass Road, which many locals still refer to as Commercial Row; some of it appeared as backdrop in Charlie Chaplin's *The Gold Rush*. Truckee is usually viewed as more of a stopoff than a destination in its own right, with a livelihood dependent on the forestry industry and the railroad. However, the town's rough, lively edge makes it as good a base as any from which to see the Lake Tahoe area, a fact that hasn't escaped the businesses beginning to exploit the commercial opportunities. There's even public transportation between the two (see below).

Practicalities

Greyhound **buses** from San Francisco stop three times a day (four times heading west) in Truckee, whence five daily TART buses connect to Tahoe City (daily 8.30am–4.45pm; $1.25; ☎530/550-1212 or 1-800/736-6365, Ⓦwww .laketahoetransit.com). Amtrak Thruway buses only drop off going west at the station on Commercial Row in the middle of town but there is one daily **train** in each direction. The **Chamber of Commerce**, 10065 Donner Pass Rd (daily 8.30am–5.30pm; ☎530/587-2757, Ⓦwww.truckee.com), has all the usual brochures and maps, as well as friendly staff; in addition, where Hwy-89 branches north off I-80, an easy to miss **Forest Service Ranger Station** (Mon–Fri 8am–4.30pm; ☎530/587-3558) offers details of camping and hiking in the surrounding countryside. To get around, rent a mountain bike for $25 a day (also kayaks, skiing and climbing gear) from The Sports Exchange, 10095 W River St (☎530/582-4520), or a car from Enterprise out at Albertson's Longs Shopping Center on Hwy-89 (☎530/550-1550, Ⓦwww.enterprise .com).

Truckee's cheapest **place to stay** is the *Cottage Hotel*, 10178 Donner Pass Rd (☎530/587-3108; ❶), central but a bit shabby with shared bathrooms. Much nicer is the *Truckee Hotel*, close to the train station at 10007 Bridge St (☎530/587-4444 or 1-800/659-6921, Ⓦwww.thetruckeehotel.com; ❸), once decorated in the grand old railroad tradition, now decked out in Victorian B&B style, as is the quieter and more lavish *Richardson House*, 10154 High St (☎530/587-5388 or 1-888/229-0365, Ⓦwww.richardsonhouse.com; ❺). In between the two in terms of comfort and price is *The River Street Inn*, a quaint brick and wood building at 10009 E River St (☎530/550-9290, Ⓕ530/582-2391; ❹). A number of low-cost **campgrounds** line the Truckee River between the town and Lake Tahoe, off Hwy-89: the closest and largest is *Granite Flat*, three miles from Truckee; others are *Goose Meadows* and *Silver Creek*, five and nine miles south respectively (all three locations ☎530/587-3558; $15).

Commercial Row has a number of good **eating** options, especially the diner-style *Coffee And...* at 10106 Donner Pass Rd (☎530/587-3123), while omelets are the specialty at the *Squeeze Inn*, 10060 Donner Pass Rd (☎530/587-9814); both places are only open until 2pm. For cheap all-day meals, try *The Truckee Diner*, on the other side of the tracks at 10144 W River St (☎530/582-6925), or *El Toro Bravo*, a standard *taqueria* at 10186 Donner Pass Rd (☎530/587-3557). The more expensive *Moody's Bistro & Lounge* in the *Truckee Hotel* (☎530/587-8688) serves upscale meat and fish such as pan-roasted wild Oregon sturgeon; and *Dragonfly*, 10118 Donner Pass Rd (☎530/587-0557), is a refreshingly modern place providing a mixture of Pacific Rim, Southeast Asian, and American cuisine on its rooftop terrace. Though the old bucket-of-blood saloons of frontier lore are long gone, there are a few good places to stop for a **drink**, including the *Bar of America* (☎530/587-3110), at the corner of Hwy-26 and Donner Pass Road, offering free live music most nights, or the *Pastime Club*, 10096 Donner Pass Rd (☎530/582-9219), which features great live blues and jazz. *OB's*, at 10046 Donner Pass Rd (☎530/587-4164), is another relaxed pub with decent food. For chocolate so good that you might consider hibernating here through a brutal Truckee winter, try the award-winning cappuccino truffles at *Sweets*, 10118 Donner Pass Rd (☎530/587-6556).

Donner Lake

Two miles west of Truckee, surrounded by alpine cliffs of silver-gray granite, **DONNER LAKE** was the site of one of the most gruesome and notorious tragedies of early California, when pioneers trapped by winter snows were forced to eat the bodies of their dead companions (see box below).

The horrific tale of the Donner party is recounted in some detail in the small **Emigrant Trail Museum** (daily: summer 9am–5pm; rest of year 10am–4pm; $3; ☎530/582-7892) – just off Donner Pass Road, three miles west of Truckee in **Donner Memorial State Park** – which shows a re-enactment of the events in the hourly 26min video that's so over-the-top most viewers will have a hard time choking back their chuckles. Outside, the **Pioneer Monument** stands on a plinth as high as the snow was deep that fateful winter of 1846 – 22 feet. From the museum, an easy nature trail winds through the forest past a memorial plaque marking the site where the majority of the Donner party built its simple cabins. Nearby, on the southeastern shore of the lake, there's a $16-a-night summer-only **campground** (reserve through ReserveAmerica ☎1-800/444-7275).

Above Donner Lake, the Southern Pacific railroad tracks climb west over the **Donner Pass** through tunnels built by Chinese laborers during the nineteenth century – still one of the main rail routes across the Sierra Nevada. For much of the way, the tracks are protected from the usually heavy winter snow by a series of wooden sheds, which you can see from across the valley, where Donner Pass Road snakes up the steep cliffs. On well-signposted Hwy-40, there's a scenic overlook where you can get that prize-winning photo of Donner Lake and possibly a glimpse beyond to Tahoe. Further on, rock climbers from the nearby Alpine Skills Institute (☎530/426-9108) can often be seen honing their talents on the 200-foot granite faces; the institute offers a variety of climbing and mountaineering courses and trips. At the crest, the road passes the Soda Springs, Sugar Bowl, and Royal Gorge **ski areas** before rejoining I-80, which runs east from Donner Pass to Reno, Nevada, and west to Sacramento.

The Donner party

The 91-member **Donner party**, named after one of the pioneer families among the group, set off for California in April 1846 from Illinois across the Great Plains, following a shortcut recommended by the first traveler's guide to the West Coast (the 1845 *Emigrant's Guide to California and Oregon*), which actually took three weeks longer than the established route. By October, they had reached what is now Reno and decided to rest a week to regain their strength for the arduous crossing of the Sierra Nevada Mountains – a delay that proved fatal. When at last they set off, early snowfall blocked their route beyond Donner Lake, and the group was forced to stop and build crude shelters, hoping that the snow would melt and allow them to complete their crossing; it didn't, and they were stuck.

Within a month, the pioneers were running out of provisions, and a party of fifteen set out across the mountains to try and reach Sutter's Fort in Sacramento. They struggled through yet another storm and, a month later, two men and five women stumbled into the fort, having survived by eating the bodies of the men who had died. A rescue party set off from Sutter's Fort immediately, only to find more of the same: thirty or so half-crazed survivors, living off the meat of their fellow travelers.

Into Nevada: Reno and around

On I-80 at the foot of the Sierra Nevada, thirty miles east of Truckee, **RENO**, **NEVADA**, has plenty of affordable places to stay and eat, making it a reasonable stopoff, especially if you enjoy gambling, as many neighboring Californians do each weekend. The town itself, apart from the stream of blazing casino neon, may not be much to look at, having sprung up out of nowhere in the middle of the desert on the hopes that the gambling industry alone could sustain its existence. Nevertheless, its setting – with the snowcapped Sierra peaks as a distant backdrop and the Truckee River winding through – is nice enough, and unlike Las Vegas, to which it is most often compared, Reno maintains a small-town feel that residents are proud of. As the locals love to say – over and over again – Reno is the biggest little town in the world. Even if you don't like to gamble, you can still pass a pleasant afternoon here ambling in the dry desert heat or visiting one of the mildly diverting museums. Reno is also another good place from which to visit Lake Tahoe, and a suitable base for exploring the evocative mining towns of **Carson City** and **Virginia City**.

Arrival and information

Reno's Cannon International **airport** (☏775/328-6400, ⓦwww.renoairport .com) is served by most major domestic carriers. RTC/Citifare (6am–1am; $1.50 flat fare, $4 day-pass; ☏775/348-0480, ⓦwww.citifare.com) bus #13 makes the twenty-minute journey from the terminals to Reno's downtown Citicenter transit center, where you can connect to many of the company's other routes. Greyhound **buses** from San Francisco, via Sacramento and Truckee, and from LA, via the Owens Valley, use the terminal at 155 Stevenson St, also used by KT Services (☏775/945-2282), which operates a daily bus to Las Vegas and Phoenix. The Amtrak *California Zephyr* **train** from Chicago stops in the center of town at 135 Commercial Row, as do Thruway buses from Sacramento. To **rent a car**, try Alamo (☏775/323-7940 or 1-800/327-9633, ⓦwww.alamo.com), Avis (☏775/785-2727 or 1-800/831-2837, ⓦwww.avis.com), or Thrifty (☏775/329-0096 or 1-800/367-2277, ⓦwww.thrifty.com), all three at the airport.

The brand new **visitor center** is located inside the Reno Town Mall at 4001 S Virginia St (Mon–Fri 8am–5pm; ☏775/827-7600 or 1-800/367-7366, ⓦwww.renolaketahoe.com). On the sixteenth floor of 1 E First St, the **Chamber of Commerce** (Mon–Fri 8am–5pm; ☏775/337-3030, ⓦwww .reno-sparkschamber.org) can also dish out advice and brochures.

Accommodation

Inexpensive **accommodation** is plentiful, but if you arrive on a weekend you should book ahead and be prepared for rates to all but double. Usually, a two-nights' stay applies on weekends, especially at the **casinos**. You can also call the **Reno–Sparks Visitor and Convention Association**'s toll-free information and reservation line (☏1-800/367-7366) for help with finding a place to stay. **Camping** is an RV experience in Reno; for tent sites, head west to the numerous campgrounds around Lake Tahoe (see p.751).

Atlantis 3800 S Virginia St ☏775/825-4700 or 1-800/723-6500, ⓦwww.atlantiscasino.com. One of the newer casinos on the scene, this hotel's coffeeshop, restaurant, and buffet – which offers mounds of a huge range of quality cuisines – represent some of the best Reno has to offer. Great rates and plush amenities for slightly less than casinos of the same class in the center of town, especially the motor-lodge rooms. **❸**

Circus Circus 500 N Sierra St ☎775/329-0711 or 1-800/648-5010, ⓦwww.circusreno.com. One of the largest and tackiest casinos, with over 1600 popular rooms – check online for rock-bottom rates at slow times. ❷

Crest Inn 525 W Fourth St ☎775/329-0808, ⓔcrestinn@aol.com. Simple downtown motel with few trimmings and low prices. ❶

Easy 8 Motel 255 W Fifth St ☎775/322-4587. Another basic and even cheaper motel just a stone's throw from the casinos. ❶

Eldorado 345 N Virginia St ☎775/786-5700 or 1-800/777-5325, ⓦwww.eldoradoreno.com. The nicer rooms are on the upper floors, those lower down are cheaper, in this bustling downtown casino. Lots of online specials. ❸

Peppermill 2707 S Virginia St ☎775/826-2121 or 1-866/821-9996, ⓦwww.peppermillreno.com. Another large new casino, slightly outside the center of town; plusher than most with special rates offered frequently. ❹

Silver Legacy 407 N Virginia St ☎775/329-4777 or 1-800/687-7733, ⓦwww.silverlegacyreno.com. The flashiest of all the Reno casinos, which plays on the mining heritage; but the constant stampede of gawkers and gamblers means actually staying here entails negotiating the crowds. Offers golf and skiing packages. ❸

Truckee River Lodge 501 W First St ☎775/786-8888 or 1-800/635-8950, ⓦwww.truckeeriverlodge.com. Non-smoking hotel near the river with an emphasis on recreation; it has its own fitness center. ❷

RENO

Rancho San Rafael Park

Wilbur D Day Museum

University of Nevada

N McCARRAN BOULEVARD

Circus Circus Casino

RTC/ Citifare Depot

National Bowling Stadium

Silver Legacy Casino

Eldorado Casino

Train Station

Harrah's Casino

Greyhound Station

Wingfield Park

National Automobile Museum

Washoe County Courthouse

E L Wiegand Gallery & Nevada Museum of Art

RESTAURANTS
Beto's	1
Harrah's	2
La Vecchia Varese	3

ACCOMMODATION
Atlantis	H
Circus Circus	A
Crest Inn	E
Easy 8 Motel	B
Eldorado	D
Peppermill	G
Silver Legacy	C
Truckee River Lodge	F

0   400 yds

Ⓖ,Ⓗ & all other restaurants covered ▼

Truckee & Sacramento

The Town

It may lack the glitz and the glamour that help make Vegas a global draw, but **Reno** is northern Nevada's number one **gambling** spot, offering a 24-hour diet of slot machines, blackjack, craps, keno, roulette, and many more ways to win and lose a fortune. Gaming was only legalized in Nevada in 1931, but silver miners in Virginia City and Gold Hill regularly tried their hands at fortune's wheel back in the mid-nineteenth century, when a deck of cards was an almost mandatory part of a miner's kit. This tradition was revived with a vengeance when Reno came into being the following century.

While nowhere near as grand as the Vegas gambling institutions (see p.337), most of Reno's **casinos** still warrant a quick tour. If you can only handle visiting a few, the best of the lot are: **Circus Circus**, 500 N Sierra St, where a small circus performs every half-hour, giving patrons a reason to look up from their dwindling savings; it runs seamlessly into **Silver Legacy**, whose main entrance is around the corner at 407 N Virginia St, which reveals a planetarium-style dome with a makeshift 120-foot mining derrick underneath, appearing to draw silver ore out of the ground and spilling cascades of coins in the process – it is joined in turn onto *Eldorado* and you can quite unwittingly wander between all three; the other main attraction for punters is **Harrah's**, a few blocks south at 219 N Center St, the classiest casino downtown with row upon row of high-stakes slot machines and the occasional famous entertainer. If you want to compare these with one of the newer establishments further out, then the best bet is to head south towards the brash opulence of **Peppermill** at 2707 S Virginia St. In order to learn more than you can glean from a solo tour of the casinos, contact the Reno–Tahoe Gaming Academy, 1313 S Virginia St (☎775/329-5665), for an overview of some of the rules of the major games followed by a behind-the-scenes **tour** of Reno's major gambling dens (hours vary; $10) – lessons are also available from $5.

Once you're ready to cash in all the casino clatter and any remaining chips for some peace and quiet, take refuge in one of Reno's many **museums**. The largest and most significant among them is the **National Automobile Museum** (The Harrah Collection), at Mill and Lake streets (Mon–Sat 9.30am–5.30pm, Sun 10am–4pm; $8; ☎775/333-9300, ⓦwww.automuseum.org), which holds the most comprehensive public display of automobiles in the western hemisphere, with more than 200 vintage and classic cars, some of them artfully arranged along re-created city streets of bygone decades. The sheer scale of the collection can't help but impress, even if you think you'd rather be pulling on the arm of a slot machine than admiring the shine on an 1892 Philion. The one time it's guaranteed to get crowded is during the Hot August Nites classic cars festival, when famous twentieth-century automobiles congregate and go on show. Those more into motifs than motors should take a look at the inventive contemporary exhibitions at the **E.L. Weigand Gallery and Nevada Museum of Art**, 160 W Liberty St (Tues–Sun 10am–5pm; $10; ☎775/329-3333, ⓦwww.nevadaart.org).

You'll find Reno's most curious trove, however, at the **Wilbur D. May Great Basin Adventure** (Mon–Sat 10am–5pm, Sun noon–5pm; ☎775/785-5961, ⓦwww.maycenter.com), which sits on the edge of **Rancho San Rafael Park**, a mile north of downtown Reno off North Sierra Street. The collection outlines the eventful life of Wilbur May (1898–1982) – a traveler, hunter, military aviator, cattle-breeder, and heir to the May depart-

If you've come to Reno to get **married**, you and your intended must be at least 18 years old and able to prove it, swear that you're not already married, and appear before a judge at the **Washoe County Court** (daily 8am–midnight; ☎775/328-3275), south of the main casino district at South Virginia and Court streets, to obtain a **marriage license** ($50). There is no waiting period or blood test required. Civil services are performed for an additional $50 at the **Commissioner for Civil Marriages**, behind the Courthouse at 195 S Sierra St (☎775/328-3461). If you want something a bit more special, however, **wedding chapels** all around the city will help you tie the knot: over the crossroads from the courthouse, the Heart of Reno, 243 S Sierra St (☎775/786-6882), does the job quickly – "No Waiting, Just Drive In" – for around $80–100, providing a pink chintzy parlor full of plastic flowers. Fork out more cash, and you get the tux and dress, and can invite a few guests. Other chapels include the Park Wedding Chapel, 136 S Virginia St (☎775/323-1770), and the Silver Bells Wedding Chapel, 628 N Virginia St (☎775/322-0420 or 1-800/221-9336). If it doesn't work out, you'll have to stay in Nevada for another six weeks before you can get a **divorce**.

ment store fortunes – with several rooms of furnishings, mounted animal heads, and plunder from his trips to Africa and South America; the museum also houses temporary exhibitions, hence admission fees vary. In summer only, the complex opens its **Great Basin Adventure** (Tues–Sat 10am–5pm, Sun noon–5pm; $5; ☎775/785-4319), where kids can pet animals, ride on ponies, shoot down a flume, and discover about Native Americans and dinosaurs.

On the other side of US-395, the University of Nevada campus hosts the **Nevada Historical Society Museum**, 1650 N Virginia St (Mon–Sat 10am–5pm; $3; ☎775/688-1190), full of items of local interest, especially Native American artifacts. Next door is the **Fleischmann Planetarium** (Mon–Fri 10am–8pm, Sat & Sun 11am–8pm; $8; ☎775/784-4811, ⊛www .planetarium.unr.nevada.edu), where, amongst the telescopes and solar system galleries, OMNIMAX-style films (2–4 shows daily; ☎775/784-4811) are projected onto a huge dome; the museum contains all four meteorites recovered in Nevada and impressive six-foot globes of earth and the moon.

Eating and nightlife

All-you-can-eat casino buffets are the order of the day for tourists in Reno, and seemingly everyone goes out and stuffs themselves to bursting. The buffets can be fun and of surprisingly good quality; we list the best of them below along with the alternatives most favored by locals, most of which are awkwardly spread over the south of the city. Tourists tend to stick to the shows in the casinos for **nightlife**, but occasionally the city holds an art and/or music festival, and there are some popular venues downtown including *Reno Live*, at Sierra and Second streets (☎775/329-1952), which claims to be the largest nightclub complex in Nevada. Check Reno's free independent weekly *Reno News and Review* for listings. There are a number of **gay and lesbian bars** in town, including the popular *Patio Bar* at 600 W Fifth St (☎775/323-6565).

Buffets

Atlantis 3800 S Virginia St ☎775/825-4700. Consistently and justifiably voted best buffet in town by locals – well worth the extra couple of bucks. The casino also boasts the moderately priced *Café Alfresco* and more upscale *Seafood Steakhouse*, which has exceptional food, wine list and service.
Circus Circus 500 Sierra St. The place to go for a buffet meal if your budget is of greater concern than your stomach, with all-you-can-eat dinners for little over $10.
Harrah's 219 N Center St ☎775/786-3232. The most lavish downtown casino buffet includes multiple entrees such as prime rib, crab leg, shrimp, and a fine Asian section for around $13 most days. Their *à la carte Café Napa* is also recommended.

Restaurants

Aloha Sushi in the Mervyns shopping center at 3338 Kietzke Lane ☎775/828-9611. A bit of a jump southeast from casino central, but reasonable and good; if you're staying for any length of time, you'll need to escape from the buffets eventually. Try their specialty mountain roll.
Bangkok Cuisine 55 Mt Rose St ☎775/322-0299. Cozy Thai family restaurant offering spicy

dinners and filling lunch specials for $5.99.
Beto's 575 W 5th St ☎775/324-0632. Excellent authentic self-service Mexican canteen, one of the best-value downtown eateries outside of the casinos.
Einstein's Quantum Café 6135 Lakeside Drive, near Virginia Lake Park ☎775/825-6611. An inexpensive vegetarian café that's a hit among locals tired of meat-dominated menus – well off course though.
La Piñata 1575 Vassar St ☎775/323-3210. Quality Mexican fare in a spacious lounge – there is a buffet every lunchtime and on Friday evenings.
La Vecchia Varese 130 West St ☎775/322-7486. Unfussy decor and an excellent, moderately priced selection of gourmet Italian dishes, with several vegetarian choices.
Liberty Belle Saloon & Restaurant 4250 S Virginia St ☎775/825-1776. Reasonably priced place famed for its prime rib with spinach salad and other meaty dishes. Established in 1958, it also houses a slot-machine collection and other memorabilia.
S.S. Super Indian Restaurant 1030 S Virginia St ☎775/322-5577. Fresh, primarily Northern Indian specialties and a daily $6 lunch buffet.

Carson City

US-395 heads south from Reno along the jagged spires of the High Sierra past Mono Lake, Mount Whitney, and Death Valley (see Chapter Five). Just thirty miles south of Reno, it briefly becomes Carson Street as it passes through **CARSON CITY**, the state capital of Nevada. Small compared to Reno, and despite the sprawling mess of fast-food joints, strip malls, and car dealerships that surround its center, it is well worth a visit, especially if you are interested in the history of mining. The city has a number of elegant buildings, excellent historical museums, and a few world-weary casinos, populated mainly by old ladies armed with buckets of quarters.

Named, somewhat indirectly, after frontier explorer Kit Carson in 1858, Carson City is still redolent with Wild West history: you'll get a good introduction at the **Nevada State Museum & Mint** at 600 N Carson St (daily 8.30am–4.30pm; $3; ☎775/687-4810). Housed in a sandstone structure built during the Civil War as the Carson Mint, the museum's exhibits deal with the geology and natural history of the Great Basin desert region, from prehistoric days up through the heyday of the 1860s, when the silver mines of the nearby Comstock Lode were at their peak. Amid the many guns and artifacts, the two best features of the museum are the reconstructed **Ghost Town**, from which a tunnel allows entry down into a full-scale model of an **underground mine**, giving some sense of the cramped and constricted conditions in which miners worked. The new **North Building** is home to the **Under One Sky** exhibition, featuring material about cowboys and Indians, natural history, and children's interactive displays.

Four blocks from the museum, on the other side of Carson Street, the impressively restored **State Capitol**, 101 N Carson St (daily 9am–5pm; free), dating from 1871, merits a look for its stylish Neoclassical architecture and the commendable stock of artifacts relating to Nevada's past housed in an upper-floor room.

The **Nevada State Railway Museum**, 2180 S Carson St (daily 8.30am–4.30pm; $2; ℡775/687-6953), just a stone's throw away from the visitor center (see below), displays carefully restored locomotives and carriages, several of them from the long since defunct but fondly remembered Virginia & Truckee Railroad, founded in the nineteenth century.

Practicalities

Greyhound **buses** stop outside the *Frontier Motel* on North Carson Street. Amtrak Thruway services from Sacramento and South Lake Tahoe stop outside the *Nugget* casino at the junction of Robinson and Carson streets. The No Stress Express ($38 one-way; ℡1-800/426-5644, ⓦwww.nostressexpress.com) can be reserved in advance for transportation between Carson City and Reno Airport. The **Convention and Visitors Bureau**, on the south side of town at 1900 S Carson St (Mon–Fri 9am–4pm, Sat & Sun 9am–3pm; ℡775/687-7410 or 1-800/638-2321, ⓦwww.visitcarsoncity.com), can help with practical details, and sells the *Kit Carson Trail Map* ($2.50), a leaflet detailing a **walking tour** of the town, taking in the main museums, the state capitol, and many of the fine 1870s Victorian wooden houses and churches on the west side.

There are a number of reasonably priced **motels** in town, among them the *Nugget Motel & Inn* at 651 N Stewart St (℡775/882-7711, ⓦwww.nuggetmotel .com; ❷) behind the *Nugget* casino, and the more colorful *Plaza Hotel*, 801 S Carson St (℡775/883-9500 or 1-888/227-1499, ⓦwww.carsoncityplaza .com; ❸), not far from the Capitol; while a little further out is the plusher *Piñon Plaza Resort Hotel and Casino* at 2171 US-50 (℡775/885-9000, ⓦwww .pinonplaza.com; ❹), a *Best Western* franchise. If exploring Carson City gives you an appetite, **places to eat** in town include *Heidi's Family Restaurant*, 1020 N Carson St (℡775/882-0486), which serves generous breakfasts and lunches, the basic *Howlin' Good BBQ & Grill*, 1701 N Carson St (℡775/885-2248), or the rather more ambient *Whiskey Creek Steakhouse & Saloon* in the *Piñon Plaza Resort* (℡775/885-9000).

Virginia City and Genoa

Much of the wealth on which Carson City – and indeed San Francisco – was built came from the silver mines of the Comstock Lode, a solid seam of pure silver discovered in 1859 underneath Mount Hamilton, fourteen miles east of Carson City off US-50. Raucous **VIRGINIA CITY** grew up on the steep slopes above the mines, and a young writer named Samuel Clemens made his way west in the 1860s with his older brother, who'd been appointed acting secretary to the governor of the Nevada Territory, to see what all the fuss was about. His descriptions of the wild life of the mining camp, and of the desperately hard work men put in to get at the valuable ore, were published years later under his adopted pseudonym, **Mark Twain**. Though Twain also spent some time in the Gold Rush towns of California's Mother Lode on the other side of the Sierra – which by then were all but abandoned – his accounts of Virginia City life, collected in *Roughing It*, give a hilarious, eyewitness account of the hard-drinking life of the frontier miners.

The miners have long since left, but Virginia City still exploits a rich vein, one which runs through the pocketbooks of tour parties bussed up here from Reno. But despite the camera-clicking throngs, there's a sense of authenticity to Virginia City missing from even the most evocative of the California mining towns. Perhaps it's the town's location, encircled by the barren Nevada Desert that so sharply contrasts with the diverse countryside of California's Gold Country, or perhaps it's the colorful advertisements that lure tourists to the many quirky museums. Then again, it could simply be the raucous spirit that seems to affect almost every sarsaparilla-sippin' tourist who sets foot here. Whatever the reason, it's hard not to get caught up in the infectious Wild West atmosphere and stay longer than you'd intended. Still, not everyone who floods into town is here for the Gold Rush nostalgia – many visitors are here to frequent the **legal brothels**, another reminder of the town's frontier days.

At the **Chamber of Commerce**, in the disused premises of the old *Crystal Bar Saloon* on the corner of Taylor and North C streets (daily 10am–4pm; ☏775/847-0311, ⓦwww.virginiacity-nv.org), you can pick up pamphlets and a self-guided walking-tour map, or you can just as easily wander around the town until you've bumped into all the sights in your own time. Historic highlights include the **Mackay Mansion Museum**, 129 South D St (daily 11am–6pm; $4; ☏775/847-0173), and **The Castle**, 70 South B St (daily late May–mid Oct 11am–5pm; closed Nov–early May; $4; ☏775/847-0766), both painstakingly preserved 1860s residences; and the **Nevada Gambling Museum**, 50 South C St (daily: April–Sept 10am–6pm; Oct–March 10am–5pm; $2; ☏775/847-9022), with its historic roulette wheel and other period game-room accessories. You can also poke your head into the **Bucket of Blood Saloon** at 1 South C St, which is delightfully crowded with period fixtures and crooked old furnishings. The mood of the era and current desire to cash in on it is summed up in **The Way It Was Museum**, 113 North C St (daily 10am–6pm; $3; ☏775/847-0766), with its collection of mining equipment, rare photos and maps, and fully stocked gift shop.

If you'd like to **stay in town**, there are a few decent options, but no Reno-style resorts. Right on the main drag, the *Silver Queen*, at 28 North C St (☏775/847-0468; ➋), and *Comstock Lodge*, at 875 South C St (☏775/847-0233; ➋), are two reasonable, if basic, options for spending the night on the main drag of an old boomtown. The converted 1861 *Chollar Mansion* B&B, 565 South D St (☏775/847-9777; ➍), provides greater comfort and amenities. For a meal, decent options include good Chinese cuisine at *Mandarin Garden*, 30 North B St (☏775/847-9288), whose outside deck affords great views, and cheaper bar food at the *Old Washoe Club*, 112 South C St (☏775/847-7210), which claims to be the town's oldest saloon.

A 35-minute train ride ($6 round-trip) from the town center on the **Virginia & Truckee Railroad** will take you the short distance of little over a mile up to the all-but-extinct town of **Gold Hill**, which consists primarily of a hotel, restaurant, and tavern of the same name (☏775/847-0111; ➌); Nevada's oldest, with good rates and atmosphere, it also lets out half a dozen more expensive lodges in ex-miner's houses around the tiny town.

South of Carson City in the Carson Valley lies another evocative Wild West scene, **GENOA**, the oldest town in Nevada. Slightly less stampeded by tourists than Virginia City, the main draw here is the curious **Mormon Station**, 2295 Main St (daily mid-May–mid-Oct 9am–5pm; free; ☏775/782-2590), a replica of the original trading post and fort built on the site in 1851. For information on walking tours in town, stop by the information counter in the **Genoa Courthouse** at 2304 Main St (daily mid-May–mid-Oct 10am–5pm; $3; ☏775/782-4325). You can stay in some comfort at *The Legend Country Inn*, 2292 Main St (☏775/783-0906, ⓦwww.legendcountryinn.com; ➏), part of a new complex mercifully built to blend in with the old architecture. Locals still congregate at the *Genoa Bar*, 2282 Main St (☎775/782-3870), which claims to be Nevada's oldest continuously operating watering hole.

Travel details

Trains

Oakland/Emeryville (for San Francisco Thruway service) to: Reno (1 daily; 6hr 35min); Sacramento (12 daily; 1hr 50min).
Reno to: Oakland/Emeryville (1 daily; 7hr 30min); Sacramento (1 daily; 5hr); Truckee (1 daily; 1hr).
Sacramento to: Oakland/Emeryville (12 daily; 1hr 40min); Reno (1 daily; 4hr 40min); Truckee (1 daily; 3hr 30min).

Buses

All buses are Greyhound unless otherwise stated.
Reno to: Las Vegas (5 daily; 17–19hr); Los Angeles (6 daily; 10hr 30min–13hr 45min);

Sacramento (9 daily; 2hr 40min–3hr 45min); San Francisco (9 daily; 5hr 10min–7hr 30min).
Reno airport to: Stateline (14 daily Tahoe Casino Express; 1hr 30min).
Sacramento to: Auburn (3 daily; 55min–1hr 20min); Grass Valley (4 daily Amtrak Thruway; 1hr 25min); Nevada City (4 daily Amtrak Thruway; 1 hr 35min); Reno (12 daily; 2hr 50min–4hr); San Francisco (13 daily; 2hr–3hr 5min); Truckee (3 daily; 2hr 40min–3hr).
San Francisco to: Auburn (3 daily; 3hr 50min–4hr 10min); Reno (11 daily; 5hr 15min–6hr 50min); Sacramento (15 daily; 2–3hr); Truckee (3 daily; 5hr 30min–5hr 55min).
South Lake Tahoe/Stateline to: Reno airport (14 daily Tahoe Casino Express; 1hr 30min).

Northern California

Highlights

❋ Russian River Valley wineries The wine tasting here is more leisurely and less commercialized than in the Napa and Sonoma valleys just to the south. See p.791

❋ Mendocino Art Center Admire, purchase, or even participate in the creative output of this friendly community art center in the quaint seaside town of Mendocino. See p.801

❋ Klamath Overlook Where the Klamath River empties into the Pacific, this overlook affords marvelous vistas at this dramatic stop on the rugged Coastal Trail. See p.818

❋ Lassen Volcanic National Park Visit this top natural wilderness, which offers steaming geysers, high-altitude lakes, exhilarating walks, and bracing camping sites. See p.829

❋ Mount Shasta This huge volcanic peak is the focal point of many legends and a haven for cross-country skiing in winter and hiking or mountaineering in summer. See p.844

❋ Lava Beds National Monument Admire the black lavic rock, crawl through tubular caves, or indulge in a spot of birdwatching at California's northernmost attraction. See p.849

△ Bald eagle, Klamath Basin National Wildlife Refuge

10

Northern California

The northern coast and interior of California covers about a third of the state, a gigantic area over 400 miles long and 300 miles wide, with a rugged rural landscape and ethic far removed from portions of the urbanized daydreams of the south. It's a schizophrenic region of a schizophrenic state, coupling volcanoes with vineyards, fog-shrouded redwoods with scorched olive trees, loggers with environmentalists, and legends of Bigfoot with movies of Ewoks. Northern Californians are tied to the land, and agriculture dominates the economy as well as the vistas. Deep-rooted logging, fishing, and cattle industries are also ever-present, even though the first two are in decline, along with the wild, crashing Pacific Coast and steady rain that supports a marijuana-farming region called the Emerald Triangle. Add only two major highways and the lack of a metropolis in favor of small, Main Street towns, and you have a region that has more in common with Oregon and Washington than Los Angeles or San Francisco. In that regard, Northern Californians have long rumbled about forming a state of their own. Indeed, in 1941 there was a proposal to form a state called Jefferson near Mount Shasta, an event that could have gained steam were it not for Japan's bombing of Pearl Harbor two days later, channeling collective energies into the war.

Immediately north of the Bay Area, the **Wine Country** might be your first – indeed your only – taste of Northern California, though it's by no means typical. The two valleys of **Napa** and **Sonoma** unfold in around thirty miles of rolling hills and premium real estate, home to the Californian wine barons and San Franciscan weekenders wanting to rough it in comfort. Napa is the reigning king of indulgence and high-caliber vintages, while Sonoma caters to a funkier set, with its interesting history and outdoor tours. The northwest corner of Sonoma County is Wine Country's other "grape escape," an area of six varieties and resorts clustered around the **Russian River** and its tributaries. Further north and towards the coast, the **Anderson Valley** in Mendocino County is gradually becoming established as the newest haven for vineyards. Another inland area that can be included in a longer itinerary is **Clear Lake**, to the north of the Wine Country.

It's the **northern coast** which provides the most appealing, and slowest, route through the region, beginning just north of Marin County and continuing for four hundred miles on Hwy-1 and US-101 along rugged bluffs and through dense forests as far as the Oregon border. The landscape varies little at first, but given time reveals tangible shifts from the flat oyster beds of **Sonoma County** to the seal and surfer breeding grounds around the coastal elegance of **Mendocino** and the big logging country further north in **Humboldt**. Trees are the big attraction up here: some thousands of years old and hundreds of feet

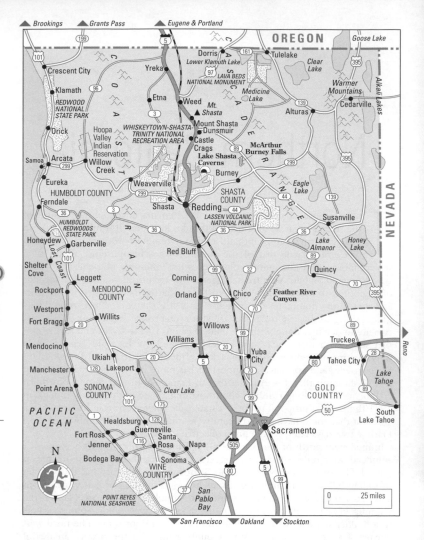

high, dominating a very sparsely populated landscape swathed in swirling mists. In summer, areas like the **Redwood National Park**, stretching into the most northerly **Del Norte County**, teem with campers and hikers, but out of season it can be an idyllic experience, coexisting with the area's woodland creatures, including, some say, Bigfoot. Although the nightlife is rarely swinging, the college town of **Arcata**, towards the top end of the northern coast, makes a lively refuge when the great outdoors begins to pall.

The **interior** is more remote still, an enchanting land whose mystery and sheer physical enormity can't help but leave a lasting impression. I-5 neatly divides the region, cutting through the forgettable Sacramento Valley north to the **Shasta Cascades**, a mountainous area of isolated towns, massive lakes, and a forbidding climate. In winter, much of this corner of the state is completely impassable, and the region's commercial activities are centered around the lower, warmer climes of the largest town and transportation hub of **Redding**. Redding, now boasting an excellent museum and iconic new bridge, is a major crossroads serving **Whiskeytown-Shasta-Trinity National Recreation Area**, **Lassen Volcanic National Park**, **McArthur-Burney Falls State Park** and, northward, the railroad towns in the shadows of towering **Mount Shasta**. Up at the top of the interior, the eerie moonlike terrain of the **Lava Beds National Monument** rewards those who make the effort to get there, and the wetlands of the **Klamath Basin**, which straddles the Oregon border, are a must for birdwatchers. In the very northeast corner of the state, rugged **Modoc County** is another paradise for admirers of the great outdoors. Unlike the Wine Country and the coast, locals all over the Shasta Cascades are actually glad to see tourists, and visitor centers take the time to explain the many outdoor recreational options. Food and lodging costs are cheap by California standards, and the efficient network of highways – by-products of the logging industry – make travel easy. Parts of the region fill up in summer, but given the sheer enormity of the forests and the plethora of lakes, waterfalls, parks, and bird sanctuaries, escaping the masses and finding peace isn't much of a task. In the winter months, you may feel like you're the only one here at all.

Some history

As with elsewhere in California, the first inhabitants of the north were **Native Americans**, whose past has all but been erased, leaving only the odd desolate reservation or crafts museum. Much later, the **Russians** figured briefly in the region's history when they had a modest nineteenth-century settlement at Fort Ross on the coast, ostensibly to protect their interests in otter hunting and fur trading, though more likely to promote territorial claims. **Mexican** explorers and maintenance costs that exceeded revenues prevented them from extending their hunting activities further south, and in the 1840s they sold the fort to the **Americans**. It was the discovery of **gold** in 1848 that really put the north on the map, and much of the countryside bears the marks of this time, dotted with abandoned mining towns, deserted since the gold ran out. Not a lot has happened since, although in the 1980s New Ageism triggered a kind of future for the region, with low land prices drawing more and more devotees up here to sample the delights of a landscape they see as rich in rural symbolism. Hollywood has also been drawn to the region, using the north as a cost-effective way to travel to another place and time. *Robin Hood*, *Gone With the Wind*, *The Birds*, *The Return of the Jedi*, and *Jurassic Park: The Lost World* are just a few examples of movies filmed amongst the frozen-in-time beauty. In more recent years the spiralling rise in Bay Area property prices has led to a small but steady movement of more mainstream folk and retirees into some areas, searching for better value for money or a spacious second home. Many die-hard locals are fearful of this influx of new homes and lifestyles spoiling the coast in particular, though the Coastal Commission tightly controls development, and farmers, so far, have resisted selling out on a large scale.

Getting around

While most people see the Wine Country on a day-trip from San Francisco, it is also feasible to take the area in before encountering the less manicured territory further north, hooking up to the coast by bus from Santa Rosa. **Public transportation** is sparse all over Northern California, and to enjoy the region you'll need to be independently mobile. Infrequent Greyhound **buses** run from San Francisco and Sacramento up and down I-5, stopping in Chico,

Redding, and Mount Shasta, and US-101, with halts in Garberville, Eureka, Arcata, and Crescent City. There is also one connection between the coast and interior in the shape of Greyhound's new Eureka–Redding service, though none of these routes solve the problem of actually getting around once you've arrived. Frankly, your best bet is a **driving tour** with a reliable car, fixing on a few points. The Wine Country can be seen pretty comprehensively in a long weekend, while the other two regions included below really need a week to get all but the sketchiest impression. Only the largest of Northern California's towns have any local bus service although for some of the remoter spots you could, perhaps, consider an organized trip, notably Green Tortoise's one-week tours – see p.50 of Basics for details.

The Wine Country

"The coldest winter I ever spent was summer in San Francisco," quipped Mark Twain. Like Twain, many visitors to San Francisco can't get over the daily fog and winds that chill even the hottest August day. Heading into the golden, arid **Napa** and **Sonoma valleys**, less than an hour's drive north of San Francisco, can feel like entering another country. Here, 29,000 acres of vineyards feeding hundreds of wineries and their upscale patrons, make the area the heart of the American wine industry in reputation, if not in volume. In truth, less than five percent of California's wine comes from the region, but what it does produce is some of America's best.

Predictably, the region is also one of America's wealthiest and most provincial, a fact that draws – and repels – a steady stream of tourists. For every grape on the vine there seems to exist a bed and breakfast or spa, and tourism is gaining on wine production as the Wine Country's leading industry. Expect clogged highways and full hotels during much of peak season (May–Oct), as well as packed tastings in the more popular wineries. The main road through Napa, Hwy-29, can begin to feel like a monotonous chain of connecting towns anchored by rustic red-brick-facade antique stores.

However, there are two sides to the Napa and Sonoma valleys. There is, of course, its prominence for serious, quality **wine** experiences. Almost all of the region's many wineries offer tours and tastings, usually for a small charge (typically $5); this often includes the wineglass or a credit towards the purchase of a bottle, although tastings for some premium estate vintages can cost a lot more. But aside from the type and flavor of the drink, wineries all differ in what they offer visitors. Some delight enologists by explaining the process of growing grapes, some excite kids with tractor rides through the vineyard, and some please thirsty patrons with generous samples. A trip after the October crushing gives the added benefit of lower hotel rates and fewer tourists, allowing more time at tastings. The second reason to come to Wine Country is the **natural landscape**. Separated by the Mayacamas Mountains, the Napa and Sonoma valleys feature some of the most beautiful geography in the state, from the Valley of the Moon to Mount St Helena. Once you've tired of sipping, check out ballooning, biking, horse riding,

Healdsburg & (101) ▲ · ▲ Mount St Helena (12) ►

Old Faithful Geyser ♦ ①

Petrified ♦
Forest · Calistoga ②

THE WINE COUNTRY

Ukiah ◄

(101)

(128)

Napa Valley

BOTHE-NAPA
STATE PARK ③ St Helena

(128)

④

⑤

⑥ Rutherford

⑦ ⑧

⑨ Oakville

Silverado Trail

Santa Rosa

(12)

ANNADEL
STATE PARK

SUGARLOAF RIDGE
STATE PARK

⑩

Sonoma Valley

Glen
Ellen

⑮ ⑭

JACK LONDON
STATE HISTORIC PARK

OAKVILLE GRADE

*Mayacamas
Mountains*

⑬

Arnold Drive

(12)

Yountville

⑪

⑫

YOUNTVILLE-NAPA (LOG ROAD)

Napa Valley

(29)

⑯

Redding ►

Sebastopol & Bodega Bay ◄

(101)

⑰ Sonoma
⑱

(12)

Napa

(121)

Petaluma

(116)

(121)

(29)

Sacramento ►

N

(101)

37

37

80

Novato

San Pablo Bay

Vallejo

780

0   5 miles

San Rafael

80

▼ San Francisco   ▼ East Bay

Carquinez Bridge

⑩

NORTHERN CALIFORNIA | The Wine Country

NAPA WINERIES			
Beringer Vineyards	3	Napa Wine Company	7
Chateau Montelena	1	Niebaum-Coppola Estate	
Clos Pégase	2	Winery & Vineyards	6
Darioush	16	Robert Mondavi	7
Domaine Chandon	11	Silver Oak Cellars	8
Goosecross	9	Stag's Leap Wine Cellars	12
The Hess Collection	13	Sterling Vineyards	2
Mumm Napa Valley	5	V. Sattui	4

SONOMA WINERIES	
Bartholomew Park Winery	17
Benziger Family Winery	15
Buena Vista Winery	17
Chateau St Jean	10
Gundlach-Bundschu	18
Mayo Family Winery	14
Ravenswood	17
Sebastiani Vineyards & Winery	17

hiking, and myriad historical sights, including Spanish missions and Jack London's homestead.

Around **Napa**, nothing is cheap, and the town itself can be quickly done with unless you want to board the over-hyped wine train. But many small towns further up the valley, particularly **St Helena**, have retained enough of their turn-of-the-century-homestead character to be a welcome relief. **Calistoga**, at the top of the valley, is famous for its hot springs, massages, and spas. On the western side of the dividing Mayacamas Mountains, the smaller backroad wineries of the Sonoma Valley reflect the more down-to-earth nature of the place, which is both more beautiful and less crowded than its neighbor to the east. The town of **Sonoma** itself is by far the most attractive of the Wine Country communities, retaining a number of fine Mission-era structures around its gracious central plaza. **Santa Rosa**, at the north end of the valley, is the region's sole urban center, handy for budget lodgings but otherwise unremarkable.

Arrival and getting around

The Wine Country region spreads north from the top of the San Francisco Bay in two parallel, thirty-mile-long valleys, **Napa** and **Sonoma**. As long as you avoid the rush-hour traffic, it's about an hour's drive from San Francisco along either of the two main routes: through Marin County via the Golden Gate Bridge and US-101, or through the East Bay via the Bay Bridge and I-80. Good highways ring the region, and a loop of the two valleys is conceivable in a day or so. Consider working against the flow of traffic by taking in Sonoma, Glen Ellen, and Santa Rosa first before crossing the Mayacamas and dropping into Calistoga, St Helena, and Napa.

As the Wine Country's attractions are spread over a fairly broad area, a **car** is pretty much essential. There are limited public bus options, however, from Golden Gate Transit (☎415/923-2000 or 707/541-2000, ⓦwww.goldengate .org), Greyhound (☎1-800/231-2222, ⓦwww.greyhound.com), Sonoma County Transit (☎707/576-7433 or 1-800/345-7433, ⓦwww.sctransit.com), and the Mendocino Transit Authority (☎707/462-1422 or 1-800/696-4682, ⓦwww.4mta.org); see "Travel details," p.857, for routes. Another option for the car-less is to sign up for a Gray Line **guided bus tour** ($70; ☎415/558-9400, ⓦwww.grayline.com) from San Francisco, which leaves from the Transbay Terminal at 9am. The tour covers both valleys, and visits three wineries, including favorites Sebastiani in downtown Sonoma and Sutter Home in St Helena, with a stop for lunch in pleasant Calistoga. To bypass San Francisco altogether, take the Sonoma Airporter (6 daily; 1hr 30min; $35; ☎707/938-4246 or 1-800/611-4246, ⓦwww.sonomaairporter.com – reservations required) from the San Francisco airport directly to Sonoma City Hall. The bus also stops at the corner of Geary Boulevard and Park Presidio in San Francisco's Richmond District, and makes six return trips to the city daily.

Blue and Gold Fleet **ferries** travel from the Ferry Building (11 daily; $9.50 one-way, $15 day-pass; ☎415/773-1188, ⓦwww.blueandgoldfleet.com) in San Francisco to Vallejo, and are met by hourly Napa Valley Transit buses (Mon–Sat; ☎1-800/696-6443), which continue on to the city of Napa and beyond. Blue and Gold also runs a Wine Country tour leaving daily from Pier 43 (daily 9.15am; $57).

The three-hour **Wine Train** ($40 ticket only, $65–140 with meal; ☎707/253-2111 or 1-800/427-4124, ⓦwww.winetrain.com) runs two or three times daily from Napa's station at 1275 McKinstry St, east of downtown. The ten-car train of restored 1950s Pullman cars chugs up the valley to St Helena, with a stop at Grgich Hills Cellar winery. The scenery en route is pleasant, but the ride is more of a wining-and-dining experience for older travelers than a means of transportation.

Cycling in the Wine Country

If you don't want to drive all day, **cycling** is a great way to get around. You can bring your own bike on Greyhound (though it costs $10, and the bike must be in a box), or rent one locally for around $25–30 per day and $120–150 per week. If renting, try Napa Valley Bike Tours, 4080 Byway East, Napa (☎707/255-3377 or 1-800/707-2453, ⓦwww.napavalleybiketours .com); Getaway Bike Shop, with two outlets at 1117 Lincoln Ave, Calistoga (☎707/942-0332 or 1-800/499-2453, ⓦwww.getawayadventures.com), and 2228 North Point Parkway, Santa Rosa (☎707/568-3040); St Helena Cyclery, 1156 Main St, St Helena (☎707/963-7736, ⓦwww.sthelenacyclery.com); or the Sonoma Cyclery, 20093 Broadway, Sonoma (☎707/935-3377, Ⓦwww .sonomavalleycyclery.com).

Both valleys are generally flat, although the peaks in between are steep enough to challenge the hardiest of hill-climbers. If the main roads through the valleys are full of cars, as they are most summer weekends, try the smaller parallel routes: the **Silverado Trail** in Napa Valley and pretty **Arnold Drive** in Sonoma Valley. For the more athletically inclined, the **Oakville Grade** between Oakville in the Napa Valley and Glen Ellen in the Sonoma Valley has challenged the world's finest riders. Check with the Santa Rosa Cycling Club (☎707/544-4803, Ⓦwww.srcc.com) for itineraries. Alternatively, plot your own route with the *Bicycle Rider Directory* (see Contexts, p.903).

Most local firms organize **tours**, providing bikes, helmets, food, and sag wagons in case you get worn out. In Calistoga, Getaway Adventures offers trips of varying lengths, and Napa Valley Bike Tours sets up more leisurely tours – highlighted by gourmet lunches – all over the Napa area; see above for contact details on both. More ambitious (and quite expensive) overnight tours are run most weekends by Backroads Bicycle Tours, 801 Cedar St, Berkeley (Mon–Fri 7am–5pm, Sat 9am–3pm; ☎510/527-1555 or 1-800/462-2848, Ⓦwww.backroads.com).

The Wine Country by air

The most exciting way to see the region is on one of the widely touted **hot-air balloon rides**. These usually lift off at dawn, and last sixty to ninety magical minutes, winding up with a Champagne brunch. The most established of the operators is Napa Valley Balloons (☎707/253-2224 or 1-800/253-2224, Ⓦwww.napavalleyballoons.com), who fly out of Yountville. Others include Balloons Above the Valley (☎707/253-2222 or 1-800/464-6824, Ⓦwww .balloonrides.com) in Napa and Sonoma County's Air Flambuoyant in Santa Rosa (☎707/838-8500 or 1-800/456-4711), who have the advantage of sending smaller groups of two to eight people aloft. The crunch comes when you realize the price – nearly $200 a head whichever company you use – but it really is worth every cent. Make reservations a week in advance, especially in summer, though with the increasing number of balloon companies, same-day drop-bys are a possibility.

If it's thrills you're looking for, consider taking to the air in a WWII-era propeller **biplane**. Vintage Aircraft Company, 23982 Arnold Drive, Sonoma (☎707/938-2444, Ⓦwww.vintageaircraft.com), operates one- or two-person flights that take in the Sonoma Valley between loops and rolls. Choose from four stomach-churning flight patterns: Scenic, Aerobatic, Kamikaze, and Dawn Patrol. Flights take fifteen to forty minutes and cost $130–295.

Information

Not surprisingly for such a tourist-dependent area, the Wine Country has a well-developed network of **tourist information** outlets, though the rivalry between the two valleys makes it next to impossible to find out anything about Sonoma when you're in Napa, and vice versa. Both the **Napa Valley Visitors Bureau**, 1310 Napa Town Center off First Street in downtown Napa (daily 9am–5pm; ☎707/226-7459, Ⓦwww.napavalley. com), and the **Sonoma Valley Visitors Bureau**, 453 1st St E at the center of Sonoma Plaza (summer daily 9am–6pm; winter daily 9am–5pm; ☎707/996-1090,

@www.sonomavalley.com), should be able to tell you all you need to know about their respective areas; the smaller towns usually have a tourist office too. If you're keen on touring the wineries, both the above places hand out basic free **maps** and sell more detailed ones ($3–5) giving the lowdown on the hundreds of producers.

Accommodation

Most people are content to visit the Wine Country as a day-trip from San Francisco, visiting a few of the wineries and maybe having a picnic or a meal before heading back to the city. But if you really want to absorb properly what the region has to offer, plan to spend at least one night here, pampering yourself in one of the many (generally pricey) **hotels** and **bed and breakfast inns** that provide the bulk of the area's accommodation options. In summer, the Sonoma Valley Visitors Bureau posts a daily list of available rooms in front of their downtown office and the Napa Valley Visitors Bureau can also help out (see above for both). During summer weekends, prices can rise as much as fifty percent, so call ahead. And from November to March, lodging prices drop considerably, often up to half-off. At peak times, rooms of all descriptions get snapped up, so if you have a hard time finding a place, make use of one of the many **accommodation services**: B&B Style (℡707/942-2888 or 1-800/995-8884, @www.bandbstyle.com) in Napa; Bed and Breakfast Inns of Napa Valley (℡707/944-4444, @www.bbinv.com); Napa Valley Reservations Unlimited (℡707/252-1985 or 1-800/251-6272, @www.napavalleyreservations.com); or the Bed and Breakfast Association of Sonoma Valley (℡707/938-9513 or 1-800/969-4667, @www.sonomabb.com).

Campers can find a pitch eight miles north of Sonoma at the Sugar Loaf Ridge State Park, 2605 Adobe Canyon Rd ($20; ℡707/833-5712), or outside Santa Rosa at the Spring Lake Regional Park, 391 Violetti Drive (May–Sept daily; Oct–April Sat & Sun; $15; ℡707/539-8092).

Hotels and motels

Astro Motel 323 Santa Rosa Ave, Santa Rosa ℡707/545-8555, @www.sterba.com/astro. No frills here at this downtown Santa Rosa motel, but some of the cheapest Wine Country rooms available. **②**

Calistoga Inn 1250 Lincoln Ave, Calistoga ℡707/942-4101, @www.calistogainn.com. Comfortable rooms with one bed, most with private bath, in a landmark building with its own restaurant and microbrewery right on the main street. **④**

Dr Wilkinson's Hot Springs 1507 Lincoln Ave, Calistoga ℡707/942-4102, @www.drwilkinson .com. Legendary health spa and hotel downtown. Choose from a variety of spacious, well-lit rooms with sparse furnishings, facing the courtyard or pool patio. Air conditioning and TV standard. **⑤**

El Bonita Motel 195 Main St, St Helena ℡707/963-3216 or 1-800/541-3284, @www .elbonita.com. Old roadside motel recently done up

in Art Deco style, with a pool and hot tub. Surrounded by a 2.5-acre garden, the rooms here contain microwaves, refrigerators, and coffee makers. **⑥**

Harvest Inn 1 Main St, St Helena ℡707/963-9463 or 1-800/950-8466, @www.harvestinn.com. English Tudor cottages at the edge of a vineyard. The place to stay if you can afford it, as the rooms are huge and loaded with perks like a down-feather bed, fireplace, and private terrace over-looking the garden or 14-acre vineyard. Two outdoor heated pools, whirlpool spas, and jogging/biking trails on-site make the just-completed $2 million renovation seem like money well spent. **⑨**

Hotel La Rose 308 Wilson St, Santa Rosa ℡707/579-3200 or 1-800/527-6738, @www .hotellarose.com. Restored lodging on Railroad Square with Internet access in each of its clean, new rooms. **⑥**

Hotel St Helena 1309 Main St, St Helena ℡707/963-4388 or 1-888/478-4355,

Ⓦ www.hotelsthelena.com. Slightly claustrophobic (or cozy, depending on your mood) country-style hotel right downtown. European breakfast included each morning. ⑦

Jack London Lodge 13740 Arnold Drive, Glen Ellen ⑦707/938-8510, Ⓦ www.jacklondonlodge .com. Modern motel near the Jack London State Park, with a good restaurant and pool. A good place to try if Napa and Sonoma hotels are booked, or if you want a truly rural setting and fine stargazing. ⑤

Métro Hôtel 508 Petaluma Blvd S, Petaluma ⑦707/773-4900, Ⓦ www.metrolodging.com. Handily placed for both the Sonoma Valley and the coast, this newly renovated hotel offers unexpected touches of European style in its decor and French café at unbeatable rates. ④

Motel 6 2760 Cleveland Ave, Santa Rosa ⑦707/546-1500 or 1-800/466-8356, Ⓦ www .motel6.com. A little distant from the main wine areas, but a decent, basic option and cheap. There's another branch down the street at 3145 Cleveland Ave. ②

Mount View Hotel and Spa 1457 Lincoln Ave, Calistoga ⑦707/942-6877 or 1-800/816-6877, Ⓦ www.mountviewspa.com. Lively Art Deco–style hotel with nightly jazz and a Cajun restaurant, *Catahoula*, on the ground floor. ⑦; cottage with patio and hot tub ⑧

Swiss Hotel 18 W Spain St, Sonoma ⑦707/938-2884, Ⓦ www.swisshotelsonoma.com. A ninety-year-old landmark building situated right on the plaza with a fine restaurant. The five cramped rooms each have a view of either the garden patio or Sonoma's plaza, and come with a four-poster queen-sized bed. ⑥

Travelodge Hotel & Suites 853 Coombs St, Napa ⑦707/942-6730 or 1-800/578-7878, Ⓦ www .travelodge.com. Standard motel chain with several fancier suites featuring Jacuzzis. Certainly the best prices in downtown Napa. ④

Triple-S Ranch 4600 Mount Home Ranch Rd, Calistoga ⑦707/942-6730. Up the hill from Calistoga, in the middle of the wilderness, these unpublicized cabins are decidedly no-frills, but clean and cheap, with a rustic steakhouse/bar on the premises. Take Hwy-128 north for one mile, turn left on Petrified Forest Road, follow it for five miles to Mount Home Road, turn right and continue one mile. ⑤

Vintage Inn 6541 Washington St, Yountville ⑦707/944-1112 or 1-800/351-1133, Ⓦ www .vintageinn.com. Huge luxury rooms in a modern hotel complex – all with fireplaces – plus swimming pool and free bike rental. Handy for Yountville's many fine restaurants, and great for

romantic getaways, though drastically overpriced. ⑨

White Sulphur Springs 3100 White Sulphur Springs Rd, west of St Helena ⑦707/963-8588, Ⓦ www.whitesulphursprings.com. A relaxing retreat from the tourism of the Napa Valley – simple rooms and plusher cottages in a rustic, newly remodeled 300-acre hillside resort, surrounded by hiking trails, with an outdoor sulfur pool, hot tub, and swimming pool. ⑤

The Wine Country Inn 1152 Lodi Lane, St Helena ⑦707/963-7077 or 1-888/465-4608, Ⓦ www .winecountryinn.com. Patios, strolling gardens, and vineyard-side swimming pool highlight this inn. The rooms are tasteful, open, and uncluttered with antiques. A fireplace comes with most rooms, some of which approach $600. ⑧

Bed and breakfasts

Ambrose Bierce House 1515 Main St, St Helena ⑦707/963-3003, Ⓦ www.ambrosebiercehouse .com. Luxury accommodations in the 1872 house once inhabited by Bierce himself (see p.777). Breakfast is washed down with complimentary champagne. ⑦

Candlelight Inn 1045 Easum Drive, Napa ⑦707/257-3717 or 1-800/624-0395, Ⓦ www .candlelightinn.com. Spacious mock-Tudor mansion with a pool in its lovely grounds and luxurious interior, featuring rooms of varying sizes. Friendly and informal atmosphere with free drinks and snacks. ⑥

Christopher's Inn 1010 Foothill Blvd, Calistoga ⑦707/942-5755 or 1-866/876-5755, Ⓦ www .christophersinn.com. Small and friendly B&B with a lovely English-style garden and comfortable rooms, one block north of the center of town. ⑦

Cottage Inn & Spa 302 1st St E, Sonoma ⑦707/996-0719 or 1-800/944-1490, Ⓦ www .cottageinnandspa.com. Owned by two interior designers, this tranquil, downtown B&B offers a hot tub and a relaxing courtyard. ⑦

Gaige House Inn 13540 Arnold Drive, Glen Ellen ⑦707/935-0237 or 1-800/935-0237, Ⓦ www .gaige.com. Beautifully restored Queen Anne farmhouse in a quiet and contemporary country setting. No children under 12 permitted. ⑨

Garnett Creek Inn 1139 Lincoln Ave, Calistoga ⑦707/942-9797, Ⓦ www.garnettcreekinn.com. Lavishly and gaily decorated old house at the Hwy-29 end of the main street, recently converted into a B&B and one of the best value in this price code. Friendly and knowledgeable innkeeper. ⑦

Kenwood Inn & Spa 10400 Sonoma Hwy, Kenwood ⑦707/833-1293 or 1-800/353-6966, Ⓦ www.kenwoodinn.com. Deluxe, beautiful, and

10

secluded Italian-villa-style B&B with a fireplace in all suites – some reach $700 in high season. **❾**
Oleander House 7433 St Helena Hwy (Hwy-29), Yountville ☏707/944-8315, ⓦwww .oleanderhouse.com. Cosy and friendly B&B in a handy mid-valley location. Quiet enough despite being on the main road, which also keeps prices a little lower. **❻**
Ramekins Bed and Breakfast Inn 450 W Spain St, Sonoma ☏707/933-0452, ⓦwww.ramekins

.com. European-style lodging above a famous cooking school so you can bank on being fed a fine breakfast. **❻**
Thistle Dew Inn 171 W Spain St, Sonoma ☏707/938-2909 or 1-800/382-7895, ⓦwww .thistledew.com. Sonoma's most raved-about B&B. The *Inn*, near Sonoma Plaza, features elegantly restored rooms, an amazing full breakfast, and free bike rental. Some rooms come with a fireplace, private hot tub, and patio. **❼**

The Napa Valley

A thirty-mile strip of gently landscaped corridors and lush hillsides, the **NAPA VALLEY** looks more like southern France than a near-neighbor of the Pacific Ocean. In spring, the valley floor is covered with brilliant wild flowers that mellow into autumnal shades by grape-harvest time. Local Native Americans named the fish-rich river which flows through the valley "Napa," meaning "plenty"; the name was adopted by Spanish missionaries in the early nineteenth century, but the natives themselves were soon wiped out. The few ranches the Spanish and Mexicans managed to establish were in turn taken over by Yankee traders, and by the 1850s, with California part of the US, the town of Napa soon became part of the Gold Rush. Its location also made it a thriving river port, sending agricultural goods to San Francisco and serving as a supply point for farmers and ranchers. The opening of White Sulphur Springs in 1852, California's first mineral-springs resort, made Napa the vacation choice for San Francisco's elite. Settlers came, too, including Jacob Beringer in 1870. The rocky, well-drained soil he saw resembled that of his hometown, Mainz, Germany, and by 1875 he and his brother had established Beringer Vineyards, today America's oldest continually operating winery. Before long, Napa was bypassed by the railroads and unable to compete with other, deep-water Bay Area ports, but the area's fine climate saved it from oblivion. The main route through the valley is Hwy-29, along which all the towns below are strung, but for a quieter alternative route between Napa and Calistoga, the **Silverado Trail** to the east is highly recommended.

Napa, Yountville, and Oakville

The town of **NAPA** itself, at the southern end of the valley, is the anomaly of the region. The highway sprawl that greets travelers is fair warning to what the rest of this 60,000-person city has to offer: but for a proud courthouse and some intriguingly decrepit old warehouses along the Napa River, it's rather lacking in character. That said, Napa is worth a quick stop to visit the **Napa Valley Visitors Bureau** (see p.000 for details). It's the most helpful in the whole valley and a good place to load up on free maps and brochures. Across the street, the Napa County Historical Society (☏707/224-1739) has free, informative materials on the region's pre-wine era. The other reason to visit is the smart new wine and arts center **COPIA**, built as the showcase for an organization founded by Robert Mondavi, at 500 1st St (Wed–Mon 10am–5pm; $12.50; ☏707/259-1600 or 1-888/512-6742, ⓦwww.copia.org). The somewhat steep entry-fee grants access to a thirty-minute video, the exclusively wine-or-food-themed art galleries, including an interesting wall display of spent matches ignited by one of the Mondavi clan, some original

Greek and Roman pottery, and the obligatory gift shop and restaurant. You can also sign up for classes and special events. Smaller attractions include the **Napa Firefighters Museum** at 1201 Main St (Wed–Sun 11am–4pm; free; ☎707/259-0609), which features an array of firefighting paraphernalia, or you might want to take in some culture at the newly refurbished **Opera House** at 1030 Main St (☎707/226-7372, ⓦwww.napavalleyoperahouse.org).

YOUNTVILLE, nine miles north on Hwy-29, is anchored by Vintage 1870, 6525 Washington St (daily 10.30am–5.30pm; ☎707/944-2451), a shopping complex in a converted winery that contains a range of touristic emporia. Aside from antique shops and a few restaurants, nothing in town exerts enough pull to merit a long stop, so push on three miles to tiny **OAKVILLE**, further north along Hwy-29. Dominated by the massive Robert Mondavi winery (see box, p.779), Oakville features a dozen top-rated wineries, and almost all of them require an appointment and charge a tasting fee, ranging from $10 for a famous Silver Oak Cabernet Sauvignon to a whopping $25 for Opus One. Besides its high-caliber wines, Oakville is known for its wonderful Oakville Grocery, an unmissable deli packed with the finest local and imported foods.

St Helena

Eighteen miles from Napa, and far more appealing, **ST HELENA** is the largest of all the antique-shop-filled villages you'll encounter heading north. Its main street, Hwy-29, is lined by some of the Wine Country's finest old buildings, many in pristine condition, and the town itself boasts some unlikely literary attractions. St Helena is also at the heart of a large concentration of wineries, and this combination of history and location make it the de facto tourism capital of Napa Valley, home to a large concentration of luxurious lodgings and restaurants, and with a chic appeal that you'll either love or hate.

If driving through, at least stop off to see the quaint Craftsman-style homes that line residential **Oak Avenue**, and also to see remnants of two unlikely past residents: Robert Louis Stevenson and Ambrose Bierce, both of whom lived in St Helena back in its days as a resort. The **Silverado Museum** (Tues–Sun noon–4pm; free; ☎707/963-3757), just off Main Street in the center of town, has a collection of over eight thousand articles relating to Stevenson, who spent just under a year in the area, honeymooning and recovering from an illness (see p.889). It's claimed to be the second most extensive collection of Stevenson artifacts in the US, though the only thing of interest to any but the most obsessed fan is a scribbled-on manuscript of *Dr Jekyll and Mr Hyde*. The other half of the building is taken up by the **Napa Valley Wine Library** (same hours), a briefly entertaining barrage of photos and clippings relating to the development of local viticulture. On the north side of town, at 1515 Main St, Bierce's former residence has been converted into the **Ambrose Bierce House** bed and breakfast (see p.775). The inn houses a very small collection of memorabilia relating to the misanthropic ghost-story writer and author of *The Devil's Dictionary*, who lived here for some fifteen years, before heading off to fight for Pancho Villa in the Mexican Revolution and mysteriously vanishing.

Calistoga and around

Beyond St Helena, towards the far northern end of the valley, the wineries become prettier and the traffic a little thinner. At the very tip of the valley, nestling at the foot of Mount St Helena, **CALISTOGA** is perhaps the most enjoyable Napa community, featuring around twenty wineries and some fancy bistros. The town, though, is better known for its mud baths and hot springs

Almost all of the Napa Valley's **wineries** offer tastings, though not all have tours. There are more than three hundred wineries in all, producing wines of a very high standard, so your taste should ultimately determine the ones you visit. The following selections are some long-standing favorites, plus a few lesser-known hopefuls. Keep in mind that the intention is for you to get a sense of a winery's product, and perhaps buy some, rather than get tipsy, so don't expect more than a sip or two of any one sort – though some wineries do sell wines by the glass. If you want to buy a bottle, particularly from the larger producers, you can usually get it cheaper in supermarkets than at the wineries themselves, unless you ship in bulk.

Beringer Vineyards 2000 Main St, St Helena ℡707/963-7115, ⓦwww.beringer.com. Napa Valley's most famous piece of architecture, the gothic "Rhine House," modeled on the ancestral Rhine Valley home of Jacob Beringer graces the cover of many a wine magazine. Expansive lawns and a grand tasting room, heavy on dark wood, make for a regal experience. Tasting and tours $5–30; daily 10am–5pm.

Chateau Montelena 1429 Tubbs Lane, 2 miles north of Calistoga ℡707/942-9105, ⓦwww .montelena.com. Smaller but highly rated winery, nestled below Mount St Helena. The Cabernet Sauvignon, in particular, is gradually acquiring a fine reputation. Tasting daily 9.30am–4pm; $10. In-depth tours with seated tasting summer 9.30am and 1.30pm, winter 2pm; $25.

Clos Pégase 1060 Dunaweal Lane, Calistoga ℡707/942-4981, ⓦwww.clospegase.com. A flamboyant upstart at the north end of the valley, this high-profile winery amalgamates fine wine and fine art, with a sculpture garden around buildings designed by postmodern architect Michael Graves. Free tours daily at 11am and 2pm; tasting daily 10.30am–5pm; $2.50–5.

Darioush 4240 Silverado Trail, northeast of Napa ℡707/257-2345, ⓦwww.darioush.com. Grandiose new winery modelled on Persepolis and contructed with stone blocks imported by the owner from his native Iran. Cabernet

Sauvignon and Shiraz are the signature wines. Tasting daily 10.30am–5pm; $10.

Domaine Chandon 1 California Drive, Yountville ℡707/944-2280, ⓦwww.chandon .com. Sparkling wines from this progeny of France's Moët & Chandon can challenge the authentic Champagnes from France. Vast and modern, this winery and gallery is popular with connoisseurs and features a highly regarded but expensive restaurant. Tasting summer daily 10am–6pm, winter daily 11am–5pm; tours 11am–5pm.

Goosecross 1119 State Lane, east of Yountville ℡707/944-1986 or 1-800/276-9210, ⓦwww .goosecross.com. It's well worth taking time to locate this friendly family-run winery, tucked away off Yountville Cross Rd. Crush-time is fun and their Chardonnay especially good. Tasting daily 10am–4pm; free.

The Hess Collection 4411 Redwood Rd, Napa ℡707/255-1144 or 1-877/707-4377, ⓦwww .hesscollection.com. This secluded winery features, in addition to its superior wines, a surprisingly good collection of modern art and a nice view of the valley. Self-guided tour. Tasting daily 10am–4pm; $5.

Mumm Napa Valley 8445 Silverado Trail, Rutherford ℡707/942-3434 or 1-800/ 686-6272, ⓦwww.mummnapavalley.com. Opened in 1986 by G.H. Mumm, France's renowned Champagne house, and Seagrams,

– and the mineral water that adorns every Californian supermarket shelf. Sam Brannan, a young Mormon entrepreneur who made a mint out of the Gold Rush, established a resort community here in 1860. In his groundbreaking speech he attempted to assert his desire to create the "Saratoga of California," modeled upon the Adirondack gem, but in the event got tongue-tied and coined the town's unique name.

Calistoga's main attraction, then as now, is the opportunity to soak in the soothing hot water that bubbles up here from deep in the earth. A multitude of **spas** and volcanic **mud baths**, together with a homely and health-conscious atmosphere, beckon city dwellers and tourists alike. The extravagant might enjoy *Dr. Wilkinson's* the sparkling wines from this beautifully situated winery are good but superseded by sweeping views of the surrounding valleys. The tours are particularly engaging and fun, led by witty and informative guides. Tasting daily 10am–5pm, $5–12; free hourly tours 10am–3pm, on the hour.

Napa Wine Company 7830-40 St Helena Hwy, Oakville ℡707/944-1710 or 1-800/848-9630, Ⓦwww.napawineco.com. Modeled on the co-operative wineries of France, the Napa Wine Company offers 25 small-vineyard owners access to state-of-the-art crushing and fermentation machinery, and also acts as a sales outlet for their vintages. The result? Five of *Wine Spectator*'s recent "Top 10 Wines." Their tasting room is one of the best – and certainly the broadest – in Wine Country; daily 10am–3.30pm; $5–20.

Niebaum-Coppola Estate Winery & Vineyards 1991 St Helena Hwy, Rutherford ℡707/968-1100 or 1-800/782-4266, Ⓦwww.niebaum-coppola.com. In 1975, Francis Ford Coppola purchased this Inglenook estate, originally established by Gustav Niebaum in 1879. Memorabilia from Coppola's movie career is on display in the entryway to the massive new wine-tasting room, featuring their signature Rubicon wine. Tasting daily 10am–5pm; $12; 90min tours at 10.30am, 12.30 and 2.30pm; $25 including tasting and glass.

Robert Mondavi 7801 St Helena Hwy, Oakville ℡707/251-4097 or 1-888/766-6328, Ⓦwww.robertmondavi.com. Long the standard-bearer for Napa Valley wines ("Bob Red" and "Bob White" are house wines at many California restaurants), they have one of the most informative and least hard-sell tours. Tours and tasting daily 10am–4.30pm, reservations recommended. Tastings from $5, tours from $25.

Silver Oak Cellars 915 Oakville Cross Rd, Oakville ℡1-800/273-8809,

Ⓦwww.silveroak.com. Lovers of Cabernet Sauvignon mustn't miss a stop at Silver Oak, the crème de la crème of the heady red that costs over $100 a bottle in some San Francisco restaurants; so the $10 fee (including glass) in the fire-warmed stone-and-wood room is not too outrageous. Tasting daily 9am–4pm; tours Mon–Fri at 1.30pm. Reservations recommended.

Stag's Leap Wine Cellars 5766 Silverado Trail, east of Yountville ℡707/944-2020 or 1-866/422-7523, Ⓦwww.stagsleapwinecellars.com. The winery that put Napa Valley on the international map by beating a bottle of Château Lafitte-Rothschild at a Paris tasting in 1976. Still quite highly rated. Tasting daily 10am–4.30pm; $10–30; tours by appointment.

Sterling Vineyards 1111 Dunaweal Lane, Calistoga ℡707/942-3344 or 1-800/726-6136, Ⓦwww.sterlingvineyards.com. Famous for the aerial tram ride that brings visitors up the 300-foot knoll to the tasting room, the view of Napa Valley from on high is gorgeous. The extravagant white mansion, modeled after a monastery on the Greek island of Mykonos, is Napa's most recognizable. Tasting their wide selection of wines on the View Terrace is a memorable experience. Aerial tram, tasting, self-guided tour 10.30am–4.30pm; $15.

V. Sattui 1111 White Lane, St Helena ℡707/963-7774, Ⓦwww.vsattui.com. Small family-owned winery right off Hwy-29 with award-winning wines – the Riesling and Gamay Rouge are particularly good. Sattui wines are only sold at the winery or through the mail. Gourmet deli next door to stock up for a picnic in the popular tree-shaded grove. Tasting daily summer 9am–6pm, winter 9am–5pm; $5.

Hot Springs, 1507 Lincoln Ave (treatments from $75; ℡707/942-4102, Ⓦwww.drwilkinson.com), a legendary health spa and hotel whose heated mineral water and volcanic ash tension–relieving treatments have been overseen by the same family for almost fifty years. *Mount View Spa*, 1457 Lincoln Ave (℡707/942-5789 or 1-800/772-8838, Ⓦwww.mountviewspa.com), can soothe you with a variety of combined herbal and mud treatments for in excess of $100 and offers shorter but cheaper hydrotherapy sessions. If swaddled luxury isn't what you're after, a number of slightly more down-to-earth establishments are spread along and off the mile-long main drag, Lincoln Avenue. *Golden Haven Hot Springs Spa and Resort*, 1713 Lake St (℡707/942-6793, Ⓦwww.goldenhaven.com), for example, offers a one-hour mud bath, hot mineral Jacuzzi, and blanket wrap for $65–74, and *Calistoga Spa*, 1006 Washington St (℡707/942-6269 or 1-866/822-5772, ⓦwww.calistogaspa.com), has similar rates. If that's still too expensive, ask a local resident to spray you down with their garden hose – although even that might cost a few bucks given Calistoga water's restorative reputation.

Calistoga has one standard tourist attraction in the shape of the **Sharpsteen Museum and Sam Brannan Cottage**, 1113 Washington St (daily 11am–4pm; suggested donation $3; ℡707/942-5911). Founded by long-serving Disney producer Ben Sharpsteen, the quaint little museum contains some of his personal effects, including his Oscar for the pearl-diving film *Ama Girls*, as well as a model of the original resort and lots of biographical material on Sam Brannan, plus a full-size re-creation of his cottage. You can check what else is going on in town and get maps at the friendly **Chamber of Commerce**, 1458 Lincoln Ave (Mon–Fri 10am–5pm, Sat 10am–4pm, Sun 11am–3pm; ℡707/942-6333, ⓦwww.calistogachamber.com).

Heading northwest out of town on Hwy-128 takes you up the ridge of the **Mayacamas**, a picturesque and steep drive that winds to the summit and spirals southwest, depositing you in Santa Rosa. More evidence of Calistoga's lively underground activity can be seen on this route at the **Old Faithful Geyser** (daily 9am–6pm; $8), two miles north of town on Tubbs Lane, which spurts boiling water sixty feet into the air at nine- to forty-minute intervals, depending on the time of year. The water source was discovered during oil-drilling here in the 1920s, when search equipment struck a force estimated to be up to a thousand pounds per square foot; the equipment was blown away and, despite heroic efforts to control it, the geyser has continued to go off like clockwork ever since. Landowners finally realized that they'd never tame it and turned it into a high-yield tourist attraction, using the same name as the famous spouter at Yellowstone National Park. Just south of the geyser, stylish Venetian artist Carlo Marchiori conducts weekly guided tours of his imaginatively decorated house, **Ca'Toga** (May–Oct Sat only 11am; $20 per person with minimum of 25 people). The Palladian villa is full of delicate whimsy – one room is painted as if you are a bird in a cage, another is adorned with painted cows – and the grounds secrete mock ruined temples, a Buddhist corner, and a shell-encrusted cave. An idea of his art can be gleaned, and tours arranged, through his gallery at 1206 Cedar St (℡707/942-3900, ⓦwww.catoga.com).

The **Petrified Forest** (daily: summer 9am–7pm; winter 9am–5pm; $6; ℡707/942-6667), located five miles west of Calistoga, is a popular local tourist trap, but there's little worth stopping here for unless you're a geologist or really into hardened wood. After an entire redwood grove was toppled during an eruption of Mount St Helena some three million years ago, the forest here was petrified by the action of the silica-laden volcanic ash as it gradually seeped into the decomposing fibers of the uprooted trees.

Mount St Helena

The clearest sign of the local volcanic unrest is the massive conical mountain that marks the north end of the Napa Valley, **MOUNT ST HELENA**, some eight miles north of Calistoga. The 4343-foot summit is worth a climb for its great views – on a very clear day you can see Point Reyes and the Pacific Coast to the west, San Francisco to the south, the towering Sierra Nevada to the east, and impressive Mount Shasta to the north. It is, however, a long steep climb (ten miles round-trip) and you need to set off early in the morning to enjoy it – take plenty of water (and maybe a bottle of local wine).

The mountain and most of the surrounding land is protected and preserved as the **Robert Louis Stevenson Park** (daily 8am–sunset; free), though the connection is fairly weak: Stevenson spent his honeymoon here in 1880 in a bunkhouse with Fanny Osborne, recuperating from tuberculosis and exploring the valley – a plaque marks the spot where his bunkhouse once stood. Little else about the park's winding roads and dense shrub growth evokes its former notoriety, though it's a pretty enough place to take a break from the wineries and have a picnic. In Stevenson's novel, *Silverado Squatters*, he describes the highlight of the honeymoon as the day he managed to taste eighteen of local wine baron Jacob Schram's Champagnes in one sitting. Quite an extravagance, especially considering that Schramsberg Champagne is held in such high esteem that Richard Nixon took a few bottles with him when he went to visit Chairman Mao.

The Sonoma Valley

On looks alone, the crescent-shaped **SONOMA VALLEY** beats Napa Valley hands down. This smaller, altogether more rustic valley curves between oak-covered mountain ranges from the small town of **Sonoma** a few miles north along Hwy-12 to the hamlet of **Glen Ellen** and **Jack London State Park**, and ends at the booming bedroom community of **Santa Rosa**. The area is known as the "Valley of the Moon," a label that's mined by tour operators for its connection to long-time resident Jack London, whose book of the same name retold a Native American legend about how, as you move through the valley, the moon seems to rise several times from behind the various peaks. The area has long been a favorite with visitors: Spain, England, Russia, and Mexico have all raised their flags in Sonoma, proclaiming it their own. The US took

NORTHERN CALIFORNIA | The Sonoma Valley

The Bear Flag Revolt

Sonoma Plaza was the sight of the **Bear Flag Revolt**, the 1846 action that propelled California into independence from Mexico, and then statehood. In this much-romanticized episode, American settlers in the region, who had long lived in uneasy peace under the Spanish and, later, Mexican rulers, were threatened with expulsion from California along with all other non-Mexican immigrants. In response, a band of thirty armed settlers – including the infamous John Fremont and Kit Carson – descended upon the disused and unguarded *presidio* at Sonoma, taking the retired and much-respected commander, Colonel Mariano Guadalupe Vallejo, as their prisoner. Ironically, Vallejo had long advocated the American annexation of California and supported the aims of his rebel captors, but he was nonetheless bundled off to Sutter's Fort in Sacramento and held there while the militant settlers declared California an independent republic. The Bear Flag, which served as the model for the current state flag, was fashioned from a "feminine undergarment and muslin petticoat" and painted with a grizzly bear and single star. Raised on Sonoma Plaza, where a small plaque marks the spot today, the Bear Flag flew over the Republic of California for a short time. Three weeks later, the US declared war on Mexico and, without firing a shot took possession of the entire Pacific Coast. While far from a frontier town now, the town once had a much wilder side and in fact gave the English language a slang word for prostitutes. Not long after the Bear Flag revolt, General Lee Hooker arrived, bringing along a group of ladies employed to cheer up the troops. The ladies soon became known as "Hooker's girls," and then simply, "hookers."

over in 1846 during the Bear Flag Revolt against Mexico in Sonoma's central plaza and annexed all of California.

Sonoma Valley's **wineries** are generally smaller and more casual than their Napa counterparts, even though the Sonoma Valley fathered the wine industry from which Napa derives its fame. Colonel Agostin Haraszthy first started planting grapes here in the 1850s, and his Buena Vista Winery in Sonoma still operates today. To see the area at its unspoiled best, get out of the car and ride across the Valley of the Moon on **horseback**. The Sonoma Cattle Co. (T707/996-8566) offers two-hour rides, weather permitting, for $60.

Sonoma

Behind a layer of somewhat touristy stores and restaurants, **SONOMA** retains a good deal of its Spanish and Mexican architecture. The town's charm emanates from the grassy square that acts as downtown's centerpiece, where visitors and locals alike linger over newspapers or lazy picnics. This is indicative of the town's welcoming and relaxed feel, although as a popular retirement spot with a median age of about fifty, it's not exactly bubbling with action.

Today, a number of historic buildings and relics preserve history in the sprawling **Sonoma State Historic Park** ($2 combined entry to all sites; all daily 10am–5pm). The restored **Mission San Francisco Solano de Sonoma** was the last and northernmost of the California missions, and the only one established in Northern California by nervous Mexican rulers fearful of expansionist Russian fur traders. Half a mile west stands the **General Vallejo Home**, the leader's ornate former residence, dominated by decorated filigreed eaves and slender Gothic-revival arched windows. The chalet-style storehouse next door has been turned into a **museum** of artifacts from the general's reign.

There's more to Sonoma than historic buildings, though, and relaxing coffee shops, great restaurants, rare bookstores, and a 1930s-era movie house ring the plaza, making Sonoma a nice town to come back to after a day in the vineyards.

Glen Ellen and Jack London State Park

Continuing north on Hwy-12, beautiful winding roads lead to the cozy hamlet of **GLEN ELLEN**, five miles from Sonoma, and more interestingly, **JACK LONDON STATE PARK** (daily 9.30am–5pm; $6 per car; T707/938-5216, Wwww.jacklondonpark.com). A half-mile up London Ranch Road past the Benziger Family winery, the state park sits on the 140 acres of ranchland the famed author of *The Call of the Wild* owned with his wife Charmian. A mile walk through the woods leads to the ruins of the **Wolf House**, which was to be the London ancestral home: "My house will be standing, act of God permitting, for a thousand years," wrote the author. But in 1913, a month before they were to move in, the house burned to the ground, sparing only the boulder frame. Mounted blueprints point out the splendor that was to be: the mansion contained a manuscript room, sleeping tower, gun room, and indoor reflecting pool. Nearby lies the final resting place of London – a red boulder from the house's ruins under which his wife sprinkled his ashes. Just off the parking lot, the **House of Happy Walls** (daily 10am–5pm; free) is a jewel of a London museum, housing an interesting collection of souvenirs he picked up traveling the globe. Manuscripts, rejection letters (over 600 before he was published the first time), and the note explaining his and Charmian's resignation from the Socialist Party fill the exhibits, along with reproductions of the Londons' rooms and plenty of photographs. A nearby trail leads past a picnic ground to **London's Cottage** (Sat & Sun noon–4pm; free), where he died. A video display gives background to his life, his wife, and the era. West of the cottage, a trail leads one mile toward the mountains and into the woods, ending at the lake London had built so he and Charmian could fish and swim. Bring a bottle of wine and soak in the sunny charm; given the hoopla of the

Sonoma wineries

Around forty fine **wineries** are scattered all over the Sonoma Valley, but there's a good concentration in a well-signposted group a mile east of Sonoma Plaza, down East Napa Street. Some are within walking distance, but often along quirky back-roads, so take a winery map from the tourist office and follow the signs closely. If you're tired of driving around, visit the handy Wine Exchange of Sonoma, 452 1st St E (daily 10am–5.30pm; ☎707/938-1794), a commercial tasting room where, for a small fee, you can sample the best wines from all over California. There is also a selection of 300 beers.

Bartholomew Park Winery 1000 Vineyard Lane ☎707/935-9511, ⓦwww .bartholomewparkwinery.com. This lavish Spanish Colonial building is surrounded by some great topiary in the gardens and extensive vineyards. The wines are relatively inexpensive vintages that appeal to the pocket and palate alike; a safe bet for buying a case. There's a good little museum, too, of regional history that also provides an introduction to local viticulture. Self-guided tours of the winery and $5 tastings daily 11am–4.30pm.

Benziger Family Winery 1883 London Ranch Rd, Glen Ellen ☎707/935-3000 or 1-888/490-2739, ⓦwww.benziger.com. Beautiful vineyard perched on the side of an extinct volcano next to Jack London State Park. $5 tram tours through the fields with emphasis on viticulture five or six times daily or self-guided tour introducing trellis techniques. Tastings daily 10am–5pm; $5–10.

Buena Vista Winery 18000 Old Winery Rd ☎707/252-7117 or 1-800/926-1266, ⓦwww .buenavistawinery.com. Oldest and grandest of the wineries, founded in 1857, whose wine is re-establishing a good reputation after some slim years. The tasting room, a restored state historical landmark, features a small art gallery. Tasting daily 10am–5pm; $5 including glass. Various tours available, ranging from free self-guided tours to a two-hour Sonoma Wine and Cheese Experience for $50.

Chateau St Jean 8555 Sonoma Hwy, Kenwood ☎707/833-4134 or 1-800/543-7572, ⓦwww .chateaustjean.com. Attractive estate with an overwhelming aroma of wine throughout the buildings. Quirky tower to climb from where you can admire the view of the surrounding countryside. Self-guided tours. Free tasting daily 10am–5pm.

Gundlach-Bundschu 2000 Denmark St, Sonoma ☎707/938-5277, ⓦwww.gundlach-bundschu.com. Set back about a mile away from the main cluster, Gun-Bun, as it's known to locals, is highly regarded, having stealthily crept up from the lower ranks of the wine league. The plain, functional building is deceptive – this is premium stuff and definitely not to be overlooked. The winery also hosts various theatrical, cinema, and musical events throughout the summer. Tasting daily 11am–4.30pm; $5. Unreserved tours Sat & Sun, weekdays by appointment.

Mayo Family Winery 13101 Arnold Drive, Glen Ellen ☎707/938-9401, ⓦwww .mayofamilywinery.com. Relatively new winery with a cozy feel and friendly welcome, matching the small-time production of under 5000 cases annually. Complimentary tasting daily 10.30am–6.30pm; barrel tasting tours Fri–Sun 2 & 4pm.

Ravenswood 18701 Gehricke Rd, Sonoma ☎707/933-2332 or 1-888/669-4679, ⓦwww .ravenswood-wine.com. Noted for their "gutsy, unapologetic" Zinfandel and advertising a "no wimpy" approach to the wine business, the staff at this unpretentious winery is particularly friendly and easygoing. Well-known to locals for its summer barbecues. Tastings daily 10am–4.30pm; $5, including 10.30am tour if you're there early enough.

Sebastiani Vineyards & Winery 389 4th St E, Sonoma ☎707/938-5532 or 1-800/888-5532, ⓦwww.sebastiani.com. One of California's oldest family wineries, only four blocks from central Sonoma, it now boasts a newly renovated hospitality center, while the rest of the estate is being returned to its original appearance. There is another tasting room on the central square at 103 W Napa St (☎707/933-3291). Free tasting and tours via tram every half-hour. Daily 10am–5pm.

Wine Country, the usually uncrowded museum and lovely park grounds feel like an oasis of tranquility.

Santa Rosa

Sixty miles due north of San Francisco on US-101, and about twenty miles from Sonoma on Hwy-12, **SANTA ROSA**, the largest town in Sonoma County, sits at the top end of the Sonoma Valley and is more or less the hub of this part of the Wine Country. It's a very different world from the indulgence of other Wine Country towns, however; much of it is given over to shopping centers and roadside malls. In an attempt to form a central pedestrian-only hub, **Historic Railroad Square** – a strip of red-brick-facade boutiques – has been developed, but it will never be mistaken for St Helena's Main Street or Sonoma Plaza. With the real estate prices higher than ever in the Bay Area, Santa Rosa is exploding with growth, making it both a bedroom community for San Francisco and site of the Wine Country's cheapest lodging, with major hotel and motel chains located around town. It also has a decent selection of restaurants and bars. Full listings of what the town has to offer can be found at the **CVB**, 9 4th St (Mon–Sat 9am–5pm, Sun 10am–5pm; ☎707/577-8674 or 1-800/404-7673, ⓦwww.visitsantarosa.com), by Railroad Square.

Probably the most interesting thing about Santa Rosa is that it was the hometown of Raymond Chandler's fictional private eye Philip Marlowe. You can kill an hour or two at the **Luther Burbank Home and Gardens**, at the junction of Santa Rosa and Sonoma avenues (gardens daily 8am–dusk; free; guided tours Tues–Sun every half-hour 10am–3.30pm; $4), where California's best-known horticulturist is remembered in the house where he lived and in the splendid gardens in which he created some of his most unusual hybrids. The **Redwood Empire Ice Arena**, 1667 W Steele Lane (☎707/546-7147), was built by *Peanuts* creator Charles Schulz as a gift to the community. The arena actually comprises two buildings: the ice skating rink and Snoopy's Gallery, a museum/gift shop of all things Peanuts (daily 10am–6pm; $8; ☎707/546-3385, ⓦwww.schulzmuseum.com) and a lasting tribute to the much-loved Schulz, who died at the turn of the millennium.

One enterprise few people would expect to find tucked away in the Wine Country is a full-blown **wildlife refuge**, yet spreading over four hundred acres of the pristine hills between the two valleys, five miles northeast of Santa Rosa, is **Safari West**, 3115 Porter Creek Rd (☎707/579-2551 or 1-800/616-2695, ⓦwww.safariwest.com). Set up in 1989 by Peter Lang, son of *Daktari* producer Otto, the refuge runs breeding programs for hundreds of rare mammal and bird species. Three-hour African-style **jeep tours** (daily 9am, noon & 4pm in summer; 10am & 2pm in winter; $58) take you through vast open compounds of herd animals, and you can wander at leisure past large cages of cheetah and primates or the leafy aviary, while expert guides supply detailed background on the furry and feathered inhabitants. You can even feed the giraffe, if you're lucky. Accommodation in genuine African luxury tents, hung on stilted wooden decks, is available for a princely $225 per unit and filling buffet meals are served in the mess tent.

Eating and drinking

Culinary satisfaction looms around every corner in the Wine Country. California cuisine is almost standard in both valleys, and freshness and innovative presentation are very much the order of the day. **Yountville**, in particular, is little more than a string of high-style restaurants, any of which is up there with the best San Francisco has to offer, with prices to match. **St Helena** and **Calistoga**, though more low-key, are both gourmet paradises. **Sonoma**, too, has its share and is strong on Italian food, while the size of **Santa Rosa** allows for a good deal of diversity. **Bars** are mostly locals' or immigrant Hispanic workers' hangouts, and nightlife nearly nonexistent, perhaps a result of the free booze on offer from the wineries.

Inexpensive restaurants, cafés, and takeouts

Armadillo's 1304 Main St, St Helena ☎707/963-8082. Good-value Mexican cuisine, such as fine quesadillas and burritos, in a brightly painted dining room.

Arrigoni's Deli 701 4th St, Santa Rosa ☎707/545-1297. The place to go for picnic supplies, serving an array of gourmet meats, cheeses, and other savories.

Bosko's Trattoria 1364 Lincoln Ave, Calistoga ☎707/942-9088. Standard Italian restaurant preparing moderately priced, fresh pasta dishes. Cheerful, and popular with families.

Café Citti 9049 Sonoma Hwy, Kenwood ☎707/833-2690. Small, inexpensive *trattoria* with great Italian food and an intimate, yet casual atmosphere.

Café Sarafornia 1413 Lincoln Ave, Calistoga ☎707/942-0555. Famous for delicious and enormous breakfasts and lunches with lines around the block on weekends. Let the owner talk your ear off.

The Coffee Garden 421 1st St W, Sonoma ☎707/996-6645. Fresh sandwiches are served on the back patio of this 150-year-old adobe, which was converted into a café with small gift shop.

Gary Chu's 611 5th St, Santa Rosa ☎707/526-5840. Large helpings of high-quality, award-winning Chinese food like jade garden beef at very reasonable prices. Closed Mondays.

La Casa 121 E Spain St, Sonoma ☎707/996-3406. Friendly, festive, and inexpensive Mexican restaurant just across from the Sonoma Mission. Enjoy an enchilada on the sunny outdoor patio.

The Model Bakery 1357 Main St, St Helena ☎707/963-8192. Local hangout serving the best bread in Napa Valley, as well as sandwiches and pizza.

Peking Palace 1001 2nd St, Napa ☎707/257-7197. Mandarin and Szechwan cuisine served up in a spacious and snazzy space in the heart of downtown Napa.

Puerto Vallerta 1473 Lincoln Ave, Calistoga ☎707/942-6563. Heaps of tasty and genuine Mexican grub can be consumed in the shady

courtyard of this establishment, tucked in beside the Cal-Mart supermarket.

Rins Thai 139 E Napa St, Sonoma ☎707/938-1462. Good range of spicy curries and other Thai favorites available at this modest new restaurant right on the main square.

The Schellville Grill 22900 Broadway, Sonoma ☎707/996-5151. No longer *Ford's Café* of yore but still an institution with locals, who flock here for the ample burgers and sandwiches, some with surprisingly imaginative touches thrown in.

Soo Yuan 1354 Lincoln Ave, Calistoga ☎707/942-9404. Good-value Mandarin and Szechwan cuisine in a small but friendly place on the main street.

Upmarket restaurants

Belle Arti 1040 Main St, Napa ☎707/255-0720. Genuine Sicilian *trattoria* at the back of a modern complex, with a spacious outdoor patio overlooking the creek.

Bouchon 6534 Washington St, Yountville ☎707/944-8037. Parisian chic and haute cuisine at high prices – the terrine de fois gras goes for $45 but most entrees are around $30.

Brannan's 1374 Lincoln Ave, Calistoga ☎707/942-2233. Pecan-stuffed quail, fresh steamed oysters, and a wonderful wooden interior make this rather expensive, high-profile catery worth a visit.

Café LaHaye 140 E Napa St, Sonoma ☎707/935-5994. Only eleven tables, and always packed for its lovely, lively interior and tasty Italian food.

Cole's Chop House 1122 Main St, Napa ☎707/224-6328. This is the place to come for huge chunks of well-prepared red meat. Very spacious inside and top service, but rather a stilted atmosphere.

Cucina Viansa 400 E 1st St, Sonoma ☎707/935-5656. Not too outrageously priced considering the small but creative and delicious selection of Italian specialties.

The General's Daughter 400 W Spain St, Sonoma ☎707/938-4004. Moderately priced California/ Mediterranean hybrid dishes like wild mushroom ravioli, salmon and asparagus, and pork tenderloin in a Victorian building formally owned by General Vallejo's daughter.

The Girl & The Fig 110 W Spain St, Sonoma ☎707/938-3634. Recently moved from Glen Ellen to the ground floor of the *Sonoma Hotel*, this well-known restaurant offers French dinners and weekend brunch from a menu as eclectic as its name and pricey to match.

Glen Ellen Inn 13670 Arnold Drive, Glen Ellen ☎707/996-6409. Husband-and-wife team cook and serve slightly pricey gourmet dishes in an intimate, romantic dining room with half a dozen tables. Daily 5.30–9.30pm.

Greystone Restaurant at the Culinary Institute of America 2555 Main St, St Helena ☎707/967-1010. California/Mediterranean cuisine served in an elegant ivy-walled mansion just outside of town, with a tastefully wacky Art Deco interior. Reasonably priced considering the delicious, large portions of chicken, duck, fish, and venison.

Kelley's No Bad Days Café 976 Pearl St, Napa ☎707/258-9666. American standards with an Asian influence constitute most of the menu at this small but lively spot, which has some outside seating.

Mustards Grill 7399 St Helena Hwy (Hwy-29), Yountville ☎707/944-2424. Credited with starting the late-1980s trend toward "grazing" food, emphasizing tapas-like tidbits rather than main meals. Reckon on spending over $20 a head and waiting for a table if you come on a weekend.

Pinot Blanc 641 Main St, St Helena ☎707/963-6191. California fusion cuisine prepared by the famous chef Sean Knight, and a nearly California-exclusive wine list.

Rutherford Grill 1180 Rutherford Rd, Rutherford ☎707/963-1920. Large portions of basic contemporary American food – the mash potatoes should not be missed – served in a handsome new dining room popular for its martinis and as a meeting place.

Tra Vigne 1050 Charter Oak Ave, St Helena ☎707/963-4444. Just north of town, but it feels as if you've been transported to Tuscany. Excellent food and fine wines served up in a lovely vine-covered courtyard or elegant dining room, but you pay for the privilege. They also have a small deli, where you can pick up picnic goodies.

Zuzu 829 Main St, Napa ☎707/224-5885. Not the place to come if ravenous, but this popular new tapas bar offers tasty fare and a good wine list in its trendy interior.

Bars

Amigos Grill and Cantina 19315 Sonoma Hwy, Sonoma ☎707/939-0743. Award-winning margaritas using your choice of one of 20 tequilas and a home-made mix.

Ana's Cantina 1205 Main St, St Helena ☎707/963-4921. Long-standing, down-to-earth saloon and Mexican restaurant with billiards and darts tournaments.

Compadres Bar and Grill 6539 Washington St, Yountville ☎707/944-2406. Outdoor patio seating and amazing martinis and margaritas, with free salsa and chips.

Downtown Joe's 902 Main St at 2nd, Napa ☎707/258-2337. One of Napa's most popular and lively spots for sandwiches, ribs, and pasta, with outdoor dining by the river and beer brewed on the premises. About the only place in town open until midnight and a good spot to meet locals.

Murphy's Irish Pub 464 1st St E, Sonoma ☎707/935-0660. Small bar with an eclectic interior and a few outdoor tables serving basic pub grub and European beers.

Third Street Aleworks 610 3rd St, Santa Rosa ☎707/523-3060. Frequent live music and hearty American grub like burgers and pizza, washed down with microbrewed ale, are the order of the day at this lively joint.

The northern coast

The fog-bound towns and windswept, craggy beaches of the **NORTHERN COAST** couldn't be farther removed from Southern California's sandy, sunny strip of ocean. Stretching north of San Francisco to the Oregon border, the northern coast is better suited for hiking than sunbathing, with a climate of cool temperatures year-round and a huge network of national, state, and regional **parks** preserving magnificent redwood trees. **Wildlife** thrives here and is always in view, from seals lounging on rocks around Goat Rock Beach in the south to elk chomping on berry bushes in the north, all against a backdrop of spectacular scenery. Far rarer fauna has been spotted up here as well: the legendary Bigfoot supposedly leaves footprints through the forest, and Ewoks once battled the Galactic Empire under the direction of *Star Wars* creator George Lucas, who used areas north of Orick as the set for *The Return of the Jedi*.

The only way to see the coast properly is on the painfully slow but visually magnificent Hwy-1, which hugs the coast for two hundred miles through the wild counties of **Sonoma** and **Mendocino**, before turning sharply inland at Legget to join US-101 and **Humboldt County**. The hundred miles of wild coastline Hwy-1 never reaches has become known, appropriately, as the **Lost Coast**, a virgin territory of campsites and trails. If you are heading for the coast from the Wine Country, a pleasant route is via the quieter wineries of the **Russian River Valley**, or you can take US-101 and detour inland further north to placid **Clear Lake**, before cutting across to Mendocino. North of here, the redwoods take over, blanketing the landscape all the way to Oregon, doubling as raw material for the huge logging industries (the prime source of employment in the area) and the region's prime tourist attraction, most notably in the **Redwood National Park**. **Eureka**, the coast's largest – and most boring – city, is neighbored by lively **Arcata**, home to **Humboldt State University** and thousands of Birkenstock sandals. The last stretch of redwood coast before the Oregon state line lies in **Del Norte County**, whose functional seat of **Crescent City** offers little to detain the visitor for long.

You'll need to be fairly independent to **get around** this region: only one Amtrak Thruway and two Greyhound buses a day travel the length of US-101, which parallels the coastal highway, but they don't link up with the coast until Eureka, far to the north. Otherwise most visitors travel by car and should, in summertime, expect legions of slow-moving campers trying to negotiate the two-lane road's hairpin curves.

The Sonoma coast and Russian River Valley

Hwy-1 twists and winds along the edge of the **SONOMA COAST** through persistent fog that, once burned off by the sun, reveals oyster beds, seal breeding grounds, and twenty-foot-high rhododendrons. A spectacular introduction to the northern coast, Sonoma County's western rim is never short on visitors due to its proximity to San Francisco. But tourist activity is confined to a few narrow corridors at the height of summer, leaving behind a network of north-coast villages and backwater wineries that for most of the year are all but asleep. The coast is colder and lonelier than the villages along the valley, and at some point most people head inland for a change of scene and a break from the pervasive fog. What both areas have in common, though, is a reluctance to change. As wealthy San Franciscans cast their eyes towards the north for potential second-home sites, the California Coastal Commission's policy of beach access for all keeps the architects at bay, making the Sonoma coast one of the few remaining undeveloped coastal areas in California; the southern third of the coast is almost entirely state beach.

At the tiny town of Jenner, Hwy-116 heads inland along the Russian River, leading to the **RUSSIAN RIVER VALLEY**, an affluent summer resort area popular for its canoeing, swimming, wineries, and gay resorts. This part of Sonoma County is also the center of the Farm Trails ecotourism effort – check out Ⓦwww.farmtrails.org for more details.

The Sonoma coast

Bodega Bay, about sixty-five miles north of San Francisco, is the first Sonoma County village you reach on Hwy-1. Pomo and Miwok Indians populated the area peacefully for centuries, until Captain Lt Juan Francisco de la Bodega y Quadra Mollineda anchored his ship in the bay and "discovered" it in 1775. Hitchcock filmed the waterside scenes for *The Birds* here; an unsettling number of them can still be found squawking down by the harbor. Not so long ago, a depleted fishing industry, a couple of restaurants, and some isolated seaside cottages were all there was to Bodega Bay, but in recent years San Franciscans have got wind of its appeal and holiday homes and modern retail developments now crowd the waterside.

If you're traveling the whole coast, Bodega Bay makes a tolerable first stop (although better beaches, weather, and services exist in Jenner, fourteen miles north). Of several **places to stay**, the *Bodega Harbor Inn*, 1345 Bodega Ave (Ⓣ707/875-3594, Ⓦwww.bodegaharborinn.com; ➍), is the best value in town, while the extremely comfortable *Bodega Coast Inn*, 521 Hwy-1 (Ⓣ707/875-2217 or 1-800/346-6999, Ⓦwww.bodegacoastinn.com; ➎), has newly renovated rooms with fireplaces. Reservations are pretty much essential in summer and on weekends throughout the year. If you don't have a reservation, the **Sonoma Coast Visitor Center** (Mon–Thurs 10am–6pm, Fri & Sat 10am–8pm, Sun 10am–7pm; Ⓣ707/875-3866, Ⓦwww.bodegabay.com), 850 Hwy-1, has information on room availability throughout the area. **Camp-sites** are available at the *Bodega Dunes Campground* (Ⓣ707/875-3483, reserve through ReserveAmerica Ⓣ1-800/444-7275; $20), two miles north of the village on Hwy-1 at the base of a windy peninsula known as **Bodega Head**, laid out across sand dunes that end in coastal cliffs behind the beach. There are **hiking** and **horseriding** trails around the dunes behind the beach – though in summer these tend to be packed with picnicking families, and for less crowded routes you should head up the coast.

If you are looking for a **restaurant**, *Brisas del Mar*, 2001 Hwy-1 (Ⓣ707/875-9190), does good inexpensive pastas and Mexican dishes, as well as seafood, while *Lucas Wharf*, 595 Hwy-1 (Ⓣ707/875-3522), specializes in crab (mid-Nov–June) and salmon (mid-May–Sept) dishes at around $20, and has a good menu of local wines. As part of the upscale *Inn at the Tides*, the equally pricey *Tides Wharf and Restaurant*, 835 Hwy-1 (Ⓣ707/875-3652), gives a good viewpoint for watching fishing boats unload their catch. Breakfasts and lunches from $6.50 and rather costlier dinners can be enjoyed at the *Sandpiper Restaurant*, 1410 Bay Flat Rd (Ⓣ707/875-2278). Nearby, at 1580 Eastshore Rd, *The Seaweed Café* (Ⓣ707/875-2700) offers a rather limited menu of pricey California cuisine. Bodega Bay Surf Shack in Pelican Plaza, 1400 Hwy-1 (Ⓣ707/875-3944), rents out bikes, kayaks, and windsurfing equipment at standard rates. For a **tour** of the bay, head over to Wil's Fishing Adventures, 1580 Eastshore Rd (Ⓣ707/875-2323; $8), where boats leave daily at 6pm, if there are enough punters, and tour the locations where *The Birds* was filmed, the area where Sir Francis Drake supposedly really landed, and Bodega Rock, home to sea lions and oceanic birds.

North of Bodega Bay to Jenner

North of Bodega Bay, along the **Sonoma Coast State Beach** (actually a series of beaches separated by rocky bluffs), the coastline coarsens and the trails become more dramatic. It's a wonderful stretch to hike – quite possible in a day for an experienced hiker – although the shale formations are often unstable and you must stick to the trails, which are actually quite demanding. Of Sonoma's thirteen miles of beaches, the finest are surfer-friendly **Salmon Creek Beach**, a couple of miles north of Bodega Bay and site of the park headquarters, and **Goat Rock Beach**, at the top of the coast. The latter offers the chance to get close to harbor seals. For **horseback riding**, *Chanslor Guest Ranch*, 2660 Hwy-1 (℡707/875-3333, ⓦwww.chanslor.com), requires a two-person minimum for their selection of rides, which range from a thirty-minute wetlands jaunt ($30 per person) to hour-long rides along Salmon Creek ($40) and on the beach of Sand Dune State Park (1hr 30min; $60). Located on the same property is a B&B (℡707/875-/875-2721; ⓞ); staying here takes ten percent off the price of a ride but is worth it only if you plan on doing a lot of riding.

Campgrounds are dotted along the coast (call ℡707/875-3483 for information), but the best **places to stay** are in the tiny seaside village of **JENNER**, which marks the turnoff for the Russian River Valley – a small, friendly place where you can stay in the salubrious cabins and cottages of *The Jenner Inn*, 10400 Hwy-1 (℡707/865-2377 or 1-800/732-2377, ⓦwww.jennerinn.com; rooms ⓞ, cottages ⓞ, and suites ⓞ), or the quaint cabins of *River's End Resort* (℡707/865-2484, ⓦwww.ilovesunsets.com; ⓞ). The **Russian River** joins the ocean in Jenner, and a massive sand spit at its mouth provides a breeding ground for harbor seals from March to June. The *Seagull Deli*, 10439 Hwy-1, provides wonderful clam chowder on a deck along the rivermouth to accompany your viewing.

Fort Ross and beyond

North of Jenner, the population evaporates and Hwy-1 turns into a slalom course of hairpin bends and steep inclines for twelve miles as far as **Fort Ross State Historic Park** (daily 8am–sunset; $6 per car), which houses the **Fort Compound** (daily 10am–4.30pm; free). At the start of the nineteenth century, San Francisco was still the northernmost limit of Spanish occupation in Alta California, and from 1812 to 1841 Russian fur traders quietly settled this part of the coast, clubbing the Californian sea otter almost to extinction, building a fort to use as a trading outpost, and growing crops for the Russian stations in Alaska. Officially they posed no territorial claims, but by the time the Spanish had gauged the extent of the settlement, the fort was heavily armed and vigilantly manned with a view to continued eastward expansion. The Russians traded here for thirty years until over-hunting and the failure of their shipbuilding efforts led them to pull out of the region. They sold the fort and chattels to one John Sutter in 1841, who moved them to his holdings in the Sacramento Valley, so all you see is an accomplished reconstruction built using the original techniques. Among the empty bunkers and storage halls, the most interesting buildings are the Russian Orthodox chapel and the commandant's house, with its fine library and wine cellar. At the entrance, a potting shed, which labors under the delusion that it is a **museum**, provides cursory details on the history of the fort, with a few maps and diagrams.

Fort Ross has a small beach and picnicking facilities, and you can **camp** just south of the park entrance at *Reef Campground* (℡707/847-3286; $15) or in **Salt Point State Park** (℡707/847-3221, reserve through ReserveAmerica

℡1-800/444-7275; $20), six miles north on Hwy-1. Two reasonable **hotel** options exist close to the two parks. *Fort Ross Lodge*, fifteen miles north of Jenner at 20705 Hwy-1 (℡707/847-3333, Ⓦwww.fortrosslodge.com; ❺), provides a VCR, microwave, coffeemaker, small refrigerator, patio, and barbecue in all rooms and some much pricier suites with hot tub. A little further north the *Timber Cove Inn*, 21780 Hwy-1 (℡707/847-3231 or 1-800/987-8319, Ⓦwww.timbercoveinn.com; ❹), is also comfortable, with splendid ocean views and an intimate **restaurant**. The restaurant at the *Salt Point Lodge*, 23255 Hwy-1 (℡707/847-3234), also serves fine seafood and steak dinners for $13–20 but the rooms are reported to be noisy.

One of Sonoma County's most accessible and beautiful beaches, part of Salt Point State Park, is at **Gerstle Cove** (daily 8am–sunset; $6 per car), which includes a paved, wheelchair-accessible path from the cove to Salt Point, past kelp beds, wave-battered rocks, and lounging harbor seals. The park's rainfall and habitat make mushrooms thrive and permits collecting, and Gerstle Cove is also a popular place for **mushroom gatherers** to park their cars and begin foraging. Ask the ranger for the sheet of guidelines when you enter the lot. Just north of Salt Point and a little inland, the **Kruse Rhododendron State Reserve** (℡707/847-3221) is a sanctuary for twenty-foot-high rhododendrons, indigenous to this part of the coast and in bloom from April to June, and you can drive through, or walk along a short trail. The beaches on this last stretch of the Sonoma coastline are usually deserted, save for a few abalone fishermen, driftwood, and the seal pups who rest here. Again, they're good for hiking and beachcombing, but stick to the trails. From here you pass tiny and inconsequential Stewart's Point before entering the Mendocino coast (see p.797).

The Russian River Valley

Hwy-116 begins at Jenner (see above) and turns sharply inland, leaving behind the cool fogs of the coast and marking the western entrance to a relatively warm and pastoral area known as the **RUSSIAN RIVER VALLEY**. The tree-lined highway follows the river's course through twenty miles of what appear to be lazy, backwater resorts but in fact are the major stomping grounds for partying weekenders from San Francisco. The valley's seat, **Guerneville**, has the most nightlife and lodging, while **Healdsburg** serves as the gatekeeper for the **wine area**, bordering US-101 and the Dry Creek and Alexander valleys.

The fortunes of the Russian River Valley have come full circle; back in the Twenties and Thirties, it was a recreational resort for well-to-do city folk who abandoned the area when newly constructed roads took them elsewhere. Drawn by low rents, city-saturated hippies started arriving in the late Sixties, and the Russian River took on a nonconformist flavor that lingers today. More recently, an injection of affluent Bay Area property seekers, many of them gay, has sustained the region's economy, and the funky mix of loggers, sheep farmers, and wealthy weekenders gives it an offbeat cachet that has restored its former popularity.

The road that snakes through the valley is dotted with campgrounds every few miles, most with sites for the asking, although during the first weekend after Labor Day, when the region hosts the **Jazz on the River Festival**, things can get a bit tight. The festival is something of a wild weekend around here and a good time to come: bands set up on Johnson's Beach by the river and in the woods for impromptu jamming sessions as well as regular scheduled events. The new late-June **Russian River Blues Festival** has proven equally popular.

Both events are now run by the same promoters in the East Bay (☎510/655-9471, ⓦwww.russianriverbluesfest.com for details).

Sonoma County Transit (☎707/576-7433, ⓦwww.sctransit.com) runs a fairly good weekday bus service (though patchy on weekends) between the Russian River resorts and Santa Rosa in the Wine Country, although to see much of the valley, you really need a car; or hire a **bike** or **kayak** from Russian River Kayak and Bicycle in Monte Rio (☎707/865-2141).

Russian River Valley wineries

The Guerneville Chamber of Commerce (see p.792) issues an excellent *Russian River Wine Road* map, which lists all the **wineries** that spread along the entire course of the Russian River – now numbering nearly a hundred. Unlike their counterparts in Napa and Sonoma, few of the wineries here either organize guided tours or charge for wine tasting. You can usually wander around at ease, guzzling as many and as much of the wines as you please. Some of the wines are of remarkably good quality, if not as well known as their Wine Country rivals. By car, you could easily travel up from the Sonoma coast and check out a couple of Russian River wineries in a day, although the infectiously slow pace may well detain you longer.

Belvedere four miles south of Healdsburg at 4035 Westside Rd ☎707/431-4442, ⓦwww.belvederewinery.com. Pleasantly situated winery with good views from the terraced garden. Live jazz on summer Saturday afternoons. Tastings daily 11am–5pm.

Dry Creek Vineyard 3770 Lambert Bridge Rd, four miles northwest of Healdsburg at corner of Dry Creek Road ☎707/433-1000 or 1-800/864-WINE, ⓦwww.drycreekvineyard.com. This family-owned operation is well known for its consistently top-notch wines – particularly the Cabernet Sauvignon and Chardonnay. Picnic facilities. Tastings daily 10.30am–4.30pm.

Ferrari Carano 8761 Dry Creek Rd, six miles northwest of Healdsburg ☎707/433-6700 or 1-800/831-0381, ⓦwww.ferrari-carano.com. One of the smartest wineries in the region, Ferrari is housed in a Neoclassical mansion with beautiful landscaped grounds. They specialise in Italian-style wines. Tastings daily 10am–5pm; $3.

Hop Kiln 6050 Westside Rd, over five miles south of Healdsburg ☎707/433-6491, ⓦwww.hopkilnwinery.com. Recently established rustic winery with a traditional atmosphere but not a snobbish attitude. Ironically a plaque marks the spot where kilns used to dry the hops when this was beer country. Tastings daily 10am–5pm.

Korbel Champagne Cellars 13250 River Rd, two miles east of Guerneville ☎707/824-7000, ⓦwww.korbel.com. The bubbly itself – America's best-selling premium Champagne

– isn't anything you couldn't find in any supermarket, but the wine and brandy are sold only from the cellars, and are of such notable quality that you'd be crazy not to swing by for a glass or two. The estate where they are produced is lovely, surrounded by hillside gardens covered in blossoming violets, coral bells, and hundreds of varieties of roses – perfect for quiet picnics. A microbrewery and upscale deli are also on the premises.

Lake Sonoma 9990 Dry Creek Rd, Geyserville ☎707/473-2999, ⓦwww.lakesonomawinery.net. In a fine elevated setting at the far end of Dry Creek Valley from Healdsburg, there is a good range of wines and a particularly fine port, as well as a microbrewery on the premises. Tastings daily 10am–5pm.

Porter Creek 8735 Westside Rd, over five miles east of Guerneville ☎707/433-6321, ⓦwww.portercreekvineyards.com. Small winery with a cottagey feel, producing all organic wines; Pinot Noir a specialty. Tastings daily 10.30am–4.30pm; closed Tues & Wed in winter.

Topolos at Russian River Vineyards 5700 Gravenstein Hwy, Forestville, five miles from Guerneville along Hwy-116 ☎707/887-1575 or 1-800/867-6567, ⓦwww.topolos.net. One of the Russian River Valley's most accessible wineries, specializing in Zinfandels. The popular on-site restaurant (☎707/887-1562) serves Greek-inspired California dishes – dine on the patio and feast your eyes on the wildflower gardens. Tastings daily 11am–5.30pm; tours by appointment.

Guerneville

The main town of the Russian River Valley, **GUERNEVILLE**, came out some time ago. No longer disguised by the tourist office as a place where "a mixture of people respect each other's lifestyles," it's quite clearly a **gay resort** and has been for the best part of twenty years: a lively retreat popular with tired city dwellers who come here to unwind. Gay men predominate during the summer, except during two **Women's Weekends** (☏707/869-9000) – in early May and late September – when many of the hotels take only women.

If you don't fancy venturing along the valley, there's plenty to keep you busy without leaving town. Weekend visitors flock here for the canoeing, swimming, and sunbathing that comprise the bulk of local activities. **Johnson's Beach**, on a placid reach of the river in the center of town, is the prime spot, with canoes, pedal boats, and tubes for rent at reasonable rates. But Guerneville's biggest natural asset is the magnificent **Armstrong Redwoods State Reserve** (☏707/869-2015; $6 per vehicle), two miles north at the top of Armstrong Woods Road – 700 acres of massive redwood trees, hiking and riding trails, and primitive camping sites. The visitor center (daily 11am–3pm) can provide trail maps: take food and water and don't stray off the trails, as the densely forested central grove is quite forbidding and very easy to get lost in. One of the best ways to see it is on horseback; Horseback Adventures (☏707/887-2939) offers guided horseback tours that range from a half-day trail ride ($40) to a three-day pack trip ($450). A natural amphitheater provides the setting for the Redwood Forest Theater, once used for dramatic and musical productions during the summer but now simply a fine spot for rustic contemplations.

The **Chamber of Commerce & Visitor Center**, 16209 1st St (daily 10am–6pm; 24hr info line ☏707/869-9000 or 1-877/644-9001, ⓦwww.russianriver.com), is welcoming and has good free maps of the area plus **accommodation** listings. As with most of the valley, B&Bs are the staple; two luxurious choices are the comfortable *Creekside Inn and Resort*, 16180 Neely Rd (☏707/869-3623 or 1-800/776-6586, ⓦwww.creeksideinn.com; ⑤), and *Applewood Inn & Restaurant*, 13555 Hwy-116 (☏707/869-9093, ⓦwww.applewoodinn.com; ⑦), which also features a highly acclaimed gourmet restaurant. Lower rates can be found at the *New Dynamic Inn*, 14030 Mill St (☏707/869-1563, ⓦwww.newdynamicinn.com; ③), a relaxed New Age establishment where "cosmic energies unite with you." *Fife's*, 16467 River Rd (☏707/869-0656 or 1-800/734-3371, ⓦwww.fifes.com; ③), is the original gay resort with a range of cabins right by the river, while *The Highlands*, 14000 Woodland Rd (☏707/869-0333; ②), also caters primarily to the gay community; both have sites for camping too. Indeed a dearth of cheap motels (unless you head east to US-101) makes **camping** the economical answer: the *Austin Creek State Recreation Area*, Armstrong Woods Road (☏707/865-2391; $15), is guaranteed RV-free, while *Johnson's Beach and Resort*, 16241 1st St, also has cabins and rooms available ($10 per vehicle plus one person, extra people $2 each; ☏707/869-2022, ⓦwww.johnsonsbeach.com; ③).

Guerneville has a good selection of reasonably priced, reliable **restaurants**, among them *Wild Jane's*, 16440 Main St (☏707/869-3600), which serves classic American/Californian cuisine and hosts live music. *Taqueria La Tapatia*, on the west side of town at 16632 Hwy-116 (☏707/869-1821), is an excellent, authentic, and cheap Mexican joint. Really, though, it's the **nightlife** that makes Guerneville a worthwhile stop. *Main Street Station*, 16280 Main St (☏707/869-0501), is a pizzeria with nightly live music, mostly jazz; while *Rainbow Cattle Co*, 16220 Main St (☏707/869-1916), is a lively gay bar that gets livelier as the night draws on. Both the *Russian River Resort* ("*Triple R*"),

16390 4th St (☎707/869-0691), and *The Eagle*, 16225 Main St (☎707/869-3400), serve alcohol and food and are also popular with the gay crowd.

Monte Rio

The small town of **MONTE RIO**, four miles west along the river from Guerneville, is definitely worth a look: a lovely, crumbling old resort town with big Victorian houses in stages of graceful dilapidation. For years it has been the entrance to the 2500-acre **Bohemian Grove**, a private park that plays host to the San Francisco–based Bohemian Club. A grown-up summer camp, its membership includes a very rich and very powerful male elite – ex-presidents, financiers, politicians, and the like. Every year in July they descend for "Bohemian Week" – the greatest men's party on earth, noted for its hijinks and high-priced hookers, away from prying cameras in the seclusion of the woods.

The most reasonable of Monte Rio's pricey **places to stay** are the lovely *Rio Villa Beach Resort*, 20292 Hwy-116 (☎707/865-1143, ⓦwww.riovilla.com; ❹), in a beautiful spot on the banks of the Russian River, and the restored *Highland Dell Resort*, 21050 River Blvd (☎707/865-2300, ⓦwww.highlanddell.com; ❹), whose gourmet restaurant is highly praised. *Huckleberry Springs Country Inn and Spa* (☎707/865-2683 or 1-800/822-2683, ⓦwww.huckleberrysprings.com; ❼) is a deluxe adult-pampering retreat with massages and a spa, just outside of town at 8105 Old Beedle Rd. If you are hungry, *Northwood Restaurant*, 19400 Hwy-116 (☎707/865-2454), serves up tasty Californian cuisine.

The lonely, narrow **Cazadero Highway** just to the west makes a nice drive from here, curving north through the wooded valley and leading back to Fort Ross on the coast. At the north end of the bridge over the Russian River in Monte Rio, **cyclists** can begin the world-renowned King Ridge–Meyers Grade ride, a 55-mile loop (and 4500 feet of climb) that heads along the Cazadero Highway and into the hills, finally descending to the coast and Hwy-1. Contact the Santa Rosa Cycling Club (☎707/544-4803, ⓦwww.srcc.com) for a complete itinerary.

Healdsburg

The peaceful modern town of **HEALDSBURG** straddles the invisible border between the Wine Country and the Russian River Valley, and in a quiet way manages to get the best of both worlds. While **Veterans Memorial Beach**, a mile south of the plaza along the banks of the Russian River, is a popular spot for swimming, picnicking, and canoeing in the summertime, there are also several dozen wineries, most of them family owned, within a few miles of the center of town. The only cultural diversion in town is the **Healdsburg Museum**, 221 Matheson St (Tues–Sun 11am–4pm; free; ☎707/431-3325, ⓦwww.healdsburgmuseum.org), which displays local history through a decent collection of Pomo Indian basketry, nineteenth-century tools and crafts, and eight thousand original photos. Romantic bed and breakfasts have sprung up all over the area, including the neighboring village of **Geyserville**, and although the town's economic well-being is almost exclusively dependent on tourism, it still manages to maintain a relaxed, backcountry feel. The Healdsburg Area **Chamber of Commerce**, 217 Healdsburg Ave (Mon–Fri 9am–5pm, Sat 9am–3pm, Sun 10am–2pm; ☎707/433-6935 or 1-800/648-9922, ⓦwww.healdsburg.org), provides winery and lodging information.

If you have the money to spend it's hard to beat the *Madrona Manor*, 1001 Westside Rd (☎707/433-4231 or 1-800/258-4003, ⓦwww.madronamanor.com; ❼), a luxurious Victorian-style **bed and breakfast** mansion, crowning a hilltop, with meticulously maintained gardens and a gourmet restaurant. The best value is the *Best Western Dry Creek Inn*, 198 Dry Creek Rd (☎707/433-0300 or 1-800/222-5784, ⓦwww.drycreekinn.com; ➍).

Of several gourmet restaurants that circle the green, wooded plaza, *Bistro Ralph*, 109 Plaza St (☎707/433-1380), with sparse modern decor and well-crafted dishes (around $20 per main course), is your best bet. If you want a cheaper meal, accompanied by fine local ale, look no further than *Bear Republic Brewing Co*, 345 Healdsburg Ave (☎707/433-2337). *Flying Goat Coffee Roastery and Café*, just off the main plaza at 324 Center St (☎707/433-9081), is a great place to unwind with a newspaper and a good cup of coffee.

Lake County and Clear Lake

An alternative route to the northern coast along Hwy-29 from the Wine Country or via Hwy-20, if coming from the I-5 north of Sacramento, is to take in often-neglected **LAKE COUNTY** and its centerpiece, **CLEAR LAKE**, the largest natural freshwater lake in California. With a basin that was lifted above sea level some fifty million years ago by the collision of the Pacific and North American crustal plates, it is also one of the most ancient lakes on the continent, possibly even the oldest. Its earliest inhabitants, attracted by the mild climate and abundance of fish, were the Pomo Indians, who traded peacefully with other tribes and remained here undisturbed until they were displaced by white settlers; now they number just two percent of the population. With a surface area of sixty-four square miles and over a hundred miles of shoreline, the lake is renowned among anglers as the best **bass-fishing** territory in the country. Mostly surrounded by rolling hills, the lake is dominated by the green twin cone of **Mount Konocti**, a 4500ft dormant volcano, which looms above its south shore. The largest city, conveniently named **Clearlake**, which occupies the southeast corner of the lake, has plenty of tourist facilities but is rather modern and faceless, so it is better to concentrate on the lakefront areas around **Lakeport** to the west and along the **North Shore**.

Clear Lake

A popular playground for vacationing middle classes up until WWII, **CLEAR LAKE** is currently undergoing a drive to reinvent itself as a holiday destination after several slim decades during which it gained an unflattering reputation among many Californians as "white trash central." Evidence of this period can still be found in the rather dowdy motels that line parts of the lakeshore, some of which have been turned into recovery houses. However, the locals are once again trying to harness the lake's undoubted natural beauty, sunny climate, and its location a little over two hours from San Francisco in order to make it an attractive destination. This effort is bolstered by promoting its suitability for all sorts of **water activities**: watersports, boating, and fishing facilities are available all around the lake. Southeast of Lakeport, the adjacent attractions of **Clear Lake State Park** and **Soda Bay** provide ample opportunities to play or simply unwind, as do the string of small resorts on the lake's **North Shore**. As the revitalisation process is still in its early stages, the visitor can easily find great deals on accommodation, dining, and entertainment: check out the Lake County Resort and Restaurant Association website at ⓦwww.lakecountyrandr.com. It is also, by Northern Californian standards, relatively easy to spend time here without your own vehicle, thanks to decent **public transport** connections once you get here: sadly the Greyhound service has been suspended but the efficient Lake Transit service (℡707/263-3334) runs frequent buses all round the lake every day except Sunday, and operates a route to Calistoga and St Helena in the Napa Valley four times a week, with an onward service to Santa Rosa on Thursdays.

Lakeport and around

The county seat of **LAKEPORT** is the older and more picturesque of Clear Lake's two towns, dating from the latter part of the nineteenth century, when settlers moved into the picturesque area as gold fever began to wane. Although the suburban sprawl along the lakefront gives the impression of a larger town, it is home to less than five thousand people. If you arrive by Hwy-29, the first point of call is the smart new **Visitor Center**, perched on a green knoll right by the highway exit ramp at 875 Lakeport Blvd (Mon–Fri 9am–5pm, Sat 10am–2pm; ℡707/263-5092 or 1-800/525-3743, ⓦwww.lakecounty.com). As well as providing the usual brochures, maps, and helpful info, it affords a splendid view across the lake. Downtown Lakeport still retains a good deal of Victorian charm with the original 1871 brick courthouse standing imperiously on the gentle slopes of the grassy main square right in the heart of town. The building is now used to house the **Lake County Museum**, 255 N Main St (Wed–Sat 10am–4pm, Sun noon–4pm; donation suggested; ℡707/263-4555). Exhibits concentrate on the area's native Indian heritage with a full-size Pomo village diorama and large collection of baskets, arrowheads, and tools.

The dozen or so blocks of Main Street on either side of the square and the roads leading down from it to the waterfront contain most of the town's facilities. For **accommodation**, it's hard to beat *Mallard House*, 970 N Main St (℡707/262-1601, ⓦwww.mallardhouse.com; ❷), a friendly English-style inn, while the posher *Lakeport English Inn*, 675 N Main St (℡707/263-4317, ⓦwww.lakeportenglishinn.com; ❻), is the best of the B&Bs around here. In the northern suburbs the *Rainbow Lodge*, 2569 Lakeshore Blvd (℡707/263-4309, ⓦwww.therainbowlodge.com; ❸), is typical of the resort motels to be found in the vicinity and has an adequate restaurant adjacent. Downtown **eating** options include *Park Place*, 50 3rd St (℡707/263-0444), which is the place for filling pastas, burgers, and steaks, and the inexpensive Chinese food at *Chopstick*, 185 N Main St (℡707/263-3310). If you want to try your hand at **fishing**, go to The King Connection, 2470 Reeves Lane (℡707/263-8856), and for boat or jet ski rental from $40 for thirty minutes contact Disney's Water Sports, 401 S Main St (℡707/263-0969, ⓦwww.disneyswatersports.com).

About six miles southeast of Lakeport two adjacent areas are worthy of exploration. The first is **Clear Lake State Park** (daily 8am–sunset; $6 per vehicle; ℡707/279-4293), whose erratically opening visitor center houses displays on the lake's cultural and natural history as well as a 700-gallon aquarium of indigenous fish. The park also offers forest trails, a swimming beach, and four developed campgrounds (book through ReserveAmerica ℡1-800/444-7275; $15–19). Right below Mount Konocti, in the protected waters between the park and Buckingham Peninsula, which almost spans the lake, **Soda Bay** is another haven for swimming and watersports. The eastern shore of the bay is blessed with soda springs, hence the name, which bubble up from shafts over 100ft deep. Indian legend claims that the bubbling waters mark the spot where Chief Konocti's daughter Lupiyoma threw herself into the lake after her father and lover were killed in battle. A number of **places to stay** line the bay, such as *Edgewater Resort*, 6420 Soda Bay Rd (℡707/279-0208 or 1-800/396-6224, ⓦwww.edgewaterresort.net; ❻), which offers tent and RV sites for $28, as well as a few spacious family cabins. Almost next door, *The Lakeside Inn*, 6330

Soda Bay Rd (☎707/279-1620; Thurs–Sun only), is a cosy English boozer serving meat pies and good ale; it is in fact an exact replica of its namesake in Southport, Lancashire, recorded in the *Guinness Book of Records* as the smallest pub in England.

Mount Konocti

Majestic **MOUNT KONOCTI**, which is clearly visible from just about anywhere on Clear Lake's circumference, is a multiple volcano, which is estimated to have first erupted some 600,000 years ago but has now been inactive for several thousand years. Indeed, geologists have declared large parts of it officially extinct. Its name comes from the Pomo Indian words "kno" and "hatai," meaning "mountain" and "woman" respectively. Unfortunately, most of the mountain is under private ownership so you cannot wander its slopes at will. Visitors can, however, gain access by permission and guided tours are conducted on selected days; call ☎707/972-1990 for information and reservations. The nearest amenities can be found at **Kelseyville** on the lower southern reaches. These include the biggest resort in the region, *Konocti Harbor Resort & Spa*, 8727 Soda Bay Rd (☎707/279-4281 or 1-800/660-5253, ⓦ www .konoctiharbor.com; ❸), which has accommodation ranging from motel-style rooms through beach cottages to VIP suites in excess of $300, as well as a spa, marina, sports facilities, restaurants, and a concert hall that attracts many famous acts.

Clearlake

Though somewhat anodyne and sprawling, with a population approaching twelve thousand, **CLEARLAKE** and the town of **Lower Lake** with which it merges do hold some interest and certainly offer plenty of amenities. Culturally speaking, the one place to see is the **Lower Lake Historical Schoolhouse Museum**, 16435 Morgan Valley Rd, Lower Lake (Wed–Sat 11am–4pm; free), which preserves one of the old grammar-school classrooms just as it was during the late nineteenth century. For the less academic-minded, **Outrageous Waters**, on the south side of Clearlake at the corner of Old State Highway and Dam Road (May–Sept daily noon–8pm; $13.95; ☎707/995-1402 or 1-877/932-3386, ⓦ www.outrageouswaters.com), is a family-orientated water park with race cars and other games to boot.

If you decide **to stay** in Clearlake, you shouldn't have any problem finding somewhere adequate and economical by the waterside. The *Lamplighter Motel*, 14165 Lakeshore Drive (☎707/994-2129; ❸), has basic rooms, while the jointly-owned *Jules Resort*, next door at no. 14195 (☎707/994-1491, ⓦ www .julesresort.com; ❹) is slightly more comfortable, even more so the *Highlands Inn* at no. 13865 (☎707/994-8982 or 1-800/300-8982, ⓦ www.high-lands .com; ❺). Decent breakfasts and simple **meals** are to be had inexpensively at the *Main Street Café*, 14084 Lakeshore Drive (☎707/994-6450), and good, filling Mexican fare at *Cabo's*, 14868 Olympic Drive (☎707/995-2162), several hundred yards back from the lakefront. Funtime Watersports at 6235 Old Hwy-53 (☎707/994-6267) rents out boats, fishing gear, and other equipment.

North Shore

Some five miles north of Clearlake, Hwy-53 ends at Hwy-20, which continues northwest along the lake's **NORTH SHORE** past a series of small resorts under the shade of white oak and pepperwood trees. The first place you come to once the road hits the lake is Clearlake Oaks, which doesn't really merit a stop, so it's best to press on towards **Glenhaven**, a couple of miles before which the *Lake Marina* resort/motel, 10215 E Hwy-20 (☎707/998-3787; ❸), offers reasonable waterfront rooms and has its own jetty. You can rent powered (4hr minimum, \$32–38) or pedal boats (\$11/hr) from nearby Blue Fish Cove, 10573 E Hwy-20 (☎707/998-1769, ⓦwww.bluefishcove.com). At **Glenhaven** itself the *Sea Breeze Resort*, 9595 Harbor Drive (☎707/998-3327, ⓦwww.seabreeze-resort.com; ❹), has quaint, nicely decorated cottages; if you are seeking a **campsite**, try *Glenhaven Beach* at 9625 E Hwy-20 (☎707/998-3406), where sites cost \$18.

There is more going on, however, up towards the lake's northwest corner, which also boasts the longest stretches of beach. Five miles beyond Glenhaven in the larger settlement of **Lucerne**, the *Riviera Motel*, 6900 E Hwy-20 (☎707/274-1032; ❷), offers bargain rooms, while *The Beachcomber Resort*, 6345 E Hwy-20 (☎707/274-6639, ⓦwww.beachcomberresort.net; ❸), has slightly higher rates and you can fish from their own pier. Tasty Mexican fare is dished up at *Pepper's*, 6269 E Hwy-20 (☎707/274-2773). Several miles further on, where Hwy-20 prepares to leave the lake behind as the shoreline dips south towards Lakeport, the pleasant town of **Nice** is the best base on the North Shore. Apart from more cheap cabins at *D&G's Last Resort*, 3796 Lakeshore Blvd (☎707/274-1289; ❷), there are a couple of attractive **B&Bs**: the unique railway-themed *Featherbed Railroad Company*, 2870 Lakeshore Blvd (☎707/274-8378 or 1-800/966-6322, ⓦwww.featherbedrailroad.com; ❺), where all the rooms are fashioned out of disused cabooses; and the more conventional *Gingerbread Cottages*, 4057 E Hwy-20 (☎707/274-0200, ⓦwww.gingerbreadcottages.com; ❺). Nice is also the most fruitful part of North Shore for **eating**: try the tasty and inexpensive American classics served all day at *The Marina Grill*, 3707 E Hwy-20 (☎707/274-9114), the fresh seafood, steaks, and pasta at the *Harbor Bar & Grill*, 4561 E Hwy-20 (☎707/274-1637), or the well-prepared fish at *The Boathouse*, 2685 Lakeshore Blvd (☎707/274-3534).

The Mendocino coast

The coast of **Mendocino County**, 150 miles north of San Francisco, is a dramatic extension of the Sonoma coastline – the headlands a bit sharper, the surf a bit rougher, but otherwise more of the same. Sea stacks form a dotted line off the coast, and there's an abundance of tidal pools, making the area a prime spot for diving and exploring on foot the secrets of the ocean. Surfers love it, too, for the waves and sandy beaches to be found between **Gualala** and **Albion**, and March brings out droves of people to watch migrating **whales**. You can find out more about what the county has to offer at the Mendocino County Alliance's website ⓦwww.goMendo.com. Tourists tend to mass in charming **Mendocino** and gritty **Fort Bragg**, leaving the other small former logging towns along Hwy-1 preserved in the salt air and welcoming to visitors. The county also thrives as a location spot for the movie industry, having featured in such illustrious titles as *East of Eden*, *Frenchman's Creek*, *Same Time Next Year*, and *The Fog*. Occasionally such films are supposed to be set on the East Coast, making use of the New England–style architecture closer to Hollywood, so watch out for any suspicious sunsets over the ocean next time you're in the theater.

If you are already on the coast, you can continue to hug it all the way via Hwy-1 as far north as Rockport when it turns east to join US-101, the last thirty miles constituting the only true wilderness left on California's rim.

The most direct route to Mendocino from the south, however, is to travel the length of the peaceful **Anderson Valley** by taking Hwy-128 north from US-101. The main coastal towns of Mendocino and Fort Bragg are connected to each other and the interior towns of **Willits** and Ukiah (both on US-101 and served by Greyhound and Amtrak Thruway) by two local **bus** operators: Mendocino Stage (☎707/964-0167) and Mendocino Transit Authority buses (☎1-800/696-4682, ⊛www.4mta.org); the latter has additional routes south to Gualala and Santa Rosa.

The coast from Gualala to Albion

The first oceanside stop of note, once you leave Sonoma County on Hwy-1, is **Gualala**, which has developed into quite an artistic community, as well as a spot for holidaymakers due to its fine stretch of sand. A handy brochure locating the dozen or so **galleries** can be found at any one of them – try the central Dolphin Gallery (☎707/884-3896, ⊛www.gualalaarts.org) in Sundstrom Mall, directly off Hwy-1. If you decide **to stay** here, look no further than the old *Gualala Hotel*, on the corner of Hwy-1 and the main plaza (☎707/884-3441 or 1-800/888-482-5252, ⊛www.thegualalahotel.com; ❷), whose cheaper rooms have shared baths. There is also a good restaurant and old-style saloon, plus you might expect some amusing antics because, at the time of writing, the management of the place was being taken over by a company named Fawlty Towers. A pricier option is the upscale *Surf Motel at Gualala* (☎707/884-3571 or 1-888/451-7873; ❺), on the opposite side of the road. Good, filling Mexican and Californian cuisine is available at *Mermaid's Garden Deli* (☎707/884-9571), 38920 Hwy-1.

Beyond Gualala the route is very appealing, as Hwy-1 climbs up through increasingly wooded hillsides that afford tantalising glimpses of the crashing waves at the frequent bends. Eventually the road straightens out somewhat as it turns inland to become the main street of nondescript **Point Arena**, fifteen miles or so north. The town does have the cheapest **motel** on this stretch of coast, however, in the *Sea Shell Inn* at 135 Main St (☎707/882-2000; ❷) and a couple of reasonable **places to eat** – try the pasta and soups at *Carlini's Café* (☎707/882-2942) or Mexican fare at *El Burrito* (☎707/882-2910), located at nos. 206 and 165 Main St respectively. A turning on the north side of town leads two miles to the impressive **Point Arena Lighthouse** (daily: summer 10am–4.30pm; winter 10am–3.30pm; $5; ☎1-877/725-4448, ⊛www.pointarenalighthouse.com). Built in 1870 and rebuilt after the San Francisco earthquake of 1906 – think of the devastating effect from such a distance – the landmark contains a small museum and the 115-foot tower is a great vantage point for viewing life at sea.

The main Hwy-1 continues north through a mixture of coastal scrub and grazing land, rejoining the ocean around **Manchester Beach State Park** (daily 8am–sunset; free); its campsite ($15) is about half a mile inland from the largely deserted strand. Further on you reach the pretty village of **Elk**, which boasts an excellent driftwood-strewn beach, and on through an extremely scenic stretch of cliffs counterpointed by sea stacks and crashing waves until it reaches **Albion**, a couple of miles north of the junction with Hwy-128. The small fishing village is only six miles south of Mendocino itself and has a couple of romantic **places to stay**; *Fensalden B&B Inn*, 33810 Navarro Ridge Rd (☎707/937-4042 or 1-800/959-3850, ⊛www.fensalden.com; ❻), offers comfortable rural surroundings and distant sea views; while the *Albion River Inn*, 3790 N Hwy-1 (☎707/937-1919 or 1-800/479-7944,

△ Giant Sequoia

@www.albionriverinn.com; ❼), perches on the edge of a cliff, and all the rooms except one face the ocean. The inn also has a first-class **restaurant**, serving pricey, wonderful food with a spectacular wine list and top service.

Mendocino

Continuing north Hwy-1 passes the kelp forests of Van Damme State Park before you reach the coast's most lauded stop, the decidedly touristy village of **MENDOCINO**. The quaint town sits on a broad-shouldered bluff with waves crashing on three sides; it's hard to find a spot here where you can't see the ocean sparkling in the distance. New England–style architecture is abundant, lending Mendo, as the locals call it, a down-home, almost cutesy air. Its appearance on the National Register of Historic Places and reputation as something of an artists' colony draw the curious up the coastal highway, and a fairly extensive network of bed and breakfasts, restaurants, and bars are more than happy to cater to their every need.

Accommodation

Room rates in Mendocino are generally high, but provided you stay away from the chintzy hotels on the waterfront, it is possible to find more reasonably priced hotels on the streets behind. The *Sea Gull Inn*, 44960 Albion St (☎707/937-5204 or 1-888/937-5204, @www.seagullbb.com; ❸), is the best of the affordable options right in the center, though the antique-filled rooms at the *Mendocino Hotel*, 45080 Main St (☎707/937-0511 or 1-800/548-0513, @www.mendocinohotel.com; ❺), are more luxurious. The biggest of the many B&Bs is the *MacCallum House Inn*, 45020 Albion St (☎707/937-0289 or 1-800/609-0492, @www.maccallumhouse.com; ❻), while the *Joshua Grindle Inn*, 44800 Little Lake Rd (☎707/937-4143 or 1-800/474-6353, @www.joshgrin .com; ❻), must rate as the friendliest and serves excellent gourmet breakfasts. One mile south of town the *Brewery Gulch Inn*, 9401 Hwy-1 (☎707/937-4752 or 1-800/578-4454, @www.brewerygulchinn.com; ❼), is a huge luxury inn made of redwood timber salvaged from the local river, and represents the top-end of the nearby options. *Mendocino Coast Accommodations* (☎707/937-5033 or 1-800/262-7801, @www.mendocinovacations.com) can also book rooms at B&Bs, hotels, cottages, and vacation homes for free. Just beyond blink-and-you'll-miss-it Caspar, halfway towards Fort Bragg on Hwy-1, *Jughandle Creek Farm* (☎707/964-4630, @www.jughandle.creek.org) has shared rooms ($27 per person), cabins ($35), and tent sites ($11); there's a $5 discount if you are willing to donate an hour's work. Staying there also allows you to explore the trails in the woods behind and participate in nature-study programmes. There's $20 **camping** at *Russian Gulch State Park* and *Van Damme State Park* (book both through ReserveAmerica ☎1-800/444-7275).

The Town

Like other small settlements along the coast, Mendocino was originally a mill site and shipping port, established in 1852 by merchants from Maine who thought the proximity to the redwoods and exposed location made it a good site for sawmill operations. The industry has now vanished, but the large community of artists has spawned craftsy commerce in the form of art galleries, gift shops, and boutique delicatessens. This preservation didn't come about by accident. The state of California traded a block of old-growth forest with the Boise–Cascade logging company in exchange for the headlands surrounding the town. The headlands became a state park, and Mendocino in turn became a living museum, with strict local ordinances mandating architectural design and upkeep.

The **visitor center**, 735 Main St (daily 11am–4pm; ☏707/937-5397), is located in **Ford House**, one of many mansions built by the Maine lumbermen in the style of their home state. The **Kelley House Museum**, 45007 Albion St (Thurs–Tues 11am–3pm; free; ☏707/937-5791), has exhibits detailing the town's role as a center for shipping redwood lumber to the miners during the Gold Rush, and conducts **walking tours** of the town on Saturday mornings at 11am – though you could do it yourself in under an hour, collecting souvenirs from the galleries as you go. Chief among them, the **Mendocino Art Center**, 45200 Little Lake St (daily 10am–5pm; ☏707/937-5818 or 1-800/653-3328, ⓦwww.mendocinoartcenter.org; free), has a revolving gallery for mainly Mendocino-based artists and runs workshops in ceramics, weaving, jewelry, and metal sculpture. The Mendocino Theater Company (☏707/937-4477) on the same premises puts on regular performances of both avant-garde and classic works.

Otherwise there's plenty to occupy you around the town, with a long stroll along the headlands topping the list. **Hiking** and **cycling** are popular, with bikes available for around $25 a day from Catch a Canoe & Bicycles, Too (☏707/937-0273 or 1-800/320-2453), just south of Mendocino at the corner of Hwy-1 and Compche–Ukiah Road. They also rent outriggers and kayaks. At the west end of Main Street, hiking trails lead out into the **Mendocino Headlands**, where you can explore the grassy cliffs and make your way down to the tide pools, next to the breaking waves. The **Russian Gulch State Park** ($6 per car; ☏707/937-5804), two miles north of town, has bike trails, beautiful fern glens, and waterfalls. Just south of town, hiking and cycling trails weave through the unusual **Van Damme State Park** ($6 per car; ☏707/937-5804), which has a **Pygmy Forest** of ancient trees, stunted to waist-height because of poor drainage and soil chemicals. The coast of the park is punctuated with sea stacks and caves, carved by the pounding surf. Two-hour sea-cave tours are available through Lost Coast Kayaking (three times daily; $50; ☏707/937-2434, ⓦwww.lostcoastkayaking.com). After a day of hiking and shopping, you may want to pamper yourself with a massage and a hot tub at one of the town's spas.

Abalone diving is extremely popular along the coast here, particularly just south of town in the small cove beside Van Damme State Park. In an attempt to thwart poaching, the practice is strictly regulated – the tasty gastropods are not available commercially, and you can only have three in your possession at any given time or collect a total of 24 in one season. In early October, four hundred hungry judges pay a substantial fee for the opportunity to help choose the best abalone chef in the annual Abalone Cookoff. The Sub-Surface Progression Dive Center, 18600 Hwy-1 (☏707/964-3793) in Fort Bragg, leads all-inclusive half-day diving expeditions for $50.

Eating, drinking, and nightlife

Of Mendocino's **restaurants**, the best and most famous is *Café Beaujolais*, 961 Ukiah St (☏707/937-5614), whose founder wrote a book on organic California cuisine and which serves up a frequently changing menu of such fare nightly. Almost next door, *955 Ukiah Street* (☏707/937-1955; closed Mon & Tues) serves $15–$20 entrees that make it even more popular with many locals. For slightly cheaper fair, try the *Mendocino Café*, 10451 Lansing St (☏707/937-0836), serving an eclectic mix of salads, pastas, and sandwiches. *Tote Féte Bakery*, behind the deli of the same name at 10450 Lansing

St (☎707/937-3383), produces delicious breads, pastries, and muffins, which you can eat outside on the tree-shaded deck. If you don't have time to visit any of the Anderson Valley wineries, Fetzer Vineyards Tasting Cellar, 45070 Main St (daily: summer 11am–6pm; winter 11am–5pm; $4; ☎707/937-6191, Ⓦwww.fetzer.com), next to the *Mendocino Hotel*, stocks its vintages for sampling or perusing. If beer's your preferred tipple, *Dick's Place*, 45070 Main St, is Mendocino's oldest bar, with all the robust conviviality you'd expect from a spit-and-sawdust saloon, while *Patterson's Pub*, 10485 Lansing St (☎707/937-4782), is another friendly joint with fine ale.

The first weekend in March brings the **Mendocino Whale Festival** (☎1-800/726-2780), a celebration of food and headland views of whales returning back to the Arctic. They can also be spotted in November, on the trip to the warmer waters of the California Baja. Although the emphasis of the two-week **Mendocino Music Festival** (☎1-800/937-2044) in the second half of July is largely on classical music and opera, some blues and jazz bands from all over the state also perform. Since 1999 Mendocino has also hosted a twelve-day **Wine and Mushroom Fest** every November – check with the tourist authorities for details.

Fort Bragg and around

FORT BRAGG, a mere nine miles north of Mendocino, is very much the blue-collar flipside to its comfortable neighbor, although some trendier enterprises are beginning to spring up. Still, for the most part, where Mendocino exists on wholefood, art, and peaceful ocean walks, Fort Bragg brings you the rib shack and tattoo parlor. The town sits beneath a perpetual cloud of steam choked out from the lumbermills of the massive Georgia Pacific Corporation, which monopolizes California's logging industry and to which Fort Bragg owes its existence. There was once a fort here, but it was only used for ten years until the 1860s when it was abandoned and the land sold off cheaply. The otherwise attractive **Noyo Harbor** (south of town on Hwy-1) is these days crammed full of as many pleasure boats as diminishing commercial-fishing craft, and the billowing smog does little to add to the charm. Nevertheless, its proximity to the more isolated reaches of the Mendocino coast, an abundance of budget accommodation, and bevy of inexpensive restaurants make it a good alternative to Mendocino.

As for things to do, you can take a quick look at the historical exhibits of the **Guest House Museum** (Tues–Sun 10am–4pm; donation suggested; ☎707/964-4251), in front of the train station at 343 Main St. A worthwhile hour or two can be spent rummaging on **Glass Beach**, a ten-minute walk north of downtown at the end of Elm Street, below an attractive overgrown headland. Used as the town's dump until the Sixties, the disposed articles have been smoothed by the ocean into a kaleidoscopic beachcomber's paradise of broken glassware and crockery fragments. For a day-trip you can amuse yourself on the **Skunk Trains** operated by the Californian Western Railroad ($35–45 round-trip, depending on type of engine; ☎707/964-6371 or 1-800/777-5865, Ⓦwww.skunktrain.com), which run twice daily during the summer months and once in the shoulder seasons from the terminus on Laurel Street, forty miles inland to the tiny halt at **Northspur** and back. Taking their name from the days when, piled up with timber from the redwood forests, they were powered by gas engines and could be smelt before they were seen, the trains now operate exclusively for the benefit of tourists. It's good fun to ride in the open observation car as it tunnels twenty miles through mountains and rumbles across a series of high bridges on its route through the towering red-woods, taking almost three and a half hours to complete the trip. A shorter ride is also possible from **Willits** (local depot ℡707/459-5248), on US-101 forty miles inland, to **Wolf Tree**, deep in the coastal range. Unfortunately the trains no longer connect Willits to Fort Bragg. Willits is the official county seat due to its central position, otherwise it's no different from other strip-development, mid-sized American towns and is hardly worth visiting. At least it can be used to access the coast, as it is served by both interstate and local buses.

A short drive or bus ride south of Fort Bragg will take you to the **Mendo-cino Coast Botanical Gardens**, 18220 N Hwy-1 (daily: summer 9am–5pm; winter 9am–4pm; $8; ℡707/964-4352, Ⓦwww.gardenbythesea.org), where you can see more or less every wild flower under the sun spread across 47 acres of prime coastal territory. It is particularly renowned for the many varieties of **rhododendron** that bloom in April and May. Heading north, the next stretch of Hwy-1 is the slowest, continuing for another twenty miles of road and windswept beach before leaving the coastline to turn inland and head over the mountains to meet US-101 at **Leggett**. Redwood country begins in earnest here: there's even a tree you can drive through (summer 8.30am–8pm; $3), though you'd do better to stay on course for the best forests further north. If you're peckish, stop for a filling all-American snack or meal at *Redwood Diner* (℡707/925-6442). Further on, just before you cross the Humboldt County line, you can pause briefly at **Confusion Hill** to see the "world's largest chainsaw sculpture."

Practicalities

Fort Bragg's **Chamber of Commerce** (Mon–Fri 9am–5pm, Sat 9am–3pm; ℡707/961-6300 or 1-800/726-2780, Ⓦwww.mendocinocoast.com) is almost directly across the street from the Guest House Museum at 332 N Main St. Most of the **motels** cluster along Hwy-1 close to the center of town, the lowest priced of which is the newly renovated *Chelsea Inn*, 763 N Main St (℡707/964-4787 or 1-800/253-9972; ❷). Other good options include the basic but clean *Tradewinds Lodge*, 400 S Main St (℡707/964-4761 or 1-800/524-2244, Ⓦwww.fortbragg.org; ❹), or the *Surf Motel*, 1220 S Main St (℡707/964-5361 or 1-800/339-5361, Ⓦwww.surfmotelfortbragg.com; ❸). **B&Bs** are naturally more upscale but cheaper than those in Mendocino: the *Grey Whale Inn B&B*, 615 N Main St (℡707/964-0640 or 1-800/382-7244, Ⓦwww.greywhaleinn.com; ❺), has great views from its rooms, while the *Colonial Inn*, 533 Fir St (℡707/964-1384 or 1-877/964-1384, Ⓦwww.colonialinnfortbragg.com; ❺), costs less and is tucked away down a quiet residential street. The *Old Coast Hotel*, 101 N Franklin (℡707/961-4488 or 1-888/468-3550, Ⓦwww.oldcoasthotel.com; ❹), has comfortable rooms in a restored 1892 building with a steak-and-seafood restaurant attached. Finally, there's camping among six miles of sandy beach and coastal pines at **MacKerricher State Park** ($20; reserve through ReserveAmerica ℡1-800/444-7275), three miles north of Fort Bragg.

Restaurants in Fort Bragg (of which there are plenty) tend to cater to the ravenous carnivore: *Jenny's Giant Burger*, 940 N Main St (℡707/964-2235), for example, is usually full of men from the mill scoffing large chunks of red meat. A more genteel option is the *Mendo Bistro*, upstairs in the converted old Union Lumber Store complex at 301 N Main St (℡707/964-4974), which serves excellent, imaginative international cuisine, including gourmet pasta dishes, at very moderate prices. Otherwise, *The Restaurant*, at 418 Main St (℡707/964-9800), has tasty fish entrees for around $20, and *Café Prima*, 124 E Laurel St

(☎707/964-5814), does elegant Swahili dishes from the chef's native Kenya. Vegetarians can take refuge in the hearty Italian offerings at *Headlands Coffee*, 120 E Laurel St (☎707/964-1987), which also serves wine, along with a full menu of espressos. For big breakfasts, try *Egghead's*, at 326 N Main St (daily 7am–2pm), which lists 41 different omelets on their menu. If you're feeling thirsty, stop in for one of the "handmade ales" at the *North Coast Brewing Company*, 444 N Main St (☎707/964-3400), voted one of the ten best breweries in the world by the Beverage Testing Institute of Chicago as part of their year-long World Beer Championships. Try the Acme California Brown Ale and the Old Rasputin Russian Imperial Stout. Free tours of the brewery itself, on the opposite side of Main Street, are conducted at 12.30pm on Saturday. If you want to work up a thirst first, Noyo Pacific Outfitters, down by the harbour at 32400 N Harbor Drive (☎707/961-0559), can rent you a kayak (from $15 for 2hr) and organise guide trips upriver or off the coast, as well as abalone-diving expeditions.

The Anderson Valley

Running diagonally northwest for nearly twenty miles from just south of its small main town of **Boonville** to within a few miles of the coast is the fertile **ANDERSON VALLEY**, an amalgam of sunny rolling hills shaded by oaks and madrones that merge into dark redwood forest. Hwy-128, connecting US-101 near Cloverdale to the coast at Albion, is the sole artery through the valley, which has a long-standing reputation as a magnet for mavericks. The original settlers were sheep farmers who saw so few outsiders between the 1880s and 1920s that they even developed their own language, **boontling**, snippets of which still survive today. A good sixth of this odd dialect was known as "nonch harpin's," meaning "objectionable talk," and largely referred to the then taboo subjects of sexual activity and bodily functions. You can see examples of boont-ling in the names of local beers and establishments, but if you want to know the full story, track down a copy of *Boontling, An American Lingo* in local stores. During the twentieth century, sheep farming gradually gave way to the cultivation of apples but, though many orchards still exist, they are fast being replaced by more lucrative vineyards, as the craze for Californian wine means this area is becoming a northern annex of the Wine Country, along with the **Yorkville Highlands**, the southeastern extension of the valley. Most of the Anderson Valley's existing wineries line Hwy-128 between the tiny settlements of **Philo** and **Navarro**. The area is also famous for the excellent beer produced at the Anderson Valley Brewing Co, 17700 Hwy-253 (tours daily 1.30 & 4pm; $5 including sampling; ☎1-800/207-2337, Ⓦ www.avbc.com), just east of the junction with Hwy-128 on the south side of Boonville. Their Hop Ottin' IPA (an example of boontling) and rich amber ales are especially delicious.

Boonville and Philo

Despite having a population of little over seven hundred, **BOONVILLE** still easily manages to be the largest town in the Anderson Valley. Strung along its widened half-mile section of Hwy-128 are some quaint shops, a hotel, and a few places to find sustenance. In terms of **accommodation**, the only place in town is the grand nineteenth-century *Boonville Hotel*, Hwy-128 at Lambert Lane (☎707/895-2210, Ⓦ www.boonvillehotel.com; ⑤), although the *Anderson Creek Inn*, under two miles northwest of town just off Anderson Valley Way (☎707/895-3091 or 1-800/552-6202, Ⓦ www.andersoncreekinn. com; ⑤) is an extremely comfy and quiet ranch-style B&B. Apart from the

Anderson Valley wineries

There are already over a dozen **wineries** dotted along the Anderson Valley, and you can expect that number to increase dramatically in the coming years. The cooler temperatures, especially at the northwest end, which sees the coastal fogs roll in, are better suited mostly to white varieties such as Gewürztraminer, Chardonnay, and Riesling, but the hardy Pinot Noir fares equally well. For further details you can contact the Mendocino Winegrowers Alliance in Ukiah (☎707/468-9886, ⊛www .mendowine.com). Most wineries have **open tastings** and there is rarely a fee, as they remain for the time being far less commercialized than their cousins further south. Here are a handful that would repay a visit:

Christine Woods Vineyards 3155 Hwy-128, about two miles south of Navarro ☎707/895-2115, ⊛www.christinewoods.com. The Chardonnay and Merlot from this family winery have received awards in Mendocino and San Francisco. All wines are made entirely from grapes grown on the estate, a relative rarity. Tastings daily 11am–5pm.

Handley 3155 Hwy-128, about two miles south of Navarro ☎1-800/733-3151, ⊛www .handleycellars.com. A fine range of white wines, dry, sweet, and sparkling are produced at this family winery. The tasting room also has a nice little collection of oriental art. Tasting daily summer 10am–6pm, winter 11am–5pm.

Husch Vineyards 4400 Hwy-128, almost three miles south of Navarro ☎707/895-3216 or 1-800/55-HUSCH, ⊛www.huschvineyards.com. Founded in 1971, this small family winery

is the oldest in the valley, and you are assured of a warm welcome at its rustic tasting room. Tastings daily 10am–6pm, 10am–5pm in winter.

Navarro Vineyards 5601 Hwy-128, three miles north of Philo ☎707/895-3686 or 1-800/537-WINE, ⊛www.navarrowine.com. This small winery specializes in Alsatian-style wines, which it only sells directly to the consumer and select restaurants. It also concocts a wicked grape juice, so even the kids can enjoy a free sip or two here. Tastings daily 10am–6pm, 11am–5pm in winter.

Roederer Estate 4501 Hwy-128, about three miles south of Navarro ☎707/895-2288, ⊛www.avwines.com. This is one of the higher-profile Mendocino wineries, specialising in sparkling vintages. Tasting daily 10am–5pm; $3.

spicy Mexican-influenced California **cuisine** on offer at the *Boonville Hotel*, you can enjoy quality bar food and **drink** your way through the entire range of Boonville beers at the *Buckhorn Saloon*, 14081 Hwy-128 (☎707/895-3369). The boontling-named *Horn of Zeese Café*, 14025 Hwy-128 (☎707/895-3525), is a good spot for filling breakfasts and snacks.

Six miles beyond Boonville, as you head northwest towards the coast, the village of **PHILO** has alternative venues to spend the night or have a meal, although it's all rather cutesy. *The Philo Pottery Inn*, 8550 Hwy-128 (☎707/895-3069, ⊛www.philopotteryinn.com; ❺), is a plush **B&B** right in the village but the best deal to be had is at the nearby *Anderson Valley Inn*, 8480 Hwy-128 (☎707/895-3325, ⊛www.avinn.com; ❸). *Libby's Restaurant*, 8651 Hwy-128 (☎707/895-2646), serves up excellent inexpensive Mexican **food**, and you can grab a sandwich or picnic ingredients from Lemon's Market (☎707/895-3552), just down the road.

A great place to take your picnic is three miles northwest to **Hendy Woods State Park** (☎707/895-3141; $6 per car), clearly signposted off Hwy-128. The park features hiking trails through two sizeable redwood groves, fishing on the Navarro River, and camping for $20 (reserve through ReserveAmerica ☎1-800/444-7275) or six-person cabins for $50. A mile or so beyond the park entrance another sign-posted left turn leads four miles up through more redwood-clad ridges to *Highland Ranch* (☎707/895-3600, ⊛www.highlandranch .com; ❾). The $285 per person overnight charge at this friendly guest ranch, set amidst a stunning 300 acres, includes a luxury detached cabin, three meals, plus all drinks and activities on offer, principally horse riding and clay-pigeon shooting.

The Humboldt coast

Of the northern coastal counties, **HUMBOLDT** is by far the most beautiful, and also the one most at odds with development. The biggest news story in recent years concerned Eureka's decision to bar chainstore-behemoth WalMart from erecting an outlet, despite the company's offer to clean up and build on a now deserted, and very polluted, stretch of waterfront. This is logging land, and the drive up US-101 gives a tour of giant sawmills fenced in by stacks of felled trees. Yet Humboldt County also contains the largest preserves of giant redwoods in the world in **Humboldt Redwoods State Park** and, north, **Redwood National Park**. Both are peaceful, otherworldly experiences not to be missed, though the absence of sunlight within the groves and mossy surface can be eerie.

Indeed, many locals hope that the forests are too creepy for visitors. Tourism, while good for business, encroaches on a lifestyle far removed from the glitz of Mendocino and Sonoma counties. Locals are worried that as more people discover the area, the rugged serve-yourself mentality here could quickly turn into a service economy. Outsiders are still welcomed but, outside of the few more touristic spots, it is definitely on the locals' terms, not the visitors. The coastal highway's inability to trace Humboldt's southern coast formerly guaranteed isolation and earned the region the name of the **Lost Coast**. The area, while still isolated, is not quite as "lost" any more thanks to the construction of an airstrip in Shelter Cove and an infusion of hotels, restaurants, and new homes.

Humboldt is perhaps most renowned for its "Emerald Triangle," which produces the majority of California's largest cash crop, **marijuana**. As the Humboldt coast's fishing and logging industries slide, more and more people have been turning to growing the stuff to make ends meet and new hydroponic techniques ensure that the potency of the ultra-thick buds is extremely high. In the 1980s, the elder Bush's administration took steps to crack down on the business with CAMP (Campaign against Marijuana Planting), sporadically sending out spotter planes to pinpoint the main growing areas. Aggressive law enforcement and a steady stream of crop-poaching has been met with a defiant, booby-trapped, and frequently armed protection of crops, and production goes on – the camouflage netting and irrigation pipes you find on sale in most stores clearly do their job.

Apart from considerable areas of clandestine agriculture, the county is almost entirely forestland. The highway rejoins the coast at **Eureka** and **Arcata**, Humboldt's two major towns and both jumping-off points for the redwoods. These "ambassadors from another time," as John Steinbeck dubbed them, are at their 300-foot best in the **Redwood National Park**, which contains three state parks and covers some 106,000 acres of skyscraping forest.

Again, **getting around** is going to be your biggest problem. Although Greyhound and Amtrak Thruway buses run the length of the county along US-101, they're hardly a satisfactory way to see the trees, and you'll need a car to make the trip worthwhile. **Hitchhiking** still goes on up here, and you'll see gaggles of locals gathered at the gas stations and freeway entrances begging for rides.

This is part necessity, as public transportation is scarce, and part lifestyle, as the region is a throwback to the kinder decades when hitching was a normal practice on American roads. Still, remember that stopping on the highways is illegal, and that no matter the kind appearance of a hitcher or driver, hitchhiking can be dangerous in the US. For information on **what's on** in Humboldt, two excellent, free county newspapers, *The Activist* and *North Coast Journal* (Ⓦwww.northcoastjournal.com), detail the local scene and people, and where to go and what to do in the area. Look out, too, for the activist Arcata-based *Greenfuse* and *Econews*, which highlight the ecological plight of Northern California's wild country.

Southern Humboldt and the Lost Coast

The inaccessibility of the Humboldt's beautiful **LOST COAST** in the south of the county is ensured by the **Kings Range**, an area of impassable cliffs that shoots up several thousand feet from the ocean, so that even a road as sinuous as Hwy-1 can't negotiate a passage through. To get there, you have to travel US-101 through deep redwood territory as far as tiny **Garberville**.

Garberville

A one-street town with a few good bars and hotels, **GARBERVILLE** is the center of the cannabis industry and a lively break from the freeway. Each week, the local paper runs a "bust-barometer," which charts the week's pot raids, and every August, the town hosts the massive two-day **Reggae on the River** festival. Tickets cost over $100; contact ☎707/923-4583 or Ⓦwww .reggaeontheriver.com by early May to reserve them.

Amtrak Thruway **buses** stop twice daily outside the *Waterwheel Restaurant* on Redwood Drive, Garberville's main street, while one daily Greyhound services connecting north to Eureka and south to San Francisco pull in around the corner on Church Street. The town's **Chamber of Commerce** (daily 10am–5pm; ☎707/923-2613 or 1-800/923-2613, Ⓦwww.garberville .org) is located in the Redwood Drive Center at 782 Redwood Drive. For what you get, much of the town's accommodation is a bit overpriced. Of a couple you might try, the *Benbow Inn*, several miles south of town at 445 Lake Benbow Drive (☎707/923-2124 or 1-800/355-3301, Ⓦwww.benbowinn .com; ❻), is a flash place for such a rural location (former guests include Eleanor Roosevelt and Herbert Hoover); the *Humboldt House Inn*, 701 Redwood Drive (☎707/923-2771 or 1-800/862-7756, Ⓦwww.bestwestern.com /humboldthouse.inn; ❺), and the more basic *Sherwood Forest Motel*, 814 Redwood Drive (☎707/923-2721, Ⓦwww.sherwoodforestmotel.com), round out the better options. The closest **campground** is seven miles south at **Benbow Lake State Recreation Area** (☎707/923-3238), while five miles further south on US-101 the **Richardson Grove State Park** in Piercy (☎707/247-3318) spreads over 1400 acres along the Eel River. Both cost $20 per site and can be reserved through ReserveAmerica (☎1-800/444-7275).

Even if you don't intend to stay in Garberville, at least stop off to sample some of the town's **restaurants** and **bars**, which turn out some of the best live bluegrass you're likely to hear in the state. Redwood Drive is lined with bars, cafés, and restaurants: the *Woodrose Café*, at no. 911 (☎707/923-3191), serves organic lunches, while *Treats Café*, at no. 764 (☎707/923-3554), offers snacks, drinks, and Internet access for 10¢ a minute. For an inexpensive eat-in or takeout meal, try *Calico's Café*, at no. 808 (☎707/923-2253). All the town bars tend to whoop it up in the evening; the noisiest of the lot is probably the *Branding Iron Saloon*, at no. 744 (☎707/923-2562), with a small cover for its nightly live music. More innocent by-products of the region's industry and subversive gifts can be obtained at The Hemp Connection, 412 Maple Lane (☎707/923-4851), on the corner of Redwood Drive.

Shelter Cove

From Garberville, via the adjoining village of **Redway**, where you can enjoy a gourmet meal on the terrace of the *Mateel Café*, 3342 Redwood Drive (☎707/923-3020), the Briceland and Shelter Cove roads wind 23 miles through territory populated by old hippies and New Agers beetling around in battered vehicles. You eventually emerge on the **Lost Coast** at **SHELTER COVE**, set in a tiny bay neatly folded between sea cliffs and headlands. First settled in the 1850s when gold was struck inland, its isolated position at the far end of the **Kings Range** kept the village small until recent years. Now, thanks to a new airstrip, weekenders arrive in their hordes and modern houses are indiscriminately dotted across the headland. Unfortunately, it's the closest real settlement to the **hiking** and **wildlife** explorations of the surrounding wilderness, which remains inhabited only by deer, river otter, mink, black bear, bald eagles, and falcons, so you might find yourself using either *Mario's Marina Motel*, 461 Machi Rd (☎707/986-7595, ⓦwww.mariosofsheltercove.com; ❹), or the *Beachcomber Inn*, 412 Machi Rd (☎707/986-7551 or 1-800/718-4789; ❸), as a **base**; the former establishment also has an adequate restaurant (☎707/986-1401) with a sea view on its extensive grounds, and rents out various seafaring equipment. The Cape Mendocino Lighthouse, on Upper Pacific Drive (late May–late Sept daily 10.30am–3.30pm; free), was reopened to the public in 1998 after being relocated from 25 miles further north, near Ferndale. The lighthouse operates limited hours during the rest of the year but you can call for a docent to come and open it up for you (☎707/986-7112) when it is closed. The 24-mile **Lost Coast Trail** runs along clifftops dotted with four primitive campgrounds ($10), all near streams and with access to black-sand beaches. Bring a tidebook, as some points of the trail are impassable at high tide. Another trail takes you to the top of **Kings Peak** which, at 4086ft, is the highest point on the continental US shoreline. Cape Mendocino can also lay claim to being the **westernmost point** of the lower 48 states.

Humboldt Redwoods State Park

The heart of redwood country begins in earnest a few miles north of Garberville, along US-101, when you enter the **HUMBOLDT RED-WOODS STATE PARK** (unrestricted entry; ☎707/946-2409, ⓦwww.humboldtredwoods.org): over 53,000 acres of predominantly virgin timber, protected from lumber companies, make this the largest of the redwood parks – though it is the least used. Thanks to the Save-the-Redwoods League, who have been acquiring land privately for the park, it continues to slowly expand year after year. At the Phillipsville exit, the serpentine **Avenue of the Giants** follows an old stagecoach road, weaving for 32 miles through trees which block all but a few strands of sunlight. This is the habitat of *sequoia sempervirens*, the coast redwood, with ancestors dating back to the days of the dinosaur. The avenue parallels US-101, adding at least thirty minutes to your travel time, but several exits to the freeway mean you won't get trapped here if traffic is intolerable. Pick up a free **Auto Tour** guide at the southern or northern entrances and, better still, stop at the **Visitor Center** (daily: summer 9am–5pm; winter 10am–4pm; ☎707/946-2263), halfway along at **Weott**, which has fascinating interpretive exhibits highlighting the redwoods, other flora and fauna, logging history, and the catastrophic 1964 flood. All along the main road, small stalls selling lumber products and refreshments dot the course of the highway, chief among them the **Chimney Tree** (daily 9am–5pm; free), a wonderfully corny gift shop built into the burnt-out base of a still-living redwood. There are three developed campgrounds ($20; reserve through ReserveAmerica ☎1-800/444-7275) within the park and a simpler environmental one ($12). *The Riverwood Inn* (☎707/943-3333; ❸), in **Phillipsville** itself, is a good rustic place to stay; the bar/restaurant showcases live bluegrass and other styles of music sporadically, serves good Mexican food, and you are assured a friendly welcome from the locals.

Honeydew and Scotia

The Avenue follows the south fork of the Eel River, eventually rejoining US-101 at **Pepperwood**. Ten miles before this junction, Mattole Road peels off to the left and provides the best **backcountry** access to the towering trees, which most visitors neglect to explore, as well as further access to the Lost Coast. A few miles after the road emerges from the forest, it passes through **HONEYDEW**, into a region thin on even small settlements. Honeydew is a postage-stamp-sized town popular with marijuana growers who appreciate its remote location – and the two hundred inches of annual rain that sustains the crops, making the town the wettest in California. If you continue up and over the treeless grazing country around **Petrolia**, you will descend to the ocean at a splendid driftwood-strewn beach just south of Cape Mendocino and are guaranteed that sheep and cattle will far outnumber fellow humans.

Back inland, any visitors awed by the majesty of the redwood forests can soon be brought back down to earth a few miles north of Pepperwood at **SCOTIA**, a one-industry town if ever there was one. In this case it is timber, and the stacks and stacks of logs that line the freeway are actually quite a sight. The Pacific Lumber Company has been here since 1869, but with the decline in the industry and the rise in environmental objections to clear-felling of native forests, the company is throwing itself at the tourist market and parts of the complex have already ceased active operations. Boasting of being "The World's Largest Redwood Mill," it attempts to win you over to the loggers' cause on self-guided **sawmill tours** (Mon–Fri 7.30am–2pm; ☎707/764-2222; free), starting at the Scotia Museum on Main Street.

Ferndale

Just over ten miles north of Scotia, you should definitely take a detour a few miles east to **FERNDALE**, unquestionably the Lost Coast's most attractive town, although with enough time on your hands an even better route is the stunningly scenic Lost Coast loop via Honeydew and Cape Mendocino. Promoting itself unabashedly as "California's best-preserved Victorian village," Ferndale certainly has its charms – for once the appealing architecture is not just confined to one quaint street but continues for blocks on either side of Main Street in a picturesque townscape of nineteenth-century houses and churches. Indeed, the entire town, which celebrated its 150th birthday in 2002, has been designated a State Historical Landmark. You can learn more about its history at the **Ferndale Museum**, 515 Shaw St (Wed–Sat 11am–4pm, Sun 1–4pm; $1), by perusing the old newspaper cuttings, documents, and photos, and trying to imagine exactly what people used to do with all the equipment on display that was once used in bygone occupations. The much more contemporary **Kinetic Sculpture Race Museum**, 581 Main St (daily

10am–5pm), within the Ferndale Art and Cultural Center, contains vehicles from the peculiar annual competition that takes place between Arcata and Ferndale (☎707/786-9259; see p.813) every Memorial Day weekend. Ferndale supports an active artistic community, so there are a disproportionate number of galleries and antique shops to browse through.

As you might expect, most of Ferndale's **accommodation** comes in the shape of stylish hotels and B&Bs, though the remote location keeps prices very reasonable. The *Victorian Inn*, 400 Ocean Ave at the corner with Main Street (☎707/786-4558 or 1-888/589-1808, ⓦwww.a-victorian-inn.com; ❺), has comfortable rooms above its classy carpeted lobby and lounge. Almost directly opposite at 315 Main St, *The Ivanhoe* (☎707/786-9000, ⓦwww.hotel-ivanhoe .com; ❺), fully refurbished in 2001, claims to be the oldest hotel in town and westernmost in the country; it also has a decent restaurant. Further along, the *Francis Creek Inn*, 577 Main St (☎707/786-9611; ❸), offers hotel comforts at motel rates. *Curley's Grill* (☎707/786-9696), inside the *Victorian Inn*, serves quality California **cuisine** plus sandwiches and cocktails, while *Poppa Joe's*, 409 Main St (☎707/786-4180), serves up downhome breakfasts and lunches. The *Candystick Fountain & Grill*, 361 Main St (☎707/786-9373), is the spot for a cheaper snack or whopping ice cream. The **entertainment** scene is appropriately low-key but you can drink in one of the hotel bars or catch a performance of the renowned Ferndale Repertory Theatre at 477 Main St (☎707/786-5483).

Eureka

Eureka may mean "I have found it!" but once you pull into the largest coastal settlement north of San Francisco you may wonder just what it was the first settlers were seeking. Near the top of the north coast of California between the Arcata and Humboldt bays, **EUREKA** feels – despite some rather attractive Victorian mansions – like an industrial, gritty, and often foggy lumbermill town, though its fishing industry carries the most economic weight, providing ninety percent of the state's catch of Pacific Ocean shrimp and Dungeness crab. There's a limited number of sights here, but the city has an abundance of cheap motels along Broadway, the type of mall-lined strip that's ubiquitous across America.

Arrival, information, and accommodation

One positive aspect of Eureka is that its **transportation** links are fairly good: Greyhound, 1603 4th St, connects Eureka to San Francisco in the south and Portland in the north twice, while Amtrak Thruway buses depart from outside *Stanton's Restaurant* on Fifth and L streets and run down to Wine Country via Willits and Ukiah. For getting around town or up the coast as far as Trinidad and south as far as Scotia, Humboldt Transit Authority, 133 V St (☎707/443-0826, ⓦwww.hta.org), has a Monday to Saturday service. The Eureka **Visitor Center** is on the southern approach to town at 2112 Broadway (June–Sept Mon–Fri 8.30am–5pm, Sat 10am–4pm, Sun 11am–4pm; Oct–May Mon–Fri 9am–5pm; ☎707/442-3738 or 1-800/356-6381, ⓦwww.eurekachamber.com).

The collection of **motels** dotted around town, mostly on the busiest through streets, make Eureka a reasonable option for a night, but nearby Arcata provides a much more laid-back environment. If you do decide to stay here, try the *Town House Motel*, 933 4th St at K (☎707/443-4536 or 1-800/445-6888, ⓦwww.visithumboldt.com/townhouse; ❸), which has clean rooms, or the even cheaper *Budget Motel*, 1140 4th St (☎707/443-7321; ❷). The *Eagle House*

▼ ⓘ, Fort Bragg & ⑥

Victorian Inn, at 139 2nd St (☎707/444-3344; ④), is a strangely deserted and cavernous Victorian relic with surprisingly clean rooms. If you want more than just a bed and a shower, head for _Abigail's Elegant Victorian Mansion B&B_, 1406 C St at 14th St (☎707/444-3144, ⓦwww.bnbweb.com/Abigails; ⑤), which, as the name suggests, recalls the opulence and splendor of a bygone era and even offers an architectural tour of the town in a Model "A" Ford. Another plush and relaxing B&B is _The Ship's Inn_ at 821 D St (☎707/443-7583 or 1-877/443-7583, ⓦwww.shipsinn.net; ⑥). **Campgrounds** line US-101 between Eureka and Arcata; the best is the _KOA_ (☎707/822-4243 or 1-800/562-3136, ⓦwww.koa.com; $25–26 per tent, RV hook-ups $35–$36.50, cabins $50), a large site with copious amenities four miles north of town at 4050 N US-101.

The City

Downtown Eureka is fairly short on charm, lit by the neon of motels and generic chain restaurants, and surrounded by rail and shipyards, although some colorful murals have brightened things up and the pretty, compact **Old Town**, bounded by C, G, First, and Third streets, at the edge of the bay, does its best to support a fledgling tourist economy. The peeling Victorian buildings and poky bars of the old sailors' district are pretty much run down – though they do have a certain seedy appeal, along with a handful of lively, mostly Italian restaurants. What few sights there are include the **Carson Mansion**, 143 M St at Second, an opulent Gothic pile built in the 1880s by William Carson, who made and lost fortunes in both timber and oil. Carson designed the project to keep his millworkers busy during a slow period in the industry. It now operates as a private gentleman's club behind its gingerbread facade, and can only be enjoyed from the street. Nearby, at 1410 2nd St, the one-room **Maritime Museum** (Tues–Sat noon–4pm; donation suggested; ☎707/444-9440) is chock-full of photos, maps, and relics from the days when Eureka was a whaling port. **Fort Humboldt State Historic Park**, 3431 Fort Ave (daily 9am–5pm; free; ☎707/445-6567), gives a look at a restored army fort and not much else, disappointing given that the army general and future president Ulysses S. Grant used it for a headquarters in 1853. Visitors with children might be rewarded by dropping in at the **Discovery Museum**, 517 3rd St (☎707/443-9694), which has hands-on kids' art and science displays, a puppet theatre, and planetarium.

The collection of Native American applied art at the **Clarke Memorial Museum**, Third and E streets (Tues–Sat 11am–4pm; free; ☎707/443-1947, Ⓦwww.clarkemuseum.org), can't hold a candle to the stuff at the **Indian Art Gallery**, 241 F St (Mon–Sat 10am–4.30pm; free; ☎707/445-8451, Ⓦwww .ncidc.org), which affords a rare opportunity for Native American artists to show and market their works in a gallery setting, and an even rarer opportunity to get your hands on some incredibly good, inexpensive silver jewelry. If dragging yourself around town for these sights doesn't appeal, you might prefer the Eureka Health and Spa, 601 5th St (☎707/445-2992), with its salt-rubs, tranquility tanks, and saunas. Completing an artistic trio, the **Morris Graves Museum of Art** at 636 F St (Thurs–Sun noon–5pm; suggested donation $3; ☎707/442-0278, Ⓦwww.humboldtarts.org) has six galleries of modern paintings and a sculpture garden. Back outdoors, LBJ Enterprises at 1707 E St (Mon–Fri 10am–4pm; ☎707/442-0339, Ⓦwww.birdjobs.com), runs enthusiastic **birdwatching** tours into the surrounding region for $50–100.

A few minutes by car from Eureka across the Samoa bridge, squashed against the Louisiana–Pacific plywood mill, the tiny community of **Samoa** is a company town that is the site of the last remaining cookhouse in the West. The **Samoa Cookhouse** (daily 7am–3.30pm & 5–9pm; ☎707/442-1659) was where the lumbermen would come to eat gargantuan meals after a day of felling redwoods, and although the oilskin tablecloths and burly workers have gone, the lumber-camp style remains, making the cookhouse somewhat of an institution. Eating massive portions of red meat at its long tables makes for an entertaining meal.

Eating and nightlife

In addition to the *Samoa Cookhouse* (see above), **eating** possibilities include the Italian restaurants in the Old Town, notably *Roy's*, 218 D St (☎707/442-4574), where entrees cost around $20, and Eureka's newest and finest dining option, *Avalon*, on the corner of 3rd and G Sts (☎707/445-0500; closed Sun & Mon), where Parisian meets Californian cuisine at a price – expect to pay at least $50 for meal and drinks. Meanwhile *The Lost Coast Brewery and Café*, 617 4th St at G Street (☎707/445-4480), serves large, hearty dishes to a rambunctious crowd of microbrew drinkers and sports fans. Further afield, *Adel's*, south of downtown at 1724 Broadway, has basic meat-and-potato meals and salads for about $10, making it a local hangout, while on the north side, *Samraat*, 1735 4th St (☎707/476-0930), is a good choice if you fancy a curry. The *Humboldt Bay Coffee Company*, 211 F St (☎707/444-3969), ranks as the coast's best coffee shop with its beautiful red-brick interior and sock-it-to-me roasts. It's open until around 9pm and often features live music. For delicious seafood and burgers, you might try *Café Waterfront*, 102 F St (☎707/443-9190), where entrees cost around $15.

Eureka has a fair sprinkling of **nightlife** venues; the most interesting is *The Vista*, tucked on the waterfront at 91 Commercial St (☎707/443-1491), which sporadically showcases hardcore and experimental punk bands from the local area and further afield. For full listings, check out the free weekly *North Coast Journal*.

Arcata

ARCATA, only seven miles up the coast from Eureka, is by far the more appealing of the two towns, centered on a grassy central plaza that flies an Earth flag under those of the US and California. Beards and Birkenstocks are the norm in this small college town, with a large community of rat-race refugees and Sixties throwbacks, whose presence is manifest in some raunchy bars and the town's earthy, mellow pace. The beaches north of town are some of the best on the north coast, white-sanded and windswept, and known for their easy hikeability and random parties. But think twice about diving head-long into the surf without a wetsuit, as the ocean in these parts remains frigid throughout the year.

The main square is the focal point of the town's shops and bars, with everything you're likely to want to see and do within easy walking distance. In the middle of the square rests a statue of President McKinley. Originally intended for nearby McKinleyville, it fell off the train on the way and stayed put in Arcata. Just east of the town center, **Humboldt State University**, with its nationally known environmental education and natural-resource management programs, attracts a decidedly liberal student body, which contributes considerably to Arcata's leftist feel. If you're interested in the college's history and programs, take a free student-led tour, which will give you much more insight than just wandering the campus's unflattering architecture. Free tours begin at the Plaza Avenue entrance on weekdays at 10am and 2pm and on Saturday at noon. Call ☎707/826-4402 for information. The **HSU Natural History Museum**, 1315 G St (Tues–Sat 10am–5pm; $2; ☎707/826-4479, ⓦwww .humboldt.edu/~natmus), houses interesting displays of fossils, live local fauna, and interactive exhibits.

At the foot of I Street, the **Arcata Marsh and Wildlife Sanctuary**, a restored former dump on 150 acres of wetland, is a peaceful place where you can lie on the boardwalk in the sun and listen to the birds. The Interpretive Center at 569 South G Street (daily 9am–5pm; ☎707/826-2359) runs **guided wildlife walks** (Sat 2pm), as does the Audubon Society, which meets at the very end of I Street at 8.30am every Saturday morning. For those who don't have time to explore the Redwood National Park, Arcata's own second-growth **community forest**, a 575-acre, beautiful spot with manageable trails and ideal picnic areas, is accessible by going east on 14th Street to Redwood Park Drive.

If you're around over Memorial Day weekend, don't miss the three-day **Kinetic Sculpture Race**, a spectacular event in which competitors use human-powered contraptions of their own devising to propel themselves over land, water, dunes, and marsh from Arcata to Ferndale; call ☎707/786-9259 for information.

Practicalities

Greyhound and Amtrak Thruway **buses** pull into the station at 925 E St, connecting with the Eureka services going north and south; there's also a Humboldt Transit Authority link with Eureka every day except Sunday. The new **California Welcome Center**, over a mile north of town just off US-101 at 1635 Heindon Rd (daily 9am–5pm; ☎707/822-3619, ⓦwww.arcatachamber .com), has free maps, brochures, and displays from all over the state, and lists of local accommodation and services.

Motels just out of town on US-101 are lower priced than the increasingly popular **bed and breakfasts**, if a little less inviting, and can usually be found for under $50 per night. Trusty *Motel 6*, at 4755 Valley West Blvd (℡707/822-7061 or 1-800/466-8356, ⓦwww.motel6.com; ❷), fills up with parents visiting for graduation at the adjacent university in May, but otherwise usually has space. You can get reasonable rooms at the *Fairwinds Motel*, 1674 G St (℡707/822-4824; ❷), though if you spend just a bit more money, the *Hotel Arcata*, 708 9th St (℡707/826-0217 or 1-800/344-1221, ⓦwww.hotelarcata .com; ❹), on the town's main square, is a far more stylish establishment. Of the B&Bs, try *The Lady Anne*, an Arcata favorite for years, located between the plaza and the college at 902 14th St (℡707/822-2797, ⓦwww.humboldt1.com/ladyanne; ❺). There are several **campgrounds** north of Arcata along the coast, but none within easy reach of town unless you've got a car. The nearest and cheapest is at **Clam Beach County Park** (℡707/445-765), eight miles north of town on US-101, where showerless sites cost $10 per car or $3 per person walk-in, making it quite a party venue for dishevelled youngsters staying long-term. See the "Around Arcata" section below for options with better facilities.

Dotted around the plaza and tangential streets, Arcata's **bars** set the town apart. The best of the bunch, *Jambalaya* at 915 H St (℡707/822-4766), is more of a restaurant with an additional nightly diet of R&B, jazz, and rock bands. *Humboldt Brews*, 856 10th St (℡707/822-2739), is a working beer factory with its own bar and low-priced restaurant, where you can sample the preferred stronger, darker brews of Northern California. There's also the relaxed café at the *Finnish County Sauna and Tubs* (℡707/822-2228), on the corner of Fifth and J streets, with live acoustic sets at the weekend and tubs in the garden for $15 an hour ($8 for 30min). Facing US-101 on 1603 G St, *Muddy Waters Coffee Company* (℡707/826-2233) supports local music with weekly free concerts and is a pleasant place to relax and mingle with students. Good **restaurants** also abound – the *Wildflower Café and Bakery*, 1604 G St (℡707/822-0360), turns out first-rate, cheap organic meals, while the *Big Blue Café*, 846 G St, is a great place to watch proceedings on the square over a fine leisurely breakfast, or you can try the excellent meat or veggie breakfast and lunch specials at *Crosswinds*, 860 10th St (℡707/826-2133). *Abruzzi*, 780 H St (℡707/826-2345), serves top-quality Italian dinners at moderate prices, while the mainly takeout *Pacific Room Noodle House*, at 359 G St (℡707/826-7604), makes delicious, inexpensive Asian dishes, which can also be consumed in its courtyard.

Around Arcata

If you've got a car, take time to explore the coastline just north of Arcata along US-101. On the way, a short detour worth making east of the highway is through the modern strip-mall town of **McKinleyville**, near Clam Beach, in order to see the world's tallest **totem pole**. The gaily decorated 160ft ex-redwood stands proudly at the back of the McKinleyville Shopping Center halfway along Central Avenue near the junction with City Center Road. If you're peckish, you can't beat the gourmet sandwiches on offer the other side of the main road at *Tastebuds*, 2011 Central Ave (℡707/839-2788).

Moonstone Beach, about twelve miles north of town, is a vast, sandy strip that, save for the odd beachcomber, remains empty during the day, and by night heats up with guitar-strumming student parties that rage for as long as the bracing climate allows. **Trinidad Harbor**, a few miles further on, is a good stop for a **meal** or drink, nose around the small shops, or just sit down by the sea wall and watch the fishing boats being tossed about beyond the harbor. Locals rave about the harbor's *Seascape Pier Restaurant* (℡707/677-3762), whose menu of fresh fish, steaks, and pasta tastes all the more delicious given its waterfront location. Similar grub at more moderate prices is to be had back up in town at the *Trinidad Bay Eatery* (☎707/677-3777), on the corner of Parker and Trinity streets. If you decide **to stay** in the area, there are several good options a little to the north: the *Trinidad Inn*, 1170 Patrick's Point Drive (☎707/677-3349, Ⓦwww.trinidadinn.com; ❸), is a lovely motel in a quiet location, while the *Emerald Forest*, 733 Patrick's Point Drive (☎707/677-3554, Ⓦwww.cabinsintheredwoods.com; ❹), offers secluded cabins and tent sites for $22. If money is no object, then one of the most romantic retreats along the entire coast is the *Lost Whale Inn*, 3452 Patrick's Point Drive (☎1-800/677-7849, Ⓦwww.lostwhaleinn.com; ❽); this luxurious and friendly B&B has an outdoor hot tub and access to a secluded little beach where seals frolic. **Patrick's Point State Park**, five miles north of Trinidad, sports an agate beach below rocky coastal bluffs, and tours of a re-created Yurok village are conducted by appointment (☎707/677-3570), although you can wander alone at will. The park also offers reasonably secluded **camping** for $20 (reserve through ReserveAmerica ☎1-800/444-7275). Several miles further on, **Big Lagoon County Park** (☎707/445-7651; day-use $2) has tent spaces for $14.

A more adventurous destination is **Hoopa Valley Indian Reservation**, sixty miles inland. In past years the site of often violent confrontation between Native Americans and whites over fishing territory, Hoopa is now seen by some as the badlands of Humboldt and few take the time to check out the valley. Although some of the youth are still to be seen hanging around listlessly, the atmosphere has been improving of late and the local casino has reopened after a period of closure due to alcohol-induced violence. If you're here in the last week in July you should make an effort to catch the All Indian Rodeo, which is held southwest of the village. Otherwise it is enough to visit the **Hoopa Tribal Museum** (Mon–Fri 8am–noon & 1–5pm, summer only Sat 10am–noon & 1–4pm; free; ☎530/493-2900) – full of crafts, baskets, and jewelry of the Hoopa (aka Natinixwe) and Yurok tribes.

To get to the reservation, take Hwy-299 west out of Arcata for forty miles until you hit **Willow Creek** – self-proclaimed gateway to **"Bigfoot Country"** – then take Hwy-96, the "Bigfoot Scenic Byway," north. Beside the Hwy-299/Hwy-96 junction, a statue of Bigfoot marks the entrance to the small **Willow Creek–China Flat Museum** (☎530/629-2653), which displays a modest collection of Indian quilts and settlers' possessions. Next door, a small **Chamber of Commerce** hut (summer only 9am–5pm; ☎530/629-2693, Ⓦwww.willowcreekchamber.com) has details of Bigfoot's escapades, and information on the **whitewater rafting** that is done on the Smith, Klamath, and Trinity rivers near here. Among the numerous rafting companies in the area, Bigfoot Rafting Company (☎530/629-2263 or 1-800/722-2223) offers guided trips from $55. Otherwise, the town comprises a handful of grocery stores, diners, and cheap **motels** such as *Bigfoot Motel*, 39116 Hwy-299

The legend of Bigfoot

Reports of giant 350- to 800-pound humanoids wandering the forests of north-western California have circulated since the late nineteenth century, fueled by long-established Indian legends, though they weren't taken seriously until 1958, when a road maintenance crew found giant footprints in a remote area near Willow Creek. Photos were taken and the **Bigfoot** story went worldwide. Since then there have been more than fifty separate sightings of Bigfoot prints. At the crossroads in Willow Creek stands a huge wooden replica of the prehistoric-looking apeman, who in recent years has added kidnapping to his list of alleged activities.

(☎530/629-4151, ⓦwww.bigfootmotel.com; ❷). Of the **eateries**, *Cinnabar Sam*, 19 Willow Way (☎530/629-3437), is the best bet for filling brekky, sandwiches, Mexican or American meals. Just north of town, the Lower Trinity Ranger Station (summer Mon–Sat 9am–4.30pm; rest of year Mon–Fri 9am–4.30pm; ☎530/629-2118) handles camping and wilderness permits for the immediate surroundings. Continue east on Hwy-299 and you'll arrive in the Weaverville/Shasta area (see p.000), where you can join the super-speedy I-5 freeway.

The Redwood National and State Parks

Way up in the top left-hand corner of California, the landscape is almost too spectacular for words, and the long drive up here is rewarded with a couple of tiny towns and thick, dense redwood forests perfect for hiking and camping. Some thirty miles north of Arcata, **Orick** marks the southernmost end of this landscape, a contiguous strip of forest jointly managed as the **REDWOOD NATIONAL AND STATE PARKS** (unrestricted access; free), a massive area that stretches up into Del Norte County at the very northernmost point of California, ending at the rather dull town of **Crescent City**. The fragmented Redwood National Park and the three state parks which plug the gaps – Prairie Creek Redwoods, Del Norte Coast Redwoods, and Jedediah Smith Redwoods – together contain some of the tallest trees in the world: the pride of California's forestland, especially between June and September when every school in the state seems to organize its summer camp here. Increasingly, and despite being designated a World Heritage Site and International Biosphere Reserve, it's becoming a controversial area where campers wake to the sound of chainsaws and huge lumber trucks roaring up and down the highway. Despite this and other sustained cutting, local loggers are still dissatisfied, claiming that they've lost much of the prime timber they relied on to make their living before the days of the parks.

One word of caution: **bears** and **mountain lions** inhabit this area, and you should heed the warnings in "Basics" on p.70.

Practicalities

The parks' 58,000 acres divide into distinct areas: **Redwood National Park**, southwest of the Orick area; the Prairie Creek **Redwood State Park**, south of the riverside town of **Klamath**; and the area in the far north around the **Del Norte** and **Jedediah Smith** state parks, in the environs of Crescent City in Del Norte County. The park **headquarters** are in Crescent City, at 1111 2nd St (summer daily 9am–5pm; winter Mon–Sat 9am–5pm; ☎707/464-6101, ⓦwww.nps.gov/redw), but the **visitor centers** and **ranger stations** throughout the parks are far better for maps and information, including up-to-date hiking conditions and the weather forecast. Most useful is the **Kuchel Visitor Center** (daily 9am–5pm; ☎707/464-6101 ext 5265), right by the southern entrance to Redwood National Park, before you get to Orick.

The two daily Greyhound **buses** that run along US-101 to Crescent City will, if asked, stop (and if you're lucky can be flagged down) along forested stretches of the highway, and there's a twice-daily Redwood Coast Transit service looping out from Crescent City and back. Still, unless you want to single out a specific area and stay there (not the best way to see the parks), you'll be stuck without a **car**.

As for accommodation, **camping** is your best bet. You can stay at the many primitive and free campgrounds all over the parks; for more comfort, head for the sites we've mentioned in the text below (all $20), along with a hostel and a few **motel/B&B** recommendations. Failing that, get onto US-101 and look for motels around Crescent City.

Orick and Tall Trees Grove

As the southernmost and most used entrance to the Redwood National Park, the Orick area is always busy. Its major attraction is **TALL TREES GROVE**, home of one of the world's tallest trees – a mightily impressive specimen that stands at some 367 feet. The tallest tree in the world, by the way, less than a foot taller, was recently discovered in an inaccessible grove in Mendocino County. The easiest way to get to the Tall Trees Grove, avoiding too much picking amongst the lush undergrowth, is to drive yourself, although you will need to get a free access permit (limited to fifty cars per day – only a problem in high summer) at the visitor center. Here you can pick up a free trail guide that explains why some redwood cutting is being done to balance the damages inflicted on old growth in the past. When you reach the parking lot, it takes about half an hour to hike down the steep trail to the grove itself and, unless you're super-fit, somewhat longer to get back up. The best view of the tallest redwood and its companions is to be had from the mostly dry riverbed nearby. Some people prefer to hike the 8.5-mile **Redwood Creek Trail** (permit needed if staying overnight in the backcountry) from near Orick: take a right off US-101 onto Bald Hills Road, then, 600 yards along, fork off to the picnic area where the trail starts. The bridge, 1.5 miles away, is passable in summer only. If you can make it from here, a bit further east another trail turns north off Bald Hills Road and winds for half a mile to **Lady Bird Johnson Grove** – a collection of trees dedicated to former US President LBJ's wife, "Lady Bird" Johnson, a big lover of flora and fauna. A mile-long self-guided trail winds through the grove of these giant patriarchs. On the western side of US-101, across from the entrance to the Redwood Creek Trail, begins the **Coastal Trail**, which follows the coastline and takes backpackers up the entire length of all three state parks. An unpaved road leads in for a few hundred yards before petering out into the hikers-only path.

In **ORICK** itself (actually two miles north of the entrance and ranger station), a couple of **stores** and **cafés**, along with two **motels**, string alongside US-101. On the right as you enter town from the south, the *Green Valley Motel* (☏707/488-2341; ➋) has bargain-rate rooms, while a little further along on the left the *Palm Motel & Café* (☏707/488-3381; ➋) also has adequate rooms and serves cheap burgers and sandwiches. You might also stop next door at the *Lumberjack* (☏707/488-5095) for a game of pool and an ice-cold beer. Three miles north of Orick, the narrow, gravel Davison Road turns coastwards for a bumpy eight miles to **Gold Bluffs Beach** where you can camp surrounded by elk. The $6-per-vehicle fee also covers Fern Canyon, visited on an easy three-quarter-mile trail, its 45-foot walls slippery with mosses, fern, and lichen.

Prairie Creek State Park

Of the three state parks within the Redwood National Park area, **PRAIRIE CREEK** is the most varied and popular. Bear and elk often roam in plain sight, and you can take a ranger-led **tour** of the wild, solidly populated redwood forest. Check with the **ranger station** (summer daily 9am–5pm; rest of year daily 10am–4pm; ☏707/464-6101 ext 5300) for details. Whether you choose to go independently, or opt for a tour, main features of the park include the meadows of **Elk Prairie** in front of the ranger station, where herds of Roosevelt elk – massive beasts weighing up to four hundred pounds – roam freely, protected from poachers. Remember that elk, like all wildlife, are unpredictable and should not be approached. Day-use is $6 per vehicle but you can park beside the road and wander at will. There's a campground ($20) on the edge of Elk Prairie, at the hub of a network of hiking trails. If you're pressed for time, there are some car-accessible routes through the woods. Just south of the ranger station, on the east side of US-101, is the entrance to **Lost Man Creek**, an unpaved 1.5-mile round-trip drive into a grove that passes by a cascade. To enter Prairie Creek Redwoods State Park, take the **Newton B. Drury Scenic Byway** off US-101 north of Lost Man Creek. Even if you're just passing through, the eight-mile byway is a worthwhile trip deep into the trees. A mile north of the ranger station, the magnificent **Big Tree Wayside** redwood, more than three hundred feet tall and, at over 21ft in diameter, one of the fattest of the coastal redwoods, overlooks the road. North of the Big Tree Wayside and before the byway rejoins US-101, the rough, gravel Coastal Drive branches off to the west following the Coastal Trail for 7.5 miles, leading to **High Bluff Overlook** and camping at **Flint Ridge**.

Prairie Creek also has a couple of **restaurants** on the southern approach on US-101. All do a good line in wild boar roasts, elk steaks, and the like, as well as a more traditional menu of burgers and breakfasts. *Rolf's Park Café* (☎707/488-3841; ❸), on US-101 by the Fern Canyon turnoff, is one of the best, with outdoor seating and German entrees, as well as motel-style **accommodation**.

Klamath and around

KLAMATH, in Del Norte County, isn't technically part of the Redwood area nor, by most definitions, does it qualify as a town, as most of the buildings were washed away when the nearby Klamath River flooded in 1964. Nonetheless, there are spectacular coastal views from trails where the Klamath River meets the ocean, famed salmon and steelhead fishing to be had in the river itself, a few decent accommodation options and, for a bit of fun, the **Trees of Mystery** (daily 9am–6pm, later in summer; $12; ☎707/482-2251 or 1-800/638-3389, ⓦwww.treesofmystery.net) on US-101, where you'll notice two huge wooden sculptures of Paul Bunyan and Babe, his blue ox. Taped stories of Bunyan's adventures emanate periodically from within the redwood stands and ethereal choral music greets you at the most impressive specimen of all, the **Cathedral Tree**, where nine trees have grown from one root structure to form a spooky circle. Enterprising Californians hold wedding services here throughout the year. A recent addition to the site, which somewhat justifies the steep entry fee, is an aerial tram, which takes you from the top of the foot trail over the forest canopy to 750ft **Ted's Ridge**. Here you are provided with binoculars to enhance your enjoyment of the ocean views to the west and tree-clad ridges and valleys to the east – from March to October look out for the active osprey nest atop one distant redwood. Back down in the gift shop, the free **End of the Trail Museum** highlights artwork from a number of the region's Indian tribes. Further south, where Hwy-169 peels off from US-101, the 725-year-old living **Tour Thru Tree** on Terwer Valley Road (daylight hours; $4) provides a cute photo opportunity. Perhaps the most spectacular scenery in Klamath is not the trees, but the ocean: take Requa Road about three quarters of a mile down to the estuary, to a point known as the **Klamath Overlook**, from where, once the fog has burnt off, there is an awe-inspiring view of the estuary meeting the sea and the rugged coastline to the south. From here, you can pick up the Coastal Trail on foot, which leads north for ten miles along some of California's most remote beach, ending at Endert's Beach in Crescent City.

Practicalities

The newly refurbished *Historic Requa Inn*, 451 Requa Rd (℡707/482-1425 or 1-866/800-8777, ⓦwww.requainn.com; ❹), offers some of the best **accommodation** around. There are simple cabins at *Woodland Villa*, a mile and a half north of Requa (℡707/482-2081 or 1-888/866-2466, ⓦwww.klamathusa.com; ❸), and small cottages with kitchenettes at *Camp Marigold* (℡707/482-3585 or 1-800/621-8513; ❷), just over one mile south of the Trees of Mystery. Three miles southeast of Klamath down Hwy-275 the *Rhode's End*, 115 Trobitz Rd, Klamath Glen (℡707/482-1654; ❹), offers B&B accommodation along the Klamath River, and the beautifully situated, spotlessly clean, and friendly *HI-Redwood National Park Hostel* several miles north of Trees of Mystery at 14480 Hwy-101 N (℡707/482-8265, ⓦwww.norcalhostels.org), has dorm beds for $16–19, whether you are a member or not, and rooms for $45. A couple of miles yet further north is the free, primitive *DeMartin* campground. Two miles west of US-101 on Klamath Beach Road, *Riverwoods Campground* (℡707/482-5591) has shady tent sites for $15 on the south bank of the Klamath River towards its mouth.

There are slim pickings in the **eating** department around Klamath, especially in the evening, but *Sis's Kitchen* (℡707/482-1408), on the southern edge of town at 301 Hwy-169, rustles up fine all-day breakfasts and other meals until the late afternoon and *Sweet Street Café*, 164 Klamath Blvd (℡707/482-3125), serves American standards throughout the day. If you want to get into some river activity, Klamath River Jet Boat Tours, 17635 Hwy-101 S (℡707/482-7775 or 1-800/887-5387, ⓦwww.jetboattours.com), runs four-hour ($45) and ninety-minute ($25) tours and can arrange guided fishing trips.

Crescent City

The northernmost outposts of the Redwood National Park, the Del Norte and Jedediah Smith state parks, sit either side of **CRESCENT CITY**, a rather forlorn place, whose most attractive buildings were wiped out by a typhoon over thirty years ago, leaving little to recommend it other than its proximity to the parks. That said, the city is the half-way point on US-101 between San Francisco (349 miles south) and Portland, Oregon (355 miles north), and is therefore often used as a rest stop so there are plenty of places to stay and eat. Greyhound buses stop at 1125 Northcrest Drive, and the **Visitor Center** is at 1001 Front St (summer daily 9am–5pm; winter Mon–Fri 9am–5pm; ℡707/464-3174 or 1-800/343-8300, ⓦwww.northerncalifornia.net).

The most popular tourist attraction is **Ocean World** (daily 9am–7pm, later in summer; $7.95; ℡707/464-4900, ⓦwww.oceanworld.com), an unmissably large complex on US-101 south of town, which has a limited range of fish and other sea creatures, but the guided tours that run every fifteen minutes are informative and give you the opportunity to handle many of the inmates. So if you fancy picking up a starfish or stroking a shark or sea lion, this is the place for you. Take an hour to visit the **Battery Point Lighthouse** (April–Sept Wed–Sun 10am–4pm; tours sporadically during low tide; $3), reached by a causeway from the western end of town. The oldest working lighthouse on the West Coast, it houses a collection of artifacts from the *Brother Jonathan*, wrecked off Point St George in the 1870s. Because of this loss, the St George Lighthouse, the tallest and most expensive in the US, was built six miles north of Crescent City. Or you could visit the old-fashioned **Main Museum**, 577 H St (May–Sept Mon–Sat 10am–4pm; $3; ☎707/464-3922), whose dusty interior conceals some Indian artifacts, quilts, old musical instruments, the lens from St George Lighthouse, historical displays and, most interesting of all, original cells from the building's earlier incarnation as the county jail.

Of several passable **motels**, try the pleasantly situated *Crescent Beach Motel*, on the beach two miles south of town at 1455 US-101 S (☎707/464-5436, ⓦwww.crescentbeachmotel.com; ❹), or the much cheaper *Gardenia Motel*, 119 L St (☎707/464-2181; ❷), which offers no frills but is in a more central location. If you want somewhere posher to stay, try *Cottage By The Sea*, 205 South A St (☎707/464-9068 or 1-877/642-2254, ⓦwww.waterfrontvacationrental .com; ❺), a smart B&B perched on a bluff overlooking the ocean – you might even spot a migrating whale from your room. For **eating**, try the pasta and vegetarian dishes at the upmarket *Bistro Gardens*, 938 K St (☎707/464-5627), or the excellent, moderately priced Italian, steak, and seafood at *Da Luciana*, 575 Hwy-101 S (☎707/465-6566). Other fine ethnic choices are the Thai and Vietnamese dishes at *Thai House*, 105 N St (☎707/464-2427), the filling Chinese at *China Hut*, 928 9th St (☎707/464-4921), or *Los Compadres*, a cheap Mexican diner opposite the marina at 457 Hwy-101 S (☎707/464-7871).

Del Norte and Jedediah Smith state parks

DEL NORTE STATE PARK, seven miles south of Crescent City, is worth visiting less for its redwood forests (you've probably had enough of them by now anyway), than its fantastic beach area and hiking trails, most of which are an easy two miles or so along the coastal ridge where the redwoods meet the sea. From May to July, wild rhododendrons and azaleas shoot up everywhere, laying a floral blanket across the park's floor. The Mill Creek **campground** (reserve through ReserveAmerica ☎1-800/444-7275; $20) here is in a lovely setting. **JEDEDIAH SMITH STATE PARK** (☎707/464-6101 ext 5113), nine miles east of Crescent City, is named after the European explorer who was the first white man to trek overland from the Mississippi to the Pacific in 1828, before being killed by Comanche tribes in Kansas in 1831. Not surprisingly, his name is everywhere: no less than eighteen separate redwood groves are dedicated to his memory. Sitting squatly on the south fork of the Smith River, the park attracts many people to canoe downstream or, more quietly, sit on the riverbank and fish. Of the hiking trails, the **Stout Grove Trail** is the most popular, a one-hour flat walk leading down to a most imposing Goliath – a 345-foot-tall, twenty-foot-diameter redwood.

If you're heading further east and can't face more highway, you could opt for the painfully slow, but scenic six-mile route that follows Howland Hill Road from Crescent City through the forest to the **Hiouchi Information Center** (May–Oct 9am–5pm; ☎707/464-5601 ext 5067) on Hwy-199, about five miles away. Branching off this are several blissfully short and easy trails (roughly half a mile) that are quieter than the routes through the major parts of the park. You can also access the **Little Bald Hills Trail** east of Hiouchi, which traces a strenuous ten-mile hike that should take about eight hours. You'll also find the *Jedediah Smith Redwoods* **campground** (reserve through ReserveAmerica ☎1-800/444-7275; $20), and picnicking facilities at the end of the Howland Hill Road. Back on the main road at 2097 Hwy-199, the *Hiouchi Motel*

(☎707/458-3041 or 1-866/446-8244, ⓦwww.hiouchi.com; ❸) has decent rooms. About ten miles further on, shortly before you leave the redwoods behind, the *Patrick Creek Lodge & Historical Inn*, 13950 Hwy-199 (☎707/457-3323, ⓦwww.patrickcreeklodge.com; ❹), is the last place to stay in California on this route; there are good single rates on the stylish rooms and an excellent but pricey restaurant. The apparent detour into Oregon on Hwy-199 to connect with I-5 back south is actually by far the quickest way to connect to the interior of Northern California from the extreme north coast.

The northern interior

As big as Ohio, yet with a population of only 250,000, the **NORTHERN INTERIOR** of California is about as remote as the state gets. Cut off from the coast by the **Shasta Cascade** range, it's a region dominated by forests, lakes, some fair-sized mountains – and two thirds of the state's precipitation. It's largely uninhabited, and, for the most part, infrequently visited, which makes a spin up here all the more worthwhile. Locals take the time to chat and point out areas to explore, and the region's efficient network of hiking trails and roads usually remains empty of traffic jams.

I-5 leads through the very middle of this near wilderness, forging straight up the **Sacramento Valley** through acres of olive and nut trees, and past the college towns of **Chico** to **Redding**: the latter makes a useful base, with cheap lodging, from where you can venture out on loop trips a day or so at a time. Most accessible, immediately west and north of Redding, the **Whiskeytown-Shasta-Trinity National Recreation Area** is a series of three lakes and forests set aside for what can be heavily subscribed public use, especially in summer when it's hard to avoid the camper vans, windsurfers, jet-skiers, and packs of happy holidaymakers. A better bet lies east at **Lassen Volcanic National Park**, a stunning alpine landscape of sulfur springs and peaks, or in the scenic environs of **Plumas County** to the southeast, between Lassen and Lake Tahoe. Traveling on state highways north of Lassen through national forests reveals numerous roadside surprises, including towering **Burney Falls** and access points to the **Pacific Crest Trail**, the 1200-mile path from Canada to Mexico.

Further north, the crowds swell a bit in the shadows of **Mount Shasta**, a 14,000-foot volcano whose reputation as both spiritual convergence point and climbing challenge brings together an interesting cast of characters in the small town of the same name. Train buffs should stop in the historical railroad town of **Dunsmuir**, just south of Shasta, and anglers will find trout streams filled to the gills all around the area. North of Shasta, the mountains and pines give way to cattle and caves, the latter part of the stunning lava fields of **Lava Beds National Monument**, the site of one of the saddest Indian wars in US history. Trails and monuments mark the battle's history, while all around the desolate plain, migrating birds rest up in the gigantic sanctuary of the **Klamath Basin** before resuming their journeys on the **Pacific Flyway**. To the east the scrubby lavic landscape gradually transforms into the heavily wooded and mountainous terrain of **Modoc County**, where out-door activities predominate.

It's the usual story with sparse **public transportation**: reasonably frequent Greyhound and Amtrak Thruway buses connect San Francisco and Sacramento to Portland via I-5, stopping off at the Sacramento Valley towns and Redding on the way, and trains from Oakland stop in Redding and Chico. However, neither route provides anything close to comprehensive access to the area, and if you're going to come here at all it should be in a **car**. Anything worth see-ing lies at least five miles from the nearest bus stop. The area is too big and the towns too far apart to make traveling by bus even faintly enjoyable.

The Sacramento Valley

The **SACRAMENTO VALLEY** lays fair claim to being California's most uninteresting region: a flat, largely agricultural corridor of small, sleepy towns and endless vistas of wheat fields and fruit trees. By far the best thing to do is pass straight through on I-5 – the half-empty, straight, and speedy freeway cuts an almost two-hundred-mile-long swathe through the region, and you could forge right ahead to the more enticing far north quite painlessly in half a day. If you're coming from San Francisco, save time by taking the I-505 byway around Sacramento.

Chico

Charming little **CHICO**, about midway between Sacramento and Redding and some twenty miles east of I-5 from the Orland exit, is a good stopoff if you don't want to attempt to cover the whole valley from top to bottom in one day, or if you're here to visit Lassen Volcanic National Park (see p.829) and need somewhere to stay. Home to **Chico State University**, a grassy institu-tion of sandal-wearing students renowned more for their devotion to partying than academic pursuits. Chico was once the grounds surrounding the mansion of General John Bidwell, one of the first men to cash in on the Gold Rush. As such, the city's traditional layout around a plaza, numerous college eateries, and surrounding expanse of parkland make it something of an oasis compared to the dusty fields and sleepy towns beyond.

Arrival, information, and getting around

Chico is right on Hwy-99. **Trains** (and Amtrak Thruway buses) stop at the unattended station at Fifth and Orange, as do Greyhound **buses**. The *Coast Starlight* train, from Los Angeles to Seattle, stops here once daily, though in the middle of the night. Greyhounds serving cities north and south along I-5 stop more frequently, three or four times a day. See schedules posted at the station.

Chico's **Chamber of Commerce**, 300 Salem St (Mon–Fri 9am–5pm, Sat 10am–3pm; ☎530/891-5556 or 1-800/852-8570, ⓦwww.chicochamber .com), has a terrific supply of information, from pamphlets outlining a historical walking tour through downtown to mountain-bike trails and swimming-hole locations nearby. They also publish updated lists of lodging options, with prices. To find out what's on, consult the free *Chico News & Review* (ⓦwww .newsreview.com), published every Thursday, or tune in to KZFR (90.1 FM) or The Point (107.5 FM), both broadcasting eclectic local-community radio.

Parking is only 25¢ an hour all over downtown during weekday business hours and free at weekends. The majority of places you are likely to want to

CHICO

Chica Creek
Nature Centre

E. 1ST AVENUE

MANGROVE AVENUE

VALLOMBROSA AVENUE

Lindo Channel

Lower
Bidwell
Park

WEST SACRAMENTO AVENUE

Bidwell
Mansion

California

State

University

Chico

CYPRESS STREET

PINE STREET

OLIVE STREET

ORIENT STREET

FLUME STREET

WALL STREET

Chico Museum Ⓖ

City
Hall

MAIN ST.

BROADWAY

SALEM STREET

City
Plaza

N

ACCOMMODATION	
L'Abri Inn	C
Days Inn	F
Esplanade	D
The Grateful Bed	B
Matador	A
Thunderbird Lodge	E

MULBERRY STREET

PARK AVENUE

Amtrak &
Greyhound

20TH STREET

FAIR STREET

9TH STREET

CHICO RIVER RD

0 ———— 900 yds

Durham ▼   Sacramento ▼

Hamilton City

Lassen Volcanic National Park

❿

RESTAURANTS					
The Brick Works	4	Franky's	14	Madison Bear Garden	8
Broadway Heights	10	Jack's Family Restaurant	11	Riley's	13
Caffé Malvina	9	Karim Restaurant	3	Sierra Nevada Brewing	
Chada Thai	6	La Hacienda Inn	1	Company	12
Chico Brewhouse	2	LaSalle's	7	Tres Hombres	5

visit are within walking distance of the town center, but the trails in Bidwell Park need to be biked to be appreciated. You can rent one for a rather steep $35 per day from Campus Bicycles right off the plaza at 330 Main St (☎530/345-2081). The shop also provides free maps for cyclists.

Accommodation

Chico has much more in the way of **accommodation** than it does in sights, though for **camping** you'll need to head to the Plumas National Forest to the east or Lassen Volcanic National Park. Motels are everywhere in town, particularly in the Main Street and Broadway area, and there are a couple of good B&Bs.

Days Inn 740 Broadway ☎530/343-3286 or 1-800/329-7466, ⓦwww.daysinn.com. Not the cheapest downtown motel but a safe-bet chain franchise and just two blocks south of the plaza, with refrigerators in rooms and a pool. ❹

The Esplanade 620 The Esplanade ☎530/345-8084, ⓦwww.now2000.com/esplanade. A particularly good-value B&B right across from the Bidwell Mansion. The beds are so high you almost need to pole-vault onto them, and tasty breakfasts are served on the back veranda. ❺

The Grateful Bed 1462 Arcadian Ave ☎530/342-2464, ⓦwww.chico.com/grateful. No tie-dye linen but a laid-back atmosphere at this plush and friendly B&B two blocks west of the Esplanade. ❹

L'Abri Inn 4350 Hwy-99 ☎530/893-0824 or 1-800/489-3319, ⓦwww.now2000.com/labri. Five miles north of town, this place comprises three rooms in a ranch-style home with a serene country atmosphere. Enjoy a sumptuous breakfast, then go out and pet the barnyard animals. ❺

The Matador Motel 1934 The Esplanade ☎530/342-7543. A pretty Spanish Revival building ten blocks north of the plaza; the tasteful rooms have individual tiling. Set around a courtyard, with palms shading one of Chico's largest pools, this is one of Northern California's best deals. ❶

Thunderbird Lodge 715 Main St ☎530/343-7911, ⓦwww.thunderbirdlodge.homestead.com. Decent motel two blocks from the plaza. Some rooms have refrigerators and coffee makers. ❷

The Town

Chico doesn't have much by way of sights, but strolling the leafy streets, college campus, and shady riverside feels great after the monotonous drive up I-5. The 1904 **Chico Museum**, housed in the former Carnegie Library at the corner of Second and Main streets (Wed–Sun noon–4pm; free; ☎530/891-4336), contains three distinct parts: a permanent historical section, a reconstruction of a Taoist temple altar, and a gallery for rotating shows. You might also try the three-story **Bidwell Mansion** at 525 The Esplanade, the continuation of Main Street (Wed–Fri noon–5pm, Sat & Sun 10am–4pm; tours on the hour until 4pm; $1; ☎530/895-6144). Built in 1868, it's an attractive enough Italian country villa, filled with family paraphernalia visited on 45-minute anecdotal tours that are reasonably interesting, though Bidwell Park (most sections open daylight hours; free) is a more pleasurable place to spend your time. Extending from the center of the town for ten miles to the northeast, this is a tongue of semi-wilderness and oak parkland where, incidentally, the first Robin Hood film, starring Errol Flynn, was made, a fair hike from Sherwood Forest. No road runs right through the park, and it is too large to cover on foot, so cycling (see bike rental, p.823) is by far the best way to explore. The most heavily used portions are around the recreation areas at One-Mile Dam and Five-Mile Dam, both reached off Vallombrosa Avenue, and Cedar Grove, reached off East Eighth Street, but a half-hour stroll into Upper Park will leave most of the regulars behind. Students frequent the **swimming holes** on Big Chico Creek in the Upper Park, including Bear Hole, Salmon Hole, and Brown's Hole, which has a small rope swing. For the holes, take Vallombrosa Avenue all the way east until it dead-ends into Manzanita Avenue. Turn left on Manzanita, and then right on Wildwood Avenue. Follow the road past the golf course, where it turns into gravel, and then on to the creek. Driving is the preferred method of getting out here, though biking the three miles from the center of town is rewarded with a cooling plunge into the creek.

Back in town, vintage American car fans will enjoy **Cruces Classic Auto Sales**, downtown on 720 Main St, a commercial showroom with a walk-through museum showing some of the really rare models that are brought here to be restored. The remodeled **Sierra Nevada Brewing Company**, 1075 E 20th St (☎530/893-3520, ⓦwww.sierranevadabrewing.com), gives free and fairly cursory twenty-minute tours of the plant (Tues–Fri & Sun 2.30pm, Sat noon–3pm); there is no official tasting as such but you can sample the ten or so brews on tap for under $5 at the brewery's bar. Those nostalgic for the innocent days of childhood will enjoy the **National Yo-Yo Museum**, 320 Broadway (Mon–Sat 10am–6pm, Sun noon–5pm; free; ☎530/892-1414, ⓦwww.nationalyoyo.org/museum), where enthusiasts enjoy showing visitors round the thousands of exhibits and photos.

The **Farmers' Market** closes off downtown every summer Thursday at 5.30pm for three hours of produce sales. Come for the almonds and other fresh nuts grown nearby. The **Gold Cup Races** at the Silver Dollar Speedway (☎530/969-7484) brings Chico's biggest weekend. The stock-car extravaganza, which takes place on the third weekend of September, also fills all area hotels.

Ten miles outside Chico, south on Hwy-99 then east on Skyway to Humburg–Honey Run Road, the **Honey Run Covered Bridge** is one of the few remaining covered bridges in California. You can't drive on it, but its position in Butte Creek Canyon over a riffling river leads to peaceful walking and swimming opportunities. Further east, the apple orchards in Paradise were used as a location for *Gone With the Wind*.

Eating and nightlife

Chico also does itself proud when it comes to **food** and the listings below are just a sample of what is on offer. If you're here in early September look out for the one-day Taste of Chico **festival**; call ☎530/345-6000 for information. Being a California State University town, there are many excellent places aimed at the younger customer, as well as a handful of lively **bars**, that feature live music by national acts. It's noticeably quieter when school's out, but on summer Friday evenings, **free concerts** by talented locals draw the crowds to the Downtown Park Plaza, beginning at 7pm.

The Brick Works 190 E 2nd St ☎530/895-7700. Chico's premier live-music spot, hosting national touring acts and local bands. On nights without live music, sample the dance club where the DJ plays either country, progressive, or alternative music.

Broadway Heights 300 Broadway ☎530/899-8075. Formerly *Jasco's*, this modern upstairs establishment dishes up moderate California cuisine and healthy snacks.

Caffé Malvina 234 W 3rd St ☎530/895-1614. Italian restaurant with moderately priced pasta and fish, plus some cheaper specials.

Chada Thai downstairs at 117b W 2nd St ☎530/342-7121. Authentic, and predominantly vegetarian, Thai cuisine at very reasonable prices, especially at lunchtime. Closed Sunday.

Chico Brewhouse 250 Cohasset Rd ☎530/894-2149. A winning combination of moderately priced California cuisine and fine beers microbrewed on site with a relaxed atmosphere and good rock soundtrack. Over a mile north of downtown via The Esplanade.

Franky's 506 Ivy St ☎530/898-9948. Inexpensive freshly made pasta and pizza, a staple diet for students and locals alike.

Jack's Family Restaurant 540 Main St ☎530/343-8383. 24-hr diner, a bit on the greasy side, but good for breakfasts and late-night munchies.

Karim Restaurant 14066 Hwy-99 ☎530/343-0593. Five miles north of town, this is the place for tasty Arabian food such as kebabs and some spicier dishes from further east.

La Hacienda Inn 2635 Esplanade ☎530/893-8270. *Bon Appetit* and *Gourmet* magazines have done features on this Mexican restaurant's special pink sauce, known to locals as "Heroin Sauce" for its addictive sweet flavor. Try it on a tostada, but be warned – you may not be able to stop.

LaSalle's 229 Broadway ☎530/893-1891. The place in Chico to down large quantities of beer, play pool, and listen to live rock bands.

Madison Bear Garden 316 W 2nd St ☎530/891-1639. A place for swigging beer with students from the nearby campus. Burgers, buffalo wings, and the like are also served.

Riley's 702 W 5th St ☎530/343-7459. Catch the ballgame on one of the many TV screens and hang out with the enthusiastic students at the most popular sports bar in Chico.

Sierra Nevada Brewing Company 1075 E 20th St ☎530/893-3520. The bar food is unexceptional, but the pale ale, porter, stout, and seasonal brews are a strong draw. There's usually jazz on Mondays and good local bands some weekends.

Tres Hombres 100 Broadway ☎530/342-0425. Large restaurant popular with students for the wide selection of margaritas. Reasonably priced burritos, quesadillas, tostadas, and tacos in a fun environment. Dinner until 10pm every night, drinks until 2am on weekends. Live jazz Sunday afternoons.

Red Bluff and Corning

The largest town in Tehama County, **RED BLUFF**, 45 miles north of Chico on Hwy-99, holds little of interest to travelers save for its proximity to Lassen Volcanic National Park. The Greyhound **bus** stops in front of the *Salt Creek Deli*, at the junction of Hwy-36 and Antelope Road (Hwy-99), but then heads into town for the junction with I-5, leaving no reliable form of public transportation into Lassen itself. Despite its favorable location on the Sacramento River, Red Bluff today is known more as a gas-and-lodging stop before the fifty-mile drive into Lassen along Hwy-36 or the push north to Redding and Mount Shasta on I-5. If you find yourself staying over, there's a reasonable selection of **motels** for $50 per night or less along Main Street – among them the *Crystal Motel*, 333 S Main St (530/527-1021, ⓦwww.redbluffcrystalmotel.com; ❷), and the *Lamplighter Lodge*, 210 S Main St (℗530/527-1150; ❷) – and a handful of diners and burger joints in town. The one classier **restaurant** is the *Raging Fork*, 500 Riverside Way (℗530/529-9453), which serves great grilled steak and ribs on its patio overlooking the river by the bridge into town. You may consider visiting the **Kelly-Grigs House Museum**, 311 Washington St (Thurs–Sun 1–4pm; donation suggested), where there's an exhibit on Ishi, "the last wild Indian," who appeared out of what is now the Ishi Wilderness in 1911 and was feted until his death in 1916. Pick up more information from the **Chamber of Commerce**, 100 Main St (Mon 8.30am–4pm, Tues–Thurs 8.30am–5pm, Fri 8.30am–4.30pm; ℗530/527-6220, or 1-800/655-6225, ⓦwww.redbluffchamberofcommerce.com). There are a number of antique shops to browse in and Gaumer's, on the I-5 side of the bridge at 78 Belle Mill Rd (Mon–Fri 9am–5pm; free; ℗530/527-6166), is really a jeweler's with an on-site **gemology museum**, displaying hundreds of precious stones, mining equipment, a lapidary workshop, and collection of corals and ammonites. The star exhibit is a sparkly 4ft-tall amethyst cave from Brazil.

If you bypass Chico and enter Tehama County from the south on I-5, an alternative stop for gas and provisions is **CORNING**, home of the celebrated **Olive Pit**, 2156 Solano St, just east off the interstate (℗530/824-4667 or 1-800/654-8374, ⓦwww.olivepit.com). This only-in-America store and restaurant sells jars of olives, olive oil, garlic, almonds, and pickles, and has a good grill and ice-cream bar as well. Martini-lovers can get bottles of olive-juice mixer, and a free tasting bar allows a trip around the world via olives – from Brine Greek wholes to Napa Valley Wine queens to French pitted and Sicilian cracked. The anchovy-stuffed greens are a must, and pint jars average $3.50–5.

Plumas County

Many visitors traveling between Lake Tahoe and the Lassen/Mount Shasta region bypass the Sacramento Valley altogether by using Hwy-89, which winds its way through sparsely populated and scenically exquisite **PLUMAS COUNTY**. Although it boasts no major set-piece attraction, with only one stoplight and constant vistas of pine-clad ridges, grassy valleys, sparkling lakes, and trout-rich rivers, the county is quintessential rural California at its best. Geographically it is significant as the meeting point of the lofty Sierra and volcanic Cascade mountain ranges. The area was home to the hunter-gatherer **Maidu Indians** before white settlers flooded into the valleys when gold frenzy took hold in the mid–nineteenth century, followed by a substantial number of Chinese. The veins of the precious metal were never as rich as those to the south, however, so the prospectors left and the **timber** industry soon took over as the prime economic factor. That too has since gone into decline, leaving farming as the prime source of income for the few inhabitants, along with a smattering of tourism.

Coming from the south, you pass through the missable golfing and retirement paradise of Graegle before Hwy-89 combines with Hwy-70 coming in from the east to form part of the **Feather River National Scenic Byway** and lead you to the county seat and commercial hub of **Quincy**, whose old town merits a wander. Further north Hwy-89 continues solo through the cattle-grazing land of the **Indian Valley**, past the lazy town of **Greenville** to the recreational area of **Lake Almanor**, within easy striking distance of Lassen Volcanic National Park, whose snow-capped peaks are visible in the distance.

Quincy

Nestled on the lower western slopes of the northernmost reaches of the Sierra montains, **QUINCY** is a pleasant town, divided by a hill into two distinct halves. Modern and functional East Quincy is not especially appealing but the blocks surrounding West Main Street in Quincy proper present some fine examples of Victorian architecture and are worth stopping to look around. Behind the grand old Neoclassical **Courthouse**, which stands proudly near the junction where the highway through town veers from West Main Street into Crescent Street, you can visit the **Plumas County Museum**, 500 Jackson St (summer only Tues–Sat 8am–5pm, Sun 11am–4pm; $2; ☎530/283-6320, ⓦwww.countyofplumas.com). Inside you will find informative displays on the area's Indian culture, the story of its settlement, and on natural history, while the grounds contain an old buggy and an authentic 1890s gold-miner's cabin.

For information, you have a choice between the **Chamber of Commerce**, 464 W Main St (Mon–Fri 9am–noon & 1–4.30pm; ☎530/283-0188 or 1-877/283-6320, ⓦwww.psln.com/qchamber), and the more comprehensive **Plumas County Visitors Bureau** on the northern edge of town at 550 Crescent St (☎530/283-6345 or 1-800/326-2247, ⓦwww.plumascounty .com). Of several **motels** around town, the best mix of location and economy is the *Gold Pan Motel*, 200 Crescent St (☎530/283-3686 or 1-800/804-6541; ❷), while among the **B&Bs** in the old town *The Feather Bed*, 542 Jackson St (☎530/283-0102 or 1-800/696-8624, ⓦwww.featherbed-inn.com; ❺), and *Ada's Place*, 562 Jackson St (☎530/283-1954, ⓦwww.adasplace.com; ❺), are both comfortable and suitably atmospheric. If you're hankering for a Wild West experience, horse riding, fishing, and hiking are all included in the cost of a night's stay at *Greenhorn Creek Guest Ranch* (☎530/283-0930 or 1-800/334-6939, ⓦwww.greenhornranch.com; ❽), twelve miles east of town, a mile and a half from the highway at 2116 Greenhorn Ranch Rd. **Eating** choices are not spectacular in Quincy but you can grab a filling breakfast or lunch at the *Court-house Café*, 525 W Main St (☎530/283-3344), bang opposite – you guessed it – the Courthouse, or enjoy a more upscale meal nearby at *Moon's* Italian steakhouse, 497 Lawrence St (☎530/283-0765). East Quincy offers a few cheap and cheerful joints such as *Round Table Pizza*, 60 E Main St (☎530/283-4545), and the *Mi Casita* Mexican, 875 E Main St (☎530/283-4755).

Northern Plumas County

Leaving Quincy behind, Hwy-70 soon peels off to the left and continues to follow the middle fork of the Feather River southwest, while Hwy-89 meanders in a northerly direction through the rich grassy meadows, ranches, and farms of the **Indian Valley** towards the old mining town of **Greenville**, 23 miles on from Quincy. A further nine miles brings you close to the western shore of **Lake Almanor**, an increasingly popular destination for boaters and families, and its main settlement of **Chester** at the northern end.

Greenville

Although it now depends more on cattle ranching and the felling of Christmas trees, sleepy **GREENVILLE** still celebrates its mining heritage every summer with the **Gold Digger Days** festival that takes place on the third weekend of July. For the rest of the year it remains in its slumbers but its quietude and idyllic countryside setting can still make a pleasant spot to break your journey. There's not much to see since the sole museum closed down several years ago, but just wandering along Main Street can give you a sense of the town's workaday past. If you stop for a bite to **eat**, the bar food at the *Way Station Dinner House & Tiki Bar* (☎530/284-6018), on the corner of the central Hwy-89/Main Street junction, or burgers and pizza from *Mountain Valley Pizza* (☎530/284-6680) at 116 Ann St (Hwy-89) will have to suffice. If you want to use the town as a base for some hiking in the surrounding picturesque **INDIAN VALLEY**, the only real and unexpected option is the English-literature-themed *Yorkshire House B&B*, 421 Main St (☎530/284-1794, ⓦwww.yorkshirehousebb.com; ❹).

Lake Almanor and Chester

LAKE ALMANOR, created in 1914 by the Great Western Power Company damming the north fork of the Feather River, stands at an elevation of 4500ft and covers fifty-two square miles, making it the largest of Plumas County's many lakes. It is also here that the Cascades and the Sierras truly meet. The clear blue waters reach a comfortable seventy-five degrees in summer, rendering it ideal for all sorts of **watersports**. Numerous resorts ring the pine-forested shoreline of the lake and most rent equipment for all sorts of water-based activities from high-speed water-skiing to leisurely fishing, as well as providing a range of **accommodation** possibilities. Several such enterprises are, in anticlockwise order: *Plumas Pines Resort*, on the west shore at 3000 Almanor Drive West, Canyon Dam (☎530/259-4343, ⓦwww.plumaspinesresort.com; ❸), which has motel-style rooms, cabins, and RV slots ($22), as well as food at its own *Boathouse Grill*; the friendly *Dorado Inn*, on the east shore at 4379 Hwy-147 (☎530/284-7790, ⓦwww.doradoinn.com; ❹), which offers great sunsets and a swimming pontoon; and on the peninsula that juts out from the north shore, *Knotty Pine Resort*, 430 Peninsula Drive (☎530/596-3348; ❸), whose half-dozen cabins are nicely situated. For **campers** there are simple sites all over the lake that are usually let on a first-come-first-served basis but some can be booked through the US Forest Service (☎1-800/280-2267, ⓦwww.ReserveUSA.com). Of the reasonable **restaurants** dotted round the lake, *BJ's BBQ & Deli*, near Hamilton Branch at 3881 Hwy-A13 (☎530/596-4210), offers good home-style prime rib and halibut, while the *Peninsula Grill* at 401 Peninsula Drive on the peninsula (☎530/596-3538) does tasty seafood, steaks, and pasta.

At the northwest corner of the lake, the only town on its shores, **CHESTER**, is a relaxed place with a splendid setting and a selection of amenities. You can get information on the whole region at the **Chamber of Commerce**, 529 Main St (Mon–Fri 9am–4pm, summer only Sat 9am–2.30pm; ☎530/258-2426 or 1-800/350-4838, ⓦwww.chester-lakealmanor.com). The town's small **museum**, showcasing local history and Maidu Indian basketry, is located inside the library at 210 First Ave (Mon–Wed & Fri 10am–1pm & 1.30pm–5.30pm, Thurs noon–5pm & 6–8pm; free; ☎530/258-2742). Of the dozen places to **stay** the *Chester Manor Motel*, 306 Main St (☎530/258-2441 or 1-888/571-4885, ⓦwww.chestormanor.com; ❷), and *Antlers Motel*, 268

Main St (☎530/258-2722 or 1-888/469-7829; ❷), are both fairly basic but reliable, while the *Cinnamon Teal* B&B, 227 Feather River Drive (☎530/258-3993; ❹), provides more ambience. Two miles east of town on Hwy-36, *North Shore Campground* (☎530/258-3376, ⊛www.northshorecampground.com) is the biggest **campsite** on the lake with tent spaces for $25. By way of **restaurants** *Carol's Ranch House*, 669 Main St (☎530/258-4226), serves good breakfasts and meaty meals, while *Arky's*, 300 Main St (☎530/258-2560), bashes out American classics and ice cream all day. *Ming's Dynasty*, 605 Main St (☎530/258-2420), provides copious portions of Chinese favorites. *Three Beans Coffee House* at 150 Main St (☎530/258-3312) is the place to head for a caffeine fix or light snack like a bagel.

Lassen Volcanic National Park

About fifty miles over gently sloping plains east from Red Bluff on Hwy-36, the 106,000 acres that make up the pine forests, crystal-green lakes, and boiling thermal pools of the **LASSEN VOLCANIC NATIONAL PARK** are one of the most unearthly parts of California. A forbidding climate, which brings up to fifty feet of snowfall each year, keeps the area pretty much uninhabited, with the roads all blocked by snow and (apart from a brief June to October season) completely deserted. It lies at the southerly limit of the Cascades, a low, broad range which stretches six hundred miles north to Mount Garibaldi in British Columbia and is characterized by high volcanoes forming part of the Pacific Circle of Fire. Dominating the park at over 10,000ft is a fine example, **Mount Lassen** itself, which – although quiet in recent years – erupted in 1914, beginning a cycle of outbursts which climaxed in 1915 when the peak blew an enormous mushroom cloud some seven miles skyward, tearing the summit into chunks that landed as far away as Reno. Although nearly ninety years of geothermal inactivity have since made the mountain a safe and fascinating place, scientists predict that of all the Californian volcanoes, Lassen is the likeliest to erupt again.

Arrival and information

Lassen is always open ($10 per vehicle for seven days, $5 per hiker or biker), but you'll have a big job ahead of you if planning to get in or around without a car. During the winter, when the roads in the park are almost always shut down due to snow, a car won't do you much good either – snowshoes and cross-country skis are popular modes of transportation. Public transportation really isn't an option, seeing as the "mail truck" of Mount Lassen Motor Transit (Mon–Sat from 8am; ☎530/529-2722) from Red Bluff only reaches **Mineral**, some eight miles short of the park's southwestern entrance. From Mineral, Hwy-89 leads through Lassen to the northern entrance at the junction of Hwy-44 and Hwy-89 near Manzanita Lake.

The Park Service has its **headquarters** in Mineral (summer daily 8am–4.30pm; winter Mon–Fri 8am–4.30pm; ☎530/595-4444, ⊛www.nps.gov/lavo), where you can get free maps and information (there's a box outside when it's closed, and they'll leave your backcountry permits here if you arrive late), including the *Lassen Park Guide*. The main **visitor center** (June–Aug daily; May & Sept Sat & Sun 9.30am–5.30pm; ☎530/595-4444 ext 5180) is at Manzanita Lake, just inside the northern entrance, and occupies the same building as the Loomis Museum (see p.832).

LASSEN VOLCANIC
NATIONAL PARK

2 miles

N

CARIBOU

WILDERNESS

Hat Creek & Burney (89)

44

Redding (89)

Chester & Quincy

Chester

Red Bluff, Mineral & Chico (89)

LASSEN NATIONAL FOREST

LASSEN
NATIONAL
FOREST

LASSEN
NATIONAL
FOREST

Widow
Lake

Butte
Lake

Cinder Cone
6907 ft

Snag
Lake

Juniper Lake
Primitive

Juniper
Lake

Horseshoe
Lake

Cluster
Lakes

Summit Lake
North

Summit Lake

Summit Lake South

Ranger
Station

PACIFIC CREST TRAIL

Warner Valley

Drakesbad Guest Ranch

Boiling
Springs
Lake

Devil's
Kitchen

Emigrant
Pass

Hot Rock

Devastated
Area

Crags Overflow

Lost Creek

NOBLES EMIGRANT TRAIL

Crags Lake

CHAOS CRAGS

Lassen Peak
10457 ft

Kings Creek

Kings
Creek

Bumpass
Hell

LITTLE
HOT
SPRINGS
AREA

Mill Creek
Falls

Lake
Helen

Southwest

i

Sulphur
Works

Ridge
Lakes

Lassen
Chalet

Brokeoff
Mountain
9235 ft

Reflection
Lake

Manzanita
Lake

Manzanita Lake

Visitor Center
and Museum

Accommodation

The only way to **stay** inside the Lassen park is to camp (see box, p.832), but even in August night temperatures can hover around freezing, and many people prefer to stay in one of the resorts and lodges that pepper the surrounding forest. To be sure of a room in the popular summer months, it pays to book well ahead.

Childs Meadow Hwy-36, nine miles southeast of southwest entrance ℡ 530/595-3383 or 1-888/595-3383, ⓦ www.childsmeadowresort.com. One of the few choices on this side of the park, scenic and friendly *Childs Meadow* offers basic motel accommodation (❸), more comfy chalet rooms ($300 for two nights), tent sites for $15, and an on-site café.

Hat Creek Resort Hwy-89, Old Station, eleven miles northeast of the northern entrance ℡ 530/335-7121, ⓦ www.hatcreekresort.com. A complex of motel units and fancier cabins with kitchens (two-day minimum stay), plus a restaurant on site. ❷

Lassen Mineral Lodge Hwy-36, Mineral, nine miles southwest of the southwest entrance on Hwy-36 ℡ 530/595-4422, ⓦ www.minerallodge .com. Unspectacular base-rate rooms and considerably more comfortable family ones for not much more. There's a general store, restaurant, and bar on site, as well as tent sites for $16. ❸

Mill Creek Park Mill Creek Road, Shingletown, fifteen miles west of the northern entrance ℡ 530/474-5384. Set amid pines and cedars, simple cabins with cold-water kitchenettes cost $35, those with hot water and bath $10 more, and space at the campground is $12. ❶

Padilla's Rim Rock Ranch Resort 13275 Hwy-89, Old Station, eleven miles northeast of the northern entrance ℡ 530/335-7114. A collection of cabins of varying standards, the best sleeping up to six ($100), dotted around a meadow. Closed November to March. ❷

Weston House Red Rock Road, Shingletown, nineteen miles west of the northern entrance ℡ 530/474-3738, ⓦ www.westonhouse.com. One of the nicest B&Bs in all of California, with six elegant rooms beautifully sited on a volcanic ridge with pool and deck, overlooking the Ishi National Wilderness Area. ❻

The Park

Unlike most other wilderness areas, you don't actually need to get out of the car to appreciate Lassen, as some of the best features are visible from the paved Hwy-89 that traverses the park. A thorough tour should take no more than a few hours. Pick up a copy of the *Road Guide: Lassen Volcanic National Park* ($5) in the visitor center.

Starting from the southwest entrance, you'll pass the trailhead to **Brokeoff Mountain**, a six-mile round-trip hike through wild flowers. Next is the **Lassen Chalet**, the only place to get food and, in winter, limited skiing facilities in the park. The first self-guiding trail is just up ahead – follow your nose and the **Sulfur Works** can be reached via a 200-foot boardwalk around its steaming fumaroles and burbling mud pots. The winding road climbs along the side of Diamond Peak before edging **Emerald Lake** and Lassen's show-stealer, **Bumpass Hell**, named after a man who lost a leg trying to cross it. This steaming valley of active pools and vents that bubbles away at a low rumble can be traversed on a flat, well-tended trail that loops three miles to boardwalks that put you right in the middle of the stinky action. Recall the fate of Mr Bumpass, however, and stay on the trails; the crusts over the thermal features are brittle and easy to break through, leaving you, literally, in hot water. Across the road from Bumpass Hell's parking lot, the trails around the icy-green glassy surface of Emerald Lake are also spectacular, though in much quieter fashion; the lake itself resembles a sheet of icy green, perfectly still and clear but for the snow-covered rock mound which rises from its center. The lake approaches swimmable temperatures only during summer.

During the few months of the year when conditions are suitable for camping, this is by far the best accommodation option. All **developed campgrounds** in the park are listed below and operate on a first-come-first-served basis, not a problem except on midsummer weekends. Most remain open July to September. Remember that Lassen is **bear country**; follow the posted precautions for food and waste storage, and make your presence known when hiking.

Primitive camping requires a free **wilderness permit** obtainable in advance from the park headquarters in Mineral (see p.829), or in person from the visitor centers and entrance stations. There is no self-registration and chosen sites must be a mile from developed campgrounds and a quarter of a mile from most specific sites of interest. In the surrounding **Lassen National Forest**, camping is permitted anywhere, though you'll need a free permit to operate a cooking stove or to light a fire; these are sometimes refused in the dry summer months. In addition, there are a couple of dozen developed sites strung along the highways within thirty miles of Lassen, most charging between $10 and $20.

Butte Lake 6100ft. In the far northeast corner of the park, accessed by Hwy-44. Can accommodate trailers and has a boat launch. $14

Juniper Lake 6800ft. In the far southeastern corner of the park, with good hiking trails nearby and swimming in the lake. Drinking water must be boiled or treated. $10

Manzanita Lake 5900ft. By far the largest of the Lassen campgrounds and the only one with a camp store (8am–8pm), firewood for sale ($6), 24-hour showers (bring quarters), and a laundry. Trailers allowed and boat launch facilities available. Rangers run interpretive programs from here. Open May 23 to snow closure. $16

Southwest 6700ft. Small tent-only campground by the southwest entrance on Hwy-89 with walk-in sites, water, and fire rings. Open year-round if you are equipped to brave it. $14

Summit Lake 6700ft. The pick of the Hwy-89 campgrounds, right in the center of the park and at the hub of numerous hiking trails. It's divided into two sections, the northern half can take trailers and is equipped with flush toilets, the southern half only vaults. There's swimming in the lake for the brave. $14–16

Warner Valley 5700ft. Off Hwy-89 in the south of the park, this is a beautiful site, but its distance from the road makes it only worth heading for if you're planning extended hiking in the region. $14

Just north of here, the road reaches its highest point (8512 feet) at the trailhead for **Lassen Peak**. The road then winds down to the flat meadows around **King's Creek**, whose trails along the winding water are popular for picnics. From roadmarker 32, a three-mile round-trip walk leads to the seventy-foot-tall **Kings Creek Falls**. At the halfway point you'll come to **Summit Lake**, a busy camping area set around a beautiful icy lake, from where you can start on the park's most manageable hiking trails. Press on further to the **Devastated Area**, where, in 1914, molten lava from Lassen poured down the valley, denuding the landscape as it went, ripping out every tree and patch of grass. Slowly the earth is recovering its green mantle, but the most vivid impression is still one of complete destruction. From here it's a gauntlet of pines to the northern entrance, site of **Manzanita Lake** and the **Loomis Museum** (summer daily 9am–5pm; winter Fri–Sun 9am–5pm; free), a memorial to Benjamin Loomis whose documentary photos of the 1914 eruption form the centerpiece of an exhibition strong on local geology – plug domes, composite cones, and cinder cones – and flora. An easy trail circles the lake, but so do many of the campers from the nearby campground: an early start is needed for any serious wildlife spotting.

Leaving Lassen, Hwy-44 heads forty miles west to Redding and I-5 or alternatively you can continue northwest on Hwy-89 one hundred miles to Mount

For a volcanic landscape, a surprisingly large proportion of the walking trails in the park are predominantly flat, and the heavily glaciated terrain to the east of the main volcanic massif is pleasingly gentle. Rangers will point you toward the **hiking routes** best suited to your ability – the park's generally high elevations will leave all but the most experienced walker short of breath, and you should stick to the shorter trails at least until you're acclimatized. For anything but the most tentative explorations, you should pick up a copy of *Lassen Trails* ($4.25) or the better, color *Hiking Trails of Lassen* ($16.50), which describe the most popular hikes.

Chaos Crags Lake (3.5 miles round-trip; 2–3hr; 800ft ascent). From the Manzanita Lake campground access road, the path leads gently up through pine and fir forest to the peaceful lake. An adventurous extension climbs a ridge of loose rock to the top of Chaos Crags, affording a view of the whole park.

Cinder Cone (13 miles round-trip; 1 day; 800ft ascent). Check with the rangers for the best seasonal starting point for this, Lassen's most spectacular hike, through the Painted Dunes and Fantastic Lava Beds before reaching Snag Lake. Can also be done as a 4hr hike from Butte Lake.

Lassen Peak (5 miles round-trip; 4hr; 2000ft ascent). A fairly strenuous hike from road marker 22 to the highest point in the park. Be prepared with water and warm clothing.

Manzanita Lake (1.5 miles; 1hr; flat). Easy trails on level ground make this one of the most popular short walks in the park.

Nobles Emigrant Trail (2.5 miles; 1–2hr; 200ft ascent). The most accessible and one of the more interesting sections of a trail forged in 1850 starts opposite the Manzanita Lake entrance station and meets Hwy-89 at marker 60. It isn't maintained, but is heavily compacted and easy going.

Paradise Meadows (3 miles round-trip; 3hr; 800ft ascent). Starting either at the Hat Creek parking area (marker 42) or marker 27, and passing Terrace Lake on the way, this hike winds up at Paradise Meadows, ablaze with wild flowers in the summer and a marvelous spot to pass an afternoon.

⑩

Shasta, stopping halfway at the breathtaking **McArthur–Burney Falls State Park** ($6 per vehicle; ☎530/335-2777). The park's centerpiece is a 129-foot waterfall, unique for the way the water spills over the rim from two different levels. A paved trail leads to the misty base and pool, and a 1.5-mile steep loop takes you downstream and then back up the other side of the pool to a bridge over the falls' headwater. The Pacific Crest Trail passes alongside nearby **Lake Briton**, and paddleboats, canoes, and rowboats can be rented at the park entrance. Plentiful **camping** amongst the black oaks is available for $15–20 a night.

Eating

For **food**, you don't have an awful lot to choose from in Lassen Volcanic National Park. There's a reasonable general store at *Manzanita Lake* campground (see box, opposite), and *Lassen Chalet* has a surprisingly good café (daily 9am–6pm), but beyond that you'll have to go outside the park and even then it's slim pickings. Some of the accommodations listed on p.831 have food. Otherwise, the *Coyote Grill* (☎530/335-7083) in tiny Old Station, eleven miles northeast of the park, does fair steaks and sandwiches.

Redding and around

At the heart of northern interior California, the sizeable modern town of **Redding** is often viewed as simply a hub for the region without much to merit dallying longer than it takes to refuel, grab a bite, or change transportation. It does, however, hold a certain degree of interest, making the most of its setting on the Sacramento River. **Shasta**, its diminiutive neighbour just to the west, a once-lively gold-mining town, provides a historical counterpoint and seems a world away from the urban sprawl nearby.

Redding

With a spreading expanse of strip malls along I-5, which have taken over from the ailing shopping center in its heart, and a concrete convention center at its gate, **REDDING** first appears to be a bit of an anomaly amidst the natural splendor of the northern interior. The region's largest city, with over 70,000 people, it has acted as a northern nexus since the late nineteenth century, when the Central Pacific Railroad came through. Today it remains, essentially, a crossroads, bulging with cookie-cutter motels and diners that service traffic heading east to Lassen, west to Whiskeytown-Shasta-Trinity National Recreation Area, north to Mount Shasta, and south to San Francisco. In recent years, however, the opening of a major museum and iconic new bridge across the central stretch of the Sacramento River have done more to detain passers-through. The one annual event that has long attracted substantial crowds is the **Kool**

April Nites classic-car meeting (☎1-800/874-7562, ⓦwww.koolaprilnites .com) on the second or third weekend of April, the only time you are likely to encounter problems finding a room.

Though fiercely hot in summer (100°F even in late September), the temperature drops forbiddingly in some of the surrounding areas in winter. Bear in mind that what looks like a mild day in Redding could turn out to be blizzard conditions a few miles up the road (and several thousand feet up a mountainside).

Arrival, getting around, and information

Considering its position at the crossroads of Northern California, **public transportation** in Redding is woefully inadequate, though at least the various modes of ground transport available all stop within easy walking distance of each other downtown. The Greyhound station is at 1321 Butte St (☎530/241-2070, ⓦwww.greyhound.com), while the local RABA **bus** system depot (☎530/241-2877, ⓦwww.ci.redding.ca.us/raba) is on California Street, the other side of the deserted shopping center, and the Amtrak station is right beside it. If you are in a hurry to get to Northern California and want to bypass the Bay Area, there are at least six United Express (☎1-800/241-6522, ⓦwww .united.com) **flight** connections daily from SFO to **Redding Municipal Airport** (☎530/224-4321), plus one or two daily from Seattle via Portland and sometimes Arcata/Eureka with Horizon Air/Alaska Air (☎1-800/547-9308, ⓦwww.horizonair.alaskaair.com). Typically, there is no public transportation from the airport (though some hotels have shuttles) and once here, you're not going to get to see much without a **car** anyway. Call Caltrans to check ahead for weather and road conditions (☎1-800/427-7623) and, if necessary, make extra provisions (de-icer, tire chains, and so on) in case of snowstorms.

The **Redding CVB**, 777 Auditorium Drive (Mon–Fri 8.30am–6pm, Sat 10am–4pm; ☎530/225-4100 or 1-800/874-7562, ⓦwww.visitredding.org), can give advice on accommodation in Redding, information on camping in the outlying areas, and details on where to rent camping equipment. For more specific information on the surrounding area and the whole of the northern interior and beyond, the new **California Welcome Center**, just off I-5 nine miles south of Redding at 1699 Hwy-273, Anderson (Mon–Fri 9am–5pm, Sat & Sun 10am–3pm; ☎530/365-7500 or 1-800/474-2782, ⓦwww .shastacascade.com), has a huge collection of maps and information, well-organized displays, and is staffed by helpful outdoor experts. As a general rule, Lassen National Volcanic Park is for hardier and more experienced hikers, and novices are pointed in the direction of the Whiskeytown-Shasta-Trinity National Recreation Area, where there are warmer climes and easier trails.

Accommodation

Motels are concentrated along Redding's old main strip, Market Street (Hwy-273), and Pine Street, while the smarter chain hotels tend to be along Hilltop Drive, Redding's newer service area east of I-5. A few B&Bs dotted around town round out the options.

Best Western Hilltop Inn 2300 Hilltop Drive ☎530/221-6100 or 1-800/336-4880, ⓦwww .bestwestern.com. This comfortable franchise – with its pool, sauna, and buffet breakfasts – succeeds in making you feel you are staying somewhere more personal than your average chain. Specials available most of the year. ❻

Deluxe Inn 1135 Market St ☎530/243-5141. This ultra-cheapie is fine for a night but hardly lives up to its name. ❶

Motel 6 1640 Hilltop Drive ☎530/221-1800 or 1-800/466-8356, ⓦwww.motel6.com. The most central of three outlets in the Redding area, as usual this one is basic but clean and efficient. ❸

Oxford Suites 1967 Hilltop Drive ℡ 530/221-0100 or 1-800/762-0133, ⓦ www.oxfordsuites .com. This great-value Californian chain offers smart and comfy suites at good rates. You can drink your two free happy-hour beverages in peace by the pool. ➍

Palisades Paradise 1200 Palisades Ave ℡ 530/223-5305, Ⓕ 223-1200. Friendly B&B with a fabulous view of the Trinity Mountains to the west across a bend in the river. Only two rooms, so book early. ➎

River Inn 1835 Park Marina Drive ℡ 530/241-9500 or 1-800/995-4341. Glorified motel, perhaps a little overpriced for the area because of its prime riverside location. ➍

Tiffany House 1510 Barbara Rd ℡ 530/244-3225, ⓦ www.bbonline.com/ca/tiffanyhouse. Just over a mile north of downtown, the *Tiffany* is a plush yet good-value B&B in a converted Victorian house, with a pricier detached cottage behind. ➎

The Town

Redding has been working hard of late on improving its image in order to tempt visitors to spend a day or two in its leafy urban environment before sampling the surrounding natural delights. Visitors are encouraged to stay in the newer areas near the freeway rather than in the dowdy old **downtown** area, which could really do with the proposed injection of cash to spruce it up. Though in no way unsafe, walking round it gives the distinct impression that it has seen better days. One place you might stop in at is the **Old City Hall Gallery**, 1313 Market St (Tues–Fri 9am–5pm, Sat 11am–3pm; free; ℡ 530/241-7320), which has rotating displays of works by local artists.

The centerpiece of the revitalisation process is the splendid new **Turtle Bay Exploration Park**, 800 Auditorium Drive (June–Sept daily 9am–5pm; Oct–May Tues–Sun 9am–5pm; $11; ℡ 530/243-8850 or 1-800/887-8532, ⓦ www.turtlebay.org), an ambitious $64 million project, which is now fully functional and has successfully combined the disparate exhibits from the site's two previous museums with plenty of new material into a fascinating inter-active whole. The new glass-and-wood structure blends seamlessly into the riverside environment and contains permanent displays on Native American culture, including a full-scale replica of an Indian bark-house, and the region's natural history and resources. The skillfully crafted **Visible River** exhibit, which allows you to enter a simulated limestone cave and view local water-creatures in a 24ft tank, creates the impression you are below a riverbank - a huge cottonwood tree even starts within the "river" and protrudes upwards into the museum. The River Lab enables you to play with natural materials and learn by experience how processes like erosion work on a large tilted table covered in sand, while the Exploration Hall and Art Gallery display changing cultural and artistic exhibitions, including detailed plans from the construction of the **Sundial Bridge** (see below). Also within the grounds, Paul Bunyan's Forest Camp includes logging and ecological displays and a summer butterfly house, while the projected 220-acre McConnell Arboretum, the last piece of the jigsaw, will conceal walking trails through oak savanna and wetlands when completed. The glass **café** at the west end of the main building gives uninterrupted views of the riverbank, which forms part of the newly extended **Sacramento River Trail**, a pleasant ten-mile loop designed for walkers and cyclists. The central stretch of the river opposite the Explora-tion Park is now dominated by the unique Sundial Bridge, designed by top Spanish architect **Santiago Calatrava**, whose other works include the arched roof of the Olympic Stadium in Athens. Opened to a great local fanfare on July 4, 2004, the gracefully curved and tapered 218ft mast at the northern end of this slim, translucent, glass-floored footbridge forms a sundial and is already becoming a true icon for the region, even the state.

Eating

Redding's **restaurants** are as ubiquitous as its motels, some of them 24-hour, many of them greasy diners or fast-food outlets, limited in appeal. There are, however, some noble exceptions.

Buz's Crab 2159 East St ☎530/243-2120. Just south of downtown, this local institution rustles up a vast range of fish and seafood delights at very moderate prices. Not to be missed.

CR Gibbs American Grille 2300 Hilltop Drive ☎530/221-2335. Part of the *Best Western* complex, this relaxed place offers pizza or classic meat and seafood dishes, which you can wash down with good draught ale or local wine.

De Mercurio's 1647 Hartnell Ave ☎530/222-1307. Hidden in a castle-shaped mall, this is Redding's most upscale restaurant, with an eclectic seasonal menu of high-quality French, Italian, and American dishes. Most entrees over $20.

The Hatchcover 202 Hemsted Drive ☎530/223-5606. Tasty steak and seafood are served on the riverside terrace at *The Hatchcover*, and there's a comfortable cocktail lounge inside.

Jack's Grill 1743 California St ☎530/241-9705. Popular restaurant which prepares fine grilled steak, and shrimp and chicken dishes for $10–15. Reservations not accepted, and though you'll probably have to wait for a table, it's well worth it. Closed Sunday.

Nannette's 1777 Market St ☎530/241-4068. A fairly chic but inexpensive bistro serving imaginative salads and main courses, combined with a quality bakery and café.

Taj Mahal 40 Hartnell Ave ☎530/221-4655. Authentic North Indian cuisine in a modern dining room; quite pricey dinner entrees, but great lunch buffet seven days a week.

Shasta

Huddling four miles west of Redding, the ghost town of **SHASTA** – not to be confused with Mount Shasta (see p.841) – is about the area's only option for historic entertainment, and it's a slim option at that. A booming gold-mining town when Redding was an insignificant dot on the map, Shasta's fortunes changed when the railroad tracks were laid to Redding in the late nineteenth century. Abandoned since then, it remains today a row of half-ruined brick buildings that were once part of a runaway prosperity, and literally the end of the road for prospectors. All roads from San Francisco, Sacramento, and other southerly points terminated at Shasta; beyond, rough and poorly marked trails made it almost impossible to find gold diggings along the Trinity, Salmon, and Upper Sacramento rivers, and diggers contented themselves with the rich pickings in the surrounding area, pushing out the local Native Americans in a brutal territorial quest for good mining land.

The **Courthouse**, on the east side of Main Street, has been turned into a museum (Wed–Sun 10am–5pm; $1), full of mining paraphernalia and paintings of past heroes, though best are the gallows at the back and the prison cells below – a grim reminder of the daily executions that went on here. The miners were a largely unruly lot, and in the main room of the Courthouse a charter lays down some basic rules of conduct:

> IV Thou shalt neither remember what thy friends do at home on the Sabbath day, lest the remembrance may not compare favorably with what thou doest here.

> VII Thou shalt not kill the body by working in the rain, even though thou shalt make enough money to buy psychic attendance. Neither shalt thou destroy thyself by "tight" nor "slewed" nor "high" nor "corned" nor "three sheets to the wind," by drinking smoothly down brandy slings, gin cocktails, whiskey punches, rum toddies and egg nogs.

From The Miners' *Ten Commandments*

The **Shasta State Historic Park** (unrestricted entry; ☎530/243-8194) straddles two blocks of Main Street, and is less grand than it sounds.

Indistinguishable ruins of brick buildings are identified by plaques as stores and hotels, and the central area, not much bigger than the average garden really, features miscellaneous mining machinery and a picnic area, along with a trail that loops around the back. On the whole, the park is a place to stretch your legs before moving further west.

Whiskeytown-Shasta-Trinity National Recreation Area

To the west and north of Redding lies the **Whiskeytown–Shasta–Trinity National Recreation Area**. Assuming the roads are open – they often get blocked off due to bad weather in winter – this huge chunk of land is open for public use daily, year-round. Its series of three impounded **lakes** – **Whiskeytown**, **Trinity**, and **Shasta** – have artificial beaches, forests, and camping facilities designed to meet the needs of anyone who has ever fancied themselves as a water-skier, sailor, or wilderness hiker. Sadly, during summer the area becomes completely congested, as windsurfers, motorboats, jet-skis, and recreational vehicles block the narrow routes which serve the lakes. But in the winter, when the weekenders have all gone, it can be supremely untouched, at least on the surface. In fact, there's an extensive system of tunnels, dams, and aqueducts directing the plentiful waters of the Sacramento River to California's Central Valley to irrigate cash crops for the huge agribusinesses. The lakes are pretty enough, but residents complain they're not a patch on the wild waters that used to flow from the mountains before the Central Valley Project came along in the 1960s.

Whiskeytown Lake

Of the three, **WHISKEYTOWN LAKE**, just beyond Shasta, is the smallest, easiest to get to, and inevitably the most popular. It is open all the time but day-use parking costs $5. Ideal for watersports, it hums with the sound of jet-skis and powerboats ripping across the still waters. Those who don't spend their holiday in a wetsuit can usually be found four-wheel-driving and pulling action-man stunts on the primitive roads all around. The best place for **camping** and **hiking** is in the **Brandy Creek** area – a hairy five-mile drive along the narrow J.F. Kennedy Memorial Drive from the main entrance and **Whiskeytown Visitor Information Center** on Hwy-299 (daily: summer 9am–6pm; winter 10am–4pm; ☏530/246-1225, ⊛www.nps.gov/whis), where you can pick up permits for primitive camping sites ($14) around the lake. There's a small store at the water's edge in Brandy Creek and three more developed campgrounds (summer $18) about a mile behind in the woods.

Trinity Lake and Weaverville

Northeast on Hwy-3 (off Hwy-299 forty miles west of Whiskeytown), **TRINITY LAKE** (officially called Clair Engle Lake, but not locally referred to as such) is much quieter, used by fewer in summer, and in winter primarily a picturesque stopoff for skiers on their way to the **Trinity Alps** area beyond, which in turn lead to the extensive **Salmon Mountains** range. There are several places to **stay** and enjoy the peaceful lapping waters or use as a base to get out onto them. Of these *Pinewood Cove*, 45110 Hwy-3 (☏530/286-2201

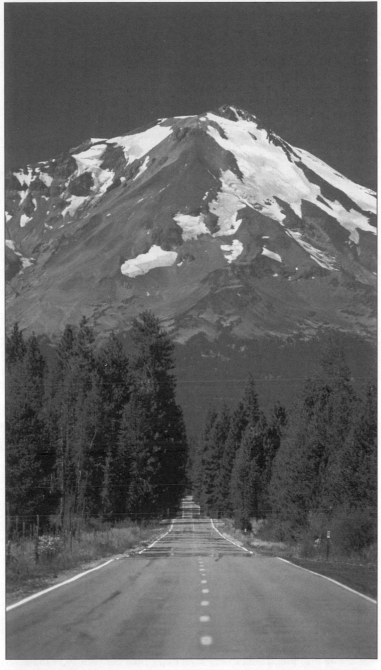

△ Mount Shasta

or 1-800/988-5253, ⓦwww.pinewoodcove.com; ⑤), rents out boats of various sizes and has $25 campsites and luxury cabins, which are unfortunately only available by the week in summer, as are the slightly more modest cabins further north at *Trinity Lake Resorts*, 45810 Hwy-3 (ⓣ1-800/255-5561, ⓦwww .trinitylakeresort.com; ⑤), which also has a full restaurant. At its southern end Lake Trinity squeezes through a narrow bottleneck to form the much slimmer and smaller Lewiston Lake, which can be reached by the backroad that cuts the corner between Hwy-299 and Hwy-3. You can camp for free on the grassy banks of the lake or stay in greater comfort at the *Old Lewiston Inn* (ⓣ1-800/286-4441, ⓦwww.theoldlewistoninn.com; ⑤) in the diminutive old mining town of Lewiston itself, on the same road.

Weaverville

Sadly, many people don't bother to stop in the small Gold Rush town of **WEAVERVILLE**, 43 miles west of Redding, where Hwy-3 branches north to Trinity Lake, while Hwy-299 continues a further one hundred miles west to Eureka (see p.810) and the coast. The town's distinctive brick buildings, fitted with exterior spiral staircases, were built to withstand fires – indeed, the fire station itself is particularly noteworthy. The main draw, though, is the **Joss House** on Main Street (Wed–Sun 10am–5pm; $2; ⓣ530/623-5284), a small Taoist temple built in 1874 by indentured Chinese mineworkers. A beautiful shrine, still in use today, it features a three-thousand-year-old altar and can be visited on a poor guided tour (last 4pm). Next door, the **J.J. Jake Jackson Museum** (May–Oct daily 10am–5pm; April, Nov & Dec daily noon–4pm; Jan–March Tues & Sat noon–4pm; free; ⓣ530/623-5211) exhibits artifacts from the Gold Rush. On the opposite side of the road look out for California's oldest still-functioning pharmacy, which stocks a brilliant selection of remedies in glass jars within original glass and wood cabinets.

You can **stay** in some style at the newly refurbished *Weaverville Hotel*, 205 Main St (ⓣ530/623-2222; ⑤), a century-old building. Alternatives include the renovated *49er Gold Country Inn*, 718 Main St (ⓣ530/623-4937, ⓦwww .goldcountryinn.com; ❸), or the friendly *Motel Trinity* (ⓣ530/623-2129 or 1-877/623-5454; ❷) on Main Street just south of Hwy-3, which has some rooms with hot tubs, but they cost twice as much as the basic ones.

For a **meal**, try the well-prepared chicken, steaks, and pasta for under $15 at the cozy *La Grange Café*, 315 Main St (ⓣ530/623-5325), or delicious Chinese food in the dark-red interior of the *Red Dragon*, 401 Main St (ⓣ530/623-30000), across from the Joss House, appropriately enough. The *New York Saloon*, 225 Main St (ⓣ530/623-3492), is a great place to mingle with the friendly locals over a glass of beer. For more information, consult the **Chamber of Commerce**, 211 Trinity Lakes Blvd, off Hwy-299 in Weaverville (summer Mon–Sat 9am–5pm; rest of year Mon–Fri 9am–4pm; ⓣ530/623-6101 or 1-800/487-4648, ⓦwww.trinitycounty.com), though these hours are somewhat erratic.

Shasta Lake

East of the other two, eight miles north of Redding, is **SHASTA LAKE**. The biggest of the three lakes – larger than the San Francisco Bay in fact – it's marred by the unsightly and enormous **Shasta Dam**, 465ft high and over half a mile long, bang in the middle. It is in fact twice the mass of the Hoover Dam and the second largest in America, made of enough concrete to send a foot-square strip round the planet several times. Built between 1938 and 1945 as part of the enormous Central Valley irrigation project, the dam backs up the

Sacramento, McCloud, and Pit rivers to form the lake, the project's northern outpost. Approached via US-151 (off I-5), you can visit the **powerhouse visitor center** (daily 9am–4pm) and take one of the free **tours** (6 daily in summer, 3–4 other seasons), though security is tight and you cannot take cameras or mobile phones with you. Still, it's an entertaining forty-five minutes' worth and the close-up views of the millions of gallons of water gushing down the face of the giant structure are memorable.

On the north side of the lake, the massive limestone formations of the **Shasta Caverns** (daily 2hr tours: June–Aug every 30min 9am–4pm; April, May, Sept hourly 9am–3pm; winter 10am, noon & 2pm; $18; ☎530/238-2341 or 1-800/795-2283, ⓦwww.lakeshastacaverns.com) are the largest in California, jutting above ground and clearly visible from the freeway. The interior, however, is something of a letdown – a fairly standard series of caves and tunnels in which stalactite and stalagmite formations are studded with crystals, flow-stone deposits, and miniature waterfalls. The admission price covers the short ferry journey from the ticket booth across an arm of Shasta Lake and the bus transfer on the other side. If you turn west instead of east at the exit to the caverns, within a couple of miles you reach two great **places to stay**. First, in the small hillside settlement of **O'Brien**, the *O'Brien Mountain Inn* (☎530/238-8026 or 1-888/799-8026, ⓦwww.obrienmountaininn.com; ❻) is a welcoming country B&B, whose star room is the detached $275 Tree House Suite on stilts over the forest. A little further on the *Bridge Bay Resort*, 10300 Bridge Bay Rd (☎530/275-3021 or 1-800/752-9669, ⓦwww.sevencrown.com; ❺), provides the only accommodation right on the lake in the shape of motel rooms, cabins, and larger suites; you can also dine with a view of the water at the resort's excellent *Tail of the Whale* restaurant. From Lake Shasta, I-5 crosses the world's highest double-deck bridge and races up towards Mount Shasta, an impressive drive against a staggering backdrop of mountains and lakes.

Mount Shasta . . . and Mount Shasta

When I first caught sight of it over the braided folds of the Sacramento Valley I was fifty miles away and afoot, alone and weary. Yet my blood turned to wine, and I have not been weary since.

John Muir, *about Mount Shasta*

The lone peak of the 14,162-foot **MOUNT SHASTA** dominates the landscape for a hundred miles all around, almost permanently snow-covered, hypnotically beautiful but menacing in its potential for destruction: it last erupted over two hundred years ago, but is still considered an active volcano. Summing up its isolated magnificence, Joaquin Miller once described it as "lonely as God and as white as a winter moon." Local lore is rich with tales of Lemurians – tall, barefoot men dressed in white robes – living inside the mountain, alongside their legendary neighbors the Yaktavians, who are said to be excellent bell-makers. Such tales have lent the mountain a bit of a Twilight Zone reputation, and numerous UFO sightings and other-worldly experiences have made Mount Shasta a center of the American **spiritualism** movement. This prominence was heightened in 1987 when 5000 people arrived to take part in the good vibes of the Harmonic Convergence, an attempt to channel the energies of sacred power spots into peace and harmony. More recently, the area hosted the Gathering of the Tribes and World Music Festival in October 2004. Not all is peaceful on the mountain, however, as hundreds of climbers annually attempt to ascend its icy heights, an activity that has resulted in deaths, usually caused from falls or from the ever-changing weather.

Just below the shadow of the behemoth sits the historic railroad town of **Dunsmuir** and, right up against the mountain, pleasant **Mount Shasta City**, a small town of shops, outfitters, spiritual bookstores, and fantastic restaurants. To the southeast, also commanding wonderful views of the mountain, is pretty little **McCloud**, while on the northern flank of the peak rests **Weed**, another tiny town that offers better views of Mount Shasta in summertime and access to Lava Beds National Monument. Further north towards the Oregon border, **Yreka** is more useful as an I-5 service stop than as a place to visit in its own right.

Arrival and information

Merely getting to Mount Shasta City without a car is a complex but rewarding journey: the nearest Greyhound **buses** will get you is Weed (see p.848 for details), seven miles north, while Amtrak **trains** stop six miles south in Dunsmuir, unfortunately in the middle of the night; from both towns, half a dozen or so daily STAGE buses (☎530/842-8295 or 1-800/247-8243) run up to the Mount Shasta Shopping Center, next to the *Black Bear Diner*, although you'll have to wait at least three hours for the first bus from Dunsmuir. STAGE also operates five daily services to McCloud. The **Chamber of Commerce**, 300 Pine St (daily: May–Sept 9am–5.30pm; Oct–April 10am–4pm; ☎530/926-4865 or 1-800/926-4865, ⓦwww.mtshastachamber.com), has a rather limited selection of brochures; you can obtain more comprehensive information on the entire county from the **Siskiyou County Visitor Bureau** (☎1-877/847-8777, ⓦwww.visitsiskiyou.org), although there is no office to visit here.

Accommodation

Mount Shasta City has no shortage of **accommodation**, and reservations should only be necessary on weekends in the height of summer. Mount Shasta Cabins & Cottages, 500 S Mount Shasta Blvd (☎530/926-5396 or 1-888/565-9422, ⓦwww.mtshastacabins.com), is a useful agency with a wide range of cabins and houses in the area. **Campgrounds** abound in the surrounding area, but few have full amenities (hot showers are vital when the mercury drops).

Hotels, motels, and B&Bs

Alpenrose Cottage Guesthouse 204 E Hinckley St ☎530/926-6724, ⓦwww.snowcrest.net/alpenrose. A top-quality and friendly hostel-style guesthouse with a relaxed atmosphere and a great deck for watching the sunset over Mount Shasta immediately behind. Only double rooms, which are let out at $30 (half-price) to lone travelers, if you are prepared to share. Follow the KOA signs a mile north on North Mount Shasta Boulevard. ❸

Best Western Tree House 111 Morgan Way ☎530/926-3101 or 1-800/545-7164, ⓦwww.bestwestern.com. One of the more attractive and intimate members of the international chain with all the usual amenities. Close to downtown too. ❺

Cold Creek Inn 724 N Mount Shasta Blvd ☎530/926-9851 or 1-800/292-9421, ⓦwww.coldcreekinn.com. Nicely refurbished motel, an easily walkable few blocks to downtown. Good value. ❸

Dream Inn 326 Chestnut St ☎530/926-1536 or 1-877/375-4744, ⓦwww.dreaminnmtshastacity.com. Very central and good-value B&B, a block east of Mount Shasta Boulevard, in a Victorian house with all the usual trappings. ❹

Mount Shasta Ranch B&B 1008 W A Barr Rd ☎530/926-3870, ⓦwww.stayinshasta.com. A stylish ranch house with spacious rooms, a hot spring, and a great view of Mount Shasta. The cheaper rooms have shared bathrooms. ❷

Travel Inn 504 S Mt Shasta Blvd ☎530/926-4617, ⓦwww.shastaweb.com/travelinn. Decent, clean motel with basic rooms at bargain rates. ❸

MOUNT SHASTA

0 — 1 mile

Weed & Yreka ▲   ▲ Black Butte   ▲ Mt Shasta

VILLAGE DRIVE
BUTTE AVE.
EVERITT MEMORIAL HIGHWAY
ROCKFELLOW DRIVE
LASSEN LANE
HINCKLEY ST.
KOA Campground ⛺ **A**
CHESTNUT ST.
PINE ST.
ALMA STREET
LAKE STREET
WASHINGTON DRIVE
ADAMS DRIVE
HILL ROAD
OLD STAGE ROAD
Big Springs Creek
B ②①
②
Mt Shasta Ranger District Office ③ **C**
④
ⓘ
McCLOUD AVE.
S. MOUNT SHASTA BLVD.
WASHINGTON DRIVE
LAKE ST.
⑤ **D**
HATCHERY LANE
State Fish Hatchery   **Sisson Museum**
Wagon Creek
Browns Lake
Cold Creek
5
OLD STAGE ROAD
OLD McCLOUD RD.
E **6**
7
N
SHASTA NATIONAL FOREST
SHASTA NATIONAL FOREST
W. REAM AVE.
F
N. SHORE ROAD

10

NORTHERN CALIFORNIA | Mount Shasta . . . and Mount Shasta

Mount Shasta Ski Park, McCloud & (89) ▶
Redding & Dunsmuir ▶

RESTAURANTS
Black Bear Diner   5
Laurie's Mountain View Café   3
Lily's   7
Mike and Tony's   6
Suda Thai   1
Tolo Grill   4
Trinity Café   2

⛺ Lake Siskiyou Camp Resort

Lake Siskiyou

MOUNT SHASTA RESORT

Box Canyon Dam

ACCOMMODATION
Alpenrose Cottage Guesthouse   A
Best Western Tree House   D
Cold Creek Inn   B
Dream Inn   C
Mount Shasta Ranch B&B   F
Travel Inn   E

Camping

The most picturesque campground in the area is the woodland *Lake Siskiyou Camp Resort* ($18; ☏530/926-2618 or 1-888/926-2618), four miles southwest of town on a lake of the same name, where you can picnic, bathe, and go boating. More **primitive sites** tend to be free if there is no piped drinking water, though creek water is often available. The most useful of these is the walk-in *Panther Meadows* (7400ft; closed in winter), high up on the mountain at the end of the Everitt Memorial Highway, though *McBride Springs* ($10; 5000ft), being lower down the same road, tends to be open for longer. The fully equipped *KOA*, 900 N Mount Shasta Blvd (☏530/926-4029 or 1-800/736-3617), a few blocks from downtown, charges $17–22 per tent site and has basic cabins from $42.50.

The Town and around

Quite rightly, few people come to Mount Shasta for its museums, but in bad weather you might visit the otherwise missable **Sisson Museum**, 1 N Old Stage Rd (daily: June–Sept 10am–4pm; April, May & Oct–Dec 1–4pm; donation suggested; ☎530/926-5508), with a few examples of native basketware, a fair bit on pioneering life in the region, and some more diverting material on the mountain itself. The brown, rainbow, and eastern brook trout in the **fish hatchery** outside (daily April–Sept 8am–4pm; free; ☎530/926-2215) can be fed on food from a vending machine.

A couple of New Age **bookstores** along North Mount Shasta Boulevard provide the key to some of the town's more offbeat activities. Golden Bough Books at no. 219 (☎530/926-3228 or 1-877/674-7282), for example, has active bulletin boards and stacks of publications exhorting you to visit a sweat lodge or get in touch with the ascended masters. They provide an ever-changing list of metaphysics, astrology, and alternative-healing options as their practitioners and followers migrate in and out of town. Shasta Vortex Adventures, 310 N Mt Shasta Blvd (☎530/926-4326), is an interesting outfit, whose primary business is providing personalised spiritual tours of the mountain but they also offer other esoteric services. For a spot of **culture**, the Stage Door, 414 N Mt Shasta Blvd (☎530/926-1050, ⓦwww.stagedoorcabaret.com), is a small theater showcasing drama and music at the back of a relaxed coffee shop. An increasing number of galleries and gift shops are sprouting up too.

Mainly, though, Mount Shasta is full of outfits hoping to help you into the **outdoors**, from trout fishing to dog sledding to, of course, mountain climbing. Competition keeps prices reasonable and the options wide open. Obviously, there are a thousand ways to climb Mount Shasta, and these are covered in the box on p.846. Otherwise, Shasta Mountain Guides, 1938 Hill Rd (☎530/926-3117, ⓦwww.shastaguides.com), arranges jeep trips up the mountain and conducts rock- and ice-climbing courses for all levels, as well as backcountry skiing trips, all from $100 per day. For real thrills, whitewater rafting trips on the churning Upper Sacramento are offered by Turtle River Rafting (☎530/926-3223 or 1-800/726-3223, ⓦwww.turtleriver.com) and River Dancers (☎530/926-3517 or 1-800/926-5002, ⓦwww.riverdancers.com), both starting at $80 a day. Train enthusiasts should check out the elegant **Shasta Sunset Dinner Train**, which departs from the nearby town of McCloud (see p.847), nine miles southeast of Mount Shasta City on Hwy-89. Cars constructed in 1916 clack along east- and west-bound routes while you sit back and enjoy a full-course meal (3 hours; from $80; ☎530/964-2142 or 1-800/733-2141, ⓦwww.shastasunset.com).

Eating

Aside from a rash of fast-food outlets towards I-5, Mount Shasta's **eating** options are largely health–conscious, with vegetarian dishes featured on almost every menu. Hardy mountain types are amply catered for, too, with plenty of opportunities to stoke up on hearty fare before hitting the mountain heights. You can stock up on picnic supplies with the hand-crafted loaves from *The Oven Bakery* at 214 N Mt Shasta Blvd.

Black Bear Diner 401 W Lake St ☎530/926-4669. Wholesome family diner, a great place for heaped breakfasts or classic American dinners.
Laurie's Mountain View Café 401 N Mt Shasta Blvd ☎530/926-4998. Simple coffeehouse serving cooked breakfasts, bagels, and pasta with, as the name suggests, views of the mountain.
Lily's 1013 S Mt Shasta Blvd ☎530/926-3372. Moderately priced and consistently good restaurant serving California cuisine, vegetarian, and

Mexican dishes. Mains cost around $15, sand-wiches around $6.

Mike and Tony's 501 S Mt Shasta Blvd ☎530/926-4792. It may not look like much, but this excellent Italian restaurant specializes in home-made ravioli. It offers good wines, figs, and goat cheese; great martinis. Dinner only; closed Tues & Wed.

Suda Thai 531 Chestnut St ☎530/926-1276. Rather upmarket Thai restaurant serving exotic delicacies, including a fine range of curries, in comfortable surroundings. Closed Mon & Tues.

Tolo Grill 107 Chestnut St ☎530/918-9901. Mostly gyros and other Hellenic faves are available at this Greek joint in a quaint corner building. Closed Tues & Wed.

Trinity Café 622 N Mt Shasta Blvd ☎530/926-6200. The best place for quality international cuisine made from local produce. The menu changes weekly and fine microbrewed ales are available on tap.

Around Mount Shasta

Apart from Mount Shasta itself and the surrounding towns covered below, there are several other natural delights to explore, which you will certainly find less well-trodden in season than the main body of the mountain. Five miles north of town, the largely treeless cone of **Black Butte** (2.5 miles; 2–3hr; 1800ft ascent), offers a more modest alternative to climbing Mount Shasta. The switchback trail to this 6325ft volcanic plug dome is hard to find without the leaflet available from the ranger station or visitor center.

If you have time, you'd also be well advised to explore the beautiful trails that climb 4000ft up to the 225-million-year-old glacier-polished granite crags at the aptly named **Castle Crags State Park** (daily 8am–dusk; $6 per car; ☎530/235-2684), thirteen miles south of Mount Shasta along I-5. Campgrounds with full amenities are available for $17 per night (book through ReserveAmerica 1-800/444-7275) and primitive ones for $9 in the often deserted 6200-acre forested park.

Mount Shasta Ski Park (☎530/926-8610 or 1-800/754-7478, Ⓦwww .skipark.com), near McCloud on Hwy-89, has yet to establish itself on the ski circuit, so its lift tickets ($35) and rental charges for skis ($22), snowboards ($30), and snowshoes ($12) are quite reasonable. In summer, it transforms into some of the best **mountain-biking** territory in the region, with marked trails following the ski runs. A day-pass is $12, and bikes can be rented for $20 a day. There's also an artificial tower for climbing ($10 per day) and chairlift rides ($10). Half a mile before the Ski Park, Shasta Cove Stables (☎1-800/662-3529) offer **horse riding** from $35 during the summer months.

On the lower slopes, keep your eyes skinned for the inedible **watermelon snow**, its bright red appearance caused by a microbe which flourishes here – think Frank Zappa, just change the color. Most importantly, be prepared for **storms** on the mountain. Bring extra food, stove fuel, a good, wind-resistant shelter, and plenty of warm clothing. And if the weather does take a turn for the worse, don't hesitate to head back down the mountain – high-elevation storms sometimes last for days, with little or no visibility.

After a day or two trudging around or up Mount Shasta, **Stewart Mineral Springs** (Mon–Thurs & Sun 10am–6pm, Fri & Sat 10am–8pm; ☎530/938-2222, Ⓦwww.stewartmineralsprings.com; ➋) at 4617 Stewart Springs Rd off I-5 just north of Weed, provides welcome relief. Individual bathing rooms in a cedar and pine forest glade soothe your aches away for $20, less if you stay in the very affordable cabins, tepees ($24), or campground ($15) here. Just before you reach the springs, you can take Parks Creek Road to the top of the ridge, from where it's a ninety-minute hike along the **Pacific Coast Trail** to Dead Fall Lakes.

Even if you are only passing through the region, you'll be tempted to tackle Mount Shasta. Ambling among the pines of the lower slopes is rewarding enough, but the assault on the summit is the main challenge – and it can be done in a day with basic equipment and some determination.

Still, it's not a climb to be taken lightly, and every year several deaths occur and numerous injuries are sustained through inexperience and over-ambition. The wise will stick to the routes prescribed by the **Mount Shasta Ranger District Office**, 204 W Alma St (June–Aug daily 8am–4.30pm; Sept–May Mon–Fri 8am–4.30pm; ☎530/926-4511), which will insist that you obtain a **wilderness permit** (also self-issued outside the office when closed and at the trailhead; $15) and enter your name in the voluntary **climbers' register** before and after your ascent.

The mountain's isolation creates its own **weather**, which can change with alarming rapidity. In early summer, when most novice attempts are made, the snow cover is complete, and crampons and an ice axe are a requirement to get a good grip; later during the season, as the snow melts, patches of loose ash and cinder appear, making the going more difficult and the chance of falling rock greater. Only at the end of summer, with most of the snow melted, is there a chance of climbing safely without equipment. There are countless equipment rental agencies in town, such as The Fifth Season, 300 N Mount Shasta Blvd (☎530/926-3606, ⓦwww.thefifthseason.com), which has the following rental prices for two/three-day trips: boots ($26), crampons and ice axe ($20), mountain tent ($50), and sleeping bag ($18). They also provide a mountain weather forecast on ☎530/926-5555. House of Ski & Board, 316 Chestnut St (☎530/926-2359, ⓦwww.shastaski.com), offers much the same at very competitive rates.

Even for fit, acclimatized climbers **the ascent**, from 7000ft to over 14,000ft, will take eight to ten utterly exhausting hours. The easiest, safest, and most popular way up is via **Avalanche Gulch** – just follow the footprints of the person in front of you. Drive up the mountain on the Everitt Memorial Highway to the **Bunny Flat** trailhead at 7000ft. A gentle hour's walk brings you to **Horse Camp**, 7900ft, a good place to acclimatize and spend the night before your ascent – there's drinking water, toilet facilities, and a knowledgeable caretaker who can offer good advice about your impending climb. The return trip is done in four or five hours, depending on the recklessness of your descent: Mount Shasta is a renowned spot for **glissading** – careering down the slopes on a jacket or strong plastic sheet – a sport best left to those proficient in ice-axe arrests, but wonderfully exhilarating nonetheless.

Dunsmuir

One example of how the Shasta area looked in the past can be seen in the hamlet of **DUNSMUIR**, which is even quainter than Mount Shasta City. Situated ten miles south of Mount Shasta on a steep hill sloping down from I-5, Dunsmuir's downtown was bypassed by the freeway, essentially freezing the community in time. Now it makes its living as a historic railroad town, and the main drag, **Dunsmuir Avenue**, is lined with restored hotels and shops, many of them taking the train theme a bit too far; expect to see shopkeepers dressed as train engineers and business names like Billy Puffer Suites. Amtrak stops at the recently spruced up railway station, its last California halt before continuing north to Oregon. The **Visitors Bureau**, near Amtrak at 4118 Pine St (Wed–Mon 10am–4pm; ☎530/235-2177 or 1-800/386-7684), has updated train and STAGE schedules, but its volunteers are rather lackadaisical about opening hours.

Dunsmuir used to bill itself as a day-trip from Shasta, but recently realized that it had a quietude and natural wonders of its own. Foremost among these are the Mossbrae and Hedge Creek **waterfalls**, along the Sacramento River Canyon, beautiful spots for walks and picnics. To reach **Mossbrae**, drive north on Dunsmuir Avenue to Scarlet Way, crossing the bridge and railroad tracks to the parking area. Follow the walking trail along the train tracks for one mile until you get to the railroad bridge. Don't cross, but continue along the tracks through the trees and the falls are ahead. **Hedge Creek Falls** are accessible via the parking area at the North Dunsmuir exit on I-5.

If you are planning **to stay**, several B&Bs ply their trade around town, the most central being *The Dunsmuir Inn*, 5423 Dunsmuir Ave (T530/235-4543 or 1-888/386-7684; ❸). A good mile further north the *Cedar Lodge*, 4201 Dunsmuir Ave (T530/235-4331, Wwww.cedarlodgedunsmuir.com; ❶), is considerably cheaper. The most unique place to stay in the area is the *Railroad Park Resort* (T530/235-4440, Wwww.rrpark.com; ❹), nearly three miles south at 100 Railroad Park Rd; most of the accommodations are fashioned out of old railway cabooses, though there are also some cabins. Dunsmuir has been developing into something of a gourmet paradise of late, with a number of new upscale **restaurants**. The *Cornerstone Bakery Café*, 5759 Dunsmuir Ave (T530/235-2620), serves upmarket California-style cuisine, while equally pricey is *Sengthong's*, 5855 Dunsmuir Ave (T530/235-4770), which is the place for quality Vietnamese. Fine imaginative seafood dishes can be enjoyed at the *Salt H2O Café*, 5740 Dunsmuir Ave (T530/235-4988), and tasty Mediterranean fare is on the menu at *Café Maddalena*, 5801 Sacramento Ave (T530/235-2725). One place you can grab a cheaper snack is at the *Pizza Factory*, 5804 Dunsmuir Ave (T530/235-4849).

McCloud

Home to the famous *Sunset Dinner Train* (see p.844 for details), **McCLOUD** is a delightful little town with stunning views of Mount Shasta and it can make another good base for the area, especially if you plan to spend much time in the Ski Park (see p.847). The only cultural diversion is the small **Heritage Junction Museum** (May–Oct Mon–Sat 11am–3pm, Sun 1–3pm; free), loaded with a haphazard collection of bric-a-brac, memorabilia and woodcutters' gear. In the **accommodation** stakes the *McCloud Hotel*, right in town at 408 Main St (T530/964-2822 or 1-800/964-2823, Wwww.mccloudhotel.com; ❺), has smart rooms in a classy restored building and a fine restaurant, while an excellent B&B option just up the road is *Stoney Brook Inn*, 309 W Colombero Drive (T530/964-2300 or 1-800/369-6118, Wwww.stoneybrookinn.com; ❷), which has some shared bathrooms and particularly good single rates. The only motel in the vicinity is the *McCloud Timber Inn*, 153 Squaw Valley Rd (T530/964-2893; ❷), which boasts an attractive location and more spacious than average rooms. For a **meal** try the fine Italian and American food at *Raymond's*, 424 Main St (T530/964-2009), or the tasty and filling Mexican dishes at the *Briar Patch Restaurant*, on the south side of Hwy-89 at 140 Squaw Valley Rd (T530/964-2700), both evenings-only. *Briar Patch* also has the town's main bar, and the owner occasionally plays live music for the customers himself. For a daytime snack *Floyd's Frosty*, 125 Broadway (T530/964-9747), is a Fifties-style joint offering chunky burgers, thick shakes, and ice cream.

There's not much to do in the town itself, but the nearby **McCloud River Falls**, five miles east on Hwy-89, is a great spot for a picnic or gentle stroll. The falls, set amidst thick woods, are divided into three distinct sections, each about one mile from the next and connected by a riverside walking trail, but also accessible by road. If you're short of time, head for the more dramatic Middle

Falls; at *Fowlers*, near the Lower Falls, there is **camping**, often free because of problems with the water supply, while the Upper Falls boast a lovely picnic area. If you continue southeast on Hwy-89, you will eventually come to the more renowned and spectacular Burney Falls and, still further, Lassen Volcanic National Park (see p.829).

Weed

A gateway town to Klamath Falls, Oregon, and the Lava Beds National Monument, **WEED** can't compete with Mount Shasta City's hip charm. But, perhaps in a form of karmic justice, it gets the better view of the peak during the summertime. Too bad the tourism board couldn't leave it at that, instead of dressing up the place as a "historic lumber town" with the groaner of a slogan, "Weed love to see you." Those responsible can be found at the **Chamber of Commerce**, 34 Main St (summer daily noon–6pm; winter Mon–Fri noon–6pm; ⊤530/938-4624, Ⓦwww.weedchamber.com), along with further information on the area. Just off Main Street at 303 Gilman Ave, **Weed Historic Lumber Town Museum** (summer daily 10am–5pm; winter by appointment; donation suggested; ⊤530/938-0550, Ⓦwww.snowcrest.net/whm) occupies the former courthouse and outlines local history, primarily that of the lumber industry; it also contains a couple of fine old vehicles. The Greyhound **bus** office is at 628 S Weed Blvd (Mon–Sat 8.30am–4pm; ⊤530/938-4454 or 1-800/231-2222) and is also the nearest stop to Mount Shasta City. There are a couple of good budget **motels** and **eateries** in town, as well as the College of the Siskiyous, which is certainly California's prettiest campus owing to its views of the peak. In town, the *Hi Lo Motel & Café*, 88 S Weed Blvd (⊤530/938-2731, Ⓦwww .hilomotel.com; ❷), has decent rooms and a café that slings hash and eggs. On the northern end of Weed Boulevard, at no. 466, the *Motel 6* branch includes a nice outdoor pool and stunning sunrise views of Mount Shasta (⊤530/938-4101 or 1-800/466-8356, Ⓦwww.motel6.com; ❸). The best place for a meal is *Hungry Moose* (⊤530/938-4060), an excellent all-day diner located at 86 N Weed Blvd, or you can chill out with a healthier snack at *Buddha Belly Kitchen*, 51 Main St (⊤530/938-4366), which has a very loungeable lounge. *Papa's Place*, 203 Main St (⊤530/938-2277), is a friendly bar where you can drink beer with the locals and get a basic snack.

Five miles outside of town, north on US-97 on the way to Oregon and Lava Beds, the **Living Memorial Sculpture Garden** experience (unrestricted entry; donation suggested) is an intriguing remembrance of the Vietnam War. Artist Dennis Smith has created ten metal sculptures illustrating different aspects of an American soldier's experience in the war. Surrounding the art are about 53,000 pine trees, one for every American killed in Vietnam. The trees, art, silence, and position under Mount Shasta add up to a very moving experience.

Yreka

There's little to justify more than an hour or two in quiet, leafy **YREKA** (pronounced "Why-reeka"), twenty-five miles north of Weed on I-5, but it makes a pleasant break. The reason most people used to come here was to ride the Yreka Western Railroad, better known as the **Blue Goose**, a 1915 Baldwin steam engine pulling attractive carriages to and from the nearby historic town of Montague, but the service is currently suspended with no immediate prospect of restarting – you could always check Ⓦwww.yrekawesternrr.com for the current status. The **Siskiyou County Museum**, 910 S Main St (summer Tues–Sat 9am–5pm; $6; ☏530/842-3836), deserves some attention, particularly the outdoor section (closes 4pm) with its historic buildings – church, houses, and shops – transported here from around the county. Finally, there's a paltry collection of gold nuggets in the **County Courthouse**, 311 4th St (Mon–Fri 8am–5pm; free).

The **Chamber of Commerce**, 117 W Miner St (summer daily 9am–5pm; winter Mon–Fri 9am–5pm; ☏530/842-1649, ⓦwww.yrekachamber.com), issues maps for a self-guided Historic Walking Tour around Yreka's numerous Victorian homes. It can also help you find accommodation, not that you'll need any with plenty of chain motels around the I-5 and independent ones such as the *Econolodge*, 526 S Main St (☏530/842-4404, ⓦwww.econolodgeyreka .com; ❷), or the *Klamath Motor Lodge*, 1111 S Main St (☏530/842-2751 or 1-800/551-7255, ⓦwww.klamathmotorlodge.com; ❸). **Eating** is best done along the street at *Nature's Kitchen*, 412 S Main St (☏530/842-1136; closed Sun), not at the cutesy *Grandma's House*, which has an unfathomable, statewide appeal to elderly Americans whose RVs fill the parking lot. You can also get inexpensive Chinese and American food in the darkened dining room of the *China Dragon*, 520 Main St (☏530/842 3444). Yreka can be reached by STAGE **bus** (☏530/842-8295 or 1-800/247-8243) from Mount Shasta, Dunsmuir, and McCloud.

A worthwhile twenty-mile detour south of Yreka along Hwy-3 takes you to charming, turn-of-the-century **Etna**, recently voted one of twenty "dream towns" by *Outside* magazine, and it certainly does not disappoint. Its other great claim to fame is as home to the Etna Brewing Company, 131 Callahan St (closed Mon & Tues; ☏530/467-5277), a tiny microbrewery producing around one thousand barrels a year for local distribution, although it's increasing reputation has led to plans for expansion. There are usually four or five of the malty real ales and other beers available to taste, each and every one a beer drinker's dream, and you can usually take an impromptu tour; tasty bar food is also available. While here, check out the Fifties soda fountain in the Scott Valley Drugstore at the top of Main Street. And if you're really struck by the place, you can **camp** for free in the town park on Diggles Street or **stay** at the basic but comfortable *Etna Motel*, 317 Collier Way (☏530/467-5388; ❷). For expert guidance of the local wilderness and the possibility of staying in a yurt, contact Rusty Coleman of Mountain Spirit Adventures (☏530/467-5444, ⓦwww .users.sisqtel.net/mtspiritad), inside his *Corrigan's* bar at 412 Main St.

Lava Beds National Monument and around

After seeing Mount Shasta, you really should push on to the **LAVA BEDS NATIONAL MONUMENT**, which commemorates a war between the US and Modoc Indians in the far northeastern corner of the state. Carved out of the huge **Modoc National Forest**, it's actually a series of volcanic caves, which you can explore, and huge black lava flows with a history as violent as the natural forces that created it.

Lava Beds is one of the most remote and forgotten – and beautiful – of California's parks, with pungent yellow rabbit-brush blooming around the burnt rocks in autumn. It's in the heart of Modoc country, a desolate outback where cowboys still ride the range, and where, as the territory of one of the last major battles with the Native Americans, there is still a suspicious relationship between the settlers and the native peoples.

Today the Lava Beds region is inhabited only by the wild deer and three million migrating ducks who easily outnumber the trickle of tourists that make it this far. To the west and north, the **Klamath Basin National Wildlife Refuge** spreads over the border into Oregon. This stop on the Pacific Flyway draws birders and hunters alike for its millions of migratory guests, hoping to catch sight of a rare eagle. In 2000–1, the area became the focus of a **controversy** that made national news after the Department of Fisheries banned the tapping of water from the basin for irrigation after a bottom-feeding fish that lives there was put on the endangered species list. This led to direct protests from farmers whose livelihood was in turn endangered, especially because the area had already been suffering from drought. Unsurprisingly, the anti-environmental Bush administration came down on the side of the farmers by declaring that there needed to be an inquiry to decide if it was legal to withhold the water supply and the Deputy Secretary of the Interior even flew out to open the sluices. Nothing has changed since.

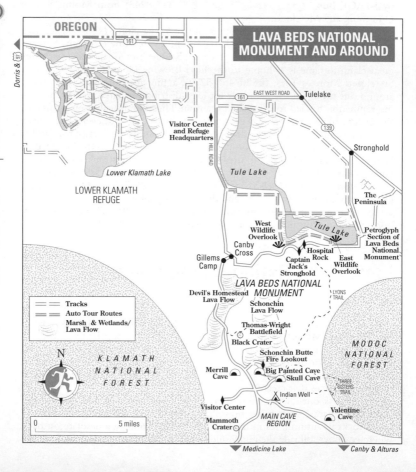

Park practicalities

Lava Beds National Monument ($10 per vehicle for seven days) is 160 miles northeast of Redding, and inaccessible without a **car**. It's a day-trip from Mount Shasta, one and a half hours away, but can be combined with camping, spelunking, and birdwatching for a much longer stay. The most tortuous route follows Hwy-89 to Bartle, then passes Medicine Lake (see p.854); the approach via Hwy-139 is easier, but the best and fastest is from Weed, following US-97 through Dorris and then via Hwy-161 through the Klamath Basin National Wildlife Refuge (see opposite).

Pick up an excellent **map** of the monument from the **visitor center**, just inside the southwestern entrance (daily: summer 8am–6pm; rest of year 8am–5pm; ☎530/667-2282, ⓦwww.nps.gov/labe). Close by, at Indian Wells, is the park's one **campground** ($10). All **wilderness camping** throughout the monument is free and no permits are necessary, but campers must pitch at least a quarter of a mile from any road, trail, or camping area, and fifty yards from any cave. Be warned, though, that elevation throughout the park ranges from 4000 to 5700 feet, and there's snow and freezing nights for most of the year, which can make camping uncomfortable.

Tulelake

The only **accommodation** near the park, and the one place to pick up supplies (the monument can only muster a soda machine), is at **TULELAKE**, fourteen miles north, which incidentally prides itself on being "the horseradish capital of the world." The near-deserted Main Street holds the extremely friendly and good-value *Fe's Bed & Breakfast*, no. 660 (☎530/667-5145 or 1-877/478-0184, ⓔelucena@cot.net; ②), while the only other option round town, the basic *Ellis Motel* (☎530/667-5342; ②), is half a mile north on Hwy-139 but not much cheaper, and should only be used as a standby. If birdwatching is your main concern and you want to stay near the Lower Klamath Refuge (see p.854), then the *Winona Lodge* (☎530/667-5158, ⓔslss@cot.net; ②) is your best bet – it also has a restaurant.

There are a couple of places to **eat** in town: *Mike and Wanda's*, just off Main Street at 423 Modoc Ave (☎530/667-3226) has filling meals in the café and bar sections and a more expensive menu in the dining room in between, while there is authentic inexpensive Mexican food at *Villapando's*, 337 Main St (☎530/667-2515). The area's top restaurant, however, is *Captain Jack's Stronghold* (☎530/664-5566), seven miles south on Hwy-139, which does good soups, steaks, and home-made pies. Nearby is the **Modoc Ranger Station** (Mon–Fri 8am–4.30pm; ☎530/667-2246, Ⓦwww.fs.fed.us/r5/modoc) with general information on the Modoc National Forest. Even if you have your own car, and it's unlikely you'll be here if you don't, you might consider taking one of the expert guided **tours** ($50–60, including lunch) conducted by Bob Galeoto of LuCena West Tours out of *Fe's B&B* (see above for contacts) in order to get the most out of the Lava Beds and Klamath Basin region.

There is one tourist attraction in town, the **Tulelake–Butte Valley Fair Museum of Local History** (Mon–Fri 9am–5pm, also Sat 9am–5pm in summer; $3), in the expansive fairgrounds at 800 S Main St. The newly created complex contains excellent displays on geological features, wildlife, history (especially the Indian wars and WWII internment), Native American culture, and current issues. The entry fee includes a one-hour interpretive **audio tour** to enhance your visit. Also within the grounds is the **Chamber of Commerce** information bureau (daily 8am–4.30pm; ☎530/667-5312, Ⓦwww.tbvfair.com). The fairgrounds host an enormous annual **fair** during the week following Labor Day in September. You can also camp on the grounds for $12 at any time.

The monument

A day spent in the **Lava Beds** is akin to exploring the innards of a volcano, scampering down hollow tubes through which molten lava once coursed. The youngest of them were formed 30,000 years ago when volcanic upwellings sent molten, basaltic magma careering across the Modoc Plateau. As the magma came into contact with cool air, it solidified, leaving a flowing molten core feeding the expanding lava field downhill. In time, the magma flow stopped and the molten lava drained out, leaving the world's largest concentration of such hollow tubes. Most remain unexplored, but where the casing has collapsed, access is possible and you are free to scramble through. Some of the caves are so small that you have to crawl along on all fours, while others are an enormous 75 feet in diameter. Some contain Native American **petroglyphs** – not to be confused with the names painted on the cave walls by J.D. Howard, one of the first white men to explore and name the caves.

Pick up the free loaner flashlights from the visitor center and begin your explorations of the caves just outside. Initially, though, entering the darkness alone can be an unnerving experience, so most people prefer to take the **free guided ranger walks** (daily Memorial Day–Labor Day). Two-to-three-hour morning walks (9am) leave from the visitor center and explore little-known sections of the monument; afternoon tours (2pm) concentrate on ninety-minute guided cave trips; and in the evening (9pm) rangers lead hour-long campfire talks and slide shows, which shift to Mushpot Cave in bad weather.

If you insist on eschewing ranger guidance, you must abide by a few **rules**. Don't go alone, wear decent shoes, and take two flashlights each. Borrowed flashlights must be returned by nightfall to ensure no one goes missing. For night explorations (the caves remain open), you'll need your own light source. Hard hats are strongly advised and can be purchased for $3.50 at the visitor center.

If caves don't do it for you, the other attraction of Lava Beds is its well-documented history. Begin at the visitor center for an exhibit on the Modoc War, including photos of its chief participants, including Modoc leader Captain Jack (see box, p.851), and scathing editorials from national papers condemning the US Army over its mission. You'll need a car to get to the northern reaches of the park, around **Captain Jack's Stronghold**, a natural fortress of craggy lava flows and shallow caves on the shores of the Old Tule

Lake. When you arrive, pick up a trail book (25¢) from the parking lot and enjoy one of two well-narrated **self-guided trails** (one half a mile, the other 1.5 miles) through a war that in many ways typified the conquest of the West. When you get here you'll see how the Modoc managed to hide and move around through the passageways of the hills. Two miles west, **Canby's Cross** marks a turning point in the war, when Captain Jack, coerced by the man who would later betray him, drew a gun during a council and murdered US General Canby and a pastor. Two miles east, the shallow lava bowl of **Hospital Rock** marks the point where one Lt Sherwood, wounded by the Modoc, was unsuccessfully tended in a makeshift field hospital towards the end of the siege on the stronghold.

Exploring the Lava Beds

Most of the interest in Lava Beds lies around the visitor center, where the largest concentration of caves can be visited on the short **Cave Loop** access road. For a confidence-building handle on your location in the twenty-five "developed" caves – less than a tenth of the known total – get the *Lava Caves Map* ($4.50) from the visitor center. New ones are discovered all the time, so the possibilities are almost endless, but for the moment, the tried and tested caves below should be enough to be going on with.

Catacombs Cave At over a mile long, this is the longest open tube in the monument, though you need perseverance, a slim body, and a cool head to get anywhere near the end. The profusion of interconnecting passageways makes it one of the most confusing; keep track of whether you are heading up- or downhill. On Cave Loop.

Golden Dome Cave The startling golden hues of the moist mossy roof lend the cave both its name and an otherworldly appearance. On Cave Loop.

Labyrinth Cave Striking geological features – lava pillars and lavacicles – and evidence of Native American habitation. At the entrance to Cave Loop.

Mushpot Cave Right by the visitor center near the start of Cave Loop, this is the most developed of the caves. It provides a good introduction, is lit during center opening hours, and has interpretive panels highlighting key features.

Skull Cave Named for Bighorn skulls found when the cave was discovered by early explorer E.L. Hopkins, this has the largest entrance of any of the lava tubes and contains ice all year-round. About two miles north of Cave Loop.

Symbol Bridge and **Big Painted Cave** (1.5-mile round-trip; almost flat). Two very worthwhile caves adjacent to each other

on a trail north of the visitor center. No flashlight is needed though one could come in handy. Some of the best examples of pictographs in the Monument – tentatively dated between 1000 AD and 1500 AD – show up as different angles of sunlight catch the rocks beside the entrance. Respecting Modoc sensibilities, make two clockwise turns before descending into a large cave, open at both ends (hence the "bridge" name), in which zigzags, squiggles, sunbursts, and human figures are picked out in grease and charcoal on pumice-washed background. Make a single anticlockwise turn on departure for Big Painted Cave, where the pictographs are less impressive. In the mid-1920s, J.D. Howard excavated a small tunnel at the very back of the cave to reveal an ice flow in a cavity fifteen feet down: with a flashlight you can scramble down there. Two miles north of Cave Loop.

Valentine Cave Interesting because it combines various characteristic cave features, such as stalactites and catacombs. The ridges at the base of the walls leading down into the deep and wide chamber almost appear to be man-made, so even are their lines. About two miles southeast of Cave Loop.

Around the monument

Small volcanic craters, buttes, spatter cones, and chimneys dot Lava Beds, but the flows which produced most of the lava tubes came from **Mammoth**

Crater on the southern perimeter of the monument, where a short path leads to a viewpoint overlooking the deep conical crater.

Underlying the most recent of Lava Beds' fabulous creations is a bed of basalt, the product of a huge shield volcano with a profile so flat it is barely noticeable. Its core is now filled by the subalpine **Medicine Lake**, ten miles southwest of Mammoth Crater. Formerly a Modoc healing center, the only therapies on offer today are fishing and swimming from the $10 campsites along the north shore. It's accessible via an unpaved road closed November to mid-May.

More volcanic spectacle lies just west at **Glass Mountain**, made almost entirely of glassy, black obsidian – source of Modoc arrowheads – but covered in fluffy, white pumice quarried for stonewashing jeans. A short and fairly easy trail leads in from the road. Just beyond the monument's northeast corner, a small outlier known as the Petroglyph Section contains **Petroglyph Point**, a three-hundred-yard-long cliff face made of "tuff," volcanic rock formed when lava flows hit Old Tule Lake. The soft rock offers some fine, but cryptic, examples of ancient art: shields, female figures, and a series of small circles thought to represent travel. The crevices are home to various bird species, especially horned owls. Pick up an interpretive leaflet at the visitor center.

East of the Petroglyphs Section, the road continues to Hwy-139 and the town of **Newell**, site of the **Tule Lake Camp**, where 110,000 people of Japanese descent, many of them American citizens, were interned without charge or trial between 1942 and 1946. There were as many as 18,000 inmates at any given time. Many of the camp buildings have been sold off to local farmers, but the wooden-sided police and military barracks remain. A simple plaque commemorates the disgraceful chapter and prays it will never be repeated, an all the more poignant message in the light of the current lengthy detention of some Islamic people for minor immigration infractions since the 2001 terrorist attacks. Nearby there was also a less-well-known camp for internees of German and Italian origin.

Perhaps the most rewarding excursion from the monument, though, is to the **Klamath Basin National Wildlife Refuge** (open daylight hours), just to the north along Hill Road (Hwy-161) leading to US-97 and spreading into Oregon. One of the last **wetlands** in California, with swathes of open water and emerging vegetation on the shoreline, it attracts an estimated eighty percent of birds following the Pacific Flyway, the major migration routes from Alaska and northern Canada to Baja California in Mexico. In spring and fall, almost a hundred species are present and the population tops a million. Bald eagles appear January to March, bringing out hundreds of photographers trying to navigate the snowy road. The most accessible reaches of the reserve are the **Lower Klamath Refuge** and **Tule Lake**, an open body of water surrounded by reeds (*tule* in Modoc). At the northwestern corner of the latter, the **visitor center** (Mon–Fri 8am–4.30pm, Sat & Sun 10am–4pm; ☏530/667-2231) rents out hunting blinds ($5); call ahead to be sure of getting one. Surprisingly, the best way of spotting the wildlife is by driving along designated routes ($3): getting out of the car and walking scares the birds off.

Heading south back towards Mount Shasta on US-97, your car will be stopped in otherwise droll **Dorris** by agriculture agents checking to see if you're transporting fruit or vegetables from out of state. Say "No" and they'll give you a nice color map to welcome you to California.

Modoc County

Occupying the far northeastern corner of California, wild and rugged **MODOC COUNTY** is bordered by equally thinly-populated areas of Oregon and Nevada, and is about as remote as it can get. Despite covering an area larger than two US states, the total population is only ten thousand, the majority of whom reside in the county seat of **Alturas**. Outside of that modest settlement, the mostly high-desert region is home to a lot more wildlife – bobcats, mule deer, antelope, elk, mountain lions, wolves, and birds such as sandhill cranes and bald eagles – than people, many of whom rely on cattle ranging and alfalfa cultivation for their livelihood. On the eastern side the imposing **Warner Mountains** divide the rest of the county from **Surprise Valley**, home to several small communities within spitting distance of the Nevada state line.

Historically the area belonged to three native tribes, the Modocs, the Paiutes, and the Pit River Indians. The creation of the Emigrant Trail, the main east–west route into Northern California, in the late 1840s, brought white settlers to the region in increasing numbers and into all-too-common confrontation with indigenous people. For the next six decades, a series of violent conflicts earned the region the title of **Bloody Ground of the Pacific**. The settlers gradually took over, though the area's control was successively bounced around from Utah Territory onto Nevada Territory and periods of attachment to California's Shasta and Siskiyou counties before Modoc County was created in 1874. It retains a frontier feel to this day and has the highest per capita gun ownership in the state, so it's no surprise that most locals and many of those who find their way here tend to occupy themselves with outdoor pursuits like hunting.

Alturas and around

Out-of-the-way **ALTURAS** is about sixty miles southeast of Tulelake via Hwy-137 and then Hwy-299, which you can also take all the way up from the Burney Falls area. Coming from Lava Beds, the black craggy rocks gradually give way to the increasingly pine-forested hills of the **Modoc National Forest**, which surround the town on three sides. The Modoc National Forest Service headquarters at 800 W 12th St (Mon–Fri 7.30am–4.30pm; ☏ 530/233-5811) provides a wealth of information on all the hiking, hunting, fishing, and camping possibilities in the region, as well as some useful maps. For more info on the town itself, visit the **Chamber of Commerce**, 522 S Main St (Mon–Fri 9am–12.30pm & 1.30–4pm; ☏ 530/233-4434, ⓦwww .alturaschamber.org). A glimpse into the region's turbulent past can be gained at the modest **Modoc County Historical Society Museum** (Tues–Sat 10am–4pm; $2; ☏ 530/233-2944), which occupies a modern building by the park at 600 S Main St; the displays concentrate on settler and Indian artifacts, as well as some of the county's natural history.

Though much of its dozen blocks are modern, Alturas, with its position by the mountains and the clear relation of the people to the land, manages to exude a Wild West atmosphere, and there is nowhere better **to stay** and soak that up than at the *Niles Hotel*, 304 S Main St (☏ 530/233-3261 or 1-877/233-5510, ⓦwww.nileshotel.com; ❹). Built in 1908, it has been refurbished to show off the original 14ft-high pressed-tin ceilings, the spacious saloon, and some of the original furnishings. A cheaper alternative, and typical of the more basic motels available, is the *Frontier Motel* at 1033 N Main St (☏ 530/233-3383; ❷). Among

eating options, the best ones to try are: *Nipa's*, 1001 N Main St (℡530/233-2520), dishes up a delightful combination of Thai and Californian cuisines in a laid-back atmosphere; *Antonio's*, 220 S Main St (℡530/233-5600), is a slightly smarter Italian restaurant, serving filling pasta, pizza, and sandwiches; and *Norma's Taqueria*, 204 W 12th St (℡530/233-5859), is the place for inexpensive and tasty Mexican fare.

Spreading out over thousands of acres south of Alturas, the **Modoc National Wildlife Refuge** (7am–sunset; free) is composed largely of unspoilt grasslands, incorporating some wetlands, and is home to many avian species, among them sandhill cranes, tundra swans, teal, pintail ducks, and warblers as well as migratory visitors such as whitefronted geese, pelicans, cormorants, and egrets. The refuge starts only a couple of miles southeast of town – take the road between the Chamber of Commerce and the museum and turn right at the first main junction, after about half a mile, which takes you right there. Around twenty miles north of town, the **Devil's Garden** is a very different type of terrain, a densely forested plateau with more wetlands and a community of some four hundred wild horses – there are trails through the excellent hiking country but you should take a good map and be careful not to stray from the paths. A little further northeast, reachable by US-395, lies **Goose Lake**, which straddles the Oregon state line. Good for fishing and other recreational activities, its largest settlement, on the east shore, is New Pine Creek, nearly all of whose facilities lie on the Oregon side – making it a good place to head to for cheaper gas. Finally, nearby **Davis Creek**, just off US-395 towards the lake, is the site of numerous obsidian mines and bucketfuls of the jagged black rocks can be carried away if you obtain a free permit from the Forest HQ in Alturas.

The Warner Mountains and Surprise Valley

Providing a dramatic backdrop to Alturas, the proud ridges of the **WARNER MOUNTAINS**, snow-capped for two-thirds of the year and prone to snowfall in any month, exert a magnetic pull on the few outsiders who venture this far. The range is divided into north and south by the valley that carries Hwy-299 east through the mountains. This road passes by the **Cedar Pass Snowpark** (℡530/233-3323, ⊛www.cedarpasssnowpark.com), where you can ski during winter weekends – all-day rope tow and T-bar tickets range from $5–15 and ski and snowboard rental is very cheap at $10 per day. It is, however, nearby **South Warner Wilderness**, part of the extensive Modoc National Forest, which presents the most fruitful territory for exploration. Here 77 miles of trails spread over more than 70,000 acres of slopes, steeper on the east side than the west, offer excellent hiking opportunities. Get maps and details from the Forest HQ in Alturas but make sure to carry provisions and all-weather gear. In the north, unpaved Rte-9 ascends over the North Warners from US-395 near Goose Lake and climbs up over **Fandango Pass**, where the old Applegate Trail and Lassen forty-niner route converge. It is passable with care in a regular car and makes for a scenic alternative route east, with arresting views of Surprise Valley along the way.

On the sunrise side of the mountains, secretive **SURPRISE VALLEY** marks the border with Nevada and is hemmed in by more barren ridges to the east. Indeed the fiercely independent types who live over here are said to prefer it if they belonged to the desert state rather than California. Hwy-299 from Alturas ends in the pleasant small town of **Cedarville**, the largest in the valley, a modest claim though that may be. Information on the whole valley can be obtained from the **Chamber of Commerce**, located in the Historic

Surprise Valley Drug Building at 519b Main St (℡530/279-2001, Ⓦwww
.hdo.net/~svcoc). Reasonable **accommodation** choices include the cutesy *J
H Metzker House B&B*, 520 Main St (℡530/279-2650; ❹), and cheaper *Sunrise Motel*, 54889 Hwy-299 (℡530/279-2161, Ⓕ530/279-6261; ❷). If you are
hungry, the *Cedarville Café & Saloon*, 415 Main St (℡530/279-6363), serves
up classic home-style breakfasts, lunches, and dinners. From Cedarville you
can branch south to even quieter Eagleville or better head north past a couple
of white alkali lakes to pay a brief visit to **Fort Bidwell**, home to a thriving
community of one hundred and fifty Paiute Indians. There you can pop into
their modern community center (flexible hours) to see a collection of rocks,
trophies, and an original peace pipe.

Travel details

Trains

Oakland to: Chico (1 daily; 4hr 8min); Dunsmuir
(1 daily; 7hr 17min); Redding (1 daily; 5hr 27min).
Redding to: Chico (1 daily; 1hr 30min); Dunsmuir
(1 daily; 1hr 50min); Oakland (1 daily; 6hr 14min).

Buses

Schedules listed below are mostly Greyhound,
combined with Amtrak Thruway where applicable.
Some routes require a transfer. See text for additional connecting local services.
Arcata to: Crescent City (2 daily; 1hr 40min);
Garberville (2 daily; 2hr); Napa (3 daily; 6hr
10min–7hr 35min); San Francisco (2 daily; 7hr
55min–8hr 20min); Santa Rosa (4 daily; 5hr
30min–6hr 5min).
Chico to: Red Bluff (6 daily; 50min–1hr 5min);
Redding (6 daily; 1hr 30min–1hr 45min);
Sacramento (3 daily; 2hr 15min); San Francisco
(1 daily; 5hr 40min); Weed (1 daily; 3hr 35min).

Eureka to: Crescent City (2 daily; 2hr); Garberville
(2 daily; 1hr 30min); San Francisco (2 daily; 7hr
20min–7hr 50min); Santa Rosa (4 daily; 5hr
15min–5hr 35min).
Redding to: Chico (6 daily; 1hr 45min); Red Bluff
(6 daily; 35–40min) Sacramento (7 daily; 2hr
40min–4hr 5min); San Francisco (4 daily; 5hr
40min–9hr 20min); Yreka (1 daily; 1hr 55min).
San Francisco to: Arcata (2 daily; 7hr 50min–8hr
5min); Chico (2 daily; 5hr 10min–5hr 55min);
Crescent City (2 daily; 9hr 30min–9hr 45min);
Eureka (2 daily; 7hr 20min–7hr 30min); Redding
(5 daily; 5hr 20min–8hr 55min); Santa Rosa (2
daily; 1hr 50min); Weed (1 daily; 9hr 35min);
Yreka (1 daily; 10hr 10min).
Santa Rosa to: Arcata (4 daily; 5hr–6hr 10min);
Crescent City (2 daily; 7hr 30min–7hr 50min);
Eureka (4 daily; 4hr 45min–5hr 35min); Garberville
(2 daily; 3hr 55min–4hr 5min); San Francisco
(2 daily; 2hr–2hr 5min).

NORTHERN CALIFORNIA | Travel details

Contexts

Contexts

The historical framework

To many people, California seems one of the least historic places on the planet. Unburdened by the past, it's a land where anything seems possible, whose inhabitants live carefree lives, wholly in and for the present moment. Its very name, appropriately for all its idealized images, is a work of fiction, free of any historical significance. The word first appeared in a popular Spanish picaresque novel of the early 1500s, *Las Sergas de Esplandián* by García de Montalvo, as the name of an island, located "very near to the terrestrial paradise" and inhabited entirely by Amazons "without any men among them."

Native peoples

For thousands of years before the arrival of Europeans, the **aboriginal peoples** of California flourished in the naturally abundant land, living fairly peacefully in tribes along the coast and in the deserts and the forested mountains. Anthropologists estimate that nearly half the native population then living within the boundaries of the present-day US were spread throughout what's now California, in small, tribal villages of a few hundred people, each with a clearly defined territory and often its own distinct language. Since there was no political or social organization beyond the immediate level of the tribe, it was not difficult for the colonizing Spaniards to divide and to conquer, effectively wiping them out – though admittedly more died because of epidemics of disease than outright genocide.

Very little remains to mark the existence of the Californian Native Americans: they had no form of written language, relatively undeveloped craft skills, and built next to nothing that would last beyond the change of seasons. About the only surviving signs of the coastal tribes are the piles of seashells and discarded arrowheads that have been found, from which anthropologists have deduced a bit about their cultures. Also, a few examples of **rock art** survive, as at the Chumash Painted Cave, near Santa Barbara on the Central Coast. Similar sorts of petroglyph figures were drawn by the Paiute Native Americans, who lived in the deserts near Death Valley, and by the Miwok from the Sierra Nevada foothills.

Discovery and early exploration

The first Europeans to set foot in California were Spanish explorers, intent on extending their colony of New Spain, which, under the 1494 Treaty of Tordesillas, included all the New World lands west of Brazil and all of North America west of the Rocky Mountains. In 1535, **Hernán Cortés**, fresh from decimating the Aztecs, headed westward in search of a short cut to Asia, which he believed to be adjacent to Mexico. Though he never reached what's now California, he set up a small colony at the southern tip of the Baja (or lower) California peninsula. Thinking it was an island, he named it Santa

Cruz, writing in his journals that he soon expected to find the imagined island of the Amazons.

The first explorer to use the name California, and to reach what's now the US state, was **Juan Cabrillo**, who sighted San Diego Harbor in 1542, and continued north along the coast to the Channel Islands off Santa Barbara. He died there six months later, persistent headwinds having made it impossible to sail any further north. His crew later made it as far north as what is now the state of Oregon, but were unable to find any safe anchorage and returned home starving and half-dead from scurvy. It was fifty years before another Spaniard braved the difficult journey: **Juan de Fuca**'s 1592 voyage caused great excitement when he claimed to have discovered the Northwest Passage, a potentially lucrative trade route across North America. It has long since turned out that there is really no such thing (de Fuca may have discovered the Puget Sound, outside Seattle), but Europeans continued to search for it for the next two hundred years.

The British explorer **Sir Francis Drake** arrived in the *Golden Hind* in 1579, taking a break from his piracy of Spanish vessels in order to make repairs. His landing spot, now called Drake's Bay, near Point Reyes north of San Francisco, had "white bancks and cliffes" that reminded him of Dover. Upon landing, he was met by a band of native Miwoks, who feted him with food and drink, and placed a feathered crown upon his head; in return, he claimed all of their lands – which he called Nova Albion (New England) – for Queen Elizabeth, supposedly leaving behind a brass plaque now on display in the Bancroft Library at the University of California.

Setting sail from Acapulco in 1602, **Sebastián Vizcaíno**, a Portuguese explorer under contract to Spain, made a more lasting impact than his predecessors, undertaking the most extensive exploration of the coast, and bestowing most of the place names that survive. In order to impress his superiors he exaggerated the value of his discoveries, describing a perfect, sheltered harbor, which he named **Monterey** in honor of his patron in Mexico. Subsequent colonizers based their efforts on these fraudulent claims (the windy bay did not live up to Vizcaáno's estimation), and the headquarters of the missions and military and administrative center of the Spanish government remained at Monterey, 100 miles south of San Francisco, for the next 75 years.

Colonization: the Spanish and the British

The Spanish occupation of California began in earnest in 1769, with a combination of military expediency (to prevent other powers from gaining a foothold) and Catholic missionary zeal (to convert the Native Americans). Father **Junípero Serra** and a company of three hundred soldiers and clergy set off from Mexico for Monterey, half of them by ship, the other half overland. In June 1770, after establishing a small mission and presidio (fort) at San Diego, the expedition arrived at Monterey, where another mission and small presidio were constructed.

The Spanish continued to build missions all along the coast, ostensibly to Catholicize the Native Americans, which they did with inquisitional fervor. The mission complexes were broadly similar, with a church and cloistered residential structure surrounded by irrigated fields, vineyards, and more extensive ranchlands. The labor of the Native American converts was co-opted: they were put to work making soap and candles, were often beaten, and never educated. Objective accounts of the missionaries' treatment of the indigenous peoples are rare, though mission registries record twice as many deaths as they do births, and their cemeteries are packed with Native American dead. Not all of the Native Americans gave up without a fight: many missions suffered from raids, and the now-ubiquitous red-tiled roofs were originally a replacement for the earlier thatch to better resist arson attacks.

Most of the mission structures that survive today were built to the designs of Serra's successor, Father **Férmin de Lasuén**, who was in charge of the missions during the period of their greatest growth. By the time of his death in 1804, a chain of twenty-one missions, each a long day's walk from its neighbors and linked by the dirt path of **El Camino Real** (The Royal Road), ran from San Diego to San Francisco.

During this time the first towns, called **pueblos**, were established in order to attract settlers to what was still a distant and undesirable territory. The first was laid out in 1777 at San Jose, south of the new mission at San Francisco. Los Angeles, the second pueblo, was established in 1781, though neither had more than a hundred inhabitants until well into the nineteenth century.

One reason for Spain's military presence in California – which consisted of four presidios all told, with twelve cannon and only two hundred soldiers – was to prevent the expansion of the small **Russian** colony based in Alaska, mostly trappers collecting beaver and otter pelts in the northwestern states of Washington and Oregon. The two countries were at peace and relations friendly, and in any case the Spanish presidios were in no position to enforce their territorial claims. In fact, they were so short of supplies and ammunition that they had to borrow the gunpowder to fire welcoming salutes whenever the two forces came into contact. Well aware of the Spanish weakness, the Russians established the outpost of **Fort Ross** in 1812, sixty miles north of San Francisco. This further undermined Spanish sovereignty over the region, though the Russians abandoned the fort in 1841, selling it to John Sutter (who features prominently in later California history; see overleaf).

The Mexican era

While Spain, France, and England were engaged in the bitter struggles of the Napoleonic Wars, the colonies of New Spain rebelled against imperial neglect, with Mexico finally gaining independence in 1821. The Mexican Republic, or the United States of Mexico as the new country called itself, governed California as a territory. However, the fifteen distinct administrations it set up lacked the money to pay for improvements and the soldiers needed to enforce the laws, and they were unable to exercise any degree of authority.

The most important effect of the Mexican era was the final **secularization** in 1834, after years of gradual diminution, of the Franciscan missions. As most of the missionaries were Spanish, under Mexican rule they had seen their position steadily eroded by the increasingly wealthy, close-knit families of the Californios – Mexican immigrants who'd been granted vast tracts of ranchland. The government's intention was that half of the missions' extensive lands should go to the Indian converts, but this was never carried out, and the few powerful families divided most of it up among themselves.

In many ways this was the most lawless and wantonly wasteful period of California's history, an era described by **Richard Henry Dana** – scion of a distinguished Boston family, who dropped out of Harvard to sail to California – in his 1840 book *Two Years Before the Mast*. Most of the agriculture and cottage industries that had developed under the missionaries disappeared, and it was a point of pride amongst the Californios not to do any work that couldn't be done from horseback. Dana's Puritan values led him to heap scorn upon the "idle and thriftless people" who made nothing for themselves. For example, the large herds of cattle that lived on the mission lands were slaughtered for their hides and sold to Yankee traders, who turned the hides into leather which they sold back to the Californios at a tidy profit. "In the hands of an enterprising people," he wrote, "what a country this might be."

The first Americans

Throughout the Mexican and Spanish eras, foreigners were legally banned from settling, and the few who showed up, mostly sick or injured sailors dropped off to regain their health, were often jailed until they proved themselves useful, either as craftsmen or as traders able to supply needed goods. In the late 1820s, the first **Americans**, without exception males, began to make their way to California, tending to fit in with the existing Mexican culture, often marrying into established families, and converting to the Catholic faith. The American presence grew slowly but surely as more and more people emigrated, still mostly by way of a three-month sea voyage around Cape Horn. Among these was **Thomas Larkin**, a New England merchant who, in 1832, set up shop in Monterey, and later instrumental in pointing the disgruntled Californios towards the more accommodating US; Larkin's wife Rachel was the first American woman on the West Coast.

The first people to make the four-month journey to California overland – in a covered wagon just as in so many Hollywood Westerns – arrived in 1841, having forged a trail over the Sierra Nevada Mountains via Truckee Pass, just north of Lake Tahoe. Soon after, hundreds of people each year were following in their tracks. In 1846, however, forty migrants, collectively known as the **Donner party**, died when they were trapped in the mountains by early winter snowfall. The immense difficulties involved in reaching California, over land and by sea, kept population levels at a minimum, and by 1846 just seven thousand people, not counting Native Americans but including all the Spanish and Mexicans, lived in the entire region.

The Mexican–American War

From the 1830s onwards – inspired by **Manifest Destiny**, the popular, almost religious, belief that the United States was meant to cover the continent from coast to coast – US government policy regarding California was to buy all of Mexico's land north of the Rio Grande, the river that now divides the US and Mexico. President Andrew Jackson was highly suspicious of British designs on the West Coast – he himself had been held as a (14-year-old) prisoner of war during the Revolutionary War of 1776 – and various diplomatic overtures were made to the Mexican Republic, all of which backfired. In April 1846, Jackson's protégé, President James Polk, offered forty million dollars for all of New Mexico and the California territory, but his simultaneous annexation of the newly independent Republic of Texas – which Mexico still claimed – resulted in the outbreak of war.

Almost all the fighting of the **Mexican–American War** took place in Texas; only one real battle was ever fought on Californian soil, at San Pasqual, northeast of San Diego, where a roving US battalion was surprised by a band of pro-Mexican Californios, who killed twenty-two soldiers and wounded another fifteen before withdrawing south into Mexico. Monterey, still the territorial capital, was captured by the US Navy without a shot fired, and in January 1847, when the rebel Californios surrendered to the US forces at Cahuenga, near Los Angeles, the Americans controlled the entire West Coast.

Just before the war began, California had made a brief foray into the field of self-government: the short-lived **Bear Flag Republic**, whose only lasting effect was to create what's still the state flag, a prowling grizzly bear with the words "California Republic" written below. In June 1846, American settlers in the Sonoma Valley took over the local presidio – long abandoned by the Mexicans – and declared California independent, which lasted for all of three weeks until the US forces took command.

The Gold Rush

As part of the Treaty of Guadalupe Hidalgo, which formally ended the war in 1848, Mexico ceded all of the Alta California territory to the US. Nine days before the signing of the accord, in the distant foothills of the Sierra Nevada Mountains, flakes of **gold** were discovered by workmen building a sawmill along the American River at Coloma, though it was months before this momentous conjunction of events became known.

At the time, California's non–Native American population was mostly concentrated in the few small towns along the coastal strip. Early rumors of gold attracted a trickle of prospectors, and, following news of their subsequent success, by the middle of 1849 – eighteen months after the initial find – men were flooding into California from all over, in the most madcap migration in world history. **Sutter's Fort**, a small agricultural community, trading post, and stage stop which had been established six years earlier by John Sutter on the banks of the American River, was overrun by miners, who headed up into the nearby foothills to make their fortune. Some did, most didn't, but in any case, within fifteen years most of the gold had been picked clean. The miners moved on or went home and their camps vanished, prompting Mark Twain to write that "in no other land, in modern times, have towns so absolutely died and disappeared as in the old mining regions of California."

Statehood

Following the US takeover after the defeat of Mexico, a **Constitutional Convention** was held at Monterey in the autumn of 1849. The men who attended were not the miners – most of whom were more interested in searching for gold – but those who had been in California for some time (about three years on average). At the time, the Territory of California extended all the way east to Utah, so the main topic of discussion was where to draw the eastern boundary of the intended state. The drawing up of a state constitution was also important, since it was the basis on which California applied for admission to the US. This constitution contained a couple of noteworthy inclusions – to protect the dignity of the manually laboring miners, **slavery** was prohibited; and to attract well-heeled **women** from the East Coast, California was the first state to recognize in legal terms the separate property of a married woman. In 1850, California was admitted to the US as the thirty-first state.

The Indian Wars

Though the US Civil War had little effect on California, many bloody battles were fought throughout the 1850s and 1860s by white settlers and US troops against the various Native American tribes whose lands the immigrants wanted. At first the government tried to move willing tribes to fairly large reservations, but as more settlers moved in the tribes were pushed onto smaller and smaller tracts. The most powerful resistance to the well-armed invaders came in the mountainous northeast of California, where a band of **Modoc** fought a long-running guerrilla war, using their superior knowledge of the terrain to evade the US troops.

Owing to a combination of disease and lack of food, as well as deliberate acts of violence, the Native American population was drastically reduced, and by 1870 almost ninety percent had been wiped out. The survivors were concentrated in small, relatively valueless reservations, where their descendants still live: the Cahuila near Palm Springs, the Paiute/Shoshone in the Owens Valley, and the Hupa on the northwest coast continue to reside near their ancestral homelands, and are naturally quite protective of their privacy.

The boom years: 1870–1900

After the Gold Rush, **San Francisco** boomed into a boisterous frontier town, exploding in population from 500 to 50,000 within five years. Though far removed from the mines themselves, the city was the main landing spot for ship-borne argonauts (as the prospectors were called), and the main supply town. Moreover, it was the place where successful miners went to blow their hard-earned cash on the whiskey and women of the **Barbary Coast**, then the raunchiest waterfront in the world, full of brothels, saloons, and opium dens. Ten years later, San Francisco enjoyed an even bigger boom as a result of the silver mines of the Comstock Lode in Nevada, owned mainly by San Franciscans, who displayed their wealth by building grand palaces and mansions on Nob Hill – still the city's most exclusive address.

The completion in 1869 of the **transcontinental railroad**, built using imported Chinese laborers, was a major turning point in the settlement of California. Whereas the trip across the country by stagecoach took at least a month, and was subject to scorching hot weather and attacks by hostile natives, the crossing could now be completed in just five days.

In 1875, when the Santa Fe Railroad reached Los Angeles (the railroad company having extracted huge bribes from local officials to ensure the budding city wasn't bypassed), there were just ten thousand people living in the whole of **Southern California**, divided equally between San Diego and Los Angeles. A rate war developed between the two rival railroads, and ticket costs dropped to as little as $1 for a one-way ticket from New York. Land speculators placed advertisements in East Coast and European papers, offering cheap land for homesteaders in towns and suburbs all over the West Coast that, as often as not, existed only on paper. By the end of the nineteenth century, thousands of people, ranging from Midwestern farmers to the East Coast elite, had moved to California to take advantage of the fertile land and mild climate.

Hollywood, the war, and after

The greatest boost to California's fortunes was, of course, the **film industry**, which moved here from the East Coast in 1911, attracted by the temperate climate in which directors could shoot outdoors year-round and by the incredibly cheap land on which large indoor studios could be built at comparatively little cost. Within three years, movies like D.W. Griffith's *Birth of a Nation* – most of which was filmed along the dry banks of the Los Angeles River – were being cranked out by the hundreds.

Hollywood, a suburb of Los Angeles that was the site of many of the early studios, and ever since the buzzword for the entire entertainment industry, has done more to promote the mystique of California as a pleasure garden landscape than any other medium, disseminating images of its glamorous lifestyles around the globe. Los Angeles still dominates the world film industry, and, increasingly, is an international center for the music business as well.

This widespread, idealized image had a magnetic effect during the **Great Depression** of the 1930s, when thousands of people from all over the country descended upon California, which was perceived to be – and for the most part was – immune to the economic downturn that crippled the rest of the US. From the Dust Bowl Midwest, entire families, who came to be known as **Okies**, packed up everything they owned and set off for the farms of the Central Valley, an epic journey captured by John Steinbeck's best-selling novel *The Grapes of Wrath*, in the photographs of Dorothea Lange, and in the baleful tunes of folksinger Woody Guthrie. Some Californians who feared losing their jobs to the incoming Okies formed vigilante groups and, with the complicity of local and state police, set up roadblocks along the main highways to prevent unemployed outsiders from entering the state.

One Depression-era initiative to alleviate the poverty, and to get the economy moving again, were the US government–sponsored **Works Progress Administration (WPA)** construction projects, ranging from restoring the California missions to building trails and park facilities, and commissioning art works like the marvelous Social Realist murals in San Francisco's Coit Tower.

Things turned around when **World War II** brought heavy industry to California, as shipyards and airplane factories sprang up, providing well-paid employment in wartime factories. After the war, most stayed on, and still today California companies – McDonnell Douglas, Lockheed, Rockwell, and General Dynamics, for example – make up the roll call of suppliers to the US military and space programs.

After the war, many of the soldiers who'd passed through on their way to the battlegrounds of the South Pacific came back to California and decided to stay on. There was plenty of well-paid work, the US government subsidized house purchases for war veterans and, most importantly, constructed the **freeways** and interstate highways that enabled land speculators to build new commuter suburbs on land that had been used for farms and citrus orchards.

The **Fifties** brought prosperity to the bulk of middle-class America (typified by President Dwight Eisenhower's goal of "two cars in every garage and a chicken in every pot"), and California, particularly San Francisco, became a nexus for alternative artists and writers, spurring an immigration of intellectuals that by the end of the decade had become manifest as the **Beat generation** – pegged "Beatniks," in honor of Sputnik, the Soviet space satellite, by San Francisco columnist Herb Caen.

The Sixties and Seventies

California remained at the forefront of youth and **social upheavals** into and throughout the **Sixties**. In a series of drug tests carried out at Stanford University – paid for by the CIA, who was interested in developing a "truth drug" for interrogation purposes – unwitting students were dosed with **LSD**. One of the guinea pigs was the writer Ken Kesey, who had just published the highly acclaimed novel *One Flew Over the Cuckoo's Nest*. Kesey quite liked the experience and soon secured a personal supply of the drug (which was still legal) and toured the West Coast to spread the word of "acid." In and around San Francisco, Kesey and his crew, the Merry Pranksters, turned on huge crowds at **Electric Kool-Aid Acid Tests** – in which LSD was diluted into bowls of the soft drink Kool-Aid – complete with psychedelic light shows and music by the Grateful Dead. The acid craze reached its height during the **Summer of Love** in 1967, when the entire Haight-Ashbury district of San Francisco seemed populated by barefoot and drugged flower children.

Within a year the superficial peace of Flower Power was shattered, as protests mounted against US involvement in the **Vietnam War**; Martin Luther King Jr and Bobby Kennedy, heroes of left-leaning youth, were both gunned down – Kennedy in Los Angeles after winning the California primary of the 1968 presidential election. The militant **Black Panthers**, a group of black radical activists based in Oakland, terrorized a white population that had earlier been supporters of the civil rights movement. By the end of the Sixties the "system," in California especially, seemed to be at breaking point, and the atrocities committed by **Charles Manson** and his "Family" seemed to signify a general collapse.

The antiwar protests, concentrated at the University of California campus in Berkeley, continued through the early **Seventies**. Emerging from the milieu of revolutionary and radical groups, the Symbionese Liberation Army, a small, well-armed, and stridently revolutionary group, set about the overthrow of the US, attracting media (and FBI) attention by murdering civil servants, robbing banks and, most famously, kidnapping 19-year-old heiress **Patty Hearst**. Amid much media attention Hearst converted to the SLA's cause, changing her name to Tanya and, for the next two years – until her capture in 1977 – she went underground, provoking national debate about her motives and beliefs.

Californian **politics**, after Watergate and the end of American involvement in Vietnam, seemed to lose whatever idealistic fervor it might once have had, and popular culture withdrew into self-satisfaction, typified by the smug harmonies of musicians like the Eagles and Jackson Browne. While the Sixties upheavals were overseen by California Governor Ronald Reagan, who was ready and willing to fight the long-haired hippies, the 1970s saw the reign of "Governor Moonbeam" Jerry Brown, under whose leadership California enacted some of the most stringent **anti-pollution** measures in the world. The state also actively encouraged the development of renewable forms of energy such as solar and wind power, and protected the entire coastline from despoliation and development. California also decriminalized the possession of under an ounce of **marijuana** (though it remains an offense to grow or sell it), and the harvesting of marijuana continues to account for over $1 billion each year, making it the number-one cash crop in the number-one agricultural region in the US.

The Eighties and Nineties

The easy-money **Eighties** of Reagonomics and the trickle-down economy, which naturally never trickled down as far as the state's poorest, crash-landed in a tangled mess. Perhaps it was fitting that the decade when greed, as many saw it, was elevated to the level of a virtue ended in disgrace. LA junk-bond king Michael Milkin was convicted of multibillion-dollar fraud, and the Savings and Loan banking scandals enmeshed such high-ranking politicos as California Senator Alan Cranston. Consequently the **Nineties** kicked off with a stagnant property market and rising unemployment.

In **Los Angeles**, the videotaped beating of black motorist Rodney King by officers of the LA Police Department, and the subsequent acquittal of those officers, sparked off destructive **rioting** in April 1992. State and federal authorities, forced into taking notice of LA's endemic poverty and violence, promised all sorts of new initiatives but achieved few concrete results. Race also dominated the year-long trial of black former football star **O.J. Simpson** – accused and finally acquitted of murdering his white ex-wife and her male friend – splitting public opinion into directly opposed camps of black and white.

All these factors combined to make the first five years of the 1990s perhaps the bleakest since the Great Depression, and **natural calamities** – regional flooding, Malibu fires and mudslides, and two dramatic earthquakes – only added to the general malaise. Mike Davis's *City of Quartz*, despite flaws and inaccuracies, served as a secular bible for the time, an artfully written work based on the inevitable doom LA was facing. And with LA's chronic interethnic hatred, natural disasters, bureaucratic inaction, and general public pessimism, it seemed that Davis was probably right.

The latter half of the decade saw **Richard Riordan**, a multimillionaire technocrat who served as LA mayor from 1992 to 2000, preside over a major **revival** in the city's economic fortunes and a restructuring of its economic base – aerospace and automotive giving way to tourism, real estate and, as always, Hollywood. New property developments attempted to revitalize deprived areas, and even crime and violence tailed off marginally. However, these improvements probably owed more to the national upswing during the Clinton years than to purely local initiatives.

San Francisco also suffered in the early Nineties; on top of AIDS-related illnesses stretching health services, the area was hit by a series of natural disasters.

An **earthquake** in October 1989 devastated much of the San Francisco Bay Area, followed two years later by a massive **fire** in the Oakland Hills which burned over two thousand homes and killed two dozen people – the third worst fire in US history.

But even more so than LA, San Francisco's economic upswing turned the city around, replacing premillennium jitters with Information Age optimism. The **Silicon Valley** industries boomed, with companies scrambling to find high-paid workers to fill their constantly growing rosters. San Jose, San Francisco's southern neighbor, surpassed the Golden Gate city in population, and even Oakland, the gritty East Bay port-town, started to receive a much needed facelift. Still, not everyone in the Bay Area was happy with the apparent prosperity. **Gentrification** threatened to turn San Francisco from a province of activism into a playground for Silicon Valley's rich young things. Housing prices rocketed sky high, and tenancy at 99 percent full, forcing out not only the city's poor, but the lower middle class as well.

Contemporary California

The optimism that had overidden many concerns at the tail end of the old millennium soon took a pummelling once the new one started. The world's computers may not have gone belly up at zero hour on Y2K, but the hi-tech industry had to come to terms with the fact it had outreached itself, becoming the biggest victim of a nationwide economic **recession** – the cause of it, in fact, according to many analysts. This immediately affected most Silicon Valley companies, which had expanded into global giants so rapidly, as they saw billions wiped off their stock values and had to offload employees faster than they had hired them. The silver lining for many who had not shared in the boom was that Bay Area **property prices** slowed for the first time in a decade, though they did not implode as some predicted. Not surprisingly, since then they have been gradually edging upwards again, as the hi-tech industry (or at least its major players) has regrouped on a more solid footing.

More gloom, literally, struck California in 2001, when gross mismanagement of the state's energy supplies led to a series of Third World–type **power cuts**, as the ailing grid system was unable to meet the enormous demands for electricity. The state was forced to fork out vast sums to import some of its shortfall in energy from other states and, although some of the management issues have been resolved, a true long-term solution to the problem has still to be found. Environmentalists maintain that there will not be a proper solution until serious money is invested in **renewable energy** sources, something the traditional lobbyists are not at all keen on.

The most important political repercussion of the power crisis, compounded by his perceived ineptitude in other areas too, was the demise of Governor **Gray Davis**. Although he had managed to get re-elected in November 2002, he failed to complete the first year of his second term, after the state Republicans contrived to force a **recall**, which amounts to a vote of confidence, in October 2003. The winner of this rather rare occurrence was Republican candidate **Arnold Schwarzenegger**, who presented himself as fiscally conservative but socially liberal (by GOP standards) and used all his Hollywood charisma to sell this image to the voters. Once enthroned in Sacramento, the "Governor", as he is known to detractors and supporters alike, set about balancing the **state budget** by cutting down on certain programs, including funding for tourism. He also implemented various initiatives aimed at raising revenue, which explains the sudden hike of day-use and camping fees in state parks, for example.

Whilst ostensibly supporting George W. Bush in public – he was a star speaker at the Republican National Convention in August 2004 – Arnie appears to be positioning himself for greater things and rumors are rife that his supporters will engineer a motion for a constitutional amendment to give foreign-born citizens the right to become President, allowing him to follow in Reagan's footsteps. Quite how such a "decadent" Hollywood figure can appeal these days to the powerful Christian Right on whose support Bush has leaned increasingly heavily is uncertain. It will certainly not have gone unnoticed in some parts of the country that Schwarzenegger openly championed **Proposition 71**, to give state funding to stem-cell research, and so helped it pass into California law on the November 2004 ballot.

The governorship notwithstanding, California remains a staunch **Democrat stronghold**, voting overwhelmingly for John Kerry in the 2004 presidential elections and returning its large majority of Democratic representatives to the US House undiminished. Indeed, one of them, **Nancy Pelosi**, has been the minority house-leader for several years and thus one of the top-ranking members of the party in Washington, DC. Meanwhile, back in San Francisco and Berkeley, political **activism** has continued to stir ever more vigorously in response to George W. Bush's hardline domestic and international policies. California Senator **Barbara Lee** bravely cast the sole vote against the resolution to use force in Afghanistan in 2001 and was one of a larger group of Democrats to vote against the Iraq resolution the following year. On the streets, San Francisco has hosted the largest antiwar demonstrations since the days of Vietnam, a beacon of progressive hope for the growing nationwide **Peace Movement** amidst all the flag waving and sabre rattling.

Throughout all of these changes, California still clings on to its aura as something of a Promised Land. Barring its complete destruction by the **Big One** (the earthquake that's destined one day to drop half of the state into the Pacific and wipe out the rest under massive tidal waves), the state seems set to continue much as it is, acting as the cornerstone of the mythical West and as the place where America reinvents itself.

Wildlife and the environment

Though popularly imagined as little more than palm trees and golden sand beaches, for sheer range of landscape, California is hard to beat. With glaciated alpine peaks and meadows, desolate desert sand dunes and flat, fertile agricultural plains, it's no wonder that Hollywood filmmakers have so often and successfully used California locations to simulate distant and exotic scenes. These diverse landscapes also support an immense variety of plant and animal life, much of which – due to the protection offered by the various state and national parks, forests, and wilderness areas – is both easily accessible and unspoiled by encroaching civilization.

Background: landscapes, geology, and earthquakes

California's landscape has been formed over millions of years through the interaction of all the main geological processes: Ice Age glaciation, erosion, earthquakes, and volcanic eruptions. The most impressive results can be seen in **Yosemite National Park**, east of San Francisco, where solid walls of granite have been sliced and shaped into unforgettable cliffs and chasms. In contrast, the sand dunes of **Death Valley** are being constantly shaped and reshaped by the dry desert winds, surrounded by foothills tinted by oxidized mineral deposits into every color of the spectrum.

Earthquakes – which earned Los Angeles the truck driver's nickname "Shakeytown" – are the most powerful expression of the volatile unrest underlying the placid surface. California sits on the Pacific "Ring of Fire," at the junction of two tectonic plates slowly drifting deep within the earth. Besides the occasional earthquake – like the 1906 quake which flattened San Francisco, or the 1994 tremor which collapsed many of LA's freeways – this instability is also the cause of California's many volcanoes. Distinguished by their symmetrical, conical shape, almost all of them are now dormant, though Mount Lassen, in Northern California, did erupt in 1914 and 1915, destroying much of the surrounding forest. Along with the boiling mud pools that accompany even the dormant volcanoes, the most attractive features of volcanic regions are the bubbling **hot springs** – pools of water that flow up from deep underground, heated to a sybaritically soothing temperature. Hot springs occur naturally all over the state, and though some have now been developed into luxurious health spas, most remain in their natural condition, where you can soak your bones *au naturel* surrounded by mountain meadows or wide-open deserts. The best of these are listed throughout the Guide.

Some of the most fantastic **wildlife** is now extinct in its natural habitat: neither the grizzly bear – a ten-foot-tall, two-ton giant that still adorns the state flag of California – nor the California condor – one of the world's largest birds, with a wingspan of over eight feet – have been seen in the Californian wilds for over half a century. But plenty more are still alive and thriving, like the otters, elephant seals, and gray whales seen all along the coast, and the chubby marmots – shy mammals often found sunning themselves on rocks in higher reaches of the mountains. Plant life is equally varied, from the brilliant but short-lived desert wildflowers to the timeless bristlecone pine trees, which live for thousands of years on the arid peaks of the Great Basin desert.

Below you will find details of the major **ecosystems** of California. The accounts are inevitably brief, as the area encompasses almost 320,000 square miles (ranging from moist coastal forests and the snow-capped Sierra Nevada peaks to Death Valley, 282 feet below sea level with an annual rainfall of two inches), and is inhabited by a multitude of species. Native to California are 54 species of cactus, 123 species of amphibian and reptile, 260 species of bird, and 27,000–28,000 species of insect. See "Books" for recommendations of more specific habitat guides. Bear in mind, also, that museums all over the state examine and exhibit the natural world in depth, notably Monterey's superb Aquarium – see p.535 for details.

The ocean

The **Pacific Ocean** determines California's climate, keeping the coastal temperatures moderate all year round. During the spring and summer, cold nutrient-rich waters rise or well up to produce cooling banks of fog and abundant crops of phytoplankton (microscopic algae). The algae nourishes creatures such as krill (small shrimps), which in their turn provide baby food for juvenile fish. This food chain provides fodder for millions of nesting **sea birds**, as well as harbor and elephant **seals**, California **sea lions**, and whales. **Gray whales**, the most common species spotted from land, were once almost hunted to the point of extinction, but have returned to the coast in large numbers. During their southward migration to their breeding grounds off Mexico, from December to January, it is easy to spot them from prominent headlands all along the coast, and most harbors have charter services offering whale-watching tours. On their way back to the Arctic Ocean, in February and March, the newborn whale pups can sometimes be seen playfully leaping out of the water, or "breaching." Look for the whale's white-plumed spout – once at the surface, it will usually blow several times in succession.

Tide pools

California's shoreline is composed of three primary ecosystems: tide pools, sandy beaches, and estuaries. To explore the **tide pools**, first consult a local newspaper to see when the low tides (two daily) will occur. Be careful of waves, don't be out too far from the shore when the tide returns, and also watch your step – there are many small lives underfoot. There are miles of beaches with tide pools, some of the best at Pacific Grove near Monterey. Here you will find **sea anemones** (they look like green zinnias), hermit crabs, purple and green shore crabs, red sponges, purple sea urchins, starfish ranging from the size of a dime to the size of a hubcap, mussels, abalone, and Chinese-hat limpets – to name a few. You may also see black **oystercatchers**, their squawking easily heard over the surf, foraging for an unwary, lips-agape mussel. Gulls and black turnstones are also common, and during the summer brown pelicans dive for fish just offshore.

The life of the tide-pool party is the **hermit crab**, who protects its soft and vulnerable hindquarters with scavenged shells, usually those of the aptly named black turban snail. Hermit crabs scurry busily around in search of a detritus snack, or scuffle with other hermit crabs over the proprietorship of vacant snail shells.

Pacific Grove is also home to large populations of **sea otters**. Unlike most marine mammals, sea otters keep themselves warm with a thick, soft coat rather than blubber. The trade in sea-otter pelts brought entrepreneurial Russian and British fur hunters to the West Coast, and by the mid-nineteenth century the otters were virtually extinct. In 1938, a small population was discovered near Big Sur, and with careful protection otters have re-established themselves in the southern part of their range. They are charming creatures with big rubbery noses and Groucho Marx moustaches. With binoculars, it's easy to spot them amongst the bobbing kelp, where they lie on their backs opening sea urchins with a rock, or sleep entwined within a seat belt of kelp which keeps them from floating away. The bulk of the population resides between Monterey Bay and the Channel Islands, but – aside from Pacific Grove – the best places to see them are Point Lobos State Park, the Seventeen-Mile Drive, and the Monterey Wharf, where, along with sea lions, they often come to beg for fish.

Many of the **seaweeds** you see growing from the rocks are edible. As one would expect from a Pacific beachfront, there are also **palms** – sea palms, with four-inch-long rubbery stems and flagella-like fronds. Their thick root-like holdfasts provide shelter for small crabs. You will also find giant **kelp** washed up on shore – harvested commercially for use in thickening ice cream.

Sand beaches

The long, golden **sandy beaches** for which California is so famous may look sterile from a distance. However, observe the margin of sand exposed as a gentle wave recedes, and you will see jetstreams of small bubbles emerge from numerous clams and mole crabs. Small shore birds called **sanderlings** race amongst the waves in search of these morsels, and sand dollars are often easy to find along the high-tide line.

The most unusual sandy-shore bathing beauties are the **northern elephant seals**, which will tolerate rocky beaches but favor soft sand mattresses for their rotund torsos. The males, or bulls, can reach lengths of over six meters and weigh upwards of four tons; the females, or cows, are petite by comparison – four meters long, and averaging a mere two thousand pounds in weight. They have large eyes, adapted for spotting fish in deep or murky waters; indeed, elephant seals are the deepest diving mammals, capable of staying under water for twenty minutes at a time, reaching depths of over four thousand feet, where the pressure is over a hundred times that at the surface. They have to dive so deeply in order to avoid the attentions of the great white sharks who lurk offshore, for whom they are a favorite meal.

Like otters, elephant seals were decimated by commercial whalers in the mid-nineteenth century for their blubber and hides. By the turn of the century less than a hundred remained, but careful protection has partially restored the California population, which is concentrated on the Channel and Farallon islands and at Año Nuevo State Park.

Elephant seals only emerge from the ocean to breed or molt; their name comes from the male's long trunk-like proboscis, through which it produces a resonant pinging sound that biologists call "trumpeting," which is how it attracts a mate. The Año Nuevo beach is the best place to observe this ritual. In December and January, the bulls haul themselves out of the water and battle for dominance. The predominant, or alpha, male will do most of the mating, siring as many as fifty young pups, one per mating, in a season. Other males fight it out at the fringes, each managing one or two couplings with the hapless, defenseless females. During this time, the beach is a seething mass of ton upon ton of blubbery seals – flopping sand over their backs to keep cool, squabbling with their neighbors while making rude snoring and belching sounds. The adults depart in March but the weaned pups hang around until May.

Different age groups of elephant seals continue to use the beach at different times throughout the summer for molting. Elephant seals are completely unafraid of people, but are huge enough to hurt or even kill you if you get in their way. Still, you're allowed to get close, except during mating season when entry into the park is restricted to ranger-guided tours.

Estuaries

Throughout California, many **estuarine** or rivermouth habitats have been filled, diked, drained, "improved" with marinas or contaminated by pollutants. Those that survive intact consist of a mixture of mud flats, exposed only at low tide, and salt marsh, together forming a critical wildlife area that provides nurseries for many kinds of invertebrates and fish, and nesting and wintering grounds for many birds. Cord grass, a dominant wetlands plant, produces five to ten times as much oxygen and nutrients per acre as does wheat.

Many interesting creatures live in the thick organic ooze, including the fat **innkeeper**, a revolting-looking pink hot-dog of a worm that sociably shares its burrow with a small crab and a fish, polychaete worms, clams, and other goodies. Most prominent of estuary birds are the **great blue herons** and **great egrets**. Estuaries are the best place to see wintering shore birds such as dunlin, dowitchers, eastern and western sandpipers, and yellowlegs. Peregrine falcons and osprey are also found here.

Important Californian estuaries include Elkhorn Slough, near Monterey, San Francisco Bay, and Bolinas Lagoon.

Coastal bluffs

Along the shore, **coastal meadows** are bright with pink and yellow sand verbena, lupines, sea rocket, sea fig, and the bright orange **California poppy**, the state flower. Slightly inland, hills are covered with coastal scrub, which consists largely of coyote brush. Coastal canyons contain broadleaf trees such as California laurel, alder, buckeye, and oaks – and a tangle of sword ferns, horsetail, and cow parsnip.

Common rainy-season canyon inhabitants include four-inch-long banana slugs and rough-skinned newts. In winter, orange-and-black **Monarch butterflies** inhabit large roosts in a few discreet locales, such as Bolinas, Monterey, and Pacific Grove. Coastal thickets also provide homes to weasels, bobcats, gray fox, raccoons, black-tailed deer, California quail, and garter snakes. **Tule elk**, a once common member of the deer family, have also been reintroduced to the wild; good places to view them are on Tomales Point at the Point Reyes National Seashore (see p.701), and inland at reserves near Bakersfield (p.383) and in the Owens Valley (p.389).

River valleys

Like most fertile **river valleys**, the Sacramento and San Joaquin valleys – jointly known as the Central Valley – have both been greatly affected by agriculture. Riparian (streamside) vegetation has been logged, wetlands drained, and streams contaminated by agricultural runoff. Despite this, the riparian habitat that does remain is prime wildlife habitat. Wood ducks, kingfishers, swallows, and warblers are common, as are gray foxes, racoons, and striped skunks. The Sacramento National Wildlife Refuge has one of the world's largest concentrations of **snow geese** during winter months. Other common winter migrants include Canada geese, green-winged and cinnamon teals, pintail, shovelers, and wigeon. These refuges are well worth a visit, but don't be alarmed by large numbers of duck hunters – the term "refuge" is a misnomer. However, most have tour routes where hunting is prohibited.

Vernal pools are a valley community unique to California. Here, hardpan soils prevent the infiltration of winter rains, creating seasonal ponds. As these ponds slowly evaporate in April and May, sharply defined concentric floral rings come into bloom. The white is meadowfoam, the blue is the violet-like downingia, and the yellow is goldfields. Swallows, meadowlarks, yellowlegs, and stilts can also be found. Jepson Prairie Nature Conservancy Reserve is the easiest to visit, south of Sacramento near the small town of Rio Vista.

Forests

Perhaps the most notable indigenous features of Californian forests are the wide expanses of **redwood** and **sequoia trees**. It's easy to confuse the coastal species, *Sequoia sempervirens*, or redwood, with the *Sequoiadendron giganteum*, or giant sequoia (pronounced *suk-oy-ah*), as both have the same fibrous reddish-brown bark. Redwoods are the world's tallest trees, sequoias have the greatest base circumference and are the largest single organisms on earth; for more on the latter, see the box on p.444. Both species can live for over two thousand years, and recent research now indicates a maximum age of 3500 years for the sequoia. Their longevity is partially due to their bark: rich in tannin, it protects the tree from fungal and insect attack and inhibits fire damage. In fact, fire is beneficial to these trees and necessary for their germination; prescribed fires are set and controlled around them. The wood of the redwoods in particular is much sought after both for its beauty – near any coastal forest you'll see signs advertising redwood burl furniture – and its resistance to decay (the bark continues to protect the tree for several hundred years after felling).

They are the only surviving members of a family of perhaps forty species of trees which, fossil records show, grew worldwide 175 million years ago. Now just a few pockets remain, and a tremendous battle between environmentalists and loggers is being waged over the remaining acres. These **virgin forests** provide homes to unique creatures such as the spotted owl and marbled murrelet.

Redwoods are a relict species, which means that they flourished in a moister climate during the Arcto-Tertiary (just after the golden age of the dinosaurs), and now occupy a much-reduced range. As the weather patterns changed, redwoods slowly retreated to their current near-coastal haunts. Today, they are found from the border with Oregon to just south of Monterey.

The floor of the redwood forest is a hushed place with little sunlight, the air suffused with a rufous glow from the bark, which gives the trees its name. One of the commonest ground covers in the redwood forest is the redwood sorrel, or oxalis, with its shamrock leaves and tubular pink flowers; ferns are also numerous. Birds are usually high in the canopy and hard to see, but you might hear the double-whistled song of the varied thrush, or the "chickadee" call from the bird of that name. Roosevelt elk, larger than the tule elk, also inhabit the humid northwest forests. Prairie Creek Redwoods State Park, near the border with Oregon, has a large herd.

Sequoias are found on the western slopes of the Sierra Nevada, most notably in Yosemite and Kings Canyon national parks – though saplings given as state gifts can be found growing all over the world.

The sequoia forest tends to be slightly more open than the redwood forest. Juvenile sequoias – say up to a thousand years old – exhibit a slender conical shape which, as the lower branches fall away, ages to the classical heavy-crowned shape with its columnar trunk. For its bulk, its cones are astonishingly small, no bigger than a hen's egg, but they live on the tree for up to thirty years before falling.

The Sierra Nevada

In the late nineteenth century, the environmental movement was founded when John Muir fell in love with the **Sierra Nevada** mountains, which he called the Range of Light. Muir fought a losing battle to save Hetch Hetchy, a valley said to be as beautiful as Yosemite, but in the process the Sierra Club was born and the move to save America's remaining wilderness began.

The Sierra mountains, which run almost the entire length of the state, have a sharp, craggy, freshly glaciated look. Many of the same conifers can be found as in the forests further west, but ponderosa and lodge-pole pines are two of the dominants, and the forests tend to be drier and more open. Lower-elevation forests contain incense cedar, sugar pine (whose eighteen-inch cones are the longest in the world), and black oak. The oaks, along with dogwood and willows, produce spectacular autumnal color. The east side is drier and has large groves of aspen, a beautiful white-barked tree with small round leaves that tremble in the wind. **Wildflowers** flourish for a few short months – shooting star, elephant's head, and wild onions in early spring, asters and yarrow later in the season.

The dominant campground scoundrels are two sorts of noisy, squawking bird: Steller's jays and Clark's nutcrackers. Black bears, who may make a raid on your campground, pose more danger to iceboxes than humans, but nonetheless you should treat them with caution. The friendly twenty-pound pot-bellied rodents that lounge around at the fringes of your encampment are **marmots**, who probably do more damage than bears: some specialize in chewing on radiator hoses of parked cars.

Other common birds include mountain chickadees, yellow-rumped warblers, white-crowned sparrows, and juncos. Deer, golden-mantled ground squirrels, and chipmunks are also plentiful.

The Great Basin

The little-known **Great Basin** stretches from the northernmost section of the state down almost to Death Valley, encompassing all of Nevada and parts of all the other bordering states. It's a land of many shrubs and few streams, and what streams do exist drain into saline lakes rather than the ocean.

Mono Lake, reflecting the 13,000-foot peaks of Yosemite National Park, is a spectacular example. Its salty waters support no fish but lots of algae, brine shrimp, and brine flies, the latter two providing a smorgasbord for nesting gulls (the term "seagull" isn't strictly correct – many gulls nest inland) and migrating phalaropes and grebes. Like many Great Basin lakes, Mono Lake has been damaged through diversion of its freshwater feeder streams to provide water for the city of Los Angeles.

Great Basin plants tolerate hot summers, cold winters, and little rain. The dominant Great Basin plant is **sagebrush**. Its dusky green leaves are wonderfully aromatic, especially after a summer thunderstorm. Other common plants include bitterbrush, desert peach, junipers, and piñon pine. Piñon cones contain tasty nuts that were a mainstay of the Paiute diet.

The **sage grouse** is one of the most distinctive Great Basin birds. These turkey-like birds feed on sage during the winter and depend on it for nesting and courtship habitat. In March and April, males gather at dancing grounds called leks, where they puff out small pink balloons on their necks, make soft drum-banging calls, and in general succeed in looking and sounding rather silly. The hens coyly scout out the talent by feigning greater interest in imaginary seeds.

Pronghorns are beautiful tawny-gold antelope seen in many places in the Great Basin. Watch for their twinkling white rumps as you drive.

Other Great Basin denizens include golden eagles, piñon jays, black-billed magpies, coyotes, feral horses and burros, black-tailed jackrabbits, and western rattlesnakes. Large concentrations of waterfowl gather at Tule Lake in northeastern California, where hundreds of wintering **bald eagles** gather in November before the cold really sets in.

The Mojave Desert

The **Mojave Desert** lies in the southeast corner of the state, near Death Valley. Like the Great Basin, the vegetation here consists primarily of drought-adapted shrubs, one of the commonest of which is creosote, with its olive-green leaves and puffy yellow flowers. Death Valley is renowned for its early spring wildflower shows. The alluvial fans are covered with desert trumpet, gravel ghost, and pebble pincushion. The quantity and timing of rainfall determines when the floral display peaks, but it's usually some time between mid-February and mid-April in the lower elevations, late April to early June higher up.

Besides shrubs, the Mojave has many interesting kinds of **cactus**. These include barrel, cottontop, cholla, and beavertail cactus, and many members of the yucca family. Yuccas have stiff, lance-like leaves with sharp tips, a conspicuous representative being the **Joshua tree** (see p.310), whose twisting arm-like branches are covered with shaggy upward-pointing leaf fronds, which can reach to thirty feet high.

Many Mojave Desert animals conserve body moisture by foraging at night, including the kit fox, wood rat, and various kinds of mice. The **kangaroo rat**, an appealing animal that hops rather than runs, has specially adapted kidneys that enable it to survive without drinking water. Other desert animals include mammals such as the Mojave ground squirrel, bighorn, and coyote; birds like the roadrunner, ash-throated flycatcher, ladder-backed woodpecker, verdin, and Lucy's warbler; and reptiles like the Mojave rattlesnake, sidewinder, and chuckwalla.

California on film

I n the early 1910s, attracted by the sunshine, cheap labor, and rich variety of California landscapes, a handful of independent movie producers left the East Coast and the stranglehold monopoly of Thomas Edison's Motion Picture Patents Company, and set up shop in the small Los Angeles suburb of Hollywood. Within a decade Hollywood had become the movie capital of the world and Southern California became the setting for everything from Keystone Kops car chases to Tom Mix Westerns, not to mention the odd Biblical epic or historic romance.

Not surprisingly, since then the list of movies set in California, and especially LA, has become almost endless. What follows are those that are the most memorable classics, make the most original use of California locations (from the vertiginous streets of San Francisco to the LA River), and reflect the state's navel-gazing fascination with itself.

Hollywood does Hollywood

The Bad and the Beautiful (Vincente Minnelli 1952). Bitter tale of the rise and fall of a ruthless Hollywood producer (Kirk Douglas), told in flashbacks by the star, writer, and director he launched and subsequently lost.

Barton Fink (Joel Coen 1991). Tinseltown in the 1940s is depicted by the Coen brothers as a dark world of greedy movie bosses, belligerent screenwriters, and murderers disguised as traveling salesmen. Allegedly based on the experience of playwright Clifford Odets.

The Big Knife (Robert Aldrich 1955). An incisive portrayal of Hollywood politics, in which a weak-willed actor can't get free from the tentacles of a hack director, despite the pleas of his wife. Based on a play by Clifford Odets and filmed like one as well.

Ed Wood (Tim Burton 1994). The ragged low-budget fringes of Fifties Hollywood are beautifully re-created in this loving tribute to the much-derided auteur of *Plan Nine from Outer Space* and *Glen or Glenda*. Gorgeously shot in black and white, with a magnificent performance

by Martin Landau as an ailing Bela Lugosi.

Get Shorty (Barry Sonnenfeld 1995). Slick Miami gangster Chili Palmer, played by John Travolta, takes up residence in Tinseltown and decides he wants to become a movie producer, in this amusing adaptation of an Elmore Leonard novel.

Gods and Monsters (Bill Condon 1998). An interesting tale of the final days of 1930s horror-film director James Whale (well-portrayed by Ian McKellen), ignored by the Hollywood elite, and slowly dying of malaise by his poolside. The title refers to a memorable Ernest Thesiger line from Whale's classic *Bride of Frankenstein*.

Good Morning, Babylon (Paolo and Vittorio Taviani 1987). Two restorers of European cathedrals find themselves in 1910s Hollywood, working to build the monstrous Babylonian set for D.W. Griffith's *Intolerance*, in this Italian story of the contribution of immigrants in early Tinseltown. Oddly enough, that same set has now been partially rebuilt in Hollywood – as part of a mall.

Hollywood on Trial (David Helpern Jr 1976). Interesting documentary offering insight about the early 1950s witch-hunts in Hollywood and the blacklisted screenwriters, actors, and directors.

Hurlyburly (Anthony Drazan 1998). David Rabe's acidic play about Hollywood players and hucksters is rendered in celluloid as a prattling pathos-fest, with much angst for Sean Penn and Chazz Palminteri, and much ironic detachment for Kevin Spacey and Garry Shandling.

In a Lonely Place (Nicholas Ray 1950). A glamourless Hollywood peopled with alcoholic former matinee idols, star-struck hat-check girls and desperate agents forms the cynical background for this devastating doomed romance between Humphrey Bogart's hot-tempered screenwriter and his elegant neighbor Gloria Grahame.

The Player (Robert Altman 1992). Tim Robbins is a studio shark who thinks a disgruntled screenwriter is out to get him; he kills the writer (at South Pasadena's Rialto Theater), steals his girlfriend, and waits for the cops to unravel it. A wickedly sharp satire about contemporary Hollywood, with some great celebrity cameos.

Singin' in the Rain (Stanley Donen & Gene Kelly 1952). A merry trip through Hollywood set during the birth of the sound era. Gene Kelly, Donald O'Connor, and Debbie Reynolds sing and dance to many classic tunes, including "Good Morning," "Moses," "Broadway Melody," and countless others.

A Star Is Born (George Cukor 1954). Based on the film *What Price Hollywood?* (see below), these adapta-tions tell the story of the rise of a starlet mirroring the demise of her Svengali. Janet Gaynor and Fredric March star in the early version, Judy Garland and James Mason in the later. Both are worthwhile, while a 1977 remake with Barbra Streisand and Kris Kristofferson runs a distant third.

Sullivan's Travels (Preston Sturges 1941). A high-spirited comedy about a director who wants to stop making schlock pictures and instead create gritty portrayals of what he thinks real life to be. The first two-thirds are great, the last third ends in mawkish fashion.

Sunset Boulevard (Billy Wilder 1950). Award-winning film about a screenwriter falling into the clutches of a long-faded silent-movie star. William Holden was near the beginning of his career, Gloria Swanson well past the end of hers. Erich von Stroheim nicely fills in as Swanson's butler, and even Cecil B. DeMille makes a cameo appearance.

What Price Hollywood? (George Cukor 1932). The template for the *A Star Is Born* movies that followed: Constance Bennett is the starlet, an ambitious waitress, and Lowell Sherman is the drunken director.

Whatever Happened to Baby Jane? (Robert Aldrich 1962). Bette Davis and Joan Crawford are former child stars who plot and scheme against one another in a rotting Malibu house. A fine slice of modern horror.

Who Framed Roger Rabbit? (Robert Zemeckis 1988). Despite being a live-action/cartoon hybrid, a revealing film about 1940s LA, where cartoon characters suffer abuse like everyone else and the big corporations seek to destroy the Red Car transit system.

LA crime stories

The Big Sleep (Howard Hawks 1946). One of the key noirs of the 1940s, with Humphrey Bogart as Philip Marlowe, and featuring a wildly confused plot that ends up being subordinate to the crackling chemistry between Bogie and Lauren Bacall.

Chinatown (Roman Polanski 1974). One of the essential films about the city. Jack Nicholson hunts down corruption in this dark criticism of the forces that animate the town: venal politicians, black-hearted land barons, crooked cops, and a morally neutered populace. Great use of locations, from Echo Park to the San Fernando Valley.

Devil in a Blue Dress (Carl Franklin 1995). Terrific modern noir, in which South Central detective Easy Rawlins (Denzel Washington) navigates the ethical squalor of elite 1940s white LA and discovers a few ugly truths about city leaders – most of which he already suspected.

Double Indemnity (Billy Wilder 1944). The prototypical film noir. Greedy insurance salesman Fred MacMurray collaborates with harpy wife Barbara Stanwyck to murder her husband and cash in on the settlement. Edward G. Robinson lurks on the sidelines as MacMurray's boss.

The Grifters (Stephen Frears 1990). A memorable film with Annette Bening, John Cusack, and Anjelica Huston playing the title characters, con artists hunting through the LA underworld looking for their next victims.

Heat (Michael Mann 1995). Stars big names like De Niro and Pacino, but this crime drama, which does include some stunning set-pieces (eg a Downtown LA shootout), is ultimately less than the sum of its parts, with a frustratingly predictable ending.

He Walked by Night (Alfred Werker/Anthony Mann 1948). Verité-style crime story set in "the fastest growing city in the nation" starts with a random cop-killing in Santa Monica and ends with a manhunt through the 700-mile subterranean city storm-drain system, stunningly shot by torch-light by peerless noir cinematographer John Alton.

Jackie Brown (Quentin Tarantino 1997). A glorious return to form for Pam Grier who, as a tough airline stewardess, plays the perfect foil for Samuel Jackson's smooth gangster. LA itself provides the dark, menacing backdrop.

The Killing of a Chinese Bookie (John Cassavetes 1976). Strange and self-indulgent, but perfectly evoking the sleazy charms of the Sunset Strip, Cassavetes' behavioral crime story about a club owner (Ben Gazzara) in hock to the mob is just one of his many great LA-based character studies.

LA Confidential (Curtis Hanson 1997). Easily the best of all the contemporary noir films, a perfectly realized adaptation of James Ellroy's novel about brutal cops, victimized prostitutes, and scheming politicians in 1950s LA. Even the good guys, Russell Crowe and Guy Pearce, are morally questionable.

The Long Goodbye (Robert Altman 1973). Altman intentionally mangles noir conventions in this Chandler adaptation, which has Elliott Gould play Marlowe as a droning schlep who wanders across a desaturated landscape of casual corruption, encountering bizarre characters like nerdy mobster Marty Augustine and Sterling Hayden as a hulking alcoholic writer. Old-time screenwriter Leigh Brackett freely changes Chandler's original ending.

One False Move (Carl Franklin 1991). A disturbing early role for Billy Bob Thornton, as a murderous hick who kills some people in an LA bungalow with his girlfriend and psychotic, nerdy colleague Pluto, then gets pursued by the LAPD and a small-town Arkansas sheriff.

Point Blank (John Boorman 1967). Engaging, somewhat pretentious flick with Lee Marvin as a hit man out for revenge. Begins and ends in Alcatraz, but in between imagines LA as an impenetrable fortress of concrete and glass.

The Postman Always Rings Twice (Tay Garnett 1946). Lana Turner and John Garfield star in this seamy – and excellent – adaptation of the James M. Cain novel, first brought to the screen as *Ossessione*,

an Italian adaptation by Luchino Visconti. Awkwardly remade by Bob Rafelson in 1981 with Jessica Lange and Jack Nicholson.

Touch of Evil (Orson Welles 1958). Supposedly set at a Mexican border town, this noir classic was actually shot in a seedy, decrepit Venice. A bizarre, baroque masterpiece with Charlton Heston playing a Mexican official, Janet Leigh as his beleaguered wife, and Welles himself as a bloated, corrupt cop addicted to candy bars.

True Romance (Tony Scott 1993). With a Quentin Tarantino plot to guide them, Patricia Arquette and Christian Slater battle creeps and gangsters amid wonderful LA locations, from seedy motels to *Rae's Diner* in Santa Monica.

Apocalyptic LA

Blade Runner (Ridley Scott 1982). While the first theatrical version flopped (thanks to a slapped-on happy ending and annoying voice-over narration), the recut director's version establishes the film as a sci-fi classic, involving a dystopic future LA where "replicants" roam the streets and soulless corporations rule from pyramidal towers.

Earthquake (Mark Robson 1974). Watch the Lake Hollywood dam collapse, people run for their lives, and chaos hold sway in the City of Angels. Originally presented in "Sensurround!"

Escape from LA (John Carpenter 1996). LA is cut off from the mainland by an earthquake and declared so "ravaged by crime and immorality" that it's been turned into a dead zone for undesirables. Sent in to stop the insurrection, Kurt Russell battles psychotic plastic surgeons in Beverly Hills and surfs a tsunami to a showdown in a netherworld Disneyland.

Falling Down (Joel Schumacher 1993). Fired defense-worker Michael Douglas tires of the traffic jams on the freeways and goes nuts in some of the city's poorer minority neighborhoods. A fitting reflection of the bleak attitudes of the time throughout LA.

Kiss Me Deadly (Robert Aldrich 1955). Perhaps the bleakest of all noirs, starring Ralph Meeker as brutal detective Mike Hammer, who tramples on friends and enemies alike in his search for the great "whatsit" – a mysterious and deadly suitcase.

Mulholland Drive (David Lynch 2001). A frightening take on the city by director Lynch, who uses non-linear storytelling to present a story of love, death, glamour, and doom – in which elfin cowboys mutter cryptic threats, elegant chanteuses lip-sync to phantom melodies, and a blue key can unlock a shocking double identity.

Strange Days (Kathryn Bigelow 1995). In a chaotic, nightmarish vision of LA, Ralph Fiennes, Angela Bassett, and Juliette Lewis run around the city screaming–in the new millennium. More interesting as a reflection of mid-1990s LA angst than as compelling cinema.

The Terminator (James Cameron 1984). Modern sci-fi classic, with Arnold Schwarzenegger as a robot from the future sent to kill the mother of an unborn rebel leader. Bravura special effects and amazing

set-pieces here were successfully followed up with the director's 1989 sequel, T2: Judgment Day, with Arnold as a good robot.

They Live (John Carpenter 1988). In this ludicrous but entertaining horror flick, a drifter living in a shanty town pitched on the outskirts of LA discovers a pair of sunglasses which allow him to see that skull-faced aliens in positions of wealth and power are subliminally encouraging the city's rampant consumerism.

Modern LA

Boyz N the Hood (John Singleton 1991). An excellent period piece that cemented the LA stereotype as a land of gangs and guns, starring Cuba Gooding Jr in his first big role, and Lawrence Fishburne as his dad.

Clueless (Amy Heckerling 1995). Jane Austen's Emma transplanted to a rich Southern California high school, with a fine performance by Alicia Silverstone as a frustrated matchmaker.

Dogtown and Z-Boys (Stacy Peralta 2002). Even if you have no interest in skateboarding, this is a fun, high-spirited look at the glory times of the sport in the mid-1970s, when a daring group of LA kids took to using the empty swimming pools of the elite as their own private skate-parks.

Ghost World (Terry Zwigoff 2001). An alienated teenager encounters LA (here, nameless) in all of its corporatized drabness, a soulless desert of identical mini-malls, cheap retro-50s diners, and desperate, lonely characters. Oddly enough, something of a dark comedy.

The Glass Shield (Charles Burnett 1995). Institutionalized racism in the LAPD is brought under the

harsh glare of Charles Burnett, who, with his masterpieces Killer of Sheep (1977) and My Brother's Wedding (1983), has long been one of the great chroniclers of black urban life in LA.

Go (Doug Liman 1999). A kinetic joyride through LA's rave subculture told from three perspectives, including Sarah Polley's botching of an aspirin-for-Ecstasy drug sale, and Jay Mohr and Scott Wolf – as two TV soap stars – stuck in a police sting operation.

The Limey (Steven Soderbergh 1999). Gangster Terence Stamp wanders into a morally adrift LA looking for his daughter's killer, and finds the burned-out husk of former hippie Peter Fonda.

Magnolia (Paul Thomas Anderson 1999). A gut-wrenching travelogue of human misery. The San Fernando Valley serves as an emotional inferno of abusive parents, victimized children, haunted memories, plaintive songs, and a curious plague of frogs.

Mayor of the Sunset Strip (George Hickenlooper 2003). Great, disturbing documentary about the titular character, a former stand-in for one of the Monkees, legendary

DJ, lounge denizen, and apparent man-child who can't seem to get his life together, despite being pals with people like David Bowie.

Mi Vida Loca (Alison Anders 1993). Depressing ensemble piece about the hard lives of Latinas in Echo Park girl-gangs and the central reason the director won a prestigious MacArthur Fellowship.

Nixon (Oliver Stone 1996. A long, dark look at the first president from Southern California, starring Anthony Hopkins, with James Woods as his henchman H.R. Haldeman.

Pulp Fiction (Quentin Tarantino 1994). A successful collection of underworld stories presented in non-linear fashion, by then-hot director Tarantino. Set against a down-at-the-heels backdrop of LA streets, bars, diners, and would-be torture chambers. The film's most famous location, the *Jackrabbit Slim's* retro-diner, was actually a studio set, not a real-life restaurant in LA.

Safe (Todd Haynes 1995). In Haynes' brilliant tale of millennial unease and corporeal paranoia, Julianne Moore plays a San Fernando Valley home-maker with seemingly little inner life and an opulent outer one, who is diagnosed with environmental sickness and finds refuge at a New Age desert retreat.

Short Cuts (Robert Altman 1993). Vaguely linked vignettes tracing the lives of LA suburbanites, from a trailer-park couple in Downey to an elite doctor in the Santa Monica Mountains. Strong ensemble cast

bolsters the intentionally fractured narrative.

Slums of Beverly Hills (Tamara Jenkins 1998). Troubled teen Natasha Lyonne deals with growing pains in a less glamorous section of town, far from Rodeo Drive, where a pill-popping cousin, manic uncle, weird neighbors, and her own expanding bustline are but a few of her worries.

Star Maps (Miguel Arteta 1997). Melodrama of immigrant life on the fringes of Hollywood. Carlos, who has grandiose dreams of movie stardom, is doing time in his father's prostitution ring, standing on street corners ostensibly selling maps to the homes of the stars, in reality selling his body for cash.

Swingers (Doug Liman 1996). Cocktail culture gets skewered in this flick about a couple of dudes who flit from club to club to eye "beautiful babies" and kibbitz like Rat Pack–era Sinatras. Many LA locales shown, such as the *Dresden Room* and *The Derby*.

To Sleep with Anger (Charles Burnett 1990). An interesting view of LA's overlooked black middle class, directed with polish by a very underrated African-American filmmaker.

Tupac and Biggie (Nick Broomfield 2002). Eye-opening documentary about the murders of rappers Tupac Shakur and Notorious B.I.G., both of whom the director suggests may have been the victims of hip-hop producer Suge Knight, along with rogue elements of the LAPD.

If you're going to San Francisco

Bullitt (Peter Yates 1968). In the minds of many filmgoers, the classic portrait of San Francisco, presented at breakneck speed in cinema's most famous car chase,

ripping up and down the city's steep hills at a frenetic, still-amazing pace. No modern special effects for this legendary sequence, either.

The Conversation (Francis Ford Coppola 1974). Opening with a mesmerizing sequence of high-tech eavesdropping in Union Square, Coppola's chilling character study of San Francisco surveillance expert Harry Caul is one of the best films of the paranoid Watergate era.

Dim Sum: A Little Bit of Heart (Wayne Wang 1985). Set among San Francisco's Chinese community, Wayne Wang's appealing comedy of manners about assimilation and family ties is a modest and rewarding treat. His earlier sleeper *Chan is Missing* (1982) also shows a Chinatown tourists don't usually see.

Dirty Harry (Don Siegel 1971). Based on the infamous case of the Zodiac Killer, Siegel's morally dubious, sequel-spawning thriller casts Clint Eastwood in his most famous role as a vigilante San Francisco cop.

Escape from Alcatraz (Don Siegel 1979). Though evocatively portrayed in *Bird Man of Alcatraz, Point Blank, The Rock*, and many others, this is the ultimate movie about San Francisco's famously unbreachable offshore penitentiary. Starring Clint Eastwood (again) as a most resourceful con.

Gimme Shelter (Albert and David Maysles 1969). Excellent documentary about the ill-fated Rolling Stones' concert at Altamont, in which Hell's Angels were hired to provide their own version of "security." Its searing look at homegrown American violence and Vietnamera chaos at the end of the 1960s includes an on-camera stabbing.

Greed (Erich von Stroheim 1924). Legendary silent masterpiece about the downfall of Polk Street dentist Doc McTeague was shot mostly on location in the Bay Area, and remains, even in its notoriously truncated version, a wonderful

time capsule of working-class San Francisco in the 1920s.

It Came from Beneath the Sea (Robert Gordon 1955). Apocalypse, San Francisco–style. One of the more memorable monster flicks of the 1950s, in which a super-sized octopus emerges from the waters of the Bay and begins scooping people up for lunch. Appealing special effects, for the time.

Petulia (Richard Lester 1968). Julie Christie is dazzling in this fragmented puzzle of a movie about a vivacious and unpredictable married woman who has an affair with a divorced doctor (George C. Scott). Set against the wittily described background of psychedelic-era San Francisco, and superbly shot by Nicolas Roeg.

Play It Again, Sam (Herbert Ross 1972). A strike in Manhattan led to one of Woody Allen's uncommon visits to the West Coast for this hilarious film about a neurotic San Francisco film critic in love with his best friend's wife and obsessed with Humphrey Bogart in *Casablanca*.

The Times of Harvey Milk (Robert Epstein 1984). This powerful and moving documentary about America's first openly gay politician chronicles his career in San Francisco and the aftermath of his 1978 assassination. Based on the book by Randy Shilts (see p.901).

Vertigo (Alfred Hitchcock 1958). Hitchcock's somber, agonized, twisted love story is the San Francisco movie nonpareil, and one of the greatest films ever made. From James Stewart's wordless drives around the city to the film's climax at the San Juan Bautista Mission, Hitchcock takes us on a mesmerizing tour of a city haunted by its past.

What's Up, Doc? (Peter Bogdanovich 1972). Madcap homage to the heyday of Hollywood screwball comedy stars Ryan O'Neal as a hapless musicologist and Barbra Streisand as the kook who drives him around the bend.

"Way out" West

Beach Blanket Bingo (William Asher 1965). A cult favorite – the epitome of sun-and-surf movies, with Frankie Avalon and Annette Funicello singing and cavorting amid hordes of wild-eyed teenagers.

Bob & Carol & Ted & Alice (Paul Mazursky 1969). Once-daring, but still funny zeitgeist satire about wife-swapping and bed-hopping in hedonistic Southern California, starring Natalie Wood, Robert Culp, Elliott Gould, and Dyan Cannon as the titular foursome.

Boogie Nights (Paul Thomas Anderson 1997). A suburban kid from Torrance hits the big time in LA – as a porn star. Mark Wahlberg, Julianne Moore, and Burt Reynolds tread through a sex-drenched San Fernando Valley landscape in the disco years.

House on Haunted Hill (William Castle 1958). Not the clumsy remake, but the ghoulish Vincent Price original, with the King of Horror as a master of ceremonies for a scary party thrown at his Hollywood Hills estate – actually, Frank Lloyd Wright's Ennis-Brown House (see p.127).

Modern Romance (Albert Brooks 1981). Brooks – the Woody Allen of the West Coast – stars in this comedy about a neurotic film editor who dumps his girlfriend and instantly regrets it. Full of early Eighties LA signifiers, from quaaludes to jogging suits to off-Hollywood parties with B-movie stars.

Point Break (Kathryn Bigelow 1991). Preposterous but kinetic crime story starring Patrick Swayze as a bank-robbing, sky-diving New Age surfer dude and Keanu Reeves as his straight-arrow FBI nemesis.

Rebel Without a Cause (Nicholas Ray 1955). Fine, brash colors and widescreen composition in this troubled-youth film, starring, of course, James Dean. A Hollywood classic with many memorable images, notably the use of the Griffith Park Observatory as a shooting location.

Repo Man (Alex Cox 1984). Emilio Estevez is a surly young punk who repossesses cars for Harry Dean Stanton. Very imaginative and fun, and darkly comic.

Sex: the Annabel Chong Story (Gough Lewis 1999). An unblinking documentary that reveals some of the seediest aspects of LA's porn business. A complex and riveting portrait, though not for the easily offended or disgusted.

Shampoo (Hal Ashby 1975). Using LA as his private playground, priapic hairdresser Warren Beatty freely acts on his formidable, though nonchalant, libido. A period piece memorable for its 1970s look.

Valley Girl (Martha Coolidge 1983). Early Nicolas Cage flick, in which he winningly plays a new-wave freak trying to woo the title character (Debra Foreman) in a clash of LA cultures. Good soundtrack, too.

Off the beaten track

The Aviator (Martin Scorsese 2004). Engaging biopic in which the brilliant but troubled mind of Howard Hughes is vividly on disply in mid-century LA, as the aircraft pioneer builds some of the world's fastest and biggest planes – including the Spruce Goose – dates teenage Hollywood starlets, and battles rival executives and politicians, all the while obsessively washing his hands and collecting jars of his own urine.

Bagdad Café (Percy Adlon 1988). Inspiring fable about a German tourist who arrives at a dusty roadside diner in the Mojave Desert and magically transforms the place with her larger-than-life charm.

The Birds (Alfred Hitchcock 1963). Set in Bodega Bay, just north of San Francisco, Hitchcock's terrifying allegory about a small town besieged by a plague of vicious birds, features indelible bird's-eye views of the Northern California coastline.

California (John Farrow 1946). Ray Milland leads a wagon train to the Land of Milk and Honey only to find the land ruled by greed and graft, in this elaborate paean to the pioneer spirit and the founding of the state. Worth seeing for its ecstatic opening montage of Californian vistas and aphorisms about the approaching Promised Land.

Citizen Kane (Orson Welles 1941). In this pinnacle of American filmmaking, director Welles successfully copies the baroque splendor and frightful vulgarity of William Randolph Hearst's legendary prison-like palace on the Central Coast, San Simeon (see p.512). Here, it's called "Xanadu" and shot in San Diego's Balboa Park (see p.237).

Faster, Pussycat! Kill! Kill! (Russ Meyer 1965). Meyer's wonderfully lurid, camp action flick unleashes a trio of depraved go-go girls upon an unsuspecting California desert. One of a kind.

Fat City (John Huston 1972). Stacy Keach and Jeff Bridges star in Huston's poignant, evocative, beautifully paced portrait of barflies, has-beens, and no-hopers on the small-time boxing circuit in Stockton, Northern California.

High Plains Drifter (Clint Eastwood 1972). Spooky Mono Lake is one of the bleak, disturbing settings for this tale of a mysterious gunslinger who comes back to a dusty burg to avenge a wrongful death – before drenching the town in blood and renaming it "Hell."

House of Sand and Fog (Vadim Perelman 2003). Jennifer Connelly is a slacker who, because she doesn't bother to open her mail, loses her Northern California coastal house to Iranian immigrant Ben Kingsley, resulting in much heart-rending Method acting, a tragic ending, and a handful of Oscar nominations.

One-Eyed Jacks (Marlon Brando 1961). Set, unusually for a Western, on the roaring shores of Monterey, where Brando tracks down Karl Malden – the bank-robbing partner who betrayed him five years earlier in Mexico – only to find him reformed and comfortably ensconced as sheriff.

Play Misty for Me (Clint Eastwood 1971). Another Monterey movie, Eastwood's directorial debut, a thriller about the consequences of a DJ's affair with a psychotic fan, was shot in Clint's home town of Carmel, and on his own two hundred acres of Monterey coastland.

Shadow of a Doubt (Alfred Hitchcock 1943). Urbane Uncle Charlie (Joseph Cotten) comes to stay with his sister's Santa Rosa family and seems to be the answer to his bored niece's prayers, until she starts to suspect that he might be a serial killer. Set in small-town Northern California.

Sideways (Alexander Payne 2004). Two vino-slurping pals take a trip into Napa wine country, one of them seeking a last fling before he gets married, the other wallowing in shame and self-pity. The golden landscapes often resemble a two-hour ad by the California tourism board.

Some Like It Hot (Billy Wilder 1959). The film some claim as the best comedy ever, set around a luxurious Florida resort that's actually San Diego's own *Hotel del Coronado* (see p.231), itself dripping with swank beachfront elegance.

The Stuntman (Richard Rush 1980). As with *Some Like It Hot*, filmed at the "Del," but with a wildly different story: a man on the run from the law takes refuge on Peter O'Toole's film set, where he is surprisingly enlisted as a stuntman in a goofy, World War II–era action flick.

Three Women (Robert Altman 1977). A fascinating, hypnotic, and unique film in which Sissy Spacek and Shelley Duvall, co-workers at a geriatric center in Desert Springs, mysteriously absorb each other's identity.

Zabriskie Point (Michelangelo Antonioni 1970). Muddled, pretentious misfire from the director that nonetheless features some promising early work by Jack Nicholson and visually interesting shots of the California desert.

California in fiction

While California may be mythologized as the ultimate stimulant for the imagination, it has inspired comparatively few travel writers, an exception being Robert Louis Stevenson, whose lively description of the Napa Valley and Mount St Helena is printed below. In contrast, floods of fiction have poured out of the state, in particular Los Angeles, over the last few decades, not only shaping perceptions of the region, but often redefining the whole course of modern American writing.

The contemporary writers featured here – Amy Tan and T. Coraghessan Boyle – are both concerned with newcomers to the state: Amy Tan with the interaction of an older generation who grew up in China with their sophisticated San Francisco daughters, and T.C. Boyle with the explosion of the Mexican population in LA, and its uneasy impact on the white elite.

Robert Louis Stevenson

Robert Louis Stevenson was born in Edinburgh in 1850, and was educated at the academy and university there. He became an ardent traveler, writing *An Inland Voyage* and *Travels with a Donkey* about his journeys through France, where he fell in love with a married American woman, Fanny Osbourne. She obtained her divorce in 1879 and Stevenson, battling with ill health, sailed to America to marry her. They took their honeymoon in the mountains of San Francisco. The result of this happy period in Stevenson's life is *Silverado Squatters*, a charming, if occasionally slight, volume about the landscape and characters of the mountains, already inflected with Stevenson's vigorous descriptive powers – and love of a good yarn. In this extract, Stevenson sets the scene of his book, and interestingly prefigures how development will change the area.

The Silverado Squatters

The scene of this little book is on a high mountain. There are, indeed, many higher; there are many of a nobler outline. It is no place of pilgrimage for the summary globe-trotter; but to one who lives upon its sides, Mount Saint Helena soon becomes a centre of interest. It is the Mont Blanc of one section of the Californian Coast Range, none of its near neighbours rising to one-half its altitude. It looks down on much green, intricate country. It feeds in the spring-time many splashing brooks. From its summit you must have an excellent lesson of geography: seeing, to the south, San Francisco Bay, with Tamalpais on the one hand and Monte Diablo on the other; to the west and thirty miles away, the open ocean; eastward, across the cornlands and thick tule swamps of Sacramento Valley, to where the Central Pacific railroad begins to climb the sides of the Sierras; and northward, for what I know, the white head of Shasta looking down on Oregon. Three counties, Napa County, Lake County, and Sonoma County, march across its cliffy shoulders. Its naked peak stands nearly four thousand five hundred feet above the sea; its sides are fringed with forest; and the soil, where it is bare, glows warm with cinnabar.

Life in its shadow goes rustically forward. Bucks, and bears, and rattlesnakes, and former mining operations, are the staple of men's talk. Agriculture has only begun to mount above the valley. And though in a few years from now the whole district may be smiling with farms, passing trains shaking the mountain to the heart, many-windowed hotels lighting up the night like factories, and a prosperous city occupying the site of sleepy Calistoga; yet in the meantime, around the foot of that mountain the silence of nature reigns in a great measure unbroken, and the people of hill and valley go sauntering about their business as in the days before the flood.

To reach Mount Saint Helena from San Francisco the traveller has twice to cross the bay: once by the busy Oakland Ferry, and again, after an hour or so of the railway, from Vallejo junction to Vallejo. Thence he takes rail once more to mount the long green strath of Napa Valley.

In all the contractions and expansions of that inland sea, the Bay of San Francisco, there can be few drearier scenes than the Vallejo Ferry. Bald shores and a low, bald islet enclose the sea; through the narrows the tide bubbles, muddy like a river. When we made the passage (bound, although yet we knew it not, for Silverado) the steamer jumped, and the black buoys were dancing in the jabble; the ocean breeze blew killing chill; and, although the upper sky was still unflecked with vapour, the sea fogs were pouring in from seaward, over the hilltops of Marin County, in one great, shapeless, silver cloud.

South Vallejo is typical of many Californian towns. It was a blunder; the site had proved untenable; and, although it is still such a young place by the scale of Europe, it has already begun to be deserted for its neighbour and namesake, North Vallejo. A long pier, a number of drinking saloons, a hotel of a great size, marshy pools where the frogs keep up their croaking, and even at high noon the entire absence of any human face or voice – these are the marks of South Vallejo. Yet there was a tall building beside the pier, labelled the Star Flour Mills; and seagoing, full-rigged ships lay close along shore, waiting for their cargo. Soon these would be plunging round the Horn, soon the flour from the Star Flour Mills would be landed on the wharves of Liverpool. For that, too, is one of England's outposts; thither, to this gaunt mill, across the Atlantic and Pacific deeps and round about the icy Horn, this crowd of great, three-masted, deep-sea ships come, bringing nothing, and return with bread.

The Frisby House, for that was the name of the hotel, was a place of fallen fortunes, like the town. It was now given up to labourers, and partly ruinous. At dinner there was the ordinary display of what is called in the west a two-bit house: the tablecloth checked red and white, the plague of flies, the wire hencoops over the dishes, the great variety and invariable vileness of the food and the rough coatless men devouring it in silence. In our bedroom, the stove would not burn, though it would smoke; and while one window would not open, the other would not shut. There was a view on a bit of empty road, a few dark houses, a donkey wandering with its shadow on a slope, and a blink of sea, with a tall ship lying anchored in the moonlight. All about that dreary inn frogs sang their ungainly chorus.

Early the next morning we mounted the hill along a wooden footway, bridging one marish spot after another. Here and there, as we ascended, we passed a house embowered in white roses. More of the bay became apparent, and soon the blue peak of Tamalpais rose above the green level of the island opposite. It told us we were still but a little way from the city of the Golden Gates, already, at that hour, beginning to awake among the sand-hills. It called to us over the waters as with the voice of a bird. Its stately head, blue as a sapphire on the paler azure of the sky, spoke to us of wider outlooks and the bright Pacific. For Tamalpais stands sentry, like a lighthouse, over the Golden Gates, between the bay and the open ocean, and looks down indifferently on both. Even as we saw and hailed it from Vallejo, seamen, far out at sea, were scanning it with shaded eyes; and, as if to answer to the thought, one of the great ships below began silently to clothe herself with white sails, homeward bound for England.

For some way beyond Vallejo the railway led us through bald green pastures. On the west the rough highlands of Marin shut off the ocean; in the midst, in long, straggling, gleaming arms, the bay died out among the grass; there were few trees and few enclosures; the sun shone wide over open uplands, the displumed hills stood clear against the sky. But by-and-by these hills began to draw nearer on either hand, and first thicket and then wood began to clothe their sides; and soon we were away from all signs of the sea's neighbourhood, mounting an inland, irrigated valley. A great variety of oaks stood, now severally, now in a becoming grove, among the fields and vineyards. The towns were compact, in about equal proportions, of bright, new wooden houses and great and growing forest trees; and the chapel bell on the engine sounded most festally that sunny Sunday, as we drew up at one green town after another, with the townsfolk trooping in their Sunday's best to see the strangers, with the sun sparkling on the clean houses, and great domes of foliage humming overhead in the breeze.

This pleasant Napa valley is, at its north end, blockaded by our mountain. There, at Calistoga, the railroad ceases, and the traveller who intends faring farther, to the Geysers or to the springs in Lake County, must cross the spurs of the mountain by stage. Thus, Mount Saint Helena is not only a summit, but frontier; and, up to the time of writing, it has stayed the progress of the iron horse.

Amy Tan

Amy Tan was born in Oakland in 1952, and first visited China in 1987. Her father, who was educated in Beijing and worked for the United States Information Service after the war, came to America in 1947. Her mother came to the United States in 1949, shortly before the Communists seized control of Shanghai. Amy Tan now lives in San Francisco and New York. Her first work of fiction, *The Joy Luck Club*, explores the nuances of Chinese-American identity through the relationships between four Chinese mothers and their American daughters, each of whom narrate their own stories, rich in detail and atmosphere. Each character's story carries inflections of their cultural identity, which is both a barrier to understanding between the two generations, and a source of shared strength. Here junior chess champion Waverly Jong takes a plunge into San Francisco's Chinatown.

The Joy Luck Club

My mother imparted her daily truths so she could help my older brothers and me rise above our circumstances. We lived in San Francisco's Chinatown. Like most of the other Chinese children who played in the back alleys of restaurants and curio shops, I didn't think we were poor. My bowl was always full, three five-course meals every day, beginning with a soup full of mysterious things I didn't want to know the names of.

We lived on Waverly Place, in a warm, clean, two-bedroom flat that sat above a small Chinese bakery specializing in steamed pastries and dim sum. In the early morning, when the alley was still quiet, I could smell fragrant red beans as they were cooked down to a pasty sweetness. By daybreak, our flat was heavy with the odor of fried sesame balls and sweet curried chicken crescents. From my bed, I would listen as my father got ready for work, then locked the door behind him, one-two-three clicks.

At the end of our two-block alley was a small sandlot playground with swings and slides well-shined down the middle with use. The play area was bordered by wood-slat benches where old-country people sat cracking roasted watermelon seeds with their golden teeth and scattering the husks to an impatient gathering of gurgling pigeons. The best playground, however, was the dark alley itself. It was crammed with daily mysteries and adventures. My brothers and I would peer into the medicinal herb shop, watching old Li dole out onto a stiff sheet of white paper the right amount of insect shells, saffron-colored seeds, and pungent leaves for his ailing customers. It was said that he once cured a woman dying of an ancestral curse that had eluded the best of American doctors. Next to the pharmacy was a printer who specialized in gold-embossed wedding invitations and festive red banners.

Farther down the street was Ping Yuen Fish Market. The front window displayed a tank crowded with doomed fish and turtles struggling to gain footing on the slimy green-tiled sides. A hand-written sign informed tourists, "Within this store, is all for food, not for pet." Inside, the butchers with their bloodstained white smocks deftly gutted the fish while customers cried out their orders and shouted, "Give me your freshest," to which the butchers always protested, "All are freshest." On less crowded market days, we would inspect the crates of live frogs and crabs which we were warned not to poke, boxes of dried cuttlefish, and row upon row of iced prawns, squid, and slippery fish. The sanddabs made me shiver each time; their eyes lay on one flattened side and reminded me of my mother's story of a careless girl who ran into a crowded street and was crushed by a cab. "Was smash flat," reported my mother.

At the corner of the alley was Hong Sing's, a four-table café with a recessed stairwell in front that led to a door marked "Tradesmen." My brothers and I believed the bad people emerged from this door at night. Tourists never went to Hong Sing's, since the menu was printed only in Chinese. A Caucasian man with a big camera once posed me and my playmates in front of the restaurant. He had us move to the side of the picture window so the photo would capture the roasted duck with its head dangling from a juice-covered rope. After he took the picture, I told him he should go into Hong Sing's and eat dinner. When he smiled and asked me what they served, I shouted, "Guts and duck's feet and octopus gizzards!" Then I ran off with my friends, shrieking with laughter as we scampered across the alley and hid in the entryway grotto of the China Gem Company, my heart pounding with hope that he would chase us.

My mother named me after the street that we lived on: Waverly Place Jong, my official name for important American documents. But my family called me Meimei, "Little Sister." I was the youngest, the only daughter. Each morning before school, my mother would twist and yank on my thick black hair until she had formed two tightly wound pigtails. One day, as she struggled to weave a hard-toothed comb through my disobedient hair, I had a sly thought.

I asked her, "Ma, what is Chinese torture?" My mother shook her head. A bobby pin was wedged between her lips. She wetted her palm and smoothed the hair above my ear, then pushed the pin in so that it nicked sharply against my scalp.

"Who say this word?" she asked without a trace of knowing how wicked I was being. I shrugged my shoulders and said, "Some boy in my class said Chinese people do Chinese torture."

"Chinese people do many things," she said simply. "Chinese people do business, do medicine, do painting. Not lazy like American people. We do torture. Best torture."

T. Coraghessan Boyle

PEN/Faulkner Award winner **T. Coraghessan Boyle** was born in Manhattan, but now lives in California; his sixth novel, *The Tortilla Curtain*, is pure LA. Its protagonist, prosperous and peaceable Delaney, lives on the leafy fringes of the city and spins out his nature column "Pilgrim at Topanga Creek," while his dynamic wife Kyra shifts real estate. Meanwhile another pilgrim has come to the creek: Cándido, an illegal Mexican immigrant, who is trying to protect his young pregnant wife América from the natural and unnatural forces around them. The initial violent encounter between the two men precipitates events that both tear at the veneer of Delaney's liberalism, satirized with easy precision by Boyle, and expose the vulnerability of LA's legions of have-nots. In this extract, Delaney's incipient fear of invasion is realized, in an unexpected and dramatic form.

The Tortilla Curtain

High up in the canyon, nestled in a fan-shaped depression dug out of the side of the western ridge by the action of some long-forgotten stream, lay the subdivision known as Arroyo Blanco Estates. It was a private community, comprising a golf course, ten tennis courts, a community center and some two hundred and fifty homes, each set on one-point-five acres and strictly conforming to the covenants, conditions and restrictions set forth in the 1973 articles of incorporation. The houses were all of the Spanish Mission style, painted in one of three prescribed shades of white, with orange tile roofs. If you wanted to paint your house sky-blue or Provençal-pink with lime-green shutters, you were perfectly welcome to move into the San Fernando Valley or to Santa Monica or anywhere else you chose, but if you bought into Arroyo Blanco Estates, your house would be white and your roof orange.

Delaney Mossbacher made his home in one of these Spanish Mission houses (floor plan #A227C, Rancho White with Navajo trim), along with his second wife, Kyra, her son, Jordan, her matching Dandie Dinmont terriers, Osbert and Sacheverell, and her Siamese cat, Dame Edith. On this particular morning, the morning that Cándido Rincón began to feel he'd lost control of his wife, Delaney was up at seven, as usual, to drip Kyra's coffee, feed Jordan his fruit, granola and hi-fiber bar and let Osbert and Sacheverell out into the yard to perform their matinal functions. He hadn't forgotten his unfortunate encounter with Cándido four days earlier – the thought of it still made his stomach clench – but the needs and wants and minor irritations of daily life had begun to push it into the background. At the moment, his attention was focused entirely on getting through the morning ritual with his customary speed and efficiency. He was nothing if not efficient.

He made a sort of game of it, counting the steps it took him to shut the windows against the coming day's heat, empty yesterday's coffee grounds into the mulch bucket, transform two kiwis, an orange, apple, banana and a handful of Bing cherries into Jordan's medley of fresh fruit, and set the table for two. He skated across the tile floor to the dishwasher, flung open the cabinets, rocketed the plates and cutlery into position on the big oak table, all the while keeping an eye on the coffee, measuring out two bowls of dog food and juicing the oranges he'd plucked from the tree in the courtyard.

Typically, he stole a moment out in the courtyard to breathe in the cool of the morning and listen to the scrub jays wake up the neighborhood, but today he was in a rush and the only sound that penetrated his consciousness was a strange excited yelp from one of the dogs – they must have found something in the fenced-in yard behind the house, a squirrel or a gopher maybe – and then he was back in the kitchen, squeezing oranges. That was what he did, every morning, regular as clockwork: squeeze oranges. After which he would dash round the house gathering up Jordan's homework, his backpack, lunchbox and baseball cap, while Kyra sipped her coffee and washed down her twelve separate vitamin and mineral supplements with half a glass of fresh-squeezed orange juice. Then it was time to drive Jordan to school, while Kyra applied her makeup, wriggled into a form-fitting skirt with matching jacket and propelled her Lexus over the crest of the canyon and into Woodland Hills, where she was the undisputed volume leader at Mike Bender Realty, Inc. And then, finally, Delaney would head back home, have a cup of herbal tea and two slices of wheat toast, dry, and let the day settle in around him.

Unless there was an accident on the freeway or a road crew out picking up or setting down their ubiquitous plastic cones, he would be back at home and sitting at his desk by nine. This was the moment he lived for, the moment his day really began. Unfailingly, no matter what pressures were brought to bear on him or what emergencies arose, he allotted the next four hours to his writing – four hours during which he could let go of the world around him, his fingers grazing lightly over the keyboard, the green glow of the monitor bathing him in its hypnotic light. He took the phone off the hook, pulled the shades and crept into the womb of language.

There, in the silence of the empty house, Delaney worked out the parameters of his monthly column for Wide Open Spaces, a naturalist's observations of the life blooming around him day by day, season by season. He called it "Pilgrim at Topanga Creek" in homage to Annie Dillard, and while he couldn't pretend to her mystical connection to things, or her verbal virtuosity either, he did feel that he stood apart from his fellow men and women, that he saw more deeply and felt more passionately – particularly about nature. And every day, from nine to one, he had the opportunity to prove it.

Of course, some days went better than others. He tried to confine himself to the flora and fauna of Topanga Canyon and the surrounding mountains, but increasingly he found himself brooding over the fate of the pupfish, the Florida manatee and the spotted owl, the ocelot, the pine marten, the panda. And how could he ignore the larger trends – overpopulation, desertification, the depletion of the seas and the forests, global warming and loss of habitat? We were all right in America, sure, but it was crazy to think you could detach yourself from the rest of the world, the world of starvation and loss and the steady relentless degradation of the environment. Five and a half billion people chewing up the resources of the planet like locusts, and only seventy-three California condors left in all the universe.

It gave him pause. It depressed him. There were days when he worked himself into such a state he could barely lift his fingers to the keys, but fortunately the good days outnumbered them, the days when he celebrated his afternoon hikes through the chaparral and into the ravines of the mist-hung mountains, and that was what people wanted – celebration, not lectures, not the strident call to ecologic arms, not the death knell and the weeping and gnashing of environmental teeth. The world was full of bad news. Why contribute more?

The sun had already begun to burn off the haze by the time Jordan scuffed into the kitchen, the cat at his heels. Jordan was six years old, dedicated to Nintendo, superheroes and baseball cards, though as far as Delaney could see he had no interest whatever in the game of baseball beyond possessing the glossy cardboard images of the players. He favored his mother facially and in the amazing lightness of his hair, which was so pale as to be nearly translucent. He might have been big for his age, or maybe he was small – Delaney had nothing to compare him to.

"Kiwi," Jordan said, thumping into his seat at the table, and that was all. Whether this was an expression of approval or distaste, Delaney couldn't tell. From the living room came the electronic voice of the morning news: Thirty-seven Chinese nationals were drowned early today when a smuggler's ship went aground just east of the Golden Gate Bridge . . . Outside, beyond the windows, there was another yelp from the dogs.

Jordan began to rotate his spoon in the bowl of fruit, a scrape and clatter accompanied by the moist sounds of mastication. Delaney, his back to the table, was scrubbing the counter in the vicinity of the stove, though any splashes of cooking oil or spatters of sauce must have been purely imaginary since he hadn't actually cooked anything. He scrubbed for the love of scrubbing. "Okay, buckaroo," he called over his shoulder, "you've got two choices today as far as your hi-fiber bar is concerned: Cranberry Nut and Boysenberry Supreme. What'll it be?"

From a mouth laden with kiwi: "Papaya Coconut."

"You got the last one yesterday."

No response.

"So what'll it be?"

Kyra insisted on the full nutritional slate for her son every morning – fresh fruit, granola with skim milk and brewer's yeast, hi-fiber bar. The child needed roughage. Vitamins. Whole grains. And breakfast, for a growing child at least, was the most important meal of the day, the foundation of all that was to come. That was how she felt. And while Delaney recognized a touch of the autocratic and perhaps even fanatic in the regimen, he by and large subscribed to it. He and Kyra had a lot in common, not only temperamentally, but in terms of their beliefs and ideals too – that was what had attracted them to each other in the first place. They were both perfectionists, for one thing. They abhorred clutter. They were joggers, nonsmokers, social drinkers, and if not full-blown vegetarians, people who were conscious of their intake of animal fats. Their memberships included the Sierra Club, Save the Children, the National Wildlife Federation and the Democratic Party. They preferred the contemporary look to Early American or kitsch. In religious matters, they were agnostic.

Delaney's question remained unanswered, but he was used to cajoling Jordan over his breakfast. He tiptoed across the room to hover behind the boy, who was playing with his spoon and chanting something under his breath. "Rookie card, rookie card," Jordan was saying, dipping into his granola without enthusiasm. "No looking now," Delaney warned, seductively tapping a foil-wrapped bar on either side of the boy's thin wilted neck, "right hand or left?"

Jordan reached up with his left hand, as Delaney knew he would, fastening on the Boysenberry Supreme bar just as Kyra, hunched over the weight of two boxes of hand-addressed envelopes – Excelsior, 500 Count – clattered into the kitchen in her heels. She made separate kissing motions in the direction of her husband and son, then slid into her chair, poured herself half a cup of coffee lightened with skim milk – for the calcium – and began sifting purposively through the envelopes.

"Why can't I have Sugar Pops or Honey Nut Cheerios like other kids? Or bacon and eggs?" Jordan pinched his voice. "Mom? Why can't I?"

Kyra gave the stock response – "You're not other kids, that's why" – and Delaney was taken back to his own childhood, a rainy night in the middle of an interminable winter, a plate of liver, onions and boiled potatoes before him.

"I hate granola," Jordan countered, and it was like a Noh play, timeless ritual.

"It's good for you."

"Yeah, sure." Jordan made an exaggerated slurping sound, sucking the milk through his teeth.

"Think of all the little children who have nothing to eat," Kyra said without looking up, and Jordan, sticking to the script, came right back at her: "Let's send them this."

Now she looked up. "Eat," she said, and the drama was over.

"Busy day?" Delaney murmured, setting Kyra's orange juice down beside the newspaper and unscrewing the childproof caps of the sturdy plastic containers that held her twelve separate vitamin and mineral supplements. He did the little things for her – out of love and consideration, sure, but also in acknowledgment of the fact that she was the chief breadwinner here, the one who went off to the office while he stayed home. Which was all right by him. He had none of those juvenile macho hang-ups about role reversal and who wore the pants and all of that – real estate was her life, and he was more than happy to help her with it, so long as he got his four hours a day at the keyboard.

Kyra lifted her eyebrows, but didn't look up. She was tucking what looked to be a small white packet into each of the envelopes in succession. "Busy?" she echoed. "Busy isn't the word for it. I'm presenting two offers this morning, both of them real low-ball, I've got a buyer with cold feet on that Calabasas property – with escrow due to close in eight days – and I'm scheduled for an open house on the Via Escobar place at one . . . is that the dogs I hear? What are they barking at?"

Delaney shrugged. Jordan had shucked the foil from his hi-fiber bar and was drifting toward the TV room with it – which meant he was going to be late for school if Delaney didn't hustle him out of there within the next two minutes. The cat, as yet unfed, rubbed up against Delaney's leg. "I don't know," he said. "They've been yapping since I let them out. Must be a squirrel or something. Or maybe Jack's dog got loose again and he's out there peeing on the fence and driving them into a frenzy."

"Anyway," Kyra went on, "it's going to be hell. And it's Carla Bayer's birthday, so after work a bunch of us – don't you think this is a cute idea?" She held up one of the packets she'd been stuffing the envelopes with. It was a three-by-five seed packet showing a spray of flowers and printed with the legend Forget-Me-Not, Compliments of Kyra Menaker-Mossbacher, Mike Bender Realty, Inc.

"Yeah, I guess," he murmured, wiping at an imaginary speck on the counter. This was her way of touching base with her clients. Every month or so, usually in connection with a holiday, she went through her mailing list (consisting of anyone she'd ever sold to or for, whether they'd relocated to Nome,

Singapore or Irkutsk or passed on into the Great Chain of Being) and sent a small reminder of her continued existence and willingness to deal. She called it "keeping the avenues open." Delaney reached down to stroke the cat. "But can't one of the secretaries do this sort of thing for you?"

"It's the personal touch that counts – and moves property. How many times do I have to tell you?"

There was a silence, during which Delaney became aware of the cartoon jingle that had replaced the voice of the news in the other room, and then, just as he was clearing Jordan's things from the table and checking the digital display on the microwave for the time – 7:32 – the morning fell apart. Or no: it was torn apart by a startled breathless shriek that rose up from beyond the windows as if out of some primal dream. This was no yip, no yelp, no bark or howl – this was something final and irrevocable, a predatory scream that took the varnish off their souls, and it froze them in place. They listened, horrified, as it rose in pitch until it choked off as suddenly as it had begun.

The aftereffect was electric. Kyra bolted up out of her chair, knocking over her coffee cup and scattering envelopes; the cat darted between Delaney's legs and vanished; Delaney dropped the plate on the floor and groped for the counter like a blind man. And then Jordan was coming through the doorway on staccato feet, his face opened up like a pale nocturnal flower: "Delaney," he gasped, "something, something—"

But Delaney was already in motion. He flung open the door and shot through the courtyard, head down, rounding the corner of the house just in time to see a dun-colored blur scaling the six-foot chainlink fence with a tense white form clamped in its jaws. His brain decoded the image: a coyote had somehow managed to get into the enclosure and seize one of the dogs, and there it was, wild nature, up and over the fence as if this were some sort of circus act. Shouting to hear himself, shouting nonsense, Delaney charged across the yard as the remaining dog (Osbert? Sacheverell?) cowered in the corner and the dun blur melded with the buckwheat, chamise and stiff high grass of the wild hillside that gave onto the wild mountains beyond.

He didn't stop to think. In two bounds he was atop the fence and dropping to the other side, absently noting the paw prints in the dust, and then he was tearing headlong through the undergrowth, leaping rocks and shrubs and dodging the spines of the yucca plants clustered like breastworks across the slope. He was running, that was all he knew. Branches raked him like claws. Burrs bit into his ankles. He kept going, pursuing a streak of motion, the odd flash of white: now he saw it, now he didn't. "Hey!" he shouted. "Hey, goddamnit!"

The hillside sloped sharply upward, rising through the colorless scrub to a clump of walnut trees and jagged basalt outcroppings that looked as if they'd poked through the ground overnight. He saw the thing suddenly, the pointed snout and yellow eyes, the high stiff leggy gait as it struggled with its burden, and it was going straight up and into the trees. He shouted again and this time the shout was answered from below. Glancing over his shoulder, he saw that Kyra was coming up the hill with her long jogger's strides, in blouse, skirt and stocking feet. Even at this distance he could recognize the look on her face – the grim set of her jaw, the flaring eyes and clamped mouth that spelled doom for whoever got in her way, whether it was a stranger who'd locked his dog in a car with the windows rolled up or the hapless seller who refused a cash-out bid. She was coming, and that spurred him on. If he could only stay close the coyote would have to drop the dog, it would have to.

By the time he reached the trees his throat was burning. Sweat stung his eyes and his arms were striped with nicks and scratches. There was no sign of the dog and he pushed on through the trees to where the slope fell away to the feet of the next hill beyond it. The brush was thicker here – six feet high and so tightly interlaced it would have taken a machete to get through it in places – and he knew, despite the drumming in his ears and the glandular rush that had him pacing and whirling and clenching and unclenching his fists, that it was looking bad. Real bad. There were a thousand bushes out there – five thousand, ten thousand – and the coyote could be crouched under any one of them.

It was watching him even now, he knew it, watching him out of slit wary eyes as he jerked back and forth, frantically scanning the mute clutter of leaf, branch and thorn, and the thought infuriated him. He shouted again, hoping to flush it out. But the coyote was too smart for him. Ears pinned back, jaws and forepaws stifling its prey, it could lie there, absolutely motionless, for hours. "Osbert!" he called out suddenly, and his voice trailed off into a hopeless bleat. "Sacheverell!"

The poor dog. It couldn't have defended itself from a rabbit. Delaney stood on his toes, strained his neck, poked angrily through the nearest bush. Long low shafts of sunlight fired the leaves in an indifferent display, as they did every morning, and he looked into the illuminated depths of that bush and felt desolate suddenly, empty, cored out with loss and helplessness.

"Osbert!" The sound seemed to erupt from him, as if he couldn't control his vocal cords. "Here, boy! Come!" Then he shouted Sacheverell's name, over and over, but there was no answer except for a distant cry from Kyra, who seemed to be way off to his left now.

All at once he wanted to smash something, tear the bushes out of the ground by their roots. This didn't have to happen. It didn't. If it wasn't for those idiots leaving food out for the coyotes as if they were nothing more than sheep with bushy tails and eyeteeth . . . and he'd warned them, time and again. You can't be heedless of your environment. You can't. Just last week he'd found half a bucket of Kentucky Fried Chicken out back of the Dagolian place – waxy red-and-white-striped cardboard with a portrait of the grinning chicken-killer himself smiling large – and he'd stood up at the bimonthly meeting of the property owners' association to say something about it. They wouldn't even listen. Coyotes, gophers, yellow jackets, rattlesnakes even – they were a pain in the ass, sure, but nature was the least of their problems. It was humans they were worried about. The Salvadorans, the Mexicans, the blacks, the gangbangers and taggers and carjackers they read about in the Metro section over their bran toast and coffee. That's why they'd abandoned the flatlands of the Valley and the hills of the Westside to live up here, outside the city limits, in the midst of all this scenic splendor.

Coyotes? Coyotes were quaint. Little demi-dogs out there howling at the sunset, another amenity like the oaks, the chaparral and the views. No, all Delaney's neighbors could talk about, back and forth and on and on as if it were the key to all existence, was gates. A gate, specifically. To be erected at the main entrance and manned by a twenty-four-hour guard to keep out those very gangbangers, taggers and carjackers they'd come here to escape. Sure. And now poor Osbert – or Sacheverell – was nothing more than breakfast.

The fools. The idiots.

Delaney picked up a stick and began to beat methodically at the bushes.

Books

California may well be the subject of more books than any other US state outside of New York or Massachusetts, and for contemporary culture it's clearly drawn the most ink. Most of the state's stories tend to revolve around the Spanish Mission era, Gold Rush, movie industry, and modern politics and mores. LA and San Francisco are predictably well covered, though other major cities appear much less often, with San Diego in particular yet to find an insightful chronicler on the order of Carey McWilliams (for LA), Herb Caen (SF), or Kevin Starr (the entire state). In the following listing, wherever a book is in print, the publisher's name is given in parentheses after the title, in the format: UK publisher; US publisher. Where books are published in only one of these countries, we have specified which one; when the same company publishes the book in both, it appears just once. The note "o/p" signifies an out-of-print title – which you may be able to find through one of the many used-book sellers in LA or on the Internet.

Travel and impressions

Umberto Eco *Travels in Hyperreality* (Harcourt Brace, US). Influential examination of the still-potent concept of "simulacra," in which reality is denigrated in favor of its crass imitation. Examples are a bit dated now, though, including a now-closed museum in Orange County that re-created the great works of art as wax figurines.

Barney Hoskyns *Beneath the Diamond Sky: Haight–Ashbury 1965–1970* (Simon & Shuster, US). A vivid account of the glory days of mid-1960s psychedelia, with evocative pictures of seminal rock bands such as the Jefferson Airplane, Grateful Dead, and Charlatans, and a narrative that describes how the hippie paradise was lost.

Robert Koenig *Mouse Tales* (Bonaventure Press). All the Disneyland dirt that's fit to print: a behind-the-scenes look at the ugly little secrets – from disenchanted workers to vermin infestations – that lurk behind the happy walls of the Magic Kingdom.

Leonard Pitt and Dale Pitt *Los Angeles A to Z* (University of California Press, US). If you're truly enthralled by the city, this is the tome for you: six-hundred pages of encyclopedic references covering everything from conquistadors to movie stars.

★ **Mark Twain** *Roughing It* (Penguin; University of California Press). Vivid tales of frontier California, particularly evocative of life in the silver mines of the 1860s Comstock Lode, where Twain got his start as a journalist and storyteller.

John Waters *Crackpot* (Fourth Estate; Random House). Odds and ends from the Pope of Trash, the mind behind cult film *Pink Flamingos*, including a personalized tour of LA.

★ **Tom Wolfe** *The Electric Kool-Aid Acid Test* (Black Swan; Bantam). Take an LSD-fueled bus trip with Ken Kesey and his Merry Pranksters as they travel through mid-1960s California, before the counterculture was discovered, and co-opted, by corporate America.

History

Oscar Zeta Acosta *Autobiography of a Brown Buffalo*, *Revolt of the Cockroach People* (Vintage). The legendary model for Hunter S. Thompson's bloated D. Gonzo, this author was in reality a trailblazing Hispanic lawyer who used all manner of colorful tactics to defend oppressed and indigent defendants. Two vivid portraits of late-1960s California, written just before the author mysteriously vanished in 1971.

★ **Mark Arax and Rick Wartzman** *The King of California: J.G. Boswell and the Making of a Secret American Empire* (Public Affairs, US). Essential reading for anyone interested in the real history of the state, focusing on how a family of Georgia farmers migrated to the San Joaquin Valley and created the nation's biggest cotton empire with hardly anyone noticing.

H.W. Brands *The Age of Gold* (Doubleday). Excellent introduction to Gold Rush–era California, highlighting the immigrants from around the world who came to mine the ore, the unexpected fortunes of a lucky few, and the political and social repercussions of this unprecedented event – the first glimmer of the Gilded Age.

Gray Brechin *Imperial San Francisco: Urban Power, Earthly Ruin* (University of California, US). Long-overdue puncturing of myths about the City of the Bay, showing how dubious mining and financial schemes led to its rise, and how its history, strangely enough, parallels that of ancient Rome and other classical cities.

James Conaway *Napa: the Story of an American Eden* (Mariner, US). Compelling story of how Napa Valley vintners attained international glory through clever science and down-and-dirty politics. A follow-up volume, *The Far Side of Eden* (Houghton Mifflin), details how fame and fortune have led to corruption and malaise.

★ **Carey McWilliams** *Southern California: an Island on the Land* (Peregrine Smith, US). The bible of Southern Californian histories, focusing on the key years between the two world wars and written by a lawyer and social activist involved in much of the drama of the time. Evocatively written and richly detailed.

★ **Harris Newmark** *Sixty Years in Southern California: 1853–1913* (Houghton Mifflin, US). One of the great nineteenth-century leaders of the Jewish community offers an insider's take on the region's politics as well as various secrets of the time.

Mark Reisner *Cadillac Desert* (Penguin). An essential guide to water problems in the American West, with special emphasis on LA's schemes to bring upstate California water to the metropolis. One of the best renderings of this sordid tale.

W.W. Robinson *Ranchos become Cities* (San Pasqual Press, US). A chronicle of the changes that turned the old Mexican rancho system into subdivided plots of land fit for real-estate speculation, urban growth, and massive profit-taking.

Kevin Starr *Inventing the Dream* (OUP). The best in a long series of sometimes captivating, sometimes aggravating books on the phenomenon known as California, this one covering the time up to the Roaring 20s. The latest, and perhaps the most uneven, *Coast of Dreams* (Knopf), puts a rosy glow around contemporary chaos.

Dale L. Walker *Bear Flag Rising: the Conquest of California, 1846* (Forge). An entertaining and painstakingly detailed account of how the US, in the name of Manifest Destiny, acquired California from Mexico.

Politics and society

Jean Baudrillard *America* (Verso). Scattered thoughts of the trendy French philosopher, whose (very) occasionally brilliant but often overreaching analysis of American pop culture, especially in LA, is undermined by factual errors.

★ **Mike Davis** *City of Quartz* (Picador; Vintage). The most important modern history of LA, in this case from a Leftist perspective, vividly covering cops, riots, politicians, movies, and architecture. Other volumes, *Ecology of Fear* and *Under the Perfect Sun* (New Press, US), respectively tell of LA's apocalyptic bent in fiction and reality, and of the corruption at the core of sunny San Diego.

Gordon DeMarco *A Short History of Los Angeles* (Lexicos US o/p). Excellent 180-page summary of the major events and phenomena that have shaped the city, with particular regard to class and racial struggles.

Joan Didion *Slouching towards Bethlehem* (Flamingo; Noonday Press). Love her or hate her, these essays from one of California's most polarizing writers take a critical look at 1960s California, from the acid culture of San Francisco to a profile of American tough guy John Wayne. In a similar style, *The White Album* (Farrar Straus & Giroux, UK) traces the West Coast characters and events that shaped the Sixties and Seventies.

Frances Fitzgerald *Cities on a Hill* (Picador; Simon & Schuster). Intelligent and sympathetic exploration of four of the odder corners of American culture, including San Francisco's Castro district.

Maxine Hong Kingston *China Men* (Picador; Vintage). A compelling history dealing with the various waves of Chinese immigrants to America, but specifically California. Interwoven with fact and myth, *China Men* examines the nature of being an American.

Lisa McGirr *Suburban Warriors: the Origins of the New American Right* (Princeton University Press, US). The tale of how once-fringe right-wing activists in Southern California rose from the ashes of the 1960s to dominate state and, later, national politics, culminating with the presidency of Ronald Reagan and his followers.

Russel Miller *Barefaced Messiah* (Sphere; Holt; both o/p). Eye-opening study of the rise of L. Ron Hubbard and Scientology, the new American religion that has its headquarters in LA and acolytes lurking everywhere.

Randy Shilts *The Mayor of Castro Street: the Life and Times of Harvey Milk* (St. Martin's, US). Overview of the life, career, and martyrdom of one of America's most famous gay-rights advocates, presented as an emblem for the rise of identity politics and social activism in 1970s California.

Danny Sugarman *Wonderland Avenue* (Abacus; Bullfinch). Publicist for The Doors and other seminal US rock bands from the late Sixties on, Sugarman delivers a raunchy autobiographical account of sex, drugs, and LA rock'n'roll.

Architecture

Reyner Banham *Los Angeles: the Architecture of Four Ecologies* (Penguin). The most lucid account of how LA's history has shaped its present form; the author's enthusiasms are infectious.

Federal Writers Project *The WPA Guide to California* (Pantheon, US). Republished 1939 guide that is a remarkable handbook to the architecture and neighborhoods of its time.

David Gebhard *Guide to Architecture in San Francisco and Northern California* (Gibbs Smith, US). Although it stops at the 1980s, this volume highlights the best and most engaging buildings of the north, to match those of the south in the author's classic *Los Angeles: the Architecture Guide* (Gibbs Smith, US).

Philip Jodidio *Contemporary Californian Architects* (Taschen). This photo-heavy glossy argues that the public and private buildings of Frank Gehry, Eric Owen Moss, Frank Israel, and Michael Rotundi, among others, are strongly influenced by the state itself.

Esther McCoy *Five California Architects* (Hennessey and Ingalls, US). The still-relevant 1960s book that first drew attention to LA's Irving Gill, an early twentieth-century forerunner of the modern style in San Diego and LA, along with other important architects who practiced in Southern California.

Richard Meier *Building the Getty* (University of California Press; Knopf). If you're a fan of this hill-top art colossus in West LA, you'll want to pick up this highly read-able account of the conception and creation of the Getty Center, as told by its architect, the high prince of modernism.

Charles Moore *The City Observed: Los Angeles* (Random House, US). Twenty-year-old volume that still merits a read for its maps, pictures, anecdotes, and recommendations to set you on your way to exploring the old-time nooks and crannies of LA.

Elizabeth Pomada, et al *Painted Ladies Revisited* (Studio Books, US). One in a series of volumes on Victorian mansions (in San Francisco and beyond) that you'll see in book-stores throughout the region, and well worth a look as a photo glossy and architecture guide.

Elizabeth A.T. Smith *Blueprints for Modern Living: History and Legacy of the Case Study Houses* (MIT Press, US). An excellent compendium of essays and articles about the built and unbuilt homes of California's renowned Case Study Program, with descriptions, diagrams, and photo-graphs of each.

Hollywood and the movies

Kenneth Anger *Hollywood Babylon* (Arrow; Bantam). A vicious yet high-spirited romp through Tinseltown's greatest scandals, written by one of the great avant-garde filmmakers. A second volume, *Hollywood Babylon II* (E.P. Dutton o/p), covers more recent times, but was hurriedly put together and not as well researched.

Robert Berger *Last Remaining Seats* (Balcony Press; Princeton Archi-tectural Press). An excellent photo guide to the extant movie palaces of Los Angeles, particularly along the Broadway corridor, including many shots of theaters that are now closed to the public.

Kevin Brownlow *Hollywood: the Pioneers* (Knopf, US). An intriguing look at the founders of American cinema in the silent era, told from the points of view of an esteemed film historian and preservationist, and a prolific writer on movie topics.

Otto Friedrich *City of Nets* (Headline o/p; University of Califor-nia Press). Descriptions of the major actors, directors, and studio bosses of the last good years of the studio sys-tem, before TV, antitrust actions, and Joe McCarthy ruined it all.

Ephraim Katz *The Film Encyclopedia* (Harper). Massive, essential reference guide for anyone interested in Hollywood, providing valuable information on the old movie companies and countless studio-system bit players, along with more contemporary figures. The first, 1980 edition is by far the best – the original author died soon after.

Clayton R. Koppes and Gregory D. Black *Hollywood Goes to War* (I.B. Tauris o/p; University of California Press). Masterly examination of the influence of World War II on the film industry – and vice versa.

Michael Munn *Hollywood Murder Casebook* (St Martin's o/p). If you really want to dive into the ugly side of Tinseltown, this is your book, examining the gory details of Hollywood murders with clinical efficiency.

Julia Phillips *You'll Never Eat Lunch in This Town Again* (Mandarin; Signet). Amusing, if somewhat self-serving, portrayal of the drugs and violence behind the Hollywood gloss.

Alain Silver and Julia Ward *Film Noir* (Overlook, US). Large-format guide to the bleak films of the 1940s to the present, and an essential title that has gone through many editions.

Jerry Stahl *Permanent Midnight* (Warner). When his employers heard star scriptwriter Stahl (*Moonlighting*, *thirtysomething*) was spending his already-huge paycheck to support his heroin and other habits, they gave him a raise to cover the difference and keep him on the job. A gritty descent into Tinseltown drug hell.

Specialist guides

Bicycle Rider Directory (Cycle America, US). Low-cost guide to do-it-yourself bicycle touring around the Bay Area and Napa and Sonoma valleys, with good fold-out route maps.

Tom Kirkendall and Vicky Spring *Bicycling the Pacific Coast* (Mountaineers Books, US). Detailed guide to the bike routes all the way along the coast from Mexico up to Canada.

John J. Lamb *San Diego Specters* (Sunbelt, US). Looking into the ghosts, poltergeists, and other assorted spooks that populate San Diego County. An intriguing counterpart to the usual sun-and-surf books about the city.

Peterson Series Field Guides *Field Guide to Western Reptiles and Amphibians/ Insects/ Pacific State Wildflowers* (all Houghton Mifflin). Excellent general field guides to the flora and fauna of California and the West Coast.

Ray Riegert *Hidden Coast of California* (Ulysses). A detailed and interesting guide to the nooks and crannies along the California state beaches and parks, told from the perspective of a recreational enthusiast who tracks down all his favorite underrated beachside gems.

Jeffery Schaffer *The Pacific Crest Trail: California* (Wilderness Press). A guide to the southern section of the trail that leads all the way from Mexico to Canada through the Sierra Nevada range.

John R. Soares *100 Classic Hikes in Northern California* (Mountaineers Books). An engaging presentation of wilderness hiking in the northern side of the state, from the Bay Area up to the Oregon border.

Tom Steinstra and Ann Marie Brown *California Hiking: the Complete Guide* (Foghorn Press, US). Dense 700-page tome detailing over 1000 hikes, from hour-long strolls to the 1700 Californian miles of the Pacific Crest Trail. Unfortunately, the trail notes and maps are limited, and the text is hardly inspirational.

★ **Walking the West Series**
Walking Southern California/ California Coast/ California's State Parks; and others (all HarperReference). Well-written paperbacks, each covering over a hundred excellent day-walks from two to twenty miles. Strong on practical details (maps, route descriptions, and so on), and boast inspiring prose and historical background.

Fiction and literature

Eve Babitz *Eve's Hollywood* (Delacorte o/p), *Slow Days, Fast Company* (Knopf o/p), *LA Woman* (Simon & Schuster o/p). Eye-opening, thinly veiled autobiographical portraits of Southern California in the 1960s and 70s, with all the drugs, sex, and rock 'n' roll you can imagine, but described in a relaxed, sometimes wistful, manner. Though all are out of print, only the first is difficult to find online.

James P. Blaylock *Land of Dreams* (Grafton o/p; Ace Books). A fantastic tale spun out as the twelve-year Solstice comes to a Northern Californian coastal town.

T. Coraghessan Boyle *The Tortilla Curtain* (Bloomsbury; Penguin). Set in LA, this novel boldly borrows its premise – a privileged white man running down a member of the city's ethnic underclass – from Tom Wolfe's *The Bonfire of the Vanities*, and develops its plot with a similar intensity.

Scott Bradfield *What's Wrong with America* (Picador). Humor and idiosyncratic absurdity combine as Bradfield explores America's malaise through an elderly woman's slide towards mental breakdown. Southern California provides the backdrop and its people the caricatured bit players.

Richard Brautigan Tacoma-born writer more often associated with the California Beat writers of the Fifties and Sixties. His surreal work seems overtly simple, but is overlaid with cultural references that question the direction the country was traveling in. His most successful book, *Trout Fishing in America* (Vintage; Dell o/p), although designed as a fishing handbook, stealthily creates a disturbing image of contemporary life. Other novels include *A Confederate General from Big Sur* (Houghton Mifflin) and *In Watermelon Sugar* (o/p).

Charles Bukowski *Post Office* (Black Sparrow). An alcohol- and sex-soaked romp through some of LA's more festering back alleys, with a mailman surrogate for Bukowski as your guide. One of several books the author wrote exploring his encounters with the city's dark side.

James M. Cain *Double Indemnity, The Postman Always Rings Twice, Mildred Pierce* (Vintage; Picador). With Raymond Chandler, the ultimate writer of dark, tough-guy novels. His entire oeuvre is excellent reading, but these three are the best explorations of LA.

★ **Raymond Chandler** *Farewell My Lovely, Lady in the Lake, The Big Sleep* (Random House; Penguin). Famous books adapted into classic movies, but Chandler's prose is still inimitable: terse, pointed, and vivid.

For guidebooks of specific relevance to travelers with **disabilities**, see p.73 of Basics.

CONTEXTS | Books

More than just detective stories (centered on gumshoe detective Philip Marlowe), these are masterpieces of fiction.

Michael Connelly *Angels Flight* (Little Brown; Orion). One of several volumes focusing on LAPD investigator Harry Bosch, whose appropriate moniker casts him as a keen observer of LA's blood-curdling mix of corruption, public scandals, and violence.

Philip K. Dick *A Scanner Darkly* (Voyager; Random House). Erratic but frequently brilliant author who, in this book, evokes the mid-1990s split between the Straights, the Dopers, and the Narks – a dizzying study of identity, authority, and drugs. Among the pick of the rest of Dick's vast legacy is *Do Androids Dream of Electric Sheep?* (Voyager; Ballantine), set in San Francisco, which gave rise to the film *Blade Runner*, set in LA.

Joan Didion *Play It as It Lays* (Flamingo; Farrar Straus & Giroux). Hollywood rendered in booze-guzzling, pill-popping, sex-craving detail. Oddly, the author went on to write the uninspired script for the third adaptation of *A Star Is Born*.

⭐ **James Ellroy** *The Black Dahlia, The Big Nowhere, LA Confidential, White Jazz* (Arrow; Warner). The LA Quartet: an excellent saga of city cops from the postwar era to the 1960s, with each novel becoming progressively more complex and elliptical in style.

John Fante *Ask the Dust* (Black Sparrow; Rebel Inc.). The third and still the best of the author's stories of itinerant poet Arturo Bandini, whose wanderings during the Depression highlight California's faded glory and struggling residents.

F. Scott Fitzgerald *The Last Tycoon* (Penguin; Macmillan). The legendary author's unfinished final work, on the power and glory of Hollywood. Intriguing reading that gives a view of the studio system at its height.

Robert Ferrigno *Horse Latitudes* (Pocket Books; Avon o/p). A drug-dealer-turned-academic begins a descent into a bizarre LA world when he encounters a corpse at his home, possibly left by his departed wife.

James Gardner *Fat City* (University of California, US). Poignant account of small-time Stockton boxing, following the initiation and fitful progress of a young hopeful and the parallel decline of an old contender. Painfully exact on the confused, murky emotions of its men as their lives stagnate in the heat of the town and the surrounding country.

Molly Giles *Iron Shoes* (Scribner). A sobering but fascinating look into the life of a Northern California woman, busy caring for her dying mother while trying to juggle the alternately absurd and dismal characters in her life.

⭐ **Dashiell Hammett** *The Four Great Novels* (Picador; Vintage); *The Maltese Falcon* (Random House, US). Seminal detective novels featuring Sam Spade, the private investigator working out of San Francisco. See also the absorbing biography of Hammett: Diane Johnson's *Dashiell Hammett: A Life* (Picador; Fawcett).

Joseph Hansen *Gravedigger* (Holt; No Exit Press). Best in a series of entertaining tales of Dave Brandstetter, a gay insurance-claims investigator, set against a vivid Southern California backdrop.

Chester Himes *If He Hollers Let Him Go* (Thunder's Mouth Press; Serpent's Tail). A fine literary introduction to mid-twentieth-century race relations in LA, narrated by one Bob Jones, whose struggles mirrored those of author Himes, who eventually ended up living in Spain.

Aldous Huxley *Ape and Essence* (Flamingo; I.R. Dee); *After Many a Summer Dies the Swan* (I.R. Dee, US). Huxley spent his last twenty years as a Hollywood screenwriter, and both these novels are products of that time. The first is an imaginative depiction of postnuclear LA, in which books are burned in Pershing Square for warmth and the *Biltmore* hotel is the site of an annual orgy; the latter is based on William Randolph Hearst, and concerns a rich, pampered figure who surrounds himself with art treasures and dwells on the meaning of life.

Christopher Isherwood *Down There on a Visit* (Noonday Press; Minerva). Incisive, involving read by a British expatriate, who penned much of his later fiction in and on Southern California.

Helen Hunt Jackson *Ramona* (New American Library; Fisher Press). Ultra-romanticized depiction of mission life that criticizes America's treatment of Indians while showing the natives to be noble savages and glorifying the Spanish exploiters. Not particularly good reading, but a valuable period piece – perhaps the most influential piece of fiction ever written about California.

★ **Jack Kerouac** *Desolation Angels* (Flamingo; Riverhead); *The Dharma Bums* (Penguin). The most influential of the Beat writers on the rampage in California. See also his first novel *On the Road* (Penguin), which has a little of San Francisco and a lot of the rest of the US.

Elmore Leonard *Get Shorty* (Penguin; Bantam). Ice-cool mobster Chili Palmer is a Miami debt collector who follows a client to Hollywood, and finds that the increasing intricacies of his own situation are translating themselves into a movie script.

David Levien *Wormwood* (Allison & Busby; Hyperion) Get a glimpse of the seamier side of the contemporary movie biz, following an up-and-coming story editor through the corporate ranks until he achieves utter exhaustion and, curiously, an addiction to absinthe.

David Lodge *Changing Places* (Penguin). Thinly disguised autobiographical tale of an English academic who spends a year teaching at UC Berkeley and finds himself in the middle of the late Sixties student upheaval.

Ross MacDonald *Black Money* (Allison & Busby; Vintage); *The Blue Hammer* (Allison & Busby; Vintage); *The Zebra-Striped Hearse* (Allison & Busby o/p; Knopf o/p); *The Doomsters*; *The Instant Enemy* (Allison & Busby, US). Following in the footsteps of Spade and Marlowe, private detective Lew Archer looks behind the glitzy masks of Southern California life to reveal the underlying nastiness of creepy sexuality and manipulation.

Armistead Maupin *Tales of the City; Further Tales of the City* (both Black Swan; HarperCollins); *More Tales of the City* (Corgi; Harper-Collins). Lively and witty soap operas detailing the sexual antics of a select group of archetypal San Francisco characters of the late Seventies and early Eighties. See also *Babycakes* (Black Swan; Harper-Collins) and *Significant Others*, which continue the story, though in more depth, and *Sure of You* (last two Black Swan; HarperCollins) – set several years later and more downbeat.

Brian Moore *The Great Victorian Collection* (Flamingo; Acacia Press). A professor dreams up a parking lot full of Victoriana, which becomes the biggest tourist attraction of Carmel, California.

Walter Mosely *Devil in a Blue Dress, A Red Death, White Butterfly, Black*

Betty, *A Little Yellow Dog, Bad Boy Brawly Brown* (Pan; Pocket Books). Excellent modern noir novels that involve black private detective Easy Rawlins, who "does favors" from his South Central base. Mosley compellingly brings to life pre-riots Watts and, later, Compton.

Kem Nunn *Tapping the Source* (Four Walls Eight Windows Press). One of the most unexpected novels to emerge from California beach culture, an eerie murder-mystery set among the surfing landscape of Orange County's Huntington Beach.

Thomas Pynchon *The Crying of Lot 49* (Vintage; HarperPerennial). Pynchon's celebrated – and most readable – excursion in modern paranoia follows the hilarious adventures of techno-freaks and potheads in Sixties California, and reveals the sexy side of stamp collecting. His later *Vineland* (Penguin) is set in Northern California.

Richard Rayner *Los Angeles without a Map* (Flamingo; Mariner Book). An English non-driving journalist goes to LA on a romantic whim and lives out movie fantasies made even more fantastic by the city itself.

John Ridley *Love is a Racket* (Knopf; Bantam). A delightful slice of Hollywood hell, in which protagonist Jeffty Kittridge, slumming through the dregs of local society and being abused by countless predators, leads us on a darkly comic journey through LA's many bleak corners.

Theodore Roszak *Flicker* (Bantam, US o/p). In a rundown LA movie house, Jonathan Gates discovers cinema and becomes obsessed by the director Max Castle – a genius of the silent era who disappeared under mysterious circumstances in the Forties – leading Gates into a labyrinthine conspiracy with its roots in medieval heresy.

Danny Santiago *Famous All over Town* (New American Library, US). Coming-of-age novel set among the street gangs of East LA, vividly depicting life in the Hispanic community.

Budd Schulberg *What Makes Sammy Run?* (Vintage). Classic anti-Hollywood vitriol by one of its insiders, a novelist and screenwriter whose acidic portrait of the movie business is unmatched.

Vikram Seth *The Golden Gate* (Faber; Vintage). A novel in verse which traces the complex social lives of a group of San Francisco yuppies.

Mona Simpson *Anywhere But Here* (Faber; Vintage). Bizarre and unforgettable saga of a young girl and her ambitious mother as they pursue LA stardom for the daughter.

Upton Sinclair *The Brass Check* (Ayer Press o/p). The failed California gubernatorial candidate and activist author vigorously criticizes LA's yellow journalism and the underhanded practices of its main figures. Sinclair also wrote *Oil!*, about the city's 1920s oil rush, and *The Goose Step*, concerning collegiate life at USC.

Terry Southern *Blue Movie* (Grove Press). Sordid, frequently hilarious take on the overlap between high-budget moviemaking and pornography, with the author's vulgar themes and characters cheerfully slashing through politically correct literary conventions.

⭐ **John Steinbeck** *The Grapes of Wrath* (Mandarin; Penguin). The classic account of a migrant family forsaking the Midwest for the Promised Land. The light-hearted but crisply observed novella, *Cannery Row*, captures daily life on the prewar Monterey waterfront, and the epic *East of Eden* (both Mandarin; Penguin), updates and resets the

Bible in the Salinas Valley and depicts three generations of family feuds.

★ **Robert Louis Stevenson** *The Silverado Squatters* (Everyman; Tuttle). Depicts the splendor of the San Francisco hills and the cast of eccentrics and immigrants that populate them, as well as the strange atmosphere of Silverado itself, a deserted former Gold Rush settlement.

Amy Tan *The Joy Luck Club* (Mandarin; Putnam). Huge bestseller in which four Chinese women – new arrivals in 1940s San Francisco – come together to play mahjong and tell their stories. They have four daughters, divided between Chinese and American identities, who also tell their stories, from childhood and from their often troubled present.

Erik Tarloff *The Man Who Wrote the Book* (Crown). Amusing look at the life of a frustrated professor at a Fresno bible college, who finds himself immersed in the seedy world of Southern California's frenetic party scene.

Michael Tolkin *The Player* (Faber; Grove Atlantic). A convincing look at the depravity and moral twilight of the filmmaking community, with special scorn for venal movie execs. Made into a classic flick by Robert Altman (see p.880).

Gore Vidal *Hollywood* (Modern Library). The fifth volume in the author's "Empire" series about emerging US power on the world stage, this one focusing on the movie industry, its interaction with Washington bigwigs, and boundless capacity for propaganda.

Evelyn Waugh *The Loved One* (Little Brown). The essential literary companion to take with you on a trip to Forest Lawn – here rendered as Whispering Glades, the apex of funerary pretension and a telling symbol of LA's postmortem status mania.

★ **Nathanael West** *The Day of the Locust* (Signet; Picador UK o/p). The best book about LA not involving detectives, an apocalyptic story of the fringe characters at the edge of the film industry, which culminates in a glorious riot and utter chaos.

Mexican-Spanish terms

California is bound to its Spanish colonial and Mexican past, a fact manifest in the profusion of Spanish place names, particularly in the south of the state. Today large numbers of people living in California speak Spanish as their first language, so it can be useful to know a few terms. Note that the double-L is pronounced like a "Y" and an "Ñ" sounds like an N and a Y run together.

abierto	open	mar	sea
agua	water	mesa	high plateau, literally "table"
alta, alto	high		
arroyo	canyon or gully	monte	mount(ain)
avenida	avenue	nevada	snowy
buena, bueno	good	norte	north
caliente	hot	obispo	bishop
calle	street, pronounced "ka-ye"	oro	gold
		parque	park
cerrado	closed	pescadero	fisherman
costa	coast	playa	beach
cruz	cross	rey	king
de	of	rio	river
del	of the	rojo	red
dorado	golden	san, santa, santo	saint
el	the	sierra	mountain range
escondido	hidden	sol	sun
fuego	fire	sur	south
grande	big	taqueria	taco stall or shop
hermosa	beautiful	tienda	shop
jolla	jewel, pronounced "hoya"	tierra	land
		tres	three
las, los	the (plural)	verde	green

For the basics, the most useful language book on the market is *Mexican Spanish: A Rough Guide Phrasebook* (Rough Guides), £3.99/$5, which covers the essential phrases and expressions, as well as dipping into grammar and providing a fuller vocabulary in dictionary format.

Rough Guides

advertiser

Rough Guides travel...

ROUGH GUIDES ADVERTISER

...music & reference

Also! More than 120 Rough Guide music CDs are available from all good book
and record stores. Listen in at www.worldmusic.net

Don't bury your head in the sand!

Take cover!

with Rough Guide Travel Insurance

Worldwide cover, for Rough Guide readers worldwide

Check the web at
www.roughguidesinsurance.com

UK: 0800 083 9507
US: 1-800 749-4922
Australia: 1 300 669 999
Worldwide: **(+44) 870 890 2843**

ROUGH GUIDES

Insurance organized by Columbus Direct. Columbus Direct are authorised and regulated by the Financial Services Authority.

Columbus Direct, 41 Southgate, Chichester, West Sussex, PO19 1ET

small print and

Index

A Rough Guide to Rough Guides

In the summer of 1981, Mark Ellingham, a recent graduate of Bristol University, was traveling around Greece and couldn't find a guidebook that really met his needs. On the one hand there were the student guides, insistent on saving every last cent, and on the other the heavyweight cultural tomes whose authors seemed to have spent more time in a research library than lounging away the afternoon at a taverna or on the beach.

In a bid to avoid getting a job, Mark and a small group of writers set about creating their own guidebook. It was a guide to Greece that aimed to combine a journalistic approach to description with a thoroughly practical approach to travelers' needs – a guide that would incorporate culture, history, and contemporary insights with a critical edge, together with up-to-date, value-for-money listings. Back in London, Mark and the team finished their Rough Guide, as they called it, and talked Routledge into publishing the book.

That first *Rough Guide to Greece*, published in 1982, was a student scheme that became a publishing phenomenon. The immediate success of the book – with numerous reprints and a Thomas Cook Prize shortlisting – spawned a series that rapidly covered dozens of destinations. Rough Guides had a ready market among low-budget backpackers, but soon also acquired a much broader and older readership that relished Rough Guides' wit and inquisitiveness as much as their enthusiastic, critical approach. Everyone wants value for money, but not at any price.

Rough Guides soon began supplementing the "rougher" information about hostels and low-budget listings with the kind of detail on restaurants and quality hotels that independent-minded visitors on any budget might expect, whether on business in New York or trekking in Thailand.

These days the guides – distributed worldwide by the Penguin Group – offer recommendations from shoestring to luxury and cover more than 200 destinations around the globe, including almost every country in the Americas and Europe, more than half of Africa and most of Asia and Australasia. Our ever-growing team of authors and photographers is spread all over the world, particularly in Europe, the USA, and Australia.

In 1994, we published the *Rough Guide to World Music* and *Rough Guide to Classical Music*, and a year later the *Rough Guide to the Internet*. All three books have become benchmark titles in their fields – which encouraged us to expand into other areas of publishing, mainly around popular culture. Rough Guides now publish:

- Travel guides to more than 200 worldwide destinations
- Dictionary phrasebooks to 22 major languages
- History guides ranging from Ireland to Islam
- Maps printed on rip-proof and waterproof Polyart™ paper
- Music guides running the gamut from Opera to Elvis
- Restaurant guides to London, New York, and San Francisco
- Reference books on topics as diverse as the Weather and Shakespeare
- Sports guides from Formula 1 to Man Utd
- Pop culture books from *Lord of the Rings* to Cult TV
- World Music CDs in association with World Music Network.

Visit **www.roughguides.com** to see our latest publications.

SMALL PRINT

Rough Guide credits

Text editor: Steven Horak
Layout: Jessica Subramanian
Cartography: Rajesh Mishra
Picture editor: Simon Bracken, Mark Thomas
Proofreader: Diane Margolis
Editorial: **London** Martin Dunford, Kate Berens, Geoff Howard, Claire Saunders, Ruth Blackmore, Gavin Thomas, Polly Thomas, Richard Lim, Clifton Wilkinson, Sally Schafer, Karoline Densley, Andy Turner, Ella O'Donnell, Keith Drew, Edward Aves, Andrew Lockett, Joe Staines, Duncan Clark, Peter Buckley, Matthew Milton, Daniel Crewe, Nikki Birrell, Chloë Thomson, Helen Marsden; **New York** Andrew Rosenberg, Richard Koss, Chris Barsanti, AnneLise Sorensen, Amy Hegarty
Design & Pictures: **London** Simon Bracken, Dan May, Diana Jarvis, Mark Thomas, Jj Luck, Harriet Mills, Chloë Roberts; **Delhi** Madhulita Mohapatra, Umesh Aggarwal, Ajay Verma, Amit Verma
Production: Julia Bovis, Sophie Hewat, Katherine Owers

Cartography: **London** Maxine Repath, Ed Wright, Katie Lloyd-Jones **Delhi** Manish Chandra, Rajesh Chhibber, Jai Prakash Mishra, Ashutosh Bharti, Animesh Pathak, Karobi Gogoi
Online: **New York** Jennifer Gold, Suzanne Welles; **Delhi** Manik Chauhan, Narender Kumar, Shekhar Jha, Rakesh Kumar, Lalit Sharma
Marketing & Publicity: **London** Richard Trillo, Niki Hanmer, David Wearn, Demelza Dallow; **New York** Geoff Colquitt, Megan Kennedy, Milena Perez; **Delhi** Reem Khokhar
Custom publishing and foreign rights: Philippa Hopkins
Finance: Gary Singh
Manager India: Punita Singh
Series editor: Mark Ellingham
PA to Managing Director: Megan McIntyre
Managing Director: Kevin Fitzgerald

Publishing information

This eighth edition published August 2005 by **Rough Guides Ltd**,
80 Strand, London WC2R 0RL
345 Hudson St, 4th Floor,
New York, NY 10014, USA
14 Local Shopping Centre, Panchsheel Park,
New Delhi 110017, India
Distributed by the Penguin Group
Penguin Books Ltd,
80 Strand, London WC2R 0RL
Penguin Putnam, Inc.
375 Hudson St, NY 10014, USA
Penguin Group (Australia)
250 Camberwell Road, Camberwell
Victoria 3124, Australia
Penguin Books Canada Ltd,
10 Alcorn Ave, Toronto, ON,
M4V 1E4, Canada
Penguin Group (New Zealand)
Cnr Rosedale and Airborne roads
Albany, Auckland, New Zealand

Typeset in Bembo and Helvetica to an original design by Henry Iles.
Printed and bound in China.
© Rough Guides 2005
Originally written and researched by Mick Sinclair.
No part of this book may be reproduced in any form without permission from the publisher except for the quotation of brief passages in reviews.
936pp includes index
A catalogue record for this book is available from the British Library.
ISBN 1-84353-428-2
The publishers and authors have done their best to ensure the accuracy and currency of all the information in **The Rough Guide to California**; however, they can accept no responsibility for any loss, injury, or inconvenience sustained by any traveler as a result of information or advice contained in the guide.

1 3 5 7 9 8 6 4 2

Help us update

We've gone to a lot of effort to ensure that the eighth edition of **The Rough Guide to California** is accurate and up to date. However, things change – places get "discovered," opening hours are notoriously fickle, restaurants and rooms raise prices or lower standards. If you feel we've got it wrong or left something out, we'd like to know, and if you can remember the address, the price, the time, the phone number, so much the better.

We'll credit all contributions, and send a copy of the next edition (or any other Rough Guide if you prefer) for the best letters. Everyone who writes to us and isn't already a subscriber will receive a copy of our full-color thrice-yearly newsletter. Please mark letters: **"Rough Guide California Update"** and send to: Rough Guides, 80 Strand, London WC2R 0RL, or Rough Guides, 4th Floor, 345 Hudson St, New York, NY 10014. Or send an email to **mail@roughguides.com**.

Have your questions answered and tell others about your trip at **www.roughguides.atinfopop.com**.

SMALL PRINT

Acknowledgments

J.D. would foremost like to thank his editor Steven Horak, who contributed much energy and determination to this book, not to mention panache. Thanks also are due to grand editor Andrew Rosenberg, J.D.'s wife and family, his travel contacts and coordinators in California, Rough Guides cartographers in both Delhi and London, including Rajesh Mishra and Katie Lloyd-Jones, Jessica Subramanian for setting the guide, Simon Bracken for taking care of the photos, and Nikki Birrell for providing administrative support.

Mark extends his warmest thanks to Laurie Armstrong at the San Francisco CVB for her constant helpfulness, as well as Rob Delamater and Tom Walton. Thanks, too, to Julie Armstrong in Monterey, Carrie Head in San Luis Obispo, Chris Taranto in Paso Robles, Christina Glynn in Santa Cruz, Lucy Steffens in Sacramento, and LaVerne Richmond in Tuolumne. Back in New York, thanks as ever to Ben, Maureen, and Karen for keeping the home fires burning; and finally, thanks to Addison Marshall for his first-class map-reading skills, enthusiasm for exploring even the most obscure sights, and of course, disco know-how.

Nick would like to thank Leona Reed in Sacramento and the ever-helpful staff at all the tourist offices on his patch, especially the following: Adel at Berkeley CVB; Bob Warren & Karen Whittaker of Shasta Cascades; Earl Hansen at Crescent City; Tony Smithers of Humboldt County; Sharon Rooney & Heidi Cusick of Mendocino County; Matt Perry of Lake County; Kimberley in Napa Valley; Joanne Steele of Siskiyou County; Lynn Saunders at Truckee; all at Pettit Gilwee, Lake Tahoe; Susanne Woodrum, Amie Rubenstein, & Steve Fogle in Sonoma County; and Margi Grant of San Mateo County. Warmest gratitude for house-sharing and all-round brotherhood in Berkeley to Clint Marsh, and for hospitality in absentia to guitar-toting landlord Laramie – keep strumming for democracy! Thanks once more for hospitality and great sounds to Eric & Nicki Taylor and family in the Gold Hills. Well done to Alexandra for making it up from LA for Labor Day weekend. Finally, deepest heartfelt thanks to Maria for keeping the western Pennsylvanian nest warm.

Paul would like to thank everyone who shared experiences, opinions, and knowledge on various research trips over the years. For this update, special thanks go to Chris Kapka for a warm welcome after long flights, and encouraging exploration of Owens Valley hot springs. Thanks as ever to Irene for holding the fort back home during my long absences and to Pharaoh for keeping her company.

The **editor** would like to thank J.D., Paul, Nick, Mark, and Greg for their many efforts and for the experience; Jessica Subramanian for tireless typesetting; Rajesh Mishra and Katie Lloyd-Jones for the excellent maps; and Simon Bracken and Mark Thomas for tracking down the photos. Thank you to Diane Margolis for meticulous proofreading; Todd Obolsky for a thorough index; Nikki Birrell and Madhu Mohapatra for their steady support; Chloe Roberts for the cover; Jeff Cramner and Stephen Timblin for their editing in a pinch; reliable Richard Koss for lending considerable aid throughout, as always; and Andrew Rosenberg for his helpful overall guidance and for stepping in, when needed, to keep it all moving along.

Readers' letters

Thanks to all the readers who took the trouble to write in with their comments and suggestions (and apologies to anyone whose name we've misspelt or omitted):

Barbara Abram, David Hew, Nadia Lee, David Masters, David Phillips, Barry Rawlinson, Andrew Sharp, Barbara Snelling, John Snelling

Photo credits

SMALL PRINT

Havasu Falls © Galen Rowell/Corbis p.354
Salt pans, Badwater, Death Valley NP © Bob Anderson p.366
Bristlecone Pines, White Mountains, Owens Valley © Paul Whitfield p.390
A&W Root Beer Drive-In, Modesto © Cindy Lewis/Car Photos/Alamy p.414
Hikers looking at Half Dome, Yosemite NP © Terry Husebye/Getty p.454
Leopard shark, Monterey Bay Aquarium © Kike Calvo/VW Pics/Visual & Written SL/Alamy p.486
Sea Lions, California coast © Corbis p.525
Victorian-inspired houses in Haight-Ashbury © Corbis p.556

Downtown San Francisco © Travel Ink p.609
San Francisco mural © Axiom/C. Caffrey p.650
Muir Woods © Rough Guides, by Nelson Hancock p.694
Lake Tahoe © Travel Ink p.706
Wells Fargo Express Office, Columbia State Historic Park © Jan Butchofsky-Houser/ Corbis p.750
Bald Eagle, Lower Klamath Falls Wildlife Refuge © Corbis p.766
Sequoia tree © Robert Harding/Gavin Hillier p.799
Highway 89 and Mount Shasta © Chuck Pefley/Alamy p.839

Index

Map entries are in color.

INDEX

O

I

INDEX

933

Map symbols

Maps are listed in the full index using colored text.

MAP SYMBOLS

------	International border	♦	Point of interest
--·--·--	Province/U.S. state border	⊥	Viewpoint
---	Chapter division boundary	♠	Museum
80	U.S. interstate	✕	Battlefield
30	U.S. highway	⌐	Dam
⊂⊃	Highway	⛷	Ski area
═══	Secondary highway	⊛	Swimming pool
═══	Local road	▣	Restaurant
▭	Pedestrianized road	◉	Accommodation
▥	Steps	⚠	Campsite
-----	Path	✈	Airport
▬▬	Railway	⊠—⊠	Gate
——	River	⊞	Hospital/medical centre
— —	Ferry route	ⓘ	Tourist information
——	Muni/Bart	⊠	Post office
— — ·	Tramline	⚲	Church (regional maps)
——	Light rail	)(	Bridge
-----	Footpath	⚑	Golf course
▪▪▪▪▪	Wall	⚑	Immigration post/border
⌂	Cave	★	Bus stop
🏛	Stately home/Palace	-Ⓜ-	Metro station
⧠	Mountain range	⊙	Statue
▲	Mountain peak	⬭	Stadium
◉	Crater	▪	Building
⚘	Waterfall	⊞	Church (town maps)
⊻	Marshland/swamp	⊞	Cemetery
⌐⌐⌐	Rocks	▨	Park
♠	Sequoia grove	▨	Forest
⚐	Lighthouse	░	Beach
🌴🌴	Oasis	▨	Marine base
⋀⋀	Spring	◩	Restricted zone